Essentials of Cognitive Neuroscience

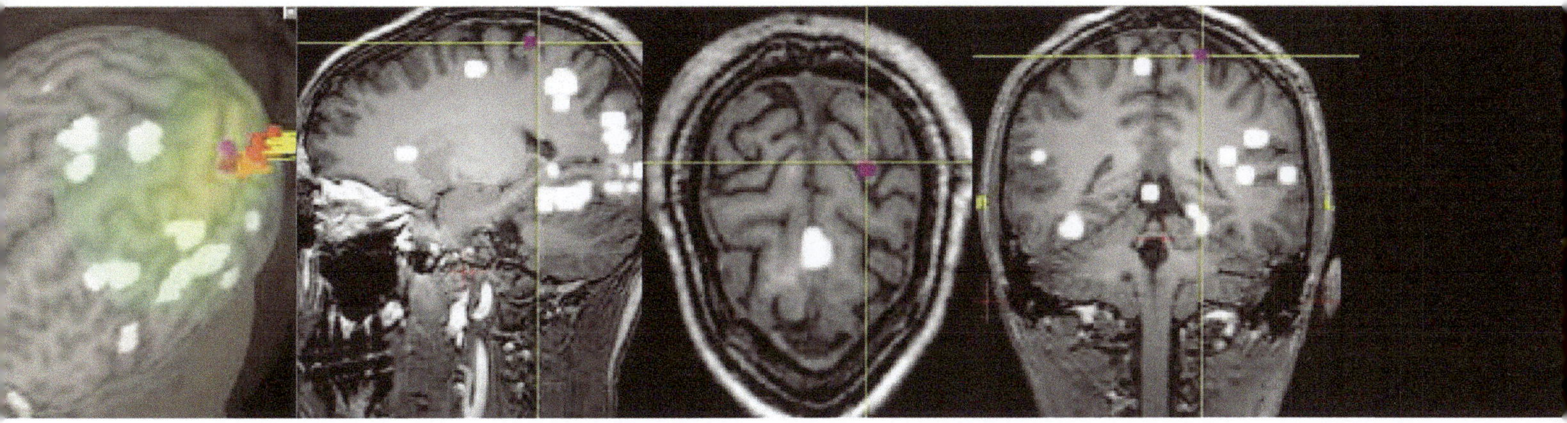

Essentials of Cognitive Neuroscience

Third Edition

BRADLEY R. POSTLE

WILEY

SENIOR EDITORIAL DIRECTOR	Justin Jeffryes
EXECUTIVE EDITOR	Todd Green
ASSISTANT EDITOR	Kelly Gomez
SENIOR EDITORIAL MANAGER	Judy Howarth
CONTENT REFINEMENT SPECIALIST	Srinivasan Kandasamy
COVER PHOTO CREDIT	© Morsa Images/Getty Images, © Abraham Gonzalez Fernandez/Getty Images, Courtesy of Rodrigo Braga and Donnisa Edmonds, Courtesy of Oliver Contier, Courtesy of Doris Tsao

This book was typeset in 9.5pt/12pt Stix Textbook with Signposting by Straive™.

Wiley is a global leader in research and education, unlocking human potential by enabling discovery, powering education, and shaping work- forces. For over 200 years, Wiley has fueled the world's knowledge ecosystem. Today, our high-impact content, platforms, and services help researchers, learners, institutions, and corporations achieve their goals in an ever-changing world. Visit us at Wiley.com.

ISBN: 978-1-394-38014-5 (PBK)
ISBN: 978-1-394-38010-7 (EPUB)
ISBN: 978-1-394-38013-8 (EPDF)

Library of Congress Cataloging-in-Publication Data

Name: Postle, Bradley R. author
Title: Essentials of cognitive neuroscience / Bradley R. Postle.
Description: Third edition. | [Hoboken] : Wiley, [2026] | Includes index.
Identifiers: LCCN 2025042613 (print) | LCCN 2025042614 (ebook) | ISBN 9781394380145 paperback | ISBN 9781394380138 adobe pdf | ISBN 9781394380107 epub
Subjects: LCSH: Cognitive neuroscience–Textbooks | Clinical neuropsychology–Textbooks
Classification: LCC QP360 .P675 2026 (print) | LCC QP360 (ebook)
LC record available at https://lccn.loc.gov/2025042613
LC ebook record available at https://lccn.loc.gov/2025042614

MWEP441464200226

Brief Contents

Contents

Preface

Does the world need another cognitive neuroscience textbook? Well, "need" is such a loaded word. What I'll try to do here is summarize my motivation for initially writing this book and, subsequently, revising it twice. In the process, I'll also try to convey the pedagogical vision behind choices about style, content, and organization.

For the past 25 years, I have taught cognitive psychology and cognitive neuroscience to undergraduate and graduate students at the University of Wisconsin–Madison. For undergraduates in the honors program, I offer a seminar that is linked to a large-enrollment lecture course on cognitive psychology. The lecture course is a survey of cognitive psychology, spanning sensation, and perception to decision-making, language, and consciousness. The honors seminar, the original impetus for this book, is populated by 15 or so students who are concurrently enrolled in the lecture course. In the seminar, which meets only once per week, for only 50 minutes (sic), we discuss the cognitive neuroscience of what's been covered in that week's cognitive psychology lectures. The modal student in this seminar has a background in experimental design and in probability and statistics for experimental psychology; only some have any formal training in biology, and fewer still in neuroscience. In this context, I have found that a textbook that attempts to cover "everything that we know" in the field is not effective – either it will be too superficial in its coverage to support substantive discussions in class or it will be inappropriately lengthy and dense, a cognitive neuroscience analogue of the >1000-page medical-school neuroscience textbook that I lugged around as a graduate student in systems neuroscience. Another approach, which is to assign papers from the primary literature, has proven to be an unsatisfactory alternative, because it results in an inordinate amount of class time being taken up with the remedial work of filling in background that the assigned papers don't cover, and explaining methods so that students can fully understand how the experiments were performed and how their results can be interpreted.

Essentials of Cognitive Neuroscience aspires to be a textbook that will support high-level, substantive engagement with the material in settings where contact hours and/or expectations for outside-of-the-classroom preparation time may be constrained. It introduces and explicates key principles and concepts in cognitive neuroscience in such a way that the reader will be equipped to critically evaluate the ever-growing body of findings that the field is generating. For some students, this knowledge will be needed for subsequent formal study, and for all readers, it will be needed to evaluate and interpret reports about cognitive neuroscience research that make their way daily into the news media and popular culture. The book seeks to do so in a style that will give the student a sense of what it's like to be a cognitive neuroscientist: when confronted with a problem, how does one proceed? How does one read and interpret research that's outside of one's subarea of specialization? How do two scientists advancing mutually incompatible models interrelate? Most importantly, what does it feel like to partake in the wonder and excitement of this most dynamic and fundamental of sciences?

To translate these aspirations into a book, I have made the following pedagogical and organizational choices:

- The introductory section is organized into three preliminary chapters, one on history and key concepts, one a primer on cellular and circuit-level neurobiology, and one an introduction to classical approaches to the study of cognitive neuroscience while introducing principles of sensation and perception. These are followed by a chapter on methods and one on prominent contemporary theoretical frameworks and computational approaches. These latter two, newly introduced for the second edition and now for the third edition, respectively, merit some additional explication.
- My own preference when teaching is to introduce methods throughout the course of the semester, at the point at which they are relevant for the research question that is being described. Thus, the first edition of this book did not include a chapter dedicated to *Methods of Cognitive Neuroscience*. When we solicited feedback from instructors who had used

the first edition, however, we learned not all share this preference. Thus, subsequent editions have included a stand-alone chapter on methods (*Chapter 4*), and any instructor following the "Postle preference" can do as I will do: omit this chapter as a stand-alone assignment during the first week of the course, and, instead, assign one or more relevant sections to supplement domain-of-cognition-themed readings the first time that a method is introduced. (Recommendations for how to do this are provided with the instructor guide.)

- Newly added for this third edition is *Chapter 5: Theoretical Frameworks and Computational Approaches*, which was necessitated to accommodate the ongoing explosion of new developments at the levels of theory and analysis, particularly in the realm of computational approaches. More specifically, if the early chapter on *The Visual System* was to be reasonably coherent (i.e., not interrupted on each page by lengthy theoretical or methodological digression), the reader would already need to be conversant with such topics as predictive coding, machine learning-derived analysis techniques, and representational similarity analysis. (And the same would be true for the early chapter on skeletomotor control for Hebbian plasticity, dynamical systems theory, reinforcement learning, recurrent neural networks, and representational geometry analysis.) Therefore, new to this third edition is a reworked *Chapter 3* that introduces "classical" concepts of sensory systems (e.g., the transduction of energy into a neural code, the receptive field, feedforward/"bottom-up" versus feedback/"top-down" signaling) so as to provide context and motivation for content from *Chapter 5*, such as why an idea like predictive coding, or a method like multivariate pattern analysis, might be valuable for supplementing (or, in some cases, supplanting) the principles adopted or developed during the first quarter century of cognitive neuroscience as a formal discipline.
- Important concepts are introduced and explained via experiments that illustrate them. These won't always be the first experiment that is credited with introducing an idea, nor even an experiment performed by the investigator or group that is credited with innovating the idea. Rather, they will be ones that I feel are particularly effective for explicating the concept in question. Further, most of the experiments that make it into this book are considered in a fair amount of depth. In doing so, I seek to model a "best practice" of the cognitive neuroscientist, one that is captured by a quote from the nineteenth-century neuroscientist David Ferrier, "In investigating reports on diseases and injuries of the brain . . . I feel obliged always to go to the fountainhead – dirty and muddy though this frequently turns out." A corollary to this point is that because cognitive neuroscientists learn about and work with key concepts via empirical findings, almost all of the figures in this book are taken directly from the primary scientific literature, just as they appear in the empirical reports or review papers in which they were published. This is also how I teach and reflects my conviction that an important skill for students to develop is how to interpret figures as they appear in scientific publications. Thus, the book contains only a minimum of figures/diagrams/cartoons that were developed expressly for pedagogical purposes.
- Because a book targeting "essentials" can't cover all of the areas of research that fall under the rubric of cognitive neuroscience, each chapter concludes with an annotated list of suggested Further Reading. Many of the listed works will provide effective entrées into an area that the book doesn't cover.
- The first edition of this book was accompanied by a companion website that included 6–12 (or so)-minute bespoke narrated audiovisual presentations contributed by over 40 experts in different areas of cognitive neuroscience. These have now been spun off from the book and are made publicly available at https://postlab.psych.wisc.edu/cognitive-neuroscience-compendium/. Through these presentations, students will hear directly from the experts themselves about either (1) an important experiment that is described in the book and that I think merits a telling from the perspective of the investigator who actually performed the study, or (2) an important area of cognitive neuroscience that can't be covered in the book but that the reader really should know about. These narrated videos generate a frisson of "what it's like" to work in this field. I am greatly indebted to my colleagues

who contributed their time and expertise to this remarkable collection. (Poignantly, those from Corkin, Eichenbaum, and Lisman capture the wisdom and energy of colleagues from whom we can no longer learn through direct interaction.)

Although conceived and written for an upper-level undergraduate readership, *Essentials of Cognitive Neuroscience* can also be used for graduate teaching. For example, one associate of mine has used it as the primary text in a general "Introduction to Cognitive Neuroscience" course in which each week a student presented a chapter to the class and led the ensuing discussion. In my graduate seminar, assigned readings from this book cover the background that every student needs to know before coming to the class, and in class we focus on more recent developments.

Those of us who are lucky enough to make a living grappling with some facet of the mind–brain problem have a responsibility to impart to our students a sense of the wonder, awe, and excitement that permeate our professional lives. I hope this book can help some of us meet this responsibility.

Acknowledgments

The efforts and/or indulgence of many made this book possible. Going back to the first edition (2015), then-lab manager Mike Starrett provided unflagging support at all stages of the writing of the first edition, from tracking down obscure, out-of-print volumes to formatting references to proofreading drafts to filming and editing the author's introduction to each chapter. "*MStarr*: We don't know how to do that . . . yet"! In the second edition, Claire Carson provided valuable help with figure production. Dan Acheson was a wise and resourceful collaborator and was responsible for much of the content that was initially on the book's companion web page, now accessible at https://postlab.psych.wisc.edu/cognitive-neuroscience-compendium/, as well as for much of the instructional support material. Dan was also a critical guide and sounding board during the writing of Chapter 19. Additional colleagues (and one spouse) who also provided valued feedback on portions of earlier editions of the book include Sue Corkin, Olivia Gosseries, Mike Koenigs, Bornali Kundu, Maryellen MacDonald, Jay McClelland, Chris Moore, Pat Mulvey, Tim Rogers, and Giulio Tononi. This time around (i.e., for the third edition), conversations with Yuri Saalmann and Ali Mohebi were particularly valuable and appreciated. I am fortunate to have worked in the company of so many smart and generous individuals. Additionally, I am grateful to graduate students from the Fall 2024 semester of Psychology 720 and undergraduate students from the Spring 2025 semester of Psychology 505 for providing valuable feedback on early drafts of much of the content that is new for this third edition.

The indulgence of colleagues and trainees in my laboratory who tolerated my engagement with this project was much appreciated, as were the substantive contributions of Jacqueline Fulvio and Jung-Woo Hur.

Colleagues who willingly gave their time and energy to contribute a *Narrated Video* for the companion Web page of the first edition (now accessible at https://postlab.psych.wisc.edu/cognitive-neuroscience-compendium/) contributed enormously to the pedagogical value of this enterprise, and I am very grateful to each of them: Dan Acheson, Andy Alexander, Chris Baker, Shaowen Bao, Morgan Barense, Rasmus Birn, Sue Corkin, Clay Curtis, Mark D'Esposito, Mingzhou Ding, Howard Eichenbaum, Olivia Gosseries, Shawn Green, Peter Hagoort, John-Dylan Haynes, Mike Koenigs, Victor Lamme, John Lisman, Bea Luna, Marcello Massimini, Yuko Munakata, Betsy Murray, Behrad Noodoust, Josef Parvizi, Sean Polyn, Mike Robinson, Tim Rogers, Bas Rokers, Vincenzo Romei, Yuri Saalmann, John Serences, Jon Simons, Heleen Slagter, Leah Somerville, Craig Stark, Mark Stokes, Jack Van Horn, Brad Voytek, and Gagan Wig. Wow! What a list!

I'm also grateful to many additional colleagues who took the time to track down and share high-resolution copies of hard-to-find images appearing as figures in this book.

The team at Wiley, and their associates, provided much-appreciated guidance, assistance, and encouragement at every stage of the process.

A book such as this is necessarily shaped by one's past experience, and I'm grateful to everyone who has guided and influenced my career in cognitive neuroscience, from pre-graduate school mentors, to professors, classmates, and lab mates at MIT, to the team in Area 9 (U. Penn instantiation) and the D'Esposito diaspora, to all the colleagues and students with whom I've interacted in the classroom, in the lab, and in the hallway, since coming to Wisconsin. Professional organizations whose members and programming have enriched my career include the Cognitive Neuroscience Society, the International Society for Behavioral Neuroscience, the Memory Disorders Research Society, the Psychonomic Society, the Society for Human Brain Mapping, and the Society for Neuroscience.

Much of the aforementioned career has been underwritten by generous support from the National Institutes of Health and the National Science Foundation, for which I am grateful. These and other funding entities in the United States and around the world, public and private, are necessary and valued contributors to all the knowledge and discoveries that are recounted on the pages that follow.

Finally, I am forever indebted to my loving family, without whose support and indulgence this book could not have been written, nor revised (twice!). Three times now, Pat Mulvey has been, as the t-shirt says, “Essentially . . . a Cognitive Neuroscience widow.”

Madison, WI
April 2025

Walkthrough of Pedagogical Features

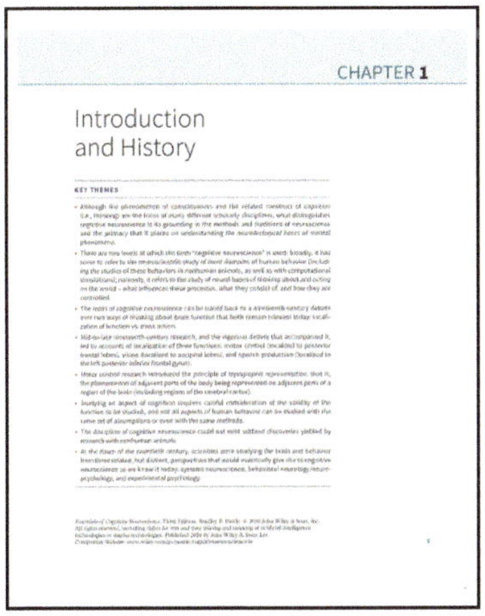

CHAPTER 1

Introduction and History

KEY THEMES

Key Themes The opening page of each chapter lists the key themes that will be introduced and explored in that chapter, to help the reader navigate the text.

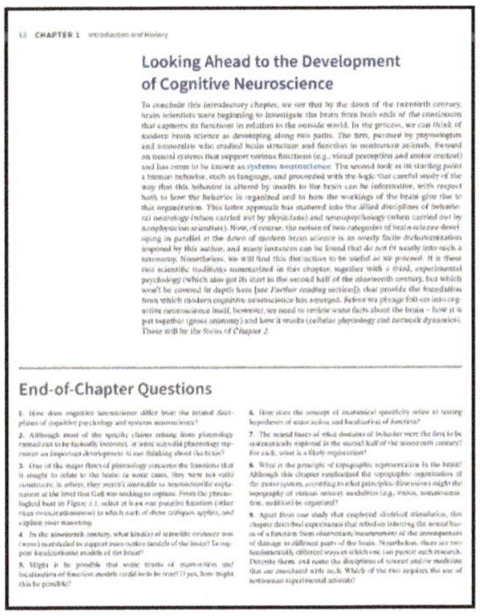

Looking Ahead to the Development of Cognitive Neuroscience

End-of-Chapter Questions

End-of-Chapter Questions The reader can use these to assess how well s/he has understood a chapter's central themes, and as a starting point for further investigations.

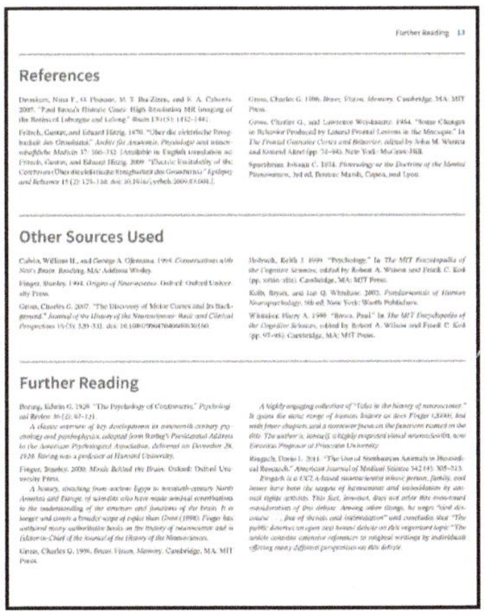

References

Other Sources Used

Further Reading

Further Reading An annotated list of readings that either elaborate on a chapter's contents, if one wants to learn more, or offer an entrée into a related topic that the chapter did not cover.

Companion Website

www.wiley.com/go/postle/cognitiveneuroscience3e

This book has a comprehensive companion website that features a number of useful resources for instructors and students alike.

FOR INSTRUCTORS

- **Instructor Notes:** These thematic notes provide deeper insights into chapter topics, exploring specific subjects in greater detail or addressing questions that diverge from the main thread of the chapter. The Finer points highlight specific details that may benefit from additional explanation or point to resources that can supplement lecture material or be used by students outside of class time
- **Test Bank:** A collection of both print and computerized questions for each chapter to help instructors create exams

Please note that the resources for instructors are password protected and can only be accessed by instructors who have registered with the site.

The Neurobiology of Thinking

INTRODUCTION TO SECTION I

The Neurobiology of Thinking

Anyone who can read these words, including you, experiences conscious awareness. What explains this? Is the conscious experience of other people "the same" as my own? Is our conscious experience qualitatively different from what may or may not be experienced by nonhuman animals? These and similar questions have fascinated some of humankind's most celebrated thinkers for as long as humans have been leaving records of what they are thinking about. They are among the most profound that a human being can ask. Not surprising, then, is the fact that questions that relate either directly or indirectly to the phenomenon consciousness and the related construct of cognition (i.e., thinking) have been taken up by many different scholarly disciplines, including philosophy, evolutionary biology, anthropology, economics, linguistics, computer science, and psychology. What distinguishes **cognitive neuroscience**, the focus of this book, from these and other disciplines, is its grounding in the methods and traditions of neuroscience, and the primacy that it places on understanding the biological bases of mental phenomena. Now it bears noting that cognitive neuroscience doesn't concern itself only with consciousness and conscious awareness. Indeed, I feel confident asserting that the vast majority of articles that have been published in, say, the *Journal of Cognitive Neuroscience* (one of many scientific journals publishing peer-reviewed reports of research in the field) don't even explicitly address the idea of consciousness, much less use the word. Nonetheless, it is also true that it can be difficult to entertain detailed thoughts about human behavior and the principles that govern it without straying into ideas such as those that opened this paragraph. This clear relationship to profound philosophical questions is one of the properties that differentiates cognitive neuroscience from other physical and biological sciences, including many other domains of neuroscience.

Like other physical and biological scientists, cognitive neuroscientists design and carry out rigorously controlled experiments that yield objective, measurable data, and seek to relate these data to mechanistic models of how a natural system works. And, as suggested above, the system studied by cognitive neuroscientists is one that is also of direct interest to scholars who study it from a very different perspective (e.g., from philosophy, from anthropology, and from **cognitive psychology**). This overlap turns out to be both a blessing and a curse. It's a blessing in that the cognitive neuroscientist can draw on ideas and observations from a vast array of rich intellectual traditions. And because they are studying questions that are fundamental to the human condition, almost any thinking person that a cognitive neuroscientist encounters is likely to be interested in what they do for a living. (Much easier, in the humble opinion of the author, to be a cognitive neuroscientist attending a social function full of strangers than, say, an economist, or a cell biologist, or a particle physicist.) The curse is found on the flip side of this coin. Because scholars in different fields are often interested in the same object of study (whether it be, say, visual perception, aesthetics, or antisocial behavior), cognitive

Essentials of Cognitive Neuroscience, Third Edition. Bradley R. Postle. Published 2026 by John Wiley & Sons, Inc.
Companion Website: www.wiley.com/go/postle/cognitiveneuroscience3e

neuroscience research can often be characterized by people working in other fields as asking the wrong question, or asking it in the wrong way, or of generating findings that are fundamentally irrelevant for understanding the question at hand. Being aware of this sociological context surrounding cognitive neuroscience is just one piece of knowledge that can be helpful in evaluating the implications and importance of any particular set of facts and ideas that will be described in this book.

Cognitive Neuroscience? or "Human Neuroscience"? or "Neuroscience-with-Direct-Implications-for-Understanding-Human-Behavior"?

How were the topics to be covered in this book selected? More importantly, when teaching cognitive neuroscience, where does one draw the line that defines the boundaries of the discipline? This is a difficult question that doesn't have a definitive answer. It's really just an accident of history that the confluence of neuroscientific methods and studies of human behavior happened first, or, at least, influentially, with domains of behavior and function that are studied by cognitive psychology (e.g., visual perception, language comprehension and production, memory), as opposed to, for example, social behavior, personality, emotion, or psychopathology. As a result, one sees the label "cognitive neuroscience" appearing earlier in the literature than, for example, **affective neuroscience** or, certainly, **social cognitive neuroscience**. As a consequence, the term "cognitive neuroscience" has come to be used in many contexts, and not always with precisely the same meaning. In one context, "cognitive neuroscience" can be used to refer to the tools and methods used to study the neural bases of human behavior (e.g., **brain** scans, recording electrical potentials at the scalp, brain stimulation). This might seem like a misnomer, however, if the behavior being studied doesn't directly relate to cognition (e.g., the study of sleep or of the maturation of various brain systems during adolescence). The label "cognitive neuroscience" can also seem like a bad fit for research that spans multiple traditional categories of brain and/or behavior. To pick one real-world example, let's consider the study of how neural systems measured with brain scans relate to performance on an economic decision-making task by high trait-anxiety vs. low trait-anxiety prisoners (all classified as "psychopaths"), and the comparison of these data with data from neurological patients with frank damage to the ventromedial prefrontal cortex. Should this be classified as cognitive neuroscience research? On one level, I hope that the answer is "yes," because we will be considering this research in *Chapter 17*! However, to do so is to not explicitly acknowledge the equally important contributions to this research from clinical psychology, from affective neuroscience, from neuroeconomics, and from behavioral neurology and neuropsychology.

In view of the above, to capture the interdisciplinary breadth of much of what we'll be considering in this book, might it perhaps have been better to entitle it "Essentials of *Human* Neuroscience"? Here the answer is an unequivocal "no," because to do so would be to exclude the fact that our understanding the neural bases of almost all domains of human behavior builds on thorough knowledge of analogous neural functioning in nonhuman animals. This is because, as we shall see in almost every chapter of this book, technical and ethical limitations of what we can measure in humans require us to draw heavily on the results of research performed with nonhuman animals. Hence, the idea, implied in the title of this section, that the most precise title for this book might be "Essentials of Neuroscience with Direct Implications for Understanding Human Behavior." Now I'm no expert in academic publishing, but I'm fairly confident that, were I to have actually proposed this title, my editor would have rejected it. If nothing else, there probably aren't many universities where one can find a course that's called "Introduction to Neuroscience with Direct Implications for Understanding Human Behavior." Nonetheless, this is probably as good a summary, in 10 words or less, of what this book hopes to cover.

And so, with these considerations in mind, we'll stick with the label "cognitive neuroscience." It's not perfect, but if one is comfortable with a reasonably broad definition of **cognition** as thinking, behaving, and the factors on which these depend, then this label will serve us reasonably well.

Introduction and History

KEY THEMES

- Although the phenomenon of consciousness and the related construct of *cognition* (i.e., thinking) are the focus of many different scholarly disciplines, what distinguishes cognitive neuroscience is its grounding in the methods and traditions of neuroscience and the primacy that it places on understanding *the neurobiological bases* of mental phenomena.
- There are two levels at which the term "cognitive neuroscience" is used: broadly, it has come to refer to the neuroscientific study of most domains of human behavior (including the studies of these behaviors in nonhuman animals, as well as with computational simulations); narrowly, it refers to the study of neural bases of *thinking* about and *acting* on the world – what influences these processes, what they consist of, and how they are controlled.
- The roots of cognitive neuroscience can be traced back to a nineteenth-century debate over two ways of thinking about brain function that both remain relevant today: localization of function vs. mass action.
- Mid-to-late nineteenth-century research, and the vigorous debate that accompanied it, led to accounts of localization of three functions: motor control (localized to posterior frontal lobes), vision (localized to occipital lobes), and speech production (localized to the left posterior inferior frontal gyrus).
- Motor control research introduced the principle of *topographic representation*, that is, the phenomenon of adjacent parts of the body being represented on adjacent parts of a region of the brain (including regions of the cerebral cortex).
- Studying an aspect of cognition requires careful consideration of the validity of the function to be studied, and not all aspects of human behavior can be studied with the same set of assumptions or even with the same methods.
- The discipline of cognitive neuroscience could not exist without discoveries yielded by research with nonhuman animals.
- At the dawn of the twentieth century, scientists were studying the brain and behavior from three related, but distinct, perspectives that would eventually give rise to cognitive neuroscience as we know it today: systems neuroscience, behavioral neurology/neuropsychology, and experimental psychology.

Companion Website: www.wiley.com/go/postle/cognitiveneuroscience3e

CONTENTS

A Brief (and Selective) History

Although the term "cognitive neuroscience" as a name for a scientific discipline has only been with us for a few decades, the field has roots that extend back thousands of years. Ancient Egyptians, Greeks, and Romans all had ideas about the corporeal bases of human thoughts and emotions, although many of these did not specify a role for the brain. In preparing the bodies of deceased nobles for the afterlife, for example, ancient Egyptians removed and discarded the brain as an early step in the mummification process. The internal organs that *were* deemed to be important were preserved in urns that were entombed along with the body. In most ancient civilizations for which there are records, up through and including Roman civilization, the heart was believed to be the organ of thought. By the time we get to Enlightenment–era Europe, however, the central importance of "neuro" for cognition was widely accepted. One highly influential (and, more recently, ridiculed) example was that of German anatomists Franz Josef Gall (1758–1828) and Johann Gaspar Spurzheim (1776–1832), who developed a highly detailed scheme, known as **phrenology**, for how they thought that the shape of different parts of the skull related to one's personality and mental capacities. The underlying premise was that the relative bigness or smallness of various parts of the brain would produce convexities or concavities in the overlying skull. A skilled phrenologist, then, could learn something about an individual by palpating that person's skull. A bulge in the eye socket (inferred from "bulgy eyes") would mean a predilection toward "language," whereas an indentation near the left ear would correspond to a relative absence of the trait of "destructiveness" (*Figure 1.1*). One can see how such a scheme, if it had any validity, would have obvious utility for diagnosing maladies of the brain, as well as for assessing personality and aptitude. (Indeed, for a period during the 1800s, it was [mis]used in this way quite extensively, particularly in England and in the United States.)

Construct Validity in Models of Cognition

For at least the past 100 years, the psychology and neuroscience communities have viewed virtually all tenets of the phrenological enterprise as being scientifically invalid. For starters, many (if not all) of the skull-to-trait assignations were based on nothing more than anecdotal observations. The attribution of a facility for "language" to bulging eyes, for example, came from Gall's observation of a classmate who had a prodigious verbal memory and protruding

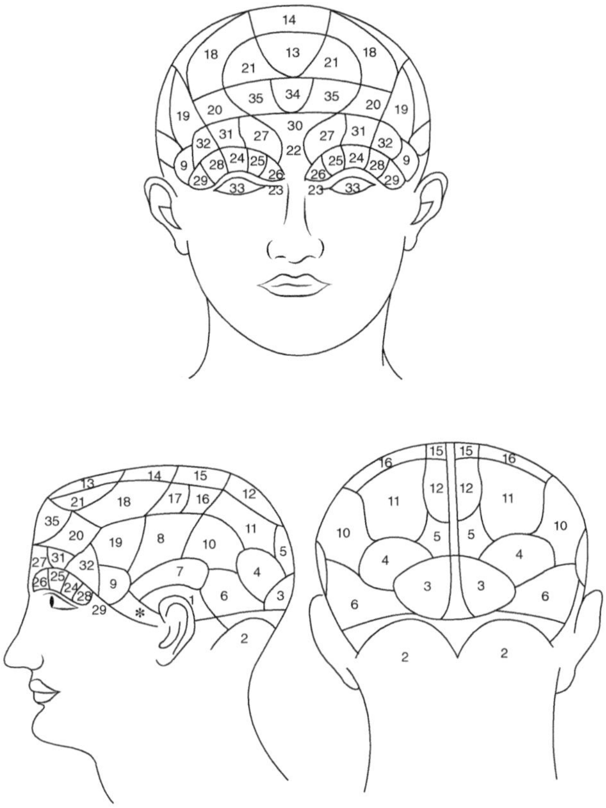

FIGURE 1.1 A phrenological map of the anatomical organization of mental faculties. They are organized into two primary categories (bold), with subcategories (underlined) under each. The first primary category is **Affective Faculties:** Propensities: * – Alimentiveness; 1 – Destructiveness; 2 – Amativeness; 3 – Philoprogenitiveness; 4 – Adhesiveness; 5 – Inhabitiveness; 6 – Combativeness; 7 – Secretiveness; 8 – Acquisitiveness; 9 – Constructiveness; Sentiments: 10 – Cautiousness; 11 – Approbativeness; 12 – Self-esteem; 13 – Benevolence; 14 – Reverence; 15 – Firmness; 16 – Conscientiousness; 17 – Hope; 18 – Marvelousness; 19 – Ideality; 20 – Mirthfulness; 21 – Imitation. The second primary category is **Intellectual Faculties:** Perceptive: 22 – Individuality; 23 – Configuration; 24 – Size; 25 – Weight and resistance; 26 – Coloring; 27 – Locality; 28 – Order; 29 – Calculation; 30 – Eventuality; 31 – Time; 32 – Tune; 33 – Language; Reflective: 34 – Comparison; 35 – Causality.

Source: Spurzheim and Johann, 1834 / Marsh, Capen & Lyon / Public Domain.

eyes (the latter presumed to be the result of a bulging frontal lobe that pushed the eyes forward). But what if Spurzheim (or you, or I) knew of a different person who had a comparable verbal memory, but who had sunken eyes? Furthermore, the very "functions" that phrenologists assigned to different parts of the scalp were derived from Gall's intuition rather than from a principled theoretical framework. Let's consider, for example, conscientiousness. Now it is true, of course, that an organism without a brain cannot exhibit conscientiousness, and, therefore, the phenomenon could not exist without a brain. However, might it not be the case that "conscientiousness" is just a label that we, as denizens of highly organized societies, have given to a certain collection of attributes characteristic of some peoples' behavior and personality? This can be illustrated from two perspectives. The first is a caveat about inferring the existence of a discrete neural correspondence to every describable aspect of behavior. For example, when a student sends me a thank-you note for having written a letter of recommendation for her, I will consider her to have displayed conscientiousness. But could it not be that this reflects the fact that she was conditioned during her upbringing to seek positive reinforcement from her parents ("You're such a good girl for writing those thank-you notes!"), and that her note to me is "merely" the product of an association that she has formed between writing a thank-you note and this reinforcement? Were this the case, it wouldn't make sense to think of conscientiousness as a discrete mental faculty. (And if there's no such faculty, then there's no "thing" to localize to a part of the brain.) The second perspective is that, as it turns out, there is a branch of psychology in which conscientiousness is a valid construct, but this is in the context of being one of the so-called "big-5" personality traits. And because each of these five traits (openness-to-experiences, conscientiousness, extraversion, agreeableness, and neuroticism) is a statistical composite derived from multiple measurements (such as responses to many-more-than-five questions on a personality assessment questionnaire), none of them can be construed as a unitary entity that might be localized to one brain system. And so, from this perspective, because conscientiousness isn't any *one* thing, it doesn't seem reasonable to expect it to localize to just one part of the brain.

The exercise of thinking through the phrenological treatment of conscientiousness highlights important principles that the scientific discipline of cognitive neuroscience shares with those from which it takes its name. Beginning with the "cognitive," a model of the neural instantiation of a cognitive function depends critically on the validity of the function that it seeks to explain. Indeed, the question of **construct validity** will be important for every domain of behavior that we consider in this book. For many of them, the formal models of the construct under study will have come from one of the "different scholarly disciplines" invoked in the *Introduction to Section I*.

From the perspective of "neuroscience," the legacy of phrenology is mixed. On the one hand, it was deeply flawed in several ways. For example, we now know that subtle, idiosyncratic variations in gross shape from one brain to another have little, if anything, to do with the "kind of person" that one is. We also recognize that the assignments of function that Gall gave to various parts of the brain (by inference, because phrenology only explicitly considered the skull) were not based on rigorous science and turned out to be altogether wrong. Despite these flaws, at the core of the phrenological enterprise, there was also a powerful idea that has continued to animate many debates about brain function up to the present day – the idea of **localization of function**.

Localization of Function vs. Mass Action The principle of localization of function refers to the idea that different aspects of brain function, such as visual perception vs. the control of our emotions vs. our talents as musicians, are governed by, and therefore localizable to, different "centers" in the brain. An analogy might be that different functions of the body – extracting oxygen from blood vs. pumping blood vs. filtering blood – are each accomplished by different organs (i.e., the lungs, the heart, and the kidneys) that are located in different parts of the body. This notion can be contrasted with an alternative idea, **mass action**, according to which a particular function can't necessarily be localized to a specific area of the brain, and, conversely, any given area of the brain can't be thought of as a "center" that is specialized for any one function. To stick with our analogy to familiar parts of the body below the neck, we can illustrate the principle of mass action by zeroing in on the kidney. The overall function of the kidney – filtering blood – is carried out in the same way by the top portion, the middle portion, and the bottom portion. To understand how the kidney does its job, one could study in detail the inner workings of only the top, or only the middle, or only the bottom of this organ, and one would learn the same thing from each. In effect, then, different zones of the kidney are "interchangeable" with respect to understanding their functions. Now project yourself back in time a few centuries to a time when what I've just written hasn't yet been discovered. It is an era when biomedical research techniques are limited, and the best tool that you have for studying the function of an organ is to damage a portion of it and then observe the consequent impact of this damage on its function. Your kidney research would indicate that damaging comparable-sized regions of the upper vs. middle vs. lower kidney has the same effect in all cases: an overall decline in the efficacy of blood filtration. Thus, you would have discovered that a principle of mass action applies to the kidney: a larger **lesion** results in a larger diminishment of the rate of blood filtration; smaller lesions result in a smaller diminishment of the rate of blood filtration; and, critically, the effects of damage to different parts of the kidney are the same.

Now, let's return to the functions of the brain. In the decades following the introduction of phrenology, and in some instances in reaction to it, scientists and physicians began pursuing the idea of localization of function in the brain with methods reflecting the maturation of the scientific method that was occurring in many branches of science, from biology to chemistry to physics. At this general level, this entailed the a priori articulation of falsifiable hypotheses (i.e., devising experiments that, if successful, can rule out previously plausible ideas and stating how various possible outcomes would be interpreted prior to performing the experiment) and the design of controlled laboratory experiments that could be replicated in other laboratories. An important advance for studies of the brain, in particular, was the careful analysis of the behavioral consequences resulting from damage to a particular brain structure. This method has come to be known as **neuropsychology**. Armed with this approach, nineteenth-century scientists began to disprove many specific localizationist claims from phrenology. Perhaps most influential were the studies of French scientist Pierre Flourens (1794–1867). A tireless critic of phrenology, Flourens did much of his experimental work with pigeons and dogs. This research was influential on two levels. First, particular experiments of Flourens disproved specific phrenological claims, such as his demonstration that damage to the **cerebellum** disrupted locomotor coordination but had no effect on amativeness (i.e., predilection for sexual arousal), as Gall's model would have predicted. Second, and at a broader level, Flourens' studies of the brain largely failed to find evidence for localization of many functions. Thus, although damage to the brain invariably produced marked disruption of behaviors associated with judging, remembering, and perceiving, these impairments seemed to occur regardless of what part of the brain had been damaged. By inference, such results seemed to indicate that all regions of the brain contributed equally to these behaviors. (Note that the same was not true of Flourens' studies of the brainstem, to which, e.g., the cerebellum belongs.) (*Figure 1.2*).

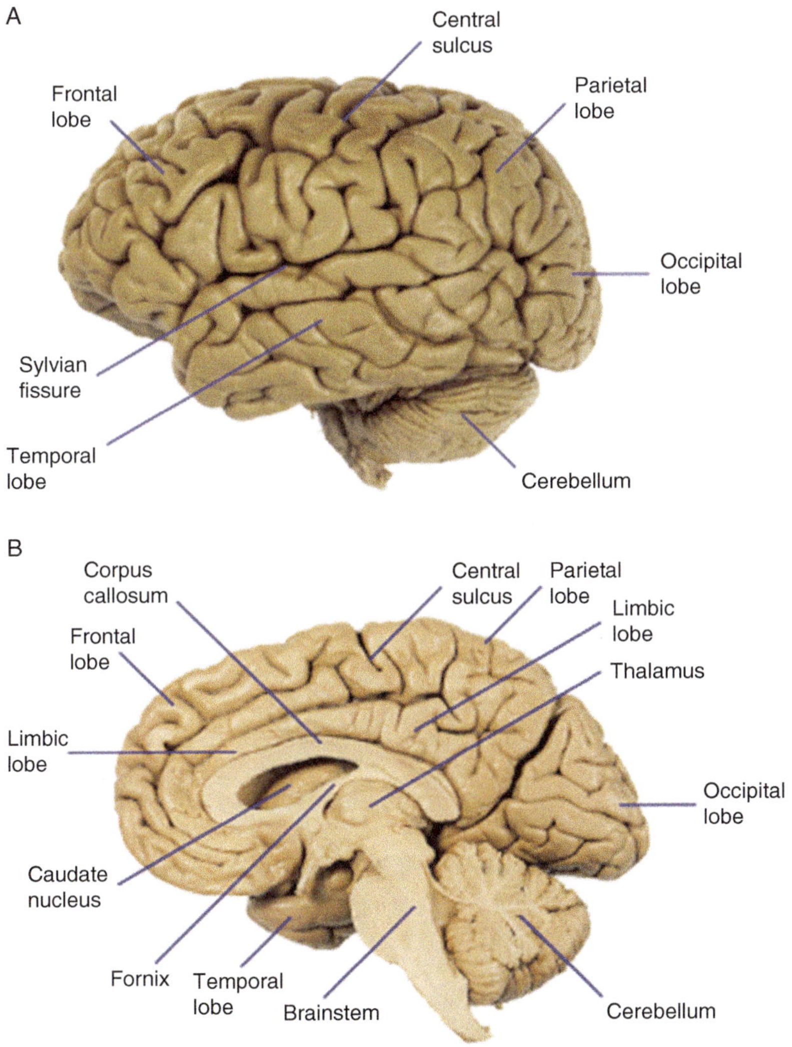

FIGURE 1.2 The human brain (see *Chapter 2* for labels and terminology). **A.** Lateral view. **B.** Medial view.

Source: Dr. Colin Chumbley / Science Source.

Another important concept to come out of the work of Flourens was derived from the fact that, over time, animals with experimental damage to a part of the cortex often recovered to presurgical levels of functioning. Because this occurred without evident repair of the damaged tissue itself, it was assumed that intact areas of the brain had taken over this function. This gave rise to the concept of **equipotentiality**, the idea that any given piece of cortical tissue had the potential to support any brain function.

Roughly 60 years prior to the preparation of the third edition of this textbook, and 130 years after the heyday of phrenology, neuroscientists Charles Gross and Lawrence Weiskrantz wrote that "The 'heroic age of our field' was opened by Gall (1835) . . . [who] stimulated the search for centers and gave the mass action-localization pendulum its first major swing" (Gross and Weiskrantz, 1964). Implied in this quote was that understanding the localization–mass action dichotomy would provide insight into understanding key contemporary problems in neuroscience. Indeed, this theme will prove to be useful for understanding many of the concepts and controversies that are prominent in contemporary cognitive neuroscience.

The First Scientifically Rigorous Demonstrations of Localization of Function Although the concepts advocated by Gall, on the one hand, and Flourens, on the other hand, still resonate today, the same cannot be said for most of the "facts" that arose from their work. Rather, it was in the mid-to-late 1800s, during what can be seen as the first return of Gross and Weiskrantz's pendulum back toward localization, that we see the emergence of principles of brain function that, at least to a first order of approximation, have held up through to the present day. These involved the functions of motor control, vision, and language.

The Localization of Motor Functions

Beginning in the 1860s, British neurologist John Hughlings Jackson (1835–1911) described the systematic trajectory of certain focal **seizures** that appear to start in the fingers and spread along the arm toward the trunk, sometimes ending with a loss of consciousness. From this distinctive pattern, which has since come to be known as the *Jacksonian march* (it's as though the seizure is "marching" along the body), Jackson proposed that the abnormal brain activity presumed to be the cause of this progression of abnormal muscle contractions begins in a part of the brain that controls the fingers, then moves continuously along the surface of the brain, progressively affecting areas that control the palm of the hand, the wrist, the forearm, and so forth. There were two important implications of Jackson's theory. The first was quite simply the proposal that the capacity for movement of the body (i.e., skeletomotor control) is a function that is localized within the brain. The second was what has come to be understood as a fundamental principle underlying the organization of function within many portions of the brain, which is that their organization can mirror the organization of the body (or, as we shall see, of a particular part of the body). Specifically, in this case, the proposal was that the area of the brain that controls the muscles of the fingers is adjacent to the area of the brain that controls the muscles of the palm, which is adjacent to the area of the brain that controls the muscles of the wrist, and so forth. Thus, the functions of what came to be known as the *motor cortex* are physically laid out on the surface of the brain in a kind of map of the body (i.e., in a **somatotopy**). In this way, the idea of a lawful, **topographic organization** of function was introduced in the void left by the (by-now-largely-discredited) arbitrary, willy-nilly scheme of the phrenologists. (The principles and characteristics of somatotopy will be considered in detail in *Chapter 3* and *Chapter 8*.)

Although the ideas that Jackson proposed were based on careful observation of patients, an idea such as the somatotopic organization of the motor cortex couldn't be definitively evaluated without either direct observation or, preferably, manipulation of the brain itself. The ability to undertake such definitive empirical investigation became possible because the Age-of-Enlightenment advances in thinking about how science should be conducted, such as the refinement of the scientific method, were being paralleled by technical advances that afforded improved experimental methods. Of particular importance was the development of methods for performing aseptic (i.e., sterile) surgery. These enabled experimenters to keep animals alive for weeks or longer after performing the **craniotomy** that was necessary to create a lesion or to manipulate the functioning of a specific part of the brain. Prior to this, infection would often limit post-surgical survival to a matter of hours or days. This technical advance had several important consequences, one of which was that it opened the way for direct stimulation of, and subsequently recording from, the brain of an intact animal (techniques that fall under the category of **neurophysiology**). Thus, it was that German physicians Gustav Fritsch (1838–1927) and Eduard Hitzig (1838–1907) reported that electrical stimulation of **anterior** portions of the cerebral cortex of a dog, in the frontal lobe, produced movements on the opposite side of the body (Fritsch and Hitzig, 1870). Noteworthy were two facts. First, comparable stimulation of a more **posterior** brain region, the parietal lobe, did not produce body movements (*Figure 1.3*). Based on this demonstration of the **anatomical specificity** of their effect, Fritsch and Hitzig explicitly challenged the applicability of equipotentiality (as had been advocated by Flourens) for skeletomotor control. Second, the part of the body affected by electrical stimulation (e.g., neck, forelimb, hind limb) varied systematically with the positioning of the stimulating electrode. This observation very directly supported Jackson's idea of a somatotopic organization of motor functions in the brain.

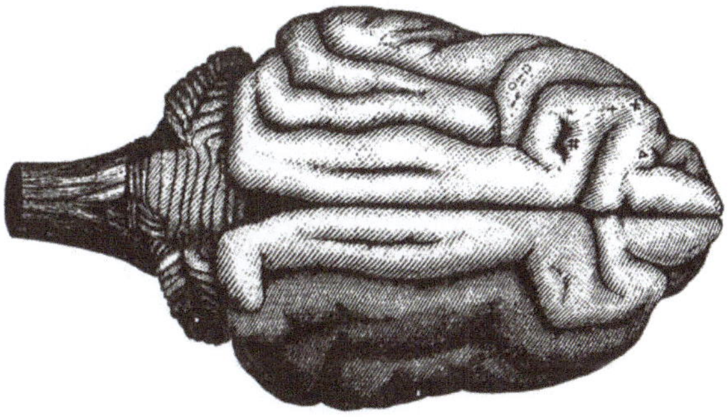

FIGURE 1.3 Illustration of a top-down view of a dog's brain, with symbols indicating, from rostral to caudal, the areas whose stimulation produced muscle contractions on the right side of the body of the neck, forelimb, and hind limb, respectively.

Source: Fritsch, Gustav, and Eduard Hitzig. 1870. "Über die elektrische Erregbarkeit des Grosshirns." *Archiv für Anatomie, Physiologie und wissenschaftliche Medicin* 37: 300–332. Public Domain.

The Localization of Visual Perception

A second function that was the focus of intense scientific investigation during this period was visual perception. Here, too, the work of Flourens had been influential. Although it had brought to light the principle of crossed lateralization of function – in that lesions of the left hemisphere produced visual impairments in the right visual field, and vice versa – it had found no evidence that this general pattern varied as a function of *where* in the hemisphere the lesion was made. That is, Flourens had failed to find evidence for localization of visual function within a **cerebral hemisphere**. As with other of his null findings, however, this one was overturned thanks to the advent of newer, better, experimental methods. In the case of vision research, the refinement of methods of experimental lesioning was the critical development that led to an important discovery. As noted earlier, the development of aseptic surgical techniques resulted in longer and healthier postsurgical survival of experimental animals than had previously been possible. This, in turn, afforded considerably more sophisticated and conclusive assessments of behavior. Indeed, for a time, it was not uncommon for a researcher to bring a lesioned animal to a scientific conference so as to demonstrate the behavioral alterations produced by a particular lesion. Perhaps for related reasons, this period also saw an increase in research with monkeys, whose brain and behavior are more comparable to those of humans than are those of, say, birds and carnivores. It is much more expensive to acquire and house monkeys relative to other species, such as birds, rodents, and carnivores. Thus, research with monkeys would not have been considered practical prior to nineteenth-century refinements of surgical techniques.

Using electrical stimulation techniques and surgical lesioning, initial research in dogs and monkeys indicated a privileged role for posterior regions in supporting visual perception. That is, whereas it had been shown conclusively that motor control did *not* depend on posterior regions, the opposite was true for vision. The final decades of the nineteenth century witnessed vociferous debate about whether the "visual centers," a characterization of British physiologist David Ferrier (1843–1928), were localized to a region of the parietal lobe or to a region of the occipital lobe (*Figure 1.4*). This research, carried out primarily in monkeys and most prominently by Ferrier, by Berlin-based physiologist Hermann Munk (1839–1912), and by London-based physiologist Edward Schäfer (1850–1935), gradually converged on the conclusion that the region whose destruction produced frank and lasting blindness – as opposed to more nuanced and transient visual deficits – was the occipital cortex. This conclusion,

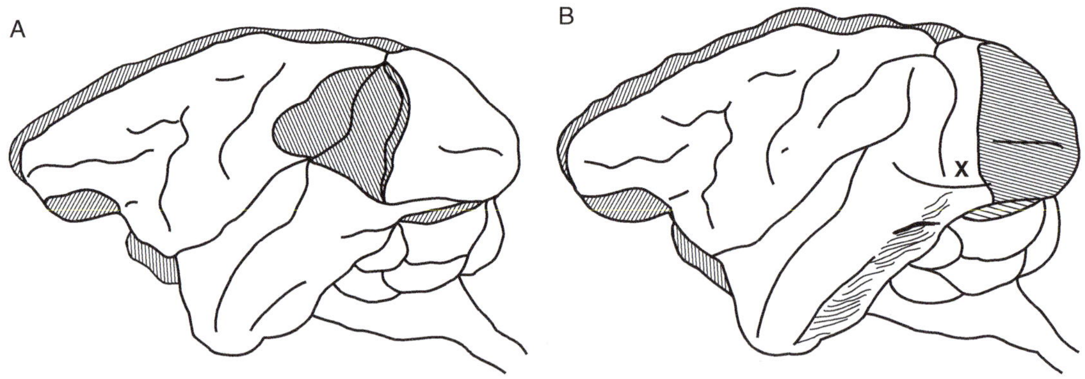

FIGURE 1.4 Two experimental lesions produced by Ferrier in experiments designed to localize the cortical locus of visual processing. Panel **A** illustrates a lesion of the parietal lobe that Ferrier interpreted in 1876 as producing lasting blindness and, a decade later, as producing only temporary blindness. Panel **B** illustrates a lesion of the occipital lobe that he interpreted as producing no visual impairments. Neuroscientist Charles Gross (1998) has marked with an X the region that we now know to represent central (i.e., foveal) vision, a topic to be explored in depth in *Chapter 4*. These lesions, and their interpretation, illustrate how difficult it was for nineteenth-century neuroscientists to localize cognitive functions in the brain.

reinforced by observations of human patients with head injuries, led to the universally accepted localization of the **primary visual cortex** to the occipital lobe.

The Localization of Speech

The last function of the brain that we will consider in this introductory chapter is language, more specifically, the ability to speak. Recall that the faculty of language had been declared by phrenologists to arise from a region of the frontal lobe directly behind the eyes. As was the case with motor control, the post-phrenology study of language began with clinical observations. In the decades prior to the 1860s, isolated reports suggested, in some cases, that damage to the left side of the brain was associated with impairments of speech, and in others, that damage to anterior portions of the brain had this effect. As these cases accumulated, the more specific idea emerged that anterior portions of the left hemisphere were important for speech. During the 1860s, French surgeon Paul Broca (1824–1880) published a series of case studies that confirmed this idea. Most celebrated was the case of the **stroke** patient "Tan," so nicknamed because this was the only sound that he could make with his mouth. (Phonetically, "tan" is pronounced in French as /tôn/.) Importantly, Tan's impairment was considered to be specific to *speech production* (i.e., talking), because he could understand and follow verbal instructions that he was given. Additionally, there wasn't any obvious paralysis of the speech apparatus, in that, despite some right-side-of-the-body motor impairment, he could eat and drink and make his famous verbal utterance. Upon Tan's death, Broca examined the patient's brain and concluded from the prominent damage that he observed (*Figure 1.5*) that the ability to speak was localized to the "posterior third of the third convolution" (a portion of the left inferior frontal gyrus that today is known as Broca's area). It's worth taking a moment to consider why Broca, rather than some of his predecessors and contemporaries who had made similar observations of patients, gets the credit for this discovery. One important factor is that Broca's reports were seen as confirming an idea that had been predicted ahead of time – a sequence of events that fit with the era's increasing emphasis on hypothesis testing as an important element of the scientific method.

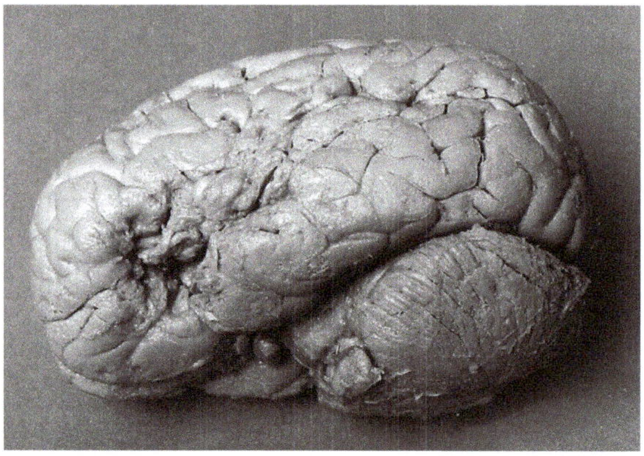

FIGURE 1.5 The left external surface of the brain of Broca's patient Tan. Note the extensive damage in the posterior inferior frontal gyrus, a region that has come to be known as Broca's area.

Source: N. F. Dronkers et al. (2007) / with permission of Oxford University Press.

What Is a Brain and What Does It Do?

As we conclude this whirlwind review of the birth of modern brain science, it is instructive to consider why *motor control*, *vision*, and *language* were among the first three functions of the brain to yield to newly developed ways of thinking about and doing science. With particular relevance to the first two, let's pose the general questions of *what is a brain*? and *what does it do*? For example, what properties do animals with brains share that living organisms without brains (trees, for example) do not? One answer is that brains confer the ability to detect changes in the environment – let's say a falling rock – and to take an appropriate action: to get out of the way. The hapless tree, on the other hand, has no means of acquiring the information that something potentially dangerous is happening nor the ability to do anything about it. So it gets crushed. Thus, the ability to see (i.e., vision) and the ability to move (i.e., skeletomotor control) are functions that are relatively easy to observe and measure. The same is not true for more nuanced examples of brain-mediated events that occur in the world. Let's take the example of writing the textbook that you're reading right now. Certainly, vision and motor control were involved. (E.g., when the author received an emailed inquiry from the publisher about writing this textbook, he used vision to read the pattern of black and white characters on the computer screen that conveyed the inquiry from the publisher.) There were also, however, many additional steps. These included judgment and decision-making (*Is it worth all the extra work to take this on? Are the terms of the contract with the publisher acceptable?*), retrieving long-term memories (*There's that great quote from Gross's chapter in the Warren & Akert book that I should use here*), making (and retrieving) new long-term memories (*Where did I put* my *copy of the* MIT Encyclopedia of the Cognitive Sciences *the last time I was working on this chapter?*), and much, much, more. These latter operations are "internal" or "mental," in the sense that they happened in the author's mind without any obvious way of seeing or measuring them. Thus, although many aspects of so-called high-**level cognition** – including decision-making and memory – are the focus of intense research in contemporary cognitive neuroscience, we shall see that the ability to define what constitutes a distinct function (analogous to vision or motor control), and the ability to localize the brain region(s) on which these functions depend, become much more complicated propositions. The principles that explain how such functions work will be less accessible to direct observation and measurement than are brain functions that are more closely tied to either the "input" of information to the brain (for which vision provides one important channel) or the "output" of the brain that is expressed via movements of the body (i.e., the actions of the organism). (However, as we shall see, there are influential perspectives on brain function as a whole that construe it as a hierarchically organized series of sensorimotor circuits, with the more abstract ones [e.g., all the processes that went into writing a textbook] having been superimposed, over the course of evolution, onto more basic ones [e.g., reflexive avoidance of a threat].)

Okay, so the neural bases of vision and motor control may have been among the first to be studied scientifically because they are easy to observe. But the same cannot be said about language. Although its production clearly has motoric components, we've already reviewed ways in which the language impairment experienced by Tan and other patients was fundamentally different than paralysis. Indeed, in ways, language can be construed as being at the opposite end of the concrete-to-abstract continuum of human faculties that spans from such "concrete" (i.e., easily observable and relatively easily measurable) functions as vision and motor control to the most abstract aspects of conscious thought. Although language is readily observable, there is also a sense in which it epitomizes abstract, high-level cognition. One reason is that language entails the use of arbitrary, abstract codes (i.e., a **natural language**) to represent meaning. Intuitively, because many of us have the sense that we "think in words," language can be viewed as "the stuff of thought" and thus epitomizes an "internal," indeed, a *cognitive*, function. And so I'm reticent to conclude that language was among the first human faculties to be studied with modern neuroscientific techniques because it is easy to observe. Instead, what I'll offer is that it is language's intuitive "specialness," and its seeming uniqueness to humans, that has made it a focus of interest for millennia. The Age of Enlightenment, then, may simply be the epoch of human history when developments in the scientific method caught up with an age-old focus of human curiosity.

Looking Ahead to the Development of Cognitive Neuroscience

To conclude this introductory chapter, we see that by the dawn of the twentieth century, brain scientists were beginning to investigate the brain from both ends of the continuum that captures its functions in relation to the outside world. In the process, we can think of modern brain science as developing along two paths. The first, pursued by physiologists and anatomists who studied brain structure and function in nonhuman animals, focused on neural *systems* that support various functions (e.g., visual perception and motor control) and has come to be known as **systems neuroscience**. The second took as its starting point a human behavior, such as language, and proceeded with the logic that careful study of the way that this behavior is altered by insults to the brain can be informative, with respect both to how the behavior is organized and to how the workings of the brain give rise to this organization. This latter approach has matured into the allied disciplines of behavioral neurology (when carried out by physicians) and neuropsychology (when carried out by nonphysician scientists). Now, of course, the notion of two categories of brain science developing in parallel at the dawn of modern brain science is an overly facile dichotomization imposed by this author, and many instances can be found that do not fit neatly into such a taxonomy. Nonetheless, we will find this distinction to be useful as we proceed. It is these two scientific traditions summarized in this chapter, together with a third, experimental psychology (which also got its start in the second half of the nineteenth century, but which won't be covered in depth here [see *Further reading* section]), that provide the foundation from which modern cognitive neuroscience has emerged. Before we plunge full-on into cognitive neuroscience itself, however, we need to review some facts about the brain – how it is put together (gross anatomy) and how it works (cellular physiology and network dynamics). These will be the focus of *Chapter 2*.

End-of-Chapter Questions

1. How does cognitive neuroscience differ from the related disciplines of cognitive psychology and systems neuroscience?

2. Although most of the specific claims arising from phrenology turned out to be factually incorrect, in what ways did phrenology represent an important development in our thinking about the brain?

3. One of the major flaws of phrenology concerns the functions that it sought to relate to the brain: in some cases, they were not valid constructs; in others, they weren't amenable to neuroscientific explanation at the level that Gall was seeking to capture. From the phrenological bust in *Figure 1.1*, select at least one putative function (other than conscientiousness) to which each of these critiques applies, and explain your reasoning.

4. In the nineteenth century, what kind(s) of scientific evidence was (were) marshaled to support mass-action models of the brain? To support localizationist models of the brain?

5. Might it be possible that some tenets of mass-action and localization-of-function models could both be true? If yes, how might this be possible?

6. How does the concept of anatomical specificity relate to testing hypotheses of mass action and localization of function?

7. The neural bases of what domains of behavior were the first to be systematically explored in the second half of the nineteenth century? For each, what is a likely explanation?

8. What is the principle of topographic representation in the brain? Although this chapter emphasized the topographic organization of the motor system, according to what principles/dimensions might the topography of various sensory modalities (e.g., vision, somatosensation, audition) be organized?

9. Apart from one study that employed electrical stimulation, this chapter described experiments that relied on inferring the neural bases of a function from observation/measurement of the consequences of damage to different parts of the brain. Nonetheless, there are two fundamentally different ways in which one can pursue such research. Describe them, and name the disciplines of science and/or medicine that are associated with each. Which of the two requires the use of nonhuman experimental animals?

References

Dronkers, Nina F., O. Plaisant, M. T. Iba-Zizen, and E. A. Cabanis. 2007. "Paul Broca's Historic Cases: High Resolution MR Imaging of the Brains of Leborgne and Lelong." *Brain* 130 (5): 1432–1441.

Fritsch, Gustav, and Eduard Hitzig. 1870. "Über die elektrische Erregbarkeit des Grosshirns." *Archiv für Anatomie, Physiologie und wissenschaftliche Medicin* 37: 300–332. [Available in English translation as: Fritsch, Gustav, and Eduard Hitzig. 2009. "Electric Excitability of the Cerebrum (Über die elektrische Erregbarkeit des Grosshirns)." *Epilepsy and Behavior* 15 (2): 123–130. doi: 10.1016/j.yebeh.2009.03.001.].

Gross, Charles G. 1998. *Brain, Vision, Memory*. Cambridge, MA: MIT Press.

Gross, Charles G., and Lawrence Weiskrantz. 1964. "Some Changes in Behavior Produced by Lateral Frontal Lesions in the Macaque." In *The Frontal Granular Cortex and Behavior*, edited by John M. Warren and Konrad Akert (pp. 74–98). New York: McGraw-Hill.

Spurzheim, Johann C. 1834. *Phrenology or the Doctrine of the Mental Phenomenon*, 3rd ed. Boston: Marsh, Capen, and Lyon.

Other Sources Used

Calvin, William H., and George A. Ojemann. 1994. *Conversations with Neil's Brain*. Reading, MA: Addison Wesley.

Finger, Stanley. 1994. *Origins of Neuroscience*. Oxford: Oxford University Press.

Gross, Charles G. 2007. "The Discovery of Motor Cortex and Its Background." *Journal of the History of the Neurosciences: Basic and Clinical Perspectives* 16 (3): 320–331. doi: 10.1080/09647040600630160.

Holyoak, Keith J. 1999. "Psychology." In *The MIT Encyclopedia of the Cognitive Sciences*, edited by Robert A. Wilson and Frank C. Keil (pp. xxxix–xlix). Cambridge, MA: MIT Press.

Kolb, Bryan, and Ian Q. Whishaw. 2003. *Fundamentals of Human Neuropsychology*, 5th ed. New York: Worth Publishers.

Whitaker, Harry A. 1999. "Broca, Paul." In *The MIT Encyclopedia of the Cognitive Sciences*, edited by Robert A. Wilson and Frank C. Keil (pp. 97–98). Cambridge, MA: MIT Press.

Further Reading

Boring, Edwin G. 1929. "The Psychology of Controversy." *Psychological Review* 36 (2): 97–121.

A classic overview of key developments in nineteenth-century psychology and psychophysics, adapted from Boring's Presidential Address to the American Psychological Association, delivered on December 28, 1928. Boring was a professor at Harvard University.

Finger, Stanley. 2000. *Minds Behind the Brain*. Oxford: Oxford University Press.

A history, stretching from ancient Egypt to twentieth-century North America and Europe, of scientists who have made seminal contributions to the understanding of the structure and functions of the brain. It is longer and covers a broader scope of topics than Gross (1998). Finger has authored many authoritative books on the history of neuroscience and is Editor-in-Chief of the Journal of the History of the Neurosciences.

Gross, Charles G. 1998. *Brain, Vision, Memory*. Cambridge, MA: MIT Press.

A highly engaging collection of "Tales in the history of neuroscience." It spans the same range of human history as does Finger (2000), but with fewer chapters and a narrower focus on the functions named in the title. The author is, himself, a highly respected visual neuroscientist, now Emeritus Professor at Princeton University.

Ringach, Dario L. 2011. "The Use of Nonhuman Animals in Biomedical Research." *American Journal of Medical Science* 342 (4): 305–313.

Ringach is a UCLA-based neuroscientist whose person, family, and house have been the targets of harassment and intimidation by animal rights activists. This fact, however, does not color this even-toned consideration of this debate. Among other things, he urges "civil discourse . . . free of threats and intimidation" and concludes that "The public deserves an open and honest debate on this important topic." The article contains extensive references to original writings by individuals offering many different perspectives on this debate.

CHAPTER 2

Principles of Organization, Structure, and Function

KEY THEMES

- The central nervous system (often abbreviated as CNS) is organized into four parts: the spinal cord, the brainstem, the cerebellum, and the cerebrum.
- The computing elements of the brain are its neurons, whose cell bodies are primarily located in the cortex, on the outside surfaces of the cerebrum and cerebellum, as well as in subcortical nuclei.
- The neocortex of the cerebrum is organized in six layers, each of which has a distinct functional role.
- The neuron has three principal components: the cell body; the branching dendrites, which receive signals from other neurons; and the projecting axon, which sends signals to other neurons.
- Neurons maintain electrical and chemical disequilibria in relation to the surrounding extracellular space, and many neuronal properties and processes can be understood in terms of the maintenance of these disequilibria.
- Neurons transmit information to other neurons via electrical action potentials that are propagated along axons.
- These electrical action potentials are converted to chemical signals – the release of neurotransmitter – at the synapse, the interface between the "sending" and the "receiving" neuron.
- Different types of neurons release different neurotransmitters, the principal "driving" neurotransmitters have either excitatory (depolarizing) or inhibitory (hyperpolarizing) effects on the postsynaptic neuron, whereas the "modulatory" neurotransmitters influence the state of the neuron and can promote longer timescale processes such as learning, or influencing the overall state of arousal of the organism.
- The net effect on a neuron of receiving different molecules of neurotransmitter that influence it at different moments in time is that its membrane potential fluctuates ("oscillates").
- The coordination and control of oscillations in different populations of neurons is an important way that the flow of information in the brain is controlled.
- The brain's representation of the visual world is dictated by the optics of the eye and, in particular, where light from the visual scene falls on the retina.
- The topography of the retina is reflected in the retinotopic organization of the primary visual cortex.

Companion Website: www.wiley.com/go/postle/cognitiveneuroscience3e

- The disproportionate retinal representation of central (i.e., foveal) vision results in its cortical magnification on the surface area of V1 of the cortex.
- A central principle for understanding the response properties of retinal photoreceptors, retinal ganglion cells, neurons of the lateral geniculate nucleus (LGN) of the thalamus, and neurons of primary visual cortex (area V1) is that of the receptive field.
- Auditory perception depends on exquisitely delicate and precise mechanical transmission in the inner ear, including the cochlea.
- The physical properties of the basilar membrane within the cochlea effect a spectral decomposition of acoustic energy, which is read out as a place code by the auditory nerve.
- Many different types of receptors are responsible for the detection of mechanical vs. thermal vs. painful sensations on the skin.
- S1 contains somatotopic maps, distributed across four Brodmann areas in the postcentral gyrus of the primate.

CONTENTS

Pep Talk

Thinking, consciousness, decision making, language – these and topics like them – are what you're expecting to learn about in this book. And you will. But for our explorations to be substantive, it's necessary that we establish a foundation of knowledge about how the brain is organized, structurally, and how it works, as well as an introduction to how measurements of brain structure and function are acquired, analyzed, and interpreted. This necessitates the present chapter (which will cover neuroanatomy and cellular and circulatory neurophysiology) and *Chapter 3* (*The Neurophysiology of Sensation and Perception*), which contain little to no consideration of behavior. Thus, the following pages may be tough sledding for some readers who, for example, may have some background in psychology but not in biology or neuroscience. But it will be good for you! And we just can't get around it. For example, understanding the physiology of the neuron is critical for interpreting neuroimaging data, because while some methods measure electrical fluctuations, others measure changes in blood oxygenation, and others measure changes in the reflectance of light. Thus, valid interpretation of data from a neuroimaging study of, say, face recognition, or emotion regulation, will depend critically on understanding what aspect of brain activity it is that is generating the signal that we are interpreting.

Later in this book, we'll see that one of the traits supported by the prefrontal cortex (PFC) is the ability to choose to engage in behavior for which the reward may not be immediate, but for which it will be worth the wait. And so, in that spirit, let's engage that PFC and dive in!

Gross Anatomy and the Organization of Systems

Brain and Central Nervous System

Like much of the rest of the body, most parts of the brain come in twos. There are two hemispheres, and within each hemisphere, there are five lobes of the **cerebrum** – four of them named after the four bones of the skull under which they lie (frontal, parietal, occipital, and temporal), plus the deep-lying limbic lobe, which is not adjacent to the skull (*Figure 1.2*). The brain belongs to the central nervous system (CNS), which also comprises the cerebellum, the spinal cord, and the motor neurons that leave the cord to innervate the muscles of the body. All of these elements derive, during development of the embryo, from the neural plate, a 2-D sheet of tissue that folds until its edges touch and merge to form the neural tube. In primates, which are bipedal, the CNS makes a right-angle bend between the midbrain and the forebrain such that, when standing erect, the spinal cord, brainstem, and midbrain are oriented vertically, and the forebrain, comprising **diencephalon** (**thalamus**) and cerebrum, is oriented horizontally. Thus, for a standing human, while the directional terms *dorsal* and *ventral* refer to the "back" and "front" of the spinal cord, they refer to the "top" and "bottom" of the brain (*Figure 2.1*).

When you look at a human brain that's been dissected out of a skull the first thing that you notice is how wrinkly it is (*Figure 1.2*, *Figure 1.4*, and *Figure 2.2*). The reason for this makes sense once you understand two facts. The first is that the computational power of the mammalian

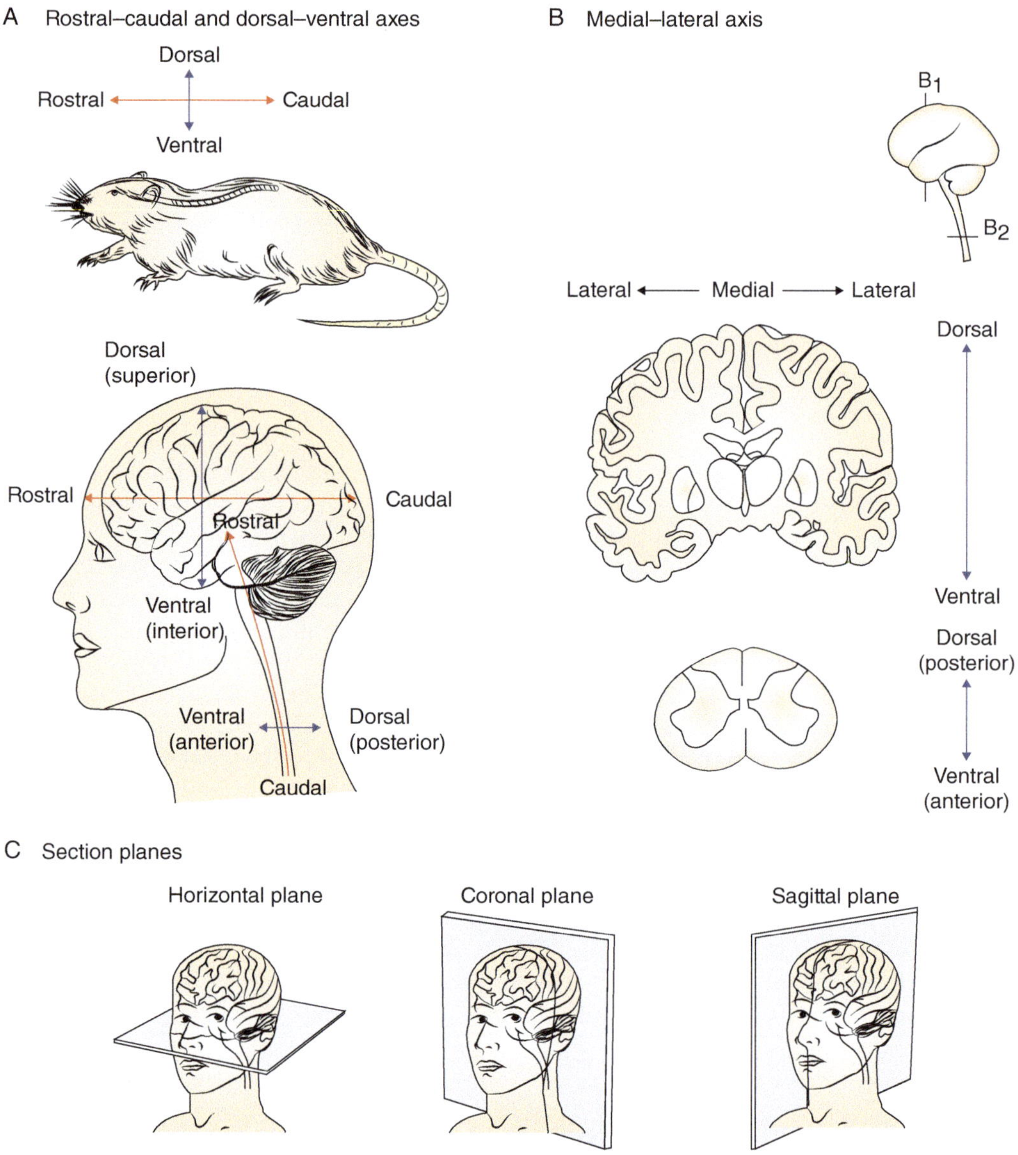

FIGURE 2.1 Terminology for anatomical orientation. **A.** The quadruped. **B.** In the bipedal human, the terminology is complicated by the right-angle bend that the neuroaxis makes between the midbrain and forebrain. **C.** The cardinal planes of section.

Source: Kandel et al., 2000 / McGraw-Hill.

brain is in the cerebral **cortex** – the thin (roughly 2.5-mm-thick) layer of tissue that covers the outside surface of the five lobes of the cerebrum – and in the cortex of two other structures, the **hippocampus** and the cerebellum. (For ease of exposition, this introductory section will focus on the cerebral cortex.) The second is that the cerebral cortex is, in effect, a 2-D sheet, with a surface area of roughly 2500 cm^2. Indeed, if one could "unfold" and flatten out the cortex, it would take roughly the same surface area as a tabloid-style newspaper. Returning to the "wrinkliness," we can now appreciate that "crumpled" might be a better descriptor: Over the course of evolution, as the computational power of the brains of vertebrate species has increased, the ever-larger cerebral cortex has needed to fold ever-tighter onto itself in order to fit inside the roughly spherical skull. The alternative for humans, evolving a thin, 50 cm × 50 cm square (or a comparably sized disk) for a skull might look okay on a creature from a sci-fi anime cartoon but would clearly be highly inefficient, particularly from the standpoint of the amount of "wiring" that would be needed to connect different parts of the brain together. In contrast, it has been calculated that the "crumpled-up" solution with which human brains have evolved yields a cerebrum that is almost optimally shaped to minimize the connection distances between its roughly 80 billion neurons, which make trillions of connections with each other.

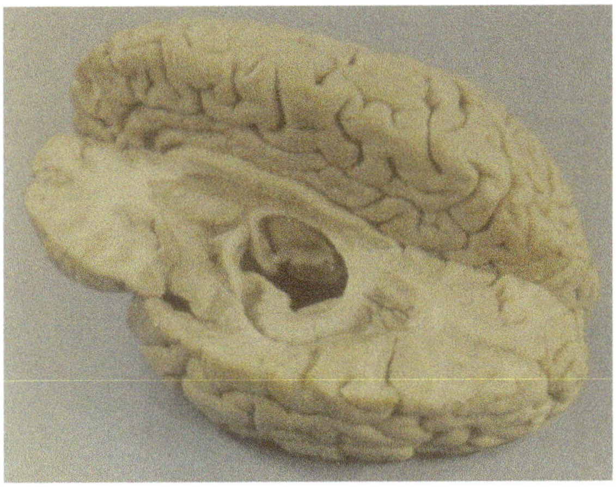

FIGURE 2.2 Human brain with dorsal half of the left hemisphere dissected away with a cut in the axial plane to reveal several subcortical anatomical features. Along the medial surface of the temporal lobe in the left hemisphere is the hippocampus, and the fibers projecting from its medial edge make up a tract called the fornix, which forms an arc as it courses rostrally from the caudal end of the hippocampus to terminate at the mammillary bodies of the hypothalamus. Immediately rostral to the rostral-most extent of the fornix, and to the rostral end of the hippocampus, is the anterior commissure, running in a mediolateral-oriented tract carrying transhemispheric axons between the anterior temporal lobes. The corpus callosum is seen in cross section along the ventral-most portion of the midline that is exposed (e.g., just dorsal to the fornix, and extending further from it both rostrally and caudally). Finally, the medial aspect of the thalamus of the right hemisphere appears as though it is immediately ventral to the arc of the fornix. The surface of the axial cut through the left hemisphere also reveals the depth of many sulci (lined with gray matter), including the intraparietal sulcus at the caudal end of this axial slice.

Source: Reproduced with permission from Warwick and Williams (1973) / Elsevier.

When the brain is sliced, one sees that the cortex looks darker (**gray matter**, although to me it looks more taupe than gray) than the **white matter** that takes up most of the volume of the brain (*Figure 2.2*). The gray matter is the aggregation of hundreds of thousands of brain cells – neurons and "supporting" cells known as **glial cells**. All neurons have a branch via which they communicate with other neurons. These branches, called **axons**, conduct electrical signals that are fundamental to how neurons communicate. Just like the electrical power lines that carry electricity from power plants to the places where the electricity is needed, axons are insulated so as to conduct electrical current efficiently. In the brain, this insulation is a cholesterol-laden substance called **myelin**, and the aggregation of millions of myelinated axons is what makes the white matter look white. As illustrated in *Figure 2.1*, there are three cardinal planes along which brains are typically sliced (either literally, for postmortem tissue, or virtually, in images of in vivo brains derived from brain scans): in vertical cross section ("coronally"), horizontal cross section ("axially"), or vertically along the long axis ("sagittally"). From the coronal section, in particular, as well as from *Figure 2.2*, one can appreciate that many of the brain's "wrinkles" are quite deep. The technical term for one such "wrinkle" is a sulcus (plural, **sulci**). Indeed, if you were to hold a dissected human brain in your hand and rotate it so that you could inspect it from every angle, you'd only be able to see about one-third of the cortical surface. Two-thirds are "hidden" along the walls of sulci, or lining the "middle" walls of each hemisphere. In inspecting a brain like this, you'd be viewing its *lateral* (i.e., "toward the outside edge") surface. Regions nearer to the center of the volume are said to be *medial*. Each "bump" and "ridge" that is visible on the surface of the intact brain is referred to as a gyrus (plural, **gyri**). The dissection featured in *Figure 2.2* was produced via an axial cut through just the left hemisphere plus a partial sagittal cut along the midline, so as to provide a "window" revealing several regions of gray matter that are medial to the cortex (i.e., deep "inside" the brain). Most of these subcortical structures are nuclei – collections of cell bodies that all perform a related function. Also visible in *Figure 2.2* are large bundles of myelinated axons. The largest, the corpus callosum, carries millions of axons projecting from one hemisphere to the other.

Let's return to the visual inspection of the intact brain that we are holding in our hands. The most obvious landmark is the midline, the gap separating the two hemispheres. From the canonical "side view" (as in *Figure 1.2*), we see the two prominent sulci that more-or-less divide the rostral from the caudal half, and we see the distinctive temporal lobe that is located ventrally and oriented parallel to the rostral–caudal axis. The sulcus that forms the dorsal boundary of the temporal lobe is the Sylvian fissure (a fissure being a really big sulcus); the sulcus that's parallel to the caudal-most portion of the Sylvian fissure, and roughly two gyri rostral to it, is the central sulcus. As its name implies, the central sulcus divides the "front half" from the "back half," more precisely, the frontal lobe from the parietal lobe. We shall see that, in functional terms, this anatomical landmark also demarcates, to a first order of approximation, the fundamental distinction of "action" (frontal) vs. "perception" (parietal, temporal, and occipital). The occipital lobe, the caudal-most in the brain, sitting "atop" the cerebellum, has the least obvious boundaries with the two lobes with which it makes contact on its lateral surface, the temporal lobe, ventrally, and the parietal lobe, dorsally.

The tissue connecting the two hemispheres is the thick band of fibers (i.e., axons) that connect neurons of the left hemisphere to those of the right, and vice versa. This is the **corpus callosum**. If one severs the corpus callosum, so as to separate the two hemispheres, one can then inspect the medial surface of either hemisphere (a so-called midsagittal view; *Figure 1.2.B*). This reveals the fifth lobe of the brain, the limbic lobe, which consists primarily of the anterior cingulate gyrus and the posterior cingulate gyrus, the gyri that surround the corpus callosum in its rostral and caudal aspects, respectively (*Figure 1.2.B* and *Figure 2.2*).

Very prominent in the middle of the brain, whether sliced axially, coronally, or sagittally, is a large gray-matter structure called the thalamus. Fittingly, the thalamus acts as a hub for the brain: all incoming sensory information (with the exception of olfaction) is relayed through the thalamus on its way to the cortex. Additionally, the thalamus acts as a node in several circuits, sometimes called "loops," in which information cycles from the cortex to the thalamus and back to the cortex again (in some cases with several other subcortical connections interposed). More details about the anatomy and functions of these "corticothalamic loops" will be considered in subsequent chapters of the book. Because it is so intricate and is organized anatomically according to the different brain systems with which it connects (e.g., the visual system, the auditory system, and the PFC), the thalamus is itself considered to be made up of several nuclei. Throughout the book, as we consider different systems and/or functions, we'll also look more closely at the relevant thalamic **nucleus** (e.g., the lateral geniculate nucleus [LGN] for initial visual processing, the pulvinar nucleus for "higher level" visual processing, the medial geniculate nucleus [MGN] for initial auditory processing, and the mediodorsal [MD] nucleus, among others, for functions of the PFC).

Finally, from any of the dissections that reveal the thalamus, one can also see the hollow chambers that take up a considerable portion of the intracranial volume. These are the **ventricles**, the largest being the lateral ventricle. In living organisms, the ventricles are filled with the **cerebrospinal fluid (CSF)** that bathes the brain on its inside (i.e., ventricular) and outside (i.e., lateral) surfaces. On the lateral surfaces, it circulates between a thin layer of tissue that lies on the surface of the cortex – the pia mater – and the arachnoid membrane, so named because it suggests the appearance of a spider web. Enclosing the arachnoid membrane is the rubbery dura mater, and, finally, there is the bone of the skull. Together, the dura, arachnoid, and pia are referred to as the meninges. (Meningitis is the infection and consequent swelling of this tissue.) The CSF is under pressure, such that it gently inflates the ventricles, and it is in continuous circulation through the ventricles and down the entire length of the spinal cord. For this reason, the CSF extracted via a procedure called a lumbar puncture (also known as a "spinal tap") can be assayed to assess certain measures of brain health. For example, elevated levels of certain proteins in the CSF may signal excessive degeneration of neurons in the brain, as happens in Alzheimer's disease.

A full appreciation of the section that you have just read would likely benefit from spending some time visiting a website with an interactive 3-D model of a brain. (In addition, I strongly encourage you to seek out an opportunity to have the hands-on experience of holding a brain and, if possible, dissecting it. Often, especially in a formal class, the dissection will be performed with the brain of a sheep. At the level of the gross anatomy, you'll find all the structures that have just been described, and the experience will generalize to any mammalian species [including humans] that you may subsequently study in more depth.)

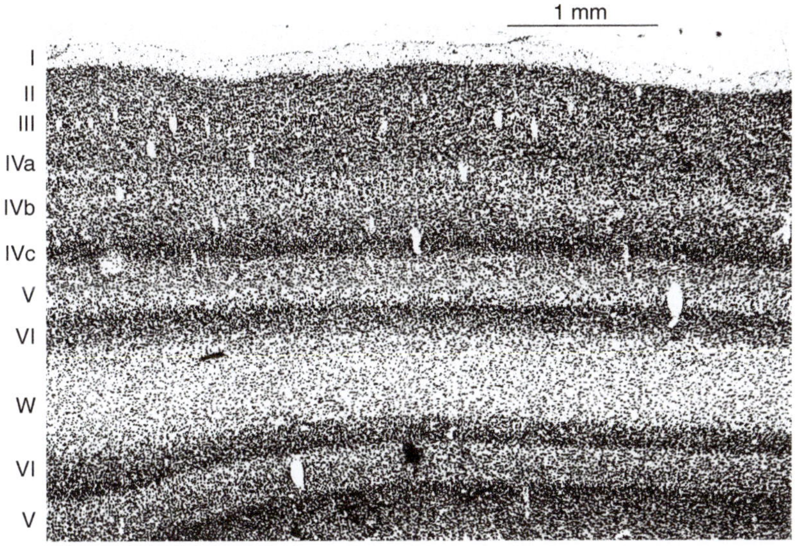

FIGURE 2.3 Cross-sectional view of cortical area V1 of the macaque, illustrating the six layers, including several subdivisions of layer IV. The tissue is from a narrow gyrus such that, at the bottom of the image, below the region of white matter (labeled "W"), one sees the deep layers of a nearby area of cortex.
Source: Reproduced with permission from Hubel and Wiesel (1977) / The Royal Society.

The Cerebral Cortex

The cerebral cortex is also referred to as neocortex, in reference to the fact that it is a relatively new feature of the CNS in evolutionary terms. It is made up of six layers, which are visible when a very thin slice of tissue is viewed under a microscope. The reason that these layers look different is that each is made up of different types of cells and/or tissues that each have a characteristic shape and packing density (*Figure 2.3*).

The central layer, layer IV, is the layer that receives input from the thalamus. Thus, in the case of primary visual cortex ("area V1"), for example, the neurons of layer IV are the first cortical neurons to begin processing signals relating to, say, the photons reflecting off this page of the book (or, alternatively, emanating from the screen you are looking at). Layers II and III have subtle differences, but for the purposes of this textbook, they can be thought of as being functionally a single layer and will often be referred to as "layer II/III." The property of layer II/III that will be emphasized here is that neurons from this layer tend to be those that send information to higher levels of the cortex. As illustrated in *Figure 2.4*, it is neurons of layer II/III of the second visual processing area ("V2") that project to a higher-level visual processing area ("V4"). (More details on what is meant by "project to" are considered in the next section, *The Neuron*; more details on the organization of the visual system are in *Chapters 3 and 6*.) Because the flow of visual information can be construed as traveling from the retina to the LGN of the thalamus, from thalamus to V1, from V1 to V2, and from V2 to V4, the layer II/III projections from V2 to V4 are considered feedforward connections. The neurons of layers V and VI tend to be those that send feedback projections to earlier levels of cortex. (Depending on the region of the brain, corticocortical feedback projections may arise predominantly from layer V or from layer VI.) Finally, neurons from layer VI (and sometimes also layer V) tend to be those that send their projections to the thalamus, or to other subcortical structures (*Figure 2.4*). (Note that this and the subsequent paragraph are referring to **pyramidal cells**, one of the two general classes of cortical neurons that will be described in more detail in the ensuing section, *The Neuron*.) (As you are seeing, although it is not universally employed, a common convention is to identify cortical layers with Roman numerals.)

As we shall see in the next paragraph, it's often convenient to refer to one layer of cortex as being "above" or "below" another (as in *layer IV is located below layer II/III*). The reason that this can be problematic, however, is evident from inspecting the cartoon of a coronal slice illustrated in *Figure 2.1.B*. If we consider the cortex located on the ventral surface of

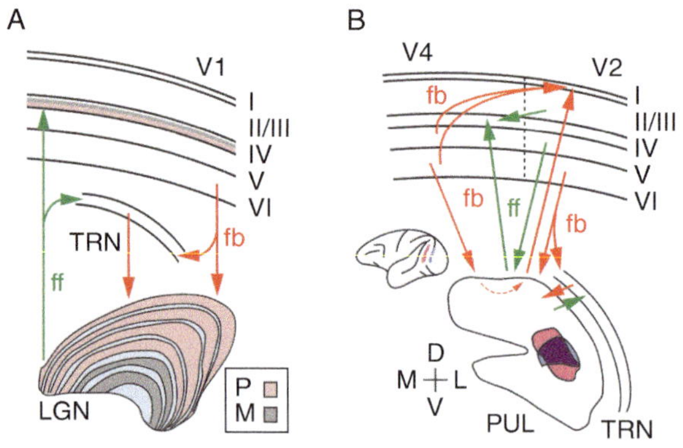

FIGURE 2.4 Schematic illustration of thalamocortical and corticocortical feedforward (ff) and feedback (fb) projections. Panel **A** illustrates the projections from the LGN (diagrammed in cross section) of the thalamus to layer IV of V1 and from layer VI of V1 back to the LGN. Note that there are six primary layers of the LGN, four containing parvocellular (P) neurons and two containing magnocellular (M) neurons (to be detailed in *Chapter 3*), and that these two types of LGN neuron project to different sublayers of cortical layer IV (to be detailed in *Chapter 6*). Also to be detailed in *Chapter 3* will be the role of the thalamic reticular nucleus (TRN), which receives collaterals from the axons carrying feedforward and feedback signals. Panel **B** illustrates the organization of feedforward and feedback pathways between two higher levels of visual cortex, areas V2 and V4. "Direct" corticocortical feedforward projections go from layer II/III of V2 to layer IV of V4. "Indirect" thalamically mediated feedforward projections go from layer V of V2 to the pulvinar nucleus of the thalamus (PUL) and then from pulvinar to layer IV of V4. Direct corticocortical feedback projections are illustrated as going from layers V and VI of V4 to layer I of V2 (the laminar specificity for this and other interareal projections varies across brain systems and across species). Indirect feedback projections go from layer VI of V4 to the pulvinar nucleus and then from pulvinar to layer I of V2. The small diagram of a lateral view of the macaque brain relates to how these data were generated and will be more easily understood after reading *Chapter 4*'s section on *tract tracing*. For now, we'll just state that it shows where cell bodies in area V4 (pink) and area V2 (blue) each send axons to an overlapping projection zone of the pulvinar nucleus of the thalamus (diagrammed in coronal section).

Source: Saalmann et al., 2011 / with permission of Elsevier.

the Sylvian fissure, and thus defining the dorsal boundary of the temporal lobe, layer II/III is, indeed, above layer IV (e.g., it is closer to the top of the page). For the cortex just dorsal to it, however, on the dorsal surface of the Sylvian fissure, the opposite is true, in that layer IV in this bit of cortex is closer to the top of the page than is layer II/III. This is a simple consequence of the fact that the "crumpled" nature of cortex means that portions of it are oriented in virtually every direction possible. A constant property of the layers of cortex, however, no matter in what part of the brain, or whether the owner of that brain is standing upright, lying on their back, or in any other orientation, is that layer II/III is always closer to the surface of the cortex and layer IV is always closer to the white matter. Thus, their positions relative to each other are most accurately referred to as being superficial (closer to the surface) or deep (further from the surface).

And what about layer I? Layer I is distinctive from all other layers of cortex in that it contains very few cell bodies. Instead, it is made up primarily of the "antennae" (dendrites) extending from neurons in deeper layers, through which they receive signals being sent by neurons in other regions. Indeed, this property of neurons with cell bodies located in one layer having dendrites that extend to another layer is common in all layers of cortex. Another important fact about cortical neurons is that, in addition to the properties of receiving thalamic input, sending feedforward projections, or sending feedback projections, many also send projections to other neurons located in the layer(s) above or below. As a result, groups of neurons that are "stacked" on top of each other (from layer II/III to layer VI) can often be characterized as forming **cortical columns**. As this designation implies, neurons tend to be more strongly interconnected with other neurons within the same column than they are with neurons that are immediately adjacent but that do not belong to the same column. This principle of "columnar organization" will be important for understanding the principles of visual information processing (*Chapter 3* and *Chapter 6*) and auditory and somatosensory information processing (*Chapter 3*) and may also be important in brain areas that process higher-level information (e.g., the PFC, which features prominently in the final section of this book). A final fact about the layers of cortex: depending on the region of the brain, corticocortical connections can terminate in layers I, II/III, and/or V.

As is the case with the section that you've just read, descriptions of the functioning of the brain will often be framed in terms of "the flow of information," or "communication between brain areas." The structural basis for this communication is the connections between neurons via the axonal projections of pyramidal neurons, such as for the feedforward and feedback connections that we have just summarized. The functional basis for this communication, to be reviewed in detail in the section The Neuron, is the release of the excitatory neurotransmitter glutamate. Note, however, that if one were to construct even a relatively simple circuit with only excitatory pyramidal cells, its activity would quickly race out of control, rendering it dysfunctional. (Indeed, this is effectively the state the brain the brain during a seizure.) Indeed, in the healthy brain, the excitatory properties of pyramidal neurons are balanced by the inhibitory properties of the second general class of cortical neuron: the interneuron, which releases the inhibitory neurotransmitter gamma-aminobutyric acid (GABA). In an artificial system, using only generic excitatory and inhibitory processing units, one could construct quite elaborate circuits that could carry out sophisticated operations. In the mammalian brain, however, even though the majority of cortical neurons release only one of two primary neurotransmitters, things are more complicated. In particular, there are several nuclei that lie outside the cerebral cortex but whose neurons project axons into it, releasing neurotransmitters other than glutamate or GABA.

Ascending Neuromodulatory Systems

Although the cerebral cortex and other components of the brain are necessary for carrying out almost all aspects of cognition that we will consider in this book, they do not function in isolation. In particular, several aspects of the functioning of neurons in cortex (and elsewhere) are influenced by the neurotransmitters norepinephrine (NE), serotonin (5-HT, from its chemical structure 5-hydroxytryptamine), dopamine (DA), and acetylcholine (ACh), each synthesized in neurons with cell bodies located in nuclei that are outside the cortex. These nuclei are each located near the midline and are arrayed along a caudal-to-rostral axis extending from the midbrain to the basal forebrain. The caudal-most of these is the locus coeruleus. (Latin for "the blue spot," so named because the accumulation of neuromelanin, a byproduct of the synthesis of NE, gives it a bluish hue.) Next are the raphe nuclei (from the Greek for "seam," because they give the appearance of holding two parts of the brainstem together), a dorsal raphe nucleus and a median raphe nucleus, which synthesize 5-HT. Rostral-most in the midbrain are the substantia nigra pars compacta (SNpc) and the ventral tegmental area (VTA), which synthesize DA. ("Substantia nigra" translates from Latin as "black substance" – DA is chemically similar to NE, and its synthesis also produces neuromelanin – "tegmentum" translates from Latin as "cover" or "lid," and the VTA is the rostral-most part of the brainstem [thus serving as its "lid"].) Rostral to the brainstem is the basal forebrain, a collection of structures at the base of the brain. Among these are the nucleus basalis of Meynert (named after a neuroanatomist) and the septal nuclei (named for their proximity to a "wall" (septum, from the Latin) separating two ventricular compartments), which synthesize ACh. What all of these nuclei have in common is that they send long and widely branching axons that "climb" into the brain and innervate several brain areas, including cerebral cortex and many subcortical structures (*Figure 2.5*). The neurotransmitters that they release each contribute to cognition in distinct ways, as we shall see in subsequent chapters. How do these and other neurotransmitters work? That's a question we'll get to in the next section.

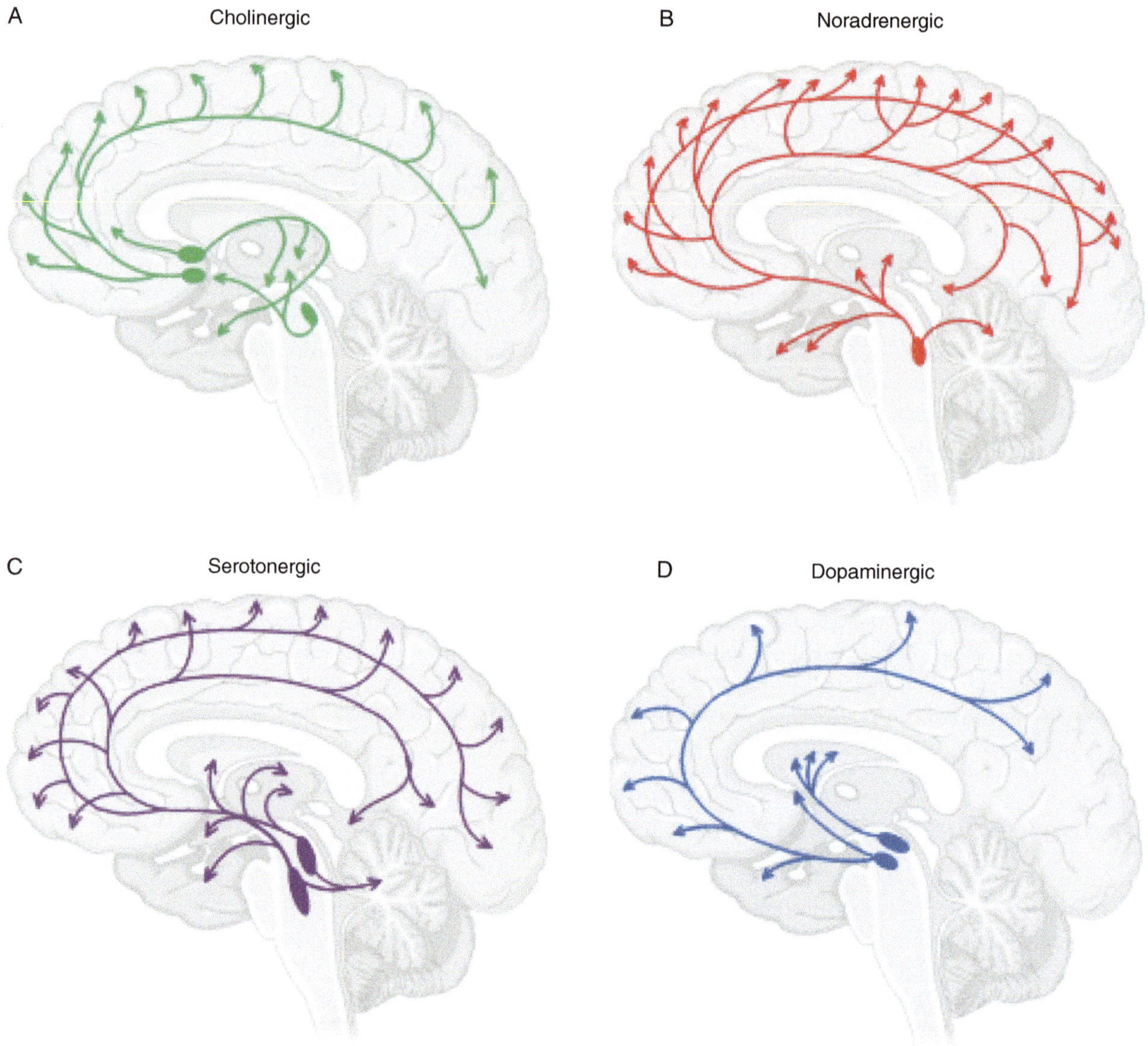

FIGURE 2.5 Nuclei and projection patterns of subcortical neuromodulatory systems. **A.** ACh – basal forebrain, including the septal nuclei (top) and basal nucleus of Meynert (bottom); as well as the brainstem pedunculopontine/laterodorsal tegmental complex. **B.** NE (also referred to as "noradrenalin") – locus coeruleus. **C.** 5-HT – dorsal (top) and median (bottom) raphe nuclei. **D.** DA – substantia nigra (top) and ventral tegmental area (bottom).

Source: (O'Callaghan, Walpola, & Shine, 2021) / The Royal Society.

The Neuron

The elements that give the brain its unique properties are the cells that make it up. Recall from earlier in this chapter that there are many, many different types of cells in the brain, and that many of these are not neurons. For the time being, however, we'll focus on just two classes of cortical neurons: pyramidal cells and interneurons. The pyramidal cell is the canonical neuron. Its large cell body (often referred to as the *soma*, from the Greek for "body") has a 3-D shape that resembles a pyramid, with antenna-like dendrites sprouting from the soma, particularly its pointy "top," and the axon leaving from the base of the cell (*Figure 2.6*). Typically, the dendrites, like the branches of a tree, spread themselves out over an area much larger than that taken up by the cell body itself (the soma being the trunk in this analogy). The function of

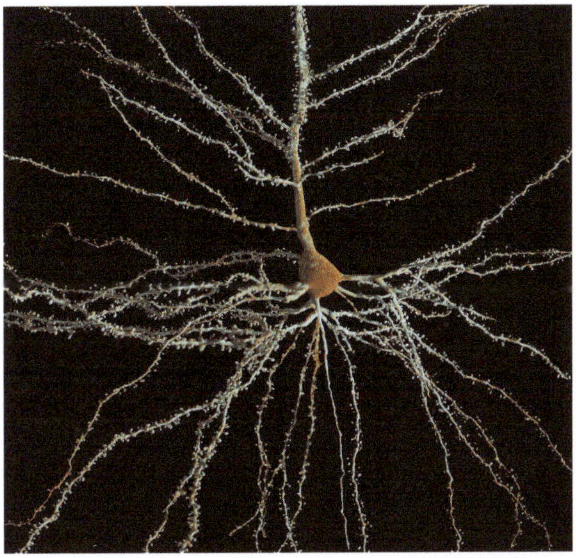

FIGURE 2.6 A pyramidal neuron from layer III of the PFC of a monkey. Branching out from the "corners" at the base of the pyramid-shaped soma are the basal dendrites, and projecting up toward the top of the page is the trunk of the apical dendrite, which will branch extensively when it reaches layer I (not shown). Each dendritic branch is studded with spines, submicron-sized protrusions at the end of which a synapse is formed with an axon. Extending from the base of the soma and projecting straight down and off the bottom of the image is this neuron's axon, distinguishable as the only process (i.e., the only "branch") that is not studded with spines. To generate this image, the neuron was first microinjected with a dye, and then images were acquired with a laser confocal microscope. For details about the method, see Dumitriu, Rodriguez, and Morrison (2011); Morrison and Baxter (2012, *Further reading*) demonstrate the use of this method to study the effects of aging in the PFC.

Source: Courtesy of John H. Morrison, PhD. Reconstruction done by The Visual MD.

dendrites is to receive messages from other neurons (i.e., it is along dendrites that connections are formed with axons from other neurons). The axon, as we've already discussed, conveys signals from the neuron in question to other neurons. (Note that it is almost never the case that a neuron makes contact with just one other neuron. Rather, axons typically have multiple branches [in some cases, thousands], each of which ends in a synaptic terminal and many of which also have synaptic varicosities along their length. The action potential propagates equally along each branch.) So let us now consider the nature of these electrical signals.

Electrical and Chemical Properties of the Neuron

It may be difficult to find a single definition of "life" that any two people would find fully acceptable. Nonetheless, one (admittedly overly reductive) stab at a definition would be a system that is able to actively maintain itself in a high-energy state. This is a definition that draws on thermodynamics, in that it invokes the general tendency for nonliving objects in our universe to dissipate (or acquire) energy so that their own level of energy matches that of the surrounding environment. As one example, food that is removed from a hot oven and left on the countertop will cool until its temperature matches that of the kitchen. Similarly, food taken out of the freezer and left on the countertop will warm up until it achieves room temperature. In terms of their temperature, these nonliving objects passively give off or take on energy until they reach an equilibrium, which is the ambient temperature of the kitchen. Neurons maintain life by maintaining a *dis*equilibrium along two dimensions, electrical and chemical. With regard to the former, a neuron in its baseline state will maintain a negative voltage of approximately −70 mV relative to the extracellular space that surrounds it. It achieves this by maintaining a lower concentration of positively charged ions relative to the extracellular space. In addition to this electrical disequilibrium, the neuron at rest maintains a chemical disequilibrium by "hoarding" a high concentration of potassium (K^+) ions relative to the extracellular space and maintaining a relatively low concentration of sodium ions (Na^+) and calcium ions (Ca^{2+}) relative to the extracellular space. (Recall that the membranes of all cells in the body are made up of a lipid bilayer that, because it repels water, separates the watery cytoplasm [and all dissolved or floating in it] inside the cell from the watery extracellular fluid [and all dissolved or floating in it].)

The consequence of the electrical and chemical imbalances in the neuron is that if a hole were to be poked in the membrane of a neuron, two events would happen: (1) the electrical gradient would be reduced by an influx of positively charged ions into the cell (including Na^+ and Ca^{2+} ions); (2) simultaneously, the chemical gradient would be reduced by an efflux of K^+ from the relatively higher K^+ concentration inside the cell. (And note that the influx of Na^+ ions from (1) would also be reducing the chemical gradient of a relatively lower concentration of Na^+ ions inside the cell.) As you might imagine, however, the workings of the neuron are much more orderly and regulated than the poking of holes. Indeed, the membrane of the neuron is punctuated with channels that can open and close, thereby allowing the passage of certain types of ions in a highly regulated manner. Most of these channels have differential permeability to different types of ions and are only activated under certain conditions. One example is the voltage-gated Na^+ channels that are concentrated at (or near, depending on the type of neuron) the **axon hillock**, the region where the bulky cell body funnels down into the long tube that is the axon. These channels are closed when the neuron is at rest (i.e., with a membrane potential of −70 mV). However, when the neuron has been sufficiently **depolarized** (e.g., the voltage raised to roughly −20 mV, the precise voltage can vary depending on cell type), these channels open and allow for the (very rapid) influx of Na^+ ions. Recall that this influx is propelled by both the electrical gradient and the chemical gradient that exist across the cell membrane. This influx of Na^+ ions gives rise to the action potential (or "spike" in neurophysiology vernacular), which is the basis for neuronal communication.

Ion Channels The membrane-spanning channels of neurons are made up of complexes of proteins that span the membrane from the intra- to extracellular space. The channel's walls are formed by several subunits, each a molecule of protein (i.e., a polypeptide chain), as is illustrated in *Figure 2.7*. A channel's specificity for one type of ion is determined by the physical size of its pore (e.g., Na^+ channels are simply too small to allow large ions or molecules (including, e.g., Ca^{2+}) to pass through), as well as by the properties of binding sites located in the pore of some channels that result in preferential permeability to some ions over others. When closed (i.e., "at rest"), the subunits making it up are twisted together, such that the pore is too narrow for anything to pass through. When activated, the channel "untwists" (due to a change in conformational state of one or more of the subunits), thereby enlarging the pore and allowing ions to pass through. Depending on the type of channel, activation is accomplished by a change of membrane voltage (such as for the voltage-gated Na^+ channels that we just considered, these are found, e.g., at the axon hillock), by the binding of a molecule of neurotransmitter to a binding site (a so-called "ligand-gated" channel), or by activation of the channel via chemical signaling from within the cell. The so-called "driving" neurotransmitters **glutamate** and **GABA**, which will be considered in detail in the upcoming section on *Different neurotransmitters and different receptors can produce different effects on the postsynaptic cell*, have their effects by activating ligand-gated channels. That is, the binding site and channel are part of the same receptor complex, and when the ligand binds at the binding site, this triggers the channel to open. An example of a third type of channel are those triggered by the neurotransmitter dopamine (DA). (There are many subclasses of DA receptor, but all work on the same principles.) The DA receptor is not part of a larger complex that includes a channel. Instead, the binding of DA to a receptor triggers a cascade of biochemical events inside the postsynaptic neuron (specifically, inside the postsynaptic terminal), and a downstream consequence of this can be the opening of a membrane-spanning channel, or some other process (often involving changing the phosphorylation state of an intracellular protein). Note that such a multistep cascade is likely to take longer to influence the voltage of a neuron than is a ligand-gated channel. This is one of the reasons that neurotransmitters such as dopamine are considered to be neuromodulators – their effect is to modulate the responsivity of the neuron to the faster-acting, "driving" effects of glutamate and GABA.

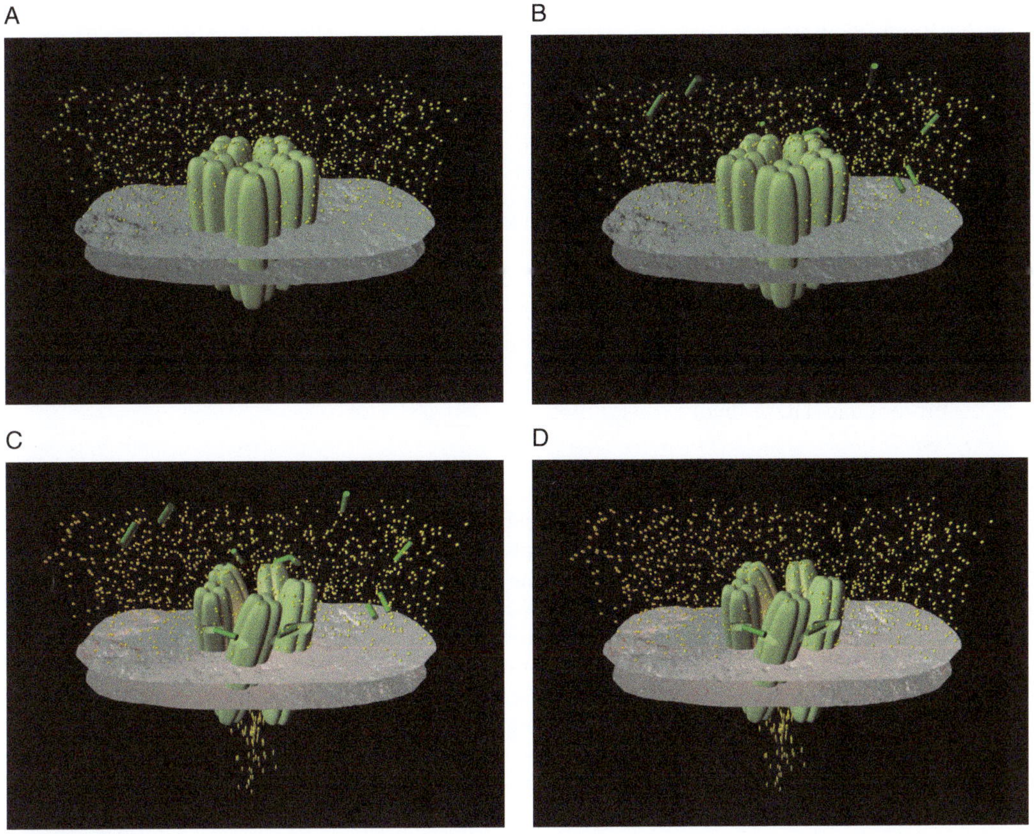

FIGURE 2.7 Four panels illustrating the effects of the neurotransmitter GABA binding with a membrane-spanning $GABA_A$ receptor (a subtype of GABA receptor). **A.** The receptor is composed of five separate proteins, each one consisting of four membrane-spanning domains (green "cigars"). As a functional unit, the receptor spans the neuronal membrane (gray planes) and provides a pathway for the inflow of ions (yellow dots represent a cloud of chloride [Cl^-] ions in the extracellular space). The receptor is shown in its resting, closed state, with no neurotransmitter bound, and no available path for ions to flow across the membrane. **B.** Shorter, darker green cylinders represent GABA molecules having been released into the synaptic cleft. (I.e., an action potential in a GABAergic neuron has triggered the release of GABA from the presynaptic terminal [not shown] into the cleft.) **C.** Binding of GABA molecules at two binding sites results in conformational change of receptor proteins (illustrated here as a mechanical twisting of subunits), which opens the pore of the receptor, thereby allowing Cl^- ions to enter the neuron. **D.** For some period of time after unbound GABA has been cleared from the synapse, the receptor remains active.

Source: Images courtesy of Mathew V. Jones, University of Wisconsin–Madison. Reproduced with permission.

How Neurons Communicate: The Action Potential A neuron initiates an action potential by taking advantage of the local depolarization produced by the influx of Na^+ ions that occurs at the axon hillock. It has to "act fast," because although this event produces a short-lived "cloud" of depolarization in the vicinity of the axon hillock, this "cloud" will quickly dissipate due to the rapid diffusion of Na^+ ions throughout the intracellular space (recall that there's a low concentration of Na^+ ions inside the cell). The neuron exploits this temporary depolarization by having another cluster of voltage-gated Na^+ channels that is "strategically" located just a little way along the axon. The channels of this cluster of receptors experience a brief pulse of depolarization from the hillock (i.e., the initial "cloud" of depolarization reaches this cluster), and they, in turn, open. Next, guess what? There's *another* cluster of voltage-gated Na^+ channels even further along the axon. This pattern repeats, and in this way, an action potential is propagated along the length of the axon until it reaches the dendrites of the next neuron. (You may be wondering, "But how did the initial depolarization that triggered the activity at the axon hillock come to pass?" Stick with me, and we'll come to that.)

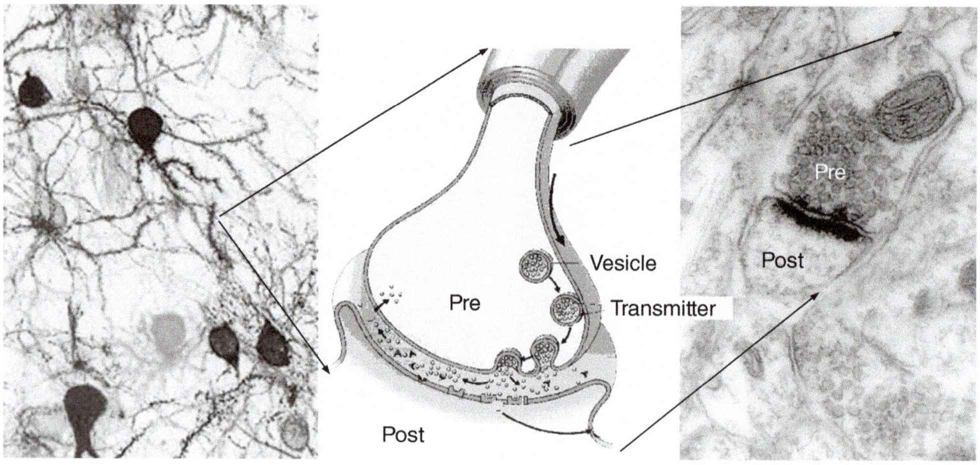

FIGURE 2.8 Left-side panel: light microscope image of neural tissue with cell bodies and processes visible. Many of the dendrites are studded with dendritic spines, including the one from which a tiny region is blown up to illustrate a synapse in the center panel. Center panel: diagram of a synapse, illustrating (with arrows) the events triggered by the arrival of an action potential: vesicles filled with neurotransmitter in the presynaptic terminal ("pre") are transported to the membrane, where they fuse with it to release neurotransmitter into the synaptic cleft; subsequently, molecules of neurotransmitter (or, depending on the type of synapse, a catabolite) are reuptaken back into the presynaptic terminal. Right-side panel: an electron microscope image of a synapse, with vesicles visible in the presynaptic terminal, and the "postsynaptic density," partly composed of membrane-spanning receptors, visible as a dark band at the postsynaptic terminal.

Source: Reproduced with permission from Buszáki, György (2006) / Oxford University Press.

When the action potential arrives in the vicinity of a dendrite from another neuron, it encounters a change in the morphology (i.e., shape) of the axon. This is a swelling of the axon into what is variously referred to as a synaptic bouton, a synaptic varicosity, or a presynaptic terminal (*Figure 2.8*). For a neural signal to pass from one cell to another, there needs to be a synapse linking them. At the presynaptic terminal, one finds the machinery necessary for converting the electrical signal of the action potential into the chemical signal that will be transmitted to the postsynaptic terminal. (Note from *Figure 2.8* that the pre- and postsynaptic cells do not touch – there is a gap [the **synaptic cleft**] between them.) That is, the electrical signal that is the action potential does *not* jump to the next neuron. Instead, the rapid depolarization triggered by the action potential opens voltage-gated calcium-ion (Ca^{2+}) channels located in the membrane of the presynaptic terminal. Not unlike Na^{+}, Ca^{2+} ions are in much higher concentration outside than inside the neuron, and thus the opening of voltage-gated Ca^{2+} channels results in an influx of Ca^{2+} ions into the presynaptic terminal. Ca^{2+} ions have a special status in the nervous system, in that they can initiate many biochemical processes within the cell. At the presynaptic terminal, the influx of Ca^{2+} ions triggers a cascade of events that result in the release of neurotransmitter into the synaptic cleft (*Figure 2.8*).

How Neurons Communicate: The Postsynaptic Consequences of Neurotransmitter Release On the postsynaptic side of the synapse, the cell membrane is studded with *neurotransmitter receptors*, each of which can bind with a molecule of the just-released neurotransmitter. This, in turn, will, depending on the type of receptor, produce one of any number of possible effects in the postsynaptic neuron. The most straightforward of these to describe, and one that's satisfactory for our present purposes, is to open a **ligand**-gated Na^{+} channel – that is, a molecule of neurotransmitter acts like a key by fitting into a special slot in the receptor and "unlocking" it, an event that causes the channel to open. With its channel now open, the receptor allows the influx of Na^{+} ions into the postsynaptic terminal of the dendrite. Thus, in this example, the binding of a molecule of neurotransmitter to a receptor has the effect of generating a small "cloud" of depolarization in the vicinity of this receptor within the postsynaptic terminal. Now, if only one such event happens, the cloud of depolarization quickly dissipates. If, however, many molecules of neurotransmitter have bound with many receptors, particularly if this has happened moreorless simultaneously at many synapses (e.g., if this neuron is on the receiving end of a volley of many action potentials arriving simultaneously from many different presynaptic neurons), then all these individual "clouds" of depolarization may combine, via their summation, to the point at which the cell's membrane voltage is raised to the neighborhood of −20 mV, in which case an action potential may be triggered in this postsynaptic neuron. (A mechanism by which the action potentials from many neurons can be coordinated to all arrive at a postsynaptic neuron at the same time is considered near the end of this chapter, in the section *Synchronous oscillation.*)

Different Neurotransmitters and Different Receptors Can Produce Different Effects on the Postsynaptic Cell The postsynaptic effects of neurotransmission that were described in the previous paragraph apply to the **excitatory neurotransmitter** glutamate binding to a particular kind of glutamate receptor called the **AMPA receptor**. (Neurotransmitter receptors are often named after chemicals that can mimic the effects of the naturally occurring ligands with which they bind preferentially. Thus, the *AMPA* receptor is named after the chemical that binds this type of glutamate receptor but not other types of glutamate receptor: α-amino-3-hydroxy-5-methyl-4-isoxazole propionic acid.) There are other glutamate receptors in the brain that work differently, and we will consider them in some detail when we discuss memory functions. **Glutamate** is released by cortical pyramidal cells, and because these are the most numerous neurons found in the cortex, glutamate is the predominant excitatory neurotransmitter in the CNS. Equally important for the functioning of the brain is **inhibitory neurotransmission**, and this is most commonly carried out by the neurotransmitter GABA. GABA is the primary neurotransmitter released by **inhibitory interneurons**, neurons whose primary function is to **hyperpolarize** neurons (i.e., to make their voltage more negative). (Because the resting potential of the neuronal membrane is negative, the convention is to say that a current whose effect is to move this potential closer to 0 mV is a depolarizing current, and a current whose effect is to move the potential further from 0 [i.e., making it more negative] is a hyperpolarizing current.) The most common GABA receptor produces its hyperpolarizing effects by opening channels that pass chloride ions (Cl^-; *Figure 2.7*), and because the extracellular concentration of Cl^- ions is considerably higher than the intracellular concentration, opening these channels results in an influx of negatively charged Cl^- ions and, thus, a negative shift in the membrane potential. The reason that this effect on the postsynaptic neuron is inhibitory is because it pulls the membrane voltage away from the trigger potential of −20 mV, thereby decreasing the probability that the neuron will fire an action potential.

Synaptic Plasticity All examples of learning, as well as of maturation in the developing organism, are outward products of synaptic plasticity, the changing of strength of synapses in response to changes in how the presynaptic neuron responds to an action potential (e.g., how much neurotransmitter it releases) and/or to how the postsynaptic neuron responds to the release of a fixed amount of neurotransmitter. We'll consider different examples of synaptic plasticity going forward, but for now, it's sufficient for us to know that it is a fundamental property of most synapses in the nervous system.

Housekeeping in the Synaptic Cleft Although the pre- and postsynaptic terminals of a synapse are very close together, there is no guarantee that any one molecule of neurotransmitter will bind with a receptor. Rather, binding is a probabilistic event, with the probability of binding influenced by many factors, including the number of molecules of neurotransmitter released by an action potential and the density of receptors in the postsynaptic membrane. It is also important to know that those molecules of neurotransmitter that do bind with a postsynaptic receptor do not enter the postsynaptic cell. Rather, after some period of time, they disengage from the receptor and float back into the synaptic cleft. The nervous system thus has to solve the problem of clearing-out the synapse after each action potential, lest the lingering molecules of neurotransmitter in the synapse continue to bind (and rebind) with receptors on the postsynaptic neuron for longer than intended. The nervous system has evolved many different solutions to this problem that are implemented at different synapses. Common to many is the process of **reuptake**, whereby molecules of neurotransmitter are taken back into the presynaptic terminal via specialized complexes of membrane-spanning proteins. Reuptake is an active process that requires energy, because it entails moving molecules of neurotransmitter from a low-concentration environment (the extracellular space) into a high-concentration environment (the presynaptic terminal). That is, it entails working against a chemical gradient. At glutamate synapses, the reuptake occurs both at the presynaptic terminal and at astrocytes that are located adjacent to the synapse. (In astrocytes, glutamate is converted into a precursor metabolite, which is transferred back to the presynaptic pyramidal cell for conversion back into glutamate.) At GABAergic synapses, the neurotransmitter is reuptaken into the presynaptic terminal by the GABA transporter. At synapses for many of the neuromodulatory transmitters, there are enzymes that either break down the molecules of neurotransmitter into smaller constituent molecules or transform them into a different molecule, the result in either case being a product that can no longer bind with the postsynaptic receptors. These now-inert molecules are then taken back into the presynaptic neuron, where they are reconverted into molecules of neurotransmitter. There are entire textbooks devoted to the details of how neurotransmitters are synthesized and metabolized (often falling under the rubric of "neuropharmacology"), and others to the details of the trafficking, release, and reuptake of neurotransmitters at the presynaptic bouton. Indeed, we'll need to revisit this in more detail in *Chapter 4*, when we consider the metabolic bases of some neuroimaging methods, but for now, we can move on.

Oscillatory Fluctuations in the Membrane Potential

Neurons Are Never Truly "At Rest"

As previously noted, the small cloud of depolarization produced by the opening of any single ligand-gated Na^+ channel typically won't, by itself, be enough to trigger an action potential, particularly when the channel is located on a distal dendritic branch, far from the cell body and its axon hillock. If this one channel were to periodically open then close, open then close, what one would observe at the cell membrane in the immediate vicinity of the receptor would be a slight depolarization – say, from −70 mV to −69 mV – followed by a return from −69 mV back to −70 mV, followed by another rise back to −69 mV, and so on. That is, the local membrane voltage would oscillate. Now, of course, we already know that the factors influencing the membrane voltage of a neuron are much more complicated than the behavior of a single ligand-gated ion channel. For starters, a single synaptic event (i.e., an action potential in the presynaptic neuron) is likely to activate hundreds, if not thousands, of individual channels. These individual depolarizing events will add together (they will "summate"). So, too, will the depolarizing effects produced by activity at other synapses. As a result, the overall effect that is experienced by the dendritic membrane will depend on the synchrony of incoming action potentials from glutamate-releasing axons. That is, if many (glutamatergic) action potentials arrive at about the same time, the aggregated depolarizing effect will be much larger than if the same number of incoming action potentials are spread out in time, because the depolarizing effect of the earliest-arriving action potentials will have started to dissipate (also referred to as "decay") before the depolarizing effect of the later-arriving ones starts to kick in. A second factor that influences fluctuations in overall membrane potential is the hyperpolarizing effects of action potentials at GABAergic synapses. What emerges from this cacophony of thousands of events at individual channels – some depolarizing and some hyperpolarizing – is an ongoing pattern of fluctuations in the dendritic membrane potential that can be measured with an electrode in the extracellular space. Because the dendritic branches from many, many neurons are located in close proximity to each other, it is typically not possible to isolate the voltage fluctuations attributable to a single neuron. Rather, what is recorded is the **local field potential (LFP)**, a reference to the fact that it's the electric field that is local to the region of tissue in close proximity to the electrode that is recording it. (The method for measuring the LFP, together with an example, is illustrated in Figure 4.7.)

Despite the fact that there can be literally hundreds of thousands of individual channels distributed across the tens to hundreds to thousands of neurons contributing to the LFP recorded by any one electrode, the LFP is nonetheless typically observed to fluctuate in an orderly oscillation. Indeed, different oscillatory frequencies, or "states," are so typical of the cortex that they've been given names. One common state is when the LFP oscillates with roughly 40 up–down cycles per second (i.e., 40 Hz); the range of oscillatory frequencies within which this falls, from roughly 30 Hz to roughly 80 Hz, is referred to as the **gamma frequency band** (or, "the gamma band," or, sometimes, in the shorthand jargon of the laboratory, just "gamma"). (This and other frequency bands are illustrated in Figure 4.11.) How can the brain orchestrate what we've just referred to as a *cacophony of individual single-channel events* into a steady, predictable up-and-down rhythm? One important factor to take into consideration is that neurons are wired up in a way that facilitates the sychronization of their oscillations. For many pyramidal cells, for example, inhibitory inputs from interneurons tend to synapse near the base of the dendrite, or even on the cell body itself. This targeting allows these inhibitory synapses to act as a kind of "gate" that either does or does not allow the depolarizing currents from more distally located glutamatergic synapses to influence the membrane voltage at the cell body. As we'll see in *Chapter 3*, the biophysical properties of some types of inhibitory interneuron make them tend to oscillate within a narrow band of frequencies in the gamma range. In this way, an inhibitory interneuron can impose a gamma-frequency oscillation on a pyramidal neuron. Furthermore, it is often the case that a group of interneurons, in addition to sending axons to local pyramidal cells, will also be "wired to each other" via axonal connections that they make with each other (i.e., they are reciprocally interconnected). As a result, the activity of these interneurons tends to be synchronized. The consequence for pyramidal neurons is that they tend to experience a regular pattern of the delivery, then dispersion, of hyperpolarizing currents.

Oscillatory Synchrony

There are many factors other than interneurons oscillating at 40 Hz that can influence the voltage of a pyramidal neuron, and a consequence of that is that the LFP invariably fluctuates in a complicated pattern that is a mixture of oscillations from many different sources. Indeed, it tends to be the case, due to principles from biophysics and from physics, that oscillations at lower frequencies are typically larger in magnitude than the relatively fast gamma oscillation. (I.e., oscillations at lower frequencies tend to fluctuate across a larger range of voltage than do oscillations at higher frequencies.) We won't go into a lot of detail here, but for the sake of illustration will pick just one such range of lower frequencies, the alpha band, which refers to oscillations in the human brain that cycle roughly 10 times per second (10 Hz). When the LFP exhibits a prominent oscillation at the alpha frequency, one can generally assume that the transmembrane voltage in the soma of a pyramidal cell in the immediate vicinity is also fluctuating at this frequency. Thus, although the average membrane potential of this neuron may be −70 mV while it is "at rest" (i.e., not firing), if one tracks it over time the membrane potential is actually oscillating between values above and below −70 mV (for this example let's say between values of −90 mV and −50 mV). Because this neuron is much more likely to reach its firing threshold (of −20 mV) when its membrane potential is in the neighborhood of −50 mV than that of −90 mV, this results in a situation in which the pyramidal neuron has, in effect, 10 "windows" per second during which it is more amenable to firing an action potential. Given this state of affairs, if a pyramidal neuron in a distal area (*X*) wants to make our example pyramidal neuron (let's call it *neuron Y*) fire an action potential, there are two things that it needs to do. First, it needs to time the delivery of its own action potential so that this action potential arrives during a depolarized phase of the membrane oscillation of *neuron Y*. Second, it needs many of its neighbors in *area X* to also send their action potentials at the same time, such that *neuron Y* receives many depolarizing impulses all at the same time. From this, it is apparent that the synchronization of membrane oscillations in different populations of neurons is a critical factor in the smooth operation of the brain. Within a local group of cells, there's a degree of synchrony between interneurons and pyramidal neurons. Across regions, the oscillations of **ensembles** of neurons can synchronize and desynchronize, depending on their need to effectively communicate. Indeed, in many contemporary models of neuronal function, such synchrony plays a critical role.

To illustrate how synchrony might be important for brain function, let's walk through a hypothetical example. Let's pretend that, while you're walking through the woods, three things happen simultaneously: (a) the sun breaks through the clouds; (b) a bird in an overhead tree takes flight; and (c) a bear comes ambling along the path in your direction. Now, because individual elements in your brain don't "know" that one of these events has more immediate relevance to you, the organism, than the other two, information about all three is propagated from the visual system to "downstream" brain systems that might implement one of three behaviors: (a) stopping to enjoy the warm caress of the sun, (b) reaching for the binoculars to watch the bird in flight, or (c) RUNNING AWAY(!). According to synchrony models, one way that the nervous system has evolved to let choice (c) be the "winner" is that action potentials carrying information about the bear are timed to arrive during a depolarized phase in the oscillation of their downstream target system, whereas action potentials carrying information about the sun and about the bird arrive during a hyperpolarized phase of their downstream targets. Thus, the information about the bear is more potent, in a neural sense, and it thereby "wins" the "competition" to control your behavior. Such coordination and control of the LFP in different regions is referred to as **phase synchronization** (*Figure 2.9*). We shall see in subsequent chapters that some psychiatric disorders might be attributable to abnormal control of synchronization between neural systems.

FIGURE 2.9 Illustration of how phase synchrony may govern the effectiveness of neural communication.

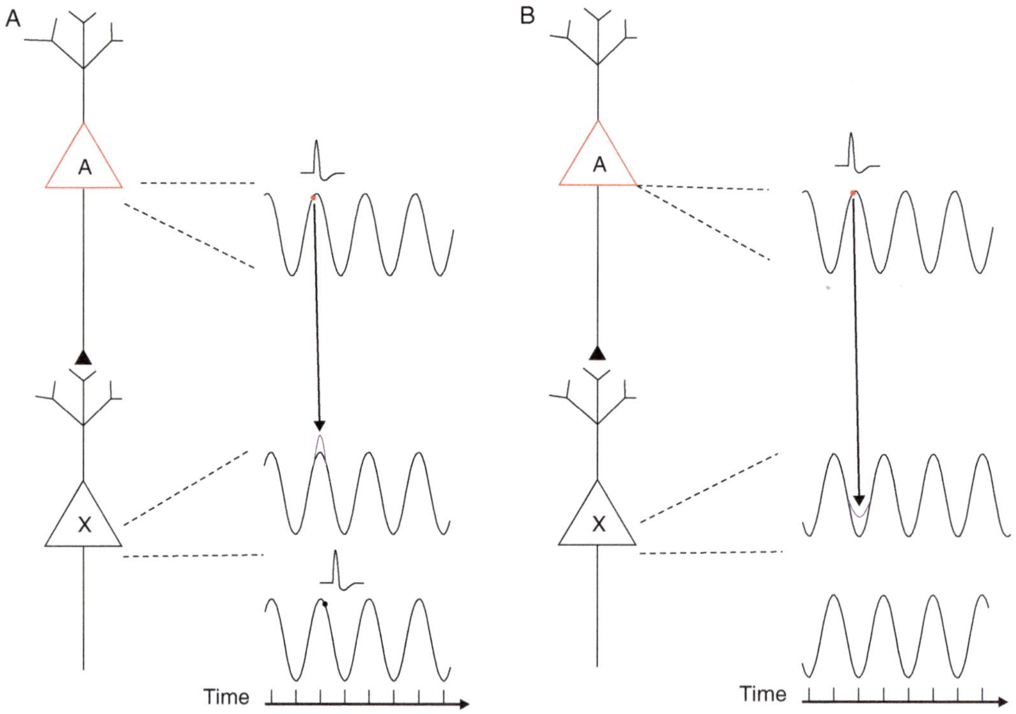

FIGURE 2.9.A Synchrony between an upstream and a downstream neuron. Neuron A and neuron X are oscillating with a phase lag of near 0 (i.e., membrane voltage of neuron A reaches the maximum depolarization point of its cycle just a fraction of a second more quickly than does neuron X). A consequence of this is that an action potential fired by neuron A (red dot superimposed on neuron A's membrane oscillation) arrives at neuron X (illustrated by arrow) just as neuron X is at its maximally depolarized state, and thus the action potential from neuron A boosts the level of depolarization of neuron X at a moment in time when neuron X is already close to threshold, thereby triggering an action potential (black dot superimposed on neuron X's membrane oscillation).

FIGURE 2.9.B A scenario in which neuron A and neuron X are oscillating out of phase with each other. Here, the action potential fired by neuron A arrives at neuron X at its maximally hyperpolarized state. Thus, although the action potential from neuron A does boost the level of depolarization of neuron X, it does so at a moment in time that it's unlikely to push neuron X above its threshold. Thus, the signal propagated by A "dies" at X and has no further influence on perception or behavior.

It should be noted that although no neuroscientist questions the existence of oscillations in membrane potentials and in the LFP, historically there have been animated debates about the extent to which these oscillations actually play a functional role in the workings of the brain. From one perspective, these oscillations could be nothing more than byproducts of the complex pattern of synaptic events experienced constantly by every neuron in the brain. This perspective might be paraphrased as *Yes, they happen, but they may not actually serve any useful function*. On the other hand, with each passing month, it seems that there are new discoveries of specific neural systems (sometimes in the visual system [*Chapter 6*], sometimes in the systems that govern skeletomotor control [*Chapter 8*], sometimes in the hippocampus [*Chapter 11*]) whose functioning seems to depend on the precise synchronization of oscillations in different ensembles of neurons. Keeping this controversy in mind, the phenomenon of neuronal oscillations is one that we will return to at several points in this book.

Organization of Sensory Systems

Up through this point, we have covered general facts that are more-or-less true anywhere in the brain (e.g., the structure and physiology of the glutamatergic pyramidal cell are, for our purposes, the same in all brain regions, as are the properties of the LFP, etc.). This final section of this chapter, however, will introduce system- and circuit-level properties that are specific to each of the three sensory modalities whose workings are the focus of *Chapter 3:* vision, audition, and somatosensation.

The Visual System

The Visual Field The visual field refers to the spatial extent of everything that you can see right now. While you're reading this page, it's likely that your visual field is largely filled by this page, with blurry images of what's behind the book (or screen) surrounding the more in-focus percept of the page itself. Note that when you pay attention to the sharpness-of-focus of your vision for words that are one or two lines above or below where you're currently reading, it's clear that your acuity falls off precipitously in all directions. The center of gaze, where your acuity is sharpest, is referred to as foveal vision because it corresponds to the part of your retina called the fovea. Now move your center of gaze over to the crease that's formed between the left and right page of the book (or to the edge of the screen . . .). Assuming that you are sitting or standing upright, and the crease is vertical, then the crease is passing through your fovea and defining the boundary between the left side and the right side of your visual field, dividing it into a left visual hemifield and a right visual hemifield. Note that this remains true regardless of the position of your eyes in your head. To demonstrate, start by holding your book in front of you and fixating the central crease (to fixate is to hold one's center of gaze on a selected location, often on an object that is stationary at that location). Now, while holding the book still and holding your head still, move your eyes as far to the left as you can, and hold them there, your center of gaze now falling on an object that's to the left of, and most likely further away than, the book. The book is still in your field of view, but it now occupies the right visual hemifield. Conversely, if you keep your center-of-gaze fixated on one point while slowly moving your head back and forth, or up and down, your visual field remains stationary. Thus, your visual field is centered on the location of gaze of your eyes, not on the orientation of your head.

The Retina and the LGN of the Thalamus Phototransduction, the process of converting light into neural signals, is accomplished by a class of cells called photoreceptors. In a sentence, these cells contain a pigmented protein called rhodopsin that, when impacted by light, undergoes a conformational change that triggers an intracellular molecular cascade that results in the closing of membrane-spanning ion channels. Thus, a type of physical energy (electromagnetic radiation with wavelengths between 400 nm and 700 nm [i.e., "visible light"]) is converted into an electrical signal (in this instance, a change in the membrane potential of the photoreceptor cell). This change in membrane potential produces currents within the complicated cellular

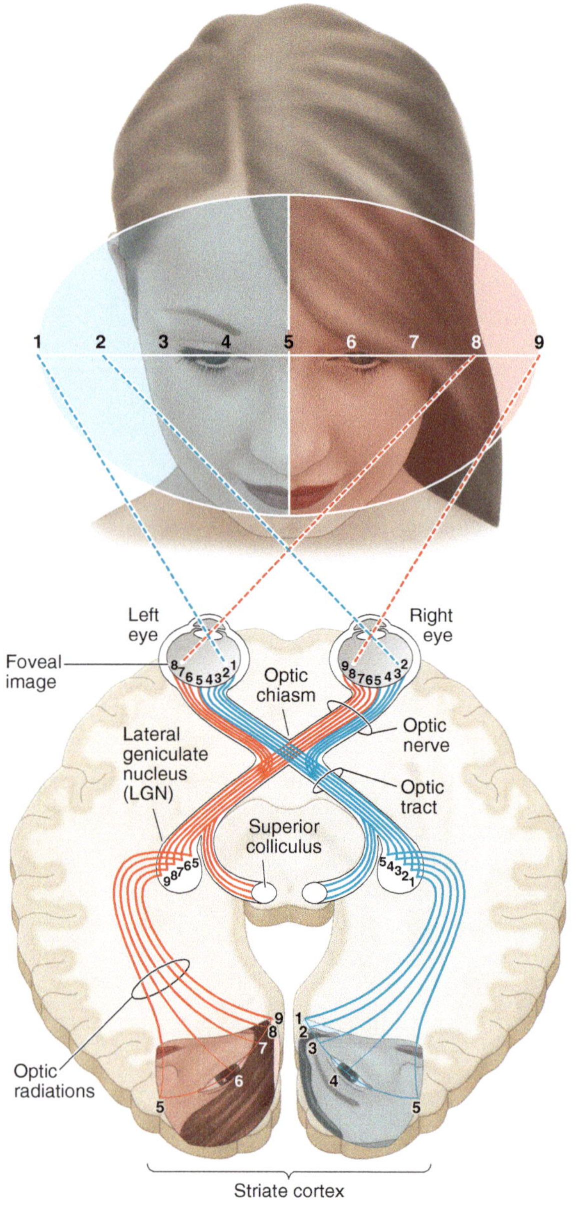

FIGURE 2.10 Illustration of the visual field, emphasizing the right (shaded red) and left (shaded blue) hemifields, and how information from these hemifields is conveyed to primary visual cortex (labeled as "striate cortex," for reasons explained in the text).

Source: Wolfe et al., 2012 / Sinauer Associates Inc.

circuitry of the retina, the end result of which is that action potentials are generated by retinal ganglion cells, the output neurons of the retina whose axons project to the LGN (*Figure 2.10*).

There are two classes of photoreceptors, cones and rods. Cones are sensitive to color, with the rhodopsin in "blue," "green," and "red" cones being preferentially sensitive to light at short, medium, and long wavelengths, respectively. Rods, on the other hand, are sensitive to this entire range of wavelengths (i.e., they are "colorblind") and contribute primarily to vision at extremely low levels of illumination, such as at night.

Although containing an array of detector elements, not unlike the grid of photodiodes in a digital camera, the packing density of photoreceptors in the retina is not uniform. Rather, at the fovea, one finds the highest density of cones, which drops off very quickly as one moves in any direction toward the periphery. For this reason, the fovea provides the highest acuity — the highest spatial resolution — of any part of the retina. This explains why, for example, we move our eyes across the page as we read: only the highest acuity portion of the retina can deliver the detail that is needed to resolve small type. The same is true for recognizing faces, for appreciating a painting, for reading road signs, and so on. As one moves away from the fovea toward the periphery, three properties begin to change. One is the progressive decrease in the density of cones. The second is that the surface area that each cone occupies on the retina increases. The third is that an increasing number of rods surround each cone. It is a consequence of the fact that there are fewer cones devoted to each square unit of surface in the periphery of the visual field that our peripheral vision is of much lower resolution than is foveal vision.

A reasonable supposition as to why the retina is organized this way comes from considering the incredible amount of processing power required to analyze information from the fovea (as will be detailed further along, beginning with the consideration of cortical magnification). If the packing density of the entire surface of the retinae were the same as that at the fovea, it's been estimated that one's optic nerves would need to be as thick as one's arms (to accommodate so many more axons), and one's primary visual cortex would need to be the size of a large room (to accommodate all the neurons needed to process so much high-resolution visual information).

Now move your eyes back to the vertical crease dividing the left vs. right pages of the book. The imaginary line that lies on top of the crease and extends to the uppermost and lowermost reaches of the visual field is called the vertical meridian of the visual field. In the same way that one can vertically divide the visual field into left vs. right hemifields, one can also divide it into upper vs. lower hemifields, a divide defined by the horizontal meridian. Together, the two meridians divide the visual field into quadrants: upper right, lower right, lower left, and upper left.

Before we start to consider how these components of the visual field are mapped onto the brain, let's try one more simple exercise. Close your left eye. Note that, with this eye closed, although your visual field is somewhat narrower than it is with both eyes open, you can still see much of the left visual hemifield. That is, *the two hemifields do* not *correspond to each of the two eyes*. Rather, each eye represents most of the visual field, with considerable overlap in the center, and only the most eccentric (i.e., farthest-from-the-center) portions of each hemifield are represented by only one eye. The reason that one eye can represent most of the visual field follows from its structure. If one thinks of the eye as a transparent globe, the retina, which is the portion of the eye that transduces light energy into neural signals, is attached to the inside surface of the half of the globe that's inside the eye socket, as though it was painted on. That is, the retina is concave. Thus, as illustrated in *Figure 2.10*, light that is emanating from the left side of the visual field strikes the right side of the retina, and light that is emanating from the right side of the visual field strikes the left side of the retina. For there to be a "one eye = one visual hemifield" arrangement, one of two things would have to be different about our eyes. Either (1) the retinae would have to be flat, instead of concave; or (2) the eyes would have to be farther apart, halfway between their present location and the temples. Indeed, animals that are "wall eyed," like most fish and birds, have two nonoverlapping visual fields.

The Retinotopic Organization of Primary Visual Cortex We concluded *Chapter 1* with three branches of science – systems neuroscience, neuropsychology, and experimental psychology – poised to make important discoveries about brain structure and function at the dawn of the twentieth century. With regard to vision, once occipital cortex was defined as its necessary substrate, the next task was to work out its organization. The fact that there is systematicity to the organization of visual cortex was soon established by neuropsychologists and neurologists whose studies of soldiers with penetrating head injuries indicated that damage to specific areas of the occipital lobe invariably produced partial blindness in the same regions of the visual field. Thus, for example, damage to dorsal regions of the right occipital lobe produced blindness in the lower-left quadrant of the visual field. A large lesion would produce a quadrantanopia – blindness in the entirety of the quadrant – or a hemianopia – blindness in one half of the visual field – whereas a smaller lesion might produce a scotoma within that quadrant. An implication of this finding was the realization that everything in the primary visual cortex is "flipped" with respect to the visual field. Things that appear to the left of the vertical meridian are initially processed in the right hemisphere of the brain, and things that appear above the horizontal meridian are initially processed in ventral portions of the occipital lobe. To understand why, we must turn to the anatomy of the visual system.

The left-right "flip" and the up-down "flip" can each be understood as resulting from the optics of the eye. For now, let's keep the left eye closed and consider just the right. The concave shape of the retina on the back of the eyeball dictates that light reflecting off stimuli appearing below the point of fixation will be projected onto the upper retina and that stimuli appearing to the right of fixation will be projected onto the left side of the retina. Because we're only considering the right eye for the moment, this left half of the retina is referred to as the nasal retina, because it is closest to the nose. (The half of the retina that is closest to the temple is the temporal retina.) And so, already in the eye, what's "up" in the world is "down" on the retina, and what's "left" in the world is "right" on the retina. This flipped state of affairs is preserved as axons from the retina project posteriorly to the thalamus. Along the way, the fibers that correspond to the nasal retina cross over to the left hemisphere, so that half of the axons from the right eye – those from the temporal retina – project to the right LGN of the thalamus, and the other half – from the nasal retina – project to the left LGN (*Figure 2.10*). Another important fact about these axons is that their trajectory preserves the layout of the retina, such that axons from adjacent retinal ganglion cells synapse onto adjacent neurons of the LGN. Similarly, adjacent neurons of the LGN project to adjacent neurons in primary visual cortex (a.k.a. V1). In this way, the spatial organization of V1 reflects the spatial organization of the retina (*Figure 2.10*). If you're looking at the trunk of a tree, green light from the leaves is reflecting onto the lower half of the retina, and the grass where the trunk meets the ground is reflecting onto the upper half of the retina. When V1 receives this information via the LGN, ventral portions of this region begin processing information about the color, texture, etc. of the leaves, whereas dorsal portions of this region begin processing information about the grass. Thus, the functional topography of V1 mirrors the functional topography of the retina. This is referred to as retinotopic organization, or *retinotopy*.

Inspection of *Figure 2.10* (and of *Figure 3.2*) identifies the fiber pathways that convey information from the retina to the cortex. Although all axons project uninterruptedly from retina to LGN, the bundles in which they travel from eye to optic chiasm are referred to as the *optic nerve*, and those in which they extend from optic chiasm to LGN are referred to as the *optic tract*. Thus, whereas the optic nerves carry eye-specific information, the optic tracts carry visual field-specific information. The LGN itself gets its name from the fact that an early anatomist thought it looked like a bent knee, and geniculate derives from Latin for "knee-like." The fibers of the optic tract terminate in one of several layers of the LGN, according to a principle that we'll return to further along this chapter. In the human, the projection from LGN to V1 runs along the dramatically curving and fanned-out optic radiations, a striking consequence of the mechanical twisting and stretching of this fiber tract brought about by the rapid growth of the brain during in utero development (*Figure 3.2*). Note that these radiations terminate along the medial surface of the occipital lobe. More specifically, the majority of them terminate inside a sulcus that runs parallel to the rostrocaudal axis of the brain, starting near the occipital pole and extending for roughly the length of the occipital lobe. This is the calcarine fissure, named after the shape that its indentation makes in the adjacent posterior horn of the lateral ventricle when viewed from a dissection similar to *Figure 2.2*. This indentation resembles the spur of a rooster's leg – in Latin, *calcar avis*.

The axial view depicted in the MR image in *Figure 3.2* is not dissimilar to the one that Italian medical student Francesco Gennari inspected, and later described in a 1782 book, noting a thick white stripe in cross-sectional views of the cortex lining the calcarine fissure. This "stripe of Gennari," as it has come to be known, was later shown to correspond to myelinated fibers coursing through layer IV of this cortex. Its primary significance for this book is that the term *striate cortex* (i.e., "striped cortex") has come to be one of the most common terms according to which this region is known. Relatedly, the visual areas beyond V1, but to which it projects, are known collectively as *extrastriate cortex*.

Another consequence of the fact that the organization of V1 is dictated by the organization of the retina is that roughly 80% of V1 is devoted to processing information from the central 10% of the retina, a simple consequence of the inhomogeneity of cone density on the retinal surface. What this means for V1 is that there is a much larger portion of cortical area devoted to processing information from the fovea than from the peripheral retina, thereby leading to the distortion of the retinal image that is "projected" onto the cortex. That is, columns of neurons are spaced the same distance apart at the rostral-most extent of the calcarine fissure as they are at the occipital pole. Thus, if there is to be a one-to-one correspondence between photoreceptors and V1 neurons (which strictly speaking, there isn't, but the approximation is fine for our purposes), it's clear why the cortical representation of the fovea, with its many more columns of neurons, covers a large area relative to the cortical representation of the periphery, with its relatively fewer columns of neurons. Such disproportionate representation of high-acuity portions of a sensory system is referred to as cortical magnification. This property is seen in other systems, prominently so in the somatosensory (further along in this chapter) and motor (*Chapter 9*) systems.

An additional implication of retinotopy for V1 neurons is that they will be sensitive to stimulation within a larger or smaller portion of the visual field, depending on what portion of the retina the neuron represents. This fundamental property of a sensory neuron is referred to as its receptive field. In V1, receptive fields are smallest at regions receiving input from the fovea and largest at regions receiving input from the periphery, properties that follow from the spatial resolution of foveal vs. peripheral regions of the retina. Because a V1 neuron's receptive field properties are determined by the region of the retina that projects to it, the most direct way to quantify the dimensions of its receptive field would be to do so in terms of the surface area of retina from which it is receiving input. Thus, as an approximation, one might estimate that a V1 neuron representing the fovea has a receptive field corresponding to a $5 \times 10^{-5}\,mm^2$ surface area of the retina, whereas a V1 neuron representing the periphery might have a receptive field corresponding to a $5 \times 10^{-4}\,mm^2$ surface area of the retina. Although these values reflect the causal factors determining V1 receptive field properties, they are neither intuitively graspable nor very meaningful with regard to the function of the primary visual cortex. Instead, it is much more useful to think of receptive field size in terms of degrees of visual angle.

The Receptive Field Two adjacent photoreceptors in the retina are likely to receive information from adjacent portions of a visual scene. For example, when you're reading the word "adjacent," there is a viewing distance at which photons reflecting off the dot over the *j* are impacting one photoreceptor, and the photons reflecting off the space between the dot and the "stick" part of the letter are impacting a photoreceptor just above it. These two photoreceptors have different receptive fields, in that they *receive* information from different portions of the visual *field*. Now, let's make the dot on the letter *j* blink on and off. If your eye were perfectly still, the photoreceptor whose receptive field is restricted to the tiny space under the dot wouldn't detect anything about the blinking dot. That's because this dot is not in this photoreceptor's receptive field. The principle of the receptive field holds for retinal ganglion cells and for neurons of the LGN and V1 (indeed, for many other areas of the brain).

One feature of V1 receptive fields is that they are larger than those of foveal photoreceptors. For example, a V1 neuron with a receptive field centered on the tiny space below the dot of the *j* might also encompass the area corresponding to the dot. The reason for this is that each V1 neuron receives input from several retinal photoreceptors (*Figure 2.11*). One consequence of such "pooling" across the inputs from several retinal photoreceptors is that a V1 neuron necessarily has a lower spatial resolution than do any of the individual photoreceptors that feed into it. A simplified way to think about this is as follows: if five photoreceptors feed into a single V1 neuron, and that V1 neuron fires each time any of these five photoreceptors signals that something has changed in its receptive field, anyone "listening" to that neuron can know when something has happened somewhere within the area covered by those five photoreceptors, but can't know precisely where within that area of five photoreceptor receptive fields the change has occurred.

There is, however, an important trade-off for the loss of spatial resolution that occurs between the retina and V1 and that is a gain in information about *what* has changed in the visual world. In effect, by sampling across the input of multiple photoreceptors, neurons in V1 can "infer" information that was not conveyed by any one photoreceptor alone. This process is already evident at the level of the retinal ganglion cell. Although it may fire robustly when a tiny spot of light is projected into the center of its receptive field, it will respond at an even higher rate (of action potentials) if that central spot is surrounded by a dark ring. This property of an "ON center" and an "OFF surround" means that the neuron signals when there is something bright in the center of its receptive field but does so even more robustly when that bright "thing" has a dark "thing" right next to it. *Figure 2.11* illustrates how this principle, by

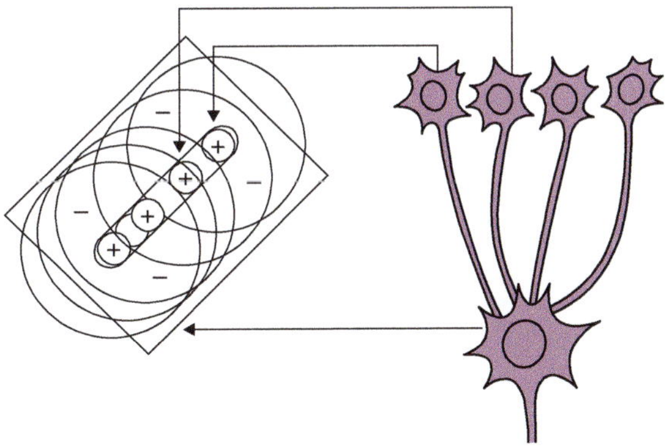

FIGURE 2.11 Constructing orientation selectivity in V1 from LGN neurons with ON center/OFF surround receptive fields. As will be detailed in *Chapter 3*, section *The V1 neuron as feature detector*, this V1 neuron receives input from four LGN neurons whose receptive fields are overlapping and whose centers are aligned along an imaginary line tilted 45° to the right of vertical. By holding a flat edge at different orientations across this array of receptive fields, you can prove to yourself that a bar of light oriented at 45° would (1) maximally excite the ON centers of each LGN neuron while (2) minimally stimulating their OFF surrounds. The consequence for the V1 neuron is that this stimulus produces the strongest net input from the LGN, thereby making it (the stimulus) optimal for eliciting a robust response from this V1 neuron.

Source: Hubel and David (1988) / John Wiley & Sons.

pooling across a series of neurons with ON center/OFF surround receptive fields, can yield an "edge detector."

To get a feel for the concept of visual angle, set down your book for a moment and fixate a point on the wall across the room. Next, hold your arms out straight to each side, as though you were about to start flapping them like wings. Now slowly move your arms toward each other, as though you were going to clap your hands with locked elbows (in the way that people do to mimic a trained seal) and stop moving them when each hand is just visible in the right and left peripheries of your field of view. A person with normal vision in both eyes will find that their arms don't get far before they have to stop. As you hold this position with arms slightly bent at each shoulder, you can think of your arms as defining a very wide angle; let's estimate it to be 170°. Next, swing your right arm into your field of view until it is pointing at the same spot that you are fixating. The imaginary line passing through your right hand and stretching from floor to ceiling defines the vertical meridian, and now your right and left arms are defining an angle that is one-half of 170°, or 85°. And so, by these rough calculations, the visual field subtends 170° of visual angle along the horizontal meridian. Finally, let's make one more observation before you relax your right arm. With your elbow straight, hold up your thumb (as if indicating "1" on Continental Europe, or signaling "I am cool" in the United States). As you stare at it, the width of the joint in the middle of the thumb subtends approximately 2° of visual angle. Having established this more functional metric of size in the visual system, we can return to receptive fields in V1. In regions of V1 representing the fovea, receptive fields can be as small as $0.5° \times 0.5°$ of visual angle, or smaller, whereas in regions of V1 representing the periphery, they can be an order of magnitude or more larger.

The Auditory System

What Is It That We Hear? Just as vision results from the transduction of energy from a relatively narrow band of the electromagnetic spectrum (what we call "visible light"), audition is the transduction of energy in the form of changes in air pressure. Many are familiar with the question *If a tree falls in a forest, but there are no animals (including humans) within one hundred miles, does it make a sound?* Auditory science tells us unequivocally that the answer is "No." Consider this: if a human were on the surface of an asteroid floating in the vacuum of space, and it were possible to wear a spacesuit that left the ears uncovered, the most violent of collisions (falling tree, exploding supernova, whatever) would not make a sound. This is because the auditory system works on the principle of detecting changes in energy in the medium making contact with the ear. In everyday life, this corresponds to the movement of molecules of the gases that make up the air that's all around us; or, when underwater, to collisions between and movement of molecules of water (plus whatever else may be dissolved in it). We will refer to this as acoustic energy. (Publicity for the sci-fi movie *Alien* had it right: "In space, no one can hear you scream.")

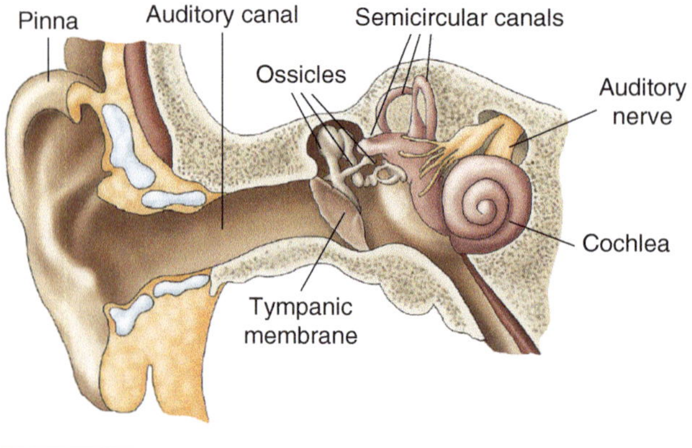

FIGURE 2.12 Major structures of the outer, middle, and inner ear.

Source: miha de / Shutterstock.com.

Mechanical Transmission and Neural Transduction From a mechanical standpoint, the steps leading to transduction of this energy are much more complicated than are those involved in the transduction of light energy. These are illustrated in *Figure 2.12*, but, in summary, a membrane in the outer ear (the tympanic membrane) vibrates in response to vibrations in the air, and its vibration is transferred through a series of tiny bones (the ossicles) to another membrane, the oval window, whose vibration produces changes of pressure in the fluid-filled cochlea. From the outside, the cochlea resembles a tube that has been rolled into a spiral. (Indeed, *cochlea* derives from the Greek for snail.) There are, in fact, three long and narrow chambers rolled up within the cochlea, and we'll focus on the (long and narrow) membrane that separates two of these chambers – the basilar membrane. The basilar membrane vibrates in response to the pressure changes caused by the "pushing" and "pulling" of the ossicles on the oval window. Note that, up to this point, what we've summarized is a series of mechanical *transfers* of energy, from vibrations in the atmosphere, through several intermediate steps, to vibrations of the basilar membrane. *Transduction* hasn't yet occurred.

Transduction of the mechanical, vibrational energy of the basilar membrane into a neural signal occurs in inner hair cells that are attached all along the long-axis of the basilar membrane. At a simplified level of description, the base of each inner hair cell is secured to the basilar membrane. At the other end of the cells are tufts of hair-like cilia extending into the fluid of the cochlea. Movement of the basilar membrane causes the cilia of inner hair cells to bend, "like tiny clumps of seaweed swept back and forth by invisible underwater currents" (Sekuler and Blake, 1985, p. 311). This back-and-forth movement produces mechanical shearing forces in the membrane of the hair cell, which, in turn, opens or closes mechanically gated ion channels. The resting potential of inner hair cells is approximately −60 mV, and the opening of these channels results in the inflow of K^+ and Ca^{2+} ions, the consequent depolarization of the cells, and the consequent release of neurotransmitter (probably glutamate) at synapses linking the base of the inner hair cell to ganglion cells of the cochlear nucleus. These ganglion cells are the first neurons of the auditory system, analogous to the retinal ganglion cells of the visual system, and they carry electrical signals about auditory information into the CNS. Together, the fibers of these cochlear ganglion cells are known as the auditory nerve. (We'll return to outer hair cells further along in this chapter.)

Two important properties of sound are its volume and pitch. Volume is encoded in this system in a fairly straightforward way: increasing the volume of a sound results in greater displacement of the oval window (i.e., "bigger" vibrations) and, consequently, in greater deflection of the basilar membrane, greater shearing forces on the cilia, greater depolarization of the inner hair cells, and, finally, the release of more glutamate onto cochlear ganglion cells. The end result is that the volume of a sound is encoded by the rate at which neurons of the cochlear nucleus fire (i.e., a rate code). To understand pitch, we have to understand another fundamental mechanical property of the basilar membrane, which is the exquisite specificity with which different regions vibrate as a function of frequency.

Spectral Decomposition Performed by the Basilar Membrane Having drawn the analogy between cochlear ganglion cells and retinal ganglion cells, it is important to note differences in how they encode information, differences that arise from fundamental differences in the physical properties of photons vs. acoustic energy. For our purposes, photons travel in a straight line, a property that our visual system exploits to detect objects regardless of where they appear in the visual field. Thus, for example, a visible rustling of leaves in a tree will produce a pattern of changing light energy on any small patch of the retina, regardless of whether one's center of gaze is directed at the tree, to the right of it, above it, or below it. Thus, retinal ganglion cells carry signals that, when pooled, create a 2-D map of space. Acoustic energy, in contrast, expands out from its source in all directions. (A commonly used metaphor is the pattern of expanding, concentric rings that result from dropping a pebble into a previously placid pond – just keep in mind that acoustic "rings" expand in 3-D, in concentric spheres.) Therefore, acoustic energy would not project in an orderly way against a 2-D receptor sheet in the way that visible light energy projects onto the retina. Consequently, the inner ear has evolved to discriminate differences in auditory stimuli along just one dimension (other than volume), and that's vibrational frequency. The physical property of vibrational frequency corresponds to the auditory percept of pitch, such that low-frequency vibrations (as produced, e.g., by a tuba) are perceived as having low pitch, and high-frequency vibrations (as produced, e.g., by a flute) are perceived as having high pitch.

Although the cochlea is a spiral structure, it's useful to think of it as a straight tube, as though it has been unrolled. The end of the tube where the oval window is located is referred to as the base. The tube is widest at this end, and it progressively narrows until it terminates at the apex. Interestingly, however, the basilar membrane within this tube is thick and narrow at the base and becomes progressively thinner and wider as one moves toward the apex. The consequence of this configuration is that different regions of the basilar membrane will vibrate preferentially to acoustic vibrations of different frequencies. In effect, the basilar membrane is tuned like a piano, with the regions near the base vibrating preferentially to the highest-frequency sounds that we can hear and regions near the apex vibrating preferentially to the lowest-frequency sounds that we can hear (*Figure 2.13*). This results in a principle for representing sounds of different frequencies with what is referred to as a place code, reflecting the fact that auditory nerve fibers arising from different *places* along the basilar membrane preferentially carry information about one relatively narrow range of frequencies. (Were it up to this author, we'd call it a "basilotopic" or "cochleotopic" encoding scheme, but as with so many things, no one consulted with him ahead of time.)

If you understand the ideas that have been described in the two previous paragraphs and accompanying figures, then you understand the concepts underlying the "spectral decomposition" referred to in this section's title. What's left for us to do is to match those concepts onto this jargony phrase. The frequency at which a signal oscillates, such as the physical vibrations that produce acoustic energy, can be characterized as falling along a continuum, or a *spectrum*, that ranges from low frequencies to high frequencies. A sound source that vibrates at just one frequency is referred to as a pure tone. (This would be represented mathematically by a sine wave.) As we've established, a pure tone with a relatively low pitch would produce a traveling wave whose largest peak occurs at a single location near the apex end of the basilar membrane, whereas a pure tone with a relatively high pitch would produce a peak at a location near the base end. A new piece of information to add to this discussion is that if we were to play both of these tones simultaneously, the resultant "combined" traveling wave would

FIGURE 2.13 Mechanical spectral decomposition of acoustic energy in the cochlea.
Source: Wolfe et al., 2012 / Oxford University Press.

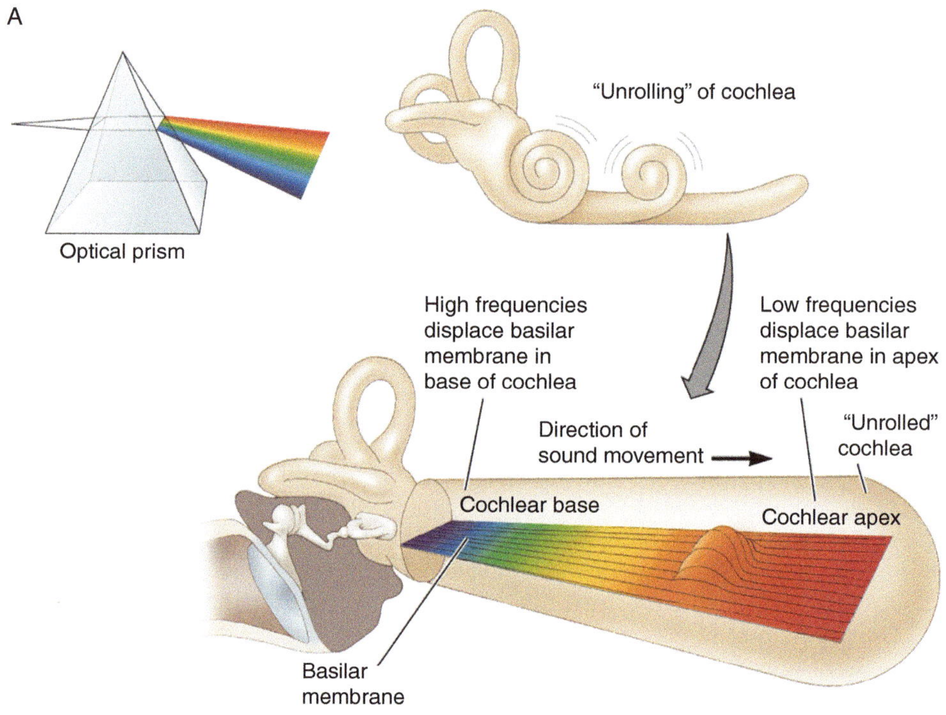

FIGURE 2.13.A On the top left is an illustration of an analogy from optics: just as a beam white light can be separated into its constituent bands of different wavelengths by shining it onto an optical prism; the basilar membrane separates the acoustic signal into vibrations at different frequencies. On the top right, it's easiest to understand the functional layout of the basilar membrane if one first imagines unrolling it. Botton: Diagram of the basilar membrane in the "unrolled" cochlea, color coded to refer back to the analogy to the optical prism.

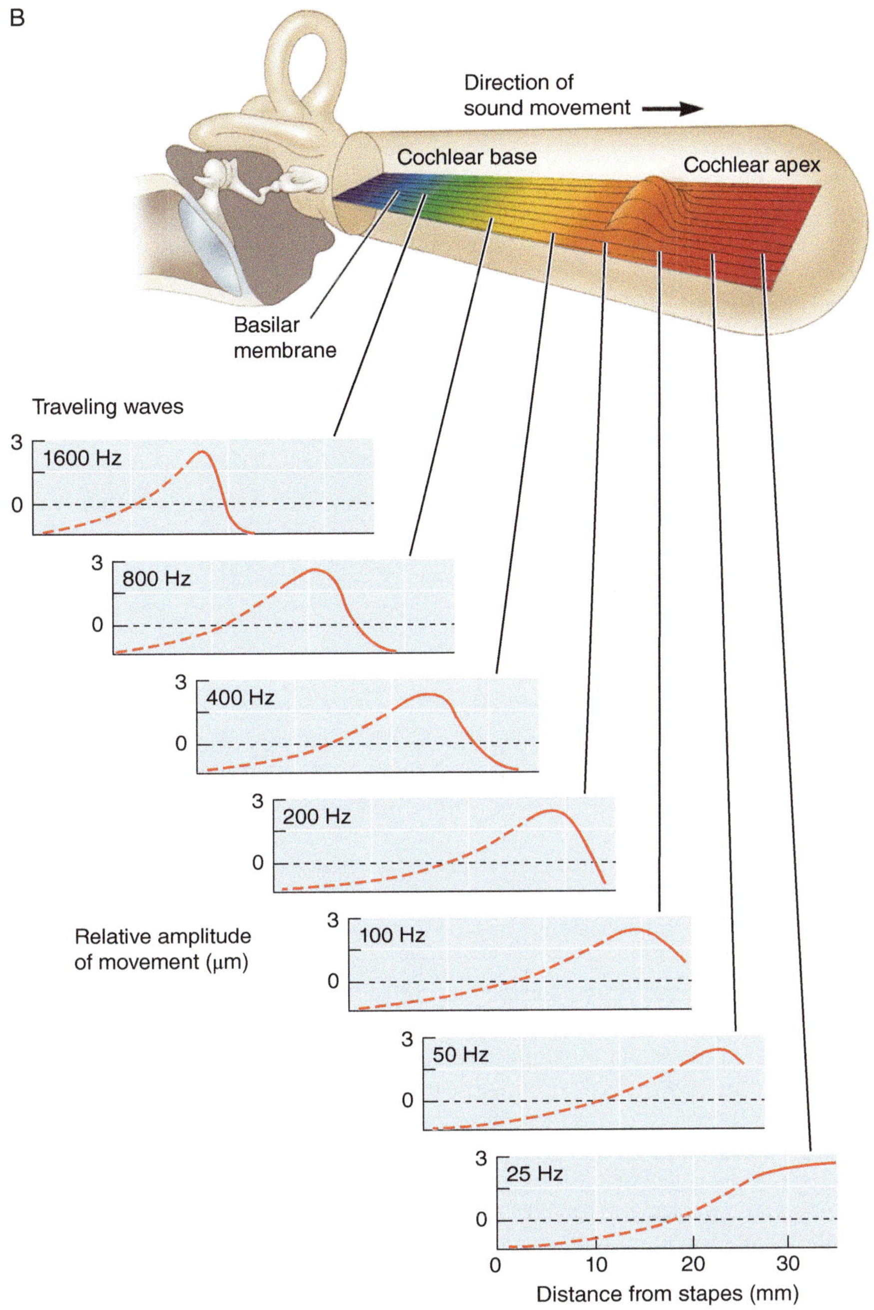

FIGURE 2.13.B Pure tones of different frequencies would produce differently shaped traveling waves on the basilar membrane, with the wave peaking progressively further from the base as frequency decreases.

produce two peaks, one at each of these two locations along the basilar membrane. Indeed, most sounds in nature are made up of a combination of many, many vibrational sources, each vibrating at a different frequency, as well as with a different amplitude. Consider for instance the human voice (a sound source that we won't consider in detail until *Chapter 19*). Speech is produced by forcing air across many flaps of tissue (the vocal cords), each of which vibrates at a different frequency; vibrations of the uvula, tongue, and lips also contribute. This mélange of vibrations at multiple frequencies is conveyed by a single complicated pattern of pushes and pulls by the oval window. This is a point that is important to emphasize: because there is only one oval window, there is no sense in which many *distinct* vibrational signals are being delivered to the cochlea from different sources. Rather, what the cochlea receives is a *single* signal in which many different frequencies are embedded. Although this amounts to a much more complicated version of our scenario of playing two pure tones simultaneously, the basilar membrane responds to it in the same way – the multiply-embedded traveling wave contains multiple peaks along the length of the basilar membrane, one corresponding to each vibrational frequency in the sound. It is in this sense that the basilar membrane can be thought of as decomposing the sound signal: the signal comes in as a single "complex waveform" in which many different vibrational frequencies are embedded, and it "leaves" the cochlea (via the auditory nerve) having been separated ("decomposed," in the parlance of signal processing) into its constituent frequencies. (Because each frequency can be represented as occurring at some point along a spectrum, the decomposition of a complex waveform into constituent frequencies can be called a "spectral decomposition.") In effect, the cochlea has performed an operation on the sound signal, via all the mechanical steps that we have just summarized, that is equivalent to a mathematical operation known as the Fourier transform that is of central importance to the analysis of neurally derived signals, and will be introduced in section *Time–Frequency Analysis, Chapter 4*.

The Somatosensory System

For the same reason that the word "soma" is used to refer to the cell body of a neuron, "somatosensation" refers to the sensory signals processed by the body, the sensations that we "feel with our skin." Colloquially this is the "sense of touch," although the surface of the skin that covers our bodies is sensitive to more than just mechanical energy.

Transduction of Mechanical and Thermal Energy, and of Pain The sensations that we "feel with our skin" result from the activation of one or several of the many types of somatosensory receptor cells embedded in the skin. These fall into three broad categories: mechanoreceptors, thermoreceptors, and pain receptors. Different mechanoreceptors are specialized for different mechanical forces that can act upon the body: pressure, texture, flutter, vibration, and stretch. Distinct thermoreceptors respond to hot and to cold. Distinct pain receptors generate the sensation of pain due to extreme temperature, due to mechanical stress (e.g., pinching or cutting the skin), or due to contact with chemicals that damage tissue (i.e., via chemosensation). In addition to these functional properties, the different types of receptors summarized here also differ in terms of various physiological properties, such as the size of receptive field and the speed of transduction and signal propagation. Each receptor is located at the end of a long process (technically, an axon) that projects past its cell body and into the spinal cord. The cell bodies of sensory receptor cells are clustered in ganglia that are spaced out along the long axis of the spinal cord. Because these ganglia are outside the spinal cord proper, these cells are classified as being a part of the peripheral nervous system (PNS; as opposed to the CNS). Indeed, unlike the prototypical CNS neuron, sensory receptor neurons do not generate action potentials at an axon hillock of the cell body. Rather, the action potential is generated in the membrane of the axon that is immediately adjacent to the receptor, and this action potential bypasses the cell body, propagating directly from the peripheral receptor into the spinal cord and then rostrally along the cord to a synapse on one of two nuclei in the brainstem. Next, the ascending sensory signal is transmitted to the ventral posterior lateral (VPL) nucleus of the thalamus and from here to the primary somatosensory cortex (S1; *Figure 2.14*). In the primate, S1 is located in the parietal cortex immediately posterior to the central sulcus. Unlike either V1 or A1, S1 is divided across four distinct Brodmann areas, some of which support different functions (*Figure 2.15*).

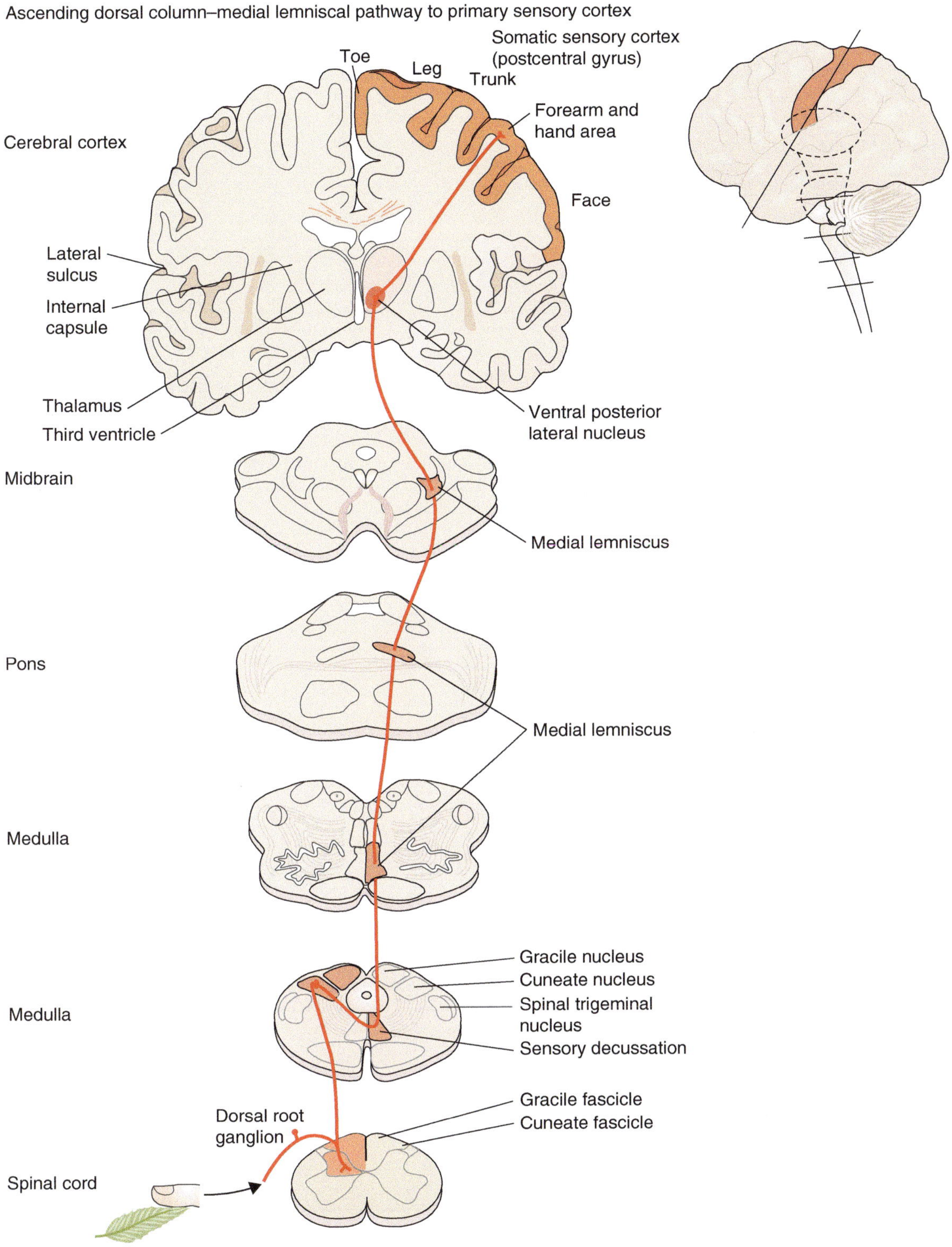

FIGURE 2.14 Somatosensory pathways from periphery to dorsal roots, ascending along dorsal spinal cord to ventral thalamus and projecting into cortex.

Source: Kandel et al., 2000 / McGraw-Hill.

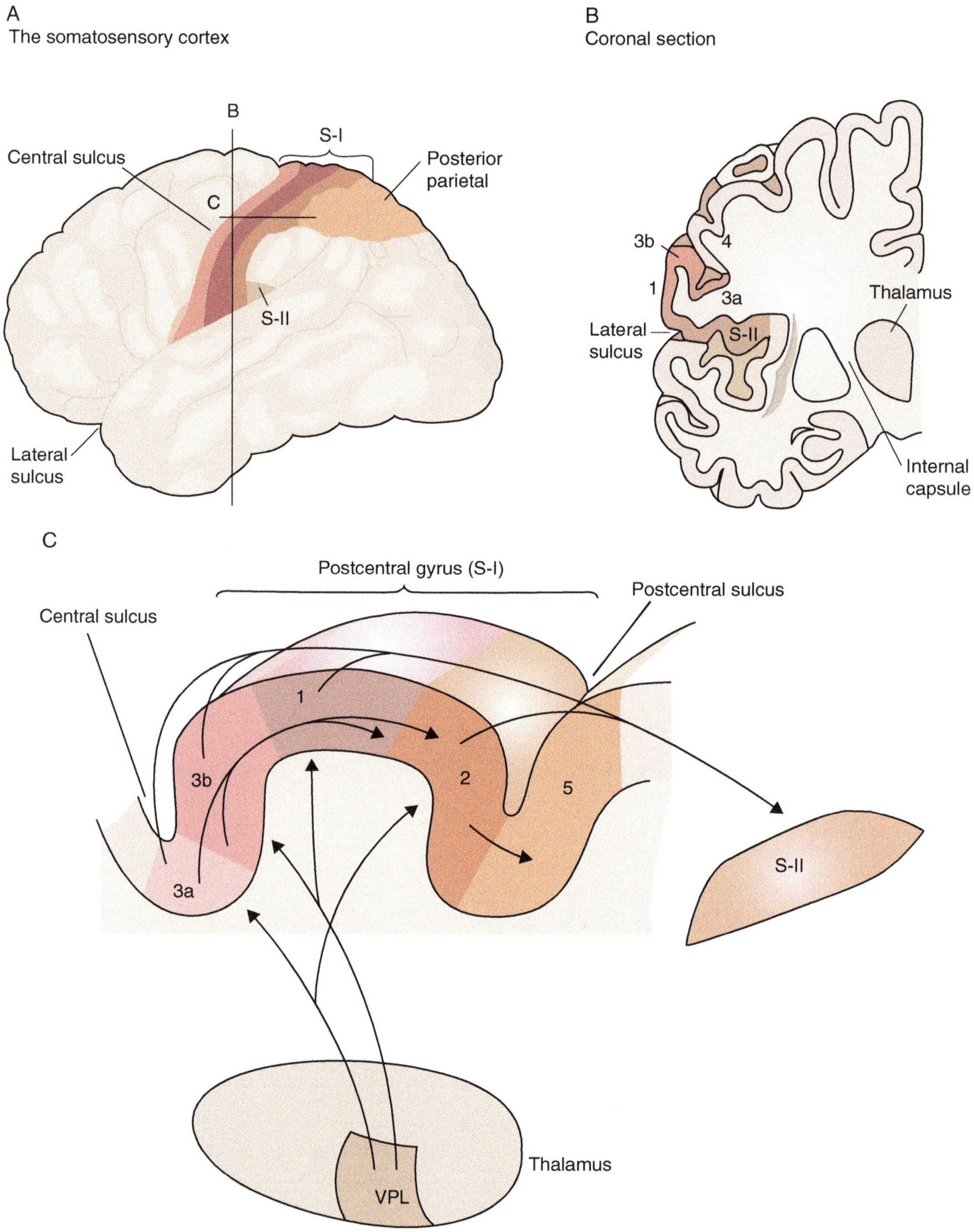

FIGURE 2.15 Somatosensory cortex, seen from three perspectives. **A.** External view of the left hemisphere, highlighting the location of S1 and S2 (here labeled "S-I" and "S-II"), and adjacent posterior parietal cortex. (Note that "lateral sulcus" is an alternate name for Sylvian fissure.) **B.** Location of S1 and S2 as viewed in coronal section. **C.** Parasagittal cross section through central sulcus and postcentral gyrus, illustrating the four Brodmann areas that make up S1. One consequence of this organization, and the circuitry schematized here, is that there is more than one somatotopic map in S1.

Source: Kandel et al., 2000 / McGraw-Hill.

Somatotopy The principle of topographic organization of sensory cortex is perhaps most intuitively demonstrated in S1: adjacent parts of the body ("soma," from the Greek) are, apart from a few necessary discontinuities, represented in adjacent regions of cortex. Although this organizational principle had been deduced from assessment of patients with focal brain lesions, it is most enduringly associated with the pioneering electrical stimulation studies of the Montreal-based neurosurgeon Wilder Penfield (1891–1976) and his colleagues. Because the brain itself is not innervated with somatosensory receptors, neurosurgery is often performed while the patient is awake, and can report what they are experiencing, and/or can be asked to perform actions that give the surgeon important moment-to-moment information about the status of the surgical intervention. Penfield was an epilepsy surgeon. His approach was guided by the dictum, still by-and-large in force today, that *no brain is better than bad brain*. That is, if a region of cortex is so dysfunctional that its periodic episodes of uncontrolled activity lead to systemic (in this context, "brain-wide") patterns of abnormal activity (i.e., seizures), the surgical removal of this epileptogenic tissue might bring an end to debilitating seizures, thereby allowing the remaining, healthy brain tissue to carry out its functions without interruption. An important corollary to this dictum, however, is that the surgeon does not want to damage cortex that supports functions that are critical for the patient's quality of life. Procedures used to abide by this corollary have led to important discoveries about brain function.

As an example, one case that Penfield and Rasmussen (1950) described was an 18-year-old male whose epilepsy was determined, upon inspection of the exposed cortex, to stem from a tumor located in the right precentral gyrus. Thus, they wrote, "The surgical problem was to remove the tumor without damage to the precentral gyrus and thus to avoid paralysis" (p. 6). (*Chapter 9* will detail the organization and function of the primary motor cortex of the precentral gyrus.) To accomplish this, they stimulated the surface of the brain at many locations that were near the region where they expected to find the "epileptogenic focus." In the process, different stimulation sites produced different responses that could be observed on the patient's body, or different verbal reports of what sensation he felt. Examples of observed effects included "Closure of the hand and pronation of the forearm" and "Dorsiflexion of the left foot." Examples of patient reports included "Contraction of my left hand and arm" (even though the doctors didn't observe any movement) and "A little of that feeling in the leg as though it were going to contract." After performing many such surgeries, Penfield and Rasmussen (1950) were able to generate the "sensory homunculus" illustrated in *Figure 2.16*. The precision of their measurements allowed them to document quantitatively the cortical magnification of various parts of the body, a feature analogous to the disproportionally larger cortical representation of the central vs. peripheral visual field in V1. Indeed, recall from section *The visual system, The retina and the LGN of the thalamus*, that the fovea has a higher packing density of photoreceptors than do peripheral parts of the retina, and that foveal receptive fields are consequently much smaller than are peripheral receptive fields. Similarly, from *Figure 2.16*, we can deduce that the skin of the lower lip is much more densely innervated with sensory receptors than is the skin of the elbow, and that, consequently, cortical receptive fields representing the lower lip (and other parts of the face, and many parts of the hand, etc.) are much smaller than are cortical receptive fields representing the elbow (and the small of the back, and the knee, etc.). The enterprising reader can appreciate this after a quick search on the internet for a full-monty view of the sculpture that interprets body-part size as being in a 1:1 relationship with the somatosensory homunculus. (As an aside, the word homunculus is Latin for "little man." In psychology and neuroscience, it is used in two contexts. Here, it refers to the representation of the human body as illustrated in *Figure 2.16*. It can also be used [often facetiously] in relation to the idea that a "little man inside our heads" is responsible for the conscious perception of sensory information, or for the coordination and control of brain activity.)

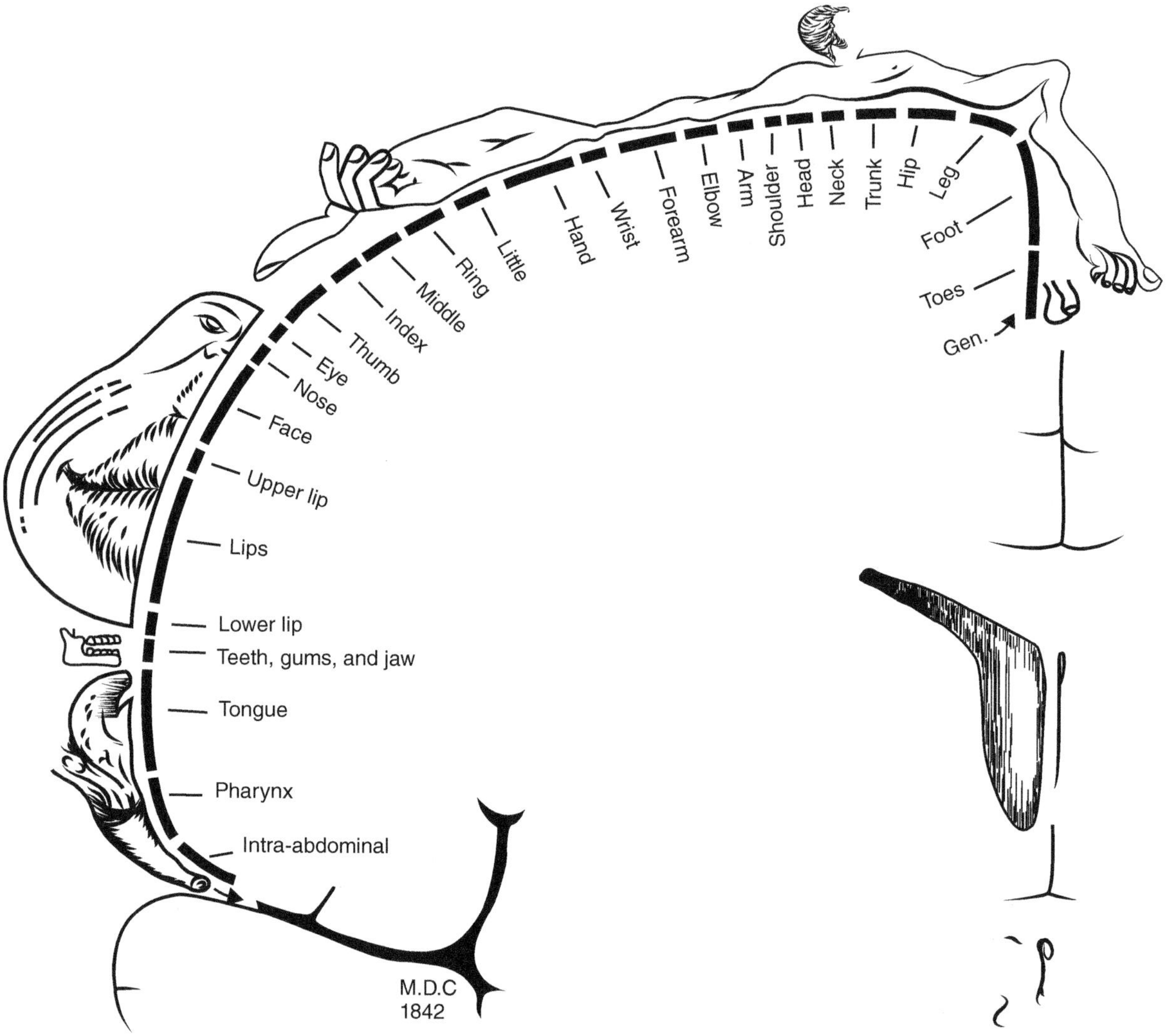

FIGURE 2.16 Depiction of the somatotopy of S1, as distributed along a paracoronal plane of section. The relative size of each body part reflects the surface area of cortex that represents it, as does the length of the line to which each label points. Two additional points are worthy of note. First, this scheme is a statistical composite derived from many individual cases. Second, this somatotopy can undergo rapid reorganization as a function of behavioral context or deafferentation (as demonstrated, e.g., by Kaas (2005, *Further reading*).

Source: Penfield et al., 1950 / Macmillan Publishers.

Complicated and Complex

The human brain is truly an amazing thing. It is made up of billions of neurons and trillions of synapses. What we have considered in this chapter only scratches the surface of all there is to know about the brain's molecular and cellular makeup, as well as the systems that transduce energy from the environment and deliver it to primary sensory cortex. However, with the facts that we have considered, and the questions we have posed, we can now start to address the question *How does the brain accomplish perception?* In so doing, we will be addressing what is meant by visual/auditory/somatosensory information processing in cortex.

But first, while all these facts about how the brain is put together and some aspects of how it works are still fresh in the mind, let's take a moment to consider a distinction made very eloquently by György Buszsáki in his 2006 book *Rhythms of the Brain*. The nuts-and-bolts facts of how cells in the brain work are, indeed, *complicated*. How this all works together to give rise to cognition, however, is not only complicated, it's *complex*. "The term 'complex' does not simply mean complicated but implies a nonlinear relationship between constituent components," and refers to properties often termed "spontaneous, endogenous, . . . self-organized, self-generated, self-assembled, and emergent" (p. 11). Stated another way, what we shall see again and again in our exploration of cognitive neuroscience is that the whole is often different from the sum of its parts.

End-of-Chapter Questions

1. In what ways does the anatomical organization of the adult brain follow from its developmental origin as the neural tube?

2. What factors explain the "crumpled-up" shape of the brain? What evolutionary pressures may have produced this shape?

3. What is a distinctive property of each layer of neocortex? Why might there be some advantages to segregating these properties/functions by layer?

4. What are the principal disequilibria maintained by the neuron that were emphasized in this chapter, and what role do they play in the generation of the action potential?

5. It can be said that neurons communicate via signals that, at one level of analysis, can be considered digital, yet from another level of analysis can be considered analog. What phenomena that were discussed in this chapter are an example of each?

6. What explains the oscillation of voltage across the cell membrane? What explains the oscillation of voltage in the LFP?

7. Although some scientists have argued that neuronal oscillations are primarily byproducts of the workings of neurons and networks of neurons (i.e., they may be "epiphenomenal"), there is a growing consensus that they may play an important role in governing the effectiveness of communication between one brain area and another. Describe the concept of phase synchronization and the role it may play in neuronal communication.

8. What is the principle of retinotopic organization? What is cortical magnification, and why does it occur?

9. What is a receptive field? How does the size of receptive fields vary as one moves from the fovea to the periphery? As one moves from retina to LGN to V1?

10. How might the mechanical properties of the cochlea result in the fact that the tuning of auditory nerve fibers broadens with increasing sound intensity?

11. What is meant by the term "spectral decomposition"? How is the operation carried out in the auditory system?

12. Which part of your body is more densely innervated with mechanoreceptors, your tongue or your forearm? What are the corresponding differences in how these two parts of your body are represented in S1 in your brain?

References

Buszáki, György. 2006. *Rhythms of the Brain*. Oxford: Oxford University Press.

Dumitriu, Dani, Alfredo Rodriguez, and John H. Morrison. 2011. "High-Throughput, Detailed, Cell-Specific Neuroanatomy of Dendritic Spines Using Microinjection and Confocal Microscopy." *Nature Protocols* 6 (9): 1391–1411. doi: 10.1038/nprot.2011.389.

Hubel, David H., and Torsten Wiesel. 1977. "Functional Architecture of Macaque Monkey Visual Cortex." *Proceedings of the Royal Society of London. Series B, Biological Sciences* 198 (1130): 1–59.

Kandel, Eric R., James H. Schwartz, and Thomas M. Jessell, eds. 2000. *Principles of Neural Science*. New York: McGraw-Hill.

Penfield, Wilder, and Theodore Rasmussen. 1950. *The Cerebral Cortex of Man. A Clinical Study of Localization of Function*. New York: Macmillan.

Saalmann, Yuri B., and Sabine Kastner. 2011. "Cognitive and Perceptual Functions of the Visual Thalamus." *Neuron* 71 (2): 209–223. doi: 10.1016/j.neuron.2011.06.027.

Sekuler, Robert, and Randolph Blake. 1985. *Perception*. New York: Alfred A. Knopf.

Warwick, Roger, and Peter L. Williams. 1973. *Gray's Anatomy. 35th*, British ed. Philadelphia, PA: W. B. Saunders.

Other Sources Used

Cooper, Jack R., Floyd E. Bloom, and Robert H. Roth. 1991. *The Biochemical Basis of Neuropharmacology*, 6th ed. New York: Oxford University Press.

Diamond, Marian C., Arnold B. Scheibel, and Lawrence M. Elson. 1985. *The Human Brain Coloring Book*. New York: Harper Perennial.

Hubel, David H. 1988. *Eye, Brain, and Vision. Scientific American Library, no. 22*. New York: W. H. Freeman.

Further Reading

Buszáki, György. 2006. *Rhythms of the Brain*. Oxford: Oxford University Press.

If there's only one book that this textbook inspires you to read, this might be it. Provides a rigorous neurophysiological and anatomical basis for much of the dynamical systems-influenced content of this book, including, for example, the final section of this chapter.

Diamond, Marian C., Arnold B. Scheibel, and Lawrence M. Elson. 1985. *The Human Brain Coloring Book*. New York: Harper Perennial.

In science, it's often said that "the best way to ensure that you understand a topic is to teach a class about it." The same might be said about neuroanatomy and drawing.

Morrison, John H., and Mark G. Baxter. 2012. "The Ageing Cortical Synapse: Hallmarks and Implications of Cognitive Decline." *Nature Reviews Neuroscience* 13 (4): 240–250. doi: 10.1038/nrn3200.

The PFC is one of the first regions of the brain to show age-related decline in healthy, middle-aged individuals. This paper shows that, in the monkey, this decline is largely due to a dramatic loss of dendritic spines in layer III, the cortical layer whose integrity is most closely tied to age-related cognitive impairment.

CHAPTER 3

The Neurophysiology of Sensation and Perception

KEY THEMES

- Individual neurons of V1 integrate input from multiple LGN neurons to construct specific features to which they respond preferentially and thereby act as feature detectors.
- At least five classes of features emerge at the level of V1: edge orientation, direction of movement, binocular disparity, end-stopping, and the representation of color, as well as an increase in acuity.
- Functional tissue imaging, which permits visualization of a large surface of cortex, has revealed that columns representing smooth transitions through the full 180° of orientation are organized in pinwheel-like configurations.
- Visual information processing does not consist of simply a serial feeding forward of signals from retina to LGN to V1, because V1 sends heavy feedback to the LGN, as do higher-level visual areas to V1.
- Functions of feedback include biasing the LGN to emphasize the orientation vs. the direction-of-movement of visual stimuli and determining how effective signals from LGN will be at driving cortical responses.
- At a broader spatial scale, the processing of incoming visual information is influenced by the magnitude of ongoing oscillations in the alpha frequency band (~8–13 Hz) of the electroencephalogram (EEG).
- Auditory perception depends on exquisitely delicate and precise mechanical transmission in the inner ear, including the cochlea.
- The physical properties of the basilar membrane within the cochlea effect a spectral decomposition of acoustic energy, which is read out as a place code by the auditory nerve.
- The multiple synaptic connections of the auditory brainstem produce the stereotyped early- and middle-latency components of the auditory-evoked potential (AEP).
- Deriving event-related potentials (ERPs) from the EEG, such as the AEP, is a powerful way to measure neural events that are difficult to isolate in the "noisy" EEG.
- Primary auditory cortex (A1), in the superior temporal gyrus, contains a 1-D tonotopic map.
- Optogenetic manipulation of S1, combined with electrophysiology, has provided insight into the functions of, and mechanisms underlying, gamma-band oscillations in the local field potential (LFP).

Companion Website: www.wiley.com/go/postle/cognitiveneuroscience3e

CONTENTS

Information Processing in Sensory Systems

As discussed in *Chapter 1*, visual perception is a function characterized by close linkage between the environment and the brain, and the same is true for audition and somatosensation. In the previous chapter, we introduced the concept of signal transduction—how information from the outside world gets converted into the electrical signals that are the language of the nervous system—now, we turn to how brain systems process these signals in ways that generate perception (including perceptual experience) and behavior. We'll start with vision.

Primary Visual Cortex – Bottom-Up Feature Detection

The V1 Neuron as Feature Detector

The anatomy of projections from retina, via lateral geniculate nucleus (LGN), to the cortex lining the calcarine fissure, combined with the systematicity of visual impairments produced by damage to the calcarine cortex, makes it clear that this region plays an important role in visual perception. By 1958, in the Johns Hopkins University laboratory of Stephen Kuffler, David Hubel (1926–2013), and Torsten Wiesel also knew, from extracellular electrophysiological experiments by themselves and others, that neurons in the LGN responded with a burst of action potentials when a small spot of light was projected in specific regions of the visual field (different regions of the LGN for neurons receiving input from retinal ganglion cells projecting from different parts of the retina). That is, LGN neurons had retinotopic receptive fields. They began studying the functions of primary visual cortex, therefore, by projecting small spots of light into the eye of a cat with an ophthalmoscope (not unlike the apparatus whose eye pieces you look through when having your vision examined by an eye doctor) while recording from neurons with the extracellular electrophysiological method that will be detailed in *Chapter 4*'s section on *Invasive recording with microelectrodes: action potentials and local field potentials*. Initially, experimental sessions during which the scientists stimulated the retina with spots of light failed to generate any responses from V1 neurons. The breakthrough discovery came when, in the process of changing slides in the ophthalmoscope, they found that a neuron responded with bursts of action potentials each time the shadow of the edge of the glass slide passed across the retina at a particular angle (*Figure 3.1*).

The importance of this discovery is that it led to a profound conceptual insight about the mechanisms whereby the primary visual cortex begins the computations that result in visual perception. More specifically, as illustrated in *Figure 2.11*, it led to the insight that neurons in primary visual cortex construct elemental features in the visual scene via the integration of information from the simpler center-surround receptive fields of LGN neurons.

Having made this initial observation, Hubel and Wiesel abandoned tiny spots of light in favor of bars of light (as can be made by cutting a long, narrow slit in a piece of cardboard and then shining a bright light through the slit and onto a projection screen). With this new stimulus, they quickly confirmed that many neurons in V1 responded robustly to a straight-line boundary defined by light on one side and darkness on the other. Importantly, for any

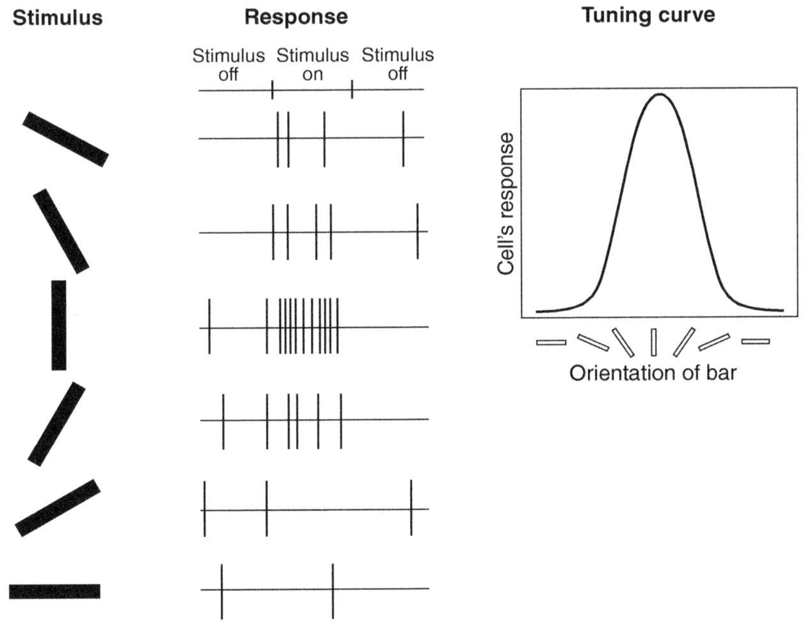

FIGURE 3.1 Orientation selectivity of a simple cell in V1, illustrated by action potentials ("Response" column) generated in response to a bar presented at each of six orientations ("Stimulus" column) and summarized in a tuning curve.

Source: Hubel and David (1988) / John Wiley & Sons.

given cell, this only occurred when that boundary was oriented (i.e., "tilted" or "slanted") in a particular direction. That is, one neuron might respond preferentially to a boundary oriented vertically, another to a boundary tilted 10° to the right of vertical, another to a boundary oriented horizontally, and so on, such that, with enough recording from enough neurons, they collected evidence that the full 180° of possible orientations was covered. The property of firing action potentials most robustly in response to a narrow range of orientations has come to be known as "orientation selectivity," or "orientation tuning," and is a hallmark property of many V1 neurons. (The term "tuning" is an analogy to the concept, from signal processing, of a tuned filter, a circuit used to separate signals in relatively narrow bands of frequencies from a broadband source.)

Orientation tuning is a specific example of a broader phenomenon that arises in V1, which is the construction of information (the "drawing of inferences," if one were to anthropomorphize) from more elemental information (e.g., the presence or absence of spots of light). Indeed, in addition to orientation, there are at least five other such "transforms" of elemental information into visual features: direction selectivity, higher acuity, binocular disparity (i.e., disparity between the images projected into the two eyes), the convergence of ON center/OFF surround and OFF center/ON surround (there are both types of LGN neurons and their convergence can give rise to more complex response properties than the 1-D orientation-tuned "simple cell" illustrated in *Figure 3.1*), and the construction of a single color axis from three cone types. A detailed consideration of how each of these transforms is computed is beyond the scope of this book. But let's briefly consider just one more example: direction of motion. Imagine receiving information that the receptive field of a neuron in the LGN is responding to visual stimulation at time t and that an LGN neuron with an immediately adjacent receptive field (let's say, 90° from vertical to the left) subsequently signals visual stimulation at time $t+1$. Voilà: a neuron receiving such time-lagged inputs from these two cells could "deduce" that an object in this part of the visual field is moving to the left. (To prove to yourself that the brain is "set up" to infer motion from temporally sequential and spatially offset events, consider the lighted marquee of a theater: a row of light bulbs lines the edges of the marquee, and flashing them rapidly, in succession, creates the illusion of a spot of light "running in circles" around the edge of the marquee.)

What might be the utility of some of the properties that emerge from processing in V1? Orientation tuning allows for the detection of edges and boundaries, a fundamental property of most objects that we encounter in the physical world. Direction selectivity is a necessary element of motion perception. Binocular disparity is used to see in depth (i.e., 3-D). Combining inputs from the two classes of LGN receptive fields can produce complex tuning properties such as responding to the end of a line (a property referred to as being "end-stopped"). Finally, with regard to color, it has been estimated that humans can distinguish among millions of hues of color, a feat that surely requires considerable processing of the initial inputs to cortex from just three types of wavelength-sensitive cones. These properties (e.g., edges, motion, binocular disparity, end-stopping, and color) can be thought of as low-level visual features that, when combined in different ways, are the constituent elements of the complex objects that we recognize and interact with, "effortlessly," during every waking moment that our eyes are open. Thus, an influential way of understanding information processing in V1 is to view these neurons as feature detectors – units in the system whose function is to signal the presence of their particular feature each time it appears in their receptive field and to pass this information forward to downstream networks in the visual system that will aggregate information from many such feature detectors to assemble a representation of what object is currently in the visual field. *Chapter 6* will give more consideration to what we know about object perception, but for now, we'll maintain our focus on the organization of V1.

Columns, Hypercolumns, and Pinwheels

A common practice during single-electrode extracellular recording sessions is having characterized the response properties of the first neuron encountered, to advance the electrode further into (or, depending on the angle of penetration, further along) the region under investigation. (In later chapters, we'll introduce the techniques of recording with a "laminar" electrode with multiple contacts along its shaft and of simultaneously recording from multiple electrodes.) The results of several perpendicular penetrations (i.e., from layer I to layer VI within a single column) led Hubel and Wiesel to conclude that neurons within a cortical column share the same orientation selectivity. (Hence the term "orientation column.") Penetrations that were parallel to the cortical surface, in contrast, revealed that adjacent columns tended to be tuned to orientations that were slightly rotated from those of the neighboring columns. This led to the proposal that primary visual cortex was organized into "hypercolumns," a hypothesized grid of orientation columns that, together, represented every possible orientation that could fall within a receptive field. Of course, to be equipped to analyze every possible feature that could occupy a receptive field, such hypercolumns would additionally need to represent all possible features (or, minimally, the constituent elements needed to construct all possible features) that could fall into this receptive field. Consistent with the idea of omni-featured hypercolumns was the fact that parallel penetrations would periodically encounter columns of neurons that did not show orientation selectivity but that did seem to process information about color. Thus, Hubel and Wiesel conjectured that each hypercolumn also contained orientation-nonselective, but chromatically tuned, neurons that are important for the perception of color.

A few decades later, advances in functional tissue imaging techniques (section *Functional tissue imaging, Chapter 4*) led to further specifications and then modifications of the hypercolumn model. It is important to note that, in their studies from the 1950s and 1960s, Hubel and Wiesel never directly observed a hypercolumn in toto. Rather, they inferred the existence of this organizing structure from after-the-fact interpretation of the results of dozens, if not hundreds, of experimental sessions. An advantage of functional tissue imaging over single-electrode recording is that it can assess the activity of a relatively large region of cortex (on the order of cm^2) all at once. A critical early discovery, triggered by the research of Margaret Wong-Riley (1989), was that superficial layers of V1, when assayed to detect activity of the enzyme cytochrome oxidase, revealed "blobs" of tissue that stained more darkly than the surrounding tissue. Cytochrome oxidase is a membrane-spanning protein found in mitochondria and is critical in the generation of adenosine triphosphate (ATP) via oxidative metabolism. Therefore, darker staining, which indicates elevated levels of cytochrome oxidase activity, is a marker for elevated activity in the cells containing it. Subsequent extracellular recordings from neurons located within blobs, by Margaret Livingstone and David Hubel, discovered these to primarily contain the orientation-nonselective, chromatically tuned neurons, as described in the previous paragraph.

More recently, optical imaging methods have revealed that, instead of being organized into cube-like modules of tissue organized in tidy rows of columns, the functional organization of V1 is more reminiscent of a series of pinwheels, with an orientation-insensitive blob at the center and several "petals" made up of orientation-selective columns of neurons emanating from it.

Inside the Pinwheel Before leaving this section, a few more words about how blobs come to be blobs, and orientation-selective regions come to be orientation-selective. There are two major classes of retinal ganglion cells (RGCs), which take their names from the *magnocellular* and *parvocellular* neurons of the LGN to which they project. (As is illustrated in *Figure 2.4* and *Figure 6.1*, layers 1 and 2 of the LGN contain magnocellular ["M"] neurons, and layers 3, 4, 5, and 6 contain parvocellular ["P"] neurons.) M RGCs have dendritic arbors that span a larger surface area and thus sample from a larger number of photoreceptors than do P RGCs. Two consequences of such broad sampling are that (1) M RGCs have relatively larger receptive fields, and (2) they do not carry color-specific information (whereas P RGCs do). M RGCs also have faster axonal conduction velocities than do P RGCs. It is magnocellular neurons (of the LGN) that project to orientation-selective regions of V1 and parvocellular neurons that project to blobs. This information will be particularly germane in *Chapter 6*, when we consider feedforward projections from V1 to different regions of extrastriate cortex, and how these regions come to have different functional specializations.

Information Processing in Primary Visual Cortex–Interactivity

At this point, the discussion from *Chapter 2* about the projection profiles of different layers of neocortex (*Figure 2.4*) becomes particularly germane. We'll begin with one of the more astounding facts about the anatomy of the visual system, one that, until this point, has been glossed over.

Feedforward and Feedback Projections of V1

Figure 3.2 illustrates the elegant sweep of the optic radiations that connect the LGN with V1. Importantly, however, an estimated 75–90% of the fibers comprising the optic radiations are traveling from V1 back to the thalamus. That is, for each axon conveying signals from the LGN to V1 (i.e., in the feedforward direction), there are anywhere from three to nine axons conveying feedback signals from V1 to LGN. One hint at why our visual systems evolved in this way has come from a series of elegant (and technically very challenging) experiments performed by London (UK)-based neuroscientist Adam Sillito and his colleagues. Their studies, summarized in *Figure 3.3*, provide evidence that ongoing activity in extrastriate and striate cortex can, in effect, shape the signals that the LGN will subsequently deliver to striate cortrex. Cudeiro and Sillito (2006) summarize the more general principle as follows: "For sensory input to be rapidly assessed and to guide the behaviour of an organism, it needs to be continually placed in the context of hypotheses formulated by higher brain centres" (p. 304).

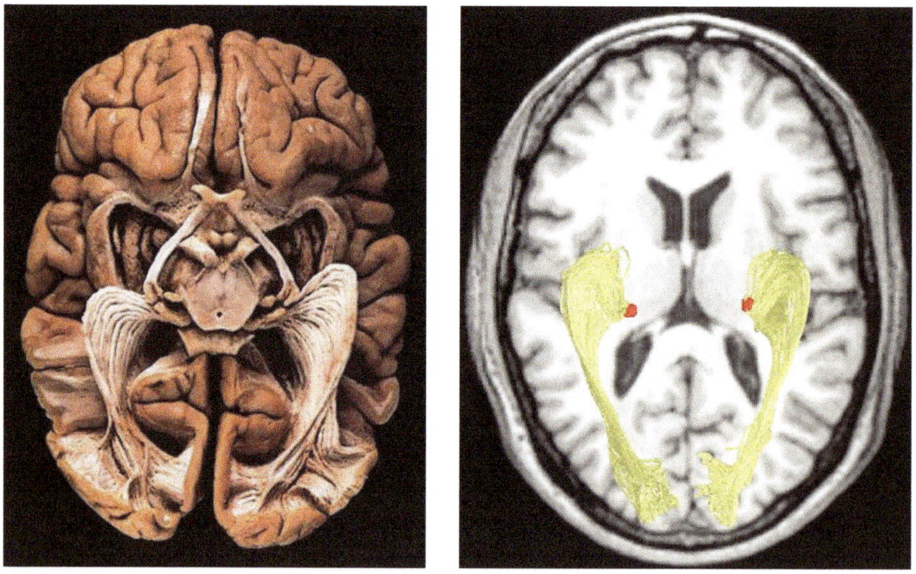

FIGURE 3.2 Image on the left shows a human brain dissected to reveal the pathways from retina, via the lateral geniculate nucleus (LGN) of the thalamus, to cortical area V1. Particularly striking are the elegant optic radiations, the myelinated fibers running between the thalamus and the primary visual cortex. To expose these pathways and structures, the anatomist dissected away tissue from the ventral surface of the brain, up to and including the ventral bank of the calcarine fissure. Thus, only the dorsal bank of the calcarine and the fibers of the optic radiations that project to it are seen here. The image on the right shows a slice from a T1-weighted anatomical MR scan (gray scale) oriented to include both the LGN (pseudocolored red) and the calcarine sulcus. Superimposed, in yellow, is an image of the path of the optic radiations, as estimated via MR-derived diffusion-tensor imaging (DTI) tractography.

Source: Reproduced from Wandell and Winawer (2011) / with permission of Elsevier.

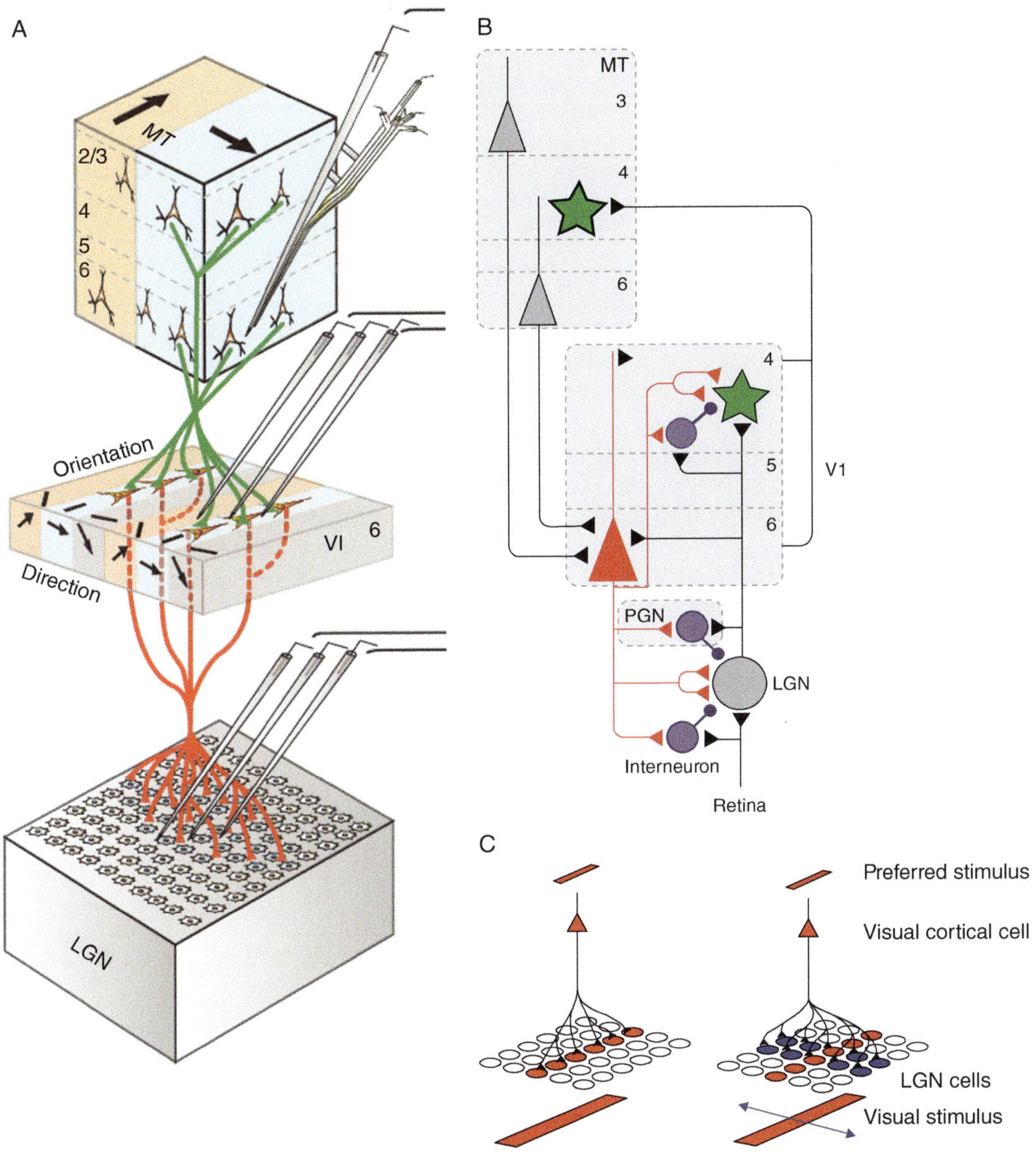

FIGURE 3.3 The role of feedback in shaping what we see. **A.** An experimental setup in which neurons with overlapping receptive fields are simultaneously recorded from in the LGN, layer VI of primary visual cortex (V1), and layer VI of the motion-sensitive region of extrastriate visual cortex known as MT. **B.** Schematic diagram of some of the circuitry that is important for motion perception. The feedforward pathway begins at the bottom of the panel, with an axon from a retinal ganglion cell projecting to and synapsing on a neuron in the LGN of the thalamus, and a branch from this axon synapsing on an adjacent inhibitory interneuron. The LGN sends its "primary" axon to a neuron in layer IV of cortical area V1 (green star), with collaterals to other cell types. The final feedforward step that is illustrated here is from V1 to MT, cartooned as axons projecting from layers VI and IV of V1 to a neuron in layer IV of MT (green star). (Note that this deviates from the "general rule" described in *Chapter 2* that corticocortical feedforward projections tend to originate from layer II/III – the brain is complicated; one can find an exception to almost all "general rules.") The principle feedback pathway illustrated here starts with projections from MT (layers 3 and 6) to a layer-VI neuron in V1, which, in turn, projects to the same LGN neuron with which we started (with collaterals to inhibitory interneurons that also synapse on our LGN neuron). (Note that these MT-to-V1 projections also deviate from the "general rule.") **C.** A schematic "zoom-in" on the LGN, illustrating a functional consequence of this bidirectional network architecture with the example of the processing of information about a bar moving through the visual field (labeled "preferred stimulus"). Depending on the balance of top-down signals from MT to V1, the output of V1-to-LGN feedback projections (schematized as just a single neuron, but in reality coming from a local population of neurons), either emphasizes the LGN's processing of the orientation of the visual stimulus (left side of panel) or its processing of the motion in which the bar is moving (right side of panel). Indeed, in the latter case, corticothalamic feedback signals can produce a "wave" of activity in LGN that precedes the arrival of the stimulus into the receptive field, in effect "preparing" the LGN with a predicted trajectory of the stimulus.

Why does this circuitry require so disproportionate a balance of feedback vs. feedforward projections? One reason is that implementing functions like the anticipatory "wave" of activity in the LGN illustrated in *Figure 3.3.C* requires a lot of circuitry. Related to this is the fact that layer VI projections to subcortical structures are much more complicated than what is illustrated in *Figure 3.4.B*. For example, the region labeled "PGN" in this figure, the perigeniculate nucleus, is part of a larger structure known as the thalamic reticular nucleus (TRN; *Figure 2.4*). Although the TRN is present in many of the photographic images in this book that include the thalamus (e.g., *Figure 1.2.B* and *Figure 2.2*), it can't actually be seen in these images due to its microscopic thinness. Unlike most subcortical nuclei, which are clumps of cell bodies whose shape often resembles a familiar object (e.g., an almond, a knee, or a tail), the TRN is a thin sheet that wraps around much of the body of the thalamus. (The familiar object that it evokes for this author is plastic kitchen wrap.) The name "reticular" derives from the fact that it is reticulated – punctuated with holes necessitated by the fact that hundreds of thousands of axons pass through it while traveling from thalamus to cortex or from cortex to thalamus. The TRN is made up exclusively of GABAergic neurons whose output, in addition to collateral projections within the TRN itself, is exclusively focused on the thalamus. As a result, the TRN is ideally suited to implement an inhibitory surround.

Corticothalamic Loops, Center-Surround Inhibition, and Signal-to-Noise Ratio To explain the concept of an inhibitory surround, let's return for a moment to the anecdote from *Chapter 2* of the encounter with the bear. This anecdote was first used to

FIGURE 3.4 A schematic interpretation of the effects of thalamic action potentials on layer IV cortical cells in V1.

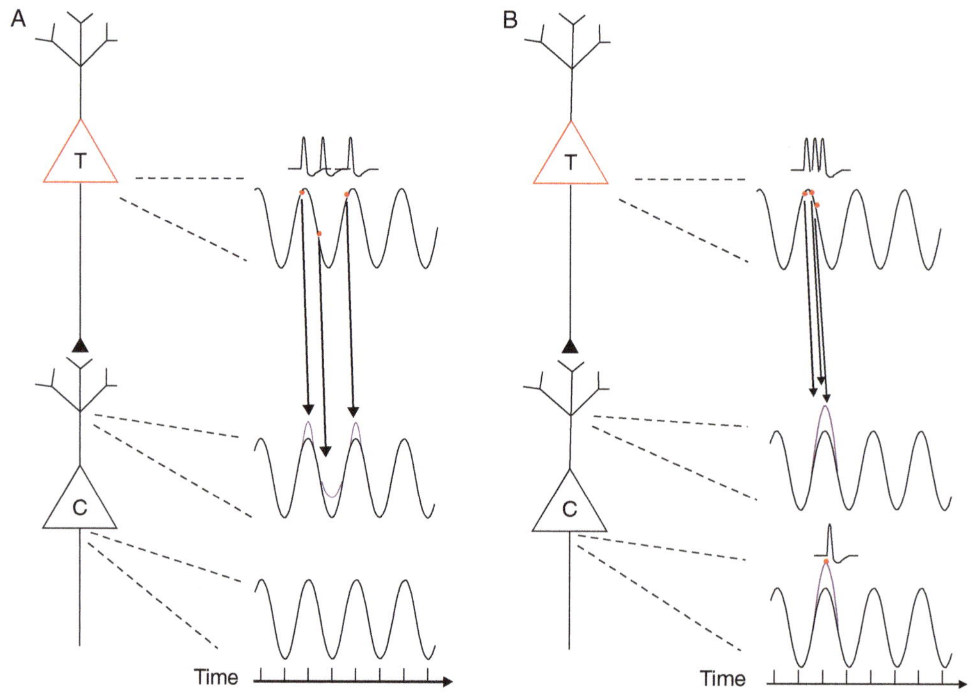

FIGURE 3.4.A A thalamic neuron (T) firing in tonic mode. Individual action potentials are sufficiently spaced out in time that, in the dendrites of the postsynaptic cortical neuron (C), the ESPS from earlier spikes dissipate by the time the next spike arrives.

FIGURE 3.4.B A thalamic neuron firing in burst mode. Here, the EPSPs from individual action potentials summate in the postsynaptic cortical neuron, and this has the effect of depolarizing this neuron above threshold.

illustrate how oscillatory synchrony might contribute to prioritizing the processing of the bear over the bird or the dappling sunlight. Another goal for the brain in this situation, however, would be to generate as sharp a representation of the bear as is possible. One way to accomplish this goal would be to minimize competition from the neural representation of other largish, hirsute quadrupeds. (Now would not be the time, e.g., to contemplate the similarities and differences of bears to, say, deer, raccoons, and dogs; as in *Hmmm. Is it really true that bears are evolutionarily more closely related to dogs than to cats?*) When a cortical neuron involved in the neural representation of the bear (let's call it neuron *A*) sends a volley of action potentials to another neuron in the hypothetical "bear network" (we'll call it *B*), a layer V or VI neuron in the same column as *A* may send a parallel volley of action potentials to a thalamic neuron (*T*) that, itself, is connected with neuron *B*. Thus, *B* receives excitatory (i.e., glutamatergic) inputs from both *A* and *T*. (This is effectively what's illustrated in the feedforward projections from V2 to V4 that are illustrated in *Figure 2.4*.) An important feature of this corticothalamic circuit is that where the *A*-to-*T* axon passes through the TRN, it sends collateral branches to TRN neurons that, in turn, project to thalamic neurons that surround *T* (but that don't synapse with *T* itself). The result is that action potentials from layer VI of cortical column *A* have the effect of inhibiting activity in thalamic neurons surrounding *T* [because excitatory collaterals from the *A*-to-*T* pathway activate TRN neurons that, in turn, release gamma-aminobutyric acid (GABA) onto these neurons]. Back in the cortex, the consequence for *B* (and, by extension, for the neural representation of the bear) is lowered activity in competing neurons (representations), due to a reduction of their excitatory thalamic "drive." A more formal way to summarize this is that engagement of this corticothalamic loop increases the signal-to-noise ratio (SNR) of the information carried by *A* and *B*. The same network dynamics described here (minus the part about the bear) have been demonstrated in studies of attention, which we will take up in *Chapter 8*. (The more general mechanism of center-surround inhibition will also be central to understanding functional contributions of the basal ganglia to motor control [*Chapter 9* and *Chapter 10*].)

And so, to return to the question of why the disproportionate ratio of corticothalamic to thalamocortical fibers in the optic radiations, another part of the answer is the implementation of cortical control of center-surround dynamics of the LGN. Note that, although the example in the previous paragraph used just one layer V or VI neuron in cortical column *A*, the inhibitory surround is, in fact, implemented by descending fibers from many neurons. A second function implemented by corticothalamic fibers, and therefore also implicated in the makeup of the optic radiations, is controlling the "thalamic wake-up call."

Setting the State of Thalamic Neurons: Tonic Mode vs. Burst Mode

Another function of corticogeniculate fibers is to modulate the effectiveness with which LGN neurons can convey signals to the cortex. They can do this because of a property of thalamic neurons that distinguishes them from most cortical pyramidal neurons: thalamic neurons can display two distinct modes of firing action potentials, tonic and burst modes. Burst-mode spiking has been referred to as "a wake-up call" from thalamus to cortex, for reasons that are evident in *Figure 3.4*: burst-mode action potentials are markedly more effective at transmitting information than are tonic-mode action potentials. Thalamic neurons move into tonic firing mode when their membrane potential is maintained at a depolarized level for 100 ms or longer and into a burst mode when maintained at a hyperpolarized level for 100 ms or longer. Research from Sillito's group, using a procedure not unlike that illustrated in *Figure 3.3.A*, has established that the layer VI neurons in V1, via projections to GABAergic neurons in the TRN and within the LGN itself, play a role in controlling whether visual information from the LGN is conveyed to V1 via tonic or bursting spike trains. Thus, in effect, the functions of some of the fibers descending from cortex to thalamus via the optic radiations enable the cortex to decide when to give itself a wake-up call.

Circularity? It Can Depend on Your Perspective On the surface, some of the phrases used in the previous two sections, such as that a "function of [layer VI of cortex] is to modulate the effectiveness with which LGN neurons can convey signals to the cortex" can sound circular. Indeed, it was physically difficult for the author to type that sentence – some stage of the process of motor preparation in his brain "knew" that it didn't sound right. When given more consideration, however, one can see that what may make one-sentence summaries of findings like these seem paradoxical is the absence of context. To interpret these findings on their own illustrates that it can be a thorny proposition to attempt to isolate discrete "processes" (or "functions") within the spectacularly complex, nonlinear system that is the brain. For example, in defining a process, where is one to stop? Take the case of the proximal control that V1 exerts over whether LGN activity emphasizes the static orientation of a stimulus or its motion (*Figure 3.3.C*). While this could be characterized as an instance of feedback control of V1 over the LGN, *Figure 3.3* illustrates that this network is embedded in a larger network that includes MT, with inputs from the latter influencing layer VI of V1.

The Relation Between Visual Processing and the Brain's Physiological State

In the 1920s, a German physician and physiologist named Hans Berger (1873–1941) began studying the electrical properties of the brain via recordings made with an electrode affixed to the scalp (i.e., as far as we know, Berger invented electroencephalography (EEG); see section *Electroencephalography, Chapter 4*). In a 1929 publication that was widely dismissed in his native country, he reported that the EEG was strongest when recorded over the occipital cortex, and that it had two key properties. First, it was characterized by "continuous oscillations in which . . . one can distinguish larger first order waves with an average duration [i.e., cycle] of 90 milliseconds and smaller second order waves of an average duration of 35 milliseconds." Thus, he was describing a complex wave form that comprised the summation of oscillations at two different frequencies. (See *Figure 4.7* for analogous properties of the local field potential [LFP] and *Figure 4.10* for the decomposition and quantification of different frequency components of the EEG signal.) He named the more prominent "first-order" rhythm *alpha* and the "second-order" rhythm *beta*. The second key property that Berger described was that the alpha rhythm of the EEG was considerably larger when the subject's eyes were closed than when they were open (*Figure 3.5*). This fact can be interpreted in at least two ways. One interpretation is that brain systems (in this case, the visual system) may slip into default "idling" states when they are not actively processing information. From this perspective, the opening of the eyes, and consequent delivery of visual information to the cortex, gives the visual system "something to do" and thereby pushes it out of its idling mode. A second interpretation is that the brain may configure itself into different states to optimize performance on the currently prioritized task. Visual perception is often (although not always) prioritized when the eyes are open. We shall also see, in *Chapter 8*, that the dynamics of alpha-band oscillations vary systematically with the control of visual attention.

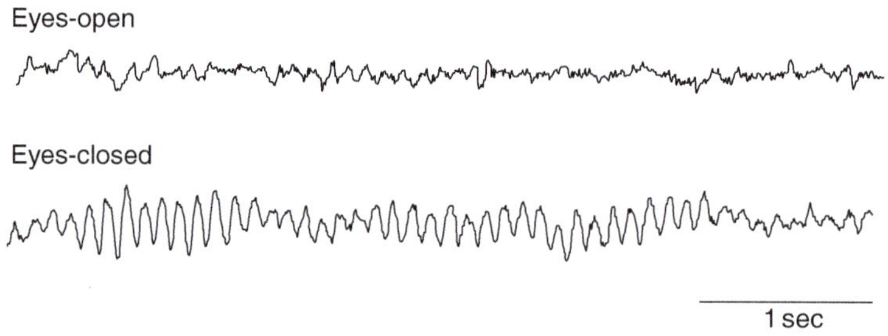

FIGURE 3.5 EEG traces illustrating the "Berger rhythm," recorded from channel O1 while the subject sits quietly with eyes open (top row) and closed (bottom row). Note how, in the eyes-closed trace, the magnitude of the alpha-band oscillation fluctuates over time, thus displaying a lower-frequency "envelope."

A contemporary experiment that can be construed as elaborating on Berger's original observations was carried out by Vincenzo Romei and colleagues in 2008, with a technique called transcranial magnetic stimulation (TMS). We will detail TMS in *Chapter 4*, but for now, suffice it to say that it uses a pulse of magnetic energy to induce a burst of electrical current in a targeted region of the brain. Romei et al. (2008) took advantage of the fact that single pulses of TMS delivered to occipital cortex can produce a perceptual phenomenon known as a phosphene – a cloud-like flash of light that a subject perceives even when the eyes are closed and covered with a blindfold (*Figure 3.6*). Phosphenes are presumed to be generated by the propagation of action potentials through the visual cortex. The generation of phosphenes with TMS is probabilistic, with the probability that any given pulse of TMS will generate a phosphene increasing with the magnitude of the TMS pulse. The procedure of Romei et al. (2008) was quite simple, in that they determined for each subject the intensity of TMS that would produce a phosphene on 50% of trials and then delivered many pulses at that intensity. After each pulse, they asked the subject to report whether or not they experienced a phosphene, and, after the experimental session, sorted trials into two categories: "Percept-yes" and "Percept-no." A final detail is that the EEG was being recorded for each subject right up until the time that TMS was delivered. Thus, upon completion of an experiment, the researchers

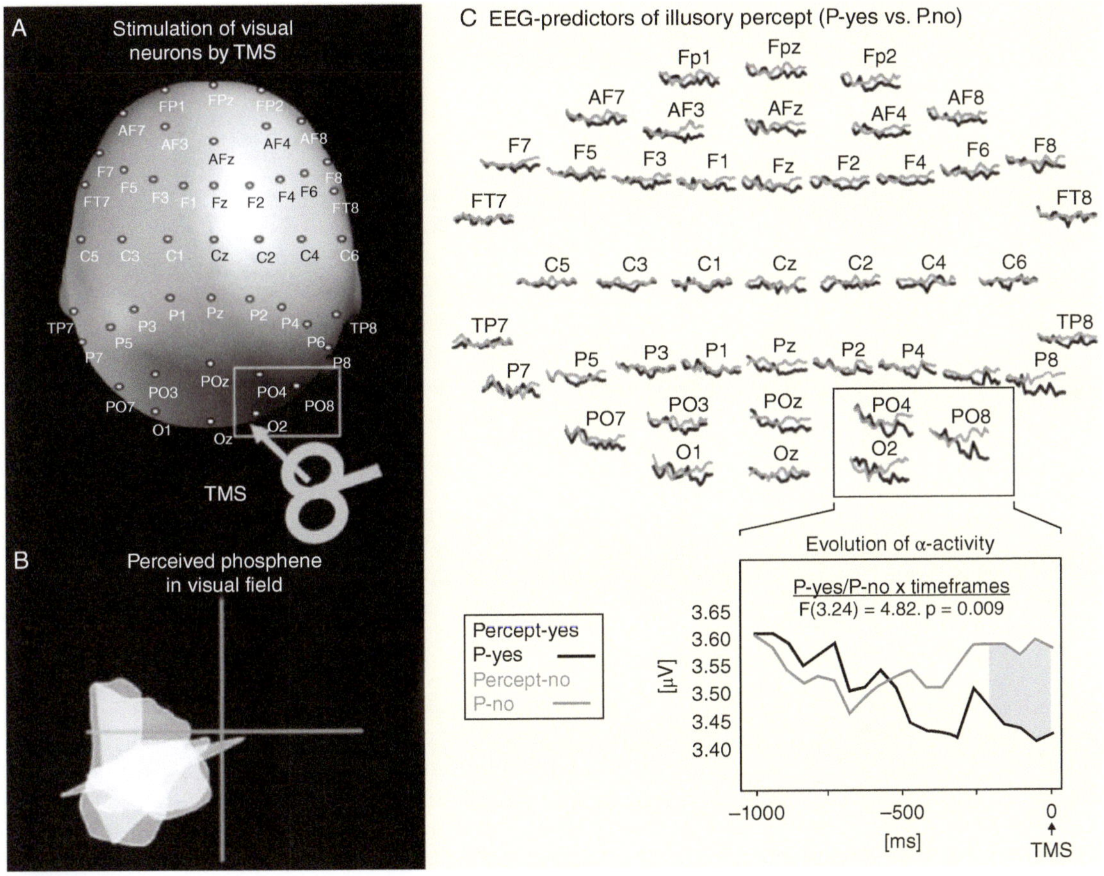

FIGURE 3.6 Methods and results from Romei et al. (2008). **A.** Illustration of the delivery of TMS to a region of the scalp medial to electrode O2, thus targeting a dorsal portion of visual cortex. (Small circles and labels correspond to EEG electrodes.) **B.** An "artist's rendering" of the shape and location of TMS-evoked phosphenes reported by subjects in this study. Note that the location in the visual field corresponds to the known functional organization of the early visual system. **C.** Illustration of the temporal evolution in the magnitude of alpha-band oscillations across the 1000 ms prior to TMS delivery on trials when subjects did (Percept-yes) vs. did not (Percept-no) report perception of a phosphene. The upper portion of this panel shows these measures at each of the electrodes illustrated in panel **A**; the lower portion of this panel shows the average of these measures from the three electrodes at which the alpha-band magnitude for the roughly 250 ms prior to TMS delivery predicted phosphene perception.

Source: Romei et al., 2008 / Oxford University Press.

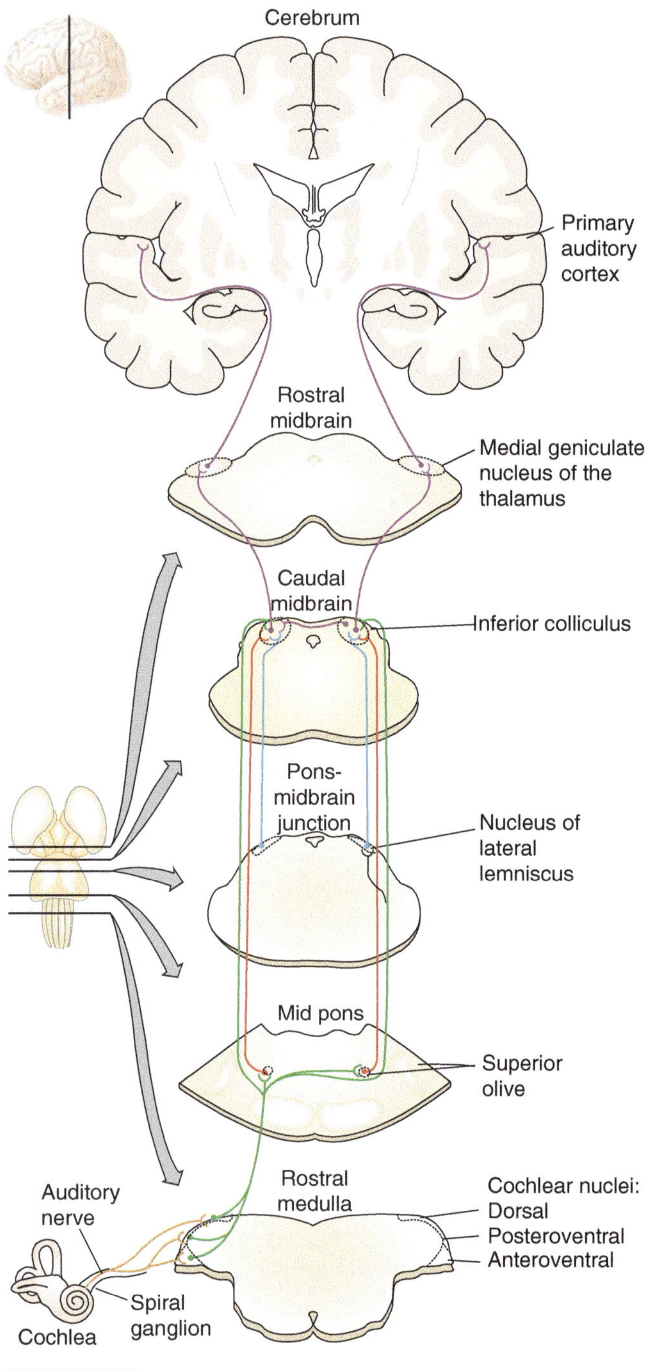

FIGURE 3.7 The auditory pathways from cochlea to cortex. On the left-hand side of the figure are three 3-D renderings of anatomical structures: the bottom is the cochlea; in the middle is a view from behind of the brainstem, midbrain, and thalamus (with cerebellum removed), and horizontal lines showing the locations of the cross-sectional slices illustrated on the right; and at the top is a view of the cerebrum, with a line indicating the level of the coronal slice. Note that there are multiple pathways, with synapses at each of the five levels of the brainstem and midbrain that are illustrated (although not every pathway synapses at each level). Pathways originating from only the left ear are shown.

Source: Wolfe et al., 2012 / Sinauer Associates Inc.

could determine whether the EEG immediately prior to the delivery of TMS differed systematically on trials when TMS did vs. did not produce a phosphene.

As illustrated in the top and bottom panels of *Figure 3.6.C*, there was, indeed, a systematic difference in the EEG that predicted whether or not the subject would experience a phosphene on each trial: on average, the magnitude of alpha-band oscillations was lower on trials when subjects did detect a phosphene than on trials when they did not. From this, the authors concluded that "momentary levels of posterior alpha-band activity [reflect . . .] distinct states of visual cortex excitability, and [. . . this] spontaneous fluctuation constitutes a visual operation mode that is activated automatically even without retinal input" (p. 2010). This study thus reinforces the idea that visual perception depends, in part, on the internally determined state of the visual system; a state that exists prior to the initial arrival of information from the outside world.

Audition

The Auditory-Evoked Response

As *Figure 3.7* illustrates, the auditory signal is processed in many subcortical structures, collectively referred to as the brainstem auditory nuclei, before arriving at primary auditory cortex, A1. Synaptic activity associated with these many nodes produces the many deflections (the "peaks") in the early-latency components of the auditory-evoked potential (AEP; *Figure 3.8*). It is in these brainstem nuclei that many of the computations are performed that allow us, among other things, to localize where a sound in the environment is coming from. Importantly, at each of these nodes, the topography of the "place code" for frequency that was established by the properties of the basilar membrane is preserved. The remarkable speed at which all of this processing takes place can be appreciated from inspection of the AEP (*Figure 3.8*), each peak of which is associated with a synaptic event (and, therefore, a stage of processing) along the auditory pathway.

To foreshadow some questions that we'll consider in future chapters, let's note that sensory-evoked responses (the AEP and its visual and somatosensory analogues) are stereotyped, stable responses that are effectively identical in all neurologically healthy individuals. This makes them very effective "tools" for studying the neural bases of many different behavioral and physiological states. To study attention, for example, one can examine how the AEP may differ on trials when one is attending to a concurrent stream of visual stimuli vs. trials when one is attending to the auditory stimuli. (E.g., does inspection of *Figure 3.9* suggest that some steps in the neural processing of sound are vs. are not influenced by attention?) To study different stages of sleep, one can examine how the AEP may differ when tones are played when the research subject is awake (and quietly resting), vs. in stage 1 (i.e., "light") sleep, vs. stage 2 (i.e., "heavy") sleep, vs. rapid-eye-movement (REM) sleep.

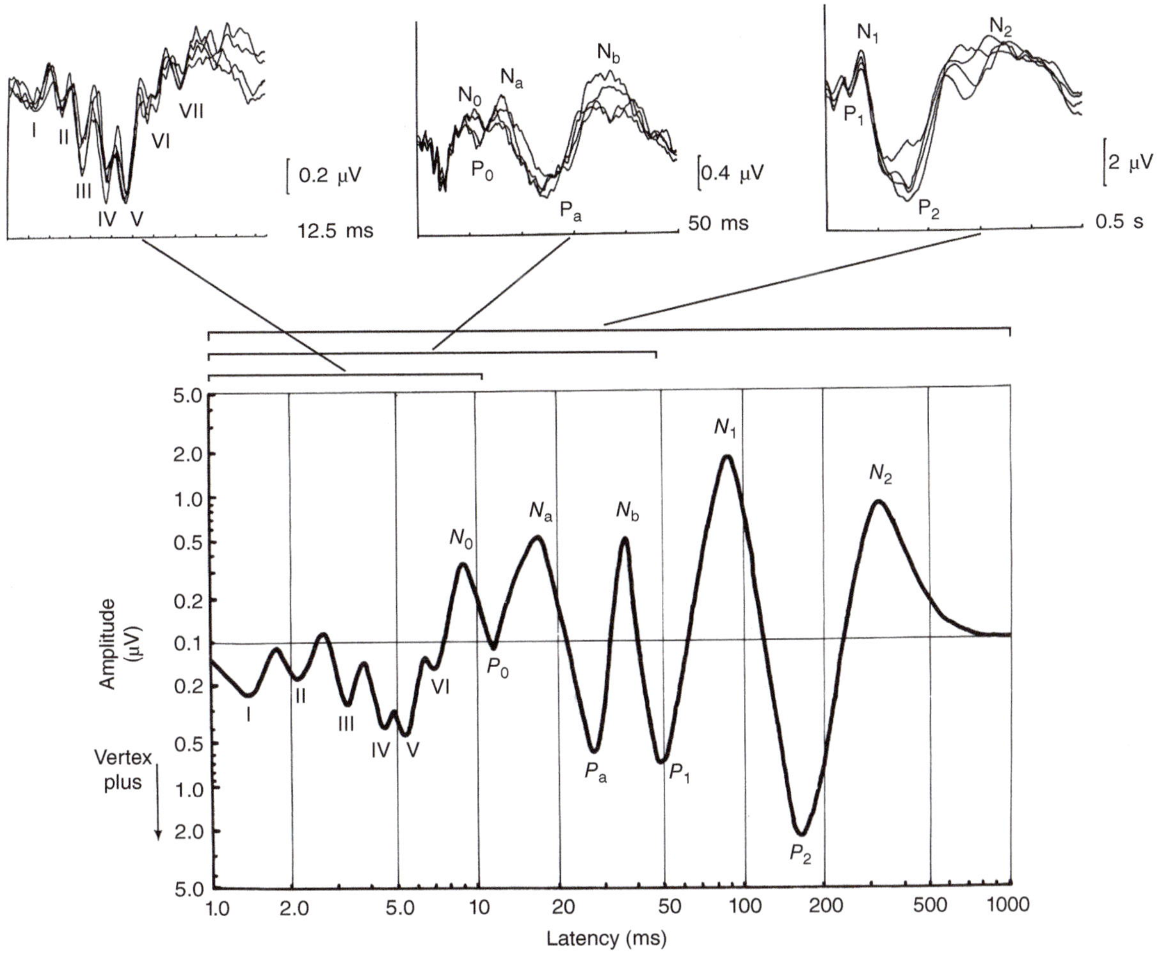

FIGURE 3.8 The auditory-evoked potential (AEP) to a 60-dB_{SPL} click of 50-μs duration. Each of the panels in the top row shows four traces, each an ERP computed by averaging the EEG from 1024 trials, and each acquired from the same subject but in four different recording sessions. (This was done to demonstrate the stability of this response within an individual.) Although each of these waveforms is time-locked to the click, each differs with regard to the length of time following the click over which the EEG traces were averaged. Thus, the panel on the left illustrates the first 12.5 ms post-click; the middle panel includes these initial 12.5 ms but also the ensuing 37.5 ms (i.e., a time span of 50 ms); the panel on the right a time span of 500 ms. Note that the scale on the vertical axis (i.e., the amplitude of the ERP) changes by an order of magnitude from the 12.5-ms time window to the 500-ms time window. These three panels correspond to what are known as the *early*, *middle*, and *long* latency components of the AEP, with the early-latency components known to correspond to processing in the auditory brainstem structures illustrated in *Figure 3.7*. The bottom panel illustrates the AEP (windowed at 1000 ms) averaged across eight individuals and accommodates the fact that these three groups of components play out on different scales of time and magnitude by plotting the "log/log" transform of the AEP (i.e., both the temporal and amplitude values are plotted on logarithmic scales).

Source: Picton et al., 1974 / with permission of Elsevier.

The Organization of Auditory Cortex In the AEP (*Figure 3.8*), the N1 and subsequent components are the first that unambiguously correspond to cortical processing. Thus, despite all the circuitry of the auditory brainstem, auditory information gets from the ear to the cortex in considerably less than 100 ms! The primary auditory cortex, A1, is located in posterior superior temporal gyrus, bilaterally, on the ventral wall of the Sylvian fissure (*Figure 3.10*). In a manner that echoes the functional organization of the primary visual cortex, the place code that originates in the cochlea is preserved all the way to A1. And although the analogy to retinotopy might make one expect that A1's functional organization would be called "basilotopy" or "cochleotopy," the standard term is tonotopy, a reference to the fact

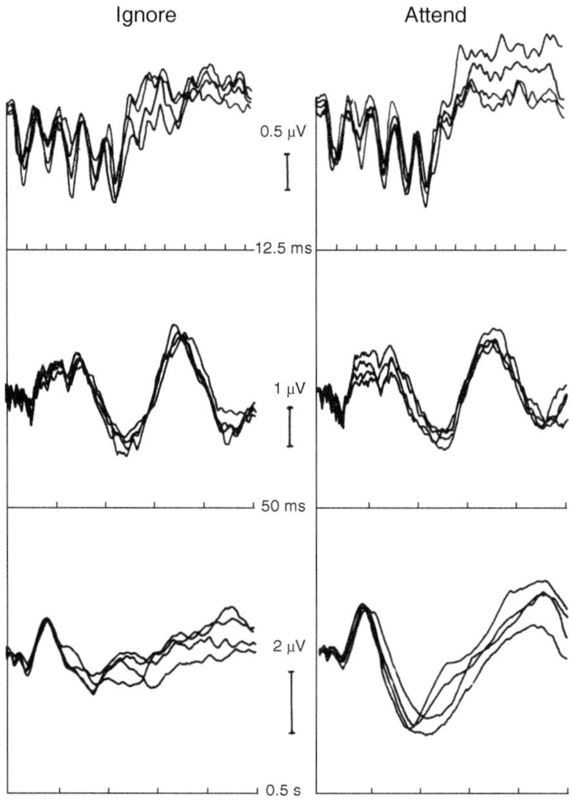

FIGURE 3.9 How attention to sound does, and doesn't, influence the AEP. Clicks (60 dB_{SPL}) were delivered once per second, and once every 5–30 seconds, the click was slightly softer. In the IGNORE condition, the subject was instructed to read a book and pay no attention to the clicks. In the ATTEND condition, they were instructed to detect each softer click and report the number detected at the end of the session. This figure illustrates the AEP to the soft click using the same three time windows as *Figure 3.8*, but here, they are arranged vertically to facilitate comparison between the IGNORE and ATTEND conditions. An effect of attention was only seen reliably on the N1 and P2 components of the AEP (bottom row). The figure illustrates two important points, one relating to the effect of attention in the ATTEND condition, and the second to the absence of detectable effects of reading in the IGNORE condition. In the ATTEND condition, because there was not an external event occurring roughly 100 ms after the click, the effects on the N1 and P2 ERP components are assumed to result from a *neural event* that was not directly evoked by an external stimulus. That is, they reflect an endogenous influence on the ERP. (We'll consider the nature of this neural event, and other attention-related ERP components, in *Chapter 9*.) The ERP from the IGNORE condition, in contrast, illustrates how trial averaging can remove components from the EEG that derive from events that one is not interested in. Note how the waveforms from the two conditions look nearly identical (apart from N1 and P2), even though only one includes reading. Reading involves regular eye movements, which produce enormous artifacts in the EEG, as well as neural processing associated with visual perception (*Chapter 3* and *Chapter 7*) and analyzing the grammar and the meaning of sentences (*Chapter 19*). However, because none of these reading-related events was time-locked to the clicks, their influence on the EEG was averaged out of these ERPs.

Source: Picton et al., 1974 / with permission of Elsevier.

that it is organized in terms of the frequency of the tone(s) being processed.[1] That is, as one moves along the long axis of the surface of A1, one finds that neurons respond to progressively higher (or lower) frequencies. (Note that A1 can be considered to have a "1-D" representation of sound, in that preferred frequency does not vary appreciably along the mediolateral axis of A1 but only along its rostrocaudal axis.) Also analogous to the visual system is the fact

[1] The scientists who carried out the pioneering studies of the electrophysiology of the auditory system are different from those who carried out the analogous studies of the visual system. They evidently used different naming conventions.

that neurons in A1 project to anatomically adjacent areas – referred to as "belt" and "parabelt" cortex – for subsequent processing. Unlike the visual system, however, the auditory cortex has systematic differences between the two hemispheres, both in terms of its anatomy and the kind of information that it processes. To provide a hint about one of the important factors behind these differences, the question of lateralization will be addressed in some detail when we consider the neural bases of speech perception in *Chapter 19*.

Top-Down Control of Auditory Transduction Before leaving the auditory system, we revisit the principle of feedback in sensory processing. Not unlike the optic radiations, which carry more axons traveling from cortex to LGN than from LGN to cortex, the auditory nerve carries more fibers projecting to the cochlea than projecting from it. Of course, an important difference between these two systems is that the cochlea is the site of transduction of acoustic energy into a neural code, more analogous to the retina than to the LGN. (The structural analogue of the LGN in the auditory system is the medial geniculate nucleus of the thalamus [MGN; *Figure 3.8*].) Indeed, while the role of top-down projections to the LGN is to implement neural filtering of the afferent visual signal, in the auditory nerve, the fibers projecting into the cochlea are directly influencing the very mechanism of transduction. They do so by synapsing on the outer hair cells, thereby controlling the behavior of these cells. Outer hair cells, although also attached to the basilar membrane at one end and sprouting cilia at the other, differ from inner hair cells in that their cilia attach to another part of the cochlea. A result of the coordinated activity of many outer hair cells, therefore, can be to sharpen the movement of the basilar membrane by dampening its vibrations on both sides of the peak of the traveling wave. In effect, the outer hair cells implement a mechanical center-surround inhibition of the movement of the basilar membrane. An important focus of ongoing research in auditory perception is determining the source and the nature of the control signals to the outer hair cells.

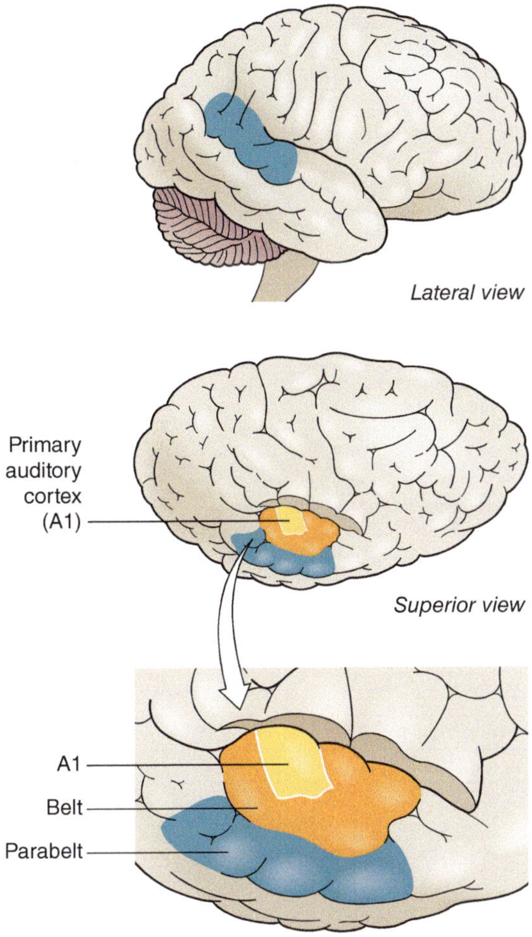

FIGURE 3.10 A1, belt, and parabelt cortex of the human auditory system (shown for the right hemisphere). Because these lie on the ventral bank of the Sylvian fissure, the overlying parietal cortex has been "cut away" to expose them in the superior view.

Somatosensation

Although most of this chapter has focused on anatomy and function in the human, here we'll switch to the rodent, for two reasons. First, many methods of neuroscience, particularly those that entail genetic manipulation, are more readily carried out in rodents (mice, in particular) than in primates. Second, it is in the "barrel system" of many species of rodent that scientists have learned a great deal about somatosensation and, more broadly, many principles of mammalian neural function.

Somatotopy in the Rodent: Barrel Cortex

Many species of rodent, including the mouse and the rat, are nocturnal and/or spend much of their time underground. For such animals, somatosensation via the whiskers is as important for navigation and exploration as is vision for humans. Indeed, an alert mouse actively explores its environment by "whisking," a rhythmic back-and-forth sweeping of the whiskers that can vary in rate from 3 to 25 or more whisks per second. There is also considerable evidence that animals coordinate whisking rate and phase (i.e., where the whiskers are in the back-and-forth cycle) with movements of the head and paws. Whisking for a rodent can be thought of as analogous to the near-constant eye movements that are characteristic of primates (human and nonhuman), something that we will consider in detail in *Chapter 9*.

The importance of whiskers to the rodent is reflected in the organization of its somatosensory cortex, in which one finds disproportionate representation of the snout, and within the "snout area" of the cortex, the distinctive barrel cortex that processes information from the whiskers (*Figure 3.11*). (A barrel refers to the cluster of neurons in Layer IV of the somatosensory cortex that all respond to the mechanical perturbation of a single whisker. [When viewed in a thin slice of tissue that exposes the 2D surface of Layer IV, these clusters resemble a top-down view of a collection of barrels.]) The elegant simplicity of this barrel system, including its "one-barrel-to-one-whisker" organization, makes it an ideal system for studying many principles of sensory processing. For example, there is considerable evidence that the phase of LFP oscillations within the barrel cortex is synchronized with the phase of whisking.

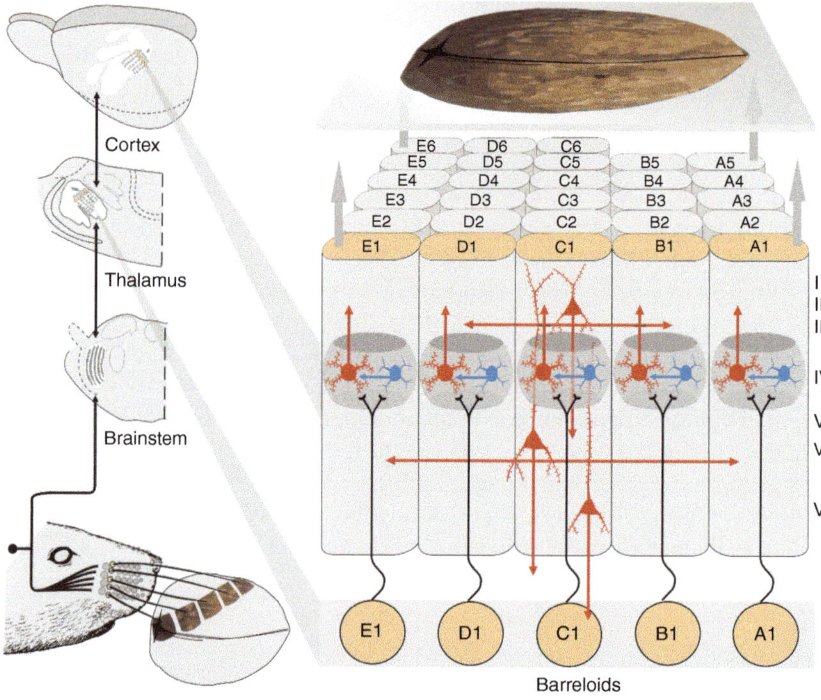

FIGURE 3.11 A diagram of the barrel system in a rodent. The column on the left illustrates a simplified rendition of the primary pathway from periphery to cortex. In the lower left, a cartoon rat is exploring an object, with the brown squares corresponding to the region of the object touched by each whisker. Each vibrissa follicle is innervated by mechanoreceptors that send their signals via the trigeminal nerve (of the PNS), in parallel, to one of many trigeminal nuclei in the brainstem (the first synapse of the system; only one nucleus illustrated here). Afferent fibers from the principal brainstem nucleus then project into the multiple "barreloids" of the VPM nucleus of the thalamus (second synapse), the arrangement of which mirrors the topography of the animal's face – that is, each barreloid receives information relating to just one whisker. Finally, thalamic afferents project into cortical area S1 (third synapse), which contains a map of the entire body surface of the animal (top left). Note that, as we have already seen with the human somatosensory homunculus, this map is distorted in a manner that corresponds to the innervation density of various parts of the animal's body. The right side of the figure illustrates more detail of the thalamocortical projection and the cortex. Thalamic afferents project into layer IV, where both excitatory (red) and inhibitory (blue) neurons make up each barrel. Also illustrated for cortical column C1 (which corresponds to whisker C1 on the animal's snout) are pyramidal cells in superficial and deep layers of cortex. Floating fancifully "above" the barrel cortex is the artist's rendition of the animal's neural representation of the object being whisked (a walnut?), which is emergent from cortical processing in S1 and downstream areas.

Source: Courtesy of Dr. Jochen Staiger.

Optogenetic Exploration of Gamma-Band Oscillations in Somatosensory Cortex

In *Chapter 2*, the phenomenon of oscillatory synchrony was introduced as a possible mechanism for organizing neural activity, such as the selection of to-be-emphasized information. The study that we will consider here, from Jessica Cardin, Marie Carlén, and colleagues in the laboratory of Christopher Moore, is noteworthy because it provides *causal*, mechanistic insight into how one type of neuronal oscillation – oscillation in the gamma frequency band – is generated. Further, it demonstrates the importance of these oscillations for the cortical processing of afferent sensory signals. It accomplishes this by using an experimental tool called optogenetics to exogenously control gamma-band oscillations in one class of neurons located in barrel cortex – fast-spiking (FS) inhibitory interneurons. In doing so, it illustrates how experimental methods that exert external control over an aspect of the brain or brain function can support stronger inferences than would have an experiment that "merely observed" the kind of activity that is described here.

Optogenetics will be considered in more detail in *Chapter 4*, section *Optogenetics*. Here are details that you need to know to follow this section. The first step is to insert DNA that codes for an opsin into a targeted type of cell. (Recall from *Chapter 2*, section *The retina and the LGN of the thalamus* that the opsin called rhodopsin is crucial for the transduction of light in the retina.) Here, the opsin used was channelrhodopsin-2 (ChR2), a cation channel activated by light of a very narrow wavelength centered at 470 nm.[2] Cardin, Carlén et al. (2009) transfected inhibitory interneurons in barrel cortex, such that shining 470 nm light has the effect of depolarizing them and causing them to spike.

The experiment by Cardin, Carlén et al. (2009) was designed to test the hypothesis that inhibitory interneurons of barrel cortex (the "blue" neurons from *Figure 3.11*) govern the gamma-band oscillations that had previously been observed in LFPs recorded from barrel cortex. The experiment proceeded in three stages. First, as illustrated in *Figure 3.12*, the authors established that their preparation gave them (a) direct optical control over these "fast spiking" (FS) interneurons and, by extension, (b) indirect inhibitory control over "regular-spiking" (RS) excitatory neurons (the "red" neurons from *Figure 3.11*). Second, they established that FS cells have a preferred oscillatory frequency in the 40–50-Hz range (*Figure 3.13*). Third, they implemented a test of the idea that "gamma oscillations . . . have a functional impact on cortical information processing by synchronizing the output of excitatory neurons" (p. 666). To do so, they imposed an oscillation at this frequency by stimulating FS cells with light pulses delivered at 40 Hz and recorded the responses of RS cells to deflections of a whisker performed at five different phases relative to the gamma cycle (*Figure 3.14.A*). The logic was that, if gamma-band oscillations serve a gating function, one should see optimal responses to afferent sensory information by layer IV excitatory neurons when that information arrives at the optimal time relative to the ongoing gamma-band oscillation in this neuron's membrane potential (*Figure 3.14.B*). The results, illustrated in *Figure 3.14.C–E*, demonstrated the predicted gating function of gamma-band oscillations, in that the response to whisker stimulation of a layer IV RS neuron was sensitive to the phase of the optically entrained LFP. That is, unless the whisker stimulation was delivered to coincide with the peak of the LFP, it lacked the magnitude of response (in spikes per trial) of the baseline response.

Why weren't optimally timed whisker stimulations stronger than the baseline? One possible answer comes from looking back at *Figure 3.11* and noting that thalamocortical axons carrying sensory signals from barreloids to barrels also send collaterals that synapse directly on layer IV interneurons. This suggests that, because the circuitry is in place to coordinate interneuron activity with the processing of the afferent sensory signal, the best that an experiment like this might be able to achieve is to push the system away from its optimal-performing regime, which is in place on "baseline" trials when no optical stimulation is being delivered.

[2] CHR2 occurs naturally in the single-celled algae *Chlamydomonas reinhardtii*, in which it serves the function of phototaxis – light-triggered movement.

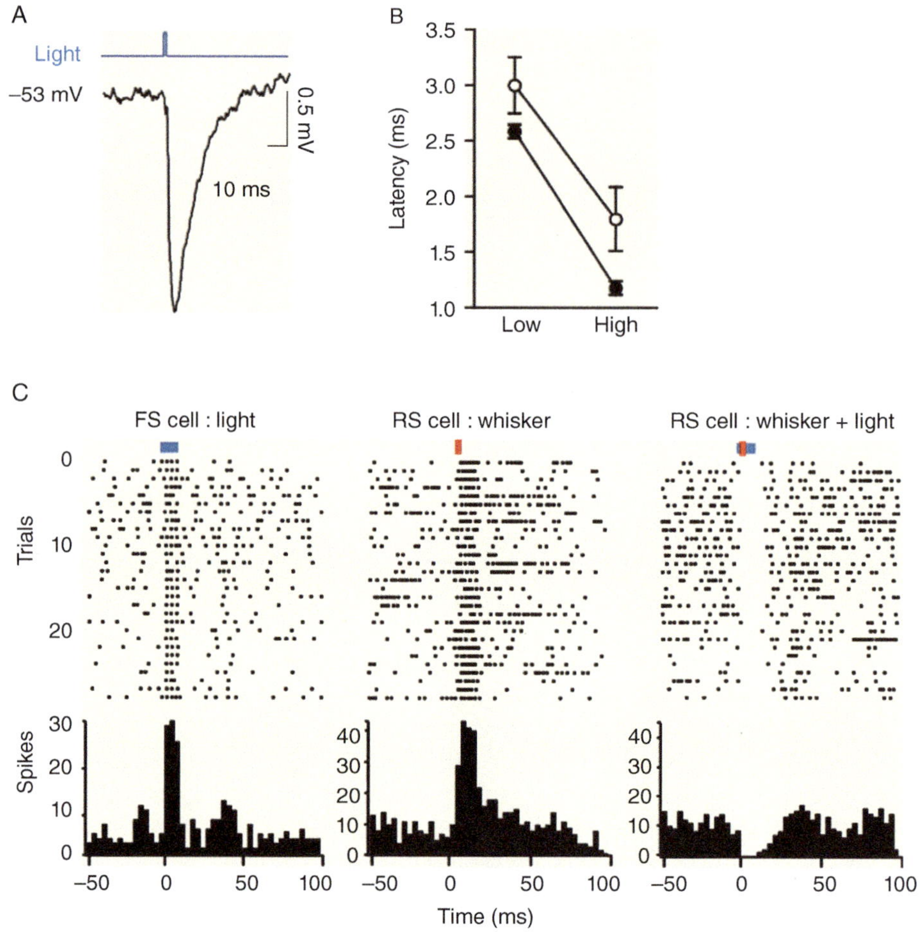

FIGURE 3.12 Electrophysiological effects of optogenetic stimulation. **A.** Intracellular recording from an RS neuron shows a near-instantaneous inhibitory postsynaptic potential (IPSP) in response to a pulse of 470-nm light onto this tissue via an optical fiber. Note that because RS neurons were not transfected, the IPSP could not have been caused directly by the light. Rather, it must have been the result of the release of GABA from transfected FS neurons onto this pyramidal cell (i.e., the pulse of light produced an action potential in one or more FS neurons). **B.** The latency between pulses of light delivered at low or high intensity and two measures: action potentials in FS neurons (filled symbols) and IPSPs in RS neurons (unfilled symbols). These data indicate that the propagation of the action potential of an interneuron, the resultant release of GABA, and the consequent postsynaptic influx of Cl^- ions in an adjacent RS neuron all transpire in less than 1 ms. **C.** A functional consequence of sustained optical stimulation of FS inhibitory interneurons is to block sensory-evoked responses in RS neurons to a whisker deflection. Left-hand panel shows sustained firing of an FS cell in layer 2/3 in response to a 10-ms light pulse (blue line). Center panel shows the response of an adjacent RS cell to a whisker deflection (red bar). Right-hand panel shows that when light is delivered coincident with whisker deflection, the result is to suppress activity in the RS neuron to below its baseline level.

Source: Cardin et al., 2009 / Springer Nature.

Proprioception

Before concluding this section, we need to introduce the somatosensory modality of **proprioception**, which refers to the sense of where different parts of the body are relative to one another. Let's think back for a moment about the earlier section of this chapter on audition and the problem of localizing the source of a sound. It was noted in passing that it is in auditory brainstem nuclei that the computations are performed that allow us to localize where a sound in the environment is coming from. In a sentence, this is accomplished by the fact that we have two detectors (i.e., two ears), and that a sound emanating from a single source will

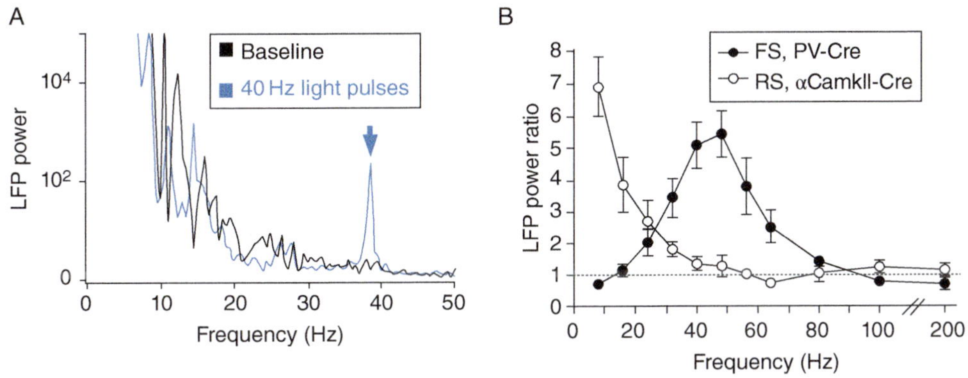

FIGURE 3.13 FS cells have a preferred oscillatory frequency in the 40–50-Hz range. **A.** A power spectrum of the LFP in barrel cortex as recorded in the absence of optical stimulation ("Baseline"; black) and during the delivery of 40-Hz light pulses (blue). **B.** Across a wide range of frequencies of optical stimulation, the LFP power ratio ($LFP_{optical\ stimulation}/LFP_{baseline}$) for transfected FS neurons (filled symbols) is highest in the 40–50-Hz range, suggesting that this is the "naturally preferred" frequency (or resonant frequency) of these cells. For comparison, in a different group of animals, RS cells (unfilled symbols) were transfected with the ChR2 gene. The highest LFP power ratio in these animals, and thus the presumed resonant frequency of RS cells, was at 8 Hz (i.e., in the theta frequency band).

Source: Cardin et al., 2009 / Springer Nature.

be sensed as having slightly different amplitudes (the interaural intensity difference, IID), and will be sensed at slightly different times (the interaural timing difference, ITD), by the two ears. One need not understand the nuts and bolts of how sound localization works to appreciate the following: a sound originating 10 feet (3 m) in front of you will produce markedly different IIDs and ITDs depending on whether your head is pointed straight ahead or whether it is turned to the side (e.g., if you are looking off to your left); yet the proverbial tiger that is stalking you is in the same location relative to your body, and so your most appropriate response is the same regardless of how your head happens to be oriented at the moment. The same is true for vision: if you are looking straight ahead, the tiger that is directly in front of you would occupy your foveal vision, whereas if your head is turned to the left, the tiger would occupy the extreme right side of your visual field. Thus, to accurately process information coming in through the ears, or through the eyes, the brain needs to know how the head is positioned relative to the torso. (And for vision, an additional factor that will receive more attention in *Chapter 9* is that the brain also needs to know the position of the eyes relative to the head.) For the head, specifically, information about the position of the head relative to the torso is provided by proprioceptive receptors located in the neck. For our purposes, these are stretch receptors that gauge the state of the neck muscles. All muscle groups in the body (including the extraocular muscles that control the position of the eyes in their sockets) are similarly equipped with stretch receptors, and so our brain gets proprioceptive information about the location (relative to adjacent body parts) of virtually every part of the body.

Where Does *Sensation* End? Where Does *Perception* Begin?

One way to think about sensory systems is from an intuitive, feedforward perspective. Take vision: photons impact the retina and are transduced into a neural signal; retinal ganglion cells carry this neural signal to the LGN; and the LGN relays this neural signal to V1, where features are detected (or, if you prefer, constructed). At one level of analysis, this is necessarily accurate: it's well established that damage to the retina and/or to various locations along the feedforward pathway from retina to cortex produces frank blindness. Additionally, in

Chapter 6, we will see how regions at higher stations of the visual system (including V4 and MT, plus many regions further downstream) construct image and object representations from the features first detected in V1. That is, extrastriate regions accomplish perception with the features first detected in V1. From this perspective, then, for vision, one may want to draw the sensation–perception boundary for vision at V1. Complicating this clear-cut, tidy demarcation, however, is the influence of feedback projections from higher regions on the functions of V1 and the LGN. That is, we have seen that many neural operations that, from one perspective, are very clearly associated with sensation are nonetheless heavily influenced by concurrent

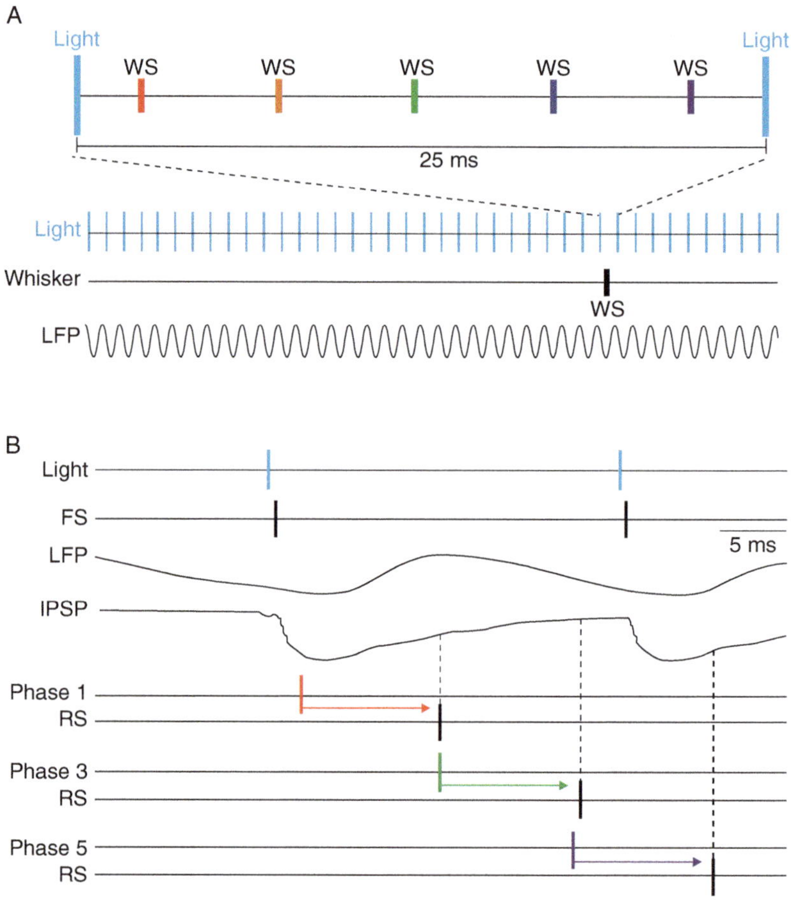

FIGURE 3.14 Optogenetically controlled gamma-band oscillations influence cortical processing of afferent sensory signals. **A.** Gamma-band oscillation is imposed by delivering light pulses at 40 Hz to ChR2-transfected FS cells, and whisker deflections (WS) are performed at five different phases relative to the gamma cycle. **B.** Schematic model of the expected effects of this procedure: the top trace shows the once-every-25 ms (i.e., 40 Hz) pulses of light; the next, the consequent action potential in FS neurons; the next, the resultant gamma-band oscillation of the LFP; and the next, the concurrent fluctuations in membrane potential experienced by a RS pyramidal cell (IPSP). An afferent signal from a WS delivered at phase 1 (red WS in panel A) would arrive at the RS cell at the point of maximal inhibition in the gamma-phase and would produce a spike roughly 10 ms later; a WS delivered at phase 3 (green) would arrive at a point of rising membrane potential and produce a spike near the peak membrane potential; and a WS delivered at phase 5 (purple) would arrive near the peak of the membrane potential, the resultant spike occurring near the trough of the membrane potential. **C.** Responses of a layer IV RS neuron to WSs in the absence of optical stimulation (baseline). **D.** Responses of the same neuron to WSs delivered at each of the five phases portrayed in *A.* **E.** Average spikes/trial for baseline (B) and each of the five phases.

Source: Cardin et al., 2009 / Springer Nature.

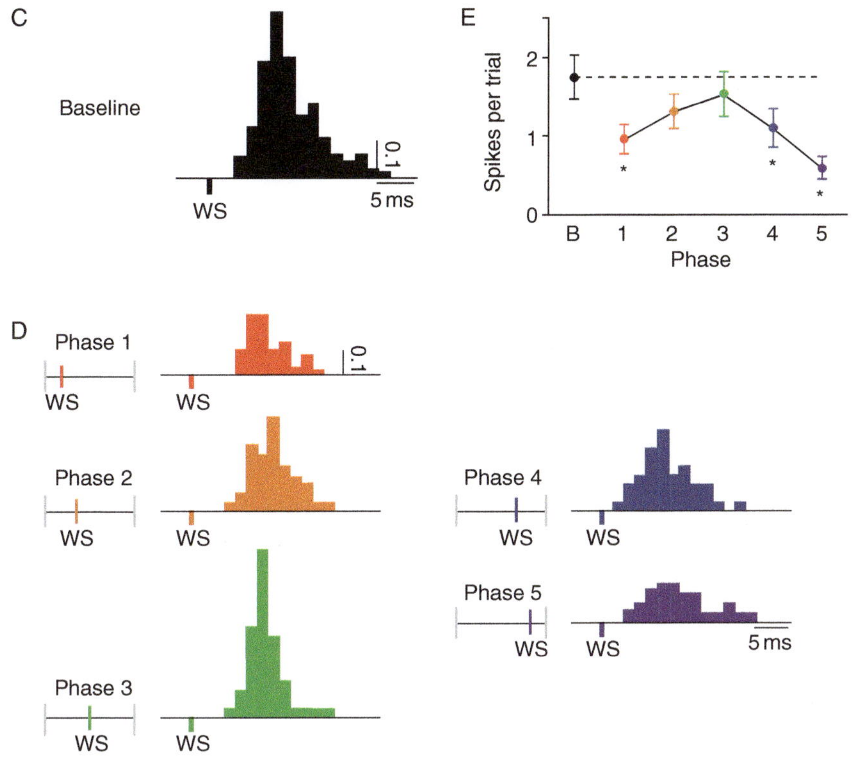

FIGURE 3.14 *(Continued)*

perceptual processing at higher levels of the system. This complicates the labeling of any given stage of processing as "belonging" to sensation or to perception. (And we shall see in subsequent chapters that top-down influences from long-term memory can influence perception in ways that are comparable to how we've just documented top-down influences of perception on sensation.) These are hallmarks of a complex system.

This and the previous chapter have introduced many of the critical "parts" – parts of the brain, neurons, and neurotransmitters – as well as some of their properties – ion channels, oscillating membrane potentials, action potentials, oscillating LFPs, emergent tuning properties, and so on. Next, we can consider how these are measured, then how the results of these measurements are analyzed and interpreted, and, in the process, start to uncover how they give rise to the complexity of the brain activity that gives rise to behavior and cognition.

End-of-Chapter Questions

1. In what sense do neurons in V1 act as feature detectors? What kinds of features are represented in V1? These features are not explicitly represented at the level of the retina or the LGN, so how do they come to be represented in V1?

2. Any of the features invoked in Question 3 can be present at any location in the visual field. How is this reflected in the "macro-level" organization of V1?

3. Provide evidence of the statement that the cortex can exert control over how the thalamus delivers sensory information to the cortex.

4. What functions are supported by feedback projections from V1 to the LGN? How, at the level of network mechanisms, are they implemented?

5. What factors influence the electroencephalogram (EEG) signal as it is measured at the scalp? What neurophysiological processes can be inferred from the EEG?

6. What is the phenomenon of alpha-band oscillations in the EEG? How do dynamics in the magnitude of these oscillations relate to visual processing?

7. How might the mechanical properties of the cochlea result in the fact that the tuning of auditory nerve fibers broadens with increasing sound intensity?

8. What is meant by the term "spectral decomposition"? How the operation carried out in the auditory system?

9. What components of the AEP are sensitive to attentional state? What can one infer from this about which stages of auditory processing are, vs. are not, influenced by attention?

10. By analogy to the retinotopic organization of V1, what is the organization of A1 relative to the acoustic signal?

11. Which part of your body is more densely innervated with mechanoreceptors, your tongue or your forearm? What are the corresponding differences in how these two parts of your body are represented in S1?

12. Rodents actively sample their environment by whisking. How is activity in barrel cortex of S1 coordinated with whisking, and what does this imply about coordination between S1 and the motoric control of the snout (from which whiskers protrude)?

References

Cudeiro, Javier, and Adam M. Sillito. 2006. "Looking Back: Corticothalamic Feedback and Early Visual Processing." *Trends in Neurosciences* 29 (6): 298–306. doi: 10.1016/j.tins.2006.05.002.

Romei, Vincenzo, Verena Brodbeck, Christoph Michel, Amir Amedi, Alvaro Pascual-Leone, and Gregor Thut. 2008. "Spontaneous Fluctuations in Posterior [alpha]-Band EEG Activity Reflect Variability in Excitability of Human Visual Areas." *Cerebral Cortex* 18 (9): 2010–2018. doi: 10.1093/cercor/bhm229.

Wong-Riley, Margaret T. T. 1989. "Cytochrome Oxidase: An Endogenous Metabolic Marker for Neuronal Activity." *Trends in Neurosciences* 12 (3): 94–101. doi: 10.1016/0166-2236(89)90165-3.

Other Sources Used

Adrian, Edgar D. 1934. "Electrical Activity of the Nervous System." *Archives of Neurology and Psychiatry* 32 (6): 1125–1136. doi: 10.1001/archneurpsyc.1934.02250120002001.

Blasdel, Gary G., and Guy Salama. 1986. "Voltage-Sensitive Dyes Reveal a Modular Organization in Monkey Striate Cortex." *Nature* 321 (6070): 579–585. doi: 10.1038/321579a0.

Bonhoeffer, Tobias, and Amiram Grinvald. 1991. "Iso-Orientation Domains in Cat Visual Cortex Are Arranged in Pinwheel-Like Patterns." *Nature* 353 (6343): 429–431. doi: 10.1038/353429a0.

Fritsch, Gustav, and Eduard Hitzig. 1870. "Über die elektrische Erregbarkeit des Grosshirns." *Archiv für Anatomie, Physiologie und wissenschaftliche Medicin* 37: 300–332. [Available in English translation as: Fritsch, Gustav, and Eduard Hitzig. 2009. "Electric excitability of the cerebrum (Über die elektrische Erregbarkeit des Grosshirns)." *Epilepsy and Behavior* 15 (2): 123–130. doi: 10.1016/j.yebeh.2009.03.001.].

Grinvald, Amiram, Edmund Lieke, Ron D. Frostig, Charles D. Gilbert, and Torsten N. Wiesel. 1986. "Functional Architecture of Cortex Revealed by Optical Imaging of Intrinsic Signals." *Nature* 324 (6095): 361–364. doi: 10.1038/324361a0.

Gross, Charles G. 1998. *Brain, Vision, Memory*. Cambridge, MA: MIT Press.

Hirsch, Sven, Johannes Reichold, Matthias Schneider, Gábor Székely, and Bruno Weber. 2012. "Topology and Hemodynamics of the Cortical Cerebrovascular System." *Journal of Cerebral Blood Flow and Metabolism* 32 (6): 952–967. doi: 10.1038/jcbfm.2012.39.

Hubel, David H. 1996. "David H. Hubel." In *Volume 1 of The History of Neuroscience in Autobiography*, edited by Larry R. Squire (pp. 294–317). Washington, DC: Society for Neuroscience. http://www.sfn.org/about/history-of-neuroscience/~/media/SfN/Documents/Autobiographies/c9.ashx.

Malmivuo, Jaakko, and Robert Plonsey. 1995. *Bioelectromagnetism: Principles and Applications of Bioelectric and Biomagnetic Fields*. New York: Oxford University Press.

Sillito, Adam M., Javier Cudeiro, and Helen E. Jones. 2006. "Always Returning: Feedback and Sensory Processing in Visual Cortex and Thalamus." *Trends in Neurosciences* 29 (6): 307–316. doi: 10.1016/j.tins.2006.05.001.

Tootell, Roger B. H., Martin S. Silverman, Eugene Switkes, and Russell L. De Valois. 1982. "Deoxyglucose Analysis of Retinotopic Organization in Primate Striate Cortex." *Science* 218 (4575): 902–904. doi: 10.1126/science.7134981.

Walsh, Vincent, and Alan Cowey. 2000. "Transcranial Magnetic Stimulation and Cognitive Neuroscience." *Nature Reviews Neuroscience* 1 (1): 73–80.

Wang, Wei, Helen E. Jones, Ian M. Andolina, Thomas E. Salt, and Adam M. Sillito. 2006. "Functional Alignment of Feedback Effects from Visual Cortex to Thalamus." *Nature Neuroscience* 9 (10): 1330–1336. doi: 10.1038/nn1768.

Further Reading

Friston, Karl. 2010. "The Free-Energy Principle: A Unified Brain Theory." *Nature Reviews Neuroscience* 11 (2): 127–138. doi: 10.1038/nrn2787.

A readable summary of many models from theoretical neuroscience addressing high-level questions of what the brain does and why it does it that way.

Glickstein, Mitchell, and David Whitteridge. 1987. "Tatsuji Inouye and the Mapping of the Visual Fields on the Human Cerebral Cortex." *Trends in Neurosciences* 10 (9): 350–353. doi: 10.1016/0166-2236(87)90066-X.

A brief history of the identification and mapping of human visual cortex, including "the brilliant contributions of a young Japanese ophthalmologist, Tatsuji Inouye, which have gone largely unrecognized."

Hubel, David H. 1988. *Eye, Brain, and Vision*. New York: Scientific American Library: Distributed by W. H. Freeman.

A summary of principles of visual neuroscience from one of the field's pioneering researchers.

Luck, Steven J. 2005. *An Introduction to the Event-related Potential Technique*. Cambridge, MA: MIT Press.

Although this book emphasizes event-related potentials (ERP), which are generated by the averaging of EEG signals that are time-locked to events of interest within trials, rather than EEG per se, it is nonetheless an excellent introduction to how EEG data are collected and processed. (Additionally, ERPs will be directly relevant for this textbook, beginning with Chapter 6.)

Rossi, Simone, Andrea Antal, Sven Bestmann, Marom Bikson, Carmen Brewer, Jürgen Brockmöller, . . . Mark Hallett. 2021. "Safety and recommendations for TMS use in healthy subjects and patient populations, with updates on training, ethical and regulatory issues: Expert Guidelines." *Clinical Neurophysiology* 132: 269–306.

The definitive, authoritative compilation of safety and ethical information relating to the use of TMS in cognitive neuroscience and clinical research. This and the previous TMS safety compendia that it updates (from1998 and 2009) derives from a Consensus Statement from workshop on "Present, Future of TMS: Safety, Ethical Guidelines" organized by the International Federation of Clinical Neurophysiology.

Walsh, Vincent, and Alvaro Pascual-Leone. 2003. *Transcranial Magnetic Stimulation: A Neurochronometrics of Mind*. Cambridge, MA: MIT Press.

A thorough, readable overview of the physics and physiology underlying TMS, and the cognitive neuroscience applications of this technique.

E. M. Wasserman, A. V. Peterchev, U. Ziemann, S. H. Lisanby, H. R. Siebner, and V. Walsh (eds.) (2021). The Oxford Handbook of Transcranial Stimulation, 2nd Edition. Oxford University Press (Oxford, U.K.). 10.1093/oxfordhb/9780198832256.013.34

A collection of authoritative reviews of many applications of transcranial stimulation (including TMS) in basic and clinical science.

Methods and Models

INTRODUCTION TO SECTION II

Methods and Models

We've had an introduction to brain, to how scientists have gone about studying it, and to some fundamentals of how neural systems operate. Part of me is raring to keep going, to dive deeper into visual perception, object recognition, and spatial cognition, into how attention helps us to prioritize all of all this information and how . . . "Slow down, Brad." Part of what makes writing a book like this a fun challenge is figuring out how to tell the reader everything that you want to tell them, and to do so in a way that solves the "everything everywhere all at once" problem. For example, consider the deeper dive into visual perception. To truly understand a reasonably comprehensive overview of this topic, the reader not only has to know about neurons and action potentials and the principle of feedforward vs. feedback signaling between LGN and V1 (i.e., what was covered in *Chapters 1–3*), they also have to understand the physics and physiological bases of functional magnetic resonance imaging (fMRI), the theoretical perspectives of predictive coding and reinforcement learning, and the kinds of interpretation supported by univariate signal intensity-based analyses vs. by multivariate pattern analysis (MVPA) vs. by representational similarity analysis (RSA). And so there are two ways to proceed. One is to "bite the bullet" and read the next two chapters straight through, and then armed with technical background knowledge, to proceed with the content that is really what this book is for. A second is to skip ahead to *Section III*, acknowledging that there will need to be a lot of back-and-forth jumping between each "cognition" chapter and these two chapters on ***Methods and Models***. (If you choose the latter, the remainder of the book is annotated with flags and links pointing to critical content in *Chapters 4* and *5*.) Neither choice is inherently better than the other, although when you get to the second half of *Chapter 16: Decision Making*, you can look back fondly to this moment and analyze the choice that you're about to make in terms of how you resolved the competing factors of the orbitofrontal cortex-based representations of value of one choice vs. the dorsal anterior cingulate cortex-based estimates of the effort associated with each. Whichever approach you choose, it's interesting to think about the fact that, unlike many other branches of the behavioral and biological sciences, cognitive neuroscience is a field that truly couldn't have existed prior to the advent of the technical advances detailed in *Chapter 4* and the conceptual advances detailed in *Chapter 5*.

Essentials of Cognitive Neuroscience, Third Edition. Bradley R. Postle. Published 2026 by John Wiley & Sons, Inc.
Companion Website: www.wiley.com/go/postle/cognitiveneuroscience3e

Methods for Cognitive Neuroscience

KEY THEMES

- Most cognitive neuroscience research employs the rationale (as well as the methods) from cognitive psychology that behavior in controlled experimental settings provides an effective, albeit indirect, way to measure mental activity.
- Neuropsychology, the study of the effects of brain lesions on behavior, can support strong inference about the *necessity* of a region's contributions to a function of interest, provided that the specificity of the effect(s) of the damage can be established.
- Many of the principles of experimental design and interpretation that apply to neuropsychology are equally important for noninvasive transcranial neurostimulation techniques, such as transcranial alternating current stimulation (tACS), transcranial direct current stimulation (tDCS), and transcranial magnetic stimulation (TMS).
- Many methods for studying the structure of the brain (i.e., neuroanatomy) exploit properties of physiological and cell biological processes.
- Depending on the exact method used to record electrical activity in the brain, one can either measure action potentials, a high-frequency proxy for action potentials referred to as multiunit activity (MUA), or oscillating field potentials at different spatial scales.
- There are two broad classes of data analysis that can be applied to signals recorded at the scalp with electroencephalography (EEG) or magnetoencephalography (MEG): event related (event-related potential [ERP] with EEG) and time–frequency. Each makes assumptions about how the signals were generated by the brain, thereby limiting the kinds of phenomena that can be measured.
- Different applications of magnetic resonance imaging (MRI) can be used to measure gross anatomy, to estimate the trajectory (and integrity) of white-matter tracts, to measure relative changes in metabolic activity (over timescales ranging from individual cognitive events to tens of minutes), and to measure the chemical makeup of different brain regions, including level of neurotransmitters and their metabolites.
- Because functional MRI (fMRI) is inherently constrained by the brain's hemodynamics, its temporal resolution is relatively poor, and its low-pass filtering qualities must be taken into account when making choices about experimental design and analysis.
- The brain is a massively interconnected nonlinear dynamical system, and neural network modeling offers one way to simulate some of these properties in ways that are simply not possible with empirical measurements of brain activity.
- Parallel distributed processing (PDP) can be an effective way to evaluate the plausibility of theoretical models about the computations underlying cognitive functions.

Companion Website: www.wiley.com/go/postle/cognitiveneuroscience3e

- Recurrent neural networks (RNNs) capture the fact that, at the moment when new input arrives, the receiving circuit hadn't been in a quiescent state "just waiting for something to do."
- Deep neural networks (DNNs) apply powerful techniques from machine learning and artificial intelligence (AI) to attain remarkably high levels of categorization of visual images, speech sounds, and other classes of stimuli. Close links between research on DNNs and on the neural bases of sensory systems (e.g., visual perception) are generating important insights leading to advancements in both fields.
- Because the brain is a massively interconnected system, analytic tools from network science, including graph theory, provide powerful ways to learn about this fundamental aspect of brain function.

CONTENTS

Behavior, Structure, Function, and Models

Studying the brain, and how its functioning gives rise to thought and behavior, requires the ability to measure behavior, anatomy, and physiology, each at several different scales, and to articulate and test models of neural computations and of mental activity that explain behavior and physiology. In order to learn about cognitive neuroscience in a substantive way, it's necessary to have an understanding of the methods that are used to acquire these measurements. The goal of this chapter, therefore, is to equip the reader with enough of an understanding of the methods used by cognitive neuroscientists that, for the remainder of the book, we won't need to go into a lengthy aside every time a new method is introduced. (On the other hand, if you would prefer not to power through this chapter right now, and would prefer to "get to the good stuff" right away, references throughout the remainder of the book have been inserted to point the reader to this chapter's description of whatever method it is that needs to be understood in order to fully understand the experiment that's being described.)

We can divide the topic of methods of cognitive neuroscience into two general categories: how a method works (i.e., the physics, physiology, and engineering on which it depends); and how the data that it generates are analyzed and interpreted. Sometimes it's not really possible to talk about one without the other, but to the extent possible, in this chapter, we'll limit ourselves to "how it works." Some topics about "how the data are analyzed and interpreted" will be introduced in *Chapter 5, Theoretical Frameworks and Computational Models*, and others will be introduced further along in the book as part of the explanation of an experiment that uses that method.

Behavior

Many neuroscientists consider the ability to move – so as to acquire food and/or to avoid becoming something else's food – to be the factor whose adaptive value has been the primary driving force behind the evolutionary development of nervous systems. Put another way, the need to act on/in the environment, and to constantly improve the efficacy with which actions are carried out, may be the driving force behind why we have such complex brains. From this, some argue that the only reason that we can see, hear, and taste, the only reason that we can entertain abstract thoughts about situations that we may never directly encounter in our lives, may be because these capacities help us carry out actions more effectively. At a more concrete and pragmatic level, because no one has figured out a way to directly measure *thinking* per se, behavior offers indirect access to mental activity, because it is an overt and measurable consequence of mental activity. Furthermore, as was noted in *Introduction to Section I*, not all neural information processing that influences cognition is accessible to conscious awareness. It is nonetheless often the case that such "unconscious" brain processes will influence behavior in systematic ways that we can measure and interpret.

Neuropsychology, Neurophysiology, and the Limits of Inference

Neuropsychology relies on the logic that one way to understand the workings of a system is to systematically damage (or inactivate) parts of it and observe how damaging each part affects the system's functioning. A neuropsychological study (sometimes also called a "lesion study") can address the question *Does* region A *make a necessary contribution to* behavior X? Note that this will be a necessary, but often not sufficient, step in addressing the broader question of *How does the brain generate* behavior X? To give a concrete example, *Chapter 1* describes how neuropsychological experimentation was used to determine definitively that visual perception is localized to the occipital lobe. Not until *Chapter 3*, however (and, chronologically, not until roughly 80 years later), did we see that electrophysiological experiments revealed *how* it is that neurons in the occipital lobe process visual information. Without the knowledge of where in the brain to record neuronal activity, however, the experiments addressing the "how" questions could never have been carried out. It's also the case that a carefully conducted neuropsychological experiment can support stronger inference about the *necessity* of a region's integrity for a particular behavior than can experiments that measure neurophysiological variables, because the latter are correlational. (E.g., one can imagine a situation in which activity in a brain area *X* varies systematically with changes in a particular behavior *B*, but that the lesioning of *X* doesn't alter *B*. [I.e., activity in *X* is correlated with *B*, but doesn't cause it.] Such a scenario could come about if the brain area in question makes a redundant contribution to the behavior, or if it is a downstream recipient of output from the region whose activity *is* necessary for that behavior.)

Many Stimulation-Based Techniques Share Inferential Principles with Neuropsychology We'll get to the technical details of different methods for neurostimulation further along in this chapter. These will include transcranial direct current stimulation (tDCS), transcranial alternating current stimulation (tACS), transcranial magnetic stimulation (TMS), and optogenetics (which was introduced in *Chapter 3*'s section Optogenetic Exploration of Gamma-Band Oscillations in Somatosensory Cortex). But it is important to note that much of the reasoning that we are applying to neuropsychology will also apply to any method that involves direct manipulation of some aspects of brain function. Indeed, *Chapter 1*'s summary of the electrical microstimulation experiments of Fritsch and Hitzig (1870; in the section on *The localization of motor functions*) offers a nice example with which to consider specificity.

The Importance of Specificity In both neuropsychology and stimulation experiments, the strength of one's conclusions depends importantly on being able to demonstrate anatomical specificity. What made the Fritsch and Hitzig (1870) experiment so powerful, for example, was the specificity with which it demonstrated that stimulation of a particular portion of the frontal lobe in the left hemisphere produced movement of the right forelimb, and that it did not produce movement of the right hind limb, nor of the left forelimb. Indeed, it was stimulation of a different, although nearby, area that selectively produced movement of the right hind limb, but no longer of the right forelimb. Had the authors limited their report to the fact that the stimulation of this left frontal region produced movement of the right forelimb, two important questions would have been left unanswered. First, *might stimulation of other regions also produce movement of the right forelimb?* Hinging on the answer to this would be an understanding of how localized is the control of the right forelimb. Second, *can stimulation of this region of the brain also produce movement of other parts of the body?* The answer to this would give an indication of how specific is the function of the brain area in question. (Note that this illustration of specificity is somewhat contrived, because simple observation would be expected to indicate whether or not other parts of the body also moved as a result of microstimulating this one region. But imagine that one was interested in a less overtly observable aspect of behavior than that of skeletomotor control. For example, *Does stimulation of this region of the brain only disrupt the ability to produce speech, or does it also disrupt verbal working memory?* [Verbal working memory is engaged, e.g., when holding an unfamiliar phone number in mind while searching for one's phone in order to dial that number.] Establishing specificity in a situation like this would require administering two (or more) tests while delivering the same stimulation protocol, and observing whether it does/does not disrupt performance on the verbal working memory task.)

These considerations can be particularly important in neuropsychological studies of humans, such as those described in *Chapter 1*'s section on *The localization of speech*, because these studies often rely on "accidents of nature," such as stroke, neurodegenerative disease, or head injury. In such studies, scientists have no control (other than patient selection) over the extent of damage in the patients that they study, neither in terms of how many structures may be damaged nor of the overall volume of tissue that is affected. When lesions are large, there can be an inherent difficulty in determining which of the damaged structures is responsible for the observed behavioral deficit. One analytic way to tackle this problem, applying the logic of the "double dissociation of function," will be introduced in *Chapter 6*.

Different Kinds of Neuropsychology Address Different Kinds of Questions

Cognitive Neuropsychology A one-sentence summary of cognitive psychology might be that it seeks to understand the organization and principles underlying different aspects of cognition. A cognitive psychologist will typically carry out an experiment by varying some independent variables (perhaps the speed at which stimuli are presented to the experimental subject or the number of stimuli concurrently presented to them) and then comparing performance at different levels of that independent variable. Cognitive neuropsychology can be thought of as a specific type of cognitive psychology in which the independent variable is the integrity of the brain. That is, the cognitive neuropsychologist will administer the same task to healthy control subjects and to neurological patients, and then compare performance between the two groups. One set of examples that we will consider in detail in *Chapter 10*, on *Visual object recognition and knowledge*, is studies of object recognition deficits observed in patients with brain damage due to a wide range of causes (e.g., blunt trauma, encephalitis, and stroke). One patient who suffered carbon monoxide poisoning retained the ability to discriminate colors, brightness, and size but was "unable to distinguish between two objects of the same luminance, wavelength, and area when the only difference between them was shape" (Benson and Greenberg, 1969). Other patients have been described as being able to copy drawings of objects with a high level of fidelity (e.g., a guitar or an owl) but unable to generate the name of these objects (Fig. 10.1). These patterns of spared vs. impaired performance were used to develop models positing a series of discrete stages of processing that support visual object recognition. Importantly, these models did not address with any detail *where* in the brain these processing stages may be implemented, just that these stages may be indicative of how object recognition is accomplished. (This is sometimes referred to as the "cognitive architecture" of object recognition.)

Experimental Neuropsychology Experimental neuropsychology is a method used to study what brain areas support a particular function, or, conversely, what functions are supported by a particular brain area. A nice example comes from Juliana Baldo and Nina Dronkers (2006), who wanted to test the hypothesis that two brain areas – left inferior parietal lobule (IPL) and left inferior frontal gyrus (IFG) – support different functions related to verbal working memory: storage vs. rehearsal, respectively. (An example of verbal working memory is when someone tells you a telephone number, and you need to remember it while you first look for your phone, then look for a quiet place to make the call – we'll consider it in detail in *Chapter 14*.) In the introduction to their study, the authors highlight the fact that their approach for recruiting patients was to identify patients with damage to one of these regions or the other, without any knowledge of the behavioral impairments that may have been caused by their stroke. An alternative approach – to start by seeking patients with a behavioral deficit in either the ability to store or to rehearse information in verbal working memory, then to see what regions had been damaged – would suffer from limitations in the ability to ascribe specific functions to these two regions. For example, had they recruited patients based on behavioral impairment, and then observed that most of the patients with a rehearsal deficit had damage in left IFG, they wouldn't be able to conclude that the left IFG is necessary for rehearsal in verbal working memory. This is because they couldn't know whether, among the population of stroke cases from which the patient selection was carried out, there may have been additional patients who had comparable damage to left IFG, but who did not have a verbal working memory impairment.

Clinical Neuropsychology For both cognitive neuropsychology and experimental neuropsychology, it's not uncommon that the researcher will develop novel behavioral tasks in order to test the question of interest. This is almost never the case, however, for clinical neuropsychology, which is concerned with patient care. Clinical neuropsychology is used for the diagnosis of a neurological or psychiatric disorder, for the assessment of the severity of a disorder, and/or for the assessment of the efficacy of a treatment and/or the rate of recovery of a patient. Therefore, a clinical neuropsychologist will almost invariably use standardized tests that have been normed on healthy subjects, typically across a range of ages, and for which an individual patient's level of performance can be used for diagnosis, staging, or assessment.

The methods of clinical neuropsychology involve having extensive knowledge of what kinds of "neuropsych tests" (as they're often known) are most appropriate for different kinds of patients, and how to interpret the results of these tests. (Because the emphasis of this book is on basic science, clinical neuropsychology won't come up very often.)[1]

How Does Behavior Relate to Mental Functions?

It is important, at this juncture, to remind ourselves that many aspects of cognition don't have to generate overt behavior. For example, you can read two words and decide whether or not they rhyme without having to say them out loud. Stated another way, we can generate phonology, and reason about it, without having to generate, nor hear, speech. (Indeed, assuming that you are not reading aloud, you may be experiencing what is informally known as "inner speech" – "covert speech" to a scientist – right now.) When behavior is covert, as it is with covert speech, mental imagery, or imagined activity, one must be careful about interpreting the results of cognitive neuroscience experiments. In particular, a form of reasoning known as "reverse inference" can often pose challenges.

Reverse inference has a formal definition in the scholarly discipline of logic, but for our purposes, we can use an example. Let's say that you are looking at the results from a functional magnetic resonance imaging (fMRI) study in which you acquired brain scans while your subjects were shown black and white drawings and asked to indicate whether each drawing depicted a living or a nonliving thing, by pressing one of two buttons. (We'll get to fMRI further along in this chapter.) The results indicate that one of the regions that showed elevated activity during task performance is a region of posterior IFG in the left hemisphere – Broca's area from *Chapter 1*. It might be tempting to conclude from this that, because Broca's area was engaged by the task, subjects must have been covertly naming the pictures. (And you would be doing so, in part, because of the "forward inference" from previous studies, in which overt speech was seen to be reliably accompanied by elevated activity in Broca's area; that, and the fact that lesion studies indicated that Broca's area is necessary for speech production.) The potential problem with this conclusion, however, is that it depends on the proposition that "Broca's area is specialized for speech production," and the consequent assumption that activity in Broca's area can mean only one thing. Another way of saying this would be to say that activity in Broca's area is specific for speech production. But what if this isn't true? Indeed, this very question was addressed in an influential review paper by Russell Poldrack (2006), who sorted through a database that contained the results from 749 neuroimaging studies that contained patterns of brain activity from 3222 experimental comparisons; 869 of these comparisons were language related, and of these, only 166 showed language-related change in activity in Broca's area. (I.e., activity in Broca's area would seem to not be a very sensitive indicator of using language.) Furthermore, of the 2353 comparisons that were not thought to emphasize language, 199 nonetheless showed a task-related change in Broca's area. (I.e., activity in Broca's area is also not specific to language.) We'll see, as we go forward, examples of analysis methods that can raise the sensitivity and the specificity of a comparison, such that reasoning from reverse inference is more tenable. But for now, we'll leave this as a cautionary tale that impels us to think critically when drawing conclusions about brain–behavior relations.

Studying the Effects of Damage to the Brain

We have already seen, in *Chapter 1*, that there are many circumstances that a scientist can either create or capitalize on to study the effects of altered brain function on behavior. Here, we'll limit ourselves to considering instances of damage incurred by an adult brain that had developed typically prior to the incident that produced the damage.

[1] Having said that, when we get to Chapter 11 and Chapter 15, we'll see that Brenda Milner, while working in a capacity of clinical neuropsychologist, made what have come to be recognized as perhaps the single biggest contributions to our understanding of the cognitive neuroscience of long-term memory and of cognitive control. The failure to award Dr. Milner (age 107 [sic] at the time of this writing) the Nobel Prize in Physiology or Medicine, in recognition of these achievements, is the most egregious scientific injustice that this author has observed over the course of his career.

Stroke For studies of human behavior, the classic source of patients with brain damage is the neurology clinic. Stroke, in which either the blockage or the rupture of an artery deprives an area of the brain of oxygenated blood for an extended period of time, results in often stereotyped patterns of cognitive and behavioral impairment that can be very similar across patients due to the fact that the vasculature of the brain, like every other part of our anatomy, is very similar across individuals. (E.g., infarction of the superior branch of the middle cerebral artery [MCA] in the left hemisphere will typically produce weakness or paralysis on the right side of the body, and often an aphasia similar to that described by Broca [*Chapter 1*, *The localization of speech*; *Figure 1.5*].) This can mean that, regardless of whether a poststroke scan may be needed for diagnostic and/or treatment purposes, the neuropsychologist may not need detailed neuroimaging to know what brain areas were likely impacted by the stroke.

Nonlocalized Trauma Brain damage can result from factors that produced damage that produces behavioral deficits that are less predictable than those resulting from stroke. *Viral encephalitis*, for example, occurs when a viral infection causes widespread swelling in the brain. (Variants of the herpes virus are often the culprit.) When the acute stage has passed and the swelling has subsided, any of a number of brain areas may turn out to have suffered irreversible damage. One notorious outcome of viral encephalitis can be damage to a subfield of the hippocampus, which, if bilateral (i.e., affecting the hippocampus in both hemispheres), can lead to a severe memory impairment. (We'll get to this starting in *Chapter 11*.) In other patients, however, the acute phase of the encephalitis can have spared the hippocampus but created lasting damage in circuits that are important for the sense of smell, or for vision, or other functions.

Environmental hypoxia/anoxia results from extended periods of time in a low-oxygen environment. (Hypoxia – access to low levels of oxygen – or anoxia – total deprivation of oxygen – can be the proximal causes of tissue damage due to stroke or other events "internal" to the body. Here, the reference is to the lack of oxygen in the breathable air.) As with encephalitis, because the impact is systemic, lasting damage can be highly variable. For example, environmental hypoxia is the cause of damage to patients who we'll consider further along in the book who have very specific impairments in the ability to name (and, perhaps, to think about) living objects in the world (but not nonliving objects), and to others who have difficulty recognizing individual faces, but not other complex and only subtly differing kinds of objects, like automobiles, or flowers.

Focal Lesions In the neurology clinic, focal lesions can result from penetrating head wounds, such as those caused by a bullet or by shrapnel in warfare, or from any of a variety of gruesome accidents that I won't review here. (Although we will take up the case of Phineas Gage in *Chapter 17*!) Depending on how circumscribed is the damage, careful assessment of patients with focal lesions can yield valuable insight about structure–function relations. One early example is that, because the Russo-Japanese war (1904–1905) has the ignoble distinction of being one of the first conflicts to feature the widespread use of high-velocity bullets, Japanese ophthalmologist Tatsuji Inouye was able to make pioneering discoveries about the organization of visual cortex – particularly retinotopy – by studying wounded veterans with visual impairments. (Among other attributes, these high-velocity bullets produced clear entry and exit wounds in the skull, which facilitated inferring the locus of brain damage despite the nonexistence of medical scanning technology.) Note that, although a stroke can produce focal lesions, there's always a concern when interpreting the effects of a stroke that it may have caused other damage in addition to the focal lesion, perhaps more diffuse damage too subtle to pick up with a brain scan. For this reason, many studies of stroke patients with damage to area X will include a control group of stroke patients with damage that spares area X, in an effort to control for possible nonspecific effects ("just from having had a stroke") contaminating the behavior of the experimental group.

In laboratories where experiments are carried out on nonhuman animals, many methods are used to disrupt brain function. Reversible methods are often used when the behavior of interest might involve learning, or periodic changing of behavior. In these studies, it can be particularly important to be able to show that normal behavior is restored when the intervention is not being applied. Methods for reversible disruption include electrical stimulation, the application of chemical agents whose effects dissipate after a finite period of time (sometimes called "behavioral pharmacology"), and cryogenic disruption (informally known as "cortical cooling"). Reversible pharmacological intervention often uses compounds that mimic the effects of neurotransmitters or other endogenous substances. Cooling takes advantage of the fact that all living tissues in warm-blooded organisms function optimally within only a narrow range of temperature. There are specific protocols whereby brain tissue can safely be cooled until its ongoing activity ceases, and with functions returning to normal once the source of the cooling is removed. Note, however, that cortical cooling entails a craniotomy and inserting the cooling device (sometimes a probe, and sometimes a coil that is positioned on a gyral surface or inside a sulcus), and so while the impairment from the cooling per se is reversible, it is not a noninvasive procedure.

Methods for producing permanent damage range from electrical (increasing the voltage in an electrode) to chemical/pharmacological (sometimes targeting, e.g., only neurons with a certain subtype of neurotransmitter receptor) to surgical intervention (sometimes referred to as "mechanical" lesions).

Noninvasive Methods to Produce "Virtual Lesions" One of the exciting, and powerful, developments that has accompanied the explosion of cognitive neuroscience over the past several decades has been the introduction and refinement of methods to alter brain function that don't require surgical intervention. Many of these methods involve controlled delivery of magnetic, electrical, or acoustic energy, and their effects are typically short-lived, limited to either the duration of the simulation itself, or to some relatively short-lived period of residual effects. Each will get its own section(s) in ensuing parts of this chapter.

Transcranial Neurostimulation

The methods summarized in this section are classified as noninvasive because they don't involve a surgical procedure.[2] Indeed, although many of them are in varying stages of consideration as potential treatments for a variety of neurological and psychiatric maladies, all are widely used to carry out studies of brain function in healthy young adults. With the exception of ultrasound, the methods that we consider here work on the basis of manipulating the electrical properties of the nervous system.

The methods that we'll summarize in this section are emblematic of a trade-off that often confronts scientists who want to study the neural bases of human cognition: although we are studying the cognition of the species that is ultimately of primary interest to most of us – Homo sapiens – we are often limited to methods that don't offer the same precision and/or resolution as do invasive methods that are often used for research carried out on nonhuman species. In the case of neurostimulation, the precision of extracranial methods is orders of magnitude more coarse than are invasive microstimulation of the kind summarized in *Chapter 1*, or of deep brain stimulation that is used as a surgically implanted treatment for conditions such as Parkinson's disease (to be discussed in detail in *Chapter 8, Skeletomotor control*). Nonetheless, these are powerful tools that have provided important insights about the neural bases of human cognition.

The Importance of Specificity (Again)

From the standpoint of the kinds of inference supported, transcranial neurostimulation techniques share with neuropsychology the characteristic that they typically afford poor anatomical specificity, a fact that imposes important constraints on experimental design. Most often, this means inclusion of a so-called "active control" condition, in which the same stimulation

---

[2]Throughout this book, we will stick with this definition of "noninvasive" because it is used in this way on a near-universal basis. One might be forgiven, however, for contemplating whether a method that deploys physical energy to influence brain function isn't, at least in some sense, "invading" the inner sanctum of the self?

parameters that were delivered to the brain area of interest are also delivered to a different area of the brain (a "control area") that is not believed to contribute to the behavior of interest. A pattern of results in which stimulation of the brain area of interest has the predicted effect on behavior, but stimulation of the control area does not have this same effect, rules out the possibility that the former may have just been a nonspecific effect of stimulation of the brain. (This is analogous to the inclusion, in a study with stroke patients, a "lesion control" group made up of patients who have also suffered strokes, but for whom the damage spares the brain area(s) of primary interest.) Depending on the experimental hypothesis, it can sometimes also be useful to include a control task.

Transcranial Electrical Stimulation

This method entails applying one large electrode (typically on the order of 5 cm × 5 cm) to a part of the cranium overlying a brain region of interest a second electrode somewhere else on the body (sometimes a different part of the cranium, sometimes a "non-brain" part of the body such as the cheek) and passing current from one – the anode – to the other – the cathode.

Transcranial Direct Current Stimulation Direct current is a steady flow of electrical current in one direction. Most batteries that power portable devices, from flashlights (a.k.a. torches) to electric lawn mowers, deliver DC power. Like a battery, tDCS has one contact (one electrode) that is the anode – from which electrons flow – and a second that is the cathode – to which electrons are drawn. Functionally, tDCS works on the basis that brain tissue located close to the anode will exhibit an increase in excitability during the application of tDCS (due to depolarization of neurons experiencing the stimulation), and for an extended period of time after tDCS has been applied. As a result, the typical expectation is that if the brain area under the anode is important for the performance of a task, performance will improve with anodal tDCS. Because the converse is true for tissue located close to the cathode, the electrode montage for a tDCS study will often place the critical electrode over the brain area of interest, and the other electrode over a non-brain part of the head, such as the cheek (see *Figure 4.1*). This avoids a situation in which it's unclear whether a tDCS-related change in behavior resulted from excitation of the region under the anode or inhibition of the region under the cathode.

tDCS is typically delivered at an intensity of 1–2 mA, and this has been estimated to produce a relatively weak electrical field that may change the membrane potential of neurons most affected by the tDCS by less than 1 mV. Therefore, the effect of tDCS on neural tissue is almost certainly a modulatory one. (I.e., it doesn't directly trigger action potentials in the neurons that it affects, but it changes the conditions under which these neurons will generate action potentials.) It's noteworthy that the behavioral effects of tDCS can extend for considerable period of time after the stimulation is no longer being delivered. The duration of these residual effects can vary from tens of minutes to more than an hour and depends on the strength and duration that tDCS is applied, as well as the cortical area being targeted. The reason for this isn't fully understood, but the assumption is that the change in some factors that influence excitability, like the density of postsynaptic receptors at certain types of synapses, must persist longer than the stimulation itself. As a result, some studies will have subjects performing one or more behavioral tasks while tDCS is being delivered (i.e., in an "online" protocol), and others will begin the behavioral testing immediately after the administration of tDCS (an "offline" protocol). With either kind of protocol, repeated measures designs that call for subjects to perform the same task(s) with different areas targeted will typically impose a separation of a day or more between tDCS sessions targeting different areas, so as to avoid the possibility that the effects of stimulation during the first session might influence the subsequent session.

There are many more variations of how tDCS can be administered, and how it can influence neural activity and behavior, than we can summarize here. The details of just one seemingly simple study, however, give a sense of some of the nuances of the method. In their study, Nivethida Thirugnanasambandam et al. (2011) delivered anodal or cathodal tDCS over primary motor cortex (M1) for 20 minutes and then assessed its effect by delivering single

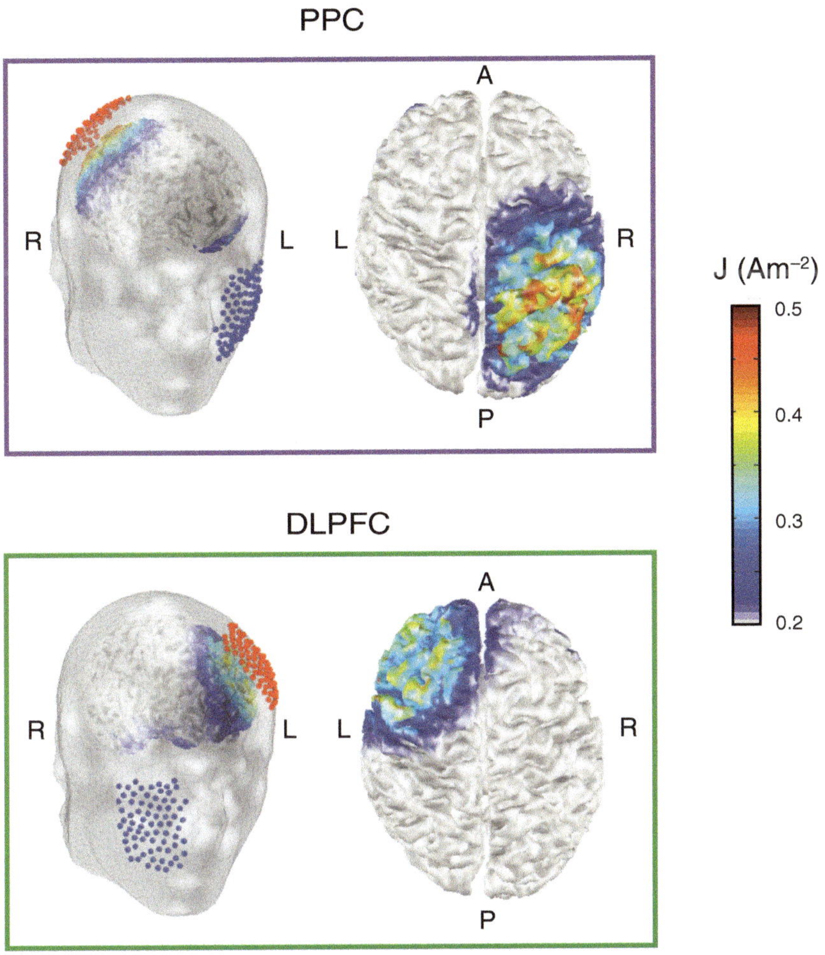

FIGURE 4.1 Illustration of electrode montages, and estimated current density distributions, from a tDCS study of working memory. Positioning of the anodes on the scalp, over the posterior parietal cortex (PPC) of the right hemisphere and over the dorsolateral prefrontal cortex (DLPFC) of the left hemisphere, is illustrated with clusters of red dots. Positioning of the cathodes, on the contralateral cheek, is illustrated with clusters of blue dots. For both montages, the current density distributions are illustrated in two formats: relative to the two electrodes on the left and superimposed on top-down views of the brain on the right. In this experiment, tDCS of PPC was hypothesized to influence task performance, and tDCS of DLPFC served as an active control condition. A = anterior; P = posterior; R = right; L = left.

Source: Wang et al., 2019 / with permission of Society for Neuroscience.

pulses of TMS to M1 and measuring the resultant electrical response in the muscles of the hand (the "motor-evoked potential," MEP). (This procedure, using TMS to evoke MEPs, is conceptually similar to the microstimulation study of Fritsch and Hitzig [1870]: it directly stimulates a region of the motor cortex and observes the resultant effect on the muscles of the body part controlled by the stimulated tissue. We'll get to the details of how it is that TMS stimulates cortical tissue further along in this section.) An important detail about the experimental procedure is that the researchers included a gap of 120 seconds after the offset of tDCS before delivering single pulses of TMS. When this 120-second gap was unfilled, the effect of anodal tDCS was to increase the amplitude of the TMS-evoked MEP, and the effect of cathodal tDCS was to decrease the amplitude of the TMS-evoked MEP. This is consistent with the expectation that tDCS will produce excitation of the region under the anode and inhibition of the region under the cathode An interesting twist, however, was that the authors included a second condition during which subjects were asked to squeeze their hands at 20% maximum possible force during the 120-second gap. Interestingly, in this "voluntary muscle contraction" (VMC) condition, the anodal tDCS-related increase in the TMS-evoked MEP was markedly reduced, as was the cathodal tDCS-related decrease in the TMS-evoked MEP.

The results from Thirugnanasambandam et al. (2011), and others like these, highlight two important points. First, the no-VMC results show directly that tDCS does, indeed, have effects on cortical excitability when it is measured directly. (I.e., if stimulation of motor cortex with identical pulses of TMS produces a larger effect in muscles of the hand when preceded by 20 minutes of anodal tDCS, it must be the case that the excitatory effect of that pulse of TMS on the targeted brain tissue was larger [and, therefore, that the targeted tissue was more excitable] in the tDCS condition.) This is often just assumed and inferred from effects of tDCS on performance of cognitive tasks (as illustrated in *Figure 4.1*), but it can be important to have direct evidence for this assumption. The second point is really two points. Most generally, the effects of tDCS are highly dependent on the state that the brain was in at the time of the stimulation. This is illustrated by the fact that VMC had the effect of blocking the effects that tDCS would have otherwise had. At a finer level of granularity, this property of state dependency is not limited to just the time that the tDCS is being delivered, as established by the fact that the VMC intervention occurred during the gap between tDCS offset and measurement of the MEPs.

The final point to make here is a caveat about the precision of targeting. Most tDCS systems come with software that estimates the current density experienced by different brain areas as a function of stimulator output and the configuration of the electrodes, as illustrated in *Figure 4.1*. Interpretation of these estimates, however, needs to be tempered by a few factors. One is that the bone of the skull has high resistance, and so half or more of the current leaving the anode does not make it through the skull and into the brain. The second is that typically the software estimating the path of current flow between the two electrodes does not have information specific to the brains of the individuals participating in that experiment. Rather, it uses assumptions about the "typical" human brain that were baked into the software long before the researchers acquired the equipment. And because different tissues and fluids (importantly, cerebrospinal fluid [CSF]) have different conductive properties, any differences between the heads of one's research subjects and the assumed "typical head" will necessarily produce error in the estimate.

Transcranial Alternating Current Stimulation tACS works on the same physical principles as does tDCS, and, indeed, many transcranial electrical stimulation devices are capable of operating in either mode. The difference is that, with tACS, the status of the two electrodes as the anode or the cathode switches back and forth several times per second. Therefore, the frequency of stimulation is an important parameter in tACS. The most common research questions that are addressed with tACS relate to endogenous oscillations in the brain. Recall that near the end of *Chapter 2,* we considered the phenomenon of oscillatory synchrony. Further along in this chapter, in the sections on *Electroencephalography (EEG)* and on *Analysis of time-varying signals*, we'll begin to see how patterns of oscillation at different frequencies are associated with different physiological states, and sometimes with different cognitive functions. In this context, tACS is often used to try to influence internally generated (i.e., endogenous) oscillations – perhaps their frequency, or their amplitude, or their phase – as a way to test hypotheses about the functional role of these properties of oscillatory dynamics. When we get to the section on EEG, we'll learn that the neurogenic (i.e., "brain-derived") electrical signals measured at the scalp are tiny, much smaller than those generated by tACS. As a consequence, the real-time effects of tACS on endogenous oscillations can only be inferred, but not measured directly. Thus, although one might hope that an effect of tACS delivered at, say, 10 Hz, might be to entrain an endogenous oscillation that typically cycles at 9.5 Hz (i.e., to "speed it up"), that's only one possibility. Another is that the endogenous oscillation and the exogenously delivered one will simply coexist. Or the tACS may weaken the endogenous oscillation, which may or may not, in turn, have an influence on the function of a region not targeted by the tACS, but that is influenced by the 9.5 Hz oscillation. Careful experimental design is needed to anticipate and rule out as many alternative scenarios as one can reasonably think of.

Transcranial Magnetic Stimulation (TMS)

Transcranial magnetic stimulation works on the principle of electromagnetic induction – the same principle at work in the turbines at electric power generation plants, or in the pickup of an electric guitar. In secondary school physics, many of us learned this as the "right-hand rule" – if you curl the fingers of your right hand and extend your thumb, current flowing in the direction that your thumb is pointing will generate a magnetic field oriented in the direction of your fingers. Conversely, electrical current will be induced in a length of conductive wire (pointing in the same orientation as your thumb) experiencing a changing magnetic field (in the same orientation as your curled fingers). With TMS, the TMS coil produces a magnetic field that, when held near the scalp, is experienced by tissue in the brain including, importantly, axons and other fibers (*Figure 4.2*). Because these fibers have the properties of conductive wire, the magnetic pulse induces a "pulse" of current in these fibers. The biophysics of cortical tissue is such that current induction is maximal at places where there are geometric changes in fiber pathways (such as where efferent axons bend at right angles to plunge into

FIGURE 4.2 Transcranial magnetic stimulation.

A

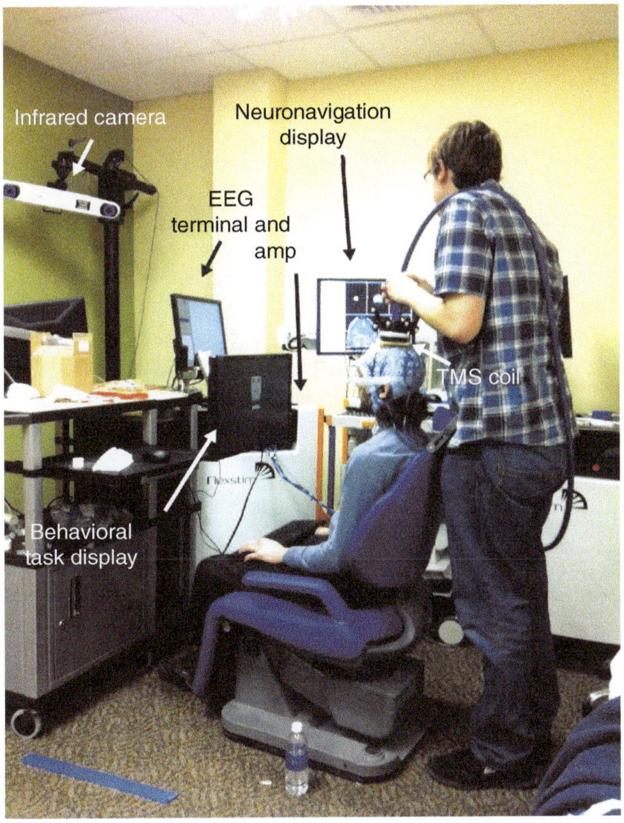

FIGURE 4.2.A An experimental setup in the author's laboratory. The subject is seated and viewing stimuli on the behavioral task display screen (responding via keyboard in his lab), and is wearing an EEG electrode cap. On his face, and on the TMS coil, are infrared-reflective beacons that are detected by the infrared camera and used to coregister the location of the TMS coil and the subject's brain, so as to compute a real-time estimate of where TMS current induction will be maximal in his brain. The experimenter uses this real-time display for "neuronavigation" – positioning the coil so as to precisely target the intended region of the brain. (The TMS stimulator, located to the right of the subject and experimenter and therefore obscured from view in this photo, is roughly the same size as the housing enclosing the EEG amplifier.)

Source: Bradley R. Postle.

B

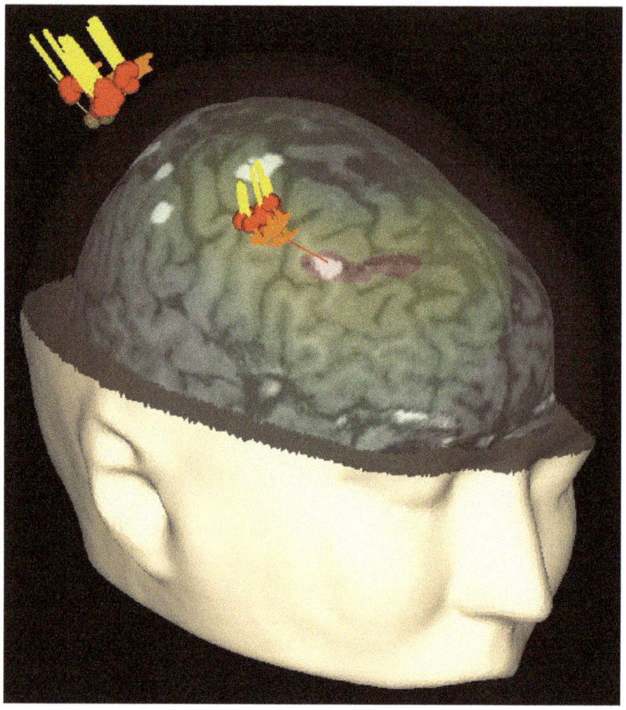

FIGURE 4.2.B An image taken from a neuronavigation display at the end of an experimental session in which hotspots of activity in DLPFC and PPC were targeted with rTMS. The 3-D head-and-brain image was derived from an fMRI experiment during which the subject performed a cognitive task, and then a thresholded statistical map from the fMRI data was merged with the T1-weighted anatomical images. In this image, the scalp and some of the cortex have been "peeled" away to expose the hotspots (white blobs), two of which were targeted with rTMS. Each red ball and yellow "spike" shows where the TMS coil was positioned on the scalp when a train of pulses was delivered, and the purple shadow covering the hotspot in the right middle frontal gyrus is the estimated focus of electromagnetic induction. The estimated extent of the weaker "penumbra" of the magnetic field is shown in green.

white matter [as happens for axons projecting to distal brain regions], or where afferent axons bend at right angles upon emerging from white matter to run parallel to the cortical surface [as happens for axons projecting from a distal area and "arriving" in Layer I of a targeted area]) and where there are discontinuities in cell membranes, such as at the axon hillock and at synaptic terminations. Thus, the effects of TMS on a region of cortex are decidedly nonspecific, in that TMS induces current in incoming fibers, in local circuitry, and in fibers exiting the region.

A TMS system consists of the "stimulator," essentially a large capacitor that can hold a large amount of electrical energy and then discharge it all at once, a cable through which the current from the stimulator travels to the coil and the coil through which the conduction of this current generates the magnetic field. Although coils come in different configurations intended for different purposes, the most common is the 70 mm "figure-of-8," with the crossing-over point of the "8" the point of maximal induction, and therefore the part of the coil used for targeting. (Because the cable and coil invariably come as one piece, the two together tend to be referred to as "the coil.")

The effects of TMS on the brain depend on the strength of the pulse, with moderately strong pulses capable of generating action potentials not only in neurons that directly experience the magnetic flux of the TMS, but also in neurons that are one or more synapses downstream from the stimulated tissue. For example, as we saw in the preceding section on tDCS, single pulses of TMS delivered to the motor cortex of humans can produce a twitch in a finger or thumb, which, as we'll see in *Chapter 8*, requires signaling across a minimum of two synapses. That is, because it is certain that the magnetic field generated by a pulse of TMS delivered at the skull does not physically reach the muscles of the hand, the only explanation for the systematic production of muscle twitches by TMS of the motor cortex is that it generates action potentials in cortical neurons that travel from the brain to the spinal cord and are sufficiently robust to trigger action potentials in the spinal motor neurons that, in turn, are the proximal cause of contraction of muscles in the hand. *Figure 20.3* illustrates the effects of single pulses of TMS on brain activity, as measured with EEG.

Although the technique often elicits questions about safety (e.g., *Can it elicit seizures?*), the method has a lengthy and well-documented history of safe application in cognitive neuroscience research (see, e.g., the report by Rossi et al. (2009) that is listed at the end of the previous chapter).

Single-Pulse TMS Although some protocols for delivering multiple TMS pulses in structured series can have the effect of disrupting brain function, and therefore behavior, this is NOT the typical effect for which TMS in single-pulse mode is chosen. Indeed, one common application effectively assumes that TMS has no influence on ongoing endogenous brain activity (i.e., the "natural" and "internally generated" activity that would be ongoing regardless of the experimental context) and so can be used as a kind of physiological probe (a "ping"). A second application is one that we've already seen in the previous chapter's section The Relation Between Visual Processing and the Brain's Physiological State. It takes advantage of the fact that, under the right conditions, single pulses of TMS delivered to different parts of the visual system can produce the percept of a flash of light.

First, the physiological probe, for which we can find an analogy from computer networking. When troubleshooting a computer network, it's common to send out a "ping" signal to determine what other computers are actively connected with the one sending out the ping. Other computers in the network will send a return ping that also indicates (in milliseconds), the amount of time that it took the ping to travel out and back. In the study by Thirugnanasambandam et al. (2011), we saw that single pulses of TMS were used to measure the excitability of cortical tissue that had been targeted with tDCS. Note that, because the effects of tDCS are modulatory, one wouldn't necessarily be able to detect any "before/after" change in the targeted tissue without probing it. Although this kind of probing could also, in principle, have been carried out by asking subjects to move their hands in a specific way and measuring whether some aspect of the movement was different after tDCS, using this kind of "behavioral challenge" can, in practice, produce noisier data, and data that are more difficult to interpret. The reason has to do with control over the stimulation of the motor cortex. Recall that we noted previously that the energy delivered by the TMS coil is identical on every trial. If, in contrast, Thirugnanasambandam et al. (2011) had used a procedure in which subjects were asked to, say, press a button every time they heard a beep, how could the scientists know whether the processing of the auditory signal was the same on each trial, and that it resulted in the delivery of an identical neural command to the motor cortex on every trial (e.g., carried by an identical number of action potentials, and with the identical latency relative to the beep)? How could they know whether the subject's attention to the task/motivation to respond was identical on each trial?

While the Thirugnanasambandam et al. (2011) study probed peripheral (i.e., "not the brain") neurophysiology, TMS can also be used to probe the physiology of the brain. This is done by measuring the TMS-evoked response via concurrent measurement of brain activity, typically with EEG or with fMRI. One study, for example, tested a hypothesis that a nucleus of the thalamus is dysfunctional in schizophrenia. Although a behavioral challenge could also have been used for this study, added to the complicating factors considered in the previous paragraph was the uncertainty about whether the overall level of compliance (or motivation, or distractability) might be different for the patients vs. the nonschizophrenic control groups.

Single-pulse TMS is also useful if one wants to study neurophysiology in different states of arousal. In *Chapter 20*, for example, we'll consider a study in which single pulses of TMS were delivered to subjects, late at night, as they transitioned from quiet wakefulness into sleep. The motivation was to test the prediction that a state of connectivity between neural circuits, hypothesized to be necessary for conscious awareness, would transform into a state of disconnectivity as people fell asleep (and, therefore, out of consciousness). Note that not only would a behavioral challenge not work for this kind of experiment, but a "sensory challenge" would also be problematic. People's eyes close when they fall asleep, and so comparing the brain's responses to flashes of light when awake vs. asleep wouldn't work. Our ears "stay open," however, so what about comparing the brain's response to tones? The complication here is that any differences in the brain response to tones during sleep vs. wake might be due to a sleep-related change in how the auditory signal is processed and transmitted from the ear to the brain, rather than to a change in the functioning of the brain per se. The physics of electromagnetic induction in contrast, are the same whether a nearby brain is awake or asleep when a pulse of current travels through a TMS coil.

A second common application of single pulses of TMS is to produce functional effects. We've already seen that single pulses of TMS delivered to the motor cortex can produce muscle twitches in the periphery, and in Chapter 3, section The Relation Between Visual Processing and the Brain's Physiological State, that single pulses of TMS delivered to the occipital cortex can produce a perceptual phenomenon known as a phosphene – a cloudlike flash of light that a subject perceives even when the eyes are closed and covered with a blindfold (*Figure 3.6*). Phosphenes are presumed to be generated by the propagation of action potentials through the visual cortex. The generation of phosphenes points out an interesting paradox about TMS, which is that although its anatomical specificity is poor, what we might consider as its "functional specificity" can be quite, well, persnickety. Simply put, it's difficult to generate visual phosphenes with TMS. The process requires a great deal of trial and error of stimulation at multiple locations on the scalp until the subject eventually reports seeing a phosphene. (On unlucky days, a subject may never see a phosphene, and eventually the experiment is aborted.) Importantly (and this also applies to generating MEPs via TMS of the motor cortex), the orientation of the coil at a particular location on the scalp also matters. Thus, even if you knew exactly where on the scalp to position the crossing-over point of the coil, you'd still need to rotate it through several orientations (relative to the scalp) to find the specific orientation for which, at that location on the scalp, a pulse of TMS will produce a phosphene. (Operationally, the orientation of the coil is described with reference to the handle [i.e., where the cable feeds into the coil] relative to a gross anatomical landmark, such as the midline.)

In addition to the positioning of the TMS coil on the scalp, the other important factor that determines its effects is the amount of energy used to generate the pulse. Although the output of a stimulator can be expressed in physical units, it almost never is. Instead, the "common currency" for reporting TMS stimulator intensity is a value normalized to the functional effects of TMS. That is, for any two healthy individuals, the physical signal intensity needed to generate a muscle twitch (when applied to the motor cortex) or a phosphene (when delivered to the visual cortex) will vary considerably. What's most important, therefore, is to ensure that the same "relative" stimulation intensity is delivered to each subject participating in the study. This will be achieved by, for example, determining the minimal stimulator intensity that will evoke a muscle twitch on 5 of 10 pulses and then increasing that intensity by, say, 15% for the experiment. In this way, although the stimulator intensity may be different for each subject, each is nonetheless experiencing TMS at "115% of motor threshold."

Repetitive (r)TMS Protocols From a functional perspective, rTMS can be delivered with the intent of disrupting the functioning of the targeted brain area (sometimes referred to as a "virtual lesion" protocol) or with the intent of enhancing the function of a targeted brain system. From a procedural perspective, it can be delivered in two general modes, offline or online.

Offline virtual-lesion protocols are similar in many respects to cathodal tDCS: TMS is delivered to a brain area for an extended period of time, and the subject then performs a behavioral task, with the assumption that functioning of the targeted area has been altered. Two common TMS protocols that are intended to produce local hypometabolism (and, consequently, a decrease in excitability) that lasts for several tens of minutes after TMS are 1 Hz rTMS and continuous theta burst (ctb)TMS. The ctbTMS stimulation protocol typically consists of triplets of pulses separated by 50 msec, delivered five times per second (i.e., a total of 15 pulses in a second), and gets its name from the fact that something that happens at a rate of 5 Hz falls within the range of 3–8 Hz, which, in the human EEG, is called the "theta band." (More on brain oscillations and their Greek-letter names in section Electroencephalography.) For reasons that aren't yet fully understood, these two virtual-lesion protocols typically produce effects with different temporal profiles. Whereas 1 Hz rTMS tends to produce hypometabolism in the targeted tissue that persists beyond the period of stimulation for roughly as long as was the duration of the stimulation (e.g., 20 minutes of 1 Hz rTMS will produce a virtual lesion that lasts for 20 minutes beyond the termination of the rTMS), a 40-second train of continuous tbTMS can produce local hypometabolism that lasts for roughly 30 minutes.

Offline enhancement protocols differ from virtual-lesion protocols primarily in terms of time scale: whereas a virtual-lesion protocol typically entails rTMS followed immediately by behavioral testing, enhancement protocols entail multiple stimulation sessions across multiple days. The logic is that whereas one session of offline rTMS will produce disruption of the cortical region that is being targeted directly, multiple sessions across days may also produce enhanced functioning in the network of regions that, together with the targeted area, contribute to the behavior of interest. Effective offline enhancement protocols have used repeated 2-second trains of 20-Hz rTMS separated by inter-train intervals of 28 seconds, as well as variants of the ctbTMS protocol described above.

An important factor to take into account with these methods is that although they generally work as summarized here, they are not "100% reliable." To be clear, assuming the TMS equipment is in good working order, at any given level of output, it will produce an identical magnetic field each time it is triggered. Similarly, for any healthy human subject, a location on the scalp can be found at which, for example, a pulse of TMS will always produce muscle contraction. Despite this, however, there will be experimental sessions for which, for example, application of a virtual-lesion protocol fails to produce a measurable alteration in behavior. The reasons for this are not well understood, and there typically won't be any clear indication from how the subject behaves, or how they say that the stimulation makes them feel. Because of this, it can be valuable to assess the effects that one's rTMS protocol actually had on brain function by, for example, recording the EEG immediately prior to and following the application of TMS, or assessing activity and/or connectivity in the region/network of interest with fMRI.

Finally, online rTMS is perhaps the most variable and context-dependent of any TMS protocol. Although some have summarized its effects as "excitatory," it's not always that straightforward. By definition, online rTMS entails delivering rTMS while the subject is engaged in a behavioral task, and a starting assumption might be that delivery of rTMS would be expected to disrupt the exquisitely tuned patterns of activity that underlie the behavior of interest. Indeed, in many studies, this is the outcome that is observed. However, there are instances in which rTMS can enhance performance. Note that, depending on the hypothesis being tested, there can be situations in which it "may not matter" whether the effects of rTMS turn out to enhance or to impair behavior. This would be an instance in which the hypothesis was that *Area X makes an important contribution to behavior A*: so long as the effect of rTMS of Area X is selective (e.g., if rTMS of Area Y does not affect the behavior of interest), either enhancement or impairment would demonstrate a role for Area X in behavior A.

And what if online rTMS has enhancing effects for some subjects in a study but impairing effects for others? Upon initial consideration, one might think that such a result would be hopelessly uninterpretable. This need not be the case, however, if concurrent physiological measures were obtained. Consider the example of a study carried out by this author's group, led by then-graduate student Massihullah Hamidi. In it, 10 Hz rTMS of a region of PPC, during the delay period of a working memory task, impaired the performance of some subjects but improved the performance of others. If considered alone, these behavioral results would have indicated that there was no interpretable effect of rTMS because the group means for the control and experimental conditions did not differ. When analyzed in conjunction with the concurrently recorded EEG, however, Hamidi et al. (2009) found that rTMS also had correspondingly opposite effects on alpha-band power in the EEG of different subjects and that these effects of rTMS on the EEG correlated with the individual differences in the effects of rTMS on behavior. (More specifically, the sign and magnitude of the effect of rTMS on behavior were inversely related to the sign and magnitude of the effect of rTMS on power in the alpha band – the larger the rTMS-associated decrease in alpha-band power, the larger the rTMS-associated improvement in behavior, and the larger the rTMS-associated increase in alpha-band power, the larger the rTMS-associated decline in behavior; Hamidi et al. [2009].)

Transcranial Ultrasound Stimulation (TUS)

This section will be very brief, because the method is still relatively new and, at the time of this writing, there have been very few studies using TUS as a tool to study the neural bases of some aspect of behavior or cognition where the primary goal isn't method development (e.g., validation of an application of TUS relative to other transcranial stimulation methods whose effect on a particular aspect of behavior is already well documented). However, considering the speed at which methods develop, it wouldn't be a surprise if TUS were to have achieved "mainstream" status by the time this book is ready for a fourth edition. This is true, in particular, because of the in-principle advantage that TUS holds over other noninvasive methods with regard to selective targeting of deep structures. (Much of what is summarized here is taken from a review by Kim Butts Pauly, Zhihai Qui, and Wynn Legon [2024].)

Ultrasound refers to acoustic energy oscillating at frequencies higher than what is audible by humans, typically >20 kHz. For TUS, these soundwaves are created by an ultrasound transducer that converts electrical energy into a pressure wave that can be spatially focused according to the geometry of the rig. Ultrasound propagates well in water but is almost fully reflected at air–tissue interfaces, and so ultrasound energy is transmitted into the body via coupling gel applied to the surface of the skin. (Anyone familiar with ultrasound-based imaging in a clinical setting, such as during prenatal care, will be familiar with "ultrasound gel".) Unlike magnetic energy, ultrasound is attenuated by the bone of the skull, and so targeting a region inside the skull requires some modeling to achieve the desired intensity of stimulation at the target regions. At the level of the physics of the method, there are several possible ways that ultrasound could interact with brain tissue. These include thermal effects (when biological tissue absorbs ultrasound energy, this energy is converted to heat), the movement of tissue (in the direction of the beam), and mechanical interaction with stretch-sensitive receptors (including many classes of ion channels). Each of these effects is sensitive to the TUS parameters of intensity, pulse duration, duty cycle, and frequency, although it is not always easy to disentangle specific effects attributable to just one of these.

Although many important details about how and why TUS produces its effects remain to be clarified, an in-principle advantage of TUS is that it can be very precisely targeted, producing, for example, contralateral limb movements in rodents, localized increases in the Blood Oxygen Level-Dependent (BOLD) signal (see section *T2*-weighted fMRI*) in several mammalian species, and even selective attenuation of somatosensory evoked potentials (i.e., as measured with EEG) generated by afferent signals passing through one but not another nucleus of the thalamus (of a pig). The reason that TUS can be so precisely targeted is that the geometry of the transducer produces what amounts to a cone of energy, with the widest part of the cone at the point of transduction (i.e., where the ultrasound waves originate) and the narrowest point of the cone focused on the intended target. Because this cone is really just the shape of the volume of space though which each ultrasound wave travels, the total amount of energy carried by each wave becomes concentrated ("focused") on smaller and smaller volumes of tissue as the wave "shrinks" in surface area, such that, for example, TUS targeting a deep nucleus of the basal ganglia will have only minimal effect on the cortical tissue through which it must pass in order to get to its target (*Figure 4.3*). (With TMS, in contrast, the magnetic energy produced by the TMS coil expands outward from the point of electromagnetic transduction, and its energy decreases with distance from this point; section *Transcranial magnetic stimulation (TMS).*) Functionally, it's believed that whether TUS has excitatory or inhibitory effects may depend the duty cycle of the stimulation protocol (i.e., the ratio of stimulation "on" vs. "off" during pulsed delivery; continuous stimulation [i.e., not pulsed] would correspond to a 100% duty cycle), although the precise parameters for this remain to be worked out.

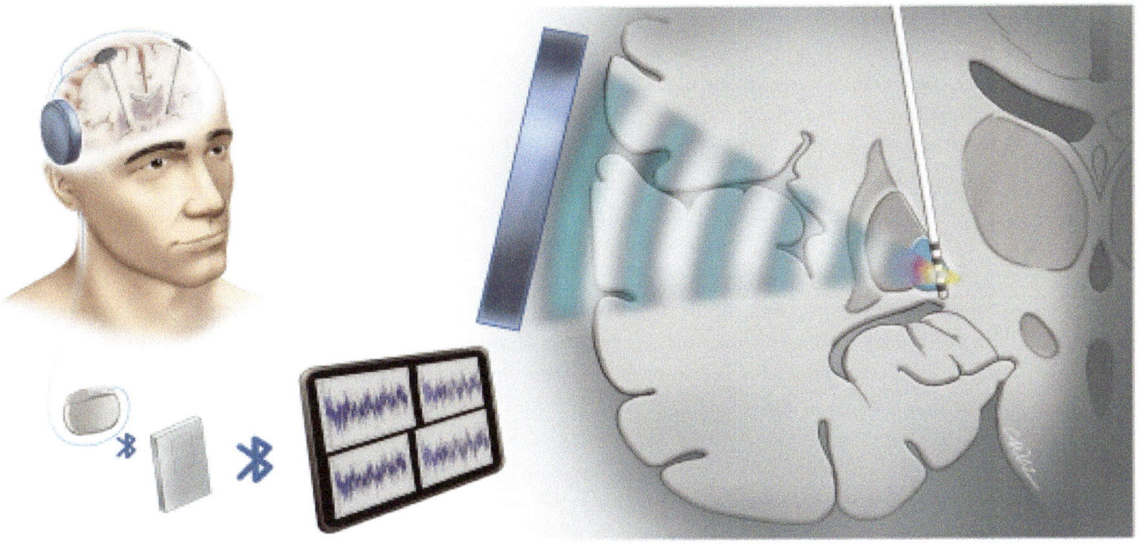

FIGURE 4.3 Transcranial ultrasound stimulation. Artist's rendition of TUS of the interior segment of the globus pallidus (GPi) in neurological patients with movement disorders. Left: Patient with bilateral deep-brain stimulation (DBS) electrodes implanted in the GPi bilaterally. Physical leads connect these electrodes with a disc-shaped unit that is surgically implanted under the scalp, which is itself connected by physical leads to the stimulator + battery unit that is surgically implanted into a flap of skin overlying the pectoral muscle of the chest. The stimulator + battery unit is Bluetooth enabled, to permit wireless transmission of neuronal signals (recorded by the DBS electrodes) to external systems. Right: Cartoon of TUS transducer delivering a focused cone of ultrasound stimulation to the GPi (Darmani et al., 2025) / Springer Nature / CC BY-NC-ND 4.0.

Anatomy and Cellular Physiology

Many of the details of gross anatomy that the reader of this book will need to understand were already covered in the first three chapters of this book and were discovered via dissection of postmortem tissue. For the contemporary cognitive neuroscientist, gross anatomy isn't as much a "discovery science" as it is a body of knowledge over which one must have considerable mastery in order to be able to interpret, for example, the effect that subtle differences in the location and/or the spatial extent of a lesion are likely to have on some domain of behavior, or whether two nearby foci of activity are part of the same or different structures.

Thematically, many methods that might be best classified as *anatomical* vs. *physiological* can be closely related, either because of physical and/or biological principles that they exploit or because of the kind of question they are used to address. For that reason, this section will jump back and forth between methods for visualizing and measuring structure (i.e., anatomy) and methods for measuring function (i.e., activity or physiology).

Techniques That Exploit the Cell Biology of the Neuron

Tract Tracing No matter how long, or multiply branched, an axon is part of just one cell. Thus, there needs to be a mechanism, for example, for proteins that are synthesized from DNA in the nucleus of the neuron to be transported to synapses at far reaches of each axonal branch. (For this author, the "gee whiz" factor is particularly high when I think of the giraffe, or of massive whales . . . .) And so, intracellular mechanisms for **axonal transport** are critical for the healthy functioning of the neuron.

Axons are microscopically small. Although bundled tracts of thousands of axons can be visible to the naked eye (e.g., the optic nerve, tract, and radiations; *Figure 3.2*), this sheds no light on the targets of individual axons. One strategy for determining precisely where axons project to is to inject a substance into a region of the brain, let the natural processes of intracellular transport "do their thing" (i.e., transport the substance from the region of uptake to other parts of the neuron), and later look for where the substance has been transported. Over the past 100 years or so, sometimes through trial and error and sometimes as a result of sophisticated understanding of cell biology, anatomists have devised many ways to address different questions about neuroanatomy. For our purposes, we can think of three categories of cell biology-based (as opposed to neuroimaging-based) neuroanatomy: anterograde transport, retrograde transport, and whole-cell staining.

Anterograde transport refers to the process of transporting substances away from the cell body and along its axon and axonal branches. Let's consider the example of using an anterograde tracer to determine whether, and how, neurons from somatosensory area S1, the first cortical stage of processing of somatosensory information, project to somatosensory area S2, the second stage in the somatosensory processing hierarchy. To do this experiment, one would inject tracer into S1 of a laboratory animal, wait for a set period of time, then sacrifice the animal, slice the brain, process the tissue, and, finally, inspect the tissue from area S2 under a microscope to observe where the tracer ended up. Such an experiment depends on several factors. First, the tracer needs to be taken up by the dendrites and/or cell bodies of the neurons of interest. Second, one needs to know the amount of time it takes for the tracer to be transported to the ends of the axon. Third, there needs to be a reliable way to detect the tracer under a microscope. With regard to the passage of time, this becomes particularly important if the tracer can "jump" the synaptic cleft and thereby be passed from one neuron to another. Exquisitely detailed studies have been performed with such tracers such that, when different animals are sacrificed at different times relative to the injection, the anatomist can determine the monosynaptic connectivity of a region, its disynaptic connectivity, and so on. With regard to detection, some tracers are visible in and of themselves, and others require the tissue to be stained or otherwise prepared so as to make the tracer visible.

Retrograde transport works in the opposite direction, transporting substances from distal parts of the axon back toward the cell body. Thus, in our example, retrograde tract tracing would entail injecting the tracer into area S2, where it is taken up at the presynaptic terminals of axons projecting to S2 and then carried "backward" along these axons to their cell bodies. *Figure 4.4* provides an illustration of how retrograde tracing can be used to determine the laminar organization of feedforward projections from S1 to S2 vs. of feedback projections from S1 to nuclei of the "somatosensory thalamus," the set of nuclei that we first considered in Chapter 3: vision, audition, and somatosensation.

Whole-Cell Staining *Whole-cell staining* is just what it sounds like. A stunningly beautiful example of one application can be admired in *Figure 2.6*. The trick with this method is to use a stain that is selective for a particular kind of cell. For example, we saw in *Chapter 3* that to study the local architecture of pyramidal vs. interneurons in primary somatosensory cortex, researchers can take advantage of the fact that one class of interneurons contains the protein parvalbumin, but other interneurons and pyramidal cells do not.

Invasive Functional Tissue Imaging The word "imaging," when used on its own, can mean different things to neuroscientists working in different branches of the field. Most cognitive neuroscientists use it to refer to noninvasive brain scanning of the kind that is used to obtain images of the human brain, whether for research or for clinical purposes, such as via magnetic resonance imaging (MRI). In this section, however, we'll review three methods that are commonly used in other branches of neuroscience, methods that entail performing a craniotomy and taking measurements directly from the tissue of interest.

The oldest of the three types of invasive functional tissue imaging that we'll review here, 2-deoxyglucose (2DG) imaging, entails the systemic administration of glucose molecules that have been tagged with a radioactive ion (such as ^{14}C) and further modified so that they can't undergo glycolysis. It exploits the fact that glycolysis is the primary source of energy for all cells in the body. Once administered, 2DG blends with naturally circulating glucose in the bloodstream, and, just like endogenous glucose, is taken up by neurons in an amount proportional to their activity. Once taken into a cell, 2DG is trapped. Upon completion of the experiment, the animal is sacrificed, and the tissue of interest is dissected out of the brain and

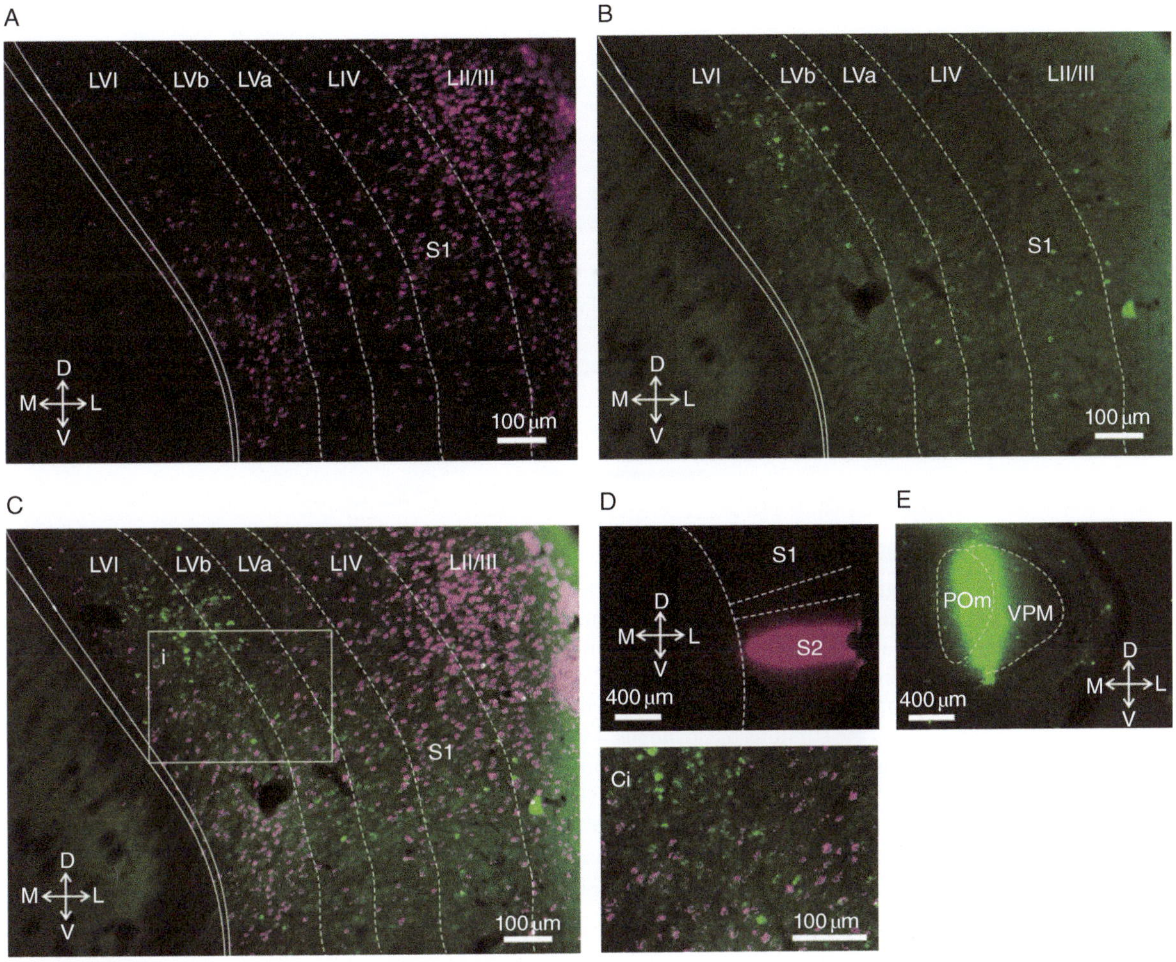

FIGURE 4.4 A neuroanatomical tracer study of the laminar organization of projections from primary somatosensory cortex (S1). To follow the logic of the experiment, look first at panel **D** – this shows the region of secondary somatosensory cortex (S2) where the (purple-colored) tracer was injected. It is a fluorescent, retrograde tracer called "Retrobeads." Panel **A** shows the distribution of labeling resulting from the injection shown in panel **D**. That is, the purple Retrobeads were taken up at presynaptic terminals in S2 (panel **D**) and retrogradely transported back to the cell bodies (panel **A**) of the neurons whose axons formed those presynaptic terminals (i.e., of the neurons whose axons projected to S2). Note that the labeling is heaviest in layer II/III of S1, meaning that it is the neurons in this layer that send the heaviest feedforward projection from S1 to S2. (Note, also, that this laminar organization is not absolute – biological systems are rarely as tidy and lawful as one might want them to be). Next, let's go to panel **E**, which illustrates the injection site of green Retrobeads into the posterior medial (POm) nucleus and ventral posterior medial (VPM) nucleus of the thalamus. The green spots concentrated in the upper left-hand corner of panel **B** are the retrograde labeling resulting from this thalamic injection. This indicates that the S1 neurons projecting to the thalamus are located primarily in layers VI and Vb. Panel **C** illustrates an overlay of **A** and **B**, to emphasize the distinct projection profiles of the superficial vs. the deep layers of S1. Panel **Ci**, a blowup of the box in panel **C**, shows the absence of "double labeling," the presence of which would have meant that individual neurons project to both S2 and the thalamus. (Addressing this question was, in fact, the primary reason that this experiment was performed.) The key in the lower left corner of each image indicates the dorsoventral and mediolateral axes.

Source: Reproduced with permission from Petrof et al. (2012) / John Wiley & Sons.

placed against a radiographic plate that detects the radiation given off by the 2DG that has been trapped in previously active neurons (a process called autoradiography). The results from a 2DG experiment are illustrated in *Figure 4.5*. (More details about the physiological bases for 2DG imaging can be found in the subsection further along in this chapter on *The metabolic demands of the action potential and of synaptic activity*.)

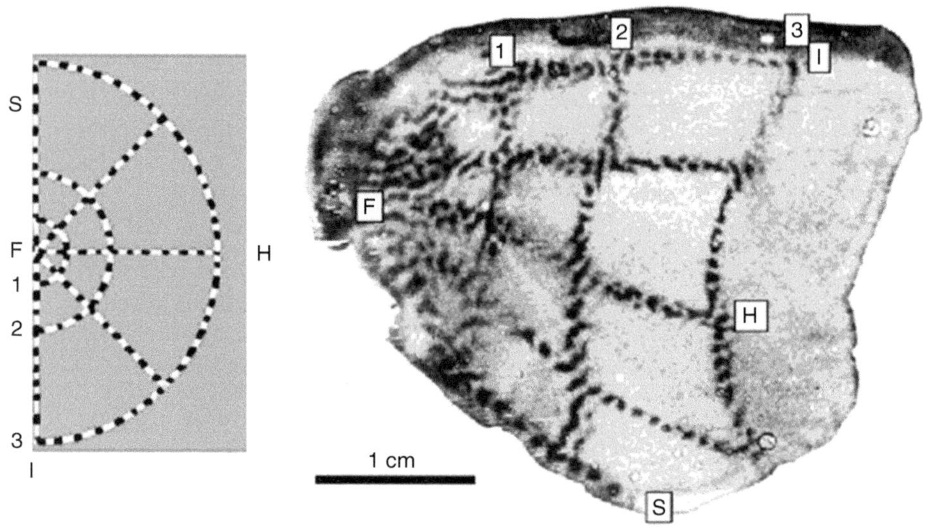

FIGURE 4.5 Retinotopic organization of V1, visualized with 14C 2DG labeling. The stimulus (left side of the figure) was presented to one eye of a monkey, with the "F" label indicating the portion projected onto the fovea, "S" and "I" indicating superior and inferior aspects of the vertical meridian, respectively, and "H" indicating the horizontal meridian. Black and white coloring on the lines and concentric circles of the stimulus flickered back and forth at a rate of three times per second, to vigorously stimulate activity in neurons of the primary visual cortex of the occipital lobe (V1) into whose receptive fields the stimulus fell. (*Chapter 4* will define these anatomical and functional properties of the visual system.) The right side of the figure shows an autoradiograph of a section of cortex dissected from primary visual cortex, with the letters (F, S, I, H) indicating the cortical representation of these demarcations of the visual field and the digits (1, 2, 3) indicating the cortical representation of the three concentric rings of the stimulus display.

Source: Reproduced with permission from Tootell et al. (1982) / American Association for the Advancement of Science - AAAS.

A second functional imaging method uses voltage-sensitive dye. It differs from 2DG in three important ways. First, it is sensitive to fluctuations in membrane voltage. Second, it gives a real-time measure of activity, whereas 2DG generates a static image (a "snapshot"). Third, voltage-sensitive dye can be used to measure cortical activity in several different conditions (e.g., responses to viewing bars that are angled at several different orientations, spanning the 180° of possible rotation). 2DG, on the other hand, requires the sacrifice of the animal after just one experimental condition. Thus, to determine the pattern of brain responses to the neural processing of six different orientations, each spaced by 30°, one would need to acquire data from (a minimum of) six animals, and then try to assemble a composite map across these.

Finally, optical imaging of intrinsic signals entails shining light of a particular wavelength on the tissue of interest, and measuring how the makeup of the reflected light changes as a function of experimental condition. The somewhat coy reference to "intrinsic signals" reflects the fact that there remains some uncertainty about all of the factors that produce changes in tissue reflectance – although the majority of the variance in the signal is due to different reflectance properties of oxygenated vs. deoxygenated blood, there may also be contributions from membrane voltage (despite the absence of externally applied dye), and even from the subtle stretching and compressing that neuronal membranes exhibit under different physiological states. (Note that there is a noninvasive variant of optical imaging – functional near infrared spectroscopy [fNIRS] – that is used with human subjects. A description of near-infrared spectroscopy comes later in this chapter, after some fundamentals of cellular and vascular physiology have been reviewed in the section on *Magnetic resonance imaging*.)

Electrophysiology

Invasive Recording with Microelectrodes: Action Potentials and Local Field Potentials

Although many methods have been devised to study the electrical properties of neurons, most have made use of some variant of the electrode. A microelectrode is a fine-tipped (of the order of 1 μ across) conductor of electricity, typically a glass micropipette filled with a conductive fluid or a platinum or tungsten wire, that can be inserted into brain tissue (thus, a "penetrating electrode") and is connected to an amplifier. Because it is conductive, it detects the changes in voltage that were detailed in *Chapter 2*. Some electrodes have multiple contacts along their shafts, the signal from each of which will feed into a different channel in the amplifier.

Many of the properties of the neuron that were described in *Chapter 2* were discovered via **intracellular recordings** obtained with in vitro methods, in which individual neurons, or more often slices of central nervous system (CNS) tissue, are surgically removed from an animal and kept alive "in a dish" by bathing them in artificial CSF. Only by recording intracellularly can one measure, for example, the activity of a single postsynaptic channel or the kinetics of voltage-gated ion channels. However, because cognitive neuroscience, by definition, concerns itself with the neural processes that underlie behaviors (that we associate with cognition), the emphasis in this book will be on **extracellular recordings** obtained in vivo – that is, recordings made outside of the cell in the brain of a living animal (*Figure 4.6*).

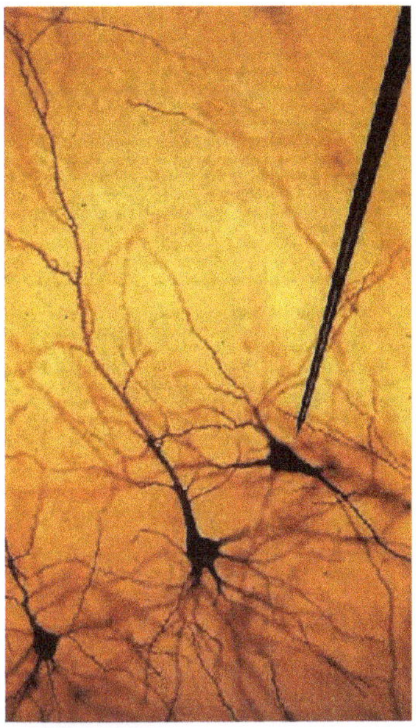

FIGURE 4.6 Extracellular electrophysiology. Photograph of a light microscope-magnified image of an extracellular microelectrode in the vicinity of a pyramidal neuron in the visual cortex of a monkey. The entire height of the image corresponds to roughly 1 mm (Hubel, 1988).

Source: Max Planck Institute for Biological Cybernetics.

Extracellular electrophysiology can measure two types of signals: action potentials and *local field potentials* (LFPs). Because action potentials are all-or-none events – an individual neuron cannot alternate between generating "big" vs. "little" action potentials – they are treated as binary events, and a standard way to quantify a neuron's activity is by its firing rate. A neuron typically has a baseline firing rate, maybe 5 "spikes per second" (i.e., 5 Hz) for a generic pyramidal cell. The neuron's involvement in a particular function, let's say visual perception, can then be assessed by determining whether this firing rate changes systematically with a systematic change in the environment, say, flashing a light in an area that the animal is looking at. Depending on the neuron, and on the state of the brain, a neuron involved in the perception of this flash of light might exhibit either an increase or a decrease from its baseline firing rate. Depending on the cell type, an activated neuron's firing rate can be anywhere from 5 to 10 Hz to upward of 200 Hz.

To record the LFP, the signal(s) from an electrode are filtered to remove contamination from individual action potentials, leaving the LFP – the aggregated fluctuation of dendritic membrane potentials from cells in the vicinity of the electrode. Importantly, action potentials from neurons that are very close to the electrode will produce large-amplitude deflections in the signal that are relatively easily detected and filtered out of the LFP recordings. Action potentials from neurons more distal to the electrode, however, produce tiny blips that are not differentiable from subtle fluctuations in the aggregated membrane potentials of nearby cells. Although these tiny blips would be expected to cancel out if they were uncorrelated with respect to one another, when a large population of neurons is firing in synchrony, this will show up as small-amplitude fluctuations across a broad band of high frequencies in the LFP recording. (The idea is that, because the synchronization of the precise moment of firing between individual neurons within a large population of neurons won't be perfect, the deflections in the LPF signal that are attributable to these individual action potentials would be offset by fractions of hundredths of milliseconds and so would show up in the LFP signal as fluctuations at higher frequencies than is generally thought to be attributable to an oscillating membrane potential. Furthermore, because these tiny fluctuations are a byproduct of the cacophony of activity from many, many sources, they do not center at any discrete frequency but rather are detected across a broad range of frequencies.) As a general rule, oscillations in the LFP signal that are higher frequency than ~120 Hz are assumed to reflect the so-called multiunit activity (MUA) in the vicinity of the electrode and are taken as a proxy for firing rate in the local population that is sampled by that electrode (*Figure 4.7*).

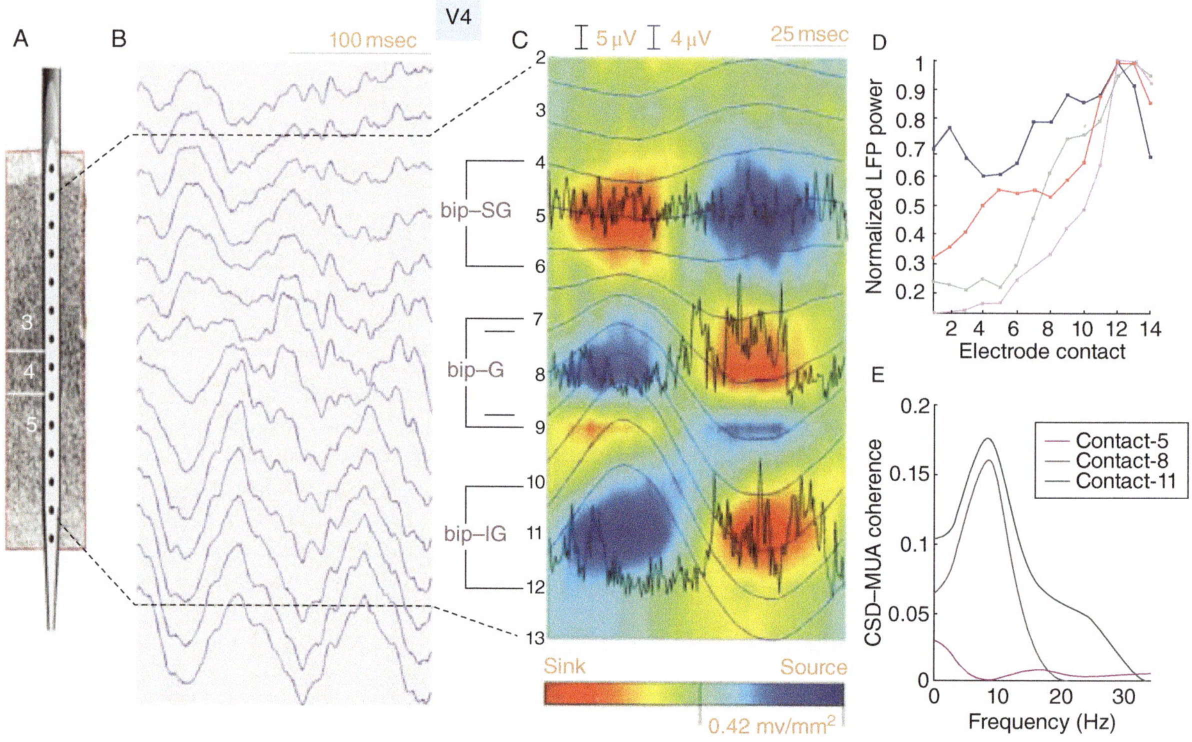

FIGURE 4.7 The local field potential (LFP). **A.** Schematic diagram showing an electrode with 14 equally spaced (by 200 μm) contacts ("3," "4," and "5" refer to layers of cortex). **B.** 200 msec of LFP recorded at each of these 14 contacts. **C.** A current source density map, computed from the pattern of LFPs in panel **B.** What this shows is the pattern, over time, of where in this cortical column current is flowing from intracellular space to extracellular space (a "source"), or from extracellular space to intracellular space (a "sink"). To compute the current source density map, bipolar recordings are needed, and "bip-SG" indicates the two contacts used to obtain these recordings in the supragranular layer, "bip-G" in the granular layer, and "bip-IG" in the infragranular layer. The jagged black traces show the MUA. The smooth blue lines are transformations of the raw LFP that we will disregard. **D.** Peak LFP power at 10 Hz (vertical axis) as a function of cortical depth (horizontal axis) from four separate recording sessions, each plotted in a different color. **E.** CSD-MUA coherence, an index of the rhythmicity of spiking at different frequencies of the LFP, of the recording session illustrated in **C.** This plot indicates that the spiking in granular and infragranular layers is most strongly "clocked" in the alpha frequency range, whereas spiking in supragranular layers is relatively unrelated to the LFP. These recordings were made in an area called "V4" (as referenced in *Figure 2.4*).

Source: Reproduced with permission from Bollimunta et al. (2008) / Society for Neuroscience.

Electrocorticography

An alternative to recording electrical activity with penetrating electrodes is to use a grid of electrodes that is positioned on the surface of the cortex, a technique called **electrocorticography** ("ECoG" [pronounced "ee-cog"] for short). Because ECoG electrodes lie on the surface of the cortex (typically beneath the thick [and electrically resistive] dura matter, i.e., "subdurally"), they lack the spatial resolution of penetrating electrodes. Additionally, they are too far from any cell bodies to measure action potentials and so can only measure field potentials. Although ECoG signals can, in principle, be measured in any species, they are particularly relevant for cognitive neuroscience when used by neurosurgeons and neurologists for presurgical planning in human patients being evaluated for neurosurgery. In cases of epilepsy that cannot be controlled with antiepileptic medication, for example, a treatment of last resort is to first isolate, then surgically remove, the tissue that is responsible for triggering systemic seizures. That is, it can sometimes be the case that only a small region of brain is responsible for initiating the disordered activity that, when it spreads to other parts of the brain, results in **grand mal** seizures. The reasoning in such cases is that if the pathological tissue can be surgically removed without causing too much "collateral damage," the patient may experience many fewer seizures. The "without causing too much collateral damage" part is key, of course, because recall from *Chapter 1* that damage to the wrong brain areas can produce, for example, irreversible paralysis, blindness, or disruption of spoken language. And so the neurosurgical removal of brain tissue is often preceded by presurgical planning, in which the surgeon places electrodes in the vicinity of the suspected focus of the seizure activity. (Depending on the circumstances, the electrodes will either be strips and/or grids of ECoG electrodes placed on the cortical surface after a partial craniotomy, or penetrating electrodes inserted through small holes drilled through the skull, a technique called stereotaxic (s)EEG; linear "strips" of ECoG electrodes can also be inserted through small holes.) The physicians then wait for the patient to have a seizure and analyze the location and timing of seizure activity at different electrodes in order to localize the area(s) responsible for initiating seizures. Because the first postimplantation seizure may not occur for several days, if the patient is willing to participate in a research study, scientists can ask the patient to perform experiments during this time. In this way, it is possible to collect ECoG data recorded from the human brain while the patient/subject is engaged in a task.

We will return to ECoG later in this chapter when we discuss analyses of phase–amplitude coupling (PAC) that can be measured in ECoG data. We'll consider detailed examples of ECoG studies in *Chapter 10* (see *Figure 10.7*) and *Chapter 19*.

Electroencephalography

The EEG is recorded from the scalp (*Figure 4.8* and *Figure 4.9*). There's a sense in which the EEG signal measured at the scalp is a kind of "macro LFP," in that it reflects the summation of many, many local cortical LFPs. This is necessarily the case, due to the conductive properties of all the tissues lying between the cortex and the scalp. Note that the changes in the membrane potential of a single neuron vary within a range spanning roughly 100 mV (e.g., from −90 to +20 mV), and the LFP, which is recorded from the extracellular space adjacent to groups of neurons, typically varies across a similar range. As measured at the scalp, however, a cortically derived electrical signal needs to additionally pass through blood vessels, CSF, meninges, skull, muscles, and skin, all of which attenuate and blur it. This has at least three implications for the EEG. First, to be detectible, the EEG necessarily reflects the summation of signals from tens of thousands (or more) neurons. (Hence, the characterization as a "macro LFP" – it pools the signals from many, many, many more neurons than does the invasively recorded LFP.) Second, the fluctuations in the membrane potential of these neurons need to be synchronized – otherwise, negative and positive potentials would cancel out each other. Finally, the EEG signal is disproportionately influenced by signal from superficial layers of cortex, with smaller contributions from deeper layers and, in most cases, only negligible contributions from subcortical structures.

Scientists studying human cognition began recording the EEG decades before the term "cognitive neuroscience" came into common usage. A big part of its appeal is that it is noninvasive and so can be measured from the same healthy young adult population that is sampled disproportionately for studies of cognitive psychology (i.e., the "convenience-sampled" population of university students). A second appeal is that, despite the attenuation of the amplitude of the extracranial EEG, its temporal properties are virtually the same as if they had been measured from within the brain, and this high temporal resolution provides exquisitely precise information about the timing of neural events. A major limitation of EEG, however, is that its spatial resolution is quite poor. This is due to three factors. First, the averaging that the signal undergoes between its source in the brain and where it is measured at the scalp means that one can't know the expanse of tissue from which it originated (e.g., strong signal from small bit of tissue or relatively weaker signal emanating from a large expanse of tissue). Second, electric current is attenuated and smeared out when it passes through biological tissue. Third, the fundamental mathematical truth that for any given pattern of signals that is measured from the surface of a sphere (e.g., electrical signals on the scalp [e.g., Figure 4.8.C], tremors on the surface of the planet), there is an infinite number of configurations of sources located within the sphere that could have produced that pattern. This is known as the **inverse problem**, and its nature is such that it can never be solved with certainty. Nonetheless, there are algorithmic approaches that estimate "solutions" to the inverse problem by

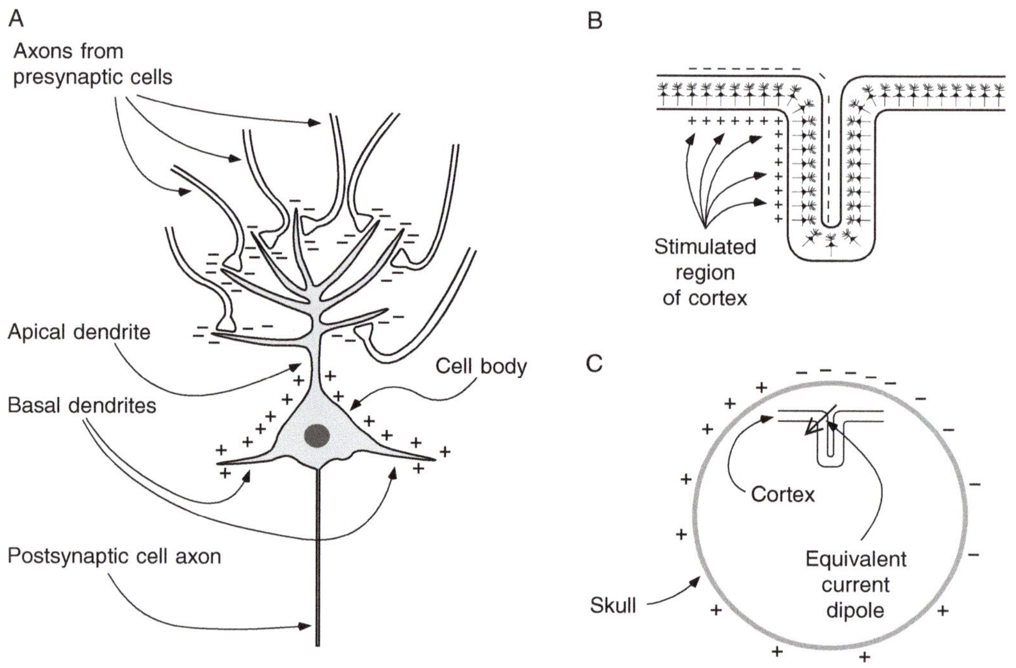

FIGURE 4.8 Principles of EEG generation. (A) Diagram of the neuron as electrical dipole. (B) Cartooned illustration of a cross section through a section of cortex, showing the alignment of pyramidal cells relative to the cortical surface. Incoming excitatory signals (represented by curved arrows) increase the amplitude of neuronal dipoles along the gyral surface (left side of image) and along one bank of a sulcus. Note that the activity in the gyrus would dominate the electrical signal measured by an electrode on the surface of the scalp, whereas activity in the sulcus would dominate the magnetic signal measured from the same location on the scalp. (C) A schematized top-down view of a skull (intended to suggest the perspective illustrated in Figure 4.9.B) showing how the aggregated signal from neurons in panel B might sum to create a single "equivalent current dipole," and how the signal from this "single source" might project onto the scalp. (This illustrates that although the true sources of electrical activity in this scenario are the thousands of individual neurons schematized in panel B, the projection onto the scalp of the current generated by these thousands of "tiny" individual dipoles can be modeled as having been generated by a single large "virtual" dipole located in the same place, and oriented as shown by the large arrow pointing down and to the left.)

Source: Luck and Steven (2005) / MIT Press.

making a variety of assumptions about which of the infinite number of possible "source solutions" is the most likely for any particular dataset.

Magnetoencephalography

Let's be clear: according to the literal definition, magnetoencephalography (MEG) is not a type of electrophysiology. However, the tight coupling of magnetic and electrical energy, as manifested by the principle of electromagnetic induction, allows us to get away with summarizing MEG in this section. MEG takes advantage of the fact that electrical activity in neural tissue, including where axons arriving from other regions arrive at dendritic fields, produces weak magnetic fields. MEG measures fluctuations in these magnetic fields with sensors that are built into a kind of helmet that is lowered over the scalp. As suggested in *Figure 4.8*, due to the orientation of neuronal dipoles in the cortex in gyri vs. in cortex lining the walls of sulci, it's generally thought that the EEG signal emphasizes activity in gyri, whereas the MEG signal emphasizes activity in sulci. (This is because the magnetic field induced by current moving radially with respect to the skull would be oriented along the surface of the skull and therefore difficult to detect. The magnetic field induced by current moving in parallel with the surface of the skull, in contrast, would be oriented radially and therefore relatively easy to detect.)

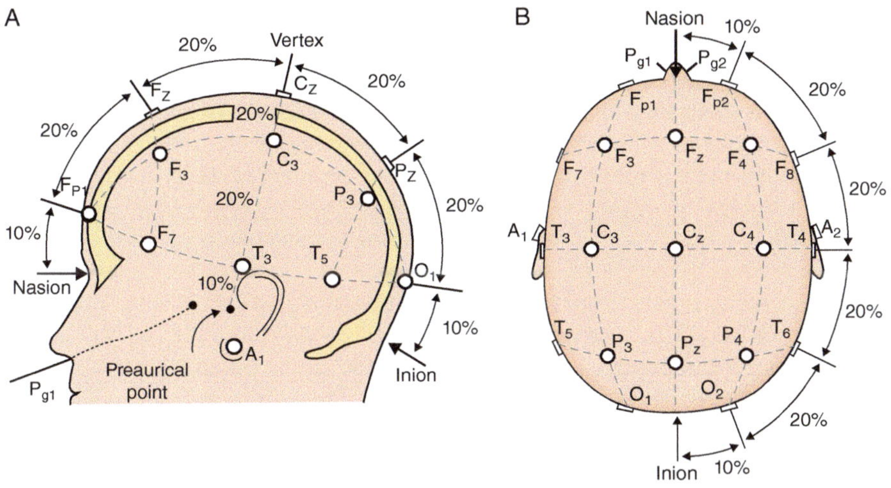

FIGURE 4.9 Placement and names of the 21 electrodes in the internationally standardized "10–20 system," as viewed from the left (**A**) and looking down on the top of the head (**B**). Reference points are the nasion, which is the indentation at the top of the nose, level with the eyes; and the inion, which is the bony lump at the base of the skull on the midline at the back of the head. From these points, the skull perimeters are measured in the transverse plane (i.e., the trajectory through O1–T5–T3–F7 in the side view) and the median plane (i.e., the trajectory through PZ–CZ–FZ in the top view). Electrode locations are determined by dividing these perimeters into 10% and 20% intervals. Since the development of this convention, the electrodes in many EEG systems now come embedded within caps that fit snugly over the subject's head (rather like a swimming cap), often with an array of 64 or 128 electrodes. High-density systems come as "nets" of 256 electrodes. EEG systems whose electrode placement doesn't correspond to the 10–20 systems will typically provide formulae in their software that will convert the system's native electrode placement scheme into 10–20 equivalents.

Source: Malmivuo et al., 1995 / Oxford University Press.

Because magnetic energy has the same temporal properties as electrical energy, MEG also boasts high temporal resolution. However, because, unlike electricity, magnetic fields do not interact with biological tissue, the MEG signal is believed to have superior spatial resolution in comparison to EEG. (The inverse problem applies to MEG just as much as it does to EEG, but the absence of any smearing by the tissue between the brain and the scalp means that estimates of sources of MEG signals have less spatial uncertainty than do source solutions with EEG data.)

Invasive Neurostimulation

Electrical Microstimulation

We were introduced to electrical microstimulation via *Chapter 1*'s consideration of Frisch and Hitzig's (1870) studies of motor control. These studies demonstrated the use of microstimulation that is most common in neuroscience: the controlled excitation of a circuit to study the effects of activity in this circuit. We'll re-encounter this method several times as we make our way through this book, including in the study of eye movement control and the control of attention, and in the study of perceptual decision making. Microstimulation can also be used to alter ongoing activity by, for example, imposing an oscillatory rhythm. Finally, microstimulation can be used to disrupt ongoing activity by either disrupting an endogenous rhythm or just overriding activity in the affected area with a strong flow of current.

Interventions using the same logic as what we've described here can also be carried out with ECoG electrodes, by, for example, passing current between adjacent electrodes in a grid or a strip that is lying on the pial surface. Technically, this should be referred to as "macrostimulation," because of the spatial scale over which it's carried out, but conceptually it fits here.

Optogenetics

The logic of optogenetics in neuroscience can be described in four steps: (1) Clone a gene that codes for a protein that one wants to have expressed in a cell. (2) Insert this strand of DNA into a target population of cells (a process called transfection). (3) Wait for a suitable period of time for the protein to be synthesized and trafficked to the part of the cell where it will have its effects. Up until this point, the words written here could have also been used to describe gene therapy. The "opto-" part, however, is what makes this such a powerful experimental tool. In the experiment that we considered in *Chapter 3*, section *Optogenetic exploration of gamma-band oscillations in somatosensory cortex*, for example, the transfected DNA coded for channelrhodopsin-2 (ChR2), a cation channel activated by light of a very narrow wavelength centered at 470 nm. (The protein occurs naturally in the single-celled algae *Chlamydomonas reinhardtii*, in which it serves the function of phototaxis – light-triggered movement.) And now, we can return to the last of our four steps: (4) Shine light of the critical wavelength on the transfected cells (e.g., 470 nm light for ChR2), thereby experimentally controlling their activity. (For neurons transfected with ChR2, shining 470 nm light has the effect of depolarizing them, thereby causing them to spike.)

To date, the technique of optogenetics has been particularly impactful in research with rodents, especially mice (see section *Optogenetic exploration of gamma-band oscillations in somatosensory cortex*, *Chapter 3*). The cell biology of mice is such that their neurons are considerably more amenable to transfection and the subsequent synthesis and trafficking of the light-sensitive protein product than is that of NHPs. For example, this author has been told about several experiments with NHPs that have been abandoned, or at least put on hold, because the expression of light-sensitive channels only occurred in a subset of the targeted population of neurons, rendering the effects of shining light weak and difficult to interpret.

Analysis of Time-Varying Signals

Once one has collected data with one of the methods reviewed in the previous section, one has to analyze them. The choice of analysis will often depend on the question that one wants to ask, but it can also be influenced by assumptions being made about how the brain works.

Event-Related Analyses

Fundamental to understanding how the workings of the brain give rise to the mind is the identification of signals that correspond to the aspect of cognition that one is studying. One complication with measuring these signals that we have already reviewed is that they are minutely small, particularly when measured at the scalp, as they are with EEG and MEG. A second complication arises from the fact that the brain is always carrying out several functions simultaneously. Because electrical signals from distinct sources summate when they coexist at the same location, this means that, when recorded at the scalp, the signal related to the process that one wants to study is invariably blended with many other signals arising from many other processes. (And in experimental terms, of course, these "other" signals constitute noise.) What are these "other" processes? They are, if not innumerable, at least too numerous to try to list here. But a very short and incomplete list could include controlling respiration, controlling heart rate, thermoregulation, maintaining postural stability, monitoring the environment for any possible unexpected change, monitoring and assessing the social environment (*how are others evaluating my behavior at this moment?*), etc. Event-related analyses offer one way to try to isolate the signal of interest from the noise in which it is embedded.

The ERP/ERF Technique Let's say that one is interested in the neural processing of an acoustic click (as we were with *Figure 3.9*, from *Chapter 3*'s section on auditory perception). How is one to isolate the click-related signal from the signals related to all the other things that the brain is doing simultaneously? In principle, one way to do this would be to record the EEG while the subject is listening to clicks, and subtract from it the signals related to respiration, heart rate, thermoregulation, etc. Ideally, this would result in a "pure" signal from which all the noise had been removed. In practice, however, this would be a flawed approach, because one can't know, a priori, the precise nature of those signals (no more than one knows a priori the precise nature of the signal in question), nor can one know with any certainty that one has subtracted out every component that is noise. Instead of subtraction, however, a solution that can yield valid results is to selectively average the data from many trials. The logic behind this approach is that if the data from each trial are aligned such that the event of interest occurs at precisely the same time in every trial (i.e., if the data are *time-locked* to this event), the average of many such trials will emphasize any components in the signal that occur at the same time in all the trials, while de-emphasizing components that either do not occur on many of the trials or do not occur at the same time relative to the event of interest. At a generic level, this is called an event-related approach. With EEG data, the processed signal resulting from this procedure will be a timeseries containing several positive-going and negative-going deflections that are each assumed to correspond to an event that occurred at the same time on each trial. Each such deflection is often referred to as an *event-related potential* (ERP), an *evoked response*, or, informally, as a *component*. When this time-locked averaging method is applied to EEG data, it's called the ERP technique, and the averaged signals that isolate processes of interest are called ERPs. With MEG, there is not a single universally used analogue to "ERP," but many use *event-related field* (ERF). (Some groups use "MEP" for "magnetic evoked potential," but this is not technically accurate, because MEG does not record electrical potentials. Additionally, its use can be confusing, because for decades the abbreviation MEP has been used for the motor-evoked potential.)

To make this concrete, we can consider the experiment illustrated in *Figure 3.9* in more detail. To create a condition in which subjects would be hearing clicks, but not attending to them, the researchers recorded the EEG while subjects read a book in an otherwise quiet room, and a standard click was played once per second, replaced at random once every 5–30 seconds with a soft click. Because reading involves many processes that are unrelated to auditory processing (including visual perception, [*Chapter 3* and *Chapter 6*], frequent eye movements [*Chapter 9*], and analyzing the grammar and the meaning of sentences [*Chapter 19*]), one might think that this choice would be counterproductive to the purposes of the experimenters. Indeed, it is surely the case that each single trial from this experiment was contaminated with more noise than it would have been without reading. However, because no reading-related process was synchronized with the onset of the soft clicks, all elements in the signal associated with reading "averaged out" when the data from several hundred trials were averaged together. Indeed, in the resultant trial-averaged timeseries illustrated in *Figure 3.8* and *Figure 3.9*, one sees a timeseries with multiple deflections (the "auditory evoked-potential" [AEP]), each associated with a discrete synaptic in the auditory brainstem.

Caveats About the ERP Technique When using the ERP technique (or evaluating ERP data), it's important to keep in mind that the time-locking step used to generate ERPs will obscure any change in task-related activity that differs from trial to trial. For example, we've already seen that the LFP captures ongoing oscillations in neural tissue. The process of generating an ERP typically removes any evidence of these oscillations. This would be fine if these oscillations only corresponded to noise that is unrelated to cognitive functioning, but what if this weren't true? Let's go back to the example of studying how the brain processes a soft click. What if it were the case that oscillations in the LFP of tissue that's involved in auditory processing are always present, whether the momentary state of the environment is filled with loud sound or if it is silent? Furthermore, what if it were the case that the amplitude of this oscillation always gets bigger the moment that auditory information gets to the brain? In this scenario, an ERP analysis would not detect this effect, even though it is clearly an effect that is related to the cognitive process that we're trying to study. This is because, in a typical experiment, the delivery of a stimulus like the soft click in our current example is jittered in time, to prevent the subject from being able to predict its precise moment of onset. A consequence of this is that the oscillation of the LFP will be random in phase on a trial-by-trial basis, and averaging these phase-random signals will remove any evidence of these oscillations. This could be thought of as a kind of "Type II error" in which the analysis failed to detect an effect of interest (*Figure 4.10*).

Perhaps a more pernicious outcome would be one in which the event-related change in the oscillation is one of phase resetting, rather than a change of amplitude. That is, what if it were the case that although the trial-by-trial phase of the oscillation in the LFP is random prior to the onset of the click, the oscillation always resets to the same moment that auditory information gets to the brain? In this scenario, an ERP analysis would remove any evidence of the oscillation during the pre-click period, but time-locked realignment of these oscillations would create the artifactual impression of an ERP that was time-locked to the onset of the click. That is, the analysis would "show" that the click started a process that hadn't been active prior to its onset, when in truth, it didn't start any new process but, rather, shifted the timing of processing that was already underway (*Figure 4.10*).

Considerations Having listed some caveats about how the ERP technique doesn't deal well with oscillations in the EEG signal, the next methods for us to introduce are ones that measure oscillatory dynamics. Before we move on to that, though, let's take a moment to consider some of the "philosophical" issues that this discussion engages ("Philosophical" in the sense of *My philosophy about how to study the brain is . . .*). An oversimplistic caricature of the ERP technique is that it assumes that a primary design principle of the brain is that it is composed of systems that are specialized for carrying out specific tasks – let's say perceiving auditory clicks, or visually presented bars – and that these systems are quiet when not actively engaged. This is sometimes summarized as treating the brain as a passive system that processes information when information is fed to it. An alternative is to construe the brain as an active system that is constantly churning, always processing information so that the organism can achieve and maintain a state that is an optimal trade-off between its goals and the current conditions in the world. (One specific theory that advances this idea is called "predictive coding" and will be considered Chapter 5.) Because living brain cells will often change the patterns of their oscillations, sometimes drastically, but they will rarely (if ever) stop oscillating, analyses that emphasize oscillations over ERPs can sometimes be construed as working from the assumption of the brain as an active system.

FIGURE 4.10 Cartooned diagrams of two hypothetical situations in which an ERP analysis would misrepresent an event-related change in oscillatory dynamics.

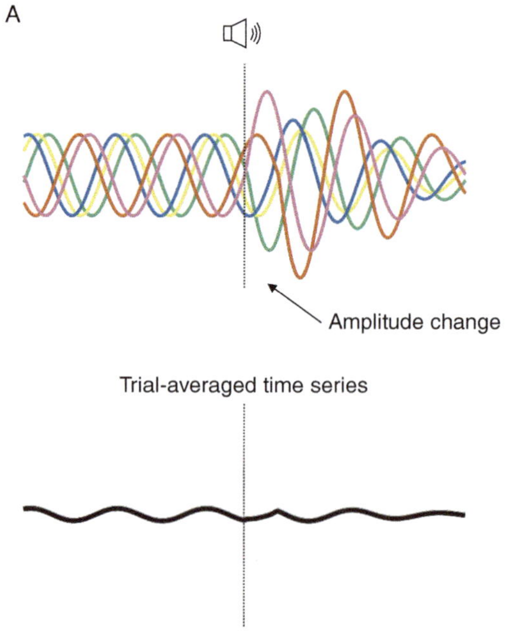

FIGURE 4.10.A Top panel illustrates hypothetical EEG signals from five trials (color-coded and superimposed) in a scenario in which an auditory click produces a change in the magnitude of the ongoing oscillation. The trial-averaged time series (below) does not show any change associated with the click.

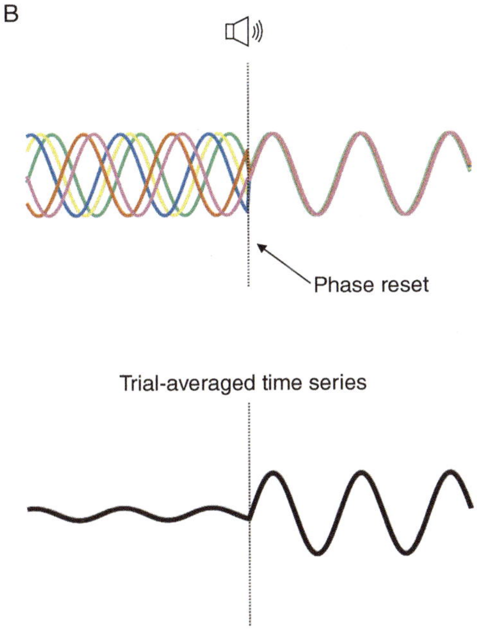

FIGURE 4.10.B Top panel illustrates five trials in which an auditory click produces a reset of the phase of the ongoing oscillation. Trial averaging (below) creates an artifactual "ERP" that does not exist in any of the individual trials.

Time-Frequency Analysis

In the early 1800s, the French mathematician Jean Baptiste Joseph Fourier (1768–1830) proposed that any fluctuating waveform, no matter how complicated, can be represented as a finite collection of sines and cosines. The mathematical operation of transforming a fluctuating time series into a collection of sinusoids has come to be known as performing a **Fourier transform**. The resultant collection of sinusoids can be represented in a **power spectrum**, as illustrated in panel D of *Figure 4.11*, and it is thus also known, in jargon, as a spectral transform. (The term "spectral transform" is also a more general term that can apply to other mathematical operations that accomplish this kind of transform, such as the Hilbert transform, or any of various wavelet transforms.) It would be difficult to overstate the impact that Fourier's theorem has had on the natural and physical sciences, and on many branches of engineering. From a practical perspective, sinusoids and power spectra can be easier to work with analytically than are complicated signals that fluctuate over time. From a conceptual standpoint, the idea that many systems can be thought of as having cyclical (or oscillatory) properties has provided many new insights for how these systems might work.

As we proceed through this book, it will be helpful to be familiar with some concepts, conventions, and terminology related to the spectral analysis of time-varying signals. In practice, a Fourier transform is often accomplished with an analytic technique called a fast Fourier transform [FFT].) *Figure 4.11* illustrates the re-representation of an EEG signal into three summary sinusoids corresponding to three narrowband ranges of frequencies – theta (4–7 Hz), alpha (8–12 Hz), and beta (15–25 Hz) – as well as the full power spectrum (*Figure 4.11.D*) and a time-frequency representation (*TFR*)[3] illustrating fluctuations in spectral power as a function of time.

[3] A convention from a software package that was in particularly widespread use in the 1990s and 2000s is to refer to a TFR as an "event-related spectral perturbation," an "ERSP".

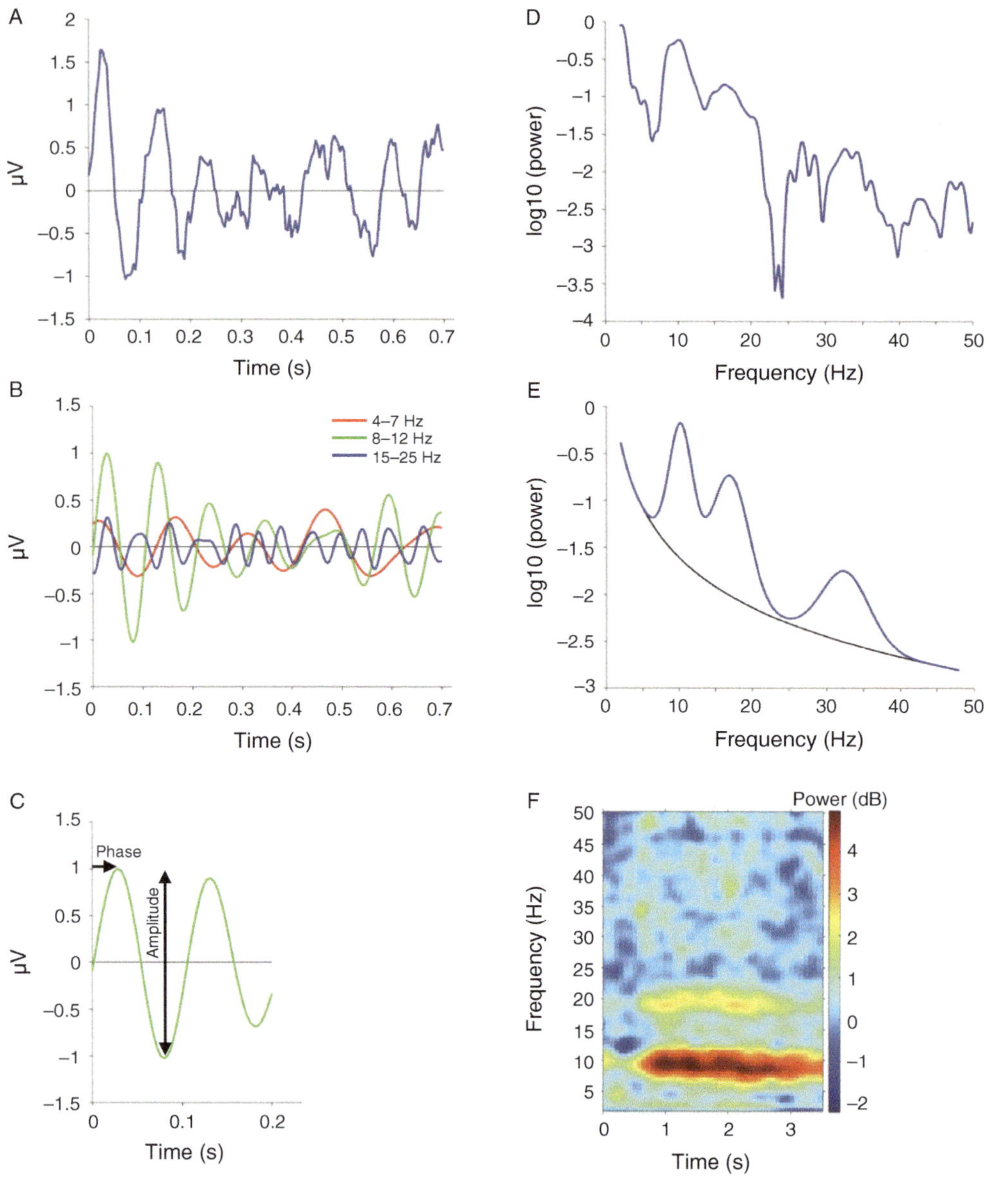

FIGURE 4.11 Spectral transform of an EEG signal. **A.** A 700-msec snippet of EEG data from electrode P1 during the delay period of a working memory task (something we'll take up in detail in *Chapter 14*). **B.** Illustration of the decomposition of the waveform in panel A into three sinusoids corresponding to three canonical narrowband ranges of frequencies. (Note that a much finer-grained set of sinusoids would be needed to represent the waveform in panel A with high fidelity.) Note that, in addition to frequency, the sinusoids illustrated here differ from one another in two other ways. One is that each differs in terms of its magnitude: the height of its peaks and the depth of its troughs. In the parlance of signal processing, the magnitude of a sinusoid is referred to as its **power**. The second is that each of the sinusoidal waves is at a different phase of its cycle at time 0. (I.e., they are shifted in phase relative to one another.) **C.** Graphical representation of phase and magnitude. Note that, because one full cycle of a sinusoid is equivalent to one complete rotation of a needle around a dial (e.g., what the second hand of an analog clock does once every 60seconds), phase can be expressed in degrees, ranging from 0° to 360°. **D.** The full complement of sinusoids required to completely represent the waveform in panel A is represented in this power spectrum. Note that in this power spectrum there is generally higher power at lower than at higher frequencies, a property characteristic of almost all spectral transforms of neural time series data. **E.** Decomposition of the power spectrum from D into oscillatory and non-oscillatory (typically referred to as "aperiodic") components. (That is, although the FFT generates the set of sinusoids needed to represent the time-varying signal in A, it need not be the case that each of these sinusoids exist among the factors that generated this signal.) This decomposition, carried out with the specparam procedure (Donoghue et al., 2020), reveals that a prominent component of the power spectrum in D is an aperiodic "1/f" component. (Additionally consideration will be given to the 1/f component of the EEG signal in Chapter 5, section *Aperiodic Activity as an Index of Excitation-Inhibition Balance.)* Superimposed on the 1/f component are what are considered to be "true oscillations," one centered at roughly 10 Hz (i.e., in the alpha band), one at roughly 18 Hz (low-beta band), and one at roughly 33 Hz (low-gamma band).) **F.** Another way to represent the spectral transform of the data from A is to, in effect, compute the Fourier transform at many narrower slices in time, and thereby illustrate the evolution of the spectral representation of the signal over time, in a time–frequency **spectrogram** (sometimes also referred to as a time–frequency representation [TFR]). Note that although frequency is represented by position relative to the vertical axis, and power by color, the TFR does not represent phase. The reason for this insensitivity to phase is that the TFR is generated by computing the spectral transform on a trial-by-trial basis, and then averaging (across trials) the power at each frequency for each time point.

Source: Figure courtesy of J. Fulvio, derived from data from Fulvio, Haegens, and Postle (2024).

Phase–Amplitude Coupling Now that we've covered some important basics of signal processing, we can return to the concept of **phase–amplitude coupling (PAC)**, which refers to the fact that sustained spiking activity in populations of neurons is often not literally an unbroken, high-frequency train of activity, but, rather, a pulsatile pattern of activity that waxes and wanes at the frequency of a prominent low-frequency component of the LFP. At the level of a single neuron, it can be seen that this comes about because a neuron tends to fire bursts of action potentials at the trough of the LFP and to fire relatively few action potentials at the peak. This makes sense if we reflect on the fact that the LFP measures the extracellular voltage, and so the trough of the LFP (i.e., the most negative part of its cycle) corresponds to the peak of the (intracellular) fluctuation of voltage of the neuron. Thus, a neuron firing at, say, 50 Hz, in a region with a prominent peak of 6 Hz in the theta band of the LFP, may fire in clusters of 6–9 action potentials spaced by just a few milliseconds each, and then pause for roughly 10 msec, then fire another burst, etc., its spiking effectively being synchronized by the LFP.

In ECoG data, PAC manifests as "stripes" in high frequencies of the TFR that are spaced by gaps in time corresponding to the frequency to which the high-frequency "stripes" are synchronized (e.g., *Figure 4.13*). The "stripes" correspond to bursts of power in the "high gamma" range (typically defined as >90 Hz), a range in which ECoG data are believed to index MUA rather than true oscillations. Thus, the *phase* in PAC refers to the phase of the low-frequency field potential that clocks the waxing and waning of the *amplitude* of the high-gamma signal (*Figure 4.12*).

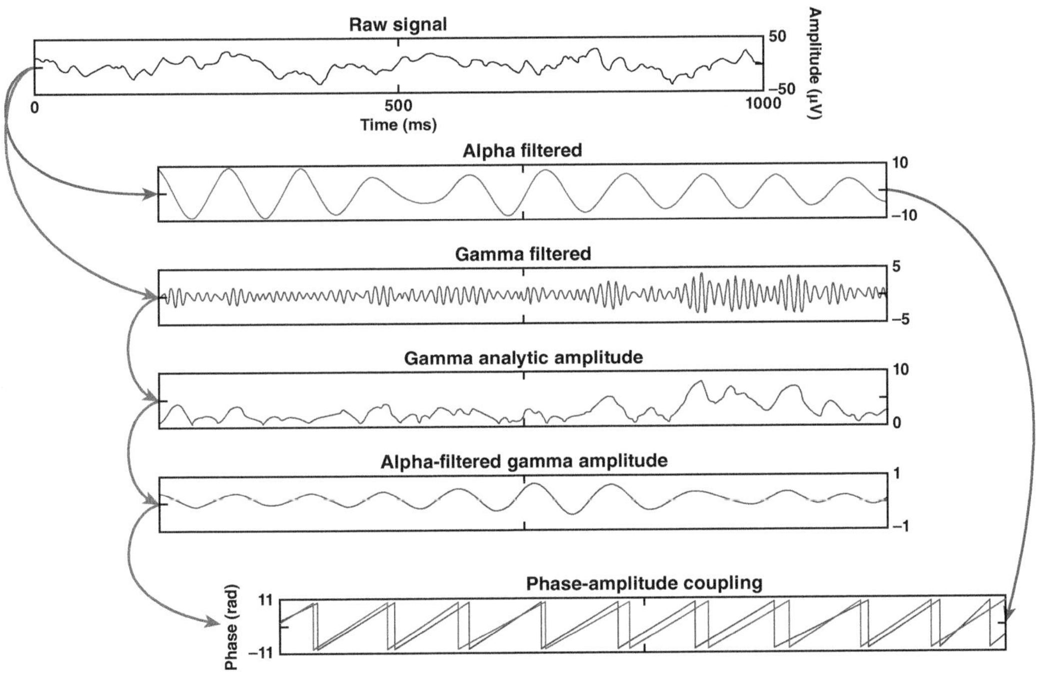

FIGURE 4.12 Data processing schematic for calculating PAC, from Voytek et al. (2010). "Raw signal" panel: self-explanatory; "alpha-filtered" panel: the raw signal band-pass filtered to isolate its components with frequencies from 8 to 12 Hz; "gamma-filtered" panel: the raw signal band-pass filtered to isolate its components with frequencies from 80 to 150 Hz; "gamma analytic amplitude" panel: the envelope of fluctuating power of the "gamma-filtered" time series; "alpha-filtered gamma amplitude": the gamma analytic amplitude band-pass filtered to isolate its components with frequencies from 8 to 12 Hz. This corresponded to the extent that high-gamma power fluctuated in the alpha frequency band. "Phase–amplitude coupling" panel: plotted together are the phase of the "alpha-filtered" component from the raw signal and the phase of the "alpha-filtered gamma amplitude." Conceptually, phase locking is the extent to which these two phase time series are "in sync."

Source: Bradley Voytek et al., 2010 / Frontiers Media / CC BY 4.0.

FIGURE 4.13 High gamma amplitude couples preferentially with different low-frequency bands as a function of brain region and behavioral task, from Voytek et al. (2010).

Source: Voytek et al., 2010 / Frontiers Media S.A / CC BY 4.0.

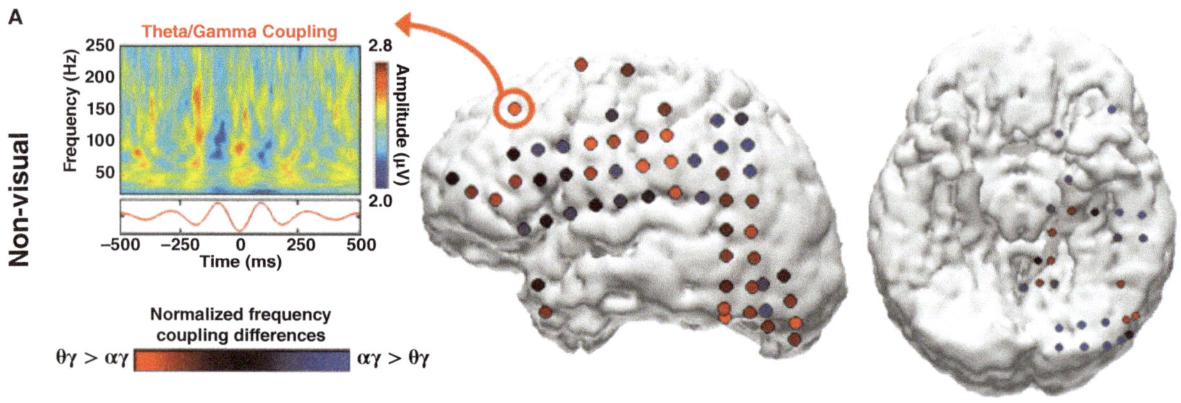

FIGURE 4.13.A "Theta PAC" at a frontal electrode during performance of a nonvisual task. The spectrogram labeled "Theta/Gamma Coupling" is a TFR aligned to a trough in the theta component of the ECoG signal, which is the red waveform below the TFR. The theta component displayed here is equivalent to the "alpha-filtered" panel in *Figure 4.12*, except that here the band-pass filtering was for a different range of frequencies (4–8 Hz), and it's averaged over all the nonvisual trials from the experiment. The "striping" of high-frequency power reflects the fact that the power at these frequencies is bursting periodically, rather than being sustained at a steady level. (Note that, because these data are trial averaged, and because the signal that is band-pass filtered from 4 to 8 Hz "speeds up" and "slows down" over time, within this range [as the relative influence of higher vs. lower frequencies within this range fluctuates], aligning the signal at any point in time during a trial will necessarily produce the "flattening out" of the waveform at more distant time points.) Although the electrodes are plotted on a single brain volume, they reflect the aggregate coverage from the two patients whose data were analyzed for this experiment.

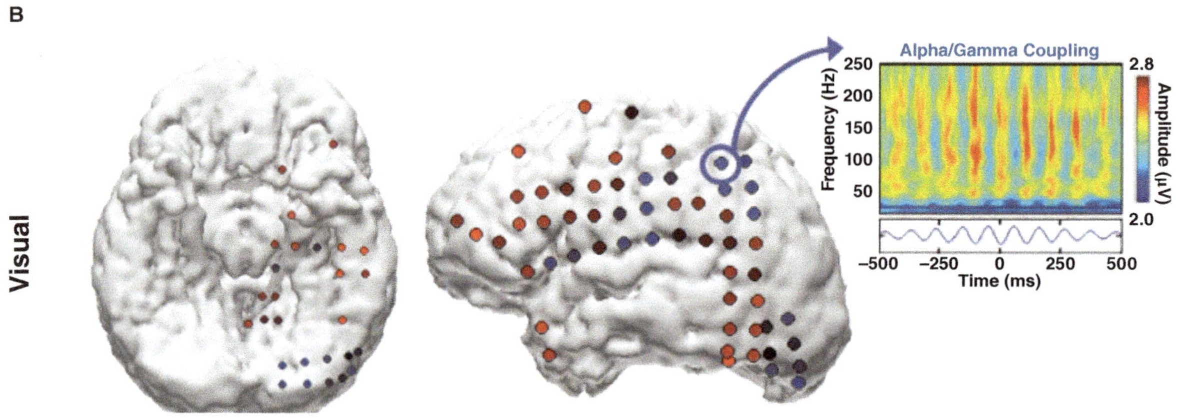

FIGURE 4.13.B "Alpha PAC" at a parietal electrode during performance of a visual task. Graphical conventions are the same as *Figure 4.13.A*; the only difference is that the low-frequency oscillation plotted under the TFR is in the alpha band (i.e., band-pass filtered from 8 to 12 Hz).

Figure 4.13 illustrates the principal finding from Voytek et al. (2010), which is that the low-frequency band that organizes high gamma (and therefore, by inference, MUA) in posterior cortical regions varies depending on whether subjects are carrying out a visual or a nonvisual task.

Finally, an implication of this section is that although ECoG offers nothing close to single-unit resolution, it can, at least under some conditions, index a proxy for spiking activity.

Other Measures of Phase Dynamics Although PAC gets its own name and its own acronym, it is one example of a broader range of ways in which one can assess the synchrony between two signals. Interareal phase synchrony refers to the extent to which oscillations in two regions are phase locked. This does not need to mean that the two signals are cycling with the same phase angle (i.e., that they are each at 0° at the same time, at 15° at the same time, etc.) but would also include the (much more frequently observed) scenario when, for example, signal A is at 15° at each instant that signal B is at 0°. In this case, the two signals would be highly synchronous despite being phase lagged relative to each other. Measures of synchrony are also not limited to oscillations of the same frequency. If signal A is oscillating at 20 Hz, for example, and signal B is oscillating at 10 Hz, one can still assess whether signal A is always at 15° when signal B is at 0°; it will just be the case that for every other cycle of A, when A is at 15° B will be at 180°. When signals at distal electrodes show a high degree of synchrony, it is assumed that one of two things is happening: either the areas giving rise to these signals are communicating with each other or a third area is exerting similar control over these two areas.

Caveats and Considerations for Spectral Analyses An important caveat about spectral analyses is that it's often the case that neuronal oscillations, whether measured intracranially or extracranially, are not sinusoidal. To some extent, this is evident from looking back-and-forth between panels A and B of *Figure 4.11*. Note how the peaks and the troughs of the raw EEG data (panel A) are alternately either flattened off or very sharp, relative to the "smoothed off" curves of the band-pass-filtered waveforms of panel B. This is what a Fourier transform does: you give it a time series and, regardless of its "true" shape, it gives you back the set of sinusoids that can be used to represent that time series. And while this transformation will be mathematically correct, one cannot assume that any given component of this transformation, in isolation, corresponds to a discrete component that exists in the original time series. *Figure 4.14* illustrates how the nature of a neuronal oscillation's deviation from purely sinusoidal can be quantified (in *Chapter 8*, *Skeletomotor control*, we'll see an example where this caveat has real-world implications for how we understand the neurophysiological mechanisms underlying the symptom-reducing effects of dopamine replacement medication on Parkinson's disease).

A second caveat relates to the hypothetical example illustrated in *Figure 4.10.B*, a scenario in which an auditory click produces a phase reset, but no change in power. Although a spectral analysis would not produce an artifactual component (as would an ERP analysis), a conventional TFR would nevertheless be insensitive to the event-related phase shift. This is simply because an analytic procedure that involves computing power on each trial and then averaging these power values across trials cannot also carry information about the phase. To detect the event-related phase shift, a different kind of analysis is required, one that ignores power but that assesses the extent to which the phase at each frequency in the spectrogram is the same or different across trials. For the scenario in *Figure 4.10.B*, intertrial phase synchrony would be low prior to the click, and then would increase markedly for the period after the reset when the phase in all trials is temporarily aligned. (And a caveat to this caveat is that if one's data contain a true ERP, that ERP would produce an artifactual increase of intertrial phase synchrony.) This measure is often referred to as intertrial coherence (ITC).

Traveling Waves

Let's start with a confession. The first time this author remembers hearing about the possibility of traveling waves as an electrophysiological phenomenon in the brain was in a lab meeting, and he scoffed (in front of all of those trainees [cringe]): *The brain is not made of some undifferentiated medium, like water in a pond, or pudding in a cup! Signals propagate via action potentials carried by axons, not as the undifferentiated expansion of energy in ever-growing concentric circles. . .* WELL, DR.-FANCY-TEXTBOOK-AUTHOR, YOU GET PARTIAL CREDIT FOR THAT ANSWER. It's true that the brain does not consist of some undifferentiated medium; however, it also turns out to be true that, by virtue of local wiring (e.g., connecting like-tuned columns within a cortical region), the propagation of signals via action potentials can, in fact, resemble an "undifferentiated expansion of energy . . ." Although *Figure 4.15* is a cartoon, it illustrates a phenomenon that we will see to be characteristic of brain function in many contexts that we will consider over the next several chapters.

To build some simple intuition, most waves that we encounter in the natural world are traveling waves. For example, the fact that ocean waves crash against the beach is a result of a traveling wave of energy. If we are in a harbor looking out to sea along a chain of equally spaced buoys, we can, in principle, track the progress of an individual cycle of a traveling wave as it makes its way to shore. A standing wave, in contrast, is most often invoked as an abstraction used to describe some repetitive motion, like the up-and-down motion of a piston in a cylinder.

FIGURE 4.14 Quantifying the shape of a neuronal oscillation.

Source: Jackson et al., 2019 / Society for Neuroscience.

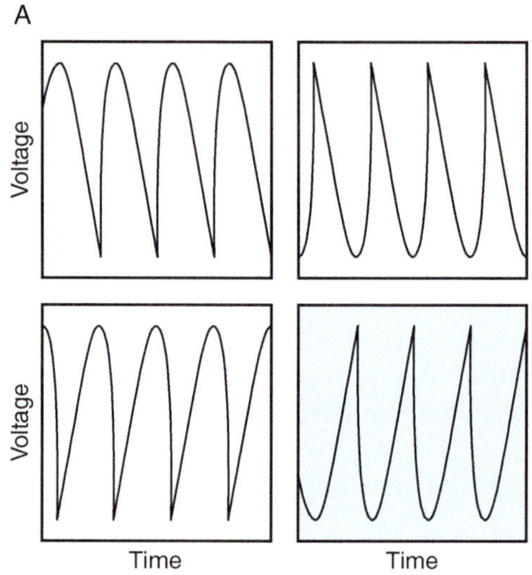

FIGURE 4.14.A Four possible ways that an oscillation can deviate from purely sinusoidal, with sharper peaks or sharper troughs accompanied by steeper rises or steeper falls. The quadrant shaded blue is the shape characteristically seen in EEG signal from electrodes C3 and C4, which emphasize signal from the underlying sensorimotor cortex (*Chapter 3*, section *Somatosensation*; *Chapter 8, Skeletomotor control*).

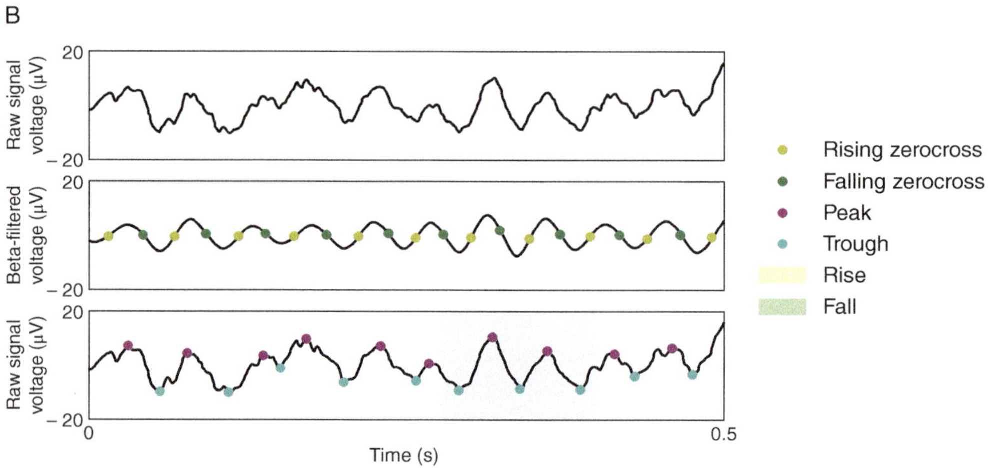

FIGURE 4.14.B Top panel: a segment of raw EEG signal. Middle panel: the signal from the top panel after being band-pass filtered to isolate its β-band component (13–30 Hz). Conceptually, the implementation of this filtering can be understood as first performing an FFT, and then extracting the range of frequencies that are of interest. Note how band-pass filtering generates a perfectly sinusoidal signal. The zero crossings are marked with lighter and darker green dots, to identify half-cycle boundaries – only one peak or trough can occur between any two of these boundaries. Bottom panel: Peaks and troughs in the original signal that lie between each zero crossing.

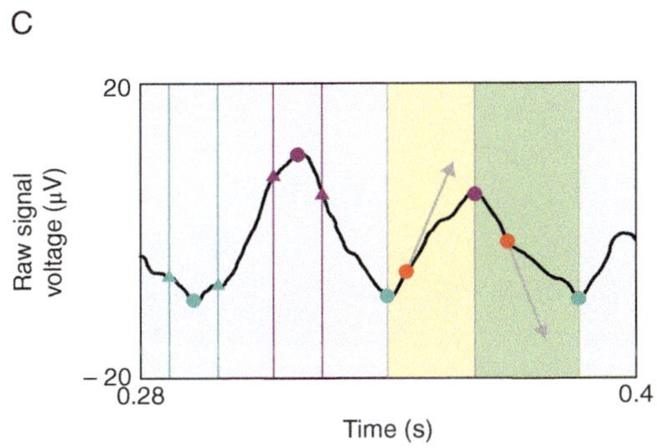

FIGURE 4.14.C Peak sharpness is calculated as the mean of the difference between the peak (purple circle) and the voltage points three samples before and after the peak (purple triangles). The trough sharpness is calculated in a similar fashion, indicated with blue circles and triangles that cycle's peak and "ending trough." The rise and fall of one cycle are highlighted in yellow and green, with the maximum slope of each illustrated with arrows.

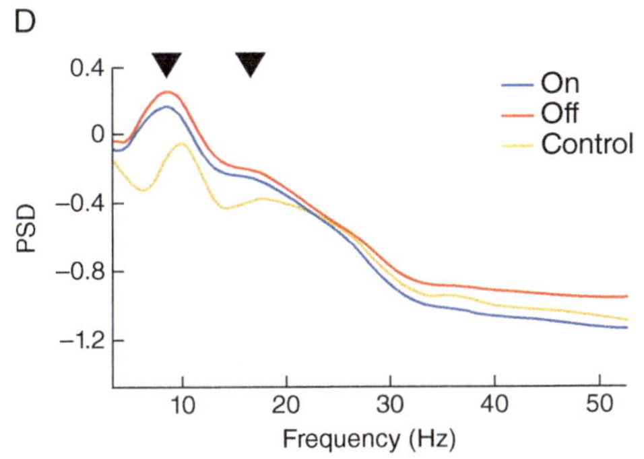

FIGURE 4.14.D The group-average power spectra (here, the "power spectral density" [PSD]) from EEG electrodes C3 and C4 from a sample of Parkinson's disease patients when they are optimally medicated with dopamine-replacement medication ("on"; blue), when they have no medication in their systems ("off"; red), and from a group of neurologically healthy control subjects (yellow). The black arrows point to peaks in the PSDs that correspond to elevated power in the alpha band and in the beta band (in the latter, the elevated power manifests as a "shoulder" in the overall trend in the PSD of decreasing power with increasing frequency). An important point made by this panel is that although the dopamine-replacement medication has a marked effect of "smoothing out" the shape of oscillations in the beta band (from the sawtoothed, asymmetric shape illustrated in the highlighted quadrant in panel A to a more sinusoidal shape), this change in shape is not captured in measures that only index power.

Magnetic Resonance Imaging

Physics and Engineering Bases

Nuclear magnetic resonance (NMR) refers to the fact that the *nucleus* of an atom (a proton, in the case of hydrogen) *resonates* at a preferred frequency in the presence of a strong *magnetic* field. For our purposes, we can understand this as owing to the fact that an "unpaired" nucleus (i.e., there is not a neutron paired up with the H atom's lonely proton) rotates. In the jargon of nuclear physics, this rotation is a "spin." NMR imaging, now commonly referred to as MRI, is based on the fact that the application of a radiofrequency (RF) pulse at just the right frequency – the resonant frequency of the H atom – can perturb its axis of rotation.

FIGURE 4.15 Cortical traveling waves.

Source: (Alamia & VanRullen, 2024) / The MIT Press.

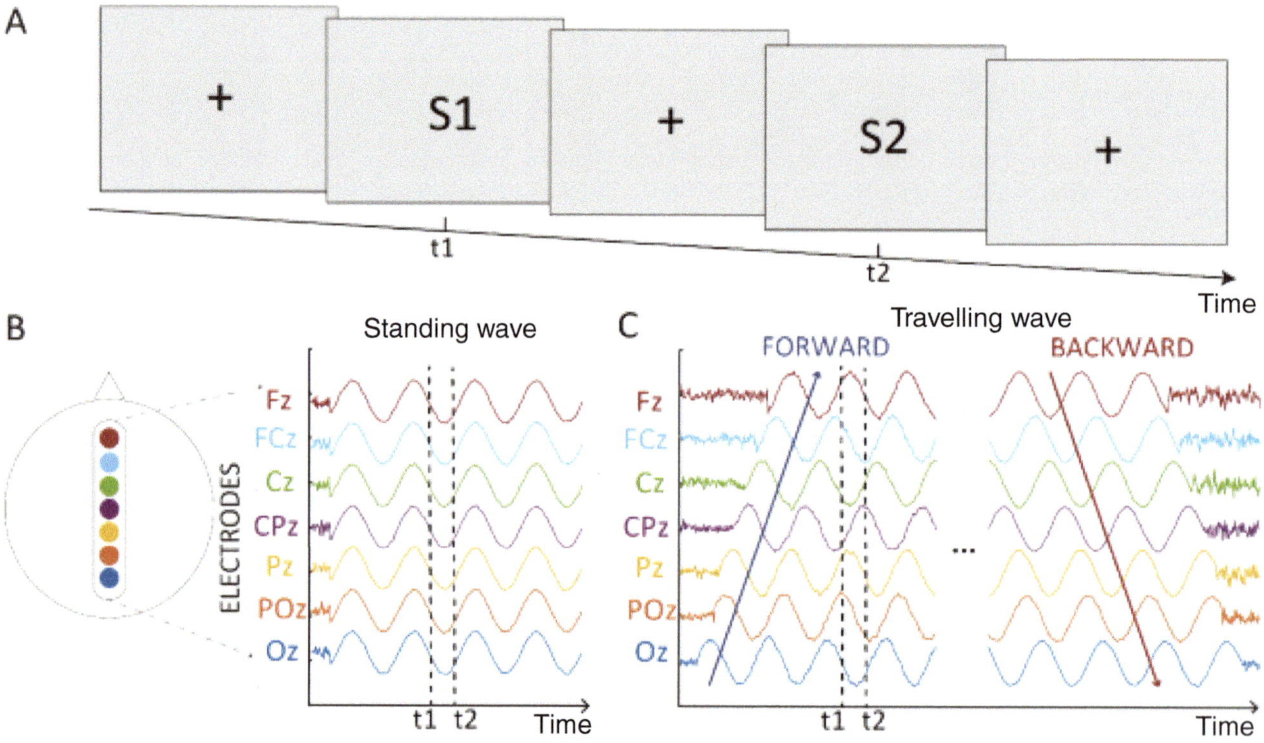

FIGURE 4.15.A Diagram of a hypothetical visual perception task in which one stimulus (S1) is presented at time *t1* and a second (S2) at *t2*.

FIGURE 4.15.B Left side of the image is a top-down view of the scalp, highlighting the electrodes in the EEG cap used in this analysis. They fall along the anterior-to-posterior axis defined by Fz–Cz–Pz from *Figure 4.9.B*. Right side of the image illustrates a standing wave as recorded at each of these electrodes. (Note that this illustrates a hypothetical single phenomenon that is either producing a uniform fluctuation of voltage across a large swath of the brain or that is emanating from a single source in a manner that its amplitude at each of these locations on the scalp is identical.)

FIGURE 4.15.C A traveling wave registered by the same electrodes from B, moving from "back to front" (i.e., "FORWARD") or from "front to back" (i.e., "BACKWARD"). Note that a consequence of this traveling wave is that the initial processing of each stimulus would occur at a different phase angle of this oscillation at each electrode (and by extension, the authors assume, the same would also likely be true for different brain regions).

Physicists and biomedical engineers figured out how to take advantage of these properties of the H atom by designing a tube big enough for a human body to slide into and running a massive amount of current through the tube so as to create a very strong magnetic field that's aligned to the long axis of the tube; this is called the "B_0" field (pronounced "bee naught"). The strength of the B_0 field is measured in units of tesla, resulting in scanners being labeled, for example, "1.5 tesla" (T), or "3T" scanners. Importantly, when a body is slid into this tube, the axes of spin of the H atoms in the body align with the "B_0" field, and this becomes their low-energy state. The reason for aligning the spin of an H atom along a known axis of rotation is that when the angle of this axis of rotation is changed by a brief "push" delivered by a pulse of RF energy, its natural tendency is to return to its initial state. (I.e., after the push, the B_0 magnetic field pulls the spin back into alignment.) This process is referred to as **relaxation**, and because relaxation amounts to the H atom transitioning from a temporarily higher-energy state back to the low-energy state of alignment with the B_0 field, it involves a release of energy. It is this energy that creates the MR image.

MRI Methods for In Vivo Anatomical Imaging

Pulses of RF energy can be delivered to the body in different configurations (e.g., number and duration of pulses; frequency of pulses), each referred to as a **pulse sequence**. Different pulse sequences influence nuclear spins in different ways, and, because of this, they can be designed to emphasize different types of tissue. Additionally, different ways of measuring the relaxation signal can yield different kinds of information about the tissue being imaged.

T1-Weighted Imaging One component of the relaxation signal, the **T1** component, is particularly well suited for distinguishing white matter from gray. This is illustrated in *Figure 3.2*, which features a "T1-weighted" image of a virtual slice through a brain. T1-weighted images ("T1 images" or, sometimes, "T1s" for short) are the most common structural MR images that one encounters in the cognitive neuroscience literature.

Voxel-Based Morphometry Voxel-based morphometry (VBM) is carried out on T1-weighted anatomical MR images to estimate the density of gray matter or the volume of a structure. Importantly, VBM calculations are made after differences in the shape of the structure in question are removed by calculating a deformation field (Ashburner and Friston, 2000). Thus, what VBM compares is T1-weighted signal intensity values in each voxel of gray matter – effectively, the average "darkness" of each voxel in group A vs. group B. Differences in VBM are often summarized as differences in "volume."

It should be noted that there is some controversy about exactly what it is that VBM measures, and the extent to which it might be sensitive to "microstructural" differences in the anatomy of different subjects. The website of a suite of neuroimaging software tools called FSL includes this caveat on its VBM page:

> *It is sometimes not possible to determine if the results you may find are the consequence of an effective reduced thickness or atrophy in the gray matter, or rather an indirect reflection of a different gyrification pattern. Indeed, it might be possible that a misalignment of the gyri/sulci or even different folding patterns may lead to the difference of gray matter distribution that you have found.*

Diffusion Tensor Imaging – In Vivo "Tract Tracing" Within tracts of myelinated axons, there are teeny gaps between each axon. As a consequence, water molecules travel much more quickly along such a bundle than across it. This motion, or *diffusion*, of water molecules can be represented as a 3-D volume (called a *tensor*) that indexes how symmetrically, or otherwise, water molecules are diffusing. Diffusion tensor imaging (DTI) uses a pulse sequence that measures the shape of diffusion tensors in different parts of the brain. A perfectly spherical tensor, said to be "isotropic," would indicate that water is diffusing freely in all directions. Fiber tracts, in contrast, produce "anisotropic" tensors shaped more like rugby footballs. By estimating the most probable route that a series of such tiny end-to-end "footballs" makes through a section of brain, one can infer the existence of a fiber tract, as illustrated in *Figure 3.2.*

Functional Magnetic Resonance Imaging

While T1-weighted and diffusion tensor images measure aspects of anatomy that are assumed to be static during the time it takes to acquire the images, the "f" in fMRI indicates that its images index the physiology of the brain. That is, it measures levels of activity that change over time. To be able to interpret fMRI data, it is necessary to understand it at several levels: the cellular processes that give rise to the activity that fMRI is measuring; the hemodynamic response that these processes trigger; and the physics of its signal.

The Metabolic Demands of the Action Potential and of Synaptic Activity The generation of an action potential entails reversing the electrical and chemical imbalances that are characteristic of the neuron at rest. How the neuron restores these imbalances turns out to be the basis for many neuroimaging techniques, including fMRI. One key mechanism is the so-called **Na^+/K^+ pump**, a membrane-spanning complex of proteins that acts as a "reverse channel." At the cost of one molecule of adenosine triphosphate (ATP) per cycle, the Na^+/K^+ pump expels three Na^+ ions and draws in two K^+ ions. Also highly energy demanding is the process of releasing molecules of neurotransmitter into the synaptic cleft (exocytosis). ATP, the "fuel" that is needed for these operations, is derived from the processing of glucose in mitochondria inside the synaptic bouton of the axon. Glucose, in turn, is delivered to cells via the bloodstream. Herein lies the linkage to the signal that is measured by fMRI: elevated activity in neurons creates a need for arterial blood, and the resultant increase of oxygenated blood to active parts of the brain is what these methods detect. (The principle is the same for all tissues of the body. Think about whether more blood flows to the muscles of your arm when you are lifting something heavy, or when your arm is just hanging by your side. Note that this section is also relevant for the 2DG method of functional tissue imaging that we have already considered in this chapter, and for some applications of **positron emission tomography [PET]**, which we will take up further along in this chapter.)

Interestingly, neurotransmitter reuptake, although a metabolically expensive process, isn't directly responsible for the consumption of ATP. Instead, it leverages electrochemical ion gradients across the membrane via a process called **cotransport**. A useful analogy is to consider a revolving door. To get it "inside," a molecule of neurotransmitter is yoked to a Na^+ ion. Now we have a situation in which the chemical gradients of the yoked components are in opposition – the low intracellular concentration of Na^+ provides an inward "pull," and the opposite is true for the neurotransmitter. It's as though two people have entered a door that's rotating counterclockwise (anticlockwise), and one (the "Na^+ ion") is pushing the door in the counterclockwise direction so as to enter, while the other (the "molecule of neurotransmitter") is pushing in the opposite way. (The role of the neurotransmitter can be played by a 2-year-old in our analogy: *No, Mommy, I don't want to go into that store!*) The stalemate is broken by adding a third "person" who is inside and who wants to leave: cotransport also entails the simultaneous transport of a molecule of K^+ along its concentration gradient and its electrical gradient, from inside the cell to outside. "Two against one," the molecule of neurotransmitter "loses," and it ends up back inside the neuron.

If cotransport "passively" takes advantage of chemical gradients, why is it metabolically expensive? The answer is that although the reuptake process itself doesn't consume ATP, its operation decreases the resting-state imbalance of a higher intracellular concentration of K^+ and higher extracellular concentration of Na^+. Thus, each cycle of the reuptake processes prompts a compensatory, energy-expending cycle of the Na^+/K^+ pump in order to restore the imbalance.

T2*-Weighted fMRI In 1990, biophysics researcher Seiji Ogawa and colleagues, working at AT&T Bell Laboratories in Murray Hill, NJ, made a breakthrough discovery: Leveraging the fact that oxygenated hemoglobin (Hb) and deoxygenated hemoglobin (dHb) have different magnetic profiles, they were able to coax from MRI a "blood oxygen level-dependent" (BOLD) signal. That is, with the right pulse sequence, they demonstrated that a different MRI measure of relaxation, called T2* (pronounced "tee-two-star"), varied with the balance between Hb and dHb. The reason that this was important comes from the principle of brain physiology that we've already seen: elevated activity in neurons creates a need for arterial blood. This is accomplished by the dilation of arterioles, and the consequent increase of arterial blood carrying Hb in the vicinity of the active cells. A distinctive feature of mammalian physiology is that this hemodynamic response is overcompensatory, in that the increased supply of Hb-rich blood exceeds the demand and, as a result, the ratio of Hb:dHb in venules carrying blood away from the capillary bed in the region of elevated activity temporarily increases (*Figure 4.16*). Neurosurgeon Wilder Penfield, who we read about in *Chapter 3*'s introduction to somatosensation, observed this with his naked eye over 70 years ago, as venous blood became redder during localized seizures (seizures being a pathological cause of increased activity).

fMRI is an extremely popular tool for cognitive neuroscience research, primarily because it offers the highest spatial resolution of any noninvasive method for measuring activity in the brain. The typical fMRI experiment includes the collection of a high-resolution T1-weighted volume, with a resolution of 0.75 mm^3 or better. The T2*-weighted data (from here on out, the "fMRI data") acquired during the same experiment are coregistered to and merged with the T1-weighted anatomical image (the "anatomicals"), thereby allowing one to see what structure(s) in the brain are generating the activity measured with fMRI. The physics of the T2*-weighted signal is such that T2*-weighted images are of lower resolution than are T1-weighted images and typically the fMRI data acquired during an experiment will have one-quarter the resolution of the anatomical data. For example, a scanning session with an anatomical resolution of 0.75 mm^3 will have a functional resolution of 3.75 mm^3. Although MRI data can be acquired as individual 2-D slices, they are more typically acquired as "full sets" of 2-D slides that, when stacked, make up a 3-D "wholebrain" image. To show "the insides" the data are often displayed as mosaics of 2-D slices that, when stacked, would reconstitute the 3-D volume of space that the physical brain occupies (see *Figure 4.17*). When one views a slice taken from an image with 0.75 mm^3 resolution, the "picture elements" (i.e., pixels) that make up the image are 0.75 mm^2. Importantly, however, with MRI, even a single slice has thickness to it, and so it is better construed as a slab. Scientists acknowledge this by referring to the "3-D pixels" that make up MRI images as "volumetric pixels," or voxels.

Although acquisition of a T1-weighted anatomical scan requires roughly 5 minutes of scanning time, the resultant image does not contain any temporal information. fMRI data, in contrast, do typically contain temporal information, because a scan typically entails the acquisition of several 3-D volumes. Let's think back to EEG for a moment. If one is acquiring EEG data with a 60-electrode cap, a 5-minute session of recorded task performance will yield data from 60 channels, each one a time series with (let's say) 1024 recorded values per second, which could be described a 2-D "slice" made up of 60 "pixels," each one of which contains a time series with (1024 time points/second * 60 seconds/minutes * 5 minutes =) 307,200 values. (EEG data are typically down-sampled to 500 Hz or less but that would still be a lot of values!) fMRI, rather than using 60 electrodes, is collected in (brain-shaped) volumes of roughly 30,000 voxels (depending on the size of the individual's head). The typical fMRI scan lasts anywhere from 4 to 10 or more minutes, with a new volume acquired roughly once every 2 seconds. (The time required to acquire a single volume of fMRI data, called the "time to repeat" [TR], will vary depending on the pulse sequence, the size of the volume being imaged, and other factors.) And so, although fMRI's sampling rate of 0.5 Hz is orders of magnitude lower than that of EEG (and, consequently, its temporal resolution is dramatically inferior to that of EEG), a 5-min-long scan with a TR of 2 seconds nonetheless acquires (0.5 time points/second * 60 seconds/minutes * 5 minutes=) 150 values per voxel.

Task-Related Functional Imaging To illustrate how MRI and fMRI data are acquired to study the activity of the brain associated with cognition, *Figure 4.17* walks us through a study of one of the simplest behaviors this author can think of, pressing a button (. . . over and over and over, once every 20 seconds). The simplicity of the task will allow us to emphasize a couple of fundamental properties of the BOLD signal that we'll need to keep in mind for every fMRI study that will be considered during the remainder of this book. First, note from *Figure 4.17.A* that this presentation of the anatomical localization of button press-related activity does not display the BOLD data themselves but, rather, the results of a statistical analysis of the data. This will be true of almost all presentations of fMRI data that one is likely to encounter. Second, note from *Figure 4.17.D* how sluggish and smeared out in time the BOLD response to the button press is. That is, although the neural activity producing the button press was probably completed by time 0.5 seconds or so, this subject's fMRI response didn't peak until time 6 seconds. And, importantly, if this fMRI response to the button press were only delayed, but not otherwise transformed, it would be expected to produce a fairly steep ramp-up at roughly time 6 seconds, and a similarly steep drop-off roughly 500 msec later. What we see, however, is a relatively shallow rise to its peak, and an equally shallow return to baseline – although we're assuming that the neural activity of interest lasted only half a second, the full-width and half maximum of this response (a common way to estimate the width of this kind of response) looks to be roughly 5 seconds long. Importantly, these "sluggish and smeared-out" qualities of the fMRI response are not due to technical limitations – the BOLD response would look like

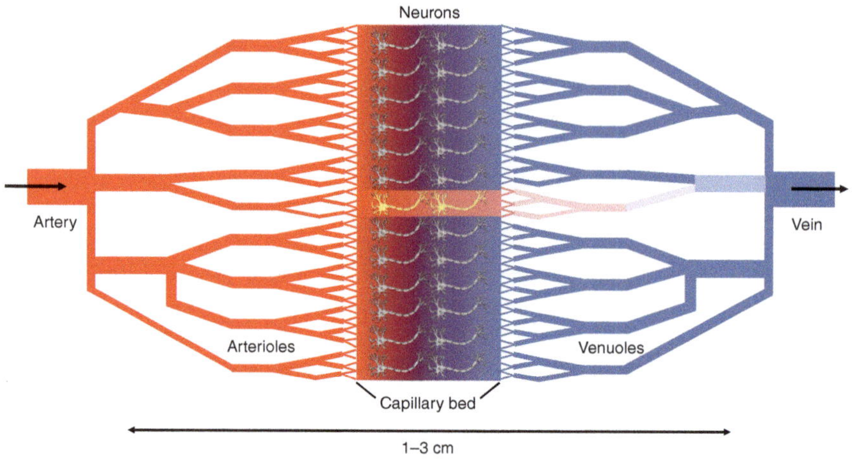

FIGURE 4.16 The hemodynamic response to neuronal activity. In this cartoon, the elevated activity of a small cluster of neurons (depicted in yellow) results in an increase in the delivery of Hb-rich blood to the local capillary bed (depicted by redder tint of capillaries), and an increase in Hb:dHb in the venules draining this blood away from the capillary bed (also depicted by a redder tint).

this regardless of whether it was sampled at 1000 Hz or 0.1 Hz. Rather, the slow rise and slow fall of the fMRI signal are consequences of the hemodynamic response to neural activity that it measures. The dilation and subsequent constriction of arterioles simply lag behind the neural signals that trigger them. Indeed, these properties of the BOLD response are so fundamental to the signal that the waveform derived in *Figure 4.17* is an empirically derived example of what is called the hemodynamic response function (HRF).

Because cognitive neuroscientists are typically interested in the activity of neurons, not in hemodynamics per se, the smearing properties of the HRF can be thought of as a filter that transforms the signal of primary interest in our experiments. More specifically, it has the properties of a low-pass filter, which render it poorly suited to tracking and resolving rapidly fluctuating signals. *Figure 4.18* gives a sense for why this is.

FIGURE 4.17 fMRI data from a 6-minute-40-second-long scan during which the subject pushed a button with each thumb, once every 20 seconds.

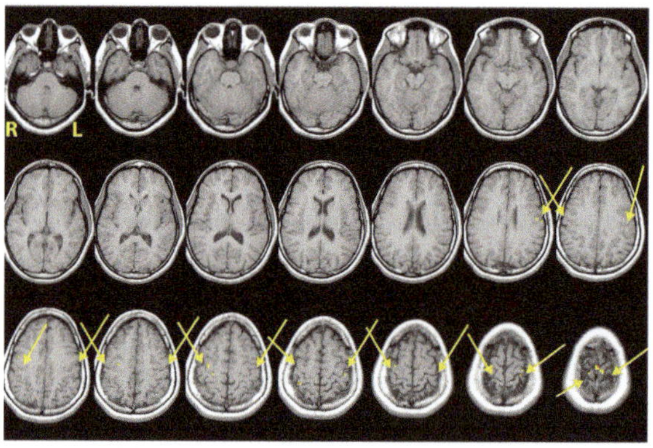

FIGURE 4.17.A Voxels in the pre- and postcentral gyrus for which the increase in fMRI signal in response to the button presses exceeded a statistical threshold appear as small yellow squares. This "thresholded statistical map" is superimposed on a T1-weighted anatomical image acquired during the same scanning session. This mosaic displays axial slices arrayed from ventralmost (upper left) to dorsalmost (lower right). Arrows point to the central sulcus in each slice in which it is visible. (Primary motor cortex is located in the precentral gyrus [*Chapter 8*], and primary somatosensory cortex is located in the postcentral gyrus [*Chapter 5*].) "R" and "L" denote "right" and "left," meaning images are displayed using radiological conventions. Note that although these data were acquired during a whole brain scan, the statistical map has been masked so that activity in only precentral and postcentral gyrus can be observed.

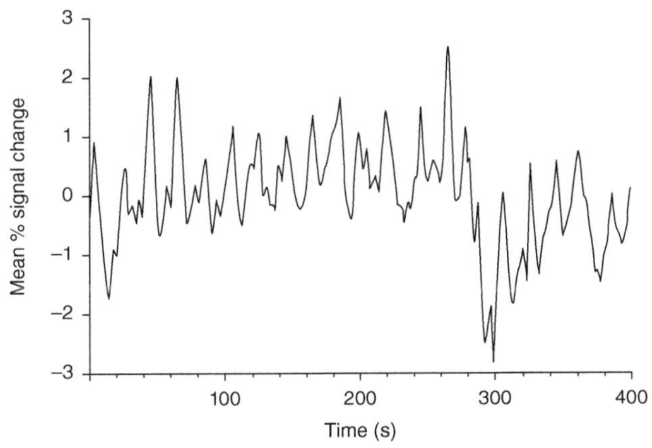

FIGURE 4.17.B BOLD signal fluctuations pooled across the voxels identified in *Figure 4.17.A*. The data have been mean-centered and scaled to units of percentage change from baseline but are otherwise "raw." A button press occurred at each of the tick marks on the time axis (except 400).

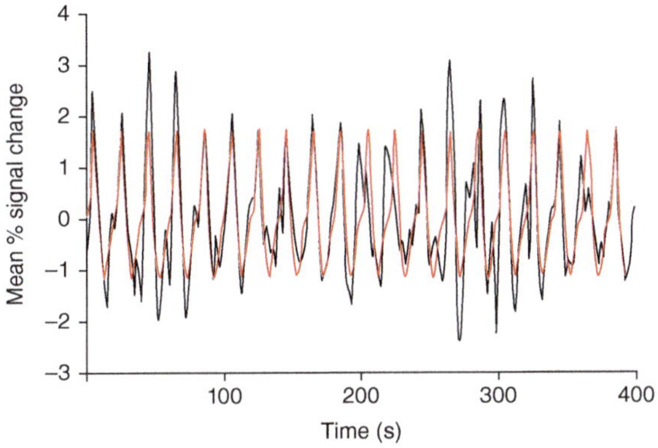

FIGURE 4.17.C Same data as *Figure 4.17.B*, but with drift removed, and an overlay (red waveform) of the fits of the statistical model to the data. With regard to "drift," the overall drop in signal at time 280 in *Figure 4.17.B* reflected some factor other than the once-every-20-seconds button press, and so was removed statistically. The independent variable in the statistical model was a series of delta functions (a.k.a. "stick functions") placed at time 0 seconds, 20 seconds, and so on up to 380 seconds – i.e., at each time point when a button press was to be executed – and convolved with a basis set of sine waves and cosine waves so as to capture the predicted shape of the HR. While the red waveform shows the least-squares best fit of the model to the data, the data themselves illustrate the trial-to-trial variability of the fMRI response to each of the 20 presumably identical events.

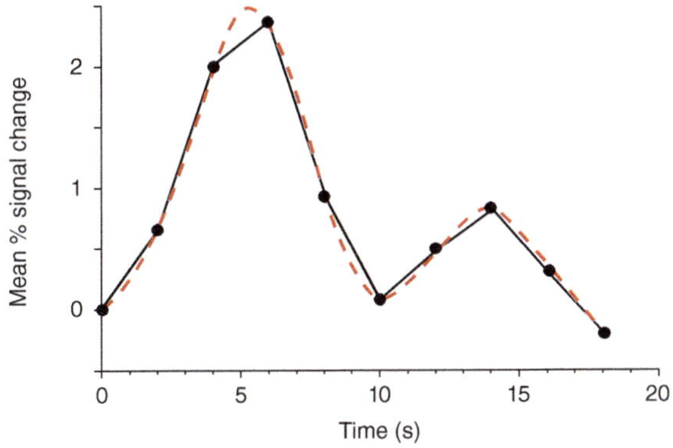

FIGURE 4.17.D In black, the trial-averaged response to a bimanual thumb press made at time 0 (i.e., the average of time segments 0–20, 20–40, . . ., 380–400 from *Figure 4.16.C*). This trial-averaged time series can be thought of as an empirically derived estimate of the HRF for this subject. In red, the HRF has been interpolated, to represent the fact that it is a continuous function, despite only being sampled at a 0.5-Hz rate in this study.

FIGURE 4.18 The lowpass filtering properties of fMRI.

Source: Adapted from Buckner & Dale (1997).

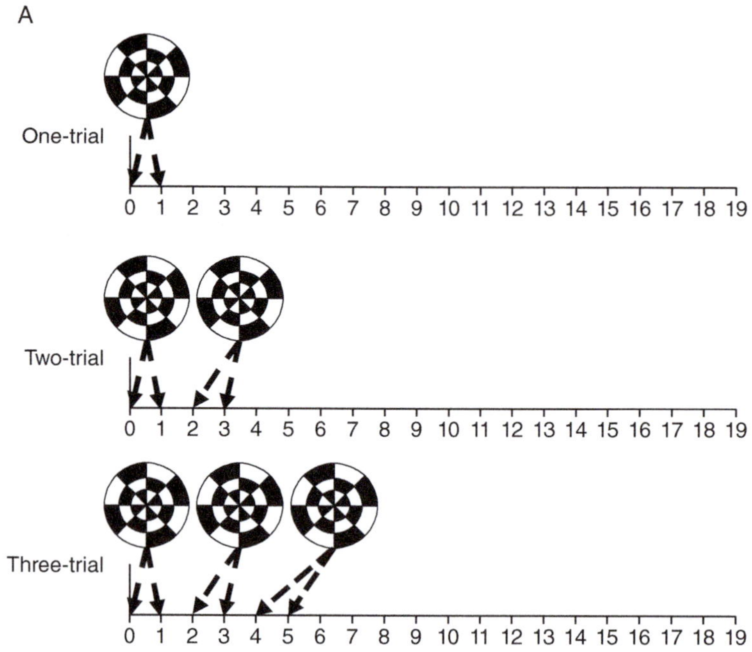

FIGURE 4.18.A Diagram of three types of trials, in which a 1-second-long visual presentation of a flickering checkerboard stimulus – chosen to evoke a strong response from visual cortex – was presented once (One-Trial), twice (Two-Trial), or three times (Three-Trial), with a 1-second intertrial interval (ITI) dividing presentations on the two- and three-event trials.

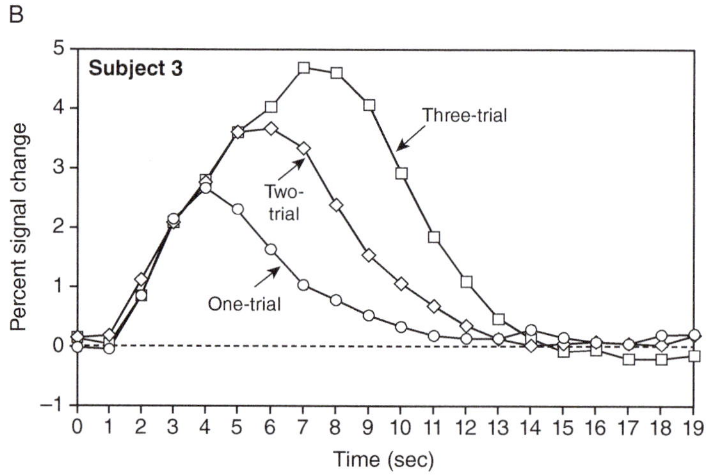

FIGURE 4.18.B The BOLD response, from the visual cortex of a single subject, from each of the three trial types, all plotted on the same graph, and all time-locked to the onset of the first checkerboard stimulus. Note that, for the Two-Trial and Three-Trial responses, although they are of higher magnitude, it's not evident that they were generated by more than one discrete event.

Functional Connectivity

Although it is a fairly general term, "functional connectivity" is most commonly used to refer to analyses in which, rather than measuring how performance of a task produces changes in activity in different regions in the brain (e.g., *Figure 4.17.A*), one measures how performance of a task produces changes in the correlation of activity between different regions. In the following section, we'll look in some detail at a method for assessing such patterns of interregional correlation, but doing so while the subject is explicitly *not* performing a task: resting state functional correlations (RSFCs). RSFCs measure the extent to which the fluctuations in activity between regions covary over an extended period of time. For functional connectivity analyses – that is, task-related patterns of correlation – the RSFC data effectively provide the baseline, because experimenters are interested in knowing whether, and if so, how, correlations between regions may strengthen (or weaken) above and beyond their baseline level of correlation. Conceptually, functional connectivity is interpreted in a manner similar to interareal phase synchrony (see earlier section on *Time–frequency analysis, other measures of phase dynamics*), in that if two or more regions show a task-related increase in functional connectivity, it is assumed that their activity is coordinated, and/or that they are sharing information. Conversely, if the functional connectivity between two areas decreases, for example, engaging in a task produces increases in activity in area A and decreases in B, and furthermore, A and B are negatively correlated; this might be interpreted as suggestive that A has an inhibitory effect on B. Importantly, as is also the case with interareal phase synchrony, changes in functional connectivity between A and B might also result from a third area, C, driving both of them (or C and D, or . . .).

Resting State Functional Correlations

Important insights into brain function, how it supports behavior, and how it varies with age and with disease state, have been gained by studying brain activity when the subject is "at rest" – awake, but not performing any experimentally controlled task. This was first reported by Marcus Raichle and colleagues at Washington University, when they observed in a meta-analysis of PET studies of a wide variety of cognition tasks that a common set of areas reliably decreased their activity in response to engagement in almost any cognitive task. (PET will be introduced in section *Tomography*.) These regions, including most prominently the posterior cingulate cortex and precuneus (on the medial surface of the parietal lobe), medial frontal cortex, and IPL, have come to be known as the default mode network (DMN), because their levels of activity are highest when no experimenter-designed task is being carried out

FIGURE 4.19 Generating an RSFC map.
Source: Adapted from Han et al., 2018.

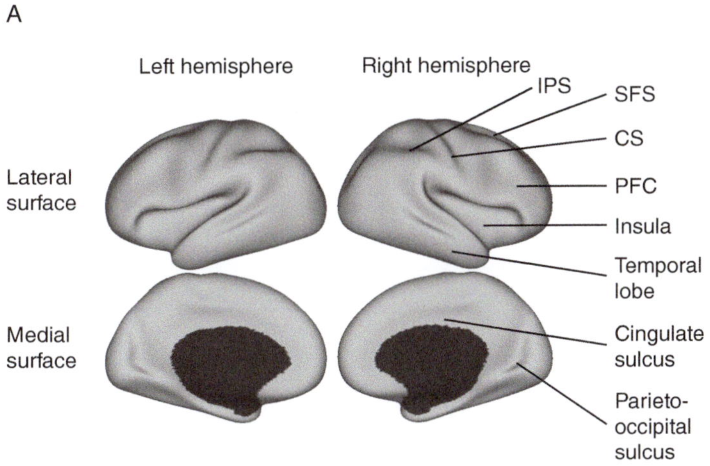

FIGURE 4.19.A An inflated anatomical volume that has been warped into atlas space, illustrating step 1. Note that in addition to exposing the insula, the inflation process has separated the dorsal bank from the ventral bank of the Sylvian fissure. Some landmarks are identified in the right-hemisphere images: CS = central sulcus; IPS = intraparietal sulcus; PFC = prefrontal cortex; SFS = superior frontal sulcus.

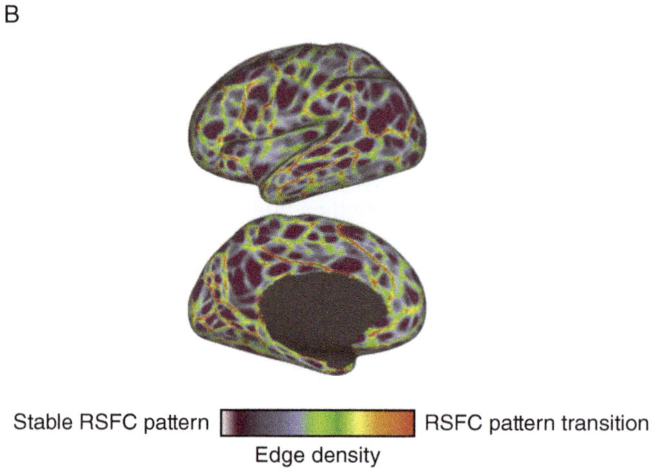

FIGURE 4.19.B RSFC-based boundary maps, with warmer colors indicating higher probability of a boundary between areas, and darker colors indicating collections of vertices with high RSFC similarity, and therefore belonging to the same area.

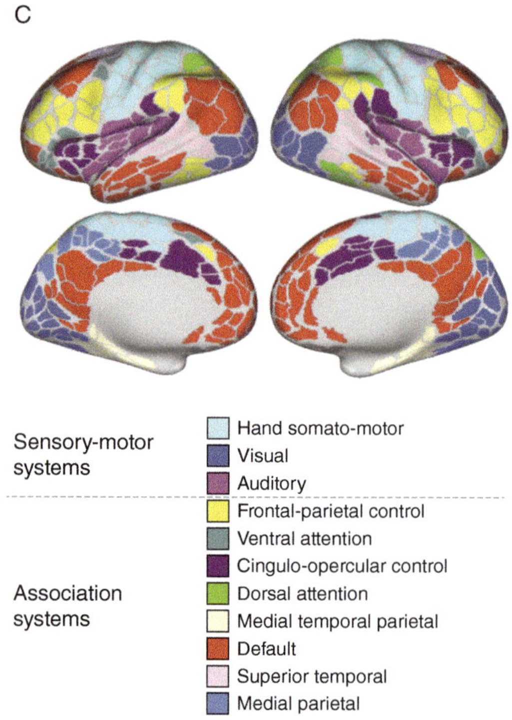

FIGURE 4.19.C RSFC parcellation into functional networks of data from 88 healthy young adults, aged 20–34 years.

(i.e., "by default"; *Figure 4.19.C*, Association System labeled "Default"). Shortly thereafter, Bharat Biswal and colleagues, then at the Medical College of Wisconsin, demonstrated with fMRI that anatomically disparate areas that increase their activity in common during performance of goal-directed tasks often also exhibit correlations in the low-frequency fluctuations (<0.1 Hz) that are typical of the brain "at rest." These two developments were initially very influential because they provided potent examples of intrinsic activity in the brain – ongoing activity that is not tied in any direct way to events in the outside world. Subsequent advances have established that RSFC can be used to "parcellate" the entire brain into networks that are often named after the domains of cognition that engage them in "task-positive" contexts. In summary, an RSFC map can be construed as reflecting "a statistical history of coactivation that [has been] sculpted over the lifespan of the individual" (Wig, 2017, p. 983).

To generate an RSFC map, MRI scanning entails acquiring a T1-weighted anatomical image of the subject's brain, and then an fMRI scan while the subject is instructed to lie still and stare at a fixation point during the entirety of the scan (here we're illustrating the procedure with the 6-minute-long scan used by Han et al. (2018)). Then, the data processing is carried out as follows:

1. Perform a virtual "inflation" of the (3-D) T1-weighted anatomical volume (*Figure 4.17.A*) to facilitate creation of a 2-D surface map of the resting state (RS) BOLD data, and the visualization of the results.
2. Transform the 3-D volume of BOLD data acquisition space into a 2-D virtual mesh that covers the inflated anatomical images. This 2-D mesh is made up of 32,000 vertices per hemisphere, each of which has a time series made up of the 180 images acquired during the fMRI scan (360 seconds of scanning with a TR of 2 seconds).
3. Compute the pairwise correlation between the time series of each vertex and that of every other surface vertex, thereby generating a 32,492 × 64,984 (32k × 64k) correlation matrix for each hemisphere.
4. Transform the correlation matrix from each subject into a common atlas space so that results can be combined across subjects.
5. Convert individual-subject correlation matrices into a group-level similarity matrix by correlating each vertex's RSFC map with that of every other vertex (e.g., two adjacent vertices that are going to end up belonging to the same region will have very similar patterns of correlation with the rest of the brain (i.e., similar correlation matrices) and so will be highly correlated in the similarity matrix).
6. Generate a gradient map by identifying abrupt transitions in the similarity matrix.
7. Apply a "watershed" edge-detection algorithm to the gradient map to convert the "abrupt transitions" into boundaries between RSFC-defined regions. Note that in the terminology of graph theory, "edge" refers to the connections between nodes (and that for RSFC, vertices act as nodes) (*Figure 4.19.B*).
8. Label the resulting RSFC-based parcellation according to the functional systems that have been identified and validated several times since their introduction in 2011. (Indeed, as we'll see throughout the book, one tension that periodically arises is whether these networks, which are typically discovered and certainly validated via analyses of resting (and, therefore, "task-free") data, are best labeled and understood according to their anatomical characteristics (e.g., the "Cingulo-Opercular Network" [CON]), their functional characteristics (e.g., the DMN) or a combination of the two (e.g., the "Frontoparietal Control Network" [FPC])).

An important development with the RSFC approach that is more recent than the research and techniques summarized here is so-called "precision imaging" (alternatively, "deep imaging"), the intensive repeated imaging of individual subjects. A special issue edited by Caterina Gratton and Rodrigo Braga (2021) is a good resource for this approach. The section of this chapter on *Network science and graph theory* will consider some of the ways that RSFC is used in cognitive neuroscience.

Magnetic Resonance Spectroscopy

Just as T2*-weighted pulse sequences take advantage of the fact that hemoglobin's magnetic resonance properties vary with its state of oxygenation, many other compounds in the world have distinct magnetic resonance profiles that can be detected and measured with MRI, including neurotransmitters and their metabolites. Magnetic resonance spectroscopy (MRS) can be used, for example, to assess the level of gamma-aminobutyric acid (GABA) in someone's visual system, or in the vicinity of their frontal eye fields. The signals from neurotransmitters and their metabolites are very weak, and so lengthy scans are required (on the order of minutes). This means that nothing approaching real-time measurement of fluctuations in the levels of, say, the synthesis or the breakdown of a certain neurotransmitter, perhaps in conjunction with task performance, is possible at this time.

Tomography

The word tomography refers to the acquisition of an image of a 2-D section through a volume, via some kind of penetrating wave. Although X-ray technology was used for medical imaging throughout the twentieth century, it was limited to the acquisition of single 2-D sections (or "slices") until the advent of computer-implemented algorithms that allowed for the effective simultaneous collection of all the slices needed to reconstruct a volume. (Note that, as is the case with MRI, although these sections are referred to as being "2-D slices," each actually has some thickness to it, and thus they might be better construed as thin "slabs.")

X-ray Computed Tomography

Computed tomography (CT) scanning is only capable of generating anatomical images and has markedly poorer spatial resolution relative to MRI, making of limited utility as a research tool for cognitive neuroscience. It is a workhorse in Emergency Medicine and Radiology departments in hospitals, however, for reasons of safety: sliding an unconscious accident victim into an MRI scanner could be catastrophic if the patient has any metal in their body (including brain), whether due to a previous injury or in the form of a medical device. Consequently, the brain images used by neurologists and neuropsychologists to estimate the damage incurred by brain-injured patients are frequently CT images acquired in the first hours after the patient's admission to the hospital.

Positron Emission Tomography

PET entails the injection of a short-lived (of the order of minutes to hours) radioactive isotope into the bloodstream, and subsequently measuring where in the body this substance accumulates. It works on the principle that the decay of the isotope releases subatomic particles called positrons, and that when a positron encounters an electron, the resultant annihilation releases two photons (gamma rays) that travel in opposite directions. The photons are detected by detectors that are arrayed in a ring around the body, and sophisticated math is performed to estimate where in space the annihilation event must have occurred in order to produce the pattern of photons detected by the scanner.

In principle, any biologically active molecule that can be rendered radioactive can be used as a PET "tracer." Thus, PET can be used to assess patterns of energy metabolism in the brain (via radiolabeled glucose, a method that can be thought of as "in vivo 2-DG imaging;" e.g., *Figure 4.4*) or patterns of activity of certain neurotransmitter systems (as with, e.g., radiolabeled dopamine agonists). For now, we'll limit our discussion to $H_2{}^{15}O$ – a.k.a. "radiolabeled water," or just "^{15}O" (pronounced "oh fifteen"). (Regardless of what kind of tracer we use, PET invariably has a low signal-to-noise ratio [SNR], which will impose constraints on experimental design, as we'll see in the next section of this chapter.) In a "cognitive activation study" (as illustrated in *Figure 4.18*), the subject lies in the scanner, with an IV in her arm. Upon the delivery of $H_2{}^{15}O$ into the bloodstream, she begins performing a cognitive task. At this point, it is useful to think back to the earlier section in this chapter on *The metabolic demands of the action potential and of synaptic activity*. In a "hearing words" task, for example, increases in the activity of the brain tissue engaged in processing this auditory information will trigger an increase in the delivery of arterial blood to this region. With $H_2{}^{15}O$ PET, such changes in regional cerebral blood flow (rCBF) are quantified as changes in "PET counts" detected by the scanner (i.e., a high number of photons emanating from a location in the brain indicates that there is a high concentration of $H_2{}^{15}O$ molecules at that location).

Because the entire brain is always consuming large amounts of arterial blood (20% of the energy consumption of the body), task-based imaging requires image subtraction in order for the results from the scanning session to be interpretable. To identify brain areas involved in "hearing words," for example, Petersen et al. (1988) acquired two scans per subject: one was an "experimental" scan acquired while the subject is fixating (visually) a point on the screen and listening to the auditory presentation of words, and the second was a "control" scan acquired while the subject was only fixating a point on the screen. Then they subtracted the resultant control image from the experimental image (*Figure 4.20*). Note that although some form of subtraction is required by most brain-measurement techniques (including EEG, MEG, fMRI, and some applications of PET) in order to effect a baseline normalization, the term "cognitive subtraction" refers to a specific experimental strategy that will come up periodically in the book, and that we will consider in more detail in the next section.

FIGURE 4.20 PET scans of word processing, illustrating the logic of image subtraction.

A

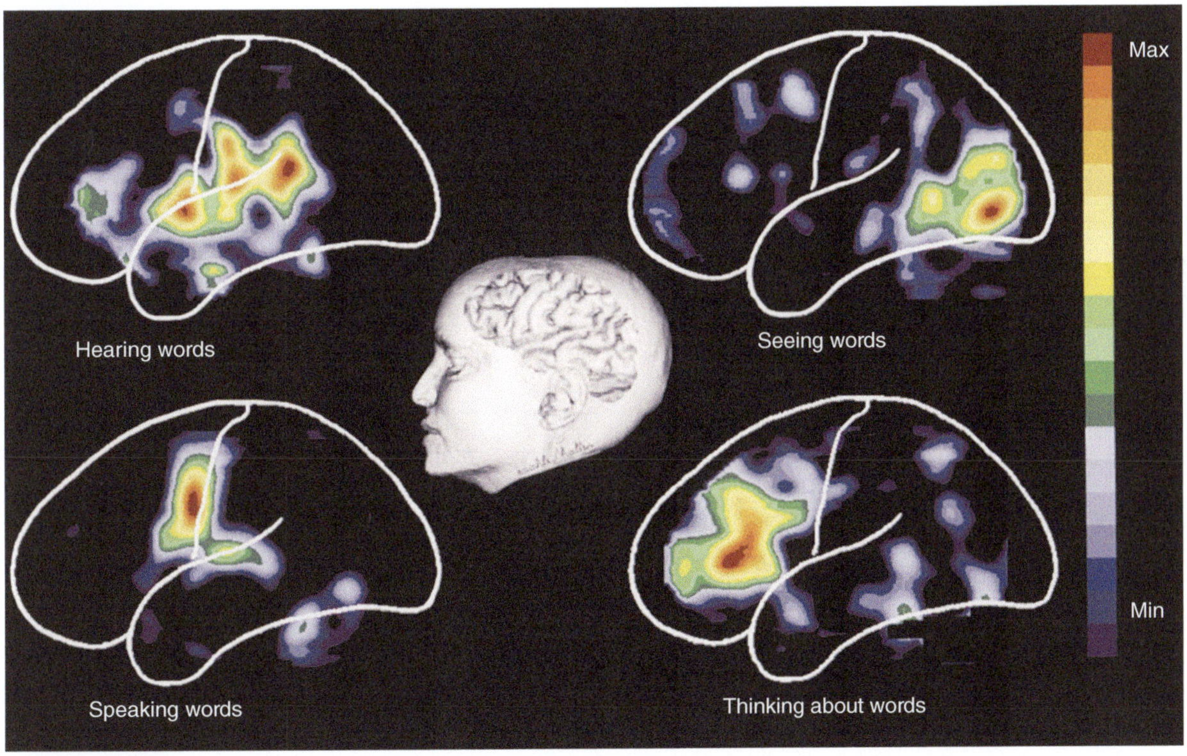

FIGURE 4.20.A PET subtraction images of rCBF when subjects perform the labeled cognitive operation vs. a matched control condition. For *Hearing words* and *Seeing words*, the contrast is vs. the fixation of a point on the screen. For *Speaking words*, the contrast is vs. *Seeing words*. For *Thinking about words*, the task was to think about a use for the presented word (e.g., for the word "cake," the subject might think "eat"), and the contrast is vs. *Speaking words*.

Source: Reproduced with permission from Petersen et al. (1988) / Springer Nature.

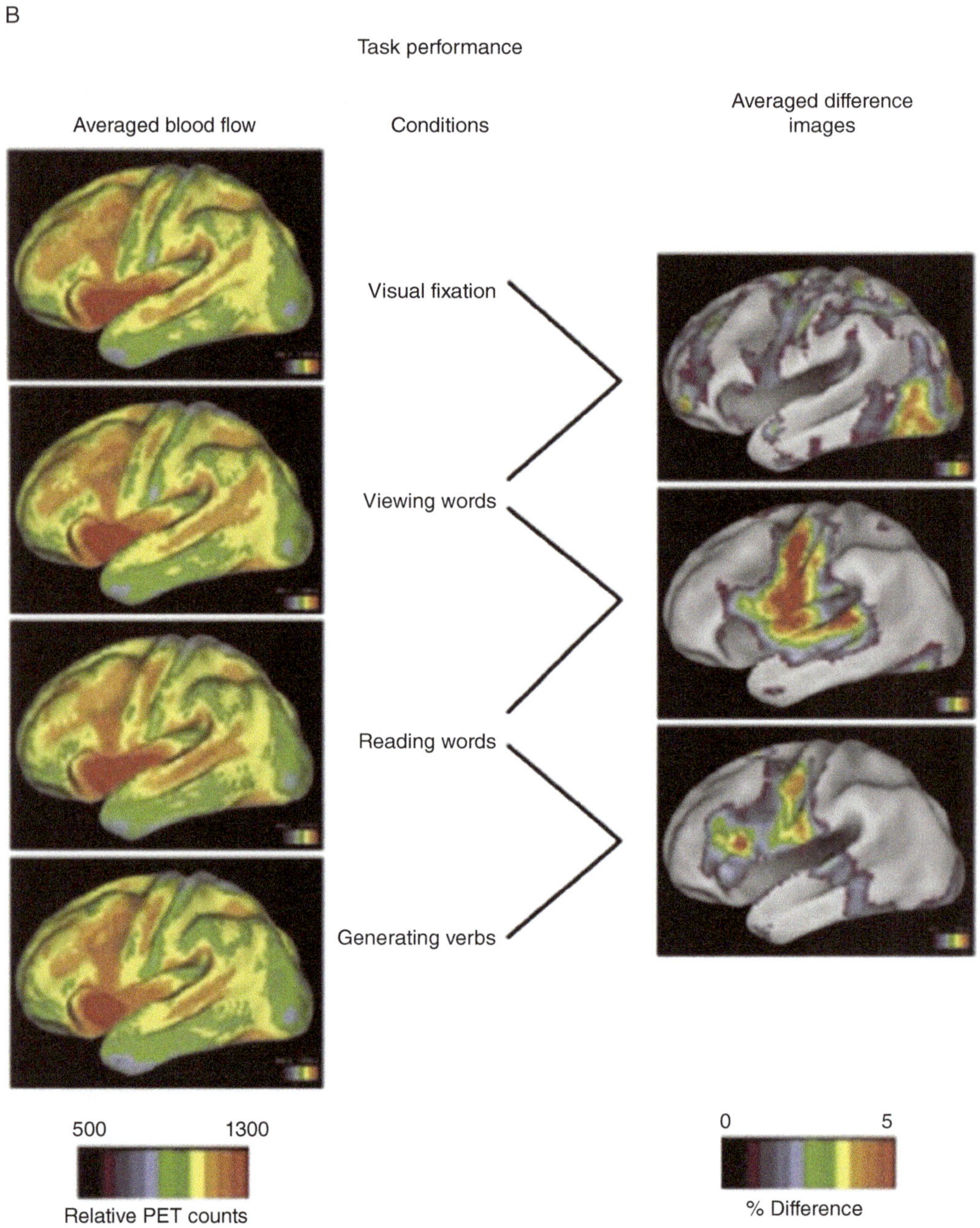

FIGURE 4.20.B A different way to represent the Petersen et al. (1988) data. The right-hand column presents three of the rCBF contrast images from *Figure 4.18.A* (now looking more "modern" because the activity maps are warped onto inflated left hemispheres). The top image is *Seeing Words*, the middle image is *Speaking Words*, and the bottom *Thinking About Words*. Note that no task-related changes in rCBF exceed 5% of the baseline level of rCBF. The left-hand column shows the unsubtracted rCBF images associated with each of the four conditions used to generate the subtraction images in the right-hand column. Try covering up the labels, as Dr. Raichle has been wont to do during presentations, and see if you think you'd be able to identify which unsubtracted rCBF image corresponds to which behavioral condition.

Source: Reproduced from Raichle et al. (2010) / with permission of Elsevier.

Near-Infrared Spectroscopy

Near-infrared light passes through the scalp, and different wavelengths are then absorbed by oxygenated vs. deoxygenated hemoglobin, thereby producing a BOLD signal. Although the optics are such that only superficial regions of cortex can be imaged, portability and ease of use relative to fMRI make it a preferred tool for pediatric neuroimaging, including by "developmental cognitive neuroscientists" who study cognition and brain development in infants. In the same way that the "f" in "fMRI" designates that it is an application of MRI that is sensitive to time-varying physiological signals, when used to study cognition, near-infrared spectroscopy is often referred to as "fNIRS".

Some Considerations for Experimental Design

The generic cognitive neuroscience experiment can be summarized (and simplified) as *recording brain activity from a subject while they perform a cognitive psychology task*. For the purposes of this consideration of experimental design, let's return to a variant of a fairly straightforward task that we've already considered: one-at-a-time visual presentation of drawings that each require a button press to indicate if they depict a living or nonliving object. This task lends itself to addressing many different kinds of questions about cognition. For example, one might use it, or a variant, to study visual perception, perceptual decision-making, categorization, semantics (i.e., the representation of meaning), or motor control. Independent of the cognitive domain of interest, however, the method that one uses to measure neural activity will constrain how the task can be designed and the data analyzed.

What if we were interested in the visual perception of these drawings? With EEG or with fMRI, we could carry out an event-related design in which we separated and averaged signals from trials presenting living vs. nonliving things, and time-locked them to stimulus onset. The EEG data could be analyzed to generate ERPs or spectrally transformed to generate TFRs. With fMRI, because of the sluggishness of the HRF, we would need to either separate each trial by 16-or-more seconds, to allow the signal to return to baseline after each trial, or randomize the order in which living and nonliving trials are presented. The benefit of randomization is that the ITI can be shortened, and so more trials can be presented during a fixed period of time; the drawback is that the effect size will be much smaller with a shorter ITI (*Figure 4.21*). With ^{15}O PET, however, the SNR is sufficiently low that only one number (per voxel) can be acquired per several-minute-long scan (e.g., "the visual cortex had an activity level of 1153 PET counts during the 6-minute-long block of performing 'living things' trials"). This necessitates the use of a block design, in which many trials of the same kind are performed in quick succession (i.e., short ITIs), and the signal is aggregated to yield one value.

Designing an experiment with a block-design procedure raises an additional set of considerations. The most obvious issue for our experiment is that a block of trials that each involves *view*, *decide*, and *press button* stages will necessarily generate brain activity that reflects more than just visual perception – it will be "contaminated" by contributions from the decision making and the button-pressing portions of each trial. Here's where cognitive subtraction comes in. One could design a control task in which, for example, a nonsense pattern of lines is presented at the beginning of each trial, and the subject judges whether the pattern is more dense on the right or left half of the image and pushes a button accordingly. The logic of this approach is that resultant subtractions of (Living – Control) and (Nonliving – Control) would reflect the differences in visual processing of viewing a real object vs. viewing a meaningless pattern of lines, but no contamination from decision-making nor from button pressing, because both the experimental and the control tasks included these, and so the signal associated with those processes would be subtracted out. One caveat from applying this logic of cognitive subtraction that should be obvious right away is that if the elements being subtracted out in an analysis aren't perfectly matched, components of them might be left over. Let's say, for example, that the left/right judgment required in the control task is simply a lot easier than the living/nonliving judgment required in the experimental task, such that the latter takes an average of 500 msec longer for the subject to complete. Assuming that the stimulus onset asynchrony (SOA) of the two tasks is identical (as it should be for any self-respecting control condition), the amount of "task" contributing to the aggregated-across-the-block signal from the experimental task will exceed that from the control task. How can one be sure, then, whether any differences that may be revealed by the (Experimental – Control) comparison are due to differences in the perception of a real object vs. a pattern, vs. some other factor, such as increased anxiety on the part of the subject of getting responses to the more difficult living/nonliving pictures incorrect, or even something as seemingly trivial as simply having spent more time on task in the experimental condition? The point of both of these possible concerns is to highlight a fundamental caveat about cognitive subtraction: the results of a cognitive-subtraction analysis are only amenable to straightforward interpretation if the two conditions *only* differ by the factor that is explicitly changed for the control task.

Another issue that we haven't addressed with our hypothetical block design, but that may be problematic, is that we've been assuming that our experimental task would consist of blocks of only living objects and blocks of only nonliving objects, in addition to blocks of the control task. After all, if we combined living and nonliving within the same block, how could we ever hope to learn about how the processing of one differs from the processing of the other? A possible problem with this, however, is the behavioral strategy that might arise from seeing only a series of living things (e.g., a cat, a tree, an inchworm, a dolphin, and so on) and pressing the "living" button each time. I'll leave it to the reader to think about why this might be problematic, and how one might try to address this concern.

Figure 4.21 also addresses a fact that is specific to the low-pass-filtering properties of the fMRI signal: the SNR of fMRI block designs is inherently superior to the SNR of fMRI event-related designs. This is evident from the fact that the magnitude of the response associated with single events in the simulation (a maximum of 1% signal change relative to baseline) is markedly smaller in magnitude than the change in signal intensity in the 144-second blocks featuring the shorter ITIs. Therefore, absent any other considerations, a block design

FIGURE 4.21 Simulations of fMRI signal in an experiment with multiple identical events (1-second long visual checkerboard presentations, as in *Figure 4.16*) and with different-length interstimulus intervals (ISI).

Source: Buckner et al., 1988 / Wolters Kluwer Health.

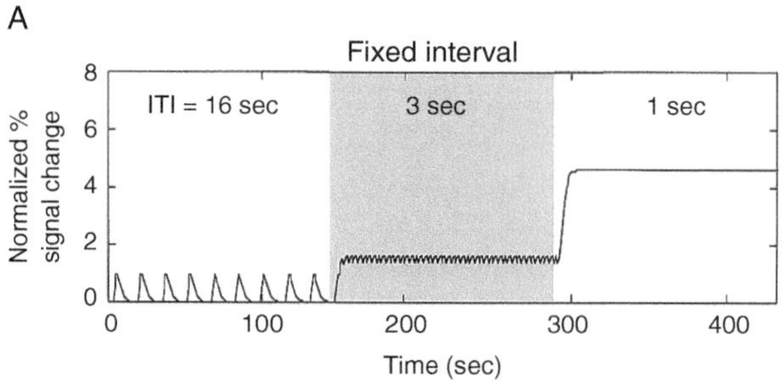

FIGURE 4.21.A fMRI signal intensity across each of three concatenated blocks of 144 seconds each, illustrating the responses to nine events separated by 15-second ISIs, to 36 events separated by 3-second ISIs, and to 72 events separated by 1-second ISIs. Note the two countervailing trends as the number of events increases and the SOA decreases: the amplitude of the average response to individual events decreases (indeed, the signal saturates and responses to individual events are no longer detectible with an ISI of 1 second), and the mean value of the signal, aggregated across each 144-second block, increases (from roughly 1% signal change, to nearly 2%, to slightly above 4%).

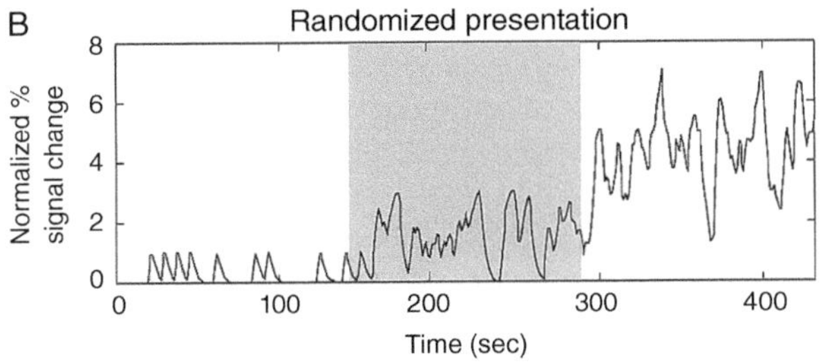

FIGURE 4.21.B Responses to the same number of events as in *Figure 4.19.A*, with the same average ISI, but with the actual ISI randomized from event to event.

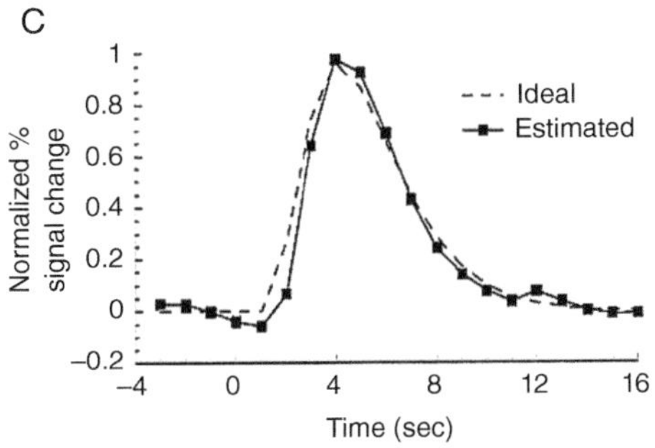

FIGURE 4.21.C An estimate of the HRF derived from the time course of the randomized ISI condition from *Figure 4.19.B*. The analysis that generated this estimate is a variant of multiple regression that has come to be known as "linear deconvolution." This estimated HRF is superimposed on the "ideal" HRF that was used to generate the responses in *Figure 4.19.A* and *Figure 4.19.B* (Burock et al., 1998).

will always generate fMRI data with greater statistical sensitivity than will an event-related design. This can be a particularly compelling factor if one is carrying out a study in which the stimuli don't lend themselves to randomization. Consider if, in our living/nonliving scenario, for example, our primary interest was in the neural bases of the decision and resulting motor response. There'd be no way to isolate the button press from the remainder of the trial, because one can't meaningfully randomize the order of picture presentations and button presses.

Pupillometry

How do you "read somebody's mind" (without measuring activity in their brain – "brain reading" is something that we'll get to in the next chapter. . .)? If you talk to a successful poker player, they'll tell you that opponents often have "tells" – gestures or expressions or reactions that, although sometimes made without awareness, can be used by a savvy observer to deduce what a person is thinking, or at least what was their initial reaction to an event. Often the culprit is the eyes, which have famously been said to act as a "window to the soul." Here, the focus is on the pupil, the dark-appearing portion of the lens that is visible on the surface of the eye, surrounded by the colored ring of the iris (which defines your eye color as brown, blue, gray, or green). The iris and the surrounding white-colored sclera are effectively opaque, making the pupil the aperture through which light reaches the retina. You already know that the pupil will dilate (grow larger) in low-light and constrict in response to bright light – reflexes that help the retina adapt to ambient lighting conditions – and you may know that it will similarly change diameter as a function of focal distance – because the aperture of the pupil also influences the optics of the eye. The reason that pupillometry (relating measurements of the diameter of the pupil to different conditions) is of interest to cognitive neuroscientists, however, is that it similarly dilates and constricts in response to internal factors, including arousal, attention, and mental effort. Indeed, a recent taxonomy proposed by Strauch et al. (2022) posits three levels of factors that influence pupil diameter: the *low* level of ambient light level and focal distance; an *intermediate* level corresponding to the stimulus and cognitively nonspecific factors of alerting and orienting (which, in the conceptualization of these authors, are partly dissociable factors that together comprise the construct of arousal); and a *high* level that relates to what they refer to as "executive functioning," and what this book will most often refer to as "cognitive control." *Figure 4.22* illustrates the nuclei and regions that instantiate each of these three levels. Many of these will become more familiar after reaching *Chapter 9, Oculomotor control and the control of attention*. (Note that the second sentence of the *Figure 4.22* legend highlights the fact that most

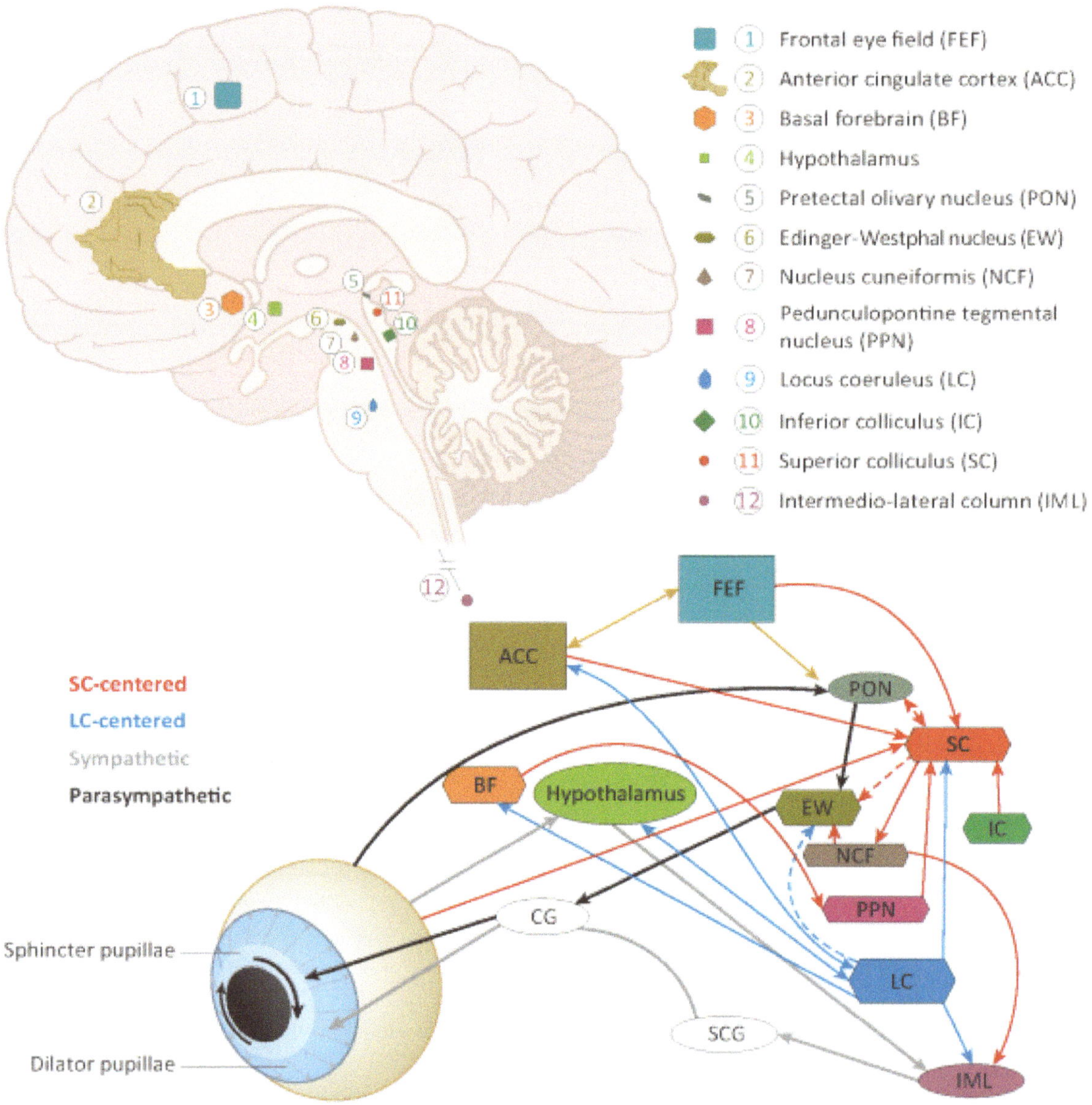

FIGURE 4.22 The neural control of pupil diameter. The most proximal influences on pupil diameter are the antagonistically related muscle groups that constrict – sphincter pupillae – and dilate – dilator pupillae – the iris. These muscles are controlled by parasympathetic and sympathetic inputs, respectively, from the ciliary ganglion (CG; located immediately caudal to the orbit of the eye) and the superior cervical ganglion (SCG; located in the cervical spinal cord). The box-and-arrow portion of this figure illustrates the taxonomy of Strauch et al. (2022), with "low" level components in ovals connected by black (parasympathetic) and gray (sympathetic) arrows and "intermediate" (hexagons) and "high" level (squares) components connected by red and blue arrows that designate assignation with the proposed locus coeruleus (LC)-linked "alerting" system or superior colliculus (SC)-linked "orienting" system. Yellow arrows denote anatomical connections that are not implicated in control of pupil diameter.

Source: (Strauch, Wang, Einhäuser, van der Stigchel, & Naber, 2022) / with permission of Elsevier.

of the verbiage in this section, including its title, is off-base in a literal sense, because the pupil itself doesn't change size or shape, rather, it's dilation vs. constriction of the iris that reveals less or more, respectively, of the pupil.)

The method for acquiring pupillometry is quite straightforward to explain, because these data come "for free" as an inherent component of eyetracking data. That is, most eyetrackers track the direction of gaze from the reflection of infrared light and infer direction of gaze from the movement of the boundary between pupil and iris/sclera. For decades, eyetracking/pupillometry data have been acquired in conjunction with EEG, and it is also now commonplace to do so during fMRI scanning. With EEG, the subject will often be stabilized with a chin rest/chin-forehead rest and the eyetracking camera placed next to the computer screen and aimed at the eye. With MRI scanning, many facilities project stimulus images into the bore of the magnet and onto a small screen that's affixed near the subject's head, then viewed in reflection off a mirror that's affixed to the RF headcoil itself. The optics are tricky, but an RF-based eyetracking system can also operate via the same setup. Alternatively, some facilities use fiberoptic goggles to display images to subjects, and these can be outfitted to also collect eyetracking data.

Computational Models and Analytic Approaches

The author has done his best in this chapter to avoid, as much as possible, straying into specific content domains (e.g., visual perception or speech production). This will be more difficult to pull off, however, in this final section, because it covers aspects of our science that are difficult to discuss without reference to the domains of cognition with which they engage. Beyond the specific examples used here to introduce them, these are approaches and ideas that have become increasingly prominent and influential during the past several years and that are playing important roles in shaping the direction of contemporary cognitive neuroscience.

Neural Network Modeling

Neural network models are computer programs composed of multiple simulated processing units (sometimes referred to as "nodes") that are interconnected so that they can pass signals from one to another. As the name implies, these networks take inspiration from what is known about operating principles of networks of neurons in the brain. In particular, individual units are built with response properties that mimic those of neurons (i.e., the functions that determine what will be the output of a unit given different levels of input), and the connections between units are designed to be able to change their weights in a manner that mimics rules of synaptic plasticity. The units in neural network models are organized into layers, the simplest being two-layer feedforward networks in which patterns of activation are presented to an input layer, and units in the input layer then each send their level of activity to the units in the output layer with which they are connected. The "feedforward" designation means that activity can only flow in one direction; a unit in the output layer cannot send signals to the input layer. The network will typically carry out some kind of transformation of the original pattern, such that the pattern of activity that emerges in the output layer is different from the pattern of activity that had been fed to the input layer. Importantly, this transformation is construed as a model for "information processing" as it is carried out by the brain system(s) being modeled.

In addition to input and output layers, most neural network models have one or more "hidden layers," so-called because they neither receive input from the (simulated) outside world nor do they send output to it. Rather, they are internal to the workings of the network, receiving input from an upstream layer and sending output to a downstream layer.

Neural network models (sometimes also referred to as "artificial neural networks," ANNs) can be designed to address scientific questions at different levels of abstraction. Here, we will consider three examples: a parallel distributed processing (PDP) model of semantic cognition; a recurrent neural network (RNN) model of visual working memory; and a deep neural network (DNN) of visual object recognition. The PDP model addresses the "high-level" question of *how is meaning represented by a large pool of undifferentiated processing units, none of which "knows" anything about the world?* The RNN model addresses *what is the representational geometry of stimulus information while it is held in "in mind"?* The DNN addresses *what are the processing steps needed to get from a "raw visual image" to the ability to categorize an object as being an animal, a boat, a car, a chair, a face, a piece of fruit, an airplane, or a table.*

A PDP Model of Picture Naming The model illustrated in *Figure 4.23* was developed to assess a theory of how the brain processes knowledge about the visual world, as operationalized by seeing an object and generating the appropriate verbal label or hearing a name and knowing what object is being referred to. It is an example of a PDP model. Its units have nonlinear response properties modeled after neurons, in that their activation level is determined by a nonlinear function, such as a sigmoid. (I.e., if the activation state of a unit is really low or really high, a small change in input won't make much difference; its midrange, in contrast, is highly sensitive to small changes in the input.) The architecture of this particular model (but not of all PDP models) differs from the *input→hidden→output* organization of the generic neural network model in that activity can be propagated in either direction so as to capture the fact that humans can process information about objects "in both directions." At a gist level, to simulate naming, a pattern of activity is input to the visual layer, and that activity propagates to the hidden layer (called the "semantic layer" in this specific model); the resultant input triggers recurrent activity within the semantic/hidden layer, the resultant pattern of which then propagates to the verbal layer, from which the resultant pattern of activity in the Names division of the verbal layer is interpreted as the network's attempt to name the object (as though it were speaking aloud). To simulate understanding a spoken word (i.e., "going in the other direction"), a pattern of activity is input to the Names subdivision of the verbal layer, activity then flows to the semantic/hidden layer, the pattern of activity resulting from recurrent activation in the semantic/hidden layer then propagates to the Perceptual, Functional, and Encyclopedic divisions of the verbal layer and to the visual layer, and the resultant patterns of

FIGURE 4.23 Architecture of the model.
Source: Adapted from Rogers et al., 2004.

A

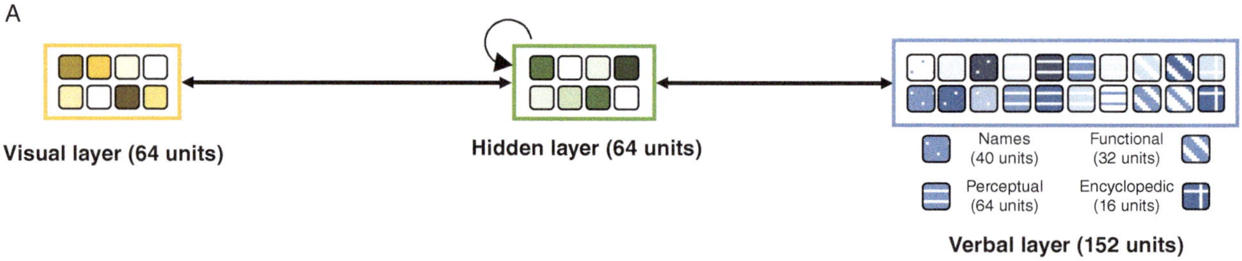

FIGURE 4.23.A 40 objects were selected as stimuli, each belonging to one of six semantic categories, three of these corresponding to living things (birds, mammals, and fruits) and three to nonliving things (vehicles, tools, household objects). The semantic properties of these stimulus items had been derived empirically by asking a group of human subjects to list attributes for each of them. Based on these "norms," the verbal layer was divided into four subdivisions, each corresponding to a category of verbal statements that can be made about an object: names, perceptual properties, functional properties, and encyclopedic properties. Within each subdivision of the verbal layer, individual units corresponded to a feature that applied to one or more of the 48 stimulus items. Units in the Names subdivision could refer to different levels of specificity (e.g., *animal*, *bird*, or *swan*); example units from the Visual Properties subdivision included *has eyes* and *has wheels*; from the Functional Properties subdivision included *can fly* and *can roll*; and from the Encyclopedic Properties subdivision included *lives in Africa* and *found in kitchen*. Within the visual layer's 64 units, each unit corresponded to a feature that had been identified in drawings that human subjects were asked to make of each of the stimulus items (e.g., *has stripes* or *is round*). In this way, the visual layer could capture similarity structure: the 64-D visual representation of, for example, the stimulus items "sparrow" and "finch" would be more similar to each other in terms of shared units than would either one be to "eagle," but the visual representations of any pair from these three would be much more similar than would be any one of them to "airplane."

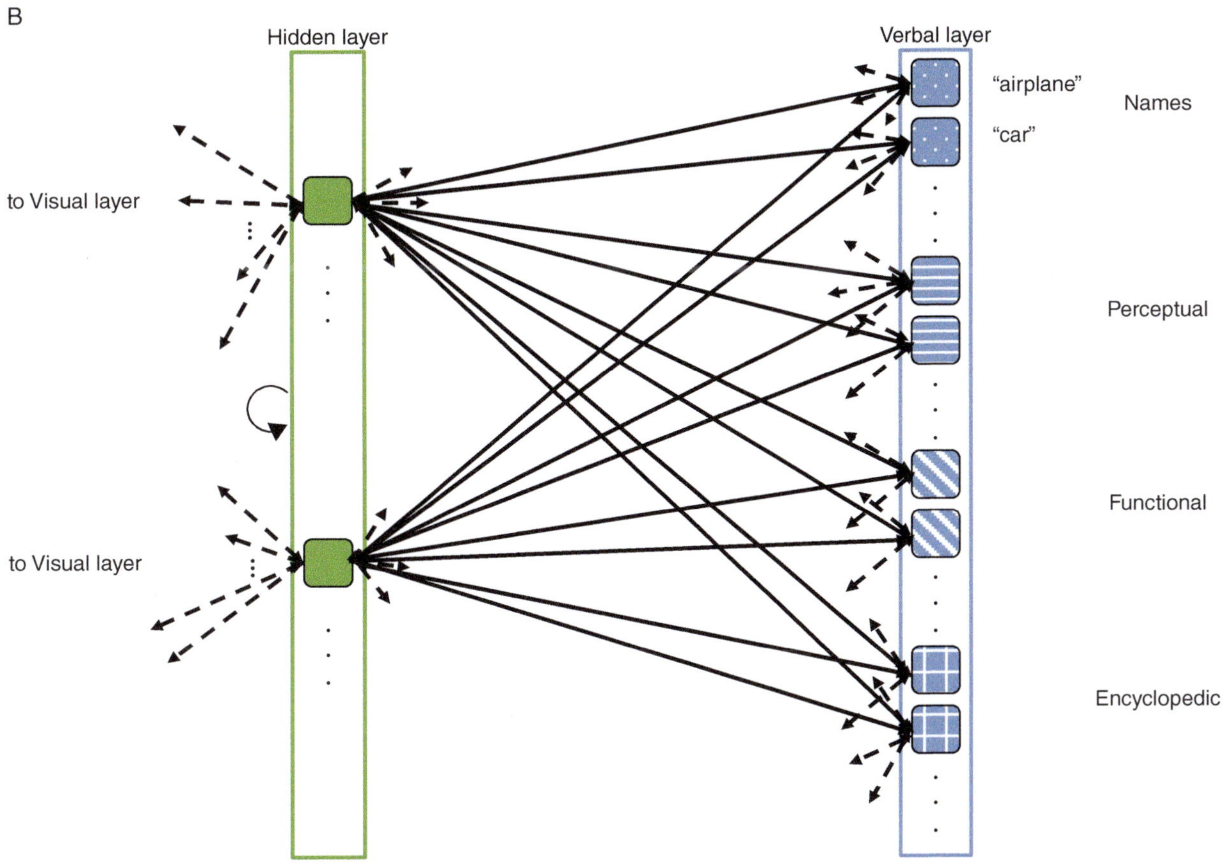

FIGURE 4.23.B Zoom-in on two units in each subdivision of the verbal layer and two units in the hidden layer, illustrating the reciprocal connection of these units, the absence of connections between units in the verbal layer, and the interconnectivity of all units within the hidden layer (indicated by arrow "circling back on itself").

activity in these subdivisions of the verbal layer and in the visual layer are interpreted as the network's attempt to "think about" the visual characteristics of the object whose name has just been spoken. A higher level of detail about the PDP model from Rogers et al. (2004) is provided in *Figure 4.23*.

The motivation for the Rogers et al. (2004) model (*Figure 4.23*) was to demonstrate the plausibility of the idea that an information processing system like the brain can carry out simple tasks that we think of as requiring knowledge about the world (e.g., answering the question *Can an ostrich fly?*) without there being explicit representations of this knowledge stored in the system. (We'll get to the context for this model, and some alternative accounts, in *Chapter 13: Semantic long-term memory*.) Importantly, it wouldn't be very compelling, nor very informative, if one were to simply build a network in which the Name unit for *ostrich* was deliberately wired up such that it would activate the Functional Properties unit for *lives in Africa* and the Visual unit for *has feathers*. Such a model would be no different than a talking doll that one can buy at a toy store. What *would* be impressive, however, and potentially informative for generating ideas about how the brain might solve the task of interest, would be if one could demonstrate that a network with the architecture described in *Figure 4.23*, starting out with no "knowledge" about what might differentiate an ostrich from an airplane, or whether or not most birds can fly, could *learn* these facts such that, with enough training, it could perform at near-human levels of accuracy. And it would be even more impressive if, once it had been so trained, it could perform at a similarly high level with new items that it had never encountered during training.

To initiate a training trial that would simulate the verbal presentation of the name "ostrich," one would set the *ostrich* unit in the Names subdivision of the Verbal layer to a value of 1, all the other units in the Names subdivision of the verbal layer to a value of 0, and then observe the resultant patterns of activation taken on by all the remaining units in the network.

(Each unit can vary in value between 0 and 1, and the resting level of activity of any unit in this model was approximately 0.19.) The next step would be to compare the final activation level in every unit in the verbal and visual layers vs. the ideal activation level that should have been produced in order for a complete representation of "ostrich" to have been activated, and to register the error (i.e., the difference between the ideal activation level and the actual activation level on that trial). (The ideal activation level for "ostrich," e.g., would have values of 1 for the nodes *animal*, *bird*, *has feathers*, *can walk*, etc., and values of 0 for such nodes as *has wheels*, *can fly*, *can roll*, and *found in kitchen*.) For each unit, the error value would be used to calculate how the weight of each connection to that unit from the semantic/hidden layer, plus the weight of each unit-to-unit connection within the semantic/hidden layer, would need to be changed in order to decrease the magnitude of the error at that unit the next time "ostrich" was presented. The final step in this trial, then, would be to deliver the "teaching signal" that actually implements these adjustments of the weights of connections within the model.

To illustrate this process at a very concrete level, let's walk through this trial again, but now starting from the perspective of the *lives in Africa* unit in the Encyclopedic properties subdivision of the verbal layer. Because the model starts out with randomized connection weights, the activation level of this unit will have only changed slightly, and in an arbitrary way, in response to the presentation of "ostrich." But let's say that on this trial, its activation level increased slightly. Important for understanding the process of training the model is to realize that, although the *ostrich* unit and the *lives in Africa* unit are not connected directly, they do connect indirectly through 64 paths, because each connects directly to every unit in the semantic/hidden layer. Because the level of activity of each unit in the semantic/hidden layer will also have changed in response to the presentation of "ostrich," the teaching signal would tend to strengthen the semantic/hidden-to-*lives in Africa* connections for the semantic/hidden units whose activation also increased. The consequence of these adjustments would be that the next time "ostrich" was spoken, the resultant activation in these critical semantic/hidden units would have a stronger influence on the activation of the *lives in Africa* unit. Taking such a restricted view of the dynamics of the model, however, misses key principles of how it works. What if one were to also consider, for example, the *ostrich*-to-semantic/hidden connections? Although at first one might assume that the connections to all semantic/hidden units that increased in activation would also be strengthened, this fails to take into account that each of those semantic/hidden units is also connected to EVERY other node in the Encyclopedic, the Perceptual, and the Functional, subdivisions of the verbal layer, as well as to the Visual layer. Thus, whether any individual *ostrich*-to-semantic/hidden connection gets strengthened or weakened will also depend on how that semantic/hidden unit's response to "ostrich" relates to the concurrent change in the activation of each of the other 215 units in those layers with which it is connected (i.e., of the *found in kitchen* unit, of the *has wheels* unit, of the *can walk* unit, of the *meows* unit, and so on). The software that's implementing the training of the network applies a gradient descent algorithm to modify each of the [(64 * 64)+(216 * 64) =] 17,920 connections involved on that trial such that, the next time "ostrich" is presented to the network, the overall error from the response of these 216 units will be smaller. The procedure for modifying these connections is referred to as the backpropagation of the error signal. (Note that, in relation to an actual human brain, which has trillions of synaptic connections, the total of 17,920 connections in this model is quite modest. Nonetheless, one can readily see how, even in such a relatively "small" network, we have to grapple with complexity of the kind invoked by Buszsáki [2006] in *Chapter 2*.)

One important property of this PDP model that will distinguish it from other ANNs is that each processing step is serial and unidirectional. To illustrate, recall that *to simulate the verbal presentation of the name "ostrich," one would set the* ostrich *unit in the Names subdivision of the Verbal layer to a value of 1, all the other units in the Names subdivision of the verbal layer to a value of 0, and then observe the resultant patterns of activation taken on by all the remaining units in the network*. One way to describe this is that the trial begins with the activation of the *ostrich* unit, upon which a wave of activation flows from the Verbal layer to the semantic/hidden layer, after which this wave of activation flows from the semantic/hidden layer to the visual layer. And we can get more precise: The chain of events is that first, the value of the ostrich unit in the Names subdivision of the Verbal layer is set to 1; second, the activation values of each of the units in the semantic/hidden layer are updated simultaneously; then third, the activation values of each of the units of the Visual layer are updated simultaneously.

Zooming back out to the overall process of carrying out this experiment, the training of the model would proceed with the serial presentation to the model of each of the remaining patterns corresponding to a feature represented in the Verbal and the Visual layers, adjusting the network's weights after each presentation. Once the full set of features had been presented, the process would start all over again, this time with a different order of presentation. Typically, a PDP model like this will be trained with hundreds or thousands of full cycles of training. Additionally, the entire process of conducting thousands of training cycles will, itself, often be carried out several times, each time starting with a new random set of initial connection weights.

How is it determined if a PDP modeling experiment has been successful? The answer will differ depending on the context, but let's consider this model from Rogers et al. (2004). As indicated earlier, the researchers' motivation for carrying out this work was to test the plausibility of a broader theory that posits, in part, that knowledge about objects may not be stored in the brain as discrete, fully encapsulated representations of, say, "ostrich-ness" or "airplane-ness," but, rather, as "nothing more" than sets of connections that link together all of an object's attributes. Thus, the fact that they could successfully train their model to simulate successful performance on a large number of cognitive tasks that depend on object knowledge (e.g., picture naming, drawing, and word-to-picture matching) was taken as evidence for the plausibility of their theory. At a more rigorous level of assessment, one important characteristic of a successful model can be its ability to generalize to new stimuli. That is, one might argue that this model's performance wouldn't have strong implications for theories of semantics if, after all those thousands of training iterations, it was only able to demonstrate a high level of performance with those same 40 items with which it had been trained. More impressive would be if one could feed the fully trained network a stimulus that it had never seen before, and it would be able to correctly answer questions about it. For example, if one were to present a set of encyclopedic, functional, and perceptual features that the network had never encountered on a single trial (corresponding to an object that it had never encountered before, like a turkey, or a helicopter), would it generate a reasonable visual representation? A second criterion that is often applied to neural network models, including PDP models, is if their behavior matches human behavior in principled ways. In *Chapter 13*, for example, we'll see how selectively "lesioning" elements in models similar to that from Rogers et al. (2004) can produce deficits in performance that resemble the deficits observed in human patients with particular patterns of brain damage.

It is important to note that although the artificial neurons in PDP models like the one we just considered draw inspiration from real neurons and have some neuron-like properties, the goal of this modeling is not intended to elucidate how neurons in the brain actually process information. Rather, as we have just seen, they typically address relatively "high-level" questions about some aspect of cognition and are interpreted in terms of how this aspect of cognition might be accomplished by a massively distributed network. The two classes of ANN that we will next introduce – recurrent neural networks (RNNs) and deep neural networks (DNNs) – are intended to more closely simulate different aspects of how biological brains function.

Recurrent Neural Networks According to some accounts, in the first decade of this century, computational neuroscience was in something of a rut. Although feedforward networks using backpropagation, such as PDP models, had led to many insights about ways in which cognitive problems could be solved at an algorithmic level, the biological implausibility of backpropagation made them ill-suited as models of mammalian brain function. A breakthrough occurred when, in 2009, David Sussillo and Larry Abbott (2009) proposed a solution to a puzzle from electrophysiological studies of skeletomotor control, which was *How can apparently chaotic spontaneous activity [which is observed prior to the execution of movement] be reorganized into the coherent patterns required to generate controlled actions?* Their solution was to build a network whose hidden layer included recurrent connections, such that once it was fed new information (for our present purposes, "given something new to do") it would continue to process this information (to "actively churn") for an extended period of time, with the strengths of connections between units adjusting in response to this recurrent activity. The technical details are beyond the scope of this book, but among the advances in this "recurrent neural network" (RNN) architecture were these two: (1) the fact that the network was trained by feeding back onto itself signals that contained information about synaptic modification within the hidden layer (i.e., it was trained, in part, by learning about its own dynamics); and (2) solving the problem of training in a network with ongoing chaotic activity that is present prior to any stimulus presentation. With regard to the second point, there's an aspect of PDP modeling that we haven't emphasized until now, and that's a sense in which they "cheat" by artificially initiating each trial of training with all the units in the network inactivated, their activity only triggered by the presentation of information to the network. In Chapter 5, section Recurrent Neural Networks, we'll take a much deeper dive into RNNs, in the context of performing a working memory task, and consider how they lend themselves to the study of "representational geometry."

Deep Neural Networks The "deep" in DNN refers to the fact that these networks employ more than one hidden layer. Unlike the RNN that we considered in the previous section, DNNs have an explicit directionality, or hierarchy, with an input layer feeding into an early processing layer, which feeds into an intermediate processing layer, and so on. Although DNNs have applications outside of computational neuroscience, the majority of research with DNNs that will be relevant for our purposes has been on the analysis of sensory signals, including visual image classification and auditory speech perception. Here we'll summarize one example of the kind of problem that DNNs are good at solving.

A pioneering demonstration of "deep learning" with a DNN was published in 2012 by Alex Krizhevsky, Ilya Sutskever, and Geoffrey Hinton[4], who trained of a deep convolutional neural network (DCNN) on 1.2 million photographic images taken from the internet (the ImageNet database – consequently, their DCNN acquired the nickname "AlexNet"), each of which had been labeled as belonging to one of 1000 different categories by human labelers. Next, they presented to the trained network 150,000 images that it had never previously processed. Performance on these 150,000 was on the order of 85% correct, which was record-setting at the time. (The performance of DNNs has gotten much better since then.) Important points to emphasize here are that the data fed to the input layer of the DCNN were not "hand-coded" with predetermined labels like "has wings" or "can roll," as had been the case in the PDP model that we considered previously. Rather, the input layer of the Krizhevsky et al. (2012) DCNN was a 256 × 256 array of sensors, each of which was fed the color and brightness value of the corresponding pixel from the image. In *Chapter 6*, we will go into detail about how DNNs have been used to study the computations underlying primate visual perception. Thus, one generalization that can often (though not always) be true is that whereas PDP models test ideas at a more abstract or conceptual level, DNNs can be used as models of neural computations at the neuron level of analysis.

Network Science and Graph Theory

Largely spurred by the discovery of the DMN and other RSFC-defined networks, for the past several years neuroscientists have been analyzing brain networks with tools originally developed in other branches of science, including mathematics, sociology, and statistics. To get a quick sense for the relevance of these other branches of science, consider the following overview from cognitive neuroscientist Gagan Wig (2017):

> *Research on complex networks has revealed that many social, biological, and man-made networks exhibit organizational properties that support efficient design and resilience to perturbation... For example, networks often contain distinct and segregated subnetworks, and effective network function is supported by maintaining subnetwork segregation while simultaneously allowing integration across the subnetworks. Excess in either direction can be harmful for a network. Too much interconnectedness between subnetworks can lead to rapid spreading of disease, and has rendered financial networks vulnerable to sudden crisis. Conversely, too much segregation between subnetworks can result in their diminished interaction or isolation, as has been argued in reference to the increasing polarization of the network of US political interactions. (p. 981)*

Many of the measures and phenomena that are commonly encountered in network neuroscience are illustrated in *Figure 4.24*.

[4]This work contributed to Hinton being awarded the Nobel Prize in Physics in 2024.

FIGURE 4.24 Elements and properties of network models.

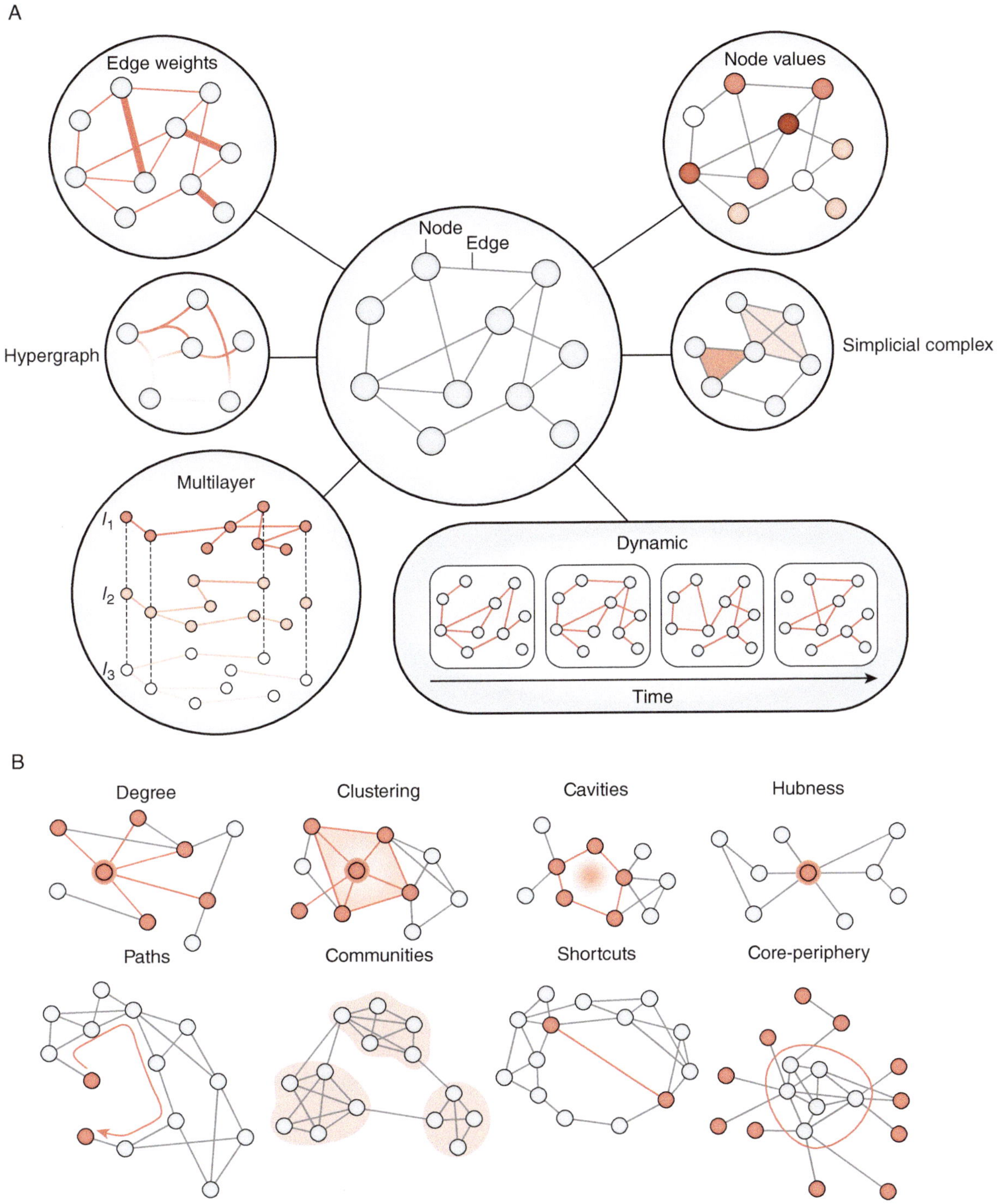

FIGURE 4.24.A Brain networks are typically represented as patterns of connections (*edges*) between neural units (*nodes*). Depending on the scale of the model, a node may represent a single neuron, a nucleus, or an entire brain region. Edges can have different weights, and nodes can have different functional properties. *Multilayer networks* can be used to represent interconnected sets of networks, and studying the *dynamic* properties of networks helps to understand the reconfiguration of network systems over time. A *hypergraph* is a graph in which a single edge can connect more than two nodes. A *simplicial complex* is a graph in which higher-order interaction terms become nodes.

FIGURE 4.24.B Common measures of interest include *degree*, the number of edges emanating from a node; *clustering*, which is related to the prevalence of triangles; *cavities*, portions of a graph where there are no edges; *hubness*, a node's influence on other nodes; *paths*, which determine the potential for information transmission; *communities*, local groups of densely interconnected nodes; *shortcuts*, a possible marker of global efficiency of information transmission; and *core-periphery structure*, which facilitates local integration of information gathered from or sent to more sparsely connected areas.

Tools from graph theory can be applied to RSFC data, as well as to functional connectivity data. With RSFC, it has been established that healthy young adult brain networks exhibit fairly segregated communities characterized by dense interactions within each community and sparser interactions between communities. With normal aging (i.e., absence of any age-related neurological disease), community segregation weakens, with relative decreases of interactions within and increases of interactions between communities. (Before the introduction of graph theory to the analysis of neuroimaging data, a similar phenomenon had already been described as a process of "dedifferentiation.") Furthermore, independent of age, individual differences in community segregation among the networks classified as "Association systems" in *Figure 4.19.C* predict cognitive ability, with greater segregation associated with superior episodic long-term memory (to be covered in *Chapter 11* and *Chapter 12*) and fluid intelligence (*Chapter 15*). Higher community segregation is also associated with better outcomes in rehabilitation after brain injury.

The examples given in the preceding paragraph treat network configuration as a trait – a set of stable properties that are characteristic of a person's brain for an extended period of time. One can also employ methods from "dynamic network neuroscience" to measure the changes in network structure that occur in real time during cognitive task performance. For example, one analysis of the data from 344 healthy individuals performing a working-memory task found that the degree of reconfiguration in networks involving the frontal cortex (frontal flexibility) was positively related to performance on the task. Measures included the probability that individual nodes changed allegiance between networks such as those illustrated in *Figure 4.19.C* during the task.

End-of-Chapter Questions

1. Why is the question of specificity so crucial for interpreting the results of a lesion study? Try to think of an example of an experimental finding for which a lack of evidence for specificity might weaken its interpretation. How might this weakness be addressed, perhaps by administering additional behavioral tasks, or by acquiring data from one or more subjects with damage to a different area of the brain?

2. For what kind of research question might tDCS be a better experimental tool than TMS? For what kind of research question might the opposite be true?

3. How can one distinguish MUA from LFP in an extracellular recording? What phenomenon, at the level of the activity of one or a group of neurons, is each of these believed to be measuring?

4. Describe the measure of PAC. Why is it of interest to cognitive neuroscientists?

5. Name a brain process that the ERP analysis technique is better able to detect and measure than a spectral analysis technique. Name a brain process for which the opposite is true.

6. What is an assumption made by the Fourier transform that is often not true of the data to which it is applied?

7. What does fMRI measure? What are the processes, at the cellular level, that can produce fluctuations in the fMRI signal?

8. What constraints do the low-pass filtering qualities of the fMRI signal impose on experimental design and analysis?

9. Summarize the three levels of factors that can influence pupil diameter. Do they correspond to different neural systems? What kinds of questions are each well suited to address?

10. How do PDP models differ from DNN models? What kinds of questions are each well suited to address?

11. What is a major feature that distinguishes RNNs from PDP models? Does one more closely emulate important properties of brain dynamics?

12. Summarize ways in which graph theory-derived measures can quantify ways in which brain function varies with individual differences in cognitive ability, and changes with age.

References

Ashburner, John, and Karl J. Friston. 2000. "Voxel-Based Morphometry—The Methods." *NeuroImage* 11 (6): 805–821. https://doi.org/10.1006/nimg.2000.0582.

Baldo, Juliana V., and Nina F. Dronkers. 2006. "The Role of Inferior Parietal and Inferior Frontal Cortex in Working Memory." *Neuropsychology* 20: 529–538.

Benson, D. Frank, and John P. Greenberg. 1969. "Visual Form Agnosia: A Specific Defect in Visual Discrimination." *Archives of Neurology* 20 (1): 82–89. doi: 10.1001/archneur.1969.00480070092010.

Bollimunta, Anil, Yonghong Chen, Charles E. Schroeder, and Mingzhou Ding. 2008. "Neuronal Mechanisms of Cortical Alpha Oscillations in Awake-Behaving Macaques." *Journal of Neuroscience* 28 (40): 9976–9988. doi: 10.1523/JNEUROSCI.2699-08.2008.

Burock, Marc A., Randy L. Buckner, Marty G. Woldorff, Bruce R. Rosen, and Anders M. Dale. 1998. "Randomized Event-Related Experimental Designs Allow for Extremely Rapid Presentation Rates Using Functional MRI." *NeuroReport* 9: 3735–3739.

Buszáki, György. 2006. *Rhythms of the Brain*. Oxford: Oxford University Press.

Butts Pauly, K., Z. Qiu, and W. Legon. 2024. "Transcranial Ultrasound Stimulation." In *The Oxford Handbook of Transcranial Stimulation*, edited by E. M. Wasserman, A. V. Peterchev, U. Ziemann, H. R. Siebner, V. Walsh, and S. H. Lisanby (pp. 251–275), 2nd ed. New York: Oxford University Press.

Darmani, Ghazaleh, Hamidreza Ramezanpour, Can Sarica, Regina Annirood, Talyta Grippe, Jean-Francois Nankoo, . . . Robert Chen. 2025. "Individualized non-invasive deep brain stimulation of the basal ganglia using transcranial ultrasound stimulation." *Nature Communications 16* (1): 2693. doi: 10.1038/s41467-025-57883-7.

Donoghue T., Haller M., Peterson E. J., Varma P., Sebastian P., Gao R., Noto T., Lara A. H., Wallis J. D., Knight R. T., Shestyuk A., and Voytek B. 2020. Parameterizing neural power spectra into periodic and aperiodic components. Nature Neuroscience, 23, 1655–1665. doi: 10.1038/s41593-020-00744-x.

Fritsch, Gustav, and Eduard Hitzig. 1870. "Über die elektrische Erregbarkeit des Grosshirns." *Archiv für Anatomie, Physiologie und wissenschaftliche Medicin* 37: 300–332.

Fulvio, J. M., S. Haegens, and B. R. Postle. 2024. "Single-pulse TMS affects working-memory performance via posterior beta-band oscillations." *Journal of Cognitive Neuroscience.* **36**: 1827–1846.

Gratton, Caterina, and Rodrigo M. Braga. 2021. "Editorial Overview: Deep Imaging of the Individual Brain: Past, Practice, and Promise." *Current Opinion in Behavioral Sciences 40*: iii–vi. doi: doi.org/10.1016/j.cobeha.2021.06.011.

Hamidi, Massihullah, Heleen A. Slagter, Giulio Tononi, and Bradley R. Postle. 2009. "Repetitive Transcranial Magnetic Stimulation Affects Behavior by Biasing Endogenous Cortical Oscillations." *Frontiers in Integrative Neuroscience* **3**: 14. doi: 10.3389/neuro.07.014.2009. PMC2707056.

Han, Liang, Neil K. Savalia, Micaela Y. Chan, Phillip F. Agres, Anupama S. Nair, and Gagan S. Wig. 2018. "Functional Parcellation of the Cerebral Cortex across the Human Adult Lifespan." *Cerebral Cortex* 28: 4403–4423.

Hubel, David H. 1988. *Eye, Brain, and Vision*. New York: Scientific American Library: Distributed by W. H. Freeman.

Jackson, Nicko, Scott R. Cole, Bradley Voytek, and Nicole C. Swann. 2019. "Characteristics of Waveform Shape in Parkinson's Disease Detected with Scalp Electroencephalography." *eNeuro* 6. doi: doi.org/10.1523/ENEURO.0151-19.2019.

Johnson, J. S., B. Kundu, A. G. Casali, and B. R. Postle. 2012. "Task dependent changes in cortical excitability and effective connectivity: A combined TMS-EEG study." *Journal of Neurophysiology* **107**: 2383–2392.

Krizhevsky, Alex, Ilya Sutskever, and Geoffrey E. Hinton. 2012. "ImageNet classification with Deep Convolutional Neural Nets." *Advances in Neural Information Processing Systems* 1: 1097–1105.

Luck, Steven J. 2005. *An Introduction to the Event-Related Potential Technique*. Cambridge, MA: MIT Press.

Malmivuo, Jaakko, and Robert Plonsey. 1995. *Bioelectromagnetism: Principles and Applications of Bioelectric and Biomagnetic Fields*. New York: Oxford University Press.

Petersen, Steven E., Peter T. Fox, Michael I. Posner, Mark Mintun, and Marcus E. Raichle. 1988. "Positron Emission Tomographic Studies of the Cortical Anatomy of Single-Word Processing." *Nature* 331 (6157): 585–589. doi: 10.1038/331585a0.

Petrof, Iraklis, Angela N. Viaene, and S. Murray Sherman. 2012. "Two Populations of Corticothalamic and Interareal Corticocortical Cells in the Subgranular Layers of the Mouse Primary Sensory Cortices." *Journal of Comparative Neurology: Research in Systems Neuroscience* 520 (8): 1678–1686. doi: 10.1002/cne.23006.

Poldrack, Russell A. 2006. "Can Cognitive Processes Be Inferred from Neuroimaging Data?." *Trends in Cognitive Sciences* 10: 59–63.

Raichle, Marcus E. 2010. "Two Views of Brain Function." *Trends in Cognitive Neuroscience* 14 (4): 180–190. doi: 10.1016/j.tics.2010.01.008.

Rogers, Timothy T., Matthew A. Lambon, Peter Garrard Ralph, Sasha Bozeat, James L. McClelland, John R. Hodges, and Karalyn Patterson. 2004. "Structure and Deterioration of Semantic Memory: A Neuropsychological and Computational Investigation." *Psychological Review* 111 (1): 205–235. doi: 10.1037/0033-295X.111.1.205.

Rossi, Simone, Mark Hallett, Paolo M. Rossini, Alvaro Pascual-Leone, and The Safety of TMS Consensus Group. 2009. "Safety, Ethical Considerations, and Application Guidelines for the Use of Transcranial Magnetic Stimulation in Clinical Practice and Research." *Clinical Neurophysiology* 120 (12): 2008–2039.

Strauch, Christoph, Chin-An Wang, Wolfgang Einhäuser, Stefan Van der Stigchel, and Marnix Naber. 2022. "Pupillometry as an Integrated Readout of Distinct Attentional Networks." *Trends in Cognitive Sciences 45*: 635–647. doi: doi.org/10.1016/j.tins.2022.05.003.

Thirugnanasambandam, Nivethida, Roland Sparing, Manuel Dafotakis, Ingo G. Meister, Walter Paulus, Michael A. Nitsche, and Gereon R. Fink. 2011. "Isometric Contraction Interferes with Transcranial Direct Current Stimulation (tDCS) Induced Plasticity – Evidence of State-Dependent Neuromodulation in Human Motor Cortex." *Restorative Neurology and Neuroscience* 29: 311–320.

Tootell, Roger B. H., Martin S. Silverman, Eugene Switkes, and Russell L. De Valois. 1982. "Deoxyglucose Analysis of Retinotopic Organization in Primate Striate Cortex." *Science* 218 (4575): 902–904. doi: 10.1126/science.7134981.

Voytek, Bradley, Ryan T. Canolty, Avgusta Shestyuk, Nathan E. Crone, Josef Parvizi, and Robert T. Knight. 2010. "Shifts in Gamma Phase-Amplitude Coupling Frequency from Theta to Alpha over Posterior Cortex During Visual Tasks." *Frontiers in Human Neurosciences* 4: 1–9.

Wang, Sisi, Sirawaj Itthipuripat, and Yixuan Ku. 2019. "Electrical Stimulation over Human Posterior Parietal Cortex Selectively Enhances the Capacity of Visual Short-Term Memory." *The Journal of Neuroscience* 39: 528–536.

Wig, Gagan. 2017. "Segregated Systems of Human Brain Networks." *Trends in Cognitive Sciences* 21: 981–996.

Other Sources Used

Aguirre, Geoffrey K., Eric Zarahn, and Mark D'Esposito. 1998. "The Variability of Human, BOLD Hemodynamic Responses." *NeuroImage* 8 (4): 360–369. doi: 10.1006/nimg.1998.0369.

Bassett, Danielle S., and Olaf Sporns. 2017. "Network Neuroscience." *Nature Neuroscience* 20: 353–364.

Bassett, Danielle S., Perry Zurn, and Joshua I. Gold. 2018. "On the Nature and Use of Models in Network Neuroscience." *Nature Reviews Neuroscience* 19: 566–578.

Biswal, Bharat, F. Zerrin Yetkin, Victor M. Haughton, and James S. Hyde. 1995. "Functional Connectivity in the Motor Cortex of Resting Human Brain Using Echo-Planar MRI." *Magnetic Resonance in Medicine* 34: 537–541.

Braun, Urs, Axel Schäfer, Henrik Walter, Susanne Erk, Nina Romanczuk-Seiferth, Leila Haddad, . . . Danielle S. Bassett. 2015. "Dynamic Reconfiguration of Frontal Brain Networks During Executive Cognition in Humans." *Proceedings of the National Academy of Sciences, USA* 112: 11678–11683.

Dale, Anders M., and Randy L. Buckner. 1997. "Selective Averaging of Rapidly Presented Individual Trials Using fMRI." *Human Brain Mapping* 5: 329–340. doi: 10.1002/(SICI)1097-0193(1997)5:5<329::AID-HBM1>3.0.CO;2-5.

Guller, Yelena, Fabio Ferrarelli, Alexander J. Shackman, Simone Sarasso, Michael J. Peterson, Frederick J. Langheim, . . . Bradley R. Postle. 2012. "Probing Thalamic Integrity in Schizophrenia Using Concurrent Transcranial Magnetic Stimulation and Functional Magnetic Resonance Imaging." *Archives of General Psychiatry* 69: 662–671.

Haxby, James V., Cheryl L. Grady, Barry Horwitz, Leslie G. Ungerleider, Mortimer Mishkin, Richard E. Carson, . . . Stanley I. Rapoport. 1991. "Dissociation of Object and Spatial Visual Processing Pathways in Human Extrastriate Cortex." *Proceedings of the National Academy of Sciences USA* 88 (5): 1621–1625. doi: 10.1073/pnas.88.5.1621.

Menon, Ravi S., and Seong-Gi Kim. 1999. "Spatial and Temporal Limits in Cognitive Neuroimaging with fMRI." *Trends in Cognitive Sciences* 3 (6): 207–215. doi: 10.1016/S1364-6613(99)01329-7.

Oztas, Emin. 2003. "Neuronal Tracing." *Neuroanatomy* 2: 2–5. http://www.neuroanatomy.org/2003/002_005.pdf.

Polanía, Rafael, Michael A. Nitsche, and Christian C. Ruff. 2018. "Studying and Modifying Brain Function with Non-invasive Brain Stimulation." *Nature Neuroscience* 21: 174–187.

Raichle, Marcus E., Ann Mary MacLeod, Abraham Z. Snyder, William J. Powers, Debra A. Gusnard, and Gordon L. Shulman. 2001. "A Default Mode of Brain Function." *Proceedings of the National Academy of Science of the United States of America* 98: 676–682.

Reinhart, Robert M. G., Josh D. Cosman, Keisuke Fukuda, and Geoffrey F. Woodman. 2017. "Using Transcranial Direct-Current Stimulation (tDCS) to Understand Cognitive Processing." *Attention, Perception, and Psychophysics* 79: 3–23.

Rogers, Timothy T., John R. Hodges, Matthew A. Lambon Ralph, and Karalyn Patterson. 2003. "Object Recognition under Semantic Impairment: The Effects of Conceptual Regularities on Perceptual Decisions." *Language and Cognitive Processes* 18 (5–6): 625–662. doi: 10.1080/01690960344000053.

Shulman, Gordon L., Julie A. Fiez, Maurizio Corbetta, Randy L. Buckner, Francis M. Miezin, Marcus E. Raichle, and Steven E. Petersen. 1997. "Common Blood Flow Changes across Visual Tasks: II. Decreases in Cerebral Cortex." *Journal of Cognitive Neuroscience* 9: 648–663.

Snyder, Abraham Z., and Marcus E. Raichle. 2012. "A Brief History of the Resting State: The Washington University Perspective." *Neuroimage* 62: 902–910.

Villringer, Arno. 2000. "Physiological Changes During Brain Activation." In *Functional MRI*, edited by C. T. W. Moonen and Peter A Bandettini (pp. 3–13). Heidelberg: Springer-Verlag.

Walsh, Vincent, and Alan Cowey. 2000. "Transcranial Magnetic Stimulation and Cognitive Neuroscience." *Nature Reviews Neuroscience* 1 (1): 73–80.

Wasserman, E. M., A. V. Peterchev, U. Ziemann, H. R. Siebner, V. Walsh, and S. H. Lisanby, eds. 2024. *The Oxford Handbook of Transcranial Stimulation*, 2nd ed. New York: Oxford University Press.

Woods, Adam J., Andrea Antal, Marom Bikson, Paulo S. Boggio, André R. Brunoni, Pablo Celnik, . . . Michael A. Nitsche. 2016. "A Technical Guide to tDCS, and Related Non-invasive Brain Stimulation Tools." *Clinical Neurophysiology* 127: 1031–1048.

Further Reading

Aguirre, G. K., and M. D'Esposito. 1999. "Experimental Design for Brain fMRI." In *Functional MRI*, edited by C. T. W. Moonen and P. A. Bandettini (pp. 369–380). Berlin: Springer-Verlag.

A comprehensive and accessible treatment of how and why the BOLD fMRI signal imposes constraints on experimental design, and of various design strategies that take these constraints into account.

Oztas, Emin. 2003. "Neuronal Tracing." *Neuroanatomy* 2: 2–5. http://www.neuroanatomy.org/2003/002_005.pdf.

A very concise overview of some of the physiology, and biochemistry, underlying anatomical tracing techniques.

Wandell, Brian A., and Jonathan Winawer. 2011. "Imaging Retinotopic Maps in the Human Brain." *Vision Research* 51 (7): 718–737. doi: 10.1016/j.visres.2010.08.004.

Nice treatment of the use of MRI for tractography. Additionally, some of the content of this paper, particularly in the section on "Functional specialization and maps," will be relevant in subsequent chapters, particularly Chapter 9.

Wasserman, E. M., A. V. Peterchev, U. Ziemann, H. R. Siebner, V. Walsh, and S. H. Lisanby, eds. 2024. *The Oxford Handbook of Transcranial Stimulation*, 2nd ed. New York: Oxford University Press.

An authoritative resource for all things transcranial stimulation.

CHAPTER 5

Theoretical Frameworks and Computational Approaches

KEY THEMES

- A memory is fundamentally an association of two (or more) previously unlinked pieces of information, and the neural bases of memory formation are believed to depend importantly on Hebbian plasticity.
- The NMDA class of glutamate receptor acts as a cell-biological coincidence detector that implements Hebbian plasticity.
- The predictive coding framework conceptualizes perception as the active process of constructing, testing, and updating internal models of the world.
- Dynamical systems theory provides a formal framework for describing how complex systems transition from one state to another and provides powerful tools for measuring and explaining the workings of the brain.
- Reinforcement learning (RL) provides a formal framework for understanding how the brain can learn about the world via trial-and-error learning and is believed to be the basis for many of the habitual behaviors that guide our daily lives in situations that don't require us to overtly "think about what to do."
- The dynamics of midbrain dopamine implement different iterations of the reward prediction error (RPE) of RL models, most notably by bursting in response to positive surprises and pausing in response to negative surprises and thereby influencing plasticity at synapses involved in the execution of the actions that produced these surprises.
- Signal intensity-based analyses of neuroimaging datasets can suffer from poor sensitivity and poor specificity, both of which are by-and-large avoided by multivariate "decoding" methods (multivariate pattern analysis; MVPA) appropriated from machine learning.
- Recurrent neural networks (RNNs) boast many advantages over other classes of artificial neural network (ANN), including that they offer a powerful and biologically plausible way of solving the credit assignment problem, and they allow for the training of a network that displays ongoing chaotic activity prior to the initiation of a trial (a biological reality not addressed by other ANN frameworks).
- An effective way to analyze high-dimensional data sets (such as, a 100D pattern of activity in the hidden layer of an RNN, or data recorded from a similarly large number of neurons) can be to apply dimensionality reduction (as, e.g., via principal component analysis [PCA]) and evaluate the resultant representational geometry of this information in a lower-dimensional subspace.

Companion Website: www.wiley.com/go/postle/cognitiveneuroscience3e

- Diffusion-decision modeling (DDM) offers a framework to analyze decision-making (including perceptual decision-making and recognition-from-memory decisions) by decomposing reaction time into non-decision and evidence-accrual stages.
- Representational similarity analysis (RSA) is a remarkably flexible type of multivariate analysis that allows one to summarize, visualize, and quantify how a region represents information, and how similar or different is this representational scheme from that of a different region.
- The 1/f component of the spectral transform of the scalp EEG corresponds, by definition, to aperiodic components in this signal, and its slope indexes the E:I balance in the tissue that is giving rise to this signal.

CONTENTS

How Are We Supposed to Think About How the Brain Works?

As made clear in *Chapter 1*, it's not possible to study how the brain gives rise to behavior and cognition in the absence of a guiding theory or framework that guides how experimental questions are conceived and framed, and how the results from these experiments are interpreted. (*Localization-of-function* vs. *mass action* was particularly prominent.) To the extent that it's possible, *Chapter 2* aspired to present "just facts" – grounding in the organization of the brain at the level of cells, circuits, and systems, and fundamentals of physiology. There's a sense in which the narrative of *Chapter 2* is not different from how one might start to go about studying inorganic phenomena, like, perhaps geology or climatology: what are the primary structural elements that need to be understood (e.g., the mineral composition of various types of rock), and what are key principles that govern how they behave (e.g., plate techtonics). *Chapter 3* took the next step of introducing how, armed with this knowledge, one goes about studying how a function of interest is carried out by the brain, and it focused on visual, auditory, and somatosensory perception. *Chapter 3* emphasized a classical *bottom-up* or *feed-forward* approach that would qualify as an "old fashioned" perspective in the view of theorist Karl Friston, who has written that "In the 20th century we thought the brain extracted knowledge from sensations" (2018, p. 1019). To be clear, Friston wouldn't dispute the validity of any of the facts about anatomy or physiology that were conveyed in that chapter. Rather, he would likely challenge the implied assumption that the "way that perception works" is that the brain is a fundamentally passive organ that "gets activated" when an event in the environment (a sound, a touch, a new pattern of light) impacts sensory receptors, which then transduce this information into an electrical code, which is then fed forward to the cortical circuits that then carry out the processing of this signal so as to identify the nature of the triggering environmental event and present the results to higher-level brain areas to interpret and, perhaps, respond to. An alternative way of thinking about "what perception is for" is introduced in this chapter's section ***Predictive coding***. Elsewhere, neuroscientist Bruno Averbeck (2025) has written "The field of systems neuroscience has been studying variations on tuning functions for over 70 years . . . [but] modern machine learning tools combined with advances in recording technology are poised to drive a new class of explanations for brain function, that will be an important advance over classical hypotheses based on static tuning function models of the brain." That is, the conceptualization of, for example, simple cells in V1 as feature detectors that are tuned for a specific element in the visual world may be limiting, at best, if we are to truly understand how the brain gives rise to visual perception. (Section *Machine learning* also follows in this chapter; also relevant to these ideas is section *Dynamical systems theory*.)

And so, although the facts that we covered in *Chapter 2* and *Chapter 3* are not wrong, an up-to-date understanding of those facts requires familiarity with contemporary theories and frameworks that guide how to situate them within a broader conceptualization of "how the brain works" and how we might best study it. What follows is a summary of theories, frameworks, conceptualizations, and approaches that will each be relevant for understanding the contemporary cognitive neuroscience of many of the categories of cognition that are covered in the remainder of this book. This chapter is organized somewhat arbitrarily as *Influential Frameworks and Constructs*; *Machine Learning and AI*; and *Analysis Methods*. (And at least one *Framework* will appear with the *Analysis Methods* because, as was the case for *Chapter 4*, this chapter is organized such that a reader can either read straight through or can refer back to one or more sections of it as each of these theories/frameworks/conceptualizations/approaches become relevant in the remainder of the book (i.e., when reading about *Perception, Attention, and Action [Section III]*; *Mental Representation [Section IV]*; or *High-Level Cognition [Section V]*.))

Influential Frameworks and Constructs

Hebbian Plasticity

A Cartoon Example of Pavlovian Conditioning What is a memory? Fundamentally, it is the association of two (or more) previously unlinked pieces of information. (Do you remember the first name of the author of this book? [No cheating!] If you do, you have associated an arbitrary name that is reasonably common in English-speaking countries with the concept of *textbook author*. My family tells the story that around the time of my birth, my older brothers wanted my parents to name me "Brent." Had they been more persuasive at that time, your answer to my question – your memory – would have been different.) To make things simple, let's consider a cartoon example of classical conditioning from Ivan Pavlov (1849–1936), whose research on the physiology of digestion had garnered the Nobel Prize in 1904. During the day-to-day of carrying out his research, Pavlov noticed that dogs in his laboratory would often begin salivating at the sight of the laboratory technician who was responsible for feeding them, even when this person was not carrying food. Formal experimentation established that the animals could be taught to associate an arbitrarily selected stimulus (e.g., the ticking of a metronome – the *conditioned stimulus* [CS]) – with the delivery of food – the *unconditioned stimulus* (UCS). The essence of the protocol was to play the metronome sound at the time of food delivery. After several such pairings, it would be sufficient to play the metronome sound, alone, and the dog would begin to salivate. In doing so, the dog was expressing a memory, because prior to the experiment, the playing of a metronome sound did not produce this behavior. Therefore, it was the influence of its recent experience that was being expressed in its behavior. If one wants to project human-like cognition onto the dog, one can speculate that hearing the metronome made the dog think of being fed (i.e., made it *remember* being fed the last time it had heard this metronome).

Hebb's Postulate If you're familiar with the history of psychology you'll know that Pavlov was far from the only scientist studying learning during the first half of the twentieth century, and that this era of "Behaviorism" was characterized by the development of many sophisticated theories of learning (e.g., Thorndike, 1911; Skinner, 1938; Hull, 1943). What distinguished the work of psychologist Donald Hebb (1904–1985) from that of many of his contemporaries, however, was the careful consideration that he gave to the question of *how might processes of the brain give rise to learning?* Indeed, in his book *The Organization of Behavior* (1949) he articulated what has come to be one of the most influential and enduring principles in neuroscience: "When an Axon of cell A is near enough to excite a cell B and repeatedly or persistently takes part in firing it, some growth process or metabolic change takes place in one or both cells such that A's efficiency, as one of the cells firing B, is increased" (p. 62). This has come to be known as "Hebb's postulate," and it has been fundamental for understanding synaptic plasticity in biological systems, as well as being the basis for learning in virtually all artificial neural network models (ANNs), including those introduced further along in this chapter (in section *Computational models and analytic approaches*).

Activity-Based Modification of Synaptic Strength Now we can return to our cartoon example of Pavlovian conditioning and bring in Hebb's postulate to consider (in a highly schematized way) how this learning to associate the CS with the UCS may have occurred at the level of neural systems. We know from *Chapter 3* that, prior to learning, the sound of the metronome generated activity in the auditory cortex of the animal. Additionally, we can safely assume that, prior to any learning, the same is not true for many other brain areas that control other functions. In particular, we can assume that neural circuits that trigger salivation would not be triggered by the sound of a metronome. However, by repeatedly pairing the sound of the metronome with the presentation of food, Pavlov created a situation in which activity in the auditory system and activity in salivary circuits occurred simultaneously. Framed in terms of our hypothetical experiment, it was a situation in which an axon carrying information about the sound of the metronome, one with a synaptic connection with a neuron in the salivary system,[1] "was made to excite [the salivary neurons] and repeatedly or persistently take part in firing them." To be clear, in our example, the auditory axon isn't *causing* the salivary neuron to fire, but the simultaneity of their activity turns out to be enough to strengthen this synapse. To understand why this is, we need to delve into the machinery of the glutamatergic synapse.

Recall from *Chapter 2*, section *How neurons communicate: the postsynaptic consequences of neurotransmitter release*, that ligand-gated Na^+ channels operate on the basis that the binding of a molecule of neurotransmitter results in the opening of a pore that allows for the influx of Na^+ ions and, consequently, depolarization of the neuron. At glutamatergic synapses, one such receptor is the alpha-amino-3-hydroxy-5-methyl-4-isoxazolepropionic acid (AMPA) receptor. (*Chapter 2*, section *Different neurotransmitters and different receptors can produce different effects on the postsynaptic cell*; if you're hazy on the details, now would be a good time to review them.) As illustrated in *Figure 5.1*, there is a second major class of glutamate receptor that often co-occurs with AMPA receptors in the same post-synaptic density, the NMDA receptor (named for *N*-methyl-D-aspartate, an experimentally derived compound that selectively binds with these, but not AMPA, receptors). The NMDA receptor differs from the AMPA receptor in that its pore is larger (and can thus pass ions that are larger than Na^+), *and* it is occupied, at rest, by a magnesium ion (Mg^{2+}). As a result, binding by glutamate, which untwists its pore, is not sufficient for the NMDA receptor to allow the influx of positively charged ions, because the Mg^{2+} ion remains in place, blocking the pore. To activate the NMDA receptor, there must be a coincidence of two events: (1) presynaptically released glutamate binds to its binding site; and (2) the postsynaptic terminal is already depolarized. A

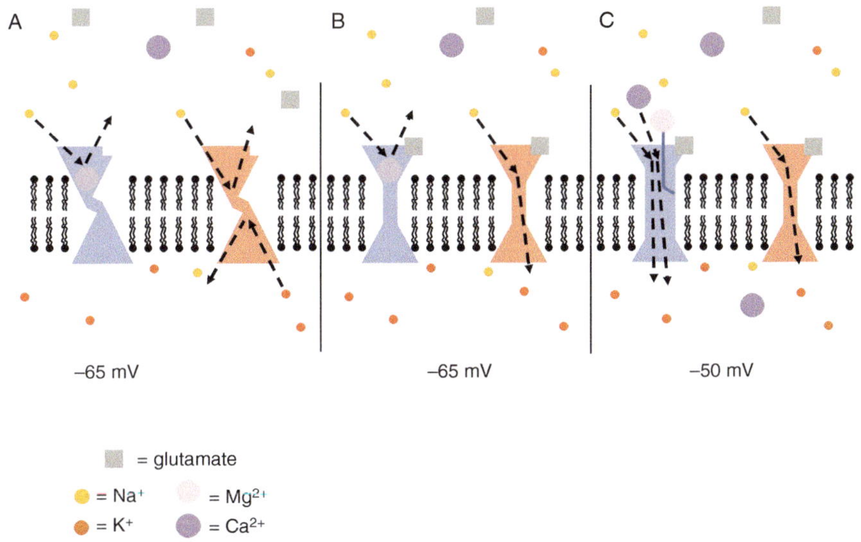

FIGURE 5.1 The two major classes of glutamate receptors. **A.** Cartoon of an NMDA receptor (blue) and an AMPA receptor (salmon), both membrane-spanning complexes of proteins that, when their binding site is not bound with a molecule of glutamate, are twisted such that ions in the extracellular and intracellular fluid cannot pass through them. Additionally, the NMDA receptor has an Mg^{2+} ion lodged in its pore. **B.** The binding of glutamate causes both of these receptors to untwist, thereby opening a pore that acts like a tube connecting the intra- and extracellular spaces. At a resting voltage of −65 mV, this allows for an influx of Na^+ ions impelled by both the electrical and chemical gradients, resulting in a depolarization of the local membrane potential. For the NMDA receptor, however, at this same resting voltage of −65 mV, the Mg^{2+} ion remains lodged in the receptor's pore (tugged by the electrical gradient). Thus, at the neuron's resting potential, binding with glutamate will not allow any ions to pass through it. **C.** As the local membrane potential begins to depolarize due to the influx of Na^+ ions through nearby AMPA channels, the net force exerted on the Mg^{2+} ion reverses, and its displacement from the channel's pore allows for the influx of positively charged ions. Importantly, because its pore is larger, the NMDA receptor also allows for the passage of Ca^{2+} ions.

[1] Where in the brain might one find such an auditory-to-salivary synapse? Probably nowhere. This is an oversimplified hypothetical example concocted to illustrate the principle of Hebbian plasticity.

depolarized state of the postsynaptic terminal has the effect of repelling the positively charged Mg^{2+} ion, thereby forcing it out of the pore, which allows for the influx of Na^{+} and, more importantly, Ca^{2+}. (Note that, although the depolarized state of the neuron would otherwise also repel these positively charged ions, this is overcome by the attractive chemical gradient.) As discussed previously, Ca^{2+} acts as a catalyst for many intracellular chemical cascades, and in the postsynaptic terminal, those cascades lead to a strengthening of the synapse.

Further detail about the intracellular events triggered by the influx of Ca^{2+} must await *Chapter 11*'s treatment of *Neural Bases of Memory*. For the present purposes, let's take another moment to emphasize the functional role of the NMDA receptor. It acts as a coincidence detector, in that it can only be activated by the coincidence of two events that implement Hebb's postulate: (1) release of glutamate by the presynaptic terminal of the synapse that is to be strengthened and (2) a prior state of depolarization of the postsynaptic terminal. In the context of our Pavlovian conditioning vignette, the presentation of food activates olfactory neurons, which, in turn, activate salivary neurons. This results in the postsynaptic depolarization in our salivary neuron of interest. If, during this time, the metronome clicks, glutamate released by auditory neurons onto their synapses with salivary neurons will activate NMDA receptors, due to the coincidence of salivary activity and auditory activity. This activation of NMDA receptors results in the influx of Ca^{2+}, which leads to the strengthening of the synapse that links the auditory with the salivary.

A final, important fact that we need to consider here is that Hebbian plasticity can work in two directions. That is, what we have been describing is a situation in which activity in neuron A that coincides with activity in neuron B leads to a strengthening of the A-to-B synapse. As we'll see in *Chapter 11*, this strengthening is referred to as long-term potentiation (LTP). It is also the case, however, that when activity in neuron A is anticorrelated with activity in neuron B, A-to-B synapses will be weakened. Thus, when action potentials in A occur shortly *after* B has been depolarized, long-term depression (LTD) of this synapse occurs. The bidirectionality of synaptic plasticity is critical for many computations carried out by the brain.

Predictive Coding

Chapter 2 and *Chapter 3* emphasized a classical view of the functioning of the nervous system. An oversimplified caricature of this classical view is that sensation and perception are accomplished by a "passive" brain that gets "activated" when an event in the environment (e.g., a sound, a touch, or a flash of light) impacts sensory receptors, which transduce this information into an electrical code and feed it forward to the circuits that begin its processing so as to accomplish perception – the localization and identification of that sound, that touch, or that visual event. Of course, we have already seen that perception isn't accomplished in a purely feedforward manner, as illustrated, for example, by *Chapter 3* sections *Information processing in primary visual cortex – interactivity* and *Top-down control of auditory transduction*. Another fact that would be difficult to reconcile with this idea of a "passive" brain that "gets activated" by signals from the environment is summarized in *Figure 4.20*, which illustrates how relatively small are the metabolic demands of, for example, "viewing words," relative to the overall energy consumption of a brain "at rest." Nonetheless, it's certainly possible to know this information and still adhere to what Friston characterized as a twentieth-century conceptualization (see section *How are we supposed to think about how the brain works?*)

It gets very math-y very fast, but for our purposes, I'm going to try to keep it in nontechnical terms. The premise of predictive coding is that the brain's modus operandi is to maintain a model (a.k.a., a set of predictions) about the current state of the outside world, and to update that model when newly gathered sensory evidence is inconsistent with it. This perspective flips the classical bottom-up/feedforward perspective of perception on its head, construing the causal direction of information processing as one of top-down signals from higher-level areas informing lower-level areas of their predictions (i.e., of what kind of signals *should* be coming from the outside world) and lower-level areas signaling mismatches between these predictions and incoming evidence (i.e., errors in the prediction), with feedforward error signals used to update the internal model. Thus, in this framework, the feedforward signals that are traditionally understood as carrying sensory information about newly detected stimuli are reframed as "after-the-fact" corrective feedback to higher-level cortex about what aspects of the visual scene are not a part of the internal model (i.e., were not predicted), and that therefore are needed to update the model. (In this text, we'll be consistent in using the terms "feedforward" and "feedback" with reference to the anatomically defined hierarchy, unless explicitly stated otherwise.) Friston (2018) summarizes this as a profound paradigm shift whereby, as conceptualized by scientists, "the brain became an organ of inference, actively constructing explanations for what's going on 'out there', beyond its sensory epithelia" (p. 1019). From the perspective of psychology and cognitive science, predictive coding has much in common with Bayesian models.

Keys for models of the neural implementation of predictive coding are accounts for how prediction signals and error signals are propagated and segregated. Recall from *Chapter 2,* section *The cerebral cortex* that the flow of visual information (in one pathway) can be construed as traveling from the retina to the LGN of the thalamus to V1 to V2 to V4. Models of predictive coding hold that, within a cortical column in any cortical region in this pathway (we can use V4), a representation of the brain's internal model (of the prediction) is maintained in deep layers, and feedback from layer V (of V4, for our example) to layers II/III (of V2) (via the connection illustrated in *Figure 2.4*) is the channel for conveying this prediction to a region closer to the sensory interface. In this feedback signal, the V4-level of stimulus representation is decomposed into the hierarchically "earlier" level of representation that V2 "can understand." In V2, feedforward input from V1 (arriving in layer IV) is then compared to the prediction that had been delivered by V4, and the error between prediction and feedforward signal is then propagated from V2 to V4 via the layer II/III-to-layer IV projection (*Figure 2.4*). This error signal also updates the predictive model encoded in V2's deep layers, and the resultant updated prediction from V2 is fed back onto V1. Laminar recordings of monkeys performing a variety of tasks relying on visual perception suggest that feedback signaling is generated by layer V pyramidal neurons whose oscillations synchronize in the 10–30 Hz range (i.e., the alpha and beta bands) and feedforward signaling by layer II/III neurons whose oscillations synchronize in the 40–90 Hz range (the gamma band). This scheme for clocking a transmission within a (relatively) narrow frequency band is referred to as using "frequency channels." One advantage of such a scheme is that, from the perspective of a cortical column in V2, it's less likely to confuse the ascending prediction-error signal from V1 and the descending prediction-update signal from V4 if the two are being carried in different frequency channels. *Figure 5.2* illustrates a different idea about the implementation of this signaling, with the feed-forward transmission of prediction errors and the feed-back of model updates reflected in forward- and backward-propagating traveling waves in the alpha band, respectively.

Note that, at the level of cortico-thalamic interactions, we've already seen a concrete manifestation of the principle of predictive coding in *Figure 3.3*, and Cudeiro and Sillito's accompanying invocation of "continually [placing sensory input] in the context of hypotheses formulated by higher brain centres" (section *Feedforward and feedback projections of V1, Chapter 3*). Here we have emphasized vision, but the principles of predictive coding have been applied to every sensory modality and are prominent, for example, in many accounts of speech perception (*Chapter 19*).

Dynamical Systems Theory

Dynamical systems theory (DST) is a branch of mathematics, prominently used in many physical sciences that describes how systems transition from one state to another. One example is the formal mathematics that describes how water transitions from solid to liquid to gaseous states with changes in temperature. Of particular interest can be the dynamics of state transitions, which are often characterized by their nonlinearity. (E.g., the fact that water remains in a solid state as the temperature increases from −5°C to −3°C and from −3°C to −1°C but transitions from solid to liquid as the temperature increases from −1°C to 1°C.) At a more abstract level, all physical systems can be represented as comprising a finite set of variables (or dimensions), and a state refers to any specific combination of values for each variable. Thus, the same set of mathematical tools can be applied to a cube of ice, or to a murmuration of starlings (which transitions from moment-to-moment through states defined by the overall volume and shape

FIGURE 5.2 A somewhat fanciful illustration of a traveling-wave implementation of predictive coding in visual perception, modified from Friston (2019); itself a commentary on Alamia and Van Rullen (2019). Superimposed on the photograph of expanding rings of waves on the surface of water is a box-and-arrow diagram of three hierarchically organized levels of cortical processing – these could be construed, for example, as corresponding to V1 ("Level 1") ➔ V4 ("Level 2") ➔ PITd ("Level 3") from the wiring diagram peeking out from under the photograph. (See *Figure 6.5.B* for a full image of this wiring diagram of the visual system.) Within each region are two nodes, corresponding to the incoming sensory signal (S) at Level 1 and to expectation ("prediction") at Level 2 and Level 3 ($\mu^{(x)}$) (in blue), and to prediction error ($\boldsymbol{\varepsilon}^{(x)}$) (in red). When sensory information arrives in layer IV of Level 1, the difference between this signal and what was expected by the system (i.e., the system's "internal model") is computed by $\boldsymbol{\varepsilon}^{(1)}$, and the resulting prediction error propagates (red arrow from Layer 1 to Layer 2) to $\mu^{(1)}$, which represents Level 2's expectation of what it will be receiving from Level 1. Next, $\boldsymbol{\varepsilon}^{(2)}$ computes the difference between the signal from $\boldsymbol{\varepsilon}^{(1)}$ and $\mu^{(1)}$, and this prediction error goes two places: it propagates to Level 3 (red arrow to $\mu^{(2)}$) and it updates Level 2's expectation (red arrow to $\mu^{(1)}$). Furthermore, when $\mu^{(2)}$ is subsequently updated by $\boldsymbol{\varepsilon}^{(3)}$, this updated expectation that is held by Level 3 propagates to Level 2 (blue arrow from $\mu^{(2)}$ to $\boldsymbol{\varepsilon}^{(2)}$). To highlight just two events from this scenario, the $\boldsymbol{\varepsilon}^{(2)}$-to-$\mu^{(2)}$ signal is a feedforward signal (from Level 2 to Level 3), and the $\mu^{(2)}$-to-$\boldsymbol{\varepsilon}^{(2)}$ signal is a feedback signal (from Level 3 to Level 2). In the context of a traveling-wave model of predictive coding, Friston (2019) invites us to visualize these events as consequences of a pebble being dropped into a flat pool of water: the initial sensory perturbation triggers an outward-spreading wave (feedforward signaling); and each time this wave encounters an object protruding from the water (the transition from one layer to another), this produces a "reflecting" wave that expands back toward where the pebble entered the water (feedback signaling). (Note that if one does not want to commit to a traveling-waves account, the metaphorical "forward waves" and "backward waves" in this diagram can be construed as stand-ins for, e.g., spiking that is coordinated in the gamma band and in the alpha/beta band, respectively.)

Source: (Friston, 2019) / PLOS / CC BY 4.0.

of the "cloud" of birds that is the flock, the distance between each bird, the direction and speed of the flock, the variation of velocity from bird-to-bird, etc.), or to patterns of activity in a nervous system. When a system is such that, despite starting from many disparate states, it tends to converge on the same end state, this end state is said to be an *attractor*, and a system with multiple attractors can be characterized as an *attractor landscape*. Consider a billiard table. The internet tells me that standard dimensions are 122 cm × 244 cm or 29,768 cm^2. This one is perfectly flat (and green) such that when you gently place a ball on any of the roughly 28,000 quadrants of 1 cm^2 of the table, the ball remains at precisely that location. (We're pretending that the remaining 1768 cm^2 of surface area corresponds to the six holes.) Now let's say that you're handed a bucket of plaster and asked to transform this flat surface into a 3D "landscape" by adding "hills" in some areas, "channels" in others, gentle slopes in others, etc., and then wait overnight for the plaster to harden. When you return the next day, there are very few 1 cm^2 quadrants on which one can set a ball without it rolling to some other location. What you have constructed is an attractor landscape – each of the many locations where the ball will come to rest is an attractor, and each 1 cm^2 quadrant from which a ball would roll into that attractor makes up part of that attractor's basin (not unlike a river's watershed). Some of your attractors are likely deeper than others, meaning that differing amounts of energy would need to be applied to move a ball out of one and into another (e.g., differing strengths of wind). The number of attractors that are present on your table is referred to as the stability of the landscape – if there's only one attractor to which a ball can roll regardless of where on the table you place it, the landscape of monostable, if there are two, it's bistable, and if there are any more than two its referred to as multistable. But before throwing out more terminology, let's relate these concepts to a fairly straightforward example from cognitive neuroscience.

The example we'll draw on here, as well as in other sections in this chapter, is visual working memory for the orientation (i.e., the "tilt") of a grating of parallel bars or for the color of that sample grating, tested with delayed recall. We use visual working memory (the focus of *Chapter 14*), for example, when a friend pulls out their phone and shows us the picture of a person that they are looking for, and we then try to help our friend find this person in a crowded room. In an fMRI study of visual working memory, led by Qing Yu and senior-authored by Yu, Panichello, Postle, and Buschman (2020), subjects first viewed one or three oriented lines, then, after an 8-second delay, were asked to reproduce from memory (i.e., to recall) the orientation of the probed item (*Figure 5.3.A*). Behavioral performance revealed marked bias in recall performance: Even though subjects saw an equivalent number of samples from each of nine values evenly spaced to span the entire range of possible orientations (i.e., from 0° to 179°), their responses clustered around two values – roughly 45° and 135° (*Figure 5.3.B*). Framed in the perspective of DST, this was a bistable landscape with attractors at 45° and 135° and repellers at 0° and 90°. Why should this be? Each subject's vision was normal, such that we can be confident that their visual perception wasn't systematically distorted in this way. (E.g., if asked to tell the time from an analog clock, they wouldn't mistakenly perceive 12:15 as looking like 12:07 or like 12:22.) Yet during the time spanning from the offset of the samples to the onset of the response display, their mental representation seems to have drifted toward these attractors. Indeed, in DST, *drift* is a parameter that indexes how strong is the "pull" of an attractor, whereas *diffusion* refers to the level of noise exhibited by the dynamics of the system. (I.e., if the system studied by Yu, Panichello, Postle, and Buschman (2020) were truly bistable, in the absence of any diffusion, every response would have been precisely "45°" or precisely "135°," with no values in between. Consider the Necker cube illusion (*Figure 5.4*) – it is considered a bistable illusion because when staring at the image in *Figure 5.4.A*, one only perceives a cube that appears to be facing up-and-to-the-left or down-and-to-the-right, but never in an intermediate pose that a real cube in the physical world would have to occupy if rotating between the poses illustrated in *Figure 5.4.B* and *Figure 5.4.C*.) Note that visual inspection of *Figure 5.3.B* suggests that the peaks at the two attractors are higher for *3O* than for *1O* trials, and *Figure 5.3.C* confirms this in two ways. Descriptively, the mean error was higher for *3O* than for *1O* trials. Analytically, the fits to a DST-based drift-diffusion model (DDM) indicated that the pull of the attractors was stronger (i.e., higher *drift*) on *3O* vs. *1O* trials, and that the performance was also noisier (i.e., higher *diffusion*) on *3O* vs. *1O* trials.

One reason for selecting the example of the Yu et al. (2020) study is how it illustrates, very concretely, the "value-added" of the DST-based analysis that we have just summarized. The Yu et al. (2020) study is actually a reanalysis of a dataset that had been collected previously by Ying Cai and colleagues (2019, 2020) to address other questions. The reanalysis was carried out to evaluate, with fMRI, a hypothesis previously articulated by Matthew Panichello, Timothy

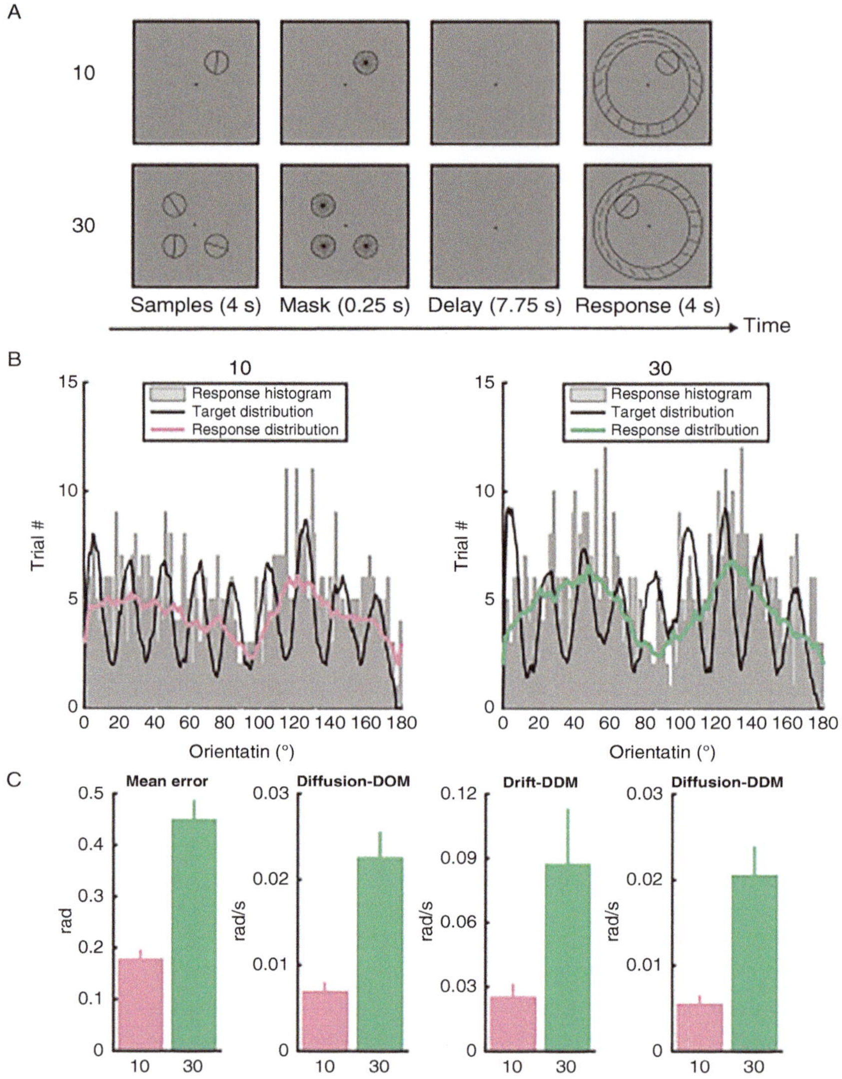

FIGURE 5.3 Dynamical drift and diffusion in visual working memory. **A.** In the *1O* condition, subjects first viewed one sample orientation (i.e., the orientation of the line within the circle), then a brief backward mask followed by a delay period, followed by a *Response* screen, which required the subject to move a cursor (via trackball) to the location on the orientation wheel corresponding to their memory of the orientation of the sample. The cursor always appeared at fixation, and the orientation of the bar located within the cue circle changed in real time to match the radial angle of the cursor as the cursor was dragged around the display. The *3O* condition presented three samples, and the location of the cue on the Response screen indicated which of the three samples was to be recalled. **B.** Histograms of the raw response distributions, by orientation, on *1O* and *3O* trials, are in gray, and the envelopes of these distributions are rendered in pink or green. The samples ("targets") were drawn randomly, with replacement, from a pool of nine equally spaced orientations, then slightly jittered (which explains why the Target Distribution resembles nine jagged peaks, rather than nine vertical lines). **C.** Plots of the descriptive data (mean error) and the parameter estimates for drift and diffusion from the DDM.

Source: (Yu, Panichello, Postle, & Buschman, 2020) / PLOS / CC BY 4.0.

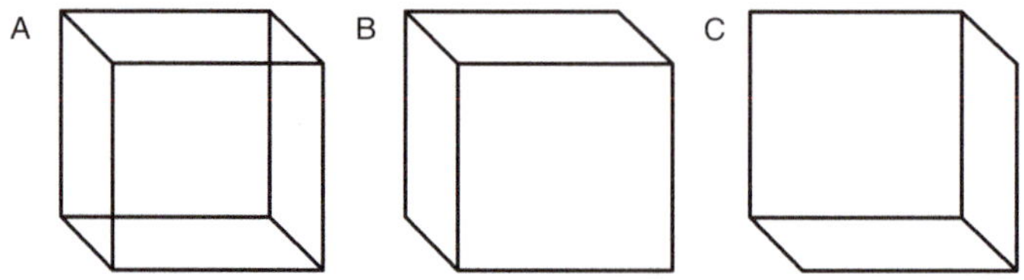

FIGURE 5.4 The Necker cube illusion exhibits perceptual bistability. That is, when staring at A, one's percept switches between a cube posed as in B or as in C but never the intermediate poses through which a solid cube held in the hand would transition if being rotated between the poses illustrated in B and C.

Buschman, and colleagues about ways that the cognitive system adjusts in the face of challenging conditions. Specifically, Panichello, DePasquale, Pillow, and Buschman (2019) had proposed that when a visual working memory task is made more difficult (e.g., by increasing the number of items to be held in memory), the system relies on its knowledge, built up over a lifetime of experience, of how the visual world is organized. (In effect: *because it's difficult for me to retain a high-fidelity record of what I saw 2 seconds ago, I'm going to bias my response with what it most likely was, based on my lifetime's history of having previously seen things similar to this.*) Following from this, the interpretation of results like those illustrated in *Figure 5.3* was as follows: (1) We can model perceiving (and remembering) orientations as representing each sample value as a location on a 1D attractor landscape that spans the space of all possible orientations (0°–180°); (2) Holding three things in mind is more difficult than holding one, and it's well-established that the precision of information held in working memory declines with the number of items being held (i.e., precision is inversely related to memory load); (3) In DST terms, this load-related decline in precision corresponds to an increase in diffusive noise; (4) A compensatory strategy adopted by the system, therefore, might be to increase reliance on prior knowledge – in DST terms, to increase the drift to attractors that were already present, but in a latent state, in the visual system. One can think of this schematically by thinking of the "response distribution" lines in *Figure 5.3.B,* as proxies for the attractor landscapes in these two conditions: If one were to flip them upside down, so that the peaks in the distributions look like attractor basins, it's as though the increased level of diffusion in the *3O* condition led to the deepening of the two attractor basins (i.e., the green "troughs" would be more pronounced than are the pink ones). In DST, the factor that determines whether the attractor landscape, at any moment in time, resembles the pink or the green is the *control parameter.*

An important point to keep in mind is that, up until this point, we have only been considering behavior. Is there evidence that the pattern illustrated in *Figure 5.3* is the result of DST principles at work in the visual system? Recall that we said previously that the visual perceptual abilities, per se, of these subjects didn't exhibit this pattern of bias. Indeed, it could be, in principle, that the pattern illustrated isn't due to neural processing in the visual system, but rather at some later stage of processing, such as deciding how to respond at the end of the trial, or in the kinematics of the motor response that the subject must make to indicate what they recall. (It's plausible, after all, that a lifetime's experience of moving cursors with trackballs has biased the motor system into executing movements in certain directions.) This is where the fMRI data come in. Yu et al. (2020) carried out a series of regression analyses, the results of which associated regions of occipital cortex with the drift parameter in the DDM modeling of the behavioral data and regions of posterior parietal and prefrontal cortex (similar to the regions highlighted, e.g., in *Figure 9.4.C*) with the diffusion parameter. Additionally, in follow up work, Yu and Postle (2021) scanned subjects performing a task similar to the one illustrated in *Figure 5.3.A*, but where the sample stimuli were rendered more difficult to perceive by displaying them for a shorter period of time, at low contrast, and superimposed on random noise. Unbeknownst to subjects, a subset of these trials presented "null" samples in which there was no orientation information (i.e., 0% contrast), but these trials nonetheless required a recall response. (Subjects had been instructed ahead of time that some of the stimuli would be difficult to see and to just give their best guess on trials when they weren't sure.) Responses on these null trials produced a pattern very similar to the one illustrated in *Figure 5.3.B* (i.e., bimodal distribution with peaks centered at 45° and 135°) and the authors used a multivariate analysis method to reconstruct, from fMRI data, the orientation information that subjects were representing in occipital cortex. (The method – multivariate inverted encoding modeling (IEM) – will be described in section *Multivariate Methods for Decoding Neural Signals.*) Importantly, the onset of these IEM reconstructions was early in the delay period, and so both the anatomical location and the timing of these results from Yu et al. (2020; 2021) provide compelling evidence that, at least in the context of working memory, the dynamics of visual processing can involve the drift toward experience-based attractors under noisy conditions (c.f., Panichello et al., 2019).

It is important to note that the work reviewed up to this point did not directly assess whether neural circuits were functioning according to principles of DST. Rather, it supported this inference by linking variation in neural activity to variation in behavioral measures that *did* follow principles of DST. Nonetheless, it's also worthy of note that these studies provide a concrete example of what Averbeck (2025) might characterize as an "advance over classical hypotheses based on static tuning function models of the brain" (see section *How are we supposed to think about how the brain works?*). (I.e., classical models, as introduced in *Chapter 2* and *Chapter 3*, would not predict that the visual system would somehow "crank up" [or down] the influence of individual orientation-tuned neurons on behavior as a function of behavioral difficulty.) Indeed, cognitive neuroscientists like Luiz Pessoa (2023) have argued that to not guide one's thinking about the brain with principles of DST is to preclude the possibility of learning how things really work because "brain functions cannot be easily isolated or attributed to individual regions. Instead, they emerge from the complex interactions within and between large-scale circuits/networks, integrating information across multiple spatial and temporal scales" (Pessoa, 2024).

Before leaving DST, it will be useful to summarize some other concepts from DST that are important for cognitive neuroscience. First, returning to the example of melting ice, we can now specify that the ambient temperature in this system is the control parameter, and the nonlinearity in the relation of the control parameter to the state of water in the immediate vicinity of 0°C is referred to as *criticality*. Several models of brain function propose that neuronal activity regimes (i.e., high-dimensional patterns of activity in one or more interconnected circuits) are optimal when they operate near the *edge of criticality* – that is, in a state where a small change to a control parameter will trigger a major change in the state of the system (e.g., holding water at −0.5°C). It has been hypothesized that putting the brain in a state near the edge of criticality enhances, for example, the ability to rapidly respond in an optimal way to anticipated but unspecified change in the environment, to maximize the potential for information transmission with minimal metabolic cost, and to optimize learning in certain contexts. (These phenomena have been compared to a tennis player who is crouched and attentively waiting to return their opponent's serve: At this moment in time they are in a state from which they can respond effectively to a fast, looming ball; much more so than two minutes previously, when they were in a different state, sitting courtside during a pause between games.) Finally, studies of the recovery of consciousness from anesthetic unconsciousness have characterized the brain as transitioning from a point that is distant from the edge of criticality to one that is nearer. (In DST terminology, the "state of the system" [e.g., a solid cube or a liquid puddle; anesthetic coma vs. conscious wakefulness] is referred to as an *order parameter*. An order parameter can be thought of as an emergent property of the system in question.)

Another aspect of brain function to which DST has been profitably applied, the last one that we'll consider here, is patterns of synchronization/desynchronization between oscillating circuits, the degree of synchronization at any moment in time also being an order parameter. This has been interpreted as an operationalization of the extent to which discrete units/circuits/systems are cooperatively sharing information (while synchronized; sometimes summarized as "integrating") vs. being "walled off from each other" (while desynchronized; sometimes summarized as "segregating"). (If you haven't already, it's time to buckle up.) Such oscillatory dynamics often display a property called *metastability*, which is characterized by *unstable attraction* – regions in an attractor landscape that initially draw the system toward them, then push it away. Such regions are referred to as *saddles*, by analogy to a horseback-riding saddle: if you look at it from the side its profile is that of an attractor basin, a ball placed at either the front or the back end will roll "downhill" to the middle; but when you now take into account its 3D shape, you see that once the ball gets the middle it will roll off either down the left or right side. A particularly powerful construct for characterizing metastability is the *Kuramoto order parameter* (KOP), an index of the temporal variance of global synchronization (i.e., the overall level of synchronization of all the signals being measured from the system, sometimes between two or more regions, often across the entire brain). Low variance (indexed by the standard deviation of the KOP [*std-KOP*]) implies that the level of synchronization is temporally stable, whereas high std-KOP implies a constantly changing level of synchronization. Indices of metastability that can be estimated from fMRI data include one that entails carrying out a spectral transform of the fMRI data and then estimating relative phase differences between regions, with an emphasis on regions that are aligned with the overall phase alignment of the brain and those that are aligned in antiphase with the overall phase alignment of the brain. (E.g., to return to the metaphor of the flock of sparrows, there's a global frequency with which the flock in its entirety [i.e., as a "single cloud"] jiggles up and down while in flight, but within the flock there will be "mini-clumps" of birds that are vibrating differently. . .) Over time, the contribution of each region to this antiphase alignment varies, and the mean temporal variance of this contribution, abbreviated as *mean-VAR*, is another signature of metastability. Finally, it is frequently observed in the brain that there is a seemingly "out of nowhere" burst of activity in one region, and that this burst triggers similar bursts elsewhere, revealing elevated connectivity between these regions. The initial burst in these cascades of activity is referred to as *ignition*, and the variability in the number and identity of regions that are subsequently "ignited" – *std-IGNITE* – is another index of metastability. Criticality can be a factor influencing these metastable dynamics. To convey a sense of the breadth of findings using tools from DST, we conclude with *Table 5.1*, a compilation from Fran Hancock, Fernando Rosas, and colleagues (2025) of findings from studies assessing indices of metastability in fMRI data.

TABLE 5.1 Investigations of metastability in functional MRI empirical studies

Study group[a]	Signature of metastability	Findings
Healthy young adults	std-KOP	Global metastability was reliable across multiple scanning sessions
Individuals with AD or MCI	std-KOP	Global metastability was reduced in people with AD or MCI compared with controls, but it was higher in people with AD than in those with MCI with concomitant reductions in cognitive performance
Individuals with AD, MCI or SCI	std-KOP	Global metastability was highest in SCI and progressively reduced in MCI and AD
Individuals with schizophrenia	std-KOP	Increased metastability in the salience network was associated with the negative symptoms of schizophrenia
People with early psychosis or schizophrenia	mean-VAR	Global and local metastability was higher in people with schizophrenia or early psychosis than in healthy controls
Healthily ageing individuals	std-IGNITE	Global metastability was lower in the older group than in the middle-aged group
Premature babies	std-IGNITE	Preterm neonates exhibited reduced metastability in the default mode, dorsal attention and the salience networks compared with neonates born at full-term
Anaesthetized macaques	std-KOP	The awake condition had higher levels of global metastability than the anaesthetized state, with different anaesthetics reducing global metastability by different degrees
Individuals with TBI	std-KOP	Global metastability was reduced in people with TBI compared with healthy control individuals, with the reductions in TBI being found in the salience network, a left-fronto-parietal network and a dorsal attention network
People practising meditation	std-IGNITE	Experienced meditators showed higher metastability during resting state than inexperience meditators

AD, Alzheimer disease; MCI, mild cognitive impairment; mean-VAR, mean variance of the leading eigenvector; SCI, subjective cognitive impairment; std-KOP, standard deviation of the Kuramoto order parameter; std-SPECT, standard deviation of the spectral radius; std-IGNITE, standard deviation of intrinsic ignition; TBI, traumatic brain injury.

[a]Unless stated otherwise, the studies involved humans.

Machine Learning and Artificial Intelligence

The first sentence in the 1959 paper that introduced the formulation "machine learning" as the words that would come to name a field of research reads: "*The studies reported here have been concerned with the programming of a digital computer to behave in a way which, if done by human beings or animals, would be described as involving the process of learning*" (Samuel, 1959, p. 211). Although machine learning has many commercial, industrial, and engineering applications, it has also had a profound impact on many aspects of cognitive neuroscience, at the levels of theory and of data analysis. Further along in this section of the chapter we will consider machine learning approaches to multivariate data analysis, and to simulating performance of cognitive tasks (in the spirit of Samuel (1959)). But first, we'll consider a branch of machine learning that has acquired the status of theoretical framework: Reinforcement Learning.

Reinforcement Learning

In their highly influential book on the topic, Richard Sutton and Andrew Bartow (2018) introduce "The Reinforcement Learning Problem" as follows:

> When an infant plays, waves its arms, or looks about, it has no explicit teacher, but it does have a direct sensorimotor connection to its environment. Exercising this connection produces a wealth of information about cause and effect, about the consequences of actions, and about what to do in order to achieve goals.
>
> (p. 1)

Further along, they specify the core properties of reinforcement learning problems, and in so doing articulate how these distinguish reinforcement learning from other approaches to learning and memory, including long-term episodic and semantic memory, which are the focus of Section IV of this book:

> Reinforcement learning is learning what to do – how to map situations to actions – so as to maximize a numerical reward signal. The learner is not told which actions to take, as in many forms of machine learning, but instead must discover which actions yield the most reward by trying them. In the most interesting and challenging cases, actions may affect not only the immediate reward but also the next situation and, through that, all subsequent rewards. These two characteristics – trial and error search and delayed reward – are the two most important distinguishing features of reinforcement learning.
>
> (Sutton and Bartow, 2018, p. 1)

Although reinforcement learning research is most typically carried out in Departments of Computer Science and Electrical Engineering or at AI Research Institutes, its intellectual origins are grounded in learning theory from twentieth century psychology, including research in the Behaviorist tradition and, more recently, Biological Psychology. Indeed, to make the concept of reinforcement learning more concrete, let's travel back in time to the 1970s.

An important development for reinforcement learning was the phenomenon of "blocking" in Pavlovian conditioning, and the Rescorla–Wagner model (Rescorla and Wagner, 1972) that was developed to explain it. To illustrate, we can carry out a fanciful thought experiment with the metronome-and-food procedure (introduced earlier in this chapter in section A cartoon example of Pavlovian conditioning): After the animal has learned the association of *metronome predicts food*, let's now introduce a second arbitrary CS, a flashing light. If we pretend, in this example, that 10 trials of presenting metronome + food had been sufficient to produce active salivation when the metronome was played alone, in our new experiment, for trials 11 through 20, we'll play the metronome and flash the light when food is presented. The critical question is, what happens if, on the 21st trial, only the light is flashed? Does it produce salivation? (I.e., has the dog now learned to also associate the light with the presentation of food?) The answer is no. In the parlance of the animal learning literature, the previous learning of the association of the metronome with food has "blocked" the association of the light with food.

Calling this effect "blocking" turns out to have been an unfortunate choice, because this emphasizes a superficial description of the effect ("it's *as though* the metronome has blocked the light), but has nothing to do with the actual mechanistic explanation. Rather, the key insight drawn by Rescorla and Wagner is that learning only happens when an event violates the animal's expectations, that is, when events don't unfold according to the animal's prediction of what should happen in a particular situation. In the parlance of reinforcement learning, this unexpected event generates a "prediction error." This prediction error serves as a "reward" for the system, and the goal of reinforcement learning algorithms is to maximize this reward. (Note that this is the "numerical reward signal" invoked by the Sutton and Bartow (2018) excerpt above.) A corollary point illustrated by the phenomenon of blocking is that the mere temporal co-occurrence of two events is not sufficient for associative learning to occur; there needs to be a plausible interpretation that one event caused, or at least predicted, the other. Next, we jump forward in time to the 1980s.

A Dopaminergic Correlate of the Reward Prediction Error By the 1980s, reinforcement learning was a burgeoning topic of research in AI, robotics, and computer science, but the potential relevance of this work for neuroscience was largely underappreciated at that time. This would change dramatically, however, when the unexpected results from motor control research being carried out by Ranulfo Romo and Wolfram Schultz finally saw the light of day.

Romo and Schultz were initially motivated by a gap in the motor-control literature: Although it had been known for at least two decades that the motor deficits of patients with Parkinson's disease (which will be detailed in *Chapter 8*) could be effectively treated with a compound that crosses the blood–brain barrier and is converted by dopaminergic neurons to dopamine (DA), no direct linkage had been made between the activity of midbrain DA neurons (see *Figure 2.5*) and motor behaviors. And to their surprise, Romo and Schultz (1990) could not find convincing evidence that activity in these neurons was linked to movement execution; instead, it seemed to relate to motivational and reward factors. As Romo later recalled: "It took us about 5 years to publish the paper because nobody was going to buy this idea that those neurons were not associated with movement, but reward" (Downey, 2006, p. 14264). Once their results finally did get published, however, it was quickly realized that these findings had profound implications for such topics as learning, motivated behavior, decision making, and addiction. One important detail, illustrated in *Figure 5.5*, is that the activity of midbrain DA neurons seemed to carry out the function of broadcasting reward prediction errors (RPE)[2] to targets in the neostriatum and cortex.

Before leaving this section on the dopaminergic RPE, it's important that we address the question "*why DA? What's so special about this particular neurotransmitter*"? Indeed, a casual sampling of everyday discourse in the popular media might give the impression that DA is some kind of magical compound that has inherently rewarding properties, the brain's equivalent to, say, the small amount of cash that parents give to their primary school-aged child as a reward for every grade of A that she brings home on her report card. But it's not, of course, about magic.[3] It's about plasticity at the synapse.

Recall that DA is a modulatory neurotransmitter. The cell biological effects of DA are such that, when mediated by D1-type receptors, they enhance membrane excitability. Thus, for neurons expressing D1-type DA receptors,[4] a positive RPE (i.e., an elevated level of DA) increases the likelihood that concurrent activity at corticostriatal synapses will have potentiating effects, whereas a negative RPE (i.e., a pause in firing that lowers the level of DA) decreases the likelihood

[2] Recall that, in reinforcement learning models, the prediction error *is* the reward. Consequently, it might seem redundant that it is commonly referred to as the "reward prediction error" (RPE). (After all, when we give a pet a treat for behaving appropriately, we don't call it a "reward treat.") The way that this author understands it is that the "reward" in RPE is shorthand for saying "a prediction error in the context of reinforcement learning," so as to distinguish it from a prediction error that occurs outside the framework of RL, such as in predictive coding. But if that's the case, why not call it a "RLPE"? This author would have done so, but no one consulted with him on this...

[3] Let's be very clear that the notion of "dopamine detox," a "thing" in some circles on the internet at the time of the preparation of this 3rd edition of this book, is fallacious.)

[4] There are also D2-type DA receptors, whose effect is to decrease excitability in the neuron, but we won't consider these in any detail until *Chapter 8: Skeletomotor Control.*

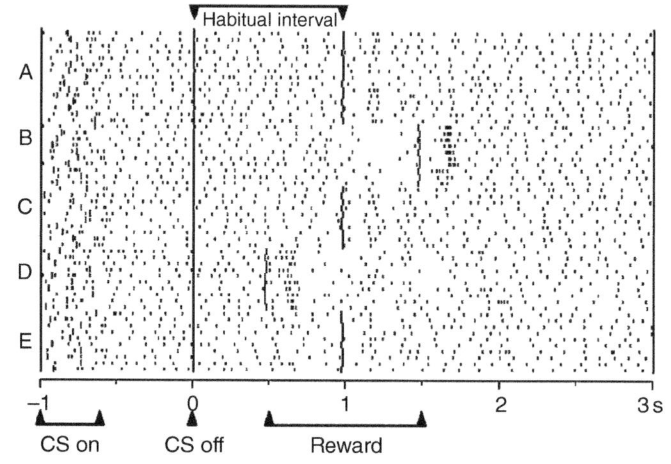

FIGURE 5.5 Activity of midbrain DA neurons as a reward prediction error (RPE) signal. Each row shows activity in a midbrain DA neuron during a trial of a well-learned Pavlovian conditioning task in which the offset of the CS is followed by a reward 1 second later (the habitual interval). (Each row is a "raster plot" in which each tick mark corresponds to an action potential. This plot illustrates a sequence of trials that are ordered from top-to-bottom along the vertical axis (such that trials in group A preceded those in group B, etc.). Note that on trials when the expected outcome occurs (groups A, C, and E), there is no change in the firing rate. When the reward is unexpectedly delayed (B), there is a brief pause in firing – a negative RPE signal – then an elevated burst upon the unexpected, later delivery – a positive RPE signal. When the reward is unexpectedly delivered early (D), there is a positive RPE – an elevated burst triggered by its delivery – followed by a negative RPE signal preceding the time of reward delivery that would have occurred on habitual trials. (Note that in addition to the rasters, the authors have added vertical lines indicating the timing of two key events: The offset of the CS (always at time 0), and thus displayed as a vertical line that spans the entirety of this set of trials; and the moment of reward delivery, with "shorter" lines indicating the duration of group A, B, C, D, and E. Note that no column of these "shorter" lines is perfectly straight, the jitter presumably reflecting slight variability in the timing of reward delivery relative to CS offset.)

Source: Annual Review of Psychology 2005 / Annual Review of Psychology.

that this same activity will have potentiating effects. Consider *Figure 5.6*, which diagrams two DA fibers (labeled "neuromodulatory axon") with en passant synaptic varicosities (i.e., "release zones") near what we can consider to be a target synapse (labeled "pre" and "post"). Indeed, if we return yet again to our schematized classical conditioning scenario, we can think of the presynaptic terminal as that of a "metronome" neuron and the postsynaptic varicosity that of a "salivation" neuron. On the very first trial during which the metronome sound and the food occur coincidentally, a positive RPE will be generated because, per the Rescorla–Wagner model, the delivery of food in conjunction with this arbitrary sound is an unexpected (and pleasant) surprise. Now, of course, the RPE is a theoretical construct – it's an event that is hypothesized to occur because there's a model that says so. But real synapses in real brains don't know about theoretical constructs. In neurophysiological terms, what happens is that a burst of activity in dopaminergic neurons in the midbrain (as illustrated in *Figure 5.5*) results in an increase in the concentration of extracellular DA in the vicinity of the two en passant varicosities that are illustrated in *Figure 5.6*,[5] and because DA has the effect, in our scenario, of enhancing membrane excitability, this has the effect of enhancing the Hebbian strengthening expected from the coincidental activity in the "pre" and the "post" synaptic cells.

Other Principles Relevant to Reinforcement Learning I realize that we just established that "it's about plasticity at the synapse." But, importantly, we didn't say that "it's *only* about plasticity at the synapse." Indeed, there are several other principles that either

[5] It can often be the case that en passant release sites do not have a matching postsynaptic varicosity, and so they have their effect by releasing their neurotransmitter into the extracellular space, such that it will diffuse to other nearby neurons that may have a receptor for the neuromodulator that they release. This is necessarily a slower and less specific mode of signaling than is releasing neurotransmitter at an axon terminal that synapses directly onto a target neuron.

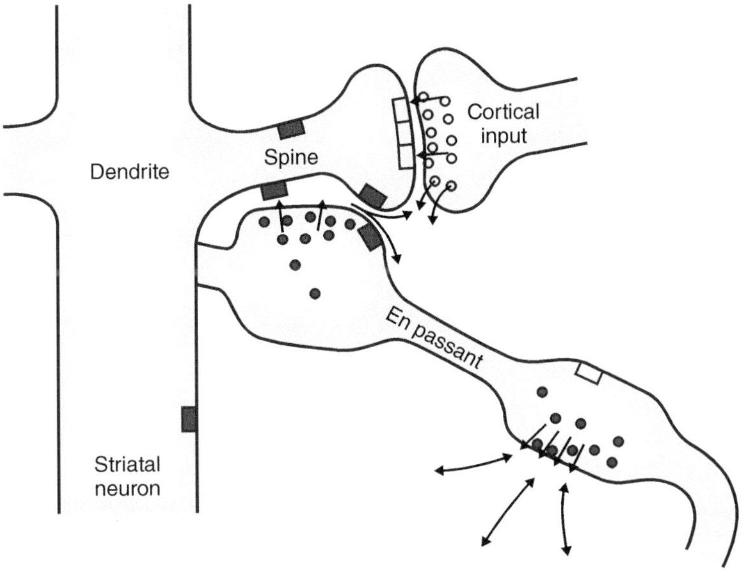

FIGURE 5.6 Diagram of axonal fibers from two neuromodulatory neurons with en passant synaptic varicosities in the vicinity of a synapse between two other neurons ("pre" and "post"). The red circle depicts the zone within which the released neuromodulatory neurotransmitter is expected to diffuse. (In the brain, this 'zone of influence' is not a 2D circle but a 3D sphere.) The term *en passant* is French for "in passing" and is used for sites of neurotransmitter release along the branch of an axon (rather than at its terminus; sometimes these varicosities are described as being "like pearls on a string").

arise from, or are addressed by, reinforcement learning that will come up at various points in the book and that we'll briefly summarize here.

- Other functions of RPE. Due to the felicitous intersection of the theoretical construct of the RPE and the neuroanatomical fact that midbrain dopaminergic neurons send their axons broadly, nonspecifically, to several forebrain regions, including the basal ganglia and the prefrontal cortex (see *Figure 2.5*),[6] midbrain DA neurons are in a privileged position to, in effect, broadcast general announcements of "heads-up!" to these brain areas, and so the RPE has been proposed to be a signal that's used by the brain for several functions, including to signpost when one "episode" of one's daily life has ended and another has begun (important for the formation and later retrieval of long-term memories; *Chapter 12*); to signal when the current strategy isn't working and it's time to switch to "Plan B" (important for cognitive control; *Chapter 15*).
- Exploitation vs. exploration. Throughout evolutionary history, most animal species have had to contend with some version of the foraging problem: *there's some food (or other valuable resource) here, but how can I be sure that there's not* more *or* better food *over there* (or perhaps, *that there will be fewer conspecifics and therefore less competition*)? From the perspective of RL, an agent is impelled to periodically "experiment" with alternative actions, in order to learn whether a larger reward might be obtained by adopting a different policy.[7]
- The credit-assignment problem. Upon receipt of a positive RPE, how does an agent know which of the several actions that it/they may have carried out in the recent (or even perhaps in the more distant) past is the one that is responsible and thus is the one to repeat in the future? Furthermore, for almost any realistic situation, there will also have been multiple actions among which the "credit" needs to be distributed. (Sutton and Bartow

[6] There is growing evidence that the timing and targeting of midbrain activity can, in some instances, be more specifically tuned than what is implied here, but these details are beyond the scope of what we can cover in this book.

[7] As a branch of machine learning, reinforcement learning problems are often framed in terms of robots or computer simulations, and the catch-all term for the entity whose behavior is being modeled (whether living or artificial) is "agent." "Policy" is the jargony word for the decision-making rule that governs the agent's behavior.

(2018) use the example of a game of tic-tack-toe. If one wins, although it was of course the most recent move that ended the game, there were also several previous moves that the agent took in order to get into the winning position.) A common approach for solving the credit-assignment problem, one that we will define when it becomes relevant, is the temporal-difference (TD) algorithm.

- Model-free vs. model-based learning and successor representations. Reinforcement learning is primarily concerned with learning how to select actions while engaged in behaviors/solving problems that involve multiple steps (as captured, e.g., by Sutton and Bartow's example of the credit-assignment problem of tic-tac-toe). Two primary classes of algorithms for selecting the appropriate action at each step are model-free and model-based learning. Model-free learning is very straightforward, and it consists of the agent building up a repository of values associated with each of multiple possible actions that could be engaged at each step of the problem[8] and, for each step, simply selecting the one with the highest value. (This is often described as "using a look-up table.") The values, called "Q values," are acquired through trial-and-error experience and are typically construed as being stored as synaptic weights in cortico-basal ganglia-thalamic circuits. (RPE-modulated synaptic plasticity, as discussed in relation to *Figure 5.6*, corresponds to the modification of a Q value.) Model-based learning, in contrast, entails in-the-moment calculation of values of various possible actions. It specifies the existence of an internal model of the problem that is being solved. Among the pros for engaging in model-based action selection are that it affords more flexibility, which can be particularly valuable in unusual situations, such as when something is unexpectedly different in an otherwise familiar situation. Among the cons for engaging in model-based action selection are that model-based action selection is slower, and computationally more expensive, than is using a model-free approach. (For a living organism, "computationally more expensive" typically equates to metabolically more expensive; thus, all other factors being equal, the computationally least-expensive solution is preferred.) In RL theory, model-free and model-based decision-making occupy two ends of a continuum, with various intermediate strategies possible. One of these, the *successor representation*, entails taking into account the values of future actions that may have to be taken depending on which immediate action is taken.

We will see that the question of the extent to which various RL algorithms are actually computed by neural systems, or, alternatively, may be mathematical formalisms that approximate, but don't literally correspond to, what the brain is doing, is a matter of active debate in many subdomains of cognitive neuroscience. Perhaps relatedly (and certainly not of unique relevance to RL) is the importance of being attentive to the extent to which similar terminology used in different scientific contexts does or does not refer to the same construct(s). In this section of this chapter, for example, someone steeped in the conventions of RL may have found the use of "action selection" to have been an awkward construction, because it's much more common in the computational neuroscience literature to use "decision making." In everyday language, however, "decision making" typically refers to the deliberative process associated with, say, deciding which candidate to vote for, or what should be the topic of the essay in my application to be admitted to university. Most would agree that these decisions are different in kind from, say, executing the seemingly "on autopilot" maneuvers that one must have taken in order to make it home from school or from work (e.g., *turn left here, turn right there*), even though one was preoccupied with a daydream during the entire commute and has the retrospective impression of "having made it home on autopilot." In this regard, an important stylistic note to raise is that this author will be careful to use the formulation "*reward* prediction error/RPE" in the context of RL-related mechanisms, but the more generic "prediction error" in the context of, for example, the feedforward signals hypothesized by predictive coding models to signal a mismatch between an internal model and sensory evidence.

[8] One unavoidable bit of jargon in this realm is variations on the word "cache": as a noun to refer to the repository; as a verb when referring to the process of creating a stored value ("to cache"); and as an adjective when referring to one of these values (a "cached" value). It's not a coincidence that this same word is used in reference to how some birds and rodents store food.

Multivariate Methods for Decoding Neural Signals

The Problem of Interpreting Images of Brain Activity Consider *Figure 4.20.A*, from Petersen, Fox, Posner, Mintun, and Raichle (1988). Although it represents one of the earliest publications of functional neuroimaging results, the analyses that produced these results are not fundamentally different from those would dominate PET and fMRI research for the next 30 years, and that are still widely in use today. That is, some variant of a general linear model (GLM) is solved at every voxel in the 3D image, by regressing activity against the experiment's independent variables, and the resultant volume of parameter estimates (typically βs or *F*-values or *t*-values) is thresholded to display the subset of voxels maximally sensitive to the parameter of interest. Although such a "signal-intensity map" can be very useful, one limitation is that it typically has only very poor specificity. For example, even if Petersen et al. (1988) had used an event-related design (see *Chapter 4,* sections *Task-related functional imaging* and *Some considerations for experimental design*), one couldn't know from inspection of the "seeing words" image whether the words being seen were nouns or verbs (or were words in English or French). Indeed, statistical maps from a study of subjects "seeing oriented lines," such as would be produced from the task illustrated in *Figure 5.3.A*, would also look quite similar to "seeing words." It is a simple fact that brain activity – whether considered at the level of a single neuron, a cortical column, a population of 100 or so neurons, a 3-mm^3 fMRI voxel containing tens of thousands of neurons, or a whole-brain fMRI volume comprising ~30,000 such voxels – is simply too complex to be "decodable" by visual inspection. In addition to the problem of poor specificity, a second issue is one of *sensitivity*. Perhaps, there's additional "unseen" activity in *Figure 4.18.A* that is also making a critical contribution to the mental operation of "seeing words" but that, for whatever reason, didn't survive thresholding. (After all, *Figure 4.18.B* reminds us that the seemingly "not active" regions in the remainder of the brain aren't inert – they're still metabolically very active.)

Another way to think about the limited interpretability of an image like the one in *Figure 4.18.A* is that the analysis-of-signal-intensity approach is inherently a univariate one. That is, when we look at the region of elevated activity in the occipital cortex as one entity, we can only watch it vary along one dimension – its signal intensity either increases or decreases. This can lead to thinking of what we're looking at as being a single thing, an "activation," and that, in turn, this "activation" is carrying out only one function. This would be a questionable assumption even if one considered just one voxel in isolation, in view of the fact that a cortical voxel contains tens of thousands of neurons. Finally, if we return to the comparison of "seeing words" vs. "seeing oriented lines," determining whether or not *these two patterns of activity look the same* isn't really what we care about. What we really want to know is *Is the brain performing the same or different computations during these two conditions?* In the decade of the 2000s, cognitive neuroscientists came to the realization that the data from the fMRI scans of even a single subject could be viewed as a high-dimensional dataset, one that can be interrogated with multivariate pattern classification techniques that had been developed and refined in machine learning since at least the 1980s.

"Decoding" fMRI Data with Multivariate Pattern analysis (MVPA) Let's consider the hypothetical dataset that contains data from just two voxels, voxel *F* and voxel *P*. On 10 trials, our subject views a line tilted left of vertical, and on 10 trials views a line tilted rightward. The first analysis that we carry out is to "collapse across" all the voxels in our dataset. That is, we average together the signal from both voxels, then compare the spatially averaged signal intensity from the 10 leftward trials vs. the spatially averaged signal from the 10 rightward trials. The bar graph in *Figure 5.7.A* illustrates that one can detect no appreciable difference between the two conditions. If we consider the two voxels separately, that is, if we determine the average signal from voxel *F* separately for the 10 leftward trials and the 10 rightward trials and do the same for voxel *P*, we can do a little bit better: keeping in mind that these are made-up data, paired *t*-tests indicate that voxel *F* shows significantly greater activity for leftward than rightward trials, and voxel *P* the converse (*Figure 5.7.A*). Nonetheless, each voxel also shows robust activity for its "less-preferred" orientation. As a consequence of this, if we were presented with data from a 21st trial, we'd have difficulty classifying it as a leftward or a rightward trial if we only knew that voxel *F*'s activity on this trial was, say, 0.6, and voxel *P*'s activity was, say, 0.7. To illustrate this, consider *Figure 5.7.C*, which shows each voxel's response on each of our 20 trials (these are the data that produced plots A and B): where, on the voxel *F* plot, would you draw the line above which you'd be confident that a trial was a leftward trial? Similarly, where would you put your discriminant line in the voxel P plot?

The two "stacks" of data points plotted in *Figure 5.7.C* are 1-D values – they only vary along a line. *Figure 5.7.D*, however, illustrates how the same data used to generate the plots in panel *C* can be redepicted as data that vary along *two* dimensions. To create the plot in *Figure 5.7.D*, all we've done is rotate the plot of voxel *P*'s activity – from panel *C* – from vertical to horizontal. That permits us to "project the data from each trial into a higher-dimensional space." (Sounds highfalutin', I know, but it *is* what we are doing; 2D *is* a higher-dimensional space than is 1D.) Put more simply, it permits us to plot what each trial's values were at the two voxels simultaneously. As a result, it's easier to decide "where to draw the line": if the hypothetical 21st trial with the value (0.6, 0.7) falls above and to the left of the discriminant line that cuts through the cloud of data points, it most likely belongs to the cloud of datapoints from leftward trials. (This can be referred to as a "decoding" analysis, because, in this simplified dataset, the "code" that has been learned is that leftward orientations are encoded with 2D values that cluster up-and-to-the-left, whereas rightward orientations are encoded with 2D values that cluster down-and-to-the-right.)

With real fMRI datasets, this same principle is applied, but the assertion that one is "projecting the data into a high-dimensional space" no longer elicits snickers, because, with, say, 1000 voxels in an ROI, one is working in 1000D space. Within this space, a machine learning algorithm would seek to find the 999D hyperplane that, like our 1D discriminant line in *Figure 5.7.D*, would provide the best discrimination between conditions A and B. In *Chapter 14: Working Memory*, for example, we will review a study by Serences, Ester, Vogel, and Awh (2009) that investigated whether the authors could decode the orientation of stimuli from primary visual cortex (V1) during the delay period of a visual working memory task. (The

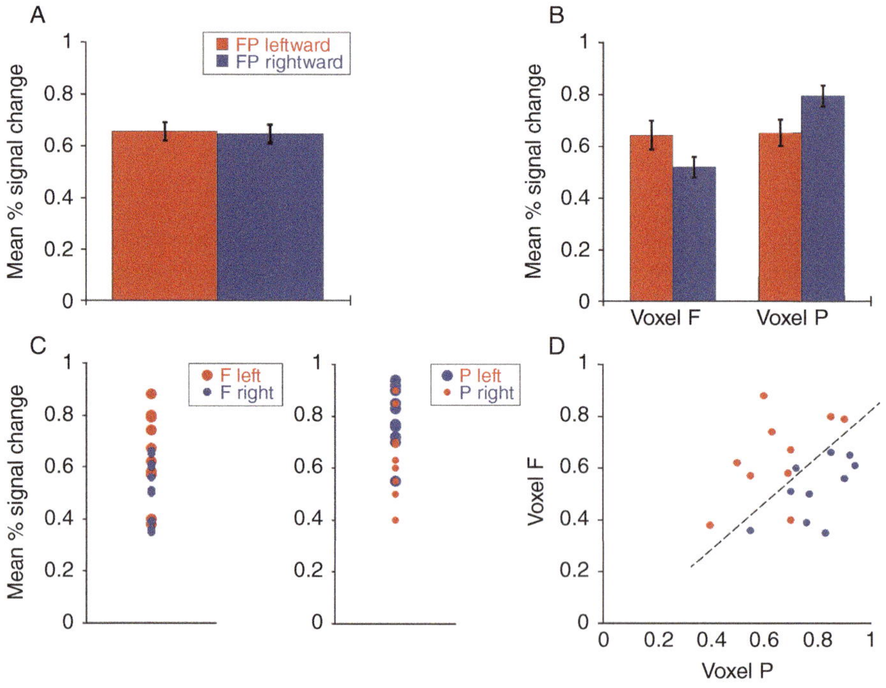

FIGURE 5.7 Improved sensitivity via MVPA. Panel **A** illustrates the data for the two conditions, averaged across voxels *F* and *P*. In panel **B**, the data are broken out by voxel. The plots in panel **C** illustrate the signal intensity from each trial, for each voxel. Panel **D** is a multivariate representation of the data from panel **C**, with a discriminant line added to illustrate how one would classify a 21st trial, depending on which side of the line it falls.

Source: © Bradley R. Postle.

task was very similar to the *1O* condition from Cai et al. (2019, 2020) (from section *Dynamical systems theory*). Serences et al. (2009) began by carrying out an activation-based analysis (i.e., solving the GLM for every voxel in V1) on the data from all eight blocks of data from each subject (1 block = 1 fMRI scan) to identify the 62 voxels in V1 that responded most strongly to viewing oriented grating stimuli. This step is referred to as *feature selection*, with each voxel in V1 being a feature to be submitted to the classification analysis. (There are technical reasons, outside the scope of this book, for not wanting to include too many features in an analysis. For this particular study, the authors settled on 62 because this was the minimum number of voxels identified by GLM in each of their subjects, and they wanted to minimize one source of potential bias by including the same number of features from each subject.) They then carried out MVPA with a classification procedure known as a Support Vector Machine (SVM) and using a procedure known as cross-validation. This sentence necessitates its own paragraph to unpack it.

First, classification. The authors first selected seven blocks with which to train their classifier. Because each block contained eight trials, this means that they fed 56 trials to the decoder (i.e., to the SVM), each labeled as 45° or 135° (the only two stimulus values in their experiment), and the decoder sought, from these 56 data points, to find the 61D hyperplane that distinguished 45° trials from 135°. (Note that each trial corresponded to a 62D vector, each dimension corresponding to the fMRI signal intensity from a voxel. Sometimes, instead of using signal intensity, MVPA is applied to vectors comprised of parameter estimates from the preceding feature-selection step.) Importantly, SVM will come up with a solution regardless of how valid it might be. (E.g., if one were to train it with data only from 45° trials, but "lie to it" and label half of these as "135°"; even though all the training data are the same, it would still generate a 61D hyperplane.) Thus, a critical step is to test this solution with the "held out" trials that had not been used for training. Testing consisted of presenting each held-out trial to the decoder, asking it to classify each as "45°" or "135°," and looking to see whether or not it performed better than chance. (For this dataset, chance-level performance was 50% correct.) Now for cross-validation. The authors used a hold-one-out cross-validation procedure in which eight decoders were trained and tested, each one with a different block of trials held out for testing. This procedure is critical because training and testing with the same data is considered "cheating" because it can produce false positive results. (A final note is that SVM is just one of many, many methods that can be used for MVPA; e.g., another commonly used approach is some form of regression, such as ridge or LASSO.)

The final step in the MVPA from Serences et al. (2009) was to treat the results from each of the eight tests produced by cross-validation as a datum, and perform a *t*-test (with seven degrees of freedom) to assess whether the decoder's performance was above chance. Success (or failure) would be interpreted as evidence that V1 does (not) represent stimulus orientation during the delay period of a visual working memory task. The results from Serences et al. (2009) are illustrated in *Figure 5.7.B*.

It is important to highlight one caveat about interpreting the results from MVPA, which is that one cannot interpret the magnitude of differences in classification accuracy as evidence for differences in the nature of the information being interrogated. To illustrate, let's look more closely at *Figure 5.7.B*. It shows that Serences et al. (2009) also included trials of visual working memory for color. Indeed, to my eye, it looks as though their orientation decoder and their color decoder both performed with roughly 60% accuracy. But let's pretend for a moment that their color decoder had actually performed at 80% accuracy; had this been the case, they would not have been able to conclude that the mental representation of color was somehow "stronger" or "sharper" than that of orientation. This is because there are many factors that can influence the accuracy of a decoder's performance, many of them a function of how the decoder works rather than due to meaningful differences in neural representation.

Reconstructing Stimulus Information with Multivariate Inverted Encoding Models (IEMs) Multivariate IEM is technically a subtype of MVPA, but it uses a forward modeling approach that is considered encoding, rather than decoding. To illustrate, we'll stick with this chapter's pedagogical workhorse: visual working memory for line orientation. With IEM, one starts with the hypothesis that any given angular value can be represented in a unique pattern of weightings across several hypothetical broadly tuned informational channels. (Here, a hypothetical informational channel can be thought of as the population-level signal that a region [let's say V1] sends to downstream areas in the visual system.) These channels are represented in the analysis with a basis set of overlapping broadly tuned functions, typically half-wave rectified sinusoids, each centered at a different angular value such that they span the full possible range of 180° of rotation. (I.e., each channel's tuning is similar to the tuning curve illustrated in *Figure 3.1*.) The model is then trained by regressing against it neural data acquired while a subject was performing visual working memory for line orientation. For fMRI, for example, the basis set's representation of the angular value of each stimulus presented to the subject is entered as a regressor into a general linear model that estimates the orientation tuning function of each voxel (sometimes referred to as the "population receptive field [pRF]") in a region of interest [ROI]). Testing of the model is carried out by inverting the matrix that maps from channel space to voxel space, then determining whether data from trials that the model has never seen generate reconstructions, in channel space, of the stimulus values used for these test trials. Successful reconstructions of test stimulus values are interpreted as reconstructions of population-level representations of these stimuli. This is formally equivalent to successful decoding. Importantly, however, because the shape of the basis functions was determined a priori and used in the training of the model, quantitative values from stimulus reconstruction can be interpreted as indices of, for example, the magnitude and the precision of a neural representation (indexed by the amplitude and width of the reconstruction, respectively [see *Figure 5.8*]).

Recall from section *Dynamical systems theory* that Yu and Postle (2021) demonstrated with IEM that subjects represent an orientation in early visual cortex even on trials of visual working memory in which no orientation information had been presented (meaning that, on these trials, they "make one up"). This is illustrated in *Figure 5.9*, which presents results from trials in which the sample was presented at high contrast (60%), low contrast (10%), and "no contrast" (i.e., 0%; labeled as "null"). Note that, although not shown in *Figure 5.6*, the authors were able to test the hypothesis that the mnemonic representations of stimuli would be stronger for high- than for low-contrast samples. This is because, unlike with MVPA, one can compare the slopes of two IEM reconstructions, so long as they were both generated by the same model. (The results indicated that the slopes of high- and low-contrast reconstructions did not differ, thereby failing to support the prediction that high-contrast sample stimuli might be represented more strongly in working memory.)

Recurrent Neural Networks

"Harnessing Chaos" In the previous chapter we emphasized the fact that Sussilo and Abbott (2009) were motivated by the neurophysiological reality that, "in the real world," a neural circuit that "has a job to do" (such as carry out an skeletomotor action), needs to overcome the fact that it is starting from a state of seemingly random ongoing activity when the motor command arrives (Chapter 4, section Recurrent Neural Networks). Now we can add the observation that, whether or not they said so explicitly, they were in effect seeking a mechanism that might play the role of setting control parameters from Dynamical Systems Theory. Here, we're going to go deeper into the nuts and bolts of RNN modeling to illustrate how it can provide novel insight about a domain of cognition with which we're growing more familiar: working memory!

RNN Modeling of Visual Working Memory The focus of much of this section will be a study in which Emilia Piwek, Mark Stokes, and Christopher Summerfield (2023) trained an RNN to perform a task that had previously been administered to nonhuman primates (NHPs) by Matthew Panichello and Timothy Buschman (2021), while extracellular recordings were obtained from several brain areas. The task was similar to the "3O" condition illustrated in *Figure 5.3*, but with three exceptions, two of them minor and one very important. The two minor differences were that two stimuli were presented as to-be-remembered samples, and the to-be-remembered information was color. The important difference was that partway through the delay period a "retrocue" was presented, telling the subject which of the two items

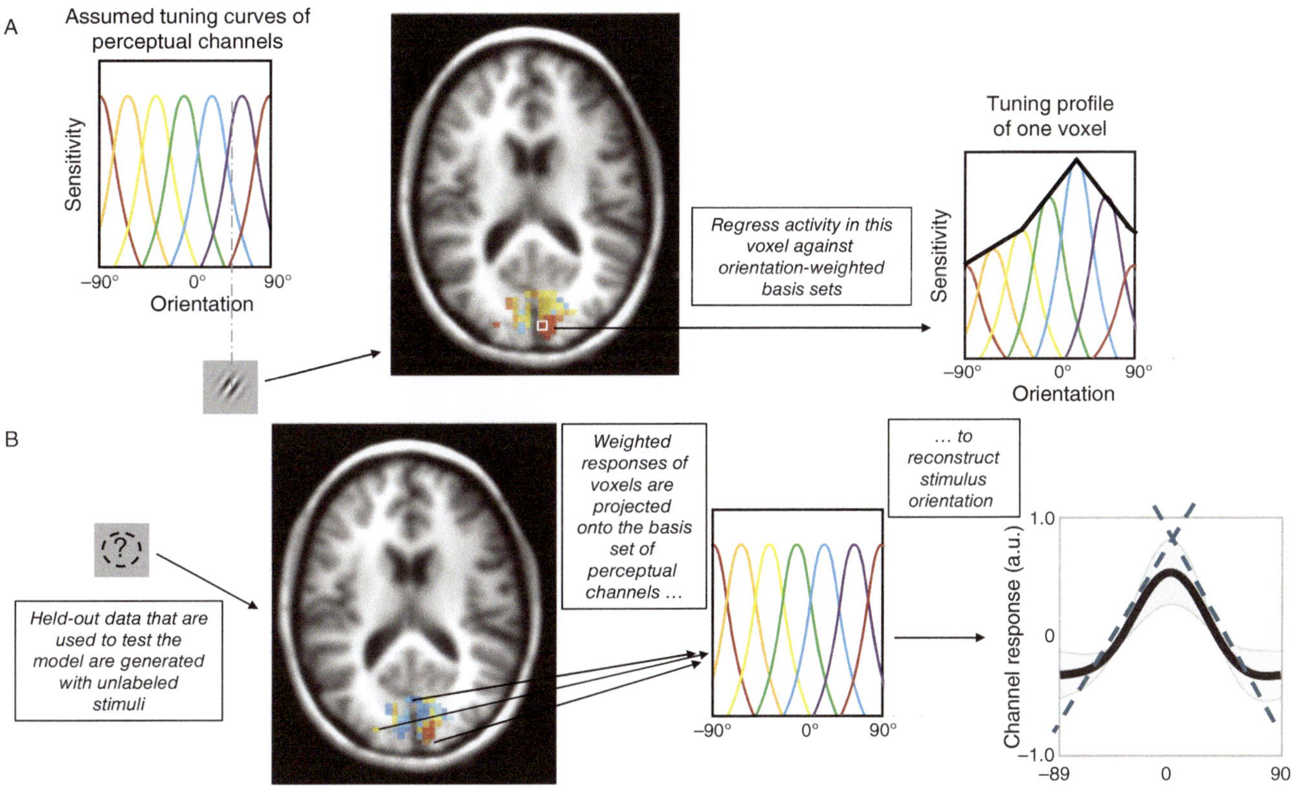

FIGURE 5.8 Multivariate inverted encoding modeling. **A**. A diagram of the procedure for training the model. On the left is the basis set of six overlapping broadly tuned basis functions, each a half-wave rectified sinusoid, each centered at a different angular value such that the basis set spans the full range of 180° of rotation. The regressor corresponding to +45° would be composed of the values of the basis functions intersected by the vertical dashed line, and then regressed onto the activity evoked by the presentation of a +45° grating, illustrated on the axial slice in the center. When the full range of stimuli has been presented, the solution of the GLM for, for example, the "tuning curve" (a.k.a. pRF) of the voxel highlighted on this axial slice might look like the profile on the right. A comparable tuning curve has been derived for every voxel in the brain (or ROI), and all are stored in a matrix of basis function-to-voxel weightings. (Note that, at this point, we have an accumulation of univariate analyses, one for each voxel.) **B**. The model is tested by presenting held-out data corresponding to the pattern of whole-brain (or ROI) activity evoked by unlabeled stimuli (also drawn from the full range of 180° of rotation; one unlabeled stimulus is represented by "?"). Let's say that we are carrying out our analysis on an ROI of 100 voxels from EVC (i.e., the subset of the voxels highlighted on the axial slice in the central panel). The analysis becomes multivariate, and an exercise in "dimensionality reduction," by inverting the basis function-to-voxel matrix and thereby projecting the signal intensity from each of the 100 voxels in our ROI onto the six dimensions of our basis set. For each stimulus, the resultant loading on the basis set is shifted such that the true orientation of the stimulus is now centered on 0°, a step that allows for averaging across trials. When the results from each trial have been so averaged, if the result is a peak, centered on 0°, that yields linear fits to its slope that are >0 (dashed lines on right side of panel), this is considered a significant reconstruction of the distributed representation of orientation.

in memory would be tested (*Figure 5.10.A*). Happily for the didactic purposes of this book, Piwek et al. (2023) explained their rationale for modeling the Panichello and Buschman (2021) task with RNNs:

> When RNNs are trained from random weights with gradient descent (rather than being endowed with coding properties by hand) they can recreate neural motifs that are observed in primates in short-term memory studies. Tools from machine learning can thus offer a normative account of how dynamic memory processes are learned through error minimization. In the current paper, we describe an example in which the activity dynamics in an RNN bear a striking resemblance to those reported in the primate brain.
>
> (p. 2/33)

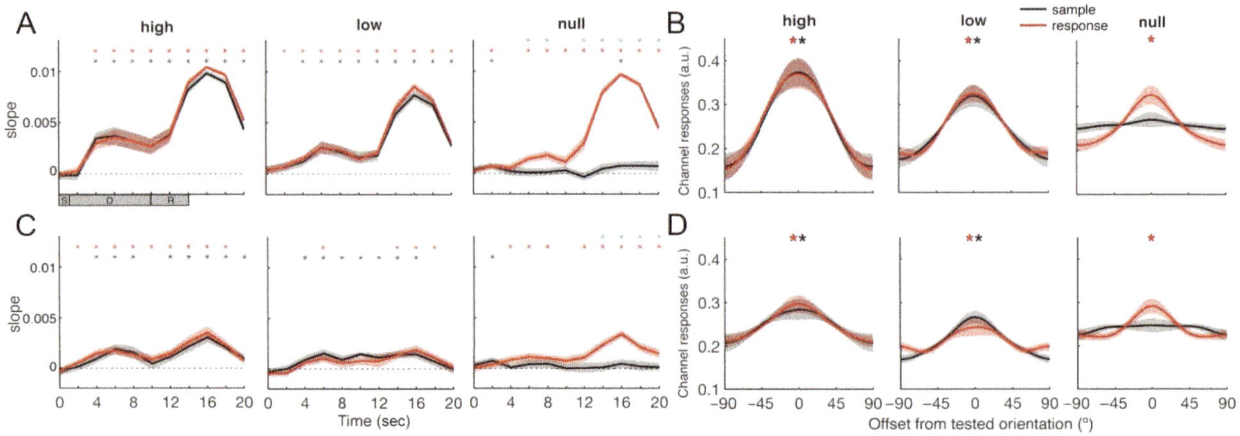

FIGURE 5.9 Multivariate inverted encoding modeling (IEM) of the representation of orientation during working memory for orientation, from Yu and Postle (2021). Sample stimuli were superimposed on random noise patterns, at one of three levels of contrast: "high" (60%); "low" (10%); or "null" (0%). (Subjects reported being unaware of null trials, meaning that they believed they were seeing stimuli drawn from a "high" or a "low" set.) **A.** Slopes from IEM reconstructions of trial-averaged activity from each timepoint of the trial, from IEMs trained on sample-evoked (black) or recall-evoked (red) data, from an ROI made up of voxels located in early visual cortex (EVC; V1, V2, V3). (I.e., the black timecourse corresponds to reconstructions from an IEM trained on sample-evoked activity, then tested on data from each timepoint in the trial [in jargonese, the IEM was "slid across the data from the entire trial"].). Gray boxes under the horizontal axis of the left-most plot indicate the time of sample presentation ("S"), delay ("D"), and recall ("R"). Black and red asterisks above each plot indicate significance of reconstruction with the sample-trained and recall-trained IEM, respectively (assessed as slopes significantly greater than 0). Green asterisks (only appearing on the "null" plots) denote a significant difference between reconstructions of the sample- and recall-trained IEMs. Note that for null trials, for which there was no stimulus information during the Sample epoch, the IEM trained on sample-evoked activity fails to reconstruct any stimulus information; this reflects the fact that it was trained on noise. **B.** Reconstructions from the "late delay period," 8–10 sec after trial onset. (I.e., the data from time 8-seconds and time 10-seconds were averaged, and IEMs tested on these averaged data.) **C.** Same as **A**, but from the intraparietal sulcus (IPS) ROI. **D.**, Same as **B**, but from the IPS ROI.

Source: Yu & Postle, 2021 / MIT Press.

(Note that, for our present purposes, the terms "working memory" and "short-term memory" are interchangeable.) By referring to a "normative account," the authors are saying that if an RNN can be trained to perform a task like this delayed-recall task, the operations by which it does so can be considered optimal, because these operations were learned and are executed by a network with a relatively simple architecture (e.g., no extraneous inputs or other sources of noise that could influence its behavior), in a network that only has to perform one task (and so isn't influenced by having to do other things at the same time), and in a network whose behavior hasn't been biased by other operations that it may have learned prior to learning how to solve this task. Furthermore, a scientist can understand precisely what are the operations carried out by the RNN to accomplish this visual working memory behavior because they know every input that the model experienced during training, and they can observe, and measure, "everything that it does" while performing the task. Consequently, this can be a very powerful approach. To fully understand how and why is going to require the introduction of several concepts, many of which will only be "quick and dirty" summaries of topics that we'll get into in more detail further along in the book. Here's a foreshadowing of what we'll cover in this introduction to RNNs, so that the reader can track their progress while working through it: *a stimulus domain with metric properties; stimulus domains represented in a continuous circular space; a bank of tuned filters; broad tuning; delivering inputs to a network; simulating chronometric time (e.g., seconds) with timesteps; precuing vs. retro-cuing; recurrence in a network; dynamics of the hidden layer of an RNN; the initial state of the untrained RNN; output: how does the network "recall" the cued color?; training via the backpropagation of the error signal; and, finally, how is it determined if training was successful?* (And that won't be the end of it, because then, to understand how activity in an RNN can be analyzed, section *Representational*

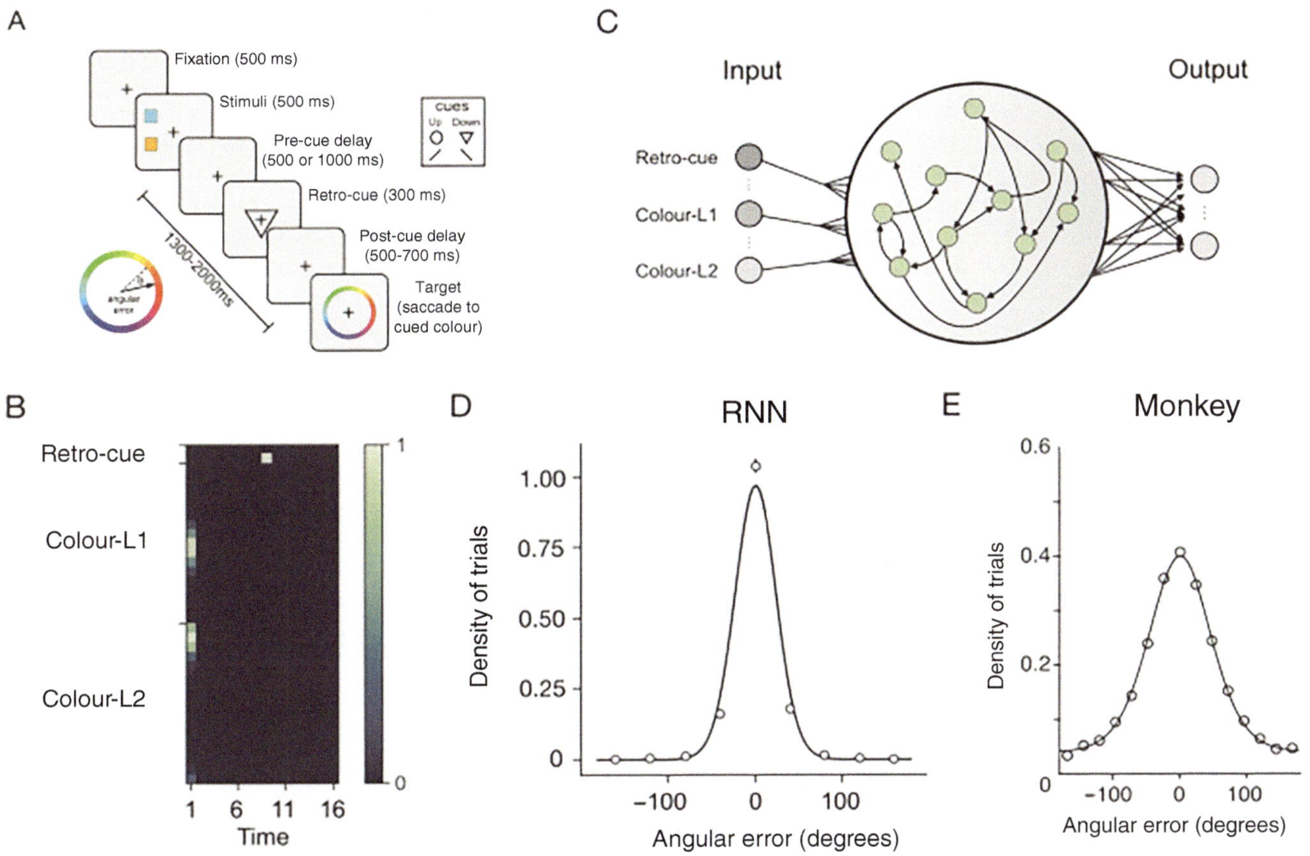

FIGURE 5.10.A Diagram of the working memory task administered to NHPs by Panichello and Buschman (2021) and simulated with RNNs by Piwek et al. (2023). The illustrated trial requires retention in working memory of the two colors during the pre-cue delay, of just the cued color during the post-cue delay, and finally recall of the cued color by making an eye movement to the matching color on the color wheel.

FIGURE 5.10.B Illustration of the pattern of activity in the input layer (see panel *C*) at each timestep of the trial. The top two rows correspond to the input units that deliver instructional cues, the next 17 rows to the color presented at the "up" location ("location 1," or L1), and the final 17 rows to the color presented in the "down" location (L2). Each of the 17 "color units" that is responsible for L1 is specialized to respond to a different section of the color wheel from panel A, and adjacent "color units" respond to similar colors (see text).

FIGURE 5.10.C Cartoon of the architecture of the RNNs trained by Piwek et al. (2023); in actuality, there were 36 units in the input layer (see panel B), 200 recurrent units in the hidden layer (rendered in green), and 17 units in the output layer.

FIGURE 5.10.D Average behavioral performance of 30 RNNs, calculated as response error. "Density of trials" (on the vertical axis) can be interpreted as reflecting proportion of responses. Each data point shows the proportion of responses for which the error fell into each of nine 40°-wide bins centered at 0°, ±40°, ±80°, ±120°, and ±160°. Note that the relative narrowness of the fitted curve indicates a high degree of precision of recall.

FIGURE 5.10.E Average behavioral performance of the two NHPs from Panichello and Buschman (2021). Note the broader distribution of response error relative to the RNNs, indicating considerably lower precision of recall for the monkeys relative to the machines.

Source: (Piwek, Stokes, & Summerfield, 2023) / PLOS /

Geometry Analysis will review this approach that is commonly used to interpret the operations carried out by the RNN.) It's going to be a lot of information, but it will be worth it!

- Stimulus domains with metric properties. To build an RNN that can simulate the performance of a working memory task, Piwek et al. (2023) constructed the three-layer network illustrated in *Figure 5.10.C*. The input layer is functionally analogous to the visual layer of the PDP model illustrated in *Figure 4.24* in that, for both networks, the activation of units in this layer simulates "showing something" to the network. However, the architecture of the input layer of the RNNs differs markedly from that of the PDP model, because this RNN is designed to represent metric properties of a dimension in the physical world, in this case, color. One characteristic of human perception of color is that, for example, yellow appears to be more similar to orange than to red, and that although a particular shade of orange and a particular shade of green can be said to be equally similar to yellow, the two can also be said to be also dissimilar from each other because the similarity of each to yellow is "coming from the opposite direction." This is captured in the color wheels illustrated in *Figure 5.10.A*. Indeed, the color wheel illustrating "angular error" shows how the distance along the wheel of, say, a particular value of yellow from a particular value of orange, can be expressed as a polar angle. One can also see that the sign of the angle measuring the yellow-to-orange distance would be the opposite for the angle separating the yellow-to-green distance (because the former is clockwise from yellow, and the latter is anticlockwise from yellow).

- Stimulus domains represented in a continuous circular space. The color wheel illustrates this property of perceptual color space, one consequence of which is that it has no discontinuities, no "beginning" or "end." (Note that this is not true of the visible portion of the electromagnetic spectrum from which color perception derives, which can be construed as "starting" at the long-wavelength boundary of infrared radiation to visible light and "ending" at the short-wavelength boundary from visible light to ultraviolet radiation.)
- A bank of tuned filters in a network. Returning to the input layer of this RNN, it contained a total of 38 units; 36 of them "color" units and two of them "instructional." (*Figure 5.10.C* only shows three units, for simplicity.) The two "instructional" units are so that the network can be informed, partway through the trial, whether it is the color of the stimulus that appeared in the top portion of the display ("up") or in the bottom portion of the display ("down") that will need to be recalled at the end of the trial. *Figure 5.10.B* shows what was the pattern of activation in the input layer at each timestep of the trial illustrated in *Figure 5.10.A*. The top two rows correspond to the instructional cues, the next 17 rows to the color presented at the up location ("location 1," or L1), and the final 17 rows to the color presented in the down location (L2). Importantly, each of the 17 "color units" that are responsible for L1 is tuned to respond to a different section of the color wheel, and adjacent "color units" respond to similar colors. For example, within this column of 17 units, the unit that is tuned to yellow is adjacent to and "just above" the unit that is tuned to orange, and it is also adjacent to, but "just below," the unit that is tuned to green. In this case, each column of 17 color-tuned units spans the full range of visible colors (i.e., the range that spans from ultraviolet to infrared) and so can be thought of as a functional subsystem for perceiving color. In engineering shorthand, such a subsystem can be referred to as a "bank of filters," and so we will refer to each 17-unit subgroup within the input layer of the RNN as a bank of tuned filters.
- Broad tuning. Quick inspection of the color wheels illustrated in *Figure 5.10.A* confirms that they contain many more than 17 distinct colors. (E.g., you can see that the larger of the two was rendered by assembling ~40 little wedges, each one a slightly different hue.) How can a bank of only 17 tuned filters enable the perception of >40 colors? The answer is, perhaps counterintuitively, by giving each of them "broad tuning." For example, consider the pinkish-red wedge that the arrow is pointing to in the larger color wheel in *Figure 5.10.A*. If one of the wedges responded to that color and ONLY that color (i.e., if it was very sharply tuned), then the network would be unable to "see" a stimulus of the hue of either of the adjacent wedges. If, however, this unit were broadly tuned, such that it responded most strongly to the pinkish-red but also, although somewhat more weakly, to the shade of the wedge that is just clockwise to it, as well as to the shade of the wedge that is just anticlockwise to it, and even more weakly to the wedges that are two positions away, one can see how 17 such broadly tuned filters could be placed at equal distances around the wheel such that any of the infinite possible shades of visible color would produce a unique pattern of activation in our bank of (broadly) tuned filters. (For an example of the classic bell-curve shape of the "tuning curve" of a broadly tuned neuron, c.f., *Figure 3.1*.)
- Delivering inputs to the network. *Figure 5.10.B* illustrates how the trial diagrammed in *Figure 5.10.A* is initiated. At timestep 1, the presentation of a cyan-colored stimulus at

location L1 is implemented by activating four units simultaneously with a bell-shaped (typically Gaussian) "bump" of activity that is highest in the middle of the bump and lower at its flanks. This corresponds to the network "seeing" cyan at location L1. Similarly, the presentation of an orange-colored stimulus at L2 is implemented by activating a different set of four units that, when activated simultaneously with a Gaussian "bump" of activation, corresponds to the network "seeing" orange at L2. (Note that this is fundamentally different from the categorical nature of units in the visual layer of the PDP model illustrated in *Figure 4.23*, for which the determination of which unit would respond to *has stripes*, for example, or to *is round*, was arbitrary [i.e., it had no topography], and it was only capable of perceiving the 64 features represented by the 64 units in that layer.)

- Simulating chronometric time (e.g., seconds) with timesteps. The simulated trial unfolds over 16 timesteps, and *Figure 5.10.B* illustrates the state of the input layer across each of them. The fact that the 36 "color units" are black for the 15 timesteps subsequent to timestep 1 corresponds to the fact that no additional stimulus information is presented during the trial. (It follows from this that, to succeed, the network must hold a representation of cyan and a representation of orange in some other part of the network from timestep 2 onward.) (For all neural networks that we will consider here, the passage of time is measured in "timesteps" rather than, say, in seconds. Each successive timestep is a static snapshot of the state of the network at that "moment in time" during performance of the task. The number of timesteps used to simulate a trial like this one is arbitrary, in that the network's performance of a trial would be expected to be the same whether the authors chose to simulate a trial with 6 timesteps, 16 timesteps, or 600 timesteps – the only difference would be the temporal granularity at which one could observe its activity.)
- Precuing vs. retrocuing. The diagram in *Figure 5.10.A* shows that the screen is blank for the 500 or 1000 msec interstimulus interval (ISI; the length of this ISI varied unpredictably from trial to trial). Accordingly, *Figure 5.10.B* shows that the level of activity in every unit in the input layer is 0 during the eight timesteps that correspond to this "pre-cue delay." At timestep 9, the activity level in the down cue unit is elevated, corresponding to the triangle retro-cue. (These instructional cues are called "retrocues" because they refer to something that happened earlier in time – if you approach a traffic light while the signal changes from green to yellow, the yellow light can be considered a "precue," because it is PREdictive of the fact that soon the light will turn red; in our example trial, in contrast, the cue is RETROdictive of the color that previously appeared at the bottom location.)

Note that if only one cue were used for "top" and one for "bottom," brain activity associated with selecting from memory the color that had appeared at the top/bottom would be confounded with activity associated with viewing a circle/triangle. For this reason, the "cues" legend in *Figure 5.10.A* shows that, in the original task administered to NHPs, "up" was indicated by either a circle or a forward slash ("/") and down by either a triangle or a backslash ("\"). (This detail was not included in the RNN simulation, which only used one input unit for "up" and one for "down.")

Now that we have an understanding of how the input layer is organized, and how stimulus information is fed into the model, we're getting closer to being able to address how this RNN can provide a "normative account of how dynamic memory processes are learned through error minimization," because this is accomplished by studying the activity in the hidden layer. So now, we proceed to the next step of understanding the RNN, which is to understand the architecture of the hidden layer. The key for doing this will be to understand what is meant by "recurrence" in RNN.

- Recurrence in a network. This week my family brought home a new puppy, so I'll draw from that for this illustration. Here goes: Imagine that I built a simple device intended to encourage good behavior by my dog. If I see the dog doing something good, I pull a lever (element A of my device). There is a string (B) that is tied to A at one end and tied to the door of a box full of doggie treats (C) at the other end. The chain of events in my simple device is that pulling A stretches B, and stretching B opens C. This is a strictly feedforward system with the causal chain A ➔ B ➔ C. A influences B, which then influences C, but there's no way for B or C to influence A. But now let's say that, after proudly demonstrating my new contraption to my spouse, she gently points out a problem with my device, which is that we don't want to over-feed the dog. One way to modify what I've already build is to add a counter to C. The counter advances every time the string is pulled and, after the string has been pulled five times, the counter pulls a new string (D), and D is connected to broomstick (E) that, when pulled, falls over and blocks A. The rationale is that when I next want to pull the lever (A) I'll be prevented from doing to until I reset E, and this will remind me not to overfeed the dog. What we have done by adding D and E is to add a "feedback loop" such that now C can influence A. "Recurrence" is a word that is used to describe a property like this, a property whereby when any element A sends a signal, not only does this trigger the chain of downstream events (A ➔ B ➔ C . . .), it also generates information about the consequence of having triggered this chain, and this information is fed back to A in a way that can influence A's subsequent behavior.

- Dynamics of the hidden layer of an RNN. The architecture of the hidden layer of an RNN is such that, at each timestep n, two things happen: first, each unit receives inputs that change its level of activation, and second, each unit then outputs a value corresponding to this new level of activation. The next timestep (timestep $n + 1$) then begins with a new set of inputs that reflect the updated values from timestep n. (Of course, this means that the inputs that initiated timestep n corresponded to the updated state of the hidden layer at the end of timestep $n - 1$). The result of this architecture is that the hidden layer of an RNN is perpetually active, always "churning" even when no external inputs are being delivered to it. This "churning," then, corresponds to the processing of information that the RNN from *Figure 5.10* carries out during the delay period of this task. Consequently, the "normative account" of how the RNN performs this working memory task will be derived from an analysis the delay-period dynamics of the hidden layer.
- The initial state of the untrained RNN. Before we can get to a definitive account of how the RNN performs the working memory task, it has to be trained. That is, the network doesn't come "off the shelf" already "knowing how" to perform the task. The only things that it "knows" prior to training is how to simulate color perception (because the organization and properties of its input layer were predetermined by the experimenter). Indeed, prior to the very first trial of training, the connections between units in the input layer and the hidden layer, the connections between units in the hidden layer, and the connections between the hidden layer and the output layer are arbitrarily randomized. (This preparation prior to the first trial of training is referred to as "initialization" of the network.) And so, if the trial that's illustrated in *Figure 5.10.A* were the first trial of training, the activation of the input layer would indeed correspond to cyan being presented to L1 and orange being presented to L2, as shown in *Figure 5.10.B*. The connections between the input layer and the hidden layer are one-way, such that the values from the input layer are fed into the hidden layer, but the hidden layer can never influence the input layer. On the first trial, these two inputs "wouldn't make sense" to the hidden layer (i.e., they wouldn't be interpreted as cyan and orange) because the hidden layer "doesn't yet know anything about the world." To elaborate, what one would want to happen – and what will happen after training – is that the input of patterns of activity corresponding to cyan and orange triggers the activity in the hidden layer to reconfigure itself so as to represent cyan and orange. Because the connection strengths in the hidden layer were initialized to be randomly determined, however, any information about the two colors is lost as soon as the input is removed, and the activity in the hidden layer just continues to churn along "meaninglessly" during the pre-cue delay. Similarly, although the down retrocue is presented via the input layer just the way it should be, the consequence of its presentation for activity in the hidden layer is negligible; it has the effect of inserting a meaningless perturbation into an already noisy and meaningless pandemonium of activity. Next, we get to the end of the trial.
- Output. How does the network "recall" the cued color? At timestep 16 (i.e., at the end of the trial), the level of activity of each of the 200 hidden units is output onto the output

layer, which is a single bank of 17 broadly tuned filters, identical to the "colour-L1" and "colour-L2" portions of the input layer of the network. On a perfect trial, after training, the effect of projecting the 200-dimensional output from the hidden layer into the output layer would be to drive the 17-D pattern of activity in the output layer to reconfigure itself to represent orange – that is, to reconfigure itself to match the pattern in the L2 input sub-layer at timestep 1. This would be an example of the RNN correctly recalling the color of the stimulus that had been presented at L2 at the beginning of the trial. Because this is the very first trial of training, however, the effect of projecting the 200-D pattern of random noise from the hidden layer into the output layer is to "push" it from its randomly initialized 17-D pattern into a different random 17-D pattern.

Note that, now that we know the full architecture of the model, we can calculate how many connections is has. Every unit in the input layer is connected to every unit in the hidden layer, and so this yields (36 * 200 =) 7200 connections. Within the hidden layer every unit is connected to every other unit, and so it contains (200 * 200 =) 40,000 connections. Finally, every hidden unit is connected with every unit in the output layer, yielding (200 * 17 =) 3400 connections. This sums to a total of 50,600 connections. (This seems like a large number, and it is, but keep in mind that the human brain is estimated to contain trillions of connections between processing units.)

- Training via the backpropagation of the error signal. The experimenters know that the response on this first trial of training was supposed to be "orange," and so, to begin training the network, they "show it" what the correct 17-D pattern in the output layer should have been, a difference is calculated between what the output should have been and what it actually was, and the resulting "difference vector" is used to slightly adjust every connection in the network. More specifically, the training procedure used by Piwek et al. (2023) was to apply what's called a "gradient descent" algorithm that slightly modifies all the connections in the network in such a way that, had the new set of connections been in place on that trial, the magnitude of the difference vector would have been slightly smaller than it actually was. This process is repeated, depending on the specific training procedure and network parameters, anywhere from hundreds to thousands to tens-of-thousands of times.

At a generic level, the procedure that we just described for training a network is referred to as backpropagation of the error signal (or "backprop" for short). Why? After each trial one can think of the difference vector as indexing the "error" in the network's performance, and the process carried out by the gradient descent algorithm to be one of "error minimization." Furthermore, if one considers the overall flow of the network as the forward propagation of information from input-to-hidden-to-output, the subsequent calculation of the error and its use to adjust connection strengths can be construed as the backward propagation of the error signal through the network (i.e., from output-to-hidden-to-input). (Note that the adjustments made on any one trial are very slight because, if they were too large, the changes applied after trial n would likely not be appropriate for trial $n + 1$ and, in fact, would make the make the difference vector for trial $n + 1$ considerably larger than it would have been had there been no correction at all after trial n. In this situation, the network would never converge to an optimal configuration of weights.)

- How is it determined if training was successful? If training is successful, the connection strengths eventually converge on a final set of 50,600 connection weights that yields a satisfactory level of recall accuracy by the network. Another way to say this, and the way in which recall performance is often measured, is that recall error will have dropped to an acceptable level. Framing behavioral improvement as a reduction in recall error also makes it easier to relate it to what we can think of as the "internal performance" of the model, because the model's performance is assessed in terms of error. Specifically, the "error vector" that is used in back propagation can be distilled into a single number referred to as the "loss" of the network's performance. It is invariably the case that loss is relatively high during the earliest stage of training and, assuming that training is successful, loss declines over training. Often it will decline exponentially across training trials, and training is considered complete when the decline in loss reaches an asymptote, or some other predetermined threshold. When training is judged to be complete, the final step is typically to cease applying the backpropagation procedure, thereby "freezing" the connection strengths in the network, and then to carry out a series of trials and record behavioral performance. This is often referred to as the "testing" stage. (One can think of this by analogy to an experimental psychology study: First one reads instructions to the subject and lets them carry out practice trials, often with feedback, and often until some criterion level of performance is achieved. Only after one is confident that the subject understands how to perform the task does one the administer the "real trials" from which interpretable data are collected.)

Figure 5.10.E illustrates the average performance of the two monkeys from Panichello and Buschman (2021), plotted as response error (i.e., for each trial, how distant from the color of the cued item was the recall response. The fact that the bell-shaped distribution of response errors is centered around 0° indicates that the animals were, indeed, reporting information about the cued color. (If they had been guessing, the distribution would have been a flat line.) However, their performance was far from perfect, as indexed by the mean absolute error of 51.8° (i.e., on an average trial their response was 51.8° distant from the precise value of the to-be-recalled color). In comparison, visual inspection of *Figure 5.10.D* suggests that the distribution of errors made by the 30 RNNs trained for this experiment was much narrower, and thus that their performance was more precise. (It is common practice to carry out RNN simulations with several models with identical architectures, but different randomly initialized patterns of weights and different sequences of training trials, to confirm the reliability of the results.) Indeed, the mean absolute error for the RNNs was 16.4°. Piwek et al. (2023) note this discrepancy in behavioral performance, and speculate that it "could be seen to reflect other sources of noise (e.g., motor error during saccadic responding) that are present in the animals but not in our models but is otherwise not consequential for our findings," adding that "increasing the noise added to network units precluded convergence" (p. 4/33). In this last statement, the authors are saying that once they had established a procedure for training networks successfully, achieving the performance illustrated in *Figure 5.10.D*, they tried repeating the procedure (on new, randomly initialized networks) but with the additional factor of injecting random noise into the network during training. The intent was to achieve a similar training profile of decreasing loss until a criterion is reached, but to do so such that the final set of 50,600 connection weights yielded poorer behavioral performance (i.e., recall precision that more closely matched the NHP performance illustrated in *Figure 5.10.E*). What they found, however, was that with the addition of noise, the networks could no longer be trained successfully, in that the loss curve never declined to the asymptotic criterion but instead would periodically jump back up to unacceptably high levels.

Analysis Methods

Representational Geometry Analysis

This section segues directly from the previous section *RNN modeling of visual working memory* and, indeed, can be construed as a continuation of it. Now that we've established some principles of how an RNN works, and how it is trained, we can turn to one of the principal reasons why they have become such a popular tool for cognitive neuroscience research: the elucidation of normative accounts of how dynamic cognitive processes are carried out. To illustrate this, we'll stay with the example of working memory and continue to draw heavily on Piwek et al. (2023). Consider the trial illustrated in *Figure 5.10.A*. Working backwards, to respond correctly at the end of this trial, the RNN needs to respond "orange." In order to do that, it must be the case that the hidden layer has retained information corresponding to orange during the roughly 1.5 seconds separating the offset of the stimuli and the onset of the color wheel. Furthermore, because the RNN can't know ahead of time whether the cue will indicate "up" or "down," it would also have had to retain information corresponding to cyan during the precue delay. One of the key questions for Piwek et al. (2023) was to understand how does a single hidden layer of the RNN retain information about two stimuli and keep these representations separated? (Panichello and Buschman (2021) had shown that several different regions in the brain of the NHP do this.) Before addressing this "two stimulus problem," we'll start by addressing the simpler question of how does the hidden layer of the RNN retain information about a single stimulus?

Recall that we said that after training "*. . . the input of patterns of activity corresponding to cyan and orange trigger the activity in the hidden layer to reconfigure itself so as to represent cyan and orange*." Logically, we know that this has to be true, based on the reasoning in the previous paragraph. However, visually inspecting the activation levels of the units of the hidden layer doesn't help us understand how it does this. For example, consider the results from a different RNN trained to perform visual working memory for grating orientation (*Figure 5.11*); its architecture is similar to that from Piwek et al. (2023), but with 100 recurrent units rather than 200. And note that, because orientation is also a continuous, circular stimulus domain, what we can learn from RNN modeling of working memory for orientation applies equally well to working memory for color, and vice versa. *Figure 5.11.C* illustrates the 100D patterns of activity in the hidden layer when it is representing 179° (i.e., nearly horizontal) and when it is representing 69°. Although these two 100D patterns are clearly different from each other, looking at them doesn't tell us how it is that with one of them the network is representing 179° and with the other, 69°. (E.g., if you were shown the 100-column panel on the left side of *Figure 5.11.C*, without the accompanying labels, you'd have no way of knowing that it corresponds to "179°." Indeed, because each RNN starts from a different randomly determined initialization pattern and is trained with unique sequences of trials, two different networks trained with identical parameters and sequences of trials would converge to different 100D patterns to represent "179°.") What *can* help us understand how the RNN represents a specific stimulus value, such as "179°," however, is to apply dimensionality reduction to the full set of 100D patterns in which it configures itself to represent the full stimulus space.

At a general level, "dimensionality reduction" refers to a technique for transforming a high-dimensional dataset into one with a smaller number of dimensions, and doing so in a way that meaningful properties of the original are retained. The resultant transformed dataset can be easier to visualize, easier to measure, and easier to understand. For example, *Figure 5.11.D* shows the result of applying a principal component analysis (PCA, a popular method for dimensionality reduction) to the 100D patterns of ISI activity from 1000 test trials. (Thus, the two arrays from *Figure 5.11.C* are two of the 1000 observations to which the PCA was applied.) As the name implies, the PCA has analytically decomposed the data into latent components that can be construed as summarizing how the hidden layer represents orientation information. (These components are "latent" in that they are not explicitly evident in the data in their native state but nonetheless define an organizing principle that allows the structure in the data to be summarized efficiently.) Indeed, for the result illustrated in *Figure 5.11.D*, diagnostics of the PCA indicate that the first two principal components (PCs) together account for 91% of the variance in hidden-layer configurations during the ISI 1 epoch, as indexed by a measure called "percentage explained variance" (PEV). This means that virtually all the stimulus information being represented by the hidden layer during ISI 1 can be represented in just the "subspace" defined by these two PCs.

What is a subspace? Mathematically, a PCA can decompose an n-dimensional dataset into a total of $n - 1$ PCs. Another way of saying this is that a PCA transforms a n-dimensional "native space" into an $n - 1$ dimensional "PC space." However, as we've already noted, during ISI 1, the vast majority of stimulus information is represented in just a small subset of the total number of PCs generated by the PCA (i.e., in PC1 and PC2). These two PCs can be said to define a 2-dimensional "subspace" within the full $n - 1$-dimensional PC space in which the data exist.

As illustrated by *Figure 5.11.D*, the PCA reveals a representational geometry that was not visible in the native space illustrated in *Figure 5.11.C*: Orientation is represented by the hidden layer on a ring-shaped manifold. (A manifold being (for our purposes) the $n - 1$ dimensional surface of an n-dimensional shape. For example, the 2D cortex can be construed as a manifold

FIGURE 5.11 The representational geometry of stimulus information represented in an RNN.

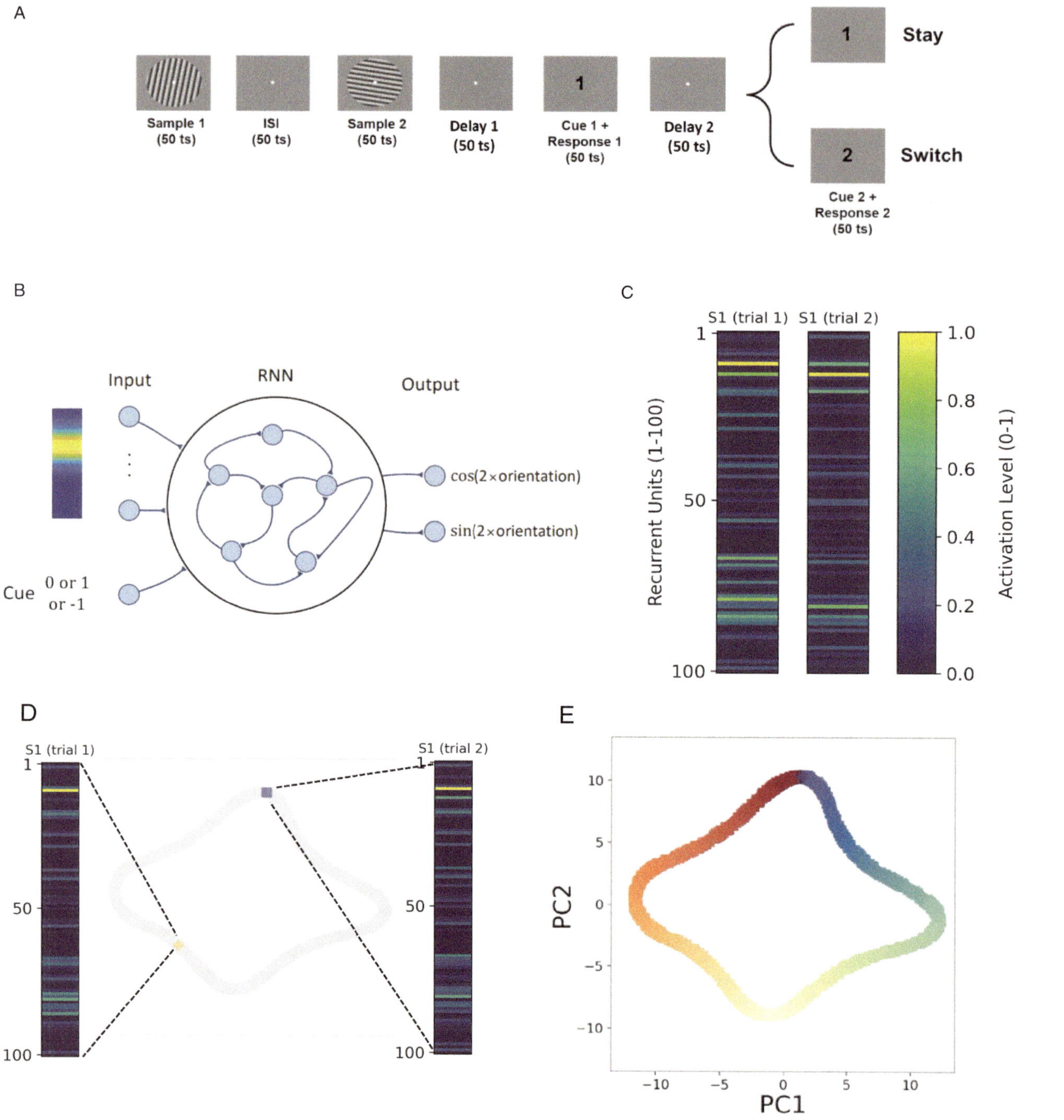

FIGURE 5.11.A Diagram of a trial from a "double serial retrocuing" test of working memory for oriented gratings, modeled after Yu, Teng, and Postle (2020). Trial epochs occurred sequentially, and each lasted 50 timesteps: central presentation of an oriented grating (*Sample 1*), interstimulus interval (*ISI*), central presentation of a second oriented grating (*Sample 2*), another ISI (*Delay 1*), first retrocued recall (*Cue 1* + *Response 1*), another ISI (Delay 2), second retrocued recall (*Cue 2* + *Response 2*; "stay"/"switch" status of Cue 2 was equiprobable and unpredictable). Note that *Figure 5.11.D* only illustrates network activity from the first ISI and Delay 1.

Source: Wan et al. (2024) / Massachusetts Institute of Technology / CC BY 4.0.

FIGURE 5.11.B Architecture of the RNN. Input layer was comprised of 32 broadly tuned orientation-selective filters that spanned the full range of 180°, plus one cue unit. Illustrated to the left of the input layer is the vector representing a sample orientation with a Gaussian bump of activity (c.f., *Figure 5.11.B*).

Source: Wan et al. (2024) / Massachusetts Institute of Technology / CC BY 4.0.

FIGURE 5.11.C Activity level during the first ISI, for two different stimulus values, in each of the 100 recurrent units in an RNN trained to perform the task illustrated in (A). The ordering of units from 1 to 100 is arbitrarily determined, but the same for both stimuli.

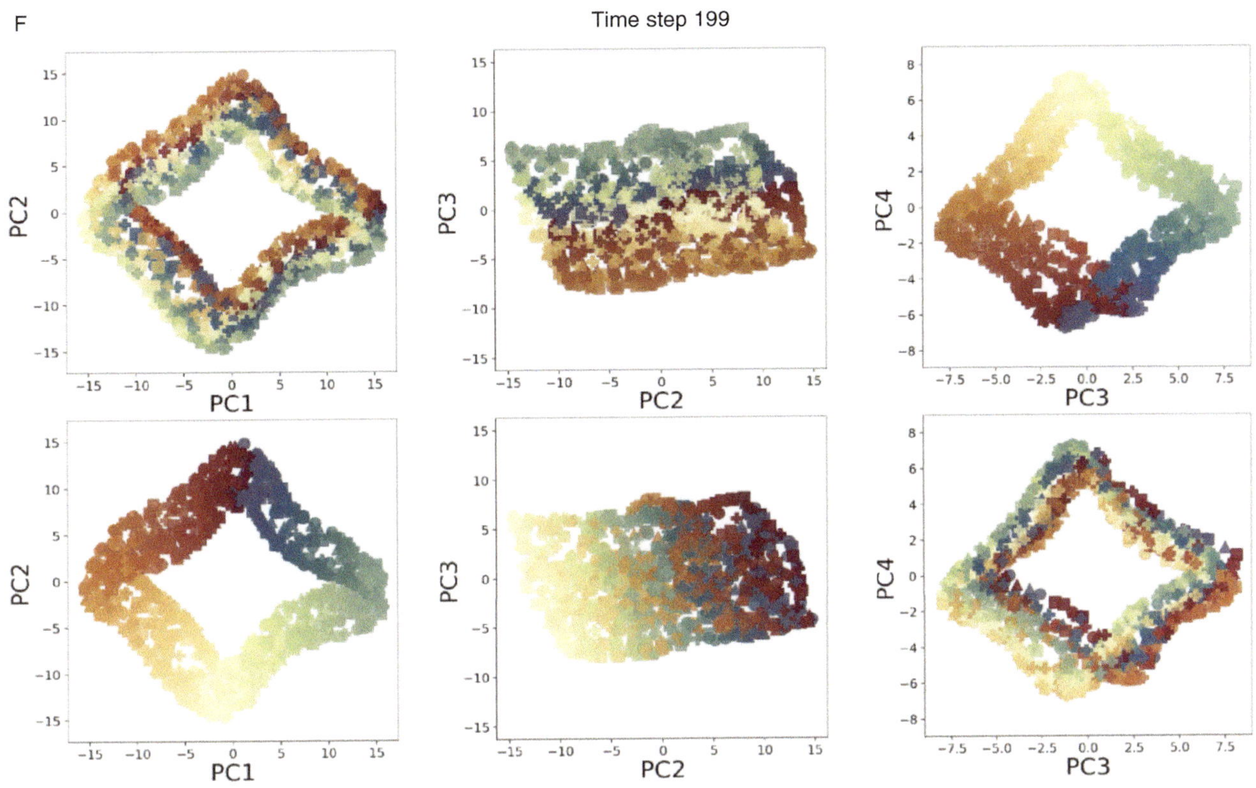

FIGURE 5.11.D The same two 100D patterns from (C), but now shown flanking the subspace defined by the first two PCs from a PCA performed on all 1000 test trials from which these two sample stimuli are exemplars (the PEV of these two PCs sums to 91%). The dotted lines illustrate, for each stimulus, the projection of each into this subspace, their values depicted as a color, as indicated in the legend. The gray outline indicates the ring manifold resulting from this dimensionality reduction – that is, the 2-D representation of the remaining 998 stimulus values submitted to the PCA. Note that here the ring manifold is rendered in a uniform gray color, to reflect the fact that the data were not labeled according to the stimulus value that they represented, and so the PCA "did not know" how or why each trial differed – this is simply the latent structure that it identified in the data.

FIGURE 5.11.E The representational geometry of stimulus information during the ISI, as revealed by PCA: a ring manifold in a 2-D subspace that preserves the topology of the physical stimulus space. This is the same manifold as illustrated in (D), but now color-coded to reflect the stimulus value from all 1000 trials that were submitted to the PCA. This visualization was constructed by projecting the 100D pattern of hidden-layer activity from the ISI from each of 1000 test trials into the subspace defined by the first two PCs from a PCA applied to the data from all test trials. (Thus, each dot corresponds to a trial and is color-coded according to the orientation being represented by the network on that trial.)

FIGURE 5.11.F The representational geometry of stimulus information during Delay 1, when two orientations are being retained by the network. As was done for the ISI (*Figure 5.11.E*), the PCA was carried out in the 1000 test trials; unlike for the ISI, however, the first four PCs were needed to cumulatively account for >90% of the variance in the data. Because Delay 1 follows the presentation of the second sample, the same data are illustrated twice, labeled according to the identity of Sample 1 in the top row and according to the identity of Sample 2 in the bottom row. Inspection of the top row indicates that Sample 1 is no longer represented in the PC1–PC2 subspace but is now represented in the PC3–PC4 subspace, and the bottom row indicates that Sample 2 is represented in the PC1–PC2 subspace. *Figure 5.11.A* and *Figure 5.11.B* based on Wan, Ardalan, Fulvio, and Postle (2024); images from *Figure 5.11.C–F* courtesy of Jung Woo Hur in the author's laboratory.

of the 3D brain; and even though color and orientation are circular dimensions, there's a technical sense in which they are a 1D array of values "covering" a 2D ring.) The image in *Figure 5.11.C* was constructed by first training the RNN on the task illustrated in *Figure 5.11.A*, then testing it on 1000 trials that drew from the full 180° range of possible stimulus values, then applying a PCA to the resultant 1000 100D patterns of hidden unit activity at a particular timestep during ISI 1. The representational geometry identified by this procedure is then visualized by "projecting into" the subspace defined by PC1 and PC2 the 100D data from each individual trial. It is important to note that the PCA applied to these data didn't "know" anything about which stimulus was presented on which trial, we added the colors after the fact. Nonetheless, as the 100-D data from each trial are projected into the PC1–PC2 subspace (*Figure 5.11.E*), one sees that each occupies a location on the ring that is adjacent to trials that presented adjacent orientations.

Now we can turn to how the network represents two stimuli simultaneously. *Figure 5.11.F* illustrates results from a PCA applied to the data from these 1000 trials at a later point in time during the trial, specifically the "Delay 1" that separates the offset of *Sample 2* from the onset of the first retrocue (i.e., "*Cue 1 + Response 1*"). Displaying these results is complicated by the fact that two stimuli are being held simultaneously, but any one image of this timestep can only be color-coded to show values corresponding to one item or to the other. So what is done in *Figure 5.11.F* is that the same data are shown twice but labeled differently in the two rows: The top row is labeled according to the value of *Sample 1,* and the bottom row is labeled according to the value of *Stimulus 2.* (An analogy might be a car-racing video game: If two of your friends are racing each other you can set up a split screen display such that at any moment in time what is being illustrated is the same moment from the same race, but from two different perspectives – one of the two images displays what friend #1 is seeing while "driving" their car and the other is displaying what friend #2 is seeing while "driving" theirs.) If we first inspect the top row of *Figure 5.11.F*, we see that *Sample 1* is no longer being represented in the subspace comprised of PC1 and PC2. It has seemingly been "pushed" into a different subspace, one comprised of PC3 and PC4. (The geometric term for this is that it has *rotated* from the PC1–PC2 subspace into the PC3–PC4 subspace.) And when we inspect the bottom row of *Figure 5.11.F*, we see that the PC1PC2 subspace is now representing *Sample 2.* Importantly, the PC1–PC2 subspace and the PC3–PC4 subspace are geometrically orthogonal with respect to each other, which means that information represented in, say, PC1–PC2 is "invisible" from the perspective of PC3–PC4. An implication of this is that information represented in PC3–PC4 won't be affected by what may or may not be represented in PC1–PC2. Thus, we can see that through training, the RNN has learned to represent distinct items in separate subspaces, one consequence of which is to minimize the likelihood that, for example, orange might "leak over" into cyan (thereby turning it brown?) (Note that a consequence of the rotation of *Sample 1* into the PC3–PC4 subspace is that the distribution of PEVs by PC is different from what we saw for the representation of a single item by the first two PCs; during delay 1.1 the PEVs for the first four PCs are 42%, 30%, 12.5%, and 8.5%.) And now, we can (finally!) get to results from Piwek et al. (2023), which we introduced in section *RNN modeling of visual working memory*, and their normative account of the simultaneous retention of two items in working memory.

Figure 5.12 illustrates results from PCAs of data from neurons in the PFC of NHPs (panel *A*, from Panichello and Buschman (2021)) and recurrent units in an RNN (panel *B*, from Piwek et al. (2023)) performing the working memory task illustrated in *Figure 5.10.A*. (And so, at a meta level, it illustrates the point that representational geometry analyses yield valuable insights when applied to data derived from physiological recordings, as well as when applied to ANNs.) The first thing to note is that, unlike for the data illustrated in *Figure 5.11.F*, the two stimuli can be decoded from the first three PCs, which means that duplicate images are not required to visualize them both. Instead, their representation can be visualized as two 2D manifolds in a single 3D space. The second thing to note is that although one can assume that the color stimuli were represented in ring manifolds (similar to *Figure 5.11*), in these two studies, the data from each trial were first sorted into four groups corresponding to equal-sized quadrants of the color wheel and averaged within each group prior to being submitted to the PCA. (Therefore, there are only four data points per stimulus in the plots in *Figure 5.12* rather than the 1000 data points in the plots in *Figure 5.11*.) To facilitate visualization of each stimulus-specific representational manifold, lines have been drawn to connect datapoints from adjacent color quadrants, and the 2D plane on which each "ring" sits is colored translucent gray. For both NHP and RNN, the plot on the left illustrates the data projected into the first three PCs of the precue delay activity, and the plot on the right the data projected into the first three PCs of the postcue delay activity.

Inspection of the pre-cue delay activity in the RNN (*Figure 5.12.A*) indicates that the *L1* item is represented in a 2D subspace primarily defined by PC1 and PC2 and the *L2* item in a 2D subspace primarily defined by PC2 and PC3. These two subspaces are orthogonal, by

FIGURE 5.12 Priority-related transformations of representational geometry in working memory.
Source: Piwek et al. (2023) / PLOS / CC BY 4.0.

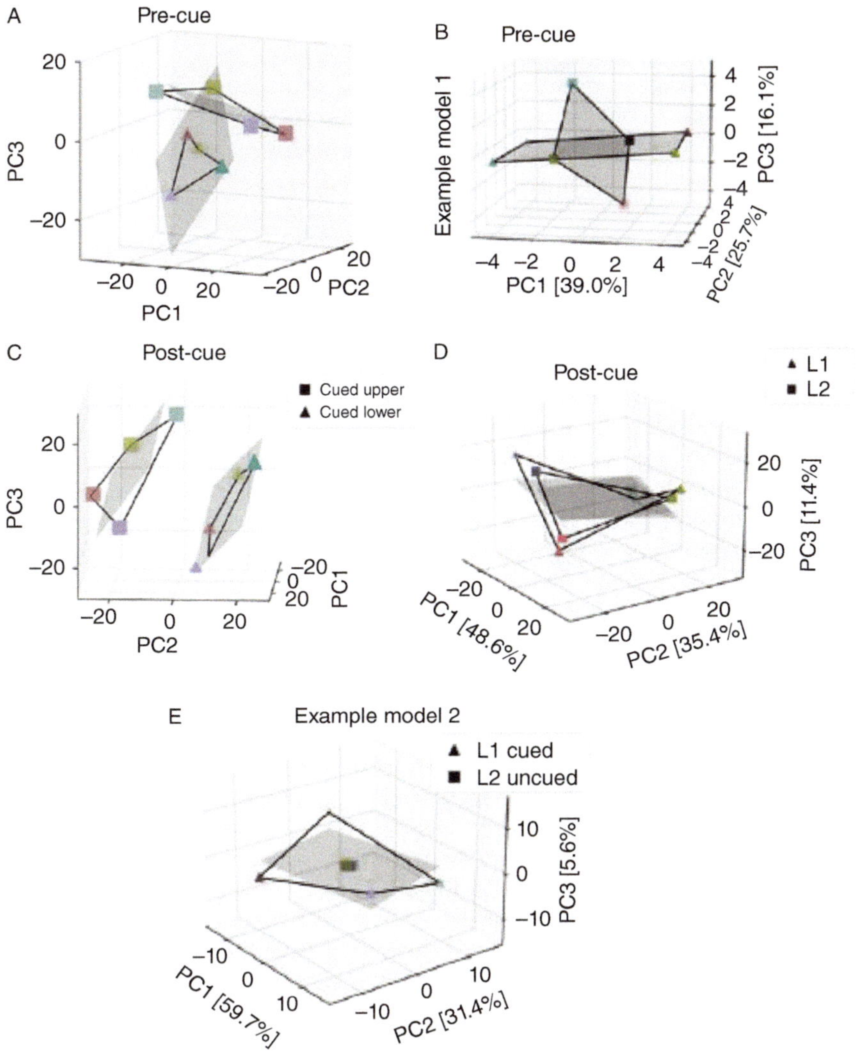

FIGURE 5.12.A Dimensionality-reduced stimulus representations during the precue delay of neuronal activity recorded from the PFC of NHPs (Panichello and Buschman, 2021). The angle separating the 2-D planes on which the stimulus-representing manifolds sit was measured to be close to 90°.

FIGURE 5.12.B Dimensionality-reduced stimulus representations during the precue delay, from the hidden layer of an RNN trained by Piwek et al. (2023). The angle separating the 2-D planes on which the stimulus-representing manifolds sit was measured to be close to 90°.

FIGURE 5.12.C The post-cue delay representation, in the PFC of NHPs, of the up stimulus on the half of the trials in the experiment in which it was cued, and of the down stimulus on the other half of the trials, when it was cued. Although this plot reflects two separate sets of trials, this illustrates that the cued item always occupies the same subspace, whether it had been presented "up" or "down," and the angle separating the 2-D planes on which the stimulus-representing manifolds sit does not differ from 0°. This suggests that, upon cuing, the prioritized item becomes represented in a communication subspace that is amenable to readout by downstream systems that will execute the response (i.e., the PFC does not directly control the direction of gaze of the eyes, and it is via an eye movement that the animal will indicates its recall of the cued item). (Note that, because this is a different PCA from the one applied to the pre-cue delay period, it cannot be known which of two possible scenarios produces this outcome: (1) upon cuing, the cued items rotates into a new subspace different from the one it occupied during the pre-cue delay, or (2) upon cuing, one of the two does not transform upon cuing, one of the two stimulus-representing subspaces takes on the function of communication subspace, and so the

(Continued)

cued item only undergoes a representational transformation on half the trials in the experiment. (E.g., if the up subspace also takes on the function of communication subspace, the up item does not undergo a representational transformation on trials when it is cued, but the down item rotates into the up subspace on trials when it is cued.)

FIGURE 5.12.D The post-cue delay representation, in the hidden layer of the RNN, of the up stimulus on half of the trials in the experiment, in which it was cued, and of the down stimulus on the other half of the trials, when it was cued. As with (C), although this plot reflects two separate sets of trials, this illustrates that the cued item always occupies the same subspace, whether it had been presented "up" or "down," and the angle separating the 2-D planes on which the stimulus-representing manifolds sit does not differ from 0°. (Indeed, for this network, the post-cue manifolds lie on the same plane. Analysis for the results from the RNNs revealed that this priority-related transformation followed "scenario B" as described in panel (C). However, neither the L1 nor the L2 subspace was inherently privileged in this regard. Rather, for some networks it was the L1 subspace that took on the role of communication subspace upon completion of training, and for others, it was the L2 subspace. Furthermore, this phenomenon of a network settling on a single privileged communication subspace was found to be dependent on the latency between retrocue and recall. That is, the pattern described here was observed for networks trained on trials with the timing as illustrated in *Figure 5.10.B*, with the retrocue presented at timestep 9. For networks trained on trials on which the retrocue was presented only one or two timesteps prior to the presentation of the recall dial, however, neither L1 nor L2 rotated into a different subspace. The authors speculated that perhaps this indicates that the phenomenon of convergence to a single privileged communication subspace confers stability in situations in which the prioritized item must be held for an extended period of time, but this additional stability may not be needed on trials when the response will follow soon after the cue.

FIGURE 5.12.E The post-cue delay representation, in the hidden layer of the RNN, of both the cued and the uncued item, on trials when the L1 item was cued. (I.e., unlike (D), this panel does show the simultaneous representation of both items.) This shows that the representation of the uncued item "shrinks," such that it becomes much less discriminable. (E.g., whereas an item that is represented in a subspace defined by PC1 and PC2 is difficult to discriminate if "viewed" from a subspace defined by PC2 and PC3 [see text], it can also be made difficult to discriminate if its manifold is shrunken so as to reduce the Euclidean distance between stimulus values even when viewed from its optimal subspace.) Piwek et al. (2023) quantified this by deriving a "color discriminability index" (CDI) from the area of the polygons formed by the datapoints in the 3D subspace and determining the mean CDI for the cued item (1294.1, arbitrary units) was significantly greater than that for uncued items (CDI = 45.46).

construction, and *Figure 5.12.A* illustrates that the two planes on which *L1* and *L2* sit intersect at nearly a right angle, the two manifolds overlapping. Despite this, this plot also nicely illustrates what was meant by the earlier statement about information in one subspace being "invisible" from an orthogonal subspace. Consider the stimulus presented at *L1*. If one wanted to know its identity on a particular trial, viewing the data as they are represented in the PC1–PC2 subspace would allow for that. (If you imagine projecting the *L1* representational manifold onto the plane defined by the PC1 and PC2 axes, you can see that its "ring" [well, its "quadrilateral"] shape would be preserved, and a cyan stimulus would be easily discriminable from, say, a yellow stimulus – they'd be separated by roughly 8 units along PC1.) Viewed from the orthogonal plane defined by the PC2 and PC3 axes, however, the *L1* representational manifold collapses onto a (1D) line roughly parallel to the PC2 axis. From this perspective, cyan and yellow occupy nearly the same location in the PC3 dimension, separated by less than a single unit along PC3 and so are very difficult to discriminate. (An analogy might be telling the time by looking at an analog clock: if the clock is hanging on the North wall and you are standing in the middle of the room, it's easy to tell where the hands are pointing [and, therefore, what time it is], but if you are standing in the frame of the doorway that's also in the North wall, you can look at the clock, but can't tell the time, because you can only see the edge of it.) Piwek et al. (2023) confirmed this intuition empirically by observing that, during the precue delay, a classifier trained to successfully decode the color of the *L1* stimulus was unable to decode the color of the *L2* stimulus, and vice versa.

Piwek et al. (2023) carried out several quantitative analyses of the dynamics of representational geometry in their RNNs. A sampling of these, which capture aspects of a normative account of the mechanisms underlying the retention of two items in working memory, followed by the cued prioritization of one of them, is illustrated in *FIGURE 5.12*. We won't consider them in depth here, but will return to them in *Chapter 14*. However, one more important concept that we do need to highlight here is that of the *communication subspace*.

Cutting Through the Chaos with Communication Subspaces Recall from section *"Harnessing Chaos"* that Sussillo and Abbott (2009) developed RNNs, in part, to address the question of how it can be that an elevated level of (chaotic) activity in the motor cortex that precedes a signal to make a movement does not result in any movement, but then a rapid transition of the pattern (but not the overall level) of this activity triggers a movement. This problem has also been considered by neurophysiologist Krishna Shenoy and colleagues, and their proposal is that premovement activity occupies a subspace of activity in the motor system that they call the "null space." The idea is that, not unlike the orthogonal subspaces discussed with reference to *Figure 5.12.A* and *Figure 5.12B*, activity in an "activity-null" subspace in motor cortex might be undetectable to downstream systems that are directly responsible for carrying out movements. Furthermore, although Sussillo and Abbott's (2009) conceptualization of pre-movement activity was that it is noise, Shenoy, Sahani, and Churchland (2013) proposed that this activity-null subspaces might act as a neural "drawing board," where motor planning can take place without influencing current behavior (including, depending on the context, holding still); and when it is time to execute a movement that had been in the planning stage, the pattern of activity corresponding to the motor plan can rotate into a "action-potent" subspace that will now be read out by the downstream systems that execute the movement. (This idea will be elaborated on in *Chapter 8: Skeletomotor Control.*)

A final point to make in this section is that this scheme of action-null and action-potent subspaces can be understood as an example of a more general phenomenon, which is that of the *communication subspace*. That is, although not all signaling between brain circuits results in action, all activity in action-potent subspaces that results in the execution of an action was necessarily communicated (either directly or indirectly) to a downstream, effector circuit.

Diffusion-Decision Modeling

One prominent development resulting from the cognitive revolution of the 1950s–1960s was the design of experimental tasks requiring speeded responses so as to use reaction time (RT) as a dependent measure with which to test models of cognitive processes. Two famous examples are Saul Sternberg's (1966) "memory scanning" task and Michael Posner's (1980) "spatial cuing" task. Let's take a moment to refresh our memory of the "Sternberg task," which presents subjects with lists of digits of varying length, then presents a single "probe" digit and asks subjects to indicate via button press ("yes" or "no") whether the probe appeared in the memory set. (I.e., it is a test of recognition from short-term memory.) When the RTs to nonmatching probes are plotted as a function of list length (a.k.a., of "memory load"), one classically sees a linear increase in RTs with a slope of ~35 msec/item. (E.g., it takes 35 msec longer to respond "no" when the memory set was *3-4-7-2* and the probe was *6* than to respond "no" when the memory set was *5-9-3* and the probe was *4*.) A way to express this mathematically is with the familiar formula $y = mx + b$, where x corresponds to the memory load (e.g., 4 or 3 from the two examples in the preceding sentence), m is 35 msec, and b is the intercept on the vertical axis.

Following from this, if, for a hypothetical subject, their RT to nonmatching probes from set-size 3 trials is 355 msec and their RT to nonmatching probes from set-size 4 trials is 390 msec, this would produce a line for which b is 250 msec. Because b is the offset that contributes to every trial's RT, regardless of set size, Sternberg's interpretation was that the values "250 msec" and "35 msec/item" correspond to two discrete (sets of) mental processes: 250 msec corresponds to all the processes that do *not* vary with memory load – visual processing of the probe, and the planning and execution of the "no" button press – and 35 msec/item corresponds to the process(es) that *does* (*do*) vary with memory load. Indeed, Sternberg (1966) proposed that the 35 msec/item process corresponded to a hypothesized "serial exhaustive scanning" operation, whereby the probe is compared to each item held in memory, one at a time, and a determination is made for each as to whether or not it matches that item. To get really granular, let's consider a single trial for this hypothetical subject for which the memory

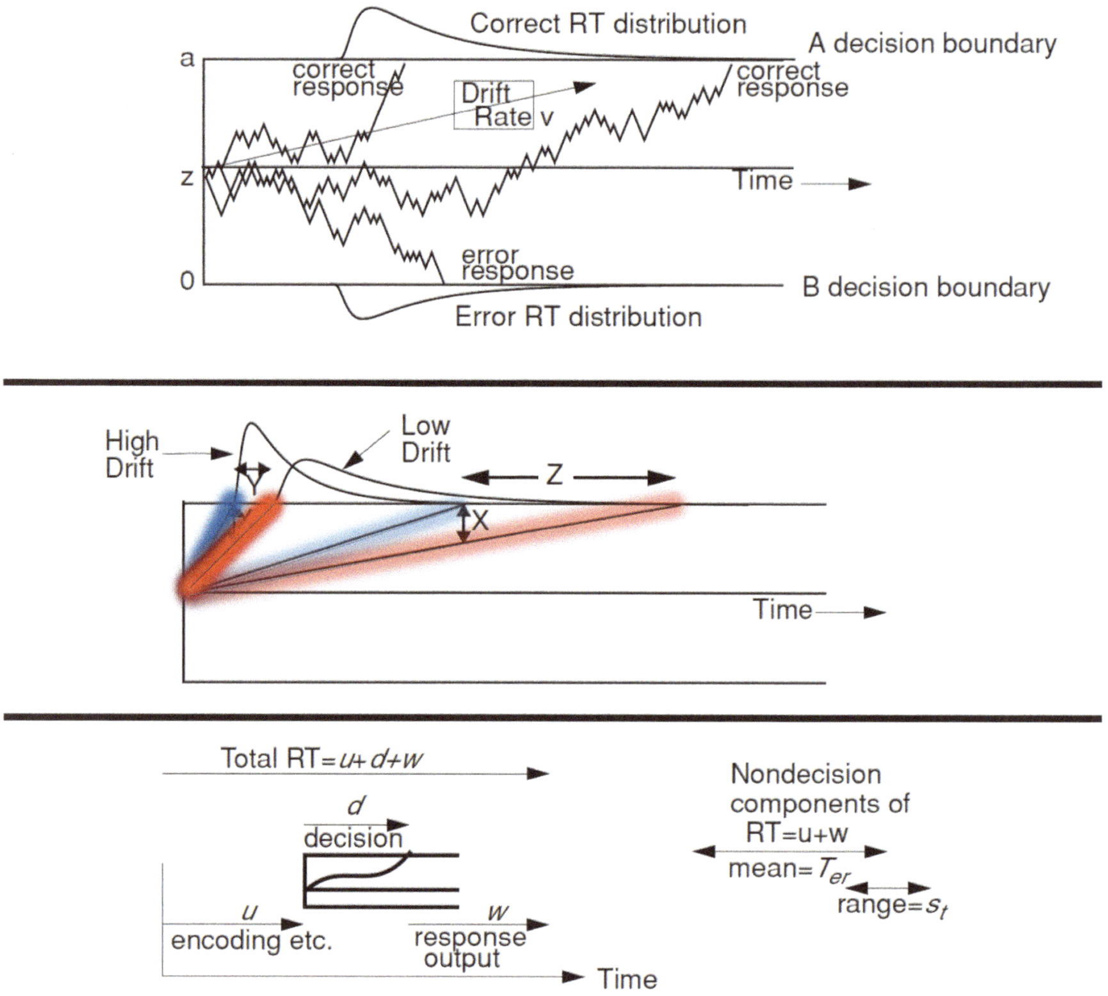

FIGURE 5.13 The accumulation of evidence in a DDM, and the model's decomposition of RT into component processes. Top: The evolution of the accumulation of information on three simulated trials, plus aggregated data, from a hypothetical subject. The drift rate (*v;* vector beginning from point z) is the parameter of the model that corresponds to the rate of accumulation of information. The accumulation process itself is implemented as a noisy random walk (specifically, a diffusion process), and so, as illustrated here, the trajectory of individual trials will differ, despite *v* holding constant. The vertical distance between the starting point (z) and the decision boundaries (a and 0) captures the amount of evidence that must accumulate for the system to decide in favor of "A" or "B". To be consistent with *Figure 5.14*, we can let "A" correspond to a *match* between the probe and an item in the memory set, and B to a *nonmatch*, in which case what is illustrated here are three trials on which a matching probe yields a relatively fast "match" decision ("correct response"), a relatively slow "match" decision (also "correct response"), and a relatively fast "nonmatch" decision ("incorrect response"). Middle: The consequence, for the RT distribution, of relatively steep vs. shallow values of *v*. Here, the lines emanating from point z illustrate the linearized trajectories of the fastest and slowest trials with a "High Drift" rate (highlighted by dark and pale blue "glow", respectively) and the fastest and slowest trials with a "Low Drift" rate highlighted by (dark and pale red "glow", respectively). Note that, for "Low Drift," not only is the mean RT longer but the tail of its distribution markedly longer (compare "Y," the difference between leading edges, to "Z," the distance between trailing edges). This is a consequence of the fact that a longer-lasting diffusion process will necessarily accrue more random error. Distributions similar to these two would be expected for recognition from short-term memory for, for example, a memory load of 1 ("High Drift") vs. a memory load of 3 "Low Drift." Bottom: The decomposition of full-trial RTs into distinct sets of processes. Whereas the top and middle panels illustrate "Total" RTs (e.g., from probe onset until button press), this panel illustrates how the duration of a trial can be broken, conceptually, into encoding processes, which necessarily precede decision processes, which necessarily precede response-related processes. In practice, the DDM decomposes "total" RT into decision and nondecision components.

Source: (Ratcliff & McKoon, 2008) / MIT Press.

set *3-4-7-2* is followed by the probe *6*. On this trial, it might be that it took 100 msec from the time when photons corresponding to the "6" on the screen impacted the retina until the transduced neural signals were perceived by the visual system as "6," then 35 msec for the cognitive system to compare *6* to *3* and determine that they don't match, 35 more msec to compare *6* to *4* and determine that they don't match, etc., and, finally, that it took 150 msec for the read-out of these four "nonmatch" determinations to be interpreted by the motor system as requiring a "no" button press, and to execute that response. Importantly, the empirical results do not allow for the adjudication between the possibilities that perception took 100 msec and motor processes took 150 msec, or that perception took 99 msec and motor processes 151 msec, or 101 msec vs. 149 msec, etc., and so these two sets of processes typically get clumped together as "non-decision time." Now, having established this important background, we can get to diffusion-decision modeling.

The diffusion-decision model (DDM[9]) was introduced in 1978 by Roger Ratcliff, in part as an alternative to Sternberg's idea of a serial search process in recognition memory. A critical difference is that DDMs assume that memory search over multiple items happens in parallel, rather than in series. To develop an intuition for how this could work, Ratcliff enlisted the metaphor of sympathetic resonance among tuning forks. The demonstration from secondary-school physics is that if two identical tuning forks are near each other, striking one will induce the second, un-struck one to also vibrate, and the auditory percept is that the volume resulting from a single strike is louder than it would have been had there not have been an unstruck fork nearby. Importantly, this effect only works if the two tuning forks are identical; if they are ever-so-slightly out of tune relative to each other (e.g., the un-struck fork is tuned to a higher or a lower pitch), the volume resulting from the fork strike will be markedly decreased. In Ratcliff's metaphor, the un-struck tuning fork is the item held in memory, the struck fork is the probe, and the elicitation of sympathetic resonance is the outcome used to decide "match" or "nonmatch." Now let's add two more "un-struck" tuning forks, and arrange them such that all three are equidistant from the probe fork. When the probe fork is struck, the vibrations in the air that emanate from it will reach each of the three un-struck forks at the same time, and so these will (or won't) begin to vibrate sympathetically at precisely the same time. Thus, the three items in memory aren't being activated serially, they are being activated in parallel (and the assessment of whether any of them is resonant with the struck fork can also happen in parallel).

But if, in the previous paragraph's example, three un-struck forks begin to vibrate (or not) in parallel, why does it take longer to make a recognition decision with a set size of 3 relative to a set size of 1? (Recall that Ratcliff (1978) didn't challenge the empirical finding that RT increases monotonically with set size, what he challenged was the explanation for what underlying mechanism might account for this pattern of behavior.) The answer to this question gets to another key element of the DDM: what it models is the accumulation of evidence over time. (Here's a very different analogy, used by Gold and Shadlen (2007), who also use the DDM framework, but in the context of perceptual decision-making [deciding whether a noisy cloud of dots is moving to the left or to the right]: "A decision, is a deliberative process that results in the commitment to a categorical proposition. An apt analogy is a judge or jury that must take time to weigh evidence for alternative interpretations and/or possible ramifications before settling on a verdict" [p. 536].) Note that the decision about whether the volume of ringing is consistent with matched or unmatched tuning forks can't be made instantaneously; rather, it requires the accumulation of evidence. Consider the fact that being exposed to only a 1 msec-long snippet of ringing wouldn't be enough to make a decision, nor would be a 2 msec-long snippet; a considerably longer span of time would be needed. And now, we need to introduce an additional variable, which is the *strength* (or, in some cases, the *quality*) of the evidence. For example, if one were to only gently tap the struck tuning fork, it would be considerably more difficult (and would require more listening time) to judge whether the untapped fork also begins to vibrate than if one were to strike it forcefully. Now, returning to the question that launched this paragraph, the explanation for the "set size effect" is comparable to the gentle-vs.-forceful tap, except now the tap remains the same, but the amount of energy absorbed by

[9] Note the ambiguity of one abbreviation referring to two types of model: drift-diffusion models (section *Dynamical systems theory*) and diffusion-decision models of decision-making being described in this section. DDMs of decision-making do not incorporate dynamical drift.

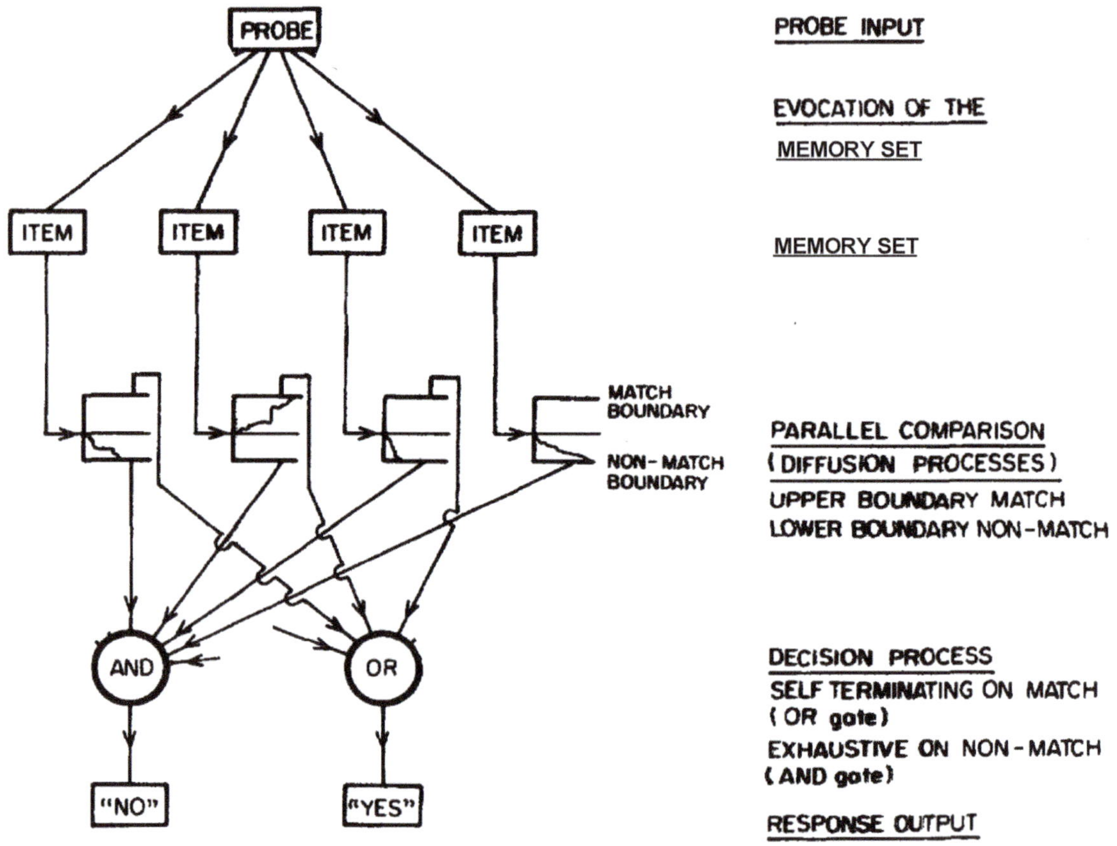

FIGURE 5.14 Configuration of DDM for recognition from memory. In this figure, the sequence of events unfolds from top-to-bottom. "PROBE INPUT" corresponds to the onset of the probe at the end of a trial (the "tapping of the tuning fork" in the sympathetic resonance metaphor). "EVOCATION OF THE MEMORY SET" corresponds to the accessing of the memory set for comparison with the probe (the "propagation of vibrational energy from struck to un-struck tuning forks"). In this illustration, the MEMORY SET contains four items. "PARALLEL COMPARISON" corresponds to the unfolding of diffusion processes playing out for each item, with the output directed to the "NO" or the "YES" decision channel depending on which boundary was crossed. DECISION PROCESS is implemented as two logic gates, the "AND" gate corresponding to a *nonmatch* decision and requiring a receipt of a "nonmatch" signal from all of the items before triggering a "NO" at the "RESPONSE OUTPUT" stage (i.e., an *exhaustive* process), the "OR" gate triggering a "YES" at the "RESPONSE OUTPUT" stage upon receiving a "match" signal from any of the items (i.e., a *self-terminating* process).
Source: (Ratcliff, 1978) / American Psychological Association.

each untapped fork decreases. That is, assuming that the fork is struck with the same force on each trial, then when this same amount of energy is apportioned among three forks, each one, if matched, would necessarily ring more faintly. Consequently, increasing the set size has the same effect as does decreasing the force of the tap – both result in a weaker signal and consequently a slower rate of evidence accumulation. *Figure 5.13* illustrates how this is operationalized by the DDM, and *Figure 5.14* illustrates how it is implemented for recognition memory. (Note the DDMs belong to a larger class of models called sequential sampling models. This reflects the fact that they model the accumulation of information as playing out across multiple discrete sampling events. This is evident in the "jaggedness" of the trajectories of the decision particle across time in the top panel of *Figure 5.13*, for which each inflection corresponds to a discrete sampling event.)

Representational Similarity Analysis

Representational Similarity Analysis (RSA) is a remarkably flexible type of multivariate analysis that allows one to summarize and visualize the principles that govern how a region represents information. For example, and as we'll see in detail, it can be used to illustrate the way in which early visual cortex represents low-level visual features, whereas higher-level areas represent categorical and/or semantic information and even to say whether a particular layer in a DNN represents visual information in a manner more similar to area X or area Y in the brain. To introduce it we'll draw on an fMRI study by Richter, Kietzmann, and de Lange (2024) that used RSA as a tool to test a hypothesis about predictive coding in the visual system. (A detailed treatment of intriguing empirical and theoretical aspects of this paper will appear in *Chapter 6*, section *Predictive coding at early levels of visual processing.*) The behavioral task was animacy judgment of images of objects (i.e., "living/nonliving?"). Each trial consisted of the presentation of a consonant letter followed by an object, and the key manipulation was that each of the eight letters in a closed set was followed by one of the eight objects from a corresponding closed set seven times more often than it was by each of the other objects. Thus, for each letter, one of the objects that could follow was the predicted object, and each of the other seven that could follow was "unexpected." The analytic goal of the investigators was to develop an objective metric for quantifying how dissimilar was each object from each of the others, such that they could estimate trial-by-trial variation of the magnitude of "unexpectedness" produced by each pairing of a letter with an unexpected object (a proxy for the magnitude of the prediction error). In addition to the fMRI-of-humans component of this experiment, Richter et al. (2024) also ran their stimulus set through a DNN, and it's RSA applied to the results from the DNN that we'll use to explain RSA.

In *Figure 5.15.A,* the authors illustrate how an expected object generates predictions at a low level of image analysis – texture, orientation, silhouette – as well as at a high level – a different token of the same type, defining constituent parts (for a guitar, a body and a neck), and how an object that is then actually "seen" can produce a large "high-level surprise" – a woman is different from a guitar (even though her torso is aligned in the same orientation as the expected image) – or a "low-level surprise – the unexpected image is a guitar but oriented differently from the expected image.

For *Figure 5.15.B,* we'll focus on the "Analysis" side of the figure, which cartoons the processing of the images through a DNN that had previously been trained to classify images from a large database. At this point, we'll clarify that although the pool of objects was limited to eight "template" images, it contained additional images that portrayed each of the template images in a different pose (e.g., the "unexpected" image of the otherwise-"predicted" guitar was oriented differently from its orientation in its predicted pose). To validate the use of the DNN as a proxy of hierarchical processing in the ventral visual stream (see *Chapter 6*, section *A functional dissociation of visual perception of what an object is vs. where it is located*), the authors confirmed that units in early layers of the DNN (including layer 2) responded preferentially to low-level visual features that corresponded to the responsivity, from the fMRI data, of voxels in V1 (a.k.a. "striate") and monosynaptically connected extrastriate cortex, whereas units at late layers of the DNN (specifically, the final image-processing layer, layer 8) represented high-level/category-selective information that corresponded to the fMRI responses in more rostral areas of the ventral visual system (i.e., to the human analogues of CIT and AIT from, e.g., *Figure 6.5*).

And now, we can get to the RSA.

RSA begins with the construction of a representational *dissimilarity* matrix (RDM), a correlation matrix that contains the representational distance between each object in a stimulus set relative to every other object. With reference to *Figure 5.15*, starting with the RDM derived from Layer 2 of the DNN, arrayed along the left-hand side of the matrix are eight images; in descending order: a woman leaning to the left; a guitar leaning to the right; a man with arms outstretched; the same woman from the top image, but now in a different pose and leaning to the right; the façade of a building; the same man, but now in a different pose; a spoon; and the same guitar, but now leaning to the right. Along the horizontal axis are the same images in the same order. To construct the matrix, we can focus on the top row, the from-the-side view of the woman (for simplicity, "template woman"). For each cell, one computes the correlation between the (high-dimensional) pattern of activity evoked by processing *template woman* in layer 2 in AlexNet with the pattern of activity evoked by processing the image in the corresponding row. (I.e., from left-to-right along the top row, the correlation with *template woman, template guitar, template man, unexpected woman, façade, unexpected man, spoon,* and *unexpected guitar.*) Importantly, because we are constructing a dissimilarity matrix, the value that goes into each cell is *1 – correlation coefficient*, so that each cell represents how distant is the representation of each item (in representational space) from all the others. Curiously, figure 4 from Richter et al. (2024) (corresponding to *Figure 5.15* in this text) doesn't include a scale

FIGURE 5.15 Representational similarity analysis.

Source: Richter et al. (2024) / PUBLIC LIBRARY OF SCIENCE (PLOS) / CC BY 4.0.

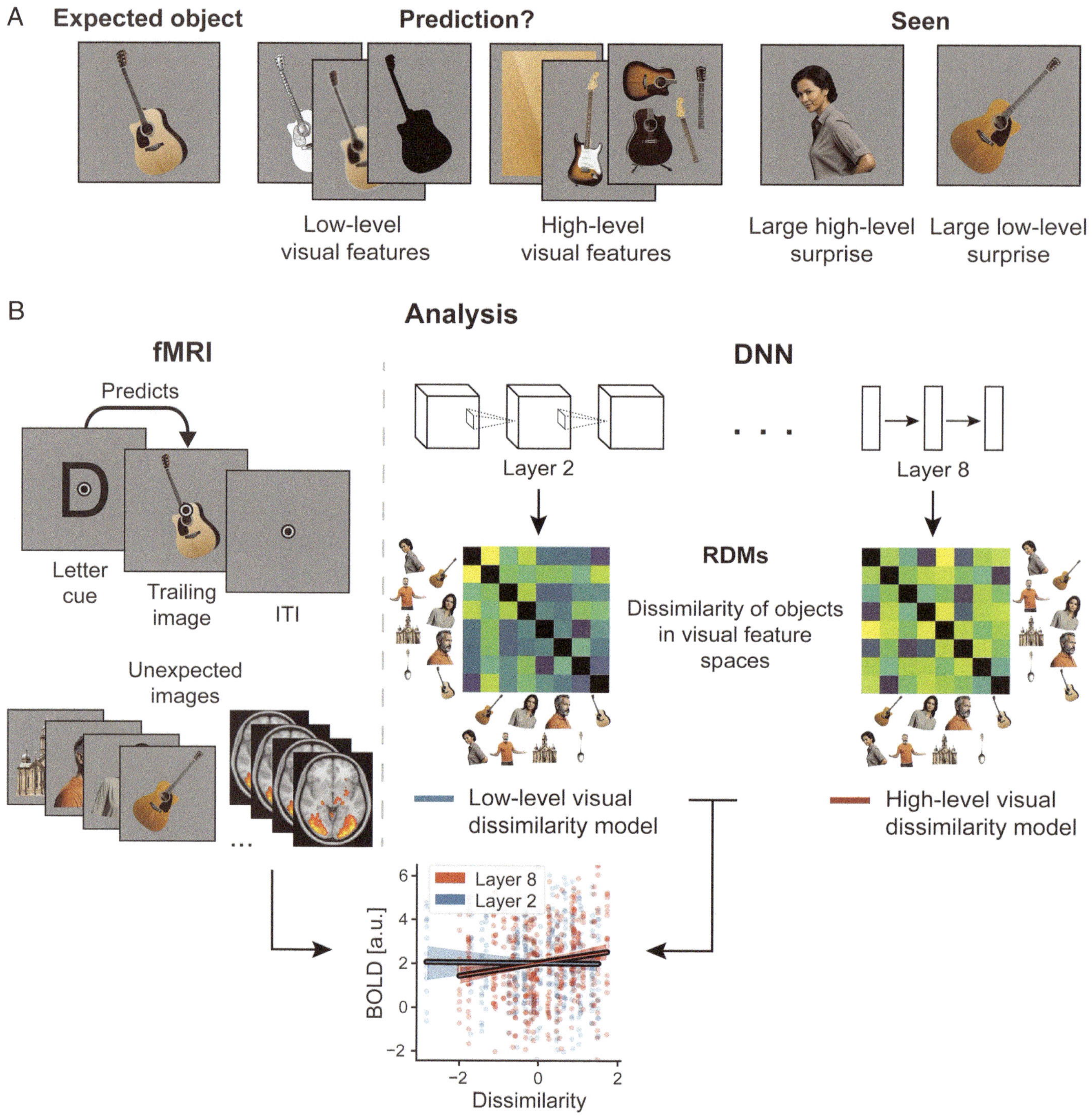

FIGURE 5.15.A The study featured in this figure was designed to compare evidence for prediction errors arising from a mismatch of low-level visual features or high-level visual features.

FIGURE 5.15.B The side of the panel titled "fMRI" illustrates a trial (top), and below it, other "unexpected" images that would also be shown as the "trailing image" following this same letter cue. The side titled "DNN" illustrates two RDMs for the stimulus set that was used for one subject. The plot on the bottom shows data from a single subject, in which the dissimilarity, on each "unexpected" trial, of that trial's item vs. that trial's predicted item is plotted twice – once using dissimilarities from Layer 2 of the DNN and once using dissimilarities from Layer 8 of the DNN. These results will be interpreted in *Chapter 6*, section *Predictive coding at early levels of visual processing*.

bar, but we can safely assume that it ranges from black = 0 to bright yellow = 1, and so the first cell is black because *template woman* correlated with *template woman* yields a correlation coefficient of 1, and *1 – 1 = 0*. Going along the row (and for each cell making comparisons relative to the preceding cell in the row), *template woman* is very dissimilar from *template guitar*, somewhat less dissimilar from *template man*, somewhat more dissimilar from *unexpected woman*, considerably more similar to *façade*, *unexpected man*, and *spoon*, and more similar still to *unexpected guitar*.

Now that we understand how the RDM captures the representation of these images in Layer 2 of the DNN, it is informative to compare it with the RDM derived from Layer 8. Starting again from the upper left, Layer 8's representation of *template woman* is (again) perfectly correlated with itself (and *1 – 1 = 0*), and its distances from *template guitar* and from *template man* are also relatively unchanged. Strikingly different between the layers of the DNN, however, is the fact that *template woman* is very similar to *unexpected woman* and dramatically different from *façade*, and although roughly unchanged with *unexpected man*, is now very dissimilar from *spoon* and *unexpected guitar*. (Note that this final comparison between Layer 2 and Layer 8 was foreshadowed in the discussion in *Figure 5.15.A*. – although the (low-level) orientation of *template woman* and *unexpected guitar* are similar, their (high-level) category memberships are very different.)

The comparison of the Layer 2 RDM vs. the Layer 8 RDM illustrates one of the important strengths of RSA, which is the ability to compare representational organization between two regions, without needing to equate the number of dimensions between the two. In its initial instantiation AlexNet was made up of 650,000 neurons, with different numbers of neurons in each layer. Nonetheless, the Layer 2 RDM can be compared with the Layer 8 RDM because the number of cells in both is determined by the number of images used in the experiment. The same principle applies to biological datasets. With fMRI data, for example, it's common to compare RDMs from different brain regions, as a way assessing evidence for representational differences.

Aperiodic Activity as an Index of Excitation-Inhibition Balance

As we've seen in, for example, *Figure 4.10*, a spectral transform of the scalp EEG characteristically contains more power at low than at high frequencies. This characteristic is, in fact, shared by many phenomena in the natural world, and it has nicknames, the most common being "1/f" (pronounced "one-over-eff") because it resembles the curve the would be produced if you plotted out the function y = 1/x, with frequency ("f") being the unit on the x-axis. As implied by another of its nicknames, "pink noise,"[10] this element of the power spectrum has traditionally been considered to be noise, because it corresponds to aperiodic components of the signal being analyzed. "Aperiodic components"? Consider *Figure 5.16.A*, from Leonard Waschke et al. (2021). What it illustrates is the average power spectra (power spectral densities; PSD) of the scalp EEG recorded from two groups of patients in each of two conditions, quiet rest and while anaesthetized. These PSDs have undergone a log/log transform which has the effect of rendering linear the aperiodic component of the EEG (which, untransformed, is curvilinear – after all, it's nickname is "1/f"). If we focus on the plot on the left ("propofol"), and only the black line (Awake condition), what we see is a downward-sloping trace that is punctuated with three bumps. Each bump corresponds to an oscillation: the one centered on ~10 Hz corresponding to alpha, the one centered on ~20 Hz to beta, and the one centered on ~30 Hz to low gamma. These are "true oscillations," in that if we were to look at the time-varying EEG traces whose spectral transform is depicted here, we would be able to see fluctuations in the trace going up-and-down at cycles of ~10/sec, ~20/sec, and ~30/sec.[11] What we

[10] Another nickname is "pink noise," because if the frequencies on the x-axis correspond to the visible portion of the electromagnetic spectrum, the light represented by this spectrum would appear pink in color.

[11] Additionally, one can see the sharp spike in the PSD at 50 Hz, from which one can surmise that these data were recorded in Germany, where co-senior author Jonas Obleser is based, and where AC power is distributed at 50 Hz; unlike the 60 Hz standard in North America.

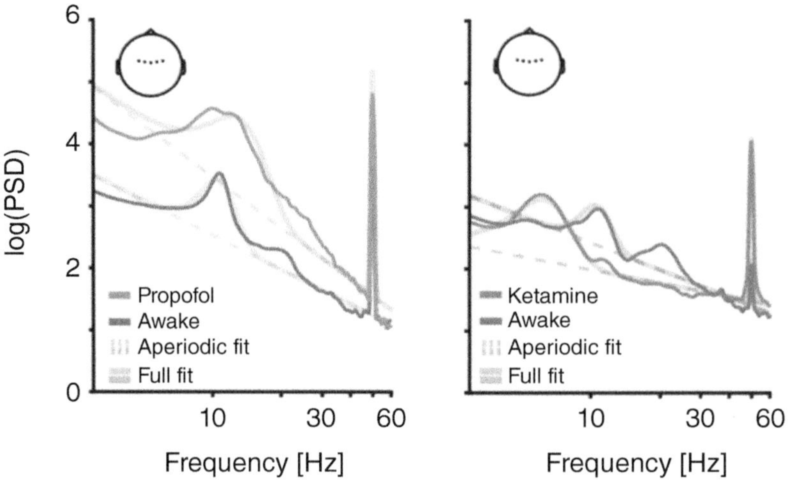

FIGURE 5.16 Anesthesia illustrates the relation between the slope of the 1/f component of the spectral transform of the EEG and E:I balance. The two plots illustrate PSDs from the resting EEG of patients before and after administration of propofol (left) or ketamine (right). Insets indicate the electrodes from which the EEG signal was taken for these analyses. Each plot shows the PSD as measured (dark gray, dark teal, dark purple) plus model fits to the aperiodic (light dashed lines) and periodic (light solid lines) components. (Note that data are plotted on a log/log scale.)

would not see, however, is a fluctuation going up-and-down at every frequency possible and at different amplitudes for each frequency. That is, there is nothing oscillating at 1/f. Rather, the 1/f component of the PSD is considered to be "aperiodic" – it reflects elements in the signal that do not fluctuate with a particular oscillatory period.

Now, we can turn our attention to the effects of anesthesia on the PSD. (Well, first, to an effect of these two anesthetic agents on brain physiology.) The two anesthetics featured in *Figure 5.16* were selected for this study because it is well established (e.g., from invasive recordings made directly in cortical tissue) that their administration decreases the balance of excitatory-to-inhibitory neurotransmission (the "E:I balance") in cortical tissue. E:I balance is a property of cortical tissue that influences excitability and is considered an important order parameter in DST models of brain function (see section *Dynamical systems theory*). And so *now,* when we reinspect *Figure 5.16,* we can note two marked effects of propofol and ketamine on the resting EEG: they disrupt the oscillatory structure of the PSD; and they change the slope of the aperiodic component of the PSD – the "1/f slope." Consequently, changes to the 1/f slope of the extracranial EEG can be used as an index of a change in the E:I balance in the tissue that is giving rise to that signal.

These Are Some of the Ways That Cognitive Neuroscientists Think About How the Brain Works

Are there more? Of course there are. But at some point, we have to stop getting ready to dive in and . . . well . . . actually dive in, right? C'mon, let's go!

End-of-Chapter Questions

1. Summarize Hebb's postulate. What neurotransmitter receptor is believed to be important in instantiating Hebb's postulate?

2. How do models of predictive coding interpret the propagation of signals from V1 to V2 (and to V4), a phenomenon that has traditionally been interpreted as the feedforward processing of the output of tuned feature detectors, a key step in the perceptual analysis of stimulus information?

3. What might be a rationale for applying analyses derived from dynamical systems theory to neuronal activity?

4. Summarize ways in which the activity of midbrain dopamine neurons seems to implement the function of the reward prediction error (RPE) from reinforcement learning (RL) theory.

5. What are functions of the RPE other than the shaping of the learning of habits?

6. In the context of a neuroimaging dataset, summarize how multivariate pattern analyses (MVPA) can yield superior sensitivity and superior selectivity relative to signal intensity-based analyses.

7. What does it mean to "decode" a neuroimaging data set?

8. How to recurrent neural networks (RNNs) differ from other artificial neural networks (ANNs), including DNs and PDP models?

9. Explain (in conceptual terms) the idea of applying a dimensionality reduction to a data set. How might the results of a dimensionality reduction lend themselves to a representational geometry analysis?

10. In what way do diffusion-decision models (DDMs) decompose behavioral reaction times into non-decision vs. evidence-accumulation components?

11. What distinguishes representational similarity analyses (RSA) from other multivariate analyses?

12. Why might it be of interest if E:I balance changes as a function of some cognitive event? Or as a function of the manipulation of some independent variable?

References

Alamia, A., and R. Van Rullen. 2019. "Alpha Oscillations and Traveling Waves: Signatures of Predictive Coding?." *PLoS Biology 17*: e3000487. doi: doi.org/10.1371/journal.pbio.3000487.

Averbeck, B. 2025. "Response to: Has AI "Killed" Marr's 'Three'-Levels Framework?." *Journal of Cognitive Neuroscience Discussion Forum*. doi: https://doi.org/10.21428/8e6ba8ef.a881ed44.

Cai, Y., A. D. Sheldon, Q. Yu, and B. R. Postle. 2019. "Overlapping and Distinct Contributions of Stimulus Location and of Spatial Context to Nonspatial Visual Short-Term Memory." *Journal of Neurophysiology 121*: 1222–1231. doi: 10.1152/jn.00062.2019.

Cai, Y., Q. Yu, A. D. Sheldon, and B. R. Postle. 2020. "The Role of Location-Context Binding in Nonspatial Visual Working Memory." *eNeuro 7*: ENEURO.0430-0420.2020 0431–0414. doi: 10.1523/ENEURO.0430-20.2020.

Downey, P. 2006. "Profile of Ranulfo Romo." *Proceedings of the National Academy of Sciences of the United States of America 103* (39): 14263–14265. doi: 10.1073/pnas.0607434103.

Friston, K. 2018. "Does Predictive Coding Have a Future?." *Nature Neuroscience 21*: 1019–1021.

Friston, K. 2019. "Waves of Prediction." *PLoS Biology 17*: e3000426. doi: doi.org/10.1371/journal.pbio.3000426.

Gold, Joshua I., and Michael, N. Shadlen. 2007. "The Neural Basis of Decision Making." *Annual Review of Neuroscience* 30: 535–574. doi: 10.1146/annurev.neuro.29.051605.113038.

Hancock, F., F. E. Rosas, A. I. Luppi, P. A. M. Mediano, J. Cabral, . . . F. E. Turkheimer. 2025. "Metastability Demystified – The Foundational Past, the Pragmatic Present and the Promising Future." *Nature Reviews Neuroscience 26*: 82–100. doi: doi.org/10.1038/s41583-024-00883-1.

Hebb, D. O. 1949. *Organization of Behavior*. New York, NY, John Wiley & Sons, Inc.

Hull, C. L. 1943. *Principles of Behavior: An Introduction to Behavior Theory*. New York: Appleton-Century.

Panichello, M. F., and T. J. Buschman. 2021. "Shared Mechanisms Underlie the Control of Working Memory and Attention." *Nature 592*: 601–605. doi: 10.1038/s41586-021-03390-w.

Panichello, M. F., B. DePasquale, J. W. Pillow, and T. J. Buschman. 2019. "Error-Correcting Dynamics in Visual Working Memory." *Nature Communications 10*: 3366. doi: 10.1038/s41467-019-11298-3.

Pessoa, L. 2023. "The Entangled Brain." *Journal of Cognitive Neuroscience 35* (3): 349–360. doi: 10.1162/jocn_a_01908.

Pessoa, L. 2024. "Is the Brain Mostly a Modular System or Do We Need Distributed Processing Frameworks?." *Journal of Cognitive Neuroscience Discussion Forum*. doi: https://doi.org/10.21428/8e6ba8ef.c1c5ff80.

Petersen, S. E., P. T. Fox, M. I. Posner, M. Mintun, and M. E. Raichle. 1988. "Positron Emission Tomographic Studies of the Cortical Anatomy of Single-Word Processing." *Nature 331*: 585–589.

Piwek, E. P., M. G. Stokes, and C. Summerfield. 2023. "A Recurrent Neural Network Model of Prefrontal Brain Activity During a Working Memory Task." *PLoS Computational Biology 19* (10): e1011555. doi: 10.1371/journal.pcbi.1011555.

Posner, M. I. 1980. "Orienting of Attention." *Quarterly Journal of Experimental Psychology* 32 (1): 3–25. doi: 10.1080/00335558008248231.

Ratcliff, Roger (1978) A theory of memory retrieval. Psychological Review *85*: 59–108.

Rescorla, R. A., and A. R. Wagner. 1972. "A theory of Pavlovian conditioning: Variations in the effectiveness of reinforcement and nonreinforcement." In *Classical Conditioning II*, edited by A. H. Black and W. F. Prokasy (pp. 64–99). Appleton-Century-Crofts.

Richter, D., T. C. Kietzmann, and F. P. de Lange. 2024. "High-Level Visual Prediction Errors in Early Visual Cortex." *PLoS Biology 22*: e3002829. doi: doi.org/10.1371/journal.pbio.3002829.

Romo, Arnulfo, and Wolfram Schultz. 1990. "Dopamine Neurons of the Monkey Midbrain: Contingencies of Responses to Active Touch During Self-Initiated Arm Movements." *Journal of Neurophysiology* 63 (3): 592–606.

Samuel, A. 1959. "Some Studies in Machine Learning Using the Game of Checkers." *IBM Journal of Research and Development 3*: 210–229. doi: 10.1147/rd.33.0210.

Serences, J. T., E. F. Ester, E. K. Vogel, and E. Awh. 2009. "Stimulus-Specific Delay Activity in Human Primary Visual Cortex." *Psychological Science 20*: 207–214.

Shenoy, K. V., M. Sahani, and M. M. Churchland. 2013. "Cortical Control of Arm Movements: A Dynamical Systems Perspective." *Annual Review of Neuroscience (Palo Alto, CA) 36*: 337–359.

Sternberg, S. 1966. "High-Speed Scanning in Human Memory." *Science 153*: 652–654. doi: 10.1126/science.153.3736.652.

Sussillo, D., and L. F. Abbott. 2009. "Generating Coherent Patterns of Activity from Chaotic Neural Networks." *Neuron 63*: 544–557. doi: 10.1016/j.neuron.2009.07.018.

Sutton, R. S., and A. G. Bartow. 2018. *Reinforcement Learning: An Introduction*, 2nd ed. Cambridge, MA: MIT Press.

Thorndike, E. L. 1911. *Animal intelligence: Experimental studies*. Macmillan Press. https://doi.org/10.5962/bhl.title.55072.

Wan, Q., A. Ardalan, J. Fulvio, and B. R. Postle. 2024. "Representing Context and Priority in Working Memory." *Journal of Cognitive Neuroscience 36*: 1374–1394. doi: 10.1162/jocn_a_02166.

Waschke, L., T. Donoghue, L. Fiedler, S. Smith, D. D. Garrett, B. Voytek, and J. Obleser. 2021. "Modality-Specific Tracking of Attention and Sensory Statistics in the Human Electrophysiological Spectral Exponent." *eLife 10*. doi: 10.7554/eLife.70068.

Yu, Q., and B. R. Postle. 2021. "The Neural Codes Underlying Internally Generated Representations in Visual Working Memory." *Journal of Cognitive Neuroscience 33*: 1142–1157. doi: 10.1162/jocn_a_01702.

Yu, Q., M. F. Panichello, B. R. Postle, and T. J. Buschman. 2020. "Delay-Period Activity in Frontal, Parietal, and Occipital Cortex Tracks Noise and Biases in Visual Working Memory." *PLoS Biology 18*: e3000854. doi: doi.org/10.1371/journal.pbio.3000854.

Other Sources Used

Brouwer, G. J., and D. J. Heeger. 2009. "Decoding and Reconstructing Color from Responses in Human Visual Cortex." *The Journal of Neuroscience 29*: 13992–14003.

Dumoulin, S. O., and B. A. Wandell. 2008. "Population Receptive Field Estimates in Human Visual Cortex." *NeuroImage 39*: 647–660.

Gao, R., E. J. Peterson, and B. Voytek. 2017. "Inferring Synaptic Excitation/Inhibition Balancer from Field Potentials." *NeuroImage 158*: 70–78.

Holroyd, C. B. 2024. "The Controllosphere: The Neural Origin of Cognitive Effort." *Psychological Review*. doi: 10.1037/rev0000467.

Kaufman, M. T., M. M. Churchland, S. I. Ryu, and K. V. Shenoy. 2014. "Cortical Activity in the Null Space: Permitting Preparation Without Movement." *Nature Neuroscience 17*: 440–448. doi: 10.1038/nn.3643.

Krizhevsky, A., I. Sutskever, and G. E. Hinton. 2012. "ImageNet Classification with Deep Convolutional Neural Nets." *Advances in Neural Information Processing Systems*: 1097–1105.

Rust, N. C., and M. R. Cohen. 2022. "Priority Coding in the Visual System." *Nature Reviews Neuroscience 23*: 377–388. doi: 10.1038/s41583-022-00582-9.

Serences, J. T., S. Saproo, M. Scolari, T. Ho, and L. T. Muftuler. 2009. "Estimating the Influence of Attention on Population Codes in Human Visual Cortex Using Voxel-Based Tuning Functions." *NeuroImage 44* (1): 223–231. doi: 10.1016/j.neuroimage.2008.07.043.

Further Reading

For this chapter only, the Further Reading section is moot, because the readings that the author thinks are most germane, plus an annotation for each, are already listed in the chapter itself.

Perception, Attention, and Action

INTRODUCTION TO SECTION III

Perception, Attention, and Action

Near the end of *Chapter 1*, we discussed the fact that brains confer the ability to detect changes in the environment and to perform actions based on this information. The chapters in this section will delve into the wondrous amount of intricate detail and organization that underlies this simple premise. As a preamble, let's briefly consider the three words in the title of this section, the concepts that they encompass, and how these classes of function relate to one another.

Perception refers to the identification of features of what is being sensed and, often, to its recognition (e.g., *Am I looking at a house cat or a raccoon? Is the voice on the telephone that of my daughter or of my wife? Does the blade of this ice skate feel sufficiently sharp as I run my finger along it? Does this milk smell as though it has gone sour, or can I drink it?*). **Attention** can refer to many things, but in the present context, it's how we mentally prioritize the perception (and related actions) of just one or a few of the multitudes of stimuli that typically clutter our environment. In *Chapter 2*, oscillatory synchrony was introduced as a mechanism for focusing one's attention on an approaching bear rather than on sunlight or on a bird. **Action** can refer to isolated acts of motor control (e.g., reaching for the computer mouse while surfing the Web, or turning one's head to see who is walking into the room), but also to goals or plans that can be abstracted from isolated movements, such as *making dinner* or *finishing my homework*.

As we saw in *Chapter 3*, perception of information in the outside world begins with the translation of information into signals that the nervous system can understand and manipulate. This is fundamental, because when you see a cat, for example, it's not the case that the photons reflecting off this animal are traveling into your brain to be projected against a "neural screen." Nor is it the case that when you smell bread baking in the oven, molecules of heated dough are entering your brain through your nose. Rather, the nervous system represents information about the seen cat and about the smelled bread with what we call a neural code. A code is a system for representing information in a format that's different from the physical properties of what's being represented. The English language is a code by which, for example, this author can convey to you, the reader, the idea of a cat without having to plop a furry, domesticated feline into your lap. Similarly, the nervous system uses a code made up of action potentials and neurotransmitters to convey information about patterns of light or the strength and quality of a smell. (It also uses a code to generate the mental image of a cat, like the one you may have just experienced a few moments ago, but we won't get to that until *Section III*.) It uses a "neural code" to trigger the click of your finger on the computer mouse, and the speed and manner (quickly and with alarm, or slowly and with insouciance) with which you turn your head toward the door. There is much about neural coding that we do not yet understand, and discovering the rules that govern it is an important goal of cognitive

Companion Website: www.wiley.com/go/postle/cognitiveneuroscience3e

neuroscience. (By analogy, without knowledge of the rules governing the English language, one wouldn't be able to understand the difference between the sentences "Dog bites man" and "Man bites dog.")

It's a matter of organizational convenience that this section presents the topics of *perception*, *attention*, and *action* in the order that it does. However, an important fact to keep in mind as one reads through these chapters is that it would be overly simplistic, to the point of being inaccurate, to think of neural information processing as proceeding in a strictly feedforward series of stages from sensation and perception to attentional selection, to action. We saw in *Chapter 2* that the cortex is wired up for the feedback as well as for the feedforward conveyance of signals, and in *Chapter 3* we began to see some of the functional consequences of this. A related point is that it would be equally inaccurate to think of the brain as "sitting passively" until a stimulus comes along to "activate it," to kick-start it into action. Instead, we'll see that a better model might be to think of a brain that is constantly "churning" along, actively representing the world, and that the perception of a newly presented stimulus corresponds to the "nudging" of this already-active system into a different state of activity. That is, the brain is a dynamic system, and the waking brain is never truly "at rest." I raise these points now in part because, even though I believe them myself, I often find myself slipping into a more straightforward, intuitively appealing way of thinking about brain function. By this intuitive account, a newly occurring stimulus evokes activity in a previously quiescent brain, and this event triggers the sensation-through-action cascade that has been previewed in this preamble. I also raise these points to be explicit about the fact that this "feedforward activation" perspective, by virtue of its intuitive appeal, offers a more straightforward way of introducing many aspects of brain function. This is evident in much of the terminology that we use to describe the brain and its functions, in figures that appear in many textbooks, and, indeed, in the order of chapters in textbooks such as this one. What we shall see in this section, however, is that a feedforward-activation view of brain function can limit one's ability to appreciate all its nuances. To give just one example, what one perceives can often be influenced, if not determined, by one's action plan.

But that's enough "pre"; let's dive in!

CHAPTER **6**

The Visual System

KEY THEMES

- The anatomical connectivity of the visual system creates a substrate for two broad classes of visual information processing: determining *what* an object is and determining *where* it is.
- Carefully designed lesion studies have localized these two categories of function to pathways projecting to the temporal and parietal cortex, respectively.
- Within this organizing principle, there is considerable cross talk and integration of information.
- Visual object recognition is accomplished via a progressive hierarchy of processing steps, beginning in V1 and extending into inferotemporal (IT) cortex.
- Although one logical terminus of such a hierarchy might be an apex level of extreme localization, with one neuron representing each object that we've encountered in our lives, the data suggest a more plausible distributed combination-coding scheme.
- Since the 1960s, the processing of faces in the temporal cortex has been a focus of interest, and a source of puzzlement, because faces seem to follow different "rules" than other types of complex objects.
- Some populations of IT neurons seem to encode "the idea of a face," rather than the identity of any one specific face, thereby demonstrating an explicit interface between perception and memory.
- Training deep neural networks (DNNs) to categorize visual images can be an effective approach for studying principles of object recognition.
- An important role for feedback is to disambiguate conflicting bottom-up signals from the early stages of the visual system.
- Not only do spontaneous fluctuations of low-frequency oscillatory dynamics influence early visual processing, but there is evidence that these can be biased in a top-down manner to control visual perception.
- Although some models of predictive coding posit the processing of prediction errors at every synapse in the visual hierarchy, some evidence suggests that predictions are preferentially evaluated at relatively high levels of stimulus representation.

CONTENTS

Familiar Principles and Processes, Applied to Higher-Level Representations

This chapter will address the question of how we recognize objects that we encounter in the world. In one sense, it will represent our first foray into the unequivocally cognitive, in that recognizing what an object is necessarily entails *thinking about* where you've seen it before and what its significance is for you (e.g., *I see my* [*spouse/friend/professor/etc.*]), or, if it's an exemplar that you've never seen before, *thinking about* how it relates to what you already know about the world (e.g., *It's the face of a man/woman/young person/old person/etc.*) and what an appropriate action when encountering such an object might be. And so, as this preamble implies (as, indeed, does the word *recognition*), this is a domain that necessarily engages memory-stored representations of knowledge about the world; the very stuff of thought.

The emphasis of this chapter will be on the sensory modality of vision, with consideration given to how information from multiple sensory modalities can interact to influence how we perceive the world. At a detailed, mechanistic level, we shall see that a principle that we examined in *Chapter 3* also underlies object recognition. In that earlier chapter, we saw that features such as orientation, depth, and direction of motion are constructed by neurons in V1 via selective sampling across inputs from LGN neurons that have much simpler response properties. At a simplified level of description, the same principle, playing out in parallel in hundreds of thousands of neurons, is believed to underlie object recognition – just the right set of features, located in just the right part of the visual field, combine to represent a complex object. Thus, there is necessarily a hierarchical element to object recognition, in that many simpler elements are combined at lower levels to construct progressively more complex representations at higher levels. This idea of many feeding into one will lead us to revisit the tension introduced in *Chapter 1*, between localization vs. mass action (reframed here as localist vs. distributed representation). We shall also see that the principle of feedback from higher to lower levels of representation, first considered in detail in *Chapter 3*, is also characteristic of the hierarchies involved in recognizing objects. This will also invoke the principle of predictive coding (*Chapter 5*, section *Predictive coding*), the idea that a neural representation of the world is already present in the brain, and that perception is the process whereby the brain uses incoming sensory inputs to update this representation.

As we have done previously, we'll start by considering the anatomical structure of the systems that support high-level vision.

Two Parallel Pathways

A Diversity of Projections from V1

You won't be surprised to learn that *Chapter 3*'s treatment of area V1, and of that region's interactions with MT, glossed over some of the intricacies both of V1's functional organization and of its feedforward projections. As is illustrated in *Figure 6.1*, there is both a direct route from V1 to MT, which carries signals primarily from the magnocellular pathway, and an indirect route, with neurons from V1 first projecting to V2 and V2 neurons projecting to MT. The indirect pathway carries information from both the magno- and parvocellular pathways, a result of the convergence in layer IV of V1 of inputs from magno- and parvocellular pathways on the neurons projecting to V2. V2, like V1, also shows heterogeneous cytochrome oxidase staining, with regions appearing as thick stripes, thin stripes, or interstripes (*Figure 6.1*). The indirect pathway from V1 to MT synapses in the thick stripe region of V2. MT, in turn, sends feedforward projections to area MST (located in *medial superior temporal* cortex in the macaque brain), which, in turn, sends feedforward projections to several areas in the posterior parietal cortex (PPC).

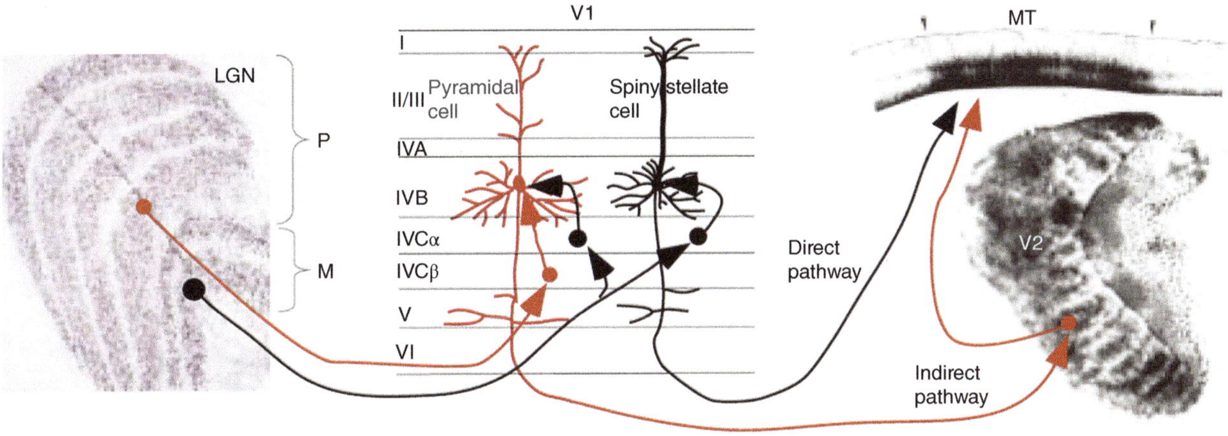

FIGURE 6.1 Dual routes from LGN to MT. The left-hand panel illustrates a cross-section through the LGN, highlighting the two layers containing magnocellular (M) neurons, and the four layers containing parvocellular (P) neurons. Superimposed in black ink is a cartooned magnocellular neuron projecting to two neurons in layer IVCα of cortical area V1. Superimposed in red ink is a cartooned parvocellular neuron projecting to a neuron in layer IVCβ of cortical area V1. Of the two IVCα neurons receiving magnocellular input, one projects to a "spiny stellate" neuron in layer IVB, which, in turn, projects directly to area MT, and the other to a pyramidal neuron in layer IVB. The layer IVCβ neuron also projects to this layer IVB pyramidal neuron, which can thus be characterized as "blending" input from both the M and P channels. The IVB pyramidal neuron projects to a neuron in the thick stripe region of cortical area V2, which, in turn, also projects to MT. This figure shows a portion of the surface area of V2 that has been stained for cytochrome oxidase. Note that immediately to the right of the thick stripe highlighted in this image is an interstripe and, to the right of the interstripe, a thin stripe. Also note that, in this image, the portion of V2 that is illustrated is shaped like a boomerang, with a clear discontinuity between it and the cortical tissue bordering it to the right. The region to the right is V1, identifiable from the small spots (i.e., *blobs*) of cytochrome oxidase staining. Finally, MT is illustrated here in cross-section, with deep layers at the bottom of the image, and has been stained to emphasize one of its distinguishing characteristics, which is heavy myelination of fibers even after they have entered the cortex. (Note that this dark staining ends abruptly near the middle of the cortex; why should that be?)

Source: Reproduced with permission from Born et al. (2001) / Elsevier.

Separate from the direct and indirect projections to MT, different populations of V1 neurons project to the thin- and interstripe regions of V2. These regions of V2, in turn, send feedforward projections to area V4 of the temporal cortex, with V4's feedforward projections extending into the inferotemporal (IT) cortex. More detail about the anatomical connectivity of the visual system appears further along in this section, but at this point, we'll focus on the fact that there are two pathways originating in V1: one that projects through the thick stripes of V2 to MT, MST, and PPC, and the second that projects through the thin- and interstripe regions of V2 to V4, and then IT. As suggested by this anatomy, there are important, and importantly dissociable, visual functions supported by the posterior parietal and inferior temporal lobes, respectively.

Insights into the visual functions of the PPC and IT have come from both of the scientific traditions highlighted at the end of *Chapter 1*: behavioral neurology/neuropsychology and systems neuroscience. Those clearly associated with the former include case studies detailing visual impairments in patients whose strokes have damaged circumscribed regions of cortex. Those clearly associated with the latter include extracellular electrophysiological studies in monkeys performing visual discrimination tasks and detailed studies of neuroanatomy. Many examples of this research will be considered further along in this chapter, but we will start examining these functions via a study performed in the late 1960s at a laboratory firmly grounded in both scientific traditions: the Laboratory of Neuropsychology at the National Institutes of Health.

A Functional Dissociation of Visual Perception of What an Object Is vs. Where It Is Located

If one were forced to choose a label for the Section of Neuropsychology (as it was then called) in the 1960s and 1970s, one would classify it as a systems neuroscience laboratory – the primary experimental approach was one of testing hypotheses about the neural bases of cognitive functions by surgically lesioning specific brain regions and assessing the effects on carefully designed behavioral tasks. Many of those in the lab, however, also had formal training in human neuropsychology, studying behavioral abnormalities in neurological patients. In this environment, a graduate student named Walter Pohl conducted a series of experiments that, in retrospect, seem to have been "made to order" for this textbook writer. I say this for three reasons: first, they illustrate an important principle of the functional organization of the visual system; second, they illustrate a key principle of inference in neuropsychological research, the double dissociation of function; and third, they illustrate the value of performing thorough, carefully controlled experiments, in that an experiment that was intended at the time as a "mere" control condition turned out to provide critical, substantive information.

The primary question of interest for Pohl was different from the one that we are currently addressing. It was motivated by the idea that "The spatial position of an object may be defined in either of two ways, [. . .] either by reference to the position of the observer himself who serves as the spatial anchor, or by reference to the position of another object which functions as an external landmark" (Pohl, 1973, p. 227). In particular, a previous study of brain-injured war veterans conducted by neuroscientist Josephine Semmes and colleagues had shown that while some had difficulty viewing a mark on a picture of a body and pointing to the corresponding location on their own body, others had difficulty following maps. The former is referred to as **egocentric localization** (i.e., using a self-centered frame of reference), and the latter as **allocentric localization** (i.e., using an other-centered frame of reference). Thus, Pohl's experiments weren't intended to be about the visual functions of PPC and IT cortex, per se, but rather about two ways of perceiving space, and using this information to act on objects in the environment. (The topic of spatial frames of reference will be revisited in greater detail in *Chapters 7–9*, on spatial cognition and skeleto- and oculomotor control, respectively.) It is the inclusion of a critical control experiment that makes them so relevant for our present purposes.

As illustrated in *Figure 6.2*, Pohl (1973) collected data from monkeys performing a "landmark discrimination" task, intended to assess the ability to judge the location of a "landmark" stimulus, and an "object discrimination" task, intended to assess visual object recognition. Depending on the experiment (four are reported in Pohl [1973], but only two are emphasized here), the monkeys had surgical lesions of PPC, IT, and prefrontal cortex, or were unoperated control subjects. The behavioral tasks, administered in a Wisconsin General Testing Apparatus (WGTA)

(*Figure 6.2.A*), were variants of the reversal learning procedure, which accommodates the fact that, unlike human research subjects, one cannot give animals verbal instructions. Instead, the rate at which an animal can learn the rules for the task by trial-and-error guessing is used as one of the primary dependent measures. In the landmark reversal task, for example, *Figure 6.2.B* illustrates what the monkey might see on the very first trial of the experiment. The food reward was always hidden in the well adjacent to the landmark stimulus. If the monkey reached correctly, it retrieved the reward, the screen was lowered, and the tray was prepared for the subsequent trial. If the monkey incorrectly reached for the well that was distant from the landmark, it would find this well to be empty. On such error trials, feedback was given on a subsequent correction trial by re-presenting to the animal the same stimulus array, but with the incorrect food well now uncovered, so that the animal could see that it contained no reward. Regardless of whether the prior trial had been performed correctly or incorrectly, on the subsequent trial, there was an equal likelihood that the landmark would appear on the right or on the left.

Each day, the monkey performed 30 trials in this fashion (not counting correction trials) until reaching a pre-determined level of performance interpreted as evidence that it had learned the rule, referred to as "learning to criterion." Criterion was set at getting at least 28 of 30 trials correct on one day's testing (i.e., ~93%), followed by a subsequent day of getting at least 24 of 30 trials correct (i.e., ~80%). The primary measure of performance was the number of errors that monkeys made before reaching this level of performance. Note that ending the experiment here, when the criterion level of performance had been reached, would leave interpretation of the results ambiguous, for two reasons. One is that this criterion for learning, although seemingly reasonable, is also arbitrary (e.g., would the outcome change if it had been set at one day of 95% correct performance followed by a second day at 90%?). Second, what if, for example, a given monkey was just "slow to catch on" to the rule, independent of the cognitive function that the task is intended to capture? (Note from *Figure 6.2.H*, for example, that, on the landmark-reversal task, the IT-lesioned group performed worse than the PPC-lesioned group on the first set of trials [i.e., the symbols plotted on the vertical axis], as, indeed, did the unoperated control animals!) As *Figure 6.2.H* and *Figure 6.2.I* illustrate, however, including a reversal element in the experimental design largely alleviates such concerns about subjectivity and experimental error. For this experiment, the reversal procedure meant that on the day after the monkey had achieved criterion-level performance, the rule was reversed, such that now the reward would be placed in the food well that was *not* adjacent to the landmark. As on day one of the experiment, the monkey now had to learn this new rule by process of trial and error. In this way, the experiment proceeded through a total of seven reversals.

The object reversal task (*Figure 6.2.E*) followed the same procedure, with the exception that the animals had to learn, on each set of trials, under which of two distinctive objects (a red striped cylinder vs. a silver cube) the reward was located.

The results from these experiments showed persuasively that PPC is selectively important for performance on the landmark task, but not for performance on the object discrimination task. Conversely, IT cortex was shown to be selectively important for the object discrimination task, but not the landmark task. The particular pattern of these results – that damage to area A affected performance on task X, but not on task Y, whereas damage to area B affected performance on task Y, but not on task X – constitutes a **double dissociation of function**. (In the context of an analysis of variance [ANOVA], it would be identified as a crossover interaction.) This was important because it supported conclusions about the specificity of the functions supported by these two brain areas. To illustrate why this is important, imagine two alternative scenarios. In one, Pohl only administers one task, the landmark task, to these three groups of monkeys. Although the larger deficit in the PPC-lesioned animals would be consistent with a more important role for PPC spatial perception, it would also be consistent with any number of equally plausible alternative interpretations. What if, for example, the true effect of the PPC lesions was to produce an incessant, loud ringing in the ears such that the animals would have difficulty holding their concentration on any difficult task for a long period of time? If this were true, it could be that the PPC-lesioned animals would also have performed worse on any similar task, including the object task. Although the true results from Pohl (1973) rule this out, this leads to the second alternative hypothetical scenario, one in which only two groups of animals were included, the PPC-lesioned and frontal-lesioned groups. In this scenario, the "loud ringing" (or any number of other nonspecific factors) could still be plausible, because it could be that the landmark task is just more difficult than the object task. Therefore, it is the demonstration that the PPC-lesioned group is not impaired on the object task *and* that a different group, the IT-lesioned group, is impaired on the object task, that supports the strong inference that the integrity of the PPC is important for the construct operationalized by the landmark task, which is allocentric spatial processing.

FIGURE 6.2 The experimental procedures used by Pohl (1973).

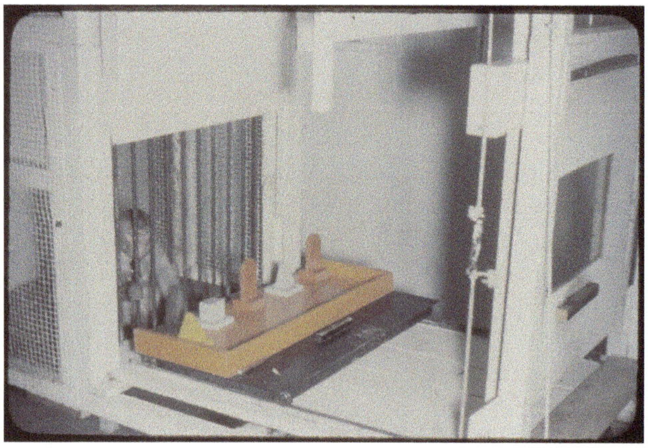

FIGURE 6.2.A Photograph of a macaque monkey performing a task in a WGTA. Note that the animal is in a cage and can interact with items on the wooden testing tray by reaching through the bars in the cage. The tray is on wheels and can be pulled away or toward the animal via ropes on pulleys. A screen can be lowered such that the animal can neither see nor reach through the bars of the cage while a trial is being prepared. On the right side of the image is a one-way mirror, through which an experimenter can observe the animal's behavior, and from where they can control screen and tray.

Source: Harlow Center for Biological Psychology, University of Wisconsin–Madison.

FIGURE 6.2.B Illustration of a two-food-well configuration of the testing tray, with a food reward being placed in one of the two wells. (Pohl (1973) used a half peanut on each trial.)

Source: Adapted from Curtis and D'Esposito, 2004.

FIGURE 6.2.C Illustration of a monkey reaching for one of the two covered food wells. Because the animal cannot see the contents of either food well, it must make its choice based on some second-order factor not related to the wells themselves (e.g., a guess, a memory of the previous trial [these would be considered "internal" factors, because they originate with the animal itself], or, as illustrated in panels **D** and **E**, the configuration of stimuli in relation to the two wells.)

Source: Curtis and D'Esposito, 2004 / Springer Nature.

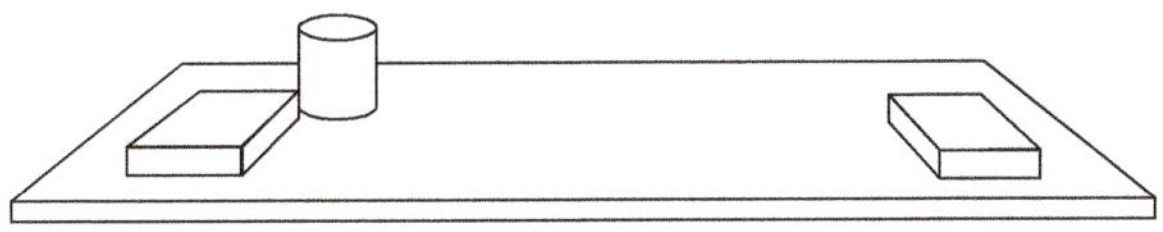

FIGURE 6.2.D The monkey's view of the testing tray during a trial of the landmark reversal (i.e., spatial discrimination) task. In the actual experiment, the landmark was a red cylinder with vertical white stripes.

Source: Pohl and Walter, 1973 / American Psychological Association.

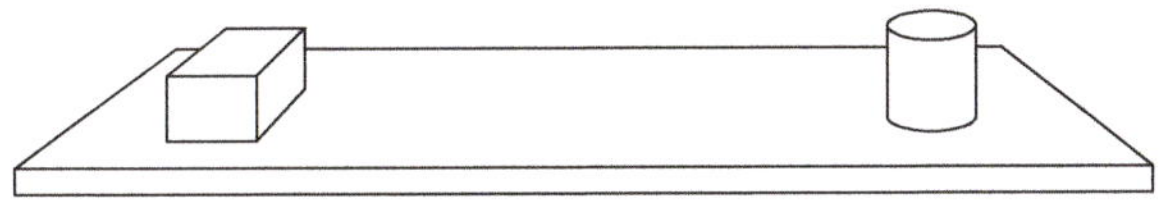

FIGURE 6.2.E The monkey's view of the testing tray during a trial of the object reversal (i.e., object discrimination) task. Each object is placed directly on top of a food well.

Source: Pohl and Walter, 1973 / American Psychological Association.

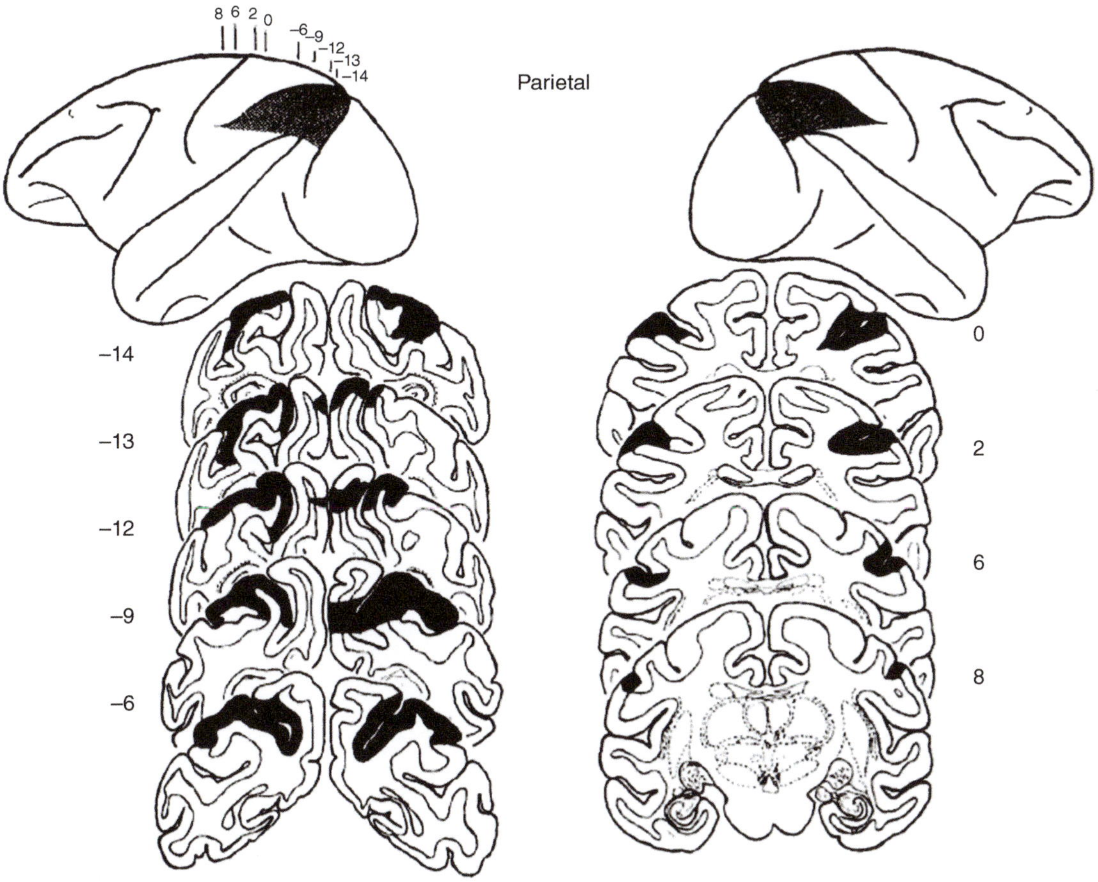

FIGURE 6.2.F Illustration of a PPC lesion. The numbers in the lateral view of the right hemisphere correspond to each of the coronal sections shown below, and also refer to the distance, in millimeters, from an origin point in an atlas of the monkey brain. Note that although the figure is labeled "parietal," great care was taken that the lesions did not invade more anterior areas known to be important for somatosensation (as detailed in *Chapter 5*).

Source: Pohl and Walter, 1973 / American Psychological Association.

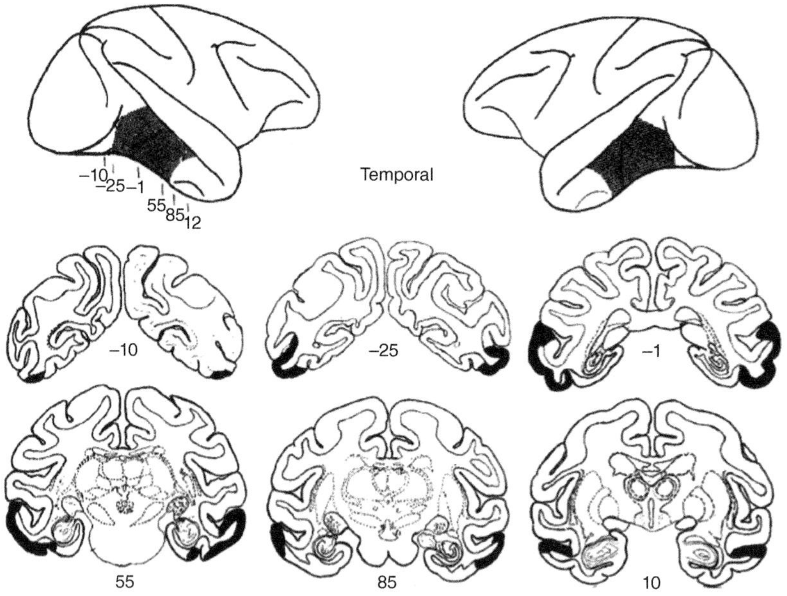

FIGURE 6.2.G Illustration of an IT lesion, same conventions as *Figure 6.2.F*.

Source: Pohl and Walter, 1973 / American Psychological Association.

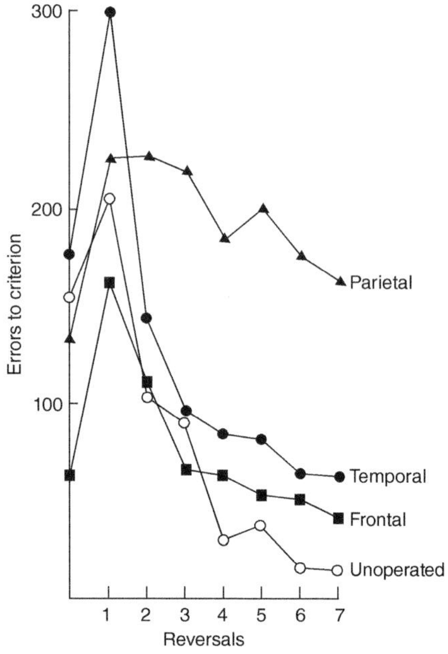

FIGURE 6.2.H Behavioral performance of monkeys from four experimental groups on the landmark reversal (i.e., spatial discrimination) task, illustrating markedly inferior performance by the parietal-lesioned animals.

Source: Pohl and Walter, 1973 / American Psychological Association.

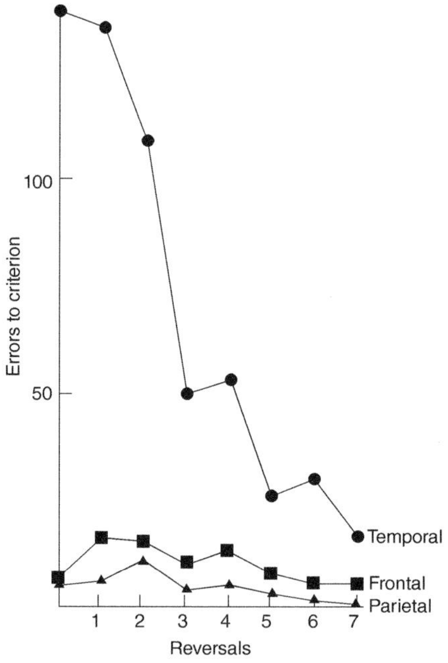

FIGURE 6.2.I Behavioral performance of monkeys from three experimental groups on the object reversal (i.e., object discrimination) task, illustrating markedly inferior performance by the inferior temporal-lesioned animals. (An unoperated control group was not included in the object reversal testing.)

Source: Pohl and Walter, 1973 / American Psychological Association.

In interpreting his findings, Pohl (1973) also drew on many previous theories and findings to advance the interpretation that regions of PPC may be "specialized for extrafoveal visual functions, as in the perception of spatial relations among objects in the visual field [. . . whereas IT cortex may be] specialized for perceptual functions related to foveal vision, as in object and pattern discrimination" (p. 238). (*Figure 6.3* illustrates what is meant by extrafoveal vs. foveal vision.)

The profound importance of the Pohl (1973) study was manifest a few years later when Pohl's mentor at the Laboratory of Neuropsychology, Mortimer Mishkin, together with colleague Leslie Ungerleider, published a thorough review of what was known about the anatomical connections of occipital-to-temporal and occipital-to-parietal cortex, about the effects of lesions to IT vs. PPC, and about the electrophysiological properties of neurons in IT vs. PPC (*Figure 6.3*), and argued that the former constituted a system for analyzing *what* an object is, and the latter a system for analyzing *where* an object is (*Figure 6.4*). This model has been highly influential in cognitive neuroscience, to the point that it has acquired two sets of nicknames, a functional one – *what* vs. *where* – and an anatomical one – *ventral stream* vs. *dorsal stream*.

FIGURE 6.3 Electrophysiological properties of neurons characteristic of the *what* and *where* systems. For both panels, the vertical and horizontal axes represent the meridia of the visual field, the intersection of the two axes thus corresponding to the fovea, and each tick mark indicating 10° of visual angle.

Source: Adapted from Curtis and D'Esposito, 2004.

A

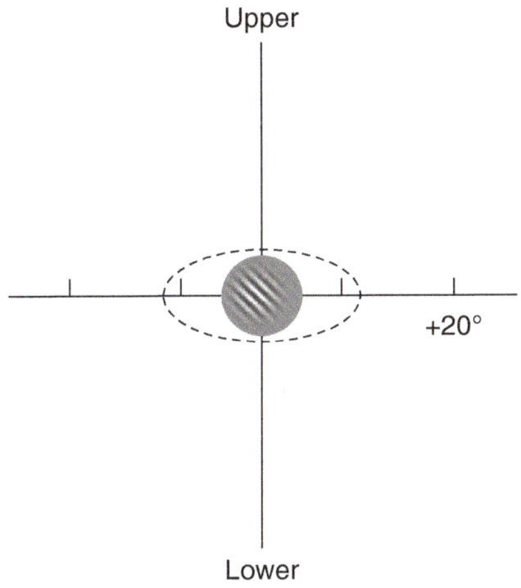

FIGURE 6.3.A For IT neurons, 60% have receptive fields (dashed oval) that span the vertical midline (i.e., they are bilateral), and the receptive fields of 100% of them include the fovea. These neurons are typically selective for particular visual features (here, an oriented grating).

B

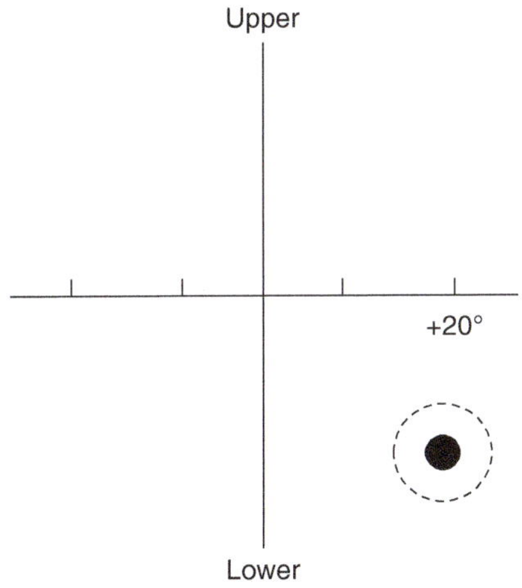

FIGURE 6.3.B For PPC neurons, the receptive fields of >60% of them are restricted to the contralateral visual field, and the receptive fields of >60% of them do NOT include the fovea. At the time, it was believed that these neurons did not show selectivity for stimulus features, meaning that a PPC neuron would respond to any stimulus falling within its receptive field. (This assumption has since been disproven for at least some regions of the PPC.)

Interconnectedness Within and Between the Two Pathways

As is often the case with conceptual models of brain function, the details of the functional organization of the visual system turn out to be much more complicated than what is suggested, for example, by *Figure 6.4*. One example relates to information carried by the M vs. the P channels from the retina through V1, and onto higher levels of the visual system. The two-parallel-pathways model seems to fit quite well with the differential projection patterns, considered earlier in this section, of neurons in thick- vs. thin- and interstripe regions of area V2. Indeed, this led some to suggest that the dorsal visual processing stream may carry primarily magnocellular signals, whereas the ventral stream may carry primarily parvocellular signals. This logic led to a research strategy that sought to exploit this presumed correspondence of the M and P channels with the dorsal and ventral pathways, respectively, by presenting stimuli under **isoluminant** conditions. That is, the stimulus display was controlled such that all objects, including the background, were presented with the same brightness (the same *luminance*), and so only differences in chrominance (i.e., color) could be used to discriminate objects from each other, and from the background. The logic was that an isoluminant display would require exclusive reliance on the ventral stream, because the dorsal stream was presumed to be dominated by the M channel. Isoluminance, therefore, might be a way to study the functions of the ventral stream while experimentally keeping the dorsal stream "offline."

Follow-up studies, however, have called the logic of testing at isoluminance into question. One persuasive line of work, by Peter Schiller and his colleagues, examined the effects of selectively lesioning one channel or the other (via small lesions in selective layers of the LGN), and then testing performance on tasks that require visual processing characteristic of the dorsal or the ventral stream. These studies did, indeed, find preferential impairment on "ventral-stream tasks" after lesions of the P system, and on "dorsal-stream tasks"

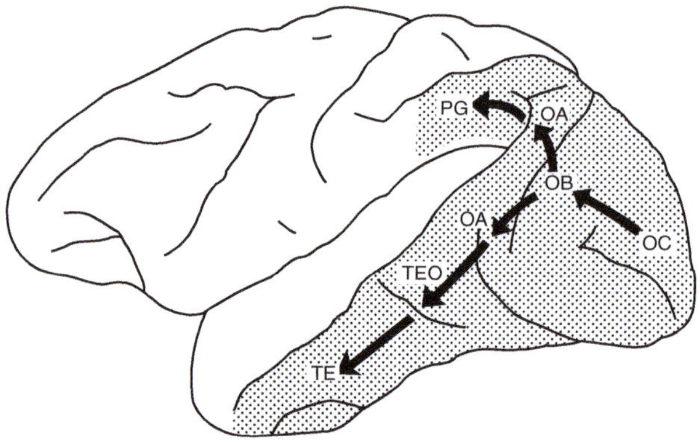

FIGURE 6.4 Schematization of the *what* and *where* pathways of the dorsal and ventral visual processing streams in the macaque monkey. The labels correspond to names given to these regions in a neuroanatomy atlas: OC is striate cortex; OB and OA are extrastriate occipital areas; PG is posterior and inferior parietal cortex; TEO and TE are IT cortex. Note that the sulcus forming the dorsal boundary of area PG is the intraparietal sulcus, which will feature prominently in chapters on attention, skeleto- and oculomotor control, and decision-making.

Source: Mishkin et al., 1983 / with permission of Elsevier.

after lesions of the M system, but the impairments were relatively subtle, not the devastating effects that one would predict from frank lesions of the temporal or parietal cortex. Thus, for example, parvocellular lesions impaired discrimination of textures with high spatial frequencies, but not those with low spatial frequencies. Magnocellular lesions, in contrast, impaired the ability to discriminate a flickering light from a steady light at high, but not low, rates of flicker. (Note that, as the rate of flicker increases, at some point, it becomes so fast that it's no longer possible to discriminate from a steady signal.) Similarly, they impaired the ability to detect a difference in the speed of motion of a small group of dots within a larger field of moving dots, but only when the difference in speed was small, and thus difficult to detect. In both cases, deficits were exacerbated when the to-be-detected stimulus was presented at low contrast (e.g., the impairment was worse for a dim light flickering against a gray background than for a bright light flickering against a black background). Schiller and colleagues concluded that the important contribution of the M and P channels is to extend the range of performance of the visual system in two dimensions – spatial frequency and temporal – under challenging conditions. Thus, the P channel extends the visual system's resolution for fine-grained discriminations of texture and color, and the M channel extends its temporal resolution.

One implication of the findings of Schiller and colleagues was that the M and P pathways each contribute to functions of both the dorsal and the ventral streams. Consistent with this is what we already saw in *Figure 6.1*, that the anatomy indicates that there is already considerable blending of inputs from magno- and parvocellular neurons at the level of V1. Additionally, as portrayed in *Figure 6.5*, we now know that there are many instances of direct, reciprocal interconnections between regions of the two streams considered to be at comparable levels of the visual processing hierarchy, such as between V4 of the ventral stream and MT of the dorsal stream.

Two final comments about the *what* vs. *where* model before we delve into the functions of the ventral stream. First, it's noteworthy that *Figure 6.4* omits the feedback projections that we already know from earlier chapters make fundamental contributions to how the brain works. This will be taken up near the end of this chapter. Second, an additional level of complexity that we won't consider in detail until *Chapter 8* (*Skeletomotor control*) hearkens back to the question raised in *Chapter 1* of *what is a function*: some argue that the dorsal stream is better construed as carrying out the function of *how* the body carries out actions in space, rather than of determining *where* objects are located in space.

Having now established some gross anatomical boundaries for the visual system, and a framework for thinking about how the functions of this system are organized (i.e., *what* vs. *where*), we can proceed to consider the question: *How does visual object recognition work?*

In the process, some of the ideas left underspecified in the preceding paragraph, such as that of the "visual processing hierarchy," will be fleshed out. For the remainder of this chapter, periodically returning to *Figure 6.5* will be helpful, and, in the process, its "subway system wiring diagram" will become progressively more familiar and, hopefully, less daunting.

FIGURE 6.5 Anatomical connectivity of the visual system.

Source: Adapted from Felleman et al., 1991.

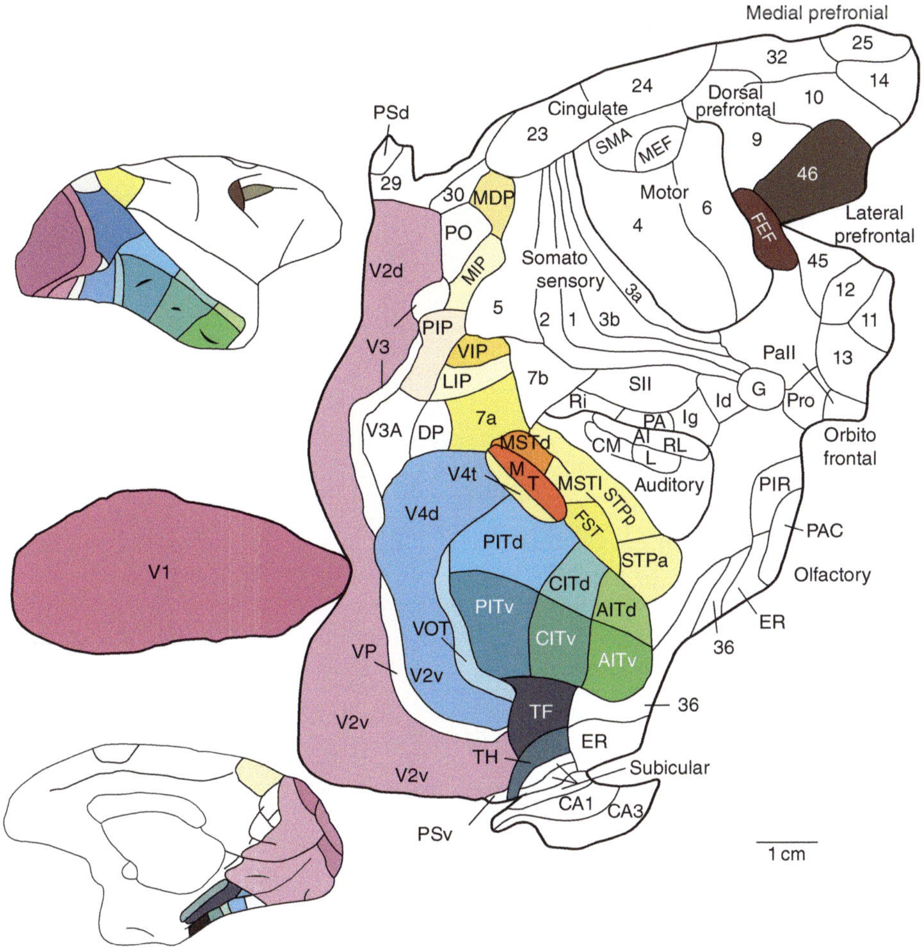

FIGURE 6.5.A Color-coded views of the right hemisphere of the macaque cerebral cortex (plus hippocampus) as seen from lateral (top-left inset) and medial (bottom-left inset) views, and as a virtual "flat map" that illustrates the entire cortical surface. To create a flat map that preserves the relative size of each region (e.g., that doesn't "stretch" or otherwise distort), it is necessary to make several virtual "cuts." Most obvious in this view is that V1 has been "cut out" along the entirety of its border with V2, with the exception of its anterior-most point on the lateral surface. The next major cut is on the medial surface, "carving" around the roughly circular boundary of cortex and non-cortex (revisiting *Figures 1.2.B* and *2.2* may be helpful here). At this point, one can imagine approaching the brain from the lateral view and reaching one hand, palm down, over the parietal cortex and down along the midline, and the other hand, palm up, under the ventral surface of the temporal lobe with fingers curling up and in along its medial surface, and then pulling up with the top hand and down with the bottom so as to "unroll" this 3-D shape and flatten it. If, in the process, one were also to gently stretch by pulling the two hands further apart, the interior of the sulci would also be exposed. It is thus, for example, that the red and yellow bands of the tissue that is not visible in the lateral view, by virtue of lying within the superior temporal sulcus, are exposed in the flat-map view. Finally, two additional cuts are needed to complete the task, each separating regions that are adjacent in the intact brain. One is a cut separating prefrontal areas 46 from 45 (running approximately along the fundus of the principal sulcus), and the second is a slit starting at the temporal pole and proceeding caudally along the medial surface, thereby artificially dividing the entorhinal cortex (ER) into two. This type of flat map is also often used to display results from functional magnetic resonance imaging (fMRI) studies of the human brain, as we shall see further along in this book.

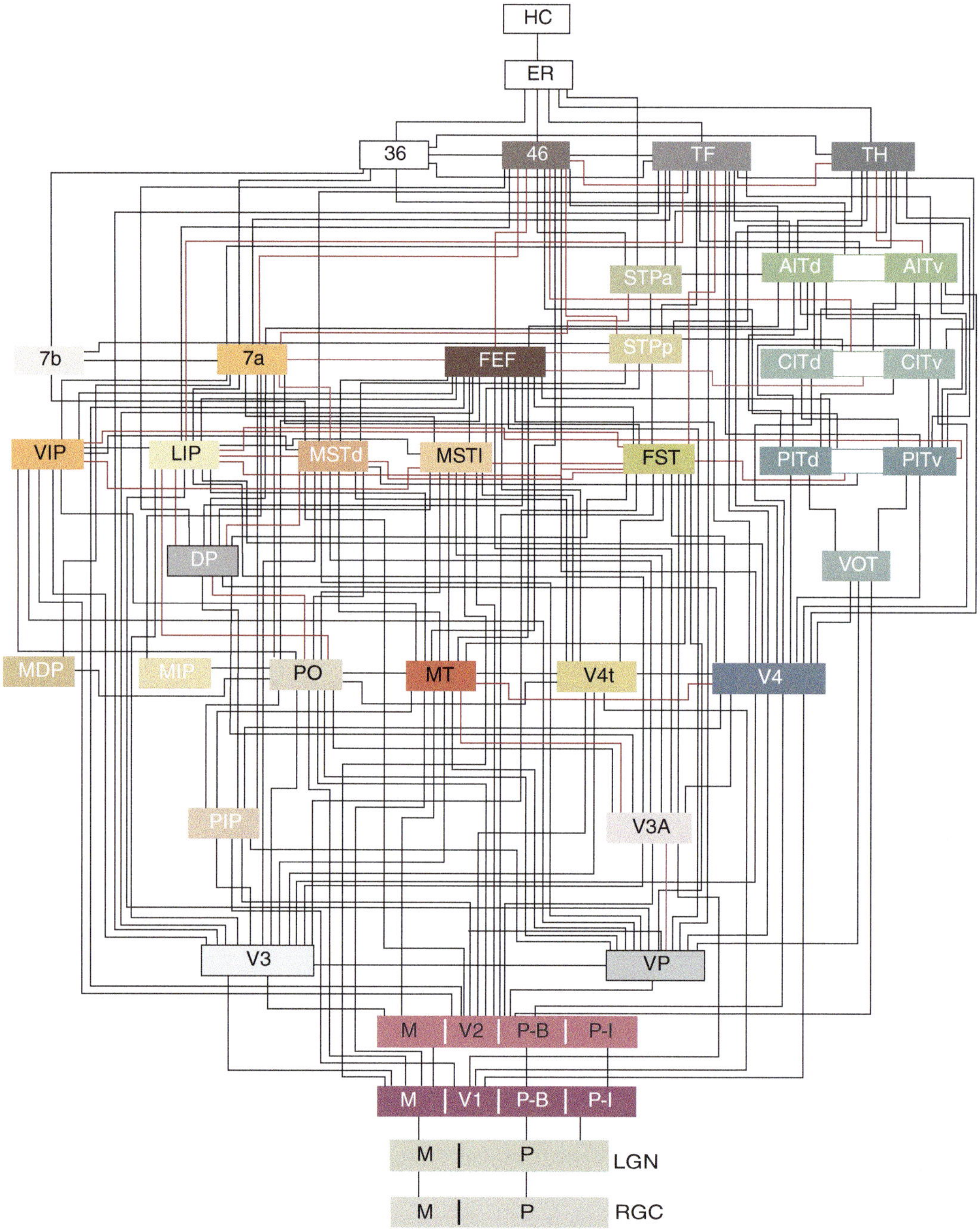

FIGURE 6.5.B Connectivity diagram of the visual system as a hierarchically organized set of interconnected regions, with each region's position in the hierarchy determined by its anatomical connectivity with all the others, as determined by laminar patterns of its inputs and outputs (see *Figure 2.4*, and associated text from *Chapter 2*). Color coding corresponds to *Figure 6.5.A*. Each line is understood to correspond to bidirectional connections between two connected regions, with feedforward connections going from lower to higher on the diagram (e.g., from MT to one of the MST subregions) and feedback connections going from higher to lower. Thus, each horizontal level of the diagram corresponds to a putative "hierarchical level of cortical processing." The bottom level is the retina, with retinal ganglion cells (RGCs) divided into M and P channels, which project to the magnocellular (M) or parvocellular (P) layers of the LGN (second level). The first two levels of cortex, V1 (purple) and V2 (pink), are each divided into sectors that carry unequivocally M or P-blob (P-B) or P-interblob (P-I) signals; connections from regions that blend these signals are labeled "V1" and "V2."

The Organization and Functions of the Ventral Visual Processing Stream

Hand Cells, Face Cells, and Grandmother Cells

Electrophysiological Recordings in Temporal Cortex By the 1960s, decades of clinical observations in humans and lesion studies in experimental animals had established that the temporal lobes play a critical role in object recognition. What remained unknown, however, was *how* this region carried out that function. *What were the mechanisms that gave rise to object recognition?* It was the pioneering studies of Hubel, Wiesel, and their colleagues, of the functions of V1 (*Chapter 3*), that provided the methodological and conceptual framework that could be applied to this question. Among the first to do so were Charles Gross and his colleagues, who began recording from neurons in IT cortex, and subsequently, the superior temporal sulcus (STS) in the monkey in the 1960s and 1970s. Because the previous literature indicated that lesions of IT cortex produced profound object recognition deficits, they began by measuring responses to a wide array of complex objects.

In a narrative reminiscent of that from Hubel and Wiesel's early experiments, Gross and colleagues initially had difficulty finding any type of object that would reliably elicit a response. Their first successful recording came when, after failing to activate a neuron with a large set of stimuli, an experimenter waved his hand in front of the display screen, and the neuron responded to it vigorously. *Figure 6.6* illustrates a series of stimuli that the researchers subsequently presented to this neuron. There is a subjective sense from this stimulus set that the closer the stimulus was to resembling a monkey's hand, the more effective it was at activating the neuron. Thus, it didn't seem to be the case that this neuron's preferred stimulus was a more "primitive," or generic shape, and that the hand just happened to have many of the same characteristics as this neuron's preferred stimulus characteristics. Rather, it seemed that this neuron's preferred stimulus was truly the hand, and other stimuli could "drive" it with more or less effectiveness as a function of how closely they resembled the hand. Another noteworthy property of this neuron was that it responded to the hand stimulus with a comparably vigorous response when it was positioned in any of many locations in the visual field. That is, it had a very large receptive field. Although this experiment did not find other neurons with the same selectivity for the hand stimulus shown in *Figure 6.6*, it did find many visually responsive neurons in IT that responded better to "complex" stimuli than to simple geometric shapes. Typically, each of these neurons had its own unique preferred stimulus. The property that IT neurons had in common, however, was large receptive fields – often larger than $10° \times 10°$ of visual angle – within which the neuron would respond equally well to its preferred stimulus. (This property was highlighted by Ungerleider and Mishkin [1982], and is illustrated in *Figure 6.3*.) One way of describing this property of an IT neuron is that its sensitivity to its preferred stimulus is relatively **invariant** to the location in which it appears.

Perhaps even more provocative than the finding of an IT neuron with responses selective to a hand was a subsequent report by this group of the results of recording from the superior

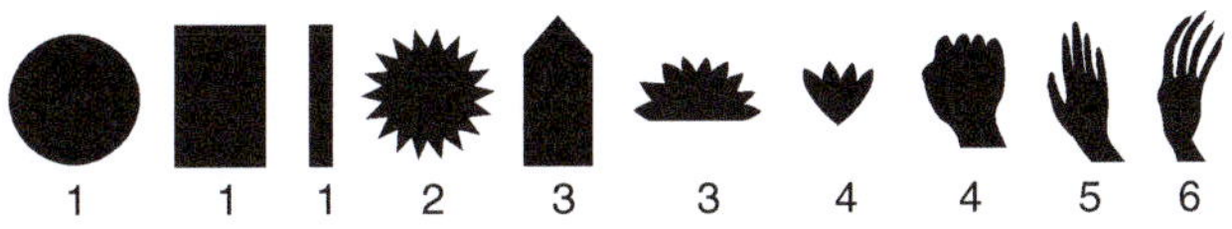

FIGURE 6.6 Examples of shapes that Gross, Rocha-Miranda, and Bender (1972) presented to a neuron in IT cortex, rank ordered by their ability to elicit activity in it, from none (1) or little (2 and 3) to maximum (6).

Source: Gross et al., 1972 / American Physiological Society.

bank of the STS. Referring back to *Figure 6.5*, this corresponds to the regions labeled STPp (superior temporal polysensory – posterior), FST (**fundus** [or "floor"] of the STS), and STPa (superior temporal polysensory – anterior). Gross and colleagues named this area the **superior temporal polysensory (STP)** area because many neurons in this area respond to stimuli from other sensory modalities in addition to visual stimuli. In one report, they found that nearly all neurons responded to visual stimuli, and of these, 21% responded to visual and auditory stimuli, 17% to visual and somesthetic stimuli, 17% to stimuli from all three modalities, and 41% exclusively to visual stimuli. The most provocative finding from this study was that a small number of neurons (7) were found that responded selectively to images of monkey and human faces. More specifically, these neurons seemed to respond to the category of *face*. For example, *Figure 6.7* illustrates a neuron that responded equally robustly to images of different monkeys' faces, as well as to an image of a human face. Psychologists make the distinction between the **type** (or category) of stimulus, such as the category of faces, and a **token**, a specific exemplar drawn from within this category, such as the face of a particular person. Thus, the "face cells" discovered by Gross and colleagues seemed to be selective for stimuli of this particular type, but not for specific tokens within this category.

The two properties of the neurons of IT and STP that we have emphasized here – a high degree of selectivity for complex stimuli and large receptive fields – were in marked contrast to the known properties of neurons from V1. Neurons in V1 respond with high specificity to well-defined, low-level features, such as a boundary or line within a narrow range of orientation or the end of a line. Additionally, within a module in V1 (i.e., within a pinwheel), there is an organization such that adjacent columns of neurons represent a smooth transition in the feature being represented. In the temporal cortex, in contrast, the hand and face cells responded to the complete shape, but, for the most part, not to its component parts. Furthermore, there was no evident topography to suggest that similar kinds of stimuli might be represented in adjacent areas of IT or STP. With regard to receptive fields, in V1, foveal receptive fields are quite small, on the order of $0.5° \times 0.5°$. The majority of neurons in the temporal cortex, in contrast, had very large receptive fields. In STP, many of the receptive fields approached the size of the entire visual field. An additional feature that distinguished these temporal cortex neurons was that they could also be invariant to the size of their preferred image.

The invariance to location and to size of visually responsive temporal-lobe neurons had two implications. The first was that the temporal cortex may contain the machinery to allow for the recognition of objects across a wide range of viewing conditions. This is a necessary property for vision in everyday life, because we rarely see an object under exactly the same viewing conditions on more than one occasion. For example, as the author sits here typing this text, he recognizes his mobile telephone lying on the desk to the left of his computer monitor. If he picks up the phone and brings it near his face, he will recognize it as the same unchanged, familiar object, despite the fact that entirely different populations of cells in the retina, LGN, and V1 are processing low-level featural information about the object when it is in these two locations. Similarly, when someone walks into the room where our protagonist is sitting and turns on the light (he's currently writing in his study at home, on an overcast day), he still recognizes the telephone despite the fact that the colors that his retina detects differ considerably depending on the level of illumination in the room. The second implication was, in effect, a "problem" for the visual system that is created by these invariances. Note that when we look at our phone, pick it up, and set it down on the other side of our monitor (or dinner plate, or whatever), one not only recognizes *what* it is but also *where* it is (*my phone is to the left of the monitor*; *my phone is near my face*; etc.). A mobile phone-tuned neuron with a large receptive field that spans the width of my computer monitor, however, won't carry information about where the phone is located. This follows from the fact that the response of this neuron is equivalent whether the phone is to the left of the monitor, to the right, or near my face. This sets up what has been referred to as the **binding problem**: *if ventral-stream neurons encode stimulus identity but not location, and if dorsal-stream neurons encode stimulus location, but not identity, how is this information brought together to create the unitary, "bound" percept that we experience of an object occupying a location in space?* The binding problem is of central interest in many branches of cognitive neuroscience. Although we will not arrive at a definitive solution to it in this chapter (nor, indeed, in this book), we will return to it periodically.

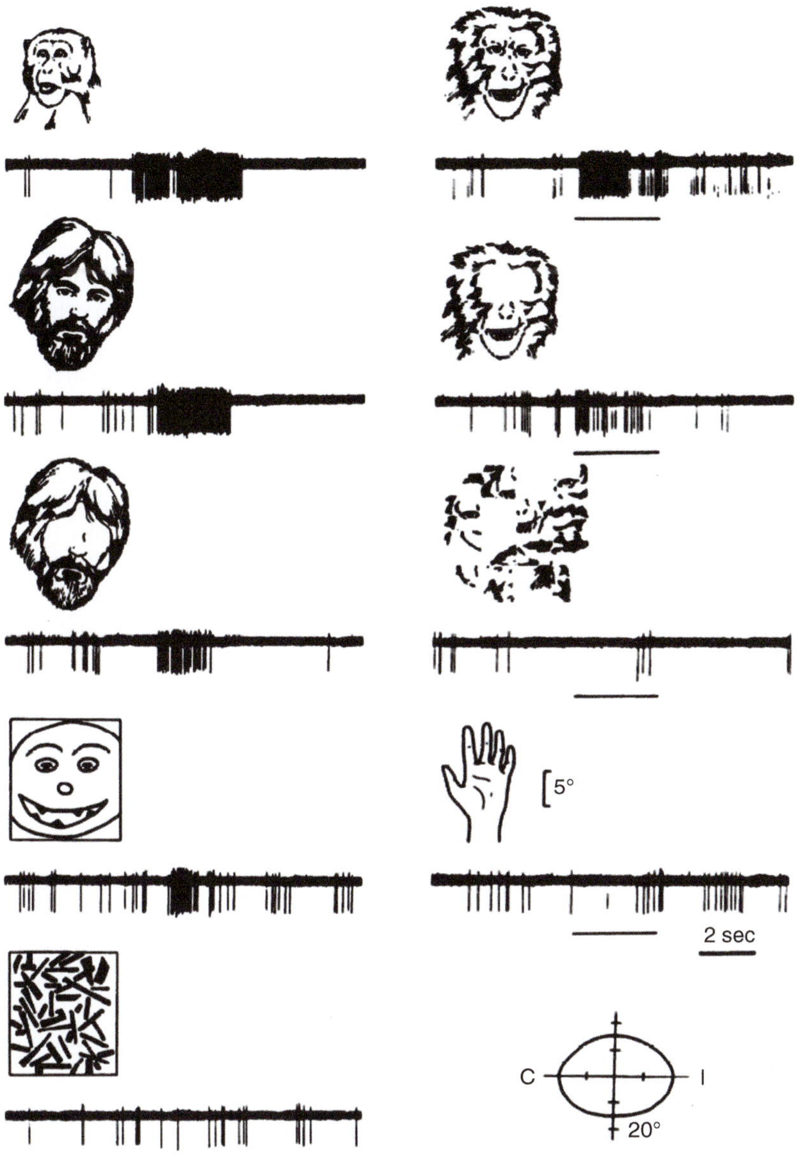

FIGURE 6.7 Responses of a face cell from area STP. Under each stimulus image is a trace from the electrode recording the neuron's activity, with each vertical bar corresponding to an action potential. Note that the neuron's response is comparably vigorous for the faces of two different monkeys and for a human face. The response is markedly weakened, though not abolished, when eyes are removed from the faces, as well as for a hand-drawn cartoon of a face. Changing the physical arrangement of the elements of an image, however, such as by scrambling the parts so that it no longer resembles a face, abolished the response. The lack of response to the hand is emblematic of the fact that this neuron did not respond to many other stimuli, ranging from bars, spots, and edges, to complex objects such as hands and brushes. The lower right illustrates the neuron's receptive field (C = contralateral; I = ipsilateral).

Source: Gross et al., 1972 / American Physiological Society.

Broader Implications of Visual Properties of Temporal Cortex Neurons

In one sense, the studies by Gross and colleagues fit well with the findings from prior decades, that lesions of the temporal lobe produced profound deficits in the ability to recognize objects. They also brought to light many thorny questions about precisely how visual object recognition is accomplished by the brain. Recall, for example, that we noted that face cells seemed to respond to any token drawn from this category, rather than to a specific face. This raises two interesting puzzles. The more concrete of the two is what supports our ability to recognize and discriminate among the tens of thousands of faces that we've encountered across our lives? This presents a puzzle because the neurons reported by Gross and colleagues didn't seem to have the specificity to support this ability. We will return to this in the next paragraph. The second question follows from the fact that these face cells seemed to signal the presence of an item from the category "face," rather than the presence of any specific face. Thus, in a sense, these neurons seemed to be conveying information about the idea of what it means to be a face – a face is the part of the body of many animals that includes the eyes, nose, and mouth; a face is associated with the individual identity of an animal more so than other parts of the body; a face conveys the mood or state of mind of the individual; and so on – rather than about the particular object being viewed. If the IT and STP are, indeed, parts of the visual object recognition system, how does one get from the low-level operations carried out in the retina, LGN, and V1 to cells in the temporal cortex processing "the idea of a face"? Processing information about "the idea of a face," if that's what these neurons were doing, involves cognitive processes that are outside the domain of vision, strictly defined. Engaging knowledge about what a face is, what it can do, how a face is typically configured, and so on falls under the rubric of semantic memory, a topic that we will address in detail in *Chapter 13*. That is, it entails accessing knowledge about the world that was already present in the brain prior to the particular instance of seeing a face that occurred during that experimental session. These are deep questions that make explicit how the study of perception is central to building an understanding of cognition. For the time being, we'll leave it that the discovery of face cells made explicit the fact that a full understanding of visual object recognition will need to take into account the interface between the processing of newly encountered information in the world with our long-term store of knowledge about the world.

Let's return now to the fact that the face cells described by Gross and colleagues did not seem to show a specificity for any individual face. The failure to find any such neurons nonetheless required scientists to confront the implications of what it would mean if they *had* found such neurons. The expectation/assumption that there will be neurons that are selective for individual faces implies a visual system in which the processing of information at each stage becomes progressively more specific until, at the highest level, there is one neuron that represents each of the millions of objects in the world that we can recognize. Such a scheme for organizing the visual system, and the existence of highly specialized "gnostic" units at the highest level, had been contemplated by the Polish neuroscientist Jerzy Konorski (1903–1973). (The term "gnostic" has its roots in the Greek word for knowledge.) It had also been caricatured and disparaged by American neurophysiologist Jerome Lettvin (1920–2011) as the "grandmother cell theory." The idea was that if there is a neuron specialized for recognizing every object with which one is familiar, among these must be a neuron that is specialized for recognizing one's grandmother.

At first blush, the grandmother cell theory might have an intuitive appeal as the logical terminus of a hierarchical system of progressively increasing specialization. To be taken seriously, however, it would need to account for (at least) two major concerns. The first is vulnerability: if the system relies on highly specialized neurons at the apex of a processing hierarchy to represent each specific token that the organism can recognize, what would happen if one or more of these neurons were to be damaged? The second is the pragmatics of **phylogeny** and **ontogeny**: how, from the perspective of evolutionary or organismal development, could a system "know" a priori how many top-level gnostic units would need to be created and "set aside" such that the organism would have enough to represent each of the distinct objects that it would encounter throughout its life?

As we have seen, the research of Gross and colleagues in IT and STP provided some clues, and stimulated many ideas, about how visual object recognition might work. To make further progress, however, it would be necessary to "close the gap" between the properties of neurons at these most advanced stages of the ventral visual pathway and those of neurons at the earliest stages of cortical processing. Thus, it is to intermediate levels of the ventral stream that we turn next.

A Hierarchy of Stimulus Representation

In the years between the early 1970s and today, many, many laboratories have performed experiments to "close the gap" between V1 and IT/STP. The picture that has emerged is generally consistent with the principle first introduced in *Chapter 3*: progressively higher levels of stimulus representation are constructed at progressively higher levels of the system by selective integration of more elemental information from earlier (or, in the terminology of a hierarchy, "lower") stages of processing. Ungerleider and Bell (2011) likened this to the process of assembling words from syllables (*Figure 6.8*), which are, themselves, assembled from an even more elemental unit of written language, individual letters. In this analogy, words correspond to high-level, complete object representations, syllables to intermediate-level conjunctions of features, and letters to low-level features (such as those detected by V1). As detailed in *Chapter 3*, simple cells in V1 respond preferentially to specific luminance-defined orientations, and complex cells can signal the termination of lines. Neurons in area V2, located one synapse downstream, can respond to corners (which can be constructed from two differently oriented line segments). Neurons in V4, which receives projections from both V1 and V2, have a wide array of response profiles: some V4 neurons respond preferentially to curved contours (as illustrated in *Figure 6.9*); some to a specific combination of a degree of curvature at a particular orientation; some to outlines of basic geometric shapes; and some to conjunctions of features, such as a line that is oriented at a particular angle *and* is of a particular color. At each of these stages, one sees that the stimulus information processed at that stage is more complicated than the information that was processed at the preceding stage(s) from which it receives feedforward inputs. Thus, one can say that neurons at higher stages in the ventral visual pathway become progressively more specialized. (E.g., while a simple cell in V1 might respond to the "leading edge" of a bar tilted 45° to the right, regardless of color, so long as the bar is darker than the background, a neuron in V4 might respond only to red bars of this orientation.) In most cases, one can see how the preferences of neurons at a particular stage of processing can be assembled, or, in some cases, inferred, from the convergence of inputs from an earlier stage. *Figure 6.9* offers an illustration of how this scheme of progressively more complex and specific stimulus representation might be engaged in the perception of a twisting tree branch. To return to the assembling-a-word analogy of visual perception (*Figure 6.8*), individual letters might be represented in V1 and V2, syllables in V4, and the "final" percept, in this case an automobile, in IT.

Figure 6.9 also illustrates the fact that, in parallel to the trend of progressively narrowing selectivity of the visual features to which a neuron will respond, neurons at progressively downstream stages of processing in the ventral stream have progressively larger receptive fields. Thus, although a neuron in V4 will respond to many fewer stimuli than will a neuron in V1, the V4 neuron will respond to its preferred stimuli when they appear in a much larger range of the visual field. As we saw in *Chapter 3*, this is a necessary byproduct of integrating over several smaller receptive fields from a lower level. It is also important to note one of the efficiencies of a feature-based hierarchical object recognition system, which is that the lower levels of the system can contribute to the perception of many, many objects. Returning

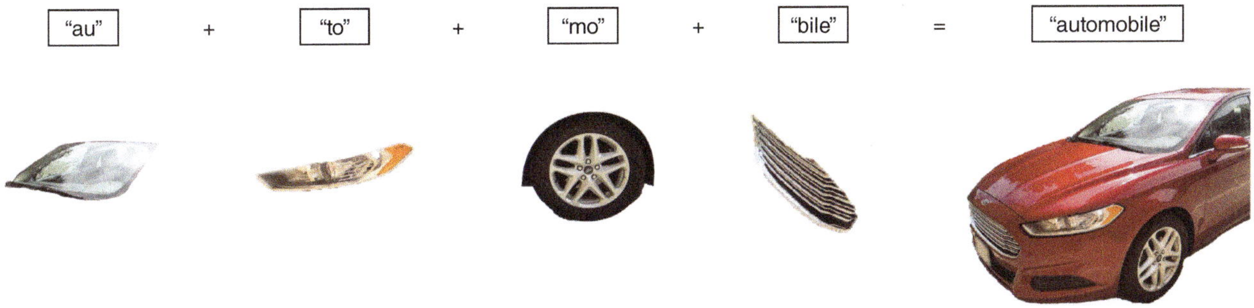

FIGURE 6.8 One analogy to object recognition is that just as words can be assembled from syllables, object representations may be assemblable from more primitive visual features.

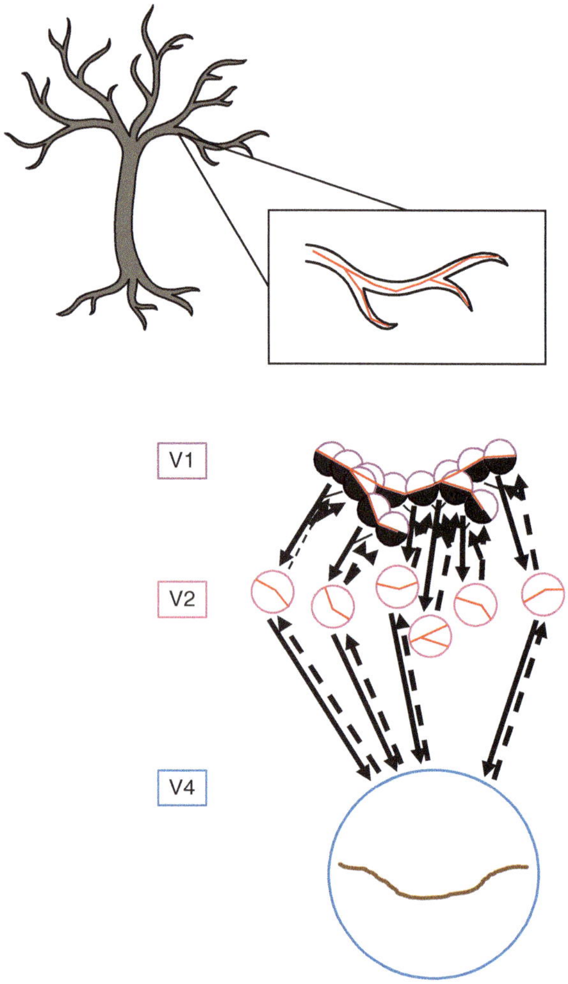

FIGURE 6.9 Hierarchical processing in the visual system. The perception of the branch of a tree (outlined with a red line in the call-out box) proceeds from the fine-grained representation of the dense orientation structure by orientation-selective neurons in V1, to the representation of corners and straight sections of varying length in V2, to a representation of the overall contour of the branch in V4. Note that receptive fields increase in size at each level of processing. Solid arrows represent the feedforward direction of information processing, and dashed arrows represent the feedback.

again to the assemble-a-word analogy (*Figure 6.8*), if the word being presented were *apple*, instead of *automobile*, the "a" and "e" feature detectors (from our fanciful V1) could also contribute to the perception of this very different word. For *apple*, the *a* would feedforward to a neuron in V4 representing the syllable *app*, and the *e* detector to a neuron in V4 representing the syllable *le*. Neurons at the level of our fanciful area V4 could also contribute to the perception of multiple words, the *mo* detector, for example, also contributing to the perception of *motion*, or *dynamo*.

Paradoxically, however, what makes for an efficient system at lower levels might lead to a hopelessly inefficient, and perhaps impossible, situation at the highest level. That is, the logical end of a hierarchical chain of progressively more specialized feature detectors is a highest level of representation at which individual neurons are each dedicated to one of the seemingly infinite number of objects that we can recognize – one for an *automobile*, one for an *apple*, one for *motion*, one for a *dynamo*, and so on, ad infinitum.

One solution to the problems articulated here is to devise a scheme for object representation that does not rely on a "grandmother level." And that's what we consider next.

Combination Coding, an Alternative to the "Grandmother Cell" A breakthrough in thinking about how object recognition might be accomplished at the highest levels came from Japanese neurophysiologist Keiji Tanaka and his colleagues at the Institute of Physical and Chemical Research (RIKEN). The key to their breakthrough came from their "reduction method" of studying stimulus selectivity in IT neurons. They made their recordings in anterior IT cortex, the regions labeled CITv and AITv (central IT, ventral portion; anterior IT, ventral portion) in *Figure 6.5*. Upon isolating a single neuron with a microelectrode, they presented the monkey with dozens of 3D objects, drawn from many categories, so as to find the complex stimulus that was most effective at driving the cell. Having done so, they next created a 2D facsimile of the 3D object via the superposition of many simple features. *Figure 6.10* illustrates this process for an IT neuron that was discovered to be most responsive to a top-down view of a tiger's head. (Presumably, in the first step of the process, the investigators presented a toy tiger and the neuron responded vigorously. Upon holding the tiger at different distances, and rotating it to present different views, they determined that the strongest responses were elicited by displaying the head from this top-down view.) The key to the 2D facsimile image is that it was assembled to be "decomposable" into progressively simpler configurations. For the tiger head, for example, the 2D facsimile image consisted of an oval (a stand-in for the shape of the head), a superimposed array of a texture of black and white bars ("stripes"), and two black rectangles (stand-ins for the ears). Critically, the investigators confirmed that the neuron's response to this 2D facsimile was comparable to its response to the tiger head itself. The "reduction" process, then, proceeded via the progressive removal, or in some cases simplification, of individual elements of the facsimile image, until reaching the point at which the neuron's response was no longer as robust as it had been to the original 3D object.

For the IT neuron featured in *Figure 6.10*, this procedure revealed that this neuron's true selectivity was not for a top-down view of a tiger's head (which would be a highly specific configuration of features indeed!) but, rather, for a simpler configuration of a white square with two superimposed black rectangles. As the investigators heroically repeated this process with hundreds of real-world 3D objects, they confirmed, again and again, that IT neurons that were initially found to respond vigorously to one of these objects were, in fact, tuned to a simpler, reduced set of generic features. Thus, the visual system may not accomplish the recognition of a top-down view of a tiger's head via a hierarchy of progressively more specialized neurons that terminates with a "top-down-view-of-a-tiger-head neuron" in a putative "grandmother cell" level at the apex of this hierarchy. Instead, the tiger's head may be recognized by the simultaneous (i.e., the "combined") activation of several tens (if not hundreds or more) of neurons that each represent a different set of features that uniquely make up this stimulus: one group of cells representing the configuration of two black rectangles superimposed on one white square, as illustrated in *Figure 6.10*, another group representing the black and white stripes, another group representing the moist, glistening skin of the nose, another group representing the whiskers, and so on. Note that, in contrast to the extreme localizationism implied by a hierarchy ending in a "grandmother level," the principle of combination coding proposed by Tanaka and colleagues has two hallmarks of a distributed system. First, there is no one place where a tiger head is represented. Instead, its representation entails the simultaneous activation of many elements that are distributed throughout the IT cortex. Second, any one of these elements can participate in the representation of many different objects. For example, although the recognition of a top-down view of the head of an otter or a warthog is sure to activate many elements not activated by the tiger, it may nonetheless activate the same IT neurons that can represent whiskers.

It is noteworthy that *faces* was the one class of stimuli that Tanaka and colleagues found that were generally not amenable to decomposition by the reduction method. That is, when an IT neuron was found that responded vigorously to a face stimulus, it was generally not possible to decompose the image into a simpler collection of features that would still drive the cell equally well. (The one exception was a single neuron described in one study for which a face could be simplified to two eyes and a nose.)

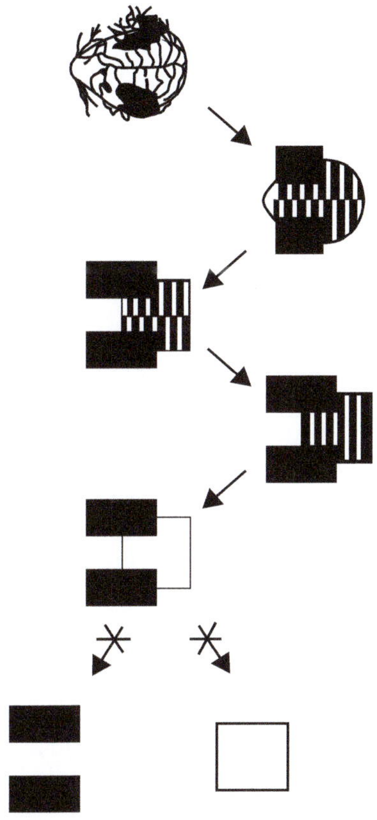

FIGURE 6.10 Tanaka's reduction method for determining the tuning properties of an IT neuron. After the neuron was determined to be maximally responsive to the top-down view of a tiger's head (top image), the investigators confirmed that it responded equally vigorously to a 2-D facsimile image comprising an oval, a pattern of black and white bars, and two black rectangles. The facsimile image was then "reduced" in a step-by-step manner until the investigators reached the simplest configuration of elements beyond which they could not further decompose the image without eliminating the neuron's response.

Source: Tanaka and Keiji, 1993 / American Association for the Advancement of Science.

A Critical Role for Feedback in the Ventral Visual Processing Stream

Using Deep Neural Networks to Understand Computations Underlying Object Recognition

In recent years, as **deep neural networks (DNNs)** have begun to approach (and, in some cases, exceed) human levels of performance on categorization tasks, scientists have begun to apply deep learning to the study of visual and auditory perception, with the rationale being that, unlike with a real nervous system, every computation carried out by a DNN can be observed and quantified (For background, see *Chapter 4*, section *Deep neural networks*.) Thus, learning how a DNN achieves levels of performance approaching that of a human or a monkey might provide novel insights about how this performance is achieved in biological systems. One study, from Yamins et al. (2014) in the laboratory of James DiCarlo at MIT, used a database of 5760 black-and-white photographic images of objects drawn from eight categories – animals, boats, cars, chairs, faces, fruits, airplanes, and tables – and presented these images to monkeys and to several different DNNs. The researchers used arrays of electrodes to record simultaneously from 168 neurons in IT while their monkeys viewed these images. Rather than "ask the monkey" to report what it had seen by requiring a behavioral response after each image, the researchers effectively "asked IT" what it was seeing by assembling a 168D vector from each image (the activity of each neuron being a dimension), and then determining whether all the images from the *animals* category tended to cluster in the same region of 168D space, if all the *boats* clustered, etc. Successful "decoding" of neural activity is achieved if a pattern classifier that has been trained on a subset of the 5760 images (let's say on 5000 of them) can successfully classify a picture that it has never seen before (one of the 760 images that was "held back" from training). For example, does it successfully classify an image of a banana as belonging to the fruit, instead of one of the other categories? (For background on this analytic approach, see *Chapter 5*, section *Multivariate methods for decoding neural signals.*)

As illustrated in panel *A* of *Figure 6.11*, the input layer of the "feedforward DCNN" from Yamins et al. (2014) was equated to the retina of the primate visual system, and each layer of the network applied a series of operations to its input. One of these is **convolution**, which

FIGURE 6.11 Methods and stimuli for the study "Evidence that recurrent circuits are critical to the ventral stream's execution of core object recognition behavior."

Source: Kar et al., 2019 / Springer Nature.

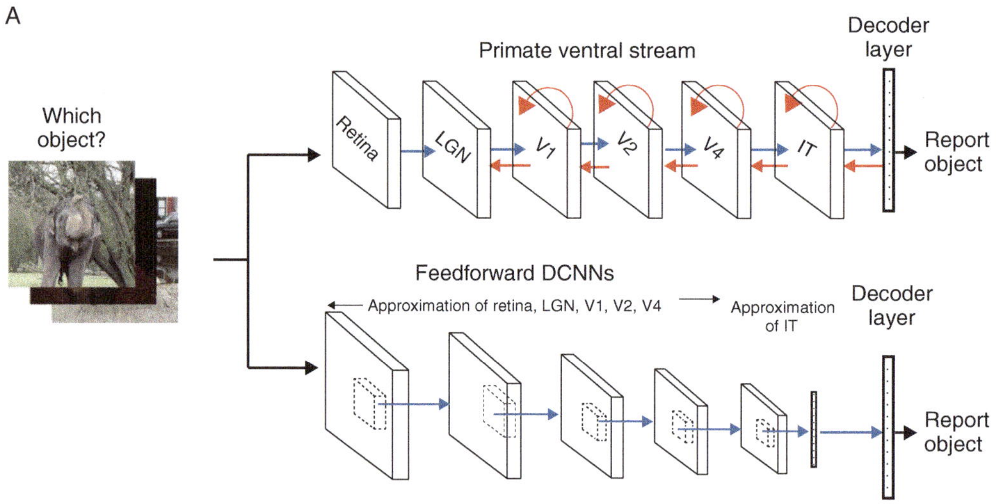

FIGURE 6.11.A The gist of the experiment was to compare image processing by neurons in the visual system of the monkey with the processing steps carried out in each layer by a DNN. On the diagrammed hierarchy of the ventral stream in the monkey, known feedforward connections are illustrated with blue arrows, known feedback connections with straight red arrows, and known lateral connections between neurons in the same regions are illustrated with curved red arrows. In the matched diagram of a "feedforward DCNN" (deep convolutional neural network), the smaller "slab" rendered with dotted lines indicates one area over which pooling will occur. That is, every unit inside that slab will converge on a single unit in the next layer. Note that the resultant decrease in the number of units in each successive layer is indicated by drawing each layer progressively smaller.

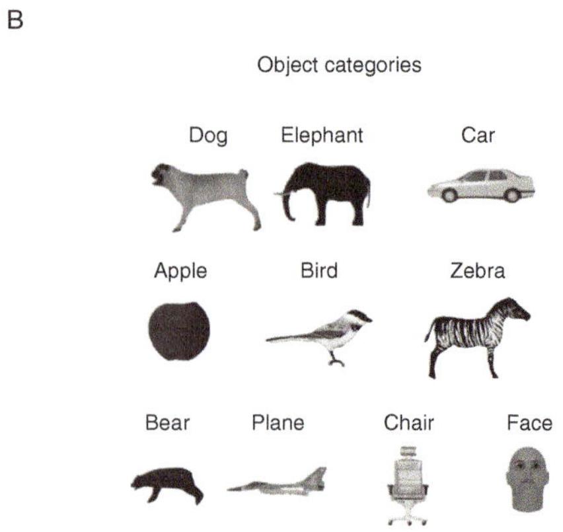

FIGURE 6.11.B The 10 categories.

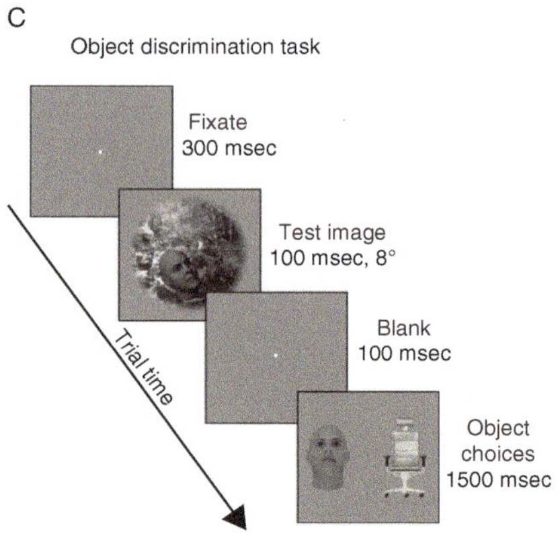

FIGURE 6.11.C The categorization task.

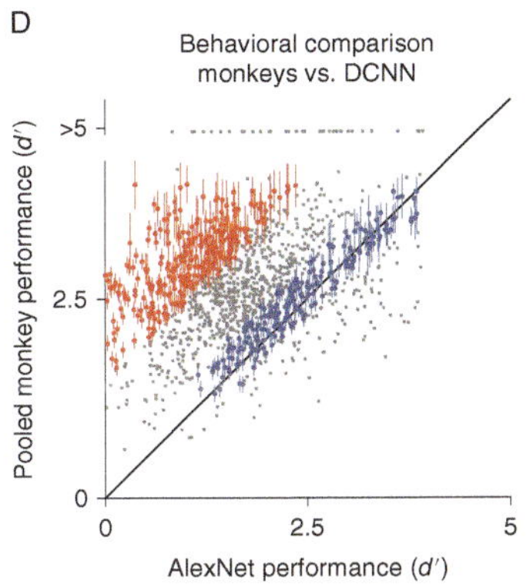

FIGURE 6.11.D Performance on each image, for the two monkeys (averaged) and for the DCNN, was computed as a *d′* value, and images for which monkeys performed at a superior level (red) were used as "challenge images," and images for which the two performed at the same level (blue) were used as "control images." (Images in gray were not used for the analyses.)

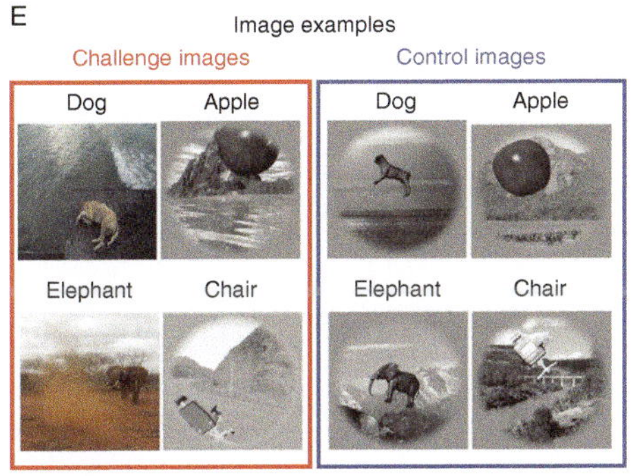

FIGURE 6.11.E Examples of images from the two groups. Note that each object was superimposed on a randomly selected "cluttered" background, to ensure that the background was not correlated with object identity, and therefore couldn't be used to help performance.

consists of applying a series of filters to the input and passing along to the next layer the output from these filters. It's conceptually very similar to the operations performed by a hypercolumn in V1: if an aspect of the stimulus matches a feature detector, the level of activity in that feature detector will increase, thereby passing along to the next layer that its preferred feature is present in the image. (Note that, for this reason, DNNs are sometimes referred to as DCNNs: deep convolutional neural networks.) Another operation applied at each layer of a DNN is called pooling, which is analogous to the increase in receptive field size when multiple neurons in V1 feed into the same neuron in V2, and when multiple neurons in V2 feed into the same neuron in V4 (*Figure 6.9*). It's a step that trades spatial resolution for integration, and the creation of more complex filters at the next layer. And this brings us back to convolution again: one of the really powerful properties of DNNs is that the filters applied during the convolution operation at each layer don't have to be prespecified, they can be learned during the training process.

Training of the DNNs in the Yamins et al. (2014) study used a procedure comparable to the one described in section *A PDP model of picture naming*, *Chapter 4*, in that after activity triggered by an image propagated through the network, the resultant pattern of activation in the output layer indicated the extent to which the DNN "wanted" to classify that image as belonging to each of the eight categories. The error between this pattern in the output layer and what the perfect answer should have been (e.g., a "1" for fruit and a "0" for every other category) was then backpropagated through the network. Importantly, as alluded to above, this error signal was used to modify the filters applied in the convolution operation at each layer.

To determine empirically what normative performance on this image database should be, Yamins et al. (2014) first used "web-based crowdsourcing methods" (presumably Amazon Mechanical Turk, or an analogue) to determine that humans can successfully classify over 90% of the images in the database. Decoding signals from monkey IT cortex yielded roughly 80% accuracy, whereas decoding signals from V4 (from which they also recorded) yielded accuracy below 70%. The best-performing DNN among those that they tried achieved a level of classification performance that was numerically higher than that of humans, almost 100% correct. A general finding from this study – and, importantly, it didn't have to turn out this way – was that the better the performance of a particular DNN, the closer the responses of units in its final layer resembled those of neurons in monkey IT when compared on an image-by-image basis. Furthermore, units in this DNN showed progressively higher levels of invariance to changes in low-level image features at progressively "deeper" layers in the network, comparable to the progression observed from V1 to V2 to V4 to IT in the monkey.

In a follow-up study, the DiCarlo group addressed a more specific question, which is whether feedback projections in the ventral visual stream play an important role in object recognition. Although there is indisputable evidence for strong reciprocal connectivity between each region in the ventral visual stream (*Figure 6.5.B*), there has been a debate about the necessity of feedback for real-time perception, based in part on the fact that the average fixation during natural viewing only lasts between 200 and 300 msec. This may not leave enough time for feedback to contribute meaningfully to the highly accurate object recognition that we all know that we experience on a moment-to-moment basis. From a different perspective, this experiment also addressed a broader point about this kind of research that may have occurred to you while reading this section: *just because a DNN* can *perform image classification at levels achieved by primates doesn't mean that it accomplishes this in the same way*. Indeed, the standard DNN architecture is exclusively feedforward, including that from Yamins et al. (2014). (And note that although the best-performing DNN identified by Yamins et al. [2014] showed unit-level responses that most closely resembled those observed in IT, the highest level of predictivity achieved was that knowing all the responses in the final layer of this DNN to a particular image predicted 48.5% of the variance of the IT response to this same image. That is, they were far from identical.)

To carry out this study, Kar et al. (2019) presented two monkeys and one DNN with a large set of images, and for each sample image followed it with two test images, requiring the observer (monkey or machine) to indicate which of the two test images belonged to the same category as the sample (*Figure 6.11.C*). After testing, they sorted the images into a group that was classified more accurately by the monkeys than by the DNN ("challenge images") and one for which monkey and DNN performance was comparable ("control images"; *Figure 6.11.D*). They had repeated the procedure from their previous study of recording from IT neurons while the monkeys viewed the images, and decoding from these recordings indicated that the time required for image classification from IT neurons was longer for challenge images (median 145 msec) than for control images (median 115 msec). This finding replicated what was known from studies of neural recordings and from behavior, and was consistent with the idea that additional processing was needed for the challenge images. The likelihood that this additional processing included "**recurrent processing**" (i.e., processing involving feedback) was suggested by the fact that the high-dimensional pattern of activity in IT evolved considerably during these additional 30 msec. That is, it didn't take longer for activity triggered by the presentation of an image to get to IT for the challenge vs. the control images; rather, once the signals arrived, it took longer for activity in IT to achieve a stable pattern. Finally, the comparison of activity patterns in the DNN vs. IT indicated that DNN predictivity of IT activity was highest, close to 50% predicted variance, for the "leading edge" of the IT response – what's often referred to as the "initial feedforward sweep" of stimulus-evoked activity – but then dropped to below 20% predicted variance by the time IT achieved its stable pattern of optimal image decoding. Thus, one way in which primate object recognition differs from image classification carried out by DNNs may be that the former depends importantly on recurrent processing (*Figure 6.11*).

One takeaway from this approach to studying visual perception is that it uses a conceptualization of what it means "to recognize something" that's different from how we have described it up until now. At the beginning of this chapter, we noted that the process of recognition necessarily entails engaging with long-term memory, with preexisting knowledge about the world. Here, although memory is involved in the sense that the DNN had to have learned from past experience (indeed, it had to be trained), successful performance doesn't entail matching perceived information to a long-term memory representation of, say, an Air France 747. Rather, it entails being able to classify this image as belonging with other airplanes, rather than with cars, or fruit, or any other category. Indeed, throughout this literature, you'll read about "classification" and "categorization," but you'll rarely encounter the word "recognition." The same is true for how activity in neurons in the temporal cortex of the monkey was processed and interpreted. As we proceed through the book, particularly when we get to *Chapter 10, Visual object recognition and knowledge*, ask yourself whether "recognizing" an image (e.g., of an Air France 747) entails anything more than concluding that it looks more similar to airplanes that you have previously seen in your life relative to the seemingly infinite number of "not-airplane" categories with you are also familiar.

Top-Down Feedback Can Disambiguate the Visual Scene Although the multiplicities of small receptive fields in the retina, LGN, and V1 that "tile" the visual field offer high acuity, they also create challenges for the visual system, one of which is known as the **aperture problem**. At a generic level, what this refers to is the fact that each neuron with a small receptive field is, in effect, viewing the visual scene through a very small aperture. (Imagine looking through the peephole in a door if the fish-eye lens has been removed from it.) *Figure 6.12* illustrates this problem for motion perception: when an irregularly shaped object is moving in one direction, the direction of motion of small portions of the edge of the object, when seen through a small aperture, can be ambiguous. The figure shows one receptive field on the neck of a deer at which at least three direction-sensitive feature detectors (each tuned for one of the directions indicated by the red and green arrows) might signal that its preferred direction of motion is occurring within this receptive field. Although this would result in a noisy, ambiguous message being sent "up the chain" to MT, we know from *Chapter 3*, section *Feedforward and feedback projections of V1*, that there is circuitry in place whereby MT can control activity in V1 and the LGN, thereby reducing this feedforward cacophony and emphasizing the motion signals that it would "prefer" to receive. Indeed, one of the points made in that earlier discussion was that, in the same way that MT can control V1 and the LGN, there must be a higher level of representation feeding back onto MT. We are now in a position to consider what that higher level of representation might be.

Recall from *Figure 6.5.B* that there are lateral interconnections between MT and V4. In our example of the running deer, then, networks in IT that have assembled the representation of the deer can feed this information back onto V4 (as well as, perhaps, laterally to area MST), V4 can then share it with MT, and MT is now equipped to "know" how to control the bottom-up flow of motion signals coming from V1. One implication of this is that, to fully perceive an object in the environment, it's probably not the case that the information flows from retina to LGN to V1, etc., all the way up to IT, and that a stable percept of the object can then persist while the activity in the regions earlier in the hierarchy returns to baseline. Rather, simultaneous activity at every stage of processing is likely needed to experience a coherent percept.

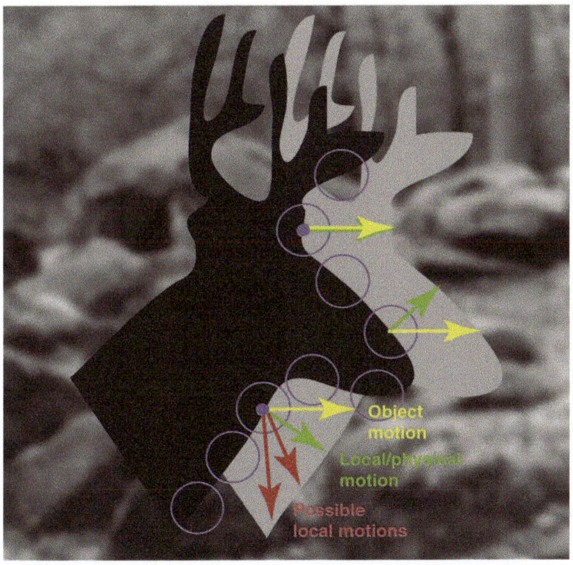

FIGURE 6.12 An example of how high-level visual object recognition is needed to influence earlier stages of visual processing. The black silhouette of the deer head represents its current location, and the gray silhouette a location it will occupy in the very near future. The purple circles represent V1 receptive fields, with yellow arrows indicating the true direction of motion of the object (i.e., of the deer), green arrows the physical motion within two receptive field "apertures," and the red arrows two other possible interpretations of the direction of motion within one of these receptive fields.

Source: Reproduced with permission from Dakin et al. (2009) / Elsevier.

Theoretical and Mechanistic Perspectives on Interactivity in Early Visual Circuits

Up through this point in this chapter, we have emphasized functional considerations of visual processing, addressing such questions as the organization of connections between visual regions, response properties of neurons in various regions, and the principle of hierarchical integration for object recognition. Here, in this final section, we'll consider some ideas about principles that govern the communication between regions.

Oscillatory Dynamics Guiding Visual Perception In general, sustained oscillations as recorded at the scalp, or from ECoG, are believed to arise from the dynamics of recurrent activity in corticothalamic circuits, and there is considerable data to suggest that oscillations in the alpha band are fundamental to functioning of the visual system. We were introduced to this in *Chapter 3*, section *The relation between visual processing and the brain's physiological state*, via the sensitivity of occipital alpha-band oscillations to eyelid closure (*Figure 3.5*) and, in turn, of transcranial magnetic stimulation (TMS)-evoked phosphene perception on endogenous fluctuations in alpha-band power (*Figure 3.6*). Evidence that alpha-band dynamics are specifically important for early visual processing comes from two additional TMS+EEG studies. In one study, Mario Rosanova et al. (2009), in the laboratory of Marcello Massimini, targeted each of three cortical areas – Brodmann's Area (BA) 19 of occipital cortex, BA 7 of parietal cortex, and BA 6 of frontal cortex – with single pulses of TMS while simultaneously recording the EEG. They reasoned that this "perturb-and-measure" approach would reveal the "natural [or resonant] frequency" of each of these regions of cortex, and their results indicated that the spectral evoked response at these three sites was most prominent at 11 Hz, 20 Hz, and 31 Hz, respectively. In a second, Jason Samaha and Olivia Gosseries, in the laboratory of Bradley Postle (2017), replicated the TMS-evoked phosphene perception procedure illustrated in *Figure 3.6*, but also targeted PPC. Their results produced a double dissociation, with pre-TMS power in the theta and alpha bands (3–11 Hz) inversely related to phosphene perception with occipital TMS, and pre-TMS power in the beta band (14–20 Hz) inversely related to phosphene perception with PPC TMS. From these TMS studies, all performed in the absence of externally presented visual stimuli, we can infer that oscillations in the alpha band are fundamental to the physiology early visual cortex. Given this, it is not surprising that there is considerable evidence that alpha-band dynamics have an important role in shaping visual perception.

As implied by results summarized in the previous paragraph, and as illustrated in *Figure 3.6*, sustained increases in alpha-band power (i.e., lasting several cycles) often have an overall inhibitory effect on stimulus processing, and, indeed, the instantaneous level of alpha-band power in a region is often taken as a proxy for cortical excitability at that moment in time. However, although the amplitude of the posterior alpha oscillation fluctuates over time, it is always present, and prominent, at posterior EEG electrodes in healthy individuals while they are awake. This leaves open the possibility that it may have functions other than "just" inhibition. Indeed, it is convenient for scientists that each individual's posterior alpha-band oscillation cycles at a stable, trait-like frequency, and there is considerable variation in "individual alpha frequency" (IAF) across the healthy population.

Because it is so prominent, and omnipresent during wakefulness, the alpha-band oscillation in early visual cortex has considerable influence on temporal aspects of visual perception. Many models propose that this is because the positive (extracellular) peak of the alpha oscillation has the effect of momentarily "shutting down" processing in neurons (due to the hyperpolarization that they experience), effectively creating highly synchronized "windows" of processing time. Considerable evidence for this comes from the two-flash discrimination task, in which a stimulus is presented for either one continuous presentation lasting from 90 to 150 msec, or for two 40 msec presentations that are separated by a gap ranging from 10 to 60 msec, and the subject's task is to identify whether they saw one flash or two. In any group of subjects, different individuals will have different discrimination thresholds, and an oft-replicated finding is that this threshold is negatively correlated with IAF. That is, the lower one's IAF, the higher one's threshold. An explanation for this is that the alpha cycle acts as an integration window, such that two events that occur within one window may be processed as though they happened at the same time, and so two distinct flashes occurring within the same alpha cycle are perceived as just one event. Because an individual with an IAF near 8 Hz has a relatively long alpha cycle (roughly 125 msec), they will necessarily experience more two-flash trials falling within the same "integration window" than would an individual with an IAF near 12 Hz (and, correspondingly, alpha cycles of roughly 85 msec). These results, and others like it, have led some to propose that even though our visual cognition feels continuous, the underlying processing that gives rise to it may actually be discretized.

The influences of alpha-band dynamics on the temporal resolution of visual perception are characterized as "bottom-up" effects, because they reflect in influence of spontaneous dynamics of the system. (Although we didn't emphasize it above, occipital TMS-evoked phosphene perception also varies with pre-TMS phase angle of the alpha-band oscillation [i.e., in addition to its sensitivity to pre-TMS power in the alpha band].) Because these oscillations are fundamental to the functioning of the early visual system, it is perhaps not surprising that the brain has developed ways to control them to optimize performance on visual tasks. One example comes from Andreas Wutz, David Melcher, and Jason Samaha (2018), who used a clever procedure that presented the same types of stimulus display on every trial, but varied with instructions whether the experimental condition encouraged integration or segregation across two briefly flashed displays (*Figure 6.13*). The authors recorded MEG during task performance and found that the group-average alpha-band frequency was significantly higher during the

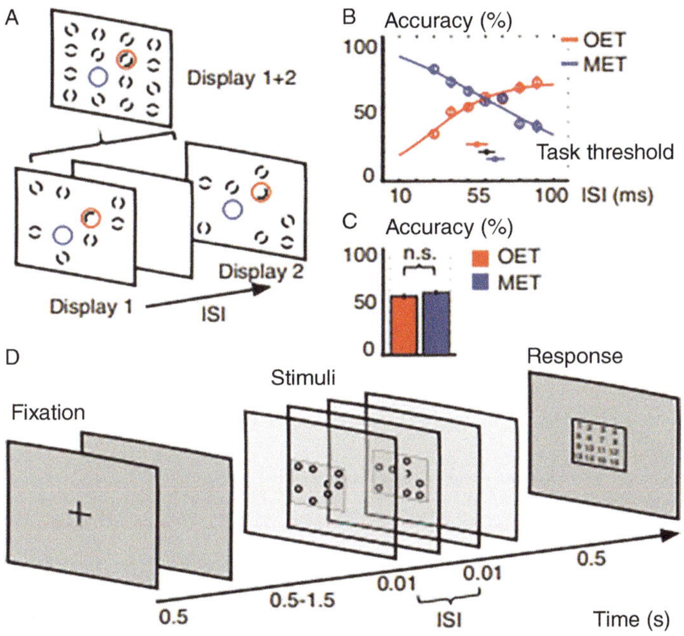

FIGURE 6.13 Diagram of visual integration/segregation task, and behavioral data, from Wutz et al. (2018). **A.** Display 1 presented an array of 15 arcs, 14 of them paired to make "gapped-circle" stimuli ("elements"), and one of them unpaired. After a delay, Display 2 also presented an array with 15 arcs, 14 of them paired to make elements appearing in locations different from Display 1, the unpaired one located so as to pair with the unpaired one from Display 1 (i.e., by integrating across the two displays, the two unpaired arcs form an "element"; indeed, the inset labeled "Display 1+2" illustrates how, on each trial, the merging of the two displays yields a 4×4 array with one missing element.) On each trial stimulus locations varied unpredictably. During blocks of "Odd Element Task" (OET) trials, subjects were to report the location in the array where the unpaired arcs had appeared (indicated with red circles in *A* [these circles were not displayed during the experiment]). During blocks of "Missing Element Task" (MET) trials, subjects were to indicate the location in the array where no element had been presented (blue circles). **B.** Behavioral data from pre-MEG session, confirming that OET performance was superior at longer ISIs (which made segregation of the two displays easier) and MET performance was superior at shorter ISIs, which made integration easier – for each subject the crossing-over point of the sigmoid fit to the two tasks was the ISI at which they were tested on both tasks during the MEG session. **C.** Accuracy from the MEG session. **D.** Timeline of each trial.

Source: (Wutz, Melcher, & Samaha, 2018) / National Academy of Sciences.

segregation than the integration task, the two separating 360 msec prior to stimulus onset and remerging 500 msec after stimulus offset (i.e., prior to the response; *Figure 6.14*). This tight temporal window was interpreted as evidence for preparatory top-down control.

In striate and extrastriate cortex, low-frequency oscillations (including in the alpha band) often manifest as traveling waves. In one study focused on the mesoscopic scale, Zachary Davis, Alexandra Busch, and colleagues in the laboratory of John Reynolds (2024) recorded from Utah arrays implanted in area MT of marmoset monkeys while they performed visual detection of sinusoidal gratings that drifted within an aperture. They identified "intrinsic traveling waves" in the alpha band that were organized into a finite set of "motifs," repeating patterns of activity characterized by the same trajectory over cortical space. Interestingly, a sweep of a motif also triggered an increase in the spiking of neurons tuned to a specific direction (i.e., each motif was feature selective). This suggests that each traveling-wave motif corresponds to a cascade of activity between anatomically distal columns of neurons that are tuned to the same direction of motion – it is a general principle across striate and extrastriate cortex that neurons in like-tuned columns are preferentially linked by excitatory connections. Furthermore, stimulus-evoked spiking and perceptual sensitivity were both enhanced on trials when a target's direction of motion was congruent with the tuning of the traveling-wave motif that was active at the time of its presentation. Analyses and accounts that focus on dynamics within a brain region, as with this careful analysis of traveling waves propagating between cortical columns within area MT, can be said to be addressing brain functioning at a mesoscopic level of analysis. There's also a sense in which, at an implicit level, studies like that of Wutz et al. (2018; *Figure 6.13* and *Figure 6.14*) can be thought of as addressing the mesoscopic scale, because they allow for the interpretation of their results as evidence that V1 dynamics act as a standing wave that gates the input of sensory information. This is the interpretation, for example, of Andrea Alamia and Rufin VanRullin (2024), who advocate for a conceptualization of the functioning of the visual system at a scale that emphasizes the importance of signaling between regions.

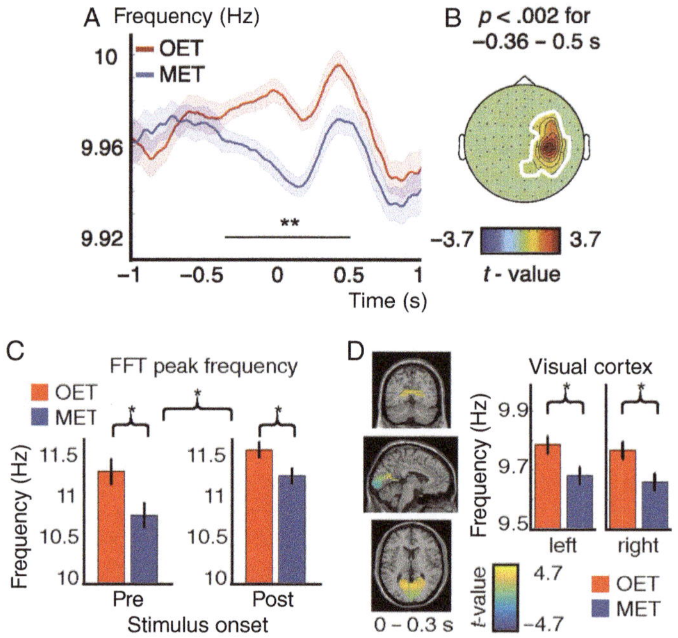

FIGURE 6.14 MEG results from Wutz et al. (2018; see Figure 6.13). **A.** Time course of the "speeding up" (for OET) and "slowing down" (for MET) of instantaneous frequency in the alpha band in anticipation of trial onset (time 0). **B.** Scalp distribution of this divergence. **C.** Peak alpha frequency for the two trial types from the 500 msec immediately prior to trial onset ("pre") and the 500 msec immediately following trial offset (post"). **D.** Source localization of signals showing significant difference for OET vs. MET contrast, from time 0 to 300 msec, plus source-localized alpha frequency by hemisphere. (Note the difference in values between **A**, **C**, and **D**, due to different filtering and different analytic procedures used to produce each.)

Source: Wutz et al. (2018) / National Academy of Sciences.

Predictive Coding at Early Levels of Visual Processing As illustrated in *Figure 5.2*, Alamia and VanRullin (2019) have proposed that traveling waves in the alpha band may be reflective of processes underlying predictive coding. In addition to computer simulations that support this model, they point to results from several studies recording intra- and extracranial electrophysiology. In one study, extracranial EEG was recorded while subjects viewed 6.25 second-long sequences of random luminance values (i.e., white noise), and forward traveling waves in the alpha band were seen to dominate. In a different dataset, in the extracranial EEG recorded during 60 second blocks of rest with eyes closed, backward traveling waves were more prominent than forward traveling waves (identified in 41.1% vs. 8.8% of 1 second epochs, respectively). Alamia and VanRullin (2019) also review similar findings that have been reported in ECoG studies. (Note that although these eyes-closed results are consistent with a predictive coding account, they can't be interpreted as strong evidence for it, because predictive coding theories posit that feedback signaling to update model predictions happens in real time during perception, effectively simultaneous with the feeding forward of prediction errors, not only during extended periods with no sensory stimulation.)

Next, we'll consider an assessment of predictive coding using fMRI. Recall from the legend accompanying *Figure 5.2* that the scheme that it illustrates could be implemented with a variety of mechanisms, including traveling waves or spiking clocked by distinct frequency channels. At a more abstract level, however, *Figure 5.2* does commit to a specific computational implementation of predictive coding, one in which "local mismatch" is computed in each receptive field at each level of the processing hierarchy. (E.g., with reference to *Figure 5.2*, in V1, there is assumed to be a unit $\varepsilon^{(1)}$ computing the error between expectation and sensory evidence for every feature-specific receptive field processing the image.) An alternative, which can thought of as a "high-level" scheme, holds that predictive coding is driven by mismatch at the level of the object (e.g., if the identity of the person entering the room is different from expected, or if the looming sound assumed be a car on the street turns out to be a motorbike on the sidewalk). To adjudicate between these two accounts, David Richter, Tim Kietzmann, and Floris de Lange (2024) scanned subjects while they viewed letter-object pairings and made animacy judgements on each object ("living"/"nonliving") with the exception of trials when the letter was a vowel, which were "no-go" trials. Each of eight consonant letters was seven times more likely to be followed by its unique paired object than by any of the other seven objects (referred to as "unexpected" in relation to this one consonant) in the closed set (*Figure 6.15*). Also included as unexpected objects were an image of the consonant's paired object, but displayed in a different orientation. Thus, each time a consonant was followed by an unexpected object, this would produce surprise, and could be primarily "high-level surprise" when it was a different object (e.g., from *Figure 5.15.A*, a woman is not a guitar) or "low-level surprise" (e.g., from *Figure 5.15.A*, the guitar is in a different orientation from the "paired" image of the guitar).

The analysis strategy was to use a DNN (specifically, the DNN used was AlexNet [see *Chapter 4*, section *Deep neural networks*]) that had been trained on a large "ecologically motivated image dataset" and feed it each of the stimuli. (There were 33 human subjects in the study, and each was tested with a unique set of eight objects [plus each object's alternative views].) First, to establish the correspondence of regions of the brain with layers of the DNN, they performed representational similarity analysis (RSA) on the fMRI data from localizer scans and on each of the eight layers of the DNN, and confirmed that both displayed a hierarchical gradient of early visual processing regions/early layers of the DNN preferentially represented low-level features, and high-level visual processing regions[1]/late layers of the DNN preferentially represented high-level features (i.e., category membership). (See *Chapter 5*, section *Representational similarity analysis*, for which the explanation of RSA uses this experiment.) Second, rather than simply analyzing the fMRI data from the animacy task (i.e., the data of primary interest) as a function of stimulus identity, the authors applied an analysis intended to be specific to surprise. They did this by estimating, for each trial, the low-level surprise and the high-level surprise generated by each unexpected item. They operationalized each trial's low-level surprise via the RSA dissimilarity between the unexpected item and that

[1]We won't get to a detailed consideration of high-level visual processing, such as object recognition, until *Chapter 10*. For the present purposes, the high-level regions identified in the fMRI data in this experiment were the human analogues of IT (*Figure 6.11.A*) and *CIT* and *AIT* (*Figure 6.5*) of the macaque.

FIGURE 6.15 Task design for study assessing the locus of processing visual prediction errors.

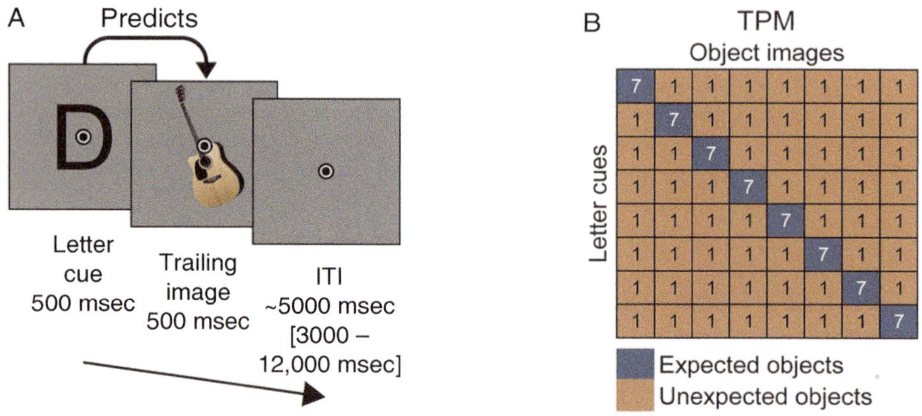

FIGURE 6.15.A The task: Subjects viewed letter-object pairings and indicated via button press whether the object was living or nonliving. (The letter had no bearing on the judgment, but had to be monitored because infrequent vowels signaled "no-go" trials on which no response was to be made.)

FIGURE 6.15.B Schematic of the transitional probability matrix (TPM), indicating how often each letter was paired with each object. (Although not labeled, each row corresponds to one of the eight consonant letters and each column to one of the eight template objects.)

consonant's expected item as represented in layer 2 of the DNN, and each trial's high-level surprise via the RSA dissimilarity between the unexpected item and that consonant's expected item as represented in layer 8 of the DNN. These values were used as regressors in the GLM with which the fMRI data were analyzed.

Remarkably, the results showed that activity in all brain areas associated with visual perception correlated with high-level, but not low-level surprise, *Figure 6.16*. These results therefore support a "high-level" account of predictive coding whereby the prediction errors that are used to update internal models of the visual world are those produced by mismatches at the level of object identity, rather than at the level of low-level features. Behaviorally, RTs were longer for unexpected items than for expected items. The authors speculate that this is consistent with the possibility that "the larger the high-level difference between what is expected and what is observed the more cycles of recurrent processing along the ventral visual stream may be necessary to solve object recognition." Importantly, in this regard, they are careful to clarify that: "we are not suggesting that visual processing in V1 primarily reflects high-level visual information, but rather that its modulation as a function of expectation reflects high-level surprise, potentially implemented by cortico-cortical feedback" (pp. 13–34).

Taking Stock

In this chapter, we enriched our understanding of early visual processing, first introduced in *Chapter 2* and *Chapter 3*. First, we detailed how anatomical and functional specialization begins very early indeed, beginning at the retina if one considers the M and P classes of RGCs, which creates a substrate for two broad classes of visual information processing: determining *what* an object is and determining *where* it is. (And we've already noted that a question for *Chapter 8* is whether *where* is perhaps better construed as *how*.) We have also seen how feedback plays an important role in controlling the processing of visual information even before it gets to the cortex. Lesion studies have confirmed, in the form of a double dissociation of function, that the temporal lobe, particularly IT cortex, contributes importantly to object recognition, and that PPC contributes to spatial processing. This chapter then made a foray into properties of visually responsive areas of the ventral stream, emphasizing the hierarchical

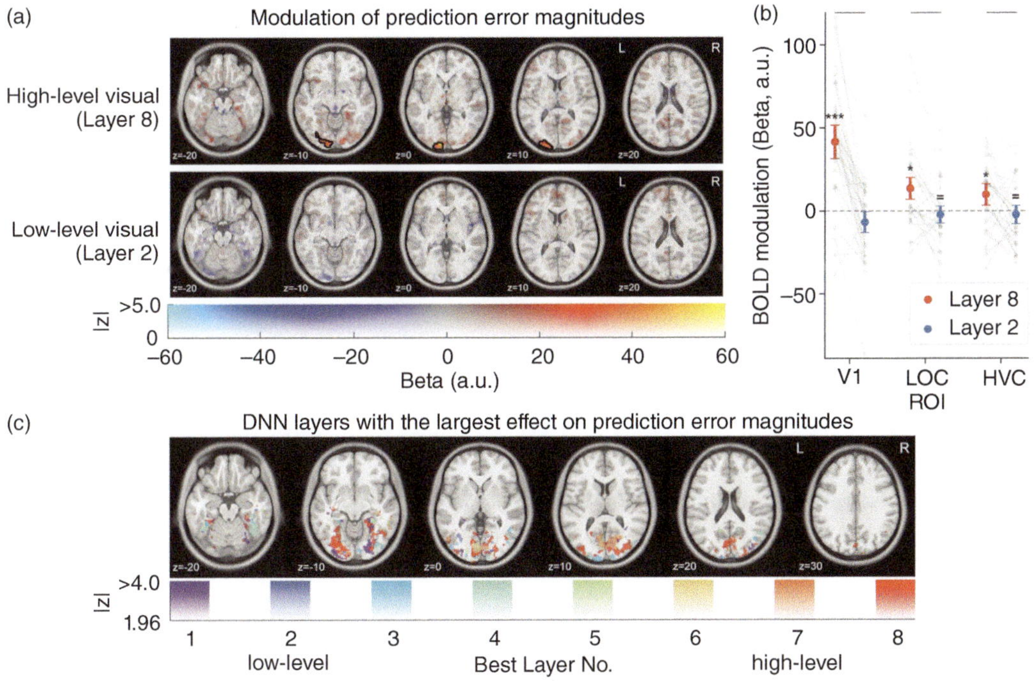

FIGURE 6.16 Prediction error magnitude scales with high-level surprise. **A.** Results from whole-brain analyses for high-level (top row) and low-level (bottom row) visual feature dissimilarity. The top row shows where surprise responses to unexpected images were increased if the image was more distant from the expected image in terms of high-level visual features. (Although this image is thresholded, the only statistically significant clusters were in the occipital cortex, outlined in black.) No evidence was found for significant modulation of sensory responses by low-level visual surprise. **B.** Group-average (red and blue) and individual subject (gray) parameter estimates from ROI-based analyses of regions identified by the localizer scan, and comprising early visual cortex ("V1"), intermediate visual processing region "LOC" (lateral occipital complex), and regions associated with high-level visual processing ("HVC"; encompassing occipito-temporal sulcus and fusiform cortex). **C.** Re-representation of results from (**B**) mapped onto the brain, color coded by which layer from the DNN did the best job explaining variance at each voxel.

Source: Richter et al. (2024) / PLOS / CC BY 4.0.

nature of object recognition. After flirting with a grandmother layer of object representation, a distributed, combination-coding scheme was seen to offer a more plausible account of stimulus processing in IT cortex. Particularly intriguing is the neural processing of faces, including the fact that faces don't seem to lend themselves to image decomposition as readily as do other complex objects. We've also seen two examples of how careful assessment of how image processing is accomplished by DNNs can be a powerful way to learn about how it is, and isn't, accomplished by biological systems. We ended with a deeper dive into the physiology and functions supported by striate and extrastriate circuits, with emphases on alpha-band dynamics and assessments through the lens(es) of predictive coding.

After the next three chapters conclude this section's emphasis on *perception*, *attention*, and *action*, *Chapter 10* will address the question (with apologies to *Chapter 4*) *Where does perception end, and where does memory begin?* As with the earlier chapter's question (which was posed about sensation vs. perception), we'll see that the boundary is a blurry one, one having more basis in the human impulse to categorize than in neurobiological or psychological principle. For example, *Chapter 10* will consider agnosias, syndromes of "perception stripped of its meaning" that result from damage to the ventral temporal lobe. It will consider the phenomenon of "category specificity" in ventral temporal cortex (e.g., the *fusiform face area*, the *parahippocampal place area*, the *extrastriate body area*, and the *visual word form area*): how did these areas come into being (nature vs. nurture); what does their existence tell us (or not) about the organization of knowledge in the brain; and, more generally, what are the limits of what we can infer if we focus on activity in only one of these areas?

End-of-Chapter Questions

1. In what sense does function follow from structure in the visual system?

2. Design an experiment that, if your hypothesis is correct, might produce evidence for a double dissociation of function. In what way would your hoped-for results support stronger inference than a single dissociation?

3. Define the functions of the *what* and *where* pathways. Summarize at least three pieces of evidence for this organizing principle of the visual system.

4. Summarize the type of image processing that occurs at each level of the ventral-stream hierarchy.

5. Define the concept of the "grandmother cell." For what reasons is it logically appealing? For what reasons, practical or theoretical, is it problematic?

6. What is a plausible alternative to a "grandmother level" of object recognition? Summarize the evidence for it.

7. Are faces processed differently than other objects by the visual system?

8. What are the similarities and differences between DNNs developed for image categorization and the primate ventral visual processing stream?

9. Although we know of the anatomical existence of feedback connections between areas in the ventral visual processing stream, what's the evidence that they play an important role in visual-scene processing?

10. Explain the distinction between the "bottom-up" influence of oscillatory dynamics on visual perception versus the "top-down" control of oscillatory dynamics to influence visual perception.

11. In the context of predictive coding in visual perception, what does it mean to hypothesize an "early locus" versus a "late locus" of the processing of prediction errors?

References

Alamia, Andrea, and Rufin VanRullen. 2019. "Alpha Oscillations and Traveling Waves: Signatures of Predictive Coding?." *PloS Biology 17*: e3000487. doi: doi.org/10.1371/journal.pbio.3000487.

Alamia, Andrea, and Rufin VanRullen. 2024. "A Traveling Waves Perspective on Temporal Binding." *Journal of Cognitive Neuroscience 36*: 721–729. doi: doi.org/10.1162/jocn_a_02004.

Born, Richard T. 2001. "Visual Processing: Parallel-er and Parallel-er." *Current Biology* 11 (14): R566–R568. doi: 10.1016/S0960-9822(01)00345-1.

Bruce, Charles, Robert Desimone, and Charles G. Gross. 1981. "Visual Properties of Neurons in a Polysensory Area in Superior Temporal Sulcus of the Macaque." *Journal of Neurophysiology* 46 (2): 369–384.

Curtis, Clayton E., and Mark D'esposito. 2004. "The Effects of Prefrontal Lesions on Working Memory Performance and Theory." *Cognitive, Affective, and Behavioral Neuroscience* 4 (4): 528–539.

Dakin, Steven C. 2009. "Vision: Thinking Globally, Acting Locally." *Current Biology* 19 (18): R851–R854. doi: 10.1016/j.cub.2009.08.021.

Davis, Zachary W., Alexandra Busch, Christopher Steward, Lyle Muller, and John Reynolds. 2024. "Horizontal Cortical Connections Shape Intrinsic Traveling Waves into Feature-Selective Motifs that Regulate Perceptual Sensitivity." *Cell Reports 43*: 114707. doi: doi.org/10.1016/j.celrep.2024.114707.

Felleman, Daniel J., and David C. Van Essen. 1991. "Distributed Hierarchical Processing in Primate Visual Cortex." *Cerebral Cortex* 1 (1): 1–47. doi: 10.1093/cercor/1.1.1.

Gross, Charles G., C. E. Rocha-Miranda, and D. B. Bender. 1972. "Visual Properties of Neurons in Inferotemporal Cortex of the Macaque." *Journal of Neurophysiology* 35 (1): 96–111.

Kar, Kohitij, Jonas Kubilius, Kailyn Schmidt, Elias B. Issa, and James J. DiCarlo. 2019. "Evidence That Recurrent Circuits are Critical to the Ventral Stream's Execution of Core Object Recognition Behavior." *Nature Neuroscience* 22: 974–983.

Mishkin, Mortimer, Leslie G. Ungerleider, and Kathleen A. Macko. 1983. "Object Vision and Spatial Vision: Two Cortical Pathways." *Trends in Neurosciences* 6: 414–417. doi: 10.1016/0166-2236(83)90190-X.

Pohl, Walter. 1973. "Dissociation of Spatial Discrimination Deficits Following Frontal and Parietal Lesions in Monkeys." *Journal of Comparative and Physiological Psychology* 82 (2): 227–239. doi: 10.1037/h0033922.

Richter, David, Tim C. Kietzmann, and Floris P. de Lange. 2024. "High-Level Visual Prediction Errors in Early Visual Cortex." *PloS Biology 22*: e3002829. doi: doi.org/10.1371/journal.pbio.3002829.

Rosanova, Mario, Adenauer Casali, Valentina Bellina, Federico Resta, Maurizio Mariotti, and Marcello Massimini. 2009. "Natural Frequencies of Human Corticothalamic Circuits." *The Journal of Neuroscience 29*: 7679–7685.

Tanaka, Keiji. 1993. "Neuronal Mechanisms of Object Recognition." *Science* 262 (5134): 685–688. doi: 10.1126/science.8235589.

Wutz, Andreas, David Melcher, and Jason Samaha. 2018. "Frequency Modulation of Neural Oscillations According to Visual Task Demands." *Proceedings of the National Academy of Science of the United States of America 115*: 1346–1351. doi: doi.org/10.1073/pnas.1713318115.

Yamins, Daniel L. K., Ha Hong, Charles F. Cadieu, Ethan A. Solomon, Darren Seibert, and James J. DiCarlo. 2014. "Performance-Optimized Hierarchical Models Predict Neural Responses in Higher Visual Cortex." *Proceedings of the National Academy of Sciences of the United States of America* 111: 8619–8624.

Other Sources Used

Blake, Randolph, and Robert Sekuler. 1985. *Perception*. New York: Alfred A. Knopf.

Gross, Charles G., D. B. Bender, and C. E. Rocha-Miranda. 1969. "Visual Receptive Fields of Neurons in Inferotemporal Cortex of the Monkey." *Science* 166 (3910): 1303–1306. doi: 10.1126/science.166.3910.1303.

Kandel, Eric R., James H. Schwartz, and Thomas M. Jessell, eds. 2000. *Principles of Neural Science*. New York: McGraw-Hill.

Kell, Alexander J. E., and Josh H. McDermott. 2019. "Deep Neural Network Models of Sensory Systems: Windows onto the Role of Task Constraints." *Current Opinion in Neurobiology* 55: 121–132.

Koenig, Lua, and Biyu J. He. 2025. "Spontaneous Slow Cortical Potentials and Brain Oscillations Independently Influence Conscious Visual Perception." *PLoS Biology 23*: e3002964. doi: doi.org/10.1371/journal.pbio.3002964.

Samaha, Jason, and Vincenzo Romei. 2024a. "Alpha-Band Brain Dynamics and Temporal Processing: An Introduction to the Special Focus." *Journal of Cognitive Neuroscience 36*: 567–571. doi: doi.org/10.1162/jocn_a_02105.

Samaha, Jason, and Vincenzo Romei. 2024b. "Alpha-Band Frequency and Temporal Windows in Perception: A Review and Living Meta-Analysis of 27 Experiments (and Counting)." *Journal of Cognitive Neuroscience 36*: 640–654. doi: doi.org/10.1162/jocn_a_02069.

Schiller, Peter H. 1993. "The Effects of V4 and Middle Temporal (MT) Area Lesions on Visual Performance in the Rhesus Monkey." *Visual Neuroscience* 10 (4): 717–746. doi: 10.1017/S0952523800005423.

Schiller, Peter H., and Nikos K. Logothetis. 1990. "The Color-Opponent and Broad-Band Channels of the Primate Visual System." *Trends in Neurosciences* 13 (10): 392–398. doi: 10.1016/0166-2236(90)90117-S.

Semmes, Josephine, Sidney Weinstein, Ghent Ghent, John S. Meyer, and Hans-Lukas Teuber. 1963. "Correlates of Impaired Orientation in Personal and Extrapersonal Space." *Brain* 86 (4): 747–772.

Tanaka, Keiji. 1996. "Inferotemporal Cortex and Object Vision." *Annual Review of Neuroscience* 19: 109–139. doi: 10.1146/annurev.ne.19.030196.000545.

Tanaka, Keiji. 1997. "Mechanisms of Visual Object Recognition: Monkey and Human Studies." *Current Opinion in Neurobiology* 7 (4): 523–529. doi: 10.1016/S0959-4388(97)80032-3.

Ungerleider, Leslie G., and Mortimer Mishkin. 1982. "Two Cortical Visual Systems." In *Analysis of Visual Behavior*, edited by David J. Ingle, Melvin A. Goodale, and Richard J. W. Mansfield (pp. 549–586). Cambridge, MA: MIT Press.

Ungerleider, Leslie G., and Anderw H. Bell. 2011. "Uncovering the Visual 'Alphabet': Advances in Our Understanding of Object Perception." *Vision Research* 51 (7): 782–799. doi: 10.1016/j.visres.2010.10.002.

Wolfe, Jeremy M., Keith R. Kleunder, Dennis M. Levi, Linda M. Bartoshuk, Rachel S. Herz, Roberta Klatzky, . . . Daniel M. Merfeld. 2012. *Sensation and Perception*, 3rd ed. Sunderland, MA: Sinauer Associates.

Wutz, Andreas, David Melcher, and Jason Samaha. 2018. "Frequency Modulation of Neural Oscillations According to Visual Task Demands." *Proceedings of the National Academy of Science of the United States of America 115*: 1346–1351. doi: doi.org/10.1073/pnas.1713318115.

Further Reading

Logothetis, Nikos K., and David L. Sheinberg. 1996. "Visual Object Recognition." *Annual Review of Neuroscience* 19: 577–621. doi: 10.1146/annurev.ne.19.030196.003045.

A very extensive review emphasizing behavioral, neuropsychological, and electrophysiological evidence for viewpoint-dependent mechanisms of object recognition, as well as for different populations of IT neurons specialized to perform different functions, such as categorization, recognizing living things, and supporting the action of object grasping.

Mishkin, Mortimer, Leslie G. Ungerleider, and Kathleen A. Macko. 1983. "Object Vision and Spatial Vision: Two Cortical Pathways." *Trends in Neurosciences* 6: 414–417. doi: 10.1016/0166-2236(83)90190-X.

A concise summary of the two-parallel-pathways model of the visual system.

Schiller, Peter H., and Nikos K. Logothetis. 1990. "The Color-Opponent and Broad-Band Channels of the Primate Visual System." *Trends in Neurosciences* 13 (10): 392–398. doi: 10.1016/0166-2236(90)90117-S.

A thorough summary, and synthesis, of the relative contributions of the M and P channels to visual perception.

Tanaka, Keiji. 1996. "Inferotemporal Cortex and Object Vision." *Annual Review of Neuroscience* 19: 109–139. doi: 10.1146/annurev.ne.19.030196.000545.

An overview of this investigator's pioneering work on the neural principles underlying object recognition in IT cortex.

Ungerleider, Leslie G., and Anderw H. Bell. 2011. "Uncovering the Visual 'Alphabet': Advances in Our Understanding of Object Perception." *Vision Research* 51 (7): 782–799. doi: 10.1016/j.visres.2010.10.002.

A remarkably comprehensive overview of the cognitive neuroscience of object recognition, ranging from nineteenth-century studies of brain and behavior (some of which we considered in Chapter 1) to an insightful critique of contemporary methods for multivariate pattern analysis of fMRI data (which we will introduce in Chapter 9).

CHAPTER 7

Spatial Cognition and Attention

KEY THEMES

- Neuropsychology can be an important tool for hypothesis generation, as evidenced by the models of attention derived from the study of unilateral neglect.
- The neglect syndrome provides evidence that attention (1) can operate within an egocentric frame of reference; (2) can be location-based or object-based; (3) may operate differently in peripersonal vs. extrapersonal space; and (4) may act to resolve competition among neural representations.
- The cortical regions whose damage produces unilateral neglect have been studied in neurologically healthy individuals with positron emission tomography (PET) and functional magnetic resonance imaging (fMRI), and show elevated activity during tasks requiring spatial- vs. object-based visual discriminations, as well as retinotopic organization.
- Neurons of posterior parietal cortex (PPC) of the dorsal visual stream integrate retinotopically encoded visual information with proprioceptive information about the position of gaze relative to the head, the head relative to the trunk, and so on, to effect coordinate transformations that are necessary for making appropriate visually guided actions with various parts of the body.
- The transformation from an egocentric to an allocentric (i.e., environment-centered) reference frame is observed in the activity of place cells in the hippocampus.
- The metaphor of attention as a spotlight highlights many of its properties: increasing the salience of one (or a few) among many stimuli; the distinction between attending to a location vs. attending to an object; the distinction between the *site* of action of attention vs. its *source*.
- ERP studies have isolated the timing, and electrophysiological signature, of the attentional selection of a visual feature.
- Extracellular electrophysiological and fMRI studies have established that spatial attention works, in part, by elevating baseline activity in the neural pathways that process information about stimuli occupying particular locations.
- An important function of attention may be to bias the neural competition for representation that results from the simultaneous perception of multiple stimuli in the environment.

Essentials of Cognitive Neuroscience, Third Edition. Bradley R. Postle. Published 2026 by John Wiley & Sons, Inc.
Companion Website: www.wiley.com/go/postle/cognitiveneuroscience3e

CONTENTS

Unilateral Neglect: A Fertile Source of Models of Spatial Cognition and Attention

Previous chapters have emphasized the importance of lesions, or other factors that perturb normal brain structure or function (e.g., electrical stimulation, optogenetic manipulation), as a tool for drawing inferences about the necessity of a brain region (or physiological phenomenon) for a particular aspect of behavior or function. In effect, the emphasis has been on the importance of perturbation methods for *hypothesis testing*. We begin this chapter by highlighting a different role that neuropsychology can play in cognitive neuroscience: brain lesions can be a fertile source for *hypothesis generation*. Stated another way, careful observation of the deficits experienced by patients with brain damage can suggest organizational principles that were not evident to introspection or observation of normal behavior. With particular relevance to our present focus, the neurological syndrome of unilateral neglect has raised many intriguing questions about the fundamental workings of spatial cognition and attention.

Unilateral Neglect: A Clinicoanatomical Primer

Unilateral neglect (sometimes referred to as "unilateral spatial neglect" or "hemispatial neglect") is a neurological syndrome in which damage in one hemisphere, typically due to a stroke that affects the right hemisphere, results in a pronounced unawareness of information from the side opposite the lesion (typically, the left side; *Figure 7.1*). The syndrome is highly heterogeneous, in that it can vary considerably from patient to patient. Nonetheless, we have to start somewhere, and we'll do so with a patient whose case is representative of many described in the literature. The patient, described by neurologist and cognitive neuroscientist Anjan Chatterjee (2003), suffered a stroke when occlusion of the right middle cerebral artery deprived portions of the posterior inferior parietal lobule (Brodmann areas [BAs] 39 and 40) and the posterior superior temporal gyrus (BA 22) of the right hemisphere of arterial blood (*Figure 7.2*). This patient's consequent neglect of the left side of her world was dramatic: when her left hand was held in front of her face, she opined that she was looking at the hand of the examining doctor; she ate only the food that was located on the right side of her plate; unswallowed food sometimes collected in the left side of her mouth; despite the disproportionate weakness of the left side of her body, when asked about why she was in the hospital she would refer to weakness in her right arm. Thus, her neglect of "the left" applied to both her own body and to stimuli in her immediate environment (e.g., the plate immediately in front of her).

Unilateral neglect can result from damage to many brain areas, including the temporoparietal junction, the frontal eye fields, and the caudate nucleus, as well as to white matter tracts that innervate these regions. Although there remains some controversy about precisely which areas must be damaged to produce neglect, *Figure 7.3* illustrates the results of one large group study.

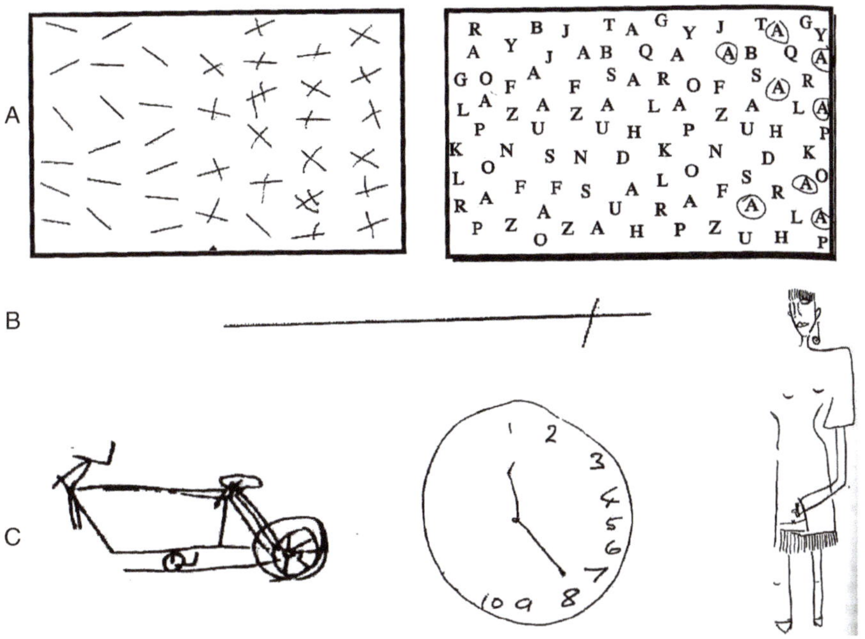

FIGURE 7.1 Patient performance on classic neuropsychological tests of neglect. **A.** One patient's performance is superior on a simple cancellation task that only requires marking each stimulus vs. on a more difficult task that requires identifying and circling targets ("A"s) among distractors (other letters). **B.** Line bisection, in which the subject was asked to mark the center point of the horizontal line. Note that for "bedside paper-and-pencil" tasks such as these, direction of gaze, orientation of body, and so on are typically not controlled. **C.** Drawing from memory. Note that neglect is evident at multiple scales, in that not only are the left side of the overall pictures of the bicycle and the woman neglected, but so too are the leftward-facing handlebar and leftward-facing pedal of the bicycle, and the left side of the handbag strap and left-sided earring of the woman. (Note that "left" is defined here in retinotopic terms, in that, e.g., the neglected handlebar and earring are both on the right in object-centered terms.)

Source: Driver et al., 2004 / MIT Press.

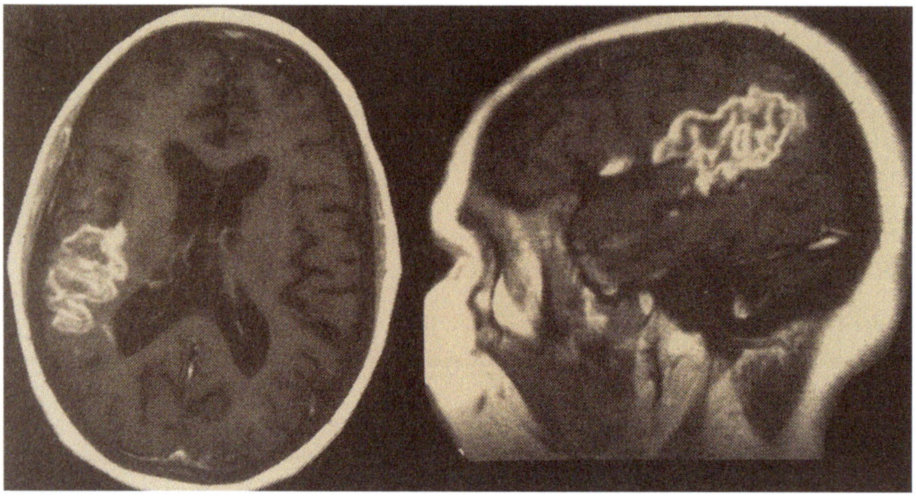

FIGURE 7.2 MR scan of unilateral neglect patient described by Chatterjee (2003), with bright regions corresponding to the damaged tissue in the right inferior parietal lobule and superior temporal gyrus. (Note that radiological convention is to display the right side of the brain on the left side of the image.)

Source: Reproduced with permission from Chatterjee (2003) / MIT Press.

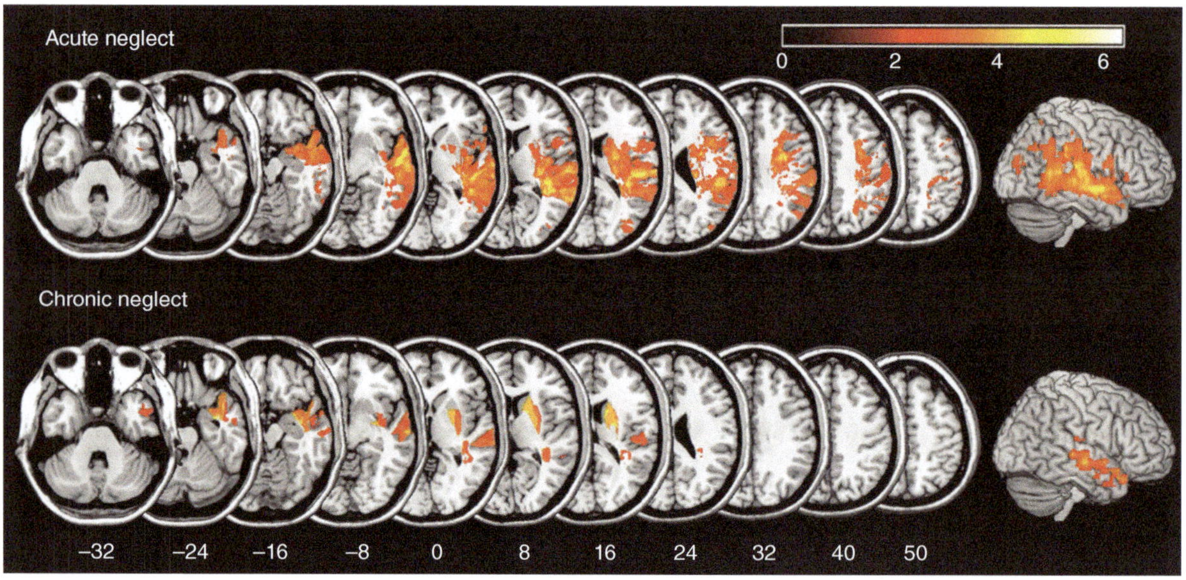

FIGURE 7.3 The neuroanatomy of unilateral neglect. This figure illustrates statistical maps of the regions most likely to be damaged in patients suffering from acute neglect (as assessed an average of 12.4 days after stroke onset) and chronic neglect (as assessed an average of 490.8 days after stroke onset). The prominence of subcortical regions in these analyses suggests important roles in spatial attention for not only gray-matter structures like the basal ganglia but also white-matter connections between cortical regions, in particular, the inferior occipitofrontal fasciculus. The results displayed here were generated by correlating lesion location (as measured on MR scans, such as those shown in *Figure 7.2*) with neglect symptoms in a sample of 54 patients with right hemisphere stroke, an approach known as voxel-based lesion-symptom mapping (VLSM). In this sample of 54 patients, 24 had neglect symptoms during the acute stage, and 8 of the 24 still exhibited neglect symptoms when reassessed in the chronic stage. Color coding indicates the *t*-value of the lesion-to-deficit correlation; numbers under the slices in the "chronic neglect" row indicate the distance (in mm) of each slice from the conventionally defined origin, along the dorsoventral (a.k.a. "*z*") axis.

Source: Reproduced with permission from Karnath et al. (2011) / Oxford University Press.

Hypotheses Arising from Clinical Observations of Neglect

Countless clinical observations such as those summarized in *Figure 7.1* have given rise to many ideas about spatial cognition and attention. Perhaps the most obvious is that humans maintain an *egocentric* reference frame that is defined with respect to the midline of the body, with the right hemisphere responsible for the representation of the left side of our body. (Furthermore, the fact that unilateral neglect of the left side of space occurs much more often after right hemisphere damage than does unilateral neglect of the right side of space after left hemisphere damage has led to the supposition, although without much additional rationale, that right hemisphere structures must allocate attention across both sides of the midline, whereas left hemisphere structures do so only for contralateral body and space.) Underlying this undisputable observation, however, is the more vexing question of *what mechanism(s) underlie this phenomenon*. Perhaps the most intuitive account is to appeal to attention, and the possibility that attention to our bodies and immediately adjacent areas is handled by posterior contralateral cortex. Although attention has many definitions, here it refers to our ability to prioritize one stream of afferent sensory information over others. (In *Figure 3.9*, e.g., we considered the effects on the auditory evoked response [AEP] of attending to visual information from a book while clicks were simultaneously presented auditorily, vs. attending to the clicks.) An alternative to attention, however, is suggested by noting that all of the examples referred to thus far – neglect of one's own hand, of food before one on a plate (or in one's mouth!), of the left side of lines on a piece of paper – can be portrayed as involving the motor system. Such observations have led to the postulation that the egocentric reference frame may arise from the intention to perform an action either with or on a part of our body. Thus, a second theme that will recur in this chapter is the debate over whether the principle of *intention* or *attention* better captures the functions of the parietal lobes. (Relatedly, in subsequent chapters, we shall consider the theoretical proposition that attention is a consequence of the intention to act – the "premotor theory" of attention.)

The *intention vs. attention* interpretation of unilateral neglect was the explicit focus of a highly influential study by Italian neuropsychologists Edoardo Bisiach and Claudio Luzzatti, who asked two stroke patients, lifelong residents of Milan, to describe their city's most famous outdoor plaza, the Piazza del Duomo. Note that these sessions took place in the hospital, and, therefore, the patients' descriptions were generated not from visual perception, but from memory. A simple, but breathtakingly insightful, manipulation that they included was to ask their patients to describe the plaza from two perspectives: first, while "facing" the cathedral from the opposite side of the plaza; and second, while "standing on the steps" of the cathedral and "looking" across the plaza at the location where they had previously been "standing." Both patients, while imagining facing the cathedral from across the plaza, named several landmarks located on its south side, which would be on one's right when standing at that location and facing east. Only one of the two patients also named three landmarks on the north side (he had named nine on the south). When imagining standing on the steps of the cathedral, and therefore imagining facing in the opposite direction (i.e., facing west), in contrast, the patients each spontaneously named several landmarks on the north side of the square (i.e., on what was now their "right"), and neglected to name any of those on the south side, despite the fact that they had named several of these just moments before (*Figure 7.4*)! Thus, it wasn't that their mental representations (i.e., their memories) had been somehow cleaved in two by their strokes. Rather, it was their ability to direct their attention to (i.e., to think about) the left side of the representation as they were mentally interrogating it at that moment. From these findings, Bisiach and Luzzatti (1978) concluded that "unilateral neglect cannot be reduced to a disorder confined to the input-output machinery of the organism interacting with its physical environment" (p. 132). That is, they argued that neglect is a disorder of attention, not intention.

In their writings, Bisiach and Luzzatti (1978) emphasized that neglect revealed a deficit in mental representation. Certainly, when the performance of their patients is compared with that of the patient illustrated in *Figure 7.1*, one sees that patients can neglect the left side of individual objects, even when their drawings suggest that they are aware that other objects and/or parts of the environment exist to the left of the object in question. This provides at

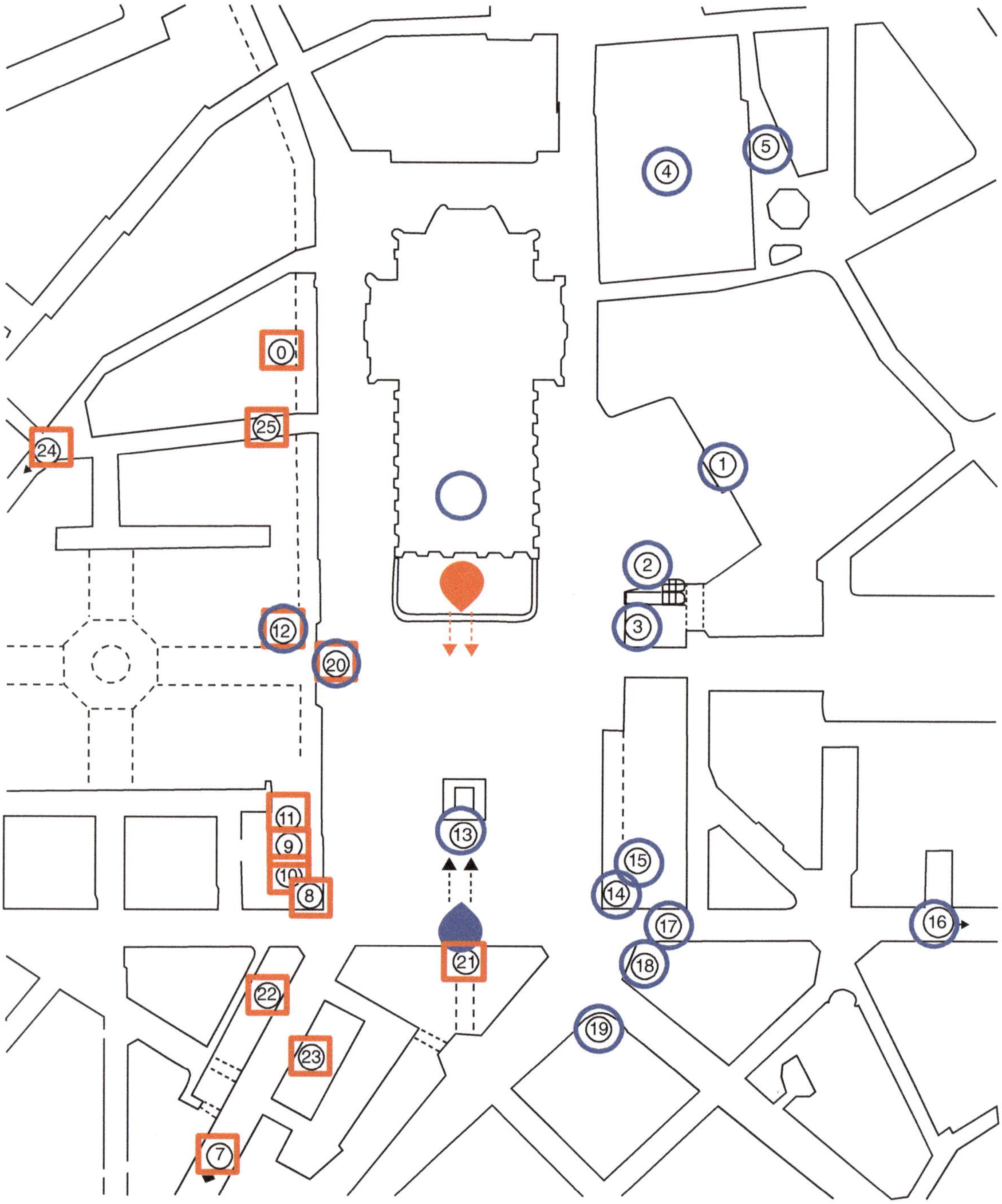

FIGURE 7.4 Landmarks named by two unilateral neglect patients of Bisiach and Luzzatti (1978). When imagining themselves looking at the cathedral from across the plaza (i.e., facing east, as cartooned by blue head and two arrows), they named the landmarks highlighted with blue circles; when imagining themselves standing on the cathedral steps and looking in the opposite direction (i.e., facing west, red head and two arrows) they named the landmarks highlighted with red squares.

Source: From Bisiach, Edoardo, and Claudio Luzzatti. 1978. "Unilateral Neglect of Representational Space." *Cortex* 14 (1): 129–133. Copyright 1978. Reproduced with permission of Elsevier.

least a hint for the existence of an *object-based attention* that operates at the level of individual objects, rather than (spatially defined) large swaths of the visual field.

Yet a different concept – that we may represent "near" vs. "far" space with different mechanisms – is illustrated by the case of a patient who very well may not have produced the same results as those reported by Bisiach and Luzzatti in 1978. This patient was a mechanic, tested in a stroke rehabilitation center in Oxford, UK. The research team first tested the patient on line bisection using the standard method: a horizontal line drawn on a piece of paper was held 45 cm from his eyes, centered on his midline, and he was asked to mark the midline with a pen. The results (from several trials, with lines of varying length) were comparable to that shown in *Figure 7.1*, demonstrating marked neglect of the left side of the line. Next, the patient was tested with lines placed on a whiteboard that was located 2.44 m distant from the patient (a distance chosen because it corresponded to the standard distance between dartboard and dart thrower that one finds in British pubs). The thickness and length of the lines were scaled up, such that they subtended roughly the same amount of visual angle as had the lines on paper from the "45 cm" test. Instead of drawing with a pen, the patient was asked to indicate the midpoint of the across-the-room lines by pointing with a light pointer (equivalent to a laser pointer, but this was 1990) or, in a cheeky follow-up test, by throwing darts at it. Whether with light pointer or darts, the patient showed no systematic bias away from the midpoint: his errors clustered near the true midpoint, and half of them fell to the left of it. Thus, this case demonstrated concretely a dissociation between the processing of **peripersonal space** – the space surrounding one's body that is within one's grasp – vs. **extrapersonal space** – those portions of perceived space that are farther than we can reach.

A final concept that we will consider here is that studies of neglect also provide compelling evidence for *competition* within the brain. **Extinction**, in the neurology clinic, refers to the fact that a patient can sometimes be aware of a single object presented on their left, but will lose awareness of it if a second item is then presented on their right. It's as though the item on the right extinguishes awareness of the item on the left.

Each of these ideas about how the brain may represent space and allocate attention will be revisited in this chapter as we consider the anatomy and physiology of spatial processing and attention in neurologically intact organisms (be they humans, monkeys, or rats).

The Functional Anatomy of the Dorsal Stream

There have been many, many important experiments using fMRI to study the neural bases of human vision. At this juncture, we'll consider just one that succinctly illustrates the two aspects of cognition that are the focus of this chapter: the representation of space and attention. In it, Ayse Saygin and Marty Sereno (2008) employed a variant of a method that is commonly used to perform retinotopic mapping – the "rotating wedge." The logic is that, while the subject fixates on a central location, a wedge shaped like a slice of pie is slowly rotated around the fixation point. The wedge looks different from the background – classically, it might contain an alternating black-and-white checkerboard pattern presented against a gray background – and the logic is simply that areas of the brain that represent a particular region of retinotopic space will only show increases of activity when the region that they represent is occupied by the wedge. Saygin and Sereno employed a clever riff on this basic logic by presenting clusters of colored dots on the entire screen, rotating the entire display around the fixation cross, and having the clusters of dots defining the wedge take on recognizable shapes (*Figure 7.5.A*). Specifically, the recognizable shapes were "point-light walker" images, created by having an actor wear a black bodysuit fitted with small lights on the arms, legs, head, and torso, and filming them as they performed a variety of actions (walking, jumping rope, etc.). Their rationale was that many areas of the brain outside low-level visual cortex are more likely to process information about "biologically relevant" stimuli than something as mundane as a checkerboard pattern.

An important factor to point out about the Saygin and Sereno (2008) results is that, while it's obvious how their experiment systematically stimulated different locations in the visual field, thereby allowing them to identify retinotopically selective parts of the visual system, there was nothing in the experiment that explicitly isolated each of the regions identified in

FIGURE 7.5 Retinotopy and attention in human occipital, temporal, parietal, and frontal cortex.
Source: Saygin and Sereno, 2008 / Oxford University Press.

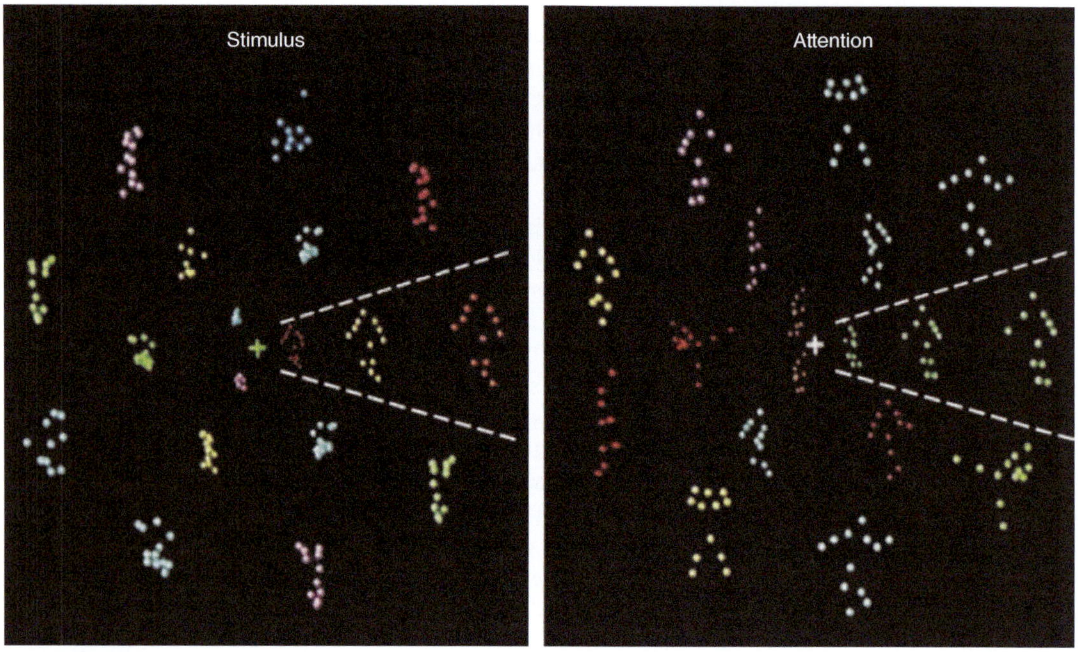

FIGURE 7.5.A A static screenshot of the stimulus displays from the two conditions. The entire display rotated about the fixation point (like a speeded-up depiction of the night sky over the course of 12 hours), with clusters continually fading in and out. In the *Stimulus* condition, the wedge was defined by clusters taking on the configuration of a point-light walker (the wedge is indicated here, for clarity of exposition, with white dotted lines that were not present during the experiment). In the *Attention* condition, all clusters took on the shape of point-light walkers, and the to-be-attended wedge was differentiated by being the only sector in which three of the same color were aligned along a single radius. In the *Stimulus* condition, the color of the fixation cross changed every second, and subjects were to report each time a change constituted a "2-back" repetition (e.g., *red-yellow-red* would be a hit, but *red-yellow-blue-red* and *red-red-yellow* would not). Note that, although the *Stimulus* condition placed heavy demands on attention, an analysis identifying regions responding to the periodic sweep of the wedge would not detect activity corresponding to steady attention to the central point on the display. The *Attention* condition, in contrast, can be construed as the attention-to-the-rotating-wedge condition, because subjects, although fixating centrally, were to respond each time the three same-color point-light walkers in the wedge were *not* all moving identically (e.g., if two were jumping rope and one was doing karate kicks).
Source: Reproduced with permission from Saygin et al. (2008) / Oxford University Press.

Figure 7.5. That is, their display didn't somehow only activate V1, then V3, then IPS2, and so on. So, how were they able to discriminate these regions and determine their boundaries? The answer is that they used their knowledge of the physiology and anatomy of the primate visual system, including the fact that retinotopic maps "reverse" at each interareal boundary. This is particularly evident along the strip of tissue extending from V3A to V7 to IPS1 to IPS2 in the right hemisphere, *Attention* image. Moving in a caudoventral-to-rostrodorsal direction, V3A's retinotopy transitions from the horizontal to upper visual field, V7's from upper to horizontal, IPS1's from horizontal to upper, and IPS2's from upper to horizontal to lower. Known anatomical landmarks were also used to determine precisely where to draw boundaries.

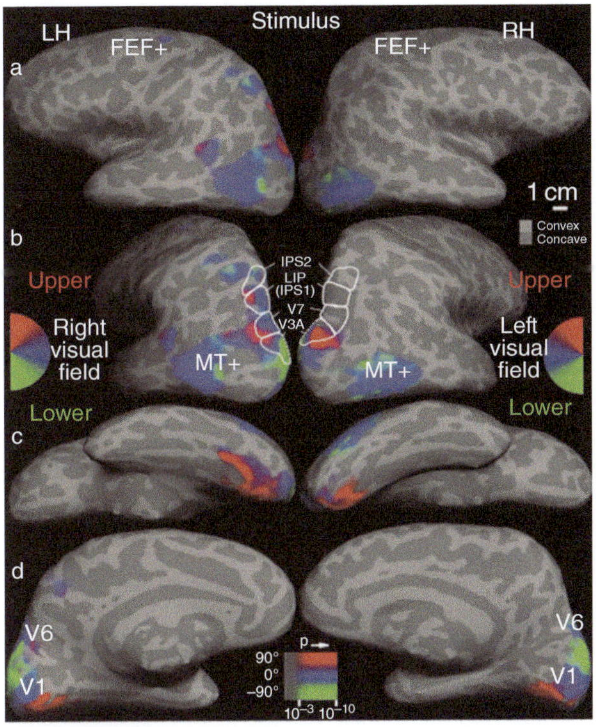

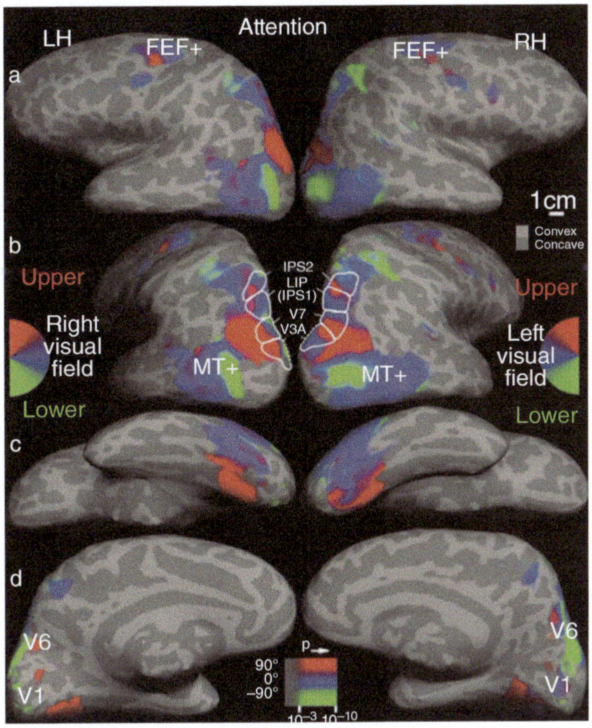

FIGURE 7.5.B Retinotopically sensitive cortex in the *Stimulus* condition, displayed on three views of an inflated hemisphere (×2, because both hemispheres are displayed); lighter gray corresponds to gyri. Superimposed on the anatomical images are patches of red-blue-green color identifying cortical regions whose activity fluctuated (either increased or decreased) each time the wedge passed through a particular region of the display, the specific color indicating the part of the visual field to which that patch of cortex was responsive (keys are located to left and right of view b for each hemisphere). Statistical significance of a region's retinotopic responses is represented by the translucency of the superimposed color. The identity of each region is labeled with white letters and, along the intraparietal sulcus (IPS), borders.

Source: Reproduced with permission from Saygin et al. (2008) / Oxford University Press.

FIGURE 7.5.C Retinotopically sensitive cortex in the *Attention* condition.

Source: Reproduced with permission from Saygin et al. (2008) / Oxford University Press.

Coordinate Transformations to Guide Action with Perception

Although *Figure 7.5* indicates that many areas of occipitoparietal cortex are organized retinotopically, they, too, follow the principle of hierarchical processing that we saw with the ventral visual processing stream in *Chapter 6*. Different from much of the ventral stream, however, is the fact that many dorsal stream regions are characterized by multisensory integration, in particular, the integration of proprioceptive with visual information. Consider the following scenarios, as narrated by your author: as I sit writing this section, occasionally lift my right hand from the keyboard to reach for the glass that is located to the right of the keyboard. (1) Sometimes I turn my head to look at the glass before reaching for it, (2) sometimes my face remains directed at the screen and I move my eyes to fixate the glass, and (3) sometimes neither head nor eyes are moved, because while both are directed toward the screen, the glass occupies the outer edge of my right visual field. In each of these three scenarios, the glass is in the same location in allocentric coordinates (i.e., it's always in the same location on the arm of the couch in my living room), yet the information that my nervous system processes about its location is different in all three. In the first two scenarios, it occupies the same retinotopic coordinates, but different head-centered coordinates, in that it is in a different location relative to my head (straight ahead in scenario 1, at "2 o'clock" in scenario 2). In the second and third scenarios, it is at the same head-centered coordinates, but in different retinotopic coordinates. And in each of these three, what ultimately matters is that the glass is located in precisely the same location relative to the hand of our narrator. What this example illustrates is that virtually all of the actions that we carry out over the course of our lives, certainly all of our sensory-guided actions, entail an ongoing process of translation between sensory-based and motor effector-based coordinate frames. To accomplish this, the nervous system needs to know the position of each part of the body relative to the others (e.g., *Are the eyes pointing right or straight ahead?*). And recall from the final section of *Chapter 5* that this proprioceptive information is supplied by muscle stretch detectors.

As we shall review here, an important function carried out by the PPC is to compute the **coordinate transformations** that are necessary to know where an object is located relative to different parts of the body. The study illustrated in *Figure 7.5* provides no insight about how these coordinate transformations are computed, because it didn't involve movement of the body. Many studies that have provided important information about these processes have come from electrophysiological recordings of neurons in the awake, behaving monkey.

Extracellular Electrophysiological Studies of Monkeys Area 7a of the PPC and the immediately superior IPS (see *Figure 6.5.A*) has been the focus of intensive investigation by neurophysiologists since the 1980s. In subsequent chapters, we will consider the role of these areas in such functions as the control of movement, the control of attention, and decision-making. Presently, however, we'll focus on the role of these regions in the integration of visual and proprioceptive information. Neurophysiologist Richard Andersen and colleagues have studied this by first finding the retinotopically defined receptive field of a neuron in PPC, then systematically varying the location at which the monkey has to fixate, all the while keeping a visual stimulus in that neuron's receptive field (*Figure 7.6*). A property of these PPC neurons that this procedure reveals is that the gain of their response is modulated by eye position. *Figure 7.6*, for example, illustrates a neuron with a retinotopic receptive field centered 20° to the right and 20° below fixation, and with the additional property that the magnitude of its response is sensitive to the position of the eyes within the head, with maximal gain when the animal is looking up and to the left. What this means is that, in effect, this neuron is processing information not just about the location of a stimulus relative to the retina but also about the location of a stimulus relative to the head. Note that, in panel B of this figure, although the stimulus is in the same retinotopic location during "Fix center" and "Fix left" displays, it is in a different location relative to the animal's head, which is in the same location for both conditions.[1]

As alluded to at the end of *Chapter 5*, coordinate transformations such as those illustrated in *Figure 7.6* are critically important, because an organism needs to know where a stimulus (say, a predator, or prey) is located relative to its body, regardless of the position of its eyes in their sockets, or of its head on its neck. It may also be the case that transformation of visual percepts into body-centered coordinates is important for our sense that our visual world, and the objects in it, are stable, despite the fact that we move our eyes an average of three times per second. This is illustrated, for example, when you watch a video shot from a camera mounted on the forehead of a downhill skier, or a mountain biker, or a surfer – if you've ever engaged in any of these activities, you know that your perceptual experience while actually doing them isn't as jerky as is the perceptual experience of watching a video captured by a head-mounted camera. The difference is that when you are actually moving through the world, your vestibular system registers all the bumps and jolts that cause your head and body to jerk around, and stretch receptors register all the rapid changes of eye position (and neck position, etc.), and the brain uses this information to "smooth out" your perceptual experience.

Data such as those illustrated in *Figure 7.6* indicate that neurons in area 7a of PPC must receive information about eye position from somatosensory cortex, in addition to retinotopic visual information. (Eye position can be computed from signals from stretch receptors that are sensitive to the state of contractedness vs. relaxedness of the muscles that control the movement of the eyes.) Evidence for such integration of information from different sensory domains, and the coordinate transformation that this allows, suggest that the PPC is well positioned to

[1] To be sure, more than just eye position is needed to effect coordinate transformation out of the retinotopic reference frame, an estimate of the distance of the target from the head being another important piece of information (Martins et al., 2024).

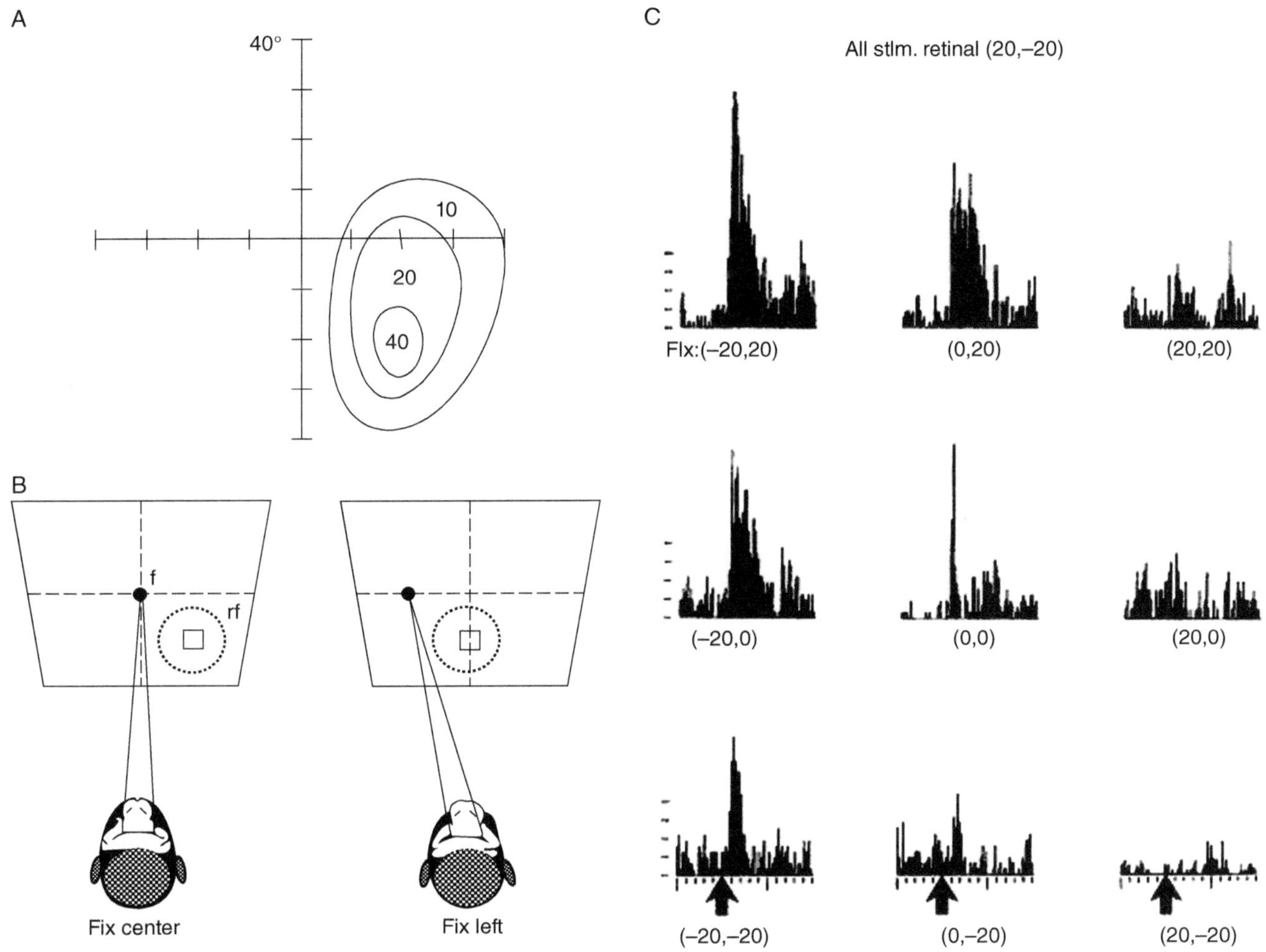

FIGURE 7.6 Eye position modulates spatial signaling of PPC neurons. **A.** Illustrates a contour plot of the receptive field of a neuron in area 7a, with the numbers indicating firing rate when the monkey is fixating centrally (corresponding to the point of intersection of the two axes) and a stimulus appears within each ring. **B.** Shows a monkey fixating on two locations, with a stimulus presented within the receptive field for both fixations. **C.** Shows the responses of this neuron to the onset of the stimulus (arrow) in its receptive field when the animal is fixating at each of nine locations.

Source: Andersen et al., 1985 / American Association for the Advancement of Science.

mediate the transition between sensory attention and motor intention. Indeed, more explicit evidence for PPC involvement in motor control comes from delayed-response tasks. In these tasks, a cue stimulus is briefly presented to identify for the subject (in the present example, a monkey, but the same procedure is also used with humans) the region on a screen to which it will need to make either an eye movement (a **saccade**) or a reaching movement. The subject has been trained, however, to withhold this movement until the offset of the fixation point, which lags behind the flash of the cue by several hundred milliseconds, or longer. (These are variants of the visual working memory tasks that featured prominently in several sections of *Chapter 5*.) One experiment from Snyder et al. (1997) identified two regions of the PPC that showed preferentially elevated delay-period activity as a function of which body part was to be used on that trial. Because the cued location was the same on both types of trial, these neurons were presumably computing information relevant to their preferred motor effector, rather than just to a sensory representation of where in space the cue had been presented. In part due to results like this, a team from a more recent incarnation of the Laboratory for Neuropsychology at the NIH has proposed the updated view of the organization of the dorsal stream that is illustrated in *Figure 7.7*. In *Chapter 8*, we will return to some implications of findings such as these for consideration of whether the dorsal stream is better construed as processing *where* a stimulus is located or as processing *how* the organism is going to interact with it.

FIGURE 7.7 An updated framework for understanding visuospatial processing (Kravitz et al., 2011).

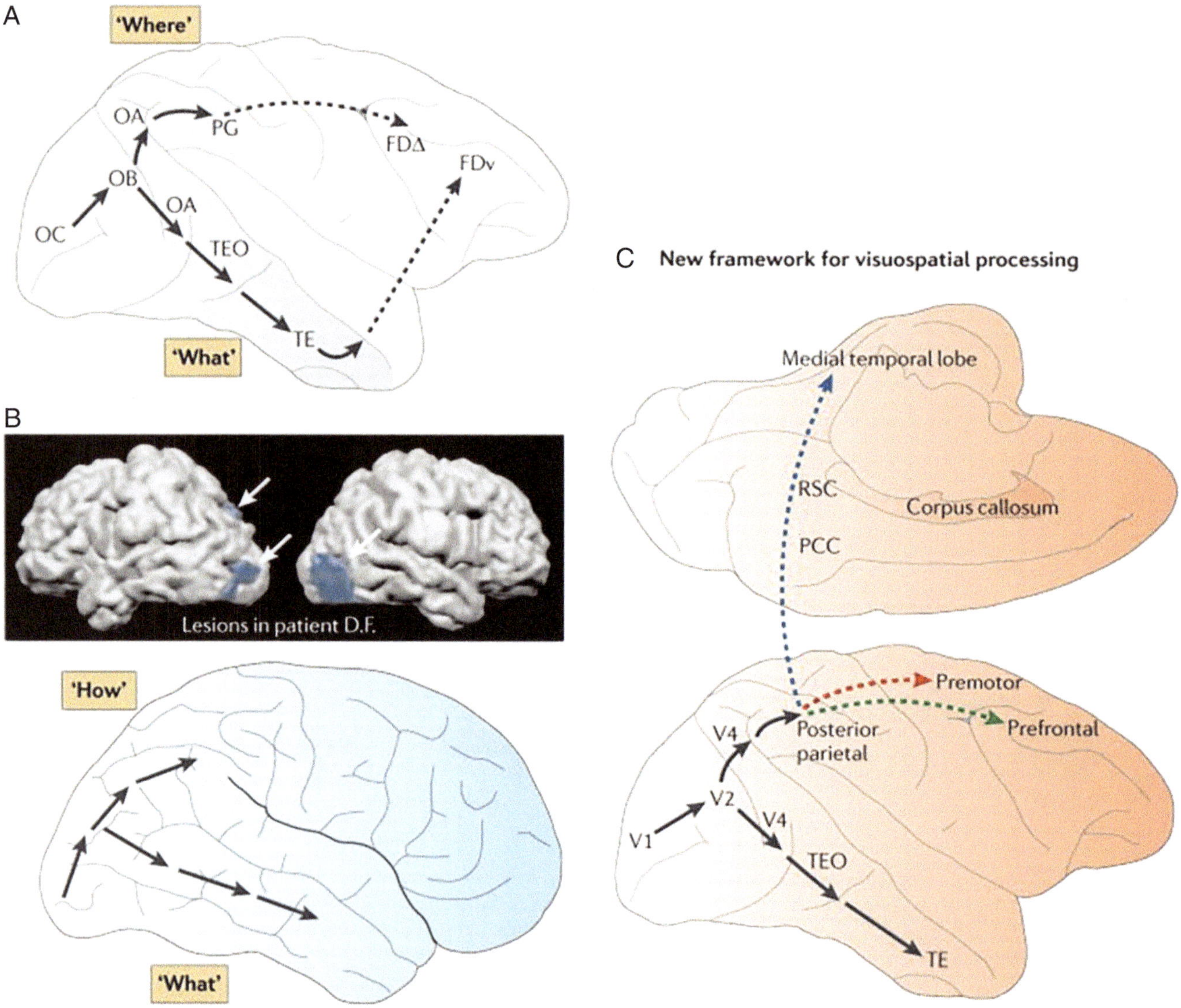

FIGURE 7.7.A The original formulation of the what-vs.-where organization of the visual system from the early 1980s, including an extension of the dorsal stream into dorsolateral prefrontal cortex (PFC; labeled here as FDΔ), and an extension of the ventral stream into a more ventral portion of PFC (FDv). (Note that this is effectively a duplication of *Figure 6.4*.)

FIGURE 7.7.B (Top) Location of lesions in the brain of patient D.F., whose ability to carry out actions in peripersonal space despite profound impairment in being able to perceive the configuration of the objects on which she could perform these actions led to the proposed reconceptualization of the dorsal stream as a "how" pathway (bottom). (Case D.F. and the proposed "what vs. how" scheme are detailed in *Chapter 8*, section *A neurological dissociation between perceiving objects and acting on them.*)

Source: Kravitz et al. (2011) / Springer Nature.

FIGURE 7.7.C The segregation of the dorsal stream into three functionally distinct pathways, one projecting to premotor cortex (see *Chapter 8*), one projecting to prefrontal cortex (see *Chapter 14*), and one projecting medially in a pathway engaging posterior cingulate cortex (PCC), retrosplenial cortex (RSP), and medial temporal cortex (MTL).

From Parietal *Space* to Medial-Temporal *Place*

Let's return for a moment to the patients of Bisiach and Luzzatti (1978; *Figure 7.4*). The fact that they were able to correctly conjure up several landmarks surrounding all sides of the Piazza, despite the fact that both required two perspectives from which to do it, means that their long-term memories contained a complete representation of this locale, one in which the position of each element relative to the others was stable – an allocentric representation. Their deficit evidently came from the fact that, in order to think about this representation, they had to do so from an egocentric perspective. First, let's consider a neural substrate for this allocentric representation of space. In the final section of this chapter, we'll take up how one might begin to address the notion of "thinking about" it.

Place Cells in the Hippocampus

Important insights about the formation of allocentric representations of space have come from research in the rat, much of it propelled by the groundbreaking research of (and, more recently, Nobel Laureate) neurophysiologist John O'Keefe and colleagues. The initial discovery was made while acquiring extracellular recordings from the dorsal hippocampus of a rat while it freely moved about, exploring an elevated maze (essentially a small tabletop with "runway" arms, and no side walls; *Figure 7.8*). What they found was that whereas some pyramidal neurons of the hippocampus responded to certain behaviors, such as grooming or sniffing and whisking, others showed a qualitatively different profile, seeming to encode where the animal was in the environment, independent of the orientation of its body. The difference was so striking that they categorized hippocampal pyramidal neurons into two groups: "the *displace* units are those whose firing pattern relates to the behavior of the animal, irrespective of where it occurs in an environment, while *place* units are those whose firing pattern is dependent on the location of the animal in an environment" (O'Keefe and Nadel, 1978, pp. 196–197; italics added). Their choice to label "displace" units in reference to the property that they did not display indicates which of the two they found more interesting.

As shown in *Figure 7.8*, "place cells," as they have come to be known, are qualitatively different from cells with body-centered receptive fields, because the fundamental piece of

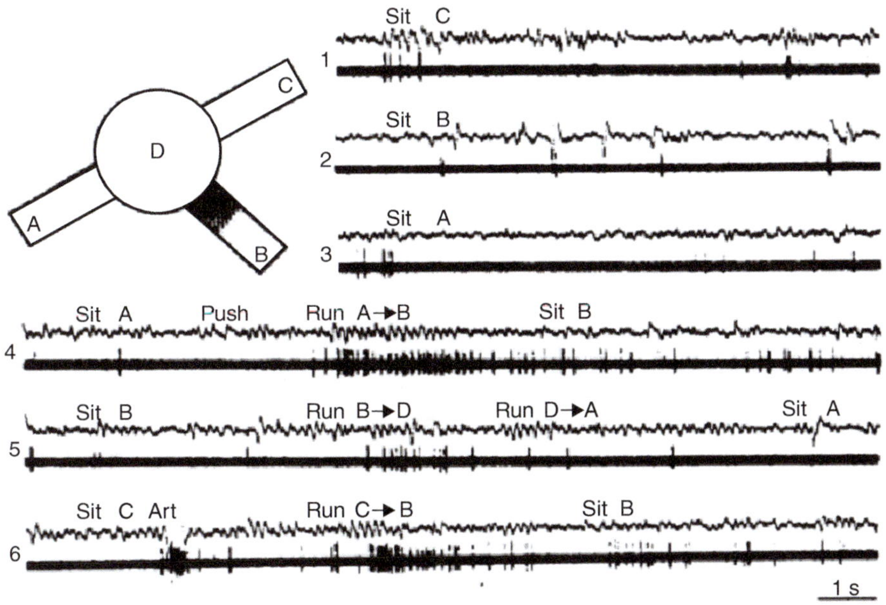

FIGURE 7.8 A place cell recorded from the dorsal hippocampus of the rat. The image on the upper left is a schematic top-down view of a three-arm maze, with the shaded area in B the location of the cell's place field. A pair of electrode traces is shown from each of six epochs of behavior, the upper the LFP (bandpass filtered to only display the theta band), the lower the spiking. Note the neuron produced place-related bursts of activity regardless of whether the animal had turned right to enter the B arm (epoch 4), turned left to enter the B arm (epoch 6), sat in the B arm (epochs 4 and 6), or was leaving the B arm (epoch 5). (The label "Art" in epoch 6 identifies an artifact in the recording.)

Source: O'Keefe et al., 1978 / Oxford University Press.

information that they represent is where the animal is located in space, not what it is currently seeing or doing. Thus, the neuron illustrated in *Figure 7.8* has a *place field* (by analogy to receptive field), in that it fires selectively whenever the animal passes through or stops in this location, regardless of the direction in which it is facing. For example, its discharge during "Run A→B" is similar to its discharge during "Run C→B," even though the former entails turning to the right and the latter turning to the left. Another interesting property is that the magnitude of this neuron's discharge, in a pattern reminiscent of the gain fields of the lateral intraparietal area (LIP), is influenced by factors other than place in and of itself. For example, the response is visibly stronger when the animal is entering the B arm than when leaving and seems to be stronger when passing through the place field than when sitting in it.

Note that, in isolation, a single place cell's output wouldn't be very informative to the organism, in that it can only signal, for example, that *I am currently in the corner of my living room near the fireplace*, or *I am* not *currently in the corner of my living room near the fireplace*. Thus, when walking around in my kitchen, say, or from my bedroom to the study, this neuron, through its silence, would be continually, implicitly, conveying that *I am* not *currently in the corner of my living room near the fireplace*. Thanks a lot. But, of course, individual neurons don't operate in isolation. Indeed, as *Figure 7.9* illustrates, a population of place cells, by each representing a different location, is ideally suited to represent an environment. Indeed, one can see how, just as is the case with receptive fields in the visual or somatosensory system, the smaller the hippocampal place field, the finer-grained the representation of that region of space.

How Does Place Come to Be Represented in the Hippocampus?

The detailed allocentric representation of a locale with which one is highly familiar (say, the Piazza del Duomo for natives of Milan) comes into existence over time, stitched together from multiple egocentric "snapshots." Only by having stood on the steps of the cathedral and looked out across the plaza, having strolled along the shops, having had a coffee at one of the outdoor cafes, and so on, could one construct a representation of how each of the discrete elements in this locale relates to one another. Because these egocentrically defined "snapshots" each depend on processing in the dorsal stream, it is reasonable to ask how it comes to pass that allocentric space is represented in a structure that lies along the rostromedial wall of the *temporal* lobe (*Figure 2.2*). From *Figure 6.5.B*, one might conjecture that the hippocampus is at the terminus of the ventral stream, located adjacent, as it is, to vAIT. Indeed, this reasoning wouldn't be incorrect; just incomplete.

Anatomical Distance vs. "Synaptic Distance" Although *Figure 6.5.A* indicates that, in terms of gross anatomy, AIT is much closer to the hippocampus than is BA 7 of the PPC, *Figure 6.5.B* indicates that, nonetheless, the two regions are equidistant from the hippocampus in terms of number of synaptic connections, each being only three synapses removed. One may wonder how it has come to pass that the PPC of the primate (including humans) is "just as close" to the hippocampus, in terms of synaptic distance, as is the AIT. To understand, it's useful to return to the rodent. In both the rodent and the primate, the hippocampus is slightly curved, like a banana. But whereas in the primate the long axis of the hippocampus parallels that of the temporal lobe, in the rodent it is oriented dorsoventrally, effectively "cupping" the caudal surface of the thalamus. Thus, in the rodent, the dorsal hippocampus (where O'Keefe and colleagues initially discovered place cells) lies directly below the cortical surface of the parietal lobe (*Figure 7.10*). Because modern-day primates and modern-day rodents can trace their evolutionary lineage back to a common rodent-like ancestor, scanning across species in *Figure 7.10* makes it seem plausible that, over the course of evolution, the primate hippocampus has "migrated" ventrorostrally from a previous dorsoventral orientation, and that it has "taken its parietal connections along with it."

Together, the hippocampus, entorhinal cortex, perirhinal cortex, and parahippocampal cortex are often referred to as the "medial temporal lobe" (MTL). Apart from speculation

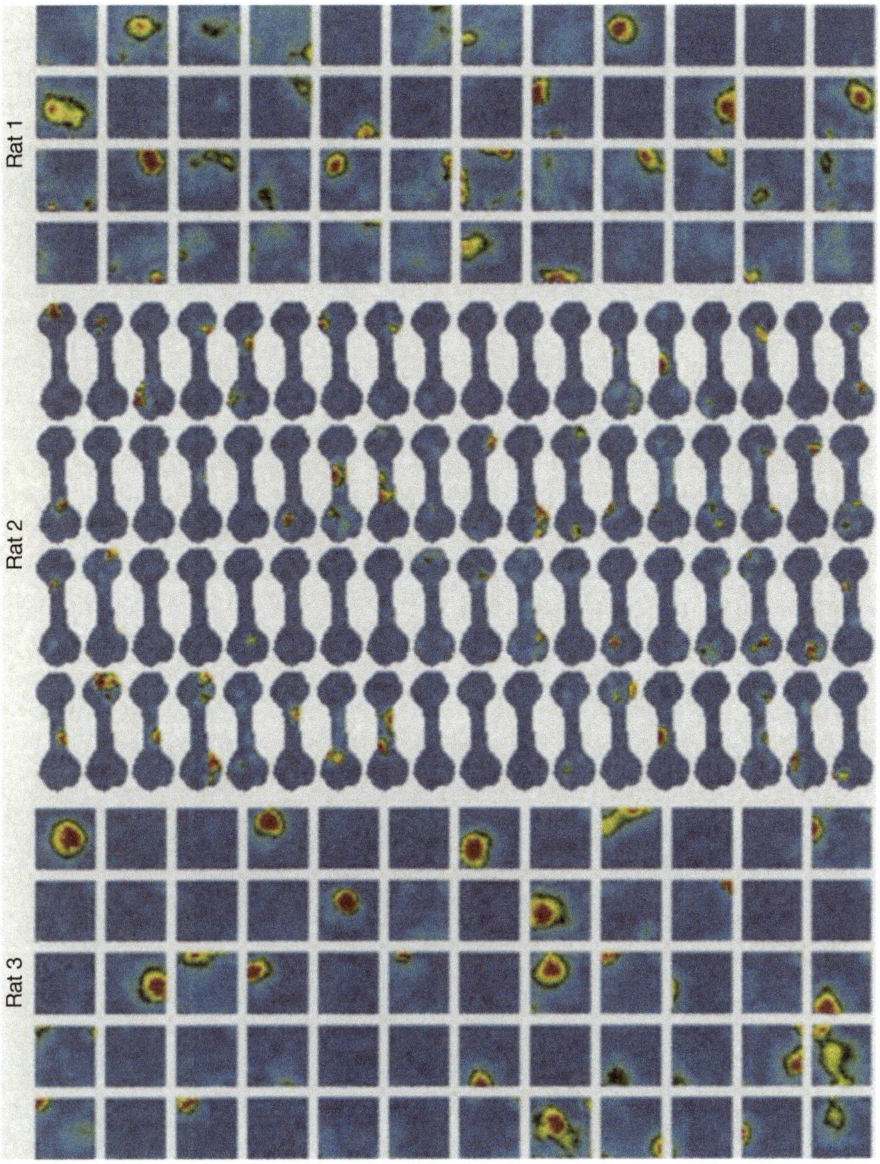

FIGURE 7.9 Place fields of multiple hippocampal pyramidal neurons from three rats. Each animal's panel shows multiple top-down views of the environment that the animal was exploring (a square-shaped enclosure for rats 1 and 3, a dumbbell-shaped enclosure for rat 2). Each individual square or dumbbell image represents the place tuning of a single neuron, the heat map indicating the neuron's firing rate at each location of the enclosure (range: blue = 0 Hz; red = ≥10 Hz). These illustrate how, by sampling across a population of place cells, the hippocampus can be thought of as having a "map" of a locale.

Source: Reproduced with permission from Wilson et al. (1994) / American Association for the Advancement of Science - AAAS.

about evolutionary changes in neuroanatomy, a practical reason to be mindful of the inter-species differences in the gross anatomy of the MTL is to not get tripped up by the different terminology used for different species. In the rodent, for example, the average size of place fields increases as one moves along the long axis of the hippocampus, from dorsal to ventral. (This is analogous to the ventral visual stream, for which the average size of retinotopic receptive fields increases in progressively more rostral regions.) Thus, it can be important to know, for example, whether a particular recording was made in dorsal hippocampus or ventral hippocampus. But this distinction is only meaningful for rodents. The analogous property

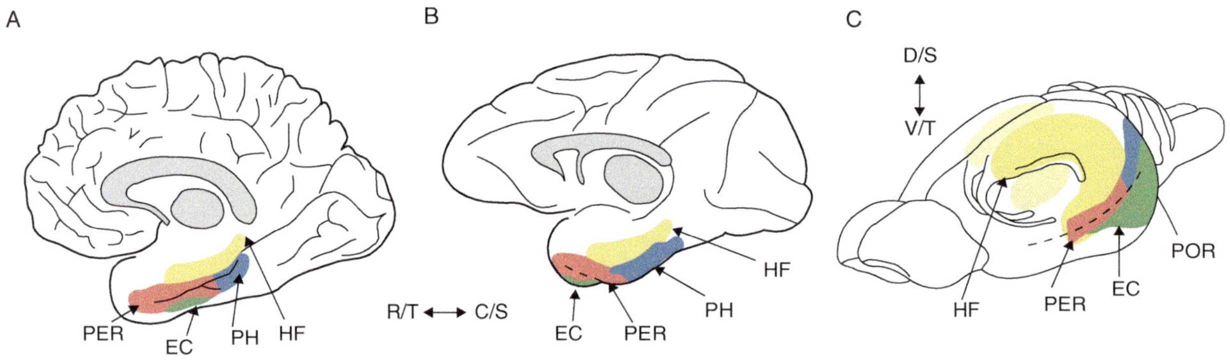

FIGURE 7.10 Location of the hippocampal formation (HF) and adjacent cortex in the human (**A**), the rhesus macaque (**B**), and the rat (**C**). The cortical areas are the perirhinal cortex (PER), the entorhinal cortex (EC), the parahippocampal cortex (PH), and, in the rat, the postrhinal cortex (POR), a homologue to primate PH. The convention for directional labels is general anatomical label/hippocampus-specific label, thus: R/T = rostral/temporal; C/S = caudal/septal; D/S = dorsal/septal; V/T = ventral/temporal. Note that area 36, which *Figure 6.5.B* shows to be a temporal-lobe target of PPC projections, corresponds to the blue-colored POR/PH in this figure. (An intriguing disorder of ego- and allo-centric processing that results from damage to this region is described by Aguirre (2003, *Further reading*).)

Source: Burwell et al., 2008 / with permission of Elsevier.

of increasing place-field size is also seen in primates, but for primates, it's in caudal/posterior hippocampus where one finds the smallest place fields, and in rostral/anterior hippocampus where they are largest.

Head-Direction Cells and Grid Cells *Figure 7.10,* having established an evolutionary "just-so story" for how spatial information from parietal cortex can come to be represented at the "apex of the ventral steam," we'll now take a closer look at some of the coordinate transformations that take place at intermediate steps along the pathway from parietal cortex to hippocampus. In primates, cortical inputs to the hippocampus come exclusively from the entorhinal cortex (colored green in *Figure 7.10.A* and *Figure 7.10.B*), and the entorhinal cortex, in turn, receives cortical input primarily from the perirhinal cortex (pink in *Figure 7.10.A* and *Figure 7.10.B*; referred to as "(area) 36" in *Figure 6.5*) and from the parahippocampal cortex (pink in *Figure 7.10.A* and *Figure 7.10.B*; referred to as "TH" and "TF" in *Figure 6.5*). Although the connections *7b→36→ER→HC*, *7a→36→ER→HC*, and *7a→TH→ER→HC* are diagrammed in *Figure 6.5.B*, there are other parietal areas that also project to perirhinal and parahippocampal cortex, but that are not included in this figure. These areas are found along the medial wall of the parietal cortex, and include a dorsal region called the precuneus and a more ventrally located region called the retrosplenial cortex. (Retrosplenial cortex gets its name from the fact that it lies immediately caudal to [thus, "behind" or "retro"] the splenium of the corpus callosum). We've already seen in section *Coordinate transformations to guide action with perception* how the translation of retinotopic information into body-centered coordinate frames requires the integration of information from different parts of the body, and the same principles are true for the construction of allocentric representations of space.

Following on the discovery of place cells in the rat in the 1970s, much of the research that has elucidated this process has been carried out, at least initially, in rodents. Among the important discoveries to come out of this work has been the characterization of "head-direction cells" in several brain areas, including in the thalamus, the striatum (of the basal ganglia), and retrosplenial cortex. These neurons, as the name implies, encode the orientation of the head relative to the body. (Recall, from *Figure 2.1*, that whereas the head of the rat is supported by a straight-line extension of the spinal cord, in primates, when standing upright, the head (and brain) "sits on top of" the spinal cord, its principal axis at right angle to the cord. Nonetheless, in all vertebrate species head direction is registered as the three degrees of freedom that define rigid-body pose: (for a primate that is "standing up straight and facing straight ahead"), pitch ("looking up or down"), yaw ("looking left or right"), and roll ("tilting left or right") (e.g., as one does when touching ear to shoulder)). Evidence for head cell-like activity has also been found in human thalamus and retrosplenial cortex. Information about the orientation of the head is important for constructing the final coordinate transformation that we'll consider in this chapter: a grid-like map of space.

In 2005, Torkel Hafting, Marianne Fyhn, and Sturla Molden, in the laboratory of May-Britt Moser and Edvard Moser, published a paper on "*Microstructure of a spatial map in the entorhinal cortex*" that has spawned a new subdiscipline in neuroscience (and a line of work that would win the Mosers the Nobel Prize). In it, they introduce the "grid cell," a neuron that integrates information about head direction and location of the body relative to landmarks in the environment. Unlike the hippocampal place cells illustrated in *Figure 7.8* and *Figure 7.9*, which represent a single location within an environment, the response field of an entorhinal grid cell covers the entire local environment. As illustrated in *Figure 7.11*, it does so by responding preferentially at each of multiple locations that are equidistant from the animal's current location within the space. A word that's often used to describe this property is "tessellation," which can be defined as the property of a surface that is covered with a repeating pattern of identically sized geometric shapes. In the case of the grid cell, it tessellates the surface of the local environment with equilateral triangles. That is, for any starting location at which the animal is currently standing, there is a grid cell that preferentially fires at that very location, *and* that will also fire preferentially if the animal moves for x steps in any of precisely six directions. These six directions are equally separated, in polar angle, from each other, and so what you get from that is a central hotspot surrounded by six hotspots that, if you connect them with imaginary lines, form a hexagon. From the perspective of the hotspot

FIGURE 7.11 Grid cells in entorhinal cortex of the rat.

Source: Hafting et al. (2005) / Springer Nature.

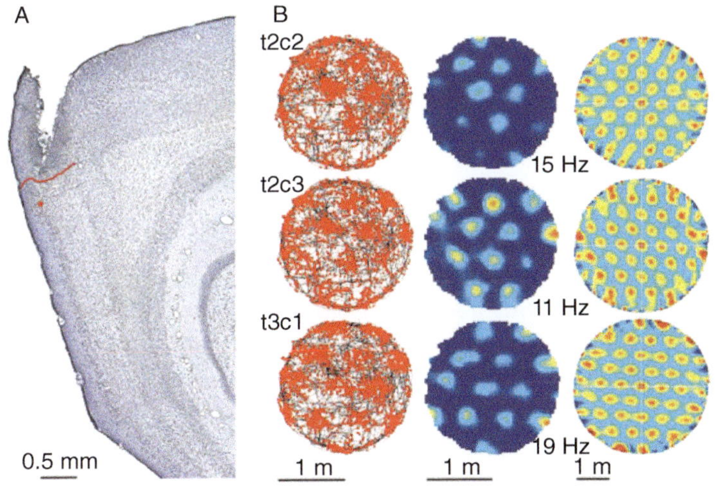

FIGURE 7.11.A Close-up of a sagittal section for dorsomedial entorhinal cortex in a rat (stained to highlight cell bodies), with a recording location in layer II/III marked with a red dot, and the boundary with postrhinal cortex (see *Figure 7.10*) marked with a red line.

FIGURE 7.11.B During a 30-minutes session, the rat from panel A explored a circular enclosure, and the first column on the left illustrates the animal's movement path (black traces) and, superimposed, the firing activity of each of three neurons (t2c2; t2c3; t3c1) recorded from the location indicated in panel A (red dots). For each neuron, the plots in the middle row illustrate the location in the enclosure of that neuron's firing fields (i.e., each circle is equivalent to a single "square" or "dumbbell" from *Figure 7.9*); color code ranges from 0 Hz (dark blue) to maximum firing rate (red). Note how, in comparison to the place cells illustrated in *Figure 7.9*, each of these neurons fires at several locations within this enclosed patch of space. The plots in the third row index spatial autocorrelation (i.e., level of similarity of the firing of that neuron at each location relative to the location marked on each plot by the dim white crosshairs), showing how each of these cells "tessellates" the space by "carving" it into virtual equilateral triangles. (See for yourself by selecting any hotspot, then drawing six "spokes" connecting it to the six nearest hotspots, then drawing six lines to connect each of these six new hotspots to its two nearest neighbors. Voila: six equilateral triangles).

at the center of the hexagon, imaginary lines connecting it to each of those six hotspots give it six "spokes." Now, if you consider all these imaginary lines together, what you've got are six equilateral triangles, which can be construed as triangular "tiles" that cover the area being represented. The reason that I only specified the length of each spoke as *x* is that, similar to the size of physical space represented by place fields in the hippocampus, the distance between a grid cell's hotspots increases systematically along the long axis of the entorhinal cortex. In rats tested on an 18 m-long track, the average interpeak distance in the dorsal-most medial entorhinal cortex was 50 cm, and systematically increased until reaching 300 cm (i.e., 3 m) in ventral-most medial entorhinal cortex.

The Neurophysiology of Sensory Attention

The deficit (of the patients of Bisiach and Luzzatti [1978]) evidently came from the fact that, in order to think about this representation, they had to do so from an egocentric perspective. It follows from this that cognition often requires us to select just a subset of the totality of information that's available to us, in order to submit this subset of information to the processing that will enable us to achieve a behavioral goal. The operations of selection and the prioritization for subsequent processing are operations ascribed to the function of attention. Among the influential late-nineteenth-century psychologists whose research and writing laid important foundations for contemporary cognitive neuroscience (see the concluding section of *Chapter 1*) was William James (1842–1910), who famously wrote that "Everyone knows what attention is. It is the taking possession by the mind, in clear and vivid form, of one out of what seem several simultaneously possible objects or trains of thought" (James, 1950, pp. 403–404). This nicely captures our intuition. The difficulty of understanding the cognitive and neural bases of attention, however, was cheekily captured by cognitive scientist Harold Pashler, who wrote roughly a century later that "no one knows what attention is, and . . . there may even not be an 'it' to be known about (although of course there might be)" (1999, p. 1). Here, we'll scratch the surface of this intriguing, notoriously slippery phenomenon that will be relevant for almost every aspect of cognition and behavior that we consider from here on out.

A Day at the Circus

The metaphor of attention as a spotlight has been a useful one for researchers, in that it captures the phenomenon of directing a resource (light) so as to prioritize one out of many possible targets. At the circus, for example, the lighting director may want the audience to attend to the diversionary pratfalls of a juggling clown, rather than to the trapeze artist who is climbing a ladder up to a high platform, but who isn't yet performing, or to the animal handler wrangling the recalcitrant tiger back into its cage, after it has jumped through the Hoop of Fire. To accomplish this, the spotlight is shined on the clown, thereby making him brighter and easier to see than the climbing acrobat or the retreating tiger. What if Clown 1 is joined by two or three additional jugglers? The area being illuminated by the spotlight can be enlarged or reduced, depending on the number of clowns performing. When it's time for the trapeze performance, the spotlight can jump from the floor, where the clowns were juggling, to a platform high overhead – the platform is currently empty, but the director wants the audience to be attending to the location onto which the trapeze artist will soon make her dramatic, graceful entrance.

This scenario captures two properties of attention that we will briefly consider here: the function of *increasing the salience* of one or more selected stimuli and the distinction between *attending to an object* vs. *attending to a location*. A third, the ability to change the aperture of attention, will be considered in *Chapter 14* (under the rubric of *capacity limitations* of working memory). A final, critical element in our circus scenario is the person who controls the spotlight, turning it on and off, and pointing it first at the clowns, then at the platform. The invocation of the spotlight operator highlights the distinction between the *site* of attention's effects (in our scenario, the clowns, then the platform), vs. the *source* of attention (the spotlight itself, which generates the bright light, and the person controlling its operation). Our present focus will be on the site of attention. We will consider the source(s) of attention in *Chapter 9*.

Attending to Locations vs. Attending to Objects

One place where we've already seen the effects of attention was in *Chapter 5*, when considering the difference in the AEP when the subject attended to a series of beeps, vs. when they read a book and ignored the beeps. In that example, because the effect of attention was to increase the magnitude of the N1 and P2 components of the AEP (*Figure 3.8*), we can say that the site of attention's effects included primary auditory cortex. And what might have caused this "amplification" of these ERP components? There are at least three plausible explanations. One is that the neurons responding to the afferent auditory information may have done so more vigorously in the count-the-beeps condition than in the book-reading condition. A second is that the level of synchrony among the neurons carrying afferent auditory information may have increased (a scenario illustrated in *Figure 4.10.B*). And a third is that more neurons may have been recruited when the subject attended to the auditory channel. (Recall, as you think about these different scenarios, that in *Chapter 2*, section *Mechanical transmission and neural transduction,* we learned that loudness is encoded in the auditory pathway by firing rate – the louder a sound, the higher the rate of firing of neurons representing that sound's "places" along the basilar membrane.)

Thus, by any of these accounts, a reasonable supposition is that paying attention to a particular sensory channel may be equivalent, in neural terms, to increasing the energy of the stimulus itself (such as by making it louder, or brighter). The phenomenon of an attention-related boost in the magnitude of sensory processing signals is also seen with the visual-evoked potential (VEP) and somatosensory-evoked potential (SEP). *Figure 7.12* illustrates a test of visual spatial attention, in that subjects fixate centrally but focus their attention on a location and wait for events to occur there. (This is referred to as covert attention. Overt attention would be to look directly at the location of interest.) From it, one can see that the effect of spatial attention on early components of the VEP is to magnify them. Further, it seems to do so in a particular way. Looking at the traces from the PO electrodes, it's as though the voltage of the *Attended* ERP at each time point was computed from the corresponding time point of the *Unattended* waveform by multiplying the latter by some constant value (perhaps 1.7 at PO7, and a value closer to 2.0 at PO8). Based on this observation, in isolation, one might hazard that attention works by applying a multiplicative gain factor to sensory information processing. We'll return to this idea in a moment, after first considering two additional pieces of evidence that complicate things a bit.

Although it's clear that we can attend to a location in space and "wait for something to happen" there, our intuitions, confirmed by decades of experimental psychology, tell us that we can also attend to an object, regardless of where it is located in space. (The author does this, for example, when proudly admiring his daughter at a gymnastics competition, despite the fact that she's surrounded by a milling gaggle of many, many other adolescent girls, all wearing similar leotards and hairstyles.) A clever ERP experiment designed by the same group featured in the previous paragraph, led by electrophysiologist Steven Hillyard, directly compared the effects of spatial attention vs. those of nonspatial feature-based attention. (For our purposes, it's simpler to start by considering single features, rather than complex objects.) In it, subjects attended to a nonspatial feature of the stimulus, its color or its direction of motion, which, from trial to trial, appeared in one of the two visual hemifields (*Figure 7.13.A*). Comparison of the VEP for the attended vs. the unattended hemifield revealed the amplification of the P1, N1, and subsequent visual-evoked components that we have already seen (compare *Figure 7.13.B* to *Figure 7.12.B*). The comparison of the attended nonspatial feature vs. the unattended nonspatial feature, in contrast, revealed an ERP component that was not "merely" an amplification of the VEP (*Figure 7.12.B*). Instead, this "selection negativity" (SN) must correspond to the enhanced processing of the critical stimulus feature (e.g., of its redness or of its horizontalness), rather than to the indiscriminate amplification of all activity in the visual system that seems to result from spatial attention. That is, it seems to reflect a neural process corresponding to the *selection* of one feature from the two-feature stimulus. It is important to

FIGURE 7.12 EEG of visual spatial attention, as studied by Di Russo, Martinez, and Hillyard (2003).

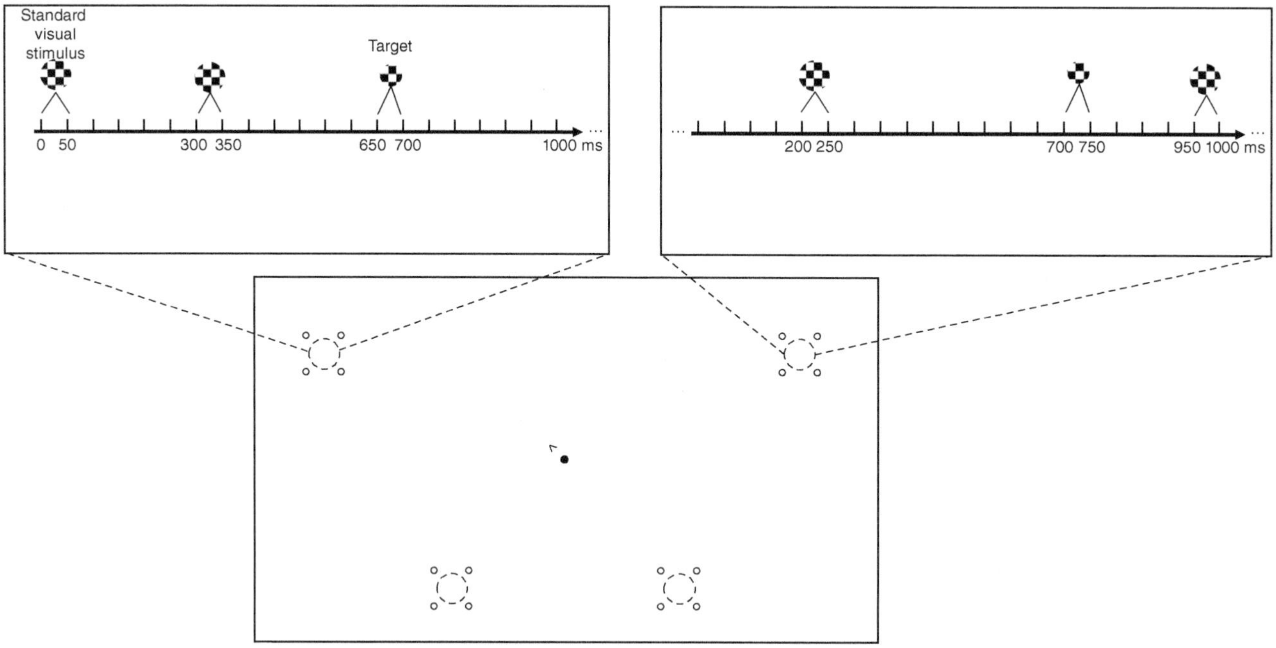

FIGURE 7.12.A The display: subjects were instructed to fixate the central dot while checkerboard stimuli flashed rapidly and randomly at two locations (illustrated here are upper left and upper right) and to count the number of infrequently appearing targets appearing in the cued location. (This is a variant of the famous Posner [1980] spatial cuing paradigm.)

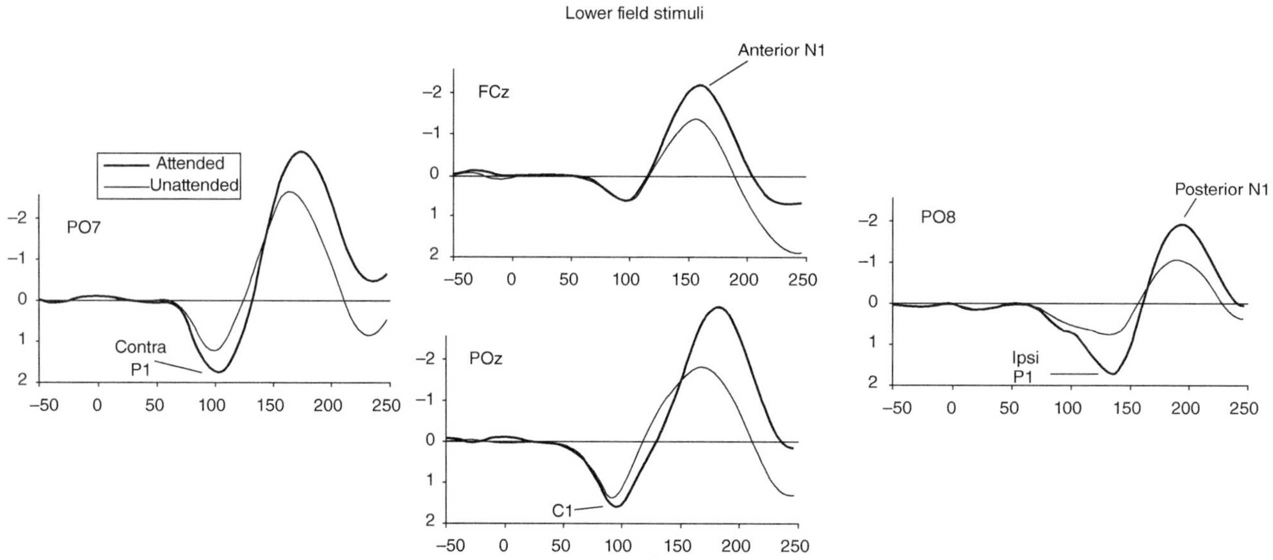

FIGURE 7.12.B ERPs associated with stimuli presented to the lower-right location, when that location was *Attended* and when it was *Unattended* (i.e., when visual presentation was identical, but subjects were attending to the left visual field location). The four plots show the signal recorded at electrodes FCz, PO8, POz, and PO7 (in relation to *Figure 3.8*, FCz is located midway between Fz and Cz, and the PO electrodes midway between the P and O electrodes).

Source: Di Russo et al., 2003 / Oxford University Press.

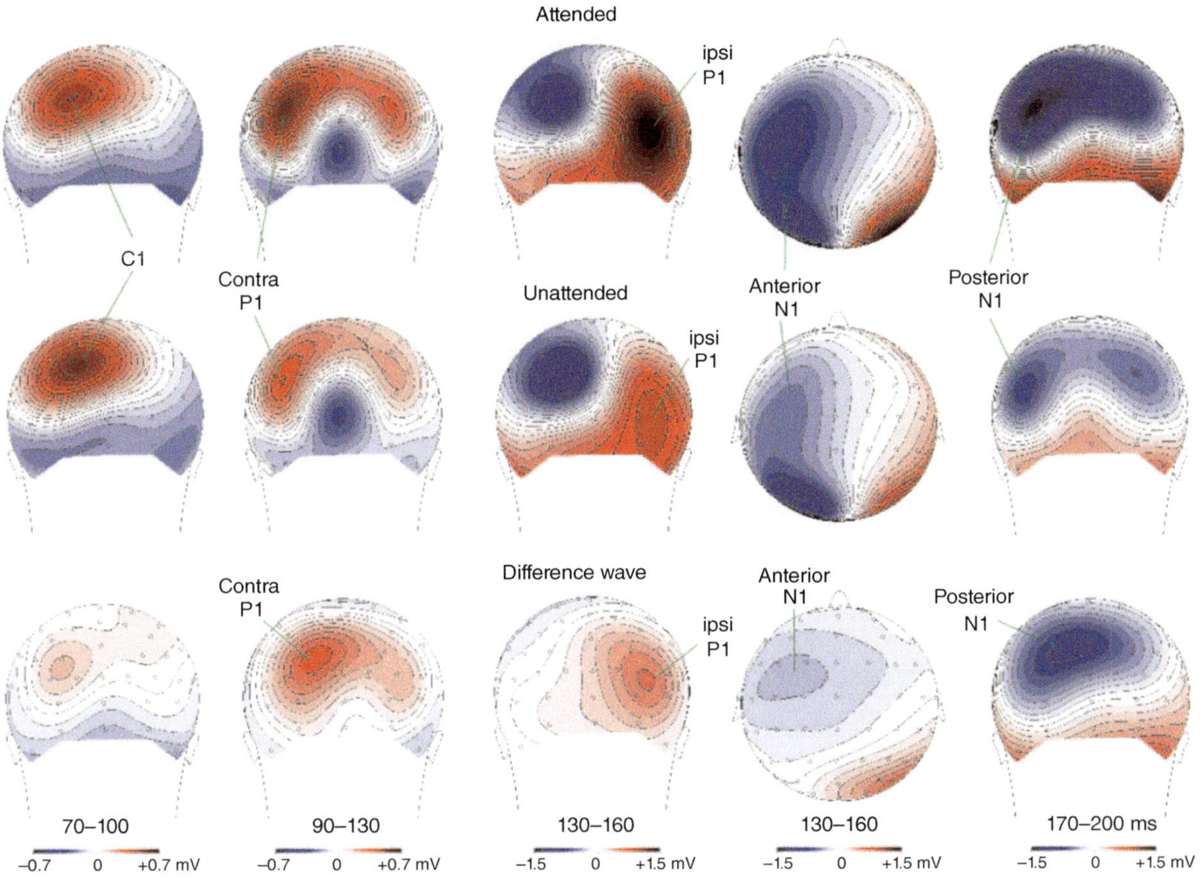

FIGURE 7.12.C Four "snapshots in time" of the ERP from *Figure 7.12.B* as is it distributed across the scalp (as viewed from behind, except fourth column from left is as viewed from above, with the nose at the top of each image). The top and middle rows show the ERP vs. baseline, the bottom row shows the subtraction images of [Attended – Unattended]. Although recorded from an array of 64 discrete electrodes, interpolation was applied to generate this continuous 2-D voltage map.

Source: Di Russo et al., 2003 / Oxford University Press.

note that although the shape and timing of the SN for attention to a color or to a direction of motion appear to be very similar, the two were extracted from electrodes on different parts of the scalp: the color SN was greatest at contralateral occipitotemporal sites, whereas the motion SN was greatest at bilateral temporal and parietal sites.

Mechanisms of Spatial Attention

Contradictory Findings from fMRI vs. EEG? Having established the distinction between location- vs. feature-based attention, let's now consider how they might work. Recall that *Figure 7.11.B* suggested a mechanism applying "multiplicative gain." *Huh?* Consider, for a moment, your mobile phone (or whatever device you kids use to listen to your "music" these days): you set the volume to a larger number and the music is louder; you set it to a smaller number and it's softer. But what about during a silent gap in the music? Whether the volume is set at *2* or at *11*, the silence will sound the same. This is because the products of [*2*0*] and of [*11*0*] are both *0*. Your volume controller only influences the gain of the signal being produced by your music player by *multiplying* it by some factor. It doesn't *add* anything to the signal. (Now look back at *Figure 7.11.B* and note how the Attended and Unattended waveforms are identical until afferent visual signals get to V1, at which point the attended vs. unattended VEPs diverge in a multiplicative manner.) An *additive* process, on the other hand, might look like what is illustrated in *Figure 7.14*. This illustrates an fMRI study of both location- and feature-based attention, the former being our interest at the moment. Note how, in *Figure 7.14*, there is an increase in fMRI signal, relative to baseline, during the *expectation* period of the task. That is, although the baseline and *expectation* periods of the task are identical with respect to visual presentation (empty gray screen) and overt behavior (fixation), the signal in brain areas representing the area of the visual field being attended to nonetheless increases when spatial attention is directed there. This phenomenon is sometimes referred to as a "baseline shift," in that "nothing has happened yet" in the *expectation* portion of the trial, and so an analysis that

FIGURE 7.13 EEG of feature-based visual attention, as studied by Anllo-Vento and Hillyard (1996).

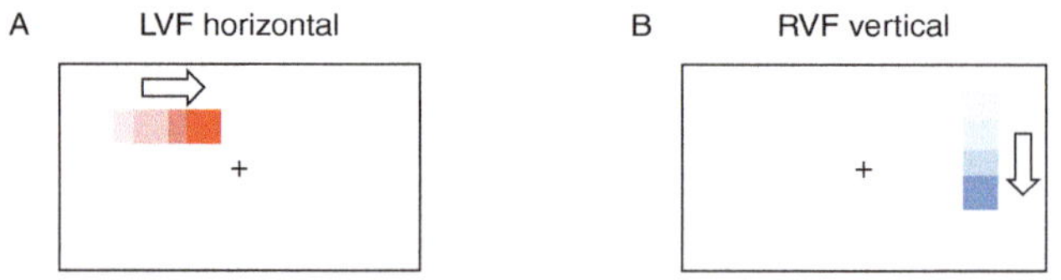

FIGURE 7.13.A There were three relevant stimulus dimensions: color (red, blue), direction of motion (horizontal, vertical), and visual field (right, left). Any of the six possible stimulus types (e.g., red horizontal motion in the LVF) could occur on each trial. On any block of trials, subjects were to indicate when the *speed* of the moving stimulus was slower than typical, but only when this slowing occurred for the instructed stimulus type (i.e., red, blue, horizontal, or vertical) in the instructed visual field.

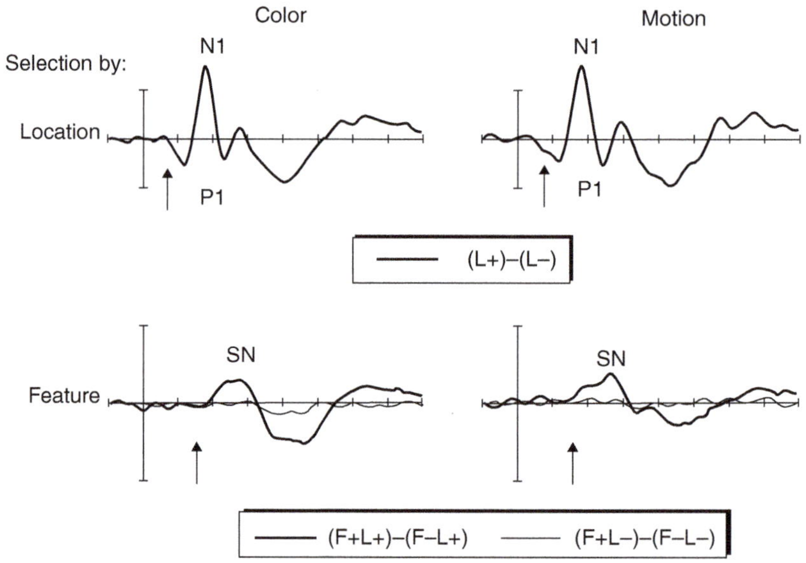

FIGURE 7.13.B ERP difference waves showing the effects of spatial attention (top row) and feature-based attention (bottom row). The waveforms in the top row are conceptually what would result if, in *Figure 7.11.B*, one were to subtract the "Unattended" (here, labeled "L–") from the "Attended" (L+) waveforms at any electrode – they illustrate the extent to which the VEP is magnified by spatial attention while the subject was attending to a color (left-hand column) or a direction of motion. In the bottom row, the waveforms drawn in heavy lines illustrate the subtraction of trials when the instructed color (or direction) was present in the attended visual field ("F+L+") vs. when the uninstructed feature was present in the attended visual field ("F–L+"), thereby emphasizing the SN component. The faint lines are the analogous subtractions from the unattended visual field. Arrows indicate the points at which attentional effects first achieved statistical significance.

Source: Anllo-Vento et al., 1996 / Springer Nature.

ignored the cognitive state of the subject ("not attending" vs. "attending") would conclude that the *expectation* period was a baseline period with a level of activity that was shifted upward.

And so the EEG studies featured in *Figure 7.12* suggest that spatial attention operates via a multiplicative mechanism, whereas the fMRI study of *Figure 7.14* suggests that spatial attention operates via an additive mechanism. Is one wrong? Of course, it's not that straightforward. We need to take into account that the two sets of experiments were intended to address different questions ("early vs. late selection" being an important question motivating the ERP studies, "biased competition" [which we'll take up presently] motivating the fMRI study), and that these two techniques are sensitive to different neurophysiological signals. Additionally, how the data are analyzed can determine what one is capable of detecting in one's data. Thus, although the ERP studies summarized here don't provide evidence for a baseline shift associated with covert spatial attention, many studies analyzing spectral elements of the EEG do find such evidence. Most prominently, covertly directing spatial attention to one visual field is known to produce a decrease in alpha-band power in the contralateral hemisphere and an increase in alpha-band power in the ipsilateral hemisphere. An ERP analysis would not detect such an effect, because alpha-band dynamics represent a major component of the "noise" that ERP averaging is intended to minimize (see section *Event-related analyses, Chapter 3,* and *Figure 3.9*). (For a study that did a head-to-head comparison of EEG/ERP vs. fMRI measures of the same subjects performing the same tasks, see Itthipuripat et al. [2019], *Further reading.*) These considerations also highlight the fact that, for some questions, to "really know what's going on," one needs to get inside the cranium.

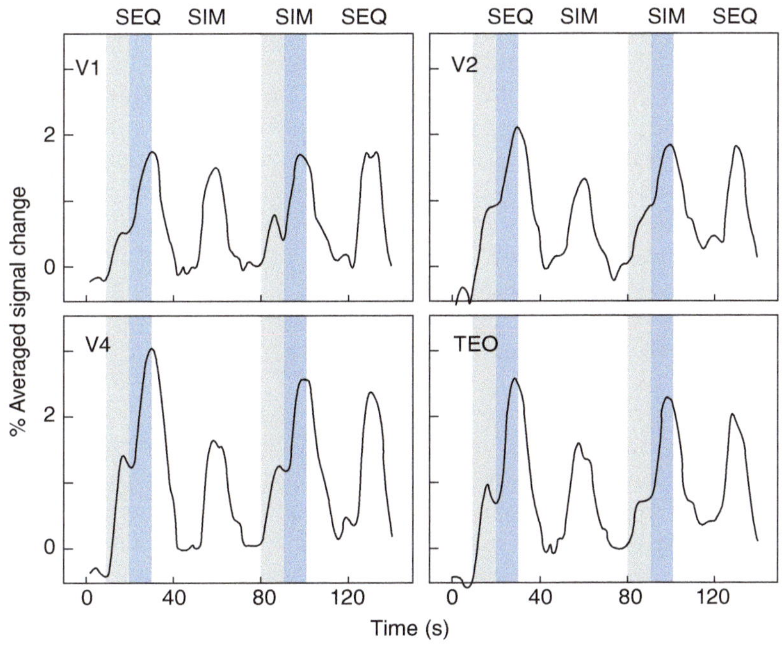

FIGURE 7.14 Visual attention studied with fMRI.

Source: Kastner et al., 1999 / with permission of Elsevier.

Effects of Attention on Neuronal Activity

Spatial Attention *Figure 7.15* illustrates a study performed in the laboratory of Robert Desimone (the neurophysiologist whose work we first encountered in *Chapter 6*, when, as a trainee of Charles Gross, he studied the visual functions of IT cortex). After Desimone joined the fabled Laboratory for Neuropsychology at the U.S. National Institutes of Health (NIH), he and his trainees carried out many pioneering studies on the neurophysiological bases of visual attention. As with studies that we've already considered, the subject (in this case, a monkey) covertly attended a specific location and waited for a predesignated target to appear there. Recordings from neurons in areas V2 and V4 clearly showed that covertly attending to a location within their receptive fields produced a sustained increase in their firing rate – a baseline shift. From these findings, the authors concluded that "visual-spatial attention operates, at least in part, by creating a preset sensory bias that modulates the initial volley of sensory information as it passes through area V4" (Luck et al., 1997, p. 41).[2]

Object-Based Attention As we near the end of this chapter, we turn to a final theme invoked by the study of unilateral neglect – the *competition* for stimulus representation inferred from the phenomenon of extinction. Evidence for such competition at the neuronal level has come from research by Desimone's group (with collaboration from the British experimental psychologist John Duncan), illustrated in *Figure 7.16*. The experiment that they carried out was modeled on visual search tasks that have been used in (human) experimental psychology for decades – you first present the target, and then an array of stimuli within which subjects must either find the target or indicate that it's not present in the search array. For the monkeys that were tested by Chelazzi et al. (1998), the task was simplified by presenting arrays of only one or two stimuli. When considering the data, the first thing to note is that these recordings were made in vAIT, the anterior-most region of the ventral visual processing stream, where, as we saw in *Chapter 6*, neurons show a high degree of preference for the conjunctions of features that define specific objects. To carry out these experiments, the researchers first isolated a neuron with an extracellular electrode and then presented many images to find one to which it responded preferentially (they refer to it as the "good" stimulus for that neuron; in *Figure 7.16*, it's the butterfly). Then they had the animal perform several kinds of trials, the results from four of which are illustrated in *Figure 7.16.B*: (1) the search array only contained one item, which matched the target, and was the "good" stimulus; (2) the search array contained two items, with the match being the "good" stimulus; (3) the search array contained two items, including the "good" stimulus, but in which the other stimulus (a "poor" stimulus for that neuron) matched the target; (4) the search array only contained one item, which matched the target, and was the "poor" stimulus for that neuron. Additionally, there were catch trials in which the target was not present in the search array (not shown). In *Figure 7.15.B*, the first 150 msec after array onset demonstrates evidence for competition between the neural representations of objects: the response to a "good" target stimulus is suppressed when it is paired with a second stimulus ("Target = good stim. in 2-stim. array") relative to when it is presented alone ("Target = good stimulus alone"). This is presumably due to **lateral inhibition** that occurs when collateral branches of neuron A's axon synapse on inhibitory interneurons located in cortical columns that are tuned for different stimulus configurations, and these interneurons, in turn, release GABA to suppress activity within that column. That is, the "initial [feedforward] volley of sensory information" associated with each of the objects in the two-item array results in the neural representations of each being activated, and these, in turn, suppress the neural representation of the other. The influence of attention is seen at the inflection, at ~175 msec, of the response to the target when it is the "good stim. in 2-stim. array" (as labeled in *Figure 7.15.B*). From that point forward, the neuron's response is identical in the "alone" and "2-stim." conditions – the suppression from the competing stimulus representation has been overcome. In the

[2] Intriguingly, recent research has shown that what we think of as our ability to allocate spatial attention to a single location over a sustained period of time (e.g., several seconds) may actually be a subjective illusion. There's a growing body of evidence from behavior and from neurophysiology, from humans and NHPs, suggesting that "sustained attention" may actually be accomplished by periodic sampling, via shifts of covert attention, among multiple regions and/or objects of potential interest, at a rate that's typically found to be in the theta band. See *Further reading*.

FIGURE 7.15 The effects of spatial attention on neural activity in the macaque visual system, as studied by Steve Luck et al. (1997).

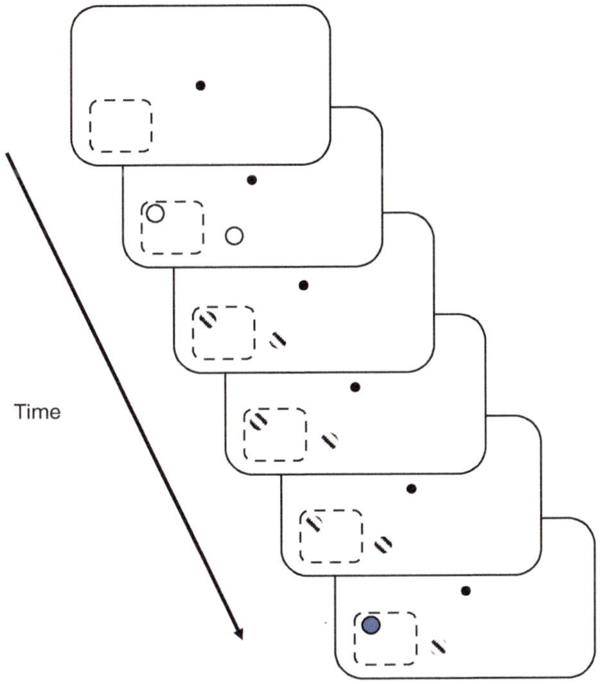

FIGURE 7.15.A The behavioral task, in which stimuli were presented sequentially or simultaneously in two "marked" locations (indicated here by unfilled circles). In different conditions, these locations were either both placed within the receptive field of the neuron in V2 or V4 that was being recorded from, or one was inside and one outside the receptive field (dashed line). At the beginning of each block of trials, the animal was cued as to which of the two marked locations was to be attended and was rewarded for indicating when the stimulus in the cued location changed. (Cartooned here is a trial in which the stimulus located inside the receptive field changes.) Of interest here is activity from neurons in conditions when one of the marked locations was located outside the receptive field.

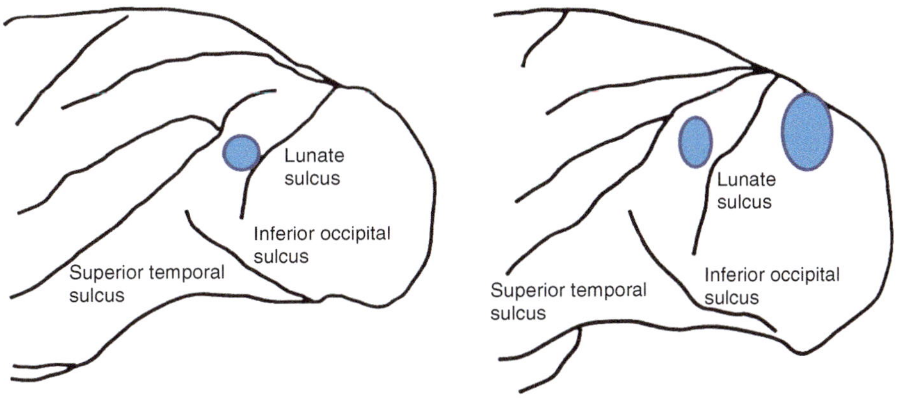

FIGURE 7.15.B Locations of electrode penetration and recording sites in two monkeys. V4 recordings were made within shaded oval regions anterior to lunate sulcus (lu) in both animals. In the animal illustrated on the right, recordings were also made in V1 (shaded oval posterior to the lunate sulcus) and in V2, reached through penetrations extending rostrally from the V1 recording site to the caudal bank of the lunate sulcus where V2 is located.

Source: Luck et al., 1997 / The American Physiological Society.

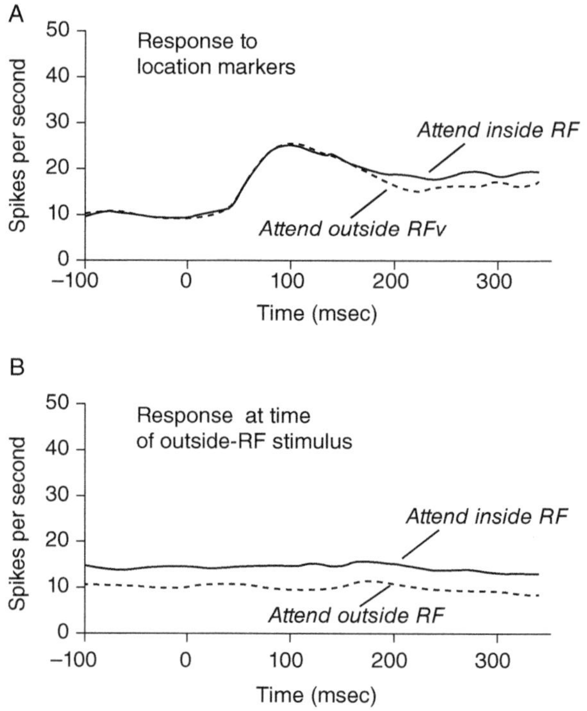

FIGURE 7.15.C Two examples of a "baseline shift" effect of spatial attention in the average firing rate of 40 V4 neurons. **A** illustrates the prestimulus period: onset of location markers occurred at time 0, and approximately 175 msec later, the neurons' firing rates diverged depending on whether attention was focused inside or outside the receptive field (RF). **B** illustrates the middle of the trial: a nontarget stimulus is presented outside the RF at time 0, when the animal is attending to a marked location inside vs. outside the RF.

Source: Luck et al., 1997 / The American Physiological Society.

parlance of Desimone and colleagues, the *competition* has been *biased* by the top-down influence of selective attention

The competition is also seen in responses when the "poor" stimulus is the target. When presented alone, the poor stimulus, by definition, barely influences the activity of the neuron. When the neuron's good stimulus is presented along with the poor target, however, the neuron initially responds to its preferred stimulus. After ~125 msec, however, the neuron's response to its preferred stimulus begins to be tamped down, presumably because the neurons representing the target have begun winning the competition, and are suppressing the neural representation of the nontarget stimulus.

These results from Chelazzi et al. (1998) suggest a neural mechanism that implements the psychological process invoked by William James 100 years before: "[Attention] implies withdrawal from some things in order to deal effectively with others" (James, 1950, p. 404). A topic to be taken up in *Chapter 9* will be: "What is the source of this biasing influence?"

Turning Our Attention to the Future

In this chapter, we started by considering how aspects of cognition that many of us take for granted (e.g., being aware that there's food on both the right *and* the left side of our dinner plate) can be severely disrupted as a result of a stroke affecting temporoparietal cortical regions and ended with a consideration of neural phenomena that may explain some of the mechanisms underlying visual awareness; mechanisms that may break down in some neurological syndromes. In the next two chapters, we'll build on what we've learned about the properties

FIGURE 7.16 Neural evidence for biased competition as a mechanism of object-based attention.

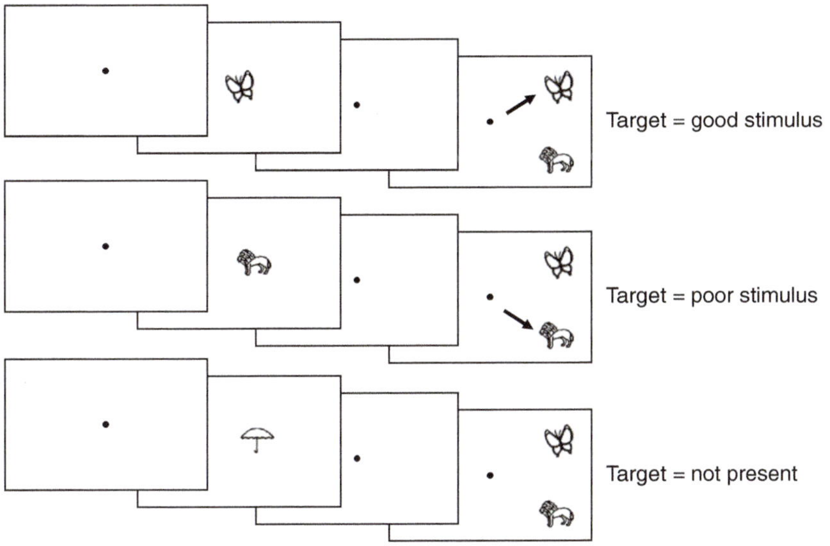

FIGURE 7.16.A The search task. The target object is presented at the beginning of the trial, and after the delay, an array of two stimuli is presented, and the monkey makes a saccade to the target (no saccade if the target is not in the array). Not shown are trials with one-item arrays, which could also be "target-present" or "target absent."

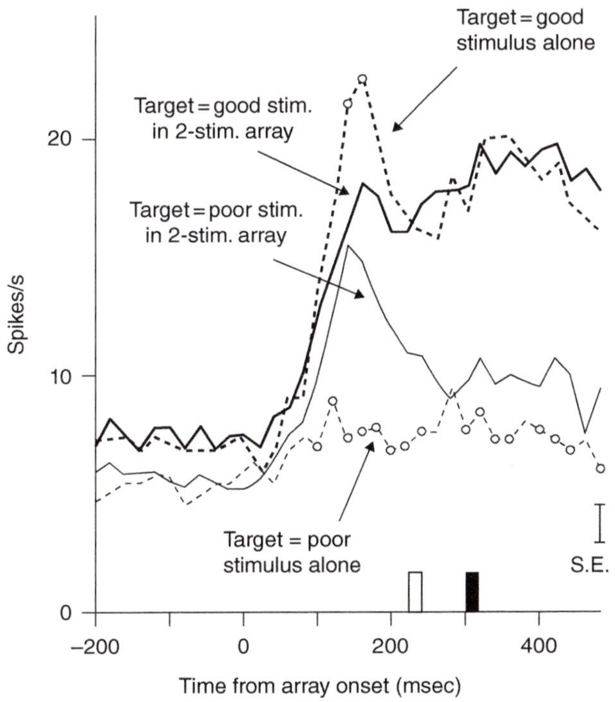

FIGURE 7.16.B A summary of the results from 58 neurons, contrasting good vs. bad targets in 2-stim.-array and 1-stim.-array ("alone") trials. Neural activity is time-locked to the onset of the search array (i.e., array appeared at time 0). Circles indicate time points for which the two good traces or the two poor traces differ statistically from each other. Unfilled and filled bars on the horizontal axis indicate average response times to one-item and two-item arrays, respectively.

Source: Chelazzi et al., 1998 / The American Physiological Society.

of the parietal cortex and of spatial cognition to introduce several new ideas about the neural organization of behavior and cognition. One, already hinted at on more than one occasion, is that an alternative way to construe the functions of the dorsal stream is that it governs *how* the body can interact with objects that necessarily occupy different locations in the environment. A second will be how parietal and frontal cortical systems coordinate with subcortical systems to produce the finely controlled actions that we execute countless times each day. A third will be to consider the source(s) of attentional control. These include the ideas that PPC and other regions support a dynamic "priority map" that helps guide attentional selection, and that the volitional vs. the reflexive control of attention are governed by different neural systems.

At a literal, and also profound, level, we are about to make our first foray across the central sulcus into the frontal lobe.

End-of-Chapter Questions

1. What symptom(s) of unilateral neglect inform ideas about the lateralization of attention; about how we process "near" vs. "far" space; about the competition for representation within the brain; and about location-based vs. object-based attention?

2. In what ways have neuroimaging studies supported, and extended, neuropsychology-based ideas about the functions of the dorsal visual processing stream?

3. Summarize the idea of a coordinate transformation. Why is this a critical principle underlying the guidance of action with perception? What evidence is there for the computation of coordinate transformations in the PPC?

4. We saw how the integration of retinotopic sensory information with eye-position information results in a coordinate transformation from retina-centered to head-centered coordinates. Using the same logic, how could the brain effect a coordinate transformation from head-centered to trunk-centered coordinates?

5. What is the difference between an egocentric vs. an allocentric representation of space? Summarize neurophysiological evidence that both are maintained in the brain.

6. In what ways is the analogy to a spotlight appropriate for understanding visual attention? Describe (at least) two aspects of attention that do not conform to this analogy.

7. How do location-based and object-based (or feature-based) attention differ neurophysiologically?

8. Summarize the evidence that biased competition may be an important principle for visual attention.

References

Andersen, Richard A., Greg K. Essick, and Ralph M. Siegel. 1985. "Encoding of Spatial Location by Posterior Parietal Neurons." *Science* 230 (4724): 456–458.

Anllo-Vento, Lourdes, and Steven A. Hillyard. 1996. "Selective Attention to the Color and Direction of Moving Stimuli: Electrophysiological Correlates of Hierarchical Feature Selection." *Perception & Psychophysics* 58 (2): 191–206. doi: 10.3758/BF03211875.

Bisiach, Edoardo, and Claudio Luzzatti. 1978. "Unilateral Neglect of Representational Space." *Cortex* 14 (1): 129–133.

Burwell, Rebecca D., and Kara L. Agster. 2008. "Anatomy of the Hippocampus and the Declarative Memory System." In *Memory Systems*, edited by Howard Eichenbaum. Vol. 3 of." In *Learning and Memory: A Comprehensive Reference*, edited by John H. Byrne 4 vols. (pp. 47–66). Oxford: Elsevier.

Chatterjee, Anjan. 2003. "Neglect: A Disorder of Spatial Attention." In *Neurological Foundations of Cognitive Neuroscience*, edited by Mark D'Esposito (pp. 1–26). Cambridge, MA: MIT Press.

Chelazzi, Leonardo, John Duncan, Earl K. Miller, and Robert Desimone. 1998. "Responses of Neurons in Inferior Temporal Cortex during Memory-Guided Visual Search." *Journal of Neurophysiology* 80 (6): 2918–2940.

Di Russo, Fracesco, Antigona Martínez, and Steven A. Hillyard. 2003. "Source Analysis of Event-Related Cortical Activity during Visuo-Spatial Attention." *Cerebral Cortex* 13 (5): 486–499. doi: 10.1093/cercor/13.5.486.

Driver, Jon, Patrik Vuilleumier, and Masud Husain. 2004. "Spatial Neglect and Extinction." In *The Cognitive Neurosciences III*, edited by Michael S Gazzaniga (pp. 589–606). Cambridge, MA: MIT Press.

James, William. 1950. *The Principles of Psychology*, vol. 1. New York: Dover. First published 1890.

Karnath, Hans-Otto, Johannes Rennig, Leif Johannsen, and Chris Rorden. 2011. "The Anatomy Underlying Acute versus Chronic Spatial Neglect: A Longitudinal Study." *Brain* 134 (3): 903–912. doi: 10.1093/brain/awq355.

Kastner, Sabine, Mark A. Pinsk, Peter De Weerd, Robert Desimone, and Leslie G. Ungerleider. 1999. "Increased Activity in Human Visual Cortex during Directed Attention in the Absence of Visual Stimulation." *Neuron* 22 (4): 751–761. doi: 10.1016/S0896-6273(00)80734-5.

Kravitz, Dwight J., Kadharbatcha S. Saleem, Baker Chris I, and Mortimer Mishkin. 2011. "A New Neural Framework for Visuospatial Processing." *Nature Reviews Neuroscience* 12: 217–230.

Luck, Steven J., Leonardo Chelazzi, Steven A. Hillyard, and Robert Desimone. 1997. "Neural Mechanisms of Spatial Selective Attention in Areas V1, V2, and V4 of Macaque Visual Cortex." *Journal of Neurophysiology* 77 (1): 24–42.

Martins, Dylan M., Joy M. Manda, Michael J. Goard, and Philip R. L. Parker. 2024. "Building Egocentric Models of Local Space from Retinal Input." *Current Biology 34* (23): R1185–R1202. doi: 10.1016/j.cub.2024.10.057.

O'Keefe, John, and Lynn Nadel. 1978. *The Hippocampus as a Cognitive Map*. Oxford: Oxford University Press.

Pashler, Harold E. 1999. *The Psychology of Attention*. Cambridge, MA: MIT Press.

Posner, Michael I. 1980. "Orienting of Attention." *Quarterly Journal of Experimental Psychology* 32 (1): 3–25. doi: 10.1080/00335558008248231.

Saygin, Ayse Pinar, and Martin I. Sereno. 2008. "Retinotopy and Attention in Human Occipital, Temporal, Parietal, and Frontal Cortex." *Cerebral Cortex* 18 (9): 2158–2168. doi: 10.1093/cercor/bhm242.

Snyder, Larry H., Aaron P. Batista, and Richard A. Andersen. 1997. "Coding of Intention in the Posterior Parietal Cortex." *Nature* 386 (6621): 167–170. doi: 10.1038/386167a0.

Torkel, Hafting, Marianne Fyhn, Sturla Molden, May-Britt Moser, and Edvard I. Moser. 2005. "Microstructure of a Spatial Map in the Entorhinal Cortex." *Nature* 436 (11): 801–806.

Other Sources Used

Burgess, Neil. 2006. "Spatial Memory: How Egocentric and Allocentric Combine." *Trends in Cognitive Sciences* 10 (12): 551–557. doi: 10.1016/j.tics.2006.10.005.

Halligan, Peter W., and John C. Marshall. 1991. "Left Neglect for Near but not Far Space in Man." *Nature* 350 (6318): 498–500. doi: 10.1038/350498a0.

Thier, Peter, and Richard A. Andersen. 1998. "Electrical Microstimulation Distinguishes Distinct Saccade-Related Areas in the Posterior Parietal Cortex." *Journal of Neurophysiology* 80 (4): 1713–1735.

Weintraub, Sandra, and M. Marsel Mesulam. 1989. "Neglect: Hemispheric Specialization, Behavioral Components and Anatomical Correlates." In *Handbook of Neuropsychology*, edited by Francois Boller and Jordan Grafman (pp. 357–374), vol. 2. Amsterdam: Elsevier.

Wilson, Matthew A., and Bruce L. McNaughton. 1994. "Reactivation of Hippocampal Ensemble Memories During Sleep." *Science* 265 (5172): 676–679. doi: 10.1126/science.8036517.

Further Reading

Aguirre, Geoffrey K. 2003. "Topographical Disorientation: A Disorder of Way-Finding Ability." In *Neurological Foundations of Cognitive Neuroscience*, edited by Mark D'Esposito (pp. 90–108). Cambridge, MA: MIT Press.

Thorough overview of the clinical aspects of this intriguing disorder, and its implications for our understanding of spatial cognition.

Burgess, Neil. 2006. "Spatial Memory: How Egocentric and Allocentric Combine." *Trends in Cognitive Science* 10 (12): 551–557. doi: 10.1016/j.tics.2006.10.005.

Synthesis of human behavioral studies of navigation and spatial representation with the neurophysiological representation of space in the rat, monkey, and human to argue that parallel, interacting ego and allocentric reference frames guide spatial cognition.

Desimone, Robert, and John Duncan. 1995. "Neural Mechanisms of Selective Visual Attention." *Annual Review of Neuroscience* 18: 193–222. doi: 10.1146/annurev.ne.18.030195.001205.

The highly influential articulation of the principle of biased competition that draws equally from theory, experimental psychology, and neurophysiology.

Fiebelkorn, I. C., and S. Kastner. 2019. "A Rhythmic Theory of Attention." *Trends in Cognitive Sciences 23*: 87–101. doi: 10.1016/j.tics.2018.11.009.

A concise summary of evidence for the idea of "sustained attention" as periodic sampling among multiple locations and/or objects.

Itthipuripat, S., T. C. Sprague, and J. T. Serences. 2019. "Functional MRI and EEG Index Complementary Attentional Modulations." *Journal of Neuroscience* 39: 6162–6179. doi: 10.1523/JNEUROSCI.2519-18.2019.

A head-to-head comparison of EEG/ERP vs. fMRI signals measured from the same individuals performing the same visual attention tasks.

Lezak, Muriel D. 1995. *Neuropsychological Assessment*, 3rd ed. New York: Oxford University Press.

This is the authoritative compendium of seemingly every neuropsychological test ever developed, how it is administered, and what behavioral and/or cognitive functions that test measures. Among these are many tests of spatial cognition and of attention.

CHAPTER 8

Skeletomotor Control

KEY THEMES

- Motor control is governed by three principal circuits: the corticospinal system that carries efferent motor commands from motor cortex to the spinal circuits that carry out motor commands; the cortico-cerebellar systems processes a copy of the efferent motor signal and feeds back to motor cortex so as to fine-tune ongoing movement; and the cortico-basal ganglia system that acts as a gate that controls the timing of movements and that selects habitual movements.
- The motor cortex plans and generates commands in abstract x, y, z coordinates, and the spinal cord translates these commands (often nonlinearly) into a set of muscle tensions needed to carry out the action.
- Despite its generally homuncular functional topography, the primary motor cortex differs from sensory analogs in that its representation of the body surface is not highly precise, and it also represents actions that are not tied to any one part of the body.
- M1 neurons have relatively broad tuning, and precise control of movement is achieved via population coding – the summation of input from thousands of units firing at varying intensities.
- Principles of representational geometry have been used to suggest that motor planning takes place in "action-null" subspaces, then rotate into "action-potent" communication subspaces in order to drive movement; and that low-dimensional "neural modes," rather than individual neurons, may be the representational building blocks of skeletomotor control.
- Neuropsychological evidence has been taken as evidence that a core function of posterior parietal cortex (PPC) may be to determine *how* visual information can be used to guide behavior.
- The unique wiring of the cerebellum makes it a key neural substrate for motor learning, fine-tuning ongoing movements, and, perhaps, encoding and refining cognitive models of the world.
- Cortico-basal ganglia-thalamic circuits govern the timing of the initiation of movement, including when a movement that's being triggered suddenly needs to be stopped.
- Common principles of network and neurochemical dynamics (including a key role for dopamine [DA]) across "affective," "cognitive," and "motoric" basal ganglia systems suggest that many principles of motor control generalize to these other domains of behavior.
- The acquisition and modification of stereotyped sequences of movements, including what we think of as habits, rely on principles of reinforcement learning.
- The discovery of mirror neurons in premotor cortex (PMC) has generated intriguing theories ranging from the understanding of actions and intentions of others, to atypical neurological development (e.g., autism spectrum disorder [ASD]), to the evolution of human culture.

Companion Website: www.wiley.com/go/postle/cognitiveneuroscience3e

CONTENTS

Our introduction to the frontal lobes came in *Chapter 1*, where we considered a nineteenth-century breakthrough in thinking about how the brain controls movement of the body, and one relating to the production of speech. The former is most relevant here. The observations of the neurologist Jackson gave rise to the idea of a somatotopic organization of the brain system controlling movement in humans. The electrical stimulation experiments of Fritsch and Hitzig, in the dog, indicated that the motor cortex was localized to the frontal cortex, and that distinct **motor effectors** contralateral to stimulation sites were represented by discrete regions within this lobe. In addition to fleshing out more details about the structure and function of the motor system, this chapter will introduce many concepts related to the control of action that will be highly germane to many of the remaining topics to be covered in this book, including *cognitive control*, *decision making*, *language*, *social behavior*, and *consciousness*. Indeed, some have argued that much of our thought and behavior, no matter how abstract and "high level," can be construed as implementations, at varying levels of abstraction, of the same principles of motor control that we will consider in detail in this chapter.

The Organization of the Motor System

The Anatomy of the Motor System

Primary motor cortex (M1) occupies the anterior bank of the central sulcus and the caudal portion of the precentral gyrus, a region classified as BA 4 that stretches from the medial wall of the hemisphere to the dorsal lip of the Sylvian fissure. In loose analogy to cortical sensory systems, there are two adjacent motor-related fields with "second-level functions," both sharing BA 6: the premotor cortex (PMC) of the rostral half of the precentral gyrus and the supplementary motor area (SMA) located superior to PMC on the lateral surface and extending into the midline, and rostral to the superior-most and medial portions of M1. Unlike with sensory systems, however, the functions of M1, PMC, and SMA aren't as hierarchically organized as are, say, V1, V2, and MT. For example, each of these three motor areas sends projections from the cortex to the areas of the spinal cord that directly trigger movement. (Thus, for simplicity, when describing general properties that apply to each, the term "motor cortex" will be used to refer nonspecifically to M1, PMC, and SMA.)

The motor cortices are a central hub in three systems that carry action-related signals. The fibers carrying the signals that descend along the ventral spinal cord to trigger movements of the body are called **motor efferents**. The other two carry motor-related signals and are considered **recurrent "circuits"** (often called "loops") in that they eventually feed back onto the frontal cortex. (I'm using scare quotes here because, although they can be thought of as circuits or loops in a very schematic summary of the motor system, when considered in detail, both are complicated systems. Another point to raise here is that although the cerebellum and basal ganglia play central roles in motor control, they are both also involved in many other domains of behavior.) Let's consider each circuit in turn.

The Corticospinal Tract

The giant pyramidal cells of layer V of motor cortex send axons that descend through the brain, funneling together as the internal capsule that passes between the (laterally located) lentiform nucleus of the basal ganglia and the (medially located) caudate nucleus and thalamus, decussating in the caudal brain stem, and descending in the ventral spinal cord as the corticospinal tract (*Figure 8.1*). Each corticospinal fiber activates motor neurons in the cord either via direct synaptic connections or, most typically, indirectly via local circuitry in the cord. Motor neurons send axons that innervate muscles, but because their cell bodies are located within the spinal cord, they are considered part of the central nervous system (CNS). Their functional organization can be considered from two perspectives: from that of the muscle, each muscle is innervated by a grouping of neurons called a motor neuron pool; from that of the individual motor neuron, it and each of the muscle fibers that it innervates make up a motor unit. Motor

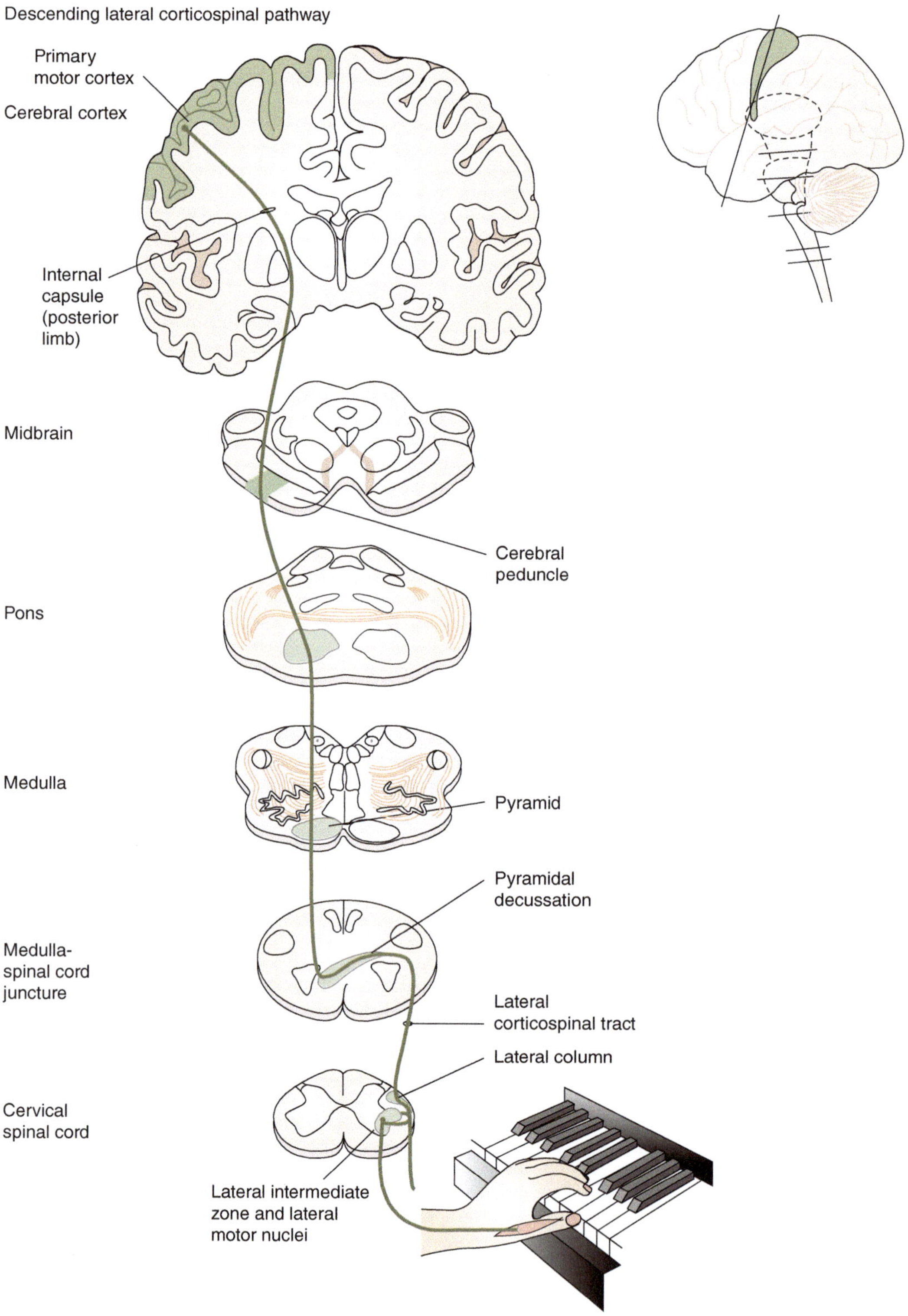

FIGURE 8.1 The descending corticospinal pathway.
Source: Kandel et al., 2000 / McGraw-Hill.

neurons release the neurotransmitter acetyl choline (ACh) at their synapses, which are often referred to as the neuromuscular junction. More details on muscles are given in the upcoming section, *The Biomechanics of Motor Control.*

The Cortico-Cerebellar Circuit

This circuit is a canonical example of the phenomenon of **efference copy**: a copy of the efferent signal is used by the cerebellum to compare the intended outcome of the outgoing motor command against information about the actual outcome (conveyed by ascending sensory signals) and, if the two don't match up, send a corrective signal back to the motor cortex so that the next movement will be more successful. The cerebellum is an intriguing structure in that it contains 50 billion of the roughly 80 billion neurons of the brain, yet, as the neurobiologist and theorist Giulio Tononi has noted, its complete removal has effectively no impact on the subjective sense of consciousness. It is made up of hundreds of thousands of parallel, modular (i.e., not interconnected) circuits that are constantly comparing motor output to sensory feedback so as to fine-tune the targeting and smooth execution of our movements, and to help us maintain postural stability. The circuit is one-way, linking the frontal cortex to the pons to cerebellar cortex to cerebellar deep nuclei to thalamus and back to the frontal cortex. The densely foliated cerebellar cortex is shaped like one half of a sawed-in-two tennis ball, but with thicker walls due to deep folds between the lobes of the cerebellar cortex, and the fibers projecting from this cortex to the deep nuclei lying near the "deepest" point of this concavity. Also projecting into the cerebellum are ascending projections carrying information about the periphery (touch on the skin, body configuration from muscle stretch receptors, and joint-position receptors) and overall body position and balance from the vestibular system. The workings and functions of the cerebellum will be considered in the upcoming section on *Cerebellum: Motor Learning, Balance, . . . and Mental Representation?*

The Cortico-Basal Ganglia-Thalamic Circuits

This circuit and its nuclei play important roles in motor control, learning, and motivated behavior, and a variety of dysfunctions within it can result in disorders ranging from Parkinson's disease (PD) (impairing movement and high-level cognition) to unilateral neglect to pathological gambling. As illustrated in *Figure 8.2*, its unidirectional circuits comprise a "direct pathway" (cortex to neostriatum to internal segment of the globus pallidus [GPi]/substantia nigra pars reticulata [SNpr] to thalamus back to cortex), an "indirect pathway" (cortex to neostriatum to external segment of the globus pallidus [GPe] to subthalamic nucleus [STN] to GPi/SNpr to thalamus back to cortex), and a "hyperdirect pathway" (cortex to STN). At the gross anatomical level, there are five relatively segregated *cortico-basal ganglia-thalamic circuits*, each associated with dissociable classes of behavior: *motor, oculomotor, dorsolateral prefrontal, lateral orbitofrontal,* and *limbic* (*Figure 8.3.A*). *Figure 8.3.B* illustrates the connectivity of the cortico-basal ganglia-thalamic motor circuit. Although the focus during this chapter will be on the motor circuit, a noteworthy property of each of these circuits is the way each integrates inputs from multiple cortical regions and funnels the integrated result back onto the originating region of the frontal cortex. Another common feature of these circuits is that the neostriatal node of each is densely innervated by dopaminergic fibers from a midbrain nucleus called the substantia nigra pars compacta (SNpc). (The distinctive black pigmentation of the substantia nigra ["black substance" in Latin], visible to the naked eye, derives from the high concentration in its neurons of the enzyme tyrosine hydroxylase, which is critical for the synthesis of DA.)

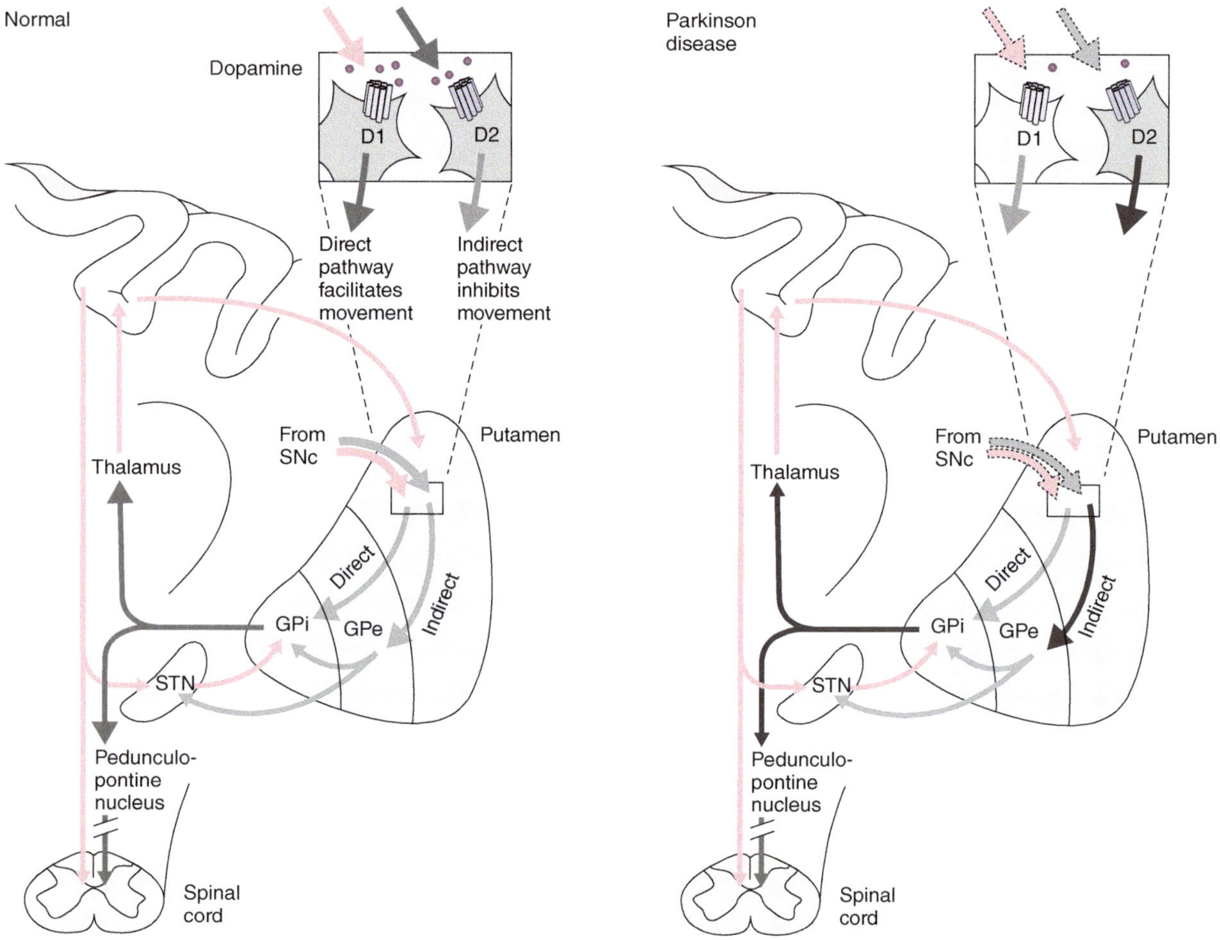

FIGURE 8.2 Schematic illustrations of the direct, indirect, and hyperdirect pathways of the basal ganglia, in the healthy ("Normal") state on the left, and in Parkinson's disease (PD) on the right. Red arrows connote excitatory pathways, gray inhibitory, and disease-related changes in PD are indicated by the dotted outlines of the "from SNc" arrows that connote a decrease of dopamine (DA) resulting from degeneration of the nigrostriatal tract, and the darker arrow illustrating the resultant increase of the influence of the indirect pathway. The hyperdirect pathway is illustrated as an arrow splitting off from the corticospinal pathway to synapse on the STN. SNc = substantia nigra pars compacta; GPe = external segment of the globus pallidus; GPi = internal segment of the globus pallidus; STN = subthalamic nucleus.

Source: Kandel et al., 2000 / McGraw-Hill.

Functional Principles of Motor Control

The Biomechanics of Motor Control

Although moving the body in a coordinated fashion is something that we do effortlessly, often "thoughtlessly," this subjective facility masks a very complicated engineering problem. To summarize just one example, the movements of our arms from almost any point A to B are remarkably straight, despite the fact that executing such movements entails the precisely coordinated, simultaneous changing of joint angles – at the shoulder and the elbow (*Figure 8.4*). How does the nervous system accomplish this?

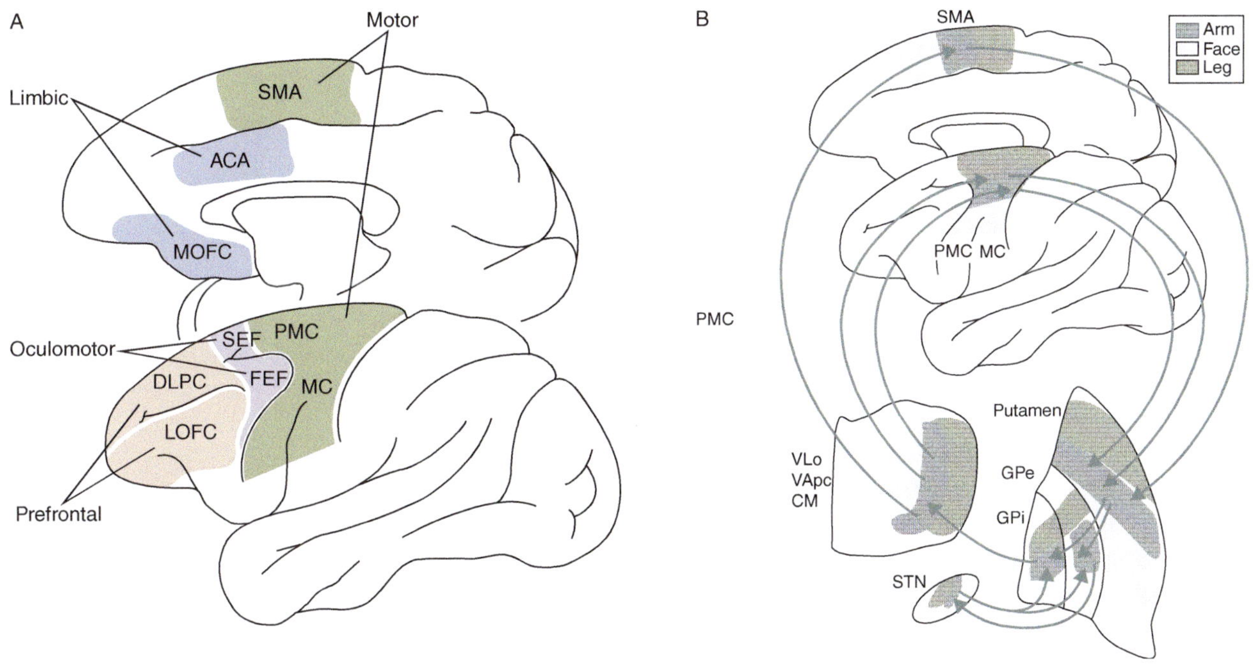

FIGURE 8.3 The five cortico-basal ganglia-thalamic circuits.

Source: Kandel et al., 2000 / McGraw-Hill. **A.** Frontal targets the five loops. ACA = anterior cingulate area; MOFC = medial orbital frontal cortex; LOFC = lateral orbitofrontal cortex. **B.** Diagram of segregation of somatotopic information at each stage of the motor circuit. GPe = external segment of the globus pallidus; GPi = internal segment of the globus pallidus; STN = subthalamic nucleus; VLo = pars oralis segment of the ventrolateral (VL) nucleus of the thalamus; VApc = parvocellular segment of the ventral anterior (VA) nucleus of the thalamus; CM = centromedian nucleus of the thalamus.

Muscles Behave Like Springs The tissue that puts the "motor" in "motor control," of course, is muscle. To move one's hand from point A to point B, it is necessary to contract the appropriate sets of muscles such that the joints that connect the bones of the arm move in the ways illustrated in the lower columns. Consider the movement from T1➔T4. Although *Figure 8.4.A* is a static image, one can easily visualize how the positions of the forearm and of the upper arm will necessarily be different when the hand is at T1 than when it is at T4. Specifically, at T1, the forearm will be closer to the chest and the upper arm "pointing more to the side," whereas at T4, the two parts of the arm will be in a "more extended" configuration, as when reaching "straight ahead." To *move* these parts of the arm from one configuration to the other, what the body must do is change the joint angles of the shoulder and elbow (identified in *Figure 8.4.A* as α and θ, respectively). At a simplified level, changing the tensions of each of the antagonistically paired biceps and triceps muscles will change the angle of the elbow, and changing the tensions of a more complicated arrangement of muscles will change the angle of the shoulder. Thus, even the relatively simple act of moving the hand from T1 to T4 requires a precise, exquisitely choreographed sequence of muscle contractions (and relaxations) that will produce a smooth, straight motion. What *Figure 8.4.C* captures very clearly is how three simple movements that would seem to be very similar to each other require a distinct choreography of transformations of joint angles and joint angular velocities.

Fortunately, the mind-bogglingly complicated sets of nonlinear computations required each time we move our bodies are simplified by a felicitous mechanical property of muscles: they behave like springs. That is, one has to only set the tensions on a set of muscles and they will "automatically" adjust to a new equilibrium point, pulling the bones to which they are attached into a new position. Therefore, in principle, each unique location in the peripersonal space of an individual, identifiable with a unique set of x, y, z coordinates, has a unique set of muscle tensions associated with it. For example, from where you are currently sitting (or standing; or reclining; or ... there is a unique set of tensions required of the muscles

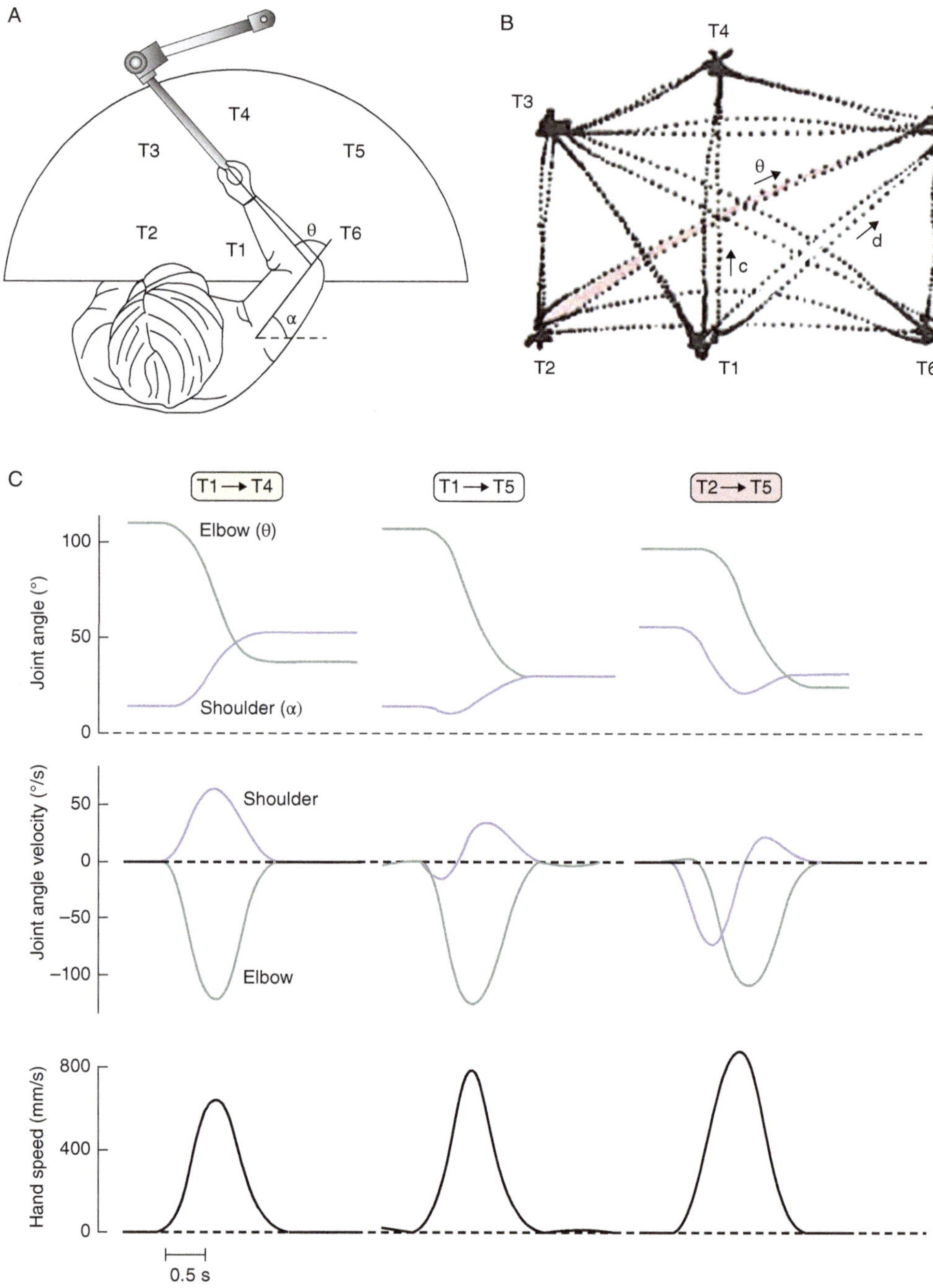

FIGURE 8.4 **A.** Top-down view of a subject grasping the handle of a manipulandum, which can be moved in a 2D plane to each of the six targets indicated on the table. **B.** Movement paths (two between each target) for a subject. **C.** Joint angle, joint angular velocity (i.e., speed at which joint angle is changing), and hand speed are plotted against time to execute each of the three movements from **B**.

Source: Kandel et al., 2000 / McGraw-Hill.

controlling your shoulder, elbow, wrist, and index finger in order for you to touch your finger to this period →. ← (Go ahead, do it. No one is watching.) And so, in principle, your cortex only needs to issue the command *Touch that period*, and the requisite muscle-tension settings will automatically deliver your index finger to that point. The nonlinear transformations of joint angles that enable your finger to travel from wherever it was to the period that you are now pointing to "just happen" as a consequence of establishing these new settings; they don't have to be explicitly calculated and commanded.

Motor Computations in the Spinal Cord If the motor cortex needs only to specify a new endpoint for, say, the index finger, what translates between the presumed command to *Go to X, Y, Z* and the resetting of muscle tensions? (I.e., to execute a movement, each muscle only experiences a change in the amount of ACh being released onto it; it can't "know" anything about points *X, Y, Z*.) The answer is that this translation happens in the networks of interneurons in the spinal cord to which most corticospinal fibers project. Evidence for this was first produced in the frog, subsequently in the rat, in an experimental preparation in which all descending skeletomotor and ascending somatosensory connections between the spinal cord and the brain are severed. Microstimulation is then applied to the portion of the spinal cord whose motor neurons innervate, say, the left forelimb. The intriguing finding is that stimulation in this single location always brings the forepaw to the same location in space, regardless of what its starting location was. The area being stimulated, therefore, is converting that burst of electrical stimulation into the new tension settings of the muscles controlling the shoulder and elbow joints that bring the limb into that position in space. Stimulate a second spot in the cord, and the limb moves to a different location. Furthermore, a property whose importance will become evident further along in this chapter is that the simultaneous stimulation of both spots moves the limb to a third location. Therefore, in effect, the motor cortex issues the general command, and the spinal cord "takes care of the details."

In addition to being able to translate cortical commands into precise settings of muscle tensions, the spinal cord also contains what are referred to as "pattern generators." Thus, for example, early-to-mid twentieth-century experiments established that if the connections between an animal's brain and spinal cord are severed, and the animal is suspended in a harness over a treadmill, it will walk with an appropriate gait when the treadmill starts moving. Not only that, its gait adjusts appropriately to treadmill speed, from a trot to a gallop to a walk. The only explanation for such demonstrations is that remarkably sophisticated sensorimotor control circuitry exists within the spinal cord itself.

Motor Cortex

Okay, so we've established that an animal can effectively walk, gallop, and trot, as appropriate, without any input from the brain. So what does the motor cortex do? (Why do we need it?) In a sentence, it controls the *volitional* movement of the body. Let's take a closer look.

The Motor Homunculus Unless you have just picked up this book for the first time, and opened to this chapter, you won't be surprised to learn that M1 has a rough somatotopic organization (as do at least four other regions in motor cortex). *Figure 8.5.A* is also taken from surgical mapping studies of Penfield and Rasmussen (1950). One important difference between the primary somatosensory and motor cortices, however, is that the latter's map lacks the same high-fidelity correspondence to different parts of the body. This is in part because the smallest unit that the motor cortex can represent corresponds to bones, rather than the surface of the skin. For example, it wouldn't make sense for M1 to represent different parts of the forearm in the way that S1 does, with a set of receptive fields that cover its entire surface. Rather, M1 represents the forearm as a unit that can be moved. Another, more fundamental, reason is that M1 represents *actions*, not just parts of the body. For example, it is often pointed out that a person's handwriting looks similar (albeit progressively sloppier) when the pen is held in the right hand vs. the left hand vs. in the mouth vs. between the toes. Thus, the representation of the shape of one's handwriting must exist in a format that is accessible by any set of effectors that need to implement it. Nonetheless, the fact that there is a mapping between different parts of M1 and different parts of the body means that the motor cortex doesn't only employ purely abstract representations like "point X, Y, Z," or the shape of one's handwriting. Rather, it clearly chooses which effector(s) will be used to carry out any particular action. Furthermore, it also controls the **kinematics** and **dynamics** of movement, such as the speed with which the arm will move, or the tightness with which the fingers will grip.

In addition to these considerations, neuroscientist Jon Kaas (2012) has proposed that if one "zooms in" from the overall somatotopic organization of M1 to look at smaller regions

FIGURE 8.5 Two versions of the motor homunculus.
Source: Gordon et al., 2023 / Springer Nature / CC BY 4.0.

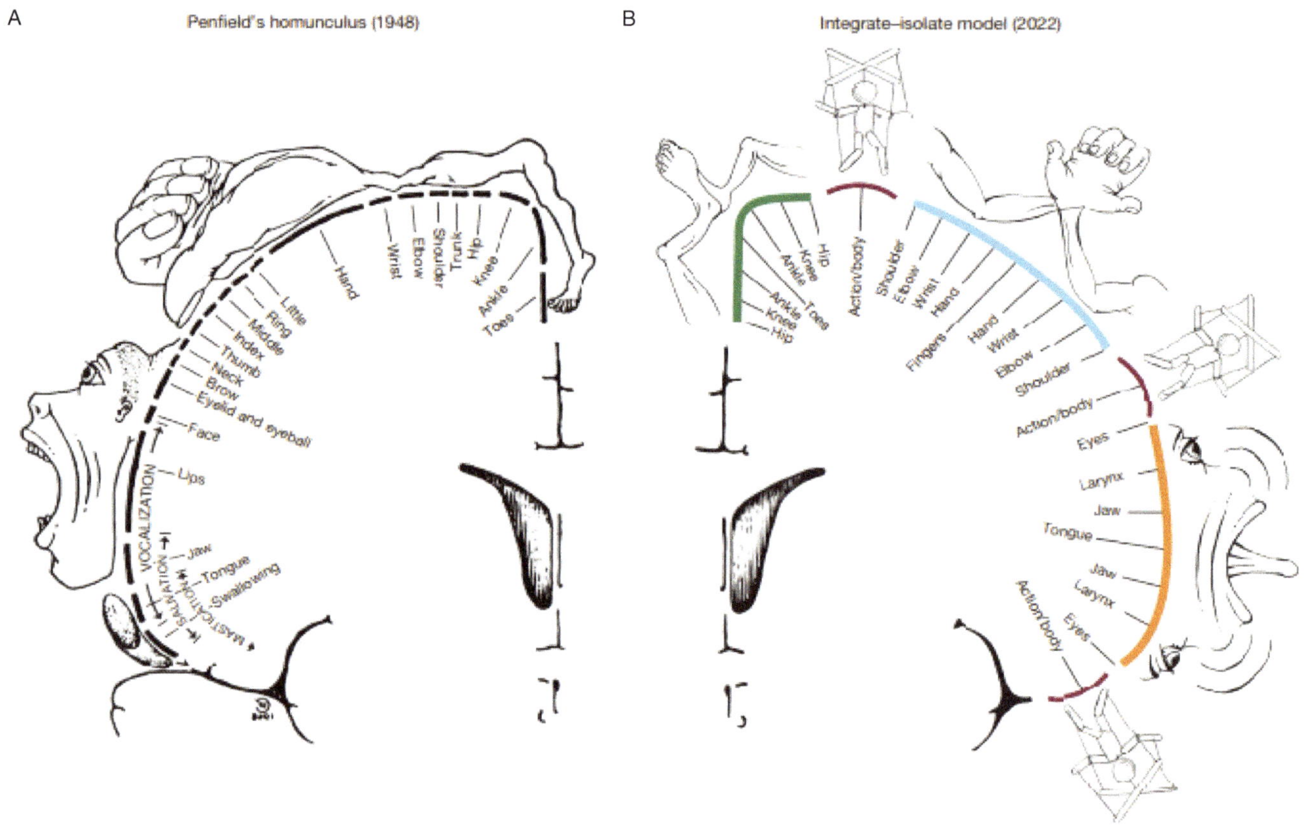

FIGURE 8.5.A The Penfield and Rassmussen (1950) motor homunculus. Same graphical conventions as *Figure 2.16*.

FIGURE 8.5.B The "integrate-isolate" organizational scheme proposed by Gordon et al. (2023) differs from the classical model in two prominent ways. First, effector-specific representations of the feet and legs, arms and hands, and face and mouth are organized in concentric rings, with the "isolated" distal body parts that are associated with fine motor control (toes, fingers, and tongue, respectively) surrounded by the lower-precision proximal parts of the respective zone of the body. Second, interspersed between each effector-specific region of M1 is an "inter-effector region" (designated by the puppet icons) that is preferentially connected with regions outside the motor system, and proposed to be involved in action planning that integrates goals and information about the internal state of the body. In the legend accompanying this figure in Gordon et al. (2023), the authors note that "As with Penfield's original drawing, this diagram is intended to illustrate organizational principles, and must not be over-interpreted as a precise map" (p. 7).

in greater detail, the coherent body map is "fractured" into clusters of cortical columns that are organized according to movement sequences, such as reaching, grasping, or shielding the head. Thus, for example, within the large expanse of cortex that we label the "hand area," there will be columns of neurons corresponding to the arm, to the wrist, and to individual fingers that, when activated in the appropriate sequence, produce the picking-up-food-and-bringing-it-to-my-mouth movement sequence that we all execute several times each day. Consistent with this idea is the more recent proposal, illustrated in *Figure 8.5.B*, that the classical effector-specific organization of the motor homunculus is interrupted by patches with strong connectivity to regions outside the motor system, including the cingulo-opercular network (e.g., *Figure 4.19.C*), which is implicated in processing information about actions at an abstract level (including error monitoring) and about the internal physiological milieu (including level of satiety, arousal, and pain). *Figure 8.6* illustrates evidence for this "integrate-isolate" organizational scheme.

Turning to PMC and SMA, how do they differ from M1? For now, we'll content ourselves with the short-hand summary that they contribute to high-level aspects of motor control, such as planning to make a movement, imagining making a movement, and coordinating motor

FIGURE 8.6 Activity profiles in M1 of two healthy young adults, as assessed with fMRI.
Source: Gordon et al., 2023 / Springer Nature / CC BY 4.0.

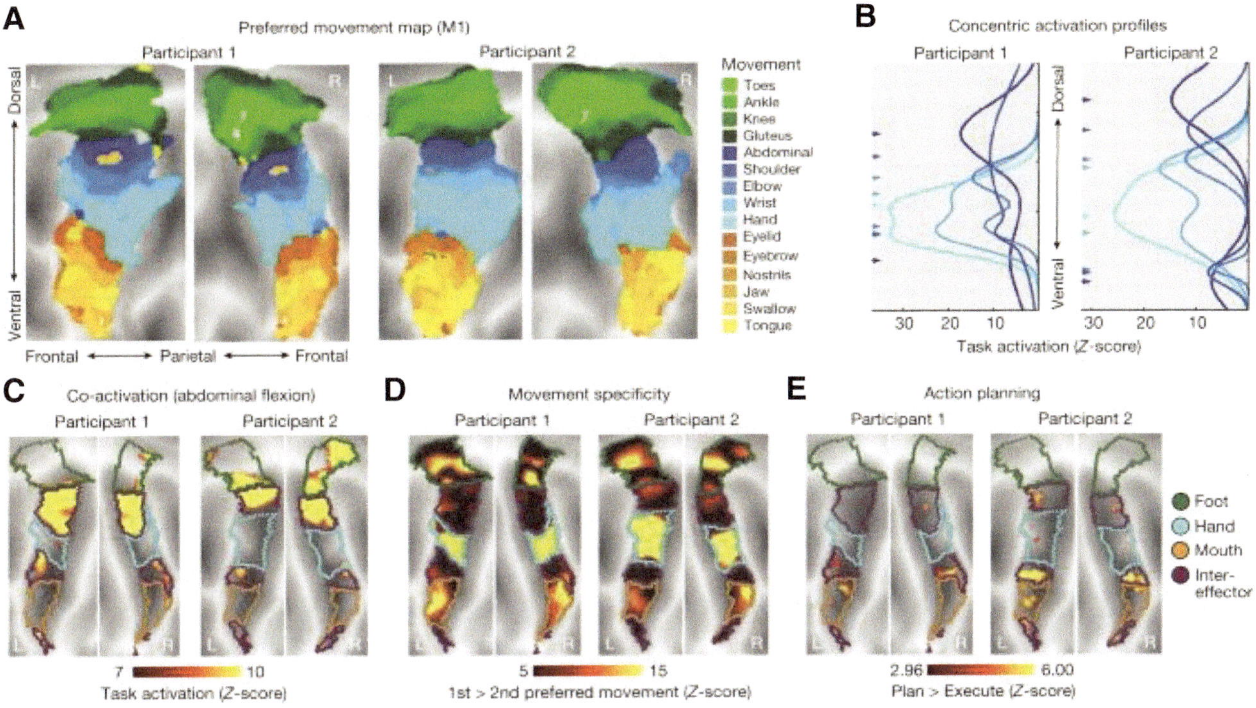

FIGURE 8.6.A Winner-take-all activation maps of M1, color-coded to show the body part whose movement produced maximal activation at each vertex. (The anatomical and fMRI data have been converted from the 3D volumes made up of voxels to 2D surface maps made up of vertices.)

FIGURE 8.6.B The concentric-circle organization of arm-and-hand representations, illustrated with fits of two-peak Gaussians to activation values from along the dorsal–ventral axes of the activation maps from A. (Note that two peaks accommodate the fact that a circle superimposed on a line crosses that line in two places.) Each fitted function corresponds to peak activations of movement of the abdominals, shoulder, elbow, wrist, and hand; the colors corresponding to the legend from A and the locations of the peaks are also marked on the vertical axis.

FIGURE 8.6.C Localization of inter-effector regions with a task requiring a low degree of fine motor control (in this case, isometric contraction of abdominal muscles; eyebrow raising was also used). Green, blue, and orange lines outline leg-foot, arm-hand, and face-mouth effector-specific regions, respectively, and purple lines outline inter-effector regions.

FIGURE 8.6.D Difference maps of activity from the preferred and second-most preferred movements of each effector-specific region, the high Z scores indicating considerable specificity within these regions, but not within the inter-effector regions.

FIGURE 8.6.E Activity evoked by an action-planning (prior to movement) is higher in inter-effector regions than in effector-specific regions.

sequences made up of many individual actions. So that's an overview of what the motor cortex does. Now, how does it work?

The Neurophysiology of Movement

EEG and LFP Correlates In the decade following Berger's discovery of the alpha rhythm (section *The Relation Between Visual Processing and the Brain's Physiological State, Chapter 3*), one of several rhythms to be discovered in the scalp EEG was the mu. Although the mu rhythm occupied the same frequency band as alpha, it differed in morphology – as a series of thin, spiky peaks surrounded by rounded troughs (suggesting the shape of the Greek letter "μ") – in topography – being maximal over central electrodes – and in function – being insensitive to perceptual factors, but being related to movement. Specifically, the amplitude of the mu rhythm is maximal when the body is at rest and begins to decline roughly two seconds prior to a movement. Such "mu desynchronizations" can be local to the cortical representation of the effector being moved, if one moves, for example, just the finger, toe, or tongue. Also prominent in the functioning of the motor system are oscillations in the beta band. Although also inversely related to motor activity, the timing of changes in the beta band tends to be much more tightly coupled to the initiation of movement. Thus, there's a sense in which both the central mu and the central beta rhythms are analogous, for skeletomotor control, to posterior alpha for visual perception, in that they reflect a state of suppression and/or "idling" in the thalamocortical system producing them. (*Figure 8.7* illustrates mu and beta, recorded intracranially from the motor cortex of a monkey performing visually guided movements of a handle from a central location to one of six radial locations [not unlike the task illustrated in *Figure 8.4*]. It also nicely illustrates how an oscillating signal can be trial-averaged to generate an ERP [as discussed in section *Analysis of Time-Varying Signals*, *Chapter 4*].)

(In the 1950s, the French neurologist/neurophysiologist Henri Gastaut [1915–1995] and his colleagues made the discovery that mu desynchronization also occurs when the subject is immobile, but watching the movements of others. As we shall see further along in this chapter, this phenomenon has acquired considerable attention of late in relation to hypotheses about the function of "mirror neurons.")

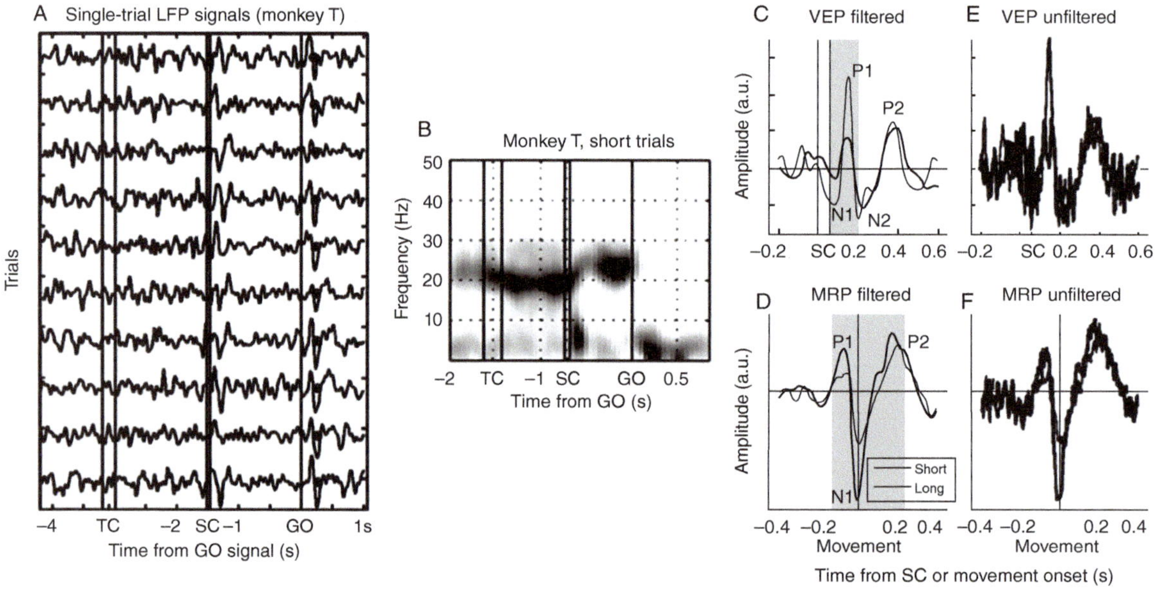

FIGURE 8.7 Movement-related dynamics in the LFP. **A.** Illustrates traces from several individual trials, bandpass filtered from 1 to 15 Hz (to emphasize the sensory- and motor-related evoked potentials), time-locked to the GO signal, and ordered by increasing RT (RT for each trial is indicated by a filled circle appearing in each trace; they are difficult to see, but occur at ~250 ms following the GO signal). The axis along the bottom of the figure shows the timeline of the task: TC is the "temporal cue" that informed the animal whether delay would be short (700 or 1000 ms, depending on the monkey) or long (1500 or 2000 ms); SC = the spatial cue, a visual cue that indicated the target to which the handle must be moved; GO = the signal to initiate movement; RT = "response time," defined as the lag between the GO signal and the instant when the handle began to move (i.e., movement-initiation time); MT = movement time, the time between the RT and the acquisition of the target. **B.** Time-frequency representation of trials from A, but without a low-pass filter. Darker color corresponds to higher power. Pre-movement power is dominated by activity in the beta band, the center frequency shifting from ~19 to ~23 Hz after the SC, then stopping abruptly with the onset of the GO signal. Brief increases in low-frequency power correspond to evoked responses. **C** and **D.** Visual-evoked potential (VEP) and movement-related potential (MRP), respectively, time-locked to SC and RT, respectively, filtered from 1 to 15 Hz. **E** and **F.** Same data as **C** and **D**, but unfiltered.

Source: Kandel et al., 2000 / McGraw-Hill.

And so, we've established from scalp and LFP recordings that the motor cortex is maintained in a functionally inactive state that is lifted just prior to the execution of a movement, that sensory signals triggering a movement are registered in this region, and that a large ERP immediately precedes the movement. Next, let's "drill down" to the level of the individual neuron.

Single-Unit Activity Reveals Population Coding Among the pyramidal cells of layer V of M1, one finds massive Betz cells, discovered by the Ukrainian anatomist Vladimir Alekseyevich Betz (1834–1894) only a few years after the pioneering microstimulation studies of Fritsch and Hitzig (1870; section *The localization of motor functions, Chapter 1*). These are the largest neurons in the nervous system, with large-diameter axons seemingly specialized to send neural impulses very rapidly and over long distances. (Subsequent research has established that many other neurons contribute to the corticospinal tract, with axons from Betz cells contributing only between 3% and 10% of the total.) The breakthrough insight about how these neurons actually generate coordinated movement had to wait another 100 years, for the research of Apostolos Georgopoulos and his colleagues.

Georgopoulos, Joyn Kalaska, Roberto Caminiti, and Joe Massey (1982) recorded from the arm area of M1 from five hemispheres of four different monkeys while they performed a "center-out" task virtually identical to the one used in the experiment featured in Figure 8.7. The results, illustrated in *Figure 8.8*, revealed another important difference between M1 and the primary sensory areas that we have studied to date: instead of narrowly tuned response properties of, for example, V1 and S1, M1 neurons had remarkably broad tuning. *Figure 8.8*, for example, illustrates a neuron whose responses are nearly indistinguishable for movements of 135°, 180°, and 225° (as, indeed, they are for movements of 45°, 0°, and 315°). Different neurons had different overall preferred directions: for example, if *Figure 8.8* illustrates a "to-the-left" neuron, others were "away-and-to-the-right" (270° being toward the animal's body), and so forth.

Upon first consideration, it's difficult to see how the activity in neurons with such broad tuning could be responsible for arm movements that we know can be much, much more fine-grained than the separated-by-45° movements required of the monkeys in this experiment. The principle must be different from what we've seen with sensory systems, for which it's customary to think of individual neurons as acting as feature detectors. Although no one really believes that a single neuron (or column) in V1 can be responsible for a single visual percept, one can nonetheless imagine, in "shorthand," that viewing a vertical line preferentially activates neurons tuned for vertical orientations, and that rotating that line ever so slightly in a clockwise direction will preferentially activate different sets of neurons tuned for precisely this slight tilt. With M1 tuning properties, however, it'd be as though the V1 cell were equally responsive to orientations from 135° to 225°. How could one construct a system with elements whose tuning is so sloppy? The answer came to the research team after they considered the entire sample of 241 neurons from which they recorded in the arm area in M1: *population coding.*

Instead of thinking of the motor system as being made up of discrete "channels," each one specialized for its own narrowly defined features, *Figure 8.8* illustrates a fundamentally different principle of neural coding. It presents a graphical representation of the response of each of the 241 neurons to each of the eight directions of motion. Each line in each of the eight, radially arrayed "explosion" plots is a vector whose length corresponds to the firing rate of a neuron during motion in that direction. (Responses of the neuron illustrated in *Figure 8.8*, therefore, correspond to one of the longish vectors at the 135°, 180°, and 225° positions, to a somewhat shorter vector at 90°, to one shorter still at 270°, and to vectors of length 0 at 45°, 0°, and 315°.) The "vectorial hypothesis" proposed by Georgopoulos and colleagues in 1983 makes the assumption that each neuron's activity on any given trial corresponds to the magnitude of its influence on the direction of movement on that trial. Now recall from mathematics that a vector is a way of representing a force that has a magnitude and a direction, and that if two or more forces are simultaneously present, their vectors can be combined and the resultant "vector sum" (or "vector average," depending on which operation one performs) will indicate what their combined effects will yield. This is what the dashed lines with arrowheads

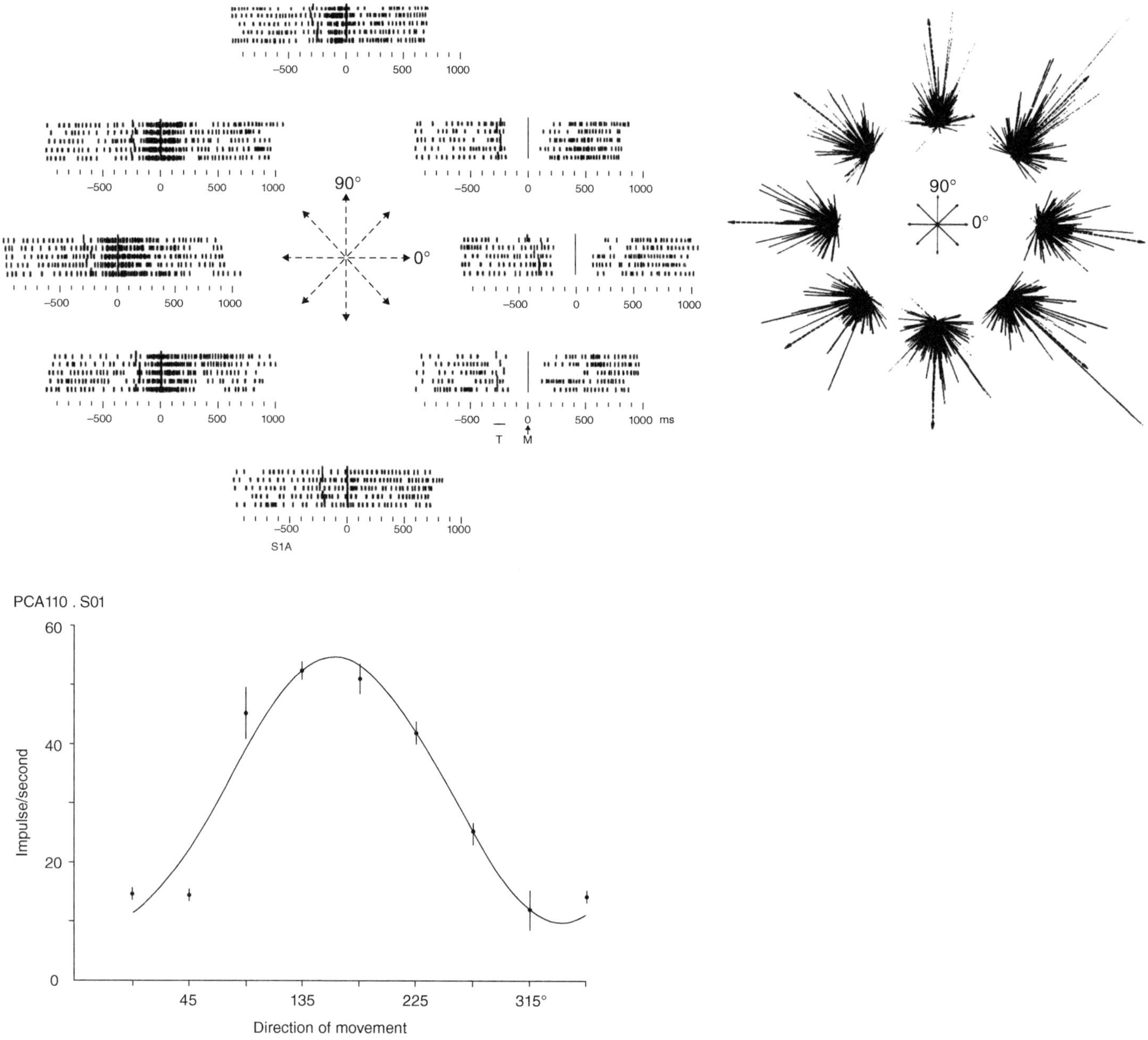

FIGURE 8.8 The electrophysiology of primary motor cortex. Top panel displays responses of a single neuron from the arm region of M1 for each of five reaches made in each of eight directions, aligned to the time of initiation of movement (arbitrarily labeled "0"). Labels under the raster plot corresponding to movement in the 315° direction indicate the time of the GO signal (labeled "T") and initiation-of-movement time (M). Bottom panel is the tuning curve derived from these data. The panel to the right is the vector representation of the activity of 241 neurons recorded from the arm region of M1, for each of eight directions of movement (center of figure). Dashed lines with arrowheads are vector sums derived from each of the eight directions of movement.

Source: Georgopoulos et al., 1982 / Society of Neuroscience.

extending from each "explosion" plot represent: the empirically derived summation of all 241 vectors in that "explosion". Given that each vector was estimated from only five or so movement trials, and that only 241 neurons were sampled out of the millions that make up motor cortex, it's astoundingly impressive that an analysis of these neural data could produce an estimated direction of motion (the eight vector sums) that so closely corresponds to the actual direction in which the monkey moved its hand on each trial (the eight arrows in the center of the plot). What Georgopoulos and colleagues accomplished was to decipher a component of the neural code for skeletomotor control! And the key insight, one to which we will return often for the remainder of this book, is that the principle underlying this function of the nervous system can only be understood by simultaneously considering the activity of a large population of neurons. Serially inspecting one after the next would never reveal it.

I can imagine that to some readers, this may seem too abstract. "*Vector summation? What, is there some little homuncular mathematician perched up on the precentral gyrus, legs dangling into the central sulcus, calculating vector sums prior to each movement?*" Nope. No need in this scheme to resort to the homunculus. Assuming that these are all layer V pyramidal cells, all located in the arm area, each neuron's action potentials travel to the same general area in the spinal cord, many of them destined for the same motor neuron pool. These action potentials all activate the very same networks of interneurons that were described in the earlier section on *Motor computations in the spinal cord*. In effect, it's as though 241 teensy weensy microelectrodes have been simultaneously lowered into the spinal cord. Recall that we saw previously that while stimulation of point A in the cord moved the forepaw to location X, Y, and stimulation of point B in the cord moved the forepaw to location X′, Y′, and simultaneous stimulation of A and B moved the forepaw to X″, Y″. Thus, the vector summation that a scientist can compute through the arduous analyses and computations summarized here turns out to be a more formal description of what we had glibly summarized earlier: the motor cortex issues the general command (in the form of a population code), and the spinal cord "takes care of the details."

One of the most exciting consequences of "cracking the code," as Georgopoulos and colleagues did with this aspect of motor cortex function, is that one can *decode* motor signals as they are generated. This has been of central importance for the development of brain–computer interface (BCI) systems that process brain signals for real-time movement of robotic limbs.

The Neural Dynamics of Motor Control Skeletomotor control is a domain of neural functioning to which the frameworks and analysis approaches summarized in *Chapter 5*, sections *Dynamical systems theory* and *representational geometry analysis* have been particularly influential. One example is the phenomenon previously raised in *Chapter 5*, section *Cutting through the chaos with communication subspaces*, which is that one typically observes elevated activity in regions of the motor system that precede the actual movement, such that the overall level of activity is often not appreciably different during pre-movement vs. movement epochs of behavior. In particular, Matthew Kaufman and colleagues (2014) in the laboratory of Krishna Shenoy have noted that such premovement activity surely has an important preparatory function, in that it is tuned for the kinematics and the dynamics of the impending movement, it predicts reaction time, and disrupting it delays the movement. They also noted that it is prevalent in PMC, present (but less prevalent) in M1, even less prevalent in the spinal cord, and absent in muscles. To explain this phenomenon, they have proposed a mechanism that is formally equivalent to the one described in *Chapter 5*, section *Cutting through the chaos with communication subspaces*: Motor preparation-related activity may unfold in an "action-null" subspace that is orthogonal to the communication subspaces via which motor commands issued by cortex are transmitted to the spinal cord and eventually to the muscles (*Figure 8.9*).

Kaufman and colleagues (2014) help us develop a simple intuition for how motor preparation in an action-null subspace could work by invoking a very simplified, hypothetical two-neuron example. It's illustrated in *Figure 8.10*, but before inspecting the figure, let's walk through the idea. In this hypothetical system, there are two neurons, *A* and *B*, that together influence behavior by sending their outputs to a target neuron, *C*, with *C* being directly responsible for the contraction of a muscle. For this thought exercise to work, one needs to keep in mind that holding still typically requires a steady level of contraction in many muscles. (To prove this to yourself, hold out your arm as though you're about to shake someone's hand, and hold it there for a few seconds. If you now let the muscles in your arm go completely flaccid, your arm will drop to your side. That's evidence that holding it still in the "shaking hands" posture requires a steady level of contraction in the muscle groups that control the position of your arm. That steady level of contraction, in turn, requires the steady delivery of a specific pattern of signals from the neurons that control those muscles.) Now, back to our toy example, let's further pretend that neuron C interprets the signals from *A* and *B* by summing their input. To track patterns of activity, we can plot neuron *A*'s level of activity on the

FIGURE 8.9 Preparatory vs. motor activity in PMC.

Source: (Kaufman, Churchland, Ryu, & Shenoy, 2014) / Frontiers Media S.A.

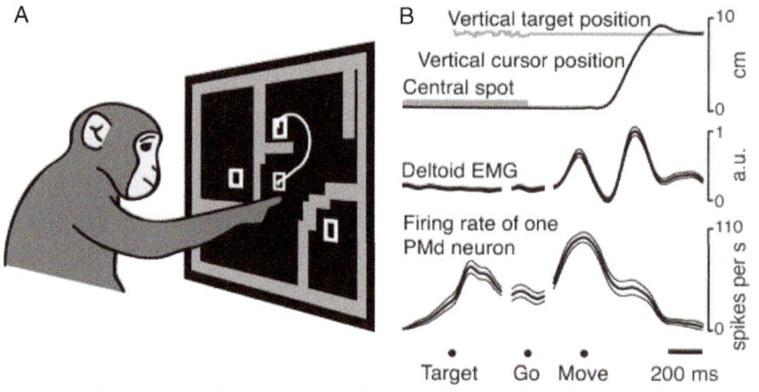

FIGURE 8.9.A Illustration of a trial in which the monkey initiates the trial by touching the start square, then a target appears together with "walls" that must be avoided and two distractors (targets that aren't valid choices because they are enclosed by walls).

FIGURE 8.9.B Top panel illustrates the location of the finger and the target along the vertical dimension, as a function of time (timing of events indicated along the bottom of the panel). Prior to target presentation, the finger is on the start square ("Central spot"), which extinguishes at time "Go," a short time after which the finger moves toward the target, slightly overshooting before acquiring it. Middle panel is the electromyogram (EMG) of the deltoid muscle, indicating no movement until after the Go signal. Bottom panel shows that, upon target onset, a neuron in dorsal PMC (PMd) begins responding vigorously, before decreasing slightly around the time of the Go signal, and then ramps up again in conjunction with the movement.

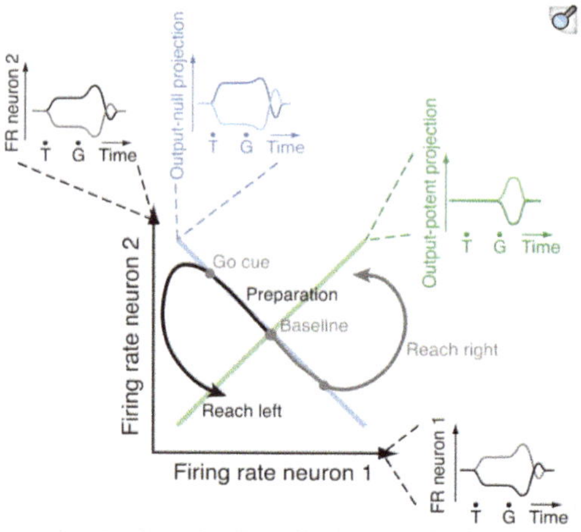

FIGURE 8.10 A hypothetical illustration of an action-null subspace. The activity of two neurons is plotted on the x and y axes, respectively. If activity values are restricted to moving along the action-null subspace (blue line), the aggregated output of these neurons remains constant. (The call-outs for two timelines of firing rates ["FR"] of neuron 1 and neuron 2 are mirror-reflections of each other: for the trial depicted with heavy lines, the activity of neuron 1 is low and that of neuron 2 is high, and the converse is true for the trial depicted with light lines.) The blue call-out represents the fact that neuron 1 and neuron 2 are changing their activity levels during the interval between target-onset (T) and go signal (G), when no movement takes place. When the activity of these two neurons rotates to an action-potent subspace (green line), however, changes of position along this subspace do result in changes to muscle-tension settings (and, therefore, to movement). Thus, the green call-out represents the fact that when in this action-potent subspace, these neurons only change their activity after the go signal. In this cartoon, when in the action-potent subspace, decreases in firing rate produce a "Reach left" and increases in firing rate produce a "Reach right."

Source: Kaufman et al. (2014) / Springer Nature.

horizontal axis of a 2D graph, and neuron *B*'s level of activity on the vertical axis. If we draw a line with a slope of −1 that intersects the *B* axis at a value of 10 and the *A* axis at a value of 10, this corresponds to a 1D subspace (defined by the function $y = -1{*}x + 10$) on which any point produces an output value of "10." (E.g., 10+0 = 10; 7+3 = 10; 1+9 = 10; . . .) If, in our toy example, an input value of "10" gets translated by neuron *C* into the "handshake pose," the instantaneous values of *A* and *B* can be constantly changing but, so long as they stay on the $y = -1{*}x + 10$ action-null subspace, neuron *C* will always receive an input of 10, and the arm will remain in that position. In this way, *A* and *B* can be involved in planning the next movement (i.e., by changing their values) without this planning activity influencing the current state of the arm. Finally, when it comes time to move the arm, we can rotate the values of *A* and *B* into a new, action-potent subspace (let's say the line $y = +1{*}x + 0$), putting us into a new regime in which changes in the values being output by *A* and *B* will result in changes to the input value being received by *C*, and this results in changes in the level of contraction of the muscle and, consequently, to movement of the arm. (I.e., in our cartoon example, neurons *A* and *B* communicate different information with neuron *C* each time they change their value while operating in the $y = +1{*}x + 0$ subspace.)

An additional point that we should make about the scenario illustrated in *Figure 8.10* is that it could also be possible for the status of the original $y = -1{*}x + 10$ subspace to change from "null" to "potent" if, instead of *A* and *B* rotating into a new subspace, *C* were to rotate into a different subspace that reads out the activity from *A* and *B* as projected onto a different plane, such as defined by the *y* and the *z* axes (rather than the *x* and *y* axes, as was previously the case). For example, from the perspective of the projection onto the (y, z) plane, the activity pattern $(y = 7, x = 3)$ would be interpreted very differently than the activity pattern $(y = 1, x = 9)$.

In addition to evidence for action-null activity, another fact that has led to the proposal of alternatives to population-coding models as described in section *Single-Unit Activity Reveals Population Coding* is the fact that many neurons in M1 and PMC, although active in a variety of contexts, are not tuned to any specific direction of movement, or other first-order movement parameters. A team led by physicist and neuroscientist Sara Solla has noted these facts, and also that neurons in the motor system are heavily interconnected. Consequently, they propose that motor control may be best understood not by studying the tuning properties of individual neurons, but rather by characterizing the relatively small number of trajectories of activity through time, which they call "neural modes," that are each followed more or less in unison by large numbers of neurons. These neural modes are characterized as being constrained by connectivity to exist on a relatively low-dimensional neural manifold. (I.e., because the activity of neurons in any population is highly correlated, any population of *n* neurons will only be able to display many fewer than *n* patterns of activity.) Empirically, neural modes are identified by dimensionality reduction techniques, such as principal component analysis (PCA) or factor analysis. Evidence consistent with this idea is illustrated in *Figure 8.11*. It shows an experiment in which, on each trial, a monkey moves a cursor to one of eight possible locations from a central starting point. *Figure 8.11.B* illustrates the trial-averaged activity, sorted by movement direction, of three individual neurons from a sample of 68 recorded simultaneously in a single session. Note that none of these three shows activity that scales parametrically with direction (as would be expected from *Figure 8.8.B*). It is presumed that neurons like these may participate in different neural modes on different trial types, and may even "jump" from one neural mode to another during the course of a trial. Consistent with the idea that the activity in this sample can be characterized by a set of neural modes, the first 10 principal components of a PCA applied to the sample of 68 neurons (each PC being interpreted as representing a mode) were sufficient to explain 70% of the variance in this sample. This suggests that many fewer than 67 modes are needed to perform this task successfully. (To frame this in a simpler system that may already be familiar, consider the RNN described in *Chapter 5*, section *Representational Geometry Analysis*, and illustrated in Figure 5.11.E. Although its hidden layer contained 100 neurons, only two principal components [out of the total of 99 generated by the PCA] were needed to explain over 90% of the variability, while the network held the representation of a single orientation. That is, although there were

FIGURE 8.11 Neural modes for the control of movement.

Source: Gallego et al., 2017 / with permission of Elsevier.

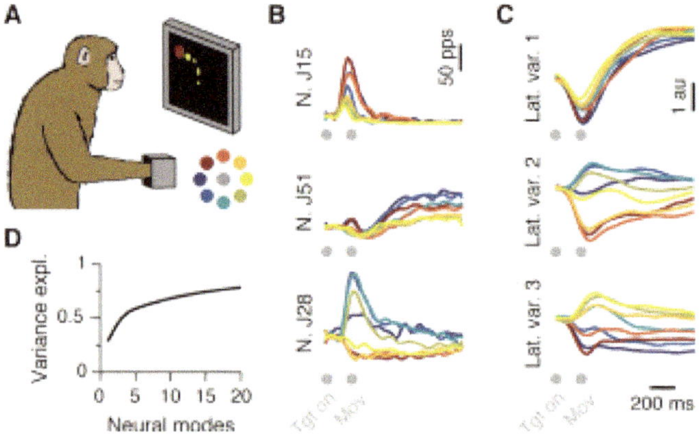

FIGURE 8.11.A Diagram of the task and the array of eight target locations.

FIGURE 8.11.B Trial-averaged time series from three neurons, sorted by movement direction. Note, for example, that for N.J51, the activity is almost identical for the targets colored orange and teal, despite these being movements in opposite directions, and that for N.J28 the activity for red-dark orange-light orange-yellow is below baseline, but markedly elevated for olive green, which is equidistant in polar angle from yellow as is yellow from light orange.

FIGURE 8.11.C Latent variables corresponding to the first three PCs.

FIGURE 8.11.D Plot of proportion variance explained in the sample of 68 neurons, as a function of neural modes (i.e., the latent variables from panel C).

99 possible principal components that could have been recruited to represent the range of 180 possible stimulus values, the activity of the network was constrained to a 2D ring manifold – only two "neural modes" were engaged.) Based on this and similar studies, the authors assert that "It is the activation of these neural modes, rather than the activity of single neurons, that provides the basic building blocks of neural dynamics and function" (Gallego, Perich, Miller, and Solla, 2017, p. 978).

Motor Control Outside of Motor Cortex

Parietal Cortex: Guiding How We Move

One of the facts made clear by motor control research is that the neural code involved in carrying out multi-step actions, such as a reach followed by a grasp followed by a pull, entails much more than the vector summation of 300 or so M1 neurons (or the engagement of just a small number of neural modes). Many regions other than M1 can contribute valuable signals for decoding movement-related neural activity, including signals related to a wide range of cognitive factors – including intention, expectation, and reward value – might be best sampled outside of traditional motor areas. "For example, PRR [parietal reach region] neural activity codes the intention to reach to an object at a particular location in space, whereas motor cortex codes the direction to move the hand" (Andersen, Musallam, and Pesaran, 2004, p. 271). The critical role of PPC for the planning and execution of visually guided action, through its contributions to sensorimotor integration and coordinate transformation, also figures prominently in the alternate framing of the ventral vs. dorsal visual pathways, which we consider next.

A Neurological Dissociation Between Perceiving Objects and Acting on Them A reassessment of the "what vs. where" framework for understanding the functional specialization of the visual system (section *A Functional Dissociation of Visual Perception of What an Object Is vs. Where It Is Located, Chapter 6*) was proposed by Canada-based researchers Melvin Goodale and David Milner after their detailed studies of a patient who developed a profound impairment in the ability to recognize objects (a form of visual agnosia, a syndrome that we will define and consider in detail in *Chapter 10*) after carbon monoxide inhalation produced extensive damage in lateral occipital BAs 18 and 19, but largely sparing V1. Despite this severe impairment, this patient (known by her initials "D.F.") seemed remarkably unimpaired when "directing accurate reaching movements toward objects in different orientations" (Goodale, Milner, Jakobson, and Carey, 1991, p. 155). (For an image of D.F.'s lesions, see *Figure 7.7.B.*) To formalize and quantify this dissociation, which was reminiscent of that demonstrated by monkeys with IT lesions in the Pohl (1973) study (section *A functional dissociation of visual perception of what an object is vs. where it is located, Chapter 6*), Goodale et al. (1991) carried out the experiment whose results are illustrated in *Figure 8.12.*

In addition to the experiment illustrated in *Figure 8.12*, Goodale et al. (1991) also carried out an experiment that looked at a second kind of visually guided action, grasping. First, subjects were asked to indicate with finger and thumb the front-to-back size of each of five plaques, ranging in shape from a 5×5 cm square to a 2.5×10 cm rectangle. These two digits were fitted with infrared light-emitting diodes so that precise measurements could be made

FIGURE 8.12 Is the dorsal stream important for processing "where" an object is, or "how" to interact with it?

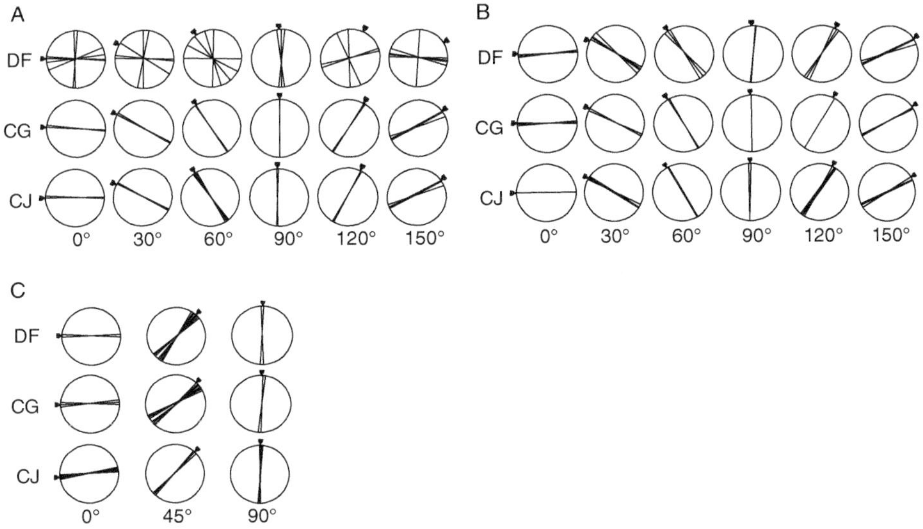

FIGURE 8.12.A Responses on five trials at each of six different orientations in a "perception" task, in which D.F. and two control subjects were asked to match the orientation of a slot in a disk that was 45 cm distant. The true orientation of each of the six is illustrated by the small arrowheads. At all angles except 90° (i.e., vertical), D.F. was profoundly impaired. (And because each trial was started with the card held at 90°, her relatively intact performance at this orientation may be artifactual.)

FIGURE 8.12.B When asked to "post" the card by reaching to insert it into the slot (as though putting a postcard into a mail slot), D.F.'s performance was nearly as precise as that of control subjects.

FIGURE 8.12.C Performance on a mental imagery version of the matching task, in which subjects were asked to close their eyes and imagine the slot at each of three orientations. This indicates that poor performance illustrated in A was not due to a misunderstanding of instructions, or some other uninteresting factor.

Source: Georgopoulos et al., 1982 / Society of Neuroscience.

of finger-to-thumb aperture. The results showed that, unlike control subjects, D.F.'s responses did not differ with shape. When asked to pick each of the shapes up, in contrast, she was just as accurate as control subjects.

In interpreting their findings, the authors conjectured that they did "not correspond to the two streams of output from primary visual cortex generally identified in the primate brain – a ventral one for object identification and a dorsal one for spatial localization [. . . instead, they] indicate separate processing systems not for different subsets of visual information, but for the different uses to which vision can be put." Therefore, to return to a theme from the previous chapter, this view has more in common with *intention* rather than *attention* interpretations of the neglect syndrome and of the functions of the parietal lobe.

The *Further Reading* list at the end of this chapter provides references to more recent installments of the lively debate about this idea that has continued more than two decades after its initial articulation. Furthermore, one possible resolution to the "where" vs. "how" debate is that both may be true. As illustrated in *Figure 7.7.C*, Dwight Kravitz, Kadharbatcha Saleem, Chris Baker, and Mortimer Mishkin (2011) have proposed that in parietal cortex the dorsal stream splits into three major pathways that provide body-centered spatial information that supports three broadly defined functions: a parieto-prefrontal pathway that supports "conscious visuospatial processing," including the endogenous control of spatial attention (a focus of *Chapter 9*) and spatial working memory (and corresponding to the classically defined "where" pathway); a parieto-premotor pathway that supports "non-conscious visuospatial processing," including visually guided action (and corresponding to Goodale and Milner's "how" pathway); and a parieto-medial temporal lobe pathway, including intermediate connections in posterior cingulate and retrosplenial regions, that supports navigation (highlighted in *Chapter 7*, section *From Parietal Space to Medial-Temporal Place*).

Cerebellum: Motor Learning, Balance, . . . and Mental Representation?

Aesthetically, the cerebellum may be the most beautiful part of the brain: the tight foliation of its cortex; the remarkably profuse, yet "flat," dendritic arbors of its Purkinje cells; the elegant simplicity of its circuitry. The cerebellum encompasses just 10% of the volume, but >50% of the neurons of the brain. As summarized previously, the cerebellum is a hub in one of the two major recurrent circuits of the motor system, serving an online error-monitoring function and feeding real-time performance information back into frontal cortex.

Cerebellar Circuitry The cerebellum is highly modular, consisting essentially of a bank of hundreds of thousands of parallel circuits that all perform the same computational operations, but each on a different, segregated channel of information. The central processing element around which cerebellar circuits are built is the Purkinje cell. These are among the largest cells in the nervous system, with massive dendritic arbors that afford an incredibly large number of synaptic connections (estimated to be as high as 200,000 per neuron!). Despite their size and extensive and intricate branching, however, these arbors only extend through a 2-D plane. A row of Purkinje cells aligned in a "strip" that is parallel to the plane of their dendritic arbors makes up a circuit (called a "microzone"), the output of which, via Purkinje cell axons, is focused on neurons of the cerebellar deep nuclei that were discussed in the introductory section of this chapter. At a simplified level, the copy of the efferent motor command is carried into the cerebellum by climbing fibers, and information about the sensory consequences of the motor action by mossy fibers. Climbing fibers are axons originating in the inferior olive in the brainstem, their name deriving from the fact that a single climbing fiber wraps around and around the basal dendrites of a single Purkinje cell, like a vine climbing a tree trunk. Climbing fibers make between 300 and 500 synaptic connections with a single Purkinje cell. Mossy fibers arise from the pons (in the brainstem), their name deriving from the distinctive "rosettes" in which they form synaptic connections with granule cells. Granule cells then send "parallel fibers" that run perpendicular to, and therefore through, the dendritic arbors of many Purkinje cells (i.e., they cut across many microzones). Individual parallel-fiber synapses on Purkinje cells are relatively weak, whereas a single action potential in a climbing fiber will reliably trigger an action potential in a Purkinje cell.

Cerebellar Functions An influential model of the computations carried out by the cerebellum, articulated by neuroscience polymath David Marr (1945–1980), and subsequently refined by electrical engineer and roboticist James Albus (1935–2011), is summarized as follows. The premise, rooted in control theory from engineering, is that the Purkinje cells in the cerebellum contain a representation of a prediction of what the effects of a movement should be (i.e., an "internal model"). The sensory report of what the consequences of the action actually were is delivered, via parallel fibers, to the cerebellum. To the extent that the internal model and the actual consequences differ, a modification is made to the cerebellar circuitry, and the results of this assessment get forwarded to the motor cortex so that it can adjust how it commands this action the next time. In effect, the idea is that the cerebellum houses one instantiation of the predictive coding models introduced in *Chapter* 5 (section *Predictive coding*). In his influential 1971 paper, Albus summarized the role for the modification of cerebellar circuits in motor learning as follows:

> It is an obvious fact that continued training in motor skills improves performance. Extended practice improves dexterity and the ability to make fine discriminations and subtle movements. This fact strongly indicates that learning has no appreciable tendency to saturate with overlearning. Rather, learning appears to asymptotically approach some ideal value. This asymptotic property of learning implies that the amount of change that takes place in the nervous system is proportional to the difference between actual performance and desired performance. A difference function in turn implies error correction, which requires a decrease in excitation upon conditions of incorrect firings. (1971, p. 52)

By the Marr–Ablus model, "desired performance" is represented by the climbing fibers, which carry the copy of the efferent motor signal. When discharge of a climbing fiber triggers an action potential in a Purkinje cell, there is a refractory period that follows, during which the Purkinje cell cannot fire another action potential. If action potentials from parallel fibers arrive during this refractory period, the consequence of this is a weakening of synapses between them and the Purkinje cell – an example of long-term depression (LTD; *Chapter 5*, section *Activity-based modification of synaptic strength*).

This modification of synaptic strength in the cerebellum is a neural instantiation of motor learning. One way to think of this process is that subtle changes in cerebellar circuitry might produce subtle changes to the length of a few of the M1 neuronal activity vectors illustrated in the vector-averaging panel of *Figure 8.8*, which, in turn, would produce an ever-so-subtle change in the endpoint of that movement the next time it is executed.

The circuitry of the cerebellum continues to fine-tune our movements throughout our lives. Evidence for this comes from the fact that damage to the cerebellum produces abnormalities in posture, gait, reaching, and other skeletomotor functions regardless of when in life the damage is incurred.

Interestingly, some channels of the cortico-cerebellar circuit link PFC with the cerebellum, and so this computational principle presumably also carries out fine-grained, online corrective processing of high-level cognitive functions, such as those mentioned in the introductory paragraph to this chapter. The Japanese neurophysiologist Masao Ito proposed an intriguing model that we can't detail here, but whereby, in addition to its internal models of motor behaviors, the cerebellum may also encode internal models "that reproduce the essential properties of mental representations in the cerebral cortex . . . [thereby providing a] mechanism by which intuition and implicit thought might function" (Ito, 2008, p. 304).

Basal Ganglia

The basal ganglia define the second major recurrent "circuit" of the motor system. The fact that their function is not limited to motor control, however, is emphasized in *Figure 8.3.A*, which shows that the skeletomotor circuit is just one of five frontocortical-basal ganglia-thalamic circuits. One major difference between the skeletomotor circuit of the basal ganglia and the other four is that its cortical efferents synapse in the putamen, whereas three of the others target different regions of the caudate nucleus, and the ACC and MOFC of the limbic circuit target the nucleus accumbens (also referred to as the "ventral striatum"). (The caudate nucleus, putamen, and nucleus accumbens together make up the neostriatum.[1]) Subsequently, each of the five circuits, although remaining segregated, bifurcates into a direct and an indirect pathway, the direct pathway linking striatum to the GPi, the GPi to thalamus, and thalamus back to cortex. Additionally, a "hyperdirect" pathway bypasses the neostriatum and projects monosynaptically from the supplementary motor area to the subthalamic nucleus.

A Subcortical Gate on Cortical Activity Although learning the wiring diagram of this circuit has been known to induce dizziness and headache, the basic operating principles are actually quite straightforward. The key to understanding its function is remembering a distinctive property of the GPi. The GPi is a tonically *active* structure. That is, its baseline state, when the circuit is not being engaged, is to steadily fire at a high frequency (~85 Hz in one study in the monkey; this will vary with species and with an animal's physiological state). Because GPi neurons are GABAergic, the default state of affairs is that the GPi maintains a steady inhibitory "clamp" on the thalamus. Now, moving one step upstream, the cells of the neostriatum that project to the GPi, called medium spiny neurons, are also GABAergic. Thus, engaging a circuit in the direct pathway has the effect of phasically inhibiting the activity of a targeted subset of neurons in the GPi, a consequence of which is to phasically lift the inhibitory clamp that these GPi neurons otherwise impose on a specific subset of neurons in the thalamus, a consequence of which is to allow these thalamic neurons to send an excitatory signal to their frontal cortical targets. In this way, the basal ganglia can be construed as "gating" cortical activity.

The Functional Anatomy and Neurochemistry of the Basal Ganglia

The Role of DA

Figure 8.2 illustrates another important component of the operation of the basal ganglia: the delivery of the neurotransmitter dopamine (DA). DA, along with norepinephrine, serotonin, and others, is classified as a neuromodulatory neurotransmitter (c.f., *Figure 2.5*). That is, it's typically not thought to convey information in the way that glutamatergic neurons do, but rather it sets the "tone" within networks, thereby biasing the way in which glutamatergic and GABAergic signals are processed. As detailed in *Chapter 5*, section *A dopaminergic correlate of the reward prediction error*, the level of DA at a synapse influences the rate of strengthening/weakening that glutamatergic and GABAergic synapses will undergo via activity-dependent plasticity. DA is synthesized in three adjacent nuclei in the midbrain. Depending on who is describing them, they are either identified as *A8*, *A9*, and *A10* or as the substantia nigra pars compacta (SNpc) and the ventral tegmental area (VTA). The SNpc (or A9) delivers DA to other nuclei of the basal ganglia, most densely to the neostriatum via the **nigrostriatal tract**; the two other nuclei project primarily to neocortex.

The influence of DA on the basal ganglia can be considered at many levels, and here we'll consider three: setting the balance between the direct and indirect pathways; the waveform shape of "sensorimotor beta"; and reinforcement learning.

[1] In the rodent there is not anatomical separation of caudate nucleus and putamen, but a single neostriatum with circuits homologous to those of the primate caudate nucleus found in the dorsomedial striatum of the rodent.

Balancing Between the Direct and Indirect Pathways

The direct and indirect pathways both originate in the neostriatum. What's illustrated in *Figure 8.2* is the fact that although all fibers of the nigrostrial tract deliver the same molecule throughout the neostriatum – DA – its effects can be either excitatory or inhibitory, depending on the zone receiving this input. How can this be? The answer is that, unlike glutamate and GABA, DA receptors are not linked to membrane-spanning channels that directly gate the passage of ions. Rather, they are second messenger-linked receptors, meaning that the binding of a molecule of DA to a DA receptor initiates a cascade of chemical events within the postsynaptic neuron, the ultimate consequences of which might be excitatory or inhibitory, depending on which second-messenger pathway is triggered. There are two classes of DA receptors: D1-type and D2-type. (D1-type DA receptors include D1 and D5, and D2-type include D2, D3, and D4.) In general, D1-type receptors produce a depolarizing effect and D2-type receptors a hyperpolarizing effect.

The neostriatum is made up of a checkerboard of compartmentalized zones that are dominated by D1-type or by D2-type receptors. The two types of zones are the basis for the direct vs. indirect pathways, because their outputs project either to the GPi or the GPe. One of the ways that we understand the influence of DA on this system is from decades of research on PD, which is characterized by progressive degeneration of the SNpc, and, therefore, a progressive lowering of DA levels in the neostriatum. Motorically, PD is associated with three cardinal clinical symptoms: resting tremor in one or more limbs, muscular rigidity, and slowness to initiate movement ("bradykinesia"). One way to understand these symptoms (and, by extension, to understand the role of DA in the healthy system) is illustrated in *Figure 8.2*: the reduction of DA in the neostriatum throws off the balance of its output, such that the descending signal of the direct pathway is weakened, and that of the indirect pathway is strengthened. (Activity in the indirect pathway is enhanced due to the reduced activation of its D2 receptors, which reduces the level of inhibition that is characteristic of the healthy state.) The consequences are two-fold: the direct pathway is less able to impose phasic inhibition on the GPi, which, in turn, reduces excitatory drive from thalamus to cortex; and the indirect pathway exerts greater inhibition on the GPe which, in turn, results in less GPe-to-GPi inhibition, which also contributes to the pathologically enhanced level of GPi-to-thalamus inhibition.

Although it seems as though we've only considered the indirect pathway in relation to its dysfunctional activity in disease states, it is, of course, the case that it has an important role in normal brain function. One is to help control movement by sending "no-go" signals to the cortex when a possible action would be a bad choice. Another important function, to be considered in the upcoming section on *Habits and reinforcement learning*, may be that of learning about the negative value of some behaviors.

The Waveform Shape of "Sensorimotor Beta"

Recall from section *The neurophysiology of movement* that the temporal dynamics, and perhaps also the central frequency, of oscillations in the beta band are tightly linked to the execution of a movement. One series of studies of this "sensorimotor beta" has been carried out in patients with PD by Coralie De Hemptinne, Phillip Starr, and colleagues. In one, field potentials from the surface of M1 were recorded with ECoG electrodes, and voltages on the scalp with EEG. The ECoG recordings were carried out while these patients were undergoing implantation of DBS electrodes, and the authors compared cortical activity when DBS was ON vs. OFF. The initially published finding was that ECoG recordings showed an atypically high level of phase–amplitude coupling (PAC) between the phase of the beta-band oscillation and high gamma power when DBS was OFF, and that the amplitude of this PAC decreased markedly when DBS was ON (de Hemptinne et al., 2015). (For a refresher on PAC, see *Chapter 4*, section *Phase–amplitude coupling*.) This was interpreted as evidence that PD motor symptoms may be caused by cortical pyramidal cells being pathologically "locked-in" to a highly synchronous pattern of firing that prevented the quick and flexible modification of large-scale patterns of activity that underlie healthy motor control. At an intuitive level, this suggested an electrophysiological correspondence to the bradykinetic aspects of PD.

The "locked-in" conceptualization of the cortical pathophysiology of PD soon had to be revised, however, when it was discovered that the atypically high levels in PAC in the DBS-off recordings weren't due to periodic bursting of MUA, the standard interpretation of the high-gamma component of PAC, but were instead an artifact of the shape of the wave forms in the cortical oscillation. Specifically, the peaks of the beta oscillation were abnormally sharp in the DBS-off condition (resembling the upper right-hand quadrant in *Figure 4.14.A*), and this resulted in the spectral transform (for our purposes, the fast Fourier transform [FFT]) needing to add power at high frequencies to be able to represent the steep slope of the rising edge of each cycle. The effect of DBS, as it turned out, was to smooth out the peaks in the beta-band oscillation (i.e., to render the slope of the rising edge of the cycle less steep). (See Cole et al. (2017) from *Further Reading*.) But what does this have to do with dopamine?

A follow-up study with scalp EEG recorded from a different group of PD patients showed similar results for DA-replacement medication: the beta-band oscillation recorded at central electrodes had an atypically saw-toothed shape when patients were OFF their medication, and a smoother, more sinusoidal shape when they were ON their medication. Other research in DBS patients (not reviewed here) has shown that one consequence of going OFF dopaminergic medication is for the peak frequency of oscillatory coherence between the GPi and STN to shift from roughly 70 Hz to roughly 20 Hz (see *Further Reading* from Brown et al. (2001)). Thus, it may be that one consequence of the elevated coherence at 20 Hz between GPi-STN when patients are OFF medication is abnormally high synchrony in the thalamic signaling to motor cortex that is gated by the GPi. From a clinical perspective, this finding may have important implications for diagnosis and tracking of disease progression, because the medication-related change in the shape of the beta-band oscillation was not accompanied by a change in beta power. That is, conventional EEG analyses that do not account for waveform shape would be insensitive to this effect.

Habits and Reinforcement Learning

For decades, the basal ganglia have been associated with "habit learning," a term that refers to the stereotyped behaviors that we engage in while carrying out everyday tasks, often multiple times each day, often with little or no awareness that we are carrying them out. Tying one's shoes, riding a bicycle, and driving a car are examples that will be familiar to most. In the framework of reinforcement learning, these are examples of model-free decision making (see *Chapter 5*, section *Other principles relevant to reinforcement learning*). Now that we're familiar with the anatomical organization of cortico-basal ganglia circuitry, we can delve more deeply into the idea that it is the synapses of cortical projections to neostriatum that are believed to be the neural substrate of Q values that are the basis of model-free decision making. Specifically, we can now return to the earlier statement that the indirect pathway may have an important role in learning the negative value of some actions. The idea is that because the indirect pathway is governed by the inhibitory effects of DA on D2 receptors, it is during the pauses in the tonic release of DA that constitute negative reward prediction errors (RPEs) (*Figure 5.5*, group *B*) that neostriatal neurons in the indirect pathway experience transient increases in excitability and, consequently, a boost in the plasticity of their synaptic connections with incoming cortical fibers. Thus, it is in conjunction with "disappointments," or situations in which outcomes are worse than expected, that reinforcement learning is strongest in the indirect pathway. In this way, future encounters with the same set of circumstances are more likely to engage an indirect pathway circuit, which has the effect of inhibiting the action(s) that these circumstances previously evoked. It follows from this fact that experiments have shown that interfering with D1 functioning impairs reward learning and interfering with D2 functioning impairs avoidance learning. (Avoidance learning will get further consideration in *Chapter 18: Emotion*.)

Cognitive Functions of the Motor System

As suggested at the beginning of this chapter, many have suggested that high-level cognition evolved over millennia as increasingly abstracted aspects of motor control. Ito's (2008) proposal of mental models represented in the cerebellum would fall into this category. Also consistent with this idea is the fact that the cortico-basal ganglia-thalamic circuits of the PFC and the ACC/LOFC operate on the same principles as does the motor circuit that we have focused on in this chapter. Two additional examples of this idea have come from neurophysiologist Giacomo Rizzolatti and his colleagues. One is the "premotor theory of attention," the idea that attention may "have evolved from"/"be a byproduct of" motor preparation. This theory will receive considerable attention in *Chapter 9: Oculomotor control and the control of attention*. In the meantime, this chapter concludes with another of Rizzolatti's conceptual innovations: mirror neurons.

Mirror Neurons

In the nonhuman primate (NHP), sector F5 is a subregion of PMC, located immediately caudal to the ventral branch of the arcuate sulcus, that has been shown in recording and microstimulation experiments to be involved in the high-level representation of actions involving the hand and the mouth. Different neurons, for example, respond selectively to grasping, tearing, or holding movements. In a study carried out by Vittorio Gallese, Luciano Fadiga, Leonardo Fogassi, and Giacomo Rizzolatti (1996), upon isolating a neuron in F5, the investigators would present the monkey with an item of food on a tray, either within or outside of the animal's reach, as well as with objects of various sizes. The size manipulation enabled distinguishing between three types of grip: "precision grip" (thumb and index finger); "prehension grip" (thumb opposite fingers to extract an object from a deep, narrow container); and "whole-hand prehension." This procedure can be construed as analogous to the procedure for determining the visual response properties of a neuron in the IT cortex by presenting it with a series of objects.

The novel innovation of this study was that the testing battery also included an experimenter performing several actions while the monkey watched: grasping a piece of food from a tray, bringing the food to their mouth, giving the food to a second experimenter, etc. Of 532 neurons recorded from F5, 92 discharged to specific actions by the monkey *and* to the observed actions of an experimenter. These were dubbed "mirror neurons." The actions that mirror neurons responded to were categorized as shown in *Table 8.1*.

TABLE 8.1 **Actions that mirror neurons responded to in Gallese et al. (1996) study**

Observed hand actions	Number of neurons
Neurons with one preferred action	
Grasping	30
Placing	7
Manipulating	7
Hands interaction	5
Holding	2
Neurons with two preferred actions	
Grasping/placing	20
Grasping/manipulating	3
Grasping/hands interaction	3
Grasping/holding	5
Grasping/grasping with the mouth	3
Placing/holding	1
Hands interaction/holding	1
Neurons with three preferred actions	
Grasping/placing/manipulating	1
Grasping/placing/holding	4

The responses summarized in *Table 8.1* were insensitive to manipulation of factors related to the animal's reference frame, such as side of the body the actions were performed, or the distance of the observed actor. Importantly, however, these neurons did not respond when their preferred action was performed as mimicry (e.g., the experimenter pretending to pick up a piece of food when there was no object on the tray; *Figure 8.13*), or when observing the same action performed with tools (forceps or pliers) instead of the hand.

In this study, 31.5% of mirror neurons were classified as being "strictly congruent," meaning that they responded preferentially to the same action, regardless of whether the animal

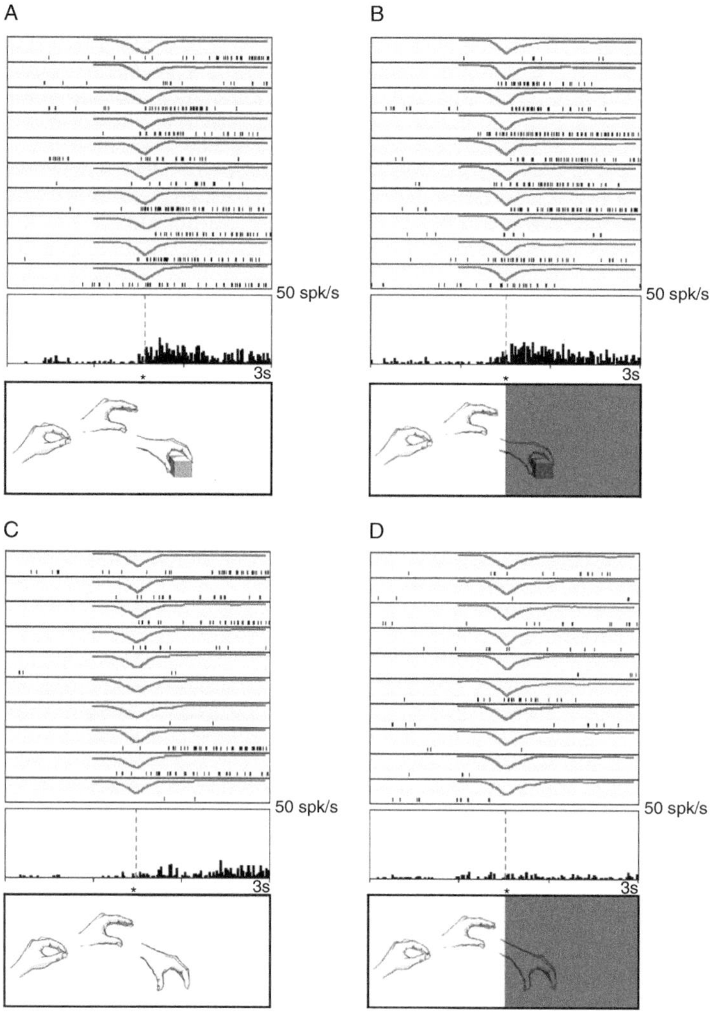

FIGURE 8.13 Mirror neurons in PMC of the monkey. Responses of an F5 neuron in a study carried out by Dr. Maria Alessandra Umiltà, in which the monkey watched while an experimenter reached to either grasp an object (panels **A** and **B**) or to mimic the same action but in the absence of the object. In between the monkey and the table on which the object was displayed was a metal frame that could either be empty (panels **A** and **C**) or hold an opaque screen, thereby blocking the monkey's view of this location (panels **B** and **D**). For all four trial types, neural activity is aligned to the moment in time when the reaching hand passed the boundary of the frame (and, therefore, became no longer visible in **B** and **D**). (The waveforms above each row of rasters illustrate the location of the hand relative to the boundary of the frame as a function of time, aligned the same as neural data.) Note how the neuron only responds to the act of grasping a physical object, not to the identical movement when the object is absent, and that it does so regardless of the presence or absence of the screen.

Source: Umiltà et al., 2001 / with permission of Elsevier.

was observing an experimenter performing the action or executing the action itself; and 61% were classified as "broadly congruent," in that the preferred observed and the preferred executed actions were similar, but not identical. For example, one such neuron responded vigorously during *observation* of a precision grip and observation of whole-hand prehension, but only responded to *execution* of a precision grip. The remainder were "noncongruent" with regard to preferred observed vs. executed action(s).

The authors suggested that mirror neurons are sensitive to the meaning of an action, rather than to its precise sensory or motoric properties. They further speculated that mirror neurons may underlie learning through imitation (prevalent in humans as well as in nonhuman primates), as well as, possibly, speech perception in humans.

Holding a Mirror Up to Nature?

In the early years of this century, mirror neurons were among the "hottest" topics of research in cognitive neuroscience. One factor driving this interest was the prospect that they offered a neural basis for many popular schools of thought in cognitive psychology, including embodied cognition, common coding theory, and the motor theory of speech perception. The last one was referenced by Gallese et al. (1996). It is a theory, first proposed in the 1960s, that an important component of speech perception is the "listener" watching the mouth of the talker, and simulating in their mind the larynx, tongue, and lip movements being made by the talker. Gallese et al. (1996) speculated that the F5 region in the monkey may bear homologies to Broca's area in the human – the region of left inferior PFC that we first encountered in *Chapter 1*, and will do so again in *Chapter 19*.

With regard to autism spectrum disorder (ASD), some have proposed that dysfunction of the mirror system underlies the disorder. One high-profile study by Mirella Dapretto et al. (2005) compared fMRI activity in typically developing adolescents vs. "high-functioning" children with ASD on tasks requiring passive observation vs. mimicking of visually presented facial expressions. The findings indicated that, although behavioral performance was comparable between the two groups, "the ASD group showed no activity in the mirror area in the pars opercularis" (Dapretto et al., 2005, p. 29). (Note that, strictly speaking, the assertion of "no activity" cannot, literally, be true. If it were, pars opercularis in these subjects would have been necrotic. Indeed, read on.) Furthermore, the authors reported that the level of activity in this region correlated negatively with ASD subjects' scores on two scales, indicating that "the greater the activity in this critical component of the [mirror neuron system] during imitation, the higher a child's level of functioning in the social domain" (pp. 29–30).

In response to this embrace of mirror neurons as a factor accounting for important human behaviors, and their pathological dysfunction, cautionary voices have been raised. These, and more recent pro-mirror neuron reviews, are listed under *Further Reading*.

It's All About Action

The principles of motor control lie at the core of understanding human behavior. On one level, this must literally be true, because we cannot *behave* without the release of ACh at the neuromuscular junction causing the contraction of muscle, nor all the steps that precede this event. At a deeper level, we have also seen that circuits identical to those responsible for the triggering of a motor command and for the fine-tuning of its execution apply those same computations to signals from prefrontal areas associated with our most abstract thoughts and our most powerful feelings. It will serve us well, therefore, as we delve further from the sensory and motor peripheries, in the exploration of "higher levels" of cognition, to be at the ready with such principles and concepts as population coding, efference copy, neuromodulatory tone, and RPE signals.

End-of-Chapter Questions

1. What is the principle of efference copy? Name two major systems that work on this principle.

2. What does it mean to say that muscles behave like springs? How does the motor system take advantage of this property?

3. In what way(s) is the motor homunculus similar to the somatosensory homunculus? In what way(s) are they different?

4. Explain how population coding across hundreds of broadly tuned units could produce exquisitely precise movements.

5. Describe the idea of activity in an action-null subspace. Why might it be a valuable feature of a motor system?

6. Describe the concept of a neural mode. How does it relate to the analytic operation of dimensionality reduction? What features of neurons in the motor system may make this system well-suited to dimensionality reduction?

7. What principle do you think better captures the function of the parietal cortex, processing *where* objects are located in the visual world, or computing *how* to act on the world based on visual input? Or, alternatively, can both be valid? Support your answer with empirical evidence.

8. How is a copy of the efferent motor signal processed in the cerebellum? What is the result?

9. What are two consequences for basal ganglia function of reducing levels of DA in the neostriatum, as occurs in PD?

10. What are the fundamental principles of reinforcement learning? In what way do these seem to be carried out by the basal ganglia nuclei?

11. What properties distinguish mirror neurons of PMC from "conventional" neurons in this region? What functions might such neurons enable?

References

Albus, James S. 1971. "A Theory of Cerebellar Function." *Mathematical Biosciences* 10 (1–2): 25–61. doi: 10.1016/0025-5564(71)90051-4.

Andersen, Richard A., Sam Musallam, and Bijan Pesaran. 2004. "Selecting the Signals for a Brain–Machine Interface." *Current Opinion in Neurobiology* 14 (6): 720–726. doi: 10.1016/j.conb.2004.10.005.

Antonioni, A., E. M. Raho, S. Straudi, E. Granieri, G. Koch, and L. Fadiga. 2024. "The Cerebellum and the Mirror Neuron System: A Matter of Inhibition? From Neurophysiological Evidence to Neuromodulatory Implications. A Narrative Review." *Neuroscience and Biobehavioral Reviews 164*: 105830. doi: doi.org/10.1016/j.neubiorev.2024.105830.

Bonini, L., C. Rotunno, E. Arcuri, and V. Gallese. 2022. "Mirror Neurons 30 Years Later: Implications and Applications." *Trends in Cognitive Sciences 26* (9): 767–781. doi: 10.1016/j.tics.2022.06.003.

Bonini, L., C. Rotunno, E. Arcuri, and V. Gallese. 2023. "The Mirror Mechanism: Linking Perception and Social Interaction." *Trends in Cognitive Sciences 27* (3): 220–221. doi: 10.1016/j.tics.2022.12.010.

Brown, Peter, Antonio Oliviero, Paolo Mazzone, Angelo Insola, Pietro Tonali, and Vincenzo Di Lazzaro. 2001. "Dopamine Dependency of Oscillations between Subthalamic Nucleus and Pallidum in Parkinson's Disease." *Journal of Neuroscience* 21 (3): 1033–1038.

Cole, S. R., R. van der Meij, E. J. Peterson, C. de Hemptinne, P. A. Starr, and B. Voytek. 2017. "Nonsinusoidal Beta Oscillations Reflect Cortical Pathophysiology in Parkinson's Disease." *Journal of Neuroscience* 37: 4830–4840.

Dapretto, Mirella, Mari S. Davies, Jennifer H. Pfeifer, Ashley A. Scott, Marian Sigman, Susan Y. Bookheimer, and Marco Iacoboni. 2005. "Understanding Emotions in Others: Mirror Neuron Dysfunction in Children with Autism Spectrum Disorders." *Nature Neuroscience* 9 (1): 28–30. doi: 10.1038/nn1611.

Fritsch, Gustav, and Eduard Hitzig. 1870. "Über die elektrische Erregbarkeit des Grosshirns." *Archiv für Anatomie, Physiologie und wissenschaftliche Medicin* 37: 300–332. [Available in English translation as: Fritsch, Gustav, and Eduard Hitzig. 2009. "Electric Excitability of the Cerebrum (Über die elektrische Erregbarkeit des Grosshirns)." *Epilepsy and Behavior* 15 (2): 123–130. doi: 10.1016/j.yebeh.2009.03.001.].

Gallego, J. A., M. G. Perich, L. E. Miller, and S. A. Solla. 2017. "Neural Manifolds for the Control of Movement." *Neuron 94*: 978–984. doi: 10.1016/j.neuron.2017.05.025.

Gallese, Vittorio, Luciano Fadiga, Leonardo Fogassi, and Giacomo Rizzolatti. 1996. "Action Recognition in the Premotor Cortex." *Brain* 119 (2): 593–609. doi: 10.1093/brain/119.2.593.

de Gelder, B. 2023. "Social Affordances, Mirror Neurons, and How to Understand the Social Brain." *Trends in Cognitive Sciences 27*: 218–219.

Georgopoulos, Apostolos P., John F. Kalaska, Roberto Caminiti, and Joe T. Massey. 1982. "On the Relations Between the Direction of Two-Dimensional Arm Movements and Cell Discharge in Primate Motor Cortex." *Journal of Neuroscience* 2 (11): 1527–1537.

Georgopoulos, Apostolos P., Roberto Caminiti, John F. Kalaska, and Joe T. Massey. 1983. "Spatial Coding of Movement: A Hypothesis Concerning the Coding of Movement Direction by Motor Cortical Populations." *Experimental Brain Research Supplementum* 7: 327–336. doi: 10.1007/978-3-642-68915-4_34.

Goodale, Melvyn A., A. David Milner, Lorna S. Jakobson, and David P. Carey. 1991. "A Neurological Dissociation between Perceiving Objects and Grasping Them." *Nature* 349 (6305): 154–156. doi: 10.1038/349154a0.

Gordon, E. M., R. J. Chauvin, A. N. Van, A. Rajesh, A. Nielsen, D. J. Newbold, . . . N. U. F. Dosenbach. 2023. "A Somato-Cognitive Action Network Alternates with Effector Regions in Motor Cortex." *Nature 617* (7960): 351–359. doi: 10.1038/s41586-023-05964-2.

de Hemptinne, C., N. Swann, J. L. Ostrem, E. S. Ryapolova-Webb, N. B. Galifianakis, and P. A. Starr. 2015. "Therapeutic Deep Brain Stimulation Reduces Cortical Phase-Amplitude Coupling in Parkinson's Disease." *Nature Neuroscience 18*: 779–786.

Ito, Masao. 2008. "Control of Mental Activities by Internal Models in the Cerebellum." *Nature Reviews Neuroscience* 9 (4): 304–313. doi: 10.1038/nrn2332.

Kaas, Jon H. 2012. "Evolution of Columns, Modules, and Domains in the Neocortex of Primates." *Proceedings of the National Academy of Sciences of the United States of America* 109 (Supplement 1): 10655–10660. doi: 10.1073/pnas.1201892109.

Kandel, Eric R., James H. Schwartz, and Thomas M. Jessell, eds. 2000. *Principles of Neural Science*. New York: McGraw-Hill.

Kilavik, Bjørg Elisabeth, Joachim Confais, Adrián Ponce-Alvarez, Markus Diesmann, and Alexa Riehle. 2010. "Evoked Potentials in Motor Cortical Local Field Potentials Reflect Task Timing and Behavioral Performance." *Journal of Neurophysiology* 104 (5): 2338–2351. doi: 10.1152/jn.00250.2010.

Kravitz, D. J., K. S. Saleem, C. I. Baker, and M. Mishkin. 2011. "A New Neural Framework for Visuospatial Processing." *Nature Reviews Neuroscience* 12: 217–230.

Penfield, Wilder, and Theodore Rasmussen. 1950. *The Cerebral Cortex of Man. A Clinical Study of Localization of Function*. New York: Macmillan.

Pohl, Walter. 1973. "Dissociation of Spatial Discrimination Deficits Following Frontal and Parietal Lesions in Monkeys." *Journal of Comparative and Physiological Psychology* 82 (2): 227–239. doi: 10.1037/h0033922.

Rescorla, R. A., and A. R. Wagner. 1972. "A Theory of Pavlovian Conditioning: Variations in the Effectiveness of Reinforcement and Nonreinforcement." In *Classical Conditioning II*, edited by A. H. Black and W. F. Prokasy (pp. 64–99). New York: Appleton-Century-Crofts.

Other Sources Used

Albus, James S. 1989. "The Marr and Albus Theories of the Cerebellum: Two Early Models of Associative Memory." In *Paper presented at COMPCON Spring '89. Thirty-fourth IEEE Computer Society International Conference: Intellectual Leverage, Digest of Papers* (pp. 577–582), vol. February 27–March 1. San Francisco, California. doi: 10.1109/CMPCON.1989.301996.

Blakeslee, Sandra. 2008. *Monkey's Thoughts Propel Robot, a Step That May Help Humans. The New York Times*. January 15. http://www.nytimes.com/2008/01/15/science/15robo.xhtml?pagewanted=all&_r=0.

Carmena, Jose M., Mikhail A. Lebedev, Roy E. Crist, Joseph E. O'Doherty, David M. Santucci, Dragan F. Dimitrov, . . . Miguel A. L. Nicolelis. 2003. "Learning to Control a Brain–Machine Interface for Reaching and Grasping by Primates." *PLoS Biology* 1 (2): e42. doi: 10.1371/journal.pbio.0000042.

Cohen, M. X., and M. J. Frank. 2009. "Neurocomputational Models of Basal Ganglia Function in Learning, Memory and Choice." *Behavioural Brain Research* 199: 141–156.

de Hemptinne, C., N. Swann, J. L. Ostrem, E. S. Ryapolova-Webb, N. B. Galifianakis, and P. A. Starr. 2015. "Therapeutic Deep Brain Stimulation Reduces Cortical Phase-Amplitude Coupling in Parkinson's Disease." *Nature Neuroscience* 18: 779–786.

Dinstein, Ilan, Cibu Thomas, Marlene Behrmann, and David J. Heeger. 2008. "A Mirror Up to Nature." *Current Biology* 18 (1): R13–R18. doi: 10.1016/j.cub.2007.11.004.

Du, J., L. M. DiNicola, P. A. Angeli, N. Saadon-Grosman, W. Sun, S. Kaiser, . . . R. L. Buckner. 2024. "Organization of the Human Cerebral Cortex Estimated within Individuals: Networks, Global Topography, and Function." *Journal of Neurophysiology 131*: 1014–1082. doi: 10.1152/jn.00308.2023.

Eccles, John C., János Szentágothai, and Masao Itō. 1967. *The Cerebellum as a Neuronal Machine*. Berlin: Springer-Verlag.

Frank, M. J. 2005. "Dynamic Dopamine Modulation in the Basal Ganglia: A Neurocomputational Account of Cognitive Deficits in Medicated and Nonmedicated Parkinsonism." *Journal of Cognitive Neuroscience* 17: 51–72.

Frank, M. J. 2011. "Computational Models of Motivated Action Selection in Corticostriatal Circuits." *Current Opinion in Neurobiology* 21: 381–386.

Gastaut, Henri J., and J. Bert. 1954. "EEG Changes During Cinematographic Presentation." *Electroencephalography and Clinical Neurophysiology* 6 (3): 433–444. doi: 10.1016/0013-4694(54)90058-9.

Georgopoulos, Apostolos P., Andrew B. Schwartz, and Ronald E. Kettner. 1986. "Neuronal Population Coding of Movement Direction." *Science* 233 (4771): 1416–1419.

Goodale, Melvyn A., and A. David Milner. 1992. "Separate Visual Pathways for Perception and Action." *Trends in Neurosciences* 15 (1): 20–25. doi: 10.1016/0166-2236(92)90344-8.

Hikida, T., K. Kimura, N Wada, K. Funabiki, and S. Nakanishi. 2010. "Distinct Roles of Synaptic Transmission in Direct and Indirect Striatal Pathways to Reward and Aversive Behavior." *Neuron* 66: 896–907.

Jackson, N., S. R. Cole, B. Voytek, and N. C. Swann. 2019. "Characteristics of Waveform Shape in Parkinson's Disease Detected with Scalp Electroencephalography." *eNeuro* 6. doi: doi.org/10.1523/ENEURO.0151-19.2019.

Jakobson, Lorna S., Y. M. Archibald, David P. Carey, and Melvyn A. Goodale. 1991. "A Kinematic Analysis of Reaching and Grasping Movements in a Patient Recovering from Optic Ataxia." *Neuropsychologia* 29 (8): 803–805. doi: 10.1016/0028-3932(91)90073-H.

Jazayeri, M., and S. Ostojic. 2021. "Interpreting Neural Computations by Examining Intrinsic and Embedding Dimensionality of Neural Activity." *Current Opinion in Neurobiology 70*: 113–120. doi: 10.1016/j.conb.2021.08.002.

Leveratto, Jean-Marc. 2009. "La revue internationale de filmologie et la genèse de la sociologie du cinéma en France." *Cinémas: revue d'études cinématographiques* 19 (2–3): 183–215. doi: 10.7202/037553ar.

Mink, J. W., and W. T. Thach. 1991. "Basal Ganglia Motor Control. I. Nonexclusive Relation of Pallidal Discharge to Five Movement Modes." *Journal of Neurophysiology* 65 (2): 273–300.

Romo, Ranulfo, and Wolfram Schultz. 1990. "Dopamine Neurons of the Monkey Midbrain: Contingencies of Responses to Active Touch during Self-Initiated Arm Movements." *Journal of Neurophysiology* 63 (3): 592–606.

Schultz, Wolfram, and Ranulfo Romo. 1990. "Dopamine Neurons of the Monkey Midbrain: Contingencies of Responses to Stimuli Eliciting Immediate Behavioral Responses." *Journal of Neurophysiology* 63 (3): 607–624.

Tononi, Giulio. 2008. "Consciousness as Integrated Information: A Provisional Manifesto." *Biological Bulletin* 215 (3): 216–242.

Umiltà, Maria Alessandra, E. Kohler, V. Gallese, L. Fogassi, L. Fadiga, C. Keysers, and G. Rizzolatti. 2001. "I Know What You Are Doing: A Neurophysiological Study." *Neuron* 31 (1): 155–165.

Umiltà, Maria Alessandra. 2000. *Premotor Area F5 and Action Recognition*. PhD diss.: University of Parma.

Further Reading

For these, the reader is directed to two opinion pieces, one entitled "A Mirror up to Nature" (Dinstein, Thomas, Behrmann, and Heeger, 2008), and a second entitled "Eight Problems for the Mirror Neuron Theory of Action Understanding in Monkeys and Humans" (Hickok, 2009), both listed

(Bonini, Rotunno, Arcuri, and Gallese, 2022)

(de Gelder, 2023)

(Bonini, Rotunno, Arcuri, & Gallese, 2023)

(Antonioni et al., 2024)

Updated dialogue about mirror neurons.

Brown, Peter, Antonio Oliviero, Paolo Mazzone, Angelo Insola, Pietro Tonali, and Vincenzo Di Lazzaro. 2001. "Dopamine Dependency of Oscillations between Subthalamic Nucleus and Pallidum in Parkinson's Disease." *Journal of Neuroscience* 21 (3): 1033–1038.

Recordings made while patients – undergoing implantation of stimulating electrodes for chronic deep brain stimulation – were ON and OFF dopaminergic medication reveal a marked change in the frequency at which these two nuclei are synchronized (i.e., DA level influences the frequency of interareal spike-field coherence).

Cole, S. R., R. van der Meij, E. J. Peterson, C. de Hemptinne, P. A. Starr, and B. Voytek. 2017. "Nonsinusoidal Beta Oscillations Reflect Cortical Pathophysiology in Parkinson's Disease." *Journal of Neuroscience* 37: 4830–4840.

Paper that reassessed ECoG data of DBS in PD and demonstrated that elevated measures of PAC were artifactually produced by the sharpness of beta-band oscillations and that the real effect of DBS is to smooth out the shape of this waveform.

Dinstein, Ilan, Cibu Thomas, Marlene Behrmann, and David J. Heeger. 2008. "A Mirror up to Nature." *Current Biology* 18 (1): R13–R18. doi: 10.1016/j.cub.2007.11.004.

A critique of the mirror neuron literature, from neurophysiological and functional perspectives, from two leading cognitive neuroscientists and their trainees.

Hickok, Gregory. 2009. "Eight Problems for the Mirror Neuron Theory of Action Understanding in Monkeys and Humans." *Journal of Cognitive Neuroscience* 21 (7): 1229–1243. doi: 10.1162/jocn.2009.21189.

The title says it all.

Hickok, Gregory. 2014. *The Myth of Mirror Neurons: The Real Neuroscience of Communication and Cognition*. New York: W. W. Norton.

An update and elaboration on the 2009 opinion piece that not only critiques the "action understanding" theory but also reviews alternative proposals about mirror neuron contributions to motor control. Some of this book's content is also relevant to the work of Hickok, and others, that is detailed in Chapter 19: Language.

Himmelbach, Marc, Rebecca Boehme, and Hans-Otto Karnath. 2012. "20 Years Later: A Second Look on D. F.'s Motor Behaviour." *Neuropsychologia* 560 (1): 139–144. doi: 10.1016/j.neuropsychologia.2011.11.011.

A comparison of more recently acquired control data with the original results from D.F. that concludes that "the widespread and popular presentation of strong dissociations between distinct visual systems seems to be exaggerated."

Jenkinson, Ned, and Peter Brown. 2011. "New Insights into the Relationship between Dopamine, Beta Oscillations, and Motor Function." *Trends in Neurosciences* 34 (12): 611–618. doi: 10.1016/j.tins.2011.09.003.

Review that nicely demonstrates how clinical research (in this case, with PD) can inform basic science-level knowledge, and vice versa.

Kravitz, Dwight J., Kadharbatcha S. Saleem, Chris I. Baker, and Mortimer Mishkin. 2011. "A New Neural Framework for Visuospatial Processing." *Nature Reviews Neuroscience* 12 (4): 217–230. doi: 10.1038/nrn3008.

A proposal that discrete anatomical pathways support the processing of spatial information in the service of where-based behavior (PPC-FEF and PFC), how-based behavior (PPC-premotor cortex), and navigation behavior (PPC-medial PPC-MTL).

Rizzolatti, G., and L. Craighero. 2004. "The Mirror-Neuron System." *Annual Review of Neuroscience* 27: 169–192. doi: 10.1146/annurev.neuro.27.070203.144230.

This review has, at the time of this writing, accrued an astounding 3588 citations in the peer-reviewed literature.

Schenk, Thomas, and Robert D. McIntosh. 2010. "Do We Have Independent Visual Streams for Perception and Action?." *Cognitive Neuroscience* 1 (1): 52–62. doi: 10.1080/17588920903388950.

A "20-years later" critical review of the what vs. how model, followed by commentary/rebuttals from many leading researchers, including Goodale and Milner.

CHAPTER 9

Oculomotor Control and the Control of Attention

KEY THEMES

- Four regions that contribute importantly to oculomotor control are the superior colliculus (SC), regions of occipital and parietal cortex (particularly V1 and LIP), regions of frontal cortex (the frontal eye field [FEF] and the supplementary eye field [SEF]), and the brainstem oculomotor nuclei that send commands to the extraocular muscles.
- Although superficial layers of the SC receive direct projections from the retina, the deep layers contain multimodal sensory neurons and movement neurons to which posterior cortical neurons project, and which, in turn, project to the brainstem oculomotor nuclei.
- FEF neurons, which project directly to the brainstem oculomotor nuclei, encode vector saccades, whereas SEF neurons encode goal-oriented saccades.
- Saccade planning and the endogenous control of attention both engage a dorsal fronto-parietal network that includes FEF and IPS/LIP.
- The reflexive, exogenous capture of attention is associated with a right hemisphere-biased ventral cortical system, including the temporal–parietal junction and the inferior PFC, regions also associated with hemispatial neglect.
- Microstimulation of monkey FEF produces retinotopically specific behavior that is equivalent to the effects of cuing the endogenous control of attention, and also produces attention-like effects in V4 neurons whose receptive fields overlap with the movement field of the stimulation site.
- MVPA has been used to demonstrate that the same systems that control eye movements are also used to control attention.
- Despite the "circuit-breaker" properties of exogenously triggered attention, individuals can adopt a behavioral strategy whereby salient distractors can be ignored, an ability supported by a subset of neurons in the FEF.

CONTENTS

Companion Website: www.wiley.com/go/postle/cognitiveneuroscience3e

Attention and Action

We have reached the final chapter of *Part 3*, themed *Sensation, perception, attention, and action*. While we have seen in previous chapters how strongly perception and attention are linked (e.g., the attentional amplification of one sensory input channel over others, the dependence on attention of experience-dependent plasticity, unilateral neglect), this chapter will emphasize even more strongly than did the previous two how closely intertwined are the constructs of attention and action. At another level, this is the last chapter for which it will be necessary to begin with an overview of the anatomy of the system of interest. We haven't, of course, covered "everything," but upon completion of this chapter, the reader will have had an introduction to all of the major systems and principles of functional neuroanatomy, and will have the foundation on which to build a more detailed understanding of the intricacies of any particular component. Similarly, if the author has done his job, we'll see in every chapter following this one – i.e., in every chapter detailing some aspect of "high-level cognition" – that the principles underlying memory storage and retrieval, cognitive control, decision making, language, emotion, and so on can be understood as variations on the principles introduced in this section on the more "concrete" functions of the brain.

Whys and Hows of Eye Movements

Let's take a moment to recall one of the reasons why the ability to move the eyes is so important: it enables the visual system to disproportionately devote processing resources and, therefore, acuity, to just a small area of the visual field. If you need detailed information about an object located 15° to the left of your current point of fixation, you can obtain it within ~300 msec by moving your center of gaze to this location. The tradeoff for the "cost" of those 300 msec is not having to drag around a visual cortex that's the size of the room that you're currently sitting in, or, alternatively, not having to survive with a visual system with uniformly horribly low resolution. Because there are some instances when a few tens of milliseconds can matter, however, we'll see that one feature of the oculomotor system is multiple pathways that control the eyes in different contexts.

Three Categories of Eye Movements

Eye movements fall into three categories: smooth pursuit, vergence shifts, and saccades. We won't spend much time considering the first two, but we will define them briefly here. If you hold out your thumb and fixate the nail, then slowly move your head from side to side, all the while maintaining fixation on your thumbnail, you are performing smooth-pursuit eye movements. (If your eyes hadn't been moving to compensate for the back-and-forth motion of your head, your thumbnail wouldn't have remained in your center of gaze.) The equivalent eye movements are generated if you now hold your head still and move your thumb back and forth. Thus, smooth-pursuit eye movements enable you to maintain fixation on an object while it, you, or both, are moving. During smooth pursuit, the two eyes move "together" (i.e., the movements of one eye are identical to those of the other). These are referred to as **conjugate eye movements**.

Vergence shifts occur when an object of interest is moving toward or away from you, and in order to fixate it with both eyes, the two must move in opposite directions: toward each other if the object is looming; away from each other if it is receding. Signals from stretch receptors on the extraocular muscles convey information about the positions of the eyes relative to each other (i.e., how parallel vs. converging). This information contributes to the perception of depth (i.e., seeing in 3-D) and of motion in depth (i.e., motion toward and away from you, as opposed to motion along a 2D surface, such as when looking at a movie screen or a computer monitor). (Importantly, although the dynamics of pupil diameter [*Chapter 4*, section *Pupillometry*] are typically measured with the same equipment, and often at the same time, as eye movements, the neural systems and cognitive constructs implicated by pupillometry and eye movements are distinct.)

The third category, saccadic eye movements, is a focus of this chapter. The word *saccade* is French for a jerky movement and was first associated with eye movements by the French ophthalmologist Emile Javal (1839–1907), who held a mirror at an angle while reading and observed that his eyes made a series of brief fixations, punctuated by abrupt conjugate movements, rather than a smooth, continuous drift across the page as most had previously assumed (and as is this author's subjective experience every time he reads words on a page). Saccades are of primary interest here because of their central importance to many domains of cognition (reading being just one of them), and because they have been used extensively in psychology and neuroscience research as an indirect measure of cognitive operations. Because monkeys cannot be verbally instructed on how to respond during performance of experimental tasks, nor can they tell you what they are thinking, saccades are a way for the animal to indicate its choice in an experiment. (E.g., *Which is the most recent item that you saw?* or *Which of these stimuli is different from the others?*) And although it would be disingenuous to suggest that training a monkey to perform a cognitive task is ever "easy," it is the case that saccadic eye movements are natural behaviors for monkeys (and humans), and choosing to use them as a dependent measure can at least give the researcher a "head start" in the training process. For humans, the saccade itself can be of fundamental interest if it is a fundamental part of the behavior of interest (e.g., reading or visual search). Additionally, scientists have devised clever ways to use eye movements to assay the dynamics of cognitive operations as they are being carried out, as opposed to, or in addition to, retrospective reports that come at the end of each trial. (E.g., whether the eyes start to drift toward word *X* or word *Y*, both displayed on a screen, can provide insight into the mental operations engaged while a person is listening to a semantically ambiguous sentence.)

The Organization of the Oculomotor System

An Overview of the Circuitry

There are many factors that can prompt an eye movement. (And here comes more author's narration:) I can decide, while taking a pause as I type this sentence, to look up at a painting hanging on the wall of my living room. My eyes can be drawn reflexively toward the source of a sound, or to a touch (say, if the cat unexpectedly jumps up onto the back of the couch that I'm sitting on). I can scan the shelves of a grocery store, looking for that particular brand of soy sauce. Much of the discussion here, however, will be framed in terms of visually guided saccades. That is, what are the steps that transpire between the detection on the retina of a visual stimulus and the saccade that brings that stimulus into foveal vision? Along the way, we'll note instances where the principles may be similar or different for other factors that can also trigger saccades.

Although the principal pathway for visual processing in most mammalian species is the retino-geniculo-striate pathway, it "wasn't always that way." In fish and amphibians, for example, the primary site of visual processing is a midbrain structure known as the optic tectum. In the mammal, the homologue is the superior colliculus (SC) ("higher hill" in Latin; the inferior colliculus of the auditory system, *Figure 3.7*, is the "lower hill"), a structure that sits immediately caudal to the thalamus on the "roof" ("tectum") of the brainstem. There is a direct, monosynaptic pathway from the retina to the SC, which will receive more consideration further along in this chapter. The SC projects to the **brainstem oculomotor nuclei**, which house the local circuitry and oculomotor neurons, analogous to the motor circuitry of the spinal cord, that process descending motor commands and send axons that innervate the extraocular muscles. Within cortex, regions contributing to oculomotor control can be divided into posterior and anterior systems, the posterior including, most prominently, V1, LIP, and V4, and the anterior comprising the frontal eye field (FEF) and the supplementary eye field (SEF, also sometimes referred to as the medial eye field [MEF] or dorsomedial frontal cortex [DMFC]). The primary distinction between the posterior and anterior systems is that the former regions project to the SC – SC lesions abolish the ability of electrical stimulation of posterior cortical areas to elicit saccades – whereas the anterior regions, although sending projections to the SC, also send projections directly to the brainstem oculomotor nuclei (*Figure 9.1*).

Let's now consider each of these major elements of the "oculomotor system" in turn. (Keep in mind that most, if not all, of the cortical areas to be discussed here can't be considered "specialized" for oculomotor control; the label "oculomotor system" is simply an economical way to say "regions in the brain that can contribute to oculomotor control.")

The Superior Colliculus

In primates, the superior colliculi (one on each side of the midline) are each about the size of a half-globe of a pea, and roughly divided into three layers: superficial, intermediate, and deep. It is the deep layers that send efferents to the brainstem oculomotor nuclei. The superficial layers receive direct input from the retina via a specialized class of retinal ganglion cells called *w* cells. The deep layers are of greater interest because they receive the cortical efferents illustrated in *Figure 9.1*, as well as sensory information from the visual, auditory, and tactile modalities. There are two interleaved populations of cells: sensory neurons that have multimodal receptive fields and that represent locations in retinotopic coordinates; and saccade neurons whose bursting activity brings the center of gaze into the receptive field of adjacent sensory neurons. Thus, the SC employs a vector code, in that activity in a certain area always produces a saccade of the same direction and magnitude.

At the rostral-most end of the SC, in the deep layers, are fixation neurons. In effect, in relation to the motor map illustrated in *Figure 9.2*, these command saccades of 0°. These neurons

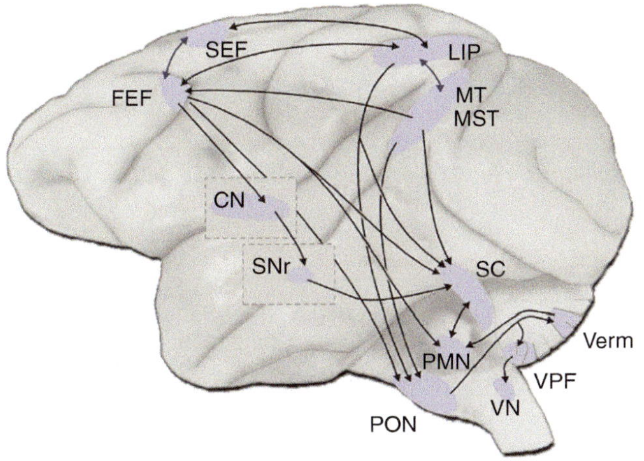

FIGURE 9.1 Important nodes and connections for oculomotor control. Note that among this diagram's simplifications are the absence of the V1 projection to SC, and the integration of LIP and FEF signals in the "oculomotor" cortico-basal ganglia-thalamic loop. CN = caudate nucleus; FEF = frontal eye field; LIP = lateral intraparietal area; MT = middle temporal area; MST = medial superior temporal area; PMN = brain stem (pre)motor nuclei (PPRF, riMLF, cMRF); PON = precerebellar pontine nuclei; SC = superior colliculus (intermediate and deep layers); SEF = supplementary eye field; SNr = substantia nigra pars reticulata; Verm = oculomotor vermis (cerebellum, lobules VI and VII); VN = vestibular nuclei; VPF = ventral paraflocculus (cerebellum).

Source: Krauzlis and Richard, 2005 / SAGE Publications.

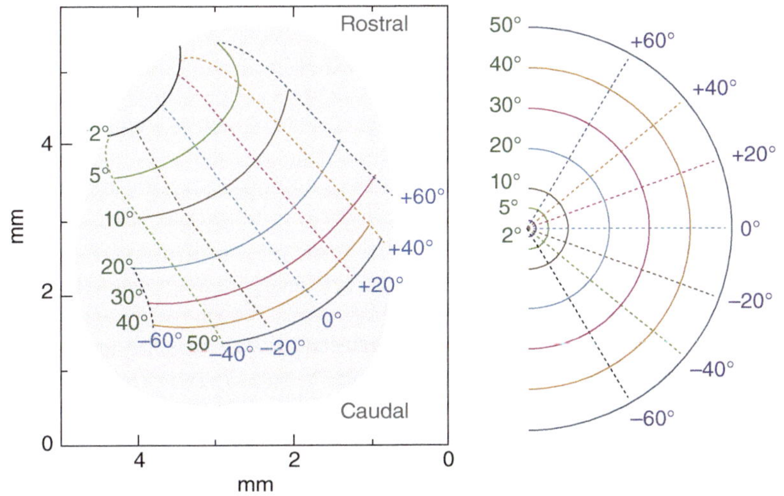

FIGURE 9.2 The functional organization of the superior colliculus (SC). Left panel: motor map in deep layers of the left SC; right panel: corresponding regions of the right visual field. Green labels correspond to saccade amplitude and blue labels to degrees of polar angle from fixation. Thus, the left panel illustrates that motor neurons in the rostral portion of the SC produce small-amplitude saccades, and neurons in progressively more caudal areas produce progressively larger-amplitude saccades. Rostral and lateral to the 2° line in the left panel (i.e., in the upper-left corner of the image) are fixation neurons.

Source: Neeraj and Husam, 2011 / Annual Reviews.

maintain a tonically elevated firing rate while one is fixating on a stationary location. (Thus, at least from the reductionist perspective of activity in the SC, the term "passive fixation" that one frequently sees in the literature is a misnomer.)

At any moment in time, most of the motor units in the deep layers of the SC are under tonic inhibition from the substantia nigra pars reticulata, an arrangement analogous to the tonic inhibition of thalamus by the GPi that we detailed in *Chapter 8*.

The Posterior System

Although neurons from layer V of V1 send projections to the SC, their contribution seems to be modulatory, rather than driving. This assessment comes from the fact that, although microstimulation of V1 can produce saccades, the currents required to do so are markedly higher than those required in other cortical areas, such as the FEF, or in the SC itself. However, cooling V1, a method that reversibly inactivates a region of cortex, has the effect of abolishing visual sensory responses in the deep layers of the SC. Also consistent with a modulatory function of V1 on the SC is the association of an oscillatory state in occipital cortex with the generation of **express saccades**.

Express saccades have a latency that can be as much as one-half that of standard saccade latency – in one study in humans, 90–135 msec after target onset for express saccades, 145–240 for standard saccades – and are often seen in response to the abrupt appearance of an unexpected stimulus. They are also readily produced experimentally with a "gap" paradigm, in which a gap of a few hundred milliseconds is inserted between the offset of the fixation point that began the trial and the onset of the target to which the subject must make a saccade. Although it would be tempting to postulate that express saccades are generated by a "short circuit" from the retina to SC to brainstem oculomotor nuclei, the anatomy would seem to argue against this, because, as far as we know, retinocollicular projections terminate exclusively in superficial layers of the SC, and these do not project directly to the deep layers. An alternative account is that "advanced motor preparation of saccadic programs" (Paré and Munoz, 1996, p. 3666) enables the cortical system to generate saccades more quickly than is typical. Consistent with this idea is the fact that express saccades are more likely to be generated on trials with elevated oscillatory synchrony in the low alpha-band range, measured at occipital EEG electrodes.

Consistent with their role in processing visual motion, the contributions of areas MT and MST to oculomotor control are particularly important for guiding smooth-pursuit movements.

As discussed in *Chapter 7* (section *Extracellular electrophysiological studies of monkeys*), the lateral intraparietal area (LIP) is involved in "cognitive" aspects of eye-movement control – carrying out coordinate transformations and representing the spatial coordinates of potential targets of fixation in the environment – functions related to this region's role in representing a priority map (section *Turning our attention to the future, Chapter 7*). Like area V1, microstimulation of neurons in LIP will drive the eyes to the location represented by the stimulated neuron's receptive field, although this may require stronger currents than other nodes in the oculomotor system.

The Frontal Eye Field

As illustrated in *Figure 9.1*, the FEF in the monkey is located in the rostral bank of the arcuate sulcus, immediately anterior to premotor cortex. Among the first to study the FEF was David Ferrier, whose involvement in nineteenth-century research on the neural bases of vision made an appearance in *Chapter 1*. Ferrier (1875) found that electrical stimulation of this region produced "turning of the eyes and head to the opposite side" (p. 424), and that a unilateral lesion impaired the abilities of the animal to orient to stimuli presented contralateral to the lesion. Based on these and other observations, he stated most presciently in 1890 that "my hypothesis is that the power of attention is intimately related to the volitional movements of the head and eyes" (Ferrier, 1890, p. 151). Consistent with this idea has been the subsequent description, in monkeys and humans, of unilateral neglect after damage to the FEF.

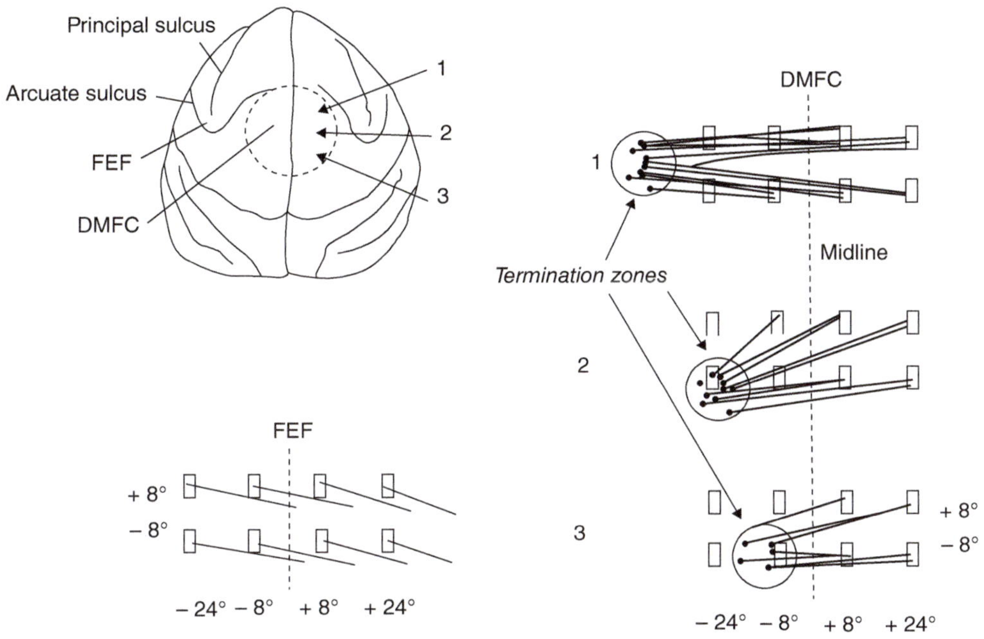

FIGURE 9.3 The effects of microstimulation of one neuron in FEF and of three neurons in SEF (referred to as DMFC by the scientist figure, the location of each indicated with an arrow, from each of eight starting fixation points).

Source: Schiller, 1998 / Psychology Press.

As indicated earlier, a distinguishing characteristic of the FEF is its low threshold for saccade generation with microstimulation. Although its organization isn't strictly retinotopic, it's generally the case that small, contralaterally directed saccades are produced by microstimulation in the ventrolateral limb of the anterior bank of the arcuate sulcus, and larger amplitude saccades by microstimulation in the dorsomedial limb. FEF encodes vector saccades, in that repeated stimulation of the same site produces a saccade of the same metrics, regardless of the starting point of the eye (*Figure 9.3*). A sustained pulse of stimulation produces a series of discrete saccades, all of the same metric. This is an interesting phenomenon that illustrates the recoding that happens in the brainstem oculomotor nuclei, because sustained microstimulation of a single location in one of these nuclei produces a very different effect – a saccade whose magnitude is linearly dependent on the duration of the stimulation train. (The same is true, of course, for the extraocular muscles: they will only contract so long as, in response to microstimulation, ACh is being released into the neuromuscular junction.)

The Supplementary Eye Field

Located dorsal and somewhat caudal to the FEF (*Figure 9.1*), the SEF lies just rostral to the SMA (*Chapter 8*). Its functions are associated with more "cognitive" aspects of oculomotor control. For example, when two targets are presented, and the monkey will receive a reward for saccading to either one (i.e., "free choice"), SEF, FEF, and LIP all show activity related to the impending choice, but that of the SEF starts earliest and is most robust. SEF activity is also prominent during the **antisaccade task**, when the rule is to make a saccade 180° opposite to the location of the target. The coding principle is also different between SEF and FEF, as is illustrated in *Figure 9.3*. While microstimulation of the FEF neuron produces a saccade with roughly the same metrics regardless of the starting point of the eyes, microstimulation of an SEF neuron always produces a saccade that lands in the same "termination zone." This is reminiscent of what we saw in the spinal cord in *Chapter 8*, where stimulation of one location will always bring the forepaw to the same location in space, regardless of its starting location.

This also highlights a terminological ambiguity caused by differing conventions among scientists studying motor systems vs. sensory systems. A functional principle that has been ascribed to the SEF is that of employing a "place code," in that activity in one set of neurons always brings the center of gaze to the same place. In this context, "place coding" is comparable in meaning to "goal-directed." Recall that in the auditory system, in contrast, the *place* in place coding refers to the place along the length of the basilar membrane from which a fiber of the auditory nerve originates (*Chapter 3*, section *The Auditory-Evoked Response*).

The Control of Eye Movements, and of Attention, in Humans

Human Oculomotor Control

A classic task for assessing oculomotor control is the oculomotor delayed-response task, in which the subject begins by fixating a central location, the to-be-acquired location is cued by a flashed stimulus, but the subject must withhold the saccade to that location until the offset of the fixation point. This temporal separation allows for the dissociation of "sensory" activity related to presentation of the cue from motor activity prompted by fixation offset. (The interpretation of "delay-period activity" sometimes observed between cue offset and fixation offset is less straightforward, as we shall see further along in this chapter, and again in *Chapter 14*.) *Figure 9.4* illustrates this task, together with examples of activity measured from the monkey and the human. Note that in the human, there is robust delay-period activity in the intraparietal sulcus (IPS; one portion of which, IPS 2 [see *Figure 7.5*], is generally thought to be homologous to LIP in the monkey), as well as at two distinct frontal foci (*Figure 9.4*, panel C). The human FEF has classically been associated with the more dorsal of the two, just rostral and ventrolateral to the point of intersection of the precentral sulcus and the superior frontal sulcus (sometimes referred to as the superior precentral sulcus [sPCS]). However, the more ventral focus of elevated activity in frontal cortex is also frequently observed. Note that although the frontal regions illustrated in *Figure 9.4* (panel C) show elevated activity during each epoch of the trial (*cue*, *delay*, *response*), these regions were identified statistically as having elevated activity during the delay period, regardless of whether or not they were differentially responsive during the *cue* and/or *response* epochs.

Human Attentional Control

Recall from *Chapter 7* that we restricted ourselves at that time to a detailed consideration of the *site* of the effects of attention, pushing off consideration of the *source* of attentional control to a later chapter. Well, *source*, your time has come.

From experimental psychology, we have long known that there are two general modes by which attention can be directed: the exogenously triggered *capture* of attention vs. the endogenously controlled *allocation* of attention. An example of an exogenously triggered capture of attention would be that you are sitting quietly, reading this book, when suddenly someone loudly, unexpectedly, bursts into the room. Your reflexive reaction is to turn your head in the direction of the noise. An example of the endogenous control of attention is when you are sitting quietly, pretending to be reading this book, but are, in fact, waiting for the imminent arrival of your roommate/boyfriend/girlfriend/spouse/whomever, and so are attending to the door, waiting for it to open at any moment.

The Endogenous Control of Attention Researchers at Washington University in St. Louis, led by neurologist Maurizio Corbetta and experimental psychologist Gordon Shulman, have used event-related fMRI to separate, for example, transient responses associated with a cue instructing the subject where to attend (i.e., to a location in the periphery) – or what to attend to (e.g., motion in a particular direction) – from the sustained activity associated with

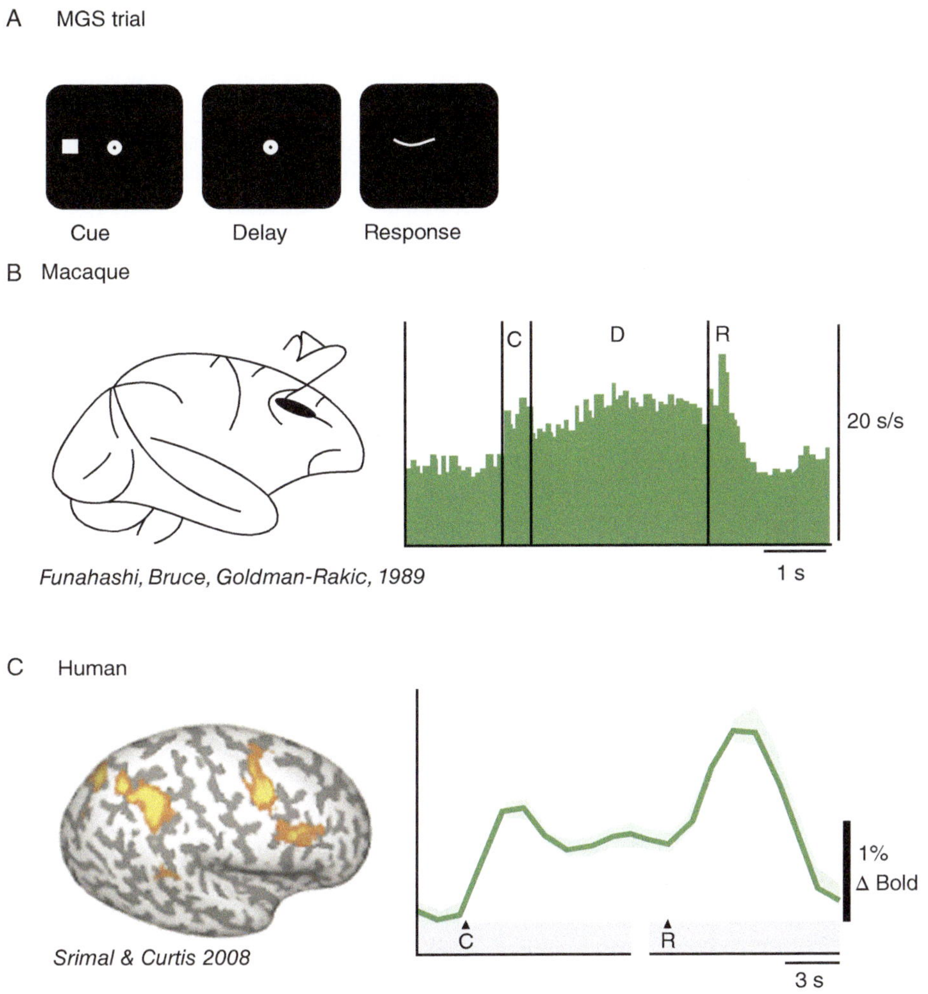

FIGURE 9.4 The delayed-saccade task (also referred to as "memory-guided saccade [MGS]" or "oculomotor delayed response [ODR]"). Panel **A** illustrates a trial, as described in the text. Panel **B** illustrates the recording location in a monkey, in this instance at the caudal end of the principal sulcus, near the rostral boundary of the FEF, and activity recorded from a neuron at this location. Panel **C** illustrates regions with elevated delay-period activity in a human performing this task in an MRI scanner. The anatomical image has been "inflated" so that sulci (darker gray) are visible. Elevated activity is observed in most of the rostral IPS. The fMRI time-series data are interrupted between cue (C) and response (R) because the researchers used variable-length delay periods in this study. Note that this analysis was performed by involving a so-called "slow event-related design," in which individual trials are spaced out, typically by 10 seconds or more. To understand why, it might be helpful to turn back to the section of *Chapter 3*, on *Some considerations for experimental design*, and *Figure 3.20*. The data from the delayed-saccade task illustrated here (i.e., in *Figure 9.4*) needed to be handled in a manner most similar to the blocks featuring nine events occurring with a 15-s ISI (*Figure 3.20.A*), to minimize smearing of responses from one of the trial to others. A "linear deconvolution" analysis of the kind illustrated in *Figure 3.20.C* is not possible with a task like this delayed-saccade task, because the elements of the task can't be presented/performed in a randomized order; that is, the Cue must always precede the Delay, which must always precede the Response.

Source: Ikkai et al., 2011 / with permission of Elsevier.

the top-down maintenance of attention at the cued location – or to the cued direction of motion. Importantly, on perceptually identical "passive viewing" trials, when subjects were told that there was no task to perform, and that they merely had to watch the screen, the transient responses in posterior occipitotemporal regions were only slightly attenuated relative to what they had been in attention-demanding trials. This was consistent with what we have already seen at *sites* of the effects of attentional selection. Activity in rostral IPS and caudal superior frontal cortex, including the FEF, however, showed a very different pattern. It was markedly attenuated, almost to baseline levels, on passive trials. Also noteworthy was the fact that virtually identical patches of cortex in superior parietal and frontal regions showed elevated activity regardless of whether the sustained attention required by a task was location-based (e.g., *Detect the onset of a target at this location*) or feature-based (e.g., *Indicate when you see motion in this direction*). This led to the conclusion, consistent with results from many other studies performed in many other laboratories, that coordinated activity in this dorsal frontoparietal network acted as a *source* of top-down attentional control (*Figure 9.5*).

How might the dorsal frontoparietal system work? At the network level, projections from deep layers of cortex in these regions likely deliver the signals that manifest in sensory processing areas as baseline shifts (in the case of location-based attention) and/or as the biasing signal that influences the competition for representation of a behaviorally relevant stimulus vs. irrelevant items. (Revisit section *Effects of attention on neuronal activity*, *Chapter 7*, if the phenomena of the baseline shift and of biased competition aren't fluently springing to mind.) And at a functional level, many researchers have proposed that elevated activity in dorsal frontoparietal cortex (*Figure 9.5*; corresponding to the Dorsal Attentional Network [DAN] as identified by RSFC [Figure 4.19]) may reflect the operation of a priority map. The idea is that the brain maintains a representation of what's currently the most relevant for behavior, whether that be a representation of the location of potentially important stimuli in the environment, a representation of current behavioral priorities, or both.

Now, let's make this more concrete. Let's say that you're new to Madison, WI, and are driving in a rental car from the airport, trying to navigate to this author's house, where you are invited for dinner. (Lucky you!) As you drive along Old University Avenue, your eyes are, of course, on the road ahead of you. In your "mind", however, are additional representations: (1) you are searching for street signs at each intersection, so as to identify "Forest St." (which should be coming up on the left); (2) you are aware of a group of people standing near a crosswalk in front of you (*What's the law here? Do I have to stop and let them cross in front of me, or will they wait for a break in the traffic?*); and (3) what's up with the car behind you that is driving right up on your @$$?!? Thus, although your eyes are, indeed, on the road, your priority map will prioritize (1) the detection of green street signs; (2) movement into the crosswalk by a pedestrian; (3) the source of potential trouble in the rearview mirror.

SUDDENLY, A BALL ROLLS OUT ONTO THE STREET IN BETWEEN TWO PARKED CARS JUST AHEAD OF YOU!

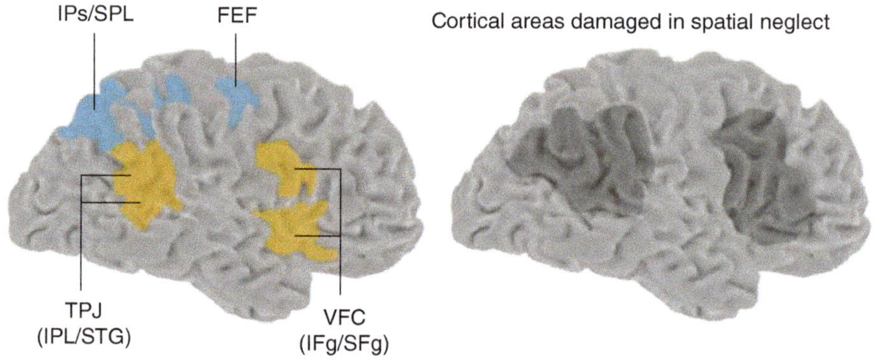

FIGURE 9.5 Two networks for the control of attention. At left, the networks associated with the endogenous (blue) vs. the exogenous (orange) control of attention. At right, regions whose damage is often associated with hemispatial neglect.

Source: Tosoni et al. (2023) / Frontiers Media S.A.

This unexpected event triggers what Corbetta and Shulman (2002) call the "circuit breaker," which overrides the influence of your current priority map on your behavior.

The Exogenous Control of Attention Exogenous control of attention occurs when something salient and unexpected occurs in the world around you, and the source is, therefore, *outside* of your brain. (The endogenous control of attention, in contrast, is considered more "cognitive," in the sense that your thoughts/plans/priorities/motivations are controlling your behavior. They are endogenous in the sense that they are generated within and maintained *inside* you, in your brain.) Corbetta and Shulman have documented that exogenous shifts of attention are associated with a right hemisphere-dominant network, ventral to the dorsal frontoparietal system, that includes the temporoparietal junction (TPJ) and the inferior frontal gyrus of the ventral prefrontal cortex (which they abbreviate as VFC). The ventral network is illustrated in orange in the brain image on the left of *Figure 9.5*. Intriguingly, Corbetta and Shulman (2002) have noted that "the anatomy of neglect . . . matches the ventral TPJ–VFC system" (p. 212). (For one independent dataset generally consistent with this view [and generated several years later], revisit *Figure 7.4*.)

Next, we turn our attention to something that many readers will have already noticed, which is that the dorsal regions highlighted in panel C of *Figure 9.4*, which illustrates activity associated with a delayed-saccade task, show a remarkable overlap with the dorsal frontoparietal system illustrated in *Figure 9.5* (as well as to the RSFC-defined dorsal attentional network [DAN]; *Figure 4.19*).

The Control of Attention via the Oculomotor System

Covert Attention

There are many times in our lives when we want to attend to something, or someone, without directly looking at it (or him, or her, or them). In high school math class, there was that cute classmate on whom you had a crush, but at whom you didn't want to stare. (Never happened to this author, but he's heard heard stories . . .) At the dinner table, one wants to convey to one's kids that one trusts them, and so doesn't want to appear to be closely monitoring their every move, yet one also wants to closely monitor their every move. (This one, your author readily confesses to . . .) These are examples of covert attention. (Overt attention is when you look directly at the object of your attention.) Sustained covert attention may be related to another attentional phenomenon, which is that there is considerable evidence from experimental psychology, and from neurophysiology, that the focus of attention jumps to the target of the next saccade tens of milliseconds prior to the initiation of the saccade itself. Therefore, might it be the case that the sustained allocation of covert attention to a location/object amounts to a "presaccadic" shift of attention, but one that does not culminate in the saccade itself?

Covert Attention as Motor Preparation? This last bit of speculation is what is posited by the **premotor theory of attention**, articulated in the 1980s by Giacomo Rizzolatti (of mirror neuron renown [Chapter 8, section *Mirror Neurons*]). It argues, in summary, that attention may fundamentally be "nothing more" [this author's quotes] than motor planning. Here's how Rizzolatti and Laila Craighero (2010) have summarized it:

> Classically, spatial attention was thought of as a dedicated supramodal control mechanism, anatomically distinct from the circuits underlying sensorimotor processing . . . [However] there is no need to postulate two control mechanisms, one for action and one for attention. According to [the premotor theory,] spatial attention does not result from a dedicated control mechanism, but derives from a weaker activation of the same frontal-parietal circuits that, in other conditions, determine motor behavior toward specific spatial locations.

Empirical Evidence for Covert Attention as Motor Preparation Tirin Moore and his colleagues, first in the laboratory of Charlie Gross, and subsequently in Moore's own lab, have carried out several experiments generating results that are broadly consistent with the premotor theory of attention. Here, we'll review one that Moore carried out with Mazyar Fallah, which specifies in considerable detail how the oculomotor control system is involved in the endogenous control of spatial attention. The first step of the experiment by Moore and Fallah (2001) was to find a neuron in FEF whose microstimulation produced a repeatable saccade to the same location (e.g., *Figure 9.3*). This is referred to as the cell's motor field (by analogy to the sensory receptive field; panel A in *Figure 9.6*). Next, the layout of the covert attention task was arranged so that the target stimulus was located in that neuron's motor field (panel B in *Figure 9.6*). In this task, the monkey had been trained to depress a lever to start the trial, and maintain central fixation while attending to the target. When the target dimmed, the monkey needed to release the lever in order to receive its reward. The dimming of the target was made difficult to detect by making the luminance change very small and very brief, by making the timing of this event unpredictable, and by including catch trials in which the target never dimmed. (On these, the monkey was rewarded for holding the lever throughout; importantly, no reward was delivered on catch trials during which the animal committed false-alarm errors by releasing the lever.) Finally, as if that wasn't already enough, most trials also featured the concurrent presentation of flashing distractors throughout the trial. (Distractors flashed on and off, one at a time, in the locations illustrated with "sunbursts" in panel B in *Figure 9.6*.)

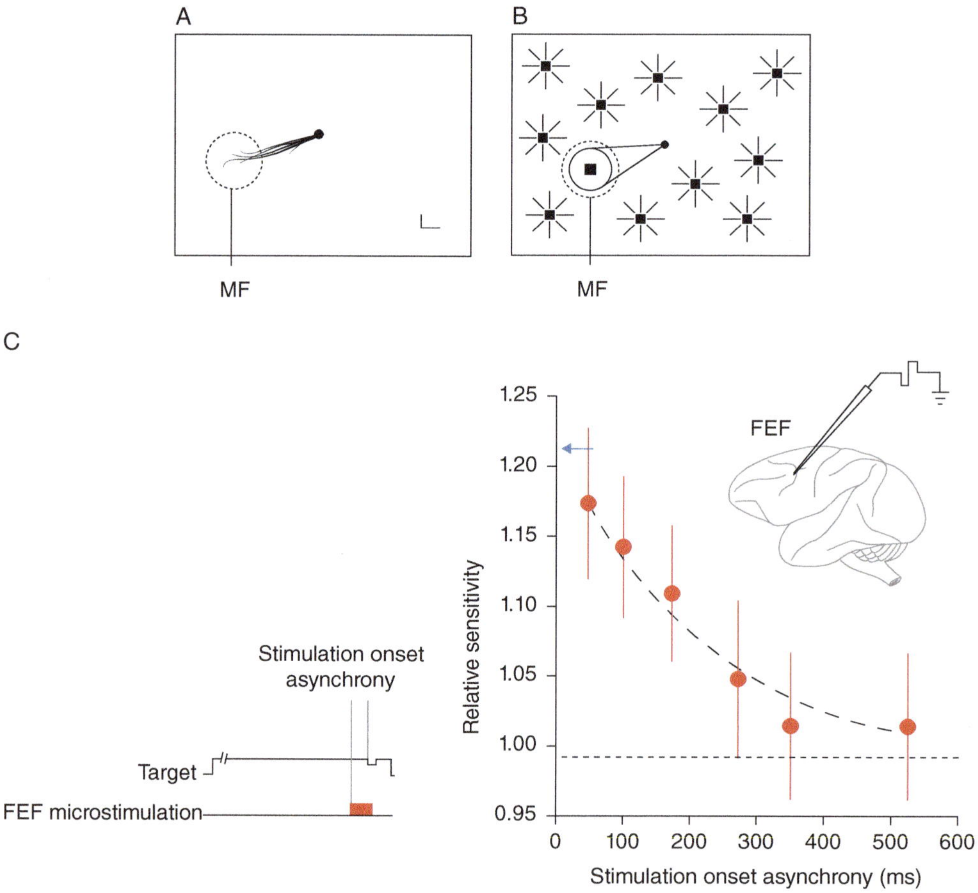

FIGURE 9.6 Electrically controlling the source of endogenous attentional control. **A.** Microstimulation of a location in the FEF of a monkey produces reliable vector saccades into a motor field (MF). **B.** The array of the visual search task is customized for that neuron such that the target location falls within this MF. **C.** Microstimulation-related improvement in performance varied monotonically with the stimulation onset asynchrony (see text).

Source: Awh et al., 2006 / with permission of Elsevier.

Now for the really compelling part. Recall that the target is positioned within the motor field of the FEF neuron. This means that, if the investigator wanted to, he could deliver a 100 msec train of ~50 μA of current and drive the eyes to the target location. Instead, they did what Tirin Moore sometimes characterizes, while giving talks, as "just tickling" the neuron, by stimulating at half the amplitude that had been determined to produce a saccade 50% of the time. That is, the stimulation was subthreshold, in that it never produced an eye movement.

But would it – drumroll please – produce a covert shift of attention?

To assess this, the investigators varied the latency between when microstimulation was applied and when the target event occurred, a parameter called the "stimulation onset asynchrony." The findings suggested that electrically "tickling" an FEF neuron does, indeed, produce an effect equivalent to a covert shift of attention, and that it does so in a timing-dependent manner: the closer in time the microstimulation was to the target event, the stronger were its attention-like effects. These results, plotted in panel C of *Figure 9.6*, express the effect of microstimulation on the animal's "relative sensitivity," which is a measure of how much smaller the magnitude of the dimming needed to be made for the monkey to perform at the same level as it did on no-stimulation trials. Thus, in effect, what the plot shows is that delivering microstimulation with a stimulation onset asynchrony of 50 msec improved the animal's performance by roughly 17.5%. For comparison, the blue arrow shows that turning off the distracting stimuli improved the monkey's performance by ~21%.

In effect, instead of overtly cuing the animal about an impending target event, as is conventionally done with variants of the "Posner (1980) task," Moore and Fallah (2001) "reached into its brain" and directly shifted the animal's attention!

Because FEF microstimulation produced attention-like effects on behavior, the inference from Moore and Fallah (2001) was that subthreshold activity in the FEF acts as a source of attentional control. To fully understand how FEF might carry out this function, the next step was to show that FEF microstimulation produces attention-like effects in activity at a site of attentional control. To do this, Moore and then-graduate student Katherine Armstrong painstakingly found FEF neurons and V4 neurons whose motor fields and receptive fields, respectively, overlapped. In this way, they were able to stimulate at a putative source of attentional control and simultaneously record from a site where attention influences visual processing. *Figure 9.7* illustrates that the effect of FEF stimulation was to boost the V4 response to a visually presented stimulus in a manner similar to the effects of selective attention that we considered in *Chapter 7*. (For example, compare the effect of FEF microstimulation in *Figure 9.7* to the effect of spatial attention in *Figure 7.11.B*.) Importantly, in this study, *the monkey was not performing a task*, other than maintaining central fixation. Thus, together with the findings from the Moore and Fallah (2001) study, Moore and Armstrong (2003) offer a remarkable demonstration of the ability to control the focus of attention via a causal manipulation of activity in the FEF, suggesting that covert eye-movement planning is an important source of the endogenous control of attention.

Where's the Attentional Controller?

Remember in *Chapter 8*, when a skeptic chimed up about "some little homuncular mathematician perched up on the precentral gyrus . . . calculating vector sums prior to each movement"? [Who invited that person, anyway?] At this point, they might chime inn again, asking sarcastically if we've placed the spotlight operator (from *Chapter 7*'s *Day at the circus*) in the FEF. Stilted rhetorical devices aside, this is a legitimate concern, and one about which the cognitive neuroscientist and, particularly, the theoretician, needs always to be mindful. *Where does this control come from? Does assigning it to the dorsal frontoparietal system make it any less mystical, any more material? Have we accomplished anything more than assigning a more specific address to the ghost in the machine?* The answer is that, in fact, in the domain of attentional control, and in many others, cognitive neuroscience has made important strides toward developing very explicit accounts of how control emerges as a consequence of network interactions. In these models, there is no one place from which control signals are generated de novo, no figurative "corner office" from which a neural executive impulsively decides to issue commands. Such models are often most convincingly achieved via computer simulations. Although such simulations invariably include some idiosyncratic choices made by the modeler that may not

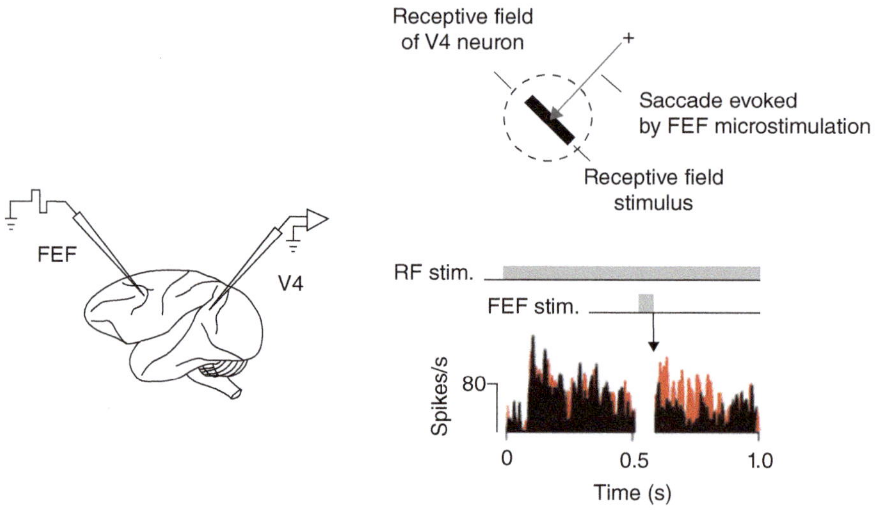

FIGURE 9.7 Generating the cause and measuring the effect of attentional control. Illustration at the top conveys the logic of the experiment: while the monkey is fixating the "+," apply subthreshold microstimulation to a location in the FEF where suprathreshold microstimulation would generate a saccade (red arrow) that would land in the receptive field of the V4 neuron that is simultaneously being recorded from (dashed circle), and evaluate the effect of this subthreshold microstimulation on the activity of this V4 neuron in response to a visual stimulus presented in that neuron's receptive field (the oriented black bar). Bottom panel is activity in the V4 neuron averaged across 10 trials when FEF microstimulation was delivered (red histogram), and 10 control trials when no FEF microstimulation was delivered (black histogram). Average activity on the two types of trials is identical from time 0 seconds, when the stimulus appears in the neuron's receptive field (RF stim.) until shortly after time 0.5 seconds, at which time the effect of FEF microstimulation is to boost the sensory-evoked response of this neuron.

Source: Awh et al., 2006 / with permission of Elsevier.

account for every detail that we (think we) know about how the brain works, their value is in demonstrating that it is possible, in principle, to understand, to describe, and to measure every step, every connection, every causal factor in a system capable of producing complex behavior. For the question of the source of attentional control, we can consider a computational model by the theoretician Fred Hamker.

The Reentry Hypothesis The goal of the Hamker (2005) model was to simulate the findings of Chelazzi, Duncan, Miller, and Desimone (1998; *Figure 7.15*) that provide an important empirical foundation for the biased-competition model of visual attention. In particular, this model provides an explicit account for how the FEF and IT act as sources of the top-down attentional control that provide the biasing signal. Additionally, by specifying and explicitly modeling the activity of different classes of neurons in the FEF, it provides a plausible scenario for how a saccade plan might be prevented from actualization in a saccade, and, thus, could also serve as the basis for sustained covert attention. (Hint: it would involve the fixation neurons.)

Figure 9.8 illustrates the architecture of the model (panel B), and the anatomical connections on which it is based (panel A). One of the features of this model, which we haven't considered up to this point, is the heterogeneity of neuronal classes within FEF. Not unlike the deep layers of the SC, within FEF, one can find visually responsive neurons, fixation neurons, visuomotor neurons, and movement neurons. Three of these are explicitly represented in the model (panel B in *Figure 9.8*), as are their temporal dynamics. Visuomovement cells in deep layers are active from stimulus onset until saccade execution. Typically, their initial response does not distinguish between a distractor and a target, but the activity decays when a distractor is in the receptive field. Movement cells are active prior to saccades and do not show any response to stimulus onset. Fixation cells decrease their activity before a planned eye movement (Hamker, 2005, pp. 433–434).

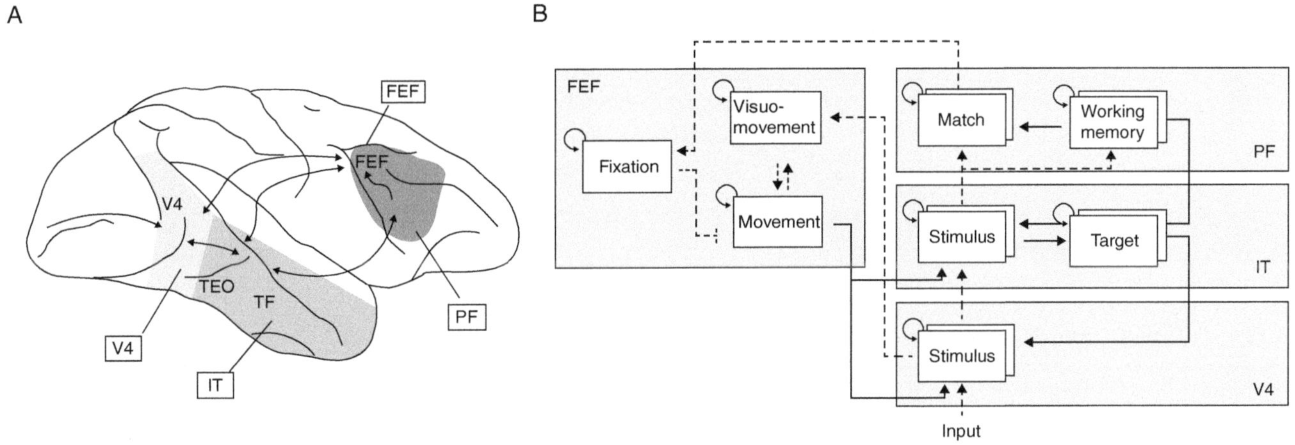

FIGURE 9.8 Illustrations from Hamker's simulation of the source of top-down control. Panel **A**, the known neural connections included in the model. Panel **B**, a schematic of the implementation of the model. Bottom-up connections are indicated in dotted arrows, feedback ("reentrant") connections in solid arrows. Each white box represents a population of neurons, "stacked" boxes indicating populations processing two stimulus features (color and form) in parallel. The "turning-back-on-itself" arrow at the upper-left corner of each of the boxes indicates that individual units within a population exert lateral inhibition on each other.
Source: Hamker and Fred, 2005 / Oxford University Press.

Now, how does this network implement attentional control? We can watch it happen, in *Figure 9.9*, on a (simulated) millisecond-by-millisecond basis. This figure can be thought of as simulating a visual search experiment like the one illustrated in *Figure 7.15*, in which the experimenters are simultaneously recording from the dendritic branches of a V4 neuron that is receiving signals from earlier stations in the visual system ("Input" plot), from the V4 neuron itself ("Gain modulated rate" plot), from a neuron in IT (plot with axis labeled "IT target firing rate"), and from an FEF movement neuron.

1. Not shown is the beginning of the trial, when initial presentation of the target object establishes the search template for that trial, which is retained in "working memory" in recurrent connections between PF and IT (between "Working memory" and "Target" populations) until the search array is presented. (For a diagram of the task, see *Figure 7.15.A.*)
2. When one stimulus of the search array appears within the simulated receptive field, increased input elevates activity within the V4 layer at roughly 60 msec. This V4 activity feeds forward to FEF, producing the initial ramp-up in the *FEF movement firing rate* that begins at ~75 msec into the trial. Note that, during the initial ramp-up of activity in V4, this activity doesn't yet differ as a function of whether or not the presented stimulus is the Target (i.e., if it is to be attended *Target = good stim.* or not *Target = bad stim.*).
3. Meanwhile, the neuron in IT does have information (from working memory) about the identity of that trial's Target, and so its early activity to the stimulus does differentiate whether or not the stimulus is the Target.
4. [First wave of *reentry*] Feedback from IT to V4 produces an initial little bump in *Target = good stim.* activity in the "Gain modulated rate" of V4 that begins just prior to 100 msec.
5. Although the receptive field of any one V4 neuron is relatively large, the aggregate result of feedforward activity from a large population of them is that visuomovement neurons in FEF that encode the region of the visual field containing the target will receive the strongest feedforward drive (a phenomenon reminiscent of population coding in M1). The visuomovement neurons in FEF receiving the strongest feedforward drive will, in turn, activate the FEF movement neurons whose movement field overlaps the location of the target. The accumulating effect of the small differential feedforward drive from V4 begins to emerge in FEF activity at ~130 msec.

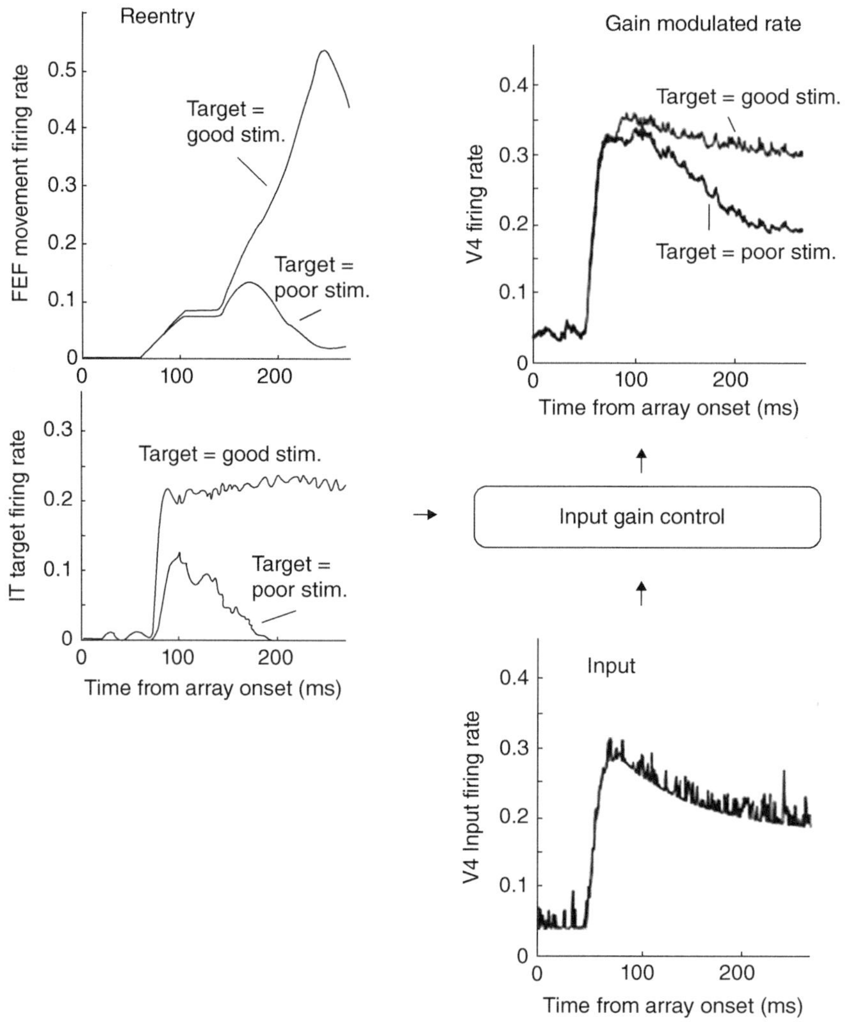

FIGURE 9.9 Multiple windows on the temporal evolution of activity occurring simultaneously at multiple stages of the simulated oculomotor system from *Figure 9.8*, for a V4 receptive field/FEF movement field processing information about a stimulus that is the V4 neuron's "good" stimulus on trials when this stimulus is the target of the visual search (Target = good stim.) vs. when it is not (Target = bad stim.; definitions in *Figure 7.15* and associated text). The "Input" box shows the stimulus-driven input to a V4 neuron from visual cortex (i.e., the aggregation of feedforward signals from V1, VP, and V3). The "Input gain control" implements the convolution of this Input signal with the "Reentry" signals from FEF and IT (i.e., it's the operation in the model that computes the effects of the reentrant signals on the Input), and the "Gain modulated rate" shows the resultant activity in V4 that feeds forward to IT.

Source: Hamker and Fred, 2005 / Oxford University Press.

6. [Second wave of *reentry*] Increasing activity in FEF movement neurons is experienced by V4 neurons as top-down feedback, and those representing features of the target, which already have a slightly elevated level of activity, benefit from this top-down boost to further increase their activity and, in turn, apply lateral inhibition to V4 neurons representing features of the nontarget stimulus.
7. These processes continue, in parallel, until a threshold is reached and a saccade to the target is triggered.

The point of walking through this example has been to show how attention-related feedback from FEF can be generated without FEF "knowing" what the search target is. Thus, no "ghost" need live in the "machine" of the FEF for this region to act as a source of top-down attentional control. More broadly, it gives a very detailed example of how the dynamic interplay of regions within a recurrently connected network can give rise to sophisticated behavior. (This is at least schematically relevant, e.g., for thinking about the recurrent activity that many believe is critical for visual object recognition, as considered in section *A critical role for feedback in the ventral visual processing stream*, *Chapter 6*.)

What we haven't done, however, is satisfactorily address the question of *Where is the attentional controller?* That is, were we to stop here, one could object that all that this exercise has done is to relocate the homunculus from the FEF to the box in *Figure 9.8* that's labeled "working memory," because it's working memory that enabled IT, in our step 3 of walking through *Figure 9.9*, to respond differentially on *Target = good stim.* vs. on *Target = bad stim.* trials. This was, after all, the event that provided the initial "nudge" of biasing the activity in the system toward ultimately producing a saccade to the Target on *Target = good stim.* trials. Fair enough. But we can't expect to do something so ambitious as banning the homunculus in just nine chapters! (We still have 11 more to go!) When we get to *Chapter 14*, *Working memory* and *Chapter 15*, *Cognitive control*, we'll return to this question, and we'll see that combining some of the properties of recurrent systems that we've considered here with mechanisms from reinforcement learning (section *Habits and reinforcement learning*, *Chapter 8*) might just enable us to ban the homunculus from working memory, too.

One final note about top-down signaling from the FEF before we move on. Although the empirical work from Moore and colleagues (2001, 2003) that we've reviewed here, and the modeling from Hamker (2005), only take into account firing rates, there is a growing body of electrophysiological evidence that dynamic changes in oscillatory phase synchrony between regions also play an important role in attentional control. For example, there's a considerable amount of research suggesting that the efficacy of FEF influence on posterior regions may depend, in part, on long-range synchrony between these regions in the beta band. This is also something that we'll consider explicitly when we get to *Chapter 15*, *Cognitive control*.

Are Oculomotor Control and Attentional Control Really the "Same Thing"?

So, we've seen evidence that FEF can act as a source of attentional control when it's electrically stimulated, and we've considered a model describing how it might come to serve this function. But is there evidence that this *is* how attention is controlled in humans? That is, can the endogenous control of attention truly be reduced to "nothing more" than covert oculomotor control? Although this is a difficult question to answer unequivocally, we'll next consider one way of addressing it.

The "Method of Visual Inspection"

As noted previously, there is a striking similarity between the dorsal frontoparietal regions activated in the delayed-saccade task of Srimal and Curtis (2008; *Figure 9.4*) and the endogenous control network of Corbetta and Shulman (2002; *Figure 9.5*). Indeed, there have been many demonstrations in the literature that tasks engaging these two categories of behavior activate overlapping regions of the brain. However, there's only so far that one can get by, in effect, saying, *See? These two patterns of activity look the same.*

"Prioritized Maps of Space in Human Frontoparietal Cortex"

And so, is the brain actually performing the same computations during the performance of tasks that require oculomotor control vs. visual attention (and, for good measure) vs. visual working memory? A study from the laboratory of Clayton Curtis at New York University addressed this question by scanning subjects with fMRI while they performed tests of "intention," "attention," and "memory." First, the authors carried out an fMRI scanning session to identify cortical regions supporting retinotopic maps of space, using a method similar to the one illustrated in *Figure 7.5.A*. The regions identified were largely overlapping with those shown in *Figure 9.4*, and they used the heuristic introduced in section *The functional anatomy of the dorsal stream, Chapter 7*; (*Figure 7.5.A*) to identify the boundaries between regions, thereby defining the regions of interest (ROIs) to be used in the second part of the experiment: IPS0; IPS1; IPS2; IPS3; superior precentral sulcus (sPCS); and inferior precentral sulcus (iPCS). (Note that sPCS, IPS3, and IPS2 make up the DAN as identified with resting state functional correlation [*Chapter 4*, section *Functional connectivity*].) In the second scanning session, subjects performed the three spatial cognition tasks. Trials for the test of motor intention began with the presentation of a central fixation point, followed by a target stimulus located anywhere from 5° to 15° of visual angle to the left or the right of fixation, and anywhere from 4° to 5° above or below the horizontal meridian. Both the target and the fixation point remained visible during a variable-length delay period, and subjects were to make a saccade to the target as soon as the fixation point disappeared. Trials for the test of spatial attention started with a fixation point flanked by one shape (a square or a circle) 5.5° to the left of fixation and the other shape to the right 5.5°, each one centered on the horizontal meridian. The fixation point was then replaced by either a square or a circle, which cued the subject to attend to the flanking shape that matched it, and count the number of times the cued flanking shape dimmed during the ensuing variable-length delay period. Trials for the test of spatial delayed recognition began with the presentation of a sample stimulus anywhere from 5° to 15° to the left or the right of fixation, and anywhere from 4° to 5° above or below the horizontal meridian. After a variable-length delay period, a probe stimulus appeared in a location that was either the same as or close to the location where the sample had appeared, and the subject indicated whether probe's location was a match or a nonmatch with that of the sample. To address the question of is the brain actually doing the same thing during the performance of these three tasks?, the authors used a clever application of MVPA and produced a remarkable result.

A common use of MVPA is as a tool for "decoding" brain activity. Consider the toy example that we worked through in *Chapter 5*, section *"Decoding" fMRI data with multivariate pattern analysis (MVPA)*. After plotting the results of 20 trials of leftward vs. rightward attention, we felt reasonably confident that we would be able to classify the identity of a 21st trial, based solely on the neural activity associated with this trial. That is, we felt reasonably confident that we could *decode* the neural activity so as to know what information it was representing. What Jerde et al. (2012) did with their data, as illustrated in *Figure 9.10*, is a step beyond "just" predicting the identity of a 21st trial drawn from the same task that produced the first 20 trials. Rather, what they did was train a classifier on *Task A*, then ask whether this classifier could also correctly decode a trial from *Task B*, a task with which it had no previous experience. Successful generalization of a decoder from one task to another would provide compelling evidence that very similar, if not identical, processes are engaged by the two tasks.

To be more concrete, let's walk through an example from the sPCS ROI. Each subject performed 64 trials of each task (32 leftward and 32 rightward). Furthermore, let's say, for the purpose of this walk-through, that the sPCS ROI contained 200 voxels. Training the classifier would then begin by generating a cloud of 32 points in 200D space that correspond to delay-period activity from each *attend-left* trial and a cloud of 31 points in this same 200D space that correspond to delay-period activity from all but one of the *attend-right* trials, and then by determining the 199D hyperplane that separates the most *attend-left* points from *attend-right* points. The effectiveness of this "fold" of training would then be tested by plotting the point in this same 200D space of the delay-period activity from the held-out trial and determining whether it falls on the correct or the incorrect side of the 199D hyperplane separating *attend-left* from *attend-right*. If this trial was classified as an attend-right trial, the test of this fold would be scored as "correct." The process would then be repeated 63 more times, each time with a different trial held out from the cloud-plotting and hyperplane-fitting (a process referred to as "k-fold cross validation"). After 64 iterations, the mean performance of the

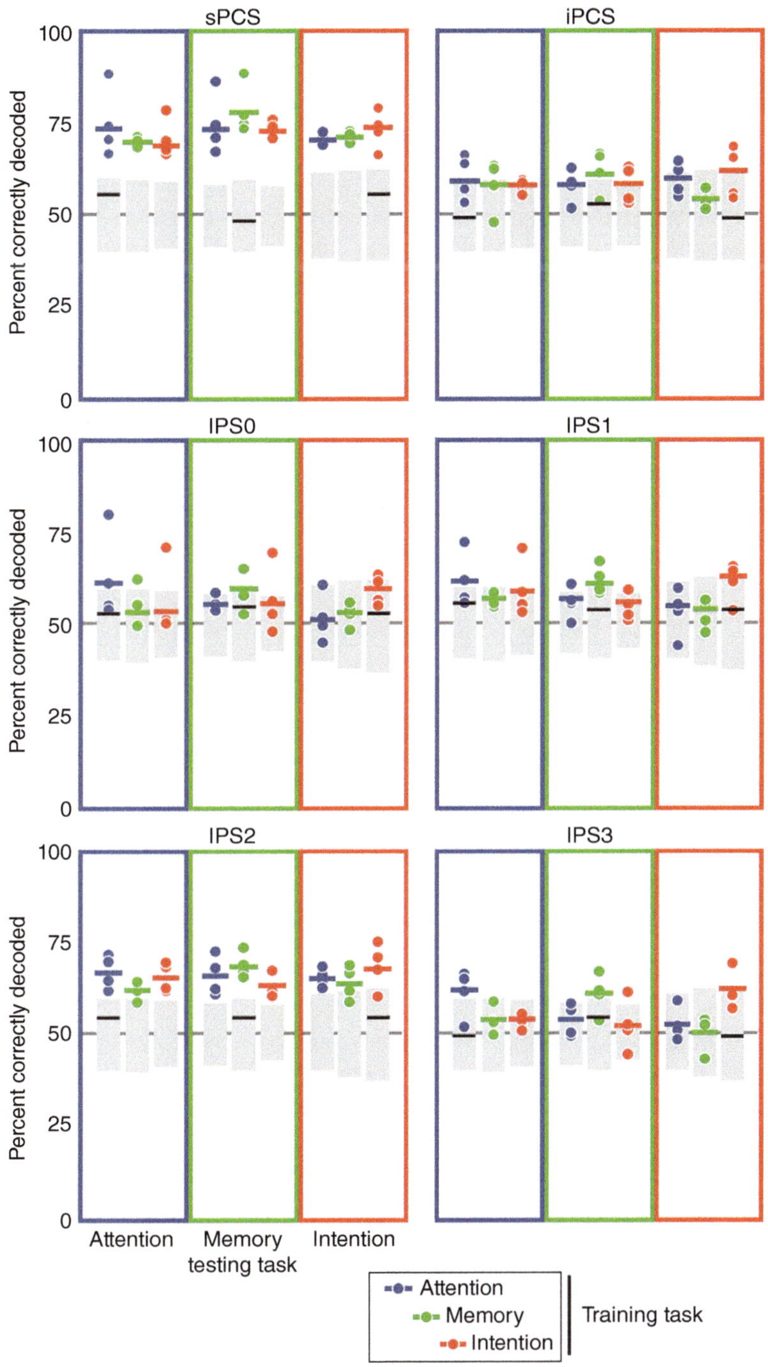

FIGURE 9.10 Classification results from Jerde et al. (2012) of data from tests of "attention," "memory," and "intention." Each dot corresponds to a subject. The color of each set of dots indicates the task used to train a classifier; the color of each rectangle around a set of dots indicates the task used to test the classifier. Thus, for example, the upper-left rectangle illustrates that, within sPCS, not only were *attention* trials decodable by the attention-trained classifier, but so, too, were *memory* trials and *intention* trials.

Source: Jerde et al., 2012 / Society of Neuroscience.

classifier (i.e., the number of correct classifications divided by 64) was calculated, and it was determined if this level of performance was better than what would be expected by chance. (Note that, in practice, the cloud-plotting and hyperplane-fitting were carried out with logistic regression.) In *Figure 9.10*, for sPCS, the mean performance for classifiers trained and tested on attention trials, using the procedure described here, is indicated for each of the four subjects in this study as a blue dot inside the blue box. The clever application referred to a few paragraphs previously is what they did next, a procedure known as cross-task decoding. First, an attention classifier was trained by plotting the data from all 64 trials of the attention task into the 200D space corresponding to the sPCS ROI, and determining the 199D hyperplane that best discriminated attend-*left* from attend-*right*. Next, the 200D point from each of the 64 memory trials was tested by determining for each whether, for example, a remember-*right* trial would be classified as belonging to the attend-*right* cloud of points (correct) or to the attend-*left* cloud of points (incorrect). In *Figure 9.11*, for sPCS, the mean performance for classifiers trained on attention trials and tested on memory trials is indicated for each of the four subjects as a green dot inside the blue box.

Now that we have a feel for the logic of the analysis of the Jerde et al. (2012) inspection of *Figure 9.10* reveals two general trends in the results. First, within-task decoding was only consistently successful in sPCS and IPS2. Second, cross-task decoding was successful only in sPCS and IPS2. This latter result is especially intriguing because it provides compelling evidence for the idea that the brain may be performing the same computations for spatial attention (and for spatial working memory) as it performs for oculomotor control, actually doing the same thing during the performance of both of these tasks. Stated another way, "oculomotor control," "spatial attentional control," and "spatial working memory" may be three verbal labels that we use in different behavioral contexts but that, in fact, engage the same underlying neural activity.

Controlling Exogenous Shifts of Attention with Endogenous Control

In noticing the similarity of patterns of activity between oculomotor and attentional tasks, what one is noticing is the coactivation of the anterior and posterior regions of the DAN. (At the risk of being too strenuously didactic, note that accounts of the DAN arise from "converging evidence" from RSFC [i.e., at rest, spontaneous fluctuations in BOLD signal are highly correlated between FEF and subregions of IPS, implying strong functional coupling] and observations of joint recruitment during various tasks recruiting covert attention and/or oculomotor control.) The final topic that we'll address in this chapter will highlight one way in which the precise attention-related functions supported by each of these two densely interconnected regions may, nonetheless, subtly differ. The control-related question of interest is the way that a subject's strategic orientation toward how to perform a task can modulate the extent to which exogenous attention can influence task performance. To elaborate in greater detail, it will be helpful to first introduce the use of the "singleton distractors" in attentional research. We'll do so by considering an experiment carried out by Panagiotis Sapountzis, Alexandra Antoniadou, and Georgia Gregoriou (2025), who recorded from FEF and LIP in NHPs performing a variant of the classic visual search task, in which the trial begins with the presentation of a search target, then, after a brief delay, an array of several stimuli is presented and the subject must find the target in the array (*Figure 9.11*).[1] Although one can find differences in terminology in this literature,[2] here we'll refer to every nontarget item in the search array as a "distractor." In this experiment there were three trial types: *singleton absent* (i.e., baseline), in which every

[1] Note that although the task featured in *Chapter 7*, section *Object-based attention*, and modeled in this chapter's section *The reentry hypothesis* was inspired by search tasks from (human) experimental psychology, the task illustrated in *Figure 9.12* is actually much more similar to the kind of task that is typically used to study visual search in humans.
[2] Indeed, with relevance to this very subfield, see the *Further* reading from Liesefeld et al. (2024) on "*Terms of debate: Consensus definitions to guide the scientific discourse on visual distraction*."

FIGURE 9.11 The visual search task from Sapountzis et al. (2025).

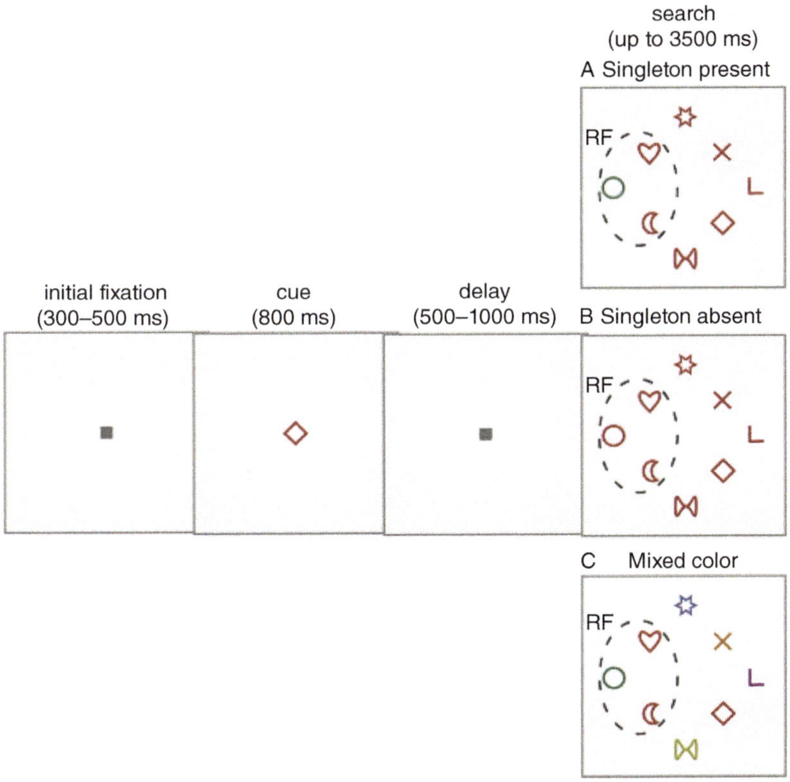

FIGURE 9.11.A Illustration of a *singleton present* search array, the singleton being rendered in green. Dotted line illustrates the spatial receptive field of a hypothetical neuron; data reported in this study were from trials in which the initial saccade was made to a location outside a cell's receptive field.

FIGURE 9.11.B Illustration of a *singleton absent* search array.

FIGURE 9.11.C Illustration of a *mixed* search array. Note how the configuration of distractors can be the same within a receptive field in *mixed* and *singleton present* trials.

item in the search array was rendered in a single color; *mixed*, in which each item in the array could appear in a different color; and *singleton present*, similar in most respects to *singleton absent*, but with one distractor appearing in a different color. One's default assumption might be that search trials that include a color singleton distractor would be more difficult and, due to exogenous attentional capture of a highly salient distractor, feature an RT cost. After all, a color singleton would be expected to "pop out," right? This is what one observes, for example, when a color singleton appears in an array in which the subject is searching for a shape singleton, and so is presumed to be operating in "singleton-detection mode." If, however, the subject adopts what's referred to as "feature-search mode," as would be expected for the task from Sapountzis et al. (2025) (*Figure 9.11*), performance on singleton present trials actually tends to be faster and more accurate.[3] This was true for the NHPs in Sapountzis et al. (2025), and the authors explain this as resulting from the color singleton effectively "announcing its irrelevance" (this author's quotes), and thereby effectively reducing the size of the search array. (I.e., it takes less time to search through an array of seven items than an array of eight items.) Although this "reduced set size" explanation makes intuitive sense, for it to be correct there would need to be an involvement of top-down control to suppress the representation of

[3]The terms "singleton detection mode" and "feature-search mode" are taken from the human experimental psychology literature, the word "mode" referring to "mode of behaving." From the perspective of cognitive control, these might be referred to adopting one or another "strategic set"; from that of dynamical systems theory these could be modeled as two order parameters.

the color singleton so as to prevent its exogenous capture. That is, mechanisms of *endogenous* control would need to be recruited to supersede the otherwise detrimental effects of *exogenous* attentional capture. The results from Sapountzis et al. (2025) suggest that a subset of neurons in FEF perform this function.

Sapountzis et al. (2025) note that, in addition to locations that correspond to behavioral priority, a neural priority map would be expected to also represent the location of perceptually salient stimuli, regardless of their priority status. Consistent with this idea, *Figure 9.12* illustrates that they found a heterogeneity of attention-related responses to the singleton distractor in both FEF and LIP, with some neurons showing an initially enhanced response to the color singleton (relative to the singleton-absent condition) followed by a suppression, a

FIGURE 9.12 Heterogeneity of attention-related responses in FEF and LIP.

Source: (Sapountzis, Antoniadou, & Gregoriou, 2025) / PLOS / CC BY 4.0.

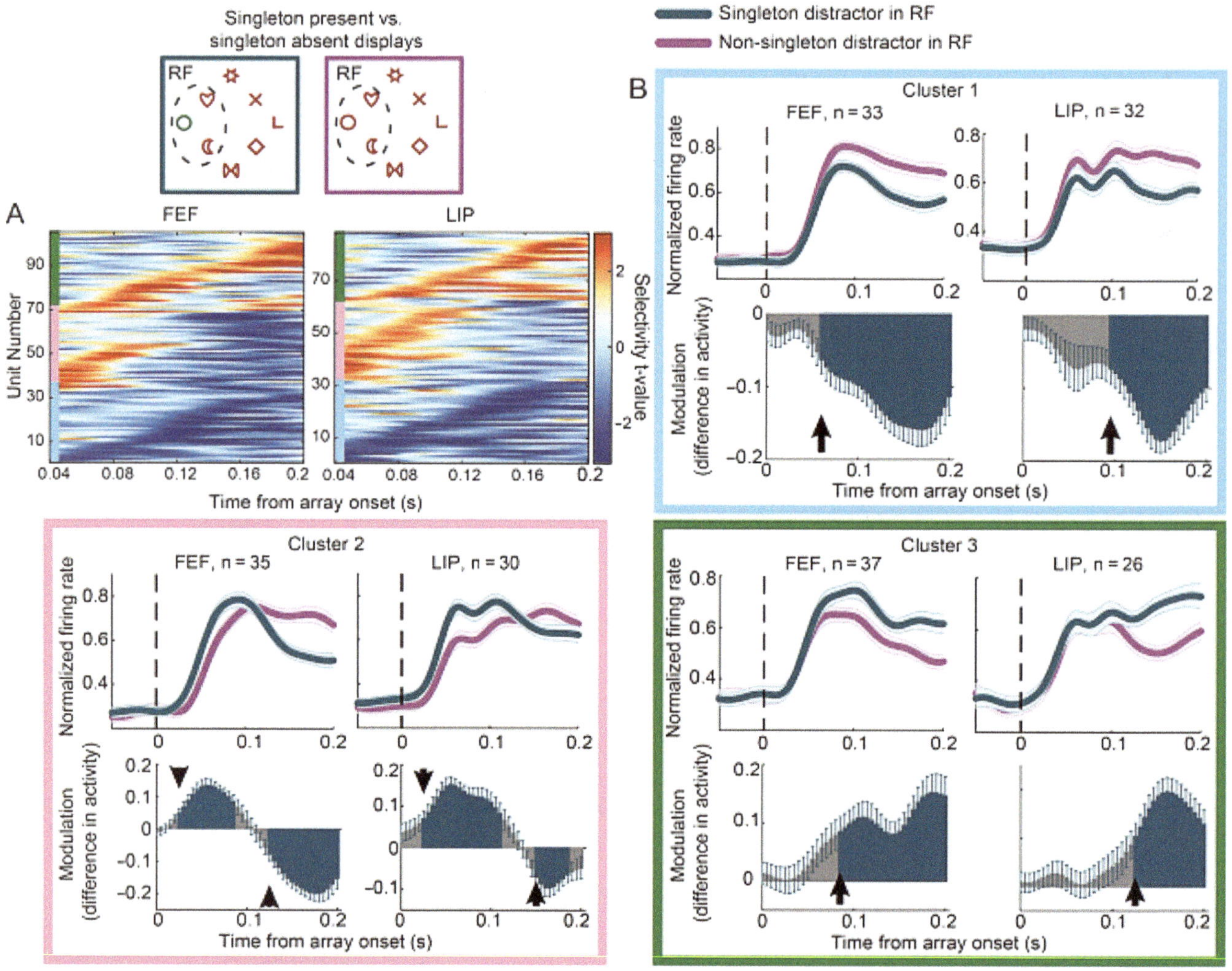

FIGURE 9.12.A Inset above data plots illustrates the two trial types being contrasted. Data plots illustrate, for FEF and LIP, responsivity of individual neurons to the color singleton, sorted into three categories (identified analytically as distinct "clusters") as designated by the color code along the vertical axis – blue, sustained suppression; pink, initial enhancement followed by suppression; green, enhancement – and sorted within category by latency of response.

FIGURE 9.12.B For each of the three categories from A, time courses of firing rates for the conditions (above), and time courses of the difference between the two conditions (below), for FEF and LIP. Arrows indicate the time at which the two time courses diverged.

second group showing initial and sustained suppression of the singleton, and a third showing initial and sustained enhancement. Interestingly, only in FEF did distractor suppression (for singleton distractors as well as for singleton-absent distractors) correlate with behavior, with stronger distractor suppression associated with faster RTs. Finally, a representational geometry analysis indicated that, in both FEF and LIP, the representation of the target (which we haven't emphasized here) and of the salient distractor "occupied a shared subspace suggesting a common substrate contributing to the formation of the priority map" (pp. 14–28).

Of Labels and Mechanisms

As humans, we tend to categorize things. Many think that doing so may be an automatic, if not obligatory, cognitive operation. (This author recently traded in his son's "hybrid" bicycle [with properties of a "street bike" and of a mountain bike] for a [expensive!] mountain bike. To a nonexpert, the two would seem to be only superficially different from each other, but to my 11-year-old expert, they're as different as a minivan from a sports car. To him, and to the bicycling community, they belong in different categories.) To our intuitions, the act of moving one's eyes vs. that of choosing to focus one's attention on object A vs. object B may feel like two different kinds of behavior. Certainly, up until quite recently, psychology and neuroscience have treated these as two different domains. But what if, as the data that we reviewed in this chapter would suggest, the very same underlying neural systems and processes are responsible for producing these two putatively different kinds of behavior? Surely, at least on the neural level, they can no longer be assigned to different categories. This is one of the reasons why so much attention, and often debate, is focused on seemingly arcane questions such as *Are PPC neurons encoding* intention *or* attention?, or *Are the attention-like results from Moore and colleagues (2001, 2003) attributable solely to the activation of sensory neurons in the FEF, or do movement neurons also contribute?* This tension about categorization, and between different levels of description, will reoccur often during the remainder of our time together. Just one example is manifested in *Figure 9.10*, which impels us to include spatial working memory in this discussion of neural mechanisms vs. psychological categories, even though we're not "supposed" to discuss it in detail until *Chapter 14.*

End-of-Chapter Questions

1. What are some important differences between the posterior and anterior oculomotor control systems?

2. There are at least three different neural codes used to encode saccade metrics at different stations of the oculomotor system. Name the three codes, and the region(s) associated with each.

3. Define the exogenous vs. the endogenous control of attention. What cortical networks are associated with each?

4. How has the development of event-related methods for fMRI been critical for the study of oculomotor control and of attention? Describe one example from each domain.

5. Summarize the data that implicate the FEF as an important *source* of attentional control.

6. How does explicit computational modeling of the network interactions underlying visual search dispel the need to locate an attentional control homunculus in dorsal frontoparietal cortex?

7. How does MVPA differ fundamentally from signal intensity-based neuroimaging data analysis methods that predominated during the 1990s and the 2000s? What advantages does MVPA offer?

8. Are "oculomotor control" and "attentional control" just two different labels that we have given to the same underlying neural mechanisms depending on the behavioral context in which they are used, or are there fundamental differences between the two? Defend your answer with data.

9. If one were to pit the endogenous control of attention against exogenously triggered shifts of attention, which would win? How might your answer be influenced if this question were in the context of an environment in which one knows that "attention-grabbing" but to-be-ignored stimuli (e.g., color singletons) will frequently appear? What brain systems are implicated?

References

Chelazzi, Leonardo, John Duncan, Earl K. Miller, and Robert Desimone. 1998. "Responses of Neurons in Inferior Temporal Cortex during Memory-Guided Visual Search." *Journal of Neurophysiology* 80 (6): 2918–2940.

Corbetta, Maurizio, and Gordon L. Shulman. 2002. "Control of Goal-Directed and Stimulus-Driven Attention in the Brain." *Nature Reviews Neuroscience* 3 (3): 201–215. doi: 10.1038/nrn755.

Ferrier, David. 1875. "The Croonian Lecture: Experiments on the Brain of Monkeys (Second Series)." *Philosophical Transactions of the Royal Society of London.* 165: 433–488. doi: 10.1098/rstl.1875.0016.

Ferrier, David. 1890. *The Croonian Lectures on Cerebral Localisation.* London: Smith, Elder and Co.

Gandhi, Neeraj J., and Husam A. Katnani. 2011. "Motor Functions of the Superior Colliculus." *Annual Review of Neuroscience* 34: 205–231. doi: 10.1146/annurev-neuro-061010-113728.

Hamker, Fred H. 2005. "The Reentry Hypothesis: The Putative Interaction of the Frontal Eye Field, Ventrolateral Prefrontal Cortex, and Areas V4, IT for Attention and Eye Movement." *Cerebral Cortex* 15 (4): 431–447. doi: 10.1093/cercor/bhh146.

Ikkai, Akiko, and Clayton E. Curtis. 2011. "Common Neural Mechanisms Supporting Spatial Working Memory." *Neuropsychologia* 49 (6): 1428–1434. doi: 10.1016/j.neuropsychologia.2010.12.020.

Jerde, Trenton A., Elisha P. Merriam, Adam C. Riggall, James H. Hedges, and Clayton E. Curtis. 2012. "Prioritized Maps of Space in Human Frontoparietal Cortex." *Journal of Neuroscience* 32 (48): 17382–17390. doi: 10.1523/JNEUROSCI.3810-12.2012.

Krauzlis, Richard J. 2005. "The Control of Voluntary Eye Movements: New Perspectives." *Neuroscientist* 11 (2): 124–137. doi: 10.1177/1073858404271196.

Liesefeld, Heinrich R., Dominique Lamy, Nicholas Gaspelin, Joy J. Geng, Dirk Kerzel, Jeffrey D Schall, . . . Jeremy Wolfe. 2024. "Terms of Debate: Consensus Definitions to Guide the Scientific Discourse on Visual Distraction." *Attention, Perception, & Psychophysics* 86 (5): 1445–1472. doi: 10.3758/s13414-023-02820-3.

Moore, Tirin, and Katherine M. Armstrong. 2003. "Selective Gating of Visual Signals by Microstimulation of Frontal Cortex." *Nature* 421 (6921): 370–373. doi: 10.1038/nature01341.

Moore, Tirin, and Mazyar Fallah. 2001. "Control of Eye Movements and Spatial Attention." *Proceedings of the National Academy of Sciences of the United States of America* 98 (3): 1273–1276. doi: 10.1073/pnas.98.3.1273.

Paré, Martin, and Douglas P. Munoz. 1996. "Saccadic Reaction Time in the Monkey: Advanced Preparation of Oculomotor Programs Is Primarily Responsible for Express Saccade Occurrence." *Journal of Neurophysiology* 76 (6): 3666–3681.

Posner, Michael I. 1980. "Orienting of Attention." *Quarterly Journal of Psychology* 32 (1): 3–25. doi: 10.1080/00335558008248231.

Rizzolatti, Giacomo, and Laila Craighero. 2010. "Premotor Theory of Attention." *Scholarpedia* 5 (1): 6311. doi: 10.4249/scholarpedia.6311.

Sapountzis, Panagiotis, Alexandra Antoniadou, and Georgia G. Gregoriou. 2025. "Diverse Neuronal Activity Patterns Contribute to the Control of Distraction in the Prefrontal and Parietal Cortex." *PLoS Biology* 23 (1): e3003008. doi: 10.1371/journal.pbio.3003008.

Schiller, Peter H. 1998. "The Neural Control of Visually Guided Eye Movements." In *Cognitive Neuroscience of Attention: A Developmental Perspective*, edited by John E Richards (pp. 3–50). Mahwah, NJ: Lawrence Erlbaum Associates.

Srimal, Riju, and Clayton E. Curtis. 2008. "Persistent Neural Activity during the Maintenance of Spatial Position in Working Memory." *NeuroImage* 39 (1): 455–468. doi: 10.1016/j.neuroimage.2007.08.040.

Other Sources Used

Awh, Edward, Katherine M Armstrong, and Tirin Moore. 2006. "Visual and Oculomotor Selection: Links, Causes and Implications for Spatial Attention." *Trends in Cognitive Sciences* 10 (3): 124–130. doi: 10.1016/j.tics.2006.01.001.

Bastos, Andre, Conrado A. Bosman, Jan-Mathijs Schoffelen, Robert Oostenveld, and Pascal Fries. 2010. "Interareal Directed Interactions and Their Modulation by Selective Attention Assessed with High Density Electrocorticography in Monkey." Presented at the annual meeting for the Society for Neuroscience, San Diego, CA, November 13–17.

Bollimunta, Anil, Yonghong Chen, Charles E Schroeder, and Mingzhou Ding. 2008. "Neuronal Mechanisms of Cortical Alpha Oscillations in Awake-Behaving Macaques." *Journal of Neuroscience* 28 (40): 9976–9988. doi: 10.1523/JNEUROSCI.2699-08.2008.

Curtis, Clayton E., and Jason D. Connolly. 2008. "Saccade Preparation Signals in the Human Frontal and Parietal Cortices." *Journal of Neurophysiology* 99 (1): 133–145.

Fischer, Burkhart, and R. Boch. 1983. "Saccadic Eye Movements After Extremely Short Reaction Times in the Monkey." *Brain Research* 260 (1): 21–26. doi: 10.1016/0006-8993(83)90760-6.

Funahashi, Shintaro, Charles J. Bruce, and Patricia S. Goldman-Rakic. 1989. "Mnemonic Coding of Visual Space in the Monkey's Dorsolateral Prefrontal Cortex." *Journal of Neurophysiology* 61 (2): 331–349.

Gaspelin, Nicholas, and Steven J. Luck. 2018. "The Role of Inhibition in Avoiding Distraction by Salient Stimuli." *Trends in Cognitive Science* 22 (1): 79–92. doi: 10.1016/j.tics.2017.11.001.

Hamilton, Antonia F. de C., and Scott T. Grafton. 2006. "Goal Representation in Human Anterior Intraparietal Sulcus." *Journal of Neuroscience* 26 (4): 1133–1137. doi: 10.1523/JNEUROSCI.4551-05.2006.

Hamm, Jordan P., Kara A. Dyckman, Lauren E. Ethridge, Jennifer E. McDowell, and Brett A. Clementz. 2010. "Preparatory Activations across a Distributed Cortical Network Determine Production of Express Saccades in Humans." *Journal of Neuroscience* 30 (21): 7350–7357. doi: 10.1523/JNEUROSCI.0785-10.2010.

Ikkai, Akiko, and Clayton E. Curtis. 2011. "Common Neural Mechanisms Supporting Spatial Working Memory." *Neuropsychologia* 49 (6): 1428–1434. doi: 10.1016/j.neuropsychologia.2010.12.020.

Javal, Louis É. 1878. "Essai sur la physiologie de la lecture." *Annales d'oculistique* 80: 61–73.

Kriegeskorte, Nikolaus, Rainer Goebel, and Peter Bandettini. 2006. "Information-Based Functional Brain Mapping." *Proceedings of the National Academy of Sciences of the United States of America* 103 (10): 3863–3868. doi: 10.1073/pnas.0600244103.

Moore, Tirin, and Mazyar Fallah. 2004. "Microstimulation of the Frontal Eye Field and Its Effects on Covert Spatial Attention." *Journal of Neurophysiology* 91 (1): 152–162. doi: 10.1152/jn.00741.

Norman, Kenneth A., Sean M. Polyn, Greg J. Detre, and James V. Haxby. 2006. "Beyond Mind-Reading: Multi-Voxel Pattern Analysis of fMRI Data." *Trends in Cognitive Sciences* 10 (9): 424–430. doi: 10.1016/j.tics.2006.07.005.

Pereira, Francisco, Tom Mitchell, and Matthew Botvinick. 2009. "Machine Learning Classifiers and fMRI: A Tutorial Overview." *NeuroImage* 45 (1–1): S199–S209. doi: 10.1016/j.neuroimage.2008.11.007.

Poldrack, Russell A. 2006. "Can Cognitive Processes Be Inferred from Neuroimaging Data?." *Trends in Cognitive Sciences* 10 (2): 59–63. doi: 10.1016/j.tics.2005.12.004.

Rizzolatti, Giacomo, Lucia Riggio, Isabella Drascola, and Carlo Umiltá. 1987. "Reorienting Attention across the Horizontal and Vertical Meridians: Evidence in Favor of a Premotor Theory of Attention." *Neuropsychologia* 25 (1–1): 31–40. doi: 10.1016/0028-3932(87)90041-8.

Shipp, Stewart. 2004. "The Brain Circuitry of Attention." *Trends in Cognitive Sciences* 8 (5): 223–230. doi: 10.1016/j.tics.2004.03.004.

Squire, Ryan F., Nicholas A. Steinmetz, and Tirin Moore. 2012. "Frontal Eye Field." *Scholarpedia* 7 (10): 5341. doi: 10.4249/scholarpedia.5341.

Further Reading

Aguirre, G. K., and M. D'Esposito. 1999. "Experimental Design for Brain fMRI." In *Functional MRI*, edited by C. T. W. Moonen and P A Bandettini (pp. 369–380). Berlin: Springer-Verlag.

A comprehensive and accessible treatment of how and why the BOLD fMRI signal imposes constraints on experimental design and of various design strategies that take these constraints into account.

Awh, Edward, Katherine M. Armstrong, and Tirin Moore. 2006. "Visual and Oculomotor Selection: Links, Causes and Implications for Spatial Attention." *Trends in Cognitive Sciences* 10 (3): 124–130. doi: 10.1016/j.tics.2006.01.001.

An accessible, concise review of the cognitive neuroscience of attention with an emphasis on its relation to oculomotor control.

Luo, Liqun, Eugenio Rodriguez, Karim Jerbi, Jean-Philippe Lachaux, Jacques Martinerie, Maurizio Corbetta, . . . A. D. (Bud) Craig. 2010. "Ten Years of Nature Reviews Neuroscience: Insights from the Highly Cited." *Nature Reviews Neuroscience* 11 (10): 718–726. doi: 10.1038/nrn2912.

A "10 years on" commentary about subsequent developments in the two-attentional-pathways model from Corbetta and Shulman, whose 2002 review introducing this idea was the most highly cited paper to appear in Nature Reviews Neuroscience that year.

Norman, Kenneth A., Sean M. Polyn, Greg J. Detre, and James V. Haxby. 2006. "Beyond Mind-Reading: Multi-Voxel Pattern Analysis of fMRI Data." *Trends in Cognitive Sciences* 10 (9): 424–430. doi: 10.1016/j.tics.2006.07.005.

An accessible review of the logic underlying many implementations of MVPA and some applications to cognitive neuroscience questions.

Pereira, Francisco, Tom Mitchell, and Matthew Botvinick. 2009. "Machine Learning Classifiers and fMRI: A Tutorial Overview." *NeuroImage* 45 (1–1): S199–S209. doi: 10.1016/j.neuroimage.2008.11.007.

An authoritative presentation of the principles of statistical machine learning that underlie many implementations of MVPA.

Poldrack, Russell A. 2006. "Can Cognitive Processes Be Inferred from Neuroimaging Data?." *Trends in Cognitive Sciences* 10 (2): 59–63. doi: 10.1016/j.tics.2005.12.004.

A prescient and thorough consideration of the logic of "reverse inference" that underlies the interpretation of functional neuroimaging data, and thereby provides a useful context from which to consider the relative advantages and limitations of univariate vs. multivariate approaches to neuroimaging data analysis. Although explicitly addressing neuroimaging, much of its argumentation is equally applicable to other types of neurophysiological data.

Rizzolatti, Giacomo, and Laila Craighero. 2010. "Premotor Theory of Attention." *Scholarpedia* 5 (1): 6311. doi: 10.4249/scholarpedia.6311.

A "23 years on" commentary about subsequent developments relevant to this theory, including the role of skeletomotor systems.

Sherman, S. Murray, and Ray W. Guillery. 2006. *Exploring the Thalamus and Its Role in Cortical Function.* Cambridge, MA: MIT Press.

Provocative text by two of the foremost authorities on the thalamus, proposing, among other ideas, that cortico-thalamo-cortical loops are the primary circuits for information transmission, with many cortico-cortical connections serving modulatory roles.

Mental Representation

INTRODUCTION TO SECTION IV

Mental Representation

In *Section III*, we covered "the inputs and the outputs." And as we've previously noted, some would contend that everything from here on out is an elaboration of the principles that we've already learned. Well . . . yes and no. One of the central features of the brain, its plasticity, means that it's constantly changing, constantly updating its models of the world. Consequently, no two instances of perceiving a stimulus are the same, because the circuits responsible for perception are always somewhat different, somewhat changed, from the previous instance. At another level, *Section III* will examine ways in which perception and action are necessarily dependent on the brain's interpretations of the *meaning* of the inputs and the outputs. This idea was summarized eloquently in a commentary by the neurophysiologist Joaquin Fuster, as follows:

> Perception is . . . based on long-term memory. Every percept of the world around us is an "interpretation" of current sensory data in the light of our experience with similar data stored in long-term memory. Thus, perception has been appropriately called the testing of hypotheses about the world. We not only remember what we perceive, but also perceive what we remember. Perceiving must essentially involve the matching of external gestalts to internalized representations in long-term memory. There cannot be an entirely new percept, because any conceivable new sensory configuration can resonate by associations of similarity or contiguity with others in long-term storage, which the new experience modifies and updates. In other words, the new experience modifies and updates previously established cortical networks. Intelligence and language, in all of their manifestations, operate in basically the same way, that is, by the activation of long-term memory networks towards the processing of intelligent behavior or speech.
>
> (Fuster, 2003, p. 737)

Long-term memory (LTM), the neural record of past experience that can influence future behavior, is the major focus of this section – how it's formed; how it's organized; how it influences cognition, perception, and action. Indeed, as an entrée into this topic, *Chapter 10* will, in effect, pick up where *Chapter 6* left off, considering how the sensation and perception of a visual object interact with preexisting representations of the category, and perhaps the particular token, of the object being perceived.

Reference

Fuster, Joaquín M. 2003. "More Than Working Memory Rides on Long-Term Memory." *Behavioral and Brain Sciences* 26 (6): 737–737. doi: 10.1017/S0140525X03300160.

CHAPTER 10

Visual Object Recognition and Knowledge

KEY THEMES

- The neurological syndrome of visual agnosia raises many puzzling, and profound, questions about the relationship between perception and knowledge representation.
- Perhaps most intriguing is the seemingly selective inability of prosopagnosic patients to discriminate among individual faces.
- Despite the insight that can be gained from careful assessment of neurological deficits, models intended to explain "what must be broken" in these patients can sometimes posit cognitive mechanisms of questionable neural validity.
- Parallel distributed processing (PDP) models suggest that meaning (and, therefore, recognition) may reside within circuits that mediate perception and interactions between perception and action systems.
- fMRI evidence for a fusiform face area (FFA) that responds more strongly to faces than to other categories of stimuli has launched several vigorous debates about the neural and cognitive organization of the ventral stream.
- The FFA may also be sensitive to perceptual expertise, by which account its response profile would be better explained in terms of nurture than nature.
- MVPA analyses indicate that face information is also represented outside the FFA, and that the FFA can represent information about non-face categories, thereby challenging strong claims of the specificity of this region for face processing.
- Despite the previous point, direct electrical stimulation of the FFA, guided by electrocorticography (ECoG), selectively distorts the phenomenology of perceiving faces, thereby confirming a causal role of the FFA in face perception.
- Decomposing images of faces into principal components (PCs) based on their image properties has revealed a principle underlying the brain's representation of faces, such that it provides a quantitative model with which to predict which synthetically generated face stimuli will drive neurons that, using conventional methods, had seemed to be highly specific to just one face.
- In the nonhuman primate, the axis-coding scheme may generalize to all object recognition (not just faces) with one axis varying according to spikiness-stubbiness and another to animacy.
- In humans, evidence for axis coding based on image properties (as assessed with fMRI) is equivocal; another approach that entails defining axes with judgements of perceived similarity suggests a role for behavioral relevance in object recognition.

Companion Website: www.wiley.com/go/postle/cognitiveneuroscience3e

CONTENTS

Although, as promised, we won't begin this chapter with an overview of the anatomy underlying the function of interest in this chapter, we will begin, as we did for *Chapter 7*, by introducing and motivating our topic with a neurological syndrome.

Visual Agnosia

In *Chapter 6*, it was noted that "By the 1960s, decades of clinical observations in humans and lesion studies in experimental animals had established that the temporal lobes play a critical role in object recognition." Particularly germane for our present interests are the visual agnosias. This is a term for which understanding the etymology is more than a historical curiosity. *Gnosis* is ancient Greek for "knowledge," and the *a-* in front of it confers negation. Thus, visual agnosia is the absence of visual knowledge. There are two broad categories of visual agnosia, a cardinal feature of both being profoundly impaired visual perception despite relatively intact visual sensation. That is, these patients aren't blind. The symptoms that make them agnosic reflect damage to cortical networks that are downstream from V1.

Apperceptive Agnosia

A case of Benson and Greenberg (1969), Mr. S., was selected by Martha Farah to introduce the syndrome in her influential (1990) book on the topic. After suffering accidental carbon monoxide (CO) poisoning, Mr. S. retained the ability to detect small differences in luminance, wavelength (i.e., color), and size. However, he was "unable to distinguish between two objects of the same luminance, wavelength, and area when the only difference between them was shape." Further, although failing to identify a safety pin, he reported that it was "silver and shiny like a watch or a nail clipper." Thus, some low-level functions of feature identification were spared, as was, indeed, an abstract understanding of the visual properties of real-world objects. Additionally, "Recent and remote memory, spontaneous speech, comprehension of spoken language and repetition were intact," indicating the absence of a general, nonspecific cognitive decline. And, most intriguingly, although "unable to name objects, pictures of objects, body parts, letters, numbers, or geometrical figures on visual confrontation, . . . he could readily identify and name objects from tactile, olfactory, or auditory cues" (Benson and Greenberg, 1969, pp. 83–85).

An interesting question to ask at this point – one that we won't try to answer right away – is whether this syndrome may arise from a disconnection between early visual processing and the knowledge of the world that's necessary to recognize objects. After all, the knowledge might still seem to be intact in this patient, in that he can access it through other sensory modalities. One caveat to accepting this interpretation, however, is that it assumes a property of the cognitive architecture that need not be true: it assumes that knowledge about the world is stored in an "amodal" format, one that is not tied to any one sensory modality. Could it not be the case that, at least to some degree, some long-term representations of knowledge remain tied to the sensory channel through which we first acquired this knowledge? In other words, might it not be the case that Mr. S.'s *visual* knowledge of objects was compromised, but his tactile knowledge, olfactory knowledge, and auditory knowledge remained intact?

Other interesting variants of apperceptive agnosia are manifested by patients who can recognize objects in optimal viewing conditions, but whose performance declines precipitously under more challenging conditions. For example, a patient may be able to recognize, say, a bicycle in a black and white line drawing, but fail at the same task if a piece of string is dropped onto the picture, or if a handful of is scattered across it (i.e., if noise is introduced to the scene). Another classic deficit is the inability to recognize an object when it is presented from a noncanonical viewpoint. Thus, the patient may be able to recognize a wheelbarrow from a side view, but not a rear view (in which the handles are "pointing at" the viewer, perpendicular to the picture plane). Such deficits clearly implicate impairment of perceptual processes that we considered in *Chapter 6,* including the disambiguating functions of top-down feedback, and, more generally, the hierarchical nature of object recognition.

FIGURE 10.1 Drawings by a patient with an associative agnosia. Four objects that patient H.J.A. could copy reasonably well, but could not correctly identify. He named the eagle "a cat sitting up", the guitar "some kind of machine ... a press", the owl "a pattern", and the bee "an animal with horns and a tail ... a rhino?"

Source: Riddoch and Humphreys, 1987 / Oxford University Press.

Associative Agnosia

This syndrome was famously characterized by neuropsychologist Hans-Lukas Teuber (1916–1977) as "appear[ing] in its purest form as a normal percept that has somehow been stripped of meaning" (Milner and Teuber, 1968, p. 293). *Figure 10.1* shows an iconic example from a patient who was able to execute highly precise copies of line drawings, yet was unable to recognize what the drawings represented. Examples such as this very strongly give the sense of a disconnection syndrome (i.e., of perception from knowledge), as considered previously. However, although this idea (and, indeed, Teuber's quote) remains prominent in the literature and textbooks, it should be noted that the perception of many of these patients is unlikely to be truly normal. For example, despite the high fidelity of the drawings in *Figure 10.1*, many patients producing copies of comparable quality have been described as doing so in a "slavish," "line-by-line" manner, and doing so "exceedingly slowly" (various authors, quoted by Farah, 1990, p. 60). Thus, the quality of the reproductions may owe more to "drawing strategies" than to truly intact visual perception.

It may be that the fundamental distinction between the two groups of patients (i.e., apperceptive vs. associative agnosic) isn't that visual perception is impaired in one and spared in the other, but that they differ with regard to where along the visual processing hierarchy their impairment is most pronounced. For example, whereas apperceptive agnosic patients try to identify objects based on low-level features (e.g., color and texture), associative agnosic patients typically try to rely on shape. Thus, for example, Farah (1990) notes that on four separate occasions she showed the associative agnosic patient L.H. a drawing of a baseball bat, and on each his incorrect guess was an object with a similar shape: a paddle, a knife, a baster, and a thermometer.

The most intriguing subset of associative agnosic patients is those whose primary deficit seems not to be with type identification, but with token individuation. And within this subset, the sub-subset whose impairment very saliently includes face recognition has claimed a disproportionate share of the attention of the visual cognition community.

Prosopagnosia

Following in the tradition of the neurologist Heinrich Lissauer (1861–1891), who coined the term agnosia, it was another neurologist, Joachim Bodamer, who, in 1947, welded on the prefix "prosopon" (from the ancient Greek for face) to characterize his patients with a selective agnosia for the recognition of faces. In the decades that followed, there have been many case studies of patients with this syndrome. In many cases, the deficit is quite striking, with the patient, for example, not recognizing his wife as she walks past the hospital bed, and not even realizing that the strange person staring at him is actually a reflection of himself in a mirror.

What over a half-century of research hasn't resolved, however, is just how specific to faces this syndrome can be. There is, for example, a report of a patient who could identify close relatives by voice, but not by face, but who had no difficulty recognizing, for example, his electric razor from among many similar-looking electric razors, his wallet from among similar wallets, and so on. Intriguing dissociations between patients have also been reported, such as one group with a face-recognition deficit but who have no difficulty recognizing facial expressions, and others showing the converse. Many other reports, however, indicate that within-category recognition of other categories can also be impaired, with animals and plants often compromised. Specific examples include an avid birdwatcher who, upon developing prosopagnosia, also lost the ability to discriminate between different species of birds. Perhaps most famous is the case of a farmer who, along with human faces, lost the ability to recognize each of the cows in his herd (who he had known, individually, by name, prior to his stroke). This and other reports gave rise to the idea that prosopagnosia and other seemingly category-specific deficits of visual perception may reflect a more general loss of perceptual expertise, an idea that we'll take up further along in this chapter.

Computational Models of Visual Object Recognition

Two Neuropsychological Traditions

Interestingly, although much of the research summarized in the preceding sections occurred in parallel to the neurophysiological study of object recognition in the monkey, including studies of face processing (*Chapter 6*), the two traditions of research proceeded largely independently of each other. One reason is that they had largely different goals. Whereas systems neuroscience, including the subfield that we can call experimental neuropsychology, prioritizes understanding how the brain works, the discipline of cognitive neuropsychology is primarily interested in how the mind works (i.e., in how the cognitive system is organized). One example of experimental neuropsychology that we have already considered include is the study by Pohl (1973), which illustrated the what/where organization of the visual system. In relation to visual agnosia, Milner and Teuber (1968) is an example of an experimental neuropsychology approach to that specific question. An example of cognitive neuropsychology, in contrast, is the influential model of object recognition from Humphreys and Riddoch (1987), depicted in *Figure 10.2*.

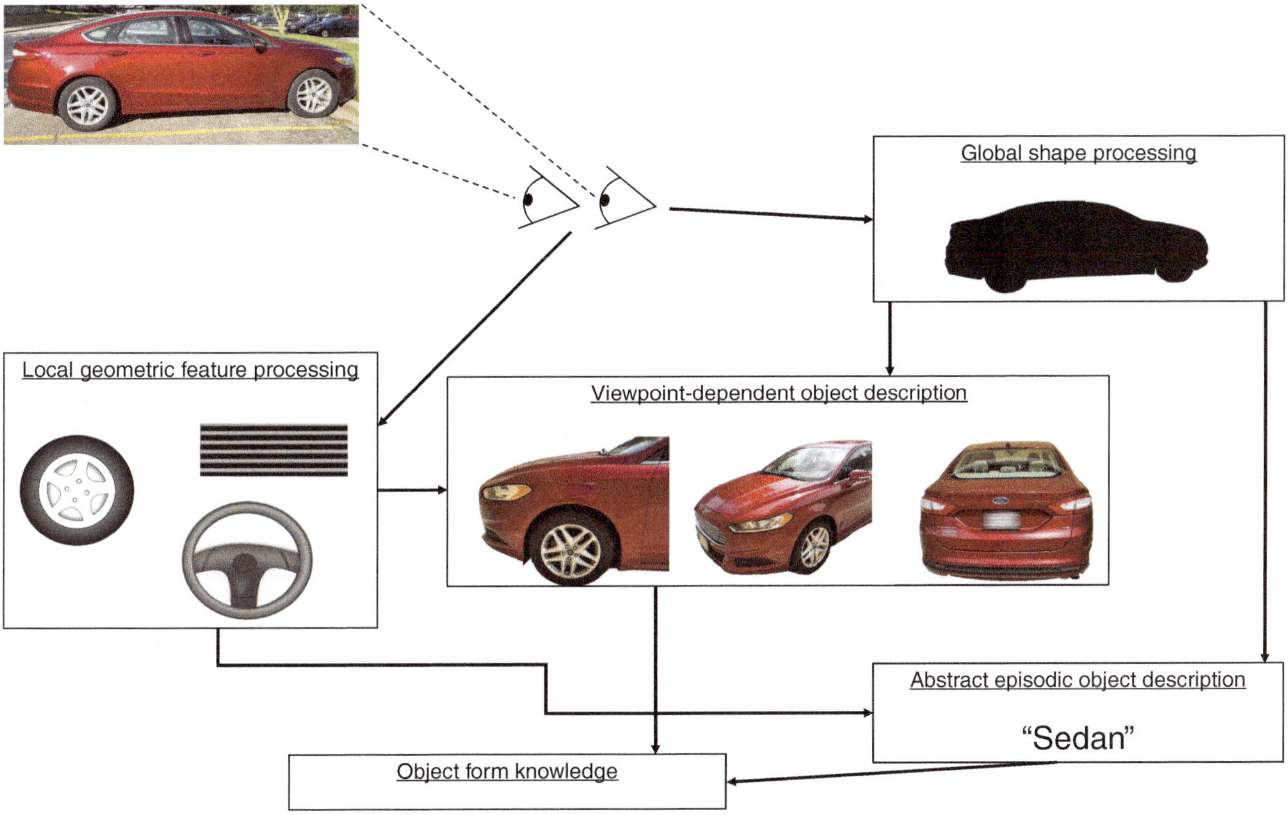

FIGURE 10.2 A cognitive neuropsychology-derived model of visual object processing.

Cognitive Neuropsychology-Influenced Models Note from *Figure 10.2* that the emphasis of this model is on stages of information processing, rather than stages of neural processing. From this perspective, although it is intended to account for object recognition deficits reported from a variety of brain-damaged patients, it addresses a level of explanation that is more closely related to cognitive psychology than to neuroscience. Thus, for example, each of the boxes in this model is inferred, rather than directly measured. They correspond to hypothesized stages of processing that were devised in order to account for one or more findings from visual agnosic patients.

To summarize, Humphreys and Riddoch (1987) offer an analogy that's evidently a popular one – searching for a book at the library in the pre-internet age. (Because your author graduated from university in 1987, it is an analogy that he understands quite well.) When one wants to find a particular book at the library, one looks it up by title or by author in the card catalog, and the card corresponding to that book indicates the specific location in the stacks (the "address") where the book will be located. (In the United States, this address is (was?) encoded via the Dewey decimal system.) To acquire the book, the library patron writes down the encoded address on a scrap of paper and then walks to the section of the library where that address is located. In this analogy, the finding of the appropriate card in the card catalog corresponds to the transduction of visual information into a neural code, and the writing of the address onto the scrap of paper is early visual processing. The scrap of paper containing the link to the book is the "abstract episodic object description," which corresponds to a higher-level visual object representation. (In the analogy, this representation is *abstract* because the Dewey code doesn't literally say "5th floor, third stack from the north wall, fourth shelf, 437 books in from the end"; nor does it have any other inherent meaning, it's just an otherwise nonsensical combination of digits that will help you find your book (e.g., "612.8/2334223) – therefore, this level of perceptual representation is posited to be without inherent meaning.) The key step in the process is recognition, when one matches the code on one's scrap of paper with the code on the spine of the sought-after book. (The code on the spine of the book corresponds to "object form knowledge" in the model.) Recognition is successfully accomplished when the patron arrives at the correct location and physically acquires the book. Phenomenologically, this corresponds to recognizing the object that one is looking at, and knowing everything that there is to know about it. (E.g., *That's my cat. Cats are quadrupedal domesticated mammals, probably bred from the lynx or ocelot or some smallish feline carnivore [etc.]. This cat's name is* Mahalia, *named after Mahalia Jackson because she's black, brown, and beige* [the cat, that is], *the title of a Duke Ellington piece (on which M.J. sang) that we were into when we "rescued" her as a kitten from that crazy cat lady's house in Billerica, MA. She's really old* [again, referring to the cat].) Associative agnosia, by this account, is caused by damage to object form knowledge. (Note that this is the interface that Fuster [2003], in the *Introduction to Section III*, refers to as "the matching of external gestalts to internalized representations in long-term memory" that is central to perception.)

Critiques of Cognitive Neuropsychology-Influenced Models Farah (1990) notes that this type of modular "symbol-manipulation" model "has appealed to many [cognitive] neuropsychologists seeking an account of associative agnosia" because it provides a framework for the intuitions of observers of the syndrome. She summarizes these, drawing on literature spanning from 1914 through 1985, as "loss of the 'stored visual memories' or '**engrams**' of objects," and disruption of "'the matching of signal to trace' . . . [and the] destruction of stored 'templates'" (pp. 96–97). However, there are at least two types of concern that one could have about such models. (And this is now this author's assessment, not a paraphrase of Martha Farah.) One is that they are not quantitative, and thus are difficult to disprove. With all models, and certainly with "verbal models" such as this, one must guard against post hoc elements that satisfy one's intuition about how a system might work. For our current discussion, make note of the fact that an explicit tenet of the Humphreys and Riddoch (1987) model, embodied in the *abstract episodic object description*, is that visual object recognition proceeds in two stages: (1) the processing of "structural" representations that have no inherent meaning, and (2) "visual semantics," the portion of long-term memory that represents meaning. A second concern about modular models is that they are often not constrained by/do not incorporate what we know about how the brain works. The model in *Figure 10.2*, for example, has no feedback from higher levels of visual processing to lower levels. Furthermore, it contains no specification that a certain kind of neuron or area of the brain (such as those we reviewed in *Chapter 6*) corresponds to any of the processing stages in the model.

PDP-Based Models Offer a Neurally Plausible Alternative for Modeling Cognitive Processes and Architectures At this juncture, a fair objection might be to point to the fact that the goal of a model such as that illustrated in *Figure 10.2* is to better understand behavior at a *cognitive* level of description, not at a *neural* level. And it is certainly true for such models that slapping "neuro-sounding" labels onto a model won't, in and of itself, confer any more legitimacy or plausibility to it. An alternative approach is offered by PDP, or "connectionist," modeling, which, although also often addressing questions at the cognitive level of description, is generally considered to generate models that are more compatible with many of the assumptions and practices of contemporary cognitive neuroscience (c.f. *Chapter 4,* section *A PDP model of picture naming*).

For this author, the really powerful implication of the model by Rogers et al. (2004), as described in *Chapter 4,* section *A PDP model of picture naming,* is the way that it encourages a radical rethinking of how object recognition works. While writing *Chapter 6*, for example, the author was feeling impelled to press "forward" (i.e., downstream) to "get to the place where recognition happens." Despite this intuitive impression, however, he may have been describing *where*, if not *how*, object recognition happens while detailing feedforward and feedback connections from V1 to V4 and MT, the lateral connections from V4 to IT, and the response profiles of neurons all along these pathways. There may not, in fact, have been a finish line to cross. (Indeed, this very conclusion will be reinforced by more recent neurophysiological work to be summarized further along in this chapter.)

The Cognitive Neuroscience Revolution in Visual Cognition

With these ideas in mind, we now return to the physiology of the ventral pathway, this time (as opposed to how we did it in *Chapter 6*) as measured with fMRI, and in humans. This next section will illustrate the truly revolutionary influence that developments in cognitive neuroscience, in this case neuroimaging, have had on fields such as object recognition and visual cognition. One example is that the divide between the cognitive neuropsychology and the neurophysiology of object recognition, which we have just reviewed, has been steadily narrowing. Indeed, it is increasingly rare today to see models of object recognition and/or visual agnosia that don't explicitly incorporate constraints from functional neuroanatomy and/or neurophysiology. In other respects, however, some longstanding debates persist, just reframed in terms of the newer technologies and the newer intellectual paradigms. Thus, for example, questions of localization-of-function vs. distributed processing remain front-and-center, as does the even older dialogue between nature and nurture.

Category Specificity in the Ventral Stream?

Are Faces Special?

"The Guns of August" You'll recall, from *Chapter 6*, the puzzling properties of neurons of temporal cortex that seemed to respond to "the idea of a face" more so than to any individual face. In the 1990s, cognitive psychologists familiar with this literature, and with the puzzling questions raised by the prosopagnosic syndrome, saw in neuroimaging an opportunity to address these problems in a new way. Prominent among these was Nancy Kanwisher, who trained as a cognitive psychologist and, early in her career, worked on a phenomenon known as repetition blindness, influentially relating it to how the brain handles the type vs.

token distinction (e.g., why is it more difficult to individuate two different flowers presented sequentially in a serial stream of stimuli than, say, a flower from a face?) (Kanwisher, 1991). Perhaps this underlies her subsequent fascination with face processing? In any event, in 1997, she, together with then-postdoctoral fellow Marvin Chun and then-undergraduate research assistant Josh McDermott (subsequently to become highly accomplished cognitive neuroscientists in their own right), published a study that spurred a subfield of cognitive neuroscience that shows no sign of slowing down 25+ years later.

"The Fusiform Face Area: A Module in Human Extrastriate Cortex Specialized for Face Perception" The experiment described in the publication with this title, by Kanwisher, McDermott, and Chun (1997), employed a block design, in which subjects viewed the serial presentation of unfamiliar faces (ID photos of Harvard undergraduates) alternating with serial presentation of control stimuli. Blocks were 30 seconds long; stimuli presented for 500 msec with an interstimulus interval of 150 msec. The experiment proceeded in three phases, the first an unapologetic "far and wide" search for regions that might respond with greater activity for faces vs. objects, the second and third more rigorous tests to replicate the phase 1 finding while ruling out potential confounds and further assessing the specificity of the regions identified in phase 1. The authors note that "Our technique of running multiple tests applied to the same region defined functionally within individual subjects provides a solution to two common problems in functional imaging: (1) the requirement to correct for multiple statistical comparisons and (2) the inevitable ambiguity in the interpretation of any study in which only two or three conditions are compared" (p. 4302).

In phase 1 of the study, 12 of 15 subjects showed significantly greater activity for faces than objects in the right fusiform gyrus, on the ventral surface of the temporal lobe, at the level of the occipitotemporal junction, and this region therefore became the focus of the subsequent scans. Phase 2, illustrated in *Figure 10.3*, panels 1B and 1C, was intended to rule out the potential confounding factors from the phase 1 study: differences in luminance between face and object stimuli, or the fact that the face, but not the object, stimuli were all exemplars drawn from the same category. Phase 3, illustrated in *Figure 10.3,* panels 2B and 2C, was intended to rule out the potential confound that the FFA was simply responding to any human body parts. Additionally, it established that FFA activity generalized to images of faces that were less easy to discriminate, and to a condition that imposed stronger attentional demands on the processing of stimuli, by requiring a decision of whether or not each stimulus matched the identity of the previous one (a so-called "1-back" task).

As illustrated in *Figure 10.3*, the results were quite striking, showing considerably higher activity in FFA to faces than to any other stimuli. Thus, they were consistent with the idea that faces receive privileged processing in this region. But is this region *specialized* for face processing? Sometime in the late 1990s, the author of this book attended a presentation by Kanwisher at a colloquium at the University of Pennsylvania. The cognitive scientist Saul Sternberg, in the audience that day, asked what to make of the fact that the region also showed elevated activity (relative to baseline) to other stimuli. Kanwisher replied (and this is a paraphrase from memory) that "there must be something to this question, because I get it almost every time I give this talk," but that quantitative superiority of response to a particular class of stimuli relative to others is a criterion often used by neurophysiologists as evidence for specificity of function. This stance will come under closer scrutiny in later portions of this chapter.

One reason that the discovery of the FFA generated so much interest was that it seemed to effect a neural test of an influential theory that had been advanced by the philosopher Jerry Fodor in his 1983 book *Modularity of Mind.* In a sentence, Fodor's idea was that some cognitive operations are "encapsulated" and "cognitively impenetrable" once launched, and thus not susceptible to influence by other factors (attention, intention, behavioral priorities, distraction, etc.) until they have run their course. Visual object recognition, as we've been emphasizing here, and auditory perception (particularly speech perception) would be two such candidate processes. Not unlike some of the cognitive neuropsychological models that we considered earlier in this chapter, Fodor's idea gave a good account of many observations

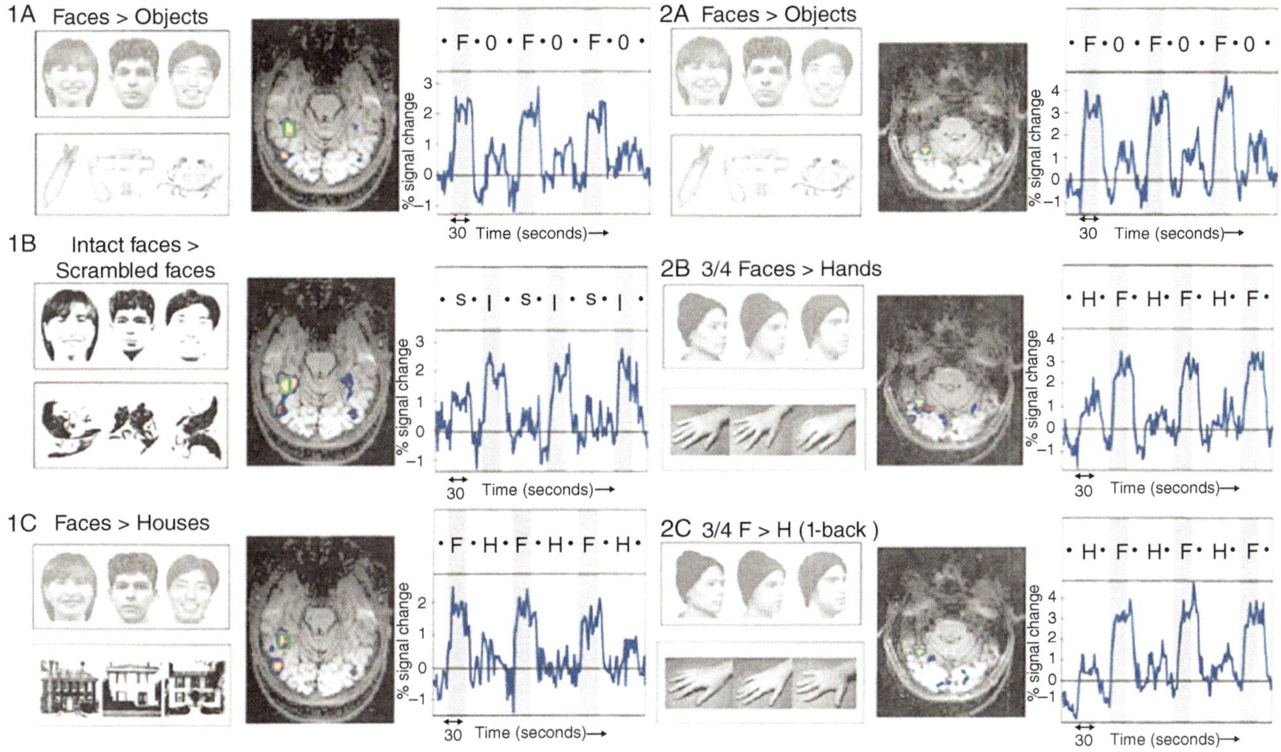

FIGURE 10.3 Examples of stimuli, fMRI statistical maps, and time series, from several assays of response properties of the FFA. The contrast illustrated in panels **1A** and **2A** (Faces > Objects) was used to define the FFA ROI, outlined in green in the axial images, each for a different individual subject. Panels **B** and **C** illustrate the statistical map generated by each of the contrasts, each for the same subject, with the green-outlined ROI from panel **A** superimposed. This procedure was repeated on the individual-subject data of five subjects, and each time series is the average from the FFA ROI of each.

Source: Reproduced with permission from Kanwisher et al. (1997) / Society for Neuroscience.

from studies of human behavior (in this case, from cognitive psychology), but, at the same time, also seemed contrary to much of what we know about how the brain works. Thus, one really intriguing aspect of the Kanwisher, McDermott, and Chun (1997) study was that it could be interpreted as a presentation of neural evidence in favor of a hypothesis that seemed contrary to how many thought that the brain works!

Questions Raised by the Kanwisher et al. (1997) Findings Now, to be clear, no one questioned the veracity of the findings by Kanwisher, McDermott, and Chun (1997). Rather, the question was, *How do we make sense out of them?* Indeed, another reason for their impact was that they gave new urgency to the longstanding puzzle presented by prosopagnosia: no one denied that the syndrome existed, but a widely accepted explanation had eluded scientists for at least 100 years. This puzzle was articulated by Hans-Lukas Teuber in an anecdote, from the "Perception" section of a chapter coauthored with Brenda Milner (Milner and Teuber, 1968). Stylistic and cultural aspects of this quote may be offensive to contemporary ears, but let's look past the dated language and focus on the substance:

> There is the familiar example of perceptual learning, on the part of a white visitor to China (or conversely, a Chinese visiting America). At first, most of the Chinese faces are indiscriminable, but, once one is fairly familiar with a few individual faces, something seems to have been learned that generalizes to all Chinese faces: "Knowing" a few makes all the others more distinguishable. Conceivably, an agnosia for faces could be due to a loss of such an acquired system of rules for classifying facial differences. Alternatively, and even more speculatively, we could assume that the initial basis for discrimination and identification of faces and of facial expressions involves

> some innate schemata onto which the subsequent, perceptual differentiations were merely imposed . . . This strong but as yet unproveable assumption would make a selective loss of capacity for identifying faces, following certain focal lesions in man, somewhat less paradoxical than it now appears to be (pp. 300–301).

The concluding sentence of Kanwisher, McDermott, and Chun (1997) echoes Teuber's reasoning: "Future studies can also evaluate whether extensive visual experience with any novel class of visual stimuli is sufficient for the development of a local region of cortex specialized for the analysis of that stimulus class, or whether cortical modules like area FF must be innately specified (Fodor, 1983)" (p. 4310).

Perceptual Expertise

Prominent among the "future studies" foreshadowed by Kanwisher, McDermott, and Chun (1997) were several led by cognitive neuroscientists Isabel Gauthier and Michael Tarr. (Tarr, like Kanwisher, started his career as a cognitive psychologist and has become increasingly "neuro" as his career has evolved.) These two and their colleagues have pursued the idea that there's "nothing special" about faces at the neural level – no genetically specified circuits responsible for their processing. Rather, faces are stimuli that we see thousands of times each day, every day, and being able to individuate them is vitally important for success in our highly social environment. Thus, for example, they have argued that it is possible that when Kanwisher, McDermott, and Chun (1997) showed different houses vs. different faces in the experiment illustrated in *Figure 10.3,* panel 1C, the two types of stimuli may have been processed differently. The house stimuli may have been processed at a more categorical level, and the faces at an individual level. (E.g., the subjects may have been thinking "there's another house, and another one, and another one, . . ." whereas they may have been scrutinizing each face to determine if it was someone they knew.) By this account, the greater activity for faces than for buildings in that experiment may have had more to do with how stimuli were processed than with what the stimuli were.

This perspective is one that emphasizes the role of expertise in perception. At the neural level, it argues, FFA may be best construed as a "fusiform expertise area." (Although no one, to my knowledge, has ever proposed the moniker "FEA." Tarr and Gauthier [2000] did try rebranding it the "flexible face area," but this never caught on.) Note that what we'll call the "expertise" account has a ready explanation for why some prosopagnosic patients also lose the ability to recognize other kinds of stimuli with which they have a high degree of expertise, such as the farmer who lost the ability to individuate his cows or the bird watcher who lost the ability to distinguish among species of bird. Gauthier and colleagues tested this idea with a clever set of studies that entailed training subjects (for some studies, healthy young individuals, for others, prosopagnosic patients) to become experts at recognizing individual tokens of a category of stimuli for which there could not exist a genetic template: Greebles.

Greeble Expertise Gauthier and Tarr (1997) developed Greebles as a class of stimuli that have many of the same properties as faces: (1) they are processed configurally – the relation between parts (for faces, distance between eyes, from nose to eyes, etc.) is critically important for recognition; (2) they show an inversion effect – it's disproportionally difficult, relative to other stimuli, to recognize them when they are upside down; (3) they tend to be classified at the individual level, rather than the category level. They can be categorized at the level of Greeble, family, gender, and individual. As illustrated in *Figure 10.4*, the fMRI data of Gauthier et al. (1999) suggest that, in contrast to Greeble novices, experts at Greeble recognition evince a statistically comparable stimulus-evoked activity for Greebles as for faces in the FFA. From this, they concluded that "The strongest interpretation suggested by our results . . . is that the face-selective area in the middle fusiform gyrus may be most appropriately described as a general substrate for subordinate-level discrimination that can be fine-tuned by experience with any object category" (p. 572).

FIGURE 10.4 FFA activity in Greeble novices vs. Greeble experts.

Source: Gauthier et al., 1999 / Springer Nature.

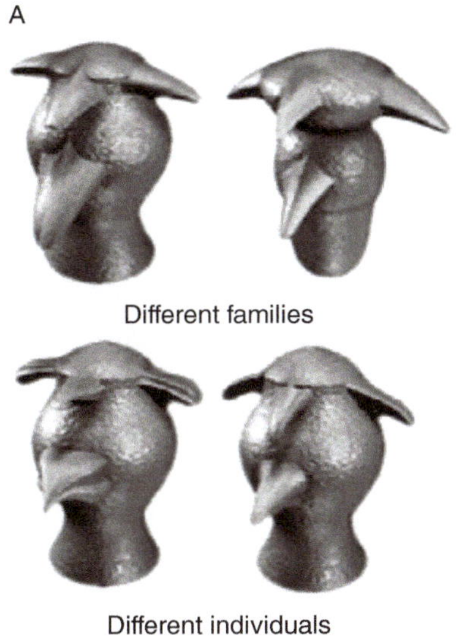

FIGURE 10.4.A Examples of Greebles. The two in the top row are from different "families," as defined by the large central part. The two at the bottom are two individuals from the same family, differing only in terms of the shapes of smaller parts. Subjects were determined to have achieved expert status with Greebles when they could distinguish two from the same family as quickly as they could distinguish two from different families.

Source: Reproduced with permission from Gauthier et al. (1999) / Springer Nature.

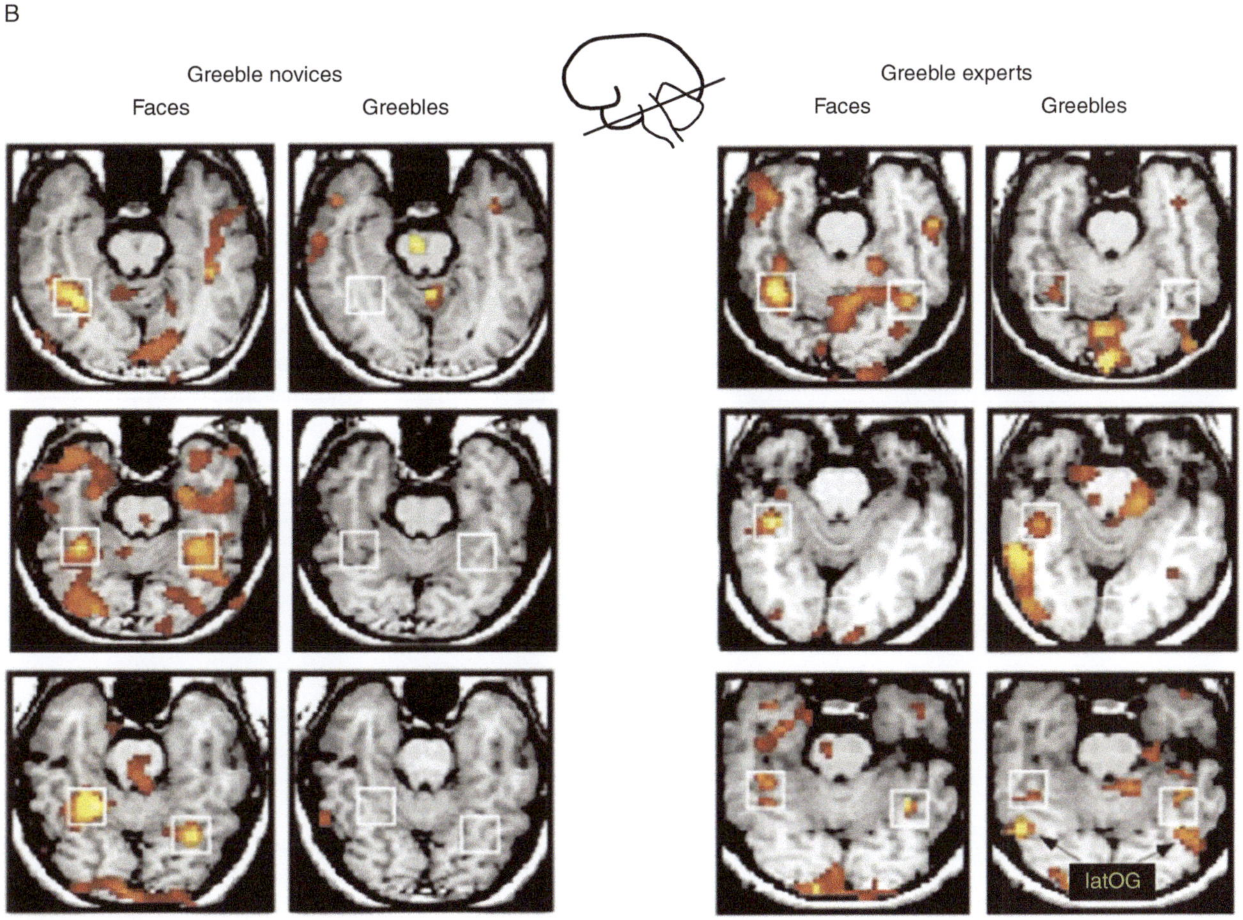

FIGURE 10.4.B Ventral temporal lobe activity, measured with fMRI, from six individuals, during passive viewing of faces vs. Greebles. White squares identify the FFA.

Source: Reproduced with permission from Gauthier et al. (1999) / Springer Nature.

Evidence for a High Degree of Specificity for Many Categories in Ventral Occipitotemporal Cortex

Quickly on the heels of the 1997 publication from Kanwisher and colleagues came a flurry of publications suggesting a further modularization of inferior temporal cortex, some of them from this same group. A *parahippocampal place area* (PPA) was discovered that responds preferentially to viewing a scene (be it a room or a landscape); an *extrastriate body area* (EBA) that responds preferentially to viewing body parts; and a *visual word-form area*. A summary of the location of these areas is provided in *Figure 10.5*. These findings, too, have not been without their skeptics: some, à la Tarr and Gauthier, have pointed to potential confounds in the studies producing the results summarized in *Figure 10.5*; others, as we'll see in the next section, have called into question the validity of the assumptions underlying the methods that produce these results.

Evidence for Highly Distributed Category Representation in Ventral Occipitotemporal Cortex

Four years after the publication of the Kanwisher, McDermott, and Chun (1997) report on face perception, James Haxby and colleagues published a study of object recognition that has also had a remarkable impact on cognitive neuroscience. In contrast to the modular models summarized in the previous paragraph, Haxby et al. (2001) proposed that "The representation of a face or object is reflected by a distinct pattern of response across a wide expanse of cortex in which both large- and small-amplitude responses carry information about object appearance," and, therefore, that "each category elicits a distinct pattern of response in ventral temporal cortex that is also evident in the cortex that responds maximally to other categories" (p. 2425). To test these ideas, they acquired fMRI while subjects viewed two blocks, each of which serially presented stimuli drawn from one of each of eight categories: faces, houses, cats, bottles, small man-made tools, shoes, chairs, and smeary "nonsense images." Next, they compared the similarity of the pattern of activity for each category in its even-numbered block vs. in its odd-numbered block, by correlating the two – that is, they assessed the extent to which knowing

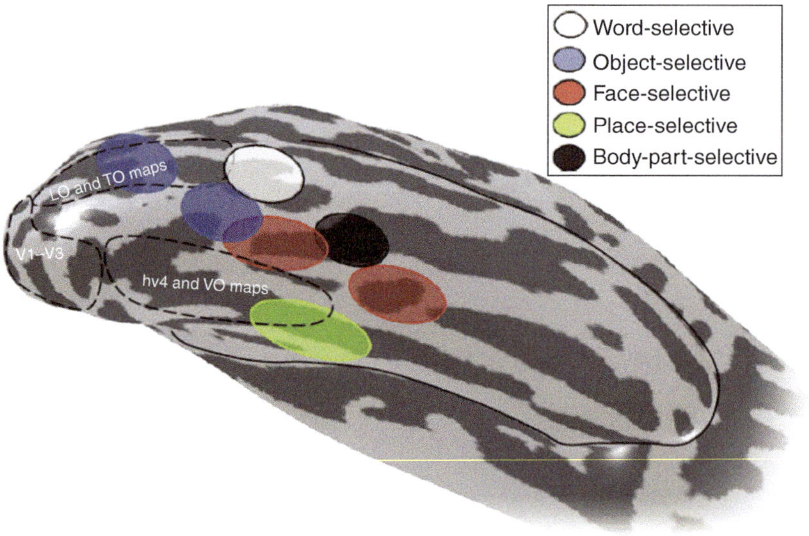

FIGURE 10.5 Juxtaposition of regions on the ventral surface of the occipital and temporal lobes that contain retinotopic maps (dashed lines and written labels) and those that have been identified as preferentially responsive (via univariate analyses) to visual stimuli from various categories.

Source: Reproduced from Wandell et al. (2011) / with permission of Elsevier.

the level of signal intensity in each voxel of ventral occipitotemporal cortex during one block predicted what that same voxel's signal intensity was in the other block. (Importantly, they did this regardless of whether any given voxel's value was large or small, positive or negative.) For comparison, they also correlated the pattern produced by the category in question against all of the other categories. (Thus, for each category, eight correlations were performed [one within-category and seven between-category], and for the experiment, eight within-category correlations and 56 between-category correlations.) This is illustrated in *Figure 10.6*, in which, for each row, the red bar represents the within-category correlation coefficient, and the dark blue the between-category coefficients. (Note that, because the correlations were computed by comparing the values of every voxel in ventral occipitotemporal cortex from one block vs. another, this was a multivariate analysis – indeed, it is considered a forerunner of the MVPA methods introduced in *Chapter 5*, section *Multivariate methods for decoding neural signals*). The results indicated that coefficients from within-category correlations were higher than those from between-category correlations for 96% of the comparisons. The fact that this analysis was successful for each stimulus category provided support for the authors' proposal that the neural representation of visual categories is broadly distributed.

MVPA Challenges Models of Modular Category Specificity Two additional analyses carried out for the Haxby et al. (2001) study went further and directly challenged the interpretation of studies supporting modular models of the neural organization of categories of information. First, redid the analyses described above, but after excluding from the dataset the voxels that responded maximally to the critical category. Thus, for faces, for example, they

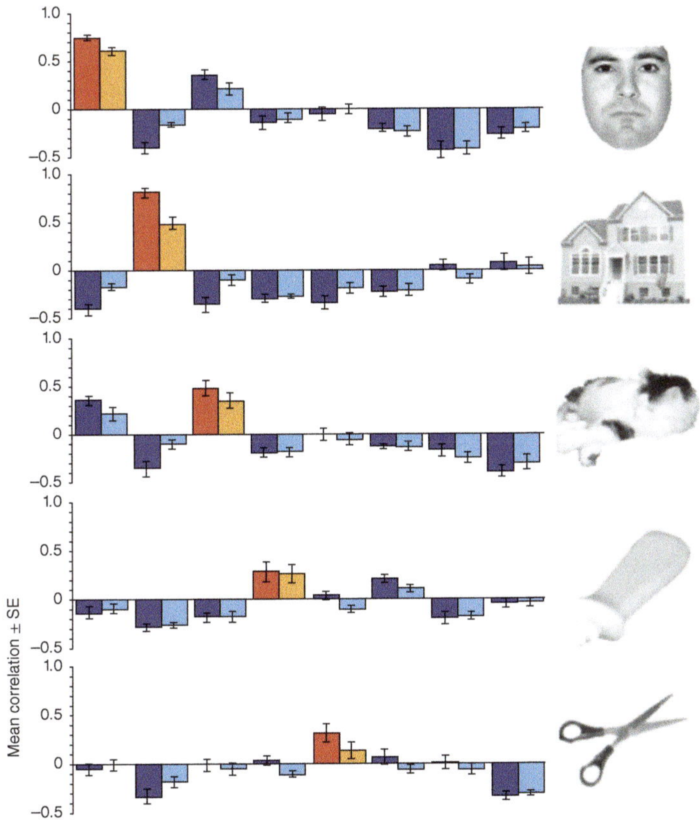

FIGURE 10.6 Correlation matrix showing within- and between-category correlations for the entirety of ventral occipitotemporal cortex that was analyzed, as well as for the same region, but with each category's maximally responsive voxels removed from the analysis. (The category *tools* is denoted by the scissors.)

Source: Reproduced with permission from Haxby et al. (2001) / American Association for the Advancement of Science - AAAS.

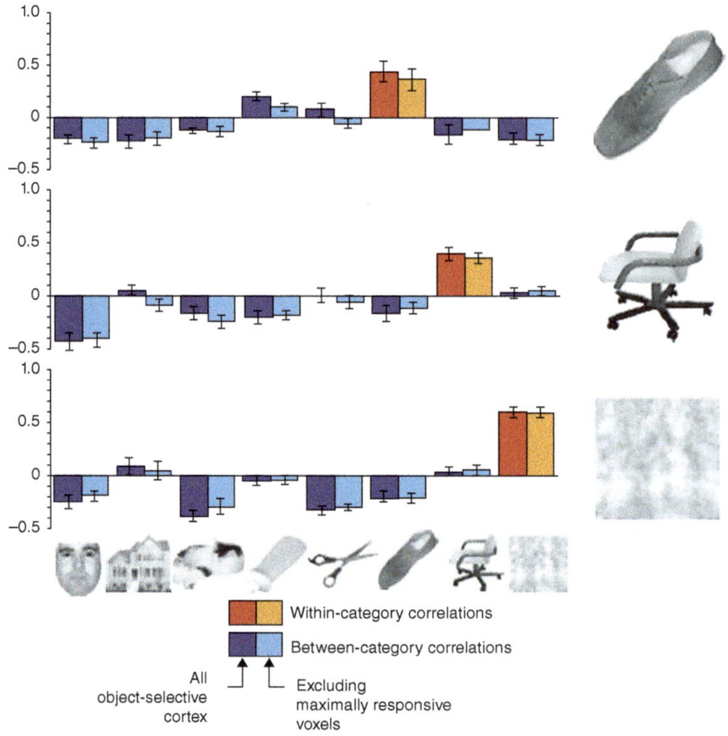

FIGURE 10.6 (Continued)

removed the voxels from the FFA before performing the within- and between-category correlations for face blocks. The outcome, as evidenced by comparison of the yellow vs. red bars in *Figure 10.6*, is that although the within-category correlation coefficients declined to varying degrees in the "excluded" datasets, they nonetheless remained higher than the between-category coefficients for 94% of comparisons. The implication of this finding is that, for faces, for example, a great deal of information about faces is represented in cortex outside of the FFA. This, therefore, might argue against the view that faces are processed in a highly modular manner.

But what about the FFA? Even if this region seems not to have "exclusive rights" to the processing of visually presented faces, it could still be "specialized" for face processing. But is it? This question hearkens back to the anecdote of Saul Sternberg's question to Nancy Kanwisher about what to make of the fact that FFA does respond, albeit with a smaller magnitude, to stimuli other than faces. To address it, Haxby et al. (2001) carried out a second set of follow-up analyses restricted to each empirically defined category-selective ROI (i.e., in the FFA, in the analogous voxels that responded maximally to houses, and so on). Within each ROI, they performed within- vs. between-category correlations for each of the other seven categories for which the ROI was not selective. That is, for example, within the FFA, does the pattern of activity evoked by one block of house stimuli better predict the pattern evoked by the second block of house stimuli than the pattern evoked by bottles, shoes, and so on? The answer was "yes," for 83% of comparisons. The same was true for six of the analogous ROIs defined with univariate methods as being selective for other categories: the house ROI supported within-category correlations (for non-house stimuli) at a rate of 93%; the tools ROI at 94%; and the cats ROI at 85%. Only the bottle ROI did not differentially represent non-bottle stimuli.

The implication of these findings is that the FFA cannot be characterized as being "specialized," or "selective," or "specific" for face processing. But might it, nonetheless, be necessary?

Convincing as the Haxby et al. (2001) analyses were at establishing the distributed nature of object representation in ventral occipitotemporal cortex, it is important to keep in mind that the data were generated in intact ventral occipitotemporal cortices. With regard to faces, for example, even though one of their analyses found evidence for face representation in cortex outside the FFA (i.e., when the FFA was excluded from the analysis), the tissue of the FFA was intact and functioning normally in the brains of their subjects when the scans were performed. Thus, the Haxby et al. (2001) findings cannot tell us whether non-FFA regions would be able to support a distributed representation of faces if the FFA were not influencing their activity when faces are being presented.

Demonstrating Necessity

The caveat at the end of the previous paragraph is a replay of a principle that we have now encountered several times: one cannot know the necessity of a region's contribution to a function without perturbing it. Thus, the next study that we will consider in this chapter employed ECoG, as well as electrical stimulation via the ECoG grid, to effect just such a focused perturbation.

The study illustrated in *Figure 10.7* was led by neurologist Josef Parvizi, in collaboration with cognitive neuroscientist Kalanit Grill-Spector (a former postdoctoral trainee of Nancy Kanwisher). Parvizi et al. (2012; *Figure 10.7*) were interested in comparing findings from fMRI with those from ECoG, and so they focused on oscillatory power in the gamma band, which is believed to be monotonically related to the BOLD signal. (Although this has been demonstrated empirically in simultaneous fMRI and LFP measurements in the monkey [e.g., Logothetis et al., 2001], it can also be deduced from what we know about these two signals: the BOLD

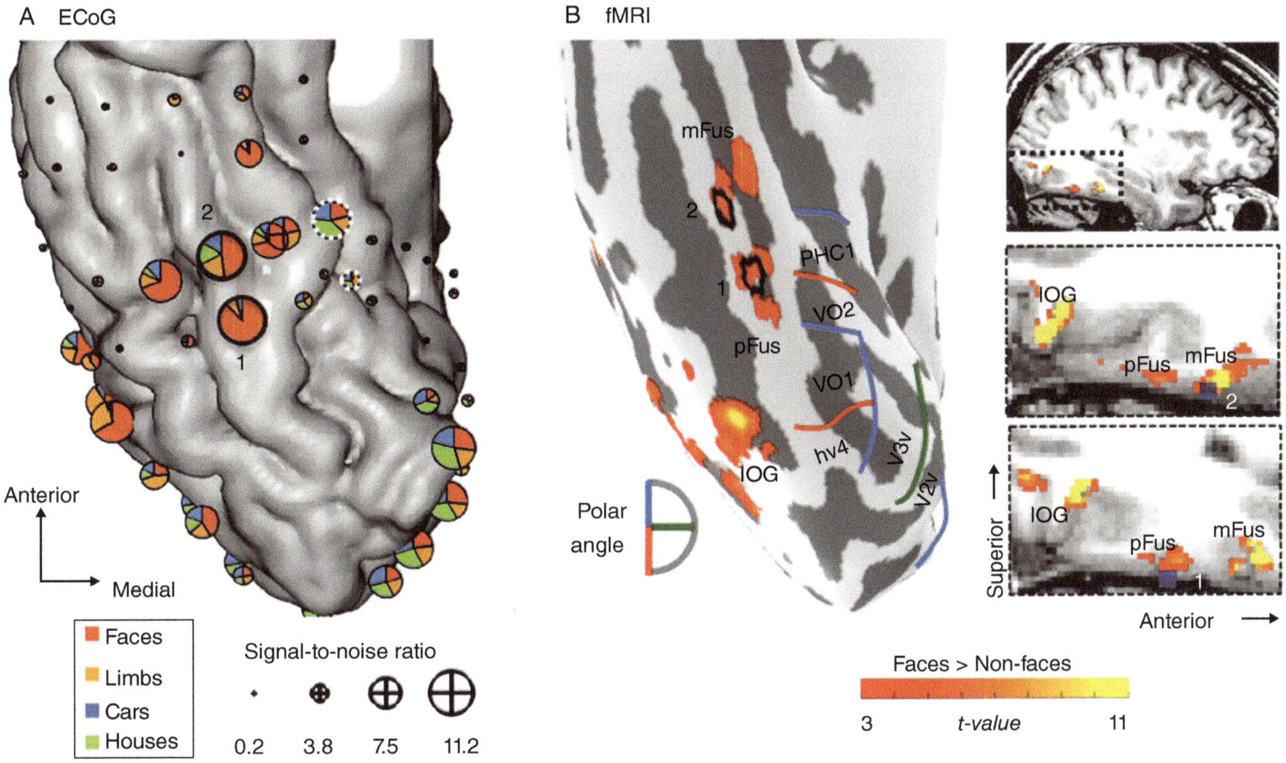

FIGURE 10.7 EcoG and electrical stimulation in the human brain. Panel **A** illustrates the layout of electrodes (black dots and pie charts) on the ventral surface of the patient's posterior right hemisphere. From their placement, one can surmise that two strips of electrodes, each containing two rows, were inserted lateral-to-medial along the ventral surface of the temporal lobe, the more posteriorly positioned one wrapping along the medial wall, and additional strips were positioned more superiorly, lateral and medial to the occipital pole. Each pie chart corresponds to an electrode that responded to one or more of the four categories of visual stimuli and is color-coded to indicate relative selectivity within these four. The size of each pie chart corresponds to the "signal-to-noise ratio," which can be understood as a normalized measure of the stimulus-specific increase in broadband power in the low- and high-gamma range (40–160 Hz) relative to the magnitude of fluctuations at this electrode at baseline. Panel **B** shows different views of regions whose univariate fMRI responses to faces exceeded responses to the other three categories, with colored lines on the inflated surface indicating retinotopically defined boundaries of the regions identified in black type. Superimposed on the inflated image in panel **B** is the location of the electrodes labeled "1" and "2" in panel **A**.

Source: Reproduced with permission from Parvizi et al. (2012) / Society for Neuroscience.

signal increases with increased metabolic demands driven by synaptic activity, and higher-frequency fluctuations in the LFP result from higher rates of synaptic activity in dendrites.) The image in panel B of *Figure 10.7* shows the location of two face-specific patches, produced with essentially the same methods as Kanwisher, McDermott, and Chun (1997). (Note from *Figure 10.3* that more than one face-selective patch was often identified in the right hemisphere of ventral occipitotemporal cortex, and this is also codified in the schematic in *Figure 10.5*.) The fMRI scan that produced the image in panel B of *Figure 10.7* was acquired prior to the surgical implantation into this same individual of the ECoG array illustrated in panel A, and, although the investigators clearly hoped for such an outcome, it was "mere luck" that, for this patient, two electrodes from the ECoG array fell directly over these two face patches.

The pie charts in panel A of *Figure 10.7* represent the results of ECoG recording while the subject viewed stimuli from four categories. Note that these results could, in principle, be interpreted as being consistent with both modularist and distributed accounts of face processing. With regard to the former, electrodes over the fusiform gyrus clearly measure stronger gamma-band responses for faces than for non-face stimuli; with regard to the latter, there are clearly prominent responses to faces, as well as to non-faces, across a large expanse of posterior occipitotemporal cortex from which recordings were obtained. The additional step taken in this study that differentiates it from studies "limited" to ECoG is that the investigators also perturbed activity in this region via stimulation – by selectively passing current between pairs of electrodes in the array. The stimulation protocol (2–4 mA delivered in alternating square-wave pulses at 50 Hz) was intended to disrupt normal functioning in the tissue between the two electrodes. In this way, with the same experimental apparatus, the investigators could both localize activity that was correlated with a function of interest and assess the necessity of the regions so identified by disrupting their activity.

Although the published report contains considerable detail and illustration relating to the ECoG results, the truly novel and consequential finding from this study, produced by the focused electrical stimulation, was so clear and striking that no statistics, indeed, no quantification, were needed. It was sufficient to post a video clip of the patient's real-time report of what he was experiencing while looking at his neurologist's face when stimulation was delivered across electrodes 1 and 2: "'You just turned into somebody else. Your face metamorphosed' (sic). When probed further, the patient reported that features appeared distorted: 'You almost look like somebody I've seen before, but somebody different. That was a trip. . . . It's almost like the shape of your face, your features drooped'" (Parvizi et al., 2012, p. 14918). The patient experienced no such perceptual metamorphoses when he attended to "Get Well Soon" helium balloons in the room, nor when he attended to the television. The video is astounding and leaves no uncertainty about the answer to our question of whether the FFA plays a causal role in face processing.

The Code for Facial Identity in the Primate Brain (!?!)

In 2006, neuroscientists Doris Tsao, Winrich Freiwald, Roger Tootell, and Margaret Livinstone (2006) published a paper entitled "A cortical region consisting entirely of face-selective cells." They made this audacious claim based on the results of a study in which they first used a method similar to that of Kanwisher, McDermott, and Chun (1997) to identify face-selective activity in the brains of monkeys, with fMRI, then recorded with extracellular electrophysiology from the hotspots identified with fMRI (see *Figure 10.8* for a similar result from a different study). What they found when they recorded from this region is, well, stated in the title of their paper. In subsequent work, Tsao and Freiwald, both in collaboration and in their own labs, have identified a total of seven face patches, along a caudal to rostral axis along the superior temporal sulcus and the inferior temporal gyrus. Previous work suggested a functional gradient along this axis, with neurons in the middle lateral (ML; "lateral" referring to the convexity of the inferior temporal gyrus) and middle fundus (MF; fundus of the superior temporal sulcus) patches showing viewpoint-specific tuning, neurons in the anterior lateral (AL) patch achieving partial viewpoint invariance, and neurons in anterior medial (AM; "wrapping onto" the ventral surface of ITG) achieving almost full viewpoint invariance. Indeed, in AM, characterized at the time as "the final output stage of IT face processing," tuning had been observed to be "sparse" [i.e., highly specific], with neurons that "encode exemplars for specific

FIGURE 10.8 Neuronal responses within face patches.

Source: Reproduced from Chang, L. et al. (2017) / with permission of Elsevier.

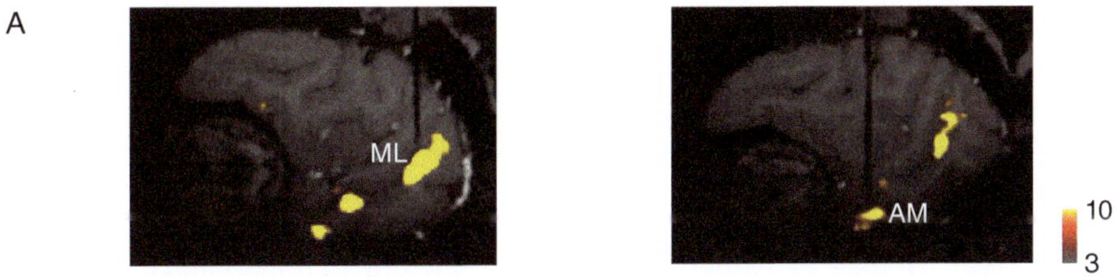

FIGURE 10.8.A fMRI activity in face patches in the temporal lobe. (Because the "shadow" of electrode tracks [caused by magnetic inhomogeneity] can be seen in ML and in AM, we can assume that these images are from a repeat scan, because images from an earlier scan would have been used for electrode targeting.)

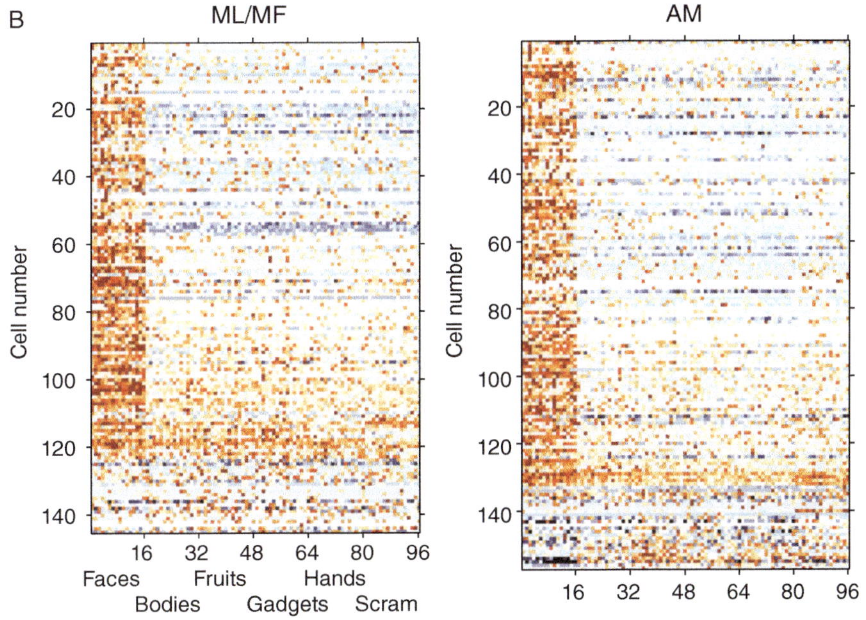

FIGURE 10.8.B Responses of neurons, averaged from 50 to 300 msec after the onset of each of 16 stimuli drawn from the categories listed along the horizontal axis of the figure. Each row corresponds to a single neuron, with warmer colors indicating higher firing rate.

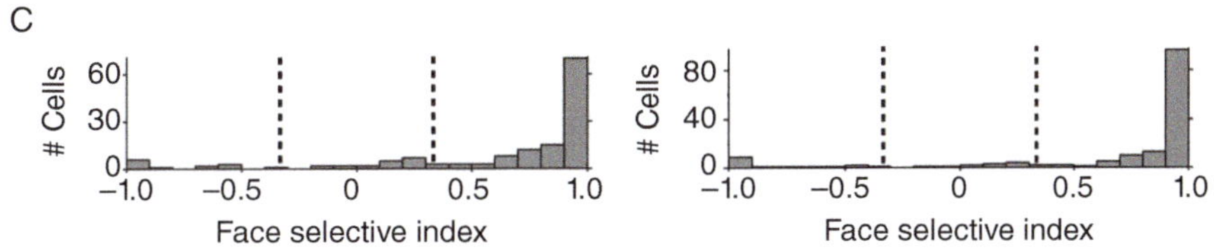

FIGURE 10.8.C Distribution of face selectivity of the neurons shown in *Figure 10.8.B*, as computed with the formula for a face selectivity index: [([mean response$_{faces}$] – [mean response$_{non\text{-}face\ objects}$])/([mean response$_{faces}$] + [mean response$_{non\text{-}face\ objects}$])]. (And so, at least for the animals in this study, these face patches didn't consist *entirely* of face-selective cells.)

individuals . . . respond[ing] to faces of only a few specific individuals, regardless of head orientation" (Chang and Tsao, 2017, p. 1013). Note that this is very different from the neurons that seem to be tuned for "the idea of a face," that we considered in *Chapter 6* (section *Broader implications of visual properties of temporal cortex neurons*). Indeed, upon first consideration, this seems much closer to the idea of the grandmother cell.

In a paper with a title perhaps as audacious as the Tsao, Friewald, and colleagues 2006 paper, Chang and Tsao (2017) presented a very sophisticated set of analyses and modeling that rule out the grandmother cell interpretation of neurons in face patch AM, thereby dramatically revising the interpretation that Tsao had given to her own previous work (e.g., Freiwald and Tsao, 2010). The key to the Chang and Tsao (2017) study was to approach the study of face processing as a quantitative problem, rather than one of engaging in a trial-and-error process of *let's-show-lots-of-stimuli-to-our-monkey-until-we-stumble-upon-one-that-this-neuron-responds-to*. Think back, for example, to the method of Tanaka and colleagues that led to the articulation of the principle of combination coding in IT (section *Combination coding, an alternative to the "grandmother cell," Chapter 6*). Although this approach led to an important conceptual breakthrough, a limitation is that it didn't provide an explanation for *why* neurons developed the seemingly arbitrary response properties that they did. For the neuron whose tuning is illustrated in *Figure 6.10*, for example, we don't know why it is that this neuron's preferred stimulus seems to be for this configuration of a white square with two superimposed black rectangles, rather than, say, just the two black rectangles, or the square with black and white stripes with two superimposed black rectangles. Phrased another way, knowing that the reduction method revealed that this neuron is just as responsive to a white square with two superimposed black rectangles as it is to a top-down view of the head of a toy tiger doesn't provide any principled basis for predicting what this neuron's level of response would be for novel stimuli never before seen by this monkey. To more fully understand how a population of neurons supports a cognitive function, one wants to know what are the rules that determine their response properties.

What Chang and Tsao (2017) did was to quantify each of 200 faces drawn from a database by identifying each of 58 landmarks on each of the faces and determining two values for each landmark: a location in a 2-D landmark-defined "face space" and a grayscale value (presumably from 0 to 255; *Figure 10.9*). With this method, I could hand you a piece of paper that had

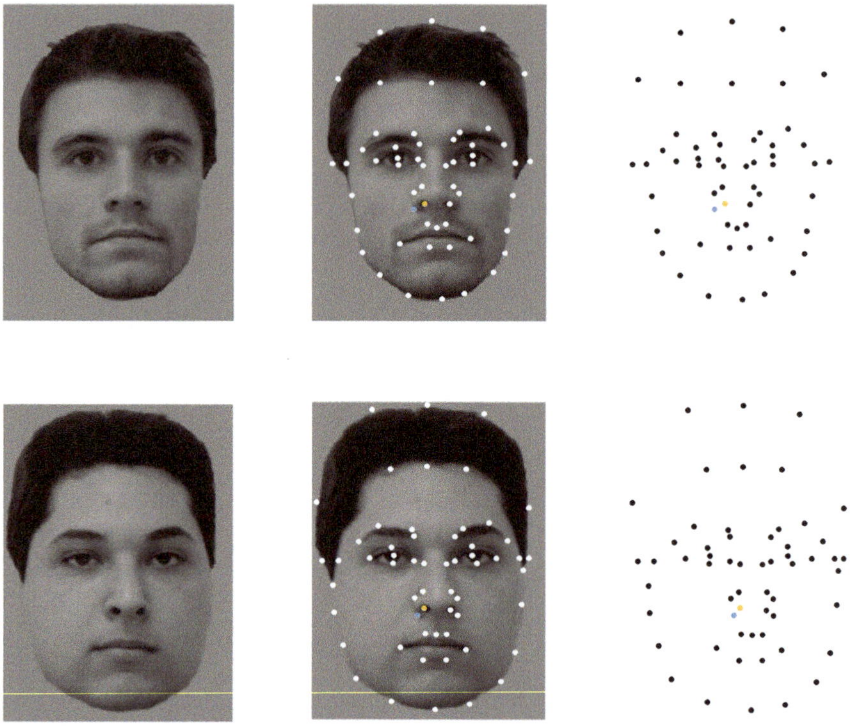

FIGURE 10.9 Quantifying what makes my face different from yours. Two faces taken from the FEI face database used by Chang and Tsao (2017) (database assembled by the Artificial Intelligence Laboratory of FEI ("Faculdade de Engenharia Industrial"), São Bernardo do Campo, São Paulo, Brazil). Each of the 200 faces was hand-labeled with 58 landmark points that corresponded to the same feature on each face. For illustrative purposes, the right-edge-of-nose landmark is colored blue, and the inside-edge-of-right-nostril landmark is colored yellow. Because the two model faces illustrated here have different shapes, the right-edge-of-nose landmark for these two will get a different location value, as well as a different grayscale value, and the same is true for each of the other 57 landmarks.

116 numbers on it – a location value and a grayscale value for each of the 58 landmarks – and you would be able to use only those 116 numbers to recreate an image of the person that these numbers correspond to, an image that that person's mother would recognize as her own child. These two values make up what Chang and Tsao (2017) referred to as the "shape" dimension and the "appearance" dimension in their matrix of digitized values for the 200 faces in their stimulus set. Next, they applied two **principal component analyses (PCA)** to this matrix, one to identify the 25 largest PCs in the shape dimension, the other to identify the 25 largest PCs in the appearance dimension, and these were used to construct a parameterized shape space. That is, by determining the 50 dimensions that are most discriminative among the 200 faces, they effected a dimensionality reduction that allowed for the conversion of each individual's location in 116-D "landmark space" to a 50-D location in "face PC space." The advantage of this step, in addition to the pragmatic benefit of reducing the size of each face file (i.e., fewer bytes are required to store a 50-D file on a computer than a 116-D file), is that it recoded face information out of the human-defined (and decidedly arbitrary) factors of the location and grayscale values of each of 58 landmarks, and into the "natural" dimensions along which each of the 200 faces actually varied in terms of their physical image properties. And, as it turns out, knowing this face PC space gives one a remarkable ability to predict what never-before-seen faces will drive a neuron, including neurons that had previously been characterized as "sparse" and therefore assumed to be narrowly tuned for the face of just one or a few individuals.

The transformation from landmark space into the face PC space effected a recoding from a human-defined code into a code that reflected the statistical distribution of the image properties of the set of 200 faces. Most of the dimensions in face PC space were "holistic," in that they captured change along a dimension that involved multiple parts of the face. For example, moving along the first shape dimension produces simultaneous changes in hairline, face width, and height of eyes. Why are we going into this level of detail about this face PC space? (*Surely*, you may be thinking to yourself, *there must be some reason other than just to develop an appreciation for the fact that Chang and Tsao are really good at math.*) The reason is that the visual system of the monkey seems to use this face PC code for the perceptual analysis of faces! That is, if Chang and Tsao (2017) first used the trial-and-error method to find which of the 200 faces a neuron responds to, they could next look up where this face fell in the face PC space and then show this neuron different morphs of this "good" face that varied along one of the 50 axes of face PC space on which this good face could sit. Before too long they'd identify which was the best axis for that neuron, and could then demonstrate (i.e., they could predict) that any face that fell along this axis in face PC space would optimally drive this neuron, and that any face that didn't fall along this axis would produce a weaker response, the amount of weakening based on the distance from the preferred axis. Impressively, this meant that even for neurons that, by traditional definition, were highly selectively tuned to just one or a few face identities, Chang and Tsao could create never-before-seen faces that would drive this putatively "sparse" neuron. Furthermore, an implication of this model is that a single grandmother unit could not uniquely represent an individual face, because an infinite number of faces can be represented along any single axis in face PC space. Rather, theoretically, you'd need activity from at least 50 neurons, one corresponding to each dimension in the face PC space, to completely represent the identity of any one person's face. In practice, with their empirically collected data, Chang and Tsao (2017) found that they needed signals from a minimum of 200 neurons in MF/ML and AM to decode face identity with a high level of accuracy.

A heuristic take-home lesson from this study is that in brain regions where physiologists find neurons that seem to be highly specific to just one unique object, or just a narrow set of variables, it is not necessarily the case that this reflects the true nature of the computations that this neuron carries out. Alternatively, it could be that the researchers simply do not know the principles underlying the activity in this brain area. (A practical consequence of this would be that they simply don't know what might be other stimuli that, if shown to this neuron, would evoke a comparable response. The conclusion would be that although this neuron's tuning may, indeed, be highly selective for stimuli whose values fall along a certain axis, its responses are not specific to just one stimulus.) A take-home for this chapter's topic of visual cognition is that the Chang and Tsao (2017) study offers a robust challenge to exemplar-based models, in which object recognition is assumed to be mediated by neurons tuned to specific objects.

Codes and Maps for the Ventral Stream

Because the primate visual system evolved in environments requiring the discrimination of many kinds of objects in addition to faces, it would seem reasonable to assume that the principles of the "axis code" proposed for face perception by Chang and Tsao (2017) (see section *The code for facial identity in the primate brain (!?!)*) might generalize. Additionally, however, because object recognition is so central to so much of cognition, it wouldn't be surprising to find important, perhaps fundamental, differences in the organization of object representation in humans in comparison to nonhuman primates?

Axis Coding of Objects in the Nonhuman Primate

It shouldn't come as a surprise that, after carrying out the work summarized in section *The code for facial identity in the primate brain (!?!)*, Doris Tsao's laboratory next tackled the broader question of object recognition. To do so, they started by presenting a large set of stimulus comparisons to a monkey, while collecting fMRI, to localize regions selective for face, body, scene, color, and disparity patches, to generate a map similar to the one illustrated (on a human brain) in *Figure 10.5*. This identified many patches showing category selectivity on the surface of the inferior temporal gyrus (ITG; i.e., areas PIT, CIT, and AIT from *Figure 6.5*), many separated by regions of tissue that did not show selectivity for any stimuli in their battery, and that they therefore referred to as "no man's land." Next, and also while collecting fMRI, they applied electrical microstimulation to one of these locations and saw that it yielded elevated activity in the immediately surrounding NML region (which they would name "NML2") as well as in two additional NML regions on the ITG, one located more posteriorly ("NML1") and more anteriorly ("NML3"). After convincing themselves, in two additional animals, that evidence for an NML network was replicable, the authors' next step was to assess the functions supported by this previously unknown set of regions.

As Bao et al. (2020) explain it, their approach was

> *"to identify the relevant shape dimensions for the NML network in a systematic way that does not depend on subjective visual inspection[1]. Until recently, this was difficult because of the lack of a computational scheme to parametrize arbitrary objects. [However, d]eep networks trained to classify objects provide a powerful solution to this problem. They allow parametrization of arbitrary objects through computation of a few thousand numbers, the unit activations in a deep layer" (p. 104).*

More specifically, they presented a stimulus set of views from 26 different perspectives of each of 51 objects to their NHP subjects and to a version of AlexNet (the same deep neural network [DNN] that featured in *Chapter 6*, section *Using deep neural networks to understand computations underlying object recognition*), then performing a PCA on the patterns of responses of units in layer fc6 of this network. The first PC corresponded roughly to images with protrusions (which the authors characterized as being "spiky") vs. those without protrusions ("stubby"), and the second PC corresponded roughly to animacy (i.e., living vs. nonliving). Furthermore, the first 50 PCs explained 85% of the variance in this layer. Next, regression analyses suggested that this DNN-defined object representation space was relevant for neurons in the NML network: On average, each NML neuron responded to seven of the 50 dimensions, and overall, the model explained 53.3% of the explainable variance in the population of NML cells from which they had recorded. Furthermore, as had been done for face-patch neurons by Chang and Tsao (2017), each NML neuron could be fit with a 50D "preferred axis" along which its activity was uniformly elevated, and to which images on orthogonal axes produced uniformly "flat" responses.

As illustrated in *Figure* 10.10, because they also had fMRI data that covered the entire temporal lobe, the authors could assess the relevance of the first two PCs pulled from layer fc6 of AlexNet. The overall pattern was that face patches responded preferentially to stubby animate

[1] Note that the methods described in *Chapter 6*, sections *Electrophysiological recordings in temporal cortex*, and *Combination coding, an alternative to the "grandmother cell"* could be characterized as "subjective visual inspection."

FIGURE 10.10 Axis coding as a general principle for object representation in IT cortex.
Source: Bao et al. (2020) / Springer Nature.

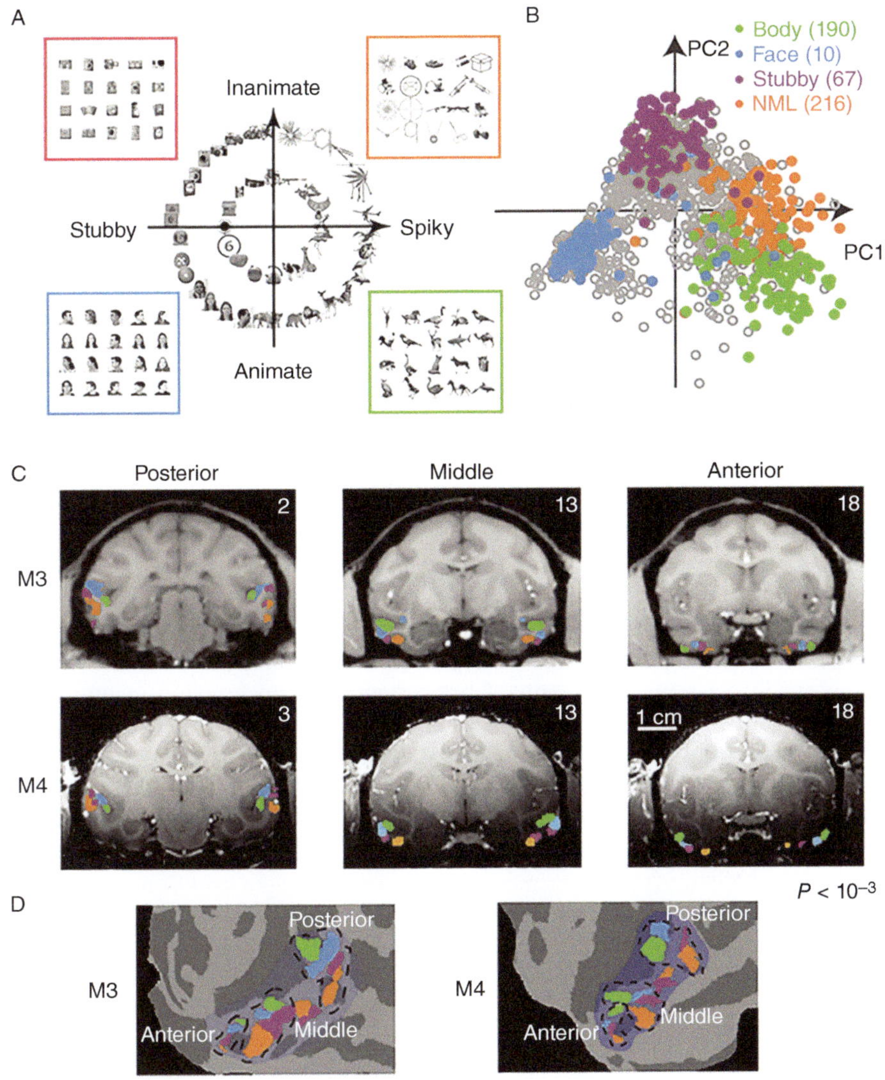

FIGURE 10.10.A Conceptual depiction of the first two Principal Components (PCs) identified by Bao et al. (2020). The first PC is a dimension that ranges from "stubby" to "spikey," and the second is a dimension that ranges from "inanimate" to "animate". The images inside the colored squares are some of those used during fMRI scanning to generate the maps illustrated in panels C. and D. The images in the two concentric circles are synthetic images, each generated to occupy precisely the location in PC1-PC2 space that they occupy relative to the two axes.

FIGURE 10.10.B Projection of all the stimuli used during electrophysiological recording sessions into the PC1-PC2 space (gray symbols), with those that elicited the top 100 strongest responses in each region color coded accordingly. (Note that the PCA was carried out on patterns of activity from AlexNet, not on neural data.) The numbers in parentheses indicate the number of neurons recorded in each area.

FIGURE 10.10.C Coronal slices at three locations along the anterior-to-posterior axis of structural MRIs of the brains of two monkeys, with the color-coded location of regions from panel A superimposed. (The numbers in the upper right of each image presumably correspond to the location (in mm) along the A-P axis in atlas space.)

FIGURE 10.10.D Same data as left hemispheres from panel C, but superimposed on anatomical flat maps of the left hemisphere.

objects, body patches to spiky animate objects, and NML patches to spiky objects regardless of location along the animacy continuum. That leaves stubby inanimate objects, what about them? (Exemplar stimuli that load on these two properties include the "@" symbol, a front-on view of a European electrical outlet [a square panel with a large circular-shaped concavity, plus two holes for the prongs], rectangular loudspeakers with no cover [and so exposing the round surfaces of the woofer and tweeter cones].) To address this question, Bao et al. (2020) carried out another set of experiments that provided evidence for – you guessed it – a fourth IT network: the "stubby network". A summary of these findings, and the overall scheme that IT cortex in the NHP can be construed as being made up of regions comprising neurons that all load in the same quadrant of a 2D space, is displayed in *Figure 10.10*. In addition to the predictions that this model makes for, for example, patterns of behavioral impairment to be expected from damage to different anatomical regions, the influence of expertise with, and/or deprivation from, certain classes of stimulus, the authors offer an updated perspective on a topic that has been prominent in this and other chapters: the nature of face processing:

> *"Our results cast the face patch system in a new light. Previously, it was thought that the face system, with its striking clustering of face-selective cells, was a unique evolutionary consequence of the importance of face recognition to primate social behaviour. Here we show that the face system arises naturally from the statistical structure of object space." (p. 107)*

(I.e., faces may not be *that* special?)

How Are Objects Represented in the Ventral Stream of the Human Primate?

It is, of course, the case that we have learned many, many otherwise unlearnable things from studies carrying out invasive measurements of brain structure and function in nonhuman animals, including NHPs. Ultimately, however, to know if a principle of neural representation (in this case, axis coding) is true for the human brain, one has to carry out experiments with humans. This is precisely what David Coggan and Frank Tong (2023) have done for axis coding, by presenting to human subjects the same stimuli that were used by Bao et al. (2020) while scanning with fMRI at 7 tesla (7T).

To be more specific about the experimental procedure, Coggan and Tong (2023) presented stimuli drawn from two sets: one from the one used by Bao et al. (2020); and one a "traditional" set of stimuli typical of what is used to identify category-selective regions in the ventral temporal lobe, drawn from the categories face, body, house, and common objects. (In the words of the authors, these were presented in "functional localizer runs to identify face-, [house-], and body selective regions in human visual cortex so that any spikiness animacy maps or NML/Stubby candidate regions could be characterized relative to these well-known object-selective cortical regions." (p. 8196)) The first thing to note about the "traditional" stimulus set is that, when presented to AlexNet, the PCA of activity in layer fc6 did not separate the images into clusters falling (roughly) into four quadrants defined by the axes of the first two PCs; rather the animacy axis separated houses from faces and bodies, and the stubby-spiky axis separated faces from bodies, but houses straddled the stubby-spiky axis and objects were diffusely positioned in PC1-PC2 space, with some individual tokens falling into each of the other three category clusters, and the mean of all objects located close to the 0,0 intersection of the two axes.

With regard to the axis-coding scheme proposed by Bao et al. (2020), the Coggan and Tong (2023) results were equivocal. Because it's easier to begin with stronger than with weaker observations, we can start with findings from the monkey (Bao et al., 2020) that were not found in the human (Coggan and Tong, 2023): the study in humans found no evidence for one or more discrete NML regions, and no evidence for one or more discrete stubby regions. To break this down, although many voxels were identified by NML and stubby localizers, the majority of these fell within the house-selective and, for NML, body-selective regions. Furthermore, there was no evidence for multiple discrete category-selective regions aligned in a roughly posterior-to-anterior manner. There were, however, also some intriguing "positive" results that suggested novel hypotheses. One of these is that at least half of the voxels in two body-selective areas (the EBA (located in occipital cortex) and the Fusiform Body Area

(FBA, located in close proximity to the FFA) were selectively responsive to just one quadrant of PC1-PC2 space, and the remainder showed high responsiveness to objects high in animacy and to stimuli high in spikiness. This raises the possibility that the selectivity for bodies of these two regions may derive from an integration of the representation of spiky things and of animate things. More generally, the fact that many voxels, although located within classical category-selective regions, showed strong selectivity along the spikiness and/or animacy axes does leave open the possibility that these factors may underlie the organization of object representation in a manner that has not yet been discovered.

Because the study by Coggan and Tong (2023) was specifically focused on hypotheses arising from a study of NHPs, it necessarily didn't take into account the many non-perceptual factors that may also influence object perception in humans. One such factor has been summarized by Oliver Contier, Chris Baker, and Martin Hebart (2024) as "behavioral goals," by which they mean how one interacts with (in some cases, how one uses) the object being viewed. They operationalized this construct via similarity judgments, offering the following explanation:

> *"perceived similarity serves as a common proxy of mental object representations underlying various behavioural goals, as the similarity relation between objects conveys much of the object knowledge and behavioural relevance across diverse perceptual and conceptual criteria. Perceived similarity is therefore ideally suited for revealing behaviourally relevant representational dimensions and how these dimensions are reflected in cortical patterns of brain activity." (p. 2 of 15; note that here the authors are using "perceive" in its metaphorical sense, as in 'what is a person's opinion about something'.)"*

To assess the hypothesis that human object perception may be organized according to behavioral goals, the authors carried out their analyses on a data set that they themselves had previously created: THINGS-data. (N.b., "THINGS" is not an acronym, it's just a word that they used a lot during the generation of the database.) THINGS-data includes images of 1854 diverse nameable manmade and natural object concepts (i.e., images of 1854 "things"), for which there are 4.7 million human judgments (Hebart et al., 2023). Importantly for our purposes, THINGS-data also includes fMRI and MEG data of subjects viewing 720 of these images. Among the 4.7 million judgments made about these objects are similarity judgments obtained with an "odd-one-out" forced-choice procedure in which the subject is presented with a target object, then indicates which of two choice objects is more similar to the target. From these measurements the authors used a procedure conceptually similar to PCA to derive 66 dimensions along which each object has a value, the totality of which captures "behaviourally relevant information, in that they support the key factors underlying arbitrary categorization behaviour and therefore underlie our ability to make sense of our visual world, to generalize, to structure our environment and to communicate our knowledge" (Contier et al., 2024; p. 2 of 16). The fMRI data were analyzed with a measure similar to the Inverted Encoding Model (IEM) described in *Chapter 5*, section *Reconstructing stimulus information with multivariate inverted encoding models (IEM)*. This resulted in a data set that contained, for each voxel, a 66D "tuning curve" (i.e., how does this voxel's activity vary as a function of different values along dimension #1? how does it vary as a function of different values along dimension #2? etc.) This approach produced the 66D "regional tuning profiles" illustrated in *Figure 10.11*.

There's a sense in which the approach taken by Contier et al. (2024; illustrated in *Figure 10.11*) is, like those Tsao's group that we reviewed in section *The code for facial identity in the primate brain (!?!)* and section *Axis coding of objects in the nonhuman primate*, is more principled, less subjective, than the piecemeal, human intuition-based processes that, over the course of a decade or more, generated the maps that are portrayed in *Figure 10.5*. Nonetheless, a question one might ask after considering *Figure 10.11* is how behavioral similarity-derived maps compare with traditionally derived category selectivity maps (c.f., *Figure 10.5*)? To answer this, Hebert et al. (2024) offer two responses, one subjective and one quantitatively derived. Subjectively, they note that their behavioral similarity-derived map includes most of early visual cortex (including V1) in addition to inferior temporal-lobe areas associated with

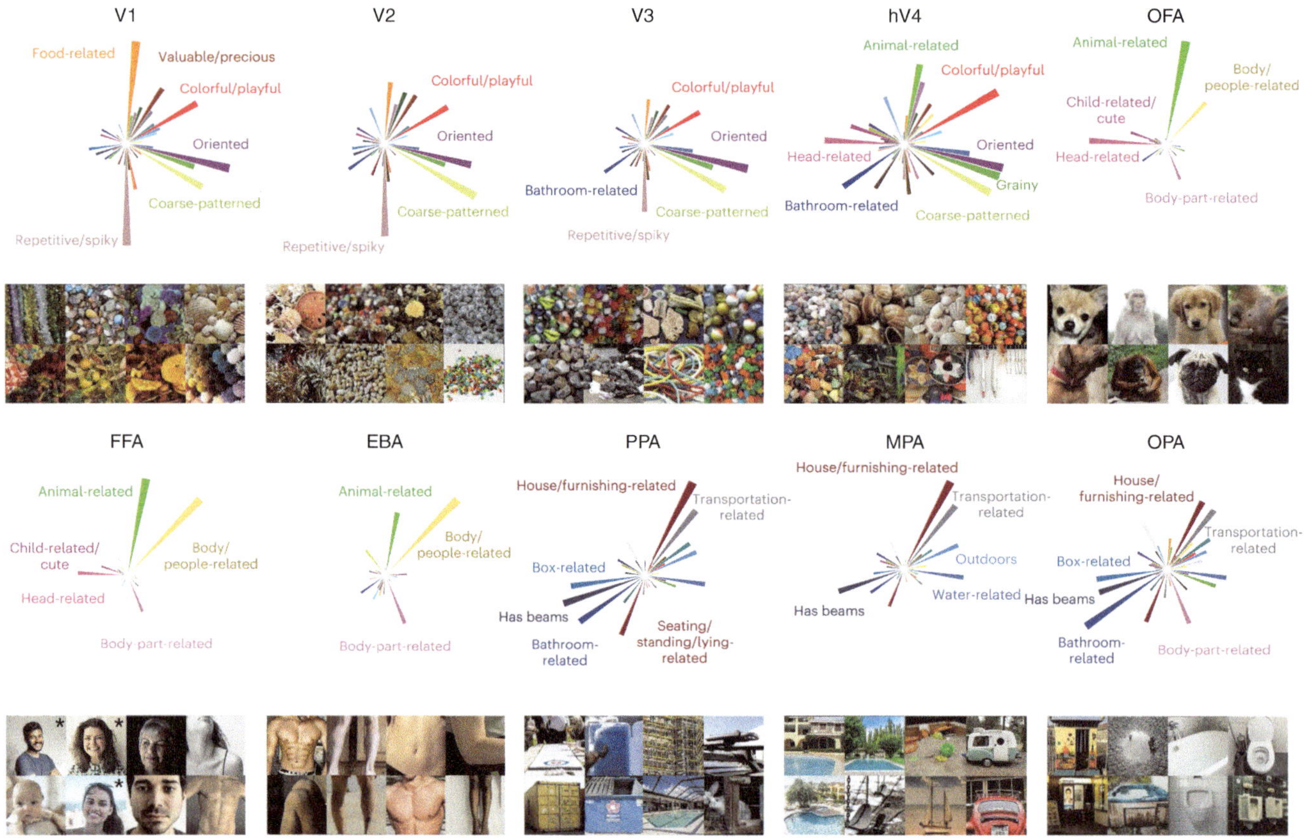

FIGURE 10.11 Behavioral similarity-based tuning profiles of several regions in the visual system. For each of the brain areas shown (labeled at the top of each two-part set of images), the colorful rose plots represent the average tuning along each of the 66 dimensions used in the encoding model, with verbal labels listed for the few dimensions with the highest weightings. The image panels below each rose plot illustrate, for that brain area, the eight images for which their image-specific 66D tuning profile is most similar to that of the regional average. For copyright reasons, all images included here (as well as in Contier et al., 2024) are not those that were used in the experiment, but were selected to be visually similar. Furthermore, images of minors for which no permission could be obtained have been replaced with images of adults (marked with asterisks).

Source: Contier et al. (2024) / Springer Nature / CC BY 4.0.

high-level image processing, whereas traditionally derived category maps primarily emphasize only the latter. Thus, Hebert et al. (2024) argue, behavioral similarity-derived maps illustrate more fully the interactive nature of visual processing. (E.g., an image that is heavily weighted on the "colorful/playful" dimension may generate a feedback-related pattern of activity in V1 that's markedly different from one that's heavily weighted on the "body/people-related" dimension. Quantitatively, they calculate that although the two approaches share a considerable proportion of variance in the fMRI signal evoked by each visual image (median = 19%; maximum = 74%), the behavioral-similarity additionally accounted for a greater amount of unique explained variance (median = 10%; maximum = 35% for behavioral-similarity vs. median = 2%; maximum = 11% for category-based).

And so, as we conclude this section, it's clear that many questions remain to be resolved. Notably, we've seen that Coggan and Tong (2023) observed that few regions that showed NML and animacy sensitivity weren't also category selective, and so they concluded that there was not a compelling reason to consider axis-coding to be an important principle underlying object perception. On the other hand, when Contier et al. (2024) observed a great deal of overlap of category-based and their version of axis-based tuning, they concluded that an axis-based scheme is to be preferred. At stake, of course, is an understanding of what are the true factors whose processing gives rise to our exquisitely precise ability to recognize and distinguish between visually perceived objects.

Playing 20 Questions with the Brain

Is anyone else dizzy? We've covered many profound questions, and in so doing have reviewed many cutting-edge techniques for modeling, measuring, and manipulating activity in the brain. One thing that comes to mind is the admonition delivered by AI pioneer Allen Newell (1973) almost 50 years ago: *You can't play 20 questions with nature and win*. Some questions about brain and behavior can never be satisfactorily addressed without formal computational modeling. This is particularly evident when one finds, as we have here, that seemingly incontrovertible evidence can be generated for each of two seemingly incompatible perspectives on how a function like face perception is carried out.

End-of-Chapter Questions

1. What factors call into question the idea that associative agnosias may reflect truly unimpaired perception "stripped of its meaning"?

2. How can prosopagnosic patients successfully navigate our modern, intensely social society?

3. Do PDP models of visual object recognition "prove" that there is no distinction between "structural" and "semantic" levels of visual representation?

4. What was it about the Kanwisher, McDermott, and Chun (1997) results that some viewed as contrary to how they thought that the brain works?

5. What are the alternative explanations of the Kanwisher et al. (1997) results proffered by Gauthier and colleagues?

6. In what sense do the findings of Haxby et al. (2001) rule out a strong version of the argument that the FFA is specialized for face processing?

7. In what sense do the findings of Parvizi et al. (2012) establish that the FFA makes necessary contributions to face processing?

8. What is the premise of the face PC code proposed by Chang and Tsao (2017), and how does it obviate the need for grandmother cells?

9. Is there evidence that the axis code proposed for face perception in NHPs generalizes to non-face objects? And/or does it generalize to the functioning of the human ventral visual stream?

10. Summarize the differences between models of human visual object perception as being organized by category versus being organized by behavioral similarity.

References

Bao, Pinglei, Liang She, Mason McGill, and Doris Y. Tsao. 2020. "A Map of Object Space in Primate Inferotemporal Cortex." *Nature* 583 (7814): 103–108. doi: 10.1038/s41586-020-2350-5.

Benson, D. Frank, and John P. Greenberg. 1969. "Visual Form Agnosia: A Specific Defect in Visual Discrimination." *Archives of Neurology* 20 (1): 82–89. doi: 10.1001/archneur.1969.00480070092010.

Chang, Le, and Doris Y. Tsao. 2017. "The Code for Facial Identity in the Primate Brain." *Cell* 169: 1013–1028.

Coggan, David D., and Frank Tong. 2023. "Spikiness and Animacy as Potential Organizing Principles of Human Ventral Visual Cortex." *Cereb Cortex* 33 (13): 8194–8217. doi: 10.1093/cercor/bhad108.

Contier, Oliver, Chris I. Baker, and Martin N. Hebart. 2024. "Distributed Representations of Behaviour-Derived Object Dimensions in the Human Visual System." *Nature Human Behaviour* 8 (11): 2179–2193. doi: 10.1038/s41562-024-01980-y.

Farah, Martha J. 1990. *Visual Agnosia*. Cambridge, MA: MIT Press.

Fodor, Jerry A. 1983. *The Modularity of Mind*. Cambridge, MA: MIT Press.

Freiwald, Winrich A., and Doris Y. Tsao. 2010. "Functional Compartmentalization and Viewpoint Generalization within the Macaque Face-Processing System." *Science* 330: 845–851.

Fuster, Joaquín M. 2003. "More Than Working Memory Rides on Long-Term Memory." *Behavioral and Brain Sciences* 26 (6): 737–737. doi: 10.1017/S0140525X03300160.

Gauthier, Isabel, and Michael J. Tarr. 1997. "Becoming a 'Greeble' Expert: Exploring Mechanisms for Face Recognition." *Vision Research* 37 (12): 1673–1682. doi: 10.1016/S0042-6989(96)00286-6.

Gauthier, Isabel, Michael J. Tarr, Adam W. Anderson, Pawel Skudlarski, and John C. Gore. 1999. "Activation of the Middle Fusiform 'Face Area' Increases with Expertise in Recognizing Novel Objects." *Nature Neuroscience* 2 (6): 568–573. doi: 10.1038/9224.

Haxby, James V., M. Ida Gobbini, Maura L. Furey, Alumit Ishai, Jennifer L. Schouten, and Pietro Pietrini. 2001. "Distributed and Overlapping Representations of Faces and Objects in Ventral Temporal Cortex." *Science* 293 (5539): 2425–2430. doi: 10.1126/science.1063736.

Hebart, Martin N., Oliver Contier, Lina Teichmann, Adam H. Rockter, Charles Y. Zheng, Alexis Kidder, . . . Chris I. Baker. 2023.

"THINGS-Data, a Multimodal Collection of Large-Scale Datasets for Investigating Object Representations in Human Brain and Behavior." *Elife* 12. doi: 10.7554/eLife.82580.

Humphreys, Glyn W., and M. Jane Riddoch. 1987. "The Fractionation of Visual Agnosia." In *Visual Object Processing: A Cognitive Neuropsychological Approach*, edited by Glyn W. Humphreys and M. Jane Riddoch (pp. 281–307). Hove, UK: Lawrence Erlbaum Associates.

Kanwisher, Nancy. 1991. "Repetition Blindness and Illusory Conjunctions: Errors in Binding Visual Types with Visual Tokens." *Journal of Experimental Psychology: Human Perception and Performance* 17 (2): 404–421. doi: 10.1037/0096-1523.17.2.404.

Kanwisher, Nancy, Josh McDermott, and Marvin M. Chun. 1997. "The Fusiform Face Area: A Module in Human Extrastriate Cortex Specialized for Face Perception." *Journal of Neuroscience* 17 (11): 4302–4311. http://www.jneurosci.org/content/17/11/4302.full.pdf+html.

Logothetis, Nikos K., Jon Pauls, Mark Augath, Torsten Trinath, and Axel Oeltermann. 2001. "Neurophysiological Investigation of the Basis of the fMRI Signal." *Nature* 412 (6843): 150–157. doi: 10.1038/35084005.

Milner, Brenda, and Hans-Lukas Teuber. 1968. "Alteration of Perception and Memory in Man: Reflections on Methods." In *Analysis of Behavioral Change*, edited by Lawrence Weiskrantz (pp. 268–375). New York: Harper and Row.

Newell, A. 1973. "You Can't Play 20 Questions with Nature and Win: Projective Comments on Papers at This Symposium." In *Visual Information Processing: Proceedings of the Eighth Annual Carnegie Symposium on Cognition*, edited by W. G. Chase. Pittsburgh: PA Academic Press.

Parvizi, Josef, Corentin Jacques, Brett L. Foster, Nathan Withoft, Vinitha Rangarajan, Kevin S. Weiner, and Kalanit Grill-Spector. 2012. "Electrical Stimulation of Human Fusiform Face-Selective Regions Distorts Face Perception." *Journal of Neuroscience* 32 (43): 14915–14920. doi: 10.1523/JNEUROSCI.2609-12.2012.

Pohl, Walter. 1973. "Dissociation of Spatial Discrimination Deficits Following Frontal and Parietal Lesions in Monkeys." *Journal of Comparative and Physiological Psychology* 82 (2): 227–239. doi: 10.1037/h0033922.

Rogers, Timothy T., Matthew A. Lambon Ralph, Peter Garrard, Sasha Bozeat, James L. McClelland, John R. Hodges, and Karalyn Patterson. 2004. "Structure and Deterioration of Semantic Memory: A Neuropsychological and Computational Investigation." *Psychological Review 111*: 205–235.

Tarr, Michael J., and Isabel Gauthier. 2000. "FFA: A Flexible Fusiform Area for Subordinate-Level Visual Processing Automatized by Expertise." *Nature Neuroscience* 8 (3): 764–769. doi: 10.1038/77666.

Tsao, Doris Y., Winrich A. Freiwald, Roger B. H. Tootell, and Margaret S. Livingstone. 2006. "A Cortical Region Consisting Entirely of Face-Selective Cells." *Science* 311: 670–674.

Other Sources Used

Bukach, Cindy M., and Jessie J. Peissig. 2010. "How Faces Become Special." In *Perceptual Expertise: Bridging Brain and Behavior*, edited by Isabel Gauthier, Michael J. Tarr, and Daniel Bub (pp. 11–40). Oxford: Oxford University Press.

Ellis, Hadyn D. 1996. "Bodamer on Prosopagnosia." In *Classic Cases in Neuropsychology*, edited by Chris Code, Claus W Wallesch, Yves Joanette, and André Roch Lecours (pp. 69–75). Hove, UK: Psychology Press.

Foster, Brett L., and Josef Parvizi. 2012. "Resting Oscillations and Cross-Frequency Coupling in the Human Posteromedial Cortex." *NeuroImage* 60 (1): 384–391. doi: 10.1016/j.neuroimage.2011.12.019.

Gross, Charles G. 1994. "Hans-Lukas Teuber: A Tribute." *Cerebral Cortex* 4 (5): 451–454. doi: 10.1093/cercor/4.5.451.

Pribram, Karl H. 1977. "Hans-Lukas Teuber: 1916–1977." *American Journal of Psychology* 90 (4): 705–707. http://www.jstor.org/stable/1421744.

Riddoch, M. Jane, and Glyn W. Humphreys. 1987. "A Case of Integrative Visual Agnosia." *Brain* 110: 1431–1462.

Rubens, Alan B., and Frank Benson. 1971. "Associative Visual Agnosia." *Archives of Neurology* 24 (4): 305–316.

Further Reading

Bastos, Andre M., W. Martin Usrey, Rick A. Adams, George R. Mangun, Pascal Fries, and Karl J. Friston. 2012. "Canonical Microcircuits for Predictive Coding." *Neuron* 76: 695–711.

A formal proposal for how cortical columns can be understood as implementing the simultaneous operations of receiving top-down signals that update the system's predictive model, bottom-up signals conveying the error computed at an earlier stage of processing, and the calculation and feedforward transmission of the error between these two incoming signals.

Brodski-Guerniero, Alla, Georg-Friedrich Paasch, Patricia Wollstadt, Ipek Özdemir, Joseph T. Lizier, and Michael Wibral. 2017. "Information-Theoretic Evidence for Predictive Coding in the Face-Processing System." *Journal of Neuroscience 37*: 8273–8283.

An empirical study testing, with MEG in healthy young adults, that face perception can be understood as a product of predictive coding. The authors start with the assumption that if an individual knows that they are in a situation in which they might see a particular stimulus, they'll "preactivate" knowledge about this stimulus to facilitate its detection if it is encountered. Analysis with an information theoretic measure called transfer entropy indicated that, during the anticipatory period preceding each stimulus, face-related information flowed from aIT to FFA and from PPG to FFA. These results are broadly consistent with the idea that face perception may be supported by the top-down signaling of predictions about faces.

Çukur, Tolga, Shinji Nishimoto, Alexander G. Huth, and Jack L. Gallant. 2013. "Attention During Natural Vision Warps Semantic Representation across the Human Brain." *Nature Neuroscience* 16 (6): 763–770. doi: 10.1038/nn.3381.

A "mind-warping" fMRI investigation of the neural bases of visual knowledge representation.

Farah, Martha J. 1990. *Visual Agnosia*. Cambridge, MA: MIT Press.

An encyclopedic synthesis of 100 years of research on the topic; be sure to look at the most recent edition, as it will contain updates on developments in this fast-moving literature since the original 1990 publication.

Fodor, Jerry A. 1985. "Précis of *The Modularity of Mind*." *Behavioral and Brain Sciences* 8 (1): 1–5. doi: 10.1017/S0140525X0001921X.

A quicker read than the 1983 monograph, plus, it is supplemented by interesting critiques from others in the field, followed by Fodor's rejoinder.

Logothetis, Nikos K. 2003. "The Underpinnings of the BOLD Functional Magnetic Resonance Imaging Signal." *Journal of Neuroscience* 23 (10): 3963–3971.

A review summarizing the relation between the LFP and BOLD signals that trade accessibility for some of the technical details packed into Logothetis et al. (2001).

Wandell, Brian A., and Jonathan Winawer. 2011. "Imaging Retinotopic Maps in the Human Brain." *Vision Research* 51 (7): 718–737. doi: 10.1016/j.visres.2010.08.004.

If you didn't look this one up after reading Chapter 2, here's another prompt. This paper presents a thorough summary of neuroimaging studies of the functional organization of the ventral stream, including category representation.

CHAPTER 11

Neural Bases of Memory

KEY THEMES

- Foundational knowledge about the organization of memory and the amnesic syndrome has resulted from the pioneering research of Brenda Milner and her associates with the patient H.M.
- The model assembled from the global amnesic syndrome is one of dissociable systems supporting declarative vs. nondeclarative vs. working memory and of dissociable processes of encoding, consolidation, storage, and retrieval.
- Hebbian learning seems to be embodied in the phenomenon of long-term potentiation (LTP) of synaptic strength, discovered by Lømo and Bliss in the 1960s and 1970s.
- It has been proposed that whereas the hippocampus supports instantaneous "one-shot learning" of any specific information that one may encounter, cortical systems support the acquisition and retention of general knowledge about "how things typically work," a process that necessarily plays out over longer spans of time.
- Two distinctive physiological properties of hippocampal neurons – place cell precession and the triggering of sharp-wave ripples – may underlie the cognitive phenomena of the representation of sequential order (as in memory for "what happened when") and LTM consolidation.
- Although an influential "standard anatomical model" has portrayed perirhinal cortex, entorhinal cortex, and hippocampus as elements of a unitary "MTL memory system," a growing body of evidence suggests that these regions support different memory-related functions, and, indeed, that their functions may not be restricted to "just memory."
- The hippocampus may support navigational prediction functions that share some functional properties with place cells and fulfill computational functions of successor representations from reinforcement learning models.
- The phenomena of memory consolidation and the more-recently characterized reconsolidation pose interesting puzzles for cognitive neuroscience, but also potential opportunities for therapeutic interventions.

CONTENTS

Essentials of Cognitive Neuroscience, Third Edition. Bradley R. Postle. Published 2026 by John Wiley & Sons, Inc.
Companion Website: www.wiley.com/go/postle/cognitiveneuroscience3e

Plasticity, Learning, and Memory

In several previous chapters, such when we considered motor learning, or the training of artificial neural networks (ANNs) by adjusting connection weights between processing units, we have touched on a fundamental property of the nervous system, which is its ability to modify itself in order to refine how it processes information about, and interacts with, the environment. (Some would say, to refine and update its representation of the outside world.) Here, finally, we will address the phenomenon of **neural plasticity**, and its behavioral and theoretical counterparts, **memory** and **learning**, head-on. We'll begin with a summary of an influential neurosurgical case that revealed many principles of human learning and memory, then consider computational and physiological models of cellular and molecular bases of these phenomena, and conclude at the systems level. This will provide a foundation for the explorations of the subsequent three chapters of the kinds of memory that we use every day: episodic, semantic, nondeclarative, and working.

The Case of H.M.

Whether in terms of raw citation counts or subjective assessment of breadth and depth of legacy, H.M. may well be the single most influential case in the history of cognitive neuroscience.

He spent his life in the vicinity of Hartford, CT, where, in 1953, at the age of 27, he underwent a neurosurgical procedure that truly shaped the course of scientific history.

Bilateral Medial Temporal Lobectomy

In the back seat of his parents' car, on the day of his fifteenth birthday, Henry Molaison was stricken by his first **grand mal epileptic seizure**. Over the next few years, his neurological condition progressively worsened, to the point where he dropped out of high school, couldn't hold down a steady job, and, by his mid-20s, was effectively housebound. For several years, he and his family had consulted with a neurosurgeon at Hartford Hospital, Dr. William Scoville, who, after exhausting other treatment strategies, proposed an experimental surgical intervention. Because EEG had failed to identify a clear focus of Henry's seizures, Scoville proposed the surgical removal of the hippocampus, known to be the most epileptogenic tissue in the brain, bilaterally. (A subsequent section summarizing the circuitry of the hippocampus will provide some insight into the epileptogenic property of the hippocampus.)

A diagram of the procedure, the surgeon's estimate of the extent of removal, and MR images acquired decades after the surgery, during the 1990s, are illustrated in *Figure 11.1*. Although the surgery was successful from the narrow perspective that it brought H.M.'s epilepsy under control, its unexpected consequences were profound and permanent: H.M. lost the ability to consciously remember anything that he experienced from that time forward, for the remaining 50+ years of his life.

FIGURE 11.1 H.M.'s lesions.

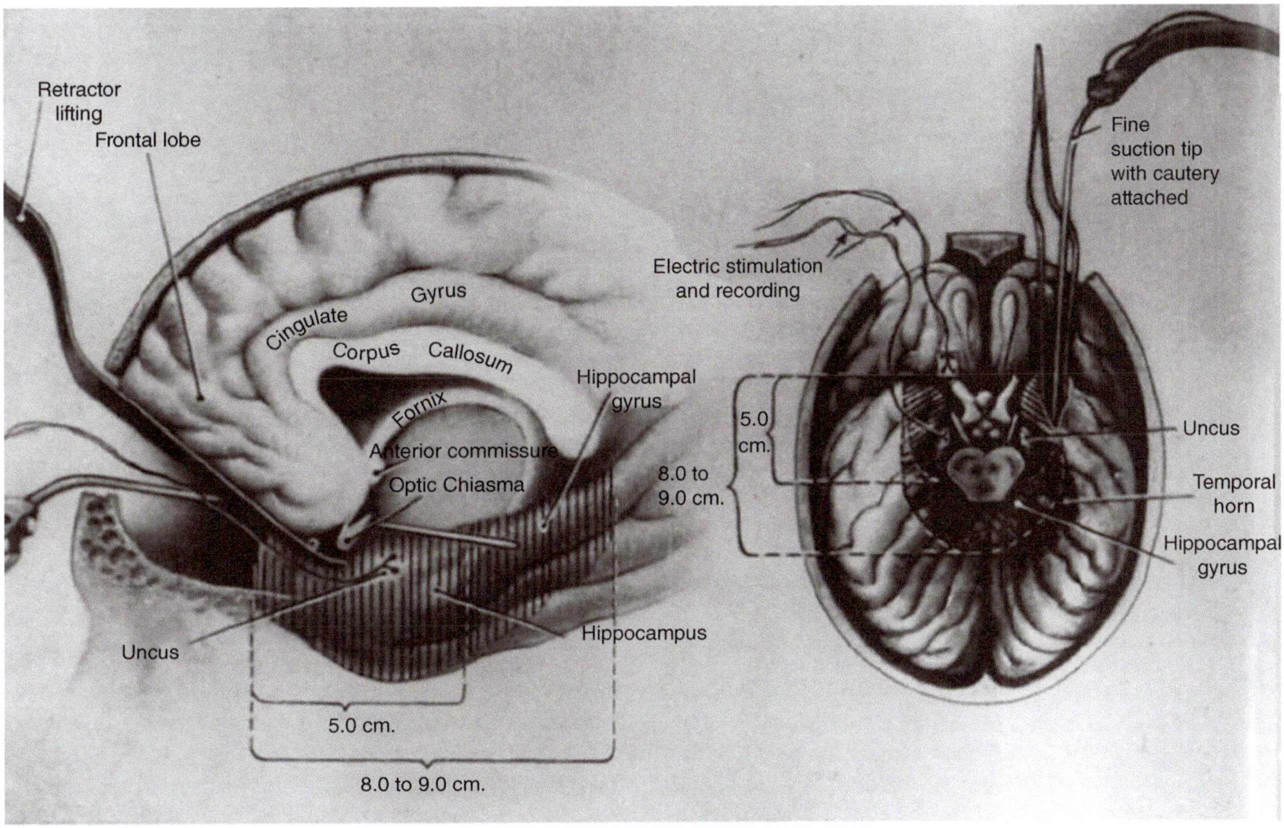

FIGURE 11.1.A Illustration of the surgical procedure, and estimated extent of removal, of H.M.'s hippocampus and adjacent structures of the medial temporal lobe (MTL).

Source: Scoville, William Beecher, and Brenda Milner. 1957. "Loss of Recent Memory after Bilateral Hippocampal Lesions." *Journal of Neurology, Neurosurgery, and Psychiatry* 20 (1): 11–21. doi: 10.1136/jnnp.20.1.11. Reproduced with permission of BMJ.

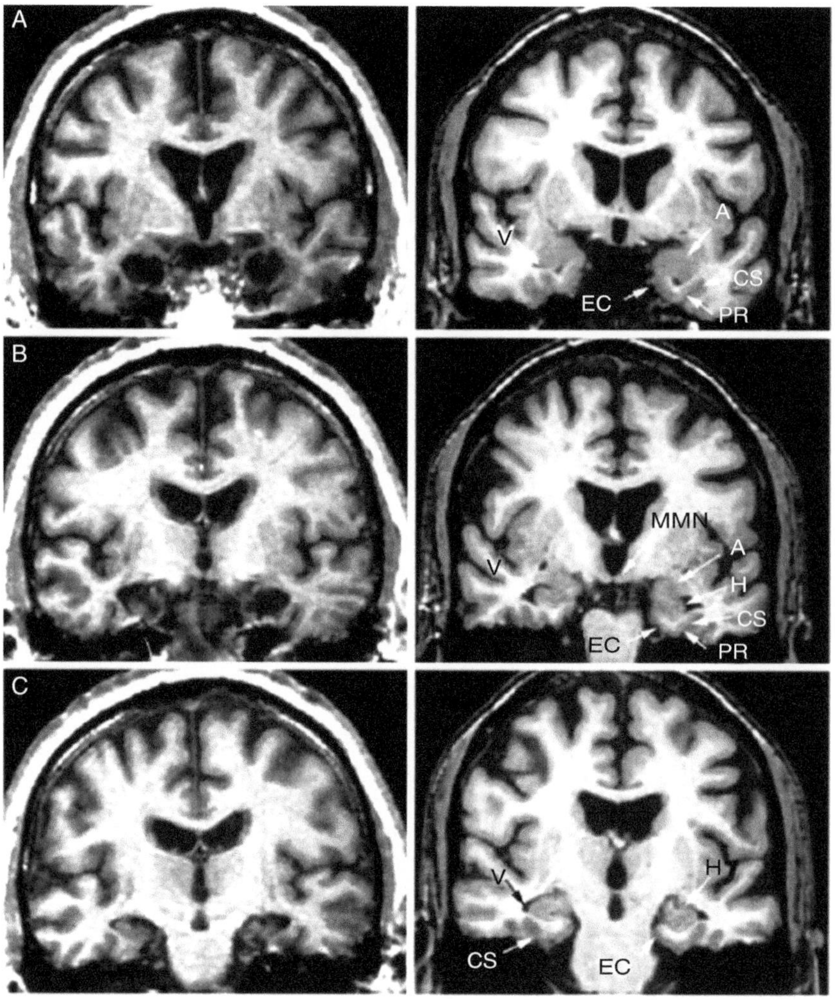

FIGURE 11.1.B T1-weighted MR images of the brain of H.M. (left-hand column) and an age- and education-matched control subject, at three progressively more caudal locations. Labels on the control images identify landmarks and regions that are damaged or missing in H.M. (A = amygdala; CS = collateral sulcus; EC = entorhinal cortex; PR = perirhinal cortex; MMN = medial mammillary nuclei; H = hippocampus; V = ventricle). At the caudal-most slice, atrophied remnants of hippocampal tissue that weren't removed by the surgery are visible. MMN, not directly affected by the surgery, are reduced in size in H.M., presumably due to the loss of afferent drive that they would typically receive from the hippocampus, via the **fornix** (see panel B).

Source: Reproduced with permission from Corkin et al. (1997) / Society for Neuroscience.

The Global Amnesic Syndrome The influence of H.M.'s case is due, in large part, to the pioneering research of Dr. Brenda Milner, a British-born and -trained neuropsychologist who has spent the majority of her scientific career at McGill University and the Montreal Neurological Institute, working with such luminaries as Wilder Penfield (who we met in section *Somatotopy, Chapter 2*) and Donald Hebb (who we met in the section on *Hebbian plasticity, Chapter 5*). Shortly after H.M.'s surgery, Scoville came across a report from Penfield and Milner detailing rare instances of profound memory impairment resulting from unilateral removal of the medial temporal lobe (MTL) and speculating that this may have resulted from the fact that the unoperated hemisphere was also, unbeknownst to them at the time of the surgery, dysfunctional. Scoville contacted Penfield to tell him about his case, and, soon thereafter, Milner traveled from Montreal to Hartford to initiate her historic series of studies. This research established several facts about the consequences of bilateral damage of the MTL:

- Within the realm of cognition, its effects are, by and large, restricted to memory. Thus, for example, H.M.'s ability to understand and produce language was unaffected by his surgery, as was his IQ, which actually increased marginally after his surgery, no doubt due to the reduction of epileptic symptoms.
- Within the realm of memory, its effects are primarily restricted to the acquisition of new memories, in that some facts acquired and memory for events that occured before the damage remain accessible. Thus, bilateral damage of the MTL produces an *anterograde amnesia* (loss of memory going forward in time).
- The comparatively less severe *retrograde amnesia* is limited to the few years immediately prior to the insult – remote memories are spared.
- Within the realm of memory acquisition, the deficit is limited to events and facts that can be consciously recalled; patients can continue to learn new skills and habits that don't require conscious recollection.
- Also spared by MTL damage is working memory (a.k.a. short-term memory), the ability to remember a telephone number while looking for your phone or, as considered in *Chapter 9*, to briefly remember the location previously occupied by a stimulus that is no longer there.

Some of these propositions have been refined and/or called into question in the ensuing years, but at this early juncture in the chapter, it will be useful to summarize them as principles whose tenets, across this and the next three chapters, we can then test and revise as appropriate.

The Organization of Memory The principles arising from the work of Milner and colleagues include the following:

1. There is a fundamental distinction between **declarative memory** (or **explicit memory**) and **nondeclarative memory** (or **implicit memory**). The former refers to consciously accessible records of facts and events and depends on the integrity of the MTL. The latter includes any example of experience-dependent plasticity that modifies a behavior in a manner that does not require conscious access for its expression and includes conditioning, motor learning, and perceptual learning.
2. Declarative memory and nondeclarative memory are both considered LTM and are distinct from working memory.
3. There is a neuroanatomical basis for dissociating the processes of encoding, storage, and retrieval in declarative memory. In the case of H.M., as presented so far, his deficit seems to be one of **encoding** – processing newly encountered information such that it can later be remembered. If either storage or retrieval were compromised, he wouldn't be able to retrieve memories from prior to his surgery. Thus, storage and retrieval would not seem to depend on the MTL.
4. Long-term declarative memories undergo a period of **consolidation**, to which the MTL contributes importantly, after which they become relatively immune to disruption by MTL damage.

The Subjective Experience of Amnesia While the cases of H.M. and many other patients have been invaluable for the scientific study of memory, they also raise profound questions that get at the core of what it means to be a sentient human being and confront us with heartbreakingly poignant conditions before which, at the present time, we are helpless.

Self-report from H.M. suggests that one phenomenological quality of anterograde amnesia is a pervasive anxiety about what may have happened just beyond the edge of the present moment:

> Right now, I'm wondering, have I done or said anything amiss? You see, at this moment everything looks clear to me, but what happened just before? . . . It's like

> waking from a dream; I just don't remember . . . Every day is alone, in itself. Whatever enjoyment I've had, whatever sorrow I've had.
>
> (Hilts, 1996, p. 138)

On another occasion, during an exchange between H.M. and researcher William Marslen-Wilson (relayed by Hilts, 1996), the patient confessed to worrying about giving the wrong answer, whether during formal testing or just in conversation:

> "It is a constant effort," Henry said. You must always "wonder how is it going to affect others? Is that the way to do it? Is it the right way?" . . . Asked if he worried about these things a lot, struggled with his thought to get right answers, he said yes, all the time. "But why?" "I don't know," said Henry. (p. 140)

The anxiety and frustration of amnesia are even more evident in Clive Wearing, a distinguished British musicologist, whose amnesia resulted from herpes encephalitis. This condition can produce severe damage to the hippocampus while leaving the rest of the brain relatively unscathed. In a clip from a television documentary, he and his wife are sitting in a city park:

Wife:	Do you know how we got here?
Wearing:	No.
Wife:	You don't remember sitting down?
Wearing:	No.
Wife:	I reckon we've been here about 10 minutes at least.
Wearing:	Well, I've no knowledge of it. My eyes only started working now . . .
Wife:	And do you feel absolutely normal?
Wearing:	Not absolutely normal, no. I'm completely confused.
Wife:	Confused?
Wearing (agitatedly):	Yes. If you've never eaten anything, never tasted anything, never touched anything, never smelled something, what right have you to assume you're alive?
Wife:	Hmm. But you are.
Wearing:	Apparently, yes. But I'd like to know what the hell's been going on!

(In making these pronouncements about his senses, it is clear that Wearing is speaking figuratively, not literally.) Thus, for Wearing, too, each waking moment feels as though he is just waking up from sleep. The journal that he keeps is filled with multiple entries that all contain variants of the same message. For example, directly under the entry "10:49 am I Am Totally Awake – First time," which appears on the first line of a page, is a second entry "11:05 am I Am Perfectly Awake – First time," and so on. When left alone in his room, the patient fills entire pages in this way with entries made at intervals ranging from 5 to 45 minutes.

These anecdotes capture an essential quality of the conscious phenomenology of the MTL amnesic patient, the near-continual impression of just having awakened from unconscious sleep. The plight of the MTL amnesic patient, then, is to be fully cognizant of, if not preoccupied by, the fact that one is *not* cognizant of the all that preceded the current moment.

Hippocampus vs. MTL?

At the time of the initial findings with H.M., and for most of the ensuing quarter century, most of the findings and principles summarized here were framed in terms of the hippocampus (e.g., "declarative memory is hippocampally dependent"). Subsequently, there has been an upswing in interest in the contributions of the neocortical regions of the MTL – the entorhinal, perirhinal, and parahippocampal cortex (PHC) – to memory functions and the extent to which each may make distinct contributions. These are questions about the organization of memory at a systems level – that is, at the level of circuits and regions of the brain and how they interact. To consider these systems-level questions in a substantive way, however, we'll first need a more detailed understanding of the cellular and molecular bases of memory formation and retention than what we've covered up to this point.

Association Through Synaptic Modification

Recall that in *Chapter 5*'s section on Hebbian plasticity, we applied Hebb's postulate to an example from Pavlovian conditioning. What we said is that there was something special about the fact that metronome-related activity in the auditory system coincided with the activity in the digestive neurons. Thus, even though the auditory activity initially had no causal role in driving the digestive neurons, something about the coincidence of their activity led to a strengthening of the ability of auditory activity to drive salivary activity. But what we didn't get into at the time was the question of *why*. What was that special something? To address this question, we'll next turn to experiments initiated in Oslo in the mid-1960s.

Long-Term Potentiation

Hippocampal Circuitry and Its Electrophysiological Investigation

For our fanciful trip to Oslo to be most profitable, we'll need to be familiar with the circuitry of the hippocampus. As illustrated in *Figure 6.5*, the hippocampus can be construed as sitting atop the cortical hierarchy, receiving highly processed inputs from the highest levels of the dorsal stream (via feedforward projections from PPC to the PHC) and the ventral stream (via feedforward projections from IT and STP to perirhinal cortex [PRC]). PHC and PRC each funnel into entorhinal cortex (EC), which then projects to hippocampus. The hippocampus is considered the top of the hierarchy because its projections don't go to yet another downstream area. Instead, after the incoming information is processed through its circuitry, the pattern of cortical convergence onto the hippocampus is inverted, and hippocampal outputs are fed back out to EC, then divergently to many of the regions of neocortex from which the input had come.

The hippocampus itself differs from six-layer neocortex in that it is, in effect, a rolled-up sheet of three-layer archicortex ("old" cortex). *Figure 11.2.A* shows the hippocampus in cross section, and *Figure 11.2.B* shows, diagramatically, that one can trace a complete circuit from the inputs from EC to the dentate gyrus (DG), through the CA fields, and then back out to cortex. This circuitry lends itself to various experimental procedures that wouldn't be feasible in other brain regions. Now we can drop in on the University of Oslo in the mid-1960s, where the electrophysiologist Per Andersen had pioneered the measurement of the "population spike" in the DG. Due to the homogeneity and relative feedforward simplicity of the circuitry, if one delivers electrical stimulation to the axons projecting from EC to the DG (the "perforant path"), a field potential recorded from the granule cell – body layer of the DG gives a straightforward measure of the aggregate strength of the connection between neurons in these two regions (*Figure 11.3*).

The breakthrough finding relating to Hebbian plasticity was first made by then-graduate student Terje Lømo, and later confirmed and codified by Lømo in collaboration with visiting British neurophysiologist Timothy Bliss. The protocol of Bliss and Lømo (1973) was to deliver high-frequency (20 Hz) trains (15 seconds in duration) of electrical pulses ("tetani") to the perforant path of an anaesthetized rabbit and measure the resultant population spike from the granule cell-body layer of the DG.

Prior to delivery of the first tetanus, the researchers measured the baseline strength of the EC–DG connection by delivering single pulses. The waveforms at the top of *Figure 11.3* show the baseline response, a negative-going potential (here, negative is plotted up) with two bumps, that then returns to baseline. Why is negative plotted up? The negative-going potential corresponds to the depolarization of granule cells (intracellular depolarization causing extracellular hyperpolarization, which is what the extracellular electrode records). The "dimple" in the middle of the depolarization wave is the population spike (after discharge, a neuron rapidly hyperpolarizes, producing a positive shift in the extracellular potential). At baseline,

FIGURE 11.2 The hippocampus in cross section.

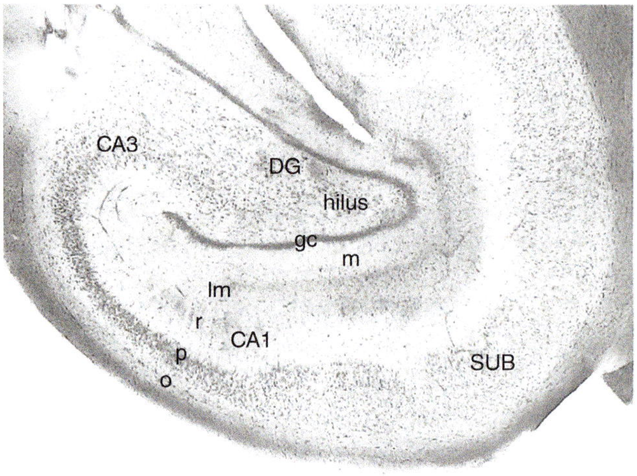

FIGURE 11.2.A Coronal section through the right hemisphere (medial on left side of image, lateral on right). DG = dentate gyrus, and within the DG, gc = granule cell layer and m = stratum moleculare. The layers of the CA fields are lm = stratum lacunosum moleculare; r = stratum radiatum; p = stratum pyramidale; o = stratum oriens. SUB = subiculum, an output station not included in *Figure 11.2.B*.

Source: Reproduced with permission from Gyorgy Buszáki et al. (2006) / Oxford University Press.

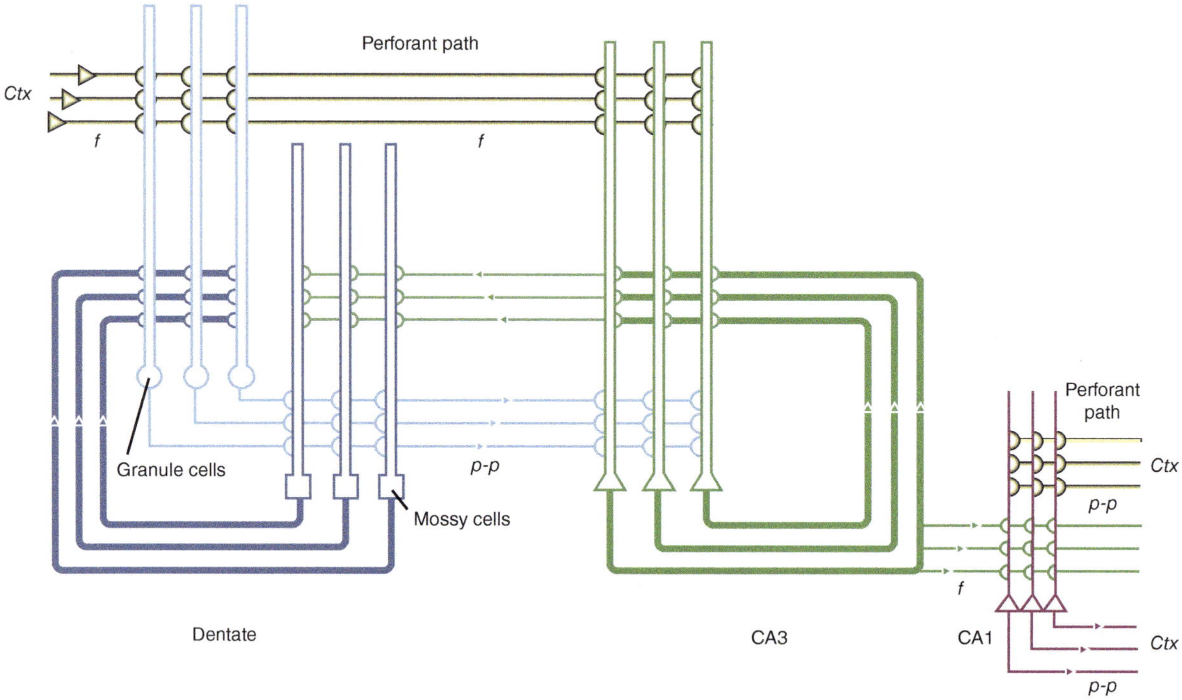

FIGURE 11.2.B A simplified wiring diagram of the circuitry in the slice if *Figure 11.2.A* was unrolled. The perforant path projects from entorhinal cortex to DG, CA3, and CA1. The projections from EC to DG are "fanning" (f; i.e., divergent), as are those from CA3 to itself (i.e., recurrent projections) and from CA3 to CA1, whereas those from EC to CA1 and from DG to CA3 are "point-to-point" (p-p).

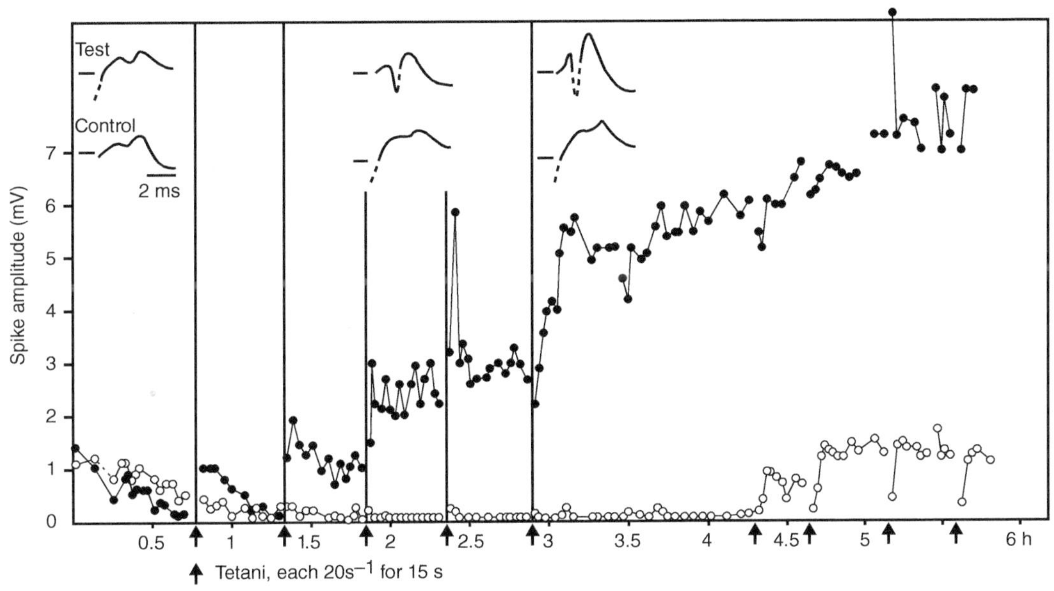

FIGURE 11.3 LTP in the DG of the hippocampus (Bliss and Lømo, 1973).

Source: Lomo and Terje (2003) / Royal Society Publishing.

very few DG neurons generate an action potential in response to single pulses to the perforant path, and so the population spike is very small. Each data point along the horizontal axis indicates the magnitude of the population spike produced by a single probing pulse (responses to the tetani themselves are not shown), and the baseline population spikes from time 0 to 0.75 hour (i.e., 45 minutes) are between 1 and 0 mV. At time 0.75 hour, a tetanus is delivered to the perforant path in the "test" hemisphere, and the population spike to subsequent probing pulses in this hemisphere is briefly elevated (filled circles), whereas the control hemisphere is largely unchanged. At time 1.35 hour, after the second tetanus, the response of the population spike is larger, and only weakens slightly, leveling off at 1 mV over the ensuing 30 minutes. At time 1.85 hours, after the third tetanus, the population spike is further strengthened to 2.5 mV. (Representative waveforms from this epoch are illustrated at the top of the figure.) Finally, just before time 3 hours, a final tetanus is delivered. From this point forward, the population spike starts to grow "on its own," without any further tetani, from a magnitude of ~3 mV to in excess of 7 mV. (The four tetani delivered after the 4-hour time point were delivered to the control hemisphere.) Critically, the potentiated state of the population spike was sustained for the next 3 hours, until the experiment was terminated. Ergo, "long-term potentiation." (After 6 hours of recording, preceded by several hours of setup and surgery, it was surely time to go to the pub!)

From these results, it was inferred (and later confirmed) that this strengthening of the population spike reflected Hebbian plasticity, because it came about after the initial pulses of the tetanus had depolarized the granule cells, such that later pulses in the tetanus generated action potentials. (Delivery of the same number of single pulses, separated in time, would not have this effect.) Thus, it was the coincidence of (upstream) perforant path activity and (downstream) granule cell firing that resulted in the strengthening (the "potentiation") of the synapse. (If you need to (re)familiarize yourself with the workings of the NMDA receptor, please (re)visit *Chapter 5*, section *Activity-based modification of synaptic strength.*)

Multiple Stages of Synaptic Strengthening Having detailed an experimental protocol for inducing LTP, here's an overview of the key events that lead to the LTP of synapses. The influx of calcium ions through NMDA receptors has both short-term and long-term consequences. In the short term (i.e., more or less instantaneously), it triggers the insertion of more AMPA receptors into the postsynaptic density. (As it turns out, postsynaptic terminals are "pre-equipped" to be strengthened rapidly, with "racks" of AMPA receptors at the ready, to be inserted into the postsynaptic density as needed.) Because the binding of neurotransmitter with a receptor is a stochastic event, adding more AMPA receptors to the postsynaptic density increases the probability that any one molecule of glutamate released into the synaptic cleft will bind with a postsynaptic receptor. The aggregate effect is that each action potential from the presynaptic neuron has a stronger influence on the postsynaptic neuron – the synapse has been potentiated.

Across a longer time span, Ca^{2+}-initiated cascades of intracellular signaling initiate the synthesis of new proteins that are necessary for new synapses to be constructed. Electron-microscopic images have documented the appearance of new dendritic spines, presumed to be forming new synapses with afferent axons, a so-called structural form of LTP.

How Might the Hippocampus Work?

I had an argument with myself (as H.M. used to say) about whether to use the word "does" or "might" in this section heading. In the end, I've concluded that "does" would imply that this question is settled to a degree that it simply is not. What follows, however, are some of the more intriguing and influential possibilities.

Fast-Encoding Hippocampus vs. Slow-Encoding Cortex

The "complementary learning systems" model was formulated by a collaboration between two PDP modelers, James McClelland and his then-student Randall O'Reilly, and hippocampal neurophysiologist Bruce McNaughton. Their model was motivated by two primary considerations, one empirical and one theoretical. The empirical consideration was the evidence for a time-limited role for the hippocampus in LTM storage. That is, the fact that retrograde memory loss is typically limited to memories acquired for the few years prior to the insult suggests either a transfer of memories from the hippocampus to cortex or a time-limited role for the hippocampus in the consolidation of cortically based long-term memories. The theoretical consideration is as follows. There are two primary functions carried out by LTM: the retention of memories for specific episodes that we have experienced; and the extraction from life experiences of general patterns about how the world works. Memories of specific episodes highly detailed and discriminable from other episodes that may have some overlapping features. (E.g., I only have one free half-hour in my entire day, and it's deadline day for submitting two letters of recommendation, one for a mentee, "A," who is applying for a faculty job, the other for a colleague, "B," who is applying for a research grant from a private foundation. Was it A or B who recently emailed to say that a one-day delay wouldn't jeopardize the evaluation of their application?) These are called **episodic memories**. The extraction of general patterns, in contrast, entails discarding details that are idiosyncratic to any one specific episode in order to extract only the general principles. (E.g., private foundation research grants tend to be smaller than research grants from government agencies, and they are often restricted to early-stage investigators.) These are called **semantic memories** and correspond to knowledge about the world that does not require reference to the episode(s) in which it was acquired.

Computational modeling has demonstrated that the formation of distinct episodic memories, an operation sometimes referred to as "pattern separation," is computationally incompatible with the abstraction across specific episodes to distill and/or update general principles, an operation sometimes referred to as "pattern completion." In particular, the rapid representation and retention of arbitrary associations, a hallmark of episodic memory, cannot be supported by a system that learns general principles by abstracting across multiple individual episodes, a necessarily slow process. The complementary learning systems model of McClelland, McNaughton, and O'Reilly (1995), therefore, proposes that the hippocampus serves as the special-purpose rapid learner of episodic memories, and the way in which these memories are periodically reinstated (i.e., in full detail, or just the important proposition that it contains) determines whether or not it will gradually migrate to the cortex as an episodic or a semantic memory.

Episodic Memory for Sequences

Figure 11.2 illustrates that the circuitry of the hippocampus includes two recurrent loops of circuitry: in addition to feeding forward to CA3, granule cells of the DG also project to mossy cells of the DG, which, in turn, project back onto the granule cells; and, in addition to feeding forward to CA1, CA3 neurons also feed back onto other CA3 neurons (as well as back onto mossy cells). Indeed, a critical detail that is not captured in this diagram is that individual CA3 axons vary in length from an astounding 150–400 mm, and each makes between 25,000 and 50,000 synapses with other neurons! This makes the CA3 layer a "giant random connection space, a requisite for combining arbitrary information" (Buszáki, 2006, p. 285). That is, it is an ideal substrate for the rapid formation of episodic memories invoked by McClelland, McNaughton, and O'Reilly (1995). The neurophysiologist and theoretician John Lisman (1944-2017) has emphasized that this recurrent circuitry, combined with the direct EC-to-CA3 projection of the perforant path, enables the hippocampus to represent two kinds of information that are critical for episodic memory: the sequence in which events occurred; and the context in which they took place.

Place Cell Precession An empirical finding that underlies Lisman's (1999) idea comes from the phenomenon of **phase precession** of the firing of hippocampal place cells, discovered by John O'Keefe, whom you'll remember from *Chapter 7* as the original discoverer of place cells (an accomplishment for which he was to be awarded the Nobel Prize in 2014). The phenomenon is cartooned in *Figure 11.4.B*. Lisman's explanation is that, because the ion channels of NMDA receptors in the CA3 and CA1 regions remain open for 100 msec or longer, the recurrent circuitry in this region can encode (via LTP) the temporal association of "location *B* comes after location *A*," and so on. Importantly, these associations are asymmetrical: although NMDA receptors at the *A*-to-*B* synapse can detect the "lagged coincidence" that A *was recently active, and* B *is now firing*, at the *B*-to-*A* synapse, the reverse cannot happen, because when *B* is firing, *A* is no longer depolarized. (Thus, although glutamate released from *B* might untwist the pores of NMDA channels in *A*, the absence of depolarization in *A* means that the Mg^{2+} blockade will remain in place.) Lisman further posits that if there is a buffer that can sustain activity in a representation over several seconds, either within the hippocampus or elsewhere, this same mechanism could also encode the sequential order of events spaced out by seconds, rather than tens of milliseconds (we'll consider data consistent with this idea from human fMRI studies in *Chapter 12*). The gist of this idea is that the mechanism observed in the phase precession of activity in hippocampal place cells (*Figure 11.4*) might underlie LTM for sequences of events.

Although not illustrated explicitly in *Figure 11.4.B*, the biophysics underlying the phase encoding of place cell activity is phase-amplitude coupling (PAC). Each of the five neurons illustrated in *Figure 11.4.B* is bursting at the trough of a gamma oscillation that is "nested" in the lower-frequency oscillation. If you revisit *Figure 4.11*, you'll note how the gamma-filtered component of the signal waxes and wanes as a function of the concurrent phase of the alpha cycle. Whereas *Figure 4.11* illustrates alpha-high gamma PAC recorded by an EcoG electrode on the cortical surface, the PAC in the hippocampus involves oscillatory gamma (~35–90 Hz) that is coordinated by the ongoing theta rhythm. Lisman's (1999) account of episodic memory recall is that each burst of activity in hippocampal PAC, rather than corresponding to a place cell as it does in *Figure 11.4.B*, corresponds to an ensemble of neurons that represent discrete propositional elements that make up the memory.

One example that Lisman (1999) uses to make concrete the connection between place cell precession in the rodent and human episodic memory retrieval is to invoke a memory of a visit to the zoo in which candy is purchased for a little boy named Jerry, but Jerry then drops the candy on the ground near the monkey cage, a monkey reaches through the bars of the cage to snatch it, and Jerry bursts into tears. (Extra credit to anyone who can dredge through John Lisman's biography to uncover the origin of this story.) If retrieval of this memory (i.e., thinking about it) were applied to *Figure 11.4.B*, N1 might correspond to an ensemble of cells representing "Jerry was given candy," N2 to "Jerry went to the monkey house," N3 to "Jerry dropped the candy," and so forth. Although these three facts are seemingly activated simultaneously while one thinks about this event (and indeed, although they activate again

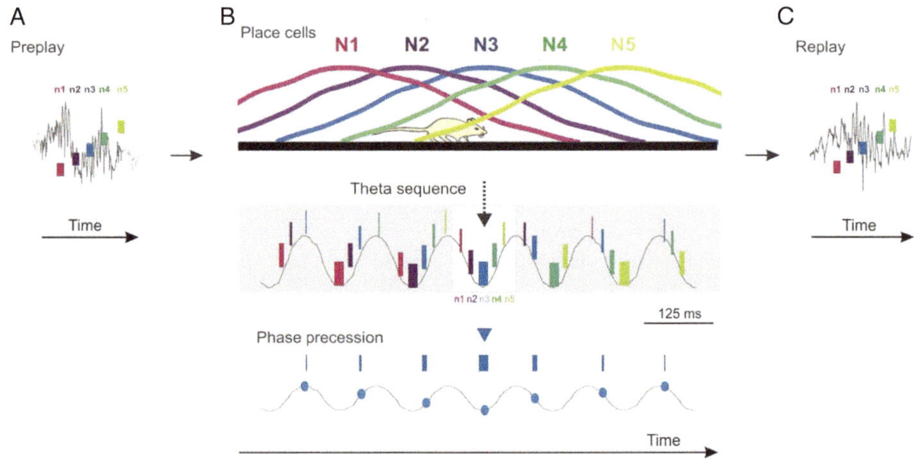

FIGURE 11.4 Phase precession of place cell firing. **A.** A sharp-wave ripple "preplaying" the sequence that will later come to represent the sequence of locations illustrated in panel **B** (see *Figure 11.4* and text for details about sharp-wave ripples). **B.** As a rat runs along a path, the hippocampal place cells representing five adjacent locations have overlapping place fields. At the moment in time captured in the top panel, when the rat is in the middle of the path, it's at the location for which neuron N3 is maximally active; it's leaving the location for which neuron N2 is maximally active, and N2's activity is beginning to decrease; and it will next be at the location for which neuron N4 is maximally active, and N4's activity is increasing. The middle panel shows how the activity of each of these five place cells (vertical bars) is not simultaneous, rather, it occurs in an unfolding sequence of bursts, the order of which corresponds to the order in which the rat will pass through these locations. Furthermore, this sequence of activity is "compressed," in that the full sequence plays through in roughly 125 msec, which is much faster than the rat is actually moving. The degree of compression is dictated by frequency of the theta rhythm, which acts like a clock in the hippocampus. The area in white is the cycle of theta occurring while the rat is at the pictured location. Note that the "location" of each neuron's burst on the theta wave (more technically, the "phase angle") indicates where the rat is (the cell bursting at the trough), where it has been (the cells bursting on the falling slope of the cycle), and where it will be (the rising slope). This phenomenon is referred to as phase encoding. In this cartoon, the rat is moving at a rate of one place field per 125 msec. Thus, if you look across time (i.e., from the leftmost cycle to the rightmost), you'll see that the phase angle of neuron N3's bursting changes from cycle to cycle: when the rat was at location "N1," N3 fired at the peak of the cycle; as the rat moved forward N3's burst "advanced" to earlier points along the cycle, firing at the trough when the rat was at location "N3," then firing progressively earlier before the trough as the animal continued forward. This phenomenon is known as "precession" and is even easier to see in the bottom panel, which illustrates the activity of only N3, across the same five cycles of theta. **C.** A sharp-wave ripple "replaying" the sequence of locations illustrated in panel B (see *Figure 11.5* and text for details about sharp-wave ripples).

Source: Adapted from Dragoi, 2013.

and again over many sequential theta cycles), the order in which they occurred is encoded in the phase of the theta cycle at which each ensemble fires. To be more mechanistic, explicit memory recall, by this scheme, would play out as follows. First, neurons of EC that represent the context of "the zoo" depolarize CA3 neurons at a subthreshold level. Second, the subset of these CA3 neurons that also receive input from the DG representing *Jerry dropped his candy* would be depolarized to their firing threshold, and their activity would represent *Jerry dropped his candy at the zoo*. This activity would, in turn, activate the CA3 representation of the puckish monkey who snatched away the candy, and so on. Note that regardless of the actual time elapsed between two sequentially occurring events, the representation of their ordinal relation would be compressed into a timescale clocked by theta-nested gamma-band oscillations in the hippocampus.

Sharp-Wave Ripples To do justice to our current understanding of memory encoding and consolidation, and, in particular, how sleep relates to these processes, we need to drill down a little bit further into hippocampal neurophysiology. When a rodent is actively moving about, exploring, rearing, sniffing, the theta rhythm dominates activity in the CA fields of the hippocampus. Whenever the animal stops moving, however, and engages in behaviors such as eating, drinking, grooming, or sleeping, theta subsides, and in its place one sees irregular bursts of "sharp-wave ripples." (During sleep, sharp-wave ripples are seen during slow-wave sleep (SWS), not rapid eye movement [REM] sleep.) As illustrated in *Figure 11.5*, sharp waves are large-amplitude negative-going deflections in the local field potential, and nested in the sharp waves are ripples – short-lived oscillatory patterns in the 100–200 Hz range. (Note that, as can be inferred from *Figure 11.5*, ripples are far too small in amplitude to be detected by ECoG methods for which power in this same frequency range is considered "high-gamma," and taken as a proxy for multiunit activity [MUA].) György Buszsáki (2015; who we first encountered at the end of *Chapter 2,* in the section entitled *Complicated and complex*) has characterized sharp-wave ripples as "the most synchronous events in the mammalian brain, associated with a robustly enhanced transient excitability in the hippocampus and its partner structures" (p. 1074). In effect, sharp-wave ripples are ideal for transferring information from the hippocampus to the neocortex, thereby, for example, providing a circuit-level mechanism for the processes considered in section *Fast-encoding hippocampus vs. slow-encoding cortex* in this chapter. An additional feature of sharp-wave ripples is that each deflection in a ripple corresponds to a spike from a different neuron. And the pattern of spiking is not arbitrary, but, rather, reflects repeating sequences of the same neurons always firing in the same sequence. Now we can return to *Figure 11.4* and explicate panels *A* and *C*, which we've ignored until now.

Starting with *Figure 11.4.C*, and consistent with an important role in consolidating memories by transferring information from the hippocampus to cortex, sharp-wave ripples are often seen to "replay" sequences of neural activity that occurred previously when the animal was in an active state. A classic example is illustrated in *Figure 11.4*, in that panel **B** shows a sequence of place cell activity that is recorded while the rat is exploring a novel environment (i.e., when it is "learning something new"). Later, when the animal is in SWS, the same sequence of N1–N2–N3–N4–N5 is observed within individual sharp-wave ripples. Because

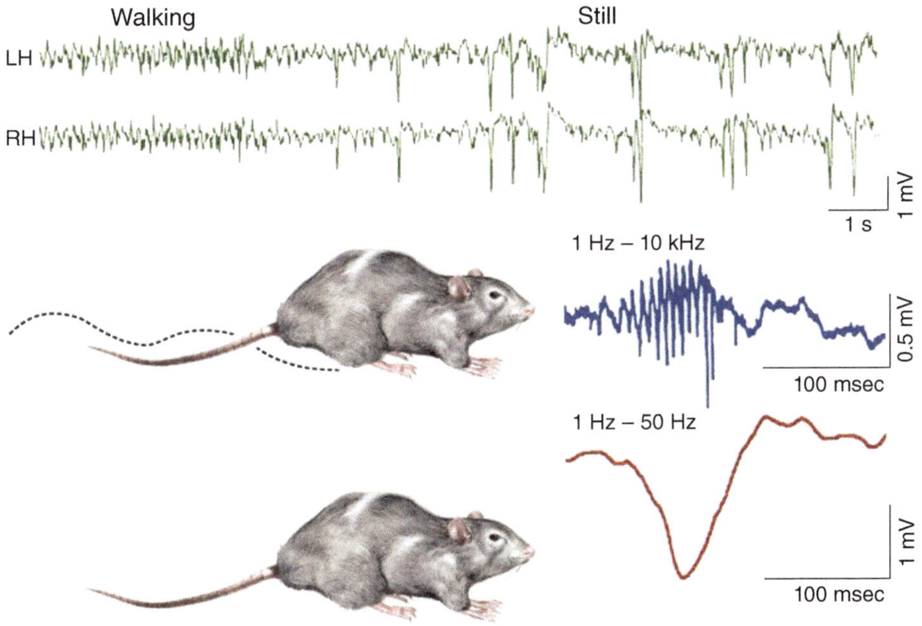

FIGURE 11.5 The hippocampal sharp-wave ripple. Green traces at the top illustrate recordings made simultaneously in CA1 in the left and right hemispheres of a rat while walking, then standing still. Sharp waves are the large-amplitude deflections during the still epoch. Red trace is a blow-up of a single sharp wave, low-pass filtered to remove evidence of ripple. Blue trace is a ripple.

Source: Reproduced with permission from Buzsaki, G. (2015) / John Wiley & Sons.

sharp-wave ripples are also characteristic of human neurophysiology (indeed, of every mammalian species in which they've been sought), they are believed to underlie the role of SWS in learning and memory. Finally, *Figure 11.4.A* – specific sequences of neuronal firing have been observed during sharp-wave ripples recorded during SWS that later turn out to be the same sequences of place cell firing that are recorded when the animal is exploring a never-before-encountered environment! The phenomenon has been termed "preplay" and is perhaps best accounted for by the proposal that the generation of self-organized sequences of activity is a natural consequence of the rapidly induced plasticity caused by sharp-wave ripples, themselves a consequence of the recurrent circuitry of CA3 and its connections with CA1. Perhaps the hippocampus is, in effect, always generating "templates" of sequential connections, and evolution has capitalized on this by learning to "harness" a "template" each time a novel sequence of events is experienced, thereby creating a mechanism for representing sequential order in long-term memories.

Episodic Memory as an Evolutionary Elaboration of Navigational Processing

For the final model of hippocampal function that we'll consider here, it will be useful to bring to mind the place cell data from *Chapter 7*, as well as *Figure 7.10*'s illustration of the dorsal location of the hippocampus in the rodent. At the level of implementation, it draws on many of the same mechanisms as Lisman's memory-for-sequences model, differing primarily in the emphasis on "how our memory came to work the way that it does." An influential account by György Buszáki uses as a starting point the fact that hippocampal place cells encode allocentric representations of space, and thus would be an effective substrate for one-dimensional (1-D) "dead reckoning" navigation (a.k.a. "route following"). 1-D maps, like that illustrated in *Figure 11.4.B*, would be sufficient to represent an episodic memory, such as Lisman's story of Jerry at the zoo (see this chapter's section on *Place cell precession*). If one adds together a sufficient number of 1-D routes, one can construct a 2-D map, and the CA3 field as a whole can be construed as a 2-D map, with distances encoded in synaptic weights. (I.e., by the same logic that Lisman uses to argue that these cells can encode asymmetric sequences of events, one would also expect stronger synaptic links between place cells representing nearby locations than between those representing distant locations.) Indeed, Buszáki has noted that CA3 probably holds many, many maps that are anatomically intermingled, thus obscuring any topography that may exist for any one map. Such 2-D maps would be used in "landmark-based" navigation (a.k.a. "map reading"), a more efficient form of navigation that has been observed in many animal species, as well as in humans. Such 2-D maps, Buszáki argues, may be the neural basis of explicit memories. Thus, the hippocampus, a region phylogenetically older than the neocortex, may have originally evolved to support navigation, foraging, and caching behaviors in our vertebrate ancestors. As the neocortex in early mammals acquired the ability to represent information other than just the minimum needed for survival and propagation of the species – such as feeding, fighting, fleeing, mating – it may have co-opted the substrate already in place in the hippocampus for the encoding and storage of information other than space.

Compatible with this "navigational origins" view is the "hippocampus as cognitive map" perspective championed by the cognitive neuroscientist Lynn Nadel, coauthor with John O'Keefe of the influential 1978 book of the same name. In a more recent review, Nadel, Hoscheidt, and Ryan (2013) add an additional level of detail by drawing on the fact that the size of hippocampal place fields in the rodent changes along a gradient from small in the dorsal to relatively large in the ventral hippocampus. They infer from this that in the rodent, the dorsal hippocampus may be more important for fine-grained spatial processing and the ventral hippocampus for what they call "context coding" (i.e., information about what a particular locale is like). In a final inferential step, they review fMRI studies of memory retrieval in the human and propose that "Retrieving detailed spatial relational information preferentially activate[s] the posterior hippocampus, whereas retrieving information about locales (or contexts) preferentially activate[s] the anterior hippocampus" (p. 22).

What Are the Cognitive Functions of the Hippocampus?

Some of the ideas reviewed in the two previous sections, such as the discovery of Hebbian plasticity in the hippocampus and the role of the hippocampus in sleep-dependent consolidation of information into LTM (via replay), fit well with the provisional principles that we listed in the earlier subsection *The organization of memory*. Others, like the putative role for the hippocampus in the retrieval of memories, might seem to be difficult to reconcile with some of the principles derived from foundational studies of H.M. and, subsequently, other patients with medial-temporal lobe amnesia. In this section, we'll revisit those principles articulated near the beginning of this chapter in light of more recent theoretical and empirical developments.

Standard Anatomical Model

After some puzzling early failures to replicate H.M.'s amnesia in nonhuman primates, by the 1980s, researchers (prominent among them teams led by Mortimer Mishkin [yes, *that* Mort Mishkin] and by Larry Squire and Stuart Zola [then Zola-Morgan]) were producing findings indicating that surgical lesioning of the amygdala and hippocampus, bilaterally, produced a marked impairment of LTM. A canonical example is illustrated in *Figure 11.6*, which shows that whereas lesions restricted to the amygdala had no effect compared to unoperated controls, lesions of hippocampus plus the overlying parahippocampal gyrus (PHG) and caudal PRC ("H^{+}") produced a marked impairment of delayed nonmatching-to-sample with delays as short as 15 seconds, and lesions of hippocampus plus PHC plus caudal *and* rostral PRC *and* EC ("H^{++}") produced an even larger impairment at 15 seconds. When the delay was extended to 60 seconds, then to 10 minutes, the rate of decline for each group (including controls) was comparable (*Figure 11.6*). It is important to note that, with the surgical aspiration methods that were used to produce these lesions, an "H" lesion that did not compromise any of the overlying tissue was not possible, due to the location of the hippocampus deep in the MTL. This detail will become important when we later consider the theoretical implications of more recent results in comparison with this "standard model." It is also important to note that the data in *Figure 11.6.C* and *Figure 11.6.D* do not show any hints that there may be qualitative differences in the impairments of any of the lesion groups; rather, they seem to show a "mass action" effect (c.f., Chapter 1, section *Localization of function vs. mass action*) whereby the magnitude of the behavioral deficit corresponds to the volume of tissue damaged.

The "standard model" that emerged from results such as those illustrated in *Figure 11.6*, supplemented by cases of human MTL amnesia, was a hierarchical organizational scheme whereby *perceptual processing* was carried out by regions "upstream of" and including anterior IT and posterior parietal areas, and the subsequent *mnemonic processing* of this information was then carried out by the PRC and PHG (and, subsequently the EC and hippocampus) into which these perceptual regions projected, the PHG, PRC, EC, and hippocampus together comprising the "MTL memory system."[1] Importantly, a strong version of this model posited that the functions carried out by each of these elements of the MTL memory system – i.e., encoding and consolidation – were equivalent.

Challenges to the Standard Anatomical Model

Newer Lesioning Methods

One possible concern about the results from Squire and Zola-Morgan (1991), hinted at in the previous section, is that they did not include a "H" condition in which the hippocampus was lesioned in a way that spared all of the overlying cortical tissue of the MTL. This means that it remained a logical possibility that none of the memory impairments illustrated in *Figure 11.6*

[1] As has been noted elsewhere, this book often adopts the visuocentric bias that is characteristic of many domains of neuroscience. The standard model also posited that auditory, somatosensory, and olfactory/gustatory processing could be construed as carrying out *perceptual* processing and transmitting the resultant perceptual information into the MTL memory system for the creation of multimodal long-term memories.

FIGURE 11.6 The "Standard Model" of a Medial Temporal Lobe Memory System.

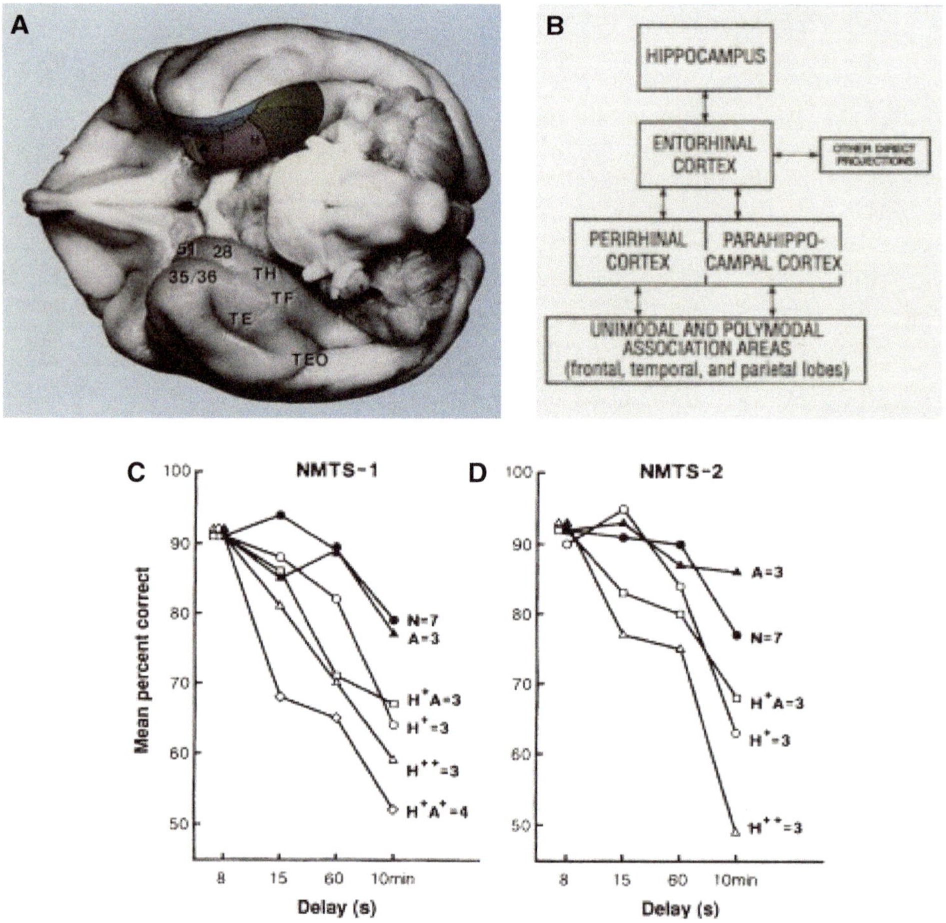

FIGURE 11.6.A Ventral view of the brain of a macaque monkey, labeled on the right hemisphere to identify neocortical regions of the ventral and medial temporal, and modified on the left hemisphere to include outlines of the underlying amygdala (A) and hippocampus (H) and with blocks of color to indicate the extent of the surgical lesions referenced in panels **C** and **D**. The labels TEO, TE, TF, and TH correspond to cytoarchitectonically identified regions – TEO and TE correspond to PIT, CIT, and AIT from Figure 6.5, TF and TE to parahippocampal cortex – 35/36 corresponds to perirhinal cortex, 28 to entorhinal cortex, 51 to the periamygdaloid cortex. The colors correspond to: H^+ (green [parahippocampal]); H^{++} (green plus blue [perirhinal] plus pink [entorhinal]); (yellow [periamygdaloid], not involved in these experiments). Note that H^+ lesions included the rostral portion of the hippocampus but spared the overlying entorhinal cortex.

Source: Squire et al. (1991) / American Association for the Advancement of Science.

FIGURE 11.6.B Diagram of the hierarchical organization of this putative "MTL memory system."

Source: Squire and Zola-Morgan (1991) / American Association for the Advancement of Science - AAAS.

FIGURE 11.6.C Results from (delayed) nonmatching to sample (NMTS) testing, session 1, at multiple delay lengths (horizontal axis), of monkeys with no surgical damage (N) or with surgical lesions as summarized in panel B: amygdala (A); H^+; H^+A; H^{++}; and H^+A^+.

Source: Squire and Zola-Morgan (1991) / American Association for the Advancement of Science - AAAS.

FIGURE 11.6.D Results from session 2, in which all of the animals from session 1 (with the exception of the H^+A^+ group) were retested one to two years later, and demonstrating that there is no evidence of recovery of function over this span of time.

Source: Squire and Zola-Morgan (1991) / American Association for the Advancement of Science - AAAS.

were due to damage to the hippocampus per se. Indeed, when Elisabeth Murray and Mort Mishkin (1998) at the NIMH's Laboratory of Neuropsychology subsequently used injections of ibotenic acid to produce lesions that were restricted to the hippocampus alone, they produced intriguing (and, for a while at least, controversial) evidence that damage restricted to the hippocampus could leave the performance of at least some LTM tasks intact!

Ibotenic acid is a glutamate agonist that, through a phenomenon called excitotoxicity, destroys neurons whose dendrites it comes into contact with. (In essence, preventing AMPA receptor pore from closing results in the influx of too much Na^+, which kills the cell.) Importantly, ibotenic acid spares so-called "fibers of passage" – axons traveling through the injection zone that neither initiate nor terminate within it, because these portions of the axon lack glutamate receptors. Mechanical lesions, in contrast, whether produced by surgical excision, heat coagulation, high electrical current, or aspiration, will destroy any fibers that pass through the lesioned area. When Murray and Mishkin produced clean "H" lesions with ibotenic acid injections, they produced results strikingly different from the earlier findings: H lesions produced no impairment on DNMS and other tests of LTM (Murray and Mishkin, 1998). Importantly, in a different set of experiments carried out in the same NIH laboratory, selective lesions of PRC and EC that spared the hippocampus had been shown to produce profound impairments on DNMS performance (Meunier et al., 1993). Although these results might at first seem confounding, an explanation comes from the fact that the DNMS with which they were produced is a test of recognition, but not a test of recall. The importance of this distinction will be a major focus of *Chapter 12: Declarative long-term memory*. For now, the main point that we'll emphasize is that these results suggest that at least some of the function(s) of neocortical components of the MTL (specifically, PRC and EC) may, indeed, be qualitatively different from those of the hippocampus.

Perceptually Challenging Behavioral Tasks The results from the two Murray-led experiments summarized in the previous paragraph challenged the idea that each region in the putative MTL memory system carried out the same function. Around the same time, in a different line of research, also pursued by Elisabeth Murray, in collaboration with David Gaffan and others, has challenged the idea that LTM is the only function carried out by the "MTL memory system." This work took the perspective that PRC, being one synapse downstream from AIT, may subserve high-level object recognition functions in addition to LTM – encoding functions. In addition to the anatomy, Murray and colleagues were motivated by computational modeling, suggesting that PRC might be particularly important for representing complex conjunctions of features. *Figure 11.7* illustrates one experiment in which monkeys first had to learn, through trial-and-error guessing, which one in each pair of stimuli was rewarded. For the test, these stimulus pairs were re-presented as they had appeared during training, along with two additional pairs per training pair that were constructed by partially morphing the two trained images together. Thus, as illustrated in *Figure 11.7.A*, the "feature ambiguity" pairs required discriminating between two stimuli that shared many features. The finding was that H- and PRC-lesioned animals did not differ when discriminating between trained stimuli, but the PRC-lesioned animals were selectively impaired on pairs with high feature ambiguity.

Importantly, Murray, Timothy Bussey, and Lisa Saksida (2007) note that PRC-lesioned animals are not impaired on just any difficult task. For example, they perform normally on tasks requiring difficult color or size discriminations. Thus, on the strength of these and other results, Murray and colleagues propose that "the perirhinal cortex participates in both perception and memory: it is important for perception because it contains mechanisms enabling the representation of complex conjunctions of features; it subserves memory because it serves as a storage site of complex stimulus representations in both the short- and long-term" (pp. 104–105).

The two previous subsections have summarized arguments that (1) the hippocampus is not needed for relatively simple object memory performance, whereas PRC and EC are; and (2) PRC performs important perceptual, in addition to mnemonic, functions. Both of these arguments represent serious challenges to the notion that the MTL can be considered a monolithic "memory system." Argument (1), in particular, may seem alarming because it challenges the longstanding assumption that the hippocampus is critical for declarative memory encoding. The next subsection summarizes some more recent proposals for how to conceive of the role of the hippocampus in cognition.

FIGURE 11.7 Memory vs. perception in the PRC.

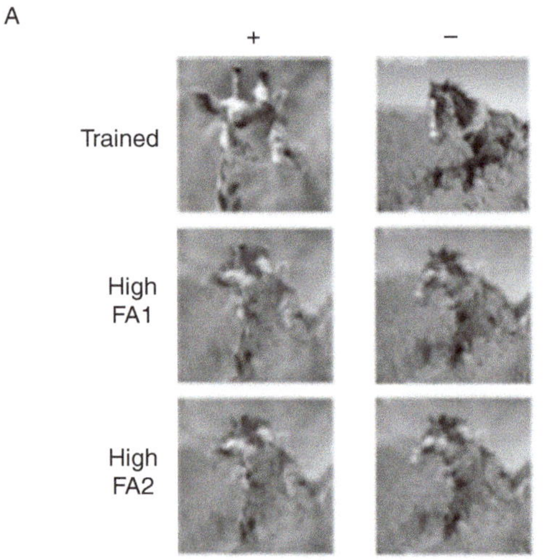

FIGURE 11.7.A On each trial, the monkey saw a pair of stimuli and had to select one. During training, the same images were always paired, and the reward contingencies were always the same. At test, the animals saw each of the training pairs, along with two variants of each pair that contained two levels of "feature ambiguity" (*High FA1* and *High FA2*).

Source: Reproduced with permission from Murray et al. (2007) / Annual Reviews.

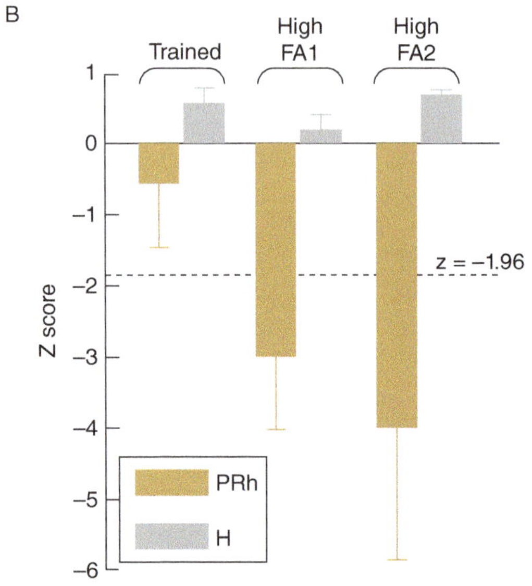

FIGURE 11.7.B Performance of animals with H vs. PRC (here, labeled "PRh") lesions on the three levels of perceptual difficulty.

Source: Murray et al., 2007 / Annual Reviews.

More-Recently Proposed Roles for the Hippocampus

One proposed reconceptualization of the hippocampus, championed by neurobiologist Howard Eichenbaum (1947-2017) and cognitive neuroscientist Neal Cohen, is that its primary function is one of *relational binding*. In brief, this theory holds that the hippocampus affects the operation of representing and learning the relations between items in the environment. This might include the arbitrary rule for written English of "*i* before *e*, except after *c*," or the concrete spatial content of something like "Zinedine Zidane struck the free kick from the left side of the field, lofting the ball over the heads of the Brazilian defenders and into the right side of the goal box, where Thierry Henry, running in unmarked, volleyed it into the back of the net." One implication of this idea is that the classical assumption that the hippocampus is not critical for STM may also need to be revisited. Indeed, recent studies have demonstrated that patients with hippocampal damage can be impaired on tests of STM for the spatial relations between items in a display, even with delays as brief as one second. Thus, from the relational binding perspective, the question isn't *How long must the information be held in memory?* But *What kind of information needs to be processed?*

A second, relatively recent, conceptualization of the function of the hippocampus is a role in what some call "mental time travel," the ability to anticipate a future event and imagine various outcomes, as well as the ability to imagine entirely made-up events. In one study, led by cognitive neuroscientist Eleanor Maguire (1970–2025), patients with bilateral hippocampal damage were asked to construct new imagined experiences, such as "Imagine you are lying on a white sandy beach in a beautiful tropical bay" and "Imagine that you are sitting in the main hall of a museum containing many exhibits." Their results indicated that the imagined experiences of the patients contained markedly less experiential richness than did those of healthy control subjects. A more detailed analysis also revealed lower "spatial coherence" (a measure of the contiguousness and spatial integrity of an imagined scene) in the performance of the patients. If the latter were at the root of the overall poor performance of the patients, these findings would be consistent with the hippocampus-as-cognitive-map framework.

A third development that postdates the articulation of what we've characterized as the standard model posits that the hippocampus may be particularly critical for recollection-based, but not familiarity-based memory retrieval. (This turns out to be key for a widely accepted explanation of the fact that performance on the DNMS can be normal despite complete bilateral hippocampal ablation (Murray and Mishkin, 1998): Many tests of recognition from LTM, including DNMS, can be solved based on familiarity alone.) Details of this "dual-processes" model will be considered in detail in *Chapter 12*, section *Familiarity vs. recollection*.

The fourth (and final) relatively recent proposal that we'll consider here shares conceptual overlap with the ideas of place-cell precession and the phase encoding of sequential information that we considered in section *Episodic memory for sequences*. Its conceptual origin, however, is of quite different provenance. It's the idea, derived from reinforcement learning (RL) models, that the hippocampus, together with the prefrontal cortex (PFC) might represent successor representations spanning a wide range of time spans. Recall from *Chapter 5*, section *Other principles relevant to reinforcement learning*, that we introduced the two extremes of model-free versus model-based mechanisms for decision making (in the context of action selection; c.f. *Chapter 8*, section *The roles of basal ganglia nuclei in the control of movement*). The successor representation affords a "middle way" of guiding behavior via the factoring-in to the decision about which immediate action to take (e.g., *turn left* at an intersection, *continue walking straight* ahead, or *turn right*?) the various future actions that will be required depending on the choice (e.g., *if I turn left here, the future actions that I'll need to take will be different than if I don't turn left and instead choose to keep going straight ahead*). Here we'll go into more detail to describe this idea from Ida Mommenejad and colleagues.

Thinking back to section *Episodic memory for sequences*, let's first recall that, in *Figure 11.4.B*, the activity at neurons N4 and N5 can be construed as predictions, in that they are signaling where the rat will be in the very near future. (E.g., if the animal's intended trajectory was going to take it through location *5′* rather than location *5*, the sequence of firing would have been N1–N2–N3–N4–N5′.) Second, recall that it was suggested that the same substrate and mechanisms underlying the phase-encoded place field activity in a rat running in a familiar maze could, in principle, also support the sequential ordering of many other kinds of information that can be retained in LTM. Thus, for example, discrete events during the Jerry-at the-zoo scenario, which would probably play out over 10 minutes or so in real life, could also be phase encoded in hippocampal theta, as could, for example, one's knowledge of key points in the lifetime of a historically significant political leader. (For an American, it might be George Washington chopping down the cherry tree as a child, commanding troops as a young officer during the "French and Indian War," commanding the Continental Army during the Revolutionary War, and serving as the first President of the newly formed United States of America – each of these time-locked to a different phase angle in the theta cycle.) For the study by Iva Brunec and Ida Mommenejad (2022) that we will summarize here, instead of selecting three different kinds of events/knowledge that each play out over different time scales, the authors drew on the fact that one can mentally represent a single event at multiple time scales.

In the experiment illustrated in *Figure 11.8*, the subjects were all residents of Toronto, and they were scanned with fMRI while virtually navigating through the city. The routes that they followed were preplanned by the subject and an experimenter, looking at a map together the day before the scanning session. The behavior that was scanned was the virtual walk from point A to point B, which subjects experienced as though they were walking along this 2–10 km-long route, with realistic 360° views assembled from first-person views from *Google street view*, and updating in real time to simulate walking along this route. The logic was that while engaged in a, say, 6-km walk through a city, a subject might simultaneously represent the trip at the level of *why am I doing this and what will I do when I arrive at my destination?* (a large-scale representation), at the level of *what are the landmarks that I'll be walking past while I'm out for this stroll?* (an intermediate scale of representation), and at the level of *how do I execute the next five steps so as to avoid that trash can?* (a small-scale representation). Note that, for this example, one can think of the large-scale representation as consisting of just one or two "chunks;" of the intermediate scale of representation as being comprised of several medium-sized chunks (i.e., one for the landmark that's 5-minutes away, a second one to get to the landmark that's 5-minutes further along the route than the first landmark, a third for the landmark that is yet another 5-minutes further from the second landmark, etc.), and of the small scale as consisting of many many small chunks (one for each "the next five steps" that will be experienced). (Such "chunks," as cartooned in *Figure 11.8.A*, can be represented in the brain as place fields or "time fields" [see legend to *Figure 11.8.B*].) Thus, this study assessed the neural bases of the idea that at any moment in time during the walking trip, a subject will be simultaneously representing multiple predictions about what's to come, one at each of several time horizons (see *Figure 11.8.A*). (In RL models, these predictions are called "successor representations.")

The analyses were carried out with a model-based representational similarity analysis (RSA) approach. At each point in time (i.e., at each TR of the fMRI scanning session), a "representational similarity matrix" (RSM) was constructed for each of several different time horizons by correlating the pattern of activity at that TR with a weighted sum of all the subsequent (i.e., "future") TRs within the given time horizon. Five time horizons were selected, implemented as five weightings on the γ parameter from an RL model of the subject's current state – 0.1, 0.6, 0.8, and 0.9 – with higher γ values extending the time horizon further into the "future state representation" (*Figure 11.8.D*). In effect, the authors determined, for several subregions

FIGURE 11.8 The hippocampus as a substrate for successor representations?

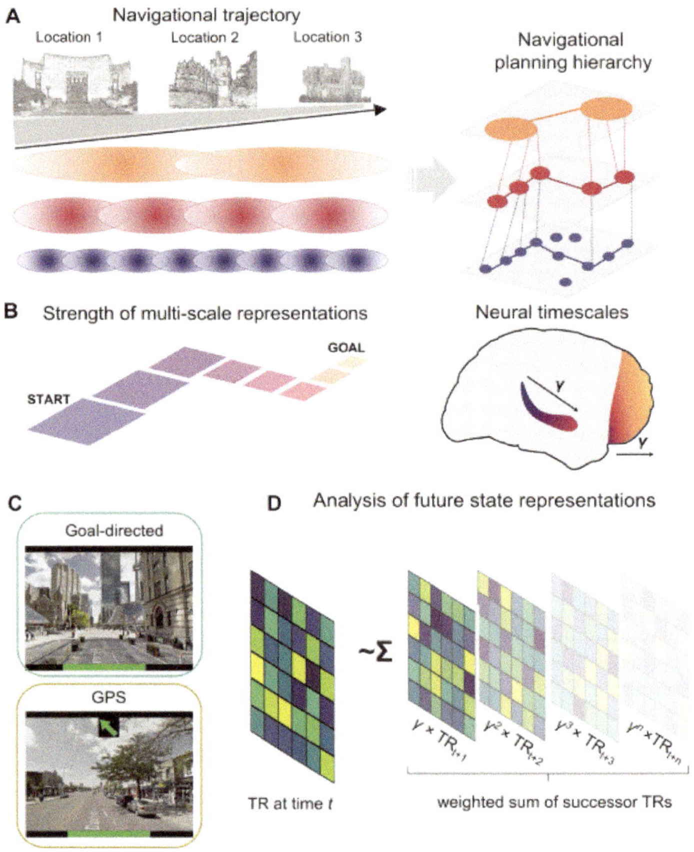

FIGURE 11.8.A Schematic representation of a walking route through a city (top), of different scales of representation that might be simultaneously represented (bottom), and of multiple hierarchically arranged levels of planning (right). Locations *1*, *2*, and *3* are prominent landmarks that a subject would pass while walking along one particular route. The largest, orange-colored "place fields" correspond to representations needed for long-range planning (e.g., thinking about the trip as a whole, thinking about what you'll do when you get to your destination; these have the longest time horizons); the intermediate-sized, pink-colored "place fields" to intermediate-scale representation (e.g., thinking about what will be the relative distances between location *1* and *2* vs. between *2* and *3*; these have intermediate-length time horizons); and the smallest, purple "place fields" to representations needed for short-term planning (e.g., "do I turn left at this next intersection or keep walking straight?"; these have short time horizons).

Source: (Brunec & Mommenejad, 2022) / The Society for Neuroscience.

FIGURE 11.8.B Illustration of the experimental prediction that predictive representations at the different scales highlighted in panel **A** will be represented along a caudal-to-rostral gradient spanning the long axis of the hippocampus and a caudal-to-rostral axis of medial PFC. (Note that in panel **A**, the units of representation were referred to as "place fields" [this author's terminology], but they can also be construed as being "time fields" in that, if one is walking at a steady pace, each unit of length along the route has a corresponding unit of time spent passing through that "place field." For more on the representation of time versus place, see Mommennejad and Howard [2018].)

Source: (Brunec & Mommenejad, 2022) / The Society for Neuroscience.

FIGURE 11.8.C The condition of primary theoretical interest was comprised of "goal-directed" walking trips in which the subject controlled their movement along the route with button presses for "turn to the left," "move straight ahead," and "turn to the right." The control condition ("GPS") was comprised of walks through unfamiliar neighborhoods in which the route was dictated by "GPS arrows," instructing the subject when to turn left, move straight ahead, or turn right, such that no navigational decision making was required during these virtual walking trips.

Source: Brunec et al. (2022) / Society for Neuroscience.

FIGURE 11.8.D Illustration of the analysis procedure, a variant of RSA. For each TR (i.e., for each whole-brain volume of data acquired), a correlation matrix was constructed by correlating that TR's activity (matrix labeled "TR at time *t*") with each of several "future state representations," each of which is itself a matrix constructed as the average of all future TRs within a given time horizon after this average has been weighted by a discount factor (γ parameter derived from an RL model; see text). Note that, relative to the TR at time *t*, all subsequent TRs can be said to be *succeeding* it in time, hence they can be called "successor TRs."

Source: (Brunec & Mommenejad, 2022) / The Society for Neuroscience.

of the hippocampus and medial (m)PFC, the similarity between a brain region's activity and an estimate of what its activity would be in the future, at each of several time scales. For each time scale, the instance of highest similarity was interpreted as the strongest representation of the brain's walking-trip-related prediction. Overall, the results were consistent with what's cartooned in *Figure 11.8.B*, which is to say that patterns of activity in posterior hippocampus were found to most closely reflect predictions with very short time horizons, those in anterior hippocampus to most closely reflect predictions with intermediate-length time horizons, and those in medial PFC to most closely reflect predictions with the longest time horizons. The authors summarize and interpret their results as follows:

> "Our proposal is that larger and more abstract scales of predictive representations in ant[erior] PFC may support planning at larger scales. This higher-level plan may be translated into gradually more granular representations in prepolar PFC, OFC [orbitofrontal cortex; not discussed here], and anterior hippocampal regions, and finer-scale trajectories are translated by hippocampal gradients to the smallest predictive horizons of place fields." (p. 308)

We can summarize Brunec and Mommenejad (2022) by noting that their account can be construed as an RL-flavored complement to the hippocampus-as-cognitive-map perspective, including the fact that it mirrors the expansion of place fields along the caudal-to-rostral axis (see section *Episodic memory as an evolutionary elaboration of navigational processing*). Furthermore, it provides a framework in which to situate the place cell activity illustrated in *Figure 11.6*. Finally, it introduces the importance of bidirectional signaling between hippocampus and PFC, a phenomenon that has been shown to be critical for many aspects of cognition.

Consolidation

The concept of consolidation has also become more complicated since the 1960s and 1970s. Consistent with the original idea of a process that yielded a time-limited role for the hippocampus in LTM, we have reviewed that McClelland, McNaughton, and O'Reilly (1995) proposed a computational basis for consolidation as the gradual integration of hippocampally based representations into the neocortex. A theoretical challenge to the idea of consolidation, however, has come in the form of the *multiple trace theory*, proposed by Lynn Nadel and neuropsychologist Morris Moscovitch. The multiple trace theory posits that each instance of memory retrieval also prompts the creation by the hippocampus of a new memory trace, such that over time, a single memory comes to be stored as multiple traces. To the extent that elements of these traces overlap, this process leads to the development of semantic knowledge that is independent of the episodes in which the information was learned. So, for example, if learning about US presidents in primary school and taking a family trip to Washington, DC, both create traces representing the proposition that *Thomas Jefferson was the third President of the United States*, repeated iterations of this process create a representation that can be retrieved independently of reference to any one of the contexts in which this information was encountered. In this way, the memory that *Thomas Jefferson was the third President of the United States* becomes a *semantic* memory. Should damage to the hippocampus be sustained several years after the learning took place, the patient would nonetheless be able to retrieve this knowledge. On this prediction, the multiple trace theory and the standard neuropsychological model are in accord. The two differ, however, in that the former holds that the specific memory of the visit to the Jefferson Memorial during the family trip to Washington, DC remains an *autobiographical episodic* memory that is dependent on the hippocampus for the remainder of the subject's life. Thus, multiple trace theory would predict that access to this autobiographical episodic memory would be severely impoverished, if not completely impossible, after extensive damage to the MTL (particularly to the hippocampus). The standard neuropsychological model, in contrast, would hold that access to remote autobiographical episodic memories would be intact. This remains a topic of vigorous and contentious debate.

Reconsolidation

The concept of consolidation got even *more* complicated in 2000, when the phenomenon of reconsolidation was discovered in the context of a fear conditioning paradigm, a variant of Pavlovian conditioning in which an initially neutral stimulus (often a tone, or sometimes the novel experimental chamber in which the conditioning occurs [referred to as the "context"]) is paired with an aversive stimulus, often an electric shock delivered through the floor. It differs from Pavlovian conditioning in that a single trial is sufficient for the animal to learn the conditioned response, which is to freeze the next time it hears the tone (or is placed back into the chamber). Although we won't consider this in detail until *Chapter 18*, plasticity that is critical for the consolidation of a conditioned fear memory has been localized to the amygdala. Evidence for this is that infusion of a protein synthesis inhibitor into the amygdala blocks the expression of the conditioned response when the animal is presented with the tone a day later. (Without the protein synthesis inhibitor, control animals freeze when they again hear the tone, and the duration of freezing is a dependent measure of how strong the memory is.)

Evidence for a reconsolidation process was produced by Karim Nader and colleagues in the laboratory of neurobiologist Joseph LeDoux when, instead of administering the protein synthesis inhibitor at the time of the learning episode, they administered it when the conditioned stimulus was re-presented, i.e., at the time of memory retrieval. The finding was that administering the protein synthesis inhibitor at the time of retrieval trial 1 did not disrupt the expression of the memory on retrieval trial 1; however, it did disrupt the expression of the memory on retrieval trial 2. This finding was controversial at first, but has since been replicated several times, in several species (including humans), and is now widely accepted. Although the mechanisms underlying reconsolidation aren't fully understood, the implication is that the act of retrieving a memory puts it into a labile state that renders it vulnerable to disruption. (Here, it might be helpful to think of, e.g., Lisman's idea for how the activation of one item in a sequence can then trigger the activation of the subsequent items.) Part of the puzzle is that the LTP underlying the memory has already been through the (or, at least, a) structural phase. Is it reversed? Or somehow overwritten? (Hang tight. One response to these questions will be preferred in Chapter 12 section "Reconsolidation" or "Reencoding"?)

Even though the neurobiological and computational details of how and why reconsolidation happens remain uncertain, the finding of Nader, Schafe, and Le Doux (2000) very quickly initiated considerable excitement about potential clinical applications. As Schwabe et al. (2012) note: "Emotionally arousing experiences are usually better remembered than neutral experiences. Although generally adaptive to survival, this emotional memory enhancement may contribute to anxiety disorders, such as posttraumatic stress disorder (PTSD)" (p. 380). Therefore, could one leverage the phenomenon of reconsolidation to develop a "pill to forget" for treating victims of trauma? The study summarized in *Figure 11.9* represents an initial step in this direction by demonstrating that a pharmacological intervention delivered at the time of retrieval of an emotional memory can, in effect, "reduce its emotionality" for subsequent retrieval episodes.

To Consolidate

Memory is of central importance to human consciousness and cognition. At the level of consciousness, it creates our sense of identity, and provides the soothing, subjectively continuous internal narrative that enables us to go about our business without constantly stopping to ask "Why am I here? What was I doing 5 minutes ago?" At an unconscious level, it shapes our habits, our proclivities and dispositions, and makes us who we are. Thus, it's not surprising that different facets of memory are the focus of such intense research activity. Nor should it be a surprise when, if a large number of really smart, really driven people are working on a similar problem, multiple answers will emerge, not all of them mutually compatible.

The next three chapters will build on the themes that we have introduced here. Not all of the controversies will be resolved, but the reader will be equipped with a good sense of what are some of the most interesting, most important problems and the ways that some of the leading scientists in the field are addressing them.

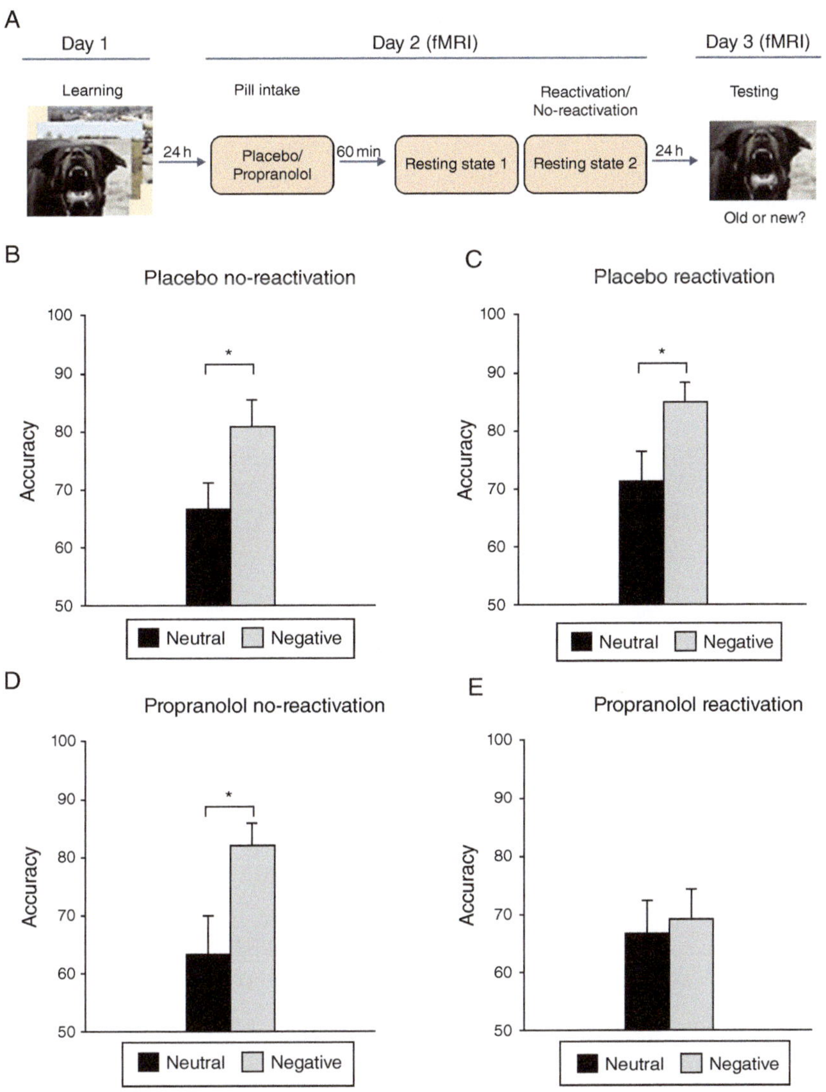

FIGURE 11.9 Weakening a consolidated emotional memory by disrupting reconsolidation. On Day 1, subjects viewed 25 emotionally negative and 25 emotionally neutral images. On Day 2, they either did or didn't receive a β-adrenergic antagonist ("beta-blocker") ("Propranolol"/"Placebo") and either were or weren't tested on their memory for the images ("Reactivation"/"No-reactivation"). (fMRI data were also acquired, but are not considered here.) On Day 3, memory for the images was tested in each of the four groups, and memory for emotionally negative images was impaired only in the "Propranolol reactivation" group. (In *Chapter 18*, we'll consider the role of norepinephrine in emotional processing.)

Source: Reproduced from Schwabe et al. (2012) / with permission of Elsevier.

End-of-Chapter Questions

1. What aspect of the global amnesic syndrome suggests a distinction between LTM encoding and LTM retrieval? Why?

2. What aspect of the global amnesic syndrome suggests a process of consolidation in LTM formation?

3. What is it like to have profound anterograde amnesia?

4. Summarize the steps of LTP induction.

5. What principles are emphasized in the Complementary Learning Systems model of McClelland, McNaughton, and O'Reilly (1995)?

6. Explain the phenomenon of phase precession in place cells. How might such a scheme also support the representation of temporal order in episodic LTM?

7. What are sharp-wave ripples, and what is their relevance for understanding consolidation of LTM?

8. Summarize the standard anatomical model of the "MTL memory system." What have been two challenges to this model?

9. What does it mean to say that the hippocampus and medial prefrontal cortex may support the computation and representation of successor representations? From what theoretical tradition does the idea of the successor representation derive, and can this perspective be related to "more traditional" models of hippocampal function?

10. What is the principal difference between the standard model of consolidation and that of the multiple trace theory? What different predictions do the two make with respect to dependence on the hippocampus of autobiographical episodic memories?

11. Summarize the evidence for a process of reconsolidation.

References

Bliss, Timothy V. P., and Terje Lømo. 1973. "Long-Lasting Potentiation of Synaptic Transmission in the Dentate Area of the Anesthetized Rabbit Following Stimulation of the Perforant Path." *Journal of Physiology* 232 (2): 331–341. http://jp.physoc.org/content/232/2/331.full.pdf+html.

Brunec, I. K., and I. Mommenejad. 2022. "Predictive Representations in Hippocampal and Prefrontal Hierarchies." *Journal of Neuroscience 42*: 299–312. doi: 10.1523/JNEUROSCI.1327-21.2021.

Buszáki, György. 2006. *Rhythms of the Brain*. Oxford: Oxford University Press.

Buszáki, György. 2015. "Hippocampal Sharp-Wave Ripple: A Cognitive Biomarker for Episodic Memory and Planning." *Hippocampus* 25: 1073–1188.

Corkin, Suzanne, David G. Amaral, R. Gilberto González, Keith A. Johnson, and Bradley T. Hyman. 1997. "H. M.'s Medial Temporal Lobe Lesion: Findings from Magnetic Resonance Imaging." *Journal of Neuroscience* 17 (10): 3964–3979. http://www.jneurosci.org/content/17/10/3964.full.pdf+html.

Dragoi, George. 2013. "Internal Operations in the Hippocampus: Single Cell and Ensemble Temporal Coding." *Frontiers in Systems Neuroscience* 7. doi: 10.3389/fnsys.2013.00046.

Hilts, Philip J. 1996. *Memory's Ghost: The Nature of Memory and the Strange Tale of Mr. M.* Touchstone edition. New York: Simon and Schuster. First published 1995.

Lisman, John E. 1999. "Relating Hippocampal Circuitry to Function: Recall of Memory Sequences by Reciprocal Dentate–CA3 Interactions." *Neuron* 22: 233–242.

Lømo, Terje. 2003. "The Discovery of Long-Term Potentiation." *Philosophical Transactions of The Royal Society of London, Series B: Biological Sciences* 358 (1432): 617–620. doi: 10.1098/rstb.2002.1226.

McClelland, James L., Bruce L. McNaughton, and Randall C. O'Reilly. 1995. "Why There Are Complementary Learning Systems in the Hippocampus and Neocortex: Insights from the Successes and Failures of Connectionist Models of Learning and Memory." *Psychological Review* 102 (3): 419–457. doi: 10.1037/0033-295X.102.3.419.

Meunier, Martine, Jocelyne Bachevalier, Mortimer Mishkin, and Elizabeth A. Murray. 1993. "Effecs on Visual Recognition of Combined and Separate Ablations of the Entorhinal and Perirhinal Cortex in Rhesus Monkeys." *Journal of Neuroscience 13*: 5418–5432.

Momennejad, Ida, and Marc W. Howard. 2018. "Predicting the Future with Multiscale Successor Representations." *bioRxiv*. doi: 10.1101/449470.

Morris, Richard G. M., E. Anderson, Gary S. Lynch, and Michael Baudry. 1986. "Selective Impairment of Learning and Blockade of Long-Term Potentiation by an N-Methyl-D-Aspartate Receptor Antagonist, AP5." *Nature* 319 (6056): 774–776. doi: 10.1038/319774a0.

Murray, Elisabeth A., and Mortimer Mishkin. 1998. "Object Recognition and Location Memory in Monkeys with Excitotoxic Lesions of the Amygdala and Hippocampus." *Journal of Neuroscience 18* (16): 6568–6582. doi: 10.1523/JNEUROSCI.18-16-06568.1998.

Murray, Elisabeth A., Timothy J. Bussey, and Lisa M. Saksida. 2007. "Visual Perception and Memory: A New View of Medial Temporal Lobe Function in Primates and Rodents." *Annual Review of Neuroscience* 30: 99–122. doi: 10.1146/annurev.neuro.29.051605.113046.

Nadel, Lynn, Siobhan Hoscheidt, and Lee R. Ryan. 2013. "Spatial Cognition and the Hippocampus: The Anterior-Posterior Axis." *Journal of Cognitive Neuroscience* 25 (1): 22–28. doi: 10.1162/jocn_a_00313.

Nader, Karim, Glenn E. Schafe, and Joseph E. Le Doux. 2000. "Fear Memories Require Protein Synthesis in the Amygdala for Reconsolidation After Retrieval." *Nature* 406 (6797): 722–726. doi: 10.1038/35021052.

O'Keefe, John, and Lynn Nadel. 1978. *The Hippocampus as a Cognitive Map*. Oxford: Oxford University Press.

Schwabe, Lars, Karim Nader, Oliver T. Wolf, Thomas Beaudry, and Jens C. Pruessner. 2012. "Neural Signature of Reconsolidation Impairments by Propranolol in Humans." *Biological Psychiatry* 71 (4): 380–386. doi: 10.1016/j.biopsych.2011.10.028.

Scoville, William Beecher, and Brenda Milner. 1957. "Loss of Recent Memory After Bilateral Hippocampal Lesions." *Journal of Neurology, Neurosurgery, and Psychiatry* 20 (1): 11–21. doi: 10.1136/jnnp.20.1.11.

Squire, Larry R., and Stuart Zola-Morgan. 1991. "The Medial Temporal Lobe Memory System." *Science* 253 (5026): 1380–1386. doi: 10.1126/science.1896849.

Other Sources Used

Baddeley, Alan D., and Elisabeth K. Warrington. 1970. "Amnesia and the Distinction between Long- and Short-Term Memory." *Journal of Verbal Learning and Verbal Behavior* 9 (2): 176–189. doi: 10.1016/S0022-5371(70)80048-2.

Brunec, Iva K., Buddhika Bellana, Jason D. Ozubko, Vincent Man, Jessica Robin, Zhong-Xu Liu, . . . Morris Moscovitch. 2018. "Multiple Scales of Representation along the Hippocampal Anteroposterior Axis in Humans." *Curr Biology 28* (13): 2129–2135.e2126. doi: 10.1016/j.cub.2018.05.016.

Cooper, Jack R., Floyd E. Bloom, and Robert H. Roth. 1991. *The Biochemical Basis of Neuropharmacology*, 6th ed. New York: Oxford University Press.

Corkin, Suzanne. 2013. *Permanent Present Tense: The Unforgettable Life of the Amnesic Patient, H.M.* New York: Basic Books.

Desimone, Robert, and Charles G. Gross. 1979. "Visual Areas in the Temporal Cortex of the Macaque." *Brain Research 178*: 363–380.

Eichenbaum, Howard, and Neal J. Cohen. 2001. *From Conditioning to Conscious Recollection: Memory Systems of the Brain*, Oxford Psychology Series. Oxford: Oxford University Press.

Fuller, Leah, and Michael E. Dailey. 2007. "Preparation of Rodent Hippocampal Slice Cultures." *Cold Spring Harbor Protocols* 2007 (10): 4848–4852. doi: 10.1101/pdb.prot4848.

Gabrieli, John D. E., M. M. Keane, Ben Z. Stanger, Margaret Kjelgaard, Suzanne Corkin, and John H. Growdon. 1994. "Dissociations among Structural-Perceptual, Lexical-Semantic, and Event-Fact Memory in Amnesia, Alzheimer's, and Normal Subjects." *Cortex* 30: 75–103.

Jarrard, Leonard E. 1989. "On the Use of Ibotenic Acid to Lesion Selectively Different Components of the Hippocampal Formation." *Journal of Neuroscience Methods* 29 (3): 251–259. doi: 10.1016/0165-0270(89)90149-0.

Milner, Brenda, Suzanne Corkin, and H.-L. Teuber. 1968. "Further Analysis of the Hippocampal Amnesic Syndrome: 14-Year Follow-Up Study of H. M." *Neuropsychologia* 6 (3): 215–234. doi: 10.1016/0028-3932(68)90021-3.

Nadel, Lynn, and Morris Moscovitch. 1997. "Memory Consolidation, Retrograde Amnesia and the Hippocampal Complex." *Current Opinion in Neurobiology* 7 (2): 217–227. doi: 10.1016/S0959-4388(97)80010-4.

Nader, Karim, and Oliver Hardt. 2009. "A Single Standard for Memory: The Case for Reconsolidation." *Nature Reviews Neuroscience* 10 (3): 224–234. doi: 10.1038/nrn2590.

Pearce, John M. S. 2001. "Ammon's Horn and the Hippocampus." *Journal of Neurology, Neurosurgery, and Psychiatry* 71 (3): 351. doi: 10.1136/jnnp.71.3.351.

Schwabe, Lars, Karim Nader, and Jens C. Pruessner. 2013. "β-Adrenergic Blockade during Reactivation Reduces the Subjective Feeling of Remembering Associated with Emotional Episodic Memories." *Biological Psychology* 92 (2): 227–232. doi: 10.1016/j.biopsycho.2012.10.003.

Squire, Larry R. 1992. "Memory and the Hippocampus: A Synthesis from Findings with Rate, Monkeys, and Humans." *Psychological Review* 99 (2): 195–231. doi: 10.1037/0033-295X.99.3.582.

Squire, Larry R., Craig E. L. Stark, and Robert E. Clark. 2004. "The Medial Temporal Lobe." *Annual Review of Neuroscience* 27: 279–306. doi: 10.1146/annurev.neuro.27.070203.144130.

Further Reading

Clelland, Claire D., M. Choi, C. Romberg, G. D. Clemenson Jr, P. Alexandra Fragniere, and Tyers . . . Tim J. Bussey. 2009. "A Functional Role for Adult Hippocampal Neurogenesis in Spatial Pattern Separation." *Science* 325 (5937): 210–213. doi: 10.1126/science.1173215.

The precise role(s) of neurogenesis – the "birth" of new neurons and their migration into the dentate gyrus – in LTM are still being worked out, but this paper captures much of the excitement and potential importance of the phenomenon.

Corkin, Suzanne. 2002. "What's New with the Amnesic Patient H. M.?." *Nature Reviews Neuroscience* 3 (2): 153–160. doi: 10.1038/nrn726.

From a student of Brenda Milner who has studied H. M. intensively from the 1960s up through the final years of his life.

Corkin, Suzanne. 2013. *Permanent Present Tense: The Unforgettable Life of the Amnesic Patient, H.* M. New York: Basic Books.

A book that with equal parts compassion and scientific acuity, alternates between the biography and tragedy of Henry Molaison, and the manifold discoveries about human memory that have resulted from research with this remarkable patient.

Dębiec, Jacek. 2012. "Memory Reconsolidation Processes and Posttraumatic Stress Disorder: Promises and Challenges of Translational Research." *Biological Psychiatry* 71 (4): 284–285. doi: 10.1016/j.biopsych.2011.12.009.

Commentary addressing the implications of the study presented in Research Spotlight 10.1.

Eichenbaum, Howard. 2013. "What H. M. Taught Us." *Journal of Cognitive Neuroscience* 25 (1): 14–21. doi: 10.1162/jocn_a_00285.

Review from a leading expert on LTM and the functions of the hippocampus.

Frankland, Paul W., Stefan Köhler, and Sheena A. Josselyn. 2013. "Hippocampal Neurogenesis and Forgetting." *Trends in Neuroscience* 36 (9): 497–503. doi: 10.1016/j.tins.2013.05.002.

MTL neurogenesis is highest early in life, and this review suggests that this may account for the phenomenon of "infantile amnesia" – our inability to remember events from the first few years of our lives.

Gaffan, David. 2002. "Against Memory Systems." *Philosophical Transactions of the Royal Society of London, Series B: Biological Sciences* 357 (1424): 1111–1121. doi: 10.1098/rstb.2002.1110.

A provocative set of arguments for a radical rethinking of LTM. I don't agree with all of it, but nonetheless always assign it to my grad seminar on the cognitive neuroscience of memory.

Luu, Paul, Orriana C. Sill, Lulu Gao, Suzanna Becker, Jan Martin Wojtowicz, and David M. Smith. 2012. "The Role of Adult Hippocampal Neurogenesis in Reducing Interference." *Behavioral Neuroscience* 126 (3): 381–391. doi: 10.1037/a0028252.

Whereas Frankland, Köhler, and Josselyn (2013) propose that MTL neurogenesis may be responsible for retroactive interference (in the very young), this paper presents a scheme whereby MTL neurogenesis in the adult may aid in the individuation of distinct episodic memories.

Murray, E. A., S. P. Wise, M. L. K. Baldwin, and K. S. Graham. 2020. *The Evolutionary Road to Human Memory*. New York: Oxford University Press.

A highly readable and authoritative book, written for a general audience, that explains all the mnemonic phenomena that we've covered in this chapter, and more, from the perspective of the authors' insightful and provocative evolutionary perspective.

Nader, Karim, and Oliver Hardt. 2009. "A Single Standard for Memory: The Case for Reconsolidation." *Nature Reviews Neuroscience* 10 (3): 224–234. doi: 10.1038/nrn2590.

A vigorous defense of the phenomenon of reconsolidation that, in the process, provides a nice review of the principles of consolidation and reconsolidation in fear conditioning.

Oudiette, Delphine, and Ken A. Paller. 2013. "Upgrading the Sleeping Brain with Targeted Memory Reactivation." *Trends in Cognitive Sciences* 17 (3): 142–149. doi: 10.1016/j.tics.2013.01.006.

A role for sleep in memory consolidation is revealed when LTM for specific items can be improved when auditory or olfactory stimuli that are associated with those items are presented to subjects while they sleep.

Postle, B. R. 2016. "The Hippocampus, Memory, and Consciousness." In *Neurology of Consciousness*, edited by S. Laureys, O. Gosseries, and G. Tononi (pp. 349–363), 2nd ed. Amsterdam: Elsevier.

A review chapter by Yours Truly that goes into more detail about the pathophysiology of amnesia and the cognitive neuroscience of long-term memory.

Declarative Long-Term Memory

KEY THEMES

- Early neuroimaging studies of LTM encoding were difficult to design, and their results were difficult to interpret, due to uncertainty over how to engage the hippocampus differentially in different conditions, and how to unconfound effects of novelty from effects of encoding per se.
- fMRI studies of the subsequent memory effect, made possible by the development of "fast" event-related techniques, have identified PFC and inferior temporal regions associated with level-of-processing manipulations as being important for successful memory encoding.
- Another important innovation in neuroimaging data analysis, particularly for studies of LTM, is methods for measuring functional connectivity between brain regions.
- Accurate interpretation of impaired vs. spared performance of anterograde amnesic patients on tests of LTM requires an understanding of the level of awareness of the learning episode that is required by the task.
- MVPA of fMRI data can be used to predict the category of information that a subject is about to recall, a feat that wouldn't be possible if contextual reinstatement was not a principle underlying recall from LTM.
- Models from cognitive psychology that posit a distinction between processes of familiarity and recollection in memory retrieval have received considerable support from cognitive neuroscience research, with the latter being explicitly linked to the hippocampus.
- Familiarity may result from a rotation of the encoding axes that represent objects (including faces) in the ventral visual stream, a process that can also be characterized as a separation of manifolds that represent unfamiliar vs. familiar exemplars from a category, such that subsequent memory-related processing of the familiar stimulus is less likely to interfere with ongoing perceptual processing of other elements in the scene that are not familiar.
- Our ongoing experience of daily life may be accompanied by a constantly ongoing process of retrieving memories whose retrieval is cued by what we are experiencing, and that serve as predictions that, when violated, generate prediction errors that are the basis of event boundaries that segment newly created memories.
- Another consequence of LTM-triggered prediction errors is that they may shift the hippocampus from a "preserve and reinforce" mode to an "update" mode, the latter of which can, somewhat paradoxically, result in the creation of false memories.
- The phenomenon of LTM-triggered prediction errors also provides an alternative account of "reconsolidation," one that relies on a multiple-trace account.

Companion Website: www.wiley.com/go/postle/cognitiveneuroscience3e

CONTENTS

The *Cognitive* Neuroscience of LTM

The previous chapter emphasized the neurobiology of memory. With that groundwork in place, this chapter will focus much more on cognitive-level questions, in many instances looking at how longstanding cognitive theories (e.g., levels of processing and contextual reinstatement) have been studied by cognitive neuroscientists.

Encoding

Neuroimaging the Hippocampus

Neuroimaging studies of LTM from the 1980s and 1990s were particularly challenging to design, and their results challenging to interpret, due to the constraints imposed by block designs. To understand why, let's think back to how the Washington University group went about studying the visual perception of words (*Figure 4.20*). They presented words, serially, for a block of 40 seconds and compared that with a 40-second block of fixation. Although one might (and some did) object that there was insufficient experimental control to support strong interpretations of what cognitive functions were engaged during the word blocks, there was little ambiguity about the control task: staring at an unchanging fixation point would produce minimal activation of the visual system relative to 1 Hz presentation of words. (And, indeed, the *words – fixation* subtraction revealed considerably higher levels of activity in ventral occipitotemporal cortex for the former than the latter.) It's not clear, however, that the same approach would work if one sought to "image the hippocampus," primarily because it's believed that this structure is "always working" – always encoding whatever is being experienced in the moment. For example, had subjects in the Petersen, Fox, Posner, Mintun, and Raichle (1988) study (see Figure 4.20) been debriefed an hour, or a day, after their scanning session, they would surely have remembered having endured the blocks of fixation as well as the blocks of word viewing. Thus, there's no reason to posit that their hippocampi would be any less (or more) active during the control than the experimental task. Would they have been differently active during the two conditions? Sure, but MVPA (and, therefore, any hope of detecting such a difference with neuroimaging) was more than a decade away.

A variant of this problem will also crop up in the section of this chapter that focuses on retrieval from LTM, and is one that was foreshadowed in the previous chapter's section on reconsolidation: even the act of retrieving information from LTM will be encoded by the hippocampus. If the darned thing never shuts off, how can one measure its function with a subtractive methodology?

Novelty-Driven "Encoding" The reasoning laid out in the previous section was invoked often in the early to mid-1990s, when a series of neuroimaging studies of encoding into LTM failed to show evidence for differential hippocampal activity during encoding vs. control blocks. One way that experimenters tried to address this problem was to reason, in effect, that *if we can't devise a condition when it is not active, perhaps we can at least devise one when it is* less *active*. To achieve this, two groups, one led by (University of Toronto) cognitive psychologist Endel Tulving and another by Chantal Stern and colleagues at the Massachusetts General Hospital (MGH) NMR Center, explicitly controlled novelty. Tulving, Markowitsch, Kapur, Habib, and Houle (1994) pre-exposed subjects to 40 color photos of complex scenes the day prior to the scanning session, and then scanned subjects on blocks that either featured the presentation of the "old" items from the day before or 40 new items that they had never seen before. Although one can imagine that the "old" condition might have generated a considerable amount of memory retrieval, what Tulving et al. (1994) emphasized was that the "new" items had greater novelty, and thus were likely to emphasize encoding processes. Their findings included greater "new" than "old" activity in the hippocampus and parahippocampal gyrus.

Stern et al. (1996) also presented 40 novel images during the experimental block, and instructed subjects to encode them for a subsequent memory test. During the control block, they presented a single image (also novel) during the entire duration of the block. Similar to the Tulving et al. (1994) findings, this study also found greater activity for the varying-identity stimuli than the repeated-identity stimulus in the posterior hippocampus and parahippocampal gyrus, as well as more posteriorly in the lingual and fusiform gyri.

In retrospect, knowing what we do now about, for example, category-preferential responses in the ventral occipitotemporal cortex (*Chapter 10*), we can surmise that at least some of the activity reported in these studies related more to visual processing than to memory encoding per se. Additionally, both explicitly confounded stimulus novelty with the mental process that they sought to engage. Thus, even at the time that these studies appeared, more impactful than their conceptual contributions was the fact that they, and a handful of other contemporaneous studies, succeeded in demonstrating differential levels of activation of the elusive hippocampus.[1] This had the effect of accelerating the pace at which the memory research community worked to develop better methods that would produce more definitive results. Indeed, two years after the Stern et al. (1996) study, two groups simultaneously published breakthrough studies of memory encoding using then-novel event-related techniques.

Subsequent Memory Effects in the PFC and in MTL Neocortex Since the early 1980s, ERP researchers had employed the following procedure to study encoding into LTM: (1) present subjects with several items, one at a time; (2) create a series of ERPs time locked to stimulus onset; (3) after the EEG recording session, administer a surprise memory test for the items that had been presented during the EEG session; (4) selectively average the ERPs according to whether each item was or was not remembered in the subsequent memory test. Any differences between the two resultant ERPs would identify a signal associated with successful vs. unsuccessful memory encoding. The logic of this approach has much to recommend it. In particular, unlike the neuroimaging studies reviewed in the previous section, subjects are performing the same task on every trial, and so this avoids the problem of whether differences in physiological signal are due to the memory-encoding processes of interest or some other factor (novelty per se, boredom, level of vigilance, etc.). The problem with the effect in the ERP literature was that it was capricious – not every lab could produce it, and even within a lab, the effect would come and go, depending on factors such as whether the subsequent memory test was a test of free recall, cued recall, or recognition. The latter was particularly puzzling because the ERP signal, of course, was collected prior to the time that the subsequent memory test would be administered. If subjects didn't even know that there was going to be a memory test, how could it be that the format of that future test would influence encoding-related activity? (*Hey, that'd be a good extra-credit question*!) The result of these problems was that interest in this approach had largely fizzled out. Until, that is, those event-related fMRI people came along . . .

In 1998, two fMRI studies of the subsequent memory effect were published, back-to-back in the journal *Science*, and the principal results of one of them, from Wagner et al. (1998), are presented in *Figure 12.1*. To fully understand it, we'll need to review some of the details. The study was designed within the levels-of-processing framework, the venerable finding from cognitive psychology that a stimulus is better remembered when one thinks about its meaning (i.e., when one processes it at a "deep" level) than when one thinks about a superficial property (i.e., processes it at a "shallow" level). The first experiment did this explicitly, presenting individual words to subjects and instructing them to either judge whether each corresponded to a living or a nonliving thing (deep processing) or, during alternate blocks, whether each was printed in upper- or lower-case type (shallow processing). A surprise memory test after the fMRI scanning session confirmed that the manipulation worked, with subjects subsequently recognizing 85% of deeply processed items vs. 47% of shallowly processed items. In the brain, regions showing greater activity on deep vs. shallow blocks included left inferior frontal gyrus (IFG) of the ventrolateral PFC and left parahippocampal and fusiform gyri on the ventral surface of the temporal lobe. The authors knew that these results wouldn't lend themselves to a straightforward interpretation because level of memory performance was confounded with cognitive process (e.g., was the effect in left IFG due to more effective encoding, per se, or to thinking about animacy vs. typography?) What they *were* useful for, however, was setting up predictions for the subsequent memory study: finding regions of overlap with the levels-of-processing results would be consistent with the idea that item-to-item fluctuations in signal intensity in these regions reflect, at least in part, moment-to-moment fluctuations in how we think about information, and these fluctuations have consequences for what we do and do not effectively encode it into LTM.

For the subsequent memory study, fMRI data were acquired while subjects viewed a total of 480 words across 6 blocks. Each block included 40 abstract words, 40 concrete words, and

[1] The imprecise phrase that was sometimes overheard was "getting the hippocampus to 'light up,'" but I hope that, at this point, reading this makes the reader cringe as much when reading it as it did the writer when typing it out.

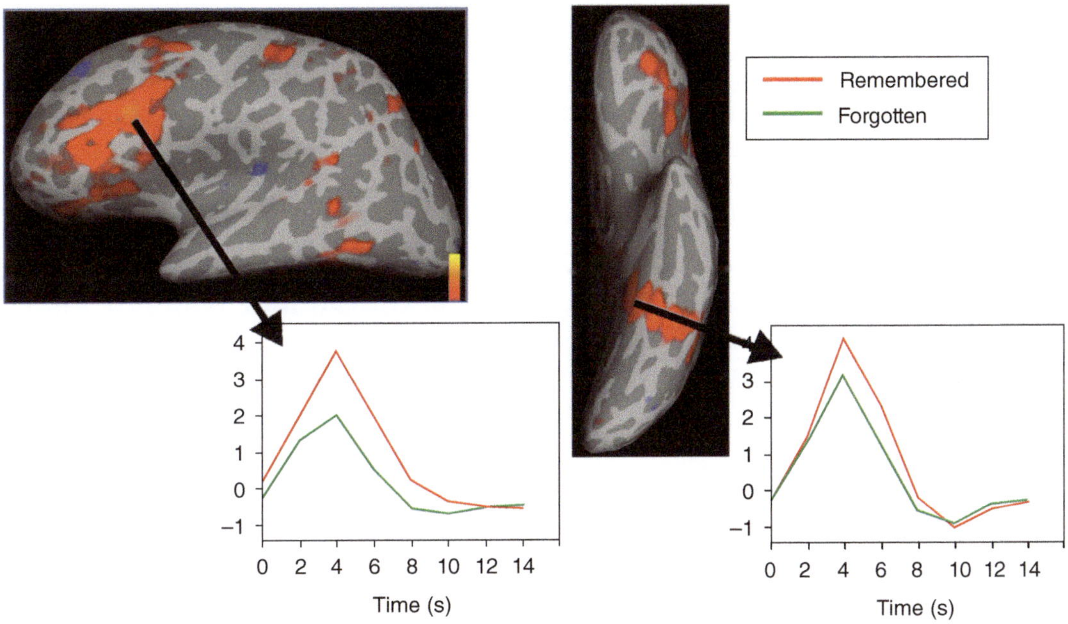

FIGURE 12.1 The subsequent memory effect reported in Wagner et al. (1998). Statistical maps, superimposed on two views of an inflated left hemisphere, show regions exhibiting higher activity for words that were later recognized with high confidence ("remembered") than for words that were later not recognized. Inset plots show the fMRI-evoked responses, estimated from the event-related analysis, from posterior IFG (left) and a region spanning parahippocampal and fusiform gyri (right; responses plotted in arbitrary units of BOLD signal intensity).

Source: Reproduced from Paller et al. (2002) / with permission of Elsevier.

40 fixation events, presented in a randomly determined order for 2 seconds each. Additionally, because the order in which words would subsequently be remembered or forgotten was expected to be random, the authors used a "fast" event-related analysis of the kind outlined in section *Some considerations for experimental design, Chapter 4.*

It is important to note that neither the Wagner et al. (1998) nor the Brewer, Zhao, Desmond, Glover, and Gabrieli (1998) study identified a "memory network," per se. Wagner et al. (1998), in their study of memory for words, identified exclusively left-hemisphere regions. Brewer et al. (1998), although using a similar subsequent-memory design and analysis, used photos of indoor and outdoor scenes, and the regions in which they found greater activity for high-confidence hits vs. misses were the parahippocampal gyrus, bilaterally, and right dorsolateral PFC. Thus, what both studies found was that item-by-item level of activity in regions that are associated with stimulus perception and processing is an important determinant of whether or not that information will later be remembered. (We'll see in *Chapter 19* that language processing is heavily biased to the left hemisphere. And we've already seen that the PHG is important for representing information about "places.") The fact that these studies both identified the magnitude of activity in their respective networks to be an important factor in subsequent memory retrieval is consistent with the idea that the strength of attentional focus may be an important determinant in LTM encoding. They are also consistent with the idea, recurring throughout this book, that ongoing fluctuations in brain state can influence the quality of cognition at any moment in time.

Incidental Encoding into LTM During a Short-Term Memory Task

Short-term memory (STM) will be the focus of *Chapter 14*, but one study of STM merits consideration here, for four reasons. First, it reinforces the idea that incidental encoding happens constantly, albeit with fluctuating efficacy, when we are awake, regardless of what behavior we're engaged in. (The didactic point being that this is true *even* when we are engaged in a task that is nominally testing something other than LTM.) The second reason for considering this study is because it illustrates the power of relating individual differences in physiological signal to individual differences in behavior. Third, it relates to a mechanism that we considered in the previous chapter's section on how the hippocampus might work. Finally, it provides an opportunity to introduce another important method for the analysis of functional neuroimaging data: task-based functional connectivity.

Signal Intensity-Based Analysis of the Subsequent Memory Effect Each trial in this study, from the laboratory of Charan Ranganath, entailed the subject viewing a sample line drawing of a novel 3-D shape (multifaceted, blocky objects), then, after a delay period varying from 7 to 13 seconds in length, indicating whether the memory probe did or did not match the sample. After the scanning session, subjects were given a surprise test of recognition of the items that had been presented as sample stimuli during the STM task, and the fMRI data were sorted as a function of subsequent LTM recognition. As illustrated in *Figure 12.2*, activity in the left dorsolateral PFC and the left hippocampus during the early delay period of the STM task predicted subsequent LTM for each item. This illustrates the point that, in principle, one should be able to find a subsequent memory effect for *any* kind of behavior, not just in experiments designed to assess LTM encoding.

Another notable feature of this study is illustrated in *Figure 12.2.B*. Here, the authors show that, on a subject-by-subject basis, the magnitude of each subject's neural subsequent-memory effect is related to his or her subsequent LTM for items that had been presented during the test of STM. Stated another way, the magnitude of the subsequent memory effect in left hippocampus predicted how well the subject would later remember items from the test of STM. Such a demonstration of **individual differences** can be powerful because it suggests that the mechanism under study might explain, at least in part, why some individuals remembered more items on the subsequent memory test and why others remembered fewer. Note that this is still (indeed, explicitly) a test of correlation, and therefore doesn't establish a causal role for, in this case, hippocampal activity. However, one could argue that such a relationship would be a necessary (though not sufficient) property of this system if it were causally related to LTM formation.

A Short-Term Memory Buffer to Bridge the Temporal Gap Between to-Be-Associated Events Recall from section *Episodic memory for sequences, Chapter 11*, that Lisman (1999) emphasized the fact that many events that we need to associate in LTM are separated in time by much longer than the ~100 ms activation time course of the CA3 NMDA receptor. Thus, although NMDA receptor dynamics could be the basis for associating location A with B and B with C as a rat runs along a path, many more than 100 ms would have elapsed, for example, between when the hapless Jerry dropped his candy and when the opportunistic monkey snatched it up. How might these two events be associated in LTM? It could be that the sustained hippocampal and prefrontal activity documented by Ranganath, Michael Cohen, and Craig Brozinsky (2005) serves this buffering function. (Interestingly, Hebb (1949; whose postulate was introduced in Chapter 5, section Hebbian plasticity) anticipated the need for such a temporary buffer, positing a "dual trace mechanism" by which transiently elevated, recurrent activity between the to-be-associated neural elements would persist until the second, structural trace [in his scheme, synaptic strengthening] would be established.)

Functional Connectivity-Based Analysis of the Subsequent Memory Effect The final reason for devoting so much space to the Ranganath et al. (2005) study is a separate analysis that was applied to this dataset, and published as a separate study by Ranganath, Aaron Heller, Cohen, Brozinsky, and Jesse Rissman (2005): a functional connectivity-based analysis of the subsequent memory effect. All of the neuroimaging studies that we have considered up to this point in this chapter used the mass-univariate approach,

FIGURE 12.2 Subsequent LTM effects in left dlPFC and left hippocampus during a test of visual STM.

Source: Ranganath et al., 2005 / MIT Press.

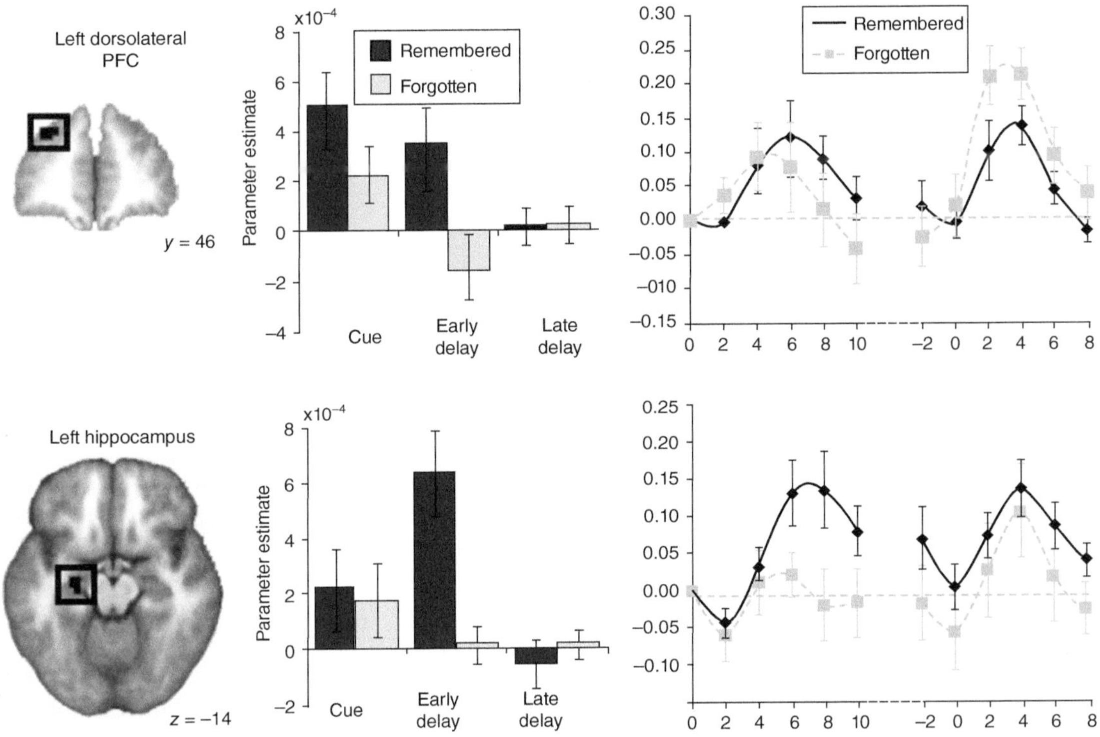

FIGURE 12.2.A Left-hand column: regions of left dlPFC (coronal view) and left hippocampus (axial view) showing the effect. Center column: bar graphs show magnitude of response during sample presentation ("Cue") and two portions of the delay period, expressed as parameter estimates from the GLM, as a function of whether they were subsequently remembered or forgotten on the surprise LTM test. Right-hand column: time series show activity (% signal change from baseline as a function of time), time locked to sample onset (first 0) and probe onset (second 0), also averaged as a function of subsequent LTM.

Source: Reproduced with permission from Ranganath et al. (2005) / MIT Press.

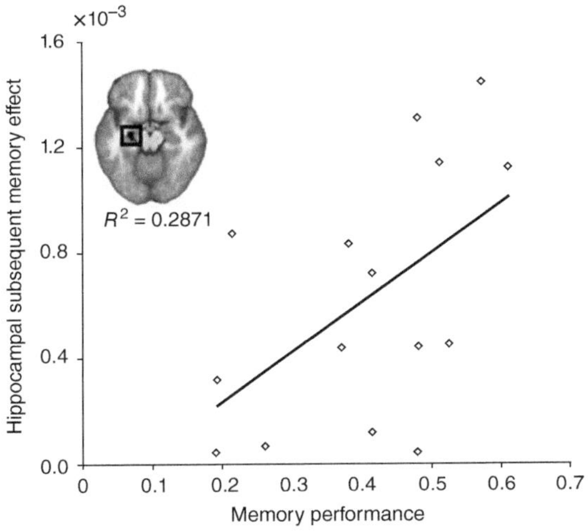

FIGURE 12.2.B Strength of early-delay hippocampal activity (vertical axis) predicts subsequent LTM performance.

Source: Reproduced with permission from Ranganath et al. (2005) / MIT Press.

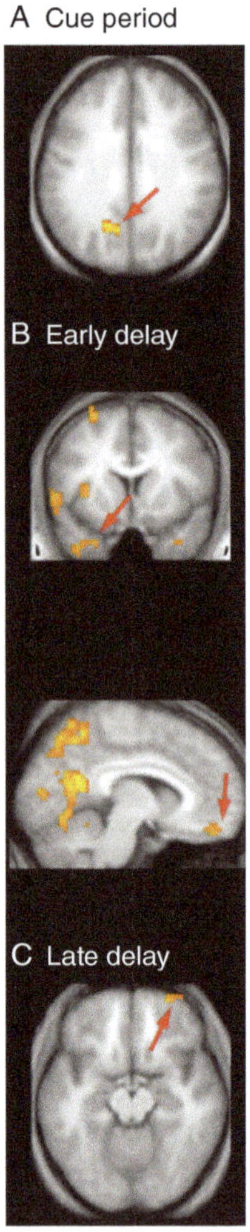

FIGURE 12.3 Seeded functional connectivity analysis, illustrating regions, by trial epoch, whose activity was more strongly correlated with the left hippocampus on trials presenting subsequently remembered vs. subsequently forgotten sample stimuli. **A.** The region correlated with fluctuations in left hippocampus activity during the stimulus presentation ("Cue") epoch of the trial. **B.** The regions correlated with fluctuations in left hippocampus during the early portion of the delay period. **C.** The region correlated with fluctuations in left hippocampus during the late portion of the delay period.

Source: Reproduced with permission from Ranganath et al. (2005) / John Wiley & Sons.

effectively identifying voxels in which greater signal intensity related to stronger memory encoding. Thus, none of them directly assayed the element that is fundamental to all contemporary models of LTM – the standard model, the multiple trace model, reconsolidation models, etc. – which is the *interaction* between MTL regions and other regions of cortex, in the encoding, consolidation, and retrieval of LTM.

The very basis of LTM is assumed to be the association of neural representations, many of them supported in anatomically distal regions. Nonetheless, the massively parallel univariate analyses used in each of the studies reviewed in the first half of this chapter could neither prove nor disprove this assumption. One way to demonstrate these associations is to measure functional connectivity (section *Functional connectivity, Chapter 4*).

Note in *Figure 12.2.A* that the authors used a "slow" event-related design (c.f., *Figure 9.4*) that partitioned variance in the fMRI signal into four epochs in the trial: cue, early delay, late delay, and probe (not shown). For the functional connectivity analysis, the loadings on each of these trial epoch-related covariates from the general linear model analysis (a.k.a. the parameter estimates, or the beta weights) were used as the data to determine which areas were functionally coupled, for each of these epochs, across trials.[2] Because the authors were specifically interested in whether there were areas for which functional connectivity with the hippocampus predicted stronger encoding into LTM, they implemented a "seeded analysis" by selecting the region of left hippocampus identified in *Figure 12.2.A*, extracting from it the early-delay parameter estimates from subsequently remembered trials, and correlating these against the early-delay parameter estimates from all other voxels in the brain. Then they did the same for subsequently forgotten trials. Finally, they determined the areas in which the correlation with the hippocampus was significantly greater on remembered than on forgotten trials. Their findings (*Figure 12.3*) provided direct evidence for something that most assumed, but that few, if any, had demonstrated directly: successful encoding was associated with enhanced functional connectivity between the hippocampus and many neocortical regions within and outside the MTL. Thus, they demonstrated that successful memory formation is associated with transient increases in cortico-hippocampal interaction.

Retrieval

In cognitive psychology, an influential framework for organizing different kinds of memory retrieval has been Tulving's (1985) distinction between *autonoetic*, *noetic*, and *anoetic* states of awareness with respect to memory retrieval. Derived from a Greek word appropriated by philosophers to refer to "mind" or "intellect," the term "noetic" in this context roughly corresponds to "knowing." Thus, autonoetic (or "self-knowing") awareness refers to an instance of memory retrieval that "is not only an objective account of what has happened or what has been seen or heard . . . [but also] necessarily involves the feeling that the present recollection is a reexperience of something that has happened before" (Wheeler, 2000, p. 597). (Note that the concept of "recollection" will take on a technical definition as the parameter in a model of recognition memory that we will consider in some detail further along in this chapter.) Noetic ("knowing") awareness can occur in two contexts. One is when retrieving information from semantic memory, for which there is not an associated "something that has happened before," the other is having a "feeling of familiarity" when encountering something or someone, but not being able to retrieve the episode in which this thing or person may have previously been encountered. ("Familiarity," too, will come up in the context of formal models of recognition memory.) Finally, the concept of anoetic ("not knowing") retrieval captures the fact that nondeclarative memory can be expressed without the individual's awareness that their performance is being influenced by a prior experience. In this section, we will consider each of these types of memory retrieval, beginning with how a misattribution of memory-test performance

[2] Note that although this procedure of task-based functional connectivity and RSFC (*Chapter 4*, section *Resting state functional correlations*) use similar analysis tools, the inferences that the two support are very different. The former addresses to how these areas interact during this particular epoch of this task, and the latter evidence for long-term statistical patterns of covariation. One analogy might be of characterizing a (task-related) state vs. a trait.

to noetic vs. anoetic memory retrieval led to erroneous conclusions about the bases of the amnesic syndrome.

Retrieval Without Awareness

In the modern era, the initial demonstrations of spared learning in amnesia were generated by Brenda Milner and her trainees and colleagues. First, in 1962, came the report of H.M.'s performance on a test of mirror tracing. This task required the subject to trace out the shape of a star on a piece of paper, while seated at an apparatus that required the paper to be viewed via its reflection off a mirror because a barrier occluded its direct observation. Although it sounds simple, it's maddeningly difficult at first, as one repeatedly watches one's own hand pushing the pencil in directions that seem to bear no relation to one's volition. Over time, however, one learns the novel sensorimotor mapping imposed by this apparatus (a kind of sensorimotor adaptation largely mediated by the cerebellum), and the number of errors declines with each trial. Impressively, H.M. also showed a steady decline in errors across trials, and, astoundingly, his first trial on day 2 of testing had many fewer errors than he had made at the beginning of day 1! By day 3, his performance on the task was near error-free, this despite the complete absence of any conscious memory of ever having performed the task. Soon thereafter, it was confirmed that H.M. demonstrated preserved motor learning on many motor performance-based tasks.

H.M. also demonstrated learning on what came to be called repetition priming tasks. For example, a set of 20 line drawings of common objects was modified to create four incomplete versions of each, with version 1 resembling a series of arbitrary dashes and marks on the page – very difficult to recognize – and each subsequent version containing progressively more details. Subjects were first shown version 1 of each image and encouraged to name it as quickly as possible. If they didn't get all 20 correct (and no individual did), they were then shown all the images from version 2, and so on, until they correctly named each drawing. H.M. correctly identified 6 from version 1, 12 from version 2, 19 from version 3, and all 20 from version 4. An hour later, he was retested on the same procedure, and this time he correctly identified 14 from version 1, 15 from version 2, and all 20 from version 3, overall making 48% fewer errors. Although this was a marked learning effect, it was characterized by Brenda Milner, Suzanne Corkin, and Hans-Lukas Teuber (1968) as "vestigial," and was smaller than that of age- and education-matched control subjects, whose improvement ranged from 52% to 93%. "All in all," they concluded, "we remain impressed with the central role of the learning impairment in these patients" (p. 233). Around this time, however, another group was interpreting very similar findings in a radically different way.

Logically, the phenomenon of relatively spared retrograde memory after bilateral damage to the MTL does not, alone, permit one to distinguish between a "consolidation block" (i.e., impaired encoding) account vs. a disordered storage or a disordered retrieval account of the consequence of MTL damage. This was illustrated most famously by neuropsychologist Elizabeth Warrington and neuroscientist Lawrence Weiskrantz, with a series of papers in the late 1960s and early 1970s. A 1974 study, for example, highlighted performance on two memory tests administered 10 minutes after the presentation of 16 words. Amnesic patients performed as well as control subjects on what the authors termed a "cued recall" task, in which the first three letters of a studied word (so-called "word stems") were presented and the subject was "required to identify the stimulus word" (p. 420). The patients were markedly impaired, however, on a test of Yes/No recognition. These results, together with evidence of disproportionate sensitivity to interference from items presented prior to or after the critical information, led Warrington and Weiskrantz (1974) to argue that MTL amnesia was better characterized by "altered control of information in storage" (p. 419), rather than a consolidation block. That is, they argued that new information "gets in there" (my quotes), but the amnesic syndrome makes it more difficult to access this information.

Subsequent research has established that the flaw in Warrington and Weiskrantz's reasoning was their failure to appreciate the distinction between noetic and anoetic states of memory retrieval. With word-stem completion, for example, it has subsequently been shown that the performance of amnesic subjects relative to control subjects depends on the precise phrasing of instructions about how to process the three-letter stems: when subjects are instructed to complete the three-letter stems to "the first word that comes to mind," and no reference is made to the prior study episode, amnesic patients often generate target words at a level that is comparable to that of control subjects. When, in contrast, they are instructed to use the three-letter stem as a cue with which to retrieve an item from the studied list, amnesic patients are typically impaired. The former procedure, which more closely resembles that used by Warrington and Weiskrantz (1974), has come to be known as word-stem completion *priming*, the latter as word-stem *cued recall*. Thus, the intact performance of amnesic patients in the Warrington and Weiskrantz (1974) study has come to be reinterpreted as an early demonstration of intact performance by amnesic subjects on a priming task, a phenomenon that falls under the rubric of *nondeclarative memory* (see Squire, 2006, *Further Reading*).

The term "priming" is a metaphor referring to priming a pump – prefilling the pipe that runs from the reservoir to the spout, such that when subsequently turned on (or activated via its handle), it will start producing fluid more quickly than it would have had it not been primed. With the psychological phenomenon of repetition priming, for example, the initial visual presentation of a stimulus makes it easier for the visual system to process that stimulus on subsequent repeat presentations. This comes about as a result of plasticity in the cortical systems that process these stimuli, regardless of whether or not there is an intact MTL to make a record of this processing that can later be explicitly recalled.

Documenting Contextual Reinstatement in the Brain

"Our results ground Tulving's speculations about mental time travel in neural fact" (Polyn, Natu, Cohen, and Norman, 2005, p. 1966).

Mic drop.

The study to which we now turn speaks directly to the neural instantiation of autonoetic retrieval. It was motivated by the idea from cognitive psychology that the British psychologist Sir Frederick Bartlett (1886–1969) had articulated in 1932, and that Tulving had codified in 1973 as "contextual reinstatement": when asked to recall a particular memory, people first activate knowledge about the general properties of the event in question, and then use this general knowledge to constrain the search for the memory of the target event. To assess the neurobiological plausibility of this "speculation," Sean Polyn, his then-graduate mentor Kenneth Norman (himself a mentee of Schacter and O'Reilly), and their colleagues devised an innovative application of multivariate pattern analysis (MVPA). The resultant publication (Polyn et al., 2005) was one among a handful of seminal publications, all published within a year or so of each other, that brought to the attention of the broader cognitive neuroscience community just how powerful this technique could be.

The Dynamics of Multivariate State Changes Underlying Behavior The experiment of Polyn et al. (2005) proceeded in three phases. The first was the study phase, during which subjects were scanned while viewing 90 stimuli, 30 drawn from each of three categories: famous people, famous locations, and common household objects. This was an incidental encoding task in that, for each stimulus, subjects were requested to indicate (a) how much they liked the famous person; (b) how much they would like to travel to the famous location; or (c) how often they use the common object. ("*But wait*," you ask, "*I thought this section was about memory retrieval. So why this study in which they scan during encoding?*" "*A perceptive question,*" I respond, "*we'll see why in a moment.*")

The second phase of the experiment was to train a neural network pattern classifier to discriminate brain activity from each of the three categories. The process of training the classifier was not different, in principle, from how Rogers, Hodges, Lambon Ralph, and Patterson (2003; section *A PDP model of picture naming, Chapter 3*) trained their PDP model to recognize verbal and visual objects: they presented it with the vector of signal intensity values produced by a given stimulus item, evaluated the network's guess as to which category the stimulus belonged to, and, when appropriate, propagated an error signal through the network that adjusted its weights such that it would be more likely to correctly classify that pattern of signal intensity values in the future. Once the classifier was fully "trained up," it could be fed the data from phase 3.

Phase 3 was a free recall session, performed in the scanner, in which subjects were simply instructed to recall as many items from the study phase as possible, by speaking into an MR-compatible microphone. Data from one subject are shown in *Figure 12.4*, and the first thing you may notice is that items were recalled in clusters: first, the subject recalled ~8 locations; then ~6 celebrities ("faces"); then ~6 objects; and so on. This kind of clustering in recall has been known to psychologists for decades and, indeed, is one of the behavioral phenomena consistent with a contextual reinstatement mechanism. What's really amazing about this figure is the relation that it reveals between this distinctive pattern of free recall performance and the concurrent fluctuations in neural activity: just prior to each "recall cluster," one can see a reconfiguration of brain activity into the pattern corresponding to that cluster's category! That is, we see the "neural *context*" associated with thinking about, let's say, famous locales, getting *reinstated* in the subject's brain just before they come out with "Taj Mahal . . . Eiffel Tower . . . Machu Pichu." Thus, an important component of autonoetic awareness in retrieval is the reconfiguration of brain activity into the state that it was in when encoding the to-be-remembered information.

Implications for "Mind Reading" . . . Well, "Brain Reading" Aside from what it tells us about memory retrieval, the Polyn et al. (2005) study garnered considerable excitement because it demonstrated a primitive form of "brain reading." Particularly intriguing was that, unlike the examples of MVPA that we've considered up to this point, in this study the experimenters were not demonstrating that a classifier could correctly guess what was the independent variable on a particular trial (e.g., "on this trial the stimulus was a picture of a cat"). Rather, their classifier was tracking the evolution of a mental *dependent* variable – memory recall – that was unaccompanied by any external cues or special instructions. I qualify it as primitive because we have to keep in mind that this demonstration occurred within a highly constrained environment in which the classifier only "knew about" three states in the world – celebrities, famous locales, and common objects. Thus, if Polyn's subjects ever thought about,

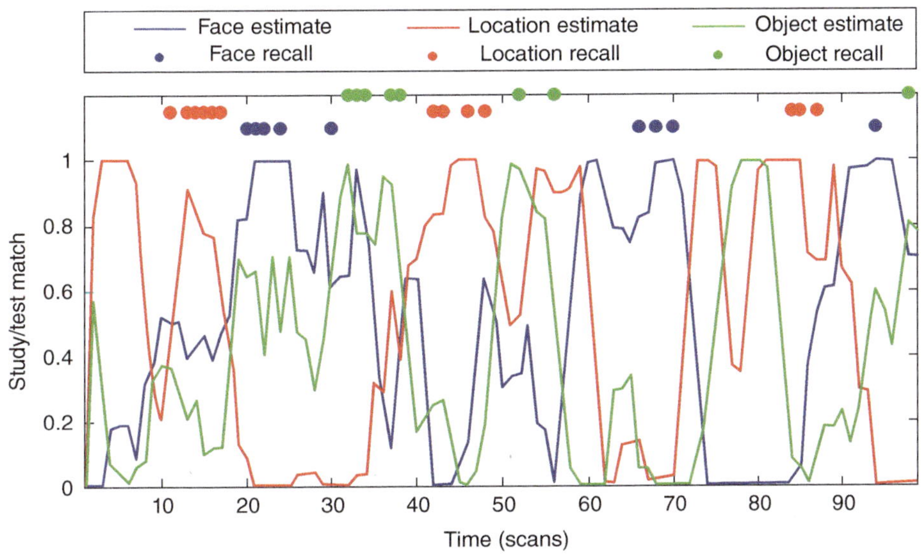

FIGURE 12.4 Contextual reinstatement during free recall. The blue, red, and green waveforms indicate, at each point in time during a scan of a single subject, the extent to which neural activity matches the pattern of neural activity independently determined to correspond to that stimulus category. Each dot indicates the recall of an item (larger dots for the recall of multiple items within the same 1.8-second volume acquisition; dots have been shifted forward in time by three TRs (i.e., 5.4 seconds) to account for the hemodynamic lag). Note how each instance of recall is preceded by brain activity taking on that category's pattern.

Source: Polyn et al., 2005 / American Association for the Advancement of Science.

I dunno, climate change, or that evening's social plans, or how physically uncomfortable they felt while lying in the scanner, the classifier would only be able to assess whether the corresponding pattern of activity was more celebrity-like, locale-like, or object-like.

Familiarity vs. Recollection

Dual-Process Models We'll conclude this chapter with a consideration of whether the theoretical distinction between autonoetic and noetic retrieval corresponds to qualitatively, or just quantitatively, different neural mechanisms. There are numerous, by and large quite similar, theoretical models from cognitive psychology that can be classified as dual-process models. These posit that free recall depends on a process called **recollection**, and that recognition memory can be supported by recollection and/or by a process called **familiarity**. According to these theories, recollection entails the retrieval of qualitative information associated with the learning episode. For example, when I recollect what I ate for dinner last night (it was my twentieth wedding anniversary! [really!]), I remember not only the scallops that I ate, but also where we sat at the restaurant, what the weather was like outside, the dress that my lovely dinner companion was wearing, etc. On a more mundane level, subjects in the Polyn et al. (2005) study, for example, would be assumed to have recollected contextual information about the moments when each of the images that they recalled had been presented at study. (E.g., perhaps, when recalling having seen an image of the actor John Wayne, they also recollected how they had rated John Wayne during the study phase.) Recollection is characterized as a relatively slow process.

Familiarity, in contrast, is a fast, quantitative memory signal that only conveys the information that one has or has not previously encountered the item in question. Let's return again to the author's personal life and engage in some mental time travel. Let's say that later today, when I need to take a break from writing, I will go jogging in my neighborhood and will encounter, walking along the sidewalk, a woman and, few minutes later, a man. As I run past the woman, I have a strong sense that I've seen her somewhere recently, but where was it? Being the omniscient narrator as well as the protagonist in this imagined anecdote, I can tell you that this woman was the waitress from last night's dinner, but that I didn't recognize her in this very different context. Subsequently, as I run past the man, I have a vague sense, but less strong, that he, too, "looks familiar." He, it turns out, drove the taxi cab that took us to the restaurant. (Or was he the driver from the ride home? . . .) Thus, familiarity can vary along the dimension of strength, whereas recollection is assumed to be an all-or-none phenomenon. (Recollected memories can, of course, contain more or less detail, but this has more to do with the stored memory than the process of retrieval, per se.)

And these two processes are assumed to work in tandem. (It's now a few hours later in the life of our author/protagonist [really].) As it turns out, I actually did go out for a run this afternoon, and although I encountered neither the waitress nor the cabbie, I did run past someone worthy of note. He was coming the other direction along the Lakeshore Path, and at first looked like just another afternoon jogger. Then, I thought, as we were passing, "that guy looks familiar." After another three or four strides, it came back to me: *His name is Charlie, he's in the Business School (Marketing Department?), and he and I used to serve together on the Graduate School Fall Competition committee.* By the dual-processes account, the visual processing of Charlie coming toward me along the path first generated a familiarity signal, which, after a few seconds of cogitation, gave way to the experience of recollection.

As stated previously, there are many dual-process models. There have also been many, many behavioral, ERP, and fMRI studies testing different facets of these models. A general pattern that has emerged from this literature is that recollection depends on the hippocampus proper, whereas familiarity is supported by neocortical regions of the MTL, particularly the perirhinal cortex. Next, we will illustrate just one narrow slice from this literature with a particularly elegant study that highlights the methods and assumptions underlying one particular model – the **receiver operating characteristic (ROC)**-based model – and a study that addresses the role of the hippocampus in these two hypothesized processes.

Dual Processes of Memory Retrieval in the Rodent One of the simplest forms of recognition test is "yes/no" recognition, in which subjects indicate whether or not they have seen the memory probe previously. In two-alternative forced choice, an old and a new item are presented together, and the subject must indicate which is old (or, in the case of delayed nonmatch-to-sample [DNMS], which is new). Although both of these procedures assess memory performance, neither addresses what underlying processes may contribute to this performance. Several procedures for estimating the relative contribution of familiarity- vs. recollection-based processes to recognition performance do so empirically. For example, in the "remember/know" procedure, instead of responding "yes" or "no" to the probe, subjects indicate whether they "remember" having seen it, in which case they are assumed to have used recollection, or whether they only "know" that they have seen it, but can't retrieve a memory of having done so, in which case they are assumed to have used familiarity. (The Wagner et al. (1998) and Brewer et al. (1998) studies with which we opened this chapter each effectively used this procedure, by asking subjects to rate their confidence for each positive response, and only using high-confidence hits in their subsequent-memory analyses.)

An alternative procedure is to derive the contribution of the two processes to recognition performance by estimating ROC curves from one's subjects. This is the approach taken by Fortin, Wright, and Eichenbaum (2004) in the study that we'll take up next.

The ROC gets its arcane name from the fact that it was first developed during World War II to understand the performance of radar operators whose difficult (and consequential) task was to observe a noisy screen on the radar receiver and to detect signals (e.g., blips corresponding to enemy aircraft) from among the noise. They faced the classic trade-off that was later formalized in signal detection theory: by setting too lenient a criterion, the operator risked issuing "false alarms" – announcing that they had detected enemy aircraft when, in fact, it was just noise – whereas, by setting too strict a criterion, they risked missing actual targets. Note that, in this scenario, the radar operator can change their performance by "setting their criterion" to be liberal or to be strict, but none of this changes the inherent signal-to-noise ratio (SNR) of the radar receiver.

Applied to recognition memory, all items that one encounters are assumed to generate some familiarity signal, and one's "mnemonic SNR" is the extent to which *old* items generate a stronger signal than *new* items. Independent of one's SNR is where one chooses to set one's criterion. The trade-off associated with different criterion settings is implemented in an ROC-based recognition test by requiring subjects to rate each recognition probe on a scale from 1 to, say, 5, with "5" corresponding to "I'm absolutely certain that I saw this previously" and "1" corresponding to "I'm certain that I did not see this previously." After collecting the data, one can then derive an ROC curve in the following way. First, set up a pair of axes like those illustrated in *Figure 12.5* with the probability of hits along the vertical axis and the probability of false alarms along the horizontal axis. Next, score the subject's data as though only their "5" responses were "yes"es, and all their other responses were "no"s. This estimates their performance at its most conservative: their hit rate will be the lowest, but so, too, will be their false-alarm rate. Next, rescore the data as though responses of "5" and "4" were "yes"es, and the others "no"s. Because the subject had assigned 4s to probes about which they had relatively high confidence, the "5s + 4s" hit rate will be higher than the "5s only" hit rate. But so, too, will be the false alarm rate. Thus, the "5s + 4s" data point will be higher along both the hits axis and the false alarms axis. The progression from most conservative to most liberal can be seen in panel D of *Figure 12.5*.

Panel A of *Figure 12.5* is an idealized plot of ROC-analyzed data from a human subject in a word-list recognition experiment. When this "asymmetric ROC" is decomposed, as in panels B and C, it can be understood as being made up of independent factors represented by each of these two: the degree of curvilinearity of the function labeled "familiarity" and the y-intercept of the function labeled "recollection" (Yonelinas, 2001). Note that overall memory performance is captured by the area under the curve, with the diagonal equivalent to chance performance.

How did Fortin and colleagues manage to get rats to give a range of five levels of confidence judgments? Let's start with their basic procedure. Rats were trained to retrieve rewards (pieces of the breakfast cereal Cheerios) buried in cups of sand that was scented with 1 of 30 distinctive household scents. Next, they learned the DNMS procedure by which, if a test scent was a new scent, they were to dig in that sand to retrieve the reward. If, on the other hand,

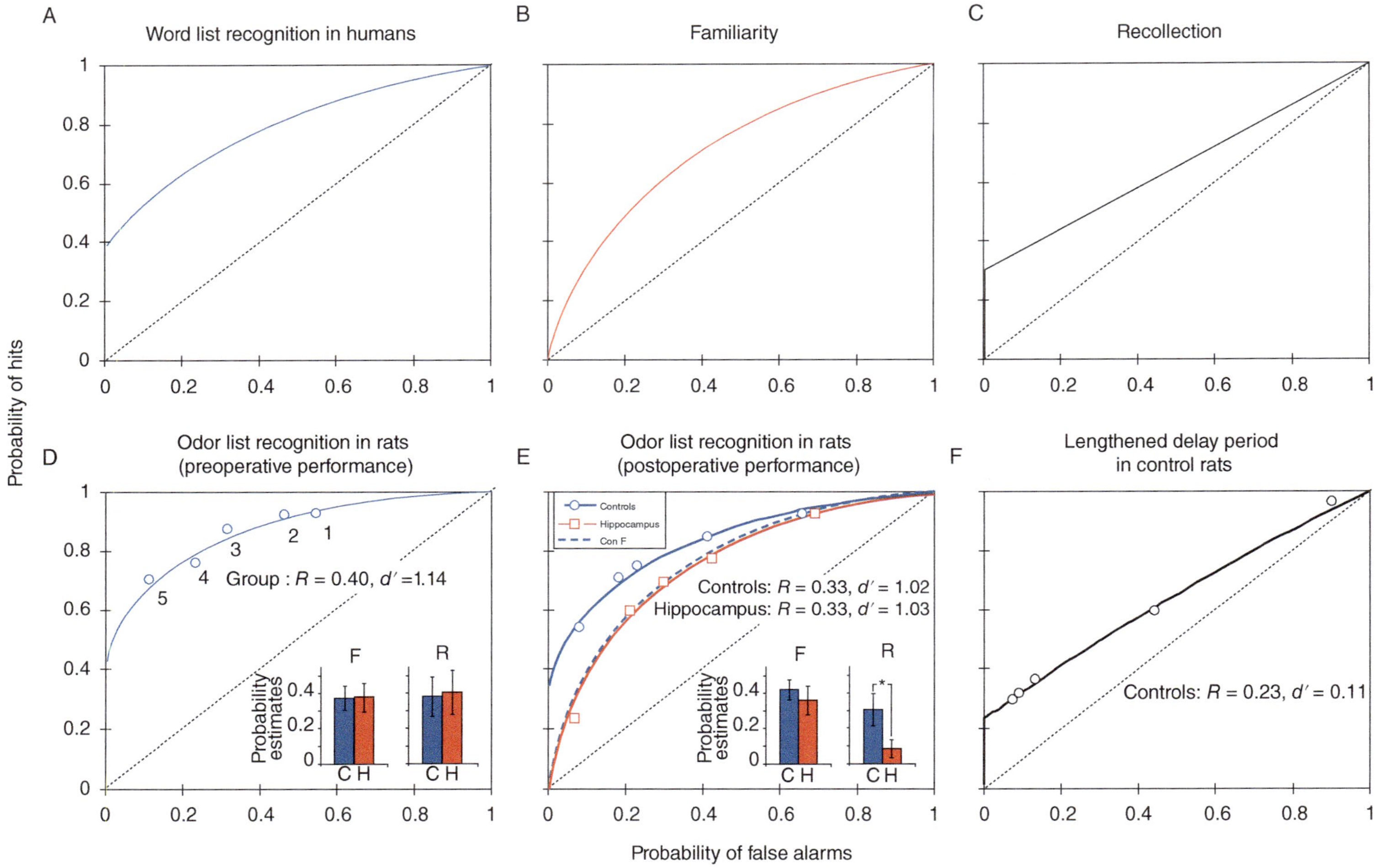

FIGURE 12.5 ROC-based dual process model of recognition, applied to humans and rats. **A.** An ROC curve derived from the recognition performance of human subjects tested on memory for a list of words. **B.** The contribution of familiarity to the performance illustrated in panel A, as estimated by dual-process model decomposition. **C.** The contribution of recollection to the performance illustrated in panel A, as estimated by dual-process model decomposition. **D.** ROC curves derived from the recognition-of-odors performance of two groups of rats prior to surgeries. Insets show model estimates of contributions of familiarity and of recollection to performance. **E.** ROC curves derived from recognition performance of the same groups of animals from 12.5.D, but now after hippocampal lesioning of one of the groups. Insets show model estimates of contributions of familiarity and of recollection to performance of each of the groups. **F.** ROC curve derived from recognition performance of the unlesioned control group from 12.5.D and E, but now after a delay of 75 minutes (results from 12.5.D and E were obtained after delays of 30 minutes).

Source: Fortin et al., 2004 / Springer Nature.

it was an old scent, the cup would not contain a reward, but the rat would be rewarded for refraining from digging and, instead, moving to the back of the cage to an alternate, empty cup to which a reward would be delivered. Different levels of bias were then created by, in effect, varying how hard the rat would have to work to receive its reward for correctly choosing "new" vs. how much food it would receive for correctly choosing "old." A liberal bias was created by making it more onerous to respond "new," by placing the same amount of sand in a taller cup, and reducing the amount of reward that it would contain. Thus, if the animal "wasn't sure" about whether a new scent was old or new, it would tend to favor an "old" response, because a "new" response required too much effort. (If, however, it was certain that the test scent was new, then the only choice was to climb and dig.) In tandem, the amount of reward delivered for correct "old" responses was increased, thereby further incentivizing this choice.

Now let's look at the results, in the bottom three panels of *Figure 12.5.* Panel D shows the preoperative performance of the animals that were to receive hippocampal lesions and of the control animals. The combined ROC of the two groups shows the standard asymmetric shape, and the model estimates (inset bar graphs) indicate comparably strong familiarity and recollection estimates for both groups. Panel E illustrates the key result: after hippocampal lesions, the estimated contribution to performance of recollection is devastated, but that of familiarity is intact. The dotted line labeled "Con F" shows the estimated performance of the control group when the contribution of recollection is algebraically removed. Finally, panel F shows the effect, in the control rats, of lengthening the delay period from 30 to 75 minutes. This manipulation removes the contribution of familiarity to their performance but leaves recollection relatively intact. Not shown in this figure is the effect of the hippocampal lesion on overall performance: the control animals at the 30-minute delay performed 73% correct, the hippocampal animals 66% correct (i.e., a modest impairment), and the control animals at the 75-minute delay performed 64% correct. (Note that while lesioning the hippocampus removes the estimated contribution of recollection to performance, increasing the delay by and large removes the estimated contribution of familiarity to performance.)

This suggests a possible solution to why the monkeys with H lesions described in the Murray, Bussey, and Saksida (2007) review (*Figure 11.8*) were not impaired on tests of DNMS: perhaps they could solve the tasks based on a familiarity signal.

What *Is* the Familiarity Signal? The data from the previous section, and from a very large number of results from many species, including human and nonhuman primates, strongly implicate neocortical areas upstream from the hippocampus as the critical substrates for the generation of the familiarity signal. But what, exactly, *is* the familiarity signal? One possibility comes (unsurprisingly) from the laboratory of Doris Tsao, of face-processing renown (cf. *Chapter 10*, sections *The code for facial identity in the primate brain (!?!)* and *Axis coding of objects in the nonhuman primate*). In this work, Liang She, Benna, Shi, Fusi, and Tsao (2024) began with the premise that "A central assumption of neuroscience is that long-term memories are represented by the same brain areas that encode sensory stimuli" (p. 861),[3] and so they set out to assess this by starting with a data set of 1036 images of monkey faces, and presented face images and videos of 36 of these daily for a minimum of one month. When unfamiliar faces were presented, axis tuning (see *Chapter 10*, section *The code for facial identity in the primate brain (!?!)*) was derived for neurons in three face patches – AM (the most anterior face patch in IT cortex; *Figure 10.8.A*), and PR and TP (located in perirhinal cortex temporal polar cortex, respectively, and both discovered subsequent to the study from Chang and Tsao (2017) from which *Figure 10.8A* was drawn) – and the investigators compared this to the tuning for familiar faces.

As illustrated in *Figure 12.6*, tuning for familiar faces was the same as that for unfamiliar faces, during the processing of the initial feedforward sweep. During this time, a decoder trained on 36 of the unfamiliar faces could reconstruct a familiar face. Subsequently, however, (and reminiscent of the time course of processing of "challenge" images in IT cortex [see *Chapter 6*, section *A critical role for feedback in the ventral visual processing stream*]), the

[3] In their paper, She et al. (2024) attribute this idea to the wrong source. The authors cited by She et al. (2024) would have been influenced by Hebb (1949).

FIGURE 12.6 Processing familiar vs. unfamiliar faces.

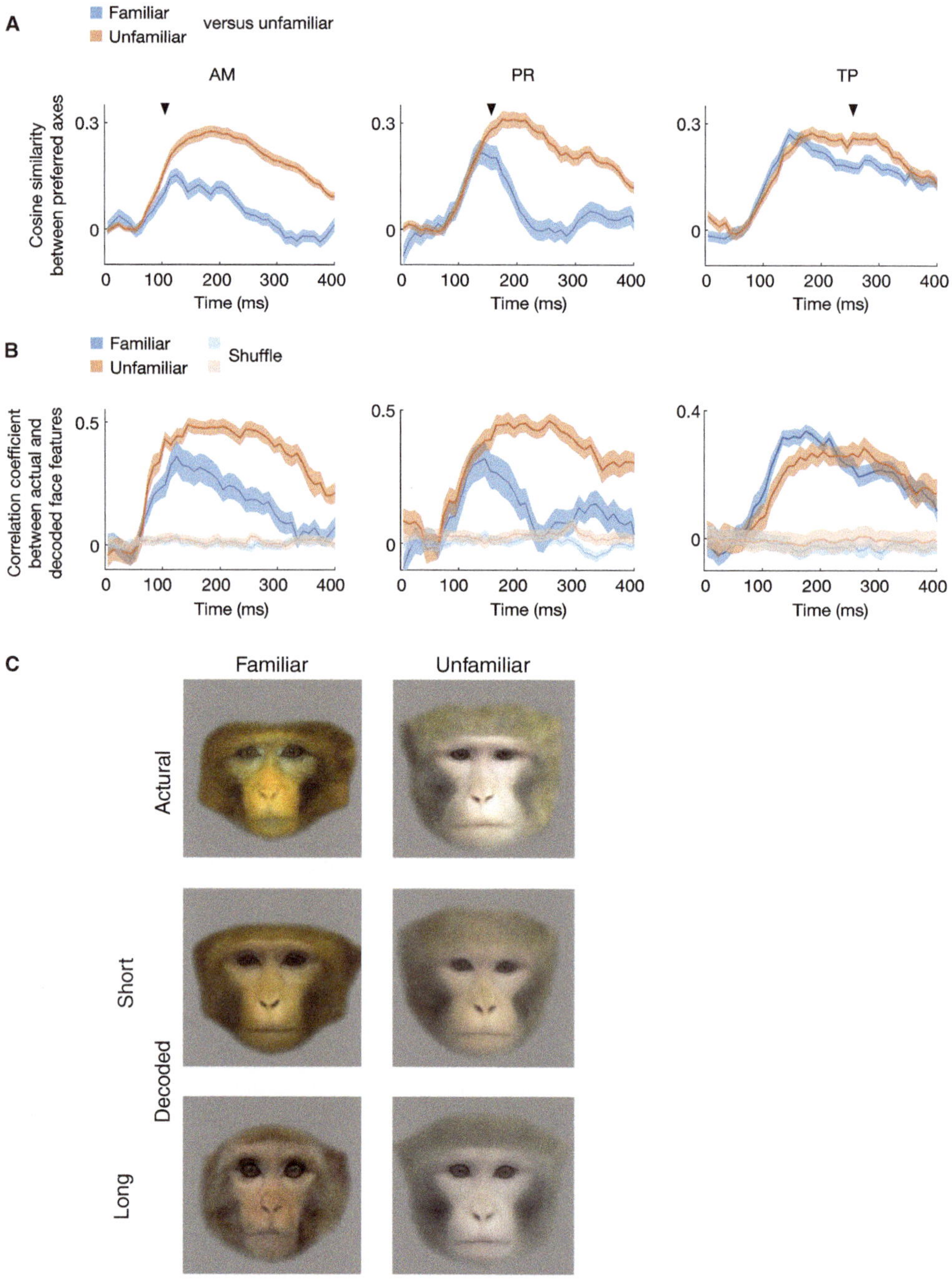

FIGURE 12.6.A Population average similarities of the tuning axes derived from 36 familiar faces (blue) and from 36 unfamiliar faces (orange) relative to the tuning axes derived from 964 different unfamiliar faces, in each of three face patches. Cosign similarity is a measure of angular difference between two subspaces, with a larger value corresponding to a smaller angle (i.e., to higher similarity), and a value of 0 corresponding to orthogonality. Black arrowheads indicate the time at which the two sets of cosign similarities began to differ significantly from each other, and the average familiar-face tuning axis is orthogonal to the average unfamiliar-face tuning axis by just over 200 msec in face patch PR and by roughly 300 msec in face patch AM.

Source: (She, Benna, Shi, Fusi, & Tsao, 2024) / Springer Nature / CC BY 4.0.

(Continued)

FIGURE 12.6.B Using a method conceptually similar to multivariate inverted encoding modeling (Chapter 5, section *Reconstructing stimulus information with multivariate inverted encoding models [IEM]*), the authors reconstructed ("decoded") monkey faces by entering neuronal activity evoked by an unfamiliar face into a regression model (one for each of the three face patches). (Conceptually, instead of the basis set of half-wave rectified sinusoids, they regressed neural activity against PCs of facial "identity" and "appearance" [see Chapter 10, section *The code for facial identity in the primate brain (!?!].*) Level of performance of this decoding procedure was assessed by calculating the correlation between the face reconstructed from neural activity and the actual face image used on that trial. Plotted here is performance, for each of the three face patches of a decoder trained at each time point by activity evoked by 964 unfamiliar faces, then tested at each time point on 36 different unfamiliar faces and 36 familiar faces.

Source: (She, Benna, Shi, Fusi, & Tsao, 2024) / Springer Nature / CC BY 4.0.

FIGURE 12.6.C Examples of the reconstruction of two faces, one unfamiliar and one familiar, using the procedure described in panel **B** with the exception that neurons from both AM and PR were used, and two decoders were used, one trained on activity during a "short"-latency epoch (120–170 msec) and one on activity during a "long"-latency epoch (220–270). Note that although the short-latency reconstruction of the familiar face appears to be very similar to the original image, the long-latency reconstruction does not, a reflection of the fact that the familiar face code has diverged considerably from the unfamiliar face code by this point in time.

Source: She et al. (2024) / Springer Nature / CC BY 4.0.

tuning properties of these neurons began to change, such that by roughly 200 msec in PR and by roughly 300 msec in AM, their preferred axis had rotated markedly (and nonlinearly, meaning that the change was a true change of tuning properties, not just, e.g., a gain modulation of tuning for unfamiliar stimuli). At this later time point, cross-category decoding was no longer successful. A control experiment in which PR was inactivated via infusion of muscimol (a GABAergic agonist that inhibits activity in the affected region) showed a reduction in the gain of responses in AM, but no change in the face tuning of AM neurons. Finally, and independent of the processing of face identity, the authors were able to decode familiarity (i.e., *this is a familiar face* vs. *this is an unfamiliar face*) with latencies that were shorter than those needed to decode identify: familiarity decoding emerged earliest in face patch ML (see *Figure. 10.8.A*) propagating in a feedforward manner to AM (latency of 95 msec), to PR (105 msec), and to TP (135 msec). This "familiarity signal" seemed to arise from the fact that the manifolds representing familiar vs. unfamiliar faces initially separated, but remained parallel (thus, in the same subspace, thereby supporting cross-category decoding). Subsequently, after this initial separation within the subspace, the familiar-face manifold rotated out of this early configuration and into a new "familiar face" subspace (inferred as a consequence of the rotation of the preferred axes of the neurons whose activity contributed to the manifold).

The authors' conclusion from these results? "We speculate that, by lifting representations of face memories into a separate subspace from that used to represent unfamiliar faces,[4] attractor-like dynamics may be built around these memories through a recurrent network to allow reconstruction of familiar face features from noisy cues without interfering with veridical representation of sensory inputs" (She et al., 2024, p. 876). That's a mouthful, but we can "decode" it with ideas introduced in *Chapter 5* (and with reference to figures from *Chapter 5*). First, "lifting representations" refers to the early separation of manifolds. By analogy, at very early latencies familiar and unfamiliar stimuli are represented on the same manifold, such as is illustrated in *Figure 5.12.D*, before the two manifolds separate, as in *Figure 5.12.C*. Note that, in *Figure 5.12.C*, a decoder aligned with the "cued upper" manifold could decode a stimulus represented on the "cued lower" manifold, and a different decoder could discriminate "upper" from "lower," although this second decoder wouldn't be able to decode stimulus identity. For the scheme proposed by She et al. (2024), replace the word "upper" with "unfamiliar" and the word "lower" with "familiar," and rename the "upper vs. lower" decoder the "familiarity decoder." Although the mechanism that prompts this early separation of manifolds is not yet

[4] Note that in just the previous paragraph your author characterized this separation as occurring within a subspace; the notion of a subspace can be a slippery thing: Where one person can interpret a condition-related separation of representational geometries as a rotation into a different subspace, if this "different subspace" isn't mathematically orthogonal to the previous one, that separation can, alternatively, be construed as a translation within the same subspace.

known, the phenomenon can be described as a state transition from a monostable to a bistable attractor landscape, with the "familiar" attractor a channel that, upon the state change, pulls the familiar tuning axes of neurons (and, therefore, the familiar-face manifold) along a trajectory that corresponds to the rotation away from the initial subspace that is occupied by all faces for the earliest few tens of msec after stimulus presentation (see *Chapter 5*, section *Dynamical systems theory*). Finally, the state transition into this bistable attractor landscape insulates ongoing perception of "veridical" elements in the visual scene from the processes that are unique to familiar faces, such as associating them with episodic and/or semantic representations in LTM (i.e., transitioning from familiarity of the face to recollection of all that is known about the face).

There is one further aspect of these findings from She et al. (2024) that is worthy of our consideration, but we'll hold off on discussing it until *Chapter 13*, section *Repetition effects and fMRI adaptation*.

Processing Long-Term Memory Across Time

What does it feel like to go through your day? The philosophical tradition of phenomenology addresses this question, in part, with the construct of the *stream of consciousness*, which provides coherence and continuity to conscious experience:

> Phenomenological analyses point to the 'width' or 'depth' of the 'living present' of consciousness: our experience of temporal[ly] enduring objects and events, as well as our experience of change and succession, would be impossible were we conscious only of that which is given in a punctual *now* and were our stream of consciousness composed of a series of isolated *now* points, like a string of pearls. (Thompson and Zahavi, 2007, p. 77; emphases added by this author)

This certainly fits with this author's subjective experience (which is reassuring!) but it also highlights a shortcoming of the memory research that we've considered up until now, because it has assessed LTM for discrete items – effectively "a series of isolated *now* points" – that were presented in lists. But "real life" is experienced as a continual stream. How does the nervous system handle this? We've seen in previous considerations of visual perception and of selective attention that the brain discretizes the moment-to-moment processing of the perceptual stream via oscillatory dynamics (e.g., *Chapter 6*, section *Oscillatory dynamics guiding visual perception*). Does LTM perhaps do something similar, albeit at longer time scales?

Incidental Encoding into LTM During "Everyday Life"

Another point to raise about the research that we've been considering up to this point is that it has emphasized what might be considered first-order neurophysiological effects, like elevated activity and/or elevated connectivity, that are associated with better encoding into LTM. But we've treated these as stochastic phenomena without considering, e.g., why it might be that for some items the level of activity in a key region is higher than it is for other items. What would be useful would be a model, or a theoretical framework, what could help us understand why these fluctuations occur, and perhaps even to predict them. For memory research, a particularly valuable set of insights and ideas has come from the study of "event cognition," the way that people tend to experience, and subsequently think about, their day-to-day experience as comprising a set of distinct events (e.g., Radvansky and Zachs, 2017). And, as we'll see, many concepts from event cognition can be related to constructs and frameworks that we're already familiar with, such as predictive coding and reinforcement learning (RL).

To get started, we can even begin with memory performance on a list of items in a laboratory experiment. Sure, the test itself may not simulate an everyday-life experience, but coming into a lab and sitting down in front of a computer to perform a task being administered by some graduate student *is* part of the lived experience of the research subject on that day. And one thing that we can assume is that that the subject's performance will show primacy and recency effects. The common interpretation of the primacy effect – the fact that memory performance tends to be higher for items that had appeared at the beginning of the list of to-be-remembered items – is that "nothing preceded these items," and so their retrieval doesn't suffer from proactive interference. Similarly, because "nothing followed" the items that had been presented last, the retrieval of those items doesn't suffer from retroactive interference. But, of course, it's not literally true that "nothing" preceded the first item on the list, because the subject experienced walking into the lab, being shown where to sit, and receiving instructions about how to perform the task (and they'll be able to recall all of this later that day). The same is true for everything that followed the final item of the list. And so for the reduced-proactive and reduced-retroactive interference accounts to hold, it must be the case that, psychologically, the beginning and end of the psychology experiment were processed as the beginning and end of an event that was distinct from what preceded it and from what followed it. This, in turn, requires us to consider the psychological (and neural) bases of event boundaries.

Several accounts of event cognition posit that prediction errors (sometimes framed as reward prediction errors [RPEs] from RL theory (e.g., Rouhani, Norman, Niv, and Bornstein, 2020), sometimes as prediction errors from predictive coding theory (Bein, Gasser, Amer, Maril, and Davachi, 2023)) are responsible for creating event boundaries. For example, Oded Bein, Camille Gasser, Tarek Amer, Anat Maril, and Lila Davachi (2023) frame contextual reinstatement, which we considered in section *Documenting contextual reinstatement in the brain*, as an example of prediction: "Stimuli in the environment serve as memory cues, leading to the reactivation of related memories . . . This reactivation of related memories encompasses reinstatement of neural activity patterns that represent our learned expectations of what is likely to happen in a particular environment" (p. 1 of 13). The extent of the match or mismatch of one's in-the-moment experience with these reinstated expectations will influence how this moment is remembered, and, in the case of a mismatch, the prediction error will generate an event boundary demarcating the beginning of what will later be remembered as a discrete event, distinct from other events that were experienced that day. This is a huge – and ever-growing – literature, and here we'll review the details from just one experiment that illustrates many of these ideas, and does so in a way that will also help tie up some conceptual loose ends left unresolved by *Chapter 11*'s section *Reconsolidation*.

Watching TikToks and Creating False Memories (O.k., they weren't actually TikToks. But they could have been.) On Day 1 of this study by Alyssa Sinclair, Grace Manalili, Iva Brunec, Alison Adcock, and Morgan Barense (2021), subjects came into the laboratory and viewed 70 brief videos, each featuring a brief narrative episode with a salient ending. (E.g., the "Baseball" video featured a crowded stadium, a rapid montage of close-ups on the faces of coaches, fans, the pitcher and the batter, then a slow-motion windup, the pitch, the swing, the sound of bat-striking-ball, and the ball flying "out of the park" for a homerun.) On Day 2 "Reactivation Phase," half of the subjects were scanned with fMRI while viewing the same 70 videos, but half of the videos were interrupted just before the final event that provided the narrative conclusion to the event. (E.g., the "Baseball" video stopped abruptly while the batter was in mid-swing, such that a first-time viewer wouldn't know if he hit the ball or struck out.) This group, the *Delay* group, returned on Day 3 for a recall test. The other half of subjects, the *Immediate* group, experienced an identical "Reactivation Phase" on Day 2, but then their recall was tested immediately after seeing the last of the 70 videos (i.e., recall on Day 2). Behavioral performance indicated that both the *Delay* group and the *Immediate* group recalled more correct details per video for videos that were interrupted during Reactivation than for videos that were replayed at full length. This result had been predicted from previous work showing that large prediction errors result in strengthening and preservation of existing memories. Intriguingly, the number of false memories per video (defined as reporting the memory of a detail that was incorrect, such as misremembering the color of the uniform worn by the pitcher in the "Baseball" video) was also increased for interrupted videos, but this effect was only observed in the *Delay* group.

To assess the neural bases of these behavioral effects, the authors carried out both univariate signal intensity-based analyses and multivariate RSA analyses on the fMRI data collected from the *Delay* group on Day 2. Intriguingly, the univariate analyses showed reversed effects for the two Reactivation conditions: For full-length videos, greater hippocampal activation was associated with a lower number of false memories; but for interrupted videos, greater hippocampal activation was associated with a higher number of false memories (*Figure 12.7.A*)! Stated another way, the absence, or presence, of a prediction error determined whether the existing memory of the video (from Day 1) would be consolidated, or updated.

Note that in this experiment, unlike model-based analyses in which data are fit to, for example, parameters from an RL model that give trial-by-trial estimates of the prediction error (e.g., Rouhani et al. 2020), in this study, there was no quantitative estimate of prediction errors, just the assumption that interrupted videos triggered a prediction error. However, what the authors were able to do was draw on the assumption that a prediction error should be associated with a transient change in a modulatory neurotransmitter that can influence processing in the forebrain.[5] Thus, they drew regions of interest (ROIs) to capture activity in the basal forebrain (a source of acetylcholine [ACh]) and the ventral tegmental area (VTA), and assessed evidence for whether the opposing trends illustrated in *Figure 12.7.A* might be modulated by activity in either of these two areas. As illustrated in *Figure 12.7.B*, this additional analysis found that both the negative relation of hippocampal activity with false memories in the Full condition and the positive relation of hippocampal activity with false memories in the Interrupted condition depended (statistically) on the level of activity in the basal forebrain. (No such effect was found for the VTA.) Therefore, these data are consistent with the idea that a prediction error-linked change in the level of ACh in the hippocampus might drive the opposing behavioral effects observed in these two conditions.

Note that, although a false memory was an error in the context of this experiment, the results illustrated in *Figure 12.7* also lend themselves to a more nuanced interpretation.

FIGURE 12.7 Reactivation and prediction in the hippocampus.
Source: (Sinclair, Manalili, Brunec, Adcock, & Barense, 2021) / National Academy of Sciences.

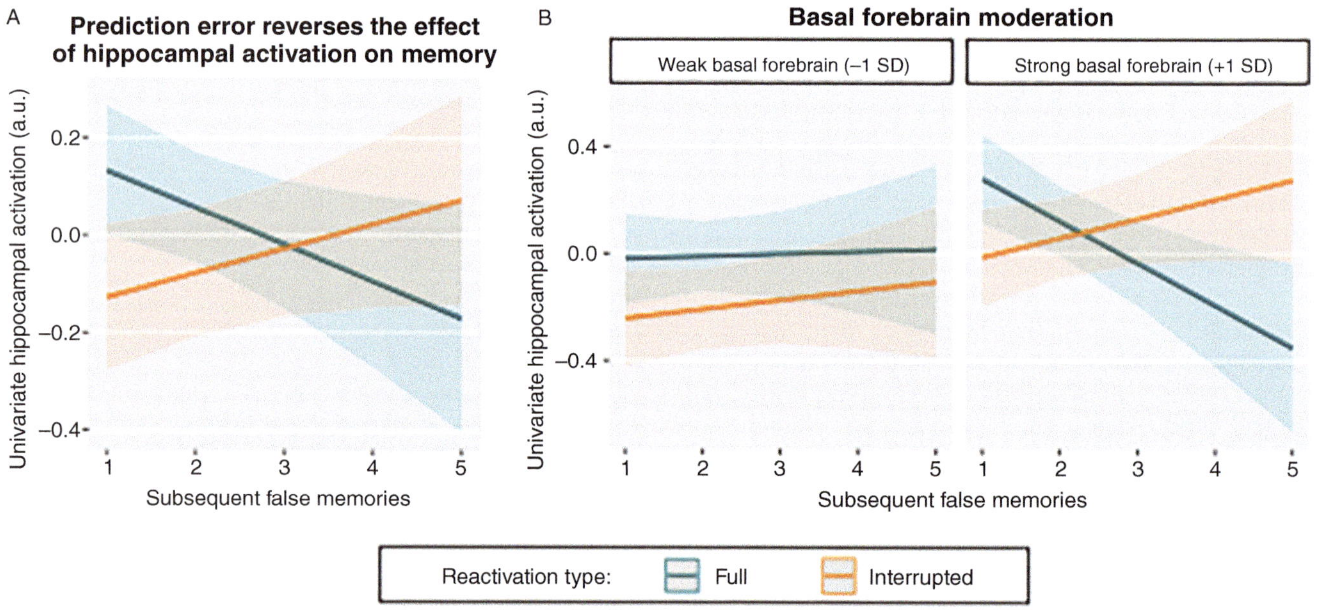

FIGURE 12.7.A Opposing relation of hippocampal activity (vertical axis) with false memory production (horizontal axis), as a function of reactivation condition.

FIGURE 12.7.B Dependence of the effect from panel A on the level of basal forebrain activity. Note that although only the lowest and highest extreme values of basal forebrain activity are shown here, the statistical analyses used that data from all trials and treated basal forebrain activity as a continuous variable.

[5] Note that up to this point in the book we have primarily discussed reward prediction errors (RPEs in relation to reinforcement learning theory) in terms of a dopaminergic signal influencing neocortical processing (see *Chapter 5*, section *A dopaminergic correlate of the reward prediction error*), but, in principle, the neuromodulator need not be dopamine (e.g., Nina Rouhani, David Clewett, and James Antony (2024) have proposed dissociable roles for dopaminergic vs. for noradrenergic RPEs in memory processing) and the target of this signal could certainly be the hippocampus.

Consider a "real life" scenario in which you walk into what should be a familiar situation, but immediately notice that this time, something is markedly different about it. In these circumstances, it would be advantageous to update your representation of this situation so as to be better prepared the next time you find yourself in it. From this perspective, the results from *Figure 12.7* might be interpreted as suggesting that the hippocampus "has a different job to do" in each of these two conditions – consolidating the extant memory in the Full condition, vs. updating this memory in the Interrupted condition, with false memories being a proxy for updating in this experiment because the design didn't provide for any new or otherwise *different* information with which the extant memory might have been updated. Here's how the authors make this point, and in so doing motivate the next analysis that we'll take up: "On the basis of our univariate findings, we proposed that during video playback, the hippocampus continually generates predictions and sustains episodic representations. If no prediction error is detected, these representations should be sustained, and the hippocampus should preserve and reinforce the memory (i.e., decreasing false memories). If a prediction error is detected, then the hippocampus should abandon ongoing predictions and prepare to update a memory (i.e., increasing false memories)" (p. 5 of 12).

To operationalize "preserving and reinforcing" vs. "abandoning" the authors used a variant of RSA in which they correlated the high-dimensional pattern of activity in the hippocampus at each point in time with the next point in time, to generate a measure of autocorrelation; the higher the autocorrelation, the more "preserving and reinforcing" the activity was assumed to be. As illustrated in *Figure 12.8*, for both conditions, autocorrelation values in the hippocampus increased monotonically over the course of each video until the end, at which point they diverged: autocorrelation values continued to climb in the Full condition, but not in the Interrupted condition. Furthermore, for the Interrupted condition, although the group-average difference in hippocampal autocorrelation during the 5 seconds following video offset vs. the 5 seconds prior to offset (the "post-video change in autocorrelation") did not differ from 0 (*Figure 12.8.C*), at the level of individual differences, a greater decline in post-video change predicted a larger number of false memories on Day 3. (The interpretation of this was that the greater the prediction error-triggered "abandonment" of the prediction formed by Day 1, the greater the evidence for prediction error-triggered "updating.") Furthermore, and reminiscent of the finding with the univariate hippocampal signal, the relation between hippocampal autocorrelation and updating was modulated by activity in the basal forebrain.

FIGURE 12.8 Autocorrelation of patterns of hippocampal activity during and after viewing short videos.
Source: Sinclair et al. (2021) / National Academy of Sciences.

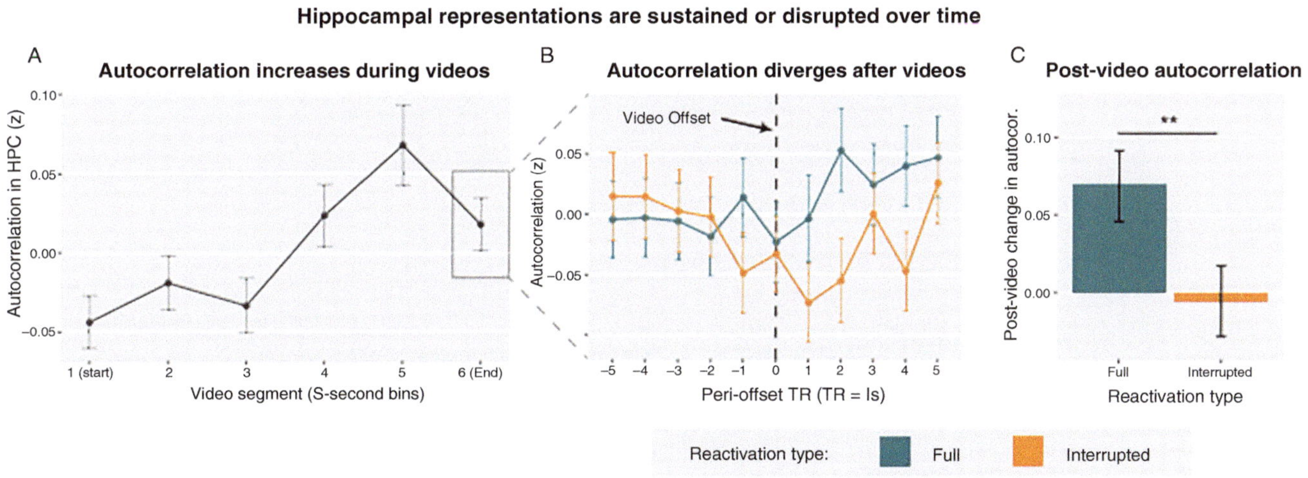

FIGURE 12.8.A Autocorrelation "ramps" over the course of the video.

FIGURE 12.8.B Autocorrelation time courses for Full vs. Interrupted videos diverge after video offset.

FIGURE 12.8.C Group average difference of post-video change in autocorrelation (5-seconds post minus 5-seconds pre).

"Reconsolidation" or "Reencoding"? A final point to emphasize about the results from Sinclair et al. (2021) is that the increase in false memories for Interrupted videos was only seen on Day 3, not immediately after the Reactivation session on Day 2. This means that the expression of the additional false memories for Interrupted videos required some time-dependent process, presumably protein synthesis (see *Chapter 11*, section *Multiple stages of synaptic strengthening*). And *this* observation brings us back to a question raised near the end of *Chapter 11,* section *Reconsolidation*, which is whether that phenomenon is somehow the result of an "undoing" of the learning on Day 1. These results, together with ideas that we have summarized earlier in this section on *Incidental encoding into LTM during "everyday life"*, suggest an alternative account: Interfering with the default tendency of the hippocampus to "preserve and reinforce," either by preventing contextual reinstatement or by introducing a prediction error, can lead to the "updating" of the memory, i.e., to creation of a new association of the information in question with a new, different, context. Consequently, when the original is presented a third time (such as in *Figure 11.9*), there is competition between the "two memories" (one associating the to-be-remembered picture with each of the two contexts), and recognition fails. Note that, by this account, there is no need to assume that retrieving a memory somehow puts it into a labile state, a hypothesized process for which, to this author's knowledge, there is no compelling neurobiological evidence.

Knowledge

That's the topic of our next chapter. Having considered the principles of how information gets into, and gets retrieved from, the brain, we next turn to how it is organized "while it sits there," waiting to be accessed and thought about.

End-of-Chapter Questions

1. Why can one not "just trial-average" stimulus-evoked fMRI signal as a function of subsequent memory performance, as can be done with ERP data?
2. Is it possible to learn anything about LTM encoding from a neuroimaging study of STM?
3. What principle of LTM formation is better captured with functional connectivity analyses than with signal intensity-based analyses?
4. What is it about the experience/expertise of London taxi drivers, and the organization of cortical projections to the hippocampus, that accounts for the pattern of structural change observed in these individuals?
5. Define autonoetic, noetic, and anoetic memory retrieval, and describe a task that would be well suited to assess each.
6. Would it be possible to document contextual reinstatement in the brain with univariate analyses of fMRI data? If your answer is 'yes,' explain how; if your answer is 'no,' explain why not.
7. Is there neural evidence for a distinction between familiarity and recollection in memory retrieval? To what kind of memory test is it assumed that only one of these can contribute, and to what can both contribute?
8. In what way does the neural evidence from monkeys viewing familiar vs. unfamiliar faces suggest that familiarity is processed by the visual system and, consequently, propagated to upstream circuits?
9. Explain the concept of an event boundary. What might be a neural basis for the creation of event boundaries?
10. In what way might the phenomenon of "reconsolidation" be better characterized as "reencoding"?

References

Bein, O., C. Gasser, T. Amer, A. Maril, and L. Davachi. 2023. "Predictions Transform Memories: How Expected Versus Unexpected Events Are Integrated or Separated in Memory." *Neuroscience & Biobehavioral Reviews 153*: 105368. doi: 10.1016/j.neubiorev.2023.105368.

Brewer, James B., Zuo Zhao, John E. Desmond, Gary H. Glover, and John D. E. Gabrieli. 1998. "Making Memories: Brain Activity that Predicts How Well Visual Experience Will Be Remembered." *Science* 281 (5380): 1185–1187. doi: 10.1126/science.281.5380.1185.

Chang., L, and D. Y. Tsao. 2017. "The Code for Facial Identity in the Primate Brain." *Cell 169*: 1013–1028.

Fortin, Norbert J., Sean P. Wright, and Howard Eichenbaum. 2004. "Recollection-Like Memory Retrieval in Rats Is Dependent on the Hippocampus." *Nature* 431 (7005): 188–191. doi: 10.1038/nature02853.

Hebb, Donald Olding. 1949. *The Organization of Behavior: A Neuropsychological Theory*. New York: Wiley and Sons.

Lisman, John E. 1999. "Relating Hippocampal Circuitry to Function: Recall of Memory Sequences by Reciprocal Dentate–CA3 Interactions." *Neuron* 22: 233–242. doi: 10.1016/S0896-6273(00)81085-5.

Milner, Brenda, Suzanne Corkin, and H.-L. Teuber. 1968. "Further Analysis of the Hippocampal Amnesic Syndrome: 14-Year Follow-Up Study of H. M." *Neuropsychologia* 6 (3): 215–234. doi: 10.1016/0028-3932(68)90021-3.

Murray, Elisabeth A., Timothy J. Bussey, and Lisa M. Saksida. 2007. "Visual Perception and Memory: A New View of Medial Temporal Lobe Function in Primates and Rodents." *Annual Review of Neuroscience* 30: 99–122. doi: 10.1146/annurev.neuro.29.051605.113046.

Petersen, Steven E., Peter T. Fox, Michael I. Posner, Mark Mintun, and Marcus E. Raichle. 1988. "Positron Emission Tomographic Studies of the Cortical Anatomy of Single-Word Processing." *Nature* 331 (6157): 585–589. doi: 10.1038/331585a0.

Polyn, Sean M., Vaidehi S. Natu, Jonathan D. Cohen, and Kenneth A. Norman. 2005. "Category-Specific Cortical Activity Precedes Retrieval during Memory Search." *Science* 310 (5756): 1963–1966. doi: 10.1126/science.1117645.

Radvansky, G. A., and J. M. Zachs. 2017. "Event Boundaries in Memory and Cognition." *Current Opinion in Behavioral Sciences 17*: 133–140. doi: 10.1016/j.cobeha.2017.08.006.

Ranganath, Charan, Michael X. Cohen, and Craig J. Brozinsky. 2005. "Working Memory Maintenance Contributes to Long-Term Memory Formation: Neural and Behavioral Evidence." *Journal of Cognitive Neuroscience* 17 (7): 994–1010. doi: 10.1162/0898929054475118.

Ranganath, Charan, Aaron Heller, Michael X. Cohen, Craig J. Brozinsky, and Jesse Rissman. 2005. "Functional Connectivity with the Hippocampus during Successful Memory Formation." *Hippocampus* 15 (8): 997–1005. doi: 10.1002/hipo.20141.

Rogers, Timothy T., John R. Hodges, Matthew A. Lambon Ralph, and Karalyn Patterson. 2003. "Object Recognition Under Semantic Impairment: The Effects of Conceptual Regularities on Perceptual Decisions." *Language & Cognitive Processes* 18 (5–6): 625–662. doi: 10.1080/01690960344000053.

Rouhani, N., D. Clewett, and J. W. Antony. 2024. "Building and Breaking the Chain: A Model of Reward Prediction Error Integration and Segmentation of Memory." *Journal of Cognitive Neuroscience 36* (11): 2401–2414. doi: 10.1162/jocn_a_02215.

Rouhani, N., K. A. Norman, Y. Niv, and A. M. Bornstein. 2020. "Reward prediction errors create event boundaries in memory." *Cognition 203*: 104269. doi: 10.1016/j.cognition.2020.104269.

She, L., M. K. Benna, Y. Shi, S. Fusi, and D. Y. Tsao. 2024. "Temporal Multiplexing of Perception and Memory Codes in IT Cortex." *Nature 629* (8013): 861–868. doi: 10.1038/s41586-024-07349-5.

Sinclair, A. H., G. M. Manalili, I. K. Brunec, R. A. Adcock, and M. D. Barense. 2021. "Prediction Errors Disrupt Hippocampal Representations and Update Episodic Memories." *Proceedings of the National Academy of Sciences of the United States of America 118* (51). doi: 10.1073/pnas.2117625118.

Stern, Chantal E., R. Suzanne Corkin, Gilberto González, Alexander R. Guimaraes, John R. Baker, Peggy J. Jennings, . . . Bruce R. Rosen. 1996. "The Hippocampal Formation Participates in Novel Picture Encoding: Evidence from Functional Magnetic Resonance Imaging." *Proceedings of the National Academy of Sciences of the United States of America* 93 (16): 8660–8665.

Thompson, E., and D. Zahavi. 2007. "Philosophical Issues: Phenomenology." In *The Cambridge Handbook of Consciousness*, edited by P. D. Zelazo, M. Moscovitch, and E. Thompson (pp. 67–88). Cambridge, UK: Cambridge University Press.

Tulving, Endel. 1985. "Memory and Consciousness." *Canadian Psychology* 26 (1): 1–12. doi: 10.1037/h0080017.

Tulving, Endel, Hans J. Markowitsch, Shitij Kapur, Reza Habib, and Sylvain Houle. 1994. "Novelty Encoding Networks in the Human Brain: Positron Emission Tomography Data." *NeuroReport* 5 (18): 2525–2528. doi: 10.1097/00001756-199412000-00030.

Wagner, Anthony D., Daniel L. Schacter, Michael Rotte, Wilma Koutstaal, Anat Maril, Anders M. Dale, . . . Randy L. Buckner. 1998. "Building Memories: Remembering and Forgetting of Verbal Experiences as Predicted by Brain Activity." *Science* 281 (5380): 1188–1191. doi: 10.1126/science.281.5380.1188.

Warrington, Elizabeth K., and Lawrence Weiskrantz. 1974. "The Effect of Prior Learning on Subsequent Retention in Amnesic Patients." *Neuropsychologia* 12 (4): 419–428. doi: 10.1016/0028-3932(74)90072-4.

Wheeler, Mark A. 2000. "Episodic Memory and Autonoetic Awareness." In *The Oxford Handbook of Memory*, edited by Endel Tulving and Fergus I. M. Craik (pp. 597–608). New York: Oxford University Press.

Yonelinas, Anderew P. 2001. "Components of Episodic Memory: The Contribution of Recollection and Familiarity." *Philosophical Transactions of the Royal Society of London, Series B: Biological Sciences* 356 (1413): 1363–1374. doi: 10.1098/rstb.2001.0939.

Other Sources Used

Gabrieli, John D. E., Margaret M. Keane, Ben Z. Stanger, Margaret M. Kjelgaard, Suzanne Corkin, and John H. Growdon. 1994. "Dissociations among Structural-Perceptual, Lexical-Semantic, and Event-Fact Memory Systems in Amnesia, Alzheimer's Disease, and Normal Subjects." *Cortex* 30 (1): 75–103. doi: 10.1016/S0010-9452(13)80325-5.

Holyoak, Keith J. 1999. "Psychology." In *The MIT Encyclopedia of the Cognitive Sciences*, edited by Robert A. Wilson and Frank C. Keil (pp. xxxix–xlix). Cambridge, MA: MIT Press.

Lee, Diane W., Troy G. Smith, Anthony D. Tramontin, Kiran K. Soma, Eliot A. Brenowitz, and Nicola S. Clayton. 2001. "Hippocampal Volume Does Not Change Seasonally in a Non Food-Storing Songbird." *NeuroReport* 12 (9): 1925–1928. doi: 10.1097/00001756-2001 07030-00031.

Moscovitch, Morris. 2000. "Theories of Memory and Consciousness." In *The Oxford Handbook of Memory*, edited by Endel Tulving and Fergus I. M. Craik (pp. 609–625). New York: Oxford University Press.

Rissman, Jesse, Adam Gazzaley, and Mark D'Esposito. 2004. "Measuring Functional Connectivity During Distinct Stages of a

Cognitive Task." *NeuroImage* 23 (2): 752–763. doi: 10.1016/j.neuroimage.2004.06.035.

Rugg, Michael D., and Kevin Allan. 2000. "Event-Related Potential Studies of Memory." In *The Oxford Handbook of Memory*, edited by Endel Tulving and Fergus I. M. Craik (pp. 521–538). New York: Oxford University Press.

Smulders, Tom V., A. D. Sasson, and Timothy J. DeVoogd. 1995. "Seasonal Variation in Hippocampal Volume in a Food-Storing Bird, the Black-Capped Chickadee." *Journal of Neurobiology* 27 (1): 15–25. doi: 10.1002/neu.480270103.

Warrington, Elizabeth K., and Lawrence Weiskrantz. 1968. "New Method of Testing Long-Term Retention with Special Reference to Amnesic Patients." *Nature* 217 (5132): 972–974. doi: 10.1038/217972a0.

Warrington, Elizabeth K., and Lawrence Weiskrantz. 1970. "The Amnesic Syndrome: Consolidation or Retrieval?." *Nature* 228 (5272): 628–630. doi: 10.1038/228628a0.

Williams, Pepper, and Michael J. Tarr. 1997. "Structural Processing and Implicit Memory for Possible and Impossible Figures." *Journal of Experimental Psychology: Learning, Memory, and Cognition* 23 (6): 1344–1361. doi: 10.1037/0278-7393.23.6.1344.

Williams, Pepper, and Michael J. Tarr. 1999. "Orientation-Specific Possibility Priming for Novel Three-Dimensional Objects." *Perception & Psychophysics* 61 (5): 963–976. doi: 10.3758/BF03206910.

Zola, Stuart M., Larry R. Squire, Edmond Teng, Lisa Stefanacci, Elizabeth A. Buffalo., and Robert E. Clark. 2000. "Impaired Recognition Memory in Monkeys after Damage Limited to the Hippocampal Region." *Journal of Neuroscience* 20 (1): 451–463.

Further Reading

Cowan, Emily, Anli Liu, Simon Henin, Sanjeev Kothare, Orrin Devinsky, and Lila Davachi. 2020. "Sleep Spindles Promote the Restructuring of Memory Representations in Ventromedial Prefrontal Cortex Through Enhanced Hippocampal-Cortical Functional Connectivity." *Journal of Neuroscience*. doi: 10.1523/JNEUROSCI.1946-19.2020.

Whereas subsequent memory designs assess item-by-item encoding processes, this study assesses consolidation processes by relating density of sleep spindles, a substrate for sharp-wave ripples, to hippocampal-neocortical connectivity at retrieval.

Norman, Kenneth A., Sean M. Polyn, Greg J. Detre, and James V. Haxby. 2006. "Beyond Mind-Reading: Multi-Voxel Pattern Analysis of fMRI Data." *Trends in Cognitive Sciences* 10 (9): 424–430. doi: 10.1016/j.tics.2006.07.005.

An accessible tutorial review on applications of MVPA decoding models in neuroimaging research.

Paller, Ken A., and Anthony D. Wagner. 2002. "Observing the Transformation of Experience into Memory." *Trends in Cognitive Sciences* 6 (2): 93–102. doi: 10.1016/S1364-6613(00)01845-3.

Review of the theoretical and ERP literatures on the subsequent memory effect that laid the groundwork for the fMRI studies detailed in this chapter.

Rissman, Jesse, and Anthony D. Wagner. 2012. "Distributed Representations in Memory: Insights from Functional Brain Imaging." *Annual Review of Psychology* 63: 101–128. doi: 10.1146/annurev-psych-120710-100344.

Review of MVPA analyses of declarative memory.

Rugg, Michael D., and Andrew P. Yonelinas. 2003. "Human Recognition Memory: A Cognitive Neuroscience Perspective." *Trends in Cognitive Sciences* 7 (7): 313–319. doi: 10.1016/S1364-6613(03)00131-1.

A good place to start if contemplating a plunge into the massive literature on the cognitive neuroscience of dual-process models of retrieval.

Serences, John T., and Sameer Saproo. 2012. "Computational Advances towards Linking BOLD and Behavior." *Neuropsychologia* 50 (4): 435–446. doi: 10.1016/j.neuropsychologia.2011.07.013.

A tutorial review that this author found to be very helpful for understanding the principles of multivariate encoding models.

Squire, Larry R. 2006. "Lost Forever or Temporarily Misplaced? The Long Debate about the Nature of Memory Impairment." *Learning and Memory* 13 (5): 522–529. doi: 10.1101/lm.310306.

A detailed, authoritative review of consolidation block vs. retrieval-based accounts of anterograde amnesia.

Yonelinas, Anderew P. 2001. "Components of Episodic Memory: The Contribution of Recollection and Familiarity." *Philosophical Transactions of the Royal Society of London, Series B: Biological Sciences* 356 (1413): 1363–1374. doi: 10.1098/rstb.2001.0939.

Detailed theoretical and quantitative background for the ROC-based dual-process model of retrieval.

CHAPTER 13

Semantic Long-Term Memory

KEY THEMES

- An intact MTL is not necessary for the preservation and retrieval of semantic memory.
- The study of patients showing (doubly dissociable) selective impairments at naming or identifying living things vs. nonliving things has given rise to three classes of theory: (1) knowledge is organized according to taxonomic categories (living vs. nonliving being the most salient); (2) knowledge is organized according to the functional modalities (e.g., visual perception of color and shape, motor sequences for manipulating tools) from which meaning derives; (3) lexical representation and access (i.e., words per se, not necessarily knowledge) is organized according to taxonomic categories.
- Important, and difficult, questions have been raised about the logical limits of what can be inferred from the results from single neuropsychological cases, as well as from demonstrations of double dissociations of function.
- The dependence on language of many experimental procedures used for testing semantic memory can complicate the interpretation of whether a particular set of neuroimaging findings reflects the processing of knowledge, per se, or reflects the language functions (often, lexical retrieval) engaged by the behavioral task.
- Attributing neuroimaging signal to knowledge vs. visual perception and/or mental imagery can also be tricky.
- fMRI adaptation, which takes advantage of the phenomenon of repetition suppression, can be an effective technique for deducing key functional properties of a targeted region of cortex.
- Research on patients with different variants of frontotemporal dementia has been characterized by debates on whether the core deficit underlying systematic patterns of cognitive decline is semantic or language based.
- Neuroimaging (both voxel-based morphometry [VBM] and activation studies) and computational modeling indicate an important role for the anterior temporal lobe in the control, if not the storage itself, of semantic memory.

CONTENTS

Companion Website: www.wiley.com/go/postle/cognitiveneuroscience3e

Knowledge in the Brain

Questions about how we represent knowledge have been at the core of formal inquiry into human cognition, and the human condition, for as far back in history as we have written records. From the perspective of cognitive neuroscience, it's one of the domains in which there is considerable contact with scholarship in the humanities and the social sciences, including anthropology, linguistics, philosophy, and cognitive development. It is also noteworthy for its relative lack of overlap with other branches of neuroscience, both because it is so difficult to study in nonhuman species and because it deals with mental faculties that other animals simply may not possess.

As we have done in other chapters, we'll outline some of the key questions by considering findings from neuropsychology. This time, however, instead of starting with an exotic "new" neurological syndrome, we'll begin with our old friend H.M.

Definitions and Basic Facts

Semantic memory is defined as memories for facts whose retrieval is not accompanied by information pertaining to how, when, or where that information was acquired – its retrieval is noetic. One of the striking findings with H.M. was that his memory for facts that he had learned prior to his surgery remained intact. So, too, did his vocabulary. Indeed, our knowledge of the meanings of words, often referred to as the **mental lexicon**, is an important subset of our semantic memory. Although it was initially believed that H.M.'s episodic memory for the distant past was intact, more recent interpretations, many of them prompted by the multiple trace theory, argue that even these were impoverished, "semanticized," and lacking the feeling of "reexperienc[ing] . . . something that has happened before." There is, however, no comparable debate about his semantic memory. For example, in 1953, H.M. was administered the Wechsler Adult Intelligence Scale (WAIS, i.e., an IQ test) as a part of preoperative cognitive testing in the run-up to his surgery. His performance on the subtests that measure lexical memory was within the normal range on that occasion, and it remained unchanged across 19 different testing sessions that were performed during the ensuing decades, through 2000. Thus, an intact MTL is not necessary for the preservation and retrieval of semantic memory.

How are semantic memories acquired? One formal account that we reviewed in *Chapter 11* is the slow cortical component of the Complementary Learning Systems models of McClelland, McNaughton, and O'Reilly (1995) (section *Fast-Encoding Hippocampus vs. Slow-Encoding Cortex*). It is generally accepted that all memories begin as episodic, and gradually transition to becoming semantic. (This view, however, is not universally held, as we shall see in just a bit.) A concrete example familiar to many readers (and one that this author has retained since the first edition of this book, because he likes it) might be one's knowledge of Barack Obama. The first time that a typical American (okay, your author) may have heard of this individual may have been while Obama was campaigning to be the president of the United States. Let's say that he first encountered the name while reading a newspaper article about the Democratic Primary race during the early months of 2008. (Obama was elected President in November 2008.) The next time our protagonist thought about Barack Obama may have been when a friend asked, "Which Democrat do you think will win the party's nomination?" To answer this question, he would have retrieved a memory of (the episode of) having read that newspaper article. Let's say that the third time our protagonist heard the name was while watching a televised debate between the candidates. At that point, would he think back to the newspaper article, or the discussion with the friend, each time the camera turned to Obama? Or would the knowledge *Black man, junior senator from Illinois, graduate of Harvard Law School,* or *Democratic candidate for President* just pop into his head noetically? If not by this third episode, shortly thereafter, repeated iterations of this process would have created a representation that can be retrieved independently of any reference to any one of the episodes in which this information was encountered. In this way, the knowledge of "Barack Obama" becomes a *semantic* memory. Should your author sustain bilateral damage to his MTL in, say, 2028 (pause here for a moment while he knocks on wood to negate this premonition), he would still be able to retrieve this knowledge after that time.

Another core fact about semantic memory is conveyed by its name: a semantic memory represents *meaning, knowledge*. Further, we know that it is organized in relation to its meaning. In the case of Barack Obama, for example, numerous experiments have demonstrated that if one is thinking about him, one can more quickly access information about John F. Kennedy (the US President from the 1960s) than if one was thinking about, say, Pelé, or John Lennon. Precisely how knowledge is organized, however, remains uncertain, and will be the question underlying much of the research that we'll review in this chapter.

And *now* we can turn to some exotic cases from cognitive neuropsychology.

Category-Specific Deficits Following Brain Damage

Animacy, or function?

Two seminal publications that have greatly influenced the contemporary study of the neural bases of semantics came from neuropsychologist Elizabeth Warrington and her colleagues in the mid-1980s. First, Warrington and McCarthy (1983) described a patient (V.E.R.) whose large left hemisphere stroke produced a massive impairment in the ability to speak or to understand spoken language, including the following of simple instructions. Nevertheless, V.E.R. was able to demonstrate some spared comprehension, in that, in response to a spoken word, she could point to a picture corresponding to the word. Her performance showed a noteworthy pattern, however, in that she produced many more correct responses when the words named flowers, animals, or foods than when they named manmade objects. Thus, she seemed to have a relative impairment of knowledge for nonliving things. The next year, Warrington and Shallice (1984) reported four patients recovering from herpes encephalitis who showed the opposite pattern: all four demonstrated worse performance with living than with nonliving words. Further, two of these patients had sufficiently spared language abilities that they could be tested on picture naming, and here the pattern was the same. One of them (J.B.R.) named 90% of the nonliving objects he was shown, but only 6% of the living objects. The second (S.B.Y.) named 75% vs. 0%. Examples of S.B.Y.'s definitions given to spoken words, in *Table 13.1*, are particularly compelling, in that they illustrate that the deficit is not a deficit of speech production, or general verbal fluency.

Together, these two studies could be construed as a double dissociation, thereby seeming to rule out any trivial reasons that one category might be inherently more difficult than the other, and therefore more vulnerable to brain trauma of any kind. What remained, of course, was to explain this intriguing pattern of findings. One interpretation is that they provide evidence that knowledge is represented according to taxonomic categories in the brain. This view might seem sensible after reading *Chapter 10*, but, of course, much of the work reviewed in *Chapter 10* was carried out considerably more recently than the 1980s and 1990s and, indeed, was influenced by what we're reviewing right here. Taxonomic explanations have been championed perhaps most vigorously by cognitive neuropsychologist Alfonso Caramazza. In one formulation of a "domain-specific knowledge hypothesis," for example, Caramazza and Shelton (1998) propose that "evolutionary pressures have resulted in specialized mechanisms for perceptually *and* conceptually distinguishing animate and inanimate kinds . . . leading to a *categorical* organization of this knowledge in the brain." We will return to this hypothesis in a bit, but first let's consider an alternative, because one of the factors that makes the domain-specific knowledge hypothesis provocative is that many investigators, including Warrington herself, have *not* interpreted these patterns of category-specific impairment as evidence for categorical organization in the brain.

Warrington and Shallice (1984) noted that patient J.B.R., for example, also showed impaired performance for several categories of nonliving objects: metals, types of cloth, musical instruments, and precious stones. Thus, perhaps the (relatively) selective impairments of knowledge for living vs. nonliving things in these patients were by-products of two different underlying factors with which the categories of living and nonliving are highly correlated. Specifically, Warrington and Shallice (1984) proposed two factors that can be construed as cardinal functions of the brain: perception and action. We primarily experience living things, they reasoned, by vision, whereas we experience inanimate objects by how we use them. Thus, patterns of relative impairment or sparing of knowledge about living or nonliving things may be a byproduct of damage to brain areas primarily involved in visual perception or in action planning. This alternative can be called a modality-specific scheme, because it posits that the organizing factor for semantics is the functional modality (e.g., vision, motor control) that a given piece of knowledge relies on.

TABLE 13.1 Example definitions to spoken words by patient S. B. Y.

Duck: an animal	*Wheelbarrow:* object used by people to take material about
Wasp: bird that flies	*Towel:* material used to dry people
Crocus: rubbish material	*Pram:* used to carry people, with wheels and a thing to sit on
Spider: a person looking for things, he was a spider for his nation or country	*Submarine:* ship that goes underneath the sea

Source: Adapted from Warrington et al., 1984.

An example of a case study that might have turned out to have been "the H.M. of semantic memory" is the patient K.C., who has been described in several studies as having a selective deficit in the encoding of episodic, but not semantic, LTM. A face-value acceptance of the findings from K.C. would require revision of the idea that all memories begin as episodic memories, and then gradually, through the process of consolidation, transition to becoming semantic. But although Endel Tulving – who unarguably occupies the highest echelon of respected and influential theoreticians of memory – has argued for this perspective very cogently (for review, see Rosenbaum et al., 2005), the absence, in the years since the initial descriptions of K.C. in the 1980s, of any additional patients presenting a similar behavioral profile, may explain the fact that this case has had negligible influence on most current views of LTM encoding. Whether or not the same is (or, will be) true of single cases in the literature on the organization of semantic memory has remained a matter of vigorous debate (with, e.g., Mahon and Caramazza (2009) arguing for the importance of single cases, and Rogers et al. (2006) calling their importance into question).

Often tied up in these debates is the more technical question of *How important is the double dissociation formed by comparing case A with case B?* This question has arisen from neural network simulations demonstrating that double dissociations can be procured from unitary computational architectures. Although the details of these arguments are beyond the scope of what we can cover in this textbook, a feel for the essence of some of these arguments is captured in a chapter from Rogers and Plaut (2002):

> apparent double dissociations even in . . . homogeneous network[s] with no assumed neuroanatomic specialisation . . . [and] double-dissociations . . . aris[ing] from damage to anatomically distinct areas that are in no way specialised to subserve the cognitive functions dissociated . . . call into question the conclusion . . . that the dissociated functions must be subserved by modules that may be damaged independently. (p. 252)

Counterarguments have pointed to simulations such as Farah and McClelland (1991), in which meaningful structure can exist, and can therefore be selectively impaired, within computational architectures that started out homogeneous before training. In view of these complications associated with cognitive neuropsychology, it is not surprising that semantic memory researchers have turned to functional neuroimaging as an important source of data. So too, now, will we.

The Neuroimaging of Knowledge

The Meaning, and Processing, of Words

Many pioneering neuroimaging studies addressing the questions that we have reviewed up to this point have come from Alex Martin and his collaborators at the National Institutes of Health (NIH). Martin trained as a neuropsychologist and spent the early part of his career studying the breakdown of language and memory functions in patients with Alzheimer's disease and HIV-AIDS. In 1989, he moved to the National Institute of Mental Health (NIMH), where he quickly fell in with Haxby, Ungerleider, and colleagues and soon began adapting their neuroimaging methods for the study of semantic memory. As a starting point, Martin considered the PET study of Petersen, Fox, Posner, Mintun, and Raichle (1988; *Figure 3.19.A* in this book), specifically the contrast that isolated verb generation and is entitled "Thinking about words." The fact that this contrast revealed greater activity in left inferior PFC (centered in BA 47) for verb generation than for either reading visually presented words or repeating auditorily presented words suggested a role for left PFC in semantic processing, independent of input modality. That is, this finding made the left inferior PFC a candidate locus for an amodal semantic store. However, Martin doubted that semantics would be localizable to this particular region of the brain, for a number of reasons. First, theories from cognitive psychology and from linguistics posited that "the meaning of a concrete noun is not unitary, but rather is composed of parts – specifically, knowledge about the physical and functional properties of the object." One would therefore predict word meanings to be anatomically distributed. Complementary to this perspective were the computational and neural canons that we have established in the previous two chapters, that long-term memories are composed of the association of the neural representations of many sensations, actions, emotions, and so on. Additionally, Martin and colleagues reasoned that "even if semantic networks were confined to a single region, the neuropsychological evidence suggested that the critical area would be the left temporal, not the left frontal, lobe" (Martin, Ungerleider, and Haxby, 2000, pp. 1023–1024).

An Aside About the Role of Language in Semantics and the Study of Semantics Note that, for each type of study that we've considered thus far in this chapter, language has been central to the theoretical motivation and/or the experimental procedures employed. Warrington and McCarthy's 1983 paper is entitled "Category Specific Access Dysphasia," **dysphasia** being an impairment in the ability to communicate following brain damage. Thus, their title appeals to the directly observable clinical presentation of the patient, rather than to the psychological construct of semantic memory. Indeed, experiment 1 from this paper reported the phenomenon that they presumably set out to study in this patient, a dissociation between her relatively spared ability to match pictures of common objects to exemplars of the objects themselves vs. a relative impairment in matching spoken words to the same objects. The subsequent several experiments then examined factors such as how the rate of presentation affected her performance, the effect of using spoken vs. written cues, and so on. It was only at experiment 10 (sic!) that the issue that this paper is famous for arose: "An incidental observation in a pilot study . . . suggested that V.E.R.'s comprehension deficits might to some extent be more severe for some taxonomic categories than others" (p. 870). The Farah and McClelland (1991) model, intended to emulate the Warrington studies, was trained, and tested, by mapping verbal labels to pictures, and vice versa. Petersen et al. (1988) studied the generation of a verb from a visually or auditorily presented noun (c.f., *Figure 4.18*), and many, many subsequent neuroimaging studies have also used linguistic material to study semantics. Perhaps this is a necessary association? Whether language is fundamental to the mental representation of knowledge, or at least to its acquisition, is a question that has occupied philosophers for centuries, and is certainly not one that we can hope to resolve in this textbook. What is important for our purposes is to be aware of this association while evaluating the research that we'll review here, and of the competing claims about the centrality of language to the impairments seen in various neurological syndromes, and to patterns of activity observed in brain imaging studies.

PET Scanning of Object Knowledge

Alex Martin's analysis of the neuropsychological literature drew heavily on the visual agnosias, which could produce selective impairment of particular stimulus attributes, such as cortical color blindness (achromatopsia) and motion blindness (akinetopsia). Thus, his first PET study, published in 1995, was designed to isolate the contributions to object knowledge of the cortical representation of the features *color* and *action*. It presented subjects with black-and-white line drawings of common objects, and in one scan asked subjects to name them, in a second, to name a color associated with that object, and in a third, to name an action that could be performed with that object. With a procedure comparable to that used by Petersen et al. (1988; *Chapter 4*, section *Positron emission tomography*), the data were analyzed by subtracting the object-naming images from both the color- and action-naming images, thereby emphasizing the processing of those two object attributes. The results, presented in *Figure 13.2*, indicated that color naming was selectively associated with activity in a region of ventral temporal cortex, just anterior to a region of ventral occipital cortex associated with color perception, and that action naming preferentially activated a broad expanse of left lateral cortex encompassing posterior middle temporal gyrus (MTG), superior temporal gyrus (STG), and posterior inferior parietal lobule (IPL). In addition to some overlap in these posterior regions, both tasks also preferentially activated a large region of left PFC and premotor cortex (PMC), with

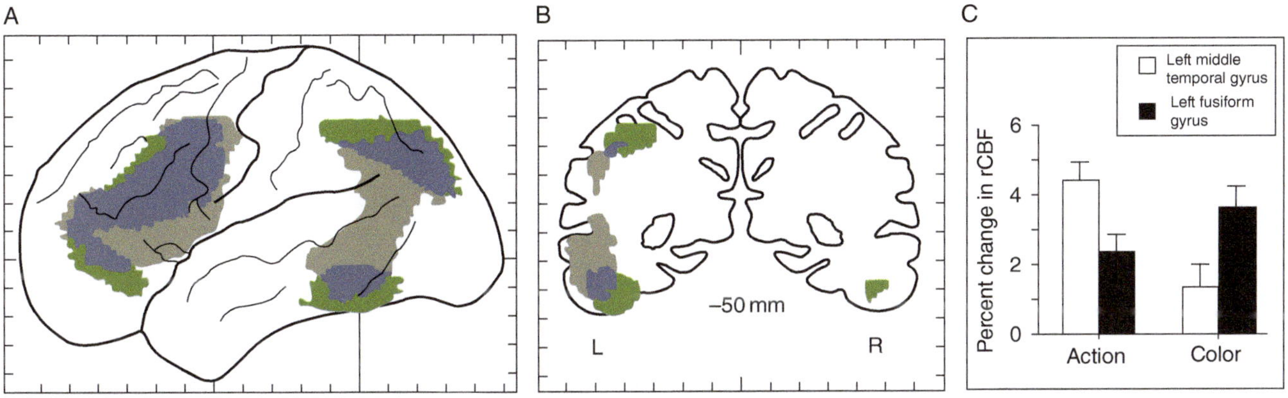

FIGURE 13.2 Superimposed subtraction images of object attribute naming from black-and-white line drawings. Green = object color generation (minus object naming); gray = object action generation (minus object naming); and blue indicates the overlap. **A.** Lateral view, with vertical line six tick marks from the right side of the image indicating the plane of section illustrated in B. **B.** Coronal slice is 50 mm posterior to the "0 mm" location, along the rostrocaudal axis of the anterior commissure. **C.** Peak magnitude of these effects in two temporal lobe regions.

Source: Martin et al., 1995 / American Association for the Advancement of Science.

the action-generation task preferentially engaging posterior inferior frontal gyrus, including Broca's area. In a second experiment, subjects performed the same tasks, but in response to written words instead of line drawings, and the results were, by and large, the same.

Martin et al. (1995) interpreted their results as evidence that "knowledge of colors and of actions is represented in discrete cortical areas . . . [that are] proximal to color and motion perceptual-processing areas" (p. 104). They further argued for a framework in which the representation of knowledge about objects is distributed among the representation of the features that make up an object, and tied to the modality that characterizes these features (e.g., the perception of chrominance and the perception of motion). Note the similarities between this perspective and the modality-specific models of Warrington and colleagues and of Farah and McClelland (1991). Indeed, consistent with the modality-specific view were the results of a second study that contrasted the silent naming of animals with the silent naming of tools (Martin, Wiggs, Ungerleider, and Haxby, 1996), effectively a PET version of the Warrington studies. The findings from this study were also consistent with a modality-specific model: naming animals was associated with greater activity in visual cortex, and naming tools with greater activity in regions that largely overlapped those identified with action generation in the 1995 study – posterior MTG and PMC. In interpreting these results, and in several subsequent studies, Martin and colleagues have argued that the tool-related activity in the posterior MTG relates to the processing of artifact motion, and that the tool-related activity in PMC corresponds to movement plans associated with object use. The involvement of PMC, in particular, has prompted the suggestion of a role for mirror neurons in the representation of tool semantics. There are also clear points of contact with the rapidly growing "embodied cognition" perspective in psychology.

To just review the results from these two PET studies as we have done up to this point, and to then move on to the next topic, would be to misrepresent this field of study. There are many conceptual nuances, and pragmatic challenges, with which one must grapple when studying a cognitive faculty as abstract as *knowledge* with a method as concrete as functional neuroimaging. Publishing in this arena often sparks vociferous debate. To get a feel for some of this nuance and challenge, let's follow the trajectory, as it were, of just one claim from the Martin et al. (1995) study, considering some of the scrutiny it has received and how it has, in turn, been critiqued and defended. The claim that we'll follow is that activity in the left fusiform gyrus is associated with the storage of color-related knowledge about objects (*Figure 13.2*). We'll begin by returning to the Martin et al. (1995) paper itself, in whose pages we can already find evidence for objections to this claim.

Knowledge Retrieval or Lexical Access?

In the discussion of their findings, Martin et al. (1995) include a footnote to reinforce the interpretation of their findings in terms of "knowledge," per se, rather than of activation of the mental lexicon.

> Findings from studies of patients with focal brain lesions argue against alternative interpretations of these activations as the sites for storage of the color and action words themselves, or of word-specific retrieval mechanisms located at sites distant from where information is stored. A patient with a color anomia can produce color words. What the patient cannot do is correctly name the colors seen or correctly answer questions about object-associated colors (the patient will respond with an inappropriate color word). To show areas of activity by functional brain imaging technologies, it is necessary for subjects to be engaged in performing a task. Thus, it might be formally more accurate to state that the activations in the temporal lobes show the sites of storage during the act of retrieval. In this sense, however, storage and retrieval cannot be distinguished. (p. 105)

Although one can't know for sure (and the author has deliberately chosen not to contact Alex Martin to confirm or deny his speculation), it is not infrequently the case that a footnote such as this gets added to a manuscript after it has gone through peer review. For example, if there's a particular point about which the author and a reviewer disagree, sometimes an editor will say something like this to the authors: "Although you disagree with this argument raised by the reviewer, you need to explicitly address it in your manuscript. In addition, if you like, you can also give your rationale for disagreeing with it." Whether or not a similar scenario played out in this instance, what is clear is that this footnote is intended to refute an alternative interpretation with which the authors strongly disagree. There are several instructive aspects to this footnote. First, it highlights the fact that, particularly in this research area, the design and interpretation of neuroimaging studies are heavily influenced by patient studies, and vice versa. Second, it highlights one of the pragmatic challenges raised by the tight coupling of language and semantics. Finally, it highlights a second alternative perspective (in addition to the domain-specificity model) to the modality-specific model: the true driver of patterns of neural activity in the left temporal lobe, such as those described here, and, by extension, of category-specific deficits in patients with lesions to these areas, may be lexical retrieval.

The lexical-retrieval view has been advocated by the husband-and-wife team of neurologists Hanna Damasio and Antonio Damasio. They have argued, from patient and neuroimaging data presented in a 1996 paper, that lateral temporal-lobe regions, although not classical language areas, make important contributions to the retrieval of words, and do so in a domain-segregated way, with lexical access to the names of people mediated by the temporal pole, to the names of animals by mid-inferior temporal gyrus wrapping onto the ventral surface of the temporal lobe, and to the names of tools by posterior MTG. They have interpreted the core deficit of patients with damage to each of these regions to be one of lexical retrieval (i.e., word finding), because the naming deficits of their patients were demonstrated after it had been determined that they understood the concept of the item in the picture. (This specific claim, incidentally, is one with which Caramazza and Shelton (1998) take issue.) Thus, Damasio, Grabowski, Tranel, Hichwa, and Damasio (1996) have argued for a different functional interpretation of the ventral temporal-lobe activity that Martin et al. (1995) attribute to color knowledge (as well as for a different functional interpretation of the area that Martin et al. (1995) attribute to action generation).

Recall that we previously noted that, in composing their title, Warrington and McCarthy (1983) emphasized the directly observable clinical presentation of their patient (dysphasia) rather than that psychological construct that the patient's clinical presentation implicated. It may be that the emphasis that the Damasios have placed on a lexical explanation for their data also derives, at least in part, from their experience in the clinic. Both are behavioral neurologists whose contributions to cognitive neuroscience have been strongly anchored by their experience and expertise in working with patients. Further along in this chapter, we'll also see that a naming interpretation has been favored by many neurologists in relation to a neurodegenerative disease that they have referred to as "primary progressive aphasia" (aphasia being an inability to use language), whereas many approaching the same disease from a psychological perspective call it "semantic dementia."

Repetition Effects and fMRI Adaptation

Recall, from *Chapter 11* and *Chapter 12*, that repetition priming is a type of nondeclarative memory in which previous exposure to a stimulus biases or facilitates the processing of that stimulus (or fragments thereof) when presented on subsequent occasions. At the neural level, a correlate of repetition priming is the repetition suppression effect, whereby neurons that responded to the initial presentation of the stimulus with an increase in firing rate respond with a smaller increase to the second and subsequent presentations. With neuroimaging, an analogous effect was shown by Randy Buckner and his mentors at Washington University with PET studies of word-stem completion, and later, more definitively, by Buckner, Anders Dale, and colleagues at the MGH NMR Center with their rapid event-related fMRI technique.

A methodological innovation that takes advantage of this phenomenon, called **fMRI adaptation**, was developed by Kalanit Grill-Spector and her then-mentor Rafael Malach. To deduce the functional properties of a region of visual cortex, one first presents a stimulus several times to produce a repetition-suppression effect. Then, one begins varying the stimulus properties along a single dimension. If the region of interest is invariant to changes along that dimension, its response will remain suppressed. If, however, it is sensitive to changes along this dimension, any change will result in a "release from adaptation" and a return to its initial level of response.

Illustrated in *Figure 13.3* is a study that employed the logic of fMRI adaptation. Subjects were presented with images of familiar objects (both living and nonliving) and asked to indicate for each, with a button press, whether or not it would fit into a shoebox. During the study phase, each of 32 items was presented on three occasions. During the test phase (the transition from study to test occurring without the subjects' knowledge), each of 64 items was presented once. Of these, 32 were repeats of the 32 study items, 16 were different exemplars of the same kind of item as the 32 (Different), and 16 were items that had not appeared among the 32 studied items (Novel).

As illustrated in *Figure 13.3*, three of the regions of interest in this study showed an identical response profile: suppressed activity for a repeated item, but a release from adaptation for a same-type-but-different-token (i.e., "Different") item. These regions, therefore, were assumed to encode the visual characteristics of stimuli, but not more abstract properties. (E.g., for a study picture of an octopus, if a region's response to a physically different picture of an octopus is not suppressed, it must be that this region doesn't register that the two physically different images correspond to the same kind of thing. The interpretation is that this region doesn't encode the meaning of "octopus-ness.") The left fusiform gyrus ROI, in contrast, showed only a partial release from adaptation. (I.e., its response to a Different stimulus showed a level of adaptation intermediate between a repeated image and a Novel image.) Thus, this region's activity registered the semantic similarity between the two images, even though their physical properties differed.

The study by Simons et al. (2003) that is illustrated in *Figure 13.3* is one of several senior authored by Daniel Schacter, a cognitive psychologist who trained with Endel Tulving and, during the 1980s and 1990s, came to be known as arguably the world's foremost authority on repetition priming. Initially, in collaboration with Randy Buckner, Schacter and his mentees performed many of the first fMRI studies of this phenomenon. Among them, this study by then-visiting scholar Jon Simons et al. (2003) was one to which Martin could refer as evidence against the possibility that the left fusiform gyrus activity produced by his color-naming condition corresponded to "just" visual imagery that did not "do any conceptual work."

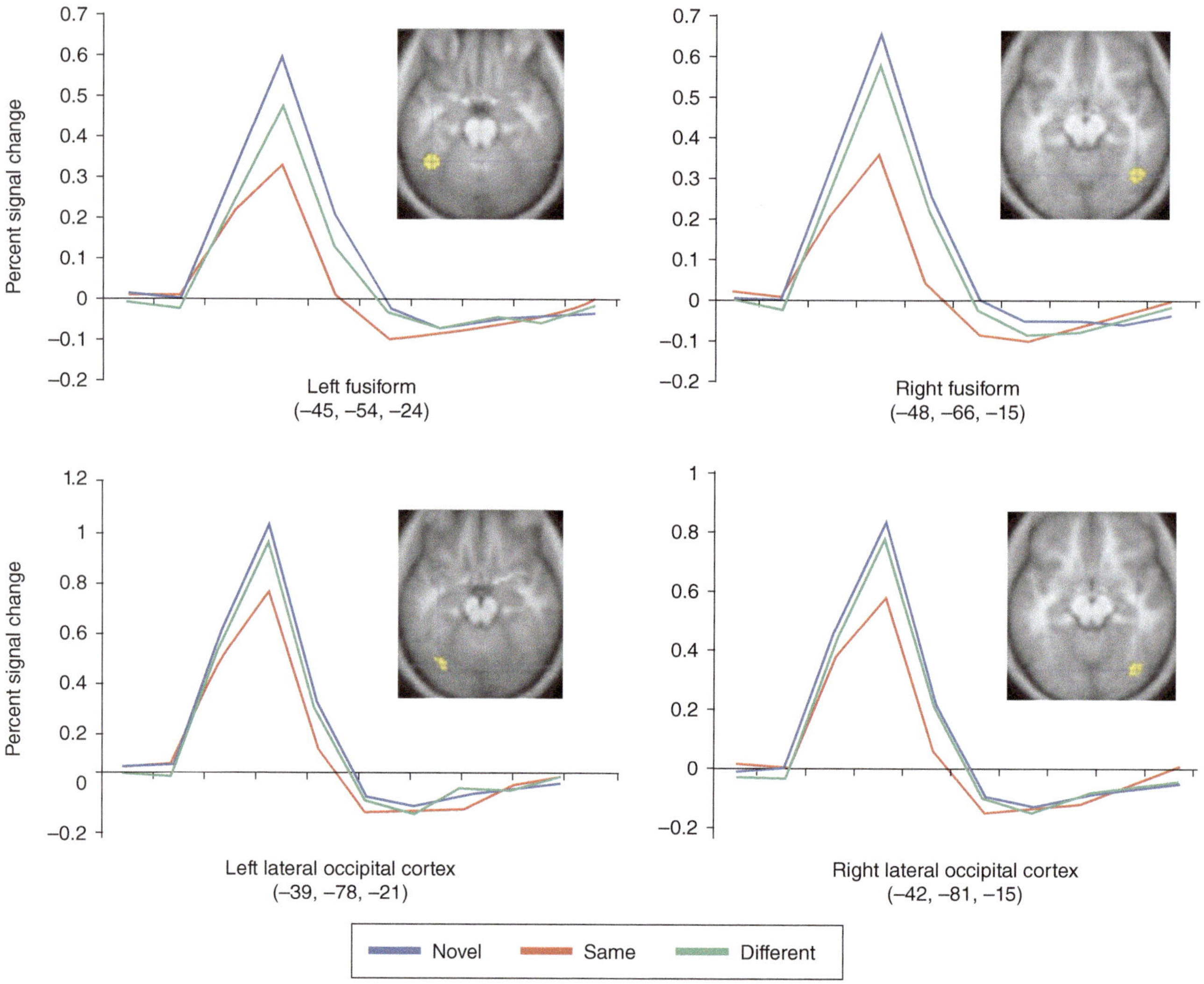

FIGURE 13.3 Repetition effects in four posterior regions. Each plot shows the fMRI stimulus-evoked response to the presentation of a picture that is being seen for the first time (Novel), is a repeat presentation of a stimulus that had already been presented on three previous occasions during the same scan (Same), or is a different exemplar of one of the already-thrice-presented items (Different).

Source: Reproduced from Simons et al. (2003) / with permission of Elsevier.

Does It Matter Whether We Understand What Causes Repetition Effects? At around the time that much of the work reviewed here was being carried out, there was, in parallel, considerable interest in understanding how fMRI repetition/adaptation effects are brought about at the level of the neuronal function. One highly cited review on the topic was written as a kind of "adversarial collaboration" commentary[1] in which Kalanit Grill-Spector, Rik Henson, and Alex Martin (2006) considered each of three candidate mechanisms: fatigue, sharpening, and facilitation. It's notable that these three authors each came from a different research domain – visual object recognition, episodic LTM (declarative and nondeclarative), and semantic memory, respectively – a fact that is emblematic of how versatile and widely used this approach has been. But the fact that underlying basis of repetition effects has

[1]The term "adversarial collaboration" is most appropriately used to describe an arrangement between two or more research groups that disagree about a particular phenomenon in which they collaboratively design an experiment that, depending on the outcome, will definitively resolve the controversy. Here the author is using it loosely to connote that these three authors had differing opinions about the neural bases of repetition suppression effects, but worked collaboratively on this review.

been uncertain also illustrates a different general point about neuroimaging research: In some cases, one does not need to fully understand the neural bases of an effect for its results to be interpretable. Consider the results from Simons et al. (2003) (*Figure 13.3*) that we just reviewed: the interpretation of a role for left fusiform cortex in visual semantics would hold regardless of whether repetition effects turned out to be exclusively due to fatigue, to sharpening, to facilitation, or to some other phenomenon that we haven't considered here. Indeed, that turns out to be fortuitous for all of the groups that we have name-checked in this section because, as was hinted at the end of section *What is the familiarity signal?, Chapter 12*, a longstanding assumption about the circumstances that produce repetition effects at the neuronal level has recently been challenged. Here's the summary from She, Benna, Shi, Fusi, and Tsao (2024):

> Previous studies have suggested that familiarity is encoded by response suppression across cells . . . Supporting this, our first experiment (a screening set consisting of familiar and unfamiliar human faces, monkey faces and objects) showed a decreased average response to familiar compared with unfamiliar faces. However, to our great surprise, data from our second experiment (1,000 unfamiliar faces interleaved with 36 familiar faces) showed a stronger mean response to familiar compared with unfamiliar stimuli . . . The two experiments had one major difference: in the first experiment the ratio of familiar to unfamiliar faces was 34:16 whereas in the second the ratio was 36:1,000 . . . Thus the expectation of familiar faces was much lower in the second experiment (p. 865).

The authors go on to note that previous studies suggested that expectation can strongly modulate response magnitudes of IT neurons, with unexpected stimuli exhibiting stronger responses. And so it may be that, although not considered by, e.g., Grill-Spector, Henson, and Martin (2006), prediction may also play a role in this phenomenon that has contributed to the study of visual semantics.

This concludes our deeper look at claims about the proposed role for the left fusiform gyrus in the storage of color-related knowledge about objects (*Figure 13.2*). The realm of nuance and challenge to which we will devote the remaining portion of this chapter is that of a neurodegenerative disease whose cognitive impairments manifest prominently in language and semantic memory.

The Progressive Loss of Knowledge

Unlike the acute-onset neurological syndromes that we have considered up until now (stroke, viral encephalitis, and, indeed, surgical excision), neurodegenerative diseases are characterized by progressive degeneration of the integrity of the affected neural systems, and in the behaviors that depend on those systems. *Dementia* refers to the progressive impairment of intellect and behavior that, over time, dramatically alters and restricts normal activities of daily living. Most dementias are of "insidious onset," medicalese for "subtle and gradual." The most common form of dementia is Alzheimer's disease, which typically initially manifests as a progressively worsening anterograde amnesia, and gradually compromises other mnemonic and other cognitive functions. Atypical dementias are a class that first manifest in domains of cognition other than episodic memory. Of interest for our present purposes is a subtype of frontotemporal dementia that has variously been called *primary progressive aphasia* or *semantic dementia*.

Primary Progressive Aphasia or Semantic Dementia, What's in a Name?

As alluded to previously, there was a period during which one's preferred label for this disease seemed to reflect, in part, the scholarly tradition from which one approached it. In the 1970s, neuropsychologists Elizabeth Warrington in the United Kingdom and Myrna Schwartz and her colleagues in Philadelphia both described cases of dementia with anomia (naming difficulty) that seemed to reveal a selective impairment of semantic memory. Subsequently, neurologists who saw similar patients in the clinic labeled the condition semantic dementia.

In parallel, in 1982, the behavioral neurologist M.-Marsel Mesulam wrote a highly influential paper describing patients with a condition he labeled "primary progressive aphasia," and that he characterized it as follows:

> Patients with Alzheimer's disease come to medical attention because of forgetfulness, usually accompanied by apathy. Misplacing personal objects, repeating questions, and forgetting recent events are among the presenting symptoms. Although the patient may forget people's names, word-finding during conversation is usually not a major problem. In contrast, patients with primary progressive aphasia come to medical attention because of the onset of word-finding difficulties, abnormal speech patterns, and prominent spelling errors. Primary progressive aphasia is diagnosed when other mental faculties, such as memory of daily events, visual and spatial skills (assessed by tests of drawing and face recognition), and behavior (assessed by a history obtained from a third party), remain relatively intact; when language is the only area of prominent dysfunction for at least the first two years of the disease; and when structural brain imaging studies do not reveal a specific lesion, other than atrophy, that can account for the language deficit. (Mesulam, 2003, pp. 1535–1536)

In this and a contemporaneous review, Mesulam and a formidable lineup of colleagues asserted (via the title of their paper) that the language impairment is the core deficit in all forms of primary progressive aphasia, and poor word comprehension is a peripheral "halo" in one subtype that they termed the fluent subtype of primary progressive aphasia. Alternatively, they argued that there is a second distinct neurodegenerative syndrome characterized by two independent factors: an aphasia due to pathology in the left hemisphere perisylvian language cortex and an associative agnosia due to pathology in the inferior temporal cortex.

In the remainder of this chapter, we will consider a series of studies advocating an alternative view, whereby the core deficit of the putatively fluent variant of primary progressive aphasia is, in fact, semantic memory. The pedagogical strategy here is analogous to what we did with the color-naming finding from Martin et al. (1995) – by zooming in for a fine-grained consideration of this particular debate, we will encounter experimental methods and lines of argumentation that illustrate broader themes about how scientists think about the neural bases of semantic memory. Much of this work that we will consider has been led by neurologist John Hodges and neuropsychologist Karalyn Patterson, both based in Cambridge, UK at the time of this work, and their colleagues and trainees, who have taken the position that semantic dementia and the fluent variant of primary progressive aphasia may be "two sides of the same coin." They have framed the debate as follows: are there "subtle nonverbal semantic deficits . . . in fPPA [(fluent primary progressive aphasia)] [that are] fundamental to the anomia and reflect, therefore, damage to an amodal semantic system associated with bilateral, though often asymmetric, anterior temporal lobe (ATL) atrophy?" Alternatively, does semantic dementia "result from a disease process that encompasses two separate neurocognitive networks – a left hemisphere language network and a bilateral fusiform network for face and object recognition – which, though jointly compromised in SD [i.e., 'semantic dementia'], can also be damaged independently?" (Adlam et al., 2006, p. 3067).

Nonverbal Deficits in Fluent Primary Progressive Aphasia?

To test between the two alternatives laid out in the previous paragraph, Adlam et al. (2006) recruited seven patients who met the diagnostic criteria of early-stage fluent primary progressive aphasia. Along with standard neuropsychological tests of language, memory, and other cognitive functions, they also administered tasks intended to probe their earlier findings that semantic dementia progressively restricts the conceptual knowledge of patients to general and typical features. Examples of these tasks are shown in *Figure 13.4*. The results of the behavioral testing indicated that, on the standardized tests, patients demonstrated a more marked verbal than nonverbal impairment. This is an oft-replicated finding and follows from the fact that these patients had been selected for meeting diagnostic criteria for fluent primary progressive aphasia. Additionally, however, results from the tests designed to assess the selective loss of specific knowledge contradicted Mesulam's assertion that "language is the only area of prominent dysfunction for at least the first two years of the disease." On the Levels of Specificity and Typicality (LOST) word-matching task (*Figure 13.4.A. AND B*), for example, the patients were selectively impaired at matching low-typical targets among close distractors. On the object-color decision task (*Figure 13.4.C*), patients were only impaired on NR > R trials, that is, when the foil was a more domain-typical color than the target. The authors interpreted these findings as evidence that fluent primary progressive aphasia/semantic dementia impairs conceptual knowledge, in addition to language functions, at early stages of the disease:

> In summary of this issue: how are we to classify patients like the ones studied here, who present with a prominent fluent, anomic aphasia and a less prominent but still significant agnosia that is modulated by concept familiarity/typicality? These patients qualify for a diagnosis of fPPA on the basis of their preserved everyday function and the predominance of their aphasia; but (i) when tested with appropriate materials, they have clear non-verbal impairments, even at this early stage, and (ii) in our (by now fairly extensive) experience, they invariably progress to a pattern that every FTD researcher would call SD. It seems more logical and more useful to label them as having mild or early-stage SD. (p. 3077)

The Locus of Damage in Fluent Primary Progressive Aphasia?

The anatomical prediction of Adlam et al. (2006), that fluent primary progressive aphasia would be characterized by degeneration focused on the anterior temporal lobe, stemmed from prior neuropathology and neuroimaging studies of patients who they had defined as having semantic dementia. Additionally, a PDP model by Rogers and McClelland (2004) suggests the existence of "a set of shared representation units that tie together all of an object's properties across different information types." After damage to or degeneration in these units, "distinctions between items that are very similar semantically tend to be lost . . . while distinctions between highly dissimilar objects are maintained" (pp. 378–379). (Note that this is the pattern of deficit observed in the patients of Adlam et al. (2006).) In contrast, most prior research explicitly performed on patients diagnosed with fluent primary progressive aphasia had assumed that the language impairments in these patients resulted from atrophy in the left hemisphere language network, particularly "perisylvian" regions of posterior STG/IPL and

FIGURE 13.4 Testing semantic impairments in fluent primary progressive aphasia/semantic dementia.

FIGURE 13.4.A AND B Two trials similar to the Levels of Specificity and Typicality (LOST) word-matching task, illustrating the manipulation of specificity, in that subjects are asked to point to the yacht (a low-typicality target from the category "boats") from among a set of close semantic distractors (**A**) and from among a set of unrelated semantic distractors (**B**). An example of a high-typicality target boat would be a sailboat.

Source: Bradley R. Postle.

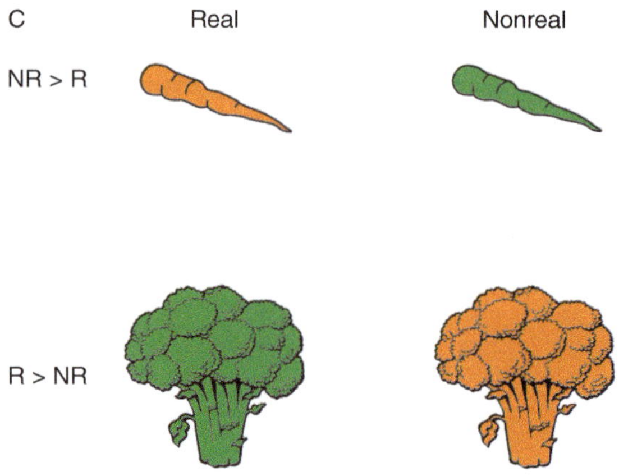

FIGURE 13.4.C Two sets of stimuli from the object-color decision task from Adlam et al. (2006). "NR > R" denotes a trial when the nonreal item has a color that is more typical of the category than the real item (i.e., vegetables are more typically green than orange; however, carrots are orange), and R > NR a trial when the real item has a color that is more typical of the category than the nonreal item (i.e., vegetables are more typically green than orange, and broccoli is green).

Source: Adapted from Adlam et al., 2006.

inferior prefrontal cortex of the left hemisphere. Further, Mesulam (2003) had argued that fluent primary progressive aphasia accompanied by associative agnosia would be expected to exhibit degeneration in the inferior occipitotemporal cortex to account for the latter.

Results from the VBM analysis performed by Adlam et al. (2006), illustrated in *Figure 13.5*, show clear evidence for bilateral degeneration in the anterior temporal lobes of these patients. Further, performance of patients on both verbal and nonverbal tasks was predicted by gray-matter density values in the left inferior temporal region marked with crosshairs in *Figure 13.5.C*, suggesting that the integrity of this region may be crucial for performance on their behavioral tests of semantic memory.

How are we to make sense of the absence of any overlap between the predictions of Mesulam (2003) on the one hand and, on the other, those of Adlam et al. (2006) with respect to which areas are expected to be compromised by fluent primary progressive aphasia? One possible answer comes from an earlier PET study of semantic dementia (Mummery et al., 1999), whose results suggested that activity in regions presumably spared the direct effects of degeneration nonetheless showed abnormal patterns of activity.

Distal Effects of Neurodegeneration

The study of Mummery et al. (1999) compared patients diagnosed with semantic dementia with age- and education-matched control subjects. Results from a VBM analysis were highly similar to those of Adlam et al. (2006; *Figure 13.5* in this book), indicating a degenerative focus in the anterior temporal lobe and, importantly, a sparing of the gray-matter integrity of the ventral surface of temporo-occipital cortex. This finding was particularly noteworthy in light of the PET results, which indicated that activity related to word matching and to picture matching was significantly reduced in patients, relative to control subjects, in the lateral and inferior temporo-occipital cortex (*Figure 13.6*). This finding suggests a way to reconcile the predictions from Mesulam (2003), on the one hand, and Adlam et al. (2006), on the other: neurodegeneration associated with fluent primary progressive aphasia/semantic dementia may directly impact the integrity of anterior temporal cortex, and this structural degeneration may lead to functional abnormalities in the inferior and lateral temporo-occipital cortex, the normal functioning of which is known to be critical for high-level visual perception and, by many accounts, the perceptual features that contribute to the semantic representation of objects.

Systems-level accounts of how disruption of ATL can lead to abnormal functioning in the visual ventral stream include the designation of this region as a critical "hub" for semantic representation (Rogers et al., 2006), and the related idea that it may be a source of "top-down modulatory input necessary for successful retrieval of semantic representations stored in posterior regions" (Martin and Chao, 2001, p. 198).

Entente Cordiale

This chapter concludes with an all-too-rare consensus resolution of a hotly debated topic in cognitive neuroscience. An important factor pushing for this outcome was the fact that the stakes in the debate about the neural and cognitive impairments of fluent primary progressive aphasia/semantic dementia have very important implications for the diagnosis and treatment of patients who are suffering from the disease. To achieve it, an international "consensus group" including all of the neurologists whose work we have highlighted here met on three different occasions. Rather than just "getting together to argue," however, they followed a systematic procedure:

The group reviewed video presentations of 12 PPA cases from different sites. A list of

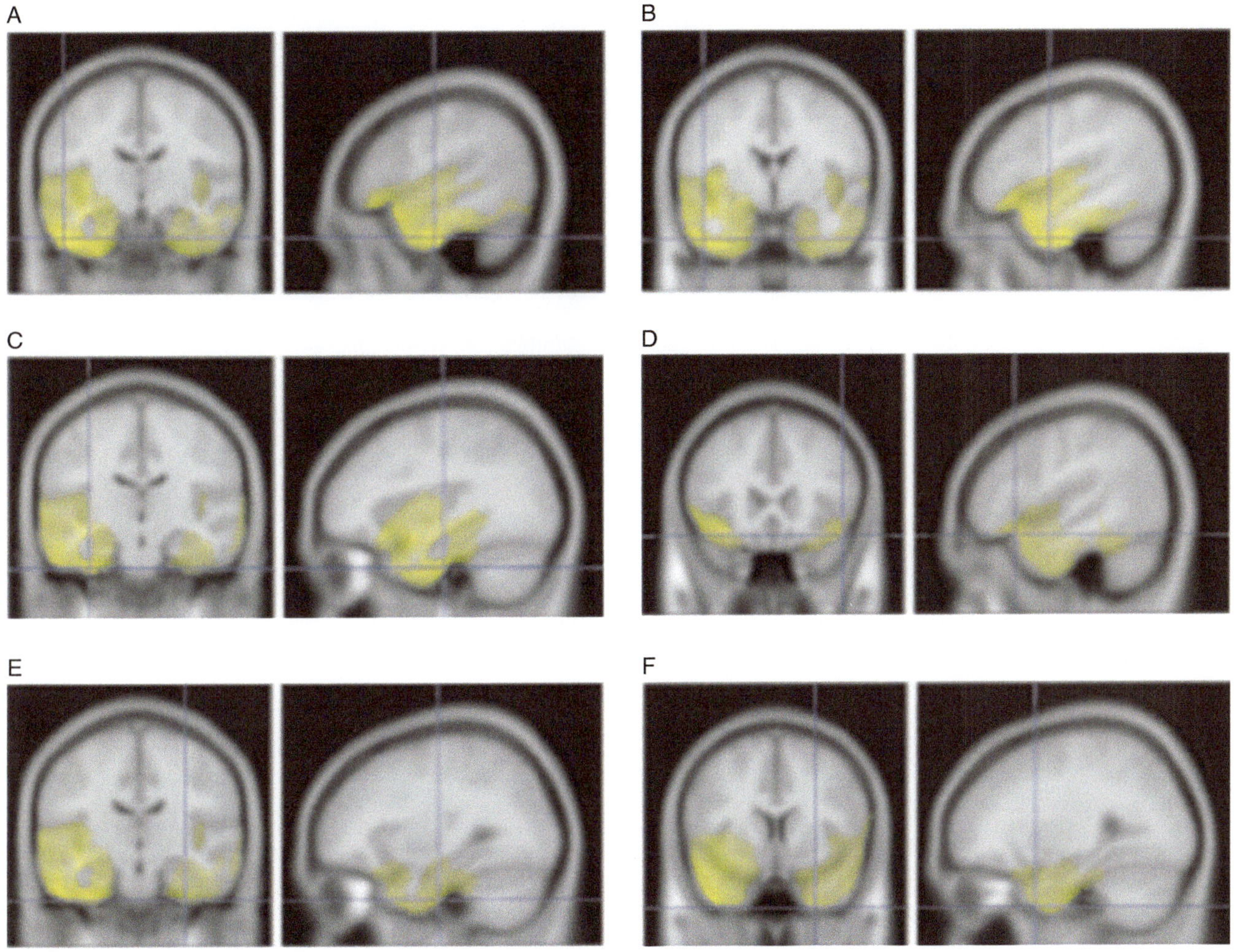

FIGURE 13.5 Results from the whole-brain VBM analysis from Adlam et al. (2006), showing extensive gray matter reduction (relative to control subjects) in each of six patients with fluent primary progressive aphasia. The crosshairs on each image indicate the peak areas of atrophy, the panels A-F corresponding to different sets of 3-D coordinates. Note that these occur in both hemispheres, and exclusively in anterior temporal lobe. Images are shown in neurological display convention (i.e., right side of coronal image corresponds to right hemisphere).

Source: Reproduced with permission from Adlam et al. (2006) / Oxford University Press.

17 salient speech and language features was provided, and each clinician rated whether specific language features were present or not. Videos included a component of spontaneous speech and various portions of formal language evaluations. The analysis of the responses revealed a high level of agreement. There were 15 clinical features in which experts agreed over 80% of the time. Thirteen of these features were included in an operationalized classification scheme listing the main features of the three most commonly recognized clinical presentations of PPA (Gorno-Tempini et al., 2011).

The three subtypes of primary progressive aphasia identified by the consensus group are nonfluent/agrammatic variant, semantic variant, and logopenic variant. It is on the existence and characteristics of the semantic variant that we have focused in this chapter, and the consensus diagnostic and classification criteria are very similar to what one would expect from the findings of Mummery et al. (1999) and Adlam et al. (2006).

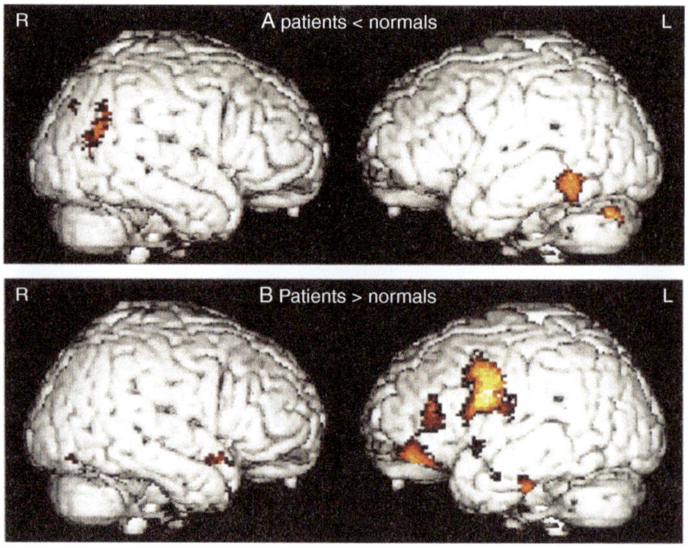

FIGURE 13.6 Difference images from PET scans comparing semantic task-related activity in semantic dementia patients vs. control subjects (Normals).

Source: Reproduced with permission from Mummery et al. (1999) / Oxford University Press.

Nuances and Challenges

We told you it would be like this! As cognitive functions become more abstract, it becomes increasingly difficult to design studies that unequivocally measure the construct of primary interest. The tradeoff, of course, is that what one gives up in reductive clarity, one gains in being able to grapple with questions that lie at the very heart of what it means to be human (from the perspective of "Je pense, donc je suis"). And even if one isn't philosophically inclined, there are pressing pragmatic reasons to better understand how to discriminate, for example, the representation of words from the representation of knowledge. Just consider the ongoing discussion and debate about whether artificial intelligence (AI) systems truly represent knowledge.

End-of-Chapter Questions

1. What are three interpretations of the fact that patients have been characterized with a selective deficit in the ability to name nonliving things and others with a selective deficit in the ability to name living things?

2. Summarize the arguments for and against placing a high level of importance on the findings from a single case study, and on the findings from two case studies that together form a double dissociation.

3. Name at least two possible explanations when a neuroimaging study finds selectively elevated activity for the naming of the color of an object relative to the naming of its shape, or of an action that one could take with that object, or some other property. What additional evidence can be drawn on to constrain the interpretation (e.g., to rule out alternative explanations)?

4. How has fMRI adaptation been used to argue for a functionally different role for the left mid-fusiform gyrus relative to its right hemisphere homolog and to areas of lateral occipital cortex?

5. How do neurodegenerative disorders, such as variants of frontotemporal dementia, differ from acute-episode neurological insults, such as stroke or viral encephalitis?

6. What pattern(s) of behavioral performance has (have) been pointed to as evidence for an inherently conceptual, as opposed to lexical, deficit in the semantic variant of primary progressive aphasia?

7. What brain area is selectively compromised in early stages of the semantic variant of primary progressive aphasia? What function, relevant to semantic dementia, is this region believed to support?

8. What are the salient differences between the consensus classifications of the nonfluent/agrammatical variant of primary progressive aphasia and the semantic variant of primary progressive aphasia? Despite these differences, how do the two differ in more fundamental ways from Alzheimer's disease?

References

Adlam, Anna-Lynne R., Karalyn Patterson, Timothy T. Rogers, Peter Nestor, Claire H. Salmond, Julio Acosta-Cabronero, and John R. Hodges. 2006. "Semantic Dementia and Fluent Primary Progressive Aphasia: Two Sides of the Same Coin?." *Brain* 129 (11): 3066–3080. doi: 10.1093/brain/awl285.

Caramazza, Alfonso, and Jennifer R. Shelton. 1998. "Domain-Specific Knowledge Systems in the Brain: The Animate–Inanimate Distinction." *Journal of Cognitive Neuroscience* 10 (1): 1–34. doi: 10.1093/neucas/4.4.399-k.

Damasio, Hanna, Thomas J. Grabowski, Daniel Tranel, Richard D. Hichwa, and Antonio R. Damasio. 1996. "A Neural Basis for Lexical Retrieval." *Nature* 380 (6574): 499–505. doi: 10.1038/380499a0.

Farah, Martha J., and James L. McClelland. 1991. "A Computational Model of Semantic Memory Impairment: Modality Specificity and Emergent Category Specificity." *Journal of Experimental Psychology: General* 120 (4): 339–357.

Farah, Martha J., Michael M. Meyer, and Patricia A. McMullen. 1996. "The Living/Nonliving Dissociation is Not an Artifact: Giving an A Priori Implausible Hypothesis a Strong Test." *Cognitive Neuropsychology* 13 (1): 137–154. doi: 10.1080/026432996382097.

Gorno-Tempini, Maria L., Argye E. Hillis, Sandra Weintraub, Andrew Kertesz, Mario F. Mendez, Stefano F. Cappa, . . . Murray Grossman. 2011. "Classification of Primary Progressive Aphasia and Its Variants." *Neurology* 76 (11): 1006–1014. doi: 10.1212/WNL.0b013e31821103e6.

Grill-Spector, Kalanit, Richard Henson, and Alex Martin. 2006. "Repetition and the Brain: Neural Models of Stimulus-Specific Effects." *Trends in Cognitive Sciences* 10 (1): 14–23. doi: 10.1016/j.tics.2005.11.006.

Mahon, Bradford Z., and Alfonso Caramazza. 2009. "Concepts and Categories: A Cognitive Neuropsychological Perspective." *Annual Review of Psychology* 60: 27–51. doi: 10.1146/annurev.psych.60.110707.163532.

Martin, Alex, and Linda L. Chao. 2001. "Semantic Memory and the Brain: Structure and Processes." *Current Opinion in Neurobiology* 11 (2): 194–201. doi: 10.1016/S0959-4388(00)00196-3.

Martin, Alex, James V. Haxby, François M. Lalonde, Cheri L. Wiggs, and Leslie G. Ungerleider. 1995. "Discrete Cortical Regions Associated with Knowledge of Color and Knowledge of Action." *Science* 270 (5233): 102–105. doi: 10.1126/science.270.5233.102.

Martin, Alex, Cheri L. Wiggs, Leslie G. Ungerleider, and James V. Haxby. 1996. "Neural Correlates of Category-Specific Knowledge." *Nature* 379 (6566): 646–652. doi: 10.1038/379649a0.

Martin, Alex, Leslie G. Ungerleider, and James V. Haxby. 2000. "Category Specificity and the Brain: The Sensory/Motor Model of Semantic Representations of Objects." In *The New Cognitive Neurosciences*, edited by Michael S. Gazzaniga (pp. 1023–1036), 2nd ed. Cambridge, MA: MIT Press.

McClelland, James L., Bruce L. McNaughton, and Randall C. O'Reilly. 1995. "Why There Are Complementary Learning Systems in the Hippocampus and Neocortex: Insights from the Successes and Failures of Connectionist Models of Learning and Memory." *Psychological Review* 102 (3): 419–457. doi: 10.1037/0033-295X.102.3.419.

Mesulam, M.-Marsel. 1982. "Slowly Progressive Aphasia without Generalized Dementia." *Annals of Neurology* 11 (6): 592–598. doi: 10.1002/ana.410110607.

Mesulam, M.-Marsel. 2003. "Primary Progressive Aphasia – A Language-Based Dementia." *New England Journal of Medicine* 346 (16): 1535–1542. doi: 10.1056/NEJMra022435.

Mummery, Catherine J., Karalyn Patterson, Richard J. Price, R. Vandenbergh, Cathy J. Price, and John R. Hodges. 1999. "Disrupted Temporal Lobe Connections in Semantic Dementia." *Brain* 122 (1): 61–73. doi: 10.1093/brain/122.1.61.

Petersen, Steven E., Peter T. Fox, Michael I. Posner, Mark Mintun, and Marcus E. Raichle. 1988. "Positron Emission Tomographic Studies of the Cortical Anatomy of Single-Word Processing." *Nature* 331 (6157): 585–589. doi: 10.1038/331585a0.

Rogers, Timothy T., and James L. McClelland. 2004. *Semantic Cognition: A Parallel Distributed Processing Approach.* Cambridge, MA: MIT Press.

Rogers, Timothy T., and David C. Plaut. 2002. "Connectionist Perspectives on Category-Specific Deficits." In *Category Specificity in Brain and Mind*, edited by Emer M. E. Forde and Glyn W. Humphreys (pp. 251–289). Hove: Psychology Press.

Rogers, Timothy T., Julia Hocking, Uta Noppeney, Andrea Mechelli, Maria Luisa Gorno-Tempini, Karalyn Patterson, and Cathy J. Price. 2006. "Anterior Temporal Cortex and Semantic Memory: Reconciling findings from Neuropsychology and Functional Imaging." *Cognitive, Affective, and Behavioral Neuroscience* 6 (3): 201–213. doi: 10.3758/CABN.6.3.201.

Rosenbaum, R. Shayna, Stefan Köhler, Daniel L. Schacter, Morris Moscovitch, Robyn Westmacott, Sandra E. Black, . . . Endel Tulving. 2005. "The Case of K. C.: Contributions of a Memory-Impaired Person to Memory Theory." *Neuropsychologia* 43 (7): 989–1021. doi: 10.1016/j.neuropsychologia.2004.10.007.

She, L., M. K. Benna, Y. Shi, S. Fusi, and D. Y. Tsao. 2024. "Temporal Multiplexing of Perception and Memory Codes in IT Cortex." *Nature 629* (8013): 861–868. doi: 10.1038/s41586-024-07349-5.

Simons, Jon S., Wilma Koutstaal, Steve Prince, Anthony D. Wagner, and Daniel L. Schacter. 2003. "Neural Mechanisms of Visual Object Priming: Evidence for Perceptual and Semantic Distinctions in Fusiform Cortex." *NeuroImage* 19 (3): 613–626. doi: 10.1016/S1053-8119(03)00096-X.

Warrington, Elizabeth K., and Rosaleen McCarthy. 1983. "Category Specific Access Dysphasia." *Brain* 106 (4): 859–878. doi: 10.1093/brain/106.4.859.

Warrington, Elizabeth K., and Tim Shallice. 1984. "Category Specific Semantic Impairments." *Brain* 107 (3): 829–853. doi: 10.1093/brain/107.3.829.

Other Sources Used

Buckner, Randy L., Julie Goodman, Marc Burock, Michael Rotte, Wilma Koutstaal, Daniel L. Schacter, . . . Anders M. Dale. 1998. "Functional-Anatomic Correlates of Object Priming in Humans Revealed by Rapid Presentation Event-Related fMRI." *Neuron* 20 (2): 285–296. doi: 10.1016/S0896-6273(00)80456-0.

Buckner, Randy L., Steven E. Petersen, Jeffrey G. Ojemann, Francis M. Miezin, Larry R. Squire, and Marcus E. Raichle. 1995. "Functional Anatomical Studies of Explicit and Implicit Memory Retrieval Tasks." *Journal of Neuroscience* 15 (1): 12–29.

Chao, Linda L., James V. Haxby, and Alex Martin. 1999. "Attribute-Based Neural Substrates in Temporal Cortex for Perceiving and Knowing about Objects." *Nature Neuroscience* 2 (10): 913–919. doi: 10.1038/13217.

Kensinger, Elizabeth A., Michael T. Ullman, and Suzanne Corkin. 2001. "Bilateral Medial Temporal Lobe Damage Does Not Affect Lexical or Grammatical Processing: Evidence from Amnesic Patient H. M." *Hippocampus* 11 (4): 347–360. doi: 10.1002/hipo.1049.

Martin, Alex. 2009. "Circuits in Mind: The Neural Foundations for Object Concepts." In *The Cognitive Neurosciences*, edited by Michael S Gazzaniga (pp. 1031–1045), 4th ed. Cambridge, MA: MIT Press.

McCarthy, Rosaleen A., and Elizabeth K. Warrington. 1988. "Evidence for Modality-Specific Meaning Systems in the Brain." *Nature* 334 (6181): 428–430. doi: 10.1038/334428a0.

Mummery, Catherine J., Karalyn Patterson, Cathy J. Price, John Ashburner, Richard S. J. Frackowiak, and John R. Hodges. 2000. "A Voxel-Based Morphometry Study of Semantic Dementia: Relationship Between Temporal Lobe Atrophy and Semantic Memory." *Annals of Neurology* 47 (1): 36–45. doi: 10.1002/1531-8249(200001)47:1<36::AID-ANA8>3.0.CO;2-L.

Paulesu, Eraldo, John Harrison, J. D. G. Simon Baron-Cohen., L Watson, J. Heather Goldstein, . . . Chris D. Frith. 1995. "The Physiology of Coloured Hearing: A PET Activation Study of Colour–Word Synaesthesia." *Brain* 118 (3): 661–676. doi: 10.1093/brain/118.3.661.

Plaut, David C. 1995. "Double Dissociation without Modularity: Evidence from Connectionist Neuropsychology." *Journal of Clinical and Experimental Neuropsychology* 17 (2): 291–321. doi: 10.1080/01688639508405124.

Schacter, Daniel L., and Randy L. Buckner. 1998. "Priming and the Brain." *Neuron* 20 (2): 185–195. doi: 10.1016/S0896-6273(00)80448-1.

Schwartz, Myrna F., Oscar S. M. Marin, and Eleanor M. Saffran. 1979. "Dissociations of Language Function in Dementia: A Case Study." *Brain and Language* 7 (3): 277–306. doi: 10.1016/0093-934X(79)90024-5.

Simner, Julia, Catherine Mulvenna, Noam Sagiv, Elias Tsakanikos, Sarah A. Witherby, Christine Fraser, . . . Jamie Ward. 2006. "Synaesthesia: The Prevalence of Atypical Cross-Modal Experiences." *Perception* 35 (8): 1024–1033. doi: 10.1068/p5469.

Warrington, Elizabeth K. 1975. "Selective Impairment of Semantic Memory." *Quarterly Journal of Experimental Psychology* 27 (4): 635–657. doi: 10.1080/14640747508400525.

Further Reading

Gorno-Tempini, Maria L., Argye E. Hillis, Sandra Weintraub, Andrew Kertesz, Mario F. Mendez, Stefano F. Cappa, . . . Murray Grossman. 2011. "Classification of Primary Progressive Aphasia and Its Variants." *Neurology* 76 (11): 1006–1014. doi: 10.1212/WNL.0b013e31821103e6.

The consensus paper on PPA and semantic dementia.

Grill-Spector, Kalanit, Richard Henson, and Alex Martin. 2006. "Repetition and the Brain: Neural Models of Stimulus-Specific Effects." *Trends in Cognitive Sciences* 10 (1): 14–23. doi: 10.1016/j.tics.2005.11.006.

No consensus, but nonetheless constructive; three scientists with different explanations for repetition effects seen with fMRI describe their models and articulate a way forward for adjudicating between them.

Lewis, Penelope A., and Simon J. Durrant. 2011. "Overlapping Memory Replay during Sleep Builds Cognitive Schemata." *Trends in Cognitive Sciences* 15 (8): 343–351. doi: 10.1016/j.tics.2011.06.004.

Proposal for how information processing during sleep may contribute to the semanticization of long-term memories.

Mahon, Bradford Z., and Alfonso Caramazza. 2009. "Concepts and Categories: A Cognitive Neuropsychological Perspective." *Annual Review of Psychology* 60: 27–51. doi: 10.1146/annurev.psych.60.110707.163532.

The perspective of two prominent advocates of the category-specific models of semantic memory.

Martin, Alex. 2007. "The Representation of Object Concepts in the Brain." *Annual Review of Psychology* 58: 25–45. doi: 10.1146/annurev.psych.57.102904.190143.

Comprehensive review from one of the leading cognitive neuroscientists of semantic memory.

Rogers, Timothy T., and James L. McClelland. 2008. "*Précis of Semantic Cognition: A Parallel Distributed Processing Approach.*" *Behavioral and Brain Sciences* 31 (6): 689–749. doi: 10.1017/S0140525X0800589X.

Précis of Rogers and McClelland's PDP model of semantic cognition, followed by many critiques by others working in the field, followed by a rejoinder from R & M.

CHAPTER **14**

Working Memory

KEY THEMES

- The terms "short-term memory" (STM) and "working memory" refer to the span of information (e.g., a telephone number, an array of objects) that one can hold in mind and use to guide behavior. Classically considered independent of MTL, although this information is quickly lost when attention is directed elsewhere, it can, in principle, be maintained indefinitely.
- "Working memory" is the more general term, because it also refers to the mental manipulation of information being held "in mind," such as performing mental arithmetic or reordering items into numerical or alphabetical order.
- From the 1940s through the 1960s, lesion findings indicated that the PFC was important for performance on tasks that required guiding behavior with working memory, but not for the short-term retention, per se, of recently encoded information.
- Despite the previous point, the 1971 extracellular electrophysiology studies reporting elevated delay-period-spanning activity of PFC neurons were interpreted by some (although not the authors themselves) as a neural correlate of the short-term retention of information.
- The conceptual integration of working memory theory from cognitive psychology with neurophysiological findings from PFC led to the development of an influential model of working memory theory, which holds the idea that PFC houses domain-segregated STM buffers.
- The superior sensitivity of MVPA over univariate analysis methods has provided compelling evidence that the short-term retention of information is supported in regions also responsible for its perception, including V1 for visual working memory.
- The superior specificity of MVPA over univariate analysis methods suggests that elevated delay-period activity, including in the PFC, does not always correspond to stimulus representation per se.
- Although "sensory recruitment" models posit that information is retained in working memory in the same neural systems that are responsible for its visual perception, RSA-based analyses suggest that the representational formats differ, with working memory becoming progressively more categorical (less "veridical") at higher levels of the cortical hierarchy.
- One function of elevated delay-period activity in the DAN is the application of mental effort.
- One function of elevated delay-period activity in lateral PFC is to control the selection and representational transformation of task-related information held in perception- and action-related brain areas.
- The ability to decode stimulus information from a brain region need not imply a storage function, because this would also be expected of regions acting as a source of the top-down control of that information.

CONTENTS

"Prolonged Perception" or "Activated LTM?"

Working memory refers to the ability to hold in mind information that's needed to achieve some immediate goal, like remembering the digits of an unfamiliar phone number until you get a chance to dial it, or remembering from the road sign that you just passed the ordering of the roads leaving the roundabout that you're about to enter. Although the order of chapters in this book by and large follows what one finds in most textbooks on cognitive psychology and cognitive neuroscience, the placement of this one is at variance with its typical placement at the transition point between a just-completed section on sensation/perception/attention and an ensuing section on LTM. This scheme, in effect, portrays working memory as "prolonged perception." The rationale for positioning this chapter here, instead of there, is twofold. First, it is increasingly the case that working memory is understood as being supported by the activation of semantic, as well as perceptual, representations. (Additionally, the idea of a role for the hippocampus in the short-term retention of at least some types of stimulus information is now widely accepted.) Thus, having an understanding of the organization and neural substrates of LTM will be important for what's to follow in this chapter. Second, short-term and working memory are closely intertwined with cognitive control, decision making, and other aspects of high-level cognition that will be the focus of the final section of this book, and so this chapter will serve as a nice transition to this final section.

Definitions

One thing to sort out before we go any further is what's meant by "immediate memory" vs. "short-term memory" vs. "working memory." Different people use these terms to mean different things, sometimes in different contexts. *Immediate memory* and *short-term memory* (STM) have a long history going back at least as far as William James and Ebbinghaus. To experimental psychologists, STM is expressed when subjects are asked to recognize or recall a small number of items more or less immediately after these items were presented. (In most contexts, the terms "immediate memory" and "STM" are synonymous, so we'll primarily use the latter.) Psychologists and neuropsychologists measure the capacity of verbal STM with variants of the digit span test, in which the subject first hears the digits "5 . . . 2" and must repeat them back to the experimenter. Assuming success, the subject next hears "7 . . . 9 . . . 4" and repeats these back. This process continues, with the span of digits increasing by one item, and the subject being given two attempts at each span, until they make an error on two consecutive attempts at the same length. The largest number of items that the subject is able to recall is referred to as their "digit span." The psychologist George Miller (1920–2012), often credited as one of the progenitors of cognitive neuroscience as a formal discipline, famously noted the high probability that this subject's span would fall within that of "the magical number 7 +/− 2."

This seems fairly straightforward, but what if, after hearing each series of digits, the subject was asked to wait 10 seconds before reciting them back? What about 10 minutes? 10 hours? At what point would their performance stop reflecting STM and instead depend on LTM? Alternatively, what if they were asked to recite the digits back immediately, but to do so in reverse order ("backward digit span")? Or to recite them back in their cardinal order, from smallest to largest (i.e., "7 . . . 9 . . . 4" becomes "4, 7, 9")? Or to mentally calculate the sum of the remembered digits and respond with that? We can begin to address some of these questions with a vignette featuring this author's go-to patient for explaining all things mnemonic:

> One of the privileges afforded graduate students at MIT's Behavioral Neuroscience Laboratory has been the opportunity to transport . . . H.M. from and to his home, a handful of hours distant, for his roughly semiannual research visit . . . The convention for H.M.'s transport was for the designated graduate student to travel with a companion, and there was never a shortage of volunteers (typically a fellow student or a postdoc) eager to take a road trip with this famous patient. On one such trip the two scientists-in-training and their charge sought to pass the time by playing a game in which each player selects a color – on this occasion, green, blue, and white – and accumulates points for each car painted in their color that passes in the opposite direction on the highway. Each player counts aloud, and the gaps between passing cars are typically filled with cheering and good-natured banter. H.M. participated fully in the game, selecting his color, accurately keeping track of his running total, and participating in the debate about whether a teal-colored car should be scored as blue, green, or neither. Indeed, on this occasion H.M. won, accruing a score of 20 first. A round of congratulations was exchanged, followed by a lull as the car rolled through the undulating central Massachusetts countryside. A few minutes later, the

> guest traveler, eager to maximize their once-in-a-lifetime opportunity to gain first-hand insight from this famous patient, asked "Henry, what are you thinking about right now?" H.M. replied that his count of white cars had now increased to 36.
>
> The driver and guest were both impressed that this patient, famously incapable of remembering virtually anything that had occurred in his life since his 1953 surgery, had accurately maintained and updated a running count of arbitrarily selected "target stimuli" across a span of several minutes, with no evident source of external support or reinforcement. The three travelers commented on this before the guest traveler redirected the conversation to a line of questions that was typical of these trips: "Do you know what today's date is?" "Do you know who the current President is?" "Do you know who we are; where we're going today?" H.M. complied with good-natured responses, as always, clearly enjoying the interaction with and attention from these young, engaged travelling companions. Very quickly, however, H.M. initiated another typical element in the driving-with-H.M. script, by steering the conversation towards a reminiscence from his youth, the portion of his life still mentally accessible after his surgery. (The story, about riding the Silver Meteor passenger train on a multi-day trip to visit an aunt in Florida, had already been told several times at that point in the trip, a product of the teller not remembering the previous tellings.) At that point, sensing a "teachable moment," the driver of the car interjected with a question of his own: "Henry, do you remember what game we were playing a few minutes ago?" No, he didn't. "It involved counting cars of different colors; do you remember what your color was?" No. "The three colors were green, blue, and white; do you remember which was yours?" No, the cues didn't help. "Do you remember who won the game?" No recollection even of the triumph that had, only a few minutes before, produced in H.M. a modest chuckle and satisfied smile. (Postle, 2009, pp. 326–327)

The main point here is that the "short" in short-term memory does not relate to the passage of time, per se. So long as H.M. continued thinking about the car-counting game, he could have maintained a memory for the number 36 (or, continued adding to it) indefinitely. *Continuous thought*, however, does seem to be a key factor for STM, as illustrated in the fact that just a few dozen seconds of thinking about other things removed any trace of memory of even the circumstances that gave rise to the number 36, not to mention the number itself. Indeed, this anecdote also illustrates that the "long" in long-term memory can't be taken at face value: The fact that both of the neurologically healthy individuals in the car *were* able to effortlessly recall all the details from the game played only a few minutes previously implies that processing in their intact MTL was critical for this outcome. One conclusion from these considerations is that the informal use of "short-term memory" to refer to memory for things that happened earlier today, or earlier this week, is neurobiologically inaccurate.[1]

Now what about "STM" vs. "working memory"? By some definitions, tasks that only require the short-term retention of a small amount of information, like the digit span task, are tests of STM, whereas tasks that require any kind of manipulation of that information, such as reordering it or performing mental arithmetic on it, are tests of working memory. A complicating factor with this definition, however, is that it implies that every test of working memory has an STM component. Additionally, some take the view that "STM" is best used only as a label for a class of tasks, but not to refer to a discrete cognitive or neural function. What we'll do is adopt the practice that is increasingly common in cognitive neuroscience, just using the term "working memory" to refer to all explicit tests of memory that can be performed without requiring a contribution from the MTL. When we want to be more specific, for example, to refer to the short-term retention of information, we'll specify "retention," or "working memory storage."

The reason for taking the time to give explicit considerations to these labels, and what they can refer to, will be evident as we start to consider the history of working memory research.

[1] It's okay, and understandable, when friends or TV newscasters misuse "STM" but, maddeningly, many neurologists and psychiatrists are also guilty of using it in this imprecise way. Confusingly, many neurobiologists studying synaptic plasticity also use "STM" to refer to the early, pre-protein-synthesis-dependent component of LTP.

Working Memory and the PFC? The Roots of a Long and Fraught Association

By the 1930s, the functions of most regions of cerebral cortex had been determined, at least to a first order of approximation, with the scientific methods that we introduced way back in *Chapter 1*. An exception to this was the prefrontal cortex (PFC), the region that, in the primate, is rostral to those in which damage produced paralysis, or other disorders of motor control. (In this chapter, unless otherwise specified, the use of "PFC" refers more specifically to the lateral PFC.) To investigate its function, Carlyle Jacobsen, at Yale University, trained two monkeys to perform a delayed-response task in an apparatus quite similar to the WGTA (Jacobsen, 1936; *Figure 6.2* in this book). After watching while one of two covered food wells was baited, the monkey waited for several seconds, during which the lowered screen blocked it from seeing or reaching the wells. When the screen was raised, the animal was given one reach with which to displace the cover and, on a correct response, retrieve the food. Pre-lesion, the animals learned to perform the task almost perfectly. After recovery from bilateral surgical removal of the frontal cortex anterior to the arcuate sulcus (i.e., these were *MASSIVE* PFC lesions), the animals' performance never deviated from chance (50% correct). That is, they were reduced to guessing. Importantly, Jacobsen included trials on which no delay was imposed between well-baiting and food retrieval. On these, performance improved dramatically, meaning that poor performance on delay trials could be ascribed to neither visual nor motoric nor motivational problems. Thus, a reasonable description of the findings might seem to be that, on delay trials, monkeys with bilateral PFC lesions could not remember which well had been baited. Jacobsen concluded that the prefrontal cortex is responsible for "immediate memory."

The idea that Jacobsen had *localized* immediate memory to the PFC was soon called into question, however, by a subsequent study performed at the same laboratory. Robert Malmo (1942) replicated the basic procedure from Jacobsen's experiment, but added the additional experimental factor of turning off the lights in the lab on one half of the trials. (The laboratory had remained illuminated throughout Jacobsen's experiment.) Remarkably, this simple manipulation had the effect of "rescuing" the performance of the PFC-lesioned monkeys, in that they performed correctly on roughly 85% of lights-off trials, despite still getting only 50% correct on lights-on trials.

Thus, even though the delayed-response task is a test of working memory, it was evidently incorrect to assume that the ability to briefly hold information in mind, per se, had been disrupted by damage to the PFC. (If it had been, then turning off the lights wouldn't have restored performance in the Malmo (1942) experiment.) Malmo (1942) attributed his findings to an increased susceptibility to interference in the monkeys after bilateral PFC removal. That is, whereas the ability to retain information over a short period of time remained intact, the ability to guide behavior with this information was compromised when other stimuli competed for attention, as would be more likely to happen in the light than in the dark. Twenty years later, in the chapter that introduced the concept and the term "working memory" to neuroscience, Karl Pribram, Ahumada, Hartog, and Roos (1964) reinforced this view, asserting that "aspects other than the trace of memory [i.e., working memory storage] were involved by the frontal procedure [i.e., were compromised by PFC lesions]: action at the time of stimulus presentation and distractability were found to be important" (p. 29).

Early Focus on Role of PFC in the Control of STM

In the wake of the Malmo (1942) study, the majority of research on behavior mediated by the PFC concentrated on the control of contents of working memory, and the control of behavior that is guided by information held in working memory. The latter was shown to be compromised, for example, when monkeys with PFC lesions were shown to be impaired on tests of delayed alternation. Delayed alternation differs from delayed response in that no to-be-remembered information is presented at the beginning of the trial. Instead, what the animal must remember is what was its response on the previous trial, whether or not that response was correct (i.e., was rewarded), and what the rules of the task are (i.e., repeat previous behavior, or alternate). On the first trial of a test of delayed alternation, the monkey sees two covered food wells and reaches to one of them (we'll call it A). Unbeknownst to the monkey, both food wells are empty on this trial (thereby guaranteeing that the choice on this first trial will be incorrect). During the ensuing delay (during which the barrier is lowered), the well that the animal has just selected is baited. This is alternation because, from the animal's point of view, it's as though the food had been in well B on the first trial. Now, on the second trial, the food will be in A. In the third trial, it will be in B, and so on. Once the task is underway, the animal needs not only to retain a memory of where the food had been on the previous trial, but also to overcome the natural tendency to return to the place where it had most recently been rewarded, a level of control of behavior that we will consider in more depth in *Chapter 15*. (In rodents, delayed alternation is often tested in a "T maze," a maze in which the animal begins each trial at the "bottom" of the T and has to run to the "top" of the T and then decide whether to turn left or right and run to the end of that arm to seek a reward.)

In humans, Lila Ghent, Mort Mishkin, and Hans-Lukas Teuber (1962) found no impairment of forward digit span performance in a group of 24 patients with PFC lesions, although they did find an impairment in a group of 20 patients with lesions in left temporoparietal cortex (more on why this may have been in *Chapter 19*). Two years later, another study revealed echoes in the humans of what the Malmo (1942) study had shown in the monkey. In it, Brenda Milner (1964) reported on the performance of PFC-lesioned patients on tests of 60-second delayed recognition. When tested with novel nonsense shapes, with no reuse of stimuli across trials (i.e., an "open set" of stimuli), performance of these patients was intact. With other types of stimuli, however, the patients were tested on closed sets, and their performance was impaired on those tests. A "closed set" refers to a stimulus pool made up of a finite number of items, such that they are reused over the course of testing. (E.g., the digit span test uses a closed set of the digits 0–9; because the test begins with a span of two, and each length is tested twice, the first four-item list in the series is necessarily composed of items that have already appeared on earlier trials of the test.) From experimental psychology, we know that the use of closed sets increases the influence of proactive interference (often abbreviated PI), a phenomenon whereby retrieval from memory "gets interfered with" by the residual traces of no-longer-relevant items from previous trials. On tests of recognition, PI can produce false-alarm responses, such that the subject incorrectly endorses a memory probe that had appeared on a previous trial, but not the current one. On tests of recall, it can produce intrusions, such that an item from a previous trial is recalled as having appeared on the current one. Because patients with PFC lesions were impaired when tested with closed sets, but not with open sets, Milner (1964) attributed their impairment on the former to the control of PI, rather than to working memory storage per se.

Thus, in the 1960s, the role of the PFC in working memory was generally understood to be one of the control of the contents of working memory, and/or the control of behavior that must be guided by the contents of working memory, rather than of the short-term retention, per se, of information. "This all changed" (well, the thinking of many researchers changed) when extracellular electrophysiological techniques were brought to the study of delay-task performance.

Single-Unit Delay-Period Activity in PFC and Thalamus

In 1971, the groups of Joaquin Fuster and Garrett Alexander and of Kisou Kubota and Hiroaki Niki published the results of recordings from neurons in the PFC while monkeys performed delayed recognition and delayed alternation. The cortical recording sites for both groups were the banks of the caudal half of the principal sulcus – many studies subsequent to those of Jacobsen and Malmo had indicated that damage restricted to just this region was sufficient to impair delay-task performance. Additionally, Fuster and Alexander (1971) also recorded in the mediodorsal (MD) nucleus of the thalamus, a thalamic hub of the lateral frontal cortico-basal ganglia-thalamic circuits labeled "DLPFC" in *Figure 8.3*.

During delayed-response performance, Fuster and Alexander found that many neurons in both PFC and MD displayed elevated firing rates that spanned the duration of the delay period, which varied in length, unpredictably, within a range of 15–65 seconds. During delayed-alternation performance, Kubota and Niki (1971) observed two classes of task-related activity: neurons with elevated activity during the delay and neurons that became active just prior to, and during, the response period. Interestingly, although both sets of authors stated explicitly that they did not interpret this activity as a correlate of working memory storage, in subsequent years, others would interpret it as such.

The Implications, and Influence, of These First Studies of PFC Electrophysiology Perhaps to a greater extent than the details of the findings, the very fact of the publication of these studies was compelling, evocative, and highly influential. At the most general level, they represented the first direct studies of brain activity underlying a behavior that was unequivocally *cognitive*. For over a century, of course, scientists had been systematically studying the effect of lesions on various aspects of cognition, but there's somehow something more compelling, more seductive, about "watching the workings of the mind" compared to inferring them from patterns of behavioral impairment. It was also true that electrophysiologists had been studying brain function for decades. But, prior to 1971, even the most ground-shattering, Nobel Prize – winning studies were being performed on the "machine-like" functions of perception and motor control – often the animals under investigation were anaesthetized and, even when not, the reports of these studies contained little to no consideration of the implications of the research for *thinking*. The two papers in question, on the other hand, didn't have to explicitly invoke "thinking"; thinking was, quite simply, what they were studying.

With regard to working memory, what seems to have made these studies so compelling was, paradoxically, an interpretation that the authors themselves explicitly discounted: some saw in them a physiological correlate of the first of two memory mechanisms that Hebb had postulated in 1949. Hebb's theory was, in fact, a dual-trace theory with the first being a "reverberatory" mechanism for "a transient 'memory' of [a] stimulus" (p. 61) that would sustain a representation until it could be encoded into a more permanent state via synaptic strengthening. The attribution of explicitly mnemonic interpretations to the 1971 findings became more prevalent when, a few years later, a highly influential model of working memory was introduced in the cognitive psychology literature.

The Multiple-Component Model of Working Memory The model of working memory proposed in 1974 by the British experimental psychologists Alan Baddeley and Graham Hitch was a response to two factors. First, in their view, contemporaneous models of STM didn't capture the fact that mental operations performed on information in conscious awareness can be carried out independently of interaction with, or influence on, LTM. (One implication from levels-of-processing theory [section *Subsequent memory effects in the PFC and MTL, Chapter* 12], for example, was that indefinite "maintenance rehearsal" of information in STM did not predict encoding into LTM. Contemporary models, in the view of Baddeley and Hitch (1974), could not accommodate this fact.) Second, they had observed that performance on each of two tasks under dual-task conditions could approach levels of performance under single-task conditions if the two engaged different domains of information, specifically verbal and visuospatial. Thus, early versions of their model called for two storage buffers (dubbed the "phonological loop" and the "visuospatial sketchpad," respectively) that could operate independently of each other and independently of LTM, although both under control of a Central Executive. This model has proven to be enormously influential, spawning a prodigious amount of research that continues through to this day.

Extracellular Electrophysiology Inspired by the Multiple-Component Model The next major development in the cognitive neuroscience of working memory was the proposal, by the neuroscientist Patricia Goldman-Rakic, that the sustained delay-period activity in the PFC of the monkey (reported by, e.g., Fuster and Alexander (1971) and Kubota and Niki (1971)) and the storage buffers of the multiple-component model of working memory from cognitive psychology were cross-species manifestations of the same fundamental mental phenomenon.

Earlier in her career, Goldman-Rakic had trained and collaborated with such luminaries as neuropsychologists Haldor Rosvold and Mortimer Mishkin and neuroanatomist Walle

Nauta. When she moved to Yale University in 1979, she was a leading authority on the anatomy, pharmacology, and functional anatomy (i.e., the effects of lesions) of the PFC. Motivated by the ongoing neurophysiological research from the groups featured earlier in this section, on the one hand, and the growing influence of the cognitive model of Baddeley and Hitch, on the other hand, she recruited a former trainee of Kubota, Shintaro Funahashi, to help her establish an electrophysiology laboratory.

The task that Funahashi, Goldman-Rakic, and colleagues used in many of their studies was the oculomotor delayed-response (ODR) task (as introduced and illustrated in *Figure 9.4*). *Figure 14.1.A* illustrates activity from a single left-hemisphere PFC neuron, recorded during several trials of ODR to each of eight locations. Note that this neuron responds selectively during trials for which a saccade to the downward (270°) target will be required. (Note that

FIGURE 14.1 Studying the organization of visual working memory with ODR tasks.

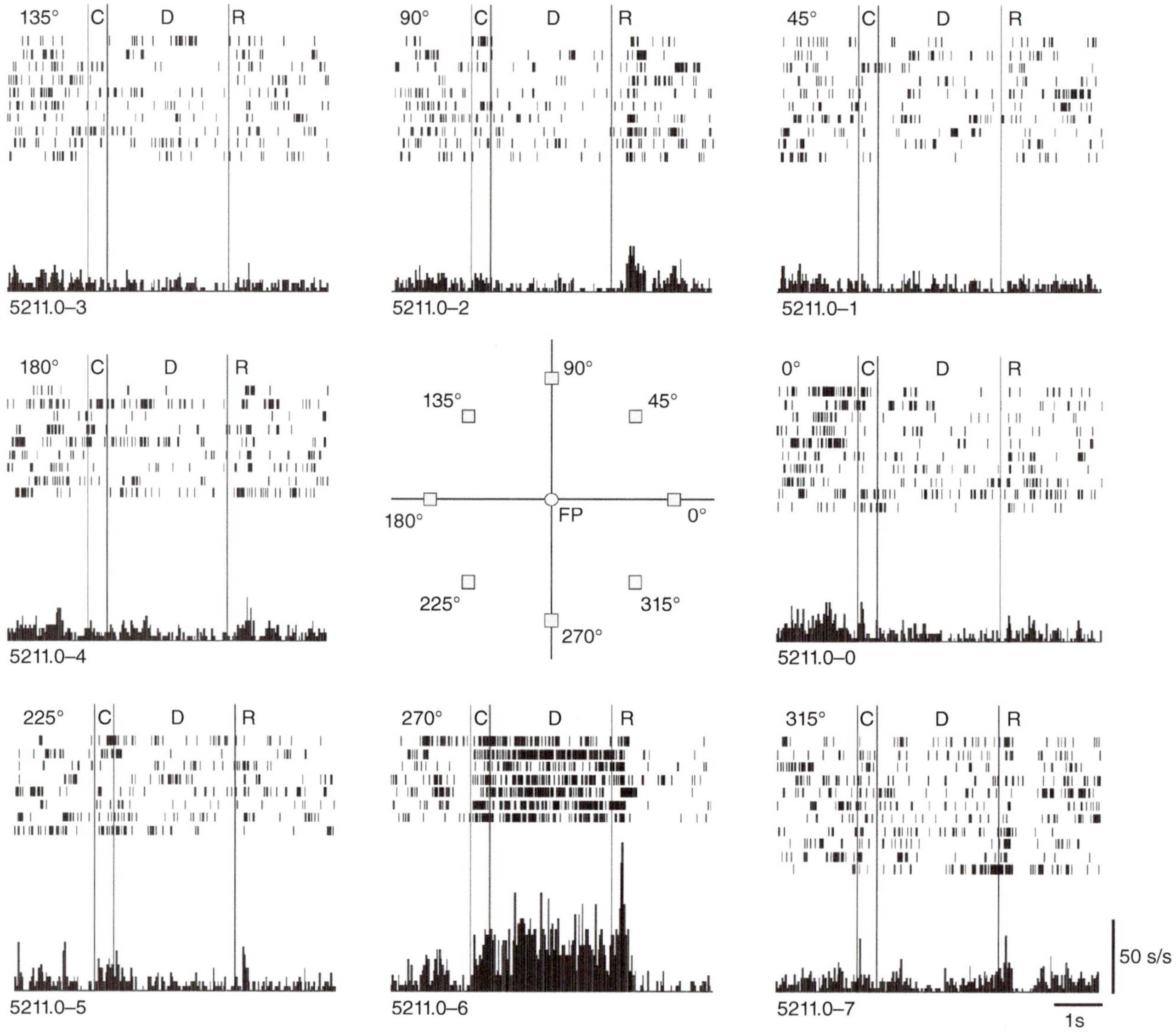

FIGURE 14.1.A The center illustrates the fixation point (FP) and the location of the eight targets, each 13° of visual angle from FP (and only visible to the animal when flashed briefly to cue a location as the target for an ODR). The plots illustrate firing rate (rows of rasters) for several trials at each location, with a histogram (below) summing up the activity.

Source: Funahashi et al., 1989 / The American Physiological Society.

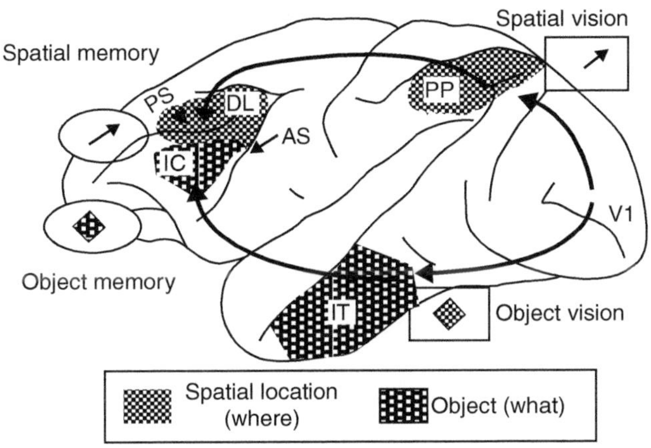

FIGURE 14.1.B Diagram, assembled from the results of many studies from Goldman-Rakic and colleagues, proposing how visual working memory may be supported by extensions into PFC of the where and what pathways. In frontal cortex: PS = principal sulcus; DL = dorsolateral; AS = arcuate sulcus; IC = inferior convexity (the gyrus ventral to the PS).

Source: Wilson et al., 1993 / American Association for the Advancement of Science.

a suggestion that it may also be conveying information during trials to other locations comes from the fact that its delay-period activity is suppressed below baseline levels on trials requiring saccades to the three upper visual field locations.) One may ask why Funahashi and colleagues found such selectivity in PFC neurons, when neither Fuster and Alexander (1971) nor Kubota and Niki (1971) did. This may have been due, in part, to changes in experimental procedures, including the finer grain of spatial discrimination required by the ODR task. It could also have to do with how the monkeys were trained, a factor that we'll consider in more depth further along.

One important contribution of Goldman-Rakic's theorizing was to suggest that the organization of the visual system into two parallel pathways (recall from *Chapter 7*, that the idea of a *what* vs. *where* organization had been introduced in the early 1980s) may extend to visual working memory, such that working memory for object identity may be dissociable from visual working memory for object locations. This idea was confirmed in subsequent experimental psychology, neuroimaging, and neuropsychological studies and led to a "fractionation" of the visuospatial sketchpad, by Baddeley and colleagues, into a "visual cache" (representing *what*) and an "inner scribe" (representing *where/how*) – a clear instance of neuroscience influencing cognitive theory.

In terms of brain organization, Goldman-Rakic's proposal is captured in *Figure 14.1.B.* There are three important points to make about this diagram. First, the heavy arrows representing the flow of information, although schematized cartoons, do reflect the anatomical bias of fibers projecting from posterior regions into PFC. Many of these pathways were discovered and characterized by Goldman-Rakic and colleagues. (We should note, however, the inaccuracy of suggesting unidirectional patterns of connectivity.) Second, the paper presenting this diagram did also report data from neurons in the inferior convexity of the PFC that showed elevated activity that was preferential for colors or faces over locations in space. Third – and this may well be the only instance in the entire book for which I have to say this – many researchers today wouldn't endorse the main point of the model illustrated in *Figure 14.1.B.* Reasons are to follow, but this has simply been such a highly influential model in the cognitive neuroscience of working memory that it couldn't not be included here.

Alternative Accounts of Delay-Period Activity in the PFC How is one to reconcile the seemingly incompatible findings between the electrophysiological findings depicted in *Figure 14.1* and the results of the lesion studies that we reviewed at the beginning of this section? Starting from the position of strongest inference, we have to accept that the lesion

FIGURE 14.2 Integration of *what* and *where* in primate prefrontal cortex.

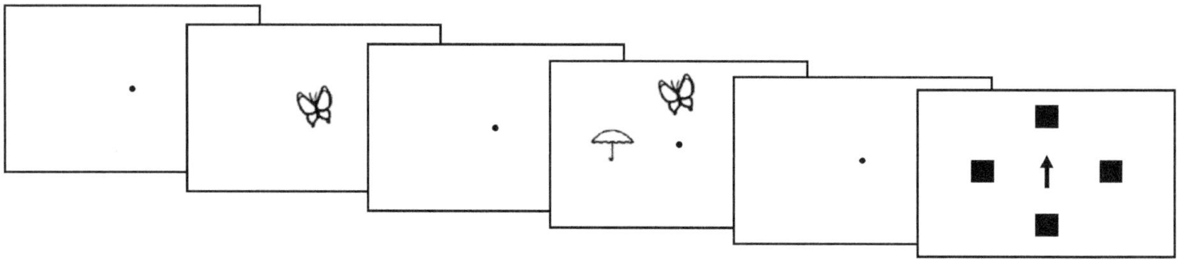

FIGURE 14.2.A An example behavioral trial of *what*-then-*where*. The trial began with the central presentation of a sample stimulus that the animal had to hold in memory across the first delay until its representation, together with a second stimulus, each in one of four possible locations. At this point, the animal had to encode the location occupied by the sample stimulus, hold this information across the second delay, and then, when the central fixation point was replaced by four target locations, make a saccade to the location that had been occupied by the sample.

Source: Rao et al., 1997 / American Association for the Advancement of Science.

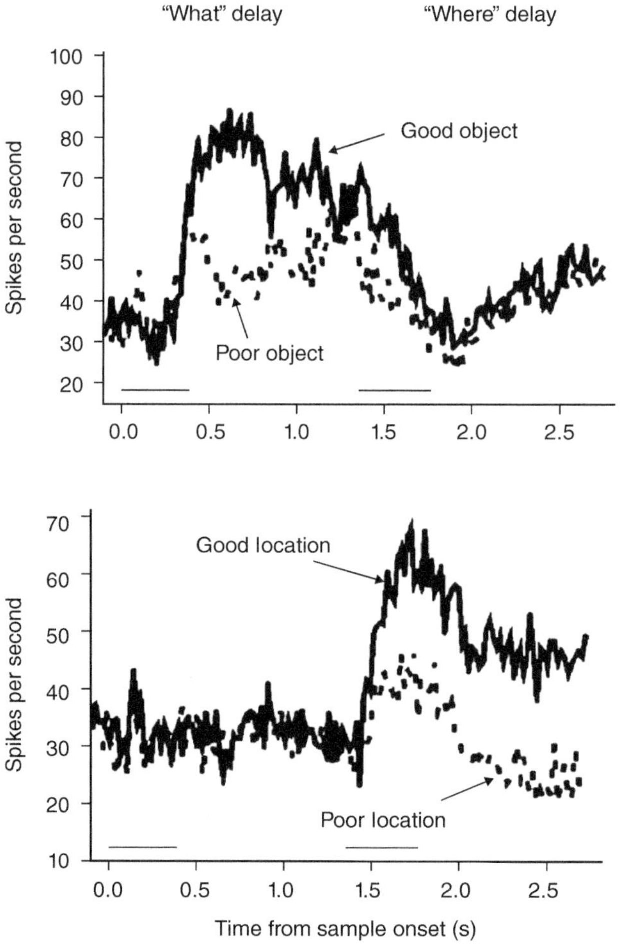

FIGURE 14.2.B Four traces from a single PFC neuron, responding to a "Good" vs. a "Poor" object (same convention as *Figure 7.15.C*), and to a "Good" vs. a "Poor" location.

Source: Rao et al., 1997 / American Association for the Advancement of Science.

studies reviewed made a strong case that performance on simple working memory tasks is by and large insensitive to the integrity of the PFC. This implies that the PFC does not play a necessary role in supporting working memory storage buffers. But if that's true, what might have been the function of the stimulus-selective delay-period activity in PFC that we just reviewed? Getting to the point where we can substantively address this question is an organizing principle for this chapter, and we'll return to it near the end of this chapter in section *Revisiting the PFC*. Next, however, we'll consider an electrophysiological study that offered an alternative interpretation of the results that Wilson, Ó Scalaidhe, and Goldman-Rakic (1993) (*Figure 14.1.B*) interpreted as evidence for a dorsal-ventral segregation of visual working memory function in lateral PFC.

The study from Chenchal Rao, Gregor Rainer, and Earl Miller (1997) was motivated by the reasoning that perhaps in the earlier work from Wilson et al. (1993), the serial training of monkeys to perform STM for one type of information, then for another, had led their PFCs to organize themselves according to the tasks that they were trained to perform. (Other studies had shown, for example, that intensive training on a color-based visual search task results in color selectivity in the frontal eye field [FEF], which is not a typical property of this region.) And so Rao et al. (1997) trained their monkeys to perform a two-step What-then-Where ODR task that required learning the spatial- and object-processing elements of the task in parallel (*Figure 14.2.A*). The results indicated that over half of the PFC neurons displaying elevated delay-period activity showed tuning for both object identity and location, and that these were topographically intermingled with those that responded only to "What" or only to "Where," with no evident dorsal–ventral segregation. This finding casts doubt on a labeled line-like organization of function in PFC, as illustrated in *Figure 14.1.B*.

Measuring Working Memory Ability in Humans

One aspect of working memory that is a focus of intensive inquiry, and debate, is the nature of its capacity limitations. We already noted at the beginning of this chapter that, for 95% of healthy young adults, digit span will be between five and nine items (i.e., "7 +/- 2"). This means that, in the general population, there is a wide range of performance on this task. The same turns out to be true for many tests of working memory and, furthermore, performance on one test of working memory correlates with performance on other such tasks, indicating that what is often referred to as a person's *working memory capacity* is a relatively stable cognitive trait. Furthermore, working memory capacity is correlated with many laboratory measures of cognitive ability (e.g., *Figure 14.3.C*), as well as with real-world outcomes like reading proficiency and scholastic achievement. From a basic-science standpoint, this implies that working memory may be a critical contributor to many aspects of high-level cognition, including those that will be covered in the final section of this book: cognitive control, decision making, and language abilities. (Thus, to understand cognitive control or decision making or language comprehension and production, one must understand working memory.) From the perspective of human factors and human performance, working memory capacity might predict, at least in part, how well-suited an individual is for a particular kind of job, or what is someone's lifetime earning potential. In the clinical realm, working memory performance can be a valuable measure in the diagnosis of disease, and/or in the tracking of recovery from neurological or psychiatric illness. For all these reasons, understanding the psychological and the neural bases of individual differences in working memory capacity has been, and continues to be, an area of intense focus.

As an aside, cognitive psychologists and cognitive neuroscientists divide working memory into two general categories: working memory for language-based and auditorily presented information (often referred to as "verbal working memory"); and working memory visually

FIGURE 14.3 Visual working memory capacity.
Source: Hakim and Vogel / PLOS / CC BY 4.0.

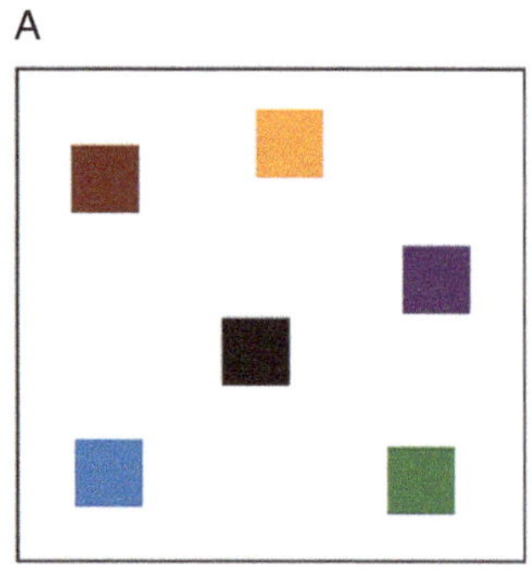

FIGURE 14.3.A A memory array at set-size 6.

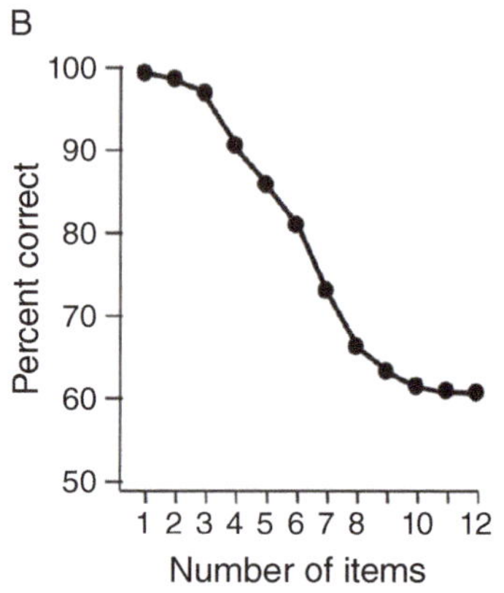

FIGURE 14.3.B Performance of a subject at multiple set sizes.

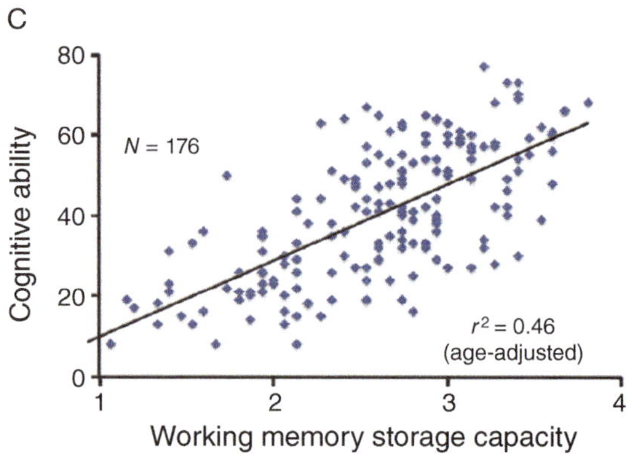

FIGURE 14.3.C Correlation of visual working memory capacity with a composite measure of cognitive ability made up of tests of processing speed, working memory, verbal learning, visual learning, attention/vigilance, reasoning/problem-solving, and social cognition. This sample includes neurologically and psychiatrically healthy adults and patients with schizophrenia. The correlations were very similar when carried out separately on the data from each of the groups, justifying their aggregation here (Johnson et al., 2013 / American Psychological Association).

presented information. Despite the periodic references to the digit span task, this chapter addresses visual working memory almost exclusively. Because verbal working memory shares considerable overlap with language (including reading and speech production), we'll postpone detailed consideration of verbal working memory until *Chapter 19*.

Slot Models of Visual Working Memory Capacity

An important development in working memory research occurred in the late 1990s when Steve Luck and his then-graduate student Ed Vogel published a series of studies in which subjects were shown a sample array of objects (colored squares in the canonical version of the task [*Figure 14.3.A*), then, after a brief delay, a test array that was either identical to the sample or differed by one feature of one of the objects (e.g., the color of one of the squares was different). (In other variants, only one test object from the array is presented, and it either is or isn't different from how it had appeared in the sample array.) In the jargon of the field, this has come to be known as a "change detection" task. There were two critical factors that were varied. The first is that arrays of many different sizes were used, varying from 1 item up to 12 or more. As *Figure 14.3.B* illustrates (and as you surely could have guessed!), performance drops off with increasing set size. Second, and more controversially, Luck and Vogel found the same pattern of performance regardless of whether the individual stimuli in the test array had only one dimension (e.g., color) or many (e.g., bars of different color, length, orientation, and size of a gap in their middle). This gave rise to the proposal that working memory capacity is constrained at the level of objects, rather than at the level of features. (I.e., because performance with arrays of, say, four items, was comparable for "4-dimension" items and for "1-dimension" items, the fact that the 4-item 4-dimension arrays contained 16 discrete features, whereas the 4-item 1-dimension arrays contained only 4, didn't seem to matter.) We'll come back to this idea of the object as the fundamental unit of visual working memory, but first, we need to flesh out the idea of a capacity limitation.

Luck and Vogel (1997) noted that another way to characterize data like those shown in *Figure 14.3.B* was to transform them from this description of accuracy at different loads into an estimate of the number of items that the subject was holding in mind at each load. To do this, they used a simple formula first introduced by the psychologist Hal Pashler that entails subtracting the false-alarm rate (FAR) from the hit rate (HR) and multiplying the result by the number of items that had been in the memory array. Let's try it by eyeballing the data from *Figure 14.3.B*. The variable used to represent capacity is k.

- at load 1, $k = [(\text{HR}\ (1.0) - \text{FAR}\ (0)) * 1] = 1$;
- at load 2, $k = [(\text{HR}\ (0.98) - \text{FAR}\ (0.02)) * 2] = 1.92$;
- at load 3, $k = [(\text{HR}\ (0.97) - \text{FAR}\ (0.03)) * 3] = 2.82$;
- at load 4, $k = [(\text{HR}\ (0.90) - \text{FAR}\ (0.1)) * 4] = 3.2$;
- at load 5, $k = [(\text{HR}\ (0.86) - \text{FAR}\ (0.14)) * 5] = 3.6$;
- at load 6, $k = [(\text{HR}\ (0.81) - \text{FAR}\ (0.19)) * 6] = 3.72$;
- at load 7, $k = [(\text{HR}\ (0.73) - \text{FAR}\ (0.27)) * 7] = 3.22$;
- at load 8, $k = [(\text{HR}\ (0.67) - \text{FAR}\ (0.33)) * 8] = 2.72$.

So the intuition is that at low loads, one is holding in mind as many items as were presented in the array, but as the set size continues to grow one reaches the point where no more items can be held in working memory, and so *k* asymptotes (or sometimes starts to decline, as is the case from this quick-and-dirty set of calculations – a common convention for determining someone's working memory capacity is to take the largest value from the range of set sizes). Estimates of working memory capacity are stable across repeated measurements, and so are considered by many to be a cognitive trait. Furthermore, as *Figure 14.3.C* illustrates, there is considerable variability across individuals. All this has led to one popular model that holds that working memory capacity limitations are due to the cognitive system having a finite number of hypothetical "slots," the number of slots that one has in one's cognitive system determining the number of items that one can hold in working memory at any one moment in time. Importantly, in many slot models, storage of information in a slot is assumed to be "all-or-none": if an item is successfully encoded into a working memory slot, it will be held with high fidelity, and there's no such thing as having only a partial or a weak representation in a slot.

The Electrophysiology of Visual Working Memory Capacity

Soon after Vogel started his own lab, he and then-graduate student Maro Machizawa described an ERP component that closely tracked estimates of *k*. They named this component the **"contralateral delay activity" (CDA)** for reasons made clear in *Figure 14.4*. The discovery of the CDA generated a great deal of interest because it seemed to track what's happening "inside people's heads" rather than on the surface of their retinas. That is, if an individual's visual STM capacity is estimated to be three items, the CDA will increase in magnitude, monotonically, as the memory array increases from 1 to 2 to 3 items (*Figure 14.4*) but then it saturates, and will remain at that magnitude for arrays of 4, 8, or 12 items, presumably because the subject can only select and remember three items out of an array, regardless of whether it contains 3 or 12 items. Importantly, the individual differences in the CDA correlate with individual differences in working memory capacity.

At the circuit level, the neuronal bases of the CDA remain poorly understood. One observation is that a sustained shift in the voltage of a signal, as is observed with the CDA, can be thought of as a "DC shift," by analogy to direct current, a constant (i.e., not alternating) current source. When the magnitude of current flow changes to a new, constant value, this is a DC shift. Thus, the load-related changes in the amplitude of the CDA may correspond to sustained increases in current flow in the neurons engaged by the task, and the CDA is considered by many to be an analogue in humans to the elevated, sustained delay-period activity recorded from neurons in the PFC of monkeys, as described earlier in this chapter. It is important to keep in mind, however, that while the neural activity reviewed early in this chapter was recorded in the PFC, the CDA is recorded from scalp electrodes positioned over parietal and occipital cortex, and is generally believed to originate from activity in these regions. In fMRI studies of visual working memory, load-sensitive activity is commonly observed both in frontal/prefrontal regions and in parietal regions. Indeed, in the same issue of the journal *Nature* in which Vogel and Machizawa introduced the CDA, Jay Todd and René Marois (2004) described an fMRI analogue: a region within the intraparietal sulcus (IPS) in which signal intensity increased with memory load up until the number of items corresponding to the subject's working memory capacity, but never exceeded this level at higher loads.

Resource Accounts of Visual Working Memory Capacity Limitations

Although the CDA and its fMRI analogs (e.g., Todd and Marois, 2004) are considered by many to be evidence for the slot model of visual working memory, this model is not universally accepted. One reason for this is due to the fact that the estimated precision of the mental representation of information begins to decline as soon as more than one item needs to be held simultaneously. Let's take our hypothetical subject whose working memory capacity was estimated to be $k = 3.72$, using the procedure described in section *Slot models of visual working*

FIGURE 14.4 Contralateral delay activity (CDA), an ERP component sensitive to STM load.
Source: Vogel et al., 2004 / Springer Nature.

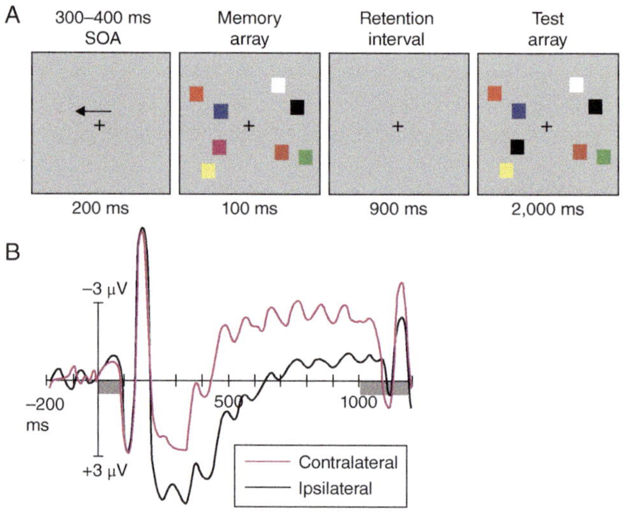

FIGURE 14.4.A Panel **A** illustrates the task, a variant of the color "change detection" task introduced in *Figure 14.4.A*. Critically, at the beginning of each trial, a cue indicates whether the array in the left or right hemisphere is to be remembered. Panel **B** shows the grand average (12 subjects) ERP recorded at parietal and occipital electrodes, first averaged within each subject across electrodes from just the right and just the left hemisphere, then averaged across trials as a function of whether the attended array was in the visual field ipsilateral or contralateral to the hemisphere. To generate the CDA (*Figure 14.4.B*, this ipsilateral signal is subtracted from the contralateral signal. The rationale is that, because subjects are fixating centrally, visual stimulation for both hemispheres is comparable, and the difference in the two waveforms should reflect the effect of the additional processing of the array in the cued hemifield (i.e., encoding it, then holding it in working memory). Note that, for both waveforms, one can count about five to six cycles of an oscillation between time 500 and 1000 ms, which would correspond to 10–12 Hz (i.e., the alpha band of the EEG). It's evidently the case that the phase reset triggered by the memory array is so potent that alpha-band oscillations aren't fully obscured by trial averaging (section *Event-related analyses, Chapter 3*).

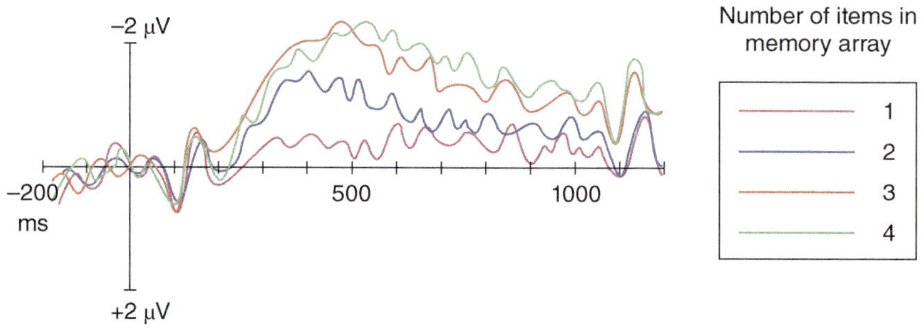

FIGURE 14.4.B The CDA at four memory loads. Beginning with load 4, the green waveform is the subtraction of the two illustrated in *Figure 14.4.A* (contralateral – ipsilateral). Note that this removes the early stimulus-evoked deflections, because they are comparable for the two hemispheres. The remaining CDAs illustrated here are for arrays of load 1, 2, and 3. An important detail to note here is that the magnitude of the CDA on load 4 trials is no different than on load 3 trials. This fits with the fact that the group-mean visual working memory capacity of this group of 12 subjects is 2.8 items.

memory capacity. Importantly, the formula used to arrive at that estimate of $k = 3.72$ relies on data from a test of *recognition*, in which the subject's response on each trial is scored as being "correct" or "incorrect" (and then sorted so as to generate a HR and FAR). If we were to slightly modify the task, however, and make it a test of recall, an additional detail would be observed.

The "change-detection" recognition task illustrated in *Figure 14.4.A* entails the presentation of an array of four items (in the cued visual field; the "memory array"), then the re-presentation of this array with, in this illustration, the square that had been pink now changed to black (the "test array"). In a variant of this procedure, one that produces behavioral results comparable to those presented in *Figure 14.3.B*, the test array can be replaced by a single test item. For example, for a trial comparable to the one illustrated in *Figure 14.4.A*, the test item would be just a single square appearing at that "third-from-the-top" location, and the square would be either pink – in which case the subject should respond "match," because the color of the test item matches what it had been in the memory array – or it would be black – in which case the subject should respond "nonmatch." (This procedure is conceptually the same as tests of "old/new" recognition in long-term memory, from *Chapter 12* section *Novelty-driven "encoding"*; it is sometimes also referred to as "yes/no recognition".) Now we can make an additional change to make this a test of recall by interrogating memory with a color wheel that appears at the "third-from-the-top" location. In effect, rather than asking *is this the color of the item that had appeared at this location?* we are now asking *what was the color of the item that had appeared in this location?* (For an example of a color wheel, see *Figure 5.10.A*.)

Now that we have converted the change detection task into a test recall, we can return to our hypothetical subject whose working memory capacity has been estimated to be $k = 3.72$. When this subject is presented with a memory array of just a single item (i.e., a load of 1), the precision of their recall will likely be very high. For the purposes of this discussion, we can pretend that we administered 100 such trials to our subject, and plotted the error of each of their responses as the histogram cartooned in *Figure 14.5.A*. This indicates that many of our subjects' recall responses were perfect (0° of error), and the majority of those that weren't perfect had a relatively small error. Stated differently, the width of the error distribution is relatively small, which corresponds to high precision. (Recall that we also encountered this convention for displaying performance on a visual working memory task in *Figure 5.10.A*; for the moment, we can disregard the caption accompanying *Figure 14.5* and just "look at the pictures".) When we test this same subject with memory arrays of two items (i.e., load of 2), it would be reasonable to assume that recall precision would be the same as it is for load of 1. After all, 2 is smaller than our subject's capacity of 3.72, and so one of the two items can be represented in one slot and the second item in a second slot, and because retention of stimulus information in a slot is hypothesized to be all-or-none, the precision of recall for load-of-2 trials should be the same as it is for load-of-1 trials. Despite this reasoning, however, the results from dozens of studies indicate that recall precision at load-of-2 is invariably lower than it is as load-of-1. (To visualize this, were we to administer 100 trials with load-of-2 to our hypothetical subject, the error histogram might look like the plot in *Figure 14.5.B* – a distribution that is decidedly broader than the one in *Figure 14.5.A*.)

Does the fact that the precision of working memory declines with load at sub-capacity levels mean that slot models are wrong? Some don't think so. Advocates of slot models have accounted for this pattern in the data with a "slots-plus-averaging" modification of the original conceptualization of the slots model. According to slots-plus-averaging, the high precision of recall at load-of-1 is due to the fact that subjects might represent the same item in multiple slots (e.g., our $k = 3.72$ individual would represent the single memory item in triplicate, with one exemplar of it in each of three slots[2]). Already at a load of 2, the number of slots that can be allocated to a single item is smaller, and because all things biological and behavioral are inherently noisy, fewer slots per item translates into greater average error. Others, however, DO

[2] How can a single person have a non-integer number of slots? (E.g., what does it mean to have 3 "full" slots plus 0.72 of a fourth?) This author has never come across a fully satisfying answer to this question, beyond the idea that an individual's *k* value is an empirical estimate and all estimates are subject to some level of noise and uncertainty.

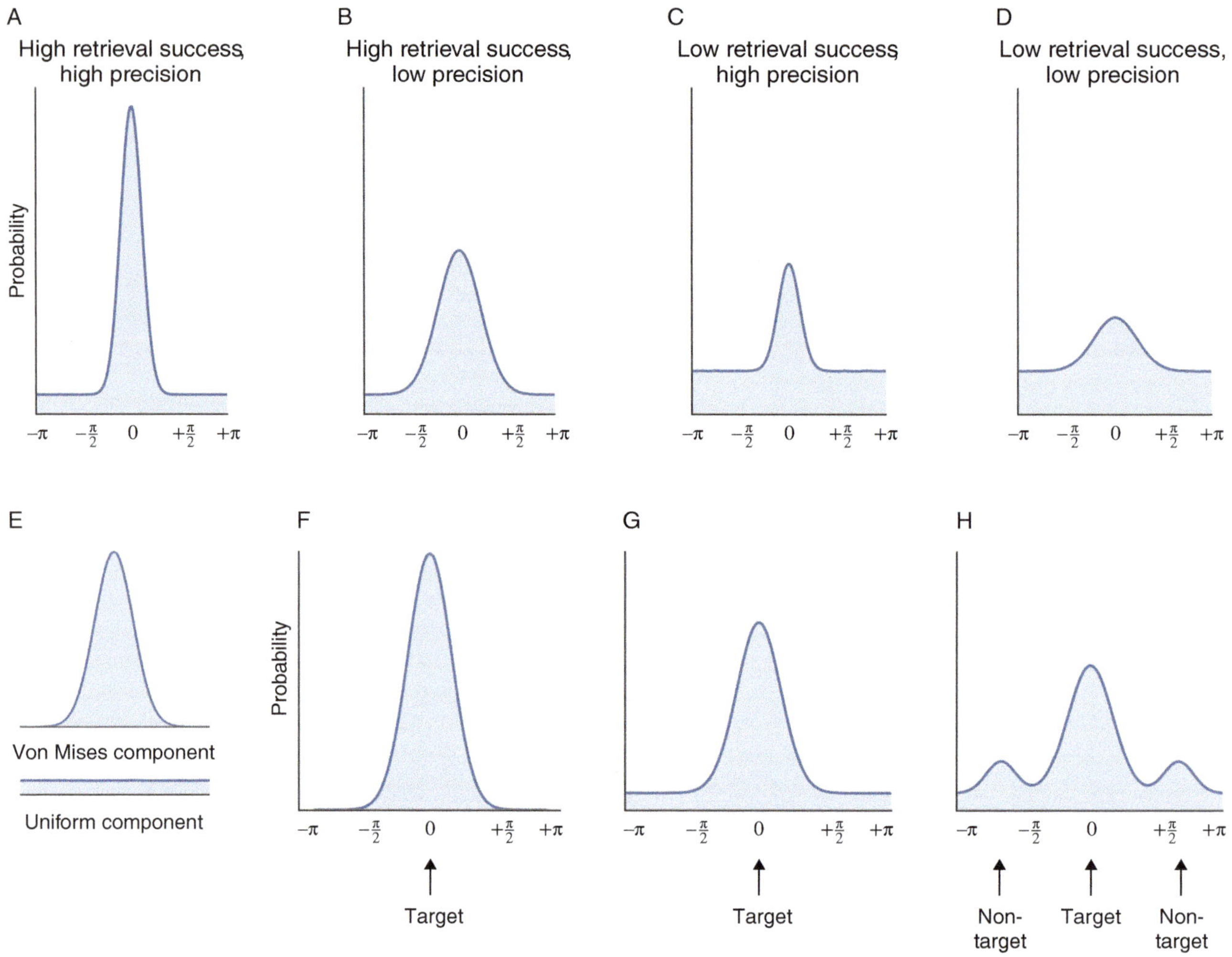

FIGURE 14.5 **A.** A plot of the data from a hypothetical subject whose responses are very precise, as captured by the narrowness of the distribution of errors. **B.** A hypothetical subject whose responses were less precise than those of the subject in A, as indicated by the broader distribution of errors. **C.** A hypothetical subject whose responses to the target were just as precise as those of the subject in A, but who also completely forgot the direction of motion on several trials, and on these trials was just guessing. A true guess is equally likely to land anywhere along the possible range of 360°, so a high rate of guessing (i.e., of forgetting) manifests as an increase in the probability of a response at every possible value. **D.** A hypothetical subject who performed really poorly – their responses, on trials when they remembered the probed item, were imprecise, and their guess rate was also high. **E.** The tendencies displayed in panels **A–D** are descriptive. For example, one way to estimate the precision of subject A's memory vs. that of subject B is to compute 1/SD of their responses. But what about subject A in comparison to subject C? It wouldn't be accurate to say that their performance was comparable just because the precision of their responses to the probed item was comparable, because this wouldn't take into account the higher rate of forgetting in subject C. To quantify everyone's performance, so that "fair comparisons" can be made across all of them, the data from each subject can be construed as a mixture of three kinds of responses: responses corresponding to the subject's memory of the direction of the probed item (called "probability of a response to the target" [P_T]), guesses (P_G), and responses mistakenly made to one of the items in the memory set that was *not* probed (responses to a nontarget [P_{NT}]). (Responses to a nontarget are illustrated in panel **H.**) What panel **E** illustrates are the parameter that fits the distribution of responses to targets and responses to nontargets (the "von Mises component"), and the parameter that fits the distribution of guesses (the "uniform component"). A von Mises distribution is the analogue of a Gaussian for stimuli that exist in a circular space, such as the 360° of possible directions of motion on a 2-D plane. The width of the fitted von Mises provides the estimate of the precision of responses, and is referred to as the "concentration parameter." **F.** Illustration of a model that only fits a von Mises function to the data. **G.** Illustration of a model that fits the data as a mixture of responses to the target, fit with a von Mises function, and of guesses, fit as a uniform distribution. **H.** Illustration of a model that fits the data as a mixture of responses to the target, of guesses, and of responses to nontargets.

Source: Franziska et al., 2016 / eLife Sciences Publications Ltd.

think that the fact that the precision of working memory declines with load at sub-capacity levels means that slot models are wrong. Indeed, some would put sub-capacity in scare quotes, because they deny that such a thing as a working-memory capacity exists. Rather, they argue that the appearance of capacity limitations is just a consequence of analyzing one's data with methods that already assume the existence of a finite number of all-or-none working memory slots. An alternative explanation – typically referred to as resource models – is that the monotonic decline in performance with increasing load is a consequence of the need for some finite resource (maybe attention?) to be spread evermore thinly across items as the memory set grows. Resource models, and an alternative method for analyzing behavioral data from working memory experiments (i.e., an alternative to estimating k), will feature prominently in the upcoming section *Increased specificity raises questions about the interpretation of elevated delay-period activity*.

Novel Insights from Multivariate Data Analysis

Your humble and devoted author has been an active researcher in the cognitive neuroscience of working memory for over 25 years (yikes!), and so one might think that this would be the easiest chapter for him to write. He certainly did. However, he has learned that insider status actually makes things more difficult, because it means being hyperaware of leaving out so much important and influential work, by so many scientists whom he really admires. (To say nothing of all the work from his own career that he REALLY admires.) But here goes . . .

The Tradition of Univariate Analyses

There was a period of time, during the 1990s and 2000s, when one could be forgiven for characterizing the functional-neuroimaging-of-human-working-memory literature as a reactive one that parroted the monkey electrophysiology literature with a lag of 3–5 years. Thus, for example, a few years after the studies by Funahashi, Bruce, and Goldman-Rakic (1989) and Wilson, Ó Scalaidhe, and Goldman-Rakic (1993) (c.f., *Figure 14.1*), neuroimaging studies appeared to confirm the gist of these findings in humans; then a few years after the Rao, Rainer, and Miller (1997) study that challenged the conclusion of Wilson, Ó Scalaidhe, and Goldman-Rakic (1993) (c.f., *Figure 14.2*), neuroimaging studies came out challenging the conclusions of the first set of neuroimaging studies; and so on. Now, of course, this would be a cynical and overly facile summary. Some examples of neuroimaging studies of working memory making important, original contributions have already been highlighted in, for example, *Figure 9.4* and *Figure 12.2*. Nonetheless, more recent developments in the field have shown that much of the neuroimaging literature based on univariate analyses may need to be reinterpreted, for two principal reasons, both deriving from advances in multivariate pattern analysis (MVPA) of fMRI datasets. The first relates to sensitivity: MVPA from several groups has now established that regions that do not show elevated levels of regionally aggregated signal intensity during the delay period of a working memory task can nonetheless be shown to be actively representing the to-be-remembered information. The second relates to specificity: MVPA has also shown that elevated delay-period signal, even when it shows properties, such as load sensitivity, that have been considered hallmarks of working memory storage, doesn't always represent the information that researchers have assumed that it does.

Multivariate Analyses of fMRI Data

Increased Sensitivity Reveals Delay-Period Storage in "Unactivated" Areas

In 2009, two groups published striking demonstrations that the active retention of information in STM can occur in regions that do not show elevated activity. One of them, from

John Serences and a team of long-time collaborators (Serences, Ester, Vogel, and Awh, 2009), was designed to test the "sensory recruitment hypothesis," the idea that the short-term retention of information may be supported, at least in part, by the very same neural systems that were responsible for their perceptual processing. (Note how this differs from the scheme, illustrated in *Figure 14.1.B*, whereby the "back of the brain" is responsible for visual perception and the "front of the brain" is responsible for working memory.) To test it, they scanned subjects performing 10-second delayed recognition in which each sample stimulus comprised a set of black oriented bars (referred to as a grating) superimposed on a colored square, and the memory probe matched the sample along both dimensions on half the trials, differing subtly by color or by orientation in the other half. (Trials were blocked by condition.)

Panel A of *Figure 14.6* shows the trial-averaged fMRI signal from the 62 most responsive voxels in V1, as defined with a (univariate) GLM analysis (analogous to *Figure 5.7*, which shows the spatially averaged response collapsed across the two voxels in that simulated dataset). Two things are noteworthy. First, the signal intensity drops to baseline during the delay period of both conditions. (This is what the word "unactivated" in the title of this subsection is referring to.) Second, it's clear by mentally superimposing the two that one wouldn't be able to discriminate orientation from color trials with these data. Panel B of this figure, however, shows that these 62 voxels evidently carried information about the sample, because Serences, Ester, Vogel, and Awh (2009) were able to discriminate 45°-oriented from 135°-oriented gratings on Remember Orientation trials and red from green on Remember Color trials.

Demonstrating stimulus-specific patterns of delay-period activity in a putatively "unactivated" part of the brain was an impressive technical feat. The real conceptual advance from this study, however, was the insightful way in which the authors tested a specific prediction of the sensory recruitment hypothesis: they trained a classifier to discriminate 45°-oriented from 135°-oriented gratings (and red from green displays) from "perception" trials – signal corresponding to the runs used to derive the ROIs, during which subjects just viewed stimuli – then used these classifiers to decode data from working memory trials. Successful decoding would necessarily mean that patterns of activity during the working memory trials were largely similar to patterns of activity measured during the perception trials. Thus, working memory for oriented gratings (or color) could be said to engage the same neural representation as the visual perception of oriented gratings (or color). Serences et al. (2009) summarized it as follows: "the sustained activation patterns observed during the delay period were similar to patterns evoked by the continuous presentation of identical sensory stimuli, which suggests that early feature-selective visual areas are recruited to maintain a 'copy' of remembered stimulus attributes, as opposed to a more abstract or categorical representation" (p. 213).

Depending on whether you were a glass-half-full or a glass-half-empty kind of person, the results from this study (and a similar one from Stephenie Harrison and Frank Tong (2009)) were either very exciting or very worrying. They were perhaps worrying from the perspective that of the hundreds (thousands?) of neuroimaging studies of working memory that had been published in the years prior to these two, almost all of them employed univariate analysis methods. How many of them may have failed to identify stimulus-related delay-period activity due to the relatively poor sensitivity of these univariate methods? On the exciting side, multivariate methods have provided researchers with novel tools to address not just *where* in the brain one can find evidence for working memory storage but also *how* these processes might work.

Increased Specificity Raises Questions About the Interpretation of Elevated Delay-Period Activity In this section, the author will immodestly summarize some research from his own group, emphasizing a study led by former postdoc Steve Emrich and former graduate student Adam Riggall. Emrich, Riggall, Josh LaRocque, and Postle (2013) scanned subjects with fMRI while they performed working memory for the direction of motion with three serially presented apertures, each containing a field of dots, colored red in one aperture, green in another, and blue in the third. On some trials, only one field of dots was moving, on some two, and on some all three. Thus, memory load was manipulated, and, indeed, results of the GLM-based univariate analysis indicated that regions of rostral IPS and several regions of PFC – caudal superior frontal gyrus and middle frontal gyrus, and more rostral regions of middle and inferior frontal gyri – demonstrated load sensitivity.

FIGURE 14.6 MVPA reveals delay-period stimulus representation in V1.

Source: Serences et al., 2009 / SAGE Publications.

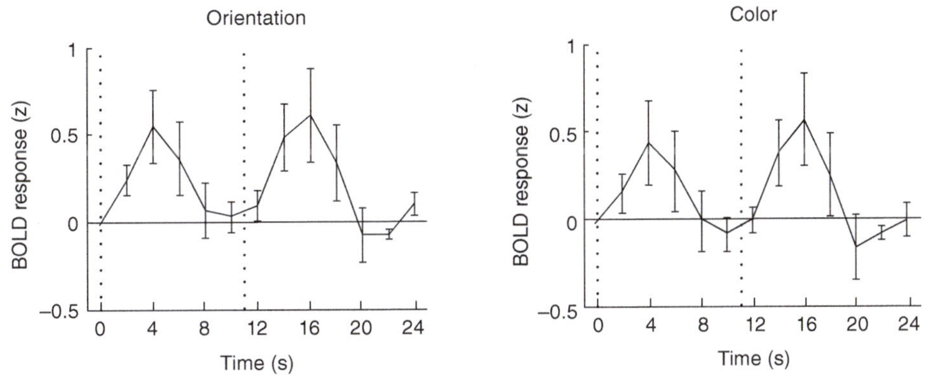

FIGURE 14.6.A Trial-averaged fMRI activity from V1 during orientation and color blocks; vertical lines indicating the onset of sample and probe stimuli. Note robust stimulus-evoked responses, but that activity drops back to baseline during the delay period.

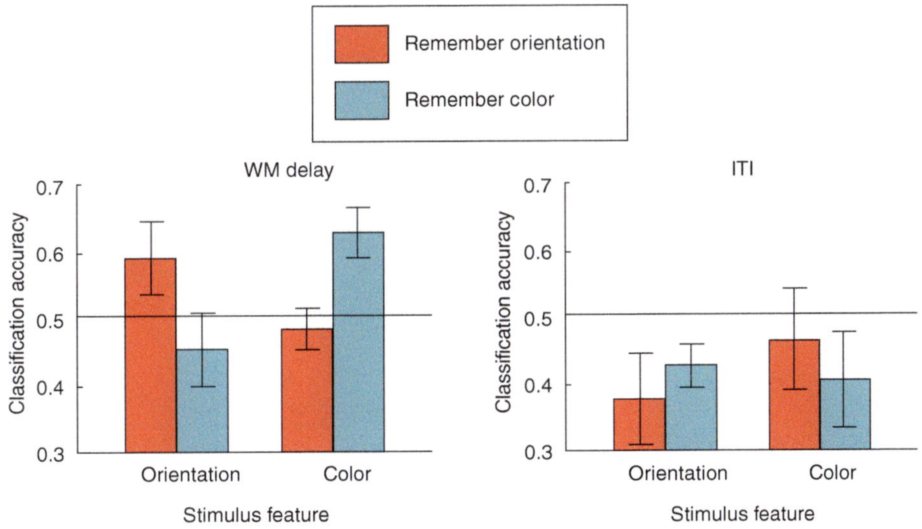

FIGURE 14.6.B Classifier performance on (or, for ITI, after) "Remember orientation" trials (red bars) and "Remember color" trials, as a function of stimulus feature being decoded. Note that the WM delay and ITI epochs were identical in length and with respect to the lag after the most recently presented stimulus (delay decoding performed on data from 4 to 10 seconds after presentation of the sample; ITI decoding from 4 to 10 seconds after presentation of the probe).

The working memory task used by Emrich et al. (2013) tested recall by presenting a dial at the end of each trial and asking the subject to rotate the needle until it pointed in the remembered direction of motion. (Sometimes this procedure is referred to as "delayed estimation.") The color of the dial indicated whether the direction of the red, the blue, or the green sample was to be recalled.

The fit of the three-factor mixture model to the behavioral performance of subjects while being scanned by Emrich et al. (2013) indicated that the precision of responses declined monotonically as memory load increased from 1 to 2 to 3 (*Figure 14.7.E*). (Additionally, P_T dropped slightly, mirrored by an increase in P_{NT}, with increasing memory load.) Note that, for comparison, there would be no way of knowing from our back-of-the-envelope conversion of performance from *Figure 14.3.B* into estimates of capacity, whether the estimates of a capacity of 1 for a one-item array, a capacity of 1.92 for a two-item array, and a capacity of

2.82 for a three-item array were accompanied by progressive declines in the quality of the working memory representations. And so one can make a case that, in certain situations, the recall/estimation procedure provides more details about the workings of working memory. It is nonetheless also important to note that, for all the conceptual and mathematical sophistication of the three-factor mixture model, it's still restricted to evaluating the subject's responses. That's why we keep saying that these measures are only a *proxy* for what we want to know, which is the nature of the mental representation(s) while they are being held in working memory – that is, during the delay period.

Among the most intriguing results from the Emrich et al. (2013) study was how MVPA decoding performance in occipital cortex tracked the load-related decline in the precision of responses. Consider the subject whose data are portrayed in red in panel E of *Figure 14.7*. For load-of-1 trials, the precision of this subject's behavioral responses was high (a concentration

FIGURE 14.7 MVPA of delayed recognition of direction of motion.

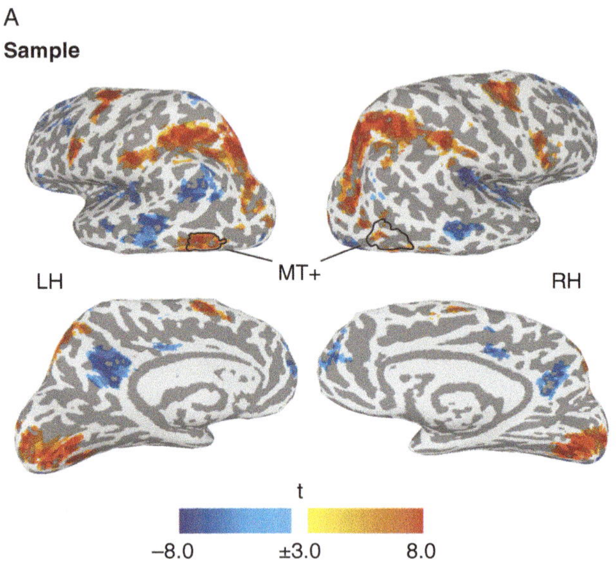

FIGURE 14.7.A Group-average univariate statistical maps of changes in fMRI activity, relative to baseline, when subjects are viewing and encoding into memory the direction of motion of a sample stimulus on a load-of-1 trial, from a study by Riggall and Postle (2012; not discussed in the text, but useful for illustrative purposes). On the lateral surface, one can see elevated activity in the occipital cortex, along the IPS, and in two patches of posterior PFC (note the similarity of these to the regions described in section *Human oculomotor control, Chapter 9*, and illustrated in *Figure 9.4*). Also note elevated activity is stronger in the left than in the right hemisphere in this sample, in MT+, which was identified in a separate localizer scan that alternated between coherently moving dots and stationary dots. On the medial surfaces, one can see strong elevated activity in calcarine and pericalcarine cortex, and in a medial frontal area that may correspond to the supplementary eye field (SEF). Finally, among the areas showing a significant decrease relative to baseline are regions associated with the default mode network: inferior parietal lobule, posterior cingulate/precuneus, and medial frontal cortex.

Source: Adam and Bradley, 2012 / Society for Neuroscience.

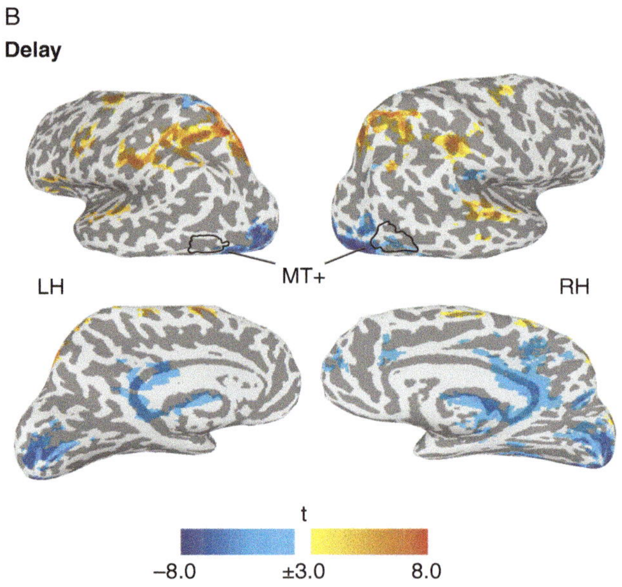

FIGURE 14.7.B Group-average univariate statistical maps of changes in fMRI activity, relative to baseline, during the delay period, when subjects are remembering the item whose encoding is illustrated in load-of-1 trial, *Figure 14.7.A*. There are two overall impressions: First, activity remains elevated in the IPS and in posterior PFC, albeit with lower statistical values; and second, activity in occipital cortex, including calcarine cortex and MT+, has declined to baseline or lower-than-baseline levels.

Source: Adam and Bradley, 2012 / Society for Neuroscience.

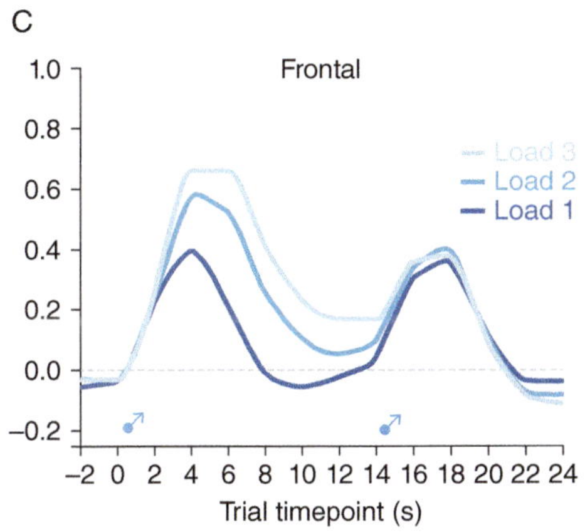

FIGURE 14.7.C Group- and trial-averaged activity from Emrich et al. (2013; i.e., the study that is described in the text) – from posterior PFC regions comparable to those shown in *Figure 14.7.B.* Note that encoding-related (4–6 seconds) and delay-related (10–15 seconds) activity shows a load effect, with higher signal intensity for higher loads. Arrow icons along the time axis indicate when moving-dot stimuli were on the screen.

Source: Emrich et al., 2013 / Society for Neuroscience.

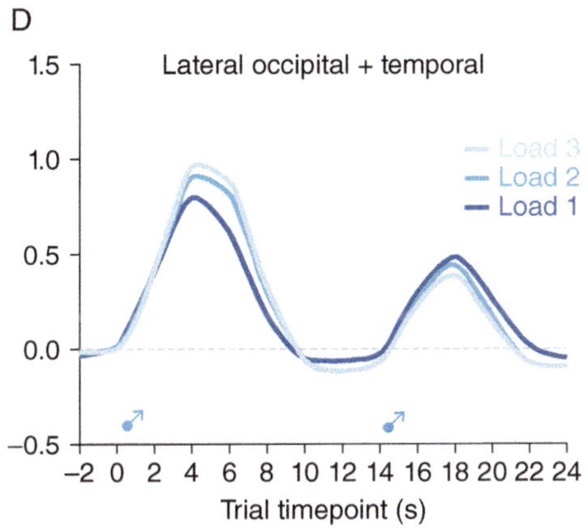

FIGURE 14.7.D Group- and trial-averaged activity from Emrich et al. (2013), from lateral occipital regions comparable to those shown in *Figure 14.7.A.* Note that although the encoding-related response is higher than that in posterior PFC, activity in these regions drops to just below baseline levels during the delay period.

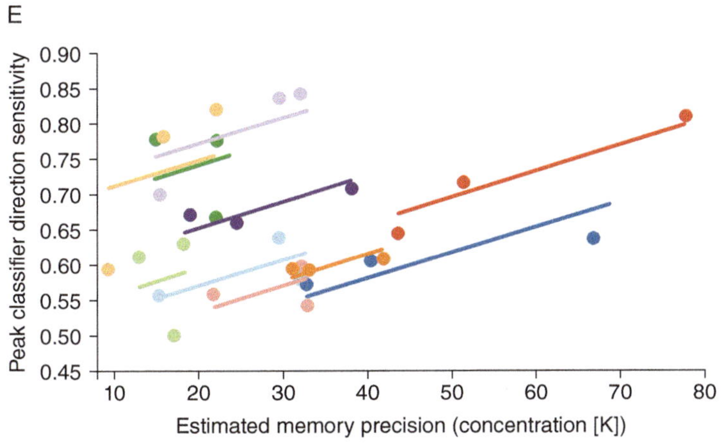

FIGURE 14.7.E Results from an analysis of covariance (ANCOVA) relating the behavioral precision of each individual subject to the fidelity of MVPA decoding of data from lateral occipital cortex at time 12 seconds (i.e., late in the delay period) from Emrich et al. (2013). Data points are color-coded by subject, with each subject's left-most point corresponding to load 3, the middle point to load 2, and the right-most point to load 1. For example, the behavioral precision (as plotted on the horizontal axis) of the subject shown in indigo is among the highest in this sample, but MVPA decoder performance for this subject starts at 65% correct and declines from there. The behavioral precision of the subject portrayed in the light violet, in contrast, is markedly lower, yet this subject's MVPA decoder performance is the highest for this sample. Despite this intersubject variability, the regression lines illustrate the common group-level effect that the load-related decline in MVPA performance relates to the load-related decline in behavioral precision with an $r^2 = 0.35$. Chance-level MVPA decoding for this analysis is 33.3%; behavioral precision is displayed as values of the concentration parameter of the three-factor mixture model illustrated in panel H of *Figure 14.5.*

parameter estimate of nearly 80; units are arbitrary), and MVPA decoding of the fMRI data from these trials was at 80% correct. For load-of-2 trials, the precision of this subject's behavioral responses declined to a concentration value of approximately 50, and MVPA decoding of the fMRI data from these trials declined to around 70% correct. For load-of-3 trials, the precision of this subject's behavioral responses declined even further, to a concentration value of about 43, and MVPA decoding of the fMRI data from these trials also declined further, to 65% correct. (*Concentration parameter* is defined in legend for panel E of *Figure 14.5*.) Although we don't understand exactly what MVPA decoding at 80% vs. 70% vs. 65% actually means in terms of the properties of a neural representation of a stimulus, we can take it as a proxy (there's that word again!) for the fidelity of the neural representation. With the caveat that this is a correlation, an interpretation of these results is that, with increasing load, the fidelity of delay-period neural representations of information declines, resulting in noisier "read-out" via end-of-trial recall.

Thus, the results from Emrich et al. (2013) indicate that not only does working memory storage of visual perceptual information take place in occipital cortex, but the fidelity of these occipital representations may also influence the precision of these memories. But what about IPS and PFC? Interestingly, in this study, MVPA decoding of stimulus information was unsuccessful in IPS and posterior PFC, the regions that showed elevated, load-sensitive delay-period activity. (Although more recent studies have shown that it can be possible to decode delay-period stimulus information from these areas, the decoding is generally weaker, and has never been shown, to this author's knowledge, with memory loads greater than 2.) If not the representation, per se, of stimulus information, what delay-period functions might account for the elevated activity in these regions? As we'll see further along, one of these is mental effort.

The Representational Format of Sensory Information Held in Visual Working Memory Studies like those illustrated in *Figure 14.6* and *Figure 14.7* (as well as, e.g., *Figure 5.9*) have been interpreted as evidence for "sensory recruitment" models of visual working memory, which posit that information is retained in working memory via the allocation of attention to the same neural systems that are responsible for the visual perception of that information when it is present in the environment.[3] A strong (and very literal) version of such a model would be that the very same circuits that are responsible for the visual perception of an object are also responsible for its representation in working memory. An alternative version holds that whereas visual perception of an object relies primarily on layers II/III and layer IV (due to its presumed preferential reliance on feedforward processing), visual working memory for the same object is relatively more reliant on layer V (a reflection of its preferential reliance on feedback processing). Here we'll consider evidence for a third account of sensory recruitment for visual working memory.

A team led by Chiapat Chunharas and anchored by Rosanne Rademaker carried out a reanalysis of data from an fMRI study that they had originally published as Rademaker, Chunharas, and Serences (2019). The experiment entailed fMRI scanning during which subjects performed two tasks with oriented-grating stimuli: a "sensory task" in which they viewed a stimulus for 9 seconds and detected slight changes in contrast that occurred unpredictably (effectively, the "attention" task from Jerde, Merriam, Riggall, Hedges, and Curtis (2012), *Figure 9.5*); and a "memory task" during which they first viewed an oriented-grating sample stimulus for 500 msec and then, after a 13-seconds delay, rotated to dial to indicate their recall of the sample orientation (a task that we have seen many times, including Serences et al. (2009), *Figure 14.6*). For the reanalyses published as Chunharas, Wolff, Hettwer, and Rademaker (2025), the authors applied several clever variants of representational similarity analysis (RSA). First, as illustrated in *Figure 14.8*, they performed "split-half" analyses in which, for both the *sensory* and the *memory* tasks, they randomly divided trials into two groups and correlated one group of trials with the other to generate representational similarity matrices (RSM). The resultant matrices, illustrated in *Figure 14.8.C*, showed interesting

[3] An alternative account would be that, once a stimulus is no longer accessible to the eyes, information about it is retained in a system, other than the visual system, that acts as a storage buffer. Some argue that this buffering function is carried out by dorsal PFC (despite the line of argumentation that will be made at the conclusion of section *Revisiting the PFC*), some that it is carried out by intraparietal sulcus (IPS), and some that it is carried out by the hippocampus.

differences between the two conditions. In particular, in early visual areas V1, V2, and V3, as well as in higher-order object-responsive region LO (named for its location in lateral occipital cortex), RSMs of the *sensory* task showed highest similarity along the diagonal, indicating that the representation of every orientation was highly distinct from that of every other orientation. And of particular relevance for our current interests, the authors characterized this pattern as evidence for "veridical" representation by these ROIs. That is, 65° was represented in a manner distinct from 50° or from 80°. For the *memory* task, in contrast, the RSMs from these same ROIs showed weaker similarity along the diagonal and a greater tendency toward for similarity to cluster into two categories: orientations from 0° to 90° tended to be similarly represented (and also more difficult to discriminate from each other); and orientations from 90° to 180° were similarly clustered. Thus, in contrast to *sensory* representations, *memory* representations were more "categorical." (There are two important details to note about orientation. The first is that they only meaningfully range from 0° to 179°, because 0° and 180° are identical, 1° and 181° are identical, etc. The second is that Chunharas et al. (2025) followed the convention that 0° corresponds to vertical, and so 1° to 89° corresponds to orientations tilted to the right of vertical, and 91°–179° corresponds to orientations tilted to the left of vertical.)

Why would the representations of orientation in early visual cortex be more categorical during working memory than during visual perception? Chunharas et al. (2025) hypothesized that these differences originate from a principle that influences the organization of most vertebrate sensory systems, which is efficient coding. In a very brief summary of this idea, we can start conceptually from the fact that different parts of the visual field are represented by neurons in V1 with differently sized spatial receptive fields, a property that varies lawfully as a function of distance from central vision. And so the representation of space in V1 is inhomogeneous. If we now consider orientation tuning, it turns out that, in adult organisms, the

FIGURE 14.8 The representational dissimilarities of stimulus information being perceived vs. being held in working memory.
Source: (Chunharas, Wolff, Hettwer, & Rademaker, 2025).

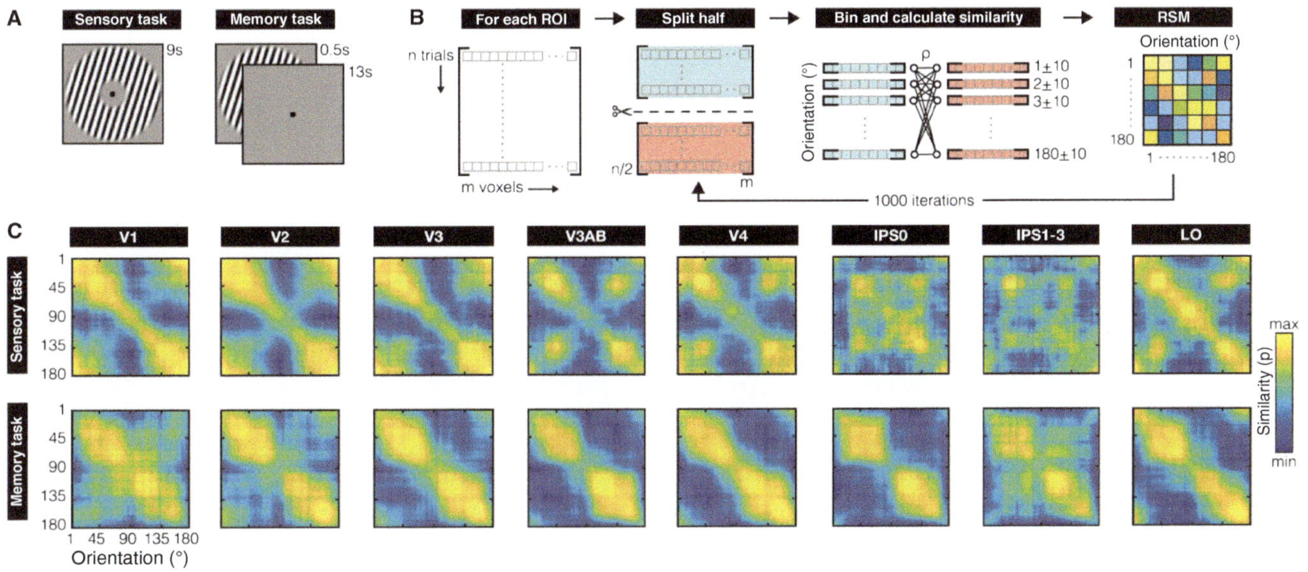

FIGURE 14.8.A Simplified diagram of the two tasks. Note that the diagram of the "memory task" does not include the recall dial with which subjects responded at the end of the trial. (For a complete diagram of the task, see Rademaker et al. (2019).)

FIGURE 14.8.B For each region of interest (ROI), RSMs were created for each subject by first randomly selecting half the trials to generate two groups, then smoothing the data by averaging, for each of 180 equally spaced orientations, the voxel patterns for every trial for which stimulus orientation was within −10° to +10°. Then, for each of the 180 degrees of orientation similarity, correlation between the two halves of data was calculated, yielding for each a Spearman correlation coefficient. This process was repeated 10,000 times (each iteration (or "fold") beginning with a new random partition of the data into two groups, and the resultant 10000 values of ρ were averaged, and an RSM was assembled.

FIGURE 14.8.C RSMs for the two tasks, in each of several ROIs.

representation of orientation is also inhomogeneous. This is because in the natural world, two orientations dominate: vertical (evolutionarily because of trees; in modern times, for humans, due to buildings, walls, doorways, poles, etc.) and horizontal (evolutionarily because of the horizon, modern times due to buildings, doors, windows, etc.). Efficient coding theory posits that a sensory system can most efficiently fulfill its functions by devoting the most resources to the features that are most prevalent in the environment, and therefore most vertebrate visual systems, and certainly primate visual systems, devote more resources to processing vertical and horizontal – the *cardinal* orientations – than to the *oblique* orientations in between. A consequence of this, as is illustrated in *Figure 14.9*, is that two very similar orientations that fall on either side of a cardinal orientation are much more perceptually discriminable than are two equally similar orientations that fall on either side of an oblique orientation. This can lead to the representation of orientation in "psychological distances" between orientations that reflect the bias imposed by the inhomogeneous orientation landscape produced by efficient coding. This, in turn, can lead to categorization, in which "everything near an oblique" gets clumped together as "left of vertical" or as "right of vertical." *Figure 14.9* illustrates how the authors used this logic to build two "theoretical" RSMs, one based on the hypothesized performance of a system sculpted by principles of efficient coding that supported veridical processing of orientations, and a second that reflected "psychological distances" that would produce categorization. These "theoretical" RDMs were then correlated with the empirical RDMs illustrated in *Figure 14.8*. For RDMs from the *sensory* task, it was found that the correlations with the veridical theoretical RDM were higher than with the categorical theoretical RDM in each of the ROIs tested. In the memory task, in contrast, the two theoretical RDMs were equally poorly correlated with the empirical RDMs in V1 and V2, but the correlations with the categorical theoretical RDMs were significantly higher in extrastriate ROIs, extending into IPS0.

Finally, the authors replicated the results obtained with theoretical RSMs with a set of "empirically derived theoretical RDMs." That is, in the place of the theoretically derived RSMs that they created based on their knowledge of how the perception textbooks say that human visual systems *should* work (i.e., *Figure 14.9*), they recruited a new set of human subjects and tested them behaviorally (i.e., no fMRI) on many trials (27,540 total trials from 17 subjects) to derive an empirical "veridical" and "categorical" RSM reflecting how the human visual system *does* work (in those 17 subjects, whose demographics matched those of the subjects scanned by Rademaker et al. (2019)). The results, illustrated in *Figure 14.10*, were consistent with what we've already seen in *Figure 14.8* and *Figure 14.9*: the neural representation of orientation during the *sensory* task was much more similar to an idealized veridical than an idealized categorical format, whereas the converse was true during the *memory* task, with categorial representation most prominent in extrastriate cortex and in IPS0 (although not achieving the threshold for significance in IPS 0).

Prior to this section, we had already seen that visual perception and visual working memory draw at least partly on common processes. For example, multivariate decoders trained on one of the two conditions can successfully decode the other (e.g., *Chapter 5*, section *Reconstructing stimulus information with multivariate inverted encoding models (IEM)*; and *Chapter 9*, section *Prioritized maps of space in human frontoparietal cortex*). What are the novel implications for "sensory recruitment" accounts of visual working memory of the results from Chunharas et al. (2025)? On one hand, they illustrate how visual working memory (for oriented gratings) is processed differently than visual perception (of the same oriented gratings), in that the former is more categorical, the latter more veridical. This means that visual working memory may not literally be "nothing more than" a prolongation of visual perception after the stimulus is no longer present in the environment. Rather, visual working memory seems to be more influenced by prior knowledge about/experience with the world than is visual perception. On the other hand, Chunharas et al. (2025) demonstrate very elegantly that the neural bases of visual working memory are nonetheless constrained by one of the most fundamental principles of visual perception, that of efficient coding.

Before leaving this section, it's also worth relating the findings and interpretations from Chunharas et al. (2025) to other frameworks that we have encountered. The first is the influence of familiarity on the neural code for object processing in the temporal lobe. Conceptually,

FIGURE 14.9 Building "theoretical RSMs" to test a hypothesis inspired by the principle of efficient coding.
Source: Chunharas et al. (2025).

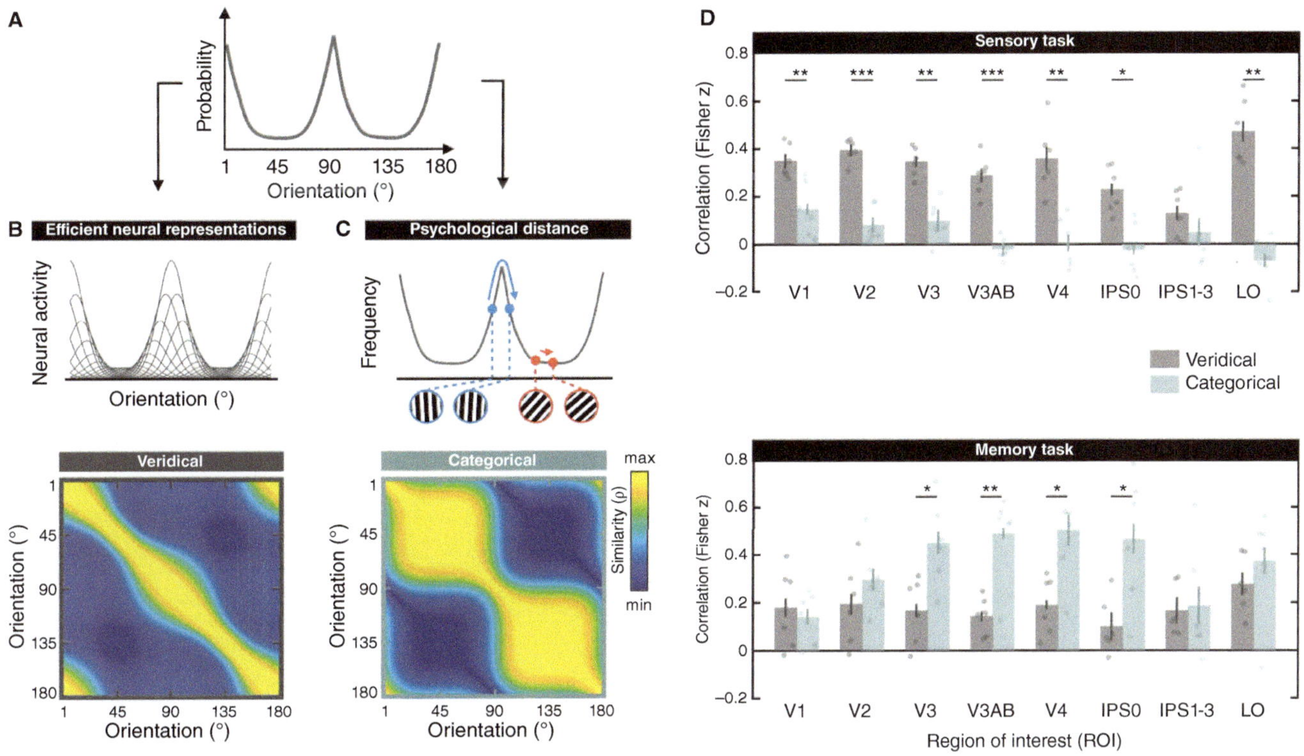

FIGURE 14.9.A Hypothetical distribution of orientations in the natural world, with peaks at the cardinal orientations of horizontal (0°/180°) and vertical (90°).

FIGURE 14.9.B "Veridical" model of visual processing as an implementation of efficient coding derived from *Figure 14.9.A*. Each von Mises curve is a hypothetical sensory processing channel, tuned for the orientation on which it is centered, and weighted by a gain factor deriving from *Figure 14.9.A*. (Note that the units of gain are expressed as "neural activity." Also note that these hypothetical tuned channels are comparable to the basis functions used for multivariate inverted encoding modeling (IEM), as illustrated in *Figure 5.8*, although the IEM basis set illustrated in *Figure 5.8* assumes equivalent gain at all orientations.) Underneath is the RSM generated by this model. The greater amplitude of responses at the cardinal orientations results in the slight "fattening" of the high correlation values along the diagonal of the matrix.

FIGURE 14.9.C "Categorical" model of visual processing that operationalizes "psychological distance," constructed as the sum of derivatives (i.e., rates of change) of differences in probability of occurrence in the environment (i.e., of the data illustrated in *Figure 14.9.A.*). The psychological distance between any two orientations corresponds to the distance along this plot that one must travel to get from one stimulus to the other, as illustrated by the two similar orientations depicted in blue and the two in red. Although the blue and red stimuli are equidistant in terms of degrees of separation, the two blue values are separated by a considerably larger psychological distance than the red. (I.e., the two blue items span a category boundary ["tilted to the left" vs. "tilted to the right"], but the two red belong to the same category ["tilted to the right"]). Underneath is the RSM generated by this model, which encodes very high similarity among all values in the "tilted to the left" category and very high similarity among all values in the "tilted to the right" category.

FIGURE 14.9.D Results of RSA of the two RSMs from *Figure 14.9.C* against the empirical RSMs from *Figure 14.8.C*. In the sensory task, the correlation in every ROI is higher for the veridical model. In the memory task, the correlation is higher for the categorical model beginning in V2, statistically so in V3, V3AB, V4, and IPS0.

the transformation of visual information into a different representational geometry when it is held in working memory (vs. when it is being perceived) is reminiscent of the familiarity-related transformation that we considered in *Chapter 12*, section *What is the familiarity signal?* Additionally, while noting that some of the details are different, the perspective from Chunharas et al. (2025) is very compatible with the one advocated by Panichello, DePasquale, Pillow, and Buschman (2019), whereby representations held in working memory drift toward attractors in the visual system, those attractors having developed as a consequence of statistical

FIGURE 14.10 Building "empirically derived theoretical RSMs" to test a hypothesis inspired by the principle of efficient coding.
Source: Chunharas et al. (2025).

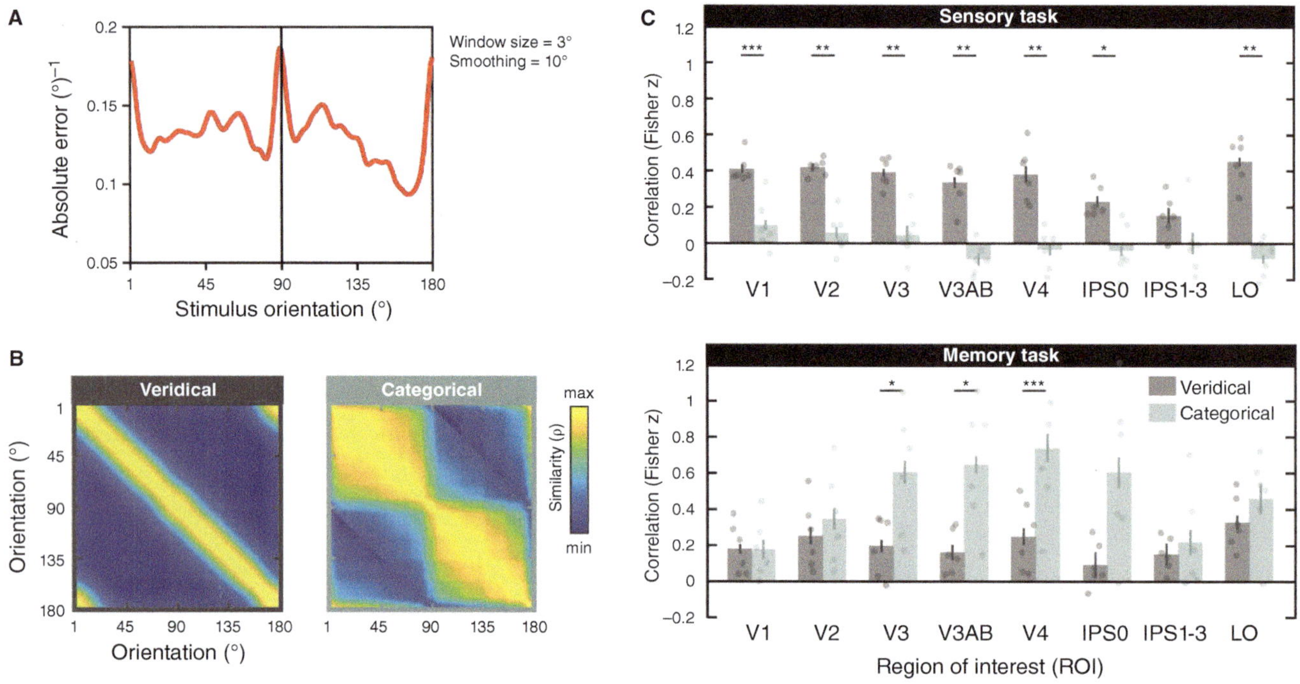

FIGURE 14.10.A Recall performance of 17 subjects (different from those whose data are shown in *Figure 14.8* and Figure *14.9*) as a function of orientation. These subjects viewed each stimulus for 200 msec and recalled it after a 2-second delay. Note that performance is expressed in units of error, but to make this plot visually similar to those from *Figure 14.8* and *Figure 14.9,* the authors have plotted the data in an inverted format (i.e., error [in °] raised to the – 1st power).

FIGURE 14.10.B Veridical and Categorical RSMs derived as in *Figure 14.9*, but now with the empirically derived data from *Figure 14.10.A*.

FIGURE 14.10.C Results of RSA of the two RSMs from *Figure 14.10.B* correlated with the empirical RSMs from *Figure 14.8.C*. In the sensory task, the correlation in every ROI is higher for the veridical model. In the memory task, the correlation is higher for the categorical model in every ROI beginning with V2, statistically so in V3, V3AB, and V4.

regularities in the visual world, as well as of the top-down influence of knowledge. Although Chunharas et al. (2025) don't frame the result from, e.g., *Figure 14.10.A*, in this way, we can do so. To convince yourself of this, just compare *Figure 14.10.A* to *Figure 5.3.B.*

The Functions of Elevated Delay-Period Activity

Early in this chapter, we saw how elevated activity in the PFC was interpreted by some as a neural correlate of an active memory trace, but then that other groups generated findings that challenged this interpretation. Then we were introduced to the contralateral delay activity (CDA), an ERP measurement of delay-period activity in the human that very closely tracks individual differences in one measure of working-memory ability – capacity – but saw that there is at least one aspect of working memory representation – precision – to which it is not sensitive. In the previous section, we've seen that MVPA has revealed that occipital regions that do not show elevated delay period activity in the fMRI signal nonetheless hold representations of the stimulus information that is being retained on that trial, whereas evidence for active stimulus representation in regions of parietal and frontal cortex that show robust elevated activity is much more equivocal. Maintaining sustained, elevated levels of activity (as illustrated in *Figure 14.1, Figure 14.2, Figure 14.4, and Figure 14.7*) is highly resource demanding, and so it must serve one or more important functions (i.e., it presumably has conferred an evolutionary advantage). In this section, we'll explore evidence for what at least some of these important functions might be.

"Trying Harder"

It makes intuitive sense that a system responsible for holding information in memory would need to "work harder" as it is given more to remember. After all, to lift a bag will require the exertion of more force when it contains two stones relative to when it contains only one, and even more when it contains three, etc. But are there additional factors, more than just "more remembering," that are engaged as memory load increases? It is certainly the case that it *feels* more effortful to hold three items in mind relative to just holding one or two, but is that feeling of effort anything different from just "more remembering?" Stated another way, is there an objective way to measure the seemingly subjective construct of mental effort? Sarah Master, in the laboratory of Clayton Curtis, has developed an ingenious way to do just that.

You'll recall the work of the Curtis group from *Chapter 9*, section *Prioritized maps of space in human frontoparietal cortex*, in which the neural activity associated with *attention* to the location of an item was compared to that for the *intention* to look at that item and to that for the *retention* in working memory of the location of that item.[4] Here, Master, Li, and Curtis (2024) developed a simple modification of the *retention* task from that experiment such that working memory for the location of a single item would require more or less effort, depending on the condition. As illustrated in *Figure 14.11*, an instructional cue informed subjects whether the impending trial would be *easy* or *difficult*.[5] The details of the task are that it required delayed discrimination of the location of a probe: After presentation of a target location, then a 12-second delay, subjects were to judge whether the location of the probe was clockwise or counterclockwise relative to where the target had been presented. For each subject, an adaptive staircase ensured that *easy* trials were just that, by presenting the probe at a distance for which the subject would be correct 90% of the time. *Difficult* trials were staircased to yield 70% correct performance. (On average, *easy* probes were 23° distant from the target location; *Difficult* probes were 5° distant from the target location.) Critically, however, every trial of the experiment required the same cognitive operation: remember the location of the target.

Figure 14.11.A illustrates that the experimental manipulation was successful: accuracy was higher and reaction times faster on *Easy* vs. *Difficult* trials. Independent evidence that *Easy* trials recruited less effort came from the concurrently measured pupillometry data: pupil size was larger on *Difficult* trials for the second half of the delay period (see *Chapter 4*, section *Pupillometry*). So far, perhaps not a big surprise, in that the objectively more difficult trials produced behavioral and pupillometric correlates of effort. But there are two points that will greatly add to the interpretability of the fMRI results (which are really impactful). The first is that because these trials were identical prior to the probe, the disparity in mental effort exerted prior to probe onset was not confounded by some "physical" factor like number of items, or luminance, or duration of presentation, or any number of other possible confounders. The second is that, even though the probe *was* physically different on *Difficult* vs. *Easy* trials, the pupillometry data confirm that the disparity in effort was present earlier in the trial (i.e., during the delay period), and so the disparity in delay-period effort can only be attributed to an endogenous factor, like volition or strategy. Now for the fMRI results.

As illustrated in *Figure 14.12.A*, the authors used independent "retinotopy" scans to identify retinotopic maps and to derive spatial receptive fields for each voxel within those maps (using methods similar to those illustrated in *Figure 7.5*). And as in previous work from Saygin

[4] The tasks from Jerde et al. (2012), in turn, were inspired by studies like the ones reviewed in section *Single-unit delay-period activity in PFC and thalamus*.

[5] Master et al. (2024) used "hard," but somehow to this author that sounds too slang-y, not science-y enough. I mean, we don't want to come across as casual and anecdotal when addressing a squishy construct like "effortfulness," right?

FIGURE 14.11 Behavioral and pupillometry correlates of effort in visual working memory.

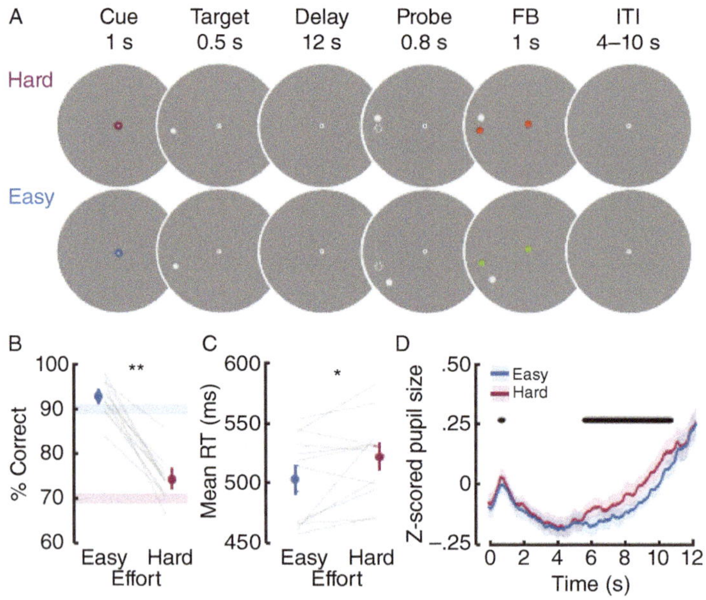

FIGURE 14.11.A Trial types were interleaved and each trial began with an instruction cue indicating, by color of fixation dot, whether the trial would be "Hard" or "Easy," followed by the presentation of the target, a delay period, and the presentation of the probe (which required a button-press response indicating that location of the probe is "clockwise" or "counterclockwise" to location or the target [for illustration, target location is portrayed with dashed circles, but no such circles actually appeared during the experiment]). Following the probe/response, feedback (FB) was given by adding to the probe display the target location in a color indicating that the subject's response was correct (green) or incorrect (red).

FIGURE 14.11.B Response accuracy, with dots + error bars illustrating the group mean and each line corresponding to an individual subject. Note that, for both conditions, mean accuracy was slightly higher than the desired target level of performance, determined by adaptive staircase algorithms that adjusted target-to-probe distance on a trial-by-trial basis (i.e., although initial thresholding was carried out ahead of time, adjustments were made throughout the experiment itself).

FIGURE 14.11.C Reaction times, indicating that responses on *Hard* trials were slower.

FIGURE 14.11.D Average pupil size (lines, with translucent ribbons indicating SE) was larger on *Hard* trials, with divergence beginning halfway across the delay period (black lines along top indicate statistically significant differences).

Source: (Master, 2024) / The Society for Neuroscience.

and Sereno (2008; *Figure 7.5*) and Jerde et al. (2012; *Chapter 9*, section *Prioritized maps of space in human frontoparietal cortex*), this identified regions of the Dorsal Attention network (DAN; *Figure 4.17.C* and *Figure 9.5*) in addition to most of the occipital cortex. For analyses, the BOLD timeseries data from each voxel were sorted on a trial-by-trial basis to identify the subset of trials in which the target stimulus appeared at a location inside the voxel's receptive field ("RF_{in}"; defined as a range within 15° of polar angle, in either direction, from the center of the receptive field). Additionally, for each voxel, trials in which the target appeared at a location 180° away from the receptive field (+/− 15° of polar angle) were labeled as "RF_{out}" trials. The results, in *Figure 14.12.B*, indicate that the delay-period activity in frontal and parietal ROIs was indeed higher for RF_{in} relative to RF_{out} trials. This effect is not as evident in occipital ROIs because, echoing was we've already seen earlier in this chapter, occipital delay-period signal intensity was not different from baseline. But the really striking result is that, in frontal and parietal ROIs, delay-period signal intensity was markedly higher on *Difficult* relative to *Easy* trials. Thus, it is indeed the case that factors other than memory load, per se, can

FIGURE 14.12 Neural correlates of effort in visual working memory.

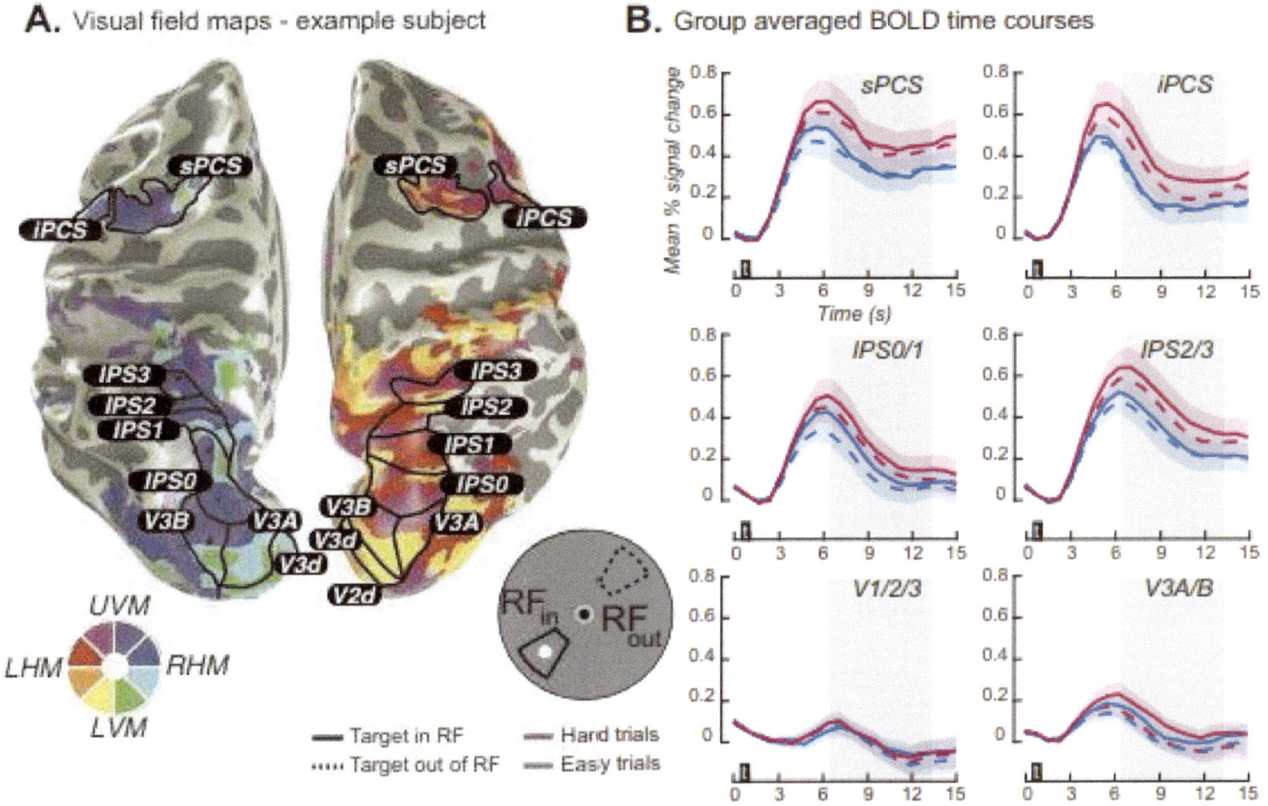

FIGURE 14.12.A Retinotopic maps identified in the independent "retinotopy" scans (see text), illustrated on two inflated hemispheres, and parcellated into ROIs. ROI labels beginning with "V" are in the occipital cortex, and are homologous with the regions of the same name in the nonhuman primate (NHP), as illustrated in *Figure 6.5*. "IPS" corresponds to IPS, and "sPCS" and "iPCS" to superior and inferior precentral sulcus, respectively, the former a universally accepted homolog of the frontal eye fields of the NHP (*Figure 9.1*), the latter a region associated with oculomotor control in the human (c.f., *Figure 9.4.C*, whose homology with the NHP brain is unclear). The circular legend references upper and lower vertical meridian (UVM, LVM) and left and right horizontal meridian (LHM, RHM), and the gray disc illustrates the hypothetical identification, for a single voxel, of a target falling within its receptive field RF_{in} and the corresponding region for which a target would be classified for that voxel as RF_{out} (see text).

FIGURE 14.12.B Trial-averaged BOLD time courses sorted by RF (RF_{in} vs. RF_{out}) and effort (*Hard* vs. *Easy*), from individual ROIs or averages across contiguous ROIs.

influence frontoparietal delay-period activity. Furthermore, these results are consistent with the possibility (the likelihood?) that *additional factors, more than just "more remembering," are engaged as memory load increases.*

Finally, we can turn to the multivariate decoding results from Master et al. (2024). For these analyses, the authors used a Bayesian decoder (developed by Reuben van Bergen and Janneke Jehee, and colleagues) that provides trial-by-trial estimates of the accuracy of the neural representation of the information being decoded (van Bergren et al., 2015; van Bergren and Jehee, 2021). The overall trend for the decoding analyses was reminiscent of what we have seen in other studies – robust decoding of delay-period activity in occipital cortex (despite the absence of elevated signal during this period) and weak-to-failed decoding from parietal and frontal regions (despite robust elevated signal) – but with a twist: the accuracy of delay-period neural representation of target location was higher on *Difficult* than on *Easy* trials. At first, this might seem paradoxical: How can it be that the neural representations were more accurate on trials in which subjects performed worse? The answer is that *difficult* trials needed to have higher-accuracy representations because the discrimination required by the probe required finer-grained representations. That is, a more fine-grained representation is needed to discriminate (from memory) stimuli that are only 5° apart, relative to stimuli that are 22° apart. And the final icing on the cake was that trial-by-trial fluctuations in decoded accuracy correlated with trial-by-trial fluctuations in signal intensity in sPCS and IPS0-3. Thus, as the authors conclude, there is compelling evidence that "effort-related feedback signals (from the DAN) sculpt population activity in the visual cortex, improving mnemonic fidelity" (Master et al., 2024; p. 1 of 12).

Revisiting the PFC

In *Chapter 5*, section *RNN modeling of visual working memory*, we introduced the RNN simulations by Emilia Piwek, Mark Stokes, and Chris Summerfield (2023) of the experiment in which Matthew Panichello and Timothy Buschman (2021) had tested working memory for the color of one of two stimuli (*Figure 5.10*) while recording from dorsolateral (dl)PFC, FEF, area 7 of posterior parietal cortex (PPC; located on the gyrus inferior to the IPS), and V4 (*Figure 14.13*). One aspect of this task that we didn't emphasize in Chapter 5, is that Panichello and Buschman (2021) designed their task to be able to compare two hypothetically distinct operations: the prioritization of one of two items currently on the screen (attentional selection) vs. the prioritization of one of two items currently held in working memory (mnemonic selection). Mnemonic selection was operationalized with trials like the one illustrated in *Figure 5.10.A*: First, two sample stimuli were presented for the animals to encode into memory; next, after a brief delay, a retrocue indicated which of the two items (the one that had appeared in the *Up* location or the one that had appeared in the *Down* location) would be tested at the end of the trial. Attentional selection was operationalized with trials that reversed this order: First, a prospective cue indicated whether the item that would appear in the *Up* or in the *Down* location was the one that would be tested; next, the two sample items were presented.[6] Panichello and Buschman (2021) emphasize that, in both trial types, the prioritization cue triggers the allocation of cognitive control, which they defined as the guidance of behavior "by controlling what, when, and how information is represented in the brain" (p. 601). That is, on the attentional selection trials the item in the *Up* location and the one in the *Down* location were equally salient, and in a no-task context would be expected to be processed in the same way by the visual system – it is due to the understanding of the behavioral relevance of the cue, and the decoding of its meaning, that the animal was able to flexibly control how the stimulus array was processed on each trial; the same considerations applied to the mnemonic selection trials.[7]

In *Chapter 5*, section *Representational geometry analysis*, we summarized the consequences of mnemonic selection on stimulus representation. Prior to cue onset, *Up* and *Down* items were represented in near-orthogonal subspaces (*Figure 5.12.A*). Following cue onset, two things happened: (1) the selected item rotated into a communication subspace so as to guide the behavioral response (*Figure 5.12.C*); and (2) (via RNN simulation) the consequence of not being selected was that the stimulus manifold collapsed such that this item could no longer be identified. These events can be construed as consequences of the application of cognitive control, and are analogous to the representational fates of the item that wins or loses the (biased) competition for representation in the visual system during a visual search task (*Chapter 7*, section *Object-based attention*; *Figure 7.15*). What we'll emphasize here is the evidence that PFC acts as a source of this control.

To assess the emergence of cognitive control, Panichello and Buschman (2021) trained a classifier to discriminate the instruction conveyed by the cue (i.e., *Up* vs. *Down*; as illustrated in *Figure 5.12.A*) in each of four areas, and found that this information emerged first in dlPFC (latency of 175 msec following cue onset), followed by FEF (245 msec), PPC (285 msec), and V4 (335 msec). This would be consistent with a control signal emerging first in dlPFC and

[6] Note that, although the authors do not emphasize this fact, the attentional selection task required holding the instruction (*Up* or *Down*) in working memory during the ISI separating it from the sample display.
[7] Consider Figure 14.6, which implies that a mere verbal instruction is enough for a subject to be able to *control* whether or not their primary visual cortex will or will not process the color of the stimulus that they are looking at!

FIGURE 14.13 Controlling selection from a visual array and from working memory for a visual array.
Source: (Panichello & Buschman, 2021) / Springer Nature.

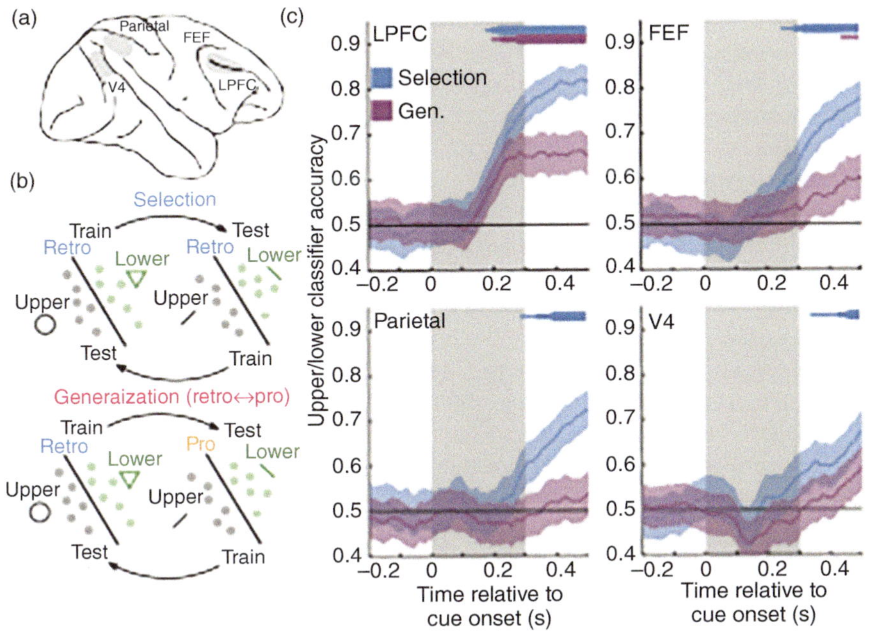

FIGURE 14.13.A The four cortical areas from which the authors made simultaneous recordings.

FIGURE 14.13.B Schematic diagram of within-trial decoding of mnemonic selection. (Note that here and in panel **C**, the authors refer to mnemonic selection as "Selection" and to cross-task decoding as "Generalization".) These diagrams illustrate the fact that two cue shapes are mapped to each instruction (circle and "/" for *Up* and inverted triangle and "\" for *Down*), such that successful decoding of *Up* from *Down* reflected decoding the instruction, and not just one symbol from another.

FIGURE 14.13.C Time courses of decoder accuracy in the four brain regions (mean and SE), illustrating that the shortest latency to achieve significant decoding of the retrocue ("Selection") was in dlPFC, and that dlPFC was the only region that supported early and robust cross-task generalization. The vertical gray band in each plot corresponds to the duration of cue presentation, and the significance of decoder performance is indicated with thin, medium, and thick lines at the top of each plot corresponding to p values < 0.05, 0.01., and 0.001, respectively.

---

then propagating in a top-down manner to other brain areas. Next, to test the hypothesis that mnemonic selection and attentional selection are accomplished via a common mechanism, they attempted to decode the prospective cue with the decoders trained on the retrospective cue (i.e., cross-task decoding by training on mnemonic selection and testing on attentional selection). Results showed successful cross-task decoding in dlPFC, equivocal evidence for cross-task decoding in FEF (for which evidence for cross-task decoding was weaker and considerably delayed), and no evidence for cross-task decoding in PPC or V4. These results thus support the idea that dlPFC can act as a domain-general controller of processing carried out in other brain areas. With this knowledge, we can now return to the question posed near the beginning of this chapter: What might have been the function of the stimulus-selective delay-period activity recorded in PFC in the studies that we reviewed near the beginning of this chapter (i.e., Fuster and Alexander, 1971; Kubota and Niki, 1971; Rao, Rainer, and Miller, 1997; and Wilson et al., 1993) (and that has subsequently been reported in many, many additional studies)? One answer is that although Wilson et al. (1993), for example, interpreted their results as reflecting activity corresponding to storage buffers of the multiple-component model (c.f., Baddeley and Hitch, 1974), they may actually have been recording from the neural instantiation of the Central Executive.

An Aside About Interpretation of Stimulus Decoding in Different Brain Regions When multivariate decoding of stimulus identity is successful in region X, it is commonplace to see this being interpreted as meaning that "there is information about the stimulus" in that region. Although this is a true statement, one should be cautious that this need not imply the stronger assumption that "copies of stimulus representations are being 'held in' region X." Consider, for example, the study from Panichello and Buschman (2021) that we reviewed in the previous section, and introduced in *Chapter 5*. Although in section *Revisiting the PFC* we emphasized the decoding of the instruction carried by the cue (*Figure 14.13*), we have also seen in *Figure 5.12.A* that the color of each of the two stimuli was represented in dlPFC. (Note that although *Figure 5.12.A* and section *Representational geometry analysis* emphasized the representational geometry of color information; we can be certain that if a region represents information in a low-dimensional ring manifold that it would support multivariate decoding of that information.) It has also been known, however, going back as far as the research from the late 1800s that we reviewed in *Chapter 1*, section *The localization of visual perception*, that large lesions of the PFC do not produce blindness, nor do they produce visual agnosias (c.f., *Chapter 10*, section *Visual Agnosia*). Therefore, we can infer that color information in the PFC does not make a necessary contribution to the perception of color, nor, in all likelihood, to short-term memory for color. What then, might be the function of the stimulus information decoded from dlPFC by Panichello and Buschman (2021), or of stimulus-specific responses observed in PFC neurons by, for example, Wilson et al. (1993) (*Figure 14.2*) and Rao et al. (1997) (*Figure 14.2*)? This author and then-postdoctoral fellow Qing Yu have offered the following possible explanation:

> In the case of a putative source of the top-down selection of one feature over another, for example, it must be the case that this selection mechanism is configured differently for each possible target of selection. Consider the spotlight metaphor. The location within a hypothetical arena that is currently the focus of illumination can be deduced from two pieces of information about the spotlight: the location of the spotlight within the 3D volume of the arena, and the spotlight's pose relative to a stable landmark (e.g., a vertical post stretching from floor to ceiling). Let's say that with a particular configuration of these values one can determine that the spotlight is illuminating a group of seats in Section L of the arena, centered on seat L35. If one were now to re-aim the spotlight so that it will illuminate a seat in Section K, the values that specify its new pose will necessarily be different. Thus, one can "decode" the seat that is being illuminated by knowing the location and the pose of the spotlight. Furthermore, if its location is fixed (let's say that the housing that holds the spotlight is welded to our vertical post, 10 meters up from the floor), there is a one-to-one relationship between a unique set of values of pose and each seat in the arena. Thus, we can obtain seat-level decoding from information relating exclusively to the configuration of the spotlight. Importantly, however, this ability to decode seat number from spotlight pose isn't equivalent to being in that seat. Thus, if the lighting technician has never explored the arena, they can't deduce from different spotlight configurations whether, for example, seat L35 or seat K16 is more comfortable to sit in, or that the occupant with season tickets for seat L34 is more polite than the occupant with season tickets for seat K15. (Postle and Yu, 2020, pp. 448–449).

Four-Score and a Handful of Years (and Counting)

We've covered research spanning from 1936 to 2025, from massive bilateral PFC lesions in NHPs to sophisticated computational simulations. Over the course of those 80+ years, we have learned a great deal about how people (and NHPs) hold information in mind for short periods of time in order to guide their behavior. One of the themes that we've emphasized – that there's an important difference between "just holding information in mind" (which does not depend on the integrity of the PFC) and performing various mental operations with, or on, that information – offers a nice segue into our next chapter, because working memory is a critical contributor to cognitive control.

End-of-Chapter Questions

1. What does the "short" in short-term memory refer to?
2. Were the interpretations that Fuster and Alexander (1971) and that Kubota and Niki (1971) gave to their electrophysiological findings consistent with the lesion data that had come before? How, or how not?
3. How did the development of the multicomponent model of working memory, from cognitive psychology, influence some people's interpretation of the findings from Question 2?
4. Summarize the findings from Funahashi, Bruce, and Goldman-Rakic (1989) and Wilson, Ó Scalaidhe, and Goldman-Rakic (1993), and how subsequent studies have been designed to evaluate and, in some cases, reinterpret them.
5. What is the CDA? What distinctive property makes it particularly interesting to students of visual working memory?
6. In what ways have recent MVPA analyses of fMRI studies of working memory raised questions about the interpretation of earlier studies analyzed with univariate methods? (Hint: sensitivity; specificity.)
7. If an fMRI scan shows that the level of activity in region X does not differ from baseline during the delay period of a working memory task, does this mean that the region is not involved in working memory storage?
8. Is elevated activity at the level of networks of neurons necessary for working memory storage? If not, what other mechanism could carry out this function?
9. Of the many regions that show working memory-related activity, which is/are most likely the exert control over the contents of working memory? Summarize evidence for your answer.

References

Baddeley, Alan D., and Graham Hitch. 1974. "Working Memory." In *The Psychology of Learning and Motivation: Advances in Research and Theory*, edited by Gordon H. Bower (pp. 47–89), vol. 8. New York: Academic Press.

van Bergen., R. S., and J. F. M. Jehee. 2021. "TAFKAP: An Improved Method for Probabilistic Decoding of Cortical Activity." *bioRxiv*. doi: 2021.03.04.433946.

van Bergen, R. S., W. J. Ma, M. S. Pratte, and J. F. M. Jehee. 2015. "Sensory Uncertainty Decoded from Visual Cortex Predicts Behavior." *Nature Neuroscience 18*: 1728–1730.

Chunharas, C., M. J. Wolff, M. D. Hettwer, and R. L. Rademaker. 2025. "A Gradual Transition Toward Categorical Representations Along the Visual Hierarchy During Working Memory, But Not Perception." *eLife*. doi: 10.7554/eLife.103347.1.

Emrich, Stephen M., Adam C. Riggall, Joshua J. LaRocque, and Bradley R. Postle. 2013. "Distributed Patterns of Activity in Sensory Cortex Reflect the Precision of Multiple Items Maintained in Visual Short-Term Memory." *Journal of Neuroscience* 33 (15): 6516–6523. doi: 10.1523/JNEUROSCI.5732-12.2013.

Funahashi, Shintaro, Charles J. Bruce, and Patricia S. Goldman-Rakic. 1989. "Mnemonic Coding of Visual Space in the Monkey's Dorsolateral Prefrontal Cortex." *Journal of Neurophysiology* 61 (2): 331–349.

Fuster, Joaquin M., and Garrett E. Alexander. 1971. "Neuron Activity Related to Short-Term Memory." *Science* 173 (3997): 652–654. doi: 10.1126/science.173.3997.652.

Ghent, Lila, Mortimer Mishkin, and Hans-Lukas Teuber. 1962. "Short-term Memory after Frontal-Lobe Injury in Man." *Journal of Comparative and Physiological Psychology* 55 (5): 705–709. doi: 10.1037/h0047520.

Hakim, N., and E. K. Vogel. 2018. "Phase-Coding Memories in Mind." *PLoS Biology* 16: e3000012.

Harrison, Stephenie A., and Frank Tong. 2009. "Decoding Reveals the Contents of Visual Working Memory in Early Visual Areas." *Nature* 458 (7238): 632–635. doi: 10.1038/nature07832.

Hebb, Donald Olding. 1949. *The Organization of Behavior: A Neuropsychological Theory*. New York: Wiley.

Jacobsen, C. F. 1936. "The Functions of the Frontal Association Areas in Monkeys." *Comparative Psychology Monographs* 13: 1–60.

Jerde, Trenton A., Elisha P. Merriam, Adam C. Riggall, James H. Hedges, and Clayton E. Curtis. 2012. "Prioritized Maps of Space in Human Frontoparietal Cortex." *Journal of Neuroscience* 32 (48): 17382–17390. doi: 10.1523/JNEUROSCI.3810-12.2012.

Johnson, M. K., R. P. McMahon, B. M. Robinson, A. N. Harvey, B. Hahn, C. J. Leonard, . . . J. M. Gold. 2013. "The Relationship Between Working Memory Capacity and Broad Measures of Cognitive Ability in Healthy Adults and People with Schizophrenia." *Neuropsychology* 27: 220–229.

Kubota, Kisou, and Hiroaki Niki. 1971. "Prefrontal Cortical Unit Activity and Delayed Alternation Performance in Monkeys." *Journal of Neurophysiology* 34 (3): 337–347.

Luck, S. J., and E. K. Vogel. 1997. "The Capacity of Visual Working Memory for Features and Conjunctions." *Nature* 390: 279–281.

Malmo, Robert B. 1942. "Interference Factors in Delayed Response in Monkeys after Removal of Frontal Lobes." *Journal of Neurophysiology* 5 (4): 295–308.

Master, S. L., S. Li, and C. E. Curtis. 2024. "Trying Harder: How Cognitive Effort Sculpts Neural Representations During Working Memory." *The Journal of Neuroscience 44*: e0060242024. doi: 10.1523/JNEUROSCI.0060-24.2024.

Milner, Brenda. 1964. "Some Effects of Frontal Lobectomy in Man." In *The Frontal Granular Cortex and Behavior*, edited by John M. Warren and Konrad Akert (pp. 313–334). New York: McGraw-Hill.

Panichello, M. F., and T. J. Buschman. 2021. "Shared Mechanisms Underlie the Control of Working Memory and Attention." *Nature 592*: 601–605. doi: 10.1038/s41586-021-03390-w.

Panichello, M. F., B. DePasquale, J. W. Pillow, and T. J. Buschman. 2019. "Error-Correcting Dynamics in Visual Working Memory." *Nature Communications 10*: 3366. doi: 10.1038/s41467-019-11298-3.

Piwek, E. P., M. G. Stokes, and C. Summerfield. 2023. "A Recurrent Neural Network Model of Prefrontal Brain Activity During a Working Memory Task." *PLoS Computational Biology 19* (10): e1011555. doi: 10.1371/journal.pcbi.1011555.

Postle, Bradley R. 2009. "The Hippocampus, Memory, and Consciousness." In *Neurology of Consciousness*, edited by Steven Laureys and Giulio Tononi (pp. 326–338). Amsterdam: Elsevier.

Postle, B. R., and Q. Yu. 2020. "Neuroimaging and the Localization of Function in Visual Cognition." *Visual Cognition 28*: 447–452. doi: doi.org/10.1080/13506285.2020.1777237.

Pribram, Karl H., Albert J. Ahumada Jr, J. Hartog, and L. Roos. 1964. "A Progress Report on the Neurological Processes Distributed by Frontal Lesions in Primates." In *The Frontal Granular Cortex and Behavior*, edited by John M. Warren and Konrad Akert (pp. 28–55). New York: McGraw-Hill.

Rademaker, R. L., C. Chunharas, and J. T. Serences. 2019. "Coexisting Representations of Sensory and Mnemonic Information in Human Visual Cortex." *Nature Neuroscience 22*: 1336–1344.

Rao, S. Chenchal, Gregor Rainer, and Earl K. Miller. 1997. "Integration of What and Where in the Primate Prefrontal Cortex." *Science* 276 (5313): 821–824. doi: 10.1126/science.276.5313.821.

Richter, F. R., R. A. Cooper, P. M. Bays, and J. S. Simons. 2016. "Distinct Neural Mechanisms Underlie the Success, Precision, and Vividness of Episodic Memory." *eLife* 5: e18260. doi: 10.7554/eLife.18260.

Riggall, Adam C., and Bradley R. Postle. 2012. "The Relationship between Working Memory Storage and Elevated Activity as Measured with Functional Magnetic Resonance Imaging." *Journal of Neuroscience* 32 (38): 12990–12998. doi: 10.1523/JNEUROSCI.1892-12.2012.

Saygin, Ayse Pinar, and Martin I. Sereno. 2008. "Retinotopy and Attention in Human Occipital, Temporal, Parietal, and Frontal Cortex." *Cerebral Cortex* 18 (9): 2158–2168. doi: 10.1093/cercor/bhm242.

Serences, John T., Edward F. Ester, Edward K. Vogel, and Edward Awh. 2009. "Stimulus-Specific Delay Activity in Human Primary Visual Cortex." *Psychological Science* 20 (2): 207–214. doi: 10.1111/j.1467-9280.2009.02276.x.

Todd, J. J., and R. Marois. 2004. "Capacity limit of visual short-term memory in human posterior parietal cortex." *Nature* 428: 751–754. doi: https://doi.org/10.1038/nature02466.

Vogel, Edward K., and Maro G. Machizawa. 2004. "Neural Activity Predicts Individual Differences in Visual Working Memory Capacity." *Nature* 428 (6984): 679–782. doi: 10.1038/nature02447.

Wilson, Fraser A. W., Séamas P. Ó. Scalaidhe, and Patricia S. Goldman-Rakic. 1993. "Dissociation of Object and Spatial Processing Domains in Primate Prefrontal Cortex." *Science* 260 (5116): 1955–1958.

Other Sources Used

Balaban, H., and R. Luria. 2019. "Using the Contralateral Delay Activity to Study Online Processing of Items Still within View." *NeuroMethods*. doi: 10.1007/7657_2019_22.

Carlisle, N. B., J. T. Arita, D. Pardo, and G. F. Woodman. 2011. "Attentional Templates in Visual Working Memory." *The Journal of Neuroscience* 31: 9315–9322.

Crowe, David A., Bruno B. Averbeck, and Matthew V. Chafee. 2010. "Rapid Sequences of Population Activity Patterns Dynamically Encode Task-Critical Spatial Information in Parietal Cortex." *Journal of Neuroscience* 30 (35): 11640–11653. doi: 10.1523/JNEUROSCI.0954-10.2010.

Emrich, S. M., N. Al-Aidroos, J. Pratt, and S. Ferber. 2009. "Visual Search Elicits the Electrophysiological Marker of Visual Working Memory." *PLoS One* 4: e8042.

Erickson, Martha A., Lauren A. Maramara, and John Lisman. 2010. "A Single Brief Burst Induces GluR1-Dependent Associative Short-Term Potentiation: A Potential Mechanism for Short-Term Memory." *Journal of Cognitive Neuroscience* 22 (11): 2530–2540. doi: 10.1162/jocn.2009.21375.

Jensen, Ole, Jack Gelfand, John Kounios, and John E. Lisman. 2002. "Oscillations in the Alpha Band (9–12 Hz) Increase with Memory Load during Retention in a Short-Term Memory Task." *Cerebral Cortex* 12 (8): 877–882. doi: 10.1093/cercor/12.8.877.

Lebedev, Mikhail A., Adam Messinger, Jerald D. Kralik, and Steven P. Wise. 2004. "Representation of Attended versus Remembered Locations in Prefrontal Cortex." *PLoS Biology* 2 (11): e365. doi: 10.1371/journal.pbio.0020365.

Masse, N. Y., G. R. Yang, H. F. Song, X.-J. Wang, and D. J. Freedman. 2019. "Circuit Mechanisms for the Maintenance and Manipulation of Information in Working Memory." *Nature Neuroscience* 22: 1159–1167. doi: 10.1038/s41593-019-0414-3.

Meyers, Ethan M., David J. Freedman, Gabriel Kreiman, Earl K. Miller, and Tomaso Poggio. 2008. "Dynamic Population Coding of Category Information in Inferior Temporal and Prefrontal Cortex." *Journal of Neurophysiology* 100 (3): 1407–1419. doi: 10.1152/jn.90248.2008.

Miller, George Armitage, Eugene Galanter, and Karl H. Pribram. 1960. *Plans and the Structure of Behavior*. New York: Holt.

Miller, Earl K., Cynthia A. Erickson, and Robert Desimone. 1996. "Neural Mechanisms of Visual Working Memory in Prefrontal Cortex of the Macaque." *Journal of Neuroscience* 16 (16): 5154–5167.

Miller, Earl K., Lin Li, and Robert Desimone. 1991. "A Neural Mechanism for Working and Recognition Memory in Inferior Temporal Cortex." *Science* 254 (5036): 1377–1379. doi: 10.1126/science.1962197.

Miller, Earl K., and Robert Desimone. 1994. "Parallel Neuronal Mechanisms for Short-Term Memory." *Science* 263 (5146): 630–522. doi: 10.1126/science.8290960.

Mongillo, Gianluigi, Omri Barak, and Misha Tsodyks. 2008. "Synaptic Theory of Working Memory." *Science* 319 (5869): 1543–1546. doi: 10.1126/science.1150769.

Nakamura, Katsuki, and Kisou Kubota. 1995. "Mnemonic Firing of Neurons in the Monkey Temporal Pole during a Visual Recognition Memory Task." *Journal of Neurophysiology* 74 (1): 162–178.

Niki, Hiroaki. 1974. "Differential Activity of Prefrontal Units during Right and Left Delayed Response Trials." *Brain Research* 70 (2): 346–349. doi: 10.1016/0006-8993(74)90324-2.

Niki, Hiroaki, and Masataka Watanabe. 1976. "Prefrontal Unit Activity and Delayed Response: Relation to Cue Location *versus* Direction of Response." *Brain Research* 105 (1): 79–88. doi: 10.1016/0006-8993(76)90924-0.

Reinhart, R. M., and G. F. Woodman. 2014. "High Stakes Trigger the Use of Multiple Memories to Enhance the Control of Attention." *Cerebral Cortex* 24: 2022–2035.

Rushworth, Matthew F. S., Philip D. Nixon, Madeline J. Eacott, and Richard E. Passingham. 1997. "Ventral Prefrontal Cortex Is Not Essential for Working Memory." *Journal of Neuroscience* 17 (12): 4829–4838.

Suzuki, Wendy A., Earl K. Miller, and Robert Desimone. 1997. "Object and Place Memory in the Macaque Entorhinal Cortex." *Journal of Neurophysiology* 78 (2): 1062–1081.

Warren, John M., and Konrad Akert, eds. 1964. *The Frontal Granular Cortex and Behavior*. New York: McGraw-Hill.

Further Reading

Meyers, Ethan, and Gabriel Kreiman. 2011. "Tutorial on Pattern Classification in Cell Recording." In *Visual Population Codes: Toward a Common Multivariate Framework for Cell Recording and Functional Imaging*, edited by Nikolaus Kriegeskorte and Gabriel Kreiman (pp. 517–538). Cambridge, MA: MIT Press.

Details on a powerful method for the retrospective MVPA of single-unit datasets.

Pasternak, Tatiana, and Mark W. Greenlee. 2005. "Working Memory in Primate Sensory Systems." *Nature Reviews Neuroscience* 6 (2): 97–107. doi: 10.1038/nrn1603.

Extensive review of evidence, from monkey neurophysiology and human psychophysics, for the sensory-recruitment hypothesis of STM.

Postle, Bradley R. 2006. "Working Memory as an Emergent Property of the Mind and Brain." *Journal of Neuroscience* 139 (1): 23–38. doi: 10.1016/j.neuroscience.2005.06.005.

Review covering much of the univariate analysis–based neuroimaging literature on human working memory that this chapter skips over.

High-Level Cognition

INTRODUCTION TO SECTION V

High-Level Cognition

Who's to say what's "high-level cognition" vs. "mental representation"? Isn't sorting out whether it was Brazil or Uruguay who won the first World Cup, or whether it was Graham Greene or Evelyn Waugh who wrote *Our Man in Havana*, high-level cognition? Sure. But they're also examples of semantic cognition. Isn't the endogenous control of attention a form of cognitive control? Of course it is. So too, as we have noted, is working memory. The labels aren't so important. The rationale behind this book's organization is that *Section II* provided a necessary foundation for exploring different facets of mental representation (i.e., *Section III*) in a substantive way, and *Sections II* and *III* have provided the background and framework needed for us to do the same with the topics to be covered here. None of them won't require a good understanding of perception, of attention, of motor control, and of memory. (Nor, for that matter, of oscillatory coherence, of fMRI, of neuropsychology, of computational modeling, and so on.) Furthermore, the chapters in this section will build on each other: principles from cognitive control will apply to decision-making, emotions, social behavior, and language; principles from decision-making will apply to emotions and social behavior; and so on.

It's THE NEURAL BASES OF HIGH-LEVEL COGNITION, people! Let's go!

CHAPTER 15

Cognitive Control

KEY THEMES

- Cognitive control refers to the ability to guide behavior and prioritize information processing in accordance with internal goals, regardless of the salience of goal-irrelevant stimuli in the environment or of goal-irrelevant behavioral choices.
- The environmental-dependency syndrome resulting from lateral PFC damage produces behavioral disinhibition that is a dramatic illustration of failures of cognitive control.
- A cardinal laboratory-based operationalization of impaired cognitive control is perseverative responding on the Wisconsin Card Sorting Test.
- ERPs from patients with lateral PFC lesions who are performing a working memory task reveal two distinctive patterns: an abnormally reduced N1 to the target stimulus, suggesting impaired attentional selection/encoding; and abnormally large medium-latency AEPs to delay-period distracting stimuli, suggesting impaired filtering of task-irrelevant information.
- A computational simulation of the A-not-B error, a perseverative response in infants attributed to an immature PFC, suggests that it may arise from ineffective top-down selection of the weaker, but behaviorally appropriate, response, rather than a failure to inhibit the stronger, but inappropriate response.
- The PFC has unique properties that may underlie its central role in cognitive control: the ability to transition between an "up" state that sustains an active pattern of activity and a "down" state during which it can update to a new pattern; heavy innervation by midbrain dopamine neurons that carry reward-related information; and extensive anatomical connectivity through which it can implement control.
- The dynamics of ascending dopamine signals, including the reward prediction error (RPE) signal, are of central importance for triggering state transitions in PFC and providing performance-related information to performance-monitoring circuits in the dorsomedial frontal cortex (dmFC).
- Rather than contributing to behavior directly, dmFC/dorsal anterior cingulate cortex (dACC) seems to track the current level of performance and acts as a governor on some aspects of PFC activity, including whether to stay in a more effortful proactive mode of control, or to revert to a reactive mode.
- The dmFC and anterior insular cortex (AI) are critical nodes in the Cingulo-Opercular Control network (CON), such that damage to only one compromises the functioning of the other. In a task that requires learning to be patient in one condition and to be impatient in another, damage to either dmFC or AI results in an inability to modify behavior in either direction, a deficit linked to an impairment in learning from negative feedback.
- A fundamental aspect of control is the ability to stop oneself from taking an action if circumstances have changed. The hyperdirect pathway in the basal ganglia plays a critical role in successful stopping.

Companion Website: www.wiley.com/go/postle/cognitiveneuroscience3e

CONTENTS

Cognitive control governs much of our day-to-day, much of the time, often in seemingly trivial ways that nonetheless add up to us conducting our daily lives much more efficiently and efficaciously. Often, we are not aware of its operation until it fails. A classic example for this writer is stepping onto the elevator in the Psychology building, lifting his eyes off the document he's reading long enough to press "5," and then going back to the document. The elevator rises, stops, the doors open, and he steps out. Only to find himself on the fourth floor. Here is how two leading researchers (one of them Earl Miller, from the previous chapter) introduced their very influential paper on the topic:

> One of the fundamental mysteries of neuroscience is how coordinated, purposeful behavior arises from the distributed activity of billions of neurons in the brain. Simple behaviors can rely on relatively straightforward interactions between the brain's input and output systems. Animals with fewer than a hundred thousand neurons (in the human brain there are 100 billion or more neurons) can approach food and avoid predators. For animals with larger brains, behavior is more flexible. But flexibility carries a cost: although our elaborate sensory and motor systems provide detailed information about the external world and make available a large repertoire of actions, this introduces greater potential for interference and confusion. The richer information we have about the world and the greater number of options for behavior require appropriate attentional, decision-making, and coordinative functions, lest uncertainty prevail. To deal with this multitude of possibilities and to curtail confusion, we have evolved mechanisms that coordinate lower-level sensory and motor processes along a common theme, an internal goal. (Miller and Cohen, 2001, pp. 167–168)

In the elevator anecdote, the internal goal of our protagonist was to get to his office (located on the fifth floor), and the detailed sensory information that was driving his behavior was being displayed on the electronic tablet in his hand. (The ubiquity of "smartphones" and other mobile gadgets in contemporary society has made the value of cognitive control in everyday life all the more apparent.) As this anecdote suggests, cognitive control often implicates the idea of inhibition – the absent-minded professor's attention focused elsewhere, he failed to inhibit the prepotent reflex of walking through the just-opened doors. Whether or not control truly engages inhibition, at a mechanistic level, will be a theme that will recur here and in subsequent chapters.

As with many other domains of human behavior, behavioral neurology has provided a rich set of cases, and theories, that provide a backdrop for contemporary thinking about cognitive control.

The Lateral Frontal-Lobe Syndrome

In reproducing the quote from Miller and Cohen (2001), above, I left out the following because I want to be careful not to advocate a "one-brain-area = one-kind-of-behavior" style of thinking. To exclude it altogether, however, would be to mischaracterize the received wisdom on this subject: "This ability for cognitive control no doubt involves neural circuitry that extends over much of the brain, but it is commonly held that the prefrontal cortex (PFC) is particularly important" (p. 168). This emphasis on the PFC derives, in part, from a large body of undeniably compelling evidence from behavioral neurology. The neurologist François Lhermitte (1921–1998) captured this succinctly in companion papers entitled *Human Autonomy and the Frontal Lobes*. "The patients' behavior was striking," he writes, "as though implicit in the environment was an order to respond to the situation in which they found themselves" (Lhermitte, Pillon, and Serdaru, 1986, p. 335). *"Human autonomy"?!? I thought this book was about neuroscience. This isn't a trick to lure us into reading a treatise on existentialism, is it?* Well, no. On the other hand, from here on out, there's not a topic that we'll consider that doesn't have clear and profound implications for what it is that makes us uniquely human.

Environmental-Dependency Syndrome

Building on the well-characterized phenomenon of **utilization behavior** – an exaggerated tendency for one's behavior to be determined by the external environment – François Lhermitte, Bernard Pillon, and Michel Serdaru (1986) carried out a study in which the experimenter simply sat opposite each subject and, with a "completely neutral and indifferent" demeanor, performed a series of gestures: common body gestures (e.g., crossing legs and tapping fingers); symbolic gestures (e.g., thumbing one's nose and military salute); manipulating objects (folding a piece of paper and putting it into an envelope, combing hair); and so on. No advance explanation or instructions were provided. The description of the response of neurologically intact individuals is not only funny, but also provides context that helps one appreciate just how striking, and profound, are the impairments of the patients. And why Lhermitte invokes autonomy in relation to the frontal-lobe syndrome:

> Normal subjects never imitated the examiner. They were unconcerned but surprised, without otherwise making the slightest remark. . . . When asked why the examiner had performed these gestures, they hesitated and replied: "To test me"; "I don't know – perhaps to see my reactions"; and so on. The answers varied little with personality or age. When the examiner asked them if it had crossed their mind to imitate him, their answer was: "No, not at all." Boys and girls between the ages of 12 and 16 reacted by laughing and calling the examiner a clown. Children between the ages of 5 and 6 . . . later [said] "The doctor was very nice, but it's funny how bad-mannered he is; he thumbed his nose at all of us." Children 2 to 4 years old sometimes took an object – a ball, for instance – and threw like the examiner [had thrown], but they were merely playing with him. (Lhermitte, Pillon, and Serdaru, 1986, p. 329)

In contrast, almost all patients with frontal-lobe damage began imitating the experimenter with their first gesture. They did this seemingly without surprise and with careful attention to detail. For example, when pretending to light a candle, no imitating patient forgot to "blow out the match." Later, when interviewed about the experiment, all patients could remember all of the gestures. Strikingly, "After being told not to imitate, most patients [nonetheless continued to] display the same IB" (p. 329). (With this study, Lhermitte, Pillon, and Serdaru were describing a "new" variant of utilization behavior: "imitation behavior" [IB].) IB was found in 28 of 29 patients with frontal lobe lesions in the study's sample. The 29th, recently diagnosed with a right frontal glioma (a tumor originating in glial cells), began to spontaneously exhibit IB 3 weeks later. Overall intellectual functioning of these patients was numerically, but not statistically, lower than that of control subjects. (In the 1940s, Hebb had reported that patients with PFC lesions can have normal IQ scores.) The frontal patients had varied damage, with inferior frontal gyrus involved in the majority of the patients. In contrast, IB was only seen in 1 of 21 non-frontal lesion control patients (and the factors behind this one patient's performance were characterized as "doubtful").

Lhermitte suggested the term "environmental-dependency syndrome" for even more exotic behavior by patients that he observed outside of the laboratory. One patient, who had undergone a large left-hemisphere frontal lobectomy to remove a glioma, was invited to the doctor's apartment. Upon walking past the bedroom and seeing the bed, the patient undressed, climbed into bed, and prepared to sleep! Subsequently, other neurologists have adopted "environmental-dependency syndrome" as a blanket term encompassing all these types of behavior. In summarizing them, two other behavioral neurologists, Robert Knight and Mark D'Esposito (2003), have noted that:

> It has been postulated that the frontal lobes may promote distance from the environment and the parietal lobes foster approach toward one's environment. Therefore, the loss of frontal inhibition may result in overactivity of the parietal lobes. Without the PFC, our autonomy in our environment would not be possible. A given stimulus would automatically call up a predetermined response regardless of context. (p. 262)

Next, let's consider how inhibition has also been implicated in a classic laboratory finding in lateral frontal-lobe patients – perseveration on the Wisconsin Card Sorting Test (WCST).

Perseveration

In the late 1950s, decades of research on the effects of various brain lesions on cognitive flexibility had yielded contradictory and equivocal results, with some studies implicating the frontal lobes, some posterior regions, and some one hemisphere over another. In 1963, this debate was resolved, and a new avenue for research opened up by a single study. Brenda Milner (of course) had the sagacity to realize that tasks that had been used in previous studies had the dual drawbacks of lacking sensitivity and lacking clearly defined psychological underpinnings. She had the insight to select a task that was likely to yield clearer results. And she had the benefit of working at the Montreal Neurological Institute (MNI), where she could test neurosurgical patients pre- and post-operatively – a repeated-measures design, of course, affording much greater statistical power.

The WCST was designed by (University of Wisconsin-based) psychologist David Grant (1916–1977) and his graduate student Esta Berg (Grant and Berg, 1948), who modeled it in part on a task by the German psychologist Egon Weigl and in part on problem-solving tasks developed for monkeys, and shown to be sensitive to frontal-lobe damage, by Grant's colleague Harry Harlow (1905–1981; developer of the Wisconsin General Testing Apparatus [WGTA; *Figure 6.2.A*]). As illustrated in *Figure 15.1*, the WCST consists of a stack of cards for which subjects must first learn, and then apply, a sorting rule. Milner tested 53 patients pre- and post-op: 18 with excisions invading dorsolateral (dl)PFC, 7 with excisions of orbitofrontal and temporal cortex, and the remainder with excisions of temporal, parietal, or temporal-parietal-occipital cortex. The average number of categories achieved decreased for the dlPFC group from pre-op (3.3) to post-op (1.4), whereas this measure was effectively unchanged for all other groups (overall mean, 4.6–4.7; for the orbitofrontal + temporal group, a slight decrease from 5.3 to 4.9). The culprit was **perseveration** (see caption to *Figure 15.1*; the term derives from Old French, and before that Latin, for *persistence* and *stubbornness*). For dlPFC patients, perseverative errors increased, from 39.5 pre-op to 51.5 post-op, whereas the average for other groups declined from 20.0 to 12.2; for the orbitofrontal + temporal group, they increased slightly from 9.3 to 12.0. Note that, when considering pre-op performance, we need

FIGURE 15.1 The WSCT, as the subject sees it. They are given the stack of 128 response cards and instructed to sort them by placing each one, at a time, under the appropriate "stimulus card" ("wherever you think it should go"), but with no further instruction. Each response card varies along three dimensions: color, shape, and number; each level of each dimension being represented across the four stimulus cards. In the example shown here, the two red crosses on the response card at the top of the stack match the *color* of the stimulus card on the left, the *number* of the next stimulus card to the right, and the *shape* of the next stimulus card to the right. The first sorting dimension is color, which the subject must learn by trial and error. The only feedback they receive throughout the task is whether each sort is "right" or "wrong." After 10 correct consecutive trials (i.e., after they have learned to sort by color), the sorting dimension is switched (without warning) to shape. After 10 correct consecutive sorts to shape, it is switched to number. The procedure continues through another full cycle of the three sorting dimensions, or until all 128 cards have been sorted. There are three dependent measures: number of categories achieved (i.e., number of dimension-changes + 1), number of perseverative errors, and number of nonperseverative errors. The former is a choice that would have been correct prior to the most recent switch.

Source: Photograph by Michael Starrett, in Bradley R Postle's laboratory.

to keep in mind that the surgeries for these patients targeted tissue that was epileptogenic, and so likely already contributing in only an impaired fashion, if at all, to task performance.

A perseverative error would seem to be one of a failure of inhibition, in that the patient "can't stop themself" from repeating a choice already known to be incorrect. Indeed, as Milner (1963) notes, "perhaps the most interesting finding after frontal-lobe injury has been the dissociation between the subject's actual responses to the stimulus-objects and his ability to verbalize what those responses should be." Many patients were "able themselves to say 'right' or 'wrong' as they placed the cards, and yet did not modify their responses accordingly" (p. 99). That is, it was literally the case for some patients that their words indicated (well, suggested) that they knew what they were supposed to do, but that they couldn't prevent themselves from nonetheless making what they knew would be an incorrect response.

When considering the effects of damage to subregions of the PFC, Milner (1963) wrote that:

> removal of the inferior and orbital portions of one frontal lobe causes no significant change, even if combined with a temporal lobectomy. One patient in seven showed a deficit in performance after such a removal, and this proportion does not differ from that showing loss after posterior excisions. In contrast to these negative results, all removals which encroached upon the superior frontal region were associated with poor performance on the sorting test. The critical lesion cannot be more precisely defined, although area 9 of Brodmann was implicated in most cases. (p. 97)

It will be worth remembering, when we get to emotions and social behavior in later chapters, that the bias in the sample of Lhermitte, Pillon, and Serdaru (1986), who showed impairments on tasks that entailed direct social interaction, was toward damage in inferior regions of PFC, whereas in the Milner (1963) study with the WCST, the procedure minimized social factors and emphasized "cold reasoning." And so, the story thus far is that a defining function of the PFC, and of cognitive control, is the overriding of prepotent responses (often summarized as "inhibition"), often triggered by environmental stimuli. Can we find physiological evidence for this?

Electrophysiology of the Frontal-Lobe Syndrome

Robert Knight is a behavioral neurologist who got his scientific training with EEG electrophysiologists Steven Hillyard and Robert Galambos, senior authors on the auditory-evoked potential (AEP) studies that we considered in *Chapter 3*. Among Knight's noteworthy contributions to cognitive neuroscience have been studies of ERPs in patients with PFC damage. Particularly relevant for us here is work that Knight carried out in the 1990s with then-graduate student Linda Chao. Chao and Knight (1995) reported that patients with lateral PFC lesions were disproportionately impaired on (5-second) delayed yes/no recognition of environmental sounds when distracting tone pips were played during the delay period. Going back to Malmo (1942), this is an oft-replicated consequence of lateral PFC damage. For a follow-up study, Chao and Knight (1998) repeated the experimental procedure, but while recording the EEG. To fully appreciate their study, it's worth taking a moment to flip back to *Figure 3.8* and refresh your memory about the organization of the AEP into early-, middle-, and long-latency components. What we're about to consider here is a masterful application of the logic, mentioned in that chapter, that "sensory evoked responses . . . are stereotyped, stable responses that are effectively identical in all neurologically healthy individuals[, making] them very effective 'tools' for studying the neural bases of many different behavioral and physiological states."

For the follow-up ERP study, Chao and Knight (1998) obtained ERPs during task performance from seven patients with unilateral damage to lateral PFC and from matched control subjects. The previous behavioral finding of exaggerated sensitivity to distraction in the PFC group was replicated. To understand why, they examined the middle-latency components of the AEP (MAEP) to the distracting tone pips, because the MAEP is known to reflect the initial cortical processing of the auditory signal. From *Figure 15.2,* one can see that several peaks in the MAEP are larger for patients than for control subjects. The proximal conclusion that can be drawn from this finding is that the patients' memory for the sample stimulus may

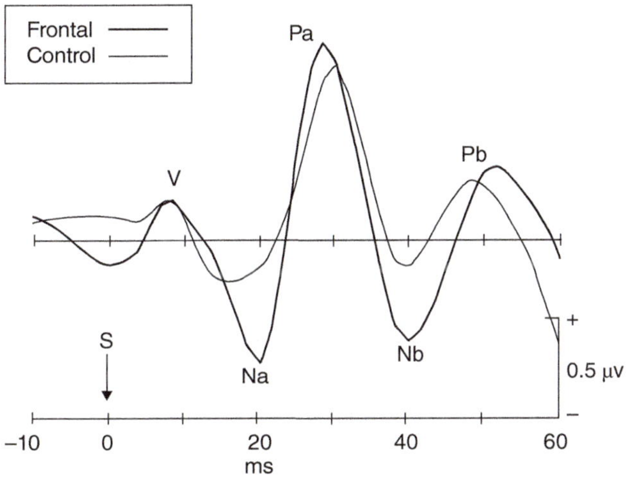

FIGURE 15.2 Auditory-evoked responses in PFC-lesioned patients performing auditory delayed recognition. The middle-latency components – MAEP – to tone pips played during the 5-second delay period of an auditory delayed-recognition task, for patients with lateral PFC lesions and control subjects.

Source: Chao et al., 1998 / The MIT Press.

have been disrupted by the abnormally high level of perceptual processing of the distracting tone pips. The inference about the mechanism that follows from this is that one function of the PFC is to control the processing of incoming sensory stimuli, such that this processing doesn't interfere with behaviorally relevant internal representations. Further evidence for this interpretation comes from the fact that, in the patients, the magnitude of the Pa component of the MAEP predicted the magnitude of their behavioral deficit. The term often used for this hypothesized mechanism is "filtering," as though the PFC imposes a filter that selectively passes only some incoming sensory information. Indeed, there's good evidence from the cat and the monkey that PFC literally controls just such a filter via its projections to the thalamic reticular nucleus (TRN; see *Chapter 3*, section *Corticothalamic loops, center-surround inhibition, and signal-to-noise ratio*, and *Figure 3.3*). In the cat, these projections have been shown to regulate the magnitude of the AEP.

A second finding from this study was seen in a long-latency component of the AEP (LAEP) to sample stimuli: The N1 was smaller across the scalp in the PFC-lesioned patients. The auditory N1 is believed to arise from the auditory association cortex, and previous research from Knight and colleagues has shown it to be disrupted in PFC patients in conjunction with impaired performance on tests of selective attention. Thus, Chao and Knight (1998) suggested that the reduced N1 in this study may have reflected an impairment in the ability of their patients "to focus attention on task-relevant stimuli" (p. 173).

Integration?

The two main findings from the study described by Chao and Knight (1998) highlight two distinct processes whose disruption may contribute to the lateral frontal-lobe syndrome: the filtering of irrelevant information and the focusing of attention on behaviorally relevant information. Do either of these mechanisms help us understand the environmental-dependency syndrome, or the phenomenon of perseveration? It's not immediately apparent to this author that they do. Whereas the Chao and Knight (1998) ERP findings relate to perceptual processing, the earlier findings that we reviewed related to the control of behavior. The environmental-dependency syndrome is characterized by a remarkable influence of external stimuli and contexts on behavior, one that supersedes the autonomous control that is central to being human. Perseveration on the WCST occurred after a behavioral set was learned and repeated (reinforced), then needed to be changed when reward contingencies changed unexpectedly.

Is it possible to unify these disparate findings under a single framework, or is cognitive control just a term that actually corresponds to a collection of task-specific proficiencies that don't share any meaningful underlying relation, apart from a common address in the lateral PFC? This is precisely the kind of question that computational modeling is good at addressing, and so it is there that we now turn our attention.

Models of Cognitive Control

Developmental Cognitive Neuroscience

The phenomenon of environmental dependency isn't restricted to behavioral neurology. Neurologically healthy adults will generate prepotent or habitual responses in inappropriate circumstances when their working memory is loaded to capacity (such as in a dual-task paradigm), or when otherwise under stress (or when intently reading something while riding on the elevator. . .). Furthermore, perseveration is also a classic feature of cognitive development. The Swiss developmental psychologist Jean Piaget (1896–1980) codified this as the "A-not-B" error, seen in infants younger than 12 months of age.

The A-Not-B Error To demonstrate the A-not-B error, a toy is placed under one of two boxes (box A) that are within reach of an infant, and she displaces the box to retrieve the toy. This is repeated several times. On the critical trial, the infant watches while the toy is now hidden under box B, but they nonetheless reach for it under box A. Sometimes on the critical trial, in a behavior reminiscent of the dissociation between verbal report and card placement described by Milner (1963), the infant will look at box B (where the toy is hidden) but nonetheless reach for box A. Piaget ascribed this error to an immature sense of "object permanence," the understanding that objects continue to exist after they disappear from view. More recently, in 1989, the developmental cognitive neuroscientist Adele Diamond, together with Patricia Goldman-Rakic (from *Chapter 14*, section *Extracellular electrophysiology inspired by the multiple-component model*), documented the phenomenon in young rhesus macaques, replicated it qualitatively in adult monkeys with dorsolateral (dl)PFC lesions, and showed the absence of the effect in adult monkeys with PPC lesions. It is known that the primate PFC is among the last brain areas to mature, and that, in the human, it (along with other brain regions) undergoes rapid development during the first few years of life. (From an "anthropology of scientists" standpoint, these findings provide an interesting example of how one's scholarly perspective can influence how one interprets data. Some have seen the PFC lesion findings as evidence that the theoretical construct of object permanence may not exist, and that the A-not-B error in young children is attributable to immature circuitry that supports a cognitive function like working memory, inhibition, or attention. Others have simply concluded that knowledge of object permanence must be supported by the PFC.)

Is the A-Not-B Error a Failure of Working Memory? The association of the A-not-B error with the PFC led to proposals that success on the task depends on working memory, and that underdeveloped working memory abilities underlie the error in infants. (Note that the Diamond and Goldman-Rakic findings were published at the same time as the latter's neurophysiological recordings from PFC, as summarized in section *Extracellular electrophysiology inspired by the multiple-component model, Chapter 14.*) The working memory view was soon challenged, however, by studies with human infants using the procedure illustrated in *Figure 15.3.A*, in which all the information needed to solve the task was always visible to the infant (i.e., no overt demands on working memory were made), yet infants still produced the A-not-B error. What *Figure 15.3.B* illustrates is a schematic of a neural network simulation carried out in the laboratory of developmental cognitive neuroscientist Yuko Munakata. In offering an explanation for the A-not-B error, it addresses several other questions that have arisen in this chapter: it provides an explicit account for why perseveration happens, and what might be the PFC mechanism that controls it; it proposes a mechanism that would unify the

FIGURE 15.3 Modeling perseveration in the A-not-B error.

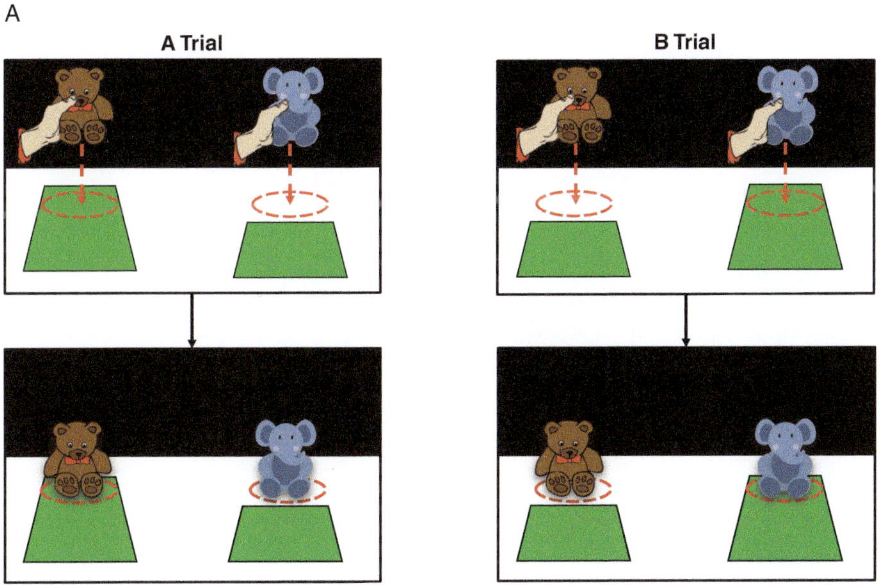

FIGURE 15.3.A An example of an experimental procedure that produces the A-not-B error in infants, even though there is no overt working memory component. Infants sit on a parent's lap and watch as two toys are placed side by side, out of reach, but one on a piece of cloth and one not on a piece of cloth. (The parent is listening to music on headphones so that they won't bias the child's performance.) The closer ends of the cloths are within reach, and the infant knows to pull on the cloth on which the toy sits in order to retrieve it. This is repeated several times. On the B trial, the cloths are switched, such that it is now the cloth on the right that should be pulled to retrieve the toy. Infants under the age of 12 months, however, commit the A-not-B error.

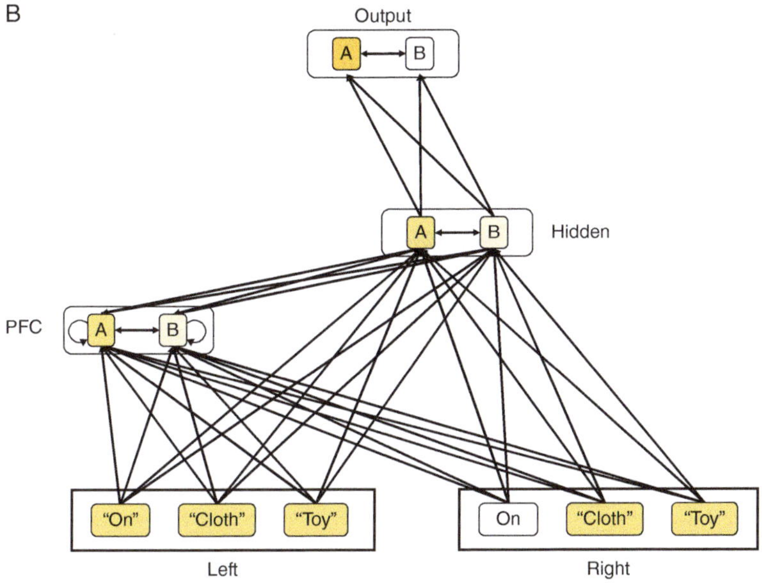

FIGURE 15.3.B Simulation of an A trial, in which stronger input on the left results in stronger activation of the *A* unit in the hidden layer, and, consequently, stronger activation of the *A* unit in the output layer. (Although the authors do not state this explicitly, the input layer can be construed as extrastriate visual areas, the hidden layer as the parietal reach area [*Chapter 7* and *Chapter 8*], and the output layer as motor cortex. The layer labeled as the PFC is what's known as a "context layer." A context layer is "off to the side," not in the direct pathway of input ➔ hidden ➔ output, but its inputs to the hidden layer can bias the activity of the latter.)

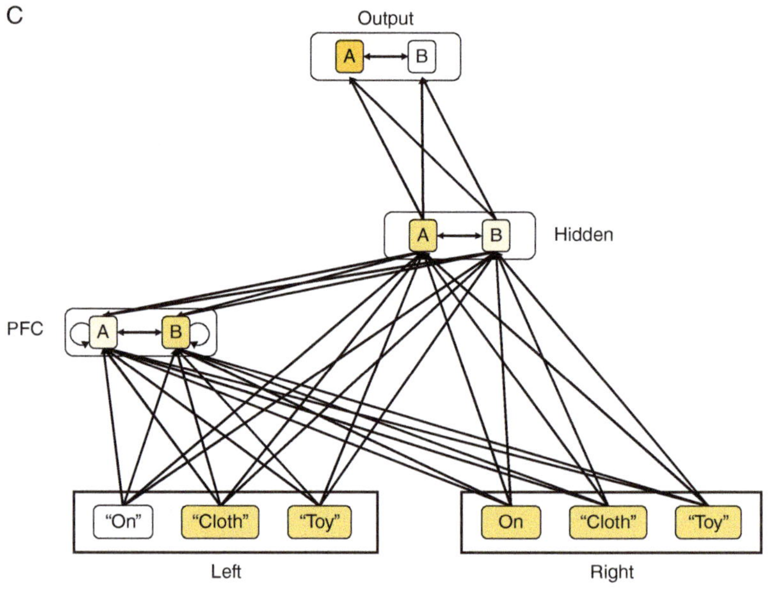

FIGURE 15.3.C Simulation of a first B trial after a series of A trials, with an immature PFC. Although the input values are higher on the right, the stronger connections between left-side inputs and the hidden layer result in stronger activation of the *A* unit in the hidden layer, and, consequently, stronger activation of the *A* unit in the output layer. The immature PFC cannot effectively bias the competition in the hidden layer.

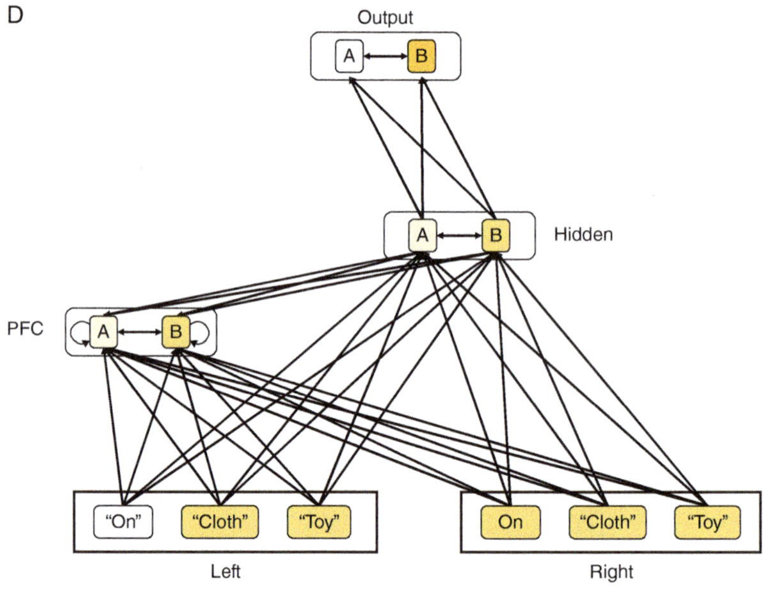

FIGURE 15.3.D Simulation of a first B trial after a series of A trials, with a matured PFC. Now, despite the stronger input-to-hidden drive from the left-side inputs, the PFC with stronger recurrent connections is able to bias the competition in the hidden layer to produce stronger activation of the *B* unit in the hidden layer, and, consequently, stronger activation of the *B* unit in the output layer.

ERP findings from Chao and Knight (1998) with the observations of perseveration and of environmental-dependency syndrome; and it offers one answer to the question of whether the lateral frontal-lobe syndrome is fundamentally one of a loss of inhibitory control.

The simulation of Stedron, Sahni, and Munakata (2005) used a neural network simulation environment created by Randall O'Reilly (of McClelland, McNaughton, and O'Reilly renown) and Munakata (2000) that is grounded in the principles of the PDP framework, and that explicitly simulates the properties of biological networks by modeling membrane potential within each unit and determining the propagation of activity from one layer to another via an equation that converts the membrane potential into an activation value (a proxy for the rate and number of action potentials). Another important feature of the model is the Hebbian strengthening of connections, which occurs when anatomically connected units are simultaneously active.

On A trials in the A-not-B task, the attributes of *Toy*, *Cloth*, and *On* are activated for the left side (i.e., A side) of the display, and the attributes of *Toy* and *Cloth* are activated for the right side (i.e., B side). As a result, units representing choice A in the hidden layer and in the PFC layer receive more activation than do those representing choice B, because $3 > 2$. Thus, choice A receives more activation in the output layer, and the correct choice is made. As this process is repeated across several trials, the connections between the left-sided input layer and the representation of A in the hidden layer, and between the representation of A in the hidden layer and the representation of A in the output layer, get strengthened by the Hebbian learning rule. This models, in a very concrete way, prepotency. A consequence of this prepotency is that, on the critical B trial, even though $2 < 3$, the strength of the drive received by the *A* unit in the output layer is greater than that received by the *B* unit in the output layer. This is because multiplying the input value of 2 by larger numbers (due to stronger connections) can yield a larger result than does multiplying a starting value of 3 by smaller numbers. End result? The model will choose output A; that is, it will perseverate. How can this problem be overcome? By top-down input from the PFC.

Unlike with the classic A-not-B task, where the toy is hidden from view under a box, success on this always-visible variant comes earlier in development: 9-month-olds perseverate with this procedure, but 11-month-olds do not. Stedron and colleagues simulated the maturation of PFC from 9 to 11 months by progressively strengthening recurrent weights between units within the PFC layer, thereby allowing it to progressively enhance its ability to sustain a representation of the input side that had a higher value, regardless of the strength of learned connections from input to hidden to output layers. Their finding was that at a certain level of PFC "maturity," the ability of this layer to sustain a representation of the correct response provided a sufficiently strong top-down boost of the hidden layer that output B was selected, despite the structural advantage of the representation of A. It is noteworthy that this simulation refutes the logic that was employed by the group that thought that, by creating a version of the task that lacked an overt memory component, it could be shown that working memory does not contribute. (And this is eight years before Luck and Vogel [2013] wrote that "visual working memory may not be a memory system per se, but may instead be a general-purpose visual representation system . . ." and here I'll add *that can implement cognitive control.*)

Generalizing Beyond Development

Implied in the Stedron, Sahni, and Munakata (2005) results (*Figure 15.3*) is something that was also implied in the chapter-opening elevator anecdote, and stated explicitly by Miller and Cohen (2001): lurking within all of us is a machinery whose default mode of operation is to respond to the most salient stimulus in the environment, or act in the most habitual, stereotyped way. Explicit in their model is the idea that cognitive control may not be implemented by inhibiting inappropriate responses but, rather, by selecting the most appropriate response and activating it to the point that it will win out over other alternatives. This is equivalent to the idea of biased competition (*Chapter 7*). Can the ERP findings of Chao and Knight (1998; *Figure 15.2*) be understood in this framework? Recall that, at a descriptive level, they suggested impairments of "filtering" and of "focusing." The former, that PFC-lesioned patients showed abnormalities in the MAEP, can be explained as a dysfunction at the *site* of cognitive (or attentional) control – a failure of sensory filtering at the level of the thalamus due to a weakened top-down signal to the TRN. The latter, manifesting as a diminished N1, could be the result of a weakened top-down selection signal. If one were striving for a unifying account of PFC function, one might posit that the same signals that were implicated in the study of Chao and Knight (1998) may also be implicated in overcoming the A-not-B error. That is, when directed to the appropriate networks in parietal and/or motor cortex, these signals could select the appropriate response over the prepotent-but-inappropriate one.

But can the "unitary mechanism" simulated in the Stedron et al. (2005) model really account for the lateral frontal-lobe syndrome in adults? There are at least a couple of arguments that one might raise. First, the A-not-B error is a behavior that infants grow out of before they can even walk. Second, that simulation is limited to a drastically impoverished and constrained environment (only 3×2 inputs; only two choices of response). How applicable can it really be to understanding the richness and complexity of adult cognition and neurological syndromes? And then there's that pesky concern that's been lurking at least since we considered the Hamker (2005) model back in *Chapter 9* – *Who is controlling the controller?* For all of the computational models that we've considered, "who" is keeping track of the rules governing the task that's being performed? For a task like the WCST, how does simply receiving the feedback "wrong," as every subject does each time the sorting dimension is surreptitiously changed, prompt us to try a different strategy? The facetious answer is that there's that "little man" inside our head, the homunculus, who knows what different parts of the brain are supposed to do in different situations and tells them how, and when, to do it. Now, of course, it's been hundreds of years since any serious scientist or philosopher may have proposed such a thing. On the other hand, the majority of contemporary models that seek to understand one aspect of cognition depend, in effect, on what Rougier et al. (2005) refer to as "some unexplained source of intelligence" (p. 7338) to do the things that the model can't. The model that we'll consider next develops the capacity for error correction and cognitive control without resorting to a homunculus, and without leaving this question unaddressed.

What Makes the PFC Special? I said earlier that I didn't want to endorse a "PFC = cognitive control" perspective, and yet we're more than halfway through this chapter, and what is the only brain area that we have discussed? Consideration of this neural network simulation by Nicolas Rougier et al. (2005) will accomplish two goals in this regard. First, it will consider some aspects of the PFC that justify this bias, by calling explicit attention to unique properties of this region and the neurons that make it up, relative to other parts of the brain. Second, it explicitly considers how the PFC must interact with other brain systems in order to accomplish cognitive control. (I.e., it can't literally do it all by itself.)

Properties of the PFC The Rougier et al. (2005) model of PFC includes three properties that distinguish it from other areas of cortex:

- Sustained activity that is robust against potentially interfering signals: PFC pyramidal neurons have the property of bistability – the ability to operate in an "up" state or a "down" state. This is partly due to the density and distribution of D1-type dopamine receptors along their dendrites, and so the state that they occupy at any point in time is influenced by dopamine levels. When in the up state, a high density of NMDA-type glutamate receptors and recurrent connections with other pyramidal cells can support sustained, elevated levels of activity, such as those illustrated in many of the figures in the opening section of *Chapter 14*.
- Capacity for rapid updating of activity patterns via bistability, that is, switching from an active maintenance mode, when one pattern of activity is sustained so as to prioritize one type of behavior, into an "updating mode," when the previous pattern is destabilized and a new pattern of activity can be established. This is effected by dopamine signals and by input from the basal ganglia, the same elements that are central to reinforcement learning (section *Habits and reinforcement learning, Chapter 8*), and turns out to be key for circumventing the homunculus problem, in that it helps "tell the PFC what to do." (And note that this scheme also offers explicit neuropharmacological and circuit-level means for effecting the otherwise-seemingly-too-abstract phenomenon of changing control settings to influence the order parameter of the system, from *Chapter 5*, section *Dynamical systems theory*).
- Capacity for PFC modulation of other cortical areas (as we have already seen in this chapter with Chao and Knight [1998], and in *Chapter 9* with FEF implementation of the endogenous control of attention).

Before returning to neural network models of cognitive control, let's get a foreshadowing of what's to come in *Chapter 16* with a snippet of an admonition from Wolfram Schultz about how to think about reward and (though he doesn't say it explicitly here) the RPE signal:

> Primary sensory systems have dedicated physical and chemical receptors that translate environmental energy and information into neural language. Thus, [their] functions . . . are governed by the laws of mechanics, optics, acoustics, and receptor binding. By contrast, there are no dedicated receptors for reward . . . [and so] the investigation of reward functions requires behavioral theories that can conceptualize the different effects of rewards on behaviors . . . Animal learning theory and microeconomics are two prominent examples of such behavioral theories. (Schultz, 2006, p. 91)

Reward, uncertainty, contingency, probability, and expected value, these don't physically exist in the world but must be constructed and represented neurally, in what Weigl (1941) called *Abstraktionsprozesse*.

Influence of the DA Reward Prediction Error on the Functions of PFC

Turning now to *Figure 15.4*, we can see that the Rougier et al. (2005) model is, for the most part, "just" a more-finely-carved-up variant of the model from Stedron, Sahni, and Munakata (2005; *Figure 15.3* in this chapter.) The finer grain of details in the input layer, for example, will enable the simulation of tasks like the WCST, in which there are multiple stimulus dimensions, and multiple levels within each dimension. For our purposes, the key qualitative difference is the little red box in the upper right, labeled "AG," for adaptive gating. This carries dopaminergic RPE signals.

Not unlike PDP models that we've considered previously, the Rougier et al. (2005) model started from scratch, knowing nothing about its world. It was trained by learning to discriminate and make decisions about stimuli via the four training tasks (see the legend to *Figure 15.4.B*). A critical fact about this process, however, is that instead of the teaching/learning process being implemented "deus ex machina," by a scientist delivering a backpropagated error signal each time they observed that the model got an answer wrong (i.e., supervised learning), it was implemented by a DA-mediated RPE in a manner that emulated what the authors knew about how this system works (i.e., unsupervised learning). Think back to the example of Pavlovian conditioning that we considered in *Chapter 5*, section *A cartoon example of Pavlovian conditioning,* and *Chapter 8*, section *Habits and reinforcement learning*. What Schultz and colleagues did in some of their studies was literally to monitor the responses of midbrain DA neurons throughout the entire process of learning a conditioned stimulus (CS)–unconditioned stimulus (US) pairing. As a result, we know, for example, that in pairings where the CS precedes the US in time (as is illustrated in *Figure 5.5*), there is initially a phasic increase in DA associated with reward delivery. (This has been interpreted by some models as signaling that "the current state is better than expected" [Montague, Dayan, and Sejnowski, 1996, p. 1944].) Over time, as the pairing is learned, the US ceases to elicit this burst of DA. (By definition, once the pairing has been learned, the arrival of the US is now expected. Thus, its delivery can no longer be characterized as being "better than expected.")

The architecture of the Rougier et al. (2005) network incorporated the fact that PFC is much more densely innervated by DA fibers than are posterior cortical regions, and as a consequence, the hidden layer corresponding to temporal and parietal cortex developed differently than did the PFC (also a context layer, as it was in the model of Stedron, Sahni, and Munakata (2005)). The hidden layer is developed to represent stimulus features, and thus the ability to discriminate between features. The PFC, in contrast, developed representations of the rules of the tasks that the network was trained on: how to select the correct name when presented with two objects that both have names; or how to decide if a medium-small-sized, yellow, vertically striped square located in the lower left of the screen is the same as or different from a small, green, vertically striped square located in the upper right if the critical dimension along which to compare the two is size. This PFC-based representation of abstract rules (there it is again, the *Abstraktionsprozesse*!) facilitated task performance by providing top-down excitation to the representations of the relevant stimulus dimension in the hidden layer of the network. We have already seen that this is one of the functions of the PFC. The new insight for us is the mechanism by which it influenced the network's performance on the WCST.

FIGURE 15.4 PFC and flexible cognitive control: rule-guided behavior without a homunculus.
Source: Rougier et al., 2005 / The National Academy of Sciences.

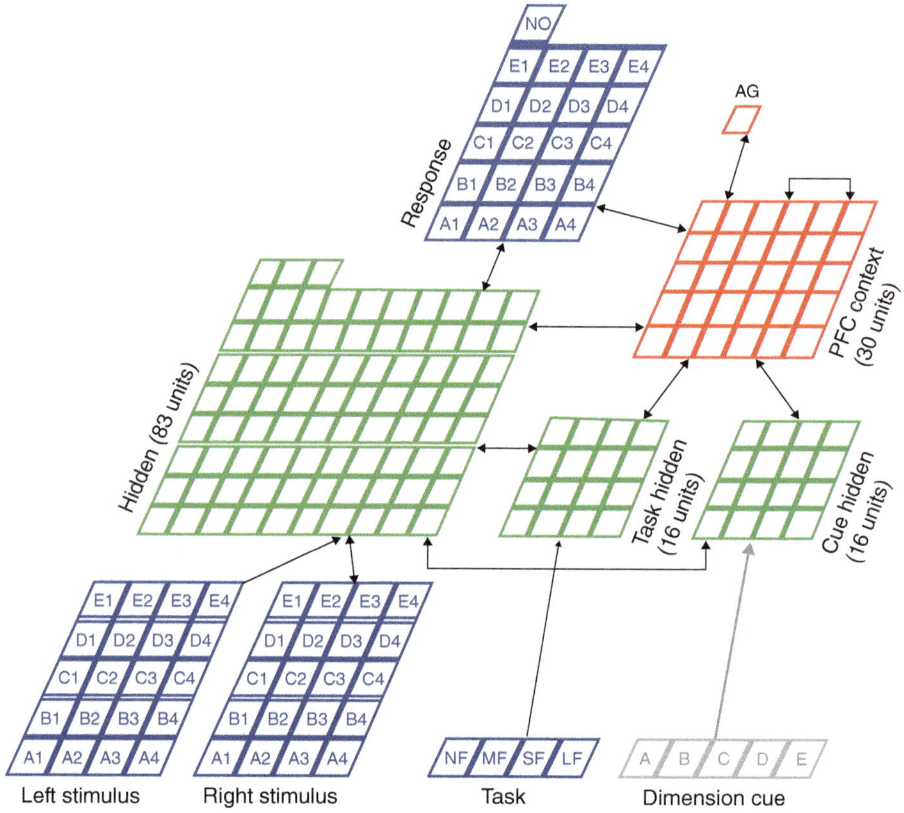

FIGURE 15.4.A The architecture of the model. "AG" is the "adaptive gating" unit, which corresponds to the ascending dopaminergic RPE signal.

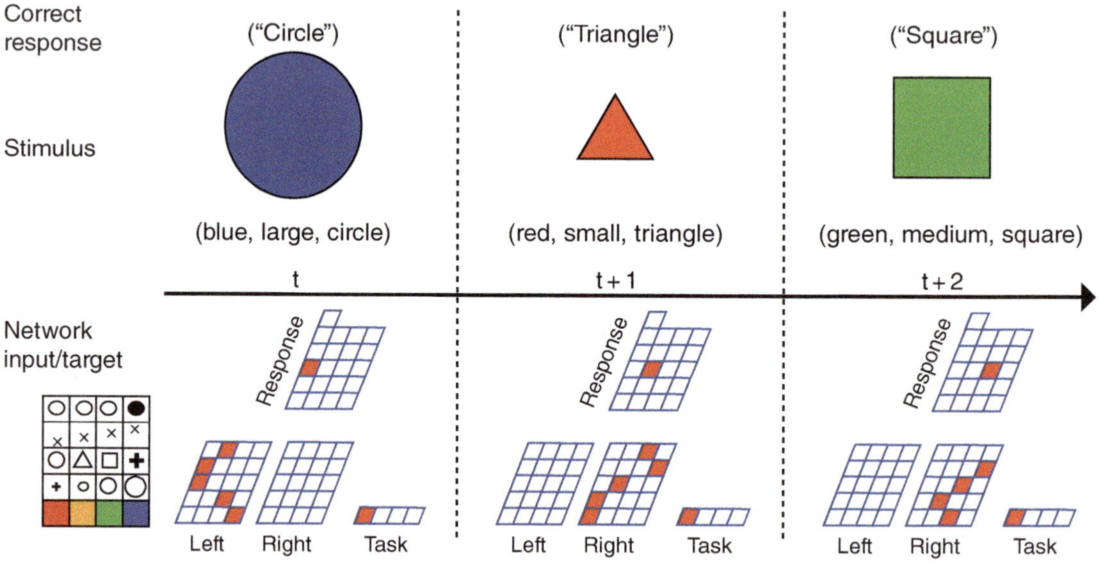

FIGURE 15.4.B Illustration of how high-dimensional inputs were fed into the model. The key in the lower left illustrates how one stimulus dimension is represented in each of the five rows of the input array – color, size, shape, location, and texture – and the columns correspond to different levels of each dimension. From left to right is an illustration of how the presentation of three consecutive stimuli (top row) would be represented and processed by the network. The "task" layer tells the model which of four tasks to perform: naming the feature in a particular stimulus dimension; determining whether two features match according to a particular stimulus dimension; indicating which item is larger; and indicating which item is smaller.

Combining an RPE Signal with a Flexible PFC to Overcome Perseveration At the end of the training process, when the model was mature, Rougier et al. (2005) introduced the WCST. The task was simulated by the feature-naming task, but minus any input to the "task" layer or to the "dimension cue" layer that would indicate which dimension was to be named. Thus, it had to rely on trial-and-error learning when presented with a medium-small, yellow, vertically striped square located in the lower left of the screen to decide whether to give the response "medium-small," "yellow," "vertical stripes," "square," or "lower left." Feedback was conveyed by the DA RPE, operationalized by the AG unit, following the dynamics described above. When, in the course of trial-and-error guessing, the network stumbled upon the correct dimension by naming the color of a stimulus, the PFC received a phasic burst of DA. And here's where the dopaminergic control of PFC bistability comes in. The response of the model's PFC to this burst of DA was to switch into its up state, in effect "locking in" its active representation of the dimension *color*. (There is considerable biophysical, neuropharmacological, and neurophysiological evidence that a phasic increase of DA can trigger such a state change in PFC pyramidal neurons.) The sustained representation of the category of *color* in the PFC, in turn, biased the competition within the hidden layer of the model in favor of representing the color of each ensuing stimulus relative to their other properties. This state of affairs persisted across the next several consecutive trials. On the switch trial, when (unbeknownst to the network) the sorting rule was changed to *shape*, the network blithely named the color of the stimulus, just as it had in the previous several trials. This time, however, it was given the feedback "incorrect." The failure to receive the expected positive feedback produced a negative RPE – a pause in the release of DA (see *Figure 5.5*), which had the effect (again, based on experimental evidence) of shunting the PFC out of its active-maintenance mode and into its updating mode. This destabilized the PFC activity pattern corresponding to the dimension of *color*, thereby permitting a different activity pattern, corresponding to a different stimulus dimension, to emerge.

One take-home from all this is that the role of the PFC in enabling flexible adaptation to unexpected changes in the environment need not be mysterious; it need not be the result of "some unexplained source of intelligence." Rather, it may result from a combination of the unique biophysical and connectivity properties of its neurons, its uniquely dense innervation by midbrain DA neurons, and the principles of reinforcement learning that are believed to be implemented by these DA neurons. It is also noteworthy that the rapid, flexible adaptation of PFC, such as emphasized in the Rougier et al. (2005) model, has more recently been characterized empirically by the application of dynamic network neuroscience analyses to fMRI data, as summarized in section *Network science and graph theory, Chapter 4.*

Controlling the Controller?

Having considered what can happen when control goes awry, and some computational principles underlying its implementation, we can now turn to the more nuanced question of, well, controlling the controller. Here's how Bill Gehring et al. (2012) have framed it: "Cognitive control functions include processes that detect when control is needed – as when performance breaks down – and processes that implement control through changes in attentional focus and other strategic adjustments" (p. 233). Up until this point, we've focused on the processes that implement control and the consequences of failures of implementation, and have seen that this work strongly implicates the dorsolateral PFC. But what about the "processes that detect when control is needed?" And, we can add to this, processes that determine *how much* control is needed. (E.g., if we infer from the results of Master et al. (2024; *Chapter 14*, section *"Trying harder."*) that at least some of the load-sensitive activity in the DAN reported by Emrich, Riggall et al. (2013; *Chapter 14*, section *Increased specificity raises questions about the interpretation of elevated delay-period activity*) reflected the allocation of effort, what signals "instructed" the DAN to exert different levels of effort at different memory loads? This would seem to be too much to ask of the RPE-switches-the-state-of-dlPFC-neurons arrangement summarized in section *Combining an RPE signal with a flexible PFC to overcome perseveration.*) A likely answer may lie in the functioning of the dorsomedial frontal cortex (dmFC), also frequently referred to as dorsal anterior cingulate cortex (dACC) in humans and in NHPs.

Error Monitoring

The ERN/Ne In the early 1990s, two research groups, one in Dortmund, Germany, and one in Ann Arbor, Michigan, reported an ERP component that corresponded to making an error on speeded reaction-time tasks. The Dortmund group, led by Michael Falkenstein, called it the Ne (error negativity), and the Ann Arbor group, led by William Gehring, called it the ERN (error-related negativity). The fact that it started out with, and, to some extent, still goes by, two names, is emblematic of the enduring lack of consensus that there has been for what process(es) it is likely to index. Here, for simplicity, we will refer to it as the ERN. As illustrated in *Figure 15.5*, the onset of the ERN occurs shortly before, or at, the moment of the erroneous button press, and peaks roughly 100 msec later. The reason for the intense interest in the ERN is captured in a continuation of the quote from Gehring et al. (2012): "Because an error is a salient marker that performance has broken down, the ERN is generally thought to reflect a process involved in evaluating the need for, or in implementing, control" (p. 233).

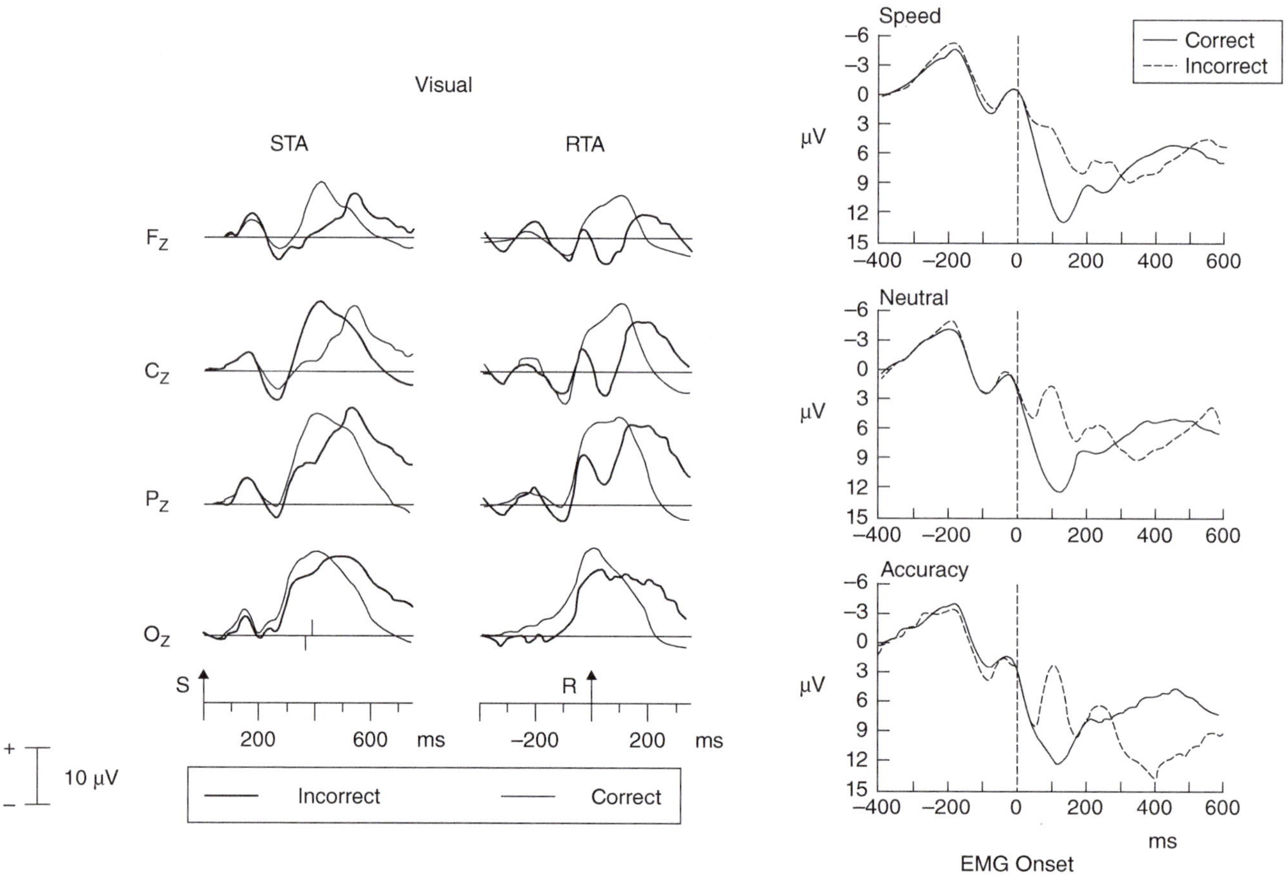

FIGURE 15.5 Two exemplars of the ERN. On the left, based on data from Falkenstein et al. (1991), are ERP waveforms aligned to stimulus onset (STA; marked by the arrow on the timeline) or to the response (RTA) in a visual discrimination task. Note that the negative-going component on incorrect trials is only detectable for the latter. (Note, too, that negative is plotted down.) On the right, based on data from Gehring et al. (1993), are ERPs from three conditions of a flanker task, time-locked to the onset of the electromyogram (EMG) of the muscles controlling the finger. (In these plots, negative is plotted up.)

Source: Gehring et al., 2012 / Oxford University Press.

Subsequent research indicates that an ERN can be generated in at least two circumstances. One, illustrated in *Figure 15.5*, is the "response ERN." The second is the "feedback ERN," which peaks 250–300 msec after the delivery of negative feedback. Some consider these to be two manifestations of activity in the same error-processing system. The response ERN, however, differs from the feedback ERN in that its timing raises the fascinating question about whether it is accompanied by awareness. We've all had the experience of making a mistake, doing something wrong, and not realizing that it was a mistake until minutes, hours, or days later. For example, "I thought that this new hairstyle was a good idea, until the barber finished and I saw the result in the mirror for the first time." Similarly, in the WCST, one can't know on a switch trial that one has made an error until being told that the just-completed action was "wrong." Here, in contrast, the question is whether, on a moment-to-moment basis, there are circumstances in which our nervous system knows that we are making a mistake even while the action is being carried out, tens if not hundreds of milliseconds before we will become aware of the error. One example is what just happened to me: in the previous sentence, I typed "errro," but didn't realize it until I saw the jumble of letters on my computer screen. This fascinating literature, full of nuance, is reviewed in the *Further reading* from Wessel (2012). (Just did it again! I typed "Wellel.")

Performance Monitoring and the dmFC

Considerable evidence, from source localization of EEG and MEG data, from recordings from nonhuman primates, and from fMRI scans of similar tasks, indicate that the ERN is likely generated in frontal midline areas generally referred to as the dorsomedial frontal cortex, a term that encompasses the posterior anterior cingulate cortex (ACC) and the pre-supplementary motor area. (Note that, in this context, the area in question is much more extensive than the "DMFC," whose oculomotor functions were illustrated in *Figure 9.3*.) Indeed, as illustrated in *Figure 15.6* and as we will review here, this region has been implicated in many types of performance-monitoring situations.

Traditionally, the dmFC has been thought of as part of the motor system, as exemplified by the organizational scheme of Picard and Strick (1996), illustrated in panel A of *Figure 15.6*. It distinguishes between a rostral cingulate zone (RCZ) activated in relation to complex motor tasks and a smaller caudal cingulate zone (CCZ) activated during simpler tasks. The near-complete overlap between these two regions and the sites of activity identified by the many studies contributing to panel B in *Figure 15.6* illustrates very concretely the idea that we have contemplated elsewhere, which is that many aspects of high-level cognition can be construed as elaborations on more basic principles of perception and action.

Panel B of *Figure 15.6* shows the results of a meta-analysis from Richard Ridderinkhof et al. (2004) of the foci of activity in neuroimaging studies that were designed to isolate one of four types of performance-monitoring phenomena.

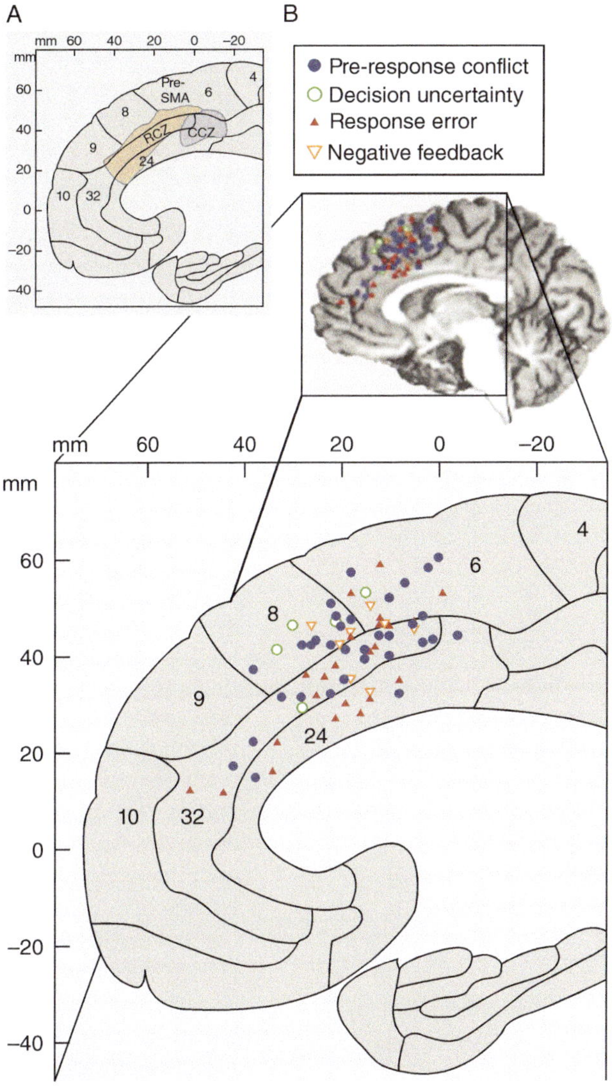

FIGURE 15.6 Performance monitoring and the dmFC. A illustrates a functional distinction proposed by Picard and Strick (1996), and B a meta-analysis from Ridderinkhof et al. (2004).

Source: Reproduced with permission from Ridderinkhof, K. et al. (2004) / American Association for the Advancement of Science - AAAS.

Pre-response Conflict Response conflict occurs when a task concurrently activates more than one response tendency, a classic example being the Stroop task, in which it's more difficult to name the color of ink in which a word is printed if the two aren't congruent. (i.e., there's more response conflict, indexed by longer reaction times, more errors, and greater activity in dmFC, when red ink is used to spell out the word "BLUE" than when it is used to spell out the word "RED" [a congruent stimulus] or the word "BOOK" [a neutral stimulus].) Response conflict processing can theoretically also occur after an incorrect response, as if a representation of the correct response, recruited too late or too weakly to influence the current trial, conflicts with the activated representation of the executed response. The canonical statement of the response conflict theory is presented in Botvinick et al. (2001).

Decision Uncertainty Also referred to as "underdetermined responding," this is operationalized by conditions requiring a choice from a set of responses, none of which is more strongly compelling, or prepotent, than the others.

Response Error This category includes the response ERN and the commission of errors on two-alternative forced-choice tasks. It is often associated with premature responses. One theory motivated by these effects draws explicitly on the dopaminergic RPE. It posits that the RCZ processes these signals in accordance with the principles of reinforcement learning to improve task performance. A place to learn more about this perspective is Clay Holroyd and Michael Coles (2002).

Negative Feedback The canonical event for this category from panel B of *Figure 15.6* is one that would produce a feedback ERN. Included in this category are trials in economic decision-making games when an unexpectedly low monetary reward is given, or when a more abstract form of negative feedback is given (like being told that a response on the WCST is "wrong"). An idea that unifies these types of trials is that they entail a comparison of expected vs. actual outcomes. Ridderinkhof et al. (2004) also note that "Similar parts of the pMFC are activated by primary reinforcers such as pain affect and pleasant tastes, suggesting that the pMFC plays a general role in coding the motivational value of external events."

Regulating Cognitive Control

Having summarized "four types of performance-monitoring phenomena" that have been described by cognitive neuroscientists, let's next make these ideas more concrete by considering two examples of how the control of behavior and cognition can go awry when the functioning of the dmFC/ACC is disrupted.

Sustained Effort The first study that we'll consider in this section is one employing the venerable antisaccade task, in which Liya Ma and colleagues (2019) in the laboratory of Stephan Everling at the University of Western Ontario studied the influence of the dorsal (d)ACC on dlPFC activity during alternating blocks of prosaccade and antisaccade performance. As illustrated in *Figure 15.7*, their task required multiple switches between runs of consecutive prosaccade and antisaccade trials, with the rule switches happening unpredictably, and with no signal, after anywhere from 15 to 25 correct trials. Therefore, this task contained elements of many tests of working memory and of cognitive control that we've already seen in this chapter and in *Chapter 14*: the need to transform the first-order stimulus–response association inherent in the visual stimulus; the frequent but unpredictable and uncued change of rules, shortly after the subject has acclimated to the current rule; frequent errors (necessitated by the uncued change of rules). *And* their experiment included cryogenic inactivation (a.k.a. "cortical cooling") of dACC, thereby effecting a test of the necessity of this region's *performance-monitoring* activity for skilled performance of this task.

The behavioral effects of cooling the dACC were marked, although perhaps different from what one might have expected, having just read the preceding section on *Performance monitoring and the dmFC*. As illustrated in *Figure 15.8*, cooling had a selective effect on antisaccade accuracy, in that performance was lower during antisaccade blocks. Notably, however, there was no evidence of an exaggerated effect on the trials immediately following a switch from one rule to the other. Rather, the effect was comparable throughout the run of antisaccade trials. In particular, there was no obvious absence of a phasic signal relating to conflict, or error, or feedback. For RT, dACC inactivation slowed saccadic RTs in both conditions, and these effects were also across-the-board, with no exaggerated effects around the time of the switch.

More generally, the dACC inactivation-related impairment of performance did not show the hallmarks classically seen with damage to the dlPFC, such as perseveration or impulsivity. Rather, the authors summarized it as one of "weakened representation of the current rule or the ability to use the rule to guide behavior" (p. 9). In effect, they reasoned that because making a speeded (pro)saccade to a target is such a prepotent response, continued "effort" is required to maintain a mode of antisaccade responding.

Do the electrophysiological results from dlPFC help make sense of these findings? Ma and colleagues (2019) recorded neural signals from dlPFC with a Utah array, and reported results from LFPs divided into four frequency bands: theta (4–8 Hz); alpha (9–12 Hz); low beta (13–20 Hz); and high beta (21–30 Hz). During baseline blocks (i.e., without inactivation), the

FIGURE 15.7 Antisaccade, rule changing, and cortical cooling.
Source: Ma et al., 2019 / PLOS / CC BY 4.0.

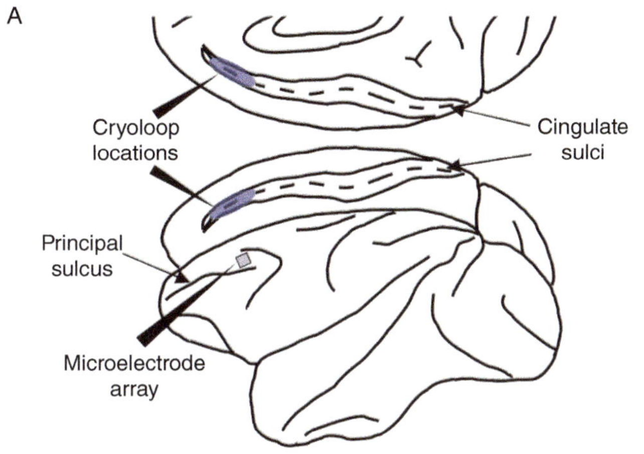

FIGURE 15.7.A Positioning of the cryoloops at the rostral end of the cingulate sulcus, bilaterally, and of the 100-contact "Utah array" in caudal dlPFC, just superior to the principal sulcus. (Note that, although not shown in this figure, the ACC of the macaque extends past and "wraps around" the genu of the corpus callosum, thus making it important to distinguish dACC from, e.g., the rostral ACC and the subgenual ACC.)

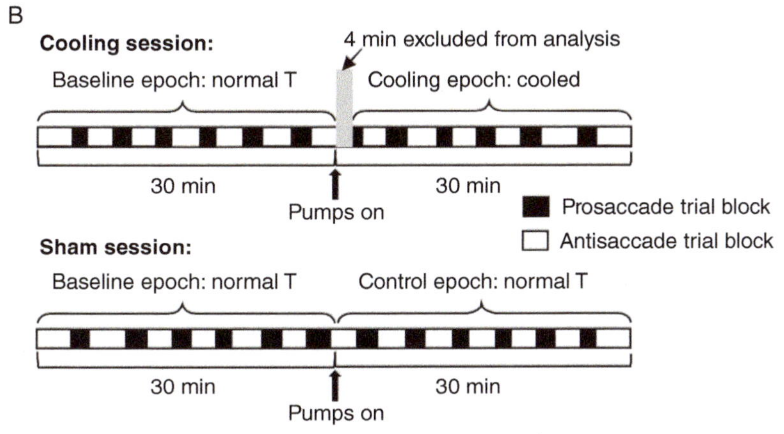

FIGURE 15.7.B The timeline of the experimental procedure.

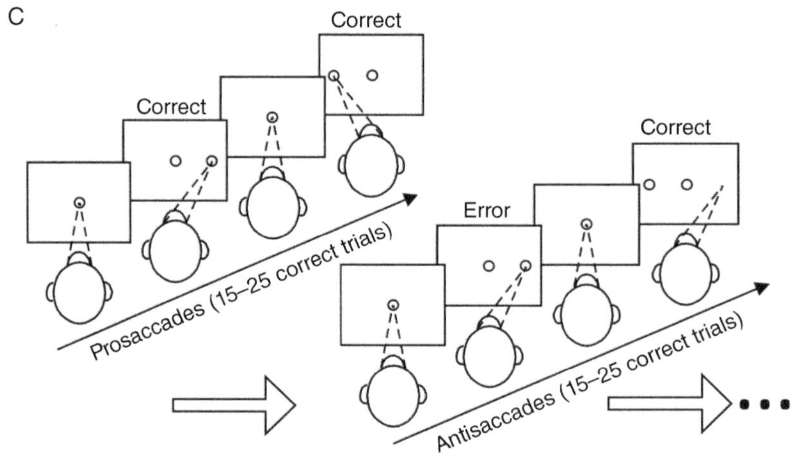

FIGURE 15.7.C Illustration of prosaccade and antisaccade trials.

most notable finding was that, for both trial types, power in the low beta-band was elevated during pretrial fixation. Furthermore, and tellingly, for correct trials, pretrial low beta was higher during anti-saccade blocks than during pro-saccade blocks, but for incorrect trials, this pattern reversed. During dACC inactivation blocks, dlPFC oscillatory power was generally lower, and reduced to baseline levels in the low-beta band, such that neither task-related nor performance-related effects were seen. Overall, these results suggested to Ma et al. (2019) a role for oscillations in the low-beta band (in dlPFC) in the representation and application of the currently relevant rule.

FIGURE 15.8 Effects of dACC cooling on pro- and antisaccade performance.
Source: Ma et al., 2019 / PLOS / CC BY 4.0.

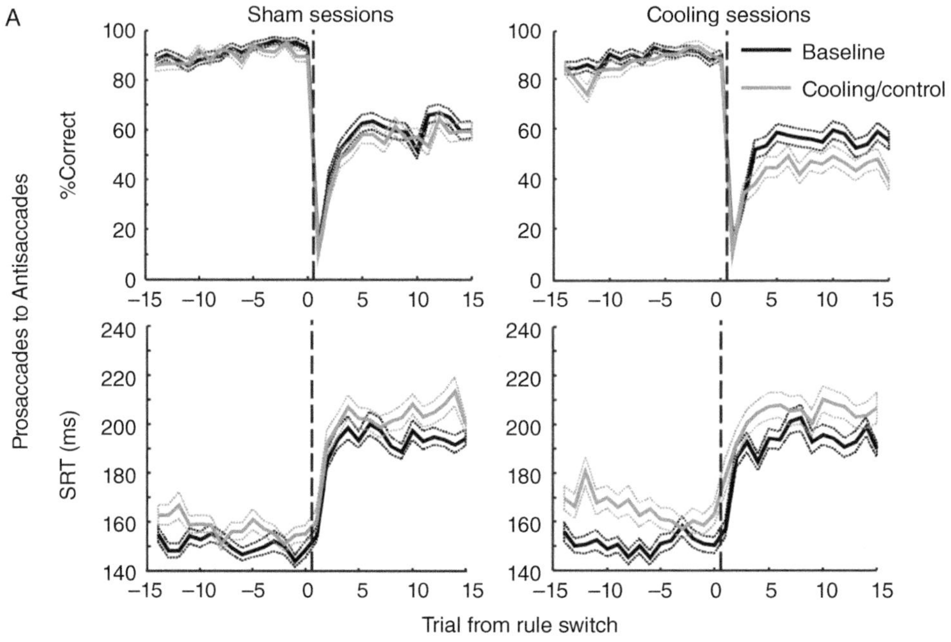

FIGURE 15.8.A Performance on the trials leading up to, and then following, a switch from the prosaccade rule to the antisaccade rule. Accuracy is plotted in the top row, and saccadic reaction time (SRT) in the bottom row.

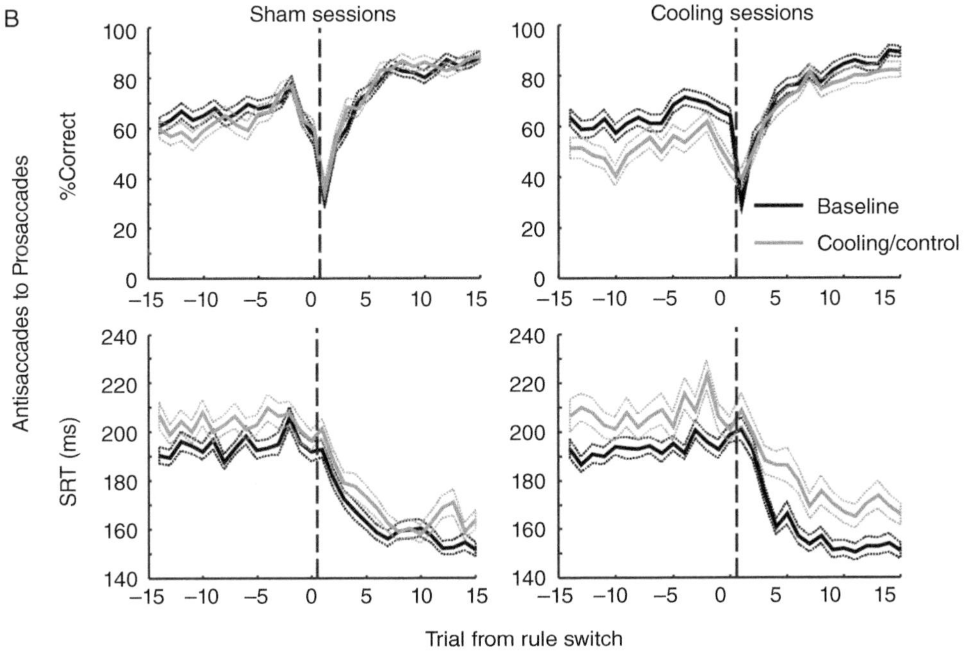

FIGURE 15.8.B Performance on the trials leading up to, and then following, a switch from the antisaccade rule to the prosaccade rule.

Cognitive neuroscientist Todd Braver has proposed that distinct frontal circuitry underlies whether one is in a state of elevated "proactive control," actively anticipating the need to counteract reflexive or otherwise prepotent tendencies, or the effects of distraction, vs. one of "reactive control," effectively waiting until response conflict, or an error, arises before engaging top-down control (e.g., Braver, 2012). Here, one interpretation of these results from Ma et al. (2019) might be that cooling has the effect of decreasing the animals' ability to sustain a state of elevated proactive control. Indeed, more intriguingly, Ma et al. (2019) speculate that "[the] antisaccade deficit may be related to a loss in the animals' ability or stamina to exert cognitive effort" (p. 23). This idea of exerting cognitive effort is reminiscent of what we saw when Master et al. (2024) manipulated the difficulty of their visual working memory task (Chapter 14, section "Trying Harder"). Relatedly, in 2013, Josef Parvizi and colleagues published a report entitled "The will to persevere induced by electrical stimulation of the human cingulate gyrus." Not unlike the approach described in the report of the patient for whom electrical stimulation of the fusiform gyrus disrupted face perception (section *Demonstrating necessity, Chapter 10*), in Parvizi et al. (2013) the authors demonstrated the effects of stimulation of the ACC with the patient's verbal reports. Here's an example, just to give you a flavor:

> It's . . . like this thing of trying to figure out your way out of, how you're going to get through something. . . . Let's say . . . if you knew you were driving your car and it was . . . one of the tires was half flat and you're only halfway there and you have no other way to turn around and go back, you have to keep going forward. That type of a, you know, feeling you have. You're like, you're like (pats chest) am I gonna, am I gonna to get through this?
>
> Am I gonna get through this? . . . I'd say . . . it was . . . a positive thing like . . . push harder, push harder, push harder to try and get through this. (Parvizi et al., 2013, p. 1361)

Dissecting Frontal Contributions to the Control of Behavior We'll close out this section on performance monitoring with a study in humans that employs a task that seems more, well, "cognitive" than the antisaccade task, and that assesses behavior with more, well, "experimental control" than unconstrained verbal report. The title of the paper is "Lesions to different regions of the frontal cortex have dissociable effects on voluntary persistence in humans." In it, Camilla van Geen, Yixin Chen, Rebecca Kazinka, Avinash R. Vaidya, Joseph Kable, and Joseph McGuire (2025) assess the constructs of persistence and cognitive effort that we've documented in several contexts – working memory (*Chapter 14*, section *"Trying harder"*), antisaccade (section *dmFC-PFC interactions*), and even while "just lying in a hospital bed" – but that we haven't yet tried to formalize. The patients recruited for this study were divided into three groups. One was comprised of patients with lesions of dmFC/dorsal (d)ACC or to anterior insula (AI; n = 8). A second group of patients had lesions of ventromedial (vm)PFC (n = 10). (vmPFC is a region that will feature prominently in *Chapter 16*'s treatment of economic decision making and *Chapter 17*'s treatment of social behavior.) Finally, a third group was a lesion control group with damage to frontal cortex ("FC," including the dlPFC; n = 10) that spared the two frontal regions of primary interest (*Figure 15.9.A*).

(Because this section has emphasized the dmFC, the dmFC/AI group merits more detailed consideration. Although AI (in the fundus of the Sylvian fissure) is not a part of the frontal lobe, it is a key node, together with dmFC/dACC, in the Cingulo-Opercular Control network (often abbreviated as "CO" or "CON"), a network originally defined via RSFC (see *Figure 4.17*, and, e.g., Kwon et al. (2025)), and that is implicated in cognitive control.[1] The dmFC/AI group assembled by van Geen et al. (2025) comprised two patients with lesions of dmFC and six with lesions of AI (the two regions being anatomically distant and fed by different arteries, and so unlikely to be damaged by the same stroke or other source of damage). For our present purposes, we can think of this dmFC/AI group as comparable to the monkeys that underwent cooling of the dACC in section *dmFC–PFC interactions*.)

The task was a willingness-to-wait task in which the goal was to earn as much money as possible during each of two 12-minute blocks of trials. Each trial began with a token worth $0.00 that, after a variable period of time, would change in value to become worth $0.10 (this

FIGURE 15.9 Frontal contributions to the willingness to wait.

Source: van Geen et al., 2025 / The Society for Neuroscience / CC BY 4.0.

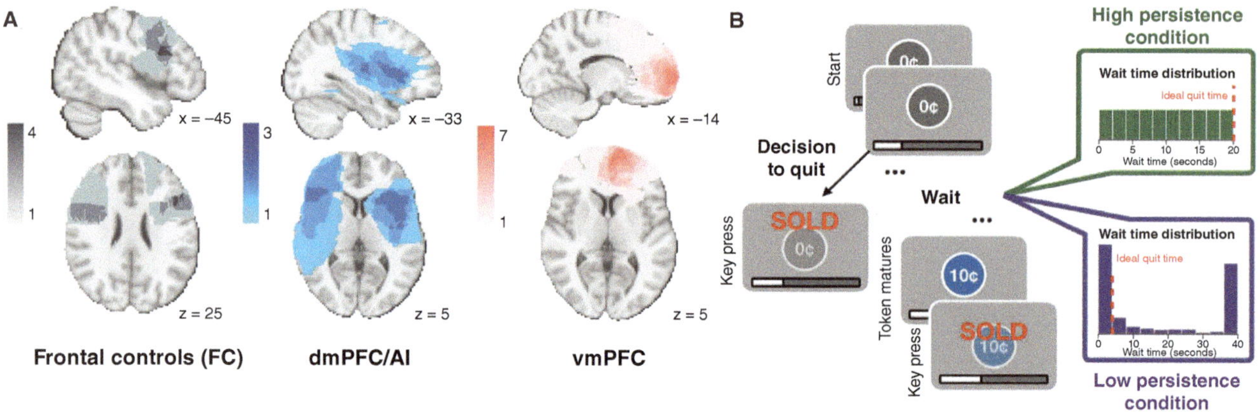

FIGURE 15.9.A Lesion overlap in the three frontal lesion groups. Note that the coordinates of the anatomical images are different for each group: the sagittal view for the FC group is very lateral, for the dmPFC/AI group is roughly midway between the lateral surface and the midline, and for the vmPFC group is close to the midline; for the axial views, the FC slice is considerably more superior than those for dmPFC/AI and vmPFC.

Source: Geen et al. (2024) / Society for Neuroscience.

FIGURE 15.9.B On the left, an illustration of what subjects see during a trial of the task, with the decision to abort a trial prior to the maturation of the token (i.e., to "quit") displaying the fact that the subject has "cashed out" their token when it had no value. Note that throughout the block, the time elapsed in the 12-minutes block was displayed by a progress bar at the bottom of the screen. On the right is a visual depiction of the sample from which each trial's wait time was randomly drawn, the vertical red dashed line indicating, for each, the optimal time within the trial to quit that trial and move on to the next one if the token has not yet matured.

Source: Geen et al. (2024) / Society for Neuroscience.

[1] At the time of the preparation of this 3rd edition of this book, the same group that has proposed the "integrate-isolate" conceptualization of the motor homunculus, based in large part on findings from RSFC, has proposed the renaming of the CO network as the "Action-Mode Network" (AMN; (Dosenbach, Raichle, and Gordon, 2025)), and a debate is underway about whether this proposed switch from an anatomy-based label to a function-based label is a good idea.

change indicated by a change of color). Trials were self-paced in that the subject could terminate a trial at any time, by doing so earning the value of the token at that moment (either $0.00 or $0.10) and immediately initiating the next trial. The reason that a subject might choose to abort a trial before earning $0.10 was that the length of time that it would take for a token to "mature" (the "wait time") varied from trial to trial, and long waits would necessarily consume larger portions of the 12-minute duration of the game. (Consider that if a token matured after 1 second, the rate of earning on that trial would be $0.10/second, but if it matured after 10 second, the rate of earning on that trial would be $0.01/second.) There were two blocks defined by different distributions of wait times. The "high-persistence" (HP) block was so named because wait times were sampled from a uniform distribution ranging from 0 to 20 second, and the optimal strategy for this block was to always wait until the token matured, regardless of wait time. For "low persistence" (LP) blocks, in contrast, wait times were sampled from a "heavy-tailed generalized Pareto distribution truncated at 40 second" (i.e., the vast majority of wait times massed at the very beginning or the very end of trials, the vast majority of "at the end" trials lasting roughly 40 second; *Figure 15.9.B*). The optimal strategy during LP blocks was to wait only 2.3 second and, if the token hadn't yet matured, to abort the trial so as to quickly move on to the next one. Neither sampling distributions nor optimal strategies were explained to subjects (just the basic rules), and how well they were able to learn the optimal strategy via trial-and-error experience was a key dependent measure. (From this perspective, the uninstructed "figure-it-out-for-yourself" aspect of this task could be thought of as similar to the WCST.)

Inspection of the descriptive statistics shows that neurologically healthy control subjects and dlPFC control subjects both learned to wait longer over the course of the HP block, and both learned to wait less long over the course of the LP block, such that, for both groups, their overall willingness to wait was higher on the HP block than on the LP block (*Figure 15.10*). The two frontal lesion groups of interest differed from the two control groups, and did so in different ways. The dmPFC/AI group showed erratic changes that are difficult to characterize as learning because they did not show a pattern of (relatively) steady change toward the

FIGURE 15.10 Frontal subregions contribute differently to the willingness to wait.

Source: van Geen et al., 2025 / The Society for Neuroscience / CC BY 4.0.

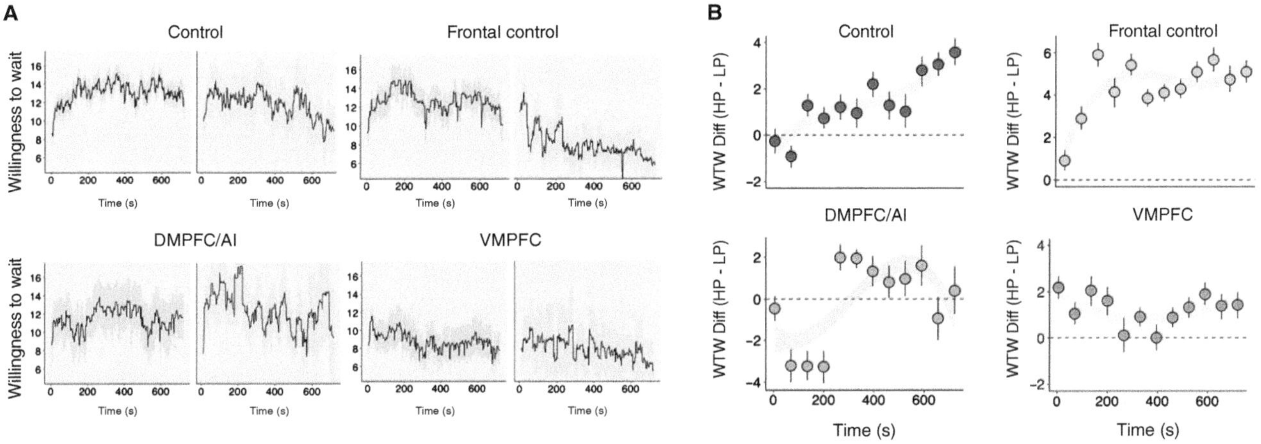

FIGURE 15.10.A Average giving-up time as a function of time in the 12-minutes (720 seconds) block, for the HP block (green) and the LP block (purple). The healthy control group, on the HP block, shows steep learning early in the block before asymptoting at a high level, and on the LP block, after an initial rise, shows a steady decline. The FC group does not differ statistically from the healthy control group. The dmPFC/AI group does not learn in either condition. The vmPFC group starts with overall lower willingness to wait, a tendency that decreases further, in both blocks, over time.

FIGURE 15.10.B Same data from panel A, but processed differently to emphasize different rates of learning. Data are averaged in 72-second bins, then willingness to wait for each LP bin is subtracted from each corresponding HP bin. The healthy controls show steady growth in the HP vs. LP difference with time. The FC group shows steeper early growth followed by a plateau. The dmPFC/AI group shows a step function, but no evidence of learning within either stage. The vmPFC group showed no evidence of change over time.

optimal behavior (sometimes followed by an asymptote), nor did their overall willingness to wait differ on HP blocks relative to LP blocks. The vmPFC group, in contrast, showed markedly shorter willingness to wait for both conditions, and in both conditions, this tendency decreased over time.

Chen, Fulford, and McGuire's (2022) model of "active persistence" is a Q-learning model that parameterizes the learning process on this task with two parameters that capture the speed of learning from positive (α) or negative (ν) feedback, respectively, (these correspond to learning from trials that earned \$0.10 vs. trials that earned \$0.00, respectively); an inverse temperature parameter (τ) that indexes "action selection noise"; a discount parameter (γ) for temporally remote rewards; and a parameter that captures participants' initial willingness to wait (η). The constructs of delay discounting and willingness-to-wait are considered trait-like aspects of one's personality that we will return to in *Chapter 16: Decision making*, *Chapter 17: Social behavior*, and *Chapter 18: Emotion*.) Fitting the data to this model revealed that the dmPFC/AI group differed from healthy controls via a lower value of the ν parameter, and the vmPFC group via a lower value of η. Thus, the fact that the pattern of behavior of these two groups differed from healthy controls in different ways is explained, in part, by the fact that they are impaired with respect to different constructs formalized by the active persistence model. Most relevant for this chapter, the dmPFC/AI patients were impaired at learning specifically from "quit" trials. One can see how the ability to process (and learn from) negative outcomes might be a basis for detecting when control is needed (section *Error monitoring: The ERN/Ne*) and, more broadly, for the functions summarized in section *Performance monitoring and the dorsomedial frontal cortex*. One can also see how disruption of this process could manifest as disruption in the "ability or stamina to exert cognitive effort" on the part of monkeys with cryogenically inactivated dACC (section *dmFC–PFC interactions*). In contrast, unpacking the finding that patients with vmPFC lesions showed an atypically reduced willingness to wait will have to wait for our considerations of value-based decision making in *Chapter 16* (see what I did there?). For now, suffice it to say that it is consistent with, as the authors note, the fact that patients with vmPFC lesions "exhibit a stronger preference for smaller-sooner reward options . . . [and that] vmPFC may play an important role in tempering impulsivity by holding a neural representation of the upcoming reward" (van Geen et al. (2025), p. 8 of 10).

Stop!

There are many, many aspects of cognitive control that we simply can't cover here, but the final one that we will cover is perhaps *the* canonical example of a principle from motor control generalizing to cognitive control: stopping. In *Chapter 8: Skeletomotor Control*, and elsewhere, we have emphasized the direct and indirect pathways of cortico-basal ganglia-thalamic circuits. It is the hyperdirect pathway, however, that will get the star treatment in this section. The hyperdirect pathway bypasses the striatum, carrying excitatory signals from cortex to subthalamic nucleus (STN), which excites the internal segment of the globus pallidus (GPi). This has the effect of increasing the GPi's inhibitory influence on the thalamus. To examine the role of the hyperdirect pathway in stopping, we need to first establish some facts about its physiology.

Figure 15.11 presents data reported by Darcy Diesburg, Jeremy Greenlee, and Jan Wessel (2021) that illustrates the fact that "sensorimotor beta" (including the signals reviewed *Chapter 8*, section *The neurophysiology of movement*) is increasingly understood to be the summation of many discrete "bursty" events, rather than a reflection of a continuous oscillatory signal. To put this figure in context, first consider *Figure 8.7*, from *Chapter 8: Skeletomotor control*. Although *Figure 8.7.B* gives the appearance of a continuous premovement oscillation centered at 20 Hz (then 25 Hz), it was assembled from averaging across many trials. *Figure 8.7.A*, in contrast, illustrates the time-varying voltage from several individual trials (i.e., "ERPs" that have not been spectrally transformed). If each of these trials were analyzed with the method used by Diesburg et al. (2021), many would expect that the beta-frequency elements in these individual trials would be shown to be bursty, rather than continuous. To whit, *Figure 15.11* presents data from patients with Parkinson's disease undergoing implantation of deep-brain

FIGURE 15.11 Motor-related beta-band activity is bursty.

Source: (Diesburg, Greenlee, & Wessel, 2021) / eLife Sciences Publications, Ltd. / CC BY 4.0.

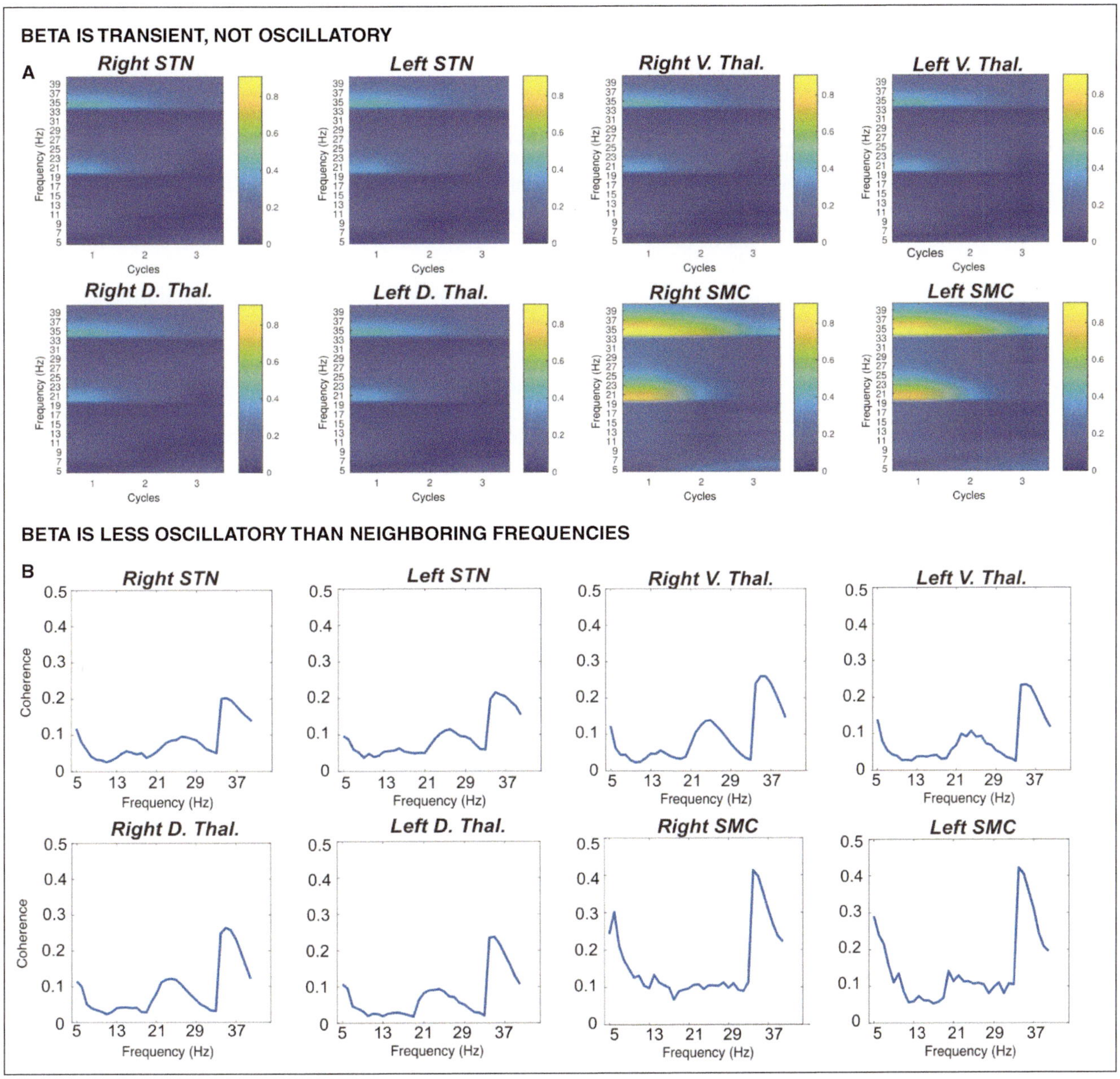

FIGURE 15.11.A Results of lagged-coherence analyses of signals from STN, ventral and dorsal thalamus, and sensorimotor cortex (SMC). The logic of this analysis is that if an oscillating signal is steady over time, its value at a given phase angle during cycle n should predict the value at that same phase angle during cycle $n+1$, $n+2$, . . . $n+\mathrm{x}$. What's evident in this panel, however, is that although coherence for 20 Hz energy is relatively high at cycle 1 (i.e., cycle $n+1$ relative to the reference cycle n), it drops off quickly thereafter and does not persist as far as cycle 3 (three cycles being one arbitrarily defined boundary for distinguishing a steady oscillation from a burst). These recordings were made during implantation of DBS electrodes, which are inserted through a burr hole that is drilled in the skull, and the subgaleal SMC recordings were made with electrode strips inserted – at the edge of the burr hole – under the scalp but on surface of the skull (just beneath the tissue called the galea aponeurotica). Thus, they are extracranial EEG recordings, albeit with higher SNR than would be expected from electrodes placed on the external surface of the scalp.

FIGURE 15.11.B Alternative display of results presented in panel **A**, emphasizing the bursty nature of fluctuations in the field potential in the beta band, in these motoric regions, relative to fluctuations at lower and higher frequencies.

stimulation (DBS) electrodes into either the STN, the thalamus, or in one case, both, to which Diesburg et al. (2021) did apply "sustained vs. burst" analyses, and the results are unequivocally supportive of a "bursty" account of sensorimotor beta.

Now, what about stopping? The concept of stopping should be familiar to all. For this author, it might be preparing to step out when the elevator doors open, but then stopping when he realizes that we're only on the 4th floor (and his destination is the 5th floor); or, when stopped at a red light, starting to lift his foot off the brake pedal in response to some visual transient, but stopping this lifting movement as soon as he realizes that the light is still red. Indeed, sometimes in this latter scenario our narrator will not only stop releasing pressure on the brake pedal, but he'll then apply even more force than he had been applying prior to the aborted lifting of the foot. In such an instance, one could say that he has "paused-then-revised" the initial intention to release the brake. And so here we will consider both the simpler scenario of "just stopping" and the more complicated scenario of "stopping-then-revising," keeping in mind that the implications of this work extend beyond the seemingly mundane processes of stopping simple finger or leg movements, or walking out of elevators: The title of one of the first papers to launch this line of research was "On the ability to *inhibit* simple *thoughts* and actions: I. Stop-signal studies of decision and memory" (Logan, 1983) (this author's emphases).

The patients reported by Diesburg et al. (2021) performed a version of the stop-signal task conceptually similar to the "STOP condition" task illustrated in *Figure 15.12*, but administered auditorily via headphones (a GO tone in left or right ear commanding a button press by the corresponding hand, followed infrequently and unpredictably by a STOP tone). The lag between

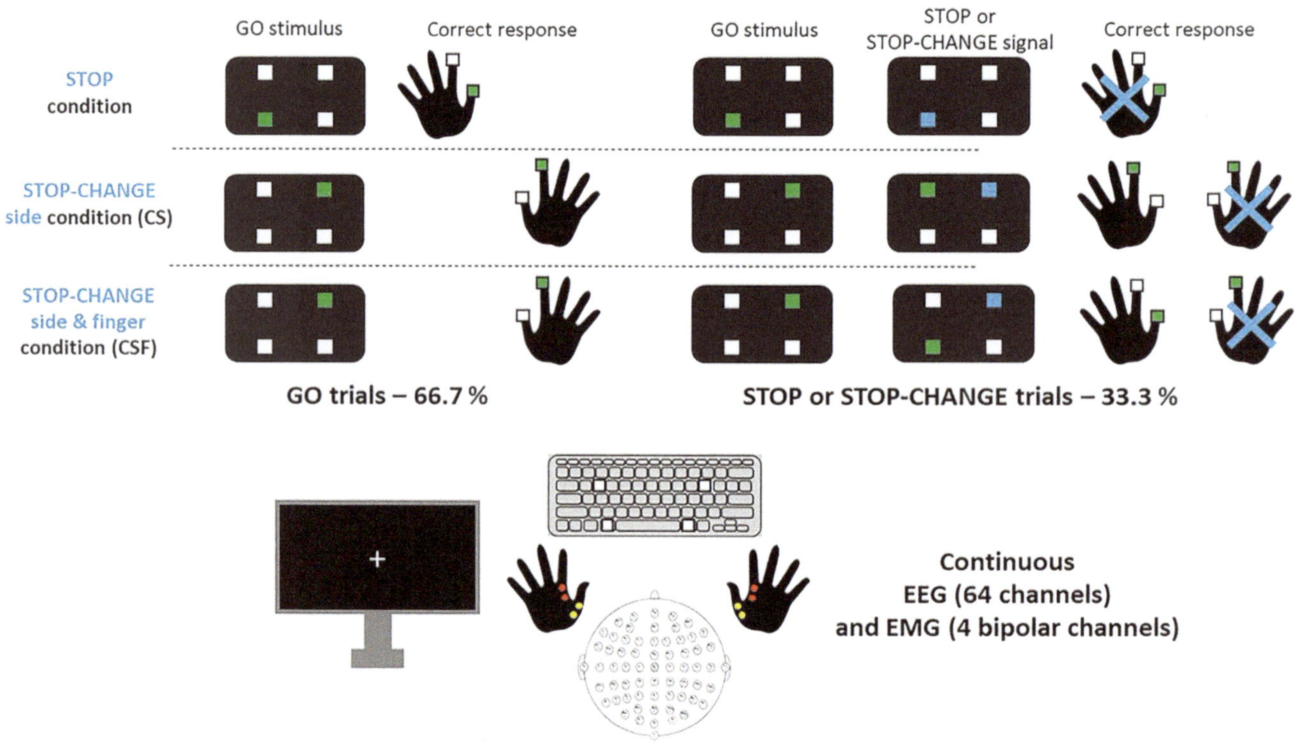

FIGURE 15.12 A variant of the stop-signal task designed to test a "pause-then-revise" model of stopping. On all trials, subjects began with fingers and thumbs of both hands poised above the keys highlighted at the bottom of the figure. On *STOP* trials, the target key was indicated by a change to green on the visual display, and on 67% of trials, pressing this key was the correct response. However, on 33% of these trials, a change of the target from green to blue indicated that the initially instructed response should be stopped (i.e., no key should be pressed). For *STOP-CHANGE side* trials and *STOP-CHANGE side and finger* trials, on 67% of trials the initially instructed response was the correct response, but on 33% of trials the subsequent change of a target square on the opposite side from white to blue indicated that the initially instructed response should be aborted and, instead, the newly instructed key should be pressed. These two differed in that "change side" trials of *STOP-CHANGE side* trials required a change of side, but not of digit, whereas "change side" trials of *STOP-CHANGE side and finger* trials required a change of side and of digit.

Source: (Hervault & Wessel, 2025) / The Society for Neuroscience.

GO and STOP signals was titrated for each patient to yield 50% failures on STOP trials. The generally accepted model of stopping in the stop-signal task conceptualizes stopping as a "horse race" between the process that was triggered by the GO signal (i.e., the motor command) and a second process triggered by the STOP signal, the outcome of the trial (i.e., failure to stop or successful stopping) determined by whichever process is completed first. (This is conceptually similar to a diffusion-decision process that unfolds as a race between, e.g., a "match" vs. a "nonmatch" decision [*Chapter 5*, section *Diffusion-decision modeling*].) At first, one might think that this is "not a fair race" because the GO process gets a head start. However, the GO process is "slower" – takes longer to complete – because it entails the translation of the GO signal into a motor command that is specific to a particular effector (e.g., to a specific digit, or a specific foot), then routing this command through the direct pathway of the basal ganglia. The STOP process, in comparison, benefits from two factors. First, shorter cortical processing time, because it does not need to be precise in the way that the GO process does; it is the same nonspecific, "global" signal every time. Second, the hyper-direct pathway that carries the stop signal is effectively a "shorter" pathway, by virtue of bypassing the neostriatum. (We know that it is *nonspecific* and *global* because, e.g., the stopping-related attenuation of a transcranial magnetic stimulation [TMS]-evoked response recorded at the hand is pronounced even when what is being stopped is the depression of a foot pedal (Hervault and Wessel, 2025) or a verbal response (Wessel et al., 2022).) The researchers who first began studying stopping in the 1980s, and who developed the race model, were experimental psychologists who didn't explicitly think through the basal ganglia-circuit considerations – that connection was made later. What they did realize, however, was that studying stopping presented a unique challenge because stopping is a process that, when successful, has no behavioral correlate. (*How do you measure the RT of a movement that... wait, there isn't any movement* to measure, because it was stopped*!*) They got around this problem by devising an analytic way to derive an estimate of a latent process called the stop-signal reaction time (SSRT), an estimate of the duration of the process that is assumed to have raced against the successfully stopped motor command. It entails varying the lag between the GO signal and the STOP signal so as to generate a distribution of RTs from failed stop trials to compare against RTs from successful go trials, and plugging these values into a formula, as detailed, for example, by Frederick Verbruggen and a cast of thousands in a consensus paper on best practices for studying stopping (Verbruggen et al., 2019).

And so Diesburg et al. (2021) demonstrated that, in subcortical structures (as well as in the extracranial EEG, not shown here), stopping is associated with an increase of beta bursting (Figure 15.13). More recently, Hervault and Wessel (2025) have used the task illustrated in *Figure 15.12* to assess a more sophisticated "pause-then-revise" model that posits that stopping is accomplished by an initial global and nonspecific "lock down" imposed on the thalamus (due to the STN-to-GPi signaling carried by the hyperdirect pathway), followed by a second and more specific command that might be to "pause-then-cancel" (Diesburg and Wessel, 2021), but might also be to "pause. . .then do something else." Their results, illustrated in *Figure 15.14*, reinforce the idea that the initial "global" stopping signal (i.e., the "pause" in "pause-then-revise") is associated with (and, by inference from work that we haven't reviewed here, causally implemented by (J. R. Wessel et al., 2022)), beta bursting of the STN, which triggers the beta bursting recorded at frontocentral (extracranial) EEG electrodes (*Figure 15.14*). The "then-revise" component of the process was indexed by two other EEG measures that we won't detail here: differences in frontal midline theta-band power and/or in the P300 ERP component, between the *STOP-CHANGE side* and *STOP-CHANGE side and finger*.

By returning to the proposition that stopping is "perhaps *the* canonical example of a principle from motor control generalizing to cognitive control." The same, or very similar, circuit-level mechanisms reviewed here are likely involved many aspects of cognitive control, as seen in the titles of two recent reviews on the topic: "Beta: Bursts of Cognition" (Lundqvist et al., 2024); and "Neural mechanisms of domain-general cognitive control (Wessel and Anderson, 2024). Examples that are considered in these reviews include the control of working memory, visual selective attention, LTM encoding, intentional forgetting of information held in LTM, resolving linguistic competition, resisting distraction, and controlling the routing of sensory and motoric information.

FIGURE 15.13 The electrophysiology of stopping.

Source: Diesburg et al. (2021) / eLife Sciences Publications, Ltd. / CC BY 4.0.

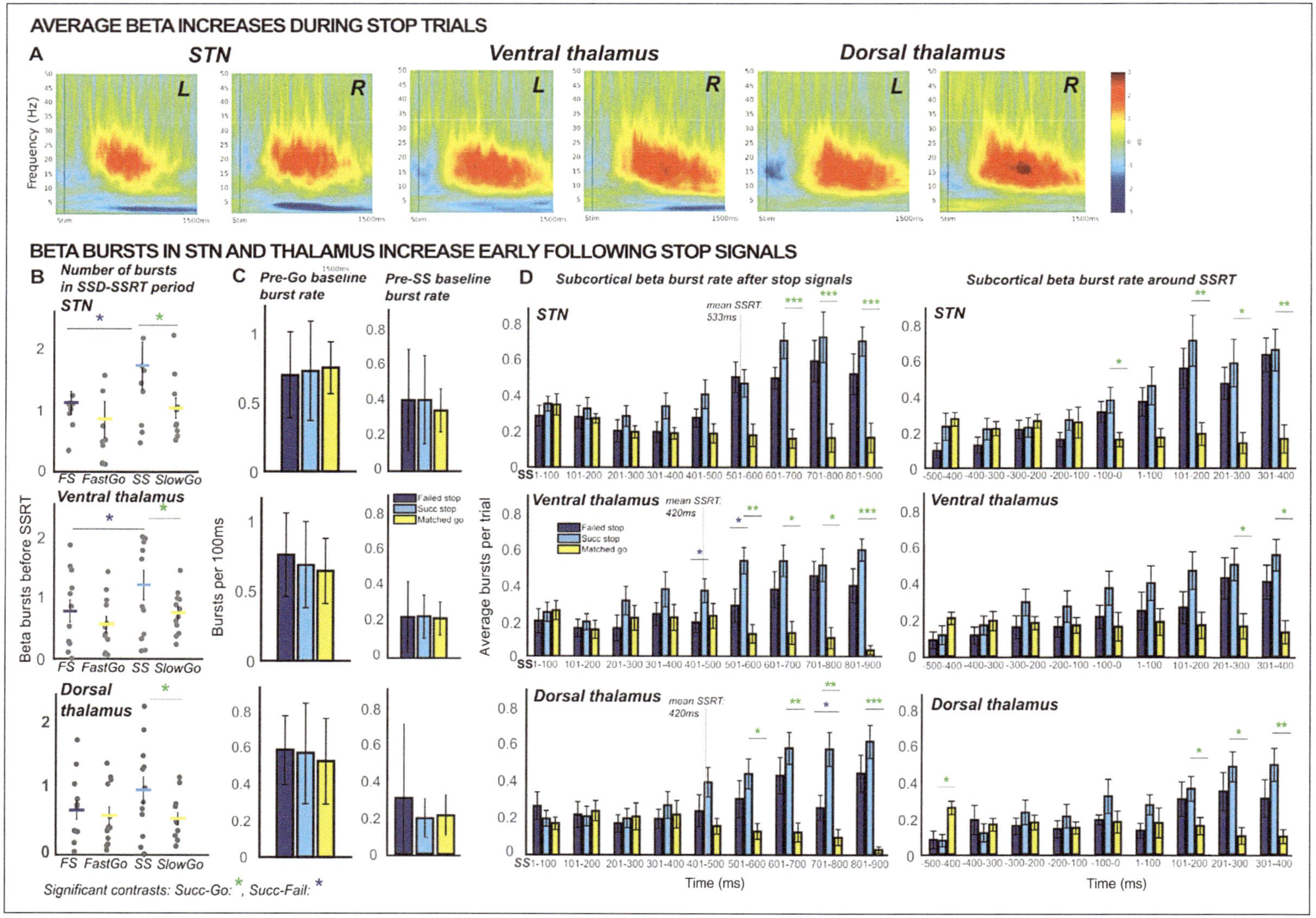

FIGURE 15.13.A Spectral differences in trial-averaged signal from successful STOPs minus correct-GO trials. Note how, due to averaging, these difference images appear to show an increase in a beta-band oscillation that persists for roughly 1000 msec (which would correspond to roughly 20 cycles).

FIGURE 15.13.B In all three subcortical regions, the number of beta bursts was higher for fast STOPs (FS) than fast correct-GOs (FastGo), and for slow STOPs (SS) than slow correct-GOs (SlowGo).

FIGURE 15.13.C Beta burst rate did not differ across conditions prior to trial onset (left-hand column), nor during lag between GO and STOP signals (right-hand column). (These aren't theoretically interesting, but are included to show that the effects in panels D and E aren't just carry-overs from pretrial differences.)

FIGURE 15.13.D Beta burst rate per 100 msec bin, time-locked to the STOP signal (time 0), was higher for successful-STOP *and* for unsuccessful-STOP than for GO trials (and higher for successful-STOPs than for unsuccessful-STOPs). Mean SSRTs are indicated with vertical lines.

FIGURE 15.13.E Same data as from panel D, but now time-locked to the estimated SSRT (time 0). Aligning the data in this way also shows beta burst rate was higher for successful-STOP *and* for unsuccessful-STOP than for GO trials (and higher for successful-STOPs than for unsuccessful-STOPs).

FIGURE 15.14 Beta bursting in the (extracranial) EEG time-locked to the stop/stop-change signal.
Source: Hervault and Wessel (2025) / The Society for Neuroscience.

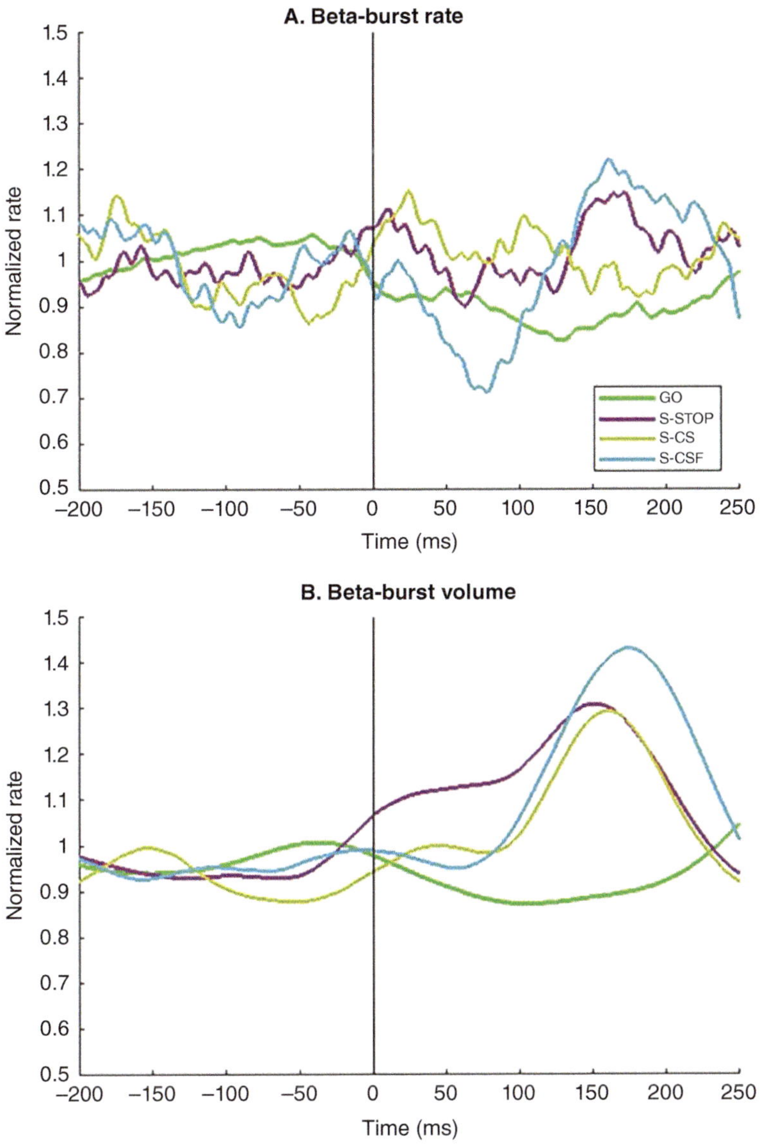

FIGURE 15.14.A Beta burst rate at electrode FCz declines subtly on *GO* trials and increases on successful *STOP* (S-STOP), *STOP-CHANGE side* (S-CS), and *STOP-CHANGE side and finger* (S-CSF) trials.

FIGURE 15.14.B Beta burst volume at electrode FCz declines subtly on *GO* trials and increases on S-STOP, S-CS, and S-CSF trials. Beta burst volume indexes the amplitude of the excursions of the burst from the baseline. Because thalamus-to-cortex communication is necessarily carried by spiking (e.g., not traveling waves), this measure can be interpreted as a proxy for the intensity of the thalamic drive on cortex (a thalamic drive fluctuating at the beta frequency evidently having an inhibitory effect; c.f., *Chapter 8*, section *The waveform shape of "sensorimotor beta"*).

Where Is the Controller?

In this chapter, we have seen that the dlPFC plays a key role in the control of cognition. Damage to this structure leads to a dramatic and debilitating behavioral disinhibition characteristic of the lateral frontal-lobe syndrome. On closer inspection, we saw that the implementation of cognitive control involves many stages, and many "players." The activity of midbrain dopamine neurons plays two roles simultaneously. Its "long game" is the shaping of habitual behaviors, while its in-the-moment role is to "nudge" the dlPFC to maintain or switch behavioral strategies. The dmFC monitors performance, processes information about conflict and errors, and likely acts as a governor on some aspects of PFC activity, including whether to stay in a more effortful proactive mode of control or to revert to a reactive mode. The unique architecture and connectivity of the PFC-basal ganglia-thalamic system enable it to "stop on a dime" and change course, as circumstances dictate.

End-of-Chapter Questions

1. Name two or three examples from your daily life that illustrate failures of cognitive control. In each case, what was it about the behavior that you *did* produce that resulted in its being expressed rather than the behavior that you should have produced? (Need a hint to get you started? Have you ever done anything "klutzy" while walking and texting on your mobile phone?)

2. What brain region is most strongly associated with cognitive control? Might there be subregional organization such that different aspects of control are preferentially carried out by different subregions?

3. Define a perseverative error on the WCST. What factors explain this distinctive failure of cognitive control? What are two possible mechanisms whereby perseverative errors are prevented in the normally functioning nervous system?

4. The study of PFC-lesioned patients with ERP has revealed two distinct loci of impaired neuronal functioning during an STM task – what are they?

5. How can models of PFC-based cognitive control rule out the logical problem of a PFC-based homunculus who decides when it's time to apply cognitive control?

6. Summarize three explanations for performance-monitoring-related activity in dorsomedial PFC.

7. In the experiment from Ma et al. (2019), monkeys that had been trained to perform both the pro-saccade and anti-saccade task performed an experiment during which the rewarded response (pro- vs. anti-) changed unpredictably over the course of a block of trials. How did inactivation of the ACC alter performance? Had the authors, instead, inactivated dorsolateral PFC, how might the alteration of performance have been different?

8. In a task that emphasizes flexible adjustment of one's "willingness to wait," what are the effects on learning and performance of lesions of dorsomedial frontal cortex (dmFC)/AI vs. vmPFC/OFC vs. dorsolateral PFC?

9. How is it possible that one can stop the intention to execute a movement when the STOP signal lags behind the GO signal by 100 msec or more?

References

Botvinick, Matthew M., Todd S. Braver, Deanna M. Barch, Cameron S. Carter, and Jonathan D. Cohen. 2001. "Conflict Monitoring and Cognitive Control." *Psychological Review* 108 (3): 624–652. doi: 10.1037/0033-295X.108.3.624.

Braver, Todd S. 2012. "The Variable Nature of Cognitive Control: A Dual Mechanisms Framework." *Trends in Cognitive Sciences* 16: 106–113.

Chao, Linda L., and Robert T. Knight. 1995. "Human Prefrontal Lesions Increase Distractibility to Irrelevant Sensory Inputs." *Neuroreport* 6 (12): 1605–1610.

Chao, Linda L., and Robert T. Knight. 1998. "Contribution of Human Prefrontal Cortex to Delay Performance." *Journal of Cognitive Neuroscience* 10 (2): 167–177. doi: 10.1162/089892998562636.

Chen, Yixin, Daniel Fulford, and Joseph McGuire. 2022. "Test-Retest Reliability of Task-Based Measures of Voluntary Persistence." *Proceedings of the Annual Meeting of the Cognitive Science Society 44*: 44.

Diamond, Adele, and Patricia S. Goldman-Rakic. 1989. "Comparison of Human Infants and Rhesus Monkeys on Piaget's A-Not-B Task: Evidence for Dependence on Dorsolateral Prefrontal Cortex." *Experimental Brain Research* 74 (1): 24–40. http://www.devcogneuro.com/Publications/Diamond&Goldman-RakicAB.pdf.

Diesburg, Darcy A., and Jan R. Wessel. 2021. "The Pause-then-Cancel Model of Human Action-Stopping: Theoretical Considerations and Empirical Evidence." *Neuroscience & Biobehavioral Reviews 129*: 17–34. doi: 10.1016/j.neubiorev.2021.07.019.

Diesburg, Darcy A., Jeremy D. W. Greenlee, and Jan R. Wessel. 2021. "Cortico-Subcortical β Burst Dynamics Underlying Movement Cancellation in Humans." *eLife 10*. doi: 10.7554/eLife.70270.

Dosenbach, Nico U. F., Marcus E. Raichle, and Evan M. Gordon. 2025. "The Brain's Action-Mode Network." *Nature Review Neuroscience 26* (3): 158–168. doi: 10.1038/s41583-024-00895-x.

Emrich, Stephen M., Adam C. Riggall, Joshua J. LaRocque, and Bradley R. Postle. 2013. "Distributed Patterns of Activity in Sensory Cortex Reflect the Precision of Multiple Items Maintained in Visual Short-Term Memory." *Journal of Neuroscience* 33 (15): 6516–6523. doi: 10.1523/JNEUROSCI.5732-12.2013.

Falkenstein, Michael, Joachim Hohnsbein, Jörg Hoormann, and L. Blanke. 1991. "Effects of Cross-Modal Divided Attention on Late ERP Components: II. Error Processing in Choice Reaction Tasks." *Electroencephalography and Clinical Neurophysiology* 78 (6): 447–455.

van Geen, Camilla, Yixin Chen, Rebecca Kazinka, Avinash R. Vaidya, Joseph W. Kable, and Joseph T. McGuire. 2025. "Lesions to Different Regions of the Frontal Cortex Have Dissociable Effects on Voluntary Persistence in Humans." *Journal of Neuroscience 45* (6). doi: 10.1523/JNEUROSCI.0068-24.2024.

Gehring, William J., Brian Goss, Michael G. H. Coles, David E. Meyer, and Emanuel Donchin. 1993. "A Neural System for Error Detection and Compensation." *Psychological Science* 4 (6): 385–390. doi: 10.1111/j.1467-9280.1993.tb00586.x.

Gehring, William J., Yanni Liu, Joseph M. Orr, and Joshua Carp. 2012. "The Error-Related Negativity (ERN/Ne)." In *The Oxford Handbook of Event-Related Potential Components*, edited by Steven J. Luck and Emily S. Kappenman (pp. 231–291). New York: Oxford University Press. doi: 10.1093/oxfordhb/9780195374148.013.0120.

Grant, David A., and Esta Berg. 1948. "A Behavioral Analysis of Degree of Reinforcement and Ease of Shifting to New Responses in a Weigl-Type Card-Sorting Problem." *Journal of Experimental Psychology* 38 (4): 404–411. doi: 10.1037/h0059831.

Hamker, Fred H. 2005. "The Reentry Hypothesis: The Putative Interaction of the Frontal Eye Field, Ventrolateral Prefrontal Cortex, and Areas V4, IT for Attention and Eye Movement." *Cerebral Cortex* 15 (4): 431–447. doi: 10.1093/cercor/bhh146.

Hervault, Mario, and Jan R. Wessel. 2025. "Common and Unique Neurophysiological Processes That Support the Stopping and Revising of Actions." *Journal of Neuroscience 45* (13). doi: 10.1523/JNEUROSCI.1537-24.2025.

Holroyd, Clay B., and Michael G. H. Coles. 2002. "The Neural Basis of Human Error Processing: Reinforcement Learning, Dopamine, and the Error-Related Negativity." *Psychological Review* 109 (4): 679–709. doi: 10.1037/0033-295X.109.4.679.

Knight, Robert T., and Mark D'Esposito. 2003. "Lateral Prefrontal Syndrome: A Disorder of Executive Control." In *Foundations of Cognitive Neuroscience*, edited by Mark D'Esposito (pp. 259–280). Cambridge, MA: MIT Press.

Kwon, Y. H., Salvo, J. J., Anderson, N. L., Edmonds, D., Holubecki, A. M., Lakshman, M., . . . Braga, R. M. (2025). Situating the salience and parietal memory networks in the context of multiple parallel distributed networks using precision functional mapping. *Cell Rep*, 44(1), 115207. doi:10.1016/j.celrep.2024.115207

Lhermitte, François, Bernard Pillon, and Michel Serdaru. 1986. "Human Autonomy and the Frontal Lobes. Part I: Imitation and Utilization Behavior: A Neuropsychological Study of 75 Patients." *Annals of Neurology* 19 (4): 326–334. doi: 10.1002/ana.410190404.

Logan, G. D. 1983. "On the ability to inhibit simple thoughts and actions: I. Stop-signal studies of decision and memory." *Journal of Experimental Psychology* 9: 585–606. doi: 10.1037/0278-7393.9.4.585.

Luck, S. J., and E. K. Vogel. 2013. "Visual working memory capacity: from psychophysics and neurobiology to individual differences." *Trends in Cognitive Sciences* 17: 391–400.

Lundqvist, M., E. K. Miller, J. Nordmark, J. Liljefors, and P. Herman. 2024. "Beta: bursts of cognition." *Trends Cogn Sci.* doi: 10.1016/j.tics.2024.03.010.

Ma, Liya, Jason L. Chan, Kevin Johnston, Stephen G. Lomber, and Stefan Everling. 2019. "Macaque Anterior Cingulate Cortex Deactivation Impairs Performance and Alters Lateral Prefrontal Oscillatory Activities in a Rule-Switching Task." *PLoS Biology* 17: e3000045. doi: doi.org/10.1371/journal.pbio.3000045.

Malmo, Robert B. 1942. "Interference Factors in Delayed Response in Monkeys after Removal of Frontal Lobes." *Journal of Neurophysiology* 5 (4): 295–308.

Master, S. L., S. Li, and C. E. Curtis. 2024. "Trying Harder: How Cognitive Effort Sculpts Neural Representations During Working Memory." *The Journal of Neuroscience* 44: e0060242024. doi: 10.1523/JNEUROSCI.0060-24.2024.

Miller, Earl K., and Jonathan D. Cohen. 2001. "An Integrative Theory of Prefrontal Cortex Function." *Annual Review of Neuroscience* 24: 167–202.

Milner, Brenda. 1963. "Effects of Different Brain Lesions on Card Sorting: The Role of the Frontal Lobes." *Archives of Neurology* 9 (1): 90–100. doi: 10.1001/archneur.1963.00460070100010.

O'Reilly, Randall C., and Yuko Munakata. 2000. *Computational Explorations in Cognitive Neuroscience: Understanding the Mind by Simulating the Brain*. Cambridge, MA, and London: MIT Press.

Parvizi, Josef, Vinitha Rangarajan, William R. Shirer, Nikita Desai, and Michael D. Greicius. 2013. "The Will to Persevere Induced by Electrical Stimulation of the Human Cingulate Gyrus." *Neuron* 80: 1359–1367.

Picard, Nathalie, and Peter L. Strick. 1996. "Motor Areas of the Medial Wall: A Review of Their Location and Functional Activation." *Cerebral Cortex* 6: 342–353. doi: 10.1093/cercor/6.3.342.

Ridderinkhof, K. Richard, Markus Ullsperger, Eveline A. Crone, and Sander Nieuwenhuis. 2004. "The Role of the Medial Frontal Cortex in Cognitive Control." *Science* 306 (5695): 443–447. doi: 10.1126/science.1100301.

Rougier, Nicolas P., David C. Noelle, Todd S. Braver, Jonathan D. Cohen, and Randall C. O'Reilly. 2005. "Prefrontal Cortex and Flexible Cognitive Control: Rules without Symbols." *Proceedings of the National Academy of Sciences of the United States of America* 102 (20): 7338–7343. doi: 10.1073/pnas.0502455102.

Schultz, Wolfram. 2006. "Behavioral Theories and the Neurophysiology of Reward." *Annual Review of Psychology* 57: 87–115. doi: 10.1146/annurev.psych.56.091103.070229.

Stedron, Jennifer Merva, Sarah Devi Sahni, and Yuko Munakata. 2005. "Common Mechanisms for Working Memory and Attention: The Case of Perseveration with Visible Solutions." *Journal of Cognitive Neuroscience* 17 (4): 623–631. doi: 10.1162/0898929053467622.

Frederick Verbruggen, Adam R. Aron, Guido Ph Band, Christian Beste, Patrick G. Bissett, Adam T. Brockett, . . . Boehler, C. Nico (2019). A Consensus Guide to Capturing the Ability to Inhibit Actions and Impulsive Behaviors in the Stop-Signal Task. *eLife, 8*. doi:10.7554/eLife.46323.

Weigl, Egon. 1941. "On the Psychology of So-Called Processes of Abstraction." Translated by Margaret J. Rioch." *Journal of Abnormal and Social Psychology* 36 (1): 3–33. doi: 10.1037/h00555440.

Wessel, Jan R., and Michael C. Anderson. 2024. "Neural Mechanisms of Domain-General Cognitive Control." *Trends in Cognitive Sciences 28* (2): 124–143. doi: 10.1016/j.tics.2023.09.008.

Wessel, Jan R., Darcy A. Diesburg, Nathan H. Chalkley, and Jeremy D. W. Greenlee. 2022. "A Causal Role for the Human Subthalamic Nucleus in Non-selective Cortico-Motor Inhibition." *Current Biology 32* (17): 3785–3791 e3783. doi: 10.1016/j.cub.2022.06.067.

Other Sources Used

Durstewitz, Daniel, Jeremy K. Seamans, and Terrence J. Sejnowski. 2000. "Dopamine-Mediated Stabilization of Delay-Period Activity in a Network Model of Prefrontal Cortex." *Journal of Neurophysiology* 83 (3): 1733–1750.

Eling, Paul, Kristianne Derckx, and Roald Maes. 2008. "On the Historical and Conceptual Background of the Wisconsin Card Sorting Test." *Brain and Cognition* 67 (3): 247–253. doi: 10.1016/j.bandc.2008.01.006.

Falkenstein, Michael, Joachim Hohnsbein, and Jörg Hoormann. 1990. "Effects of Errors in Choice Reaction Tasks on the ERP under Focused and Divided Attention." In *Physiological Brain Research*, vol. 1, edited by Cornelis Henri Marie Brunia, Anthony W. K. Gaillard, and A. Kok, 192–195. Tilburg, NL: Tilburg University Press.

Harlow, Harry F. 1949. "The Formation of Learning Sets." *Psychological Review* 56: 51–65.

Lhermitte, François. 1986. "Human Autonomy and the Frontal Lobes. Part II: Patient Behavior in Complex and Social Situations: The 'Environmental Dependency Syndrome." *Annals of Neurology* 19 (4): 335–343. doi: 10.1002/ana.410190405.

Lisman, John E., Jean-Marc Fellous, and Xiao-Jing Wang. 1998. "A Role for NMDA-Receptor Channels in Working Memory." *Nature Neuroscience* 1 (4): 273–275. doi: 10.1038/1086.

MacLeod, Colin M. 1991. "Half a Century of Research on the Stroop Effect: An Integrative Review." *Psychological Bulletin* 109 (2): 163–203. doi: 10.1037/0033-2909.109.2.163.

Miller, Earl K., and Timothy J. Buschman. 2013. "Cortical Circuits for the Control of Attention." *Current Opinion in Neurobiology* 23 (2): 216–222. doi: 10.1016/j.conb.2012.11.011.

Montague, P. Read, Peter Dayan, and Terrence J. Sejnowski. 1996. "A Framework for Mesencephalic Dopamine Systems Based on Predictive Hebbian Learning." *Journal of Neuroscience* 16 (5): 1936–1947.

Settlage, Paul, Myra Zable, and Harry F. Harlow. 1948. "Problem Solution by Monkeys Following Bilateral Removal of the Prefrontal Areas: VI. Performance on Tests Requiring Contradictory Reactions to Similar and to Identical Stimuli." *Journal of Experimental Psychology* 38 (1): 50–65. doi: 10.1037/h0054430.

Skinner, James E., and Charles D. Yingling. 1976. "Regulation of Slow Potential Shifts in Nucleus Reticularis Thalami by the Mesencephalic Reticular Formation and the Frontal Granular Cortex." *Electroencephalography and Clinical Neurophysiology* 40 (3): 288–296. doi: 10.1016/0013-4694(76)90152-8.

Yingling, Charles D., and James E. Skinner. 1976. "Selective Regulation of Thalamic Sensory Relay Nuclei by Nucleus Reticularis Thalami." *Electroencephalography and Clinical Neurophysiology* 41 (5): 476–482. doi: 10.1016/0013-4694(76)90059-6.

Zable, Myra, and Harry F. Harlow. 1946. "The Performance of Rhesus Monkeys on Series of Object-Quality and Positional Discriminations and Discrimination Reversals." *Journal of Comparative Psychology* 39 (1): 13–23. doi: 10.1037/h0056082.

Further Reading

Knight, Robert T., and Mark D'Esposito. 2003. "Lateral Prefrontal Syndrome: A Disorder of Executive Control." In *Neurological Foundations of Cognitive Neuroscience*, edited by Mark D'Esposito (pp. 259–280). Cambridge, MA: MIT Press.

An authoritative review, from two behavioral neurologists, of the clinical presentation, and theoretical interpretations, of patients with damage to the lateral PFC.

Miller, Earl K., and Jonathan D. Cohen. 2001. "An Integrative Theory of Prefrontal Cortex Function." *Annual Review of Neuroscience* 24: 167–202.

Paper that really set the agenda for cognitive control research for the first decade of the new millennium.

Miller, Earl K., and Timothy J. Buschman. 2013. "Cortical Circuits for the Control of Attention." *Current Opinion in Neurobiology* 23 (2): 216–222. doi: 10.1016/j.conb.2012.11.011.

Summary of evidence, from human and monkey research, of the key role for interareal oscillatory synchrony as a mechanism for cognitive control.

Passingham, Richard E., and Steven P. Wise. 2012. *The Neurobiology of the Prefrontal Cortex.* Oxford: Oxford University Press.

A systematic, focused, theory of frontal-lobe function, including a unique and provocative evolutionary focus, from two leading students of its anatomy, physiology, and function.

Stuss, Donald T., and Robert T. Knight, eds. 2013. *Principles of Frontal Lobe Function*, 2nd ed. New York: Oxford University Press.

An exhaustive collection of chapters from many of the world's authorities on the myriad functions of the PFC.

Wessel, Jan R. 2012. "Error Awareness and the Error-Related Negativity: Evaluating the First Decade of Evidence." *Frontiers in Human Neuroscience* 6: 88. doi: 10.3389/fnhum.2012.00088.

Review of the nuanced and fascinating literature on the role of awareness in performance monitoring and the ERN.

CHAPTER 16

Decision Making

KEY THEMES

- Three classes of decisions that are each studied differently, and may be differently implemented by the brain, are perceptual decisions, value-based decisions (the focus of neuroeconomics), and foraging decisions.
- Microstimulation of MT influences the decisions that monkeys make about the visually perceived direction of motion.
- Signal detection theory and diffusion-decision modeling (DDM) interpret the activity of LIP neurons as representing the buildup of evidence in a decision variable.
- Neural signals that track the accumulation of evidence also index the subjective sense of confidence about a decision.
- DDMs capture in exquisite detail how the dynamics of interactions between basal ganglia nuclei control the timing of the activity that implements a decision.
- In a value-based oculomotor decision task, LIP neurons can represent the value of a saccade, raising the possibility that the representation of a motor value map, rather than an attentional priority map, may be the fundamental function of the oculomotor system.
- Extracellular electrophysiology in the monkey implicates orbital and ventromedial PFC (OFC) in the representation of the "common currency" that underlies behavioral economic theory.
- The choice of whether or not to do something (whether or not to "accept an offer") is influenced by the value to be gained, as well as by the value associated with a similar offer made in the past (represented in OFC), and by the effort that would need to be expended if the offer were accepted.
- In contrast to explicit two-alternative forced choice decision, foraging entails the weighing of different factors – the value of exploiting vs. the value of exploring, conditioned by the cost of exploring – to decide how to guide behavior.

CONTENTS

Companion Website: www.wiley.com/go/postle/cognitiveneuroscience3e

Between Perception and Action

The simplest sensorimotor event is the reflex – the patellar tendon of your knee is tapped by the doctor's mallet, and your leg kicks out. This response to a stimulus involves just one synapse in the CNS: the stretch receptor in your quadriceps muscle makes a synaptic connection, in the spinal cord, directly onto a motor neuron which, in turn, commands a contraction of the quadriceps muscle. This circuit is called a reflex arc, and its action does not entail any kind of decision. Once initiated, its outcome is known with certainty. It is a deterministic system.

For behaviors that qualify as cognitive, on the other hand, all actions can be said to be the result of a decision. Most are not deterministic: given the same stimulus inputs, an individual may respond to it in different ways, depending on the context, the current state of any of many systems in his brain, and recent history with the same or similar types of stimuli.

There are three domains of decision making that we will consider here. **Perceptual decisions** are closely related to the processes of recognition – "snap" decisions by which we classify what kind of thing we are seeing (or hearing, or feeling, or . . .) and then take the appropriate action – *If that pedestrian is walking out into the street, I will apply my brakes; if she is standing still, I will continue driving past the crosswalk.* **Value-based decisions** are the purview of **neuroeconomics** – *Out of the (seemingly) hundreds of choices on the shelves, which bottle of red wine will I select to purchase and bring home to enjoy with dinner?* The third domain, **foraging decisions**, evokes (for this author, at least) that timeless question posed by the British punk rock band The Clash: *Should I stay or should I go?* That is, *Do I remain where I am to* exploit *the resources currently before me, or do I set out to* explore *new opportunities?* (This is yet another question that makes important contact with reinforcement learning models.)

We begin with perceptual decision making – *was the overall direction of motion within that cloud of dots moving up or down?* We'll begin, as we have in other domains of cognitive neuroscience, by considering the "laws of . . . optics . . . and receptor binding" From this starting point, how far will we get in our understanding of this behavior, and its neural underpinnings, before, as Wolfram Schultz admonished in the previous chapter, we need to turn to the behavioral sciences, particularly psychology and economics, for models that will help us understand even this simplest of decision-making behaviors?

Perceptual Decision Making

Microstimulation of MT

Decisions about sensory stimuli are a scientifically tractable place to start because one can systematically vary properties of the inputs and determine how this variation influences the decision, thereby gaining important knowledge about how the decision-making process works. A highly influential example of such an experiment, performed in the laboratory of neurophysiologist William Newsome, is illustrated in *Figure 16.1*. Newsome, Britten, and Movshon (1989) had previously studied the relationship between the activity of neurons in MT and a monkey's decision about whether the overall, integrated motion signal from a cloud of randomly moving dots (referred to as the "global" motion of the cloud, to distinguish it from the "local" motion of any one dot) was in one direction or another. Intriguingly, they found that the stimulus-related activity of some individual MT neurons was as good as, and in some cases even better than, the performance of the monkey! As a next step, to establish the causal role of MT neurons tuned to a specific direction of motion in the animal's decisions about motion in that direction, they performed the experiment illustrated in *Figure 16.1*.

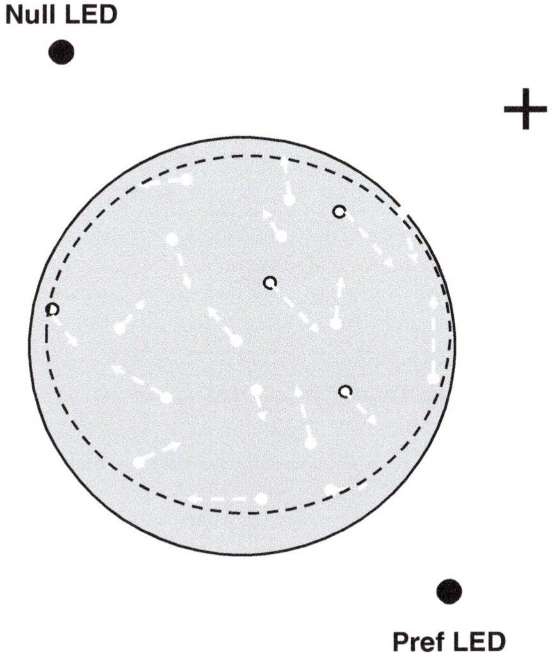

FIGURE 16.1 Influencing perceptual decisions with microstimulation. Diagram of the task, in which the directional tuning of an MT neuron was first determined (in this illustration, down and to the right), and then the monkey performed several trials in which random dot motion (RDM) was presented in a stimulus aperture that covered the neuron's receptive field (dotted circle). For each, the animal made a forced choice as to whether the global direction of motion was toward the location marked "Pref LED," or toward the "Null LED," and indicated its decision with a saccade made to that LED. The strength of the motion signal was controlled by varying the percentage of dots all moving in the same direction, such that a 25% "correlation" meant that 25% of the dots were moving in the neuron's preferred (Pref) direction, and a −8% correlation that 8% of the dots were moving in the neuron's anti-preferred (Null) direction. (This cartoon shows a display in which the four highlighted dots are producing a 21% correlation.) On a randomly determined subset of trials, microstimulation was delivered to the neuron.

The results were striking. Let's first consider just one data point in panel A of *Figure 16.2* – the *no stimulation* trials when the RDM stimulus contained 0% correlated motion. On these trials, there was no global motion, and the animal decided *Pref* on roughly half the trials (visual inspection suggests roughly 55% of these trials). Now look at its performance on the perceptually identical trials when microstimulation was delivered to an MT neuron tuned to detect motion in the *Pref* direction: on *stimulation* trials, the monkey decided *Pref* much more often, somewhere between 65% and 70% of the time. The same is true, qualitatively, at every level of stimulus signal strength, when there was true global motion in one of the two directions.

When thinking about the effect of microstimulation for one stimulus type (e.g., 0% correlation), it might be easier to think about it in terms of "How does microstimulation influence the monkey's decision?" Answer: it biases the animal to give more *Pref* responses. But this leads to additional questions whose answers are less straightforward. For example, does this mean that microstimulation makes the monkey *perceive* more of the stimuli as having motion in the preferred direction? Of course, we can't know this with any certainty, and so this makes characterization of the effects of microstimulation in terms of the animal's performance seem somehow subjective and less than satisfying. For this reason, even though on a stimulus-by-stimulus basis the effect of microstimulation is to move each data point "up" relative to the ordinate, a more useful way to quantify its effects is in terms of how it shifts the animal's psychometric curve along the abscissa. The reason is that this allows the effects of microstimulation to be quantified in terms of the physical properties of the stimulus that was varied in order to derive this curve. Thus, for the stimulation site depicted in the upper panel of *Figure 16.2*, microstimulation was equivalent to adding 7.7% dots moving in the preferred direction to each stimulus display. For the site in the lower panel, the effect was much larger, corresponding to a shift of 20.1% correlated dots in the preferred direction. (Note that, for both sites illustrated, particularly the one in the lower panel, there also seems to be some distortion to the shape of the psychometric function. What might explain this?)

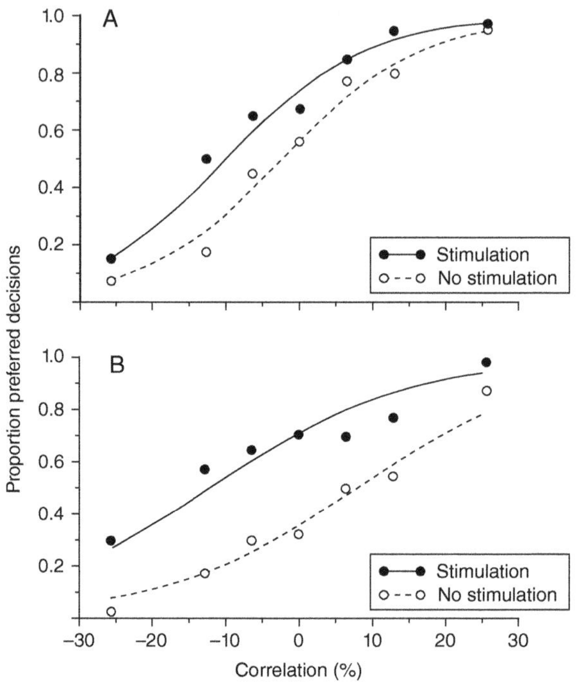

FIGURE 16.2 The results of varying the strength of the motion signal, and of microstimulation, at two stimulation sites within MT (one stimulation site is illustrated in (**A**), the other in (**B**). The data are plotted as the animal's choice (expressed as the proportion of saccades made to the Pref LED) as a function of motion signal strength (Correlation).

Source: Salzman et al., 1990 / Springer Nature.

Part of the importance of the Salzman, Britten, and Newsome (1990) study was that it prescribed a well-understood circuit in which perceptual decision making could be studied in greater depth: first, the microstimulation results indicated that MT is, indeed, causally involved in perceptual decision making (about motion); second, the task was, in effect, a visually guided eye-movement task. "This link," as Gold and Shadlen (2007) point out, "enables investigators to treat the decision as a problem of movement selection" (p. 545)[1]. Because the eye-movement command would have to pass through FEF and/or SC, the logical next area to investigate in the perceptual decision-making process, one that links MT with these two oculomotor control centers, was the lateral intraparietal area (LIP).

Recording, and Microstimulating, in LIP

Because LIP is two synapses downstream from MT, the question is whether its contribution to the perceptual decision task reflects perceptual processing, decision making, or motor planning and execution. In keeping with the idea of treating the decision as a problem of movement selection, the procedure for studying neurons in LIP is to place one of the two saccade targets inside the neuron's motor field (i.e., not the aperture displaying the RDM). With this procedure, it turns out to be fairly straightforward to rule out a perceptual role for LIP, simply by examining trials that present RDM containing 0% correlated motion. On roughly half of these trials, a saccade will be made into the motor field of the neuron being recorded from, and on the other half, it will be made away from it. If the neuron's function were perceptual in nature, its response would be the same for both decisions, because on all trials the stimulus is identical. However, this is not what is observed. Instead, for the former, the neuron shows a gradual increase in firing rate until the time of the saccade, and for the latter, it shows a suppressed level of activity until after the saccade. Interpretation of the ramp-up observed on trials when the saccade will come into the neuron's motor field, however, is more complicated. One possibility is that it corresponds to an accumulation of information related to the decision. The alternative is that it represents motor preparation, the decision having already been made elsewhere. Is it possible to rule out one of these two accounts?

Initial evidence that activity in LIP may correspond to the buildup of decision-related information comes from the rate of increase in activity that is observed as a function of stimulus strength: on trials in which the RDM contains a larger percentage of correlated motion, the increase in firing rate is steeper than it is on trials presenting weaker directional information. Does this steeper increase in firing rate result in the animal reaching its decision more quickly? It turns out that it does, as can be determined by making a change to the experimental procedure: rather than having the animal make a response after a fixed-length, longish delay, allow it to respond as quickly as possible, incentivizing speed by providing larger rewards for quicker responses. The first thing one notices on the speeded variant of the task is that response time (RT) is slower for stimuli that provide weaker directional information. This pattern in the behavior is also seen in the activity of LIP neurons (*Figure 16.3*).

Modeling Perceptual Decision Making

A Psychological Model (Signal Detection Theory)

The framework used by Joshua Gold and Michael Shadlen (2007) to formalize perceptual decision making is signal detection theory (SDT), operationalized via diffusion-decision modeling (DDM; *Chapter 5*, section *Diffusion-decision modeling*). We can reprint here the quote from Gold and Shadlen that first appeared in that section: "A decision," they write, "is a deliberative process that results in the commitment to a categorical proposition. An apt analogy is a judge or jury that must take time to weigh evidence for alternative interpretations and/or possible ramifications before settling on a verdict" (p. 536). The key factors to understand, from this perspective, are

[1]This quote highlights a noteworthy terminological ambiguity: the same actions that might characterized from a theory-neutral perspective as "movement selection" are characterized from the perspective of reinforcement-learning (RL) theory as "decisions"/"decision-making".

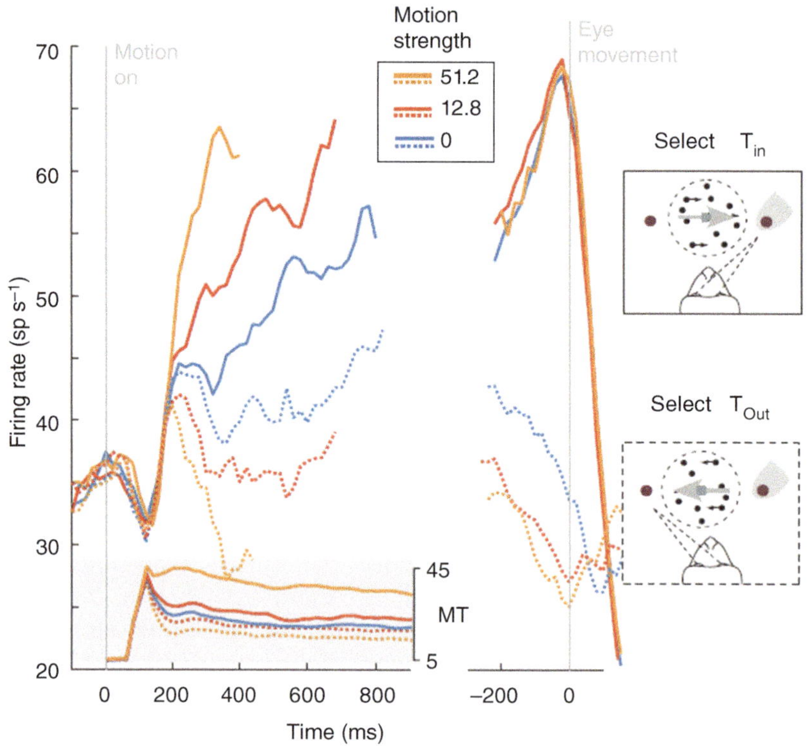

FIGURE 16.3 Activity in LIP, displayed as peristimulus time histograms (PSTHs), in speeded RDM direction decision task, as a function of motion strength and whether the direction selected corresponds to a saccade made into the neuron's motor field ("Select T_{in}"; solid lines) or away from the neuron's motor field ("Select T_{out}"; dotted lines). Data on the left are aligned to trial onset, and on the right are aligned to saccade onset. Inset, in shaded box in lower left, is activity in an MT neuron tuned for motion in the Select T_{in} direction.

Source: Gold et al., 2007 / Annual Reviews.

how the deliberative process works, and how it is translated into commitment. In *Figure 16.3*, the neural correlate of the deliberative process is captured by the evolution of any two same-colored PSTHs, which are interpreted as reflecting the temporal evolution of evidence for a *Select* T_{in} vs. a *Select* T_{out} decision. The sum of these two processes, running in parallel, is the decision variable, which Gold and Shadlen (2007) note "is not tied to the (possibly fleeting) appearance of stimuli [what they refer to as 'momentary evidence'] but spans the time from the first pieces of relevant information to the final choice" (p. 538) (i.e., accumulated evidence from the DDM; e.g., *Figure 5.13*). In this regard, the concept of the decision variable can be understood in relation to working memory, as can the sustained, elevated activity in LIP illustrated in *Figure 16.3*.

Regardless of stimulus strength, the theory predicts that the decision variable must achieve a certain value before a decision is made, and this would seem to correspond to when LIP neurons representing the decision (i.e., "Select T_{in}" from *Figure 16.3*) reach a firing rate of 70 Hz. Because LIP neurons achieve this level of activity with RDM displays containing no global direction information, they (and the hypothesized **decision variable**) must be receiving additional information apart from what is fed forward from MT. SDT holds that this additional information corresponds to expectations that have been built up over past experience ("prior probabilities" in terms of Bayesian statistics) and information about the reward value of the choice. More generally, one might think of it in terms of the predictive coding framework (*Chapter 5*, section *Predictive coding*) – where there is insufficient sensory evidence, behavior will be governed by the brain's current model of the environment.

To assess the neural bases of these hypothesized processes, Hanks, Ditterich, and Shadlen (2006) took a page from the book of Shadlen's postdoctoral mentor, William Newsome, and compared the effects of microstimulation delivered to MT vs. to LIP. They fit a DDM to the behavioral data from the monkeys and found that microstimulation of MT had the effect of steepening the drift rate in the model, thereby biasing decisions in favor of the direction preferred by the stimulated neurons. Quantitatively, the model indicated that MT microstimulation had an effect comparable to adding 9.3% correlated motion to the RDM display. (In the DDM, it increased the drift rate.) Microstimulation of LIP, in contrast, had an effect comparable to handicapping the "race" between *choose left* and *choose right*, by moving the decision variable corresponding to the location of microstimulation 16.9% closer to the decision boundary. Other studies, in which microstimulation was applied to the frontal eye field (FEF), have similarly produced results consistent with a role for FEF in evidence accumulation.

A Circuit Model of Spiking Neurons The model from Lo and Wang (2006) is a biophysically inspired spiking network model (*Figure 16.4*). That is, for even the most explicitly *neural* of the neural network models that we encountered in the previous two chapters (i.e., Rougier, Noelle, Braver, Cohen, and O'Reilly, 2005; Stedron, Sahni, and Munakata, 2005),

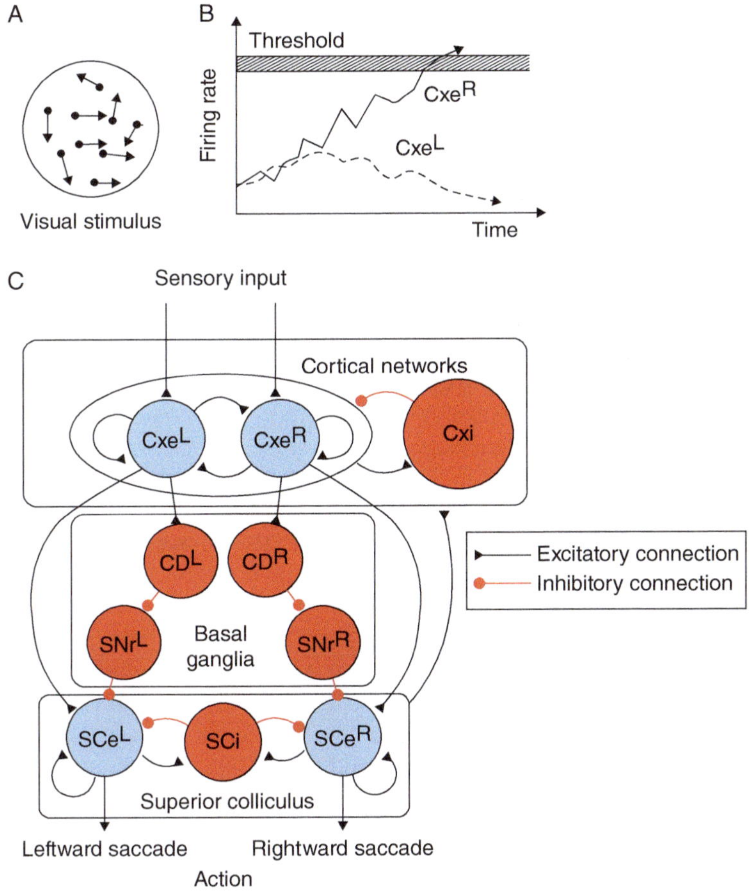

FIGURE 16.4 Corticobasal ganglia circuit mechanism for a decision threshold in reaction time tasks. **A.** Schematic of the RDM display. **B.** A schematic representation of the random walk in a DDM followed by two cortical populations (Cxe^L and Cxe^R), which we can think of as LIP neurons representing Select T_{in} and Select T_{out} from *Figure 16.3*. Commitment occurs (i.e., a saccade is generated) as soon as one of the population firing rates reaches the threshold. **C.** Schematic model architecture. Neural pools in the cortical network integrate sensory information and also compete against each other. They project to both the superior colliculus (SCe^L and SCe^R) and the caudate nucleus (CD^L and CD^R). Blue, populations of excitatory neurons; red, populations of inhibitory neurons. Each population is simulated by noisy spiking leaky integrate-and-fire neurons.

Source: Lo et al., 2006 / Springer Nature.

activation is passed from node to node as varying levels of an analog signal. Spiking network models, in contrast, explicitly simulate the analog-to-digital conversion that happens in biological neurons – the summation of postsynaptic currents that depolarize the neuron to the point of triggering the firing of one or more action potentials – then the "D to A" conversion at the synapse. When circuits in such models are recurrently connected with excitatory connections, they can achieve self-sustained stable states of activity within that circuit or, in this model from Lo and Wang (2006), evidence accumulation via "slow reverberatory network dynamics mediated by NMDA receptors" (p. 956) within and between the two modeled area LIPs (right and left hemisphere, commanding a leftward or rightward saccade, respectively). Ultimately, the decision is executed by burst neurons in the superior colliculus (SC). The commitment is achieved through a dynamic interplay between direct cortical input onto the SC and a basal ganglia-mediated input from cortex to caudate nucleus to substantia nigra pars reticulata (SNpr) to SC. The location of the threshold (i.e., how high the firing rate in LIP needs to get) is determined by the strength of synapses from cortex onto the caudate nucleus. This is because although LIP has a direct input to the SC, the excitatory influence of this input is counteracted by the tonic inhibition from the SNpr. (Here's a sentence from section *The superior colliculus, Chapter 9,* to refresh our memory about this detail from the oculomotor control system: *at any moment in time, most of the motor units in the deep layers of the superior colliculus are under tonic inhibition from the substantia nigra pars reticulata, an arrangement analogous to the tonic inhibition of thalamus by the GPi that we detailed in Chapter 8.*) Thus, a major conceptual contribution of the Lo and Wang (2006) model was to map the construct of the velocity of the decision variable from the DDM (i.e., its speed and its direction) to the dynamic interplay of activity in LIP, and of the construct from the DDM of starting distance from the threshold for commitment to a decision to the strength of corticostriatal synapses.

Controversy and Complications

Would you be surprised to learn that, in this realm of cognitive neuroscience, with important implications for questions like how we drive, or how we make choices as consumers, or how we carry out mental deliberation – there might be some controversy? Here, we'll briefly summarize some debates that have arisen since the publication of the work summarized in section *Modeling perceptual decision making.*

The necessity of LIP for perceptual decision making was called into question when it was reported that pharmacologically inactivating LIP in the monkey; Katz, Yates, Pillow, and Huk, 2016), or either posterior parietal cortex (PPC) or the Frontal Orienting Field (FOF)[2] in the rat (Yartsev, Hanks, Yoon, and Brody, 2018), had any appreciable effect on decision-making performance. Furthermore, in their study in rats, Michael Yartsev et al. (2018) demonstrated that it was pharmacological inactivation of a different region, the anterior dorsal striatum (ADS)[3], that disrupted perceptual decision-making performance. "The ADS," they reasoned, "is . . . ideally positioned to participate in evidence accumulation as part of its established role in action selection" (Yartsev et al., 2018, p. 2 of 24).

There are several points to be considered here. First, ramping activity consistent with an evidence accumulation process (c.f., *Figure 16.3*) has been reported in many brain areas, including each of those inactivated by Yartsev et al. (2018). Thus, at least implicitly, these authors are making the point that "not every area that shows activity correlated with a particular function can be assumed to be causally contributing to that function" (this author's quotes). Furthermore (and more interestingly), a strong interpretation of the inactivation results from Katz et al. (2016) and from Yartsev et al. (2018) is that it is in circuits responsible for the motoric consequences of a perceptual decision that one will find the activity that is necessary for the evidence accumulation that is assumed to be the basis for the decision. Note that this is a somewhat paradoxical proposition, because although if offers an explanation

[2] FOF is considered a rodent homologue of the primate FEF.

[3] In the rodent, the striatum is not anatomically divided into caudate nucleus and putamen, but the ADS is generally considered to be homologous to the head of the caudate nucleus in the primate.

for why inactivation of putatively sensory areas (PPC and FOF) did not disrupt performance, it is also consistent with the logic of the procedure described by Gold and Shadlen (2007) as "enabl[ing] investigators to treat the decision as a problem of movement selection" (p. 454); that is, a procedure that explicitly relied on a motoric interpretation of activity in LIP. (We'll also see another complication with the "action rather than perception" account in the next paragraph.) Finally, the two studies that we summarized in the previous paragraph invite us to consider inferences that can be drawn from inactivation results vs. microstimulation results. The title of the paper from Yartsev et al. (2018) is "Causal contribution and dynamical encoding in the striatum during evidence accumulation," and Katz et al. (2016), in discussing their results, state that "Our results reveal a dissociation between decision-related activity in LIP and the causal role of such activity in decision making" (p. 287). The message is that disruption of the functioning of a region supports inferences about the necessity of that region's activity for a cognitive function of interest. Although this is true, it does not speak to the fact that microstimulation (as used, e.g., by Hanks et al., 2006) also supports strong inference about having *causally* influenced perceptual decision-making performance. Interpreting the results of microstimulation experiments can be complicated (c.f., Katz et al., 2016), but so, too, is interpreting the implications of null results (i.e. failures to show that inactivation of LIP disrupts decision-making performance).[4]

Another twist in our understanding of the contributions of LIP to perceptual decision making has come from Yang Zhou and David Freedman (2019), who also noted that most research on perceptual decision making has been carried out in the context of tasks that emphasize "deciding where to move." What if, instead, they asked, LIP was assessed in a test of "deciding what you are looking at" (p. 180)? To do this, Zhou and Freedman (2019) trained their monkeys to perform a motion-direction categorization task – five directions in one 180° arc, and five in the other – and a motion-direction discrimination task comparable to the ones illustrated in *Figure 16.1* and *Figure 16.3*. Then they infused muscimol into LIP in one hemisphere to determine the effect of pharmacologically inactivating LIP on task performance. An important difference from the previous tasks, however, was that they varied whether it was the saccade with which the monkey indicated its decision that would be directed into the affected receptive field, or the stimulus about which the monkey was making its decision that would be presented in the affected receptive field. Their results indicated that inactivation of LIP had a much larger effect on performance on trials when the stimulus was presented in the impaired receptive field than when the decision-guided movement had to be made into the bad receptive field. Thus, they concluded that "LIP plays an important role in visually based perceptual and categorical decisions, with preferential involvement in stimulus evaluation compared with motor-planning aspects of such decisions" (p. 181).

Confidence in Decision Making

As we saw in *Chapter 15*, feedback from our actions is important both for controlling our behavior in the moment (as demonstrated, e.g., with the WCST; section *Perseveration* and section *Influence of the DA reward prediction error on the functions of PFC*) and for learning (as demonstrated, e.g., in the willingness-to-wait task; section *Dissecting Frontal Contributions to the Control of Behavior*). But what about situations in which no external feedback is available? It is believed that, in such situations, one's confidence can be an important factor in guiding decision making. Here we'll review one aspect of how confidence can be studied in the context of the now-familiar discrimination-of-direction-of-motion task.

In parallel with the research summarized in the previous section, all of it carried out in nonhuman animal models, research in humans with electroencephalography (EEG) and magnetoencephalography (MEG) has also identified neural correlates of perceptual decision making. One of these is a positive-going component recorded at centro-parietal electrodes,

[4]In principle, "necessity" and "causality" are two different concepts. Whether one or the other of these methods—inactivation vs. microstimulation—is better suited, a priori, to demonstrate either of these properties, is an interesting and important question.

known as the CPP. Wei Dou et al. (2024), in the laboratory of Jason Samaha, have noted that the CPP "behaves as an accumulating decision variable that predicts evidence quality, RT [reaction time], accuracy, and confidence" (p. 270), and were intrigued in particular about the latter, because confidence is not a variable that is accounted for in classical applications of DDM (as introduced in *Chapter 5*, section *Diffusion-decision modeling*; and as reviewed, e.g., in section *Modeling perceptual decision making*). To assess the influence of confidence on the CPP, they carried out experiments requiring a left-right discrimination about an RDM, and varied motion coherence across several levels. The behavioral results showed that reaction time (RT), accuracy, and confidence each varied monotonically with motion coherence (i.e., as coherence increased, RT decreased, accuracy increased, and confidence increased). Furthermore, as illustrated in *Figure 16.5*, the steepness of the CPP (taken as a neural correlate of the drift rate) was sensitive to each of these factors. Importantly, although RT, accuracy, and confidence are all correlated, the authors were able to show a statistically unique contribution of confidence. Thus, it may be that, not unlike effort (see *Chapter 14*, section *"Trying harder"*), confidence is a subjective state that manifests in neural activity as modulation of the signals that are critical for carrying out the behavior in question. Indeed, this is how it's framed in a "highlight" summary of a study carried out more recently in monkeys by Ariel Zylberberg and Michael Shadlen (2025): "Choice, reaction time, and confidence may be represented by the same population of neurons."

Deciding *When* to Move

In section *Controversy and complications* we saw that the details of how one administers a perceptual decision-making task can influence the extent to which it can be shown to emphasize "*what* you see" vs. "*where* you move." Next, although the task that we consider will also entail dot-motion discrimination, the process under study is yet a different dimension of decision making: deciding *when* to move.

The Roles of Basal Ganglia Nuclei in the Control of Movement The title of a paper describing a study carried out in monkeys by David Thura and Paul Cisek (2017) provides a concise one-sentence summary of the take-home point of this section: "The basal ganglia do not select reach targets but control the urgency of commitment." In particular, the authors found that whereas neurons in PMC and M1 exhibited strong preparatory encoding of the target of an impending reach, such evidence was considerably weaker and delayed in time in the GPi and GPe. Instead, the activity in these basal ganglia nuclei was closely tied to the timing of movement execution via what they characterized as an "urgency signal" that modulated the gain of activity in cortical areas, seemingly determining the rate of build-up of the preparatory activity until it reached a threshold. To consider these mechanisms in detail, we'll turn to a 2025 study in which Nadja Ging-Jehli and colleagues in the laboratory of Michael Frank fit data from human neurosurgical patients to decision diffusion models (DDM, see *Chapter 5*, section *Diffusion-decision modeling*).

Figure 16.6.C illustrates the task from Ging-Jehli et al. (2025) in which patients with neurological movement disorders (Parkinson's disease or dystonia) viewed a display of moving dots and indicated, with a button press, whether the majority of dots was moving leftward or rightward (relative to vertical). Difficulty was manipulated via two orthogonal factors: *discriminability* (operationalized as the ratio of dots moving in one direction relative to the other [a.k.a., motion coherence]) and *conflict* (operationalized as the angular distance of the directions of motion from vertical). Coherence is a perceptual factor akin to contrast, with, for example, neurons in MT responding at a higher rate to the same direction of motion under high- vs. low-coherence conditions – within a classical DDM framework, coherence is positively related to drift rate. Conflict, on the other hand, is considered to be a cognitive factor, because even under conditions of high coherence, subjects have more difficulty indicating their binary decision when the direction is close to the category boundary. (E.g., although

FIGURE 16.5 The influence of confidence on the CPP during perceptual decision making.

Source: (Dou et al., 2024) / Association for Psychological Science / CC BY-NC 4.0.

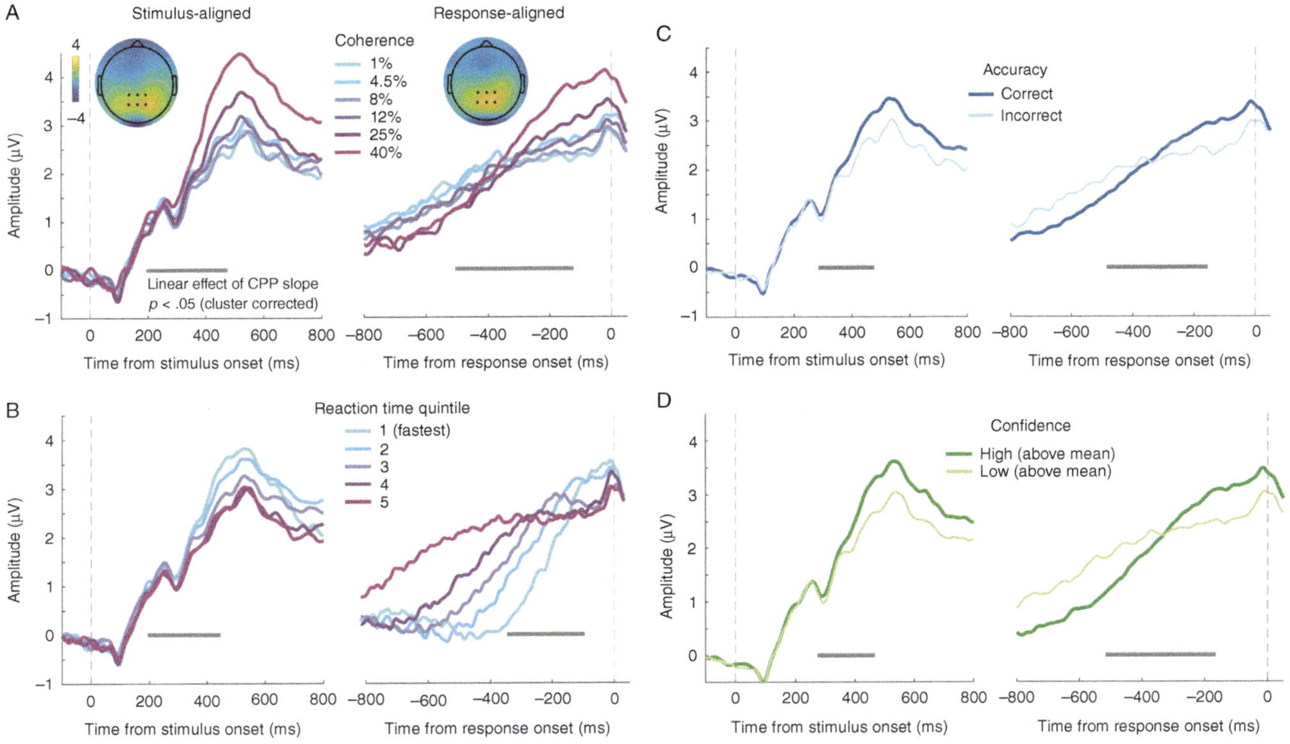

FIGURE 16.5.A The group average CPP plotted as a function of motion coherence of the RDM. Data in the left-hand panel are time-locked to stimulus onset, and in the right panel to the button-press response. The horizontal gray bar that is level with the 0 value on the vertical axis indicates time points when the effect of coherence on CPP slope was statistically significant. Insets show scalp topography of the ERP measured 250–450 msec after stimulus onset (left) and −510 to −130 msec prior to the response (right).

FIGURE 16.5.B The group average CPP plotted as a function of RT. (All conventions same as panel **A**.)

FIGURE 16.5.C The group average CPP plotted as a function of accuracy. (All conventions same as panel **A**.)

FIGURE 16.5.D The group average CPP plotted as a function of confidence. Subjects made the "right-left" response (yielding the data in panels **B** and **D**) with their right hand, and after each response indicated confidence on a 1–4 scale with their left hand. (All conventions same as panel **A**.)

both panels in the left-hand column of *Figure 16.6.C* illustrate trials with equally high coherence, subjects have more difficulty responding "left" on the trial displayed in the bottom panel because its direction of motion is close to vertical, which is the category boundary between "left" and "right.") *Figure 16.6.A* and *Figure 16.6.B* illustrate the theoretical factors hypothesized to account for basal ganglia contributions to motor control: the classical DDM decomposition of RT into the latent variables of nondecision time and the drifting accumulation of evidence that pushes the system over a decision threshold (*Figure 16.6.A*, c.f., *Figure 5.13*); and the modification of the classical DDM to accommodate a phenomenon that has been added to the DDM to help it better fit empirical data – "collapsing decision boundaries"

FIGURE 16.6 DDM dynamics and the dot-motion task from Ging-Jehli et al. (2025).

Source: (Ging-Jehli et al., 2025) / PLOS / CC BY 4.0.

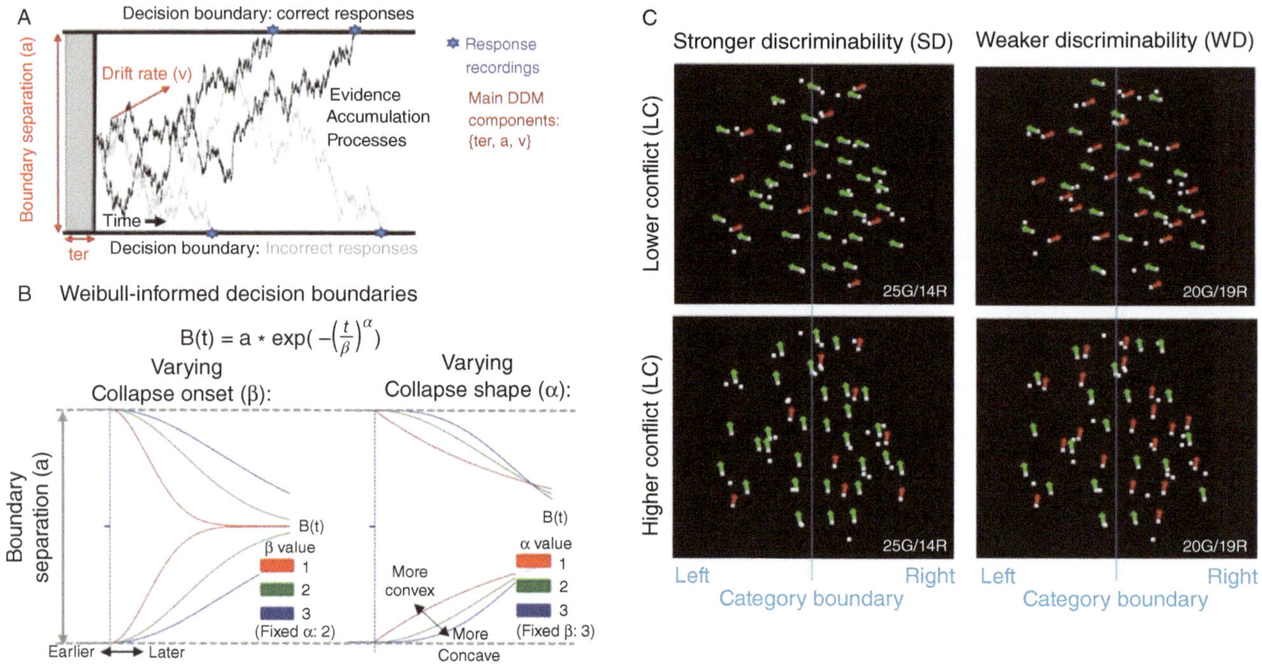

FIGURE 16.6.A The dynamics of four trials as modeled by a classical DDM with fixed decision boundaries ("ter" stands for *Time for sensory Encoding and Response execution*, referred to as nondecision time in *Chapter 5*, section *Diffusion-decision modeling*).

FIGURE 16.6.B The "Weibull-informed" DDM modified to account for collapsing decision boundaries. (The Weibull distribution is a formal tool for estimating how long a process will last.) The panel labeled "Varying collapse onset (β)" illustrates the time course of collapse of the decision boundary at three values of the β parameter, which parameterizes the onset of collapse; the panel labeled "Varying collapse shape (α)" illustrates the time course of collapse at three values of the α parameter, which parameterizes to the trajectory (along the convex-concave dimension) of the collapse.

FIGURE 16.6.C Illustration of each trial type in the 2 (discriminability) × 2 (conflict) design of the dot-motion task. Green and red arrows are used here to illustrate leftward and rightward direction of motion (respectively), and the dashed blue line to illustrate the decision boundary, but none of these appeared in the actual task.

Source: Ging-Jehli et al. (2025) / PUBLIC LIBRARY OF SCIENCE (PLOS) / CC BY 4.0.

(*Figure 16.6.B.*; that is, in some circumstances the best explanation of performance is that "it's not that evidence continued accumulating, rather, the process 'got tired of waiting' and brought the decision threshold closer to the level of accumulated evidence").

Behavioral results showed higher overall accuracy for strong vs. weak discriminability trials (mean difference of 8.3%), and although RTs were faster overall for correct responses (mean difference: −100 ms), correct responses were slower for high-conflict than for low-conflict trials. Fits of these behavioral data to the modified DDM indicated that whereas stronger discriminability was associated with higher drift rates, higher conflict was associated with a prolongation of the collapse of the decision boundary, due to a combination of delayed collapse onset and the trajectory of the collapse being more concave (*Figure 16.7*; that is, the trajectory of the time course of the collapse of decision boundaries can vary). Next, by adding trial-by-trial measures of theta-band power as neural regressors into the modified DDM (*Figure 16.8.A*), the authors were able to associate different aspects of the dynamics of these latent variables with patterns of activity in different basal ganglia nuclei. Beginning with strong perceptual discriminability, for STN, theta-band power was positively related to the greater concavity of the boundary collapse (as captured by the α parameter of the DDM) on SD-HC trials, and, to a lesser extent, to the more rapid onset of boundary collapse (as captured by the β parameter of the DDM) on SD-HC trials. For the GPe, decreases

FIGURE 16.7 Decision making under varying levels of perceptual discriminability and cognitive conflict, from Ging-Jehli et al. (2025).

Source: Ging-Jehli et al. (2025) / PLOS / CC BY 4.0.

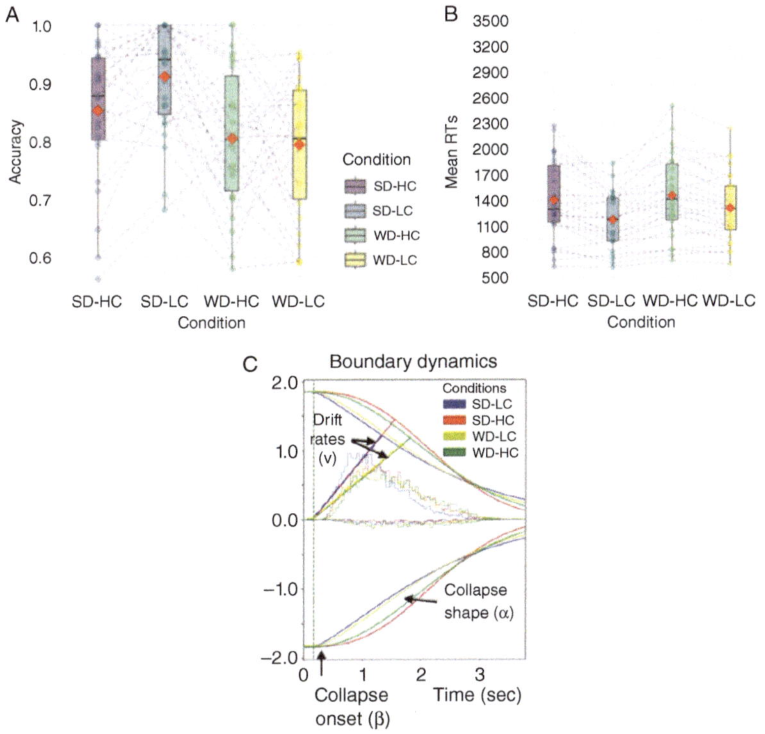

FIGURE 16.7.A Descriptive statistics: accuracy by trial type: strong discriminability-low conflict (SD-LC); strong discriminability-high conflict (SD-HC); weak-discriminability-low conflict (WD-LC); weak discriminability-high conflict (WD-HC). Group-averaged data are displayed as boxplots with means indicated by red diamonds. Data from individual subjects are connected by dotted lines.

FIGURE 16.7.B Descriptive statistics: Reaction time (RT) broken out by trial type (abbreviations and plotting conventions same as panel **A**.)

FIGURE 16.7.C Behavioral data fit to the DDM with collapsing decision boundaries. The "blocky" lines are the outlines of histograms of RTs, by trial type (note that the relatively small number of error trials makes the four histograms that are "pointing down" impossible to discriminate). The trial- and group-averaged drift rates indicate that the rate of evidence accumulation was higher for strong- than weak-discriminability trials, but is insensitive to the level of conflict. Turning to the collapsing decision boundaries, the shape parameter (α) was more concave for higher- than lower-conflict trials, and more so with strong- than weak-discriminability. Collapse onset (β) was marginally delayed for higher than lower-conflict trials. The vertical axis indicates "units of accumulated evidence" – a measure of distance in evidence space that does not have an inherent unit and depends on the scaling of other model parameters.

in theta-band power on SD-HC trials were associated with markedly more rapid onset of the boundary collapse (*Figure 16.8.B*). Thus, in conditions of high perceptual discriminability, whereas the function of STN could be summarized as promotion of more cautious and accurate decision making under high conflict, that of the GPe could be summarized as hurrying the commitment to a decision under low conflict (i.e., when there's "no point in waiting longer" to accumulate more information). Under conditions of weak perceptual discriminability, the role of the STN was considerably reduced, with GPe playing a more prominent role in slowing or speeding decisions as a function of conflict (*Figure 16.8.C*). For the GPi, regardless of condition, increases in theta-band power were associated with delaying the onset of boundary collapse.

FIGURE 16.8 DDM analysis of the contribution of basal ganglia nuclei to decision-making dynamics. **Source:** Ging-Jehli et al. (2025) / PLOS / CC BY 4.0.

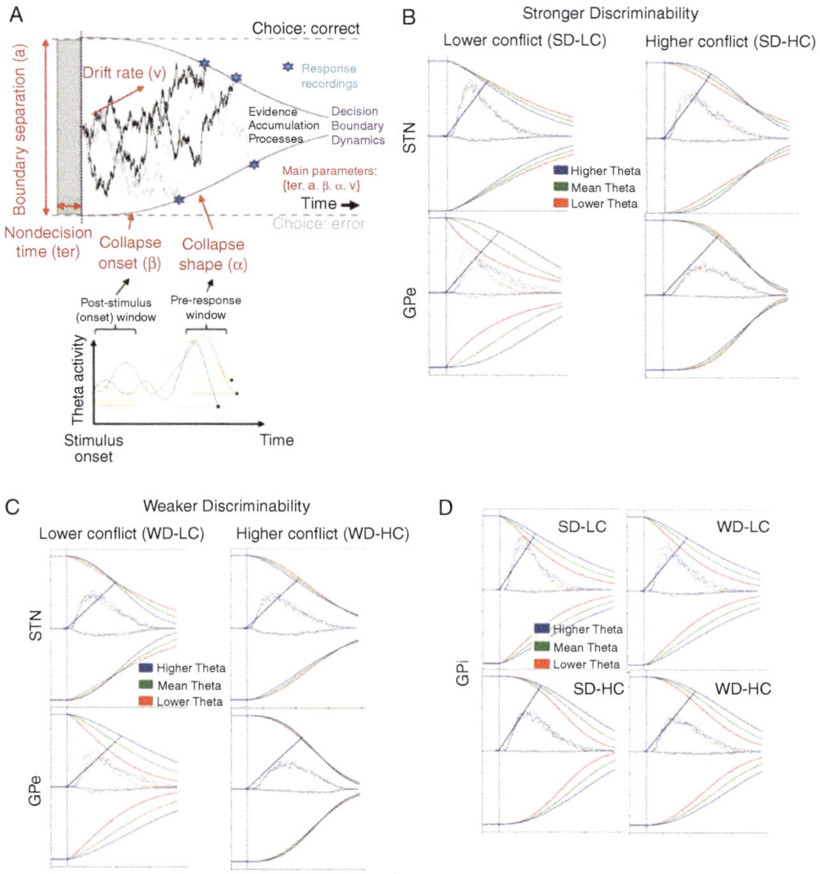

FIGURE 16.8.A Schematic illustration of how neural data are incorporated into the modified DDM, with the bottom plot indicating that theta-band power from the 500 msec following stimulus onset, from each of the three nuclei (color coded), is used to estimate the β parameter, and theta-band power from the 500 msec preceding the response is used (also from each of the three nuclei) to estimate the α parameter.

FIGURE 16.8.B Under strong perceptual discriminability: the influence of the STN and the GPe, at three levels of theta-band power, on drift rate and boundary dynamics at two levels of conflict.

FIGURE 16.8.C Under weak perceptual discriminability: the influence of the STN and the GPe, at three levels of theta-band power, on drift rate and boundary dynamics at two levels of conflict.

FIGURE 16.8.D In all four conditions, the effect of increased theta-band power in GPi was to slow the response by delaying the onset of the collapse of the decision boundary.

There's a sense in which the study that we've just summarized could be construed as addressing what some might consider rather "low level" details about the precise timing of finger movements. However, framing the timing of motor execution as a decision-making problem emphasizes the agency and choice that are fundamental to skeletomotor control, and illustrates, again, how an aspect of high-level cognition can be understood as an elaboration of principles from motor control. It also provides a novel perspective on a behavioral phenomenon that is characteristic of patients with Parkinson's disease, as well as of toddlers who are just learning to walk: freezing while trying to walk through an open doorway. If one is approaching an open doorway in a straight line, there's no obvious need for a change of the kinematics of one's gait, because there are no obstacles to avoid. However, if the relative narrowness (and/or lowness) of a doorway is processed as something akin to a "high conflict" condition (a la Ging-Jehli et al., 2025), the effect on dysfunctional or developing basal ganglia circuits may be an exaggerated prolongation of the onset of the collapse of decision boundaries.[5]

Why Do I Have to Decide?

Up until now in this chapter, and really in the entire book, we've given little-to-no consideration to what is the reason that human and nonhuman research subjects even bother to perform hundreds (for humans) or thousands of trials in these cognitive neuroscience experiments that, no matter how clever and insightful in their motivation and design, are invariably quite repetitive and boring for the subject. They do it, of course, for the rewards that they receive for diligent compliance with instructions/rules, and for accurate performance. This falls under the rubric of "value-based decision making," and it is to this that we next turn our attention.

Value-Based Decision Making

> Most decision theories – from expected utility theory in economics (von Neumann and Morgenstern, 1944) to prospect theory in psychology (Kahneman and Tversky, 1979) to reinforcement learning theories in computer science (Sutton and Barto, 1998) – share a core conclusion. Decision makers integrate the various dimensions of an option into a single measure of its idiosyncratic subjective value and then choose the option that is most valuable. Comparisons between different kinds of options rely on this abstract measure of subjective value, a kind of "common currency" for choice. That humans can in fact compare apples to oranges when they buy fruit is evidence for this abstract common scale. (Kable and Glimcher, 2009, p. 734)

Thus, the quest for the common currency will be an important theme underlying this section of this chapter.

From the outset, value-based decision making would seem to be different in kind from the perceptual decision making that we just covered. Whereas the latter entails a decision about the objective state of the world – either the dots were drifting up or they were drifting down – the former is inherently subjective – if you randomly select two people and present them with the same choice, one can prefer the apple and one can prefer the orange, and neither of these choices can be said to be wrong. This is also called economic choice, as the quote from Kable and Glimcher indicates, and economists have studied this aspect of behavior for decades. In the context of this textbook, what we'll be discussing has come to be referred to as neuroeconomics. To get started, we'll begin with an experimental procedure that shares many surface characteristics with the perceptual decision-making studies that we have just reviewed, and that measures neural activity in familiar territory.

---

[5] For this author, these considerations also suggest a possible neural correlate of nonpathological behaviors that are best classified as "social". In particular, have you ever noticed how, when the elevator doors open, the person standing next to you will hesitate to step out of the elevator until you begin to move? Or how, when stopped at a red light on a multi-lane road, the driver of the car in the lane next to you will sometimes wait for you to start moving before they do? Might these be demonstrations of a kind of elevated "social conflict," one that we may not be overtly aware of but whose existence peeks out during these mundane interactions?

The Influence of Expected Value on Activity in LIP

This study by Michael Platt and Paul Glimcher (1999), two prominent figures in neuroeconomics research, was designed from the perspective that "nearly all theories require the decision maker to have some knowledge of two environmental variables: the gain expected to result from an action and the probability that the expected gain will be realized." In expected-value theory, for example, "a rational decision-maker should multiply expected gain by the probability of gain to establish an expected value for each course of action, and then should choose the option with the highest expected value" (p. 233). To evaluate this idea, they trained monkeys to fixate centrally while two target stimuli were presented in the periphery, one always in the movement field of the LIP neuron being recorded. Upon offset of the fixation point, the monkey was rewarded for making a saccade to either target (i.e., it was a "free choice"). For the first block of trials, the amount of juice reward associated with each of the targets (i.e., the gain) was identical. Subsequently, the gain associated with each target was modified, such that selection of one yielded 0.15 ml of juice, and the other 0.05 ml. These gains were switched between the targets, on a block-by-block basis, such that across several blocks of trials, each LIP neuron was recorded under perceptually identical conditions, but when the expected gain of selecting the target in its movement field was relatively high or relatively low.

The results, illustrated in *Figure 16.9.A*, revealed a marked difference in the response profile of LIP neurons for high-gain vs. low-gain decisions, with the former showing elevated activity even prior to target onset. (One can speculate that, even prior to target onset, the animal had "already made up its mind.") Note, however, that this was no longer true at the time of response. It is also important to note that the monkeys did not always simply choose the target with the highest expected gain. Rather, they followed the "matching law," a tendency for animals to allocate their choices in direct proportion to the rewards provided by each choice. (That is, they chose 0.15 ml on 75% of the trials, and 0.05 ml on 25% of the trials.) As a result, Platt and Glimcher (1999) were able to compute an estimate of the animal's valuation of each

FIGURE 16.9 Activity of a single LIP neuron (identified as CH980304) from kinematically identical saccades made into its movement field, but at two levels of expected gain (0.15 ml vs. 0.05 ml of juice).

Source: Platt et al., 1999 / Springer Nature.

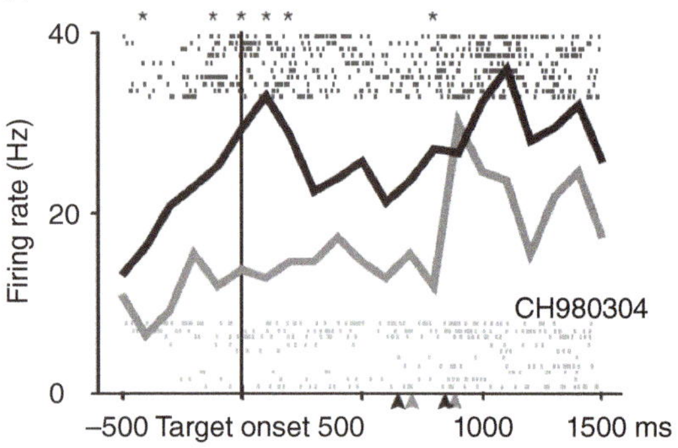

FIGURE 16.9.A Average activity, time-locked to target onset, for high (black) and low (gray) expected-value trials. Arrows along the timeline indicate, sequentially, and for each trial type, the average time of fixation offset and of saccade initiation. Asterisks indicate 100-ms bins in which firing rate differed significantly at the two levels of expected gain. Note that fixation onset preceded target onset by 500 ms.

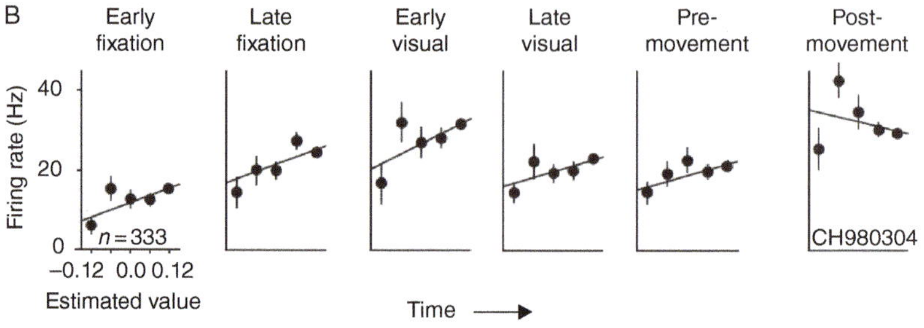

FIGURE 16.9.B Activity from the same neuron, divided into 200-ms samples, and plotted as a function of expected value, for movements into the neuron's response field.

response on a trial-by-trial basis (i.e., that response's expected value) by applying a formula from a formal theory of behavioral decision making – melioration theory – that took into account the animal's choices over the 10 preceding trials. *Figure 16.9.B* shows that activity in this LIP neuron related to expected value during all epochs of the trial, including the two that preceded target onset, with the exception of the "postmovement" epoch (which was actually time-locked to the initiation of the saccade).

Decision Variables Emergent from Motor Plans

Thus, to recap what we've learned in LIP, Shadlen and colleagues have shown that neurons in this region participate in the accumulation of evidence – the deliberation – toward a perceptual decision (*Figure 16.3*), with Zhou and Freedman (2019) clarifying that this activity is more related to sensory evaluation than to motor planning. In the study just summarized, Platt and Glimcher (1999) have shown that, in a free-choice task that varies gains over time, LIP neurons can also represent the value of eye movements. One consequence of the latter, and related, findings is that some have proposed a reframed conception of the frontoparietal oculomotor complex. Rather than this system representing a priority map (*Chapter 9*; section *The endogenous control of attention*) – which is a fundamentally attention-based construal of brain function – perhaps it represents a "saccade value" map – a fundamentally neuroeconomic construal of brain function. In-depth consideration of the relative merits of these two perspectives is beyond the scope of this book. However, there is one additional conclusion from this literature that will help us wrap up where we've been and push off toward our next destination. Studies of value-based decision making in parietal cortex have established that the representations of value found in LIP are limited to the value of decisions about where to move the eyes. Thus, by analogy to what we saw with perceptual decision making, value can be represented in the networks that will effect the value-based action. A further implication of this fact is that LIP does not seem to represent the common currency that is, in some sense, a Holy Grail of neuroeconomics. For that, neuroeconomic Sir Galahads have been more successful in the orbital and ventromedial PFC (sometimes summarized as "orbitomedial PFC" [omPFC]).

Common Currency in the omPFC

It is well established in behavioral neurology that lesions of the omPFC impair choice behavior in many domains, including eating disorders, abnormal gambling, and, more generally, erratic decision making. (omPFC, as referred to in this section, is comparable to vmPFC from *Chapter 15*, section *Dissecting frontal contributions to the control of behavior*.) In the monkey, extracellular recordings in omPFC have revealed neurons that encode particular flavors in a manner that is modulated by satiety. That is, a neuron may "prefer" raisins to pieces of apple, but its responses decrease in intensity as the animal gets closer to having eaten its fill of raisins. Thus, omPFC is a logical place to look for the representation of a common currency. Before we can start looking, though, we need to establish some definitions.

Transitivity, Value Transitivity, and Menu Invariance A key property conferred by a common currency is *transitivity*. Let's return to my wine selecting dilemma from the beginning of this chapter, but simplify it, such that on one trip to my neighborhood wine shop (enigmatically named "Mike's," even though it's owned by someone named Pat) there are only two varieties available, and I select bottle A over bottle B. Then, on a subsequent visit, the shop has sold out of A and has replaced it with C. Given this choice, I select B over C. On a third visit, if I find only A and C on the shelf, I will choose A. (To do otherwise would be to show "erratic decision making.") Another property conferred by a common currency is that the value of one item can be expressed in terms of a quantity of any other, what economists call *value transitivity*. Thus, let's also say that my wine preferences are similar in proportion to those of the monkey whose juice preferences are illustrated in

Figure 16.10.C. According to the principle of value transitivity, if Mike's started selling wine B in bottles holding 1.3 times the volume (but at the same price), I'd be equally happy with a 975-ml bottle of B as with a 750-ml bottle of A. And for the same reason, I'd be equally happy, for the same price, leaving the shop with four bottles of C as with one bottle of A. In the jargon of economics, the term "menu" refers to a set of choices. Thus, the A vs. B choice is a menu, and the B vs. C choice is a different menu. For a neural implementation of a common currency to be effective, it needs to display "menu invariance," which means that, assuming equal levels of satiety, the level of activity representing B will be the same whether it is on the A–B menu or on the B–C menu.

Now we're ready for the next two courses on our menu.

Evidence from the Nonhuman Primate *Figure 16.10.D* summarizes evidence, from a study by Camillo Padoa-Schioppa and John Assad (2008), that OFC represents a common currency. The neuron illustrated in the top row represents one type of menu invariance, in that its representation of the offer value for C is the same whether it's being offered against A or against B. The neuron illustrated in the middle row encodes the value of the choice that the animal made, regardless of which two juices were "on the menu." The neuron illustrated in the third row represents a different type of menu invariance, taste B, regardless of what else is "on the menu."

There are two details about the experimental procedure employed by Padoa-Schioppa and Assad (2008) that are worth highlighting before we move on. First, the spatial layout of offers was randomized across each experiment, such that the responses illustrated in *Figure 16.10.D* were invariant with regard to the retinotopic location of the representation of an offer and to the metrics of the saccade required to make a choice. In this way, the activity in OFC seems to differ from that in LIP, or in M1 and PMd, in that, for the latter, "value modulates responses that are sensory or motor in nature . . . [whereas] neurons in the OFC encode economic value per se, independently of visuomotor contingencies" (Padoa-Schioppa and Assad, 2008, p. 101). The second detail is that, over the course of their experiment, they used 11 different juices, recombined into 23 different juice triplets. Thus, their findings are unlikely to be stimulus specific.

Why the OFC? In interpreting their findings, Padoa-Schioppa and Assad (2008) note that "Current anatomical maps divide the medial and orbital prefrontal cortices into 22 distinct brain areas, organized in two mostly segregated networks. In the orbital [not the medial] network (including 13 m and the surrounding areas [*Figure 16.10.B*]), anatomical input from all sensory modalities converges with anatomical input from limbic areas including the amygdala. The orbital network thus seems well placed to compute a quantity such as subjective value" (p. 100).

Value- and Effort-Based Decision Making in Humans In the perceptual decision-making tasks that we reviewed in the first part of this chapter, each trial required a categorical decision. In the experiment from Padoa-Schioppa and Assad (2008; *Figure 16.10.A*), the animals chose from among two offers. But another common scenario requiring value-based decision making in daily life is deciding whether or not to engage with an opportunity that presents itself – that is, to decide "yes" or "no" with respect to a single option. Such scenarios often require weighing the tradeoff between the expected gain from choosing to engage in an activity vs. the effort that would need to be expended. One's assessment of this reward vs. effort tradeoff yields the subjective value of the choice that is on offer. This kind of value- and effort-based decision is operationalized in the task illustrated in *Figure 16.11.A*, in which on each trial the subject views an apple tree stimulus, with the number of apples in the tree indicating the amount of reward on offer, and the height of the yellow mark on the trunk of the tree indicating how much physical effort would need to be exerted in order to obtain this reward. (Specifically, prior to the task itself, subjects squeeze a dynamometer with one hand, as hard as they can, and then during the task, the effort required for each trial's "work offer" is conveyed as a proportion

FIGURE 16.10 The representation of economic value in the OFC is invariant for changes of menu.

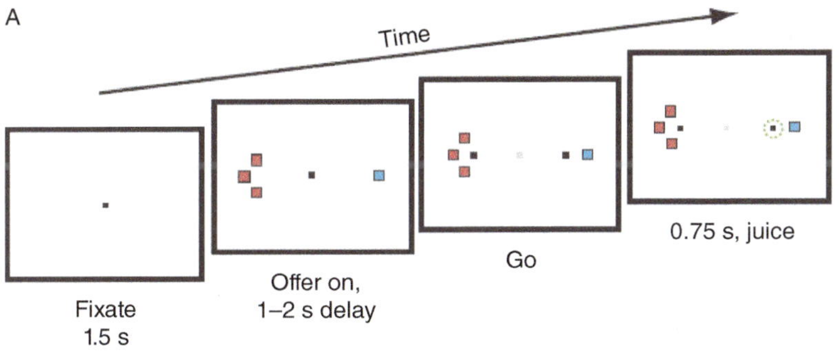

FIGURE 16.10.A On each trial, the monkey is made an offer that varies in terms of quantity and quality; in this case, three drops of agua frescas-flavored juice or one drop of peppermint tea. It indicated its choice by making a saccade to one of the two targets.

Source: Padoa-Schioppa, 2008 / Springer Nature.

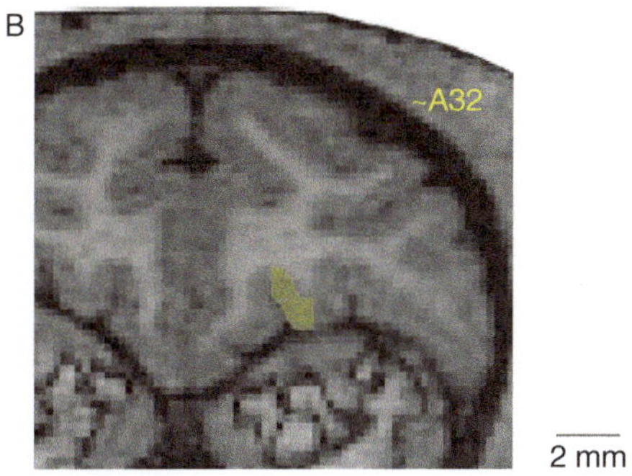

FIGURE 16.10.B Coronal slice of an MRI, with yellow shading indicating the location of area 13 m from which recordings were made. Note the orbits of the eyes, immediately ventral to this portion of cortex.

Source: Reproduced with permission from Padoa-Schioppa et al. (2008) / Springer Nature / CC BY 4.0.

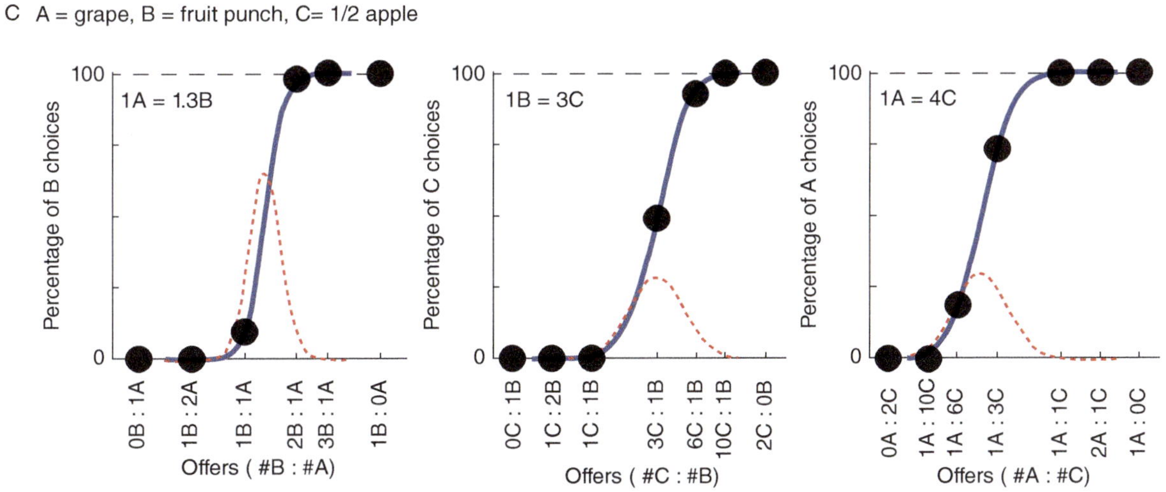

FIGURE 16.10.C Example of choice patterns from a session, featuring the three juices listed at top. This monkey liked grape juice better than fruit punch, and fruit punch better than apple juice diluted with equal parts of water (thus, "1/2 apple"). Estimation from the sigmoid fit indicates that the monkey valued 1 unit of A the same as 1.3 units of B, 1 unit of B the same as 3 units of C, and 1 unit of A the same as 4 units of C. The dotted red lines illustrate the underlying normal distributions, their width indicating the variability in these estimates.

Source: Padoa-Schioppa, 2008 / Springer Nature.

of that person's maximal exertable strength.) This task was administered by Colin Hoy, Coralie de Hemptinne, and colleagues (2024) to a group of patients with Parkinson's disease undergoing the implantation of electrodes for deep brain stimulation (DBS) of the subthalamic nucleus (STN) or the internal segment of the globus pallidus (GPi; collapsed into one "BG" for analyses), as well as a strip of four ECoG contacts placed in the subdural space over the orbitofrontal cortex (OFC; *Figure 16.11.B* and *Figure 16.11.C*; part of an "investigational, bidirectional device

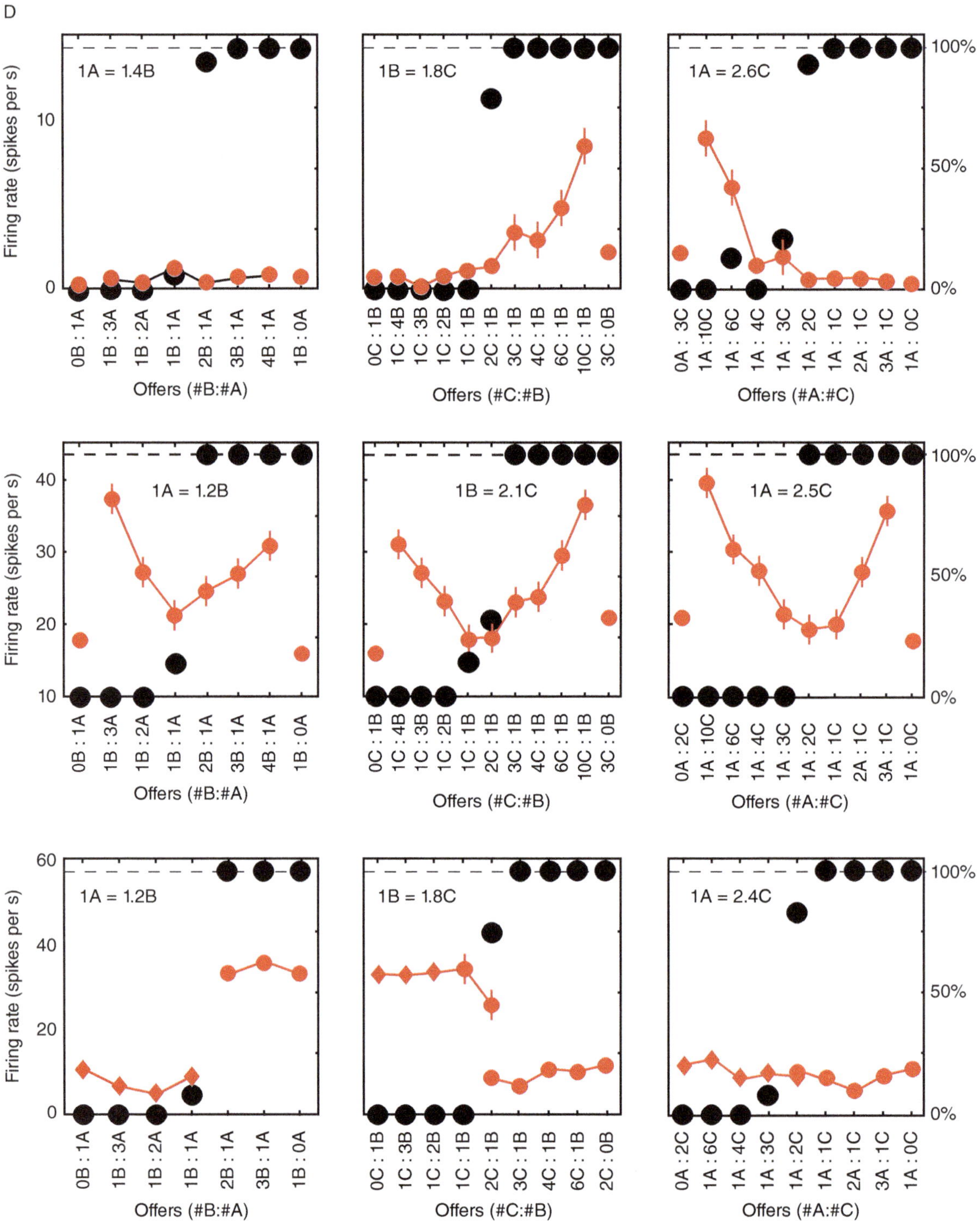

FIGURE 16.10.D Examples of three types of neurons in OFC. Each row of plots corresponds to a single neuron, with black dots indicating choices, with same conventions as *Figure 16.10.C*, except the ordinate for choices is on right side of each plot. Red dots represent firing rate. Neuron in top row encodes offer value C. Neuron in middle row encodes the "chosen value" (i.e., the difference in value between the chosen and unchosen offers, independent of the juice pair. Neuron in the bottom row encodes taste B, independent of pairing.

Source: Padoa-Schioppa, 2008 / Springer Nature.

FIGURE 16.11 Deciding whether the reward is worth the effort.

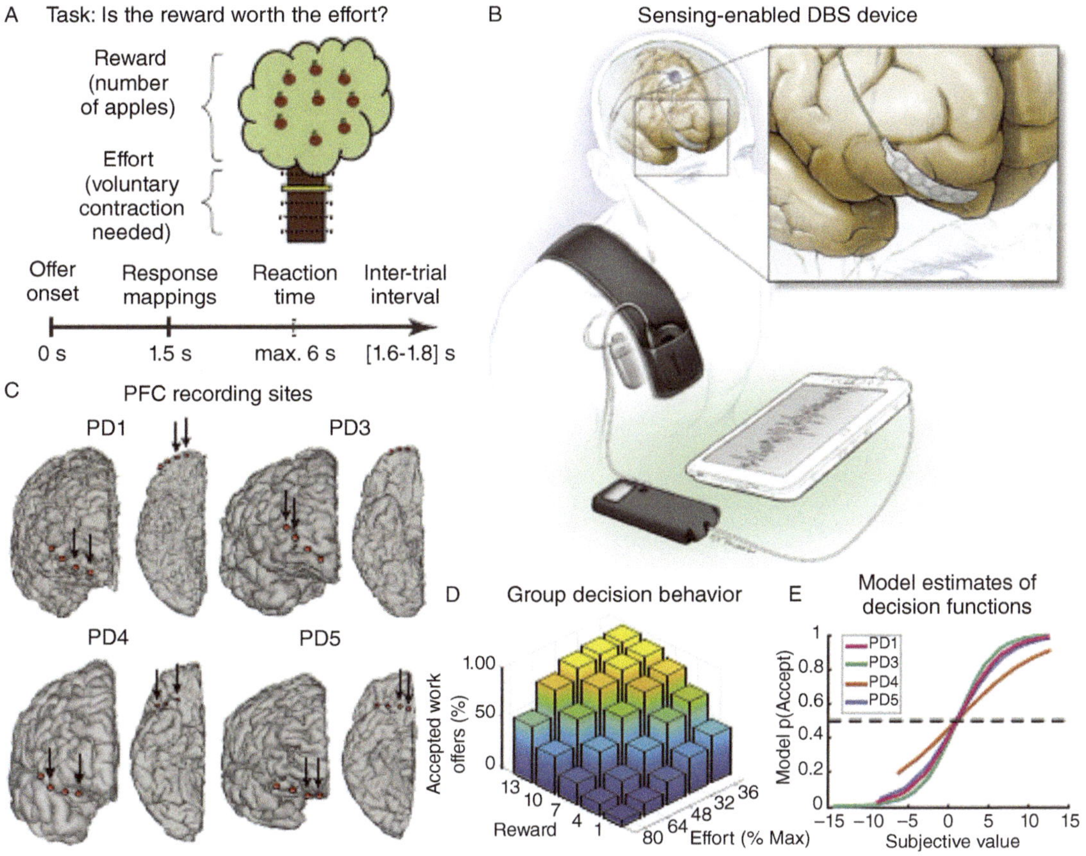

FIGURE 16.11.A Illustration of a trial from the task.

Source: (Hoy et al., 2024) / National Academy of Sciences.

FIGURE 16.11.B Illustration of the DBS (targeting STN or GPi [not shown]) and ECoG (targeting OFC) system. The electrodes are connected to a pulse generator that is surgically implanted over the pectoralis muscle, and that can communicate (for control of stimulation or for read-out of neural signals) with a device strapped to the exterior of the chest.

Source: (Hoy et al., 2024) / National Academy of Sciences / CC BY 4.0.

FIGURE 16.11.C Location of ECoG strips in each of the four Parkinson's disease patients in this study. Arrows indicate recording contact pairs.

Source: (Hoy et al., 2024) / National Academy of Sciences / CC BY 4.0.

FIGURE 16.11.D Group average summary of descriptive behavioral results, showing percentage accepted work offers as a function of reward given (number of apples) and effort required (percentage of maximum hand squeeze).

Source: (Hoy et al., 2024) / National Academy of Sciences.

FIGURE 16.11.E Modeled estimates of the subjective value of each offer (as estimated from reward and effort) plotted as a function of that trial's reward and effort, for each subject. (Note that each subject's behavior followed a sigmoid function, thus suggesting a way in which value-based decision making can be related to perceptual decision making (c.f., Figure 16.2.))

Source: (Hoy et al., 2024) / National Academy of Sciences.

allow[ing] both delivery of therapeutic stimulation and chronic recording of field potentials" p. 7 of 10). Behavioral results showed the expected pattern of an interaction of the tendency to accept more high- than low-reward offers and to accept fewer high- than low-effort offers (*Figure 16.11.D* and *Figure 16.11.E*). Interestingly, however, analyses did not find any neural signal correlating with model-based estimates of subjective value. Rather, what was found was

FIGURE 16.12 Relating neural signals to the representation of value and of effort.

Source: (Hoy et al., 2024) / National Academy of Sciences.

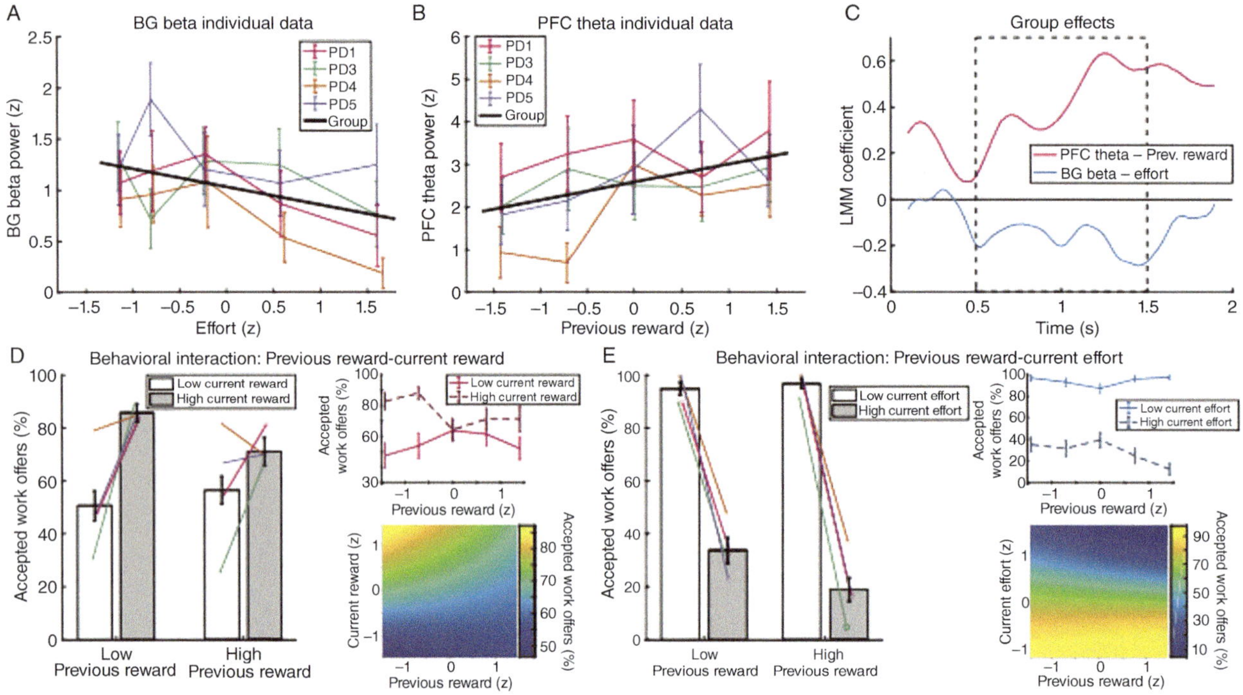

FIGURE 16.12.A Beta-band power in STN and GPi of the BG decreased as a function of effort.

FIGURE 16.12.B Theta-band power in OFC increased as a function of reward from the previous trial.

FIGURE 16.12.C Temporal evolution during the trial of the fits to a generalized linear mixed model (LMM) of the data summarized in panels **A** and **B**. Dashed lines denote time period used for hypothesis testing.

FIGURE 16.12.D Influence of the magnitude of the previous trial's reward on the choice made on the current trial, as a function of magnitude of current trial's *reward*. Effects are illustrated for individual subjects, with trial's binned as "high" or "low" (left-hand plot); and at the group level, showing that the previous trial's influence is larger when current trial's level of reward is low (for descriptive data, upper-right plot); and in the solution of the LMM when other factors are held constant (lower-right plot).

FIGURE 16.12.E Influence of the magnitude of the previous trial's reward on the choice made on the current trial, as a function of magnitude of current trial's *effort*. (Conventions are the same as panel **D**.)

a negative relation between beta-band power in the BG and the level of effort required on the current trial, and a positive relation between theta-band power in the OFC and the size of the reward on the previous trial (*Figure 16.12, Figure 16.12.A, Figure 16.12.B, and Figure 16.12.C*).

These results provide novel insights about two constructs that have received a considerable amount of attention in this and the previous chapter: value and effort. We can start with value, and how it was processed by the OFC. The contribution of OFC to value-based decision making is seen from the fact that, at the behavioral level, the magnitude of the reward from the previous trial (i.e., the factor represented by theta-band power in the OFC) biased the influence of both the current trial's reward and the current trial's effort on the decision to accept or reject that trial's offer (*Figure 16.12.D* and *Figure 16.12.E*). Note that, because the influence of the previous trial's reward only emerged when the current trial was underway (as hinted at in the time course of model fits shown in *Figure 16.12.C*), this is unlikely to have been an effect of a "working memory" sustained from the previous trial. Rather, it seems to have been a reinstatement of information from the previous trial, in OFC, to contribute to the current decision. (We will see something similar in *Chapter 17*, section *"How much can I trust you?"*, where it is framed as the computation from reinforcement learning of solving the credit-assignment problem.)

FIGURE 16.13 Stimulating OFC during value- and effort-based decision making.

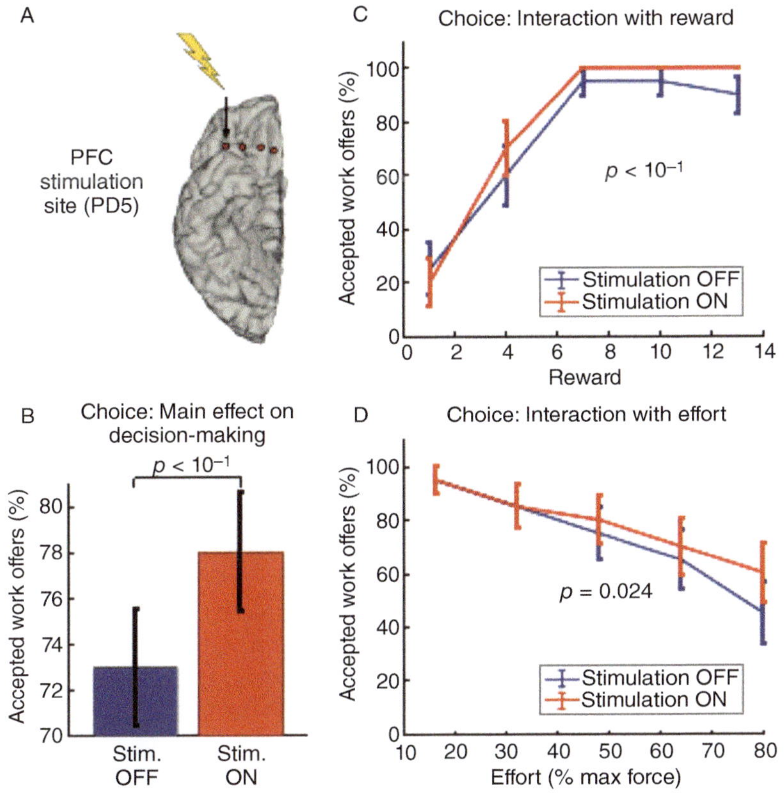

FIGURE 16.13.A The site of stimulation in subject PD5.

Source: (Hoy et al., 2024) / National Academy of Sciences / CC BY 4.0.

FIGURE 16.13.B OFC stimulation increased the overall percentage of accepted work offers.

Source: (Hoy et al., 2024) / National Academy of Sciences.

FIGURE 16.13.C OFC stimulation increased the percentage of accepted work offers at all but the lowest level of reward.

Source: (Hoy et al., 2024) / National Academy of Sciences.

FIGURE 16.13.D OFC stimulation increased the percentage of accepted work offers at higher levels of effort.

Source: (Hoy et al., 2024) / National Academy of Sciences.

An additional, and very intriguing, set of results was generated by Hoy and de Hemptinne et al. (2024) when they stimulated the OFC in one patient (PD 5) via the ECoG strip.[6] OFC stimulation had the effect of increasing the number of accepted work offers, particularly at higher levels of reward and at higher levels of effort (*Figure 16.13*). Although not shown in *Figure 16.13*, the stimulation also had the effect of increasing the point of subjective indifference. That is, stimulation of OFC had the effect of shifting to the left the sigmoid describing this patient's behavior as a function of subjective value (*Figure 16.11.E*). If we take a moment to think back to *Figure 16.2*, for those results we concluded that the effect of stimulation of MT on the perceptual decision was comparable to if one had added more coherently moving dots to the display (i.e., strengthening the "quality" of the evidence [cf., *Chapter 5*, section

[6]The stimulation procedure was similar to the one described in *Chapter 10*, section *Demonstrating necessity*, with the exception that whereas the goal of Parvizi et al. (2012) was to disrupt normal functioning of the targeted region, here the goal was to enhance the function of the targeted area. Thus, "Stimulation was delivered at an amplitude below a threshold of detectability and without motor effects" (Hoy, de Hemptinne, et al. (2024), p. 5 of 10).

Diffusion-decision modeling]). Here, the suggestion is that the effect of stimulation of OFC is equivalent to making the current offer seem more valuable (i.e., enhancing its subjective value).

Together, the results from Hoy, de Hemptinne et al. (2024) are consistent with a broad literature indicating an important role for OFC in reward learning and value-based decision making. Indeed, both the evidence for representation of value on the previous trial and the boosting effect of stimulation on the willingness to accept work offers suggest possible explanations for the low levels of "willingness to wait" that were seen in vmPFC-lesioned patients in *Chapter 15*, section *Dissecting frontal contributions to the control of behavior*. What we did not see in Hoy, de Hemptinne et al. (2024), however, was evidence, comparable to that from Padoa-Schioppa and Assad (2008), of activity corresponding to the "Holy Grail" of neuroeconomics: an explicit representation of subjective value in OFC. For that, we will have to wait for *Chapter 17, Social Behavior*.

And what are implications of the results from Hoy, de Hemptine et al. (2024) for our understanding of the influence of effort on decision making? Behaviorally (and not surprisingly), they confirm the intuition that, when given the choice, people will choose to avoid exerting physical effort. This isn't just a trivial observation. For example, one group has suggested it as a framework from which to understand age-related changes in how people move: "Slowing of Movements in Healthy Aging as a Rational Economic Response to an Elevated Effort Landscape" (Summerside, Courter, Shadmehr, and Ahmed, 2024). And although we can't cover it here in any detail, there's also good evidence that, given the choice, people will also choose to avoid the exertion of mental effort.[7] (Recall that we learned about neural correlates of mental effort in *Chapter 14*, section *"Trying harder"*, in the context of a task in which subjects were not given the choice of whether or not to engage on individual trials.) Neurally, the data from *Figure 16.12* indicate that beta-band power in the STN and GPi decreases with increased effort. This is probably best understood not as a direct correlate of the processing of effort, per se, but rather as a consequence of what we just discussed – the reluctance to engage. That is, from this chapter's section *The roles of basal ganglia nuclei in the control of movement*, and from *Chapter 15*, section *Stop!*, that oscillatory dynamics in these nuclei correspond to whether, and if so, when, a movement will be executed. Note, however, that in the studies detailed in those sections, the behavior of primary interest (to the research subjects, as well as to the experimenters) was the speed and accuracy of the button press itself, and so highly time-resolved measures of oscillatory dynamics in these nuclei could be related to precise measures of the kinematics of the movement, or to the DDM model parameters fit to those data. For this study from Hoy, de Hemptine et al. (2024), in contrast, the emphasis is on the rather more high-level question of whether or not to accept a work offer. Thus, the cortical computations being gated by STN and GPi in this task can't be inferred with the same specificity. (What *would* be very interesting and informative with regard to the processing of effort in this task would be electrophysiological data from dmFC, a fact that leads very nicely into the final section of this chapter.)

Foraging

This third category of decision making invoked at the beginning of this chapter shares some qualities with the value- and effort-based decision-making task that we just considered (i.e., as illustrated in *Figure 16.11*), in that both must factor in the effort associated with a choice. An important difference with foraging problems, however, is that with foraging, neither the value nor the effort of the alternative choice is known with any certainty. There's a great deal of overlap between behavioral economics, psychological decision theory, and studies of group dynamics and optimal foraging behavior carried out under such disciplinary rubrics as anthropology, ecology, zoology, and dynamical systems research. For example, the latter contributed importantly to many of the reviews by Glimcher and colleagues that we drew

[7] See section *Further Reading* for suggestions.

on in the previous section. Here, we'll consider one perspective that will give a feel for how this approach differs from the two that we have considered up to this point. Its consideration will also (once again) emphasize the overlap between the domains of "decision making" and "cognitive control."

For much of his career, cognitive neuroscientist Matthew Rushworth has explored the functions of the dorsomedial frontal cortex (dmFC), including the anterior cingulate cortex (ACC). Based on his training and many of his early studies, it's fair to say that he has approached this work from the perspective that this region is important for high-level motor control and response selection. (For our purposes, a perspective similar to that ascribed to Picard and Strick [1996]) in *Chapter 15*, section *Performance monitoring and the dmFC.*) In more recent work, Rushworth and colleagues have emphasized that while the majority of behavioral economics and neuroeconomics studies entail choices between two or more options, across evolutionary history, primates have often been confronted with a different kind of decision. In particular, an organism often has to choose between remaining in the place where it is and exploiting the resources that are directly accessible, vs. moving on to explore the environment for new, potentially more rewarding, opportunities. This foraging perspective, they argue, has implications for how one interprets activity in the dmFC, in particular.

In binary-choice decision-making tasks, dmFC signals are most often inversely related to the value difference between the chosen and unchosen options. This is what was illustrated in *Chapter 15, Figure 15.6*, in that difficult, or high-conflict, choices are associated with strong responses from dmFC. The alternative account from the foraging perspective, however, is that the error/difficulty/conflict accounts of this region's function may be artifacts of the two-alternative forced-choice tasks with which the majority of decision-making research is carried out. When assessed in foraging situations, dmFC signal strength is seen not to represent the unchosen option (and, therefore, a conflict), but, instead, to represent the relative benefit of exploring. One consequence of this view is that there may, in fact, be more than one common currency that guides decision making. By the foraging account, the research that we reviewed in the previous section that points to common currency representation in vmPFC/OFC, is valid, and its conclusions are generally solid. In addition, however, it argues that qualitatively different information may govern foraging decisions. In a foraging context there are three critical factors: the value of exploiting the option that one has encountered ("encounter value"), the potential value of exploring and finding something better ("search value"); and the energetic cost of embarking on the search ("search cost"; this is comparable to effort as considered in section *Value- and effort-based decision making in humans*). These three factors do not seem to be represented in the vmPFC/OFC, but are represented in the dmFC. (Additionally, search cost may also be represented/processed in frontopolar cortex [Bogdanov, Bustamante, Devine, Sheldon, and Otto, 2025].) To date, there is no consensus about whether a foraging-influenced model might account for presumed functions of the dmFC that have, from other theoretical perspectives, been framed in terms of error, difficulty, and/or conflict.

Next Stop

The South Shore of Long Island, a suburb of New York City, is so densely populated that what were once discrete villages have long since merged into mile upon mile of, to an outsider's eye, unbroken suburban landscape. Although different towns have their own distinct character, without signs along the road (or announcements by the Long Island Rail Road conductor), one wouldn't know when one was leaving one town and entering another. The same might be said of *Chapters 16*, *17*, and *18* – each will have a different emphasis, but the transitions between them are arbitrary, and wouldn't be noticeable without explicit chapter breaks. Prominent in the landscape of each are the estimation and representation of value, the influence of social interactions, and interactions between medial frontal cortex and subcortical structures. So, keep the facts and principles that we've just covered close at hand.

End-of-Chapter Questions

1. What are the three different types of decisions that we need to make, and what distinguishes each?

2. How has microstimulation informed our understanding of perceptual decision making about the direction of motion in RDM displays?

3. How does the behavior of neurons in LIP relate to drift-diffusion models of perceptual decision making?

4. How is confidence manifested in neural signals related to perceptual decision making?

5. Do the basal ganglia dynamics detailed in section *The roles of basal ganglia nuclei in the control of movement* relate to those in *Chapter 15*, section *Stop!*? Defend your answer with reference to functions of specific basal ganglia nuclei.

6. Why is the activity of LIP neurons so different on two-alternative forced-choice trials, requiring identical saccades, when the task is an RDM perceptual decision task vs. when it is a free choice between different levels of expected gain?

7. How do the concepts of transitivity, value transitivity, and menu invariance relate to the idea of a common currency? In what brain areas are all these properties observed?

8. Based on influence of the level of effort required on value-based decision making in the study by Hoy, de Hemptine et al. (2024; as illustrated in *Figure 16.11.D*), how do you predict that subjects in the study by Master et al. (2024; *Chapter 14*, section *"Trying harder"*) would have behaved if offered differing amounts of money prior to each trial, and the option to skip trials that they didn't want to perform? How might signal intensity in the DAN have fluctuated in relation to signals in OFC?

9. Inspection of *Figure 16.12.D* suggests that a low-value reward on the previous trial increased the likelihood of accepting a high-value reward on the current trial. Explain why this might be, incorporating into your answer what we know about the effects of stimulation of OFC (as illustrated in *Figure 16.13*).

10. How do foraging decisions differ fundamentally from perceptual and value-based decisions? What brain area is implicated in the control of foraging?

References

Bogdanov, M., L. A. Bustamante, S. Devine, S. Sheldon, and A. R. Otto. 2025. "Noninvasive Brain Stimulation over the Frontopolar Cortex Promotes Willingness to Exert Cognitive Effort in a Foraging-Like Sequential Choice Task." *The Journal of Neuroscience 45* (10). doi: 10.1523/JNEUROSCI.0647-24.2024.

Donner, Tobias H., Markus Siegel, Pascal Fries, and Andreas K. Engel. 2009. "Buildup of Choice-Predictive Activity in Human Motor Cortex during Perceptual Decision Making." *Current Biology* 19 (18): 1581–1585. doi: 10.1016/j.cub.2009.07.066.

Dou, W., L. J. Martinez Arango, O. G. Castaneda, L. Arellano, E. McIntyre, C. Yballa, and J. Samaha. 2024. "Neural Signatures of Evidence Accumulation Encode Subjective Perceptual Confidence Independent of Performance." *Psychological Science 35* (7): 760–779. doi: 10.1177/09567976241246561.

Ging-Jehli, N., J. F. Cavanagh, M. Ahn, D. J. Segar, W. F. Asaad, and M. J. Frank. 2025. "Basal ganglia components have distinct computational roles in decision-making dynamics under conflict and uncertainty." *PLoS Biology 23*: e3002978. doi: doi.org/10.1371/journal.pbio.3002978.

Gold, Joshua I., and Michael N. Shadlen. 2007. "The Neural Basis of Decision Making." *Annual Review of Neuroscience* 30: 535–574. doi: 10.1146/annurev.neuro.29.051605.113038.

Hanks, Timothy D., Jochen Ditterich, and Michael N. Shadlen. 2006. "Microstimulation of Macaque Area LIP Affects Decision-Making in a Motion Discrimination Task." *Nature Neuroscience* 9 (5): 682–689. doi: 10.1038/nn1683.

Holroyd, C. B. 2024. "The Controllosphere: The neural origin of cognitive effort." *Psychological Review*. doi: 10.1037/rev0000467.

Hoy, C. W., C. de Hemptinne, S. S. Wang, C. J. Harmer, M. A. J. Apps, M. Husain, . . . S. Little. 2024. "Beta and theta oscillations track effort and previous reward in the human basal ganglia and prefrontal cortex during decision making." *Proceedings of the National Academy of Sciences of the United States of America 121*: e2322869121. doi: doi.org/10.1073/pnas.2322869121.

Jamadar, S. D., A. Behler, H Deery, and M. Breakspear. 2025. "The metabolic costs of cognition." *Trends in Cognitive Sciences*. doi: 10.1016/j.tics.2024.11.010.

Kable, Joseph W., and Paul W. Glimcher. 2009. "The Neurobiology of Decision: Consensus and Controversy." *Neuron* 63 (6): 733–745. doi: 10.1016/j.neuron.2009.09.003.

Kahneman, Daniel, and Amos Tversky. 1979. "Prospect Theory: An Analysis of Decision Under Risk." *Econometrica* 47 (2): 263–291. doi: 10.2307/1914185.

Katz, L. N., J. L. Yates, J. W. Pillow, and A. C. Huk. 2016. "Dissociated functional significance of decision-related activity in the primate dorsal stream." *Nature 535* (7611): 285–288. doi: 10.1038/nature18617.

Lo, Chung-Chuan, and Xiao-Jing Wang. 2006. "Cortico–Basal Ganglia Circuit Mechanism for a Decision Threshold in Reaction Time Tasks." *Nature Neuroscience* 9 (7): 956–963. doi: 10.1038/nn1722.

von Neumann, John, and Oskar Morgenstern. 1944. *Theory of Games and Economic Behavior*. Princeton, NJ: Princeton University Press.

Newsome, William T., Kenneth H. Britten, and Anthony Movshon. 1989. "Neuronal Correlates of a Perceptual Decision." *Nature* 341 (6237): 52–54. doi: 10.1038/341052a0.

Padoa-Schioppa, Camillo, and John A. Assad. 2008. "The Representation of Economic Value in the Orbitofrontal Cortex Is Invariant for Changes of Menu." *Nature Neuroscience* 11 (1): 95–102. doi: 10.1038/nn2020.

Parvizi, J., C. Jacques, B. L. Foster, N. Withoft, V. Rangarajan, K. S. Weiner, and K. Grill-Spector. 2012. "Electrical stimulation of human fusiform face-selective regions distorts face perception." *The Journal of Neuroscience 32*: 14915–14920.

Picard, Nathalie, and Peter L. Strick. 1996. "Motor Areas of the Medial Wall: A Review of Their Location and Functional Activation." *Cerebral Cortex* 6: 342–353. doi: 10.1093/cercor/6.3.342.

Platt, Michael L., and Paul W. Glimcher. 1999. "Neural Correlates of Decision Variables in Parietal Cortex." *Nature* 400 (6741): 233–238. doi: 10.1038/22268.

Rougier, Nicolas P., David C. Noelle, Todd S. Braver, Jonathan D. Cohen, and Randall C. O'Reilly. 2005. "Prefrontal Cortex and Flexible Cognitive Control: Rules Without Symbols." *Proceedings of the National Academy of Sciences of the United States of America* 102 (20): 7338–7343. doi: 10.1073/pnas.0502455102.

Salzman, C. Daniel, Kenneth H. Britten, and William T. Newsome. 1990. "Cortical Microstimulation Influences Perceptual Judgements of Motion Direction." *Nature* 346 (6280): 174–177. doi: 10.1038/346174a0.

Stedron, Jennifer Merva, Sarah Devi Sahni, and Yuko Munakata. 2005. "Common Mechanisms for Working Memory and Attention: The Case of Perseveration with Visible Solutions." *Journal of Cognitive Neuroscience* 17 (4): 623–631. doi: 10.1162/0898929053467622.

Summerside, E. M., R. J. Courter, R. Shadmehr, and A. A. Ahmed. 2024. "Slowing of Movements in Healthy Aging as a Rational Economic Response to an Elevated Effort Landscape." *The Journal of Neuroscience 44* (15). doi: 10.1523/JNEUROSCI.1596-23.2024.

Sutton, Richard S., and Andrew G. Barto. 1998. *Reinforcement Learning: An Introduction*. Cambridge, MA: MIT Press.

Thura, D., and P. Cisek. 2017. "The Basal Ganglia Do Not Select Reach Targets But Control the Urgency of Commitment." *Neuron 95*: 1160–1170. dx.doi.org/10.1016/j.neuron.2017.07.039.

Yartsev, M. M., T. D. Hanks, A. M. Yoon, and C. D. Brody. 2018. "Causal Contribution and Dynamical Encoding in the Striatum During Evidence Accumulation." *eLife* 7: e34929. doi: doi.org/10.7554/eLife.34929.

Zhou, Y., and D. J. Freedman. 2019. "Posterior Parietal Cortex Plays a Causal Role in Perceptual and Categorical Decisions." *Science* 365: 180–185.

Zylberberg, A., and M. N. Shadlen. 2025. "A Population Representation of the Confidence in a Decision in the Parietal Cortex." *Cell Reports 44* (4): 115526. doi: 10.1016/j.celrep.2025.115526.

Other Sources Used

Gold, Joshua I., and Michael N. Shadlen. 2000. "Representation of a Perceptual Decision in Developing Oculomotor Commands." *Nature* 404 (6776): 390–394. doi: 10.1038/35006062.

Gold, Joshua I., and Michael N. Shadlen. 2001. "Neural Computations that Underlie Decisions about Sensory Stimuli." *Trends in Cognitive Sciences* 5 (1): 10–16. doi: 10.1016/S1364-6613(00)01567-9.

Kolling, Nils, Timothy E. J. Behrens, Rogier B. Mars, and Matthew F. S. Rushworth. 2012. "Neural Mechanisms of Foraging." *Science* 336 (6077): 95–98. doi: 10.1126/science.1216930.

Öngür, Dost, and Joel L. Price. 2000. "The Organization of Networks within the Orbital and Medial Prefrontal Cortex of Rats, Monkeys and Humans." *Cerebral Cortex* 10 (3): 206–219. doi: 10.1093/cercor/10.3.206.

Padoa-Schioppa, Camillo, and John A. Assad. 2006. "Neurons in the Orbitofrontal Cortex Encode Economic Value." *Nature* 441 (7090): 223–226. doi: 10.1038/nature04676.

Ratcliff, Roger, Anil Cherian, and Mark Segraves. 2003. "A Comparison of Macaque Behavior and Superior Colliculus Neuronal Activity to Predictions from Models of Two-Choice Decisions." *Journal of Neurophysiology* 90 (3): 1392–1407. doi: 10.1152/jn.01049.2002.

Ratcliff, Roger, and Jeffrey N. Rouder. 1998. "Modeling Response Times for Two-Choice Decisions." *Psychological Science* 9 (5): 347–356. doi: 10.1111/1467-9280.00067.

Rushworth, Matthew F. S., Nils Kolling, Jérôme Sallet, and Rogier B. Mars. 2012. "Valuation and Decision-Making in Frontal Cortex: One or Many Serial or Parallel Systems?." *Current Opinion in Neurobiology* 22 (6): 946–955. doi: 10.1016/j.conb.2012.04.011.

Shadlen, Michael N., and William T. Newsome. 1996. "Motion Perception: Seeing and Deciding." *Proceedings of the National Academy of Sciences of the United States of America* 93 (2): 628–633. doi: 10.1073/pnas.93.2.628.

Shadlen, Michael N., and William T. Newsome. 2001. "Neural Basis of a Perceptual Decision in the Parietal Cortex (Area LIP) of the Rhesus Monkey." *Journal of Neurophysiology* 86 (4): 1916–1936.

Wang, X.-J. 2008. "Decision Making in Recurrent Neuronal Circuits." *Neuron* 60: 215–234.

Further Reading

Ebitz, R. Becket, and Benjamin Hayden. 2016. "Dorsal Anterior Cingulate: a Rorschach test for cognitive neuroscience." *Nature Neuroscience* 19: 1278–1279. doi: 10.1038/nn.4387.

A "News and Views" overview accompanying two more recent articulations of the foraging vs. conflict interpretations of ACC function.

Glimcher, Paul W. 2010. *Foundations of Neuroeconomic Analysis.* Oxford: Oxford University Press.

As of this writing, the definitive statement of the development, current status, and future potential of neuroeconomics.

Gold, Joshua I., and Michael N. Shadlen. 2007. "The Neural Basis of Decision Making." *Annual Review of Neuroscience* 30: 535–574. doi: 10.1146/annurev.neuro.29.051605.113038.

Authoritative review of visual perceptual decision making, including thorough treatment of application of SDT.

Kable, Joseph W., and Paul W. Glimcher. 2009. "The Neurobiology of Decision: Consensus and Controversy." *Neuron* 63 (6): 733–745. doi: 10.1016/j.neuron.2009.09.003.

A broad-ranging and synthetic overview of neuroeconomics.

Rushworth, Matthew F. S., Nils Kolling, Jérôme Sallet, and Rogier B. Mars. 2012. "Valuation and Decision-Making in Frontal Cortex: One or Many Serial or Parallel Systems?." *Current Opinion in Neurobiology* 22 (6): 946–955. doi: 10.1016/j.conb.2012.04.011.

A comprehensive summary of the foraging perspective of the role of dmFC in control and decision making.

Schultz, Wolfram. 2013. "Updating Dopamine Reward Signals." *Current Opinion in Neurobiology* 23 (2): 229–238. doi: 10.1016/j.conb.2012.11.012.

Introduced in the previous chapter, but central to decision making, the most up-to-date statement, at the time of this writing, of our understanding of dopamine reward signals.

Shenhav, Amitai, Mark A. Straccia, Jonathan D. Cohen, and Matthew M. Botvinick. 2014. "Anterior Cingulate Engagement in a Foraging Context Reflects Choice Difficulty, Not Foraging Value." *Nature Neuroscience* 17: 1249–1254. doi: 10.1038/nn.3771.

A response to the foraging interpretation of cognitive control-related functions of dmFC. (Holroyd, 2024; Jamadar, Behler, Deery, and Breakspear, 2025)

Frank, M. J. 2025. "Adaptive cost-benefit control fueled by striatal dopamine." *Annual Review of Neuroscience* 48: 1–22. doi: 10.1146/annurev-neuro-112723- 025228.

Provides an overview of recent research on the complexities of DA signaling in relation to decision making and motivated behavior, and summarizes an argument for a role for the basal ganglia in action selection, not just timing.

CHAPTER 17

Social Behavior

KEY THEMES

- The concept of a common currency for decision making (which allows one to, e.g., choose between apples and oranges) also applies to the evaluation of other people.
- The case of Phineas Gage, whose medial PFC was destroyed in a freak rock-blasting accident, and whose personality was dramatically altered as a consequence, highlights the role of this region in controlling social behavior.
- Neural abnormalities in the vmPFC and its connections to medial temporal regions may be a factor in the "psychiatric" condition of psychopathy.
- Neuroscientific study of "theory of mind" (ToM), the ability to represent the thoughts and motivations of others, is an informative lens through which to observe how scientists go about studying the neural bases of social behavior – the methods, the theoretical perspectives, the complications, and the controversies.
- One hotly contested conceptual battleground has been whether the functions of the right temporoparietal junction (RTPJ) are better characterized as being specific to ToM and moral decision making, or more generally recruited by tasks requiring attentional reorienting and, perhaps, the comparison of internal models of the world with external sensory evidence.
- Insight into *why* RTPJ is involved in social cognition has been provided by resting state functional correlation (RSFC) analyses of human subjects scanned with precision fMRI at 7T.
- People make decisions differently when they are interacting with other people vs. when they are interacting with machines, and neural correlates of this phenomenon implicate many systems associated with value-based decision making.
- Observing the behavior of others – an inherently social act – can be an important way to learn new information, even if we only observe others' actions but not the outcome(s) of those actions. Model-based analysis of fMRI provides evidence that different kinds of error prediction signals, processed by different brain areas at different times during learning, may underlie this otherwise perplexing phenomenon.

CONTENTS

Companion Website: www.wiley.com/go/postle/cognitiveneuroscience3e

The Role of vmPFC in the Control of Social Cognition

To provide an explicit transition between *Chapter 15, Decision making*, we'll begin with what is considered to be among the first direct evidence for a common-currency representation of value in the human. It fits in this chapter (i.e., SOCIAL BEHAVIOR) because the basis of the value being studied is inherently social.

Common Currency for Money and Social Reward

Prior to this study by David Smith, Benjamin Hayden, Trong-Kha Truong, Allen Song, Michael Platt, and Scott Huettel (2010), Platt's group had previously performed a clever study of decision making with stimuli that were socially relevant for their male monkeys. Not unlike the Padoa-Schioppa and Assad (2008) study (Chapter 16, section Evidence from the nonhuman primate), Robert Deaner, Amit Khera, and Michael Platt (2005) derived value transitivity in its subjects via a "pay-per-view" scheme in which male monkeys evaluated offers pitting juice against the opportunity to view images of the backsides of female monkeys in estrus, or against the opportunity to view images of male monkeys from the same colony and with a known dominance status relative to the animal in the study. Then, in a follow-up to the monkey pay-per-view study, Platt's group established (to no one's surprise) that heterosexual university-aged human males will trade small amounts of money or expend effort to view photographs of attractive females.

Building on this context, Smith et al. (2010) carried out a two-part study on 26 self-reported heterosexual males, ranging in age from 18 to 28. First, during fMRI scanning, subjects passively viewed faces of young adult women varying in attractiveness from "very attractive" to "very unattractive," and of images of paper money that varied in value from \$5 to –\$5 (*Figure 17.1.A*). (Attractiveness ratings were made by an independent group of raters on >2000

FIGURE 17.1 Common currency for money and social reward in human vmPFC.

Source: Reproduced with permission from Smith et al. (2010) / Society for Neuroscience.

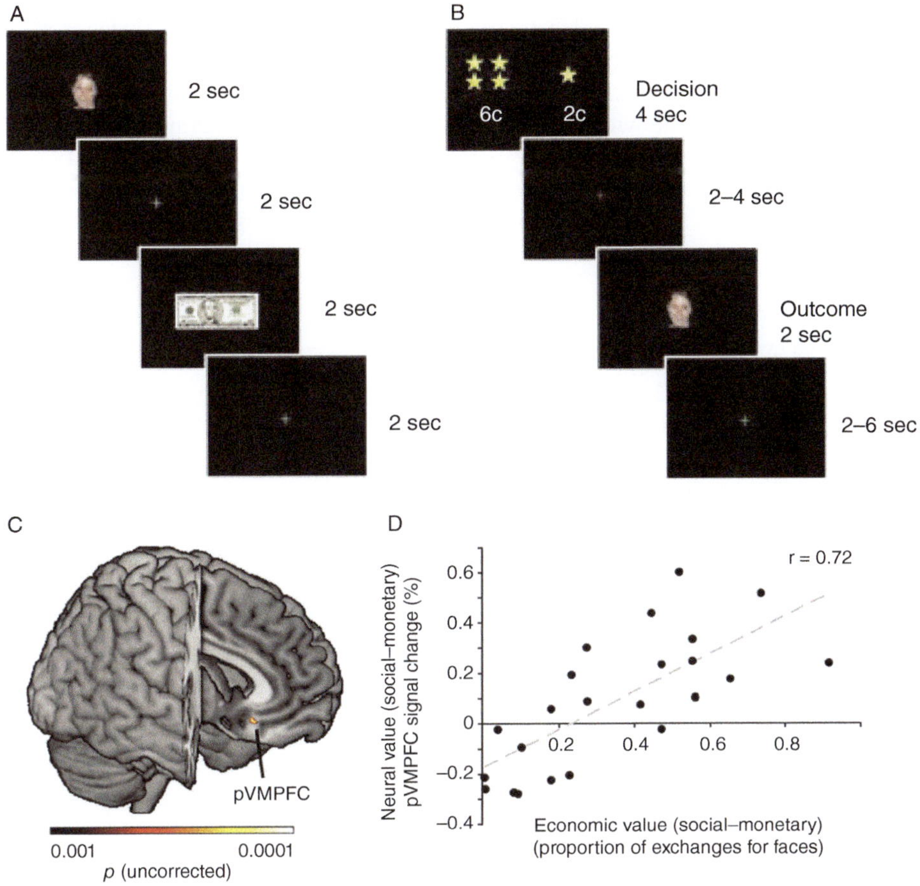

FIGURE 17.1.A AND B The first portion of the fMRI study (**A**) entailed no overt decision making, just passive viewing of images of faces that varied in attractiveness, and images of currency that varied in magnitude. The second portion (**B**) was an economic exchange task in which subjects chose, for each offer, whether to spend a larger sum of money or a smaller sum of money to view a more or less attractive face (indicated by the number of stars), respectively.

FIGURE 17.1.C Activity in posterior vmPFC that, during passive viewing, predicts individual differences in subsequently derived estimates of willingness to exchange money to view attractive faces.

FIGURE 17.1.D Correlation of the neural representation of value in OFC (y axis; from region in panel **C**) with willingness to exchange money to view an attractive face (derived from post-scan economic exchange task).

images, rumored to have been downloaded from the website www.hotornot.com.) Notably, as hinted at previously, no overt task was performed during this session. The rationale for this first stage was to determine whether neural representations of decision values are computed even when no overt decision is being made. Next, immediately following the acquisition of fMRI images, while still lying in the scanner, subjects participated in an economic exchange task formally identical to that of Padoa-Schioppa and Assad (2008), but instead of choosing between less volume of a more-preferred juice vs. more volume of a less-preferred juice, on each trial, subjects chose between spending more money to view a "more-preferred" face vs. spending less money to view a "less-preferred" face. (In *Figure 17.1.B*, four stars correspond to "most attractive," and one star to "least attractive.")

Results from the economic exchange task revealed considerable individual variability in each subject's value transitivity scale – each person's "willingness to pay" (WTP) to view a more attractive face ranged from 0 to 6.4 cents/star. The authors also computed a related measure, the proportion of offers on which the subject was willing to exchange more money to view a more attractive face. This is the measure represented on the abscissa of the plot in *Figure 17.1.D.* On the ordinate is a measure of neural activity derived from the passive viewing task, computed to operationalize the extent to which brain activity "preferred" faces over money, or vice versa, with the contrast ([4-star face – 1-star face] – [large-monetary gains – large-monetary losses]). As illustrated in *Figure 17.1.C*, the one region in the brain in which this neural measure of social value predicted individual differences in value transitivity scale was located in posterior vmPFC.[1]

Phineas Gage

If there's a neurological patient who might challenge H.M.'s status as most cited case in the brain sciences, it's Phineas Gage. The fantastic nature of his accident and injury, and its profound behavioral consequences, ensures that he appears in every textbook and in more than his fair share of introductory slides in scientific presentations.

Horrible Accident In 1848, Gage was the foreman of a crew that was blasting rock to create a route through the mountains of south-central Vermont for a new line for the Rutland and Burlington Railroad. At that time, this entailed drilling a deep, narrow hole into the rock, filling it with blasting powder, then a fuse, then sand, compressing the charge with a metal tamping iron (of, say, 3′7″ in length and 1.25″ in diameter; and did we say fashioned out of *metal*?), then presumably walking a long distance away, and yelling something like "Fire in the hole!" before lighting the fuse. An article from the *Boston Post* picks up the story from here:

> Horrible Accident – As Phineas P. Gage, a foreman on the railroad in Cavendish, was yesterday engaged in tamping for a blast, the power exploded, carrying an iron instrument through his head an inch and a fourth in circumference and three feet and eight inches [*sic*] in length, which he was using at the time. The iron entered on the side of this face, shattering the upper jaw [*sic*], and passing back of the left eye, and out at the top of the head.
>
> The most singular circumstance connected with the melancholy affair is that he was alive at two o'clock this afternoon [i.e., on the following day], and in full possession of his reason, and free from pain – Ludlow, Vt., Union. (September 21, 1848)

(Everything qualified with a "*sic*" is not strictly accurate; but what's an inch here or there?) Most singular indeed. And the fact that he was to live for not just a day after the accident, but for nearly 12 additional years, and that a detailed assessment was made of the lasting consequences of his injuries, means that contemporary scientists have gone to great lengths to reconstruct the damage likely incurred by his brain (*Figure 17.2* and *Figure 17.3*).

Sequelae Why all the fuss? Here's the most-quoted section from the first thorough account in the medical literature of the behavioral consequences of Gage's injury, published eight years after his death:

> The equilibrium or balance, so to speak, between his intellectual faculties and animal propensities, seems to have been destroyed. He is fitful, irreverent, indulging at times in the grossest profanity (which was not previously his custom), manifesting but little deference for his fellows, impatient of restraint or advice when it conflicts with his desires, at times pertinaciously obstinate, yet capricious and vacillating, and

[1] An implication of this is that "the male gaze" may be explainable, at least in part, through principles of value-based decision making. If it makes one feel uncomfortable to consider this aspect of human behavior in such crass and transactional terms, best to not look up some of the Platt group's more recent work suggesting that the gaze patterns of nonhuman primates looking at photos of (human) political candidates can predict election outcomes (Jiang, Huttunen, Belkaya, and Platt, preprint 2024).

FIGURE 17.2 Daguerreotype of Phineas Gage, taken years after his accident, holding the tamping iron that was "his constant companion for the remainder of his life."

Source: Warren Anatomical Museum / Wikimedia Commons / CC BY-SA 3.

> devising many plans of future operations, which are no sooner arranged than they are abandoned in turn for others appearing more feasible. A child in his intellectual capacity and manifestations, he has the animal passions of a strong man. Previous to his injury, although untrained in the schools, he possessed a well-balanced mind, and was looked upon by those who knew him as a shrewd, smart businessman, very energetic and persistent in executing all his plans of operation. In this regard his mind was radically changed, so decidedly that his friends and acquaintances said he was 'no longer Gage.' (Harlow, 1868, pp. 339–340)

The extent to which North American scientific culture was underdeveloped at that time, relative to that of Europe, is evident in the fact that it was decades before the scientific community (1) first learned of this case, then (2) fully accepted the veracity of its details, and finally (3) incorporated it into models of the behavioral functions of the medial PFC. (In 1877, David Ferrier [who we first encountered in section *The localization of visual perception, Chapter* 1] wrote to the chair of Harvard's Department of Psychology to inquire about reports he had heard about this case. His letter included the following observation, too rich to not share: "In investigating reports on diseases and injuries of the brain, I am constantly amazed at the inexactitude and distortion to which they are subject by men who have some pet theory to support. The facts suffer so frightfully that I feel obliged always to go to the fountainhead–dirty and muddy though this frequently turns out" [Macmillan, 2000, p. 464].)

Contemporary Behavioral Neurology

Marsel Mesulam (1985) has summarized the frontal cortex as being organized into three divisions: motor–premotor, paralimbic, and heteromodal. It is the paralimbic that has been most strongly associated with social behavior. Comprising anterior cingulate and caudal orbitofrontal regions, it is characterized by a cytoarchitecture that is transitional from evolutionarily older archicortex of the hippocampus and piriform cortex of the olfactory system, at one boundary, and six-layer "granular" neocortex at the other. (Note that the caudal orbitofrontal component of paralimbic cortex corresponds to the ventromedial [vm]PFC that featured

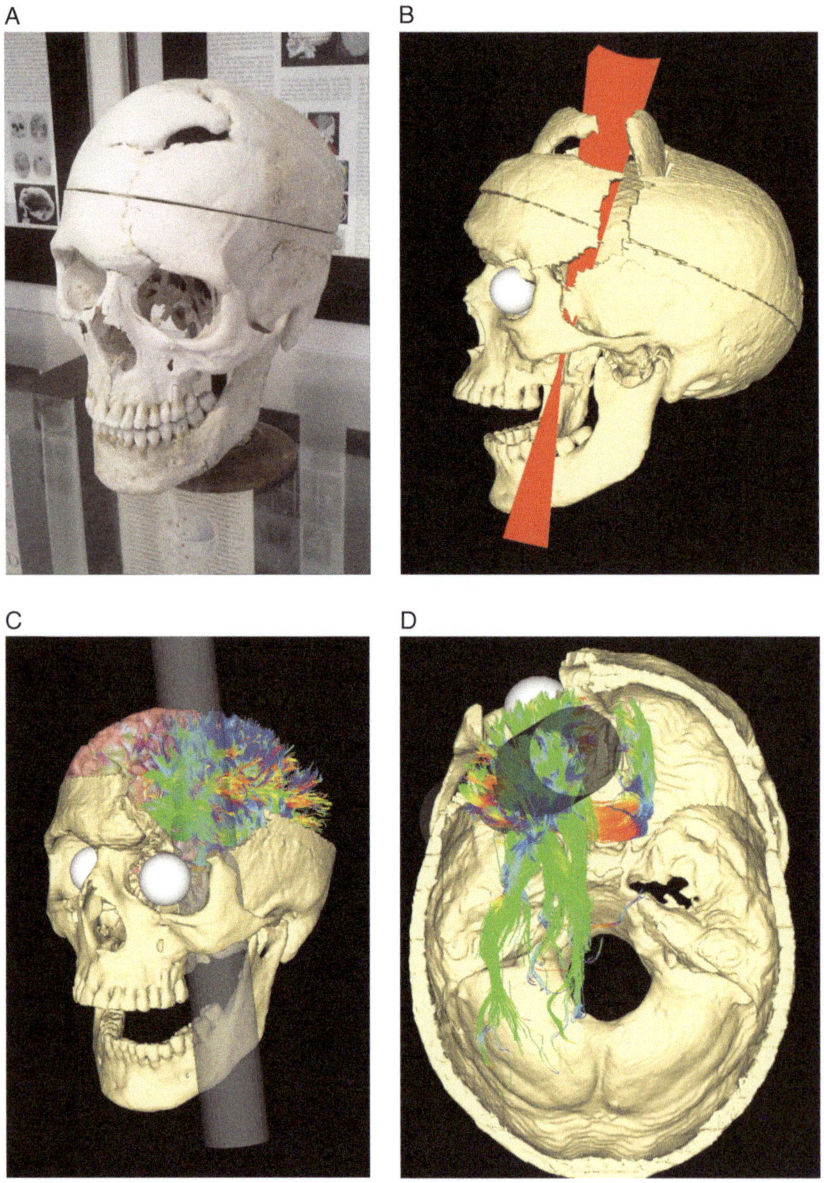

FIGURE 17.3 Reconstruction of damage to Phineas Gage's brain. **A.** The skull of Phineas Gage is on display at the Warren Anatomical Museum at Harvard Medical School. **B.** The set of possible rod trajectory centroids, estimated from CT scans of the skull. **C.** A rendering of the Gage skull with the best-fit rod trajectory and example fiber pathways in the left hemisphere intersected by the rod. **D.** Same data as **C**, but rendered in radiological conventions, and portrayed as though viewed from the underside, with a reconstruction of the ventral surface of the brain. Gray shading is the estimate of frank lesion to the left frontal lobe (note that circle within this region indicates the actual diameter of the tamping iron). Fiber pathways estimated to have been severed by the path of the tamping iron are illustrated with colors representing the orientation of the tract (e.g., green is parallel to the Y dimension, yellow-red to X, and blue to Z).

Source: Reproduced with permission from Van Horn et al. (2012) / PUBLIC LIBRARY OF SCIENCE (PLOS) / CC BY 4.0.

prominently in section *Common currency for money and social reward.*) In an editorial that accompanied the publication of the two reports from Lhermitte, Pillon, and Serdaru (1986) that we considered in section *The lateral frontal-lobe syndrome, Chapter* 15, Mesulam (1986) notes that input from regions processing internal physiological states and "extensively preprocessed sensory information . . . suggests that [paralimbic] areas should be of crucial importance for channeling drive and emotion to appropriate targets in the environment . . ." Then, with explicit reference to social behavior, he continues:

> Experimental lesions in the paralimbic component of the frontal lobe also interfere with social interactions. In social animals such as monkeys, group bonds heavily rely on specific aggressive and submissive displays, grooming behavior, and vocalizations. Success depends on directing the proper behavior to the proper individual in the proper context. Animals with orbitofrontal lesions show a severe disruption of these conspecific affective and affiliative behaviors and eventually experience social isolation . . . These experiments provide a model for the socially maladaptive and emotionally inappropriate behaviors seen after frontal lobe damage and support the contention that these behaviors emerge after involvement of the paralimbic component in the frontal lobe (pp. 322–323).

Linking Neurological and Psychiatric Approaches to Social Behavior

Consistent with the perspective represented in the preceding quote is work from Michael Koenigs and his colleagues who have studied both patients with lesions of the vmPFC, and incarcerated inmates who have been diagnosed with psychopathy. Psychopathy is a psychiatric condition associated with callous and impulsive antisocial behavior, and the rationale behind some of Koenigs' research is that "For decades, neurologists have noted that the personality changes accompanying vmPFC damage (e.g., lack of empathy, irresponsibility, and poor decision making) bear striking resemblance to hallmark psychopathic personality traits," to the extent that "the personality changes associated with vmPFC damage have been dubbed 'pseudopsychopathy' and 'acquired sociopathy' " (Motzkin, Newman, Kiehl, and Koenigs, 2012, p. 17348). Prompted by this similarity, Koenigs teamed up with clinical psychologist Joseph Newman to administer tests of economic decision making to incarcerated criminals with diagnoses of psychopathy. Their tasks, like many we considered in *Chapter 16*, comprised a series of offers. However, these offers, like the "prisoner's dilemma" and other assessments from game theory that some readers may be familiar with, were designed to assess the extent to which people's behavior in social situations can deviate from what a rational choice should be. Their findings (Koenigs, Kruepke, and Newman, 2010) indicated that psychopaths, like patients with vmPFC lesions, were disproportionately sensitive to offers that are perceived as unfair – that is, how fairly one thinks one is being treated by another person, and/or one's assessment of the motives of that person, influences how one reasons about money. The next step was to see if their brains showed evidence of abnormality in the vmPFC. Enter Kent Kiehl.

Kiehl (profiled in Seabrook, 2008, *Further Reading*) has a mobile MRI scanner, built into a trailer that can be towed around North America, and well-worked-out specifications for how the local contractor is to pour the concrete slab in the prison yard to provide the needed stability for the scanner. On the strength of their behavioral findings, Koenigs and Newman teamed up with Kiehl to set up his scanner on the grounds of a prison and enroll incarcerated psychopaths. The first of their findings, illustrated in *Figure 17.4*, emphasizes the message also evident in *Figure 17.3*, which is that we can't lose sight of the fact that no region of the brain does anything in isolation – understanding connections is central to understanding function. Here's how Julian Motzkin et al. (2012) set it up:

> Both the amygdala and precuneus/PCC are densely and reciprocally connected with vmPFC . . . and both areas have been associated with reduced activity in psychopathy . . . Moreover, the interactions between vmPFC and these areas are thought to subserve key functions related to psychopathy. vmPFC–amygdala interactions are thought to underlie aspects of emotion regulation, aggression, and stimulus-reinforcement associations [we'll get to these in *Chapter 18*], while vmPFC–precuneus/PCC interactions are thought to underlie aspects of self-reflective processing. (p. 17348)

For the study, they recruited prison inmates who did and did not have a diagnosis of psychopathy, and acquired T1-weighted MRI, diffusion tensor imaging (DTI), and resting-state fMRI data (section *Diffusion tensor imaging – in vivo "tract tracing"; T1-weighted imaging; Resting state functional correlations, Chapter 4*). *Figure 17.4* illustrates the connectivity results, which do, indeed, implicate some of the tracts also estimated to have been compromised by Phineas Gage's injury.

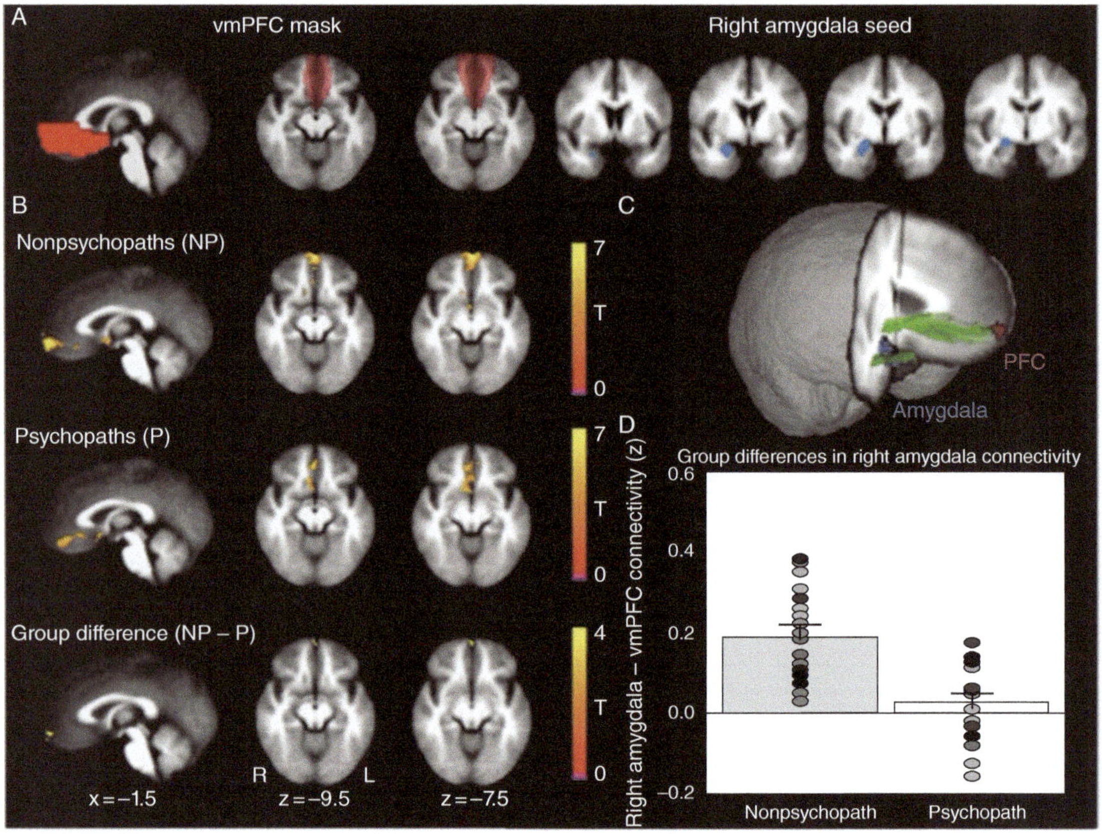

FIGURE 17.4 Amygdala–vmPFC connectivity differs between psychopathic and nonpsychopathic incarcerated inmates. **A.** Illustrates the amygdala seed and vmPFC mask used for resting-state connectivity analysis. **B.** Illustrates regions of significant resting-state functional correlation in the two groups, and the difference map. Similarly, decreased functional connectivity was found between medial parietal cortex and vmPFC. **C.** Illustrates the path of the uncinate fasciculus, the primary end, shown by DTI to be compromised in the psychopath group. **D.** Shows individual subject values that went into **B.**

Source: Reproduced with permission from Motzkin et al. (2012) / Society for Neuroscience.

Theory of Mind

One concept that is central to many accounts of cognitive development, and of adult social cognition, is the theory of mind (ToM). As described by Helen Gallagher and Christopher Frith (2003), "It underpins our ability to deceive, cooperate and empathize, and to read others' body language. It also enables us to accurately anticipate other people's behavior, almost as if we had read their minds" (p. 77). The ToM literature is considered in this section because the core questions underlying many claims, and debates, within this subfield of social neuroscience have relevance to other subfields of social neuroscience and, more broadly, to other areas of cognitive neuroscience. An additional reason that this literature is of interest to many is the widely (although not universally) held view that impairments of ToM may underlie one or more variants of **autism spectrum disorder** (ASD).

The ToM Network

ToM reasoning has been theorized to require two representational steps. First, one must represent another person as an individual. Second, one must represent that person's mental states. This second stage – engaging in mentation about the thoughts, motivations, and knowledge of another – is referred to as "mentalizing." Many neuroimaging studies of ToM have used a story comprehension procedure in which subjects read brief vignettes, answering a question about each, and the contrast of interest compares activity associated with stories that required ToM mentalization vs. stories that did not. In their 2003 review, Gallagher and Frith emphasize three regions, each contributing differently to performance on theory-of-mind tasks. Two of these are in the temporal lobes, and the authors suggest that these aren't involved in mentalizing per se, but perhaps in functions that are necessary precursor steps. To the right posterior superior temporal sulcus they ascribe "understanding the meaning of stories and cartoons involving people, with or without the requirement to mentalize . . . understanding causality and intentionality . . . the attribution of intentions to the movements of geometric shapes . . . and taking the self-perspective" (pp. 80–81). They note that this region has also been associated with the perception of biological motion, including movements of the hands, body, lips, and eyes. To the temporal poles, they ascribe retrieval of semantic and episodic memory that can be critical for succeeding on a ToM task. The anterior paracingulate cortex, in contrast, is argued to be recruited for tasks in which subjects take "an 'intentional stance', which is to treat a system as an agent, attributing to it beliefs and goals" (p. 79). This is seen, for example, when the subject is playing the game "rock, paper, scissors" (in the UK, "stone, paper, scissors") in two conditions, one in which they believe that the opponent is a computer (in which the anterior paracingulate cortex is not engaged), and the second in which they believe that the opponent is a human being outside the scanner (in which case the anterior paracingulate cortex is engaged). (This anterior paracingulate region corresponds closely to the "medial PFC" [MPFC] region that another group routinely identifies with its "ToM localizer" task.)

An Aside About Anterior Paracingulate Cortex There is a fascinating variant of frontotemporal dementia (FTD), the same category of disease that produces primary progressive aphasia of the semantic subtype (a.k.a. semantic dementia; section *The progressive loss of knowledge, Chapter 13*), which prominently affects the medial frontal cortex, including vmPFC and anterior paracingulate cortex, in addition to a focal region of the anterior insular cortex, deep within the Sylvian fissure. It is referred to as the behavioral variant of FTD (bvFTD), and manifests as a progressive decline in control over emotion, social behavior, personal conduct, and decision making (see Seeley, Zhou, and Kim, 2012, *Further Reading*).

The Temporoparietal Junction (TPJ) In an influential, and controversial, paper, Rebecca Saxe and her then-PhD advisor Nancy Kanwisher challenged the localization conclusions of Frith and colleagues with regard to ToM mentalizing (Saxe and Kanwisher, 2003). In this and subsequent papers, Saxe and colleagues have argued, instead, for a critical role for the temporoparietal junction (TPJ; the same region that Gallagher and Frith (2003) refer to as the posterior superior temporal sulcus) in ToM mentalizing. Saxe and Kanwisher (2003) noted that previous studies, including some by Frith and colleagues, relied on the practice from developmental psychology of using "false belief" stories as the gold standard for assessing ToM. An example of a false belief scenario, adapted from Gallagher and Frith (2003), is as follows: *(1) Chris knows that the chocolates have been moved from the drawer to the cupboard. (2) He also knows that Helen does not know that they were moved. (3) Chris knows that Helen wants a chocolate. (4) Chris predicts Helen will look for a chocolate in the* _______. Children younger than age 4, as well as patients with developmental disabilities, including some patients with ASD, will mistakenly answer that Chris thinks that Helen will look in the cupboard, which is interpreted as an inability to comprehend that Helen has a false belief about the location of the chocolate. That is, an inability to understand the world from Helen's perspective. With regard to the TPJ, what Gallagher and Frith (2003) have argued, in effect, is that TPJ plays a role in proposition 3, understanding that Helen wants a chocolate, but not in understanding proposition 4.

Now, back to Saxe and Kanwisher (2003). They questioned what they characterized as an overreliance on false belief scenarios to engage ToM mentalizing, and developed a procedure for an fMRI study that used many different contrasts. Experiment 1 contrasted ToM stories vs. mechanical inference stories and vs. human action stories. A group analysis indicated greater activity for ToM than mechanical inference stories in five regions: left and right TPJ; left and right anterior superior temporal sulcus; and precuneus. At the single-subject level, activity in TPJ was greater for ToM stories vs. mechanical inference stories in 22 of 25 subjects (bilaterally in 14, left in 5, and right in 3). Importantly, for 14 subjects, the authors also performed a localizer scan for the extrastriate body area (EBA; see *Figure 10.5*), and found that although this region was anatomically adjacent to the TPJ, it did not respond to ToM stories. Thus, they reasoned that TPJ does not merely respond to the physical presence of a person. Experiment 2 from Saxe and Kanwisher (2003) contrasted activity associated with (1) false belief stories, (2) false photograph stories, (3) desires, (4) inanimate descriptions, and (5) physical people. Desire stories were designed to describe the character's goals or intentions, and thereby to also rely on ToM mentalizing. The findings from Experiment 2 largely mirrored those from Experiment 1, with the additional fact that desire stories also produced elevated activity in TPJ.

In a follow-up study, Saxe and Powell (2006) note in the Introduction that:

> Research suggests that infants and young children understand mental-state concepts like desires, goals, perceptions, and feelings . . . However, not until the age of 4 do children seem to understand concepts like belief – concepts that require understanding that mental representations of the world may differ from the way the world really is. Developmental psychologists have therefore hypothesized that the later-developing system for representing the specific (representational) contents of mental states, such as beliefs, is a distinct component of human understanding of other minds. (p. 692)

Thus, for this study, they hypothesized that if the late-developing component of ToM – what we've been calling "ToM mentalizing" – remains distinct in adulthood, then they would identify one or more brain regions recruited for ToM mentalizing stories, but not for stories invoking mental-state concepts such as those listed in the previous quote. Their findings indicated that TPJ responded specifically to ToM mentalizing stories, whereas more posterior regions, in the supramarginal gyrus of the inferior parietal lobule, responded preferentially to stories invoking mental state concepts.

Challenges to the Specificity of TPJ for ToM Why, at the beginning of this section, did the author characterize this work as controversial? One reason relates to the point that was raised in section *Construct validity in models of cognition, Chapter 1* – many feel that such complex and nuanced mental constructs as conscientiousness and ToM are very unlikely to be localizable to just one or a small handful of regions. At a psychological level, Decety and Lamm (2007) have noted that "Most if not all of the concepts used in social psychology emanate from our folk psychology; we are prisoners of words. Theory of mind, perspective-taking, empathy – these are all complex psychological constructs that cannot be directly mapped to unique single computational mechanisms, and the functions that they attempt to describe [must be] underpinned by a network of areas" (p. 584). From a different perspective, that of systems neuroscience, the portrayal of TPJ as specific for ToM mentalizing smacks of a strongly modular view of the brain that's almost phrenological.

What's at stake in this debate isn't just whether ToM mentalizing "activates" area X or area Y in the brain, but a deeper question that relates to the age-old question of "nature vs. nurture." From the "nature" perspective, evidence that the TPJ may be specialized for ToM mentalizing is taken by some to be consistent with nativist theories in cognitive development, and the idea that ToM may be a trait with which we are born, and which matures to take its place in the mind at around 4 years of age. From the "nurture" perspective, psychological abilities such as ToM mentalizing are portrayed as emerging, through learning, from a general-purpose architecture that's neither specialized for, nor specific to, any one function. This latter perspective is also articulated by Decety and Lamm (2007): "activation in the TPJ during social cognition may . . . rely on a lower-level computational mechanism involved in generating, testing, and correcting internal predictions about external sensory events" (p. 583). More specifically, Decety and Lamm have proposed that "social cognition has gradually arisen from general pervasive perception-action coupling mechanisms" (p. 580) and that a function of the TPJ may be "compar[ing] internal predictions with actual external events" (p. 581).

Note that, in many ways, these objections are reminiscent of some that we considered in relation to the debate about whether the fusiform face area (FFA) is specialized for face processing (*Chapter 10*). Indeed, a 2008 paper from "social cognitive and affective neuroscientist" Jason Mitchell is clearly motivated by his concerns about strong claims of specificity for activity in TPJ. In the paper's Introduction, Mitchell notes that

> The preferential response of this region during belief stories has prompted claims that "temporo-parietal junction is selectively involved in reasoning about the contents of other people's minds" (Saxe and Kanwisher, 2003, p. 1835); "the response of the RTPJ is highly specific to the attribution of mental states" (Saxe and Wexler, 2005, p. 1397); and "the BOLD response in the RTPJ is associated with a highly specific cognitive function . . . the ability to attribute thoughts to another person" (Saxe and Powell, 2006, p. 697).
>
> He then goes on to say:
>
> Although this research has done an exhaustive job of demonstrating that RTPJ contributes to social cognition only when perceivers must infer the beliefs of another person, it has, importantly, neglected substantial evidence that this region may also subserve a set of attentional processes that are not specific to social contexts. In a literature that has developed in parallel with the work of Saxe and colleagues, researchers have repeatedly observed increased RTPJ activity when perceivers must break their current attentional set to reorient to task relevant stimuli (p. 262).

What Mitchell is referring to here is the "circuit breaker" in the Corbetta and Shulman (2002) model that we reviewed in some detail in *Chapter 9*, section *Human attentional control.* In this regard, Mitchell (2008), Decety and Lamm (2007), and others have noted that RTPJ is a key region whose damage often produces hemispatial neglect (see, e.g., *Figure 7.2* and *Figure 7.3*).

To investigate this overlap, Mitchell (2008) closely followed procedures used previously by Saxe and colleagues, most notably using Saxe's "ToM localizer" task (which she shared with him for this purpose), and then interrogating the so-identified "ToM regions" with an attention cuing task. The ToM localizer contrasts story comprehension for false belief scenarios that require ToM mentalization with story comprehension for "false photograph" scenarios, the latter requiring subjects to represent the false content of a physical representation, such as a photograph or map, that doesn't contain any "person" content. The spatial cuing task is a speeded target detection task in which a cue that precedes the target by a variable period of time informs subjects where the target will appear. On a small proportion of trials, the cue is invalid, thereby requiring a reorientation of attention to the unexpected target location (Posner, 1980).

Mitchell's finding was that the RTPJ, but not other regions identified by the ToM localizer (medial PFC, precuneus, superior frontal gyrus), showed elevated responses on all trials of the attentional cuing task, and disproportionately large responses on invalidly cued trials. His conclusion was unflinching:

> These results not only undermine the assertion that RTPJ is selective for inferring the beliefs of other people, but are also incompatible with any strong claim that this region participates selectively in social cognition, broadly construed. Greater activation in RTPJ was observed on a simple attentional cueing task in which no other people were relevant to the task: participants merely pressed 1 of 2 keys to indicate the location in which a target asterisk appeared. In so demonstrating that RTPJ activity is not selective for social cognition, the current results suggest that theory of mind and attentional reorienting may both require a solution to the same computational problem. That is, the observation that the same RTPJ region is engaged by these two tasks suggests the recruitment of a cognitive process that contributes to both belief attribution and attentional reorienting. Although the current study does not specify the exact nature of this shared process, it does suggest the need to develop a better

> conceptual account of what computational problems might jointly be faced by belief attribution and attentional reorienting and, subsequently, to test hypotheses about the processes that are deployed by the human mind to solve this particular cognitive challenge. (p. 268)

Challenges to the Challenges to the Specificity of TPJ for ToM

In the ensuing years, Saxe and colleagues carried out several studies that pointed to an important role for RTPJ in TOM. In one, Jonathan Scholz, Christina Triantafyllou, Susan Whitfield-Gabrieli, Emery Brown, and Rebecca Saxe (2009) replicated the methods of Mitchell (2008), but in a scanner featuring a higher magnetic field (3 tesla ["3T"], as opposed to the 1.5T scanners that Mitchell and Saxe's group had previously used). The higher magnetic field strength allowed Scholz et al. (2009) to acquire higher resolution data (1.6 × 1.6 × 2.4 mm voxels; as contrasted with the 3.75 × 3.75 × 6 mm of Mitchell (2008) and of previous studies from Saxe's group). The results replicated Mitchell's (2008) finding that ToM-defined regions were sensitive to the valid–invalid contrast in the spatial attention task, and that spatial attention-defined regions were sensitive to the ToM contrast, but they determined that there was only a small amount of overlap (<10%) in voxels identified in the ToM localizer and the attention reorientation localizer, and found no evidence of correlation of voxel activity across the two tasks.

Several studies addressed TOM from the perspective of moral judgment. Jorie Koster-Hale, Rebecca Saxe, James Dungan, and Liane Young (2013) motivate this choice as follows:

> The distinction between intentional and accidental acts is particularly salient in the case of moral cognition. Adults typically judge the same harmful act (e.g., putting poison in a drink, failing to help someone who is hurt, making an insensitive remark) to be more morally wrong and more deserving of punishment when committed intentionally vs. accidentally . . . These moral judgments depend on individuals' ability to consider another person's beliefs, intentions, and knowledge, and emerge relatively late in childhood, around age 6–7 years. (p. 5648)

A 2010 study by Liane Young, Joan Camprodon, Marc Hauser, Alvaro Pascual-Leone, and Rebecca Saxe used TMS applied via two different protocols to test for evidence that RTPJ plays a causal role in moral reasoning. The first stage in the procedure was to identify the brain regions that they wanted to target with TMS by scanning subjects with fMRI while they performed the ToM localizer. Next, on a subsequent day, the subjects came to the TMS laboratory and were fitted with infrared markers that allowed for the coregistration of their skull with the computer's digital image of the skull. As a result, when the experimenters touched a part of a subject's skull with an infrared-detectable wand, the computer image of the subject's skull would also be "touched" by an image of a virtual wand. Next, in the computer's 3-D image of the head (and all that was inside it), they could virtually "peel away" the skull to visualize where the wand was located relative to the subject's brain. Thus, with knowledge of the shape of the magnetic field produced by the "wand" (i.e., by the TMS stimulator), the researchers could position the TMS coil on the scalp such that its pulses would stimulate the area that they wanted to target. This approach is sometimes referred to as "frameless stereotaxy," in that it uses the same logic as stereotaxic surgery. (In stereotaxic surgery, a patient is scanned while wearing a cage-like frame over their head, and the subsequent surgery is also performed while they are wearing the cage, so that the location of unseen brain regions can be calculated in reference to the invariant spatial relation between the brain and the frame.)

Young et al. (2010) used two TMS protocols, which they referred to as "offline" and "online." The logic of offline TMS was to produce a virtual lesion with a prolonged train of

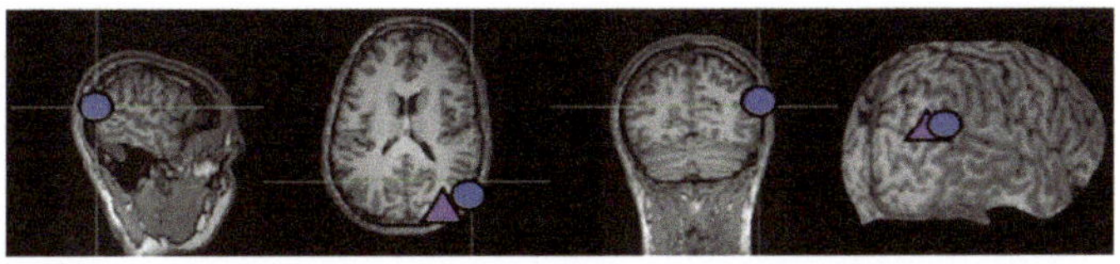

FIGURE 17.5 From Young et al. (2010): The targets for TMS of RTPJ (blue circle) and a control region (purple triangle), on the brain of a single representative subject, from each of three 2D slices, and on a 3D reconstruction of the subject's brain. Note that the 3D image (appearing on the far right of this figure) has been "peeled" (in the way that one removes layers of an onion) to the depth of the target – this is what the investigator sees when positioning the TMS coil during an experiment (c.f. Figure 4.2).

TMS pulses delivered at 1 Hz, in their case for 25 minutes (see section *"Virtual lesion" TMS protocols, Chapter 4*). This approach is "offline" in the sense that low-frequency TMS is delivered first, and then the subject performs the task during the ensuing 25 minutes – TMS is not delivered simultaneously with task performance.

The logic of "online" TMS, in contrast, was analogous to that of stimulation protocols that we have considered previously: it is delivered simultaneously with task performance and, importantly, can target specific epochs of a trial, leaving the others unaffected (section *High-frequency repetitive (r)TMS, Chapter 4*).

The study crossed three factors in each of two experiments: intention of the protagonist (malicious, neutral); outcome suffered by the recipient of the action (harm, no harm); TMS (RTPJ, control area). In both experiments, the story that each subject heard included four sections – "background," "foreshadow," "intention," and "action" – followed by a judgment in which the experimental subject rated the protagonist's actions on a permissible-to-forbidden rating scale. The inclusion of an "active stimulation" control region, which for this study was a region of parietal cortex located 5 cm posterior to the RTPJ, allowed the authors to evaluate whether any result that they might find by applying rTMS to RTPJ could be explained as a nonspecific result of simply applying magnetic stimulation to the brain. (Another type of control condition that is sometimes used in TMS studies, so-called "sham" stimulation that produces the sounds and tapping sensation of TMS, is not as effective a control, because it does not deliver any stimulation to the brain.)

Both studies (offline and online) found the same result, which is that TMS delivered to the RTPJ selectively altered judgments on the malicious-intent stories for which the outcome was no harm. For these stories, rTMS to the RTPJ, but not the control area, had the effect of making subjects judge the action of the protagonist as being more "permissible" than they did when TMS was delivered to the control area. In the online study, a 500-ms train of 10 Hz TMS was delivered simultaneously to the onset of the moral judgment question, meaning that this effect could be isolated to the judgment itself, not to some other factor, like comprehension of the protagonist's intention.

These findings, therefore, revealed a necessary contribution of RTPJ and, possibly, other regions functionally coupled with it (i.e., having elevated functional connectivity with RTPJ), for moral reasoning. It is particularly striking that the TMS effects were seen in just this one cell of the experimental design, meaning, among other things, that rTMS did not also affect judgments for scenarios when the protagonist had ill intent *and* something bad happened. This suggests that RTPJ contributes most importantly to assessing morally ambiguous situations, in which there is a mismatch between intent and outcome.

Note, however, that the results of Young et al. (2010) did not speak to the possible specificity of this region's function in relation to moral judgment vs. other aspects of cognition. In particular, the authors did not assess the effects of rTMS on attentional reorienting. Indeed, there have been several studies of spatial attention (that, in turn, did not test ToM) that have shown clear effects on attention when TMS is delivered to RTPJ. Thus, it's a reasonable assumption that, had Young et al. (2010) included a test of attentional reorienting, they would have found effects on this task, too. (This observation, in turn, must be qualified by the fact that the volume of tissue affected by TMS is sufficiently large – of the order of a cubic centimeter or so – that if the true organization of the brain were such that ToM functions and attentional reorienting functions were segregated in a strict but anatomically adjacent way, the coarse resolution of rTMS would make it impossible to target just one of these regions.)

Fast-forward a decade and a half, and a study employing the relatively recently developed approach of "precision imaging" (a.k.a., "deep imaging"; see Chapter 4, section *Resting state functional correlations*) may have resolved the conundrum of multiple functions ascribed to the RTPJ.

A Network-Level Resolution of the TPJ Debate?

A debate about the function(s) of a single area will always be incomplete, in that no brain area can be construed as "working in total isolation." With regard to the RTPJ, this was illustrated when the team of Donnisa Edmunds and colleagues (2024), led by Rodrigo Braga, carried out RSFC analyses on the data from six subjects who had been scanned on 6–35 5-minutes runs, at 7T, as part of the Natural Scenes data set ("A massive 7T fMRI dataset to bridge cognitive neuroscience and artificial intelligence" [Allen et al., 2022]). Conceptually, Edmunds et al. (2024) started from previous work (e.g., from Jessica Andrews-Hannah and colleagues in the laboratory of Randy Buckner (2010)) suggesting that the Default Mode Network (DMN, see *Chapter 4*, section *Resting state functional correlations*) is better understood as being comprised of two distinct networks – DN-A and DN-B – and that in many regions elements of the two occupy adjacent and sometimes interdigitated subregions. Furthermore, a previous study from Lauren DiNicola, Braga, and Buckner (2020) had previously shown, with fMRI at 3T, that DN-B closely overlaps with activity evoked by ToM tasks. But why, one might ask, might ToM be more strongly associated with DN-B than DN-A? (Similarly, earlier work focused only on RTPJ wasn't able to address the question "why are *these* voxels within RTPJ more important for ToM than *those* voxels?.") Because Edmunds et al. (2024) used data collected at a higher magnetic field strength (i.e., at 7T), however, were able to identify and discriminate extensions of the DN subnetworks into portions of the anterior medial temporal lobe (MTL) that had not been identified at 3T.

As an initial step, Edmunds et al. (2024) first validated their ability, with the data collected at 7T, to identify and distinguish between DN-A and DN-B using conventional methods similar to those used, e.g., by DiNicola et al. (2020). This included carrying out a "surface parcellation" that is comparable to the preprocessing step of "transforming the 3-D volume of BOLD data acquisition space into a 2-D virtual mesh," as described in *Chapter 4*, section *Resting state functional correlations*. As illustrated in *Figure 17.6*, results from the 7T data were comparable to those previously obtained at 3T, including finding nonoverlapping regions in the TPJ.

The results that provide answers to the "why DN-B?" and "why *those* RTPJ voxels?" questions came from the analyses focused on the MTL. As illustrated in *Figure 17.7*, DN-B was found to include unique regions in the anterior MTL, including amygdala (more specifically, the basolateral [BLA] and medial nuclei of the amygdala) and entorhinal cortex. We will have to wait until *Chapter 18: Emotion*, for an in-depth treatment of the amygdala, but for our present purposes, we can summarize it as a structure that is important for the analysis of visually perceived information containing social cues, including assessment of the trustworthiness of an interlocutor. Thus, although we can't explain, from *Figure 17.6*, why each blue or yellow patch appears exactly where it does, what we *can* say is that it is likely for the particular subregions of the RTPJ that have been associated with ToM, that they have this property because they are part of a functional network that includes a region that contributes crucially to many aspects of social cognition.

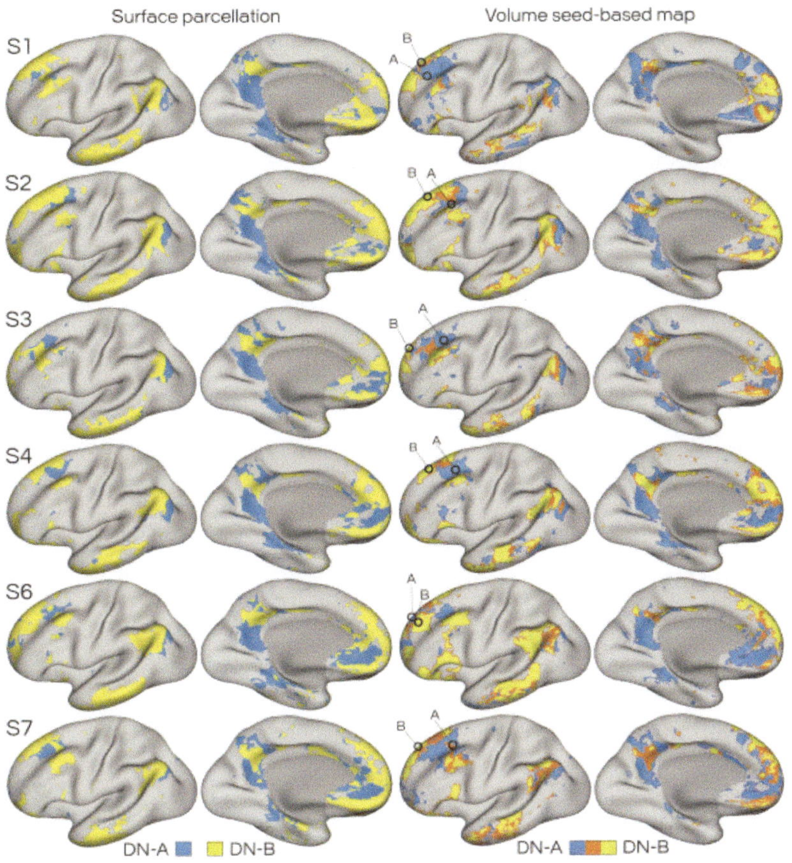

FIGURE 17.6 RSFC maps of two subnetworks of the Default Mode Network, emphasizing the cortical mantle, generated from fMRI data acquired at 7T. The left-hand column shows lateral and medial views of DN-A and DN-B in each of seven subjects, derived from data preprocessed with surface parcellation (the more conventional approach). The method used here produced winner-take-all maps. The right-hand column shows results from the same subjects, but generated with volumetric data, the preprocessed format from which the detailed MTL maps shown in *Figure 17.7* would be derived. Here, the results of the "volumetric" RSFC maps are projected onto the surface to allow comparison with the surface-parcellated data (and thereby validating the use of volumetric data for the MTL-focused analyses). Note that these analyses differ from those used with the surface-parcellated data in that they show areas of overlap (in orange) between the two subnetworks. Unfilled circles indicate the location of a priori-defined seed regions used to derive the "volumetric" RSFC maps.

Source: (Edmonds et al., 2024) / American Association for the Advancement of Science - AAAS.

Social Influences on Decision Making and Learning

We have previously alluded to the fact that individuals often behave differently when they are in a group of conspecifics, or when they think that they are being watched, vs. when they think that they are alone. Here are two demonstrations of this phenomenon.

"How Much Can I Trust You?"

One example of this comes from work by Amrita Lamba, Matthew Nassar, and Oriel FeldmanHall (2023), who scanned subjects with fMRI while they played the Trust Game. On each trial the subject started out with $10 and had to decide how much to "invest" – that is, how much to give to a partner (whom they had never met, and whom they were told had themself previously been a subject in the same study [i.e., a fellow Brown University undergraduate]). The amount of

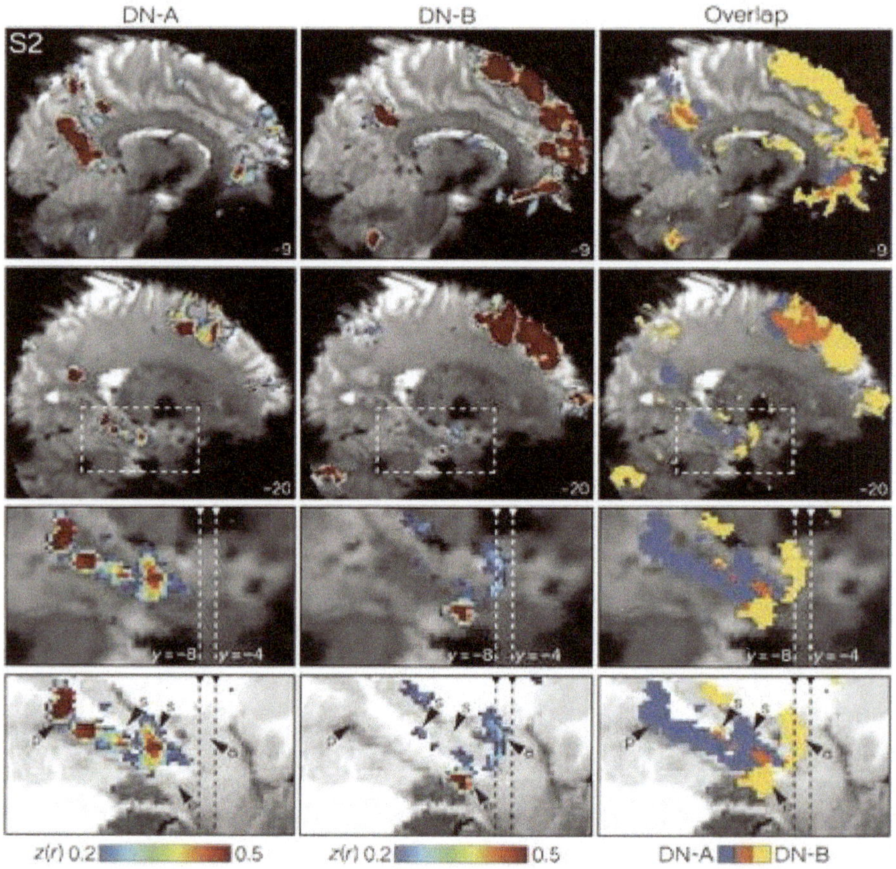

FIGURE 17.7 RSFC maps of two subnetworks of the Default Mode Network, emphasizing the medial temporal lobe. This figure illustrates data from a single subject, the left-hand column corresponding to DN-A, the central column to DN-B, and the third column to the overlap of the two. The top three rows display the RSFC data superimposed on the T2*-weighted fMRI data from which the RSFC maps were derived. Although this format obscures anatomical detail, it is sometimes used, as it is here, to illustrate the true spatial resolution from which the overlying statistical maps were derived. (Typically, the anatomical scans on which statistical data are overlaid, such as the T1-weighted images on the bottom row in this figure, are acquired at considerably higher resolution than are the functional data.) The top row displays a sagittal slice near the midline, so as to illustrate the midline parietal and frontal regions that are the most-referenced regions of the DMN. (To be precise, this slice is 9 mm to the left of the midline, as indicated by the "-9" in the lower right-hand corner.) The second row displays a more lateral section (20 mm left of the midline), selected because it roughly captures the long-axis of the hippocampus as well as the amygdala; the dashed box outlining the portion of this image that will be magnified in the bottom two rows. The y coordinates in the third row indicate locations that are 4 and 8 mm posterior to the anterior commissure (which, at the midline, is the 0,0,0 coordinate in 3D brain atlas space). The bottom row identifies important landmarks and structures, from caudal to rostral: p, parahippocampal cortex; s, subiculum of the hippocampus; e, entorhinal cortex; a, amygdala.

Source: Edmunds et al. (2024) / American Association for the Advancement of Science.

money was then doubled, and the partner then decided how much of the newly doubled amount of money to give back to the subject. Prior to each trial, the subject was shown the photograph of one of four faces, and the cover story was that each of these four individuals, when they had been in the laboratory, had filled out a form indicating how much money they would return to a future player as a function of varying sizes of investment. In reality, each of the four faces had been predetermined by the experimenters to follow one of four reward distributions: that of a high-reward partner who always returned more than the subject initially invested, that of a low-reward partner who always returned less than the subject had invested, and those of a neutral and a random partner, each of whom would return a roughly equivalent "break-even" amount, and who served as controls in some of the analyses. A final twist in the design, and the one that makes it particularly germane at this point in this chapter, is that in addition to the four human partners, subjects would also play this game with four slot machines, each identified by a different color and

FIGURE 17.8 Solving the credit assignment problem when interacting with people vs. with slot machines.
Source: (Lamba, Nassar, & FeldmanHall, 2023) / eLife Sciences Publications, Ltd / CC BY 4.0.

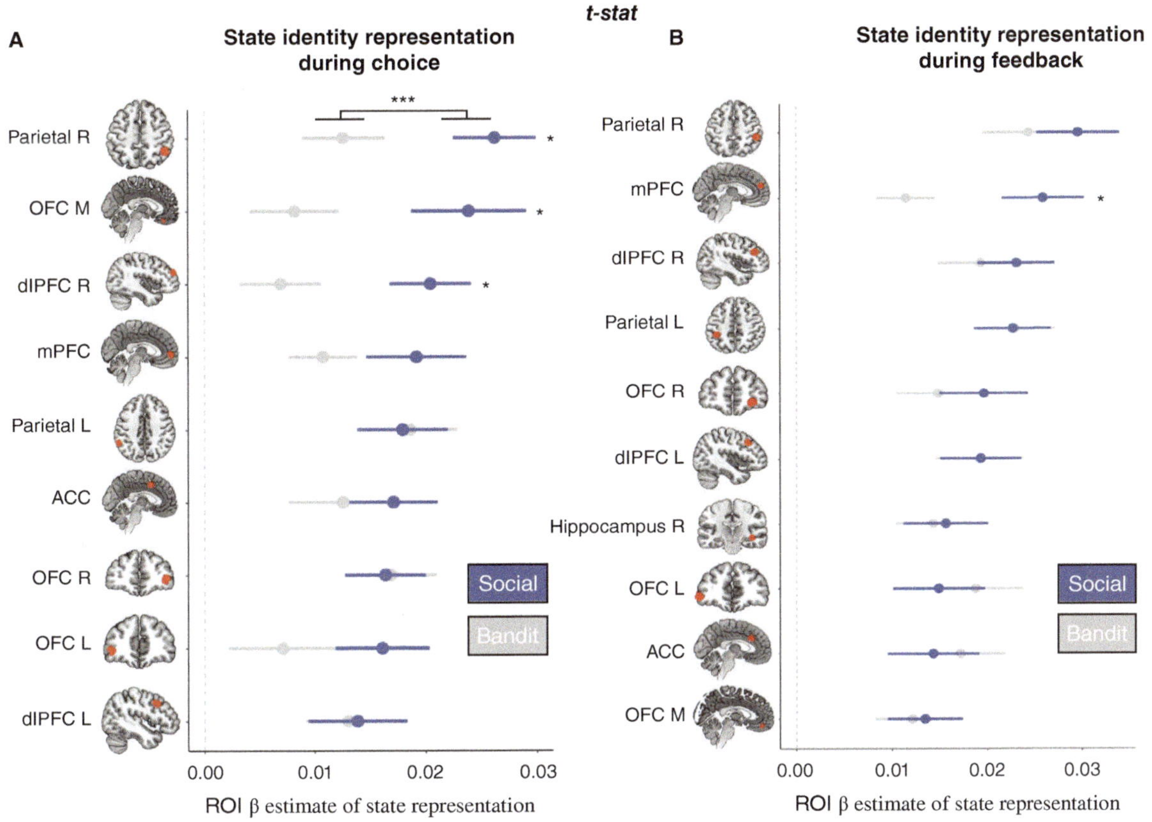

FIGURE 17.8.A The strength of stimulus representation while deciding how much to invest. For each of the ROIs displayed, each identified via a searchlight analysis, the strength of the representation of which-is-the-partner-with-whom-I'm-currently-interacting ("state identity representation") is plotted for trials involving interactions with human partners ("Social") and for trials involving interactions with a slot machine ("Bandit").

FIGURE 17.8.B The strength of stimulus representation while receiving feedback about the results of an investment.

each programmed to pay off at a different rate. (The four slot machines matched the "high," "low," "neutral," and "random" levels of the human partners).

At a descriptive level, a summary of how subjects performed differently when they thought they were partnered with fellow research subjects vs. when they thought they were partnered with a slot machine is straightforward: For the low-reward partner, subjects learned more quickly, and ultimately invested less, with a human partner than with a stingy slot machine; for the high-reward partner, in contrast, subjects learned more quickly, and ultimately invested more, with a human partner than with a generous slot machine. A reason for this "social" effect was provided by fitting the data to a reinforcement learning (RL) model, which indicated that subjects were more precise in attributing investment outcomes to a partner – formalized by RL as solving the credit assignment problem – when that partner was human. To investigate the neural bases of this, the authors reasoned that successful solution of the credit assignment problem requires the ability to link temporally separated actions with the consequences of those actions (i.e., the "outcomes"). Thus, the precision of credit assignment may depend on representing different outcomes (different "states," a distinct one associated with each partner) distinctly, and then reinstating the appropriate "state representation" when the time comes again to make a decision with the same partner. Using an RSA-based analysis to operationalize the precision of neural states (c.f., *Chapter 4*, section *Representational similarity analysis*; also *Chapter 11*, section *More-recently proposed roles for the hippocampus*), the results indicated that many of the brain areas that we have associated with value-based decision making and with social cognition showed stronger state representations during trials involving human partners than during trials involving slot machines (*Figure 17.8*).

Observational Learning

In the final section of this chapter, we'll consider another aspect of social behavior, which is learning by observing the behavior of others. Although we learn many things about how the world works through direct trial and error, it can often be more efficient, and sometimes safer, to watch how others approach a novel situation and, as the expression has it, "learn from their mistakes." Formally, these two types of learning are called "experiential" and "observational," and the latter is inherently social. On an intuitive level, it makes sense that we can learn from observing the experiences of others, and each of us can immediately think of several examples. (Here's a simple one. You are hungry and go to the lobby in your building where the vending machines are located. There are two machines, and as you arrive you see that someone else has put money into machine A, and is now cursing and kicking the machine because it took her money but didn't deliver the item that she selected, nor will it return her money. As a result of this observation of the behavior of another, which vending machine are you going to use, A or B?) As we shall now see, however, the way that observational learning works can be nonintuitive.

In this chapter's final study that we will consider in detail, Burke, Tobler, Baddeley, and Schultz (2010) scanned subjects with fMRI while they performed a probabilistic learning task. On each block of trials, three pairs of randomly selected fractal stimuli were presented, and the subject had to learn, for each pair, which of the two was associated with a positive outcome, and which with a negative outcome. (On "gain" blocks, the positive outcome was gaining 10 points for selecting the correct stimulus and gaining 0 points for the incorrect one; on "loss" blocks, the positive outcome was losing 0 points for selecting the correct stimulus and losing 10 points for selecting the incorrect one.) To capture some of the "noise" and variation that exist in the natural world, these reward contingencies were probabilistic, rather than absolute: during *gain* blocks, the "good" stimulus delivered the reward on 80% of trials, but the contingencies were reversed on the remaining 20% of trials; during *loss* blocks, the same probabilities applied. Trial types were blocked such that the subject performed a series of *gain* trials during one several minute-long scan, and then a series of *loss* trials during the next.

Here's the social/observational part. On the day of the scan, it was arranged that a few minutes after the true research subject arrived to be scanned, a second individual who was actually a part of the research team (a "confederate") arrived and also sat in the waiting room, pretending to be a second research subject. A second experimenter then came into the room (playing the role of the experimenter) and explained to both that they would be playing the same casino-style gambling-machine game – trying to win the most points and lose the least. It was also explained that, while playing the game, one of the two would be in the MRI scanner (always the true research subject) and the other would be in a testing room. They would take turns, and each would be able to observe how the other was playing. Then, a digital photo of each was taken, and it was further explained that the photo of the person currently taking a turn would be displayed on the screen.

The sequence of a trial is illustrated in *Figure 17.9.A–C*. In addition to the blocking of *gain* and *loss* trials, the critical experimental factor was the amount of social information available to the research subject: none (*Individual learning*); some (*Action only*, in which the subject could observe the confederate's choice, but not the outcome of that choice); and all (*Action + outcome*). One might expect (at least this author did) that observing only another's choice, but not the outcome of that choice, would be of little-to-no use to an individual. Afterall, how could one "learn from another's mistakes" without the knowledge of whether or not that person's choice turned out to be a mistake? (In the vending machine example, if you watched the person put their money in the machine, but then stepped outside to make a phone call and, when you returned to the lobby, they were no longer there, how could having seen them put their money into the machine, but not having seen them lose that money, possibly help you make a better decision?)

FIGURE 17.9 Experiential and observational learning.

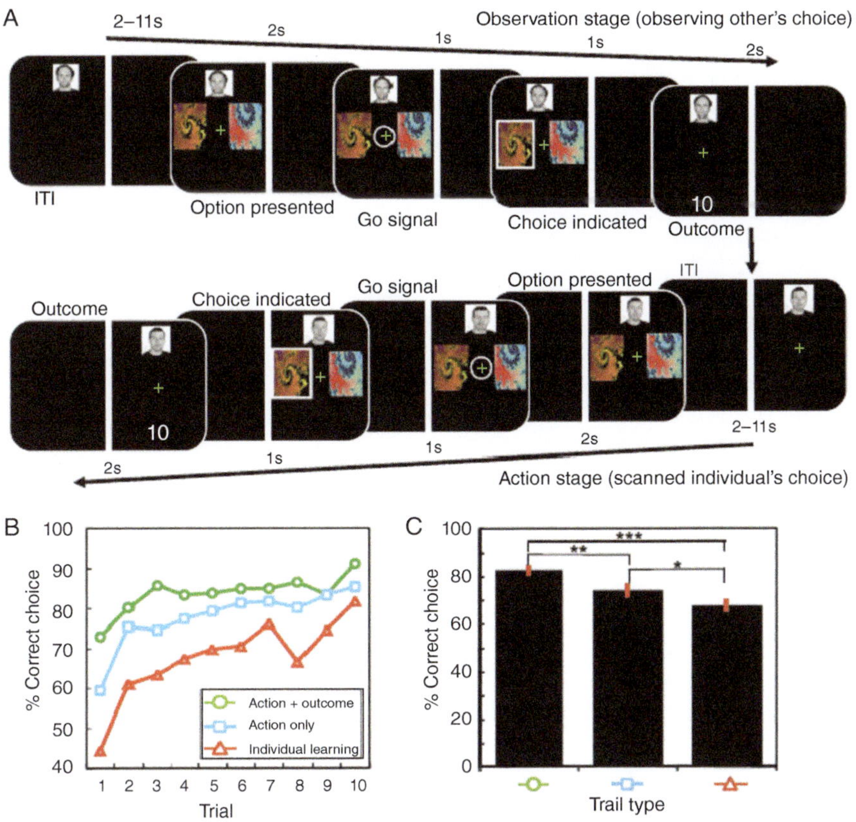

FIGURE 17.9.A–C Panel **A** illustrates the series of events on a single trial. First, in the *Observation stage*, the subject watched as the confederate's options were presented, and then as the confederate received the go signal, made his choice, and was informed of the outcome (in this illustration, he won 10 points). Next, in the *Action stage*, the subject went through the same sequence. On *Individual learning* trials, the subject only experienced the *Action stage*; on *Action-only* trials, the subject observed all the sequences of the confederate's trial (i.e., the *Observation stage*), with the exception that the outcome was not presented. During each session, the same pair of stimuli was presented for each *Individual learning* trial, a different pair for each *Action-only* trial, and still a different pair for each *Action + outcome* trial. Panel **B** illustrates, with a single subject's performance, that even beginning with the first trial, having knowledge of another's action, even without knowing what the outcome of the action was, aided performance markedly. Panel **C** shows aggregated group performance in the three learning conditions.

Source: Burke et al., 2010 / PNAS Group.

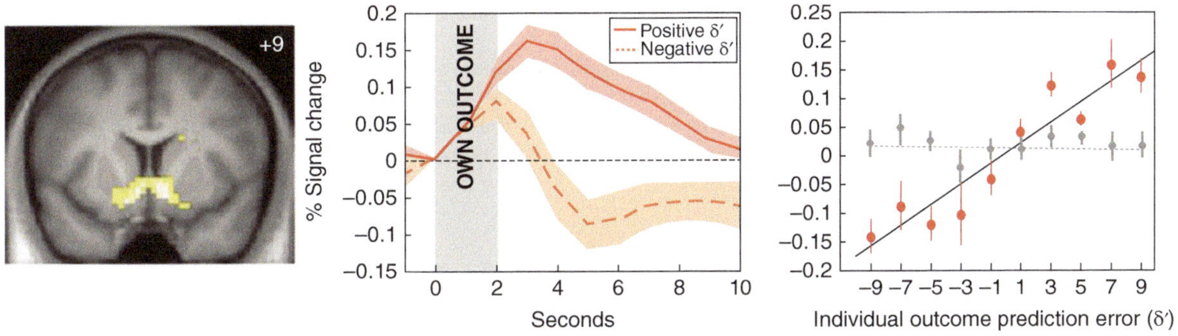

FIGURE 17.9.D The region correlating with RPEs from the model was the nucleus accumbens of the ventral striatum. The center panel shows activity from this region, time locked to the *Outcome* epoch of the *Action stage* from panel **A**, sorted into trials estimated by the model to produce a positive RPE or a negative RPE. The panel on the right illustrates the correlation between the model's estimates of individual outcome prediction error on each of the 10 trials of the session and the fMRI response from the corresponding trials, in the nucleus accumbens (red symbols). Note that, because all trial types had an *Outcome* stage, this analysis included trials from all three trial types. To demonstrate that social and nonsocial learning are integrated in this outcome prediction error in the nucleus accumbens, the gray symbols show the same regression with expected outcome prediction errors, but when social information was removed from the model on *Action only* and *Action + outcome* trials.

Source: Burke et al., 2010 / National Academy of Sciences.

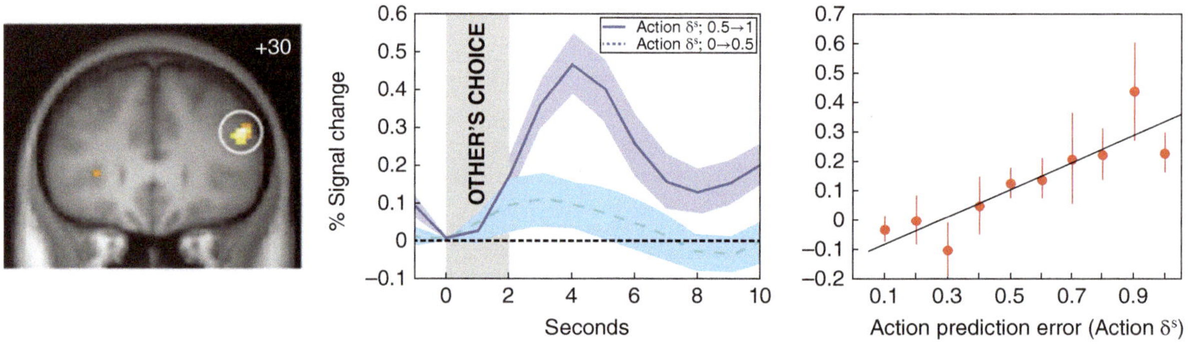

FIGURE 17.9.E The region correlating with the *action prediction error* signal from the model was the dorsolateral PFC. The center panel shows activity from this region, time locked to the *Choice indicated* epoch of the *Observation stage* from panel **A**, sorted into trials estimated by the model to produce a large *action prediction error* and a small *action prediction error*. The panel on the right illustrates the correlation between the model's estimate of *action prediction errors* and the fMRI response from the corresponding trials in the dorsolateral PFC.

Source: Burke et al., 2010 / National Academy of Sciences.

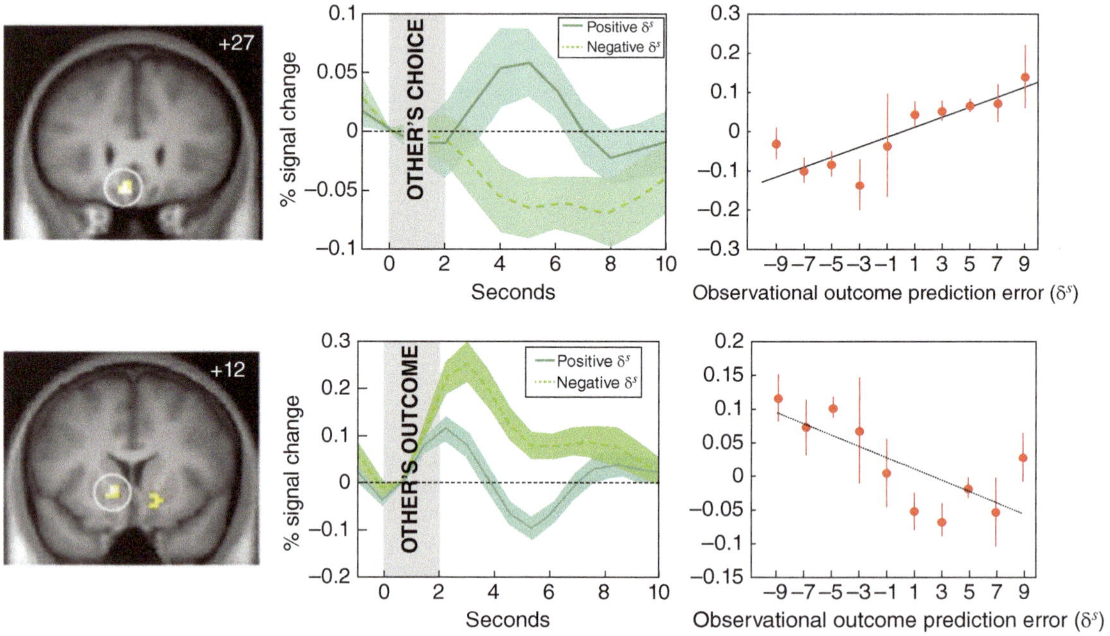

FIGURE 17.9.F The regions correlating with *observational-outcome prediction errors* from the model were the ventromedial PFC (top row) and the nucleus accumbens (bottom row), the two responding in opposite directions. The center panel shows activity from the two regions, time locked to the *Outcome* epoch of the *Observation stage* of panel **A**, sorted into trials estimated by the model to produce a positive *observational-outcome prediction error* and a negative *observational-outcome prediction error*. The panel on the right illustrates the correlation between the model's estimate of *observational-outcome prediction errors* and the fMRI response from the corresponding trials in the two regions.

Source: Burke et al., 2010 / National Academy of Sciences.

Predicting the Outcome of Someone Else's Actions

Although there is no obvious, intuitive reason why a subject should learn more quickly when they can observe the choices of another, but not the outcomes of those choices, there are RL algorithms that can explain it. The senior author of the Burke et al. (2010) study is Wolfram Schultz, whose discovery and characterization of the dopaminergic reward prediction error (RPE) signal, together with Ranulfo Romo, was detailed in section *A dopaminergic correlate of the reward prediction error, Chapter 5* (Romo and Schultz, 1990). It was true to form, then, that Burke et al. (2010) proposed that human observational learning may be achieved by applying two newly hypothesized variants of RPE signals. They implemented this idea in a RL model

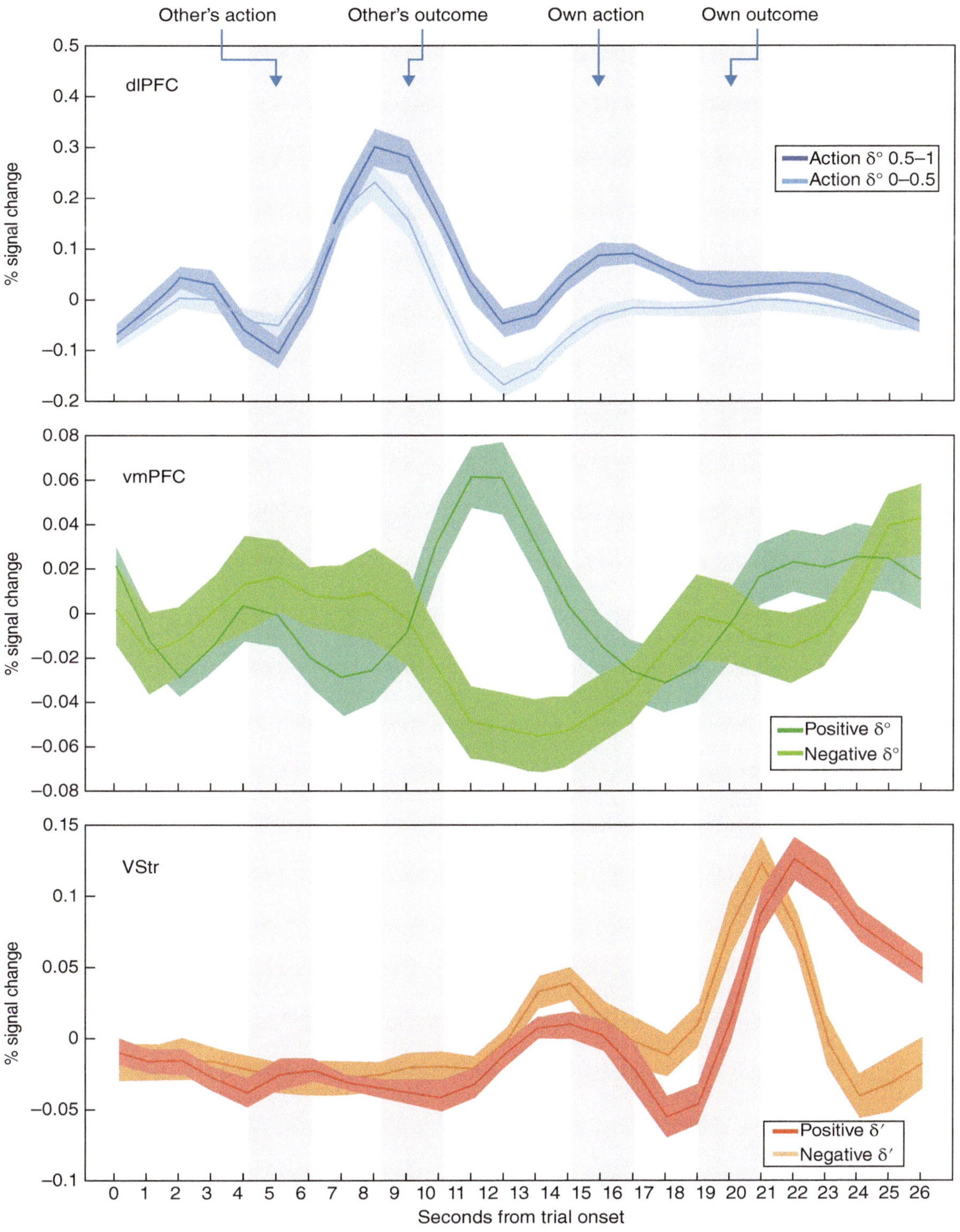

FIGURE 17.9.G The full-trial group- and trial-averaged fMRI time series from the three ROIs illustrated earlier in this figure. This panel provides a simultaneous presentation of the timing of each of the error prediction–related effects in the context of the full length of the trial, and of each of the ROIs implicated in these different facets of observation learning. ("VStr" = ventral striatum, the gross-anatomical location of the nucleus accumbens.)

Source: Burke et al., 2010 / National Academy of Sciences.

that, like we saw in section *"How much can I trust you?"*, is intended to address the credit assignment problem – in this case, that of learning which actions are the best to take in different circumstances when the outcome of the action (and, therefore, its rewarding value) won't be known until some later point in time.

When considering observational learning, the authors noted that the behavior of subjects differs as a function of whether or not the outcome of the confederate's choice is visible. If we consider *Figure 17.9.A–C*, for example, on *Action-only* trials, subjects much more frequently imitated the confederate's behavior than they did on *Action + outcome* trials. This confirmed that subjects "adaptively used available information in the different conditions," and led the authors to reason that a process of observing another's actions and combining this knowledge with one's own experience "can be thought of as a two-stage learning process; first, observing the action of another player biases the observer to imitate that action (at least on early trials), and second, the outcome of the observer's own action refines the values associated with each stimulus" (p. 14432). On *Action + outcome* trials, the authors posited an analogous two-stage process, but with the second stage corresponding to observing the outcome of the confederate's choice.

The mechanisms that Burke et al. (2010) proposed to implement the first stage of learning in these two two-stage processes were previously undescribed variants of RPEs. On *Action-only* trials, they hypothesized that an "action prediction error" would signal the extent to which the confederate's choice differed from what the observer expected the confederate to do. Because, unlike rewarded choices, simple motor actions do not have inherently rewarding or punishing values, they posited that action prediction errors could vary in magnitude, but not in sign (i.e., a so-called "unsigned" RPE[2]). On *Action + outcome* trials, they hypothesized that an "observational outcome prediction error" would have the same properties as the RPE that we have already learned about, but would be based on "vicarious" rewards, in that they pertained to the confederate, and could never have been obtained by the observer. (This is related to the concept of "fictive learning.")

To assess the neurobiological reality of these hypothesized RPEs, Burke et al. (2010) first fit their model to the behavioral data from the subjects who were scanned while performing the task illustrated in *Figure 17.9.A*. Next, they used the resultant parameter estimates, corresponding to *reward prediction errors*, *action prediction errors*, and *observational-outcome prediction errors*, as regressors with which to analyze the fMRI data. This approach to neuroimaging data analysis is known as a "model-based" analysis. The rationale behind model-based fMRI (as in the study that we are currently considering) is that if there's no clear intuitive understanding of a certain pattern of behavior, conventional analyses of fMRI scans of this poorly understood behavior wouldn't provide any new insight about it. All they would show is where in the brain there are changes in activity associated with something that we don't understand. If, on the other hand, this behavioral phenomenon can be understood via a formal model, with parameters that we can understand, determining that there are areas of the brain whose activity covaries with the parameter estimates from the model can help us understand the neural implementation of the mechanisms described by the model. This is how Burke et al. (2010) analyzed the fMRI data from their study, as illustrated in *Figure 17.9*.

The results from the *observational-outcome prediction errors*, that two different regions showed opposite effects to the same prediction error signal, allow us to make a broader point. Although the results from *Figure 17.9.D–F* show results in different regions, it's not believed to be the case that, for example, RPE signals were delivered in a targeted manner to the nucleus accumbens, whereas *action prediction errors* were delivered in a targeted manner to dorsolateral PFC. Rather, each of these prediction errors is assumed to have been delivered via the same "nonspecific broadcast" from midbrain dopaminergic neurons. The differential patterns of activity result from the fact that brain areas that are processing information about reward, or about another's actions, or about the outcome of another's actions, will respond differentially to this dopaminergic signal when they are processing information about the task. (E.g., if dorsolateral PFC "doesn't care" about reward, nor about the rewarding consequences for someone else of the outcome of that person's actions, the dopaminergic prediction error related to these events won't change its activity. Recall that DA's effects are modulatory, not driving.)

A fun and speculative note to end this chapter is the interpretation of the opposing effects that the *observational-outcome prediction error* had on vmPFC vs. on nucleus accumbens. In particular, the sign reversal of the signal in nucleus accumbens means that a positive

[2]In *Chapter 12*, section *Incidental encoding into LTM during "everyday life,"* we made passing reference (also in a footnote) to a RL-based model that makes use of unsigned RPEs in event segmentation (Rouhani, Clewett, and Antony, 2024).

observational-outcome prediction error occurs when viewing another person lose. Although the Burke et al. (2010) model did not have an a priori prediction about this finding, the authors speculate that this may suggest that "it [is] . . . rewarding to view the misfortunes of others" (p. 14435). (Author's thought bubble: Isn't there a German word for that? . . . Oh yeah, *Schadenfreude*!)

End-of-Chapter Questions

1. Explain how the concept of "menu-invariance" (from economics [and neuroeconomics]) extends to social behavior, including what brain area/s is/are implicated.

2. In what ways do findings from contemporary behavioral neurology support the conclusions drawn from the case of Phineas Gage?

3. Does the vmPFC act alone in the control of social behavior? What evidence supports your answer?

4. What brain regions have been implicated as part of a "ToM network"? What function(s) have been ascribed to different components of this network?

5. What are the two differing accounts of the function(s) supported by the right TJP in relation to social behavior? What fundamental theoretical perspectives underlie these two accounts?

6. What are the three different experimental protocols for using TMS to study neural function? (Note: only two are considered in this chapter.)

7. How have resting state functional connectivity (RSFC) analyses helped to address the controversy about the role of right TJP in social cognition?

8. What construct from reinforcement learning is implicated in the fact that humans make decisions differently when they are interacting with another human vs. when they are interacting with a machine? What are the neural correlates of this "humanness effect," and what brain regions are implicated?

9. What is the circumstance when a model-based analysis of fMRI may be preferred over the univariate or multivariate approaches that we have emphasized up until this point in the book?

10. How might it be that learning is improved when one can observe the actions of others, but not the outcomes of these actions? Be specific about the proposed neurobiological mechanism(s).

References

Allen, E. J., G. St-Yves, Y. Wu, J. L. Breedlove, J. S. Prince, L. T. Dowdle, . . . K. Kay. 2022. "A Massive 7T fMRI Dataset to Bridge Cognitive Neuroscience and Artificial Intelligence." *Nature Neuroscience 25* (1): 116–126. doi: 10.1038/s41593-021-00962-x.

Andrews-Hannah, J. R., J. S. Reidler, J. Sepulcre, R. Poulin, and R. L. Buckner. 2010. "Functional-Anatomic Fractionation of the Brain's Default Network." *Neuron 65*: 550–562. doi: 10.1016/j.neuron.2010.02.005.

Burke, Christopher J., Philippe N. Tobler, Michelle Baddeley, and Wolfram Schultz. 2010. "Neural Mechanisms of Observational Learning." *Proceedings of the National Academy of Sciences of the United States of America* 107 (32): 14431–14436. doi: 10.1073/pnas.1003111107.

Corbetta, Maurizio, and Gordon L. Shulman. 2002. "Control of Goal-Directed and Stimulus-Driven Attention in the Brain." *Nature Reviews Neuroscience* 3 (3): 201–215. doi: 10.1038/nrn755.

Deaner, Robert O., Amit V. Khera, and Michael L. Platt. 2005. "Monkeys Pay Per View: Adaptive Valuation of Social Images by Rhesus Macaques." *Current Biology* 15 (6): 543–548. doi: 10.1016/j.cub.2005.01.044.

Decety, Jean, and Claus Lamm. 2007. "The Role of the Right Temporoparietal Junction in Social Interaction: How Low-Level Computational Processes Contribute to Meta-Cognition." *The Neuroscientist* 13 (6): 580–593. doi: 10.1177/1073858407304654.

DiNicola, L. M., R. M. Braga, and R. L. Buckner. 2020. "Parallel Distributed Networks Dissociate Episodic and Social Functions within the Individual." *Journal of Neurophysiology 123* (3): 1144–1179. doi: 10.1152/jn.00529.2019.

Edmonds, D., J. J. Salvo, N. Anderson, M. Lakshman, Q. Yang, K. Kay, . . . R. M. Braga. 2024. "The human social cognitive network contains multiple regions within the amygdala." *Science Advances 10* (47): eadp0453. doi: 10.1126/sciadv.adp0453.

Gallagher, Helen L., and Christopher D. Frith. 2003. "Functional Imaging of 'Theory of Mind'." *Trends in Cognitive Sciences* 7 (2): 77–83. doi: 10.1016/S1364-6613(02)00025-6.

Harlow, John Martyn. 1868. "Recovery from the Passage of an Iron Bar through the Head." *Bulletin of the Massachusetts Medical Society* 2: 327–347.

Horn, Van, John Darrell, Andrei Irimia, Carinna M. Torgerson, Micah C. Chambers, Ron Kikinis, and Arthur W. Toga. 2012. "Mapping Connectivity Damage in the Case of Phineas Gage." *PLoS One* 7 (5): e37454. doi: 10.1371/journal.pone.0037454.

Jiang, Y., Huttunen, A., Belkaya, N., and Platt, M. L. (preprint 2024). Monkeys predict US elections. *bioRxiv*. https://www.biorxiv.org/content/10.1101/2024.09.17.613526v2

Koenigs, Michael, Michael Kruepke, and Joseph P. Newman. 2010. "Economic Decision-Making in Psychopathy: A Comparison with Ventromedial Prefrontal Lesion Patients." *Neuropsychologia* 48 (7): 2198–2204. doi: 10.1016/j.neuropsychologia.2010.04.012.

Koster-Hale, Jorie, Rebecca Saxe, James Dungan, and Liane L. Young. 2013. "Decoding Moral Judgments from Neural Representations of Intentions." *Proceedings of the National Academy of Sciences of the United States of America* 110 (14): 5648–5653. doi: 10.1073/pnas.1207992110.

Lamba, A., M. R. Nassar, and O. FeldmanHall. 2023. "Prefrontal Cortex State Representations Shape Human Credit Assignment." *eLife 12*. doi: 10.7554/eLife.84888.

Lhermitte, François, Bernard Pillon, and M. Serdaru. 1986. "Human Autonomy and the Frontal Lobes. Part I: Imitation and Utilization Behavior: A Neuropsychological Study of 75 Patients." *Annals of Neurology* 19 (4): 326–334. doi: 10.1002/ana.410190404.

Macmillan, Malcolm. 2000. *An Odd Kind of Fame: Stories of Phineas Gage*. Cambridge, MA: MIT Press.

Mesulam, M.-Marsel. 1985. "Patterns in Behavioral Neuroanatomy: Association Areas, the Limbic System, and Hemispheric Specialization." In *Principles of Behavioral Neurology*, edited by M.-Marsel Mesulam, Vol. 26 of *Contemporary Neurology Series* (pp. 1–70). Philadelphia, PA: F. A. Davis.

Mesulam, M.-Marsel. 1986. "Frontal Cortex and Behavior." *Annals of Neurology* 19 (4): 320–325. doi: 10.1002/ana.410190403.

Mitchell, Jason P. 2008. "Activity in Right Temporo-Parietal Junction Is Not Selective for Theory-of-Mind." *Cerebral Cortex* 18 (2): 262–271. doi: 10.1093/cercor/bhm051.

Motzkin, Julian C., Joseph P. Newman, Kent A. Kiehl, and Michael Koenigs. 2012. "Reduced Prefrontal Connectivity in Psychopathy." *Journal of Neuroscience* 31 (48): 17348–17357.

Padoa-Schioppa, Camillo, and John A. Assad. 2008. "The Representation of Economic Value in the Orbitofrontal Cortex Is Invariant for Changes of Menu." *Nature Neuroscience* 11 (1): 95–102.

Posner, Michael I. 1980. "Orienting of Attention." *Quarterly Journal of Experimental Psychology* 32 (1): 3–25. doi: 10.1080/00335558008248231.

Romo, R., and W. Schultz. 1990. "Dopamine Neurons of the Monkey Midbrain: Contingencies of Responses to Stimuli Eliciting Immediate Behavioral Responses." *Journal of Neurophysiology 63*: 607–624.

Rouhani, N., D. Clewett, and J. W. Antony. 2024. "Building and Breaking the Chain: A Model of Reward Prediction Error Integration and Segmentation of Memory." *Journal of Cognitive Neuroscience 36* (11): 2401–2414. doi: 10.1162/jocn_a_02215.

Saxe, Rebecca, and Nancy Kanwisher. 2003. "People Thinking about Thinking People: The Role of the Temporo-Parietal Junction in 'Theory of Mind'." *NeuroImage* 19 (4): 1835–1842. doi: 10.1016/S1053-8119(03)00230-1.

Saxe, Rebecca, and Lindsey J. Powell. 2006. "It's the Thought That Counts: Specific Brain Regions for One Component of Theory of Mind." *Psychological Science* 17 (8): 692–699. doi: 10.1111/j.1467-9280.2006.01768.x.

Saxe, R., and A. Wexler. 2005. "Making sense of another mind: the role of the right temporo-parietal junction." *Neuropsychologia* 43 (10): 1391–1399. doi: 10.1016/j.neuropsychologia.2005.02.013.

Scholz, Jonathan, Christina Triantafyllou, Susan Whitfield-Gabrieli, Emery N. Brown, and Rebecca Saxe. 2009. "Distinct Regions of Right Temporo-Parietal Junction Are Selective for Theory of Mind and Exogenous Attention." *PLoS One* 4 (3): e4869. doi: 10.1371/journal.pone.0004869.

Smith, David V., Benjamin Y. Hayden, Trong-Kha Truong, Allen W. Song, Michael L. Platt, and Scott A. Huettel. 2010. "Distinct Value Signals in Anterior and Posterior Ventromedial Prefrontal Cortex." *Journal of Neuroscience* 30 (7): 2490–2495. doi: 10.1523/JNEUROSCI.3319-09.2010.

Young, Liane, Joan Albert Camprodon, Marc Hauser, Alvaro Pascual-Leone, and Rebecca Saxe. 2010. "Disruption of the Right Temporoparietal Junction with Transcranial Magnetic Stimulation Reduces the Role of Beliefs in Moral Judgments." *Proceedings of the National Academy of Sciences of the United States of America* 107 (15): 6753–6758. doi: 10.1073/pnas.0914826107.

Other Sources Used

Dunne, Simon, and John P. O'Doherty. 2013. "Insights from the Application of Computational Neuroimaging to Social Neuroscience." *Current Opinion in Neurobiology* 23 (3): 387–392. doi: 10.1016/j.conb.2013.02.007.

Feredoes, Eva, and Bradley R. Postle. 2007. "Localization of Load Sensitivity of Working Memory Storage: Quantitatively and Qualitatively Discrepant Results Yielded by Single-Subject and Group-Averaged Approaches to fMRI Group Analysis." *NeuroImage* 35 (2): 881–903. doi: 10.1016/j.neuroimage.2006.12.029.

Fletcher, Paul C., Francesca G. Happé, S. C. Uta Frith, Ray J. Baker, Richard S. J. Dolan, Frackowiak, and Christopher D. Frith. 1995. "Other Minds in the Brain: A Functional Imaging Study of 'Theory of Mind' in Story Comprehension." *Cognition* 57 (2): 109–128. doi: 10.1016/0010-0277(95)00692-R.

Kobayashi, Shunsuke, and Wolfram Schultz. 2008. "Influence of Reward Delays on Responses of Dopamine Neurons." *Journal of Neuroscience* 28 (31): 7837–7846. doi: 10.1523/JNEUROSCI.1600-08.2008.

Ly, M., J. C. Motzkin, C. L. Philippi, G. R. Kirk, J. P. Newman, K. A. Kiehl, and M. Koenigs. 2012. "Cortical thinning in Psychopathy." *American Journal of Psychiatry* 169 (7): 743–749. doi: 10.1176/appi.ajp.2012.11111627.

Michaelson, Laura, Alejandro de la Vega, Christopher H. Chatham, and Yuko Munakata. 2013. "Delaying Gratification Depends on Social Trust." *Frontiers in Psychology* 4: 355. doi: 10.3389/fpsyg.2013.00355.

Passingham, Richard E., and Steven P. Wise. 2012. *The Neurobiology of the Prefrontal Cortex: Anatomy, Evolution, and the Origin of Insight*. Oxford: Oxford University Press.

Smith, Christopher T., and Charlotte A. Boettiger. 2012. "Age Modulates the Effect of COMT Genotype on Delay Discounting Behavior." *Psychopharmacology* 222 (4): 609–617. doi: 10.1007/s00213-012-2653-9.

Winstanley, Catharine A., Jeffrey W. Dalley, David E. H. Theobald, and Trevor W. Robbins. 2003. "Global 5-HT Depletion Attenuates the Ability of Amphetamine to Decrease Impulsive Choice on a Delay-Discounting Task in Rats." *Psychopharmacology* 170 (3): 320–331. doi: 10.1007/s00213-003-1546-3.

Scholz, Jonathan, Christina Triantafyllou, Susan Whitfield-Gabrieli, Emery N. Brown, and Rebecca Saxe. 2009. "Distinct Regions of Right Temporo-Parietal Junction Are Selective for Theory of Mind and Exogenous Attention." *PLoS One* 4 (3): e4869. doi: 10.1371/journal.pone.0004869.

Somerville, Leah H., Rebecca M. Jones, Erika J. Ruberry, Jonathan P. Dyke, Gary Glover, and B. J. Casey. 2013. "The Medial Prefrontal Cortex and the Emergence of Self-Conscious Emotion in Adolescence." *Psychological Science* 24 (8): 1554–1562. doi: 10.1177/0956797613475633.

Further Reading

Adolphs, Ralph. 2010. "Conceptual Challenges and Directions for Social Neuroscience." *Neuron* 65 (6): 752–767. doi: 10.1016/j.neuron.2010.03.006.

One of the leading figures in social neuroscience considers the challenges confronting, and promises awaiting, this field.

Amodio, David M. 2010. "Can Neuroscience Advance Social Psychological Theory? Social Neuroscience for the Behavioral Social Psychologist." *Social Cognition* 28 (6): 695–716. doi: 10.1521/soco.2010.28.6.695.

A perspective on the value, or otherwise, of bringing neuroscience methods into the traditionally behavioral field of social psychology.

Kennedy, Daniel P., and Ralph Adolphs. 2012. "The Social Brain in Psychiatric and Neurological Disorders." *Trends in Cognitive Sciences* 16 (11): 559–572. doi: 10.1016/j.tics.2012.09.006.

Psychiatric and neurological disorders have informed the concept of the social brain, and the authors argue that the social brain, and its dysfunction and recovery, must be understood not in terms of specific structures, but rather in terms of their interaction in large-scale networks.

Macmillan, Malcolm. 2000. *An Odd Kind of Fame: Stories of Phineas Gage*. Cambridge, MA: MIT Press.

Engrossing, thoughtful account of all things Gage, covering Gage's personal history, cultural history, history of science, and implications of the case for cognitive neuroscience, including an emphasis on the localization–mass action debate that reigned over the decades surrounding the turn of the twentieth century.

Seabrook, John. 2008. "Suffering Souls: The Search for the Roots of Psychopathy." *New Yorker* (November 10). http://www.newyorker.com/reporting/2008/11/10/081110fa_fact_seabrook.

Interesting profile of cognitive neuroscientist and psychopathy researcher Kent Kiehl.

Seeley, William W., Juan Zhou, and Eun-Joo Kim. 2012. "Frontotemporal Dementia: What Can the Behavioral Variant Teach Us about Human Brain Organization?." *The Neuroscientist* 18 (4): 373–385. doi: 10.1177/1073858411410354.

This review provides entrée into a fascinating (ongoing) scientific detective story about the causes of this insidious disease, which prominently compromises social behavior, personal conduct, and decision making.

CHAPTER 18

Emotion

KEY THEMES

- Neuropsychological and neuroimaging data suggest that the amygdala performs a kind of implicit, quick-and-dirty triage of visual stimuli, signaling, for example, whether or not faces look trustworthy, whether they belong to a certain race, or whether they are expressing an emotion. The evidence further suggests that the amygdala's "decision rules" are learned and can therefore change with experience.
- Scientific interest in the amygdala was triggered by the drastic and bizarre changes in behavior associated with surgically produced Klüver–Bucy syndrome.
- Intensive study of Pavlovian fear conditioning has yielded detailed knowledge, at the circuit and molecular level, of the plastic change in the amygdala that underlies acquisition and expression of conditioned fear.
- The emotional component of declarative memories also seems to depend on the amygdala and, in particular, its influence on norepinephrine levels via its outputs to the locus coeruleus.
- From a neurobiological perspective, emotions may derive from the activity of systems related to survival, and perhaps to the underlying assessment that a stimulus or situation is safe to approach, or best to avoid.
- The extinction of a fear memory depends on new learning in the amygdala, but also on top-down input from ventromedial PFC (infralimbic [IL] cortex in the rat).
- Unlike conditioned memories, which are implicit and long-lasting, our current emotional state is amenable to real-time volitional control. The mechanisms by which we implement this control are the same as those used for the control of other domains of cognition.
- Many types of psychopathology (post-traumatic stress disorder, depression, and anxiety disorder) are characterized by abnormal neural correlates of emotion regulation.
- One's awareness of the factors that are influencing one's emotional state may be an important determinant of one's ability to regulate their effects.

CONTENTS

Companion Website: www.wiley.com/go/postle/cognitiveneuroscience3e

What Is an Emotion?

The Oxford English Dictionary defines *emotion* as "any strong mental or instinctive feeling, as pleasure, grief, hope, fear, etc., deriving esp. from one's circumstances, mood, or relationship with others . . ." and goes on to specify that it refers to "instinctive feeling as distinguished from reasoning or knowledge." Not very helpful if we want to study it scientifically. If we strip away from this definition examples of different kinds of emotions (grief, hope, fear), we're left with what it's not (reasoning, knowledge), and a few alternative words (feeling, mood) that would, themselves, need definition. From one perspective, this illustrates the principle that knowledge, fundamentally, may arise from "nothing more" than associations between the sensory and the motor (c.f., section *A PDP model of picture naming*, *Chapter 4;* also *Chapter 10* and *Chapter 13*). On the other hand, we *know* that emotions exist, and we know what it feels like to experience them. So how can we define and operationalize this aspect of our mental lives in such a way that it can be studied with the methods of cognitive neuroscience?

Here's how two prominent groups have done so.

Approach/Withdrawal

One perspective from which we can start to operationalize emotion comes from psychology, and the distinction between approach vs. withdrawal behaviors. As framed by Richard Davidson and Wil Irwin (1999):

> The approach system facilitates appetitive behavior and generates certain types of positive affect that are approach-related, for example, enthusiasm, pride, etc. . . . This form of positive affect is usually generated in the context of moving toward a desired goal . . . a second neural system [is] concerned with the implementation of withdrawal. This system facilitates the withdrawal of an individual from sources of aversive stimulation and generates certain forms of negative affect that are withdrawal-related. For example, both fear and disgust are associated with increasing the distance between the organism and a source of aversive stimulation (pp. 12–13).

From "Feeling Words" to Neural Systems

An alternative, though not necessarily incompatible, way to operationalize emotion is to acknowledge the linkage between the subjective experience of emotions and survival-related systems in the brain, but then to only study the latter. Thus, Joseph LeDoux (2012b) has argued that the clearest way to make meaningful progress in understanding emotions and their regulation is to be explicit that the relevant systems whose neurobiological bases can be studied are "circuits involved in defense, maintenance of energy and nutritional supplies, fluid balance, thermoregulation, and reproduction. These survival circuits and their adaptive functions are conserved to a significant degree . . . across mammalian species, including humans" (p. 654). He further argues that it is important that we not conflate these circuits and functions with the "feeling words" that we use to describe the subjective experience of emotion: fear, anger, love, sadness, jealousy, and so on.

> By focusing on survival functions instantiated in conserved circuits, key phenomena relevant to emotions and feelings are discussed with the natural direction of brain evolution in mind (by asking to what extent are functions and circuits that are present in other mammals also present in humans) rather than by looking backward, and anthropomorphically, into evolutionary history (by asking whether human emotions/feelings have counterparts in other animals) (p. 654).

At the Nexus of Perception and Social Cognition

As we make our way through this chapter, we'll see that these two perspectives inform several themes that will be important as we consider the neural bases of emotion. One is the influence of social context on many aspects of cognition that we've already considered in depth, including perception, memory encoding and retrieval, and decision making. Another is how we control *emotional* aspects of our thinking. A third, and related, theme is the influence of the implicit vs. the explicit on our emotional state and our ability to control it. Let's start with the interaction of the social with the perceptual.

Trustworthiness

Trustworthiness is a variable that is frequently manipulated in studies of social behavior (c.f. *Chapter 17*, section *"How much can I trust you?"*). For neuroscientists, this is in part because one way that humans judge the trustworthiness of another is by studying the other's face,[1] and

[1] "You can tell a lot about a person by looking them in the eyes." That must be a line from at least one movie. . .

the neural bases of face processing are relatively well understood. Here, the nexus of trustworthiness and face processing will facilitate our introduction of a neural structure that will be front-and-center in this chapter: the amygdala.

A Role for the Amygdala in the Processing of Trustworthiness

Neuropsychological Evidence A seminal study linking the amygdala to judgments of trustworthiness came from the team of Ralph Adolphs, Daniel Tranel, and Antonio Damasio (1998), who reported on judgments of approachability and trustworthiness in three patients with bilateral amygdala lesions. The findings, illustrated in *Figure 18.1*, showed that the patients tended to judge all faces to be approachable and trustworthy, even those belonging to the 50 most negative faces, as rated by an independent group of individuals. Recall from *Chapter 11* that the amygdala is located in the medial temporal lobe, just rostral, medial, and superior to the rostral end of the hippocampus. Although it is in close anatomical proximity to ventral anterior IT cortex, it has not typically been considered a part of the visual system (a point that is germane to the findings of this study, and many others to follow). Strikingly, the patients described by Adolphs, Tranel, and Damasio (1998) did not differ from healthy control subjects when making the same judgments based on *verbal* descriptions of different individuals. Thus, the impairment seems tied to the visual modality. Based on this finding, the authors proposed that "The amygdala appears necessary to trigger the retrieval of information on the basis of

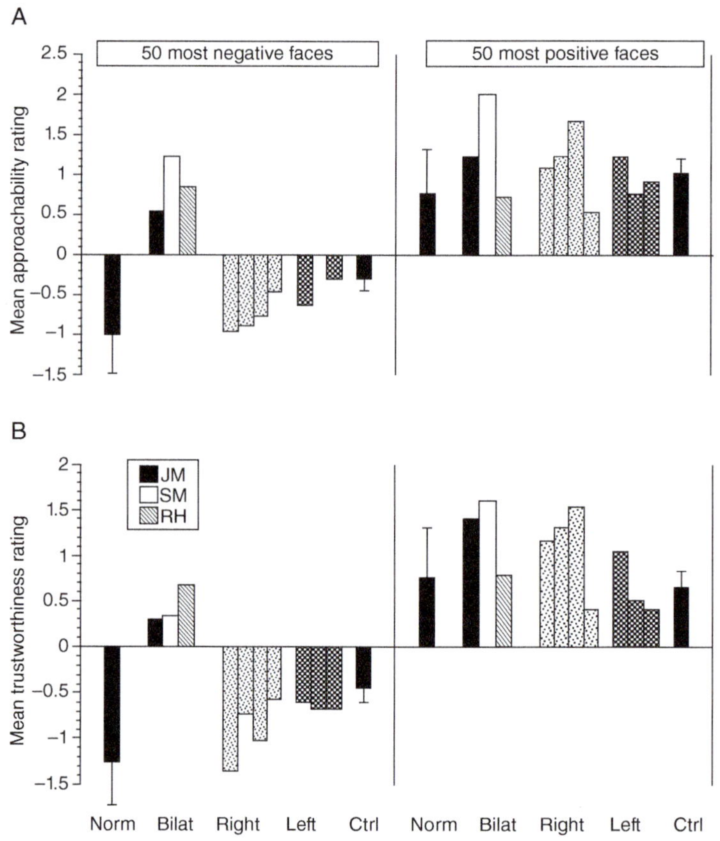

FIGURE 18.1 Performance of three patients with bilateral amygdala lesions (Bilat) – relative to neurologically healthy control subjects (Norm), unilateral right or left amygdala lesion patients, and non-amygdala lesion control subjects (Ctrl) – on rating the approachability **(A)** and trustworthiness **(B)** of 50 visually presented faces rated "most negative," and 50 "most positive," by an independent group.

Source: Adolphs et al., 1998 / Springer Nature.

prior social experience or innate bias in regard to certain classes of faces" (p. 472). By this account, the social information itself is stored elsewhere, and accessible via other channels, such as spoken language.

fMRI Evidence Several fMRI studies prompted by the Adolphs, Tranel, and Damasio (1998) finding have shown that the magnitude of amygdala responses to faces corresponds to judgments of the trustworthiness of each face. Remarkably, one such study has shown that the correlation is stronger between the amygdala of an individual and the group-average ratings of trustworthiness made by 129 unscanned subjects than it is for that individual's own ratings of trustworthiness (Engell, Haxby, and Todorov, 2007; *Figure 18.2*)! I know; it also took this author a while to wrap his brain around this finding. How could a person's brain show a response that corresponds more closely to a group-average judgment (made by a group of total strangers!) than to their own judgment? The answer to this question requires us to keep in mind that this finding only pertained to one region within this person's brain. As Engell, Haxby, and Todorov (2007) note, their finding is "consistent with the notion that the amygdala is involved in the initial automatic assessments of trustworthiness based on facial features, but that other neural systems, which are more closely linked to idiosyncratic perception, modulate the amygdala's influence on behavior" (p. 1516).

A final note about this study is that Engell et al. (2007) told their subjects that they were participating in a face memory experiment and made no mention of trustworthiness prior to the scanning session. Then, with the same logic as a subsequent-memory study (section *Subsequent memory effects in the PFC and the MTL neocortex, Chapter 12*), and of the study of *Common currency for money and social reward* (*Chapter 17*), the researchers measured behavioral correlates of the actual mental construct of interest, in this case trustworthiness judgments, after the scanning session. This means that the activity measured in their scans corresponded to what could be characterized as "implicit trustworthiness judgments." That is, the subjects presumably weren't thinking to themselves *Is this person trustworthy?* as they viewed each

FIGURE 18.2 Amygdala responses to visually presented faces correlate with "consensus" judgments of trustworthiness.

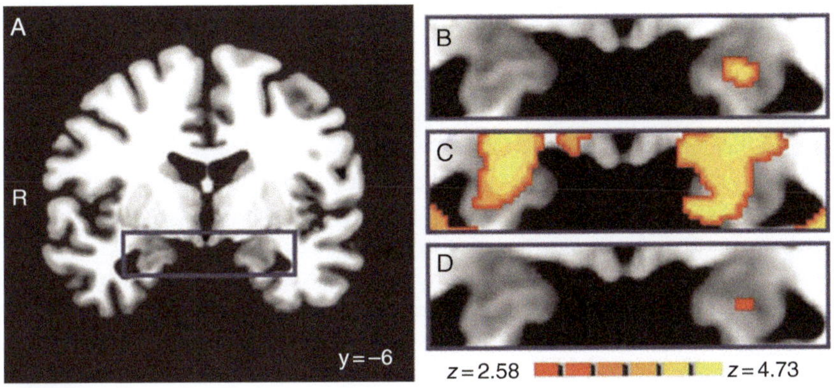

FIGURE 18.2.A Coronal section with a rectangle indicating the area that is magnified in **B–D**. The black regions immediately lateral to each amygdala are the temporal horns of the lateral ventricles.

FIGURE 18.2.B The correlation of individual judgments of trustworthiness (acquired in the post-scanning test) with amygdala activity.

FIGURE 18.2.C Correlation of "consensus" judgments of trustworthiness, the average across 129 subjects who were not scanned, with amygdala activity.

FIGURE 18.2.D Correlation with individual judgments after partialling out variance shared between individual and consensus judgments.

Source: Reproduced with permission from Engell et al. (2007) / MIT Press.

face; they were just trying to memorize them. Nonetheless, a part of their brain was responding to each face in a way that very strongly mirrored how they would later judge trustworthiness when asked to do so explicitly.

If we relate the findings and interpretation of the Engell, Haxby, and Todorov (2007) study to those of Adolphs, Tranel, and Damasio (1998), a decidedly visual role for the amygdala emerges. Recall that the patients with bilateral amygdala lesions were not impaired at making approachability and trustworthiness judgments when they listened to brief spoken biographies of hypothetical individuals. Thus, despite what we earlier said about the amygdala not being considered a part of the visual system, the operation performed here seems to be a fundamentally visuoperceptual one: it may be that the amygdala detects visually perceived configurations of physical properties that can be used to classify other people according to any number of categories, including their moral character, and the emotion that they are currently experiencing. By this view, the amygdala may carry out fast, unconscious, "triage" operations on incoming sensory information, upon which this initial classification, this "early-warning signal," is fed to relevant cortical areas that can then engage in more deliberative processing.

Implicit Information Processing by the Amygdala One question for us to keep in mind as we proceed through this chapter is whether this function of the amygdala is limited to vision. For example, what if one presented to subjects the voices of different individuals, all speaking the same sentence, such that physical properties like timbre and emotional inflection, but not the semantic content of the speech, would vary as a function of moral character? Would the amygdala also implicitly classify this auditory information as a function of trustworthiness? We'll get a sense of the modality specificity of the amygdala in the next section, when we consider its functional anatomy in detail. But before leaving the assessment of *trustworthiness*, another important question to ask is whether this phenomenon of implicit social "judgment," of unconscious classification of people that we encounter, generalizes to other dimensions along which one can evaluate other people.

Neural Bases of Racial Stereotyping The implicit association test (IAT) is widely used by social psychologists to measure implicit social judgments, such as the judgments of trustworthiness illustrated in *Figure 18.1* and *Figure 18.2*. A study of racial bias by affective neuroscientist Elizabeth Phelps and colleagues. (2000) used a design similar to that of Engell, Haxby, and Todorov (2007) – first scan, then obtain behavioral measures of the subjects' evaluation of the stimuli and see if the latter relate to the former – with the important difference that the post-scan behavioral measures included a test of implicit cognition, in addition to a test of explicit cognition.

Research subjects in experiment 1 of Phelps et al. (2000) were White Americans who were told they were participating in a memory study. During scanning, they viewed photographs of nine White male faces and nine Black male faces. After the scan, subjects were first administered an IAT during which they made interleaved speeded judgments of whether a face was Black or White (race classification) and whether a word was good or bad (word classification). The logic of the IAT is to vary the classification-to-response-button mapping, such that on some blocks the race classification maps Black to left and White to right, and on others the mapping is reversed. Independently, the word-classification mapping to the same two buttons is also varied, such that one can then compare the RT for endorsing a good word as "good" when the same button was required for classifying a face as Black, vs. the RT for endorsing a good word as "good" when that button was required for classifying a face as White. The oft-replicated finding is that White Americans show an implicit bias, in that they are slower to endorse good words as "good" when the same button is associated with Black faces. Notably, this effect is statistically independent of one's professed, explicit stance with regard to racial equality.

Experiment 1 of Phelps et al. (2000) did, indeed, replicate the standard finding of an implicit negative association between Black faces and positive words. This was despite the fact that the subjects also were rated with a mean of 1.89 on the Modern Racism Scale, a test of explicit racial attitudes that was administered after the IAT. The scale ranges from 1 (strongly pro-Black) to 6 (strongly anti-Black). Comparison of the behavioral vs. fMRI data showed that the magnitude of implicit anti-Black bias in an individual's IAT score was positively correlated with the extent to which the amygdala response in that subject was greater for Black than

White faces. There was no evidence for a similar relationship between performance on the Modern Racism Scale and amygdala responsivity.

In experiment 2, Phelps et al. (2000) repeated their experimental procedure, but with the faces of famous and positively regarded Black and White men. For these stimuli, the IAT revealed diminished evidence for differential association of Black vs. White faces with positive words, and these scores no longer correlated with amygdala responses. Because experiment 1 used unfamiliar faces and experiment 2 famous faces, these findings were interpreted as evidence that the fast, implicit social categorization performed by the amygdala is learned, rather than hardwired.

We will return to the study of amygdala processing of implicit bias later in this chapter, when we consider the volitional control of emotion. At present, however, we will pursue a different theme, which is that the principles of plasticity and learning in the amygdala seem to play a prominent role in this region's functions. Indeed, we've reached a point where, having linked a handful of intriguing findings to the activity of this neural structure, we really need to learn more about the structure itself – its afferents, its internal anatomy and physiology, and its efferents.

The Amygdala

Klüver–Bucy Syndrome

The idea that the amygdala plays a central role in emotion processing has its roots in the work of the German-born, US-based experimental psychologist Heinrich Klüver (1897–1979) and the American neurosurgeon Paul Bucy (1904–1992). Klüver had pursued the first three years of his doctoral research at the University of Hamburg under the mentorship of Max Wertheimer (1880–1943), a founder of the tradition of **Gestalt psychology**. After immigrating to the United States in 1923, he received his PhD from Stanford University in 1924 for research on visual imagery ("eidetic vision") in children (presumably getting credit for work done in Hamburg). Soon thereafter, he began to compare his findings in children with subjective experiences produced by consuming the dried tops of the cactus *Lophophora williamsii* (a.k.a. peyote), which contains the psychoactive compound mescaline. These early studies of self-experimentation led to subsequent studies of the effects of mescaline on the behavior of monkeys, and this led Klüver to Paul Bucy.

Of particular interest to Klüver was the observation that mescaline produced chewing and licking behaviors, as well as seizures, in monkeys, and these suggested a type of seizure that the neurologist John Hughlings Jackson had named "uncinate fits." These seizures, implicating the temporal lobe terminations of the uncinate fasciculus (*Figure 17.4*), are characterized by hallucinations of taste and odor, no doubt a consequence of the involvement of the vmPFC (connected via the uncinate fasciculus with anterior medial temporal lobe) in olfactory and gustatory processing. Klüver's goal, therefore, was to determine whether lesions of the medial temporal lobes would produce comparable effects, thereby localizing the circuitry responsible for mescaline's psychoactive effects. He enlisted Bucy, a neurosurgeon, to perform the surgical lesions. Although Klüver wanted Bucy to restrict the region to the uncus (adjacent to the piriform cortex, see *Chapter 17*), Bucy "felt he couldn't perform such an operation and decided to take out the whole temporal lobe" (Nahm and Pribram, 1998, p. 9). The syndrome that resulted, which was exacerbated by an equivalent surgical removal in the other hemisphere, was dramatic, and characterized by five cardinal symptoms: (1) "psychic blindness" (later to be known as associative agnosia [*Chapter 10*]); (2) "tameness" (i.e., docility); (3) hyperorality, characterized by putting nearly everything in the mouth to "explore" it (this has been reported to include such obviously hazardous items as lighted cigarettes); (4) dietary changes, including hyperphagia (an extreme drive to consume food); and (5) hypersexuality, including the mounting of animals from different species. Anecdotal reports also indicated that the monkeys lost their fear of snakes and of humans, the former of which is believed to be innate.

In the 1950s, research by Lawrence Weiskrantz (later to mentor Charles Gross, and of "Warrington and Weiskrantz [1974]" renown [section *Retrieval without awareness,*

Chapter 12]) localized most of the symptoms of the Klüver–Bucy syndrome to the amygdala and established the idea that this structure was important for processing the rewarding or punishing value of stimuli. This set the stage for enormously influential breakthroughs from studies of the role of the amygdala in Pavlovian fear conditioning.

Pavlovian Fear Conditioning

Induction Recall from section *A cartoon example of Pavlovian conditioning, Chapter 5,* that Pavlovian conditioning entails pairing an unconditioned stimulus (US) with a conditioned stimulus (CS), in temporal contiguity, until an association between the two is learned, at which time the CS, alone, will produce the conditioned response. In the classic fear conditioning protocol (carried out with rats), the CS is an auditory tone, and the unconditioned stimulus is a footshock. ("Footshock" is such a commonly used protocol that this formulation has become an accepted word in the literature.) Decades of intensive research, beginning in the 1980s, have established in exquisite detail the mechanisms underlying fear conditioning in mammals. For the following summary to make sense, you should first familiarize yourself with the circuitry of the amygdala and of its afferents and efferents by studying *Figure 18.3.*

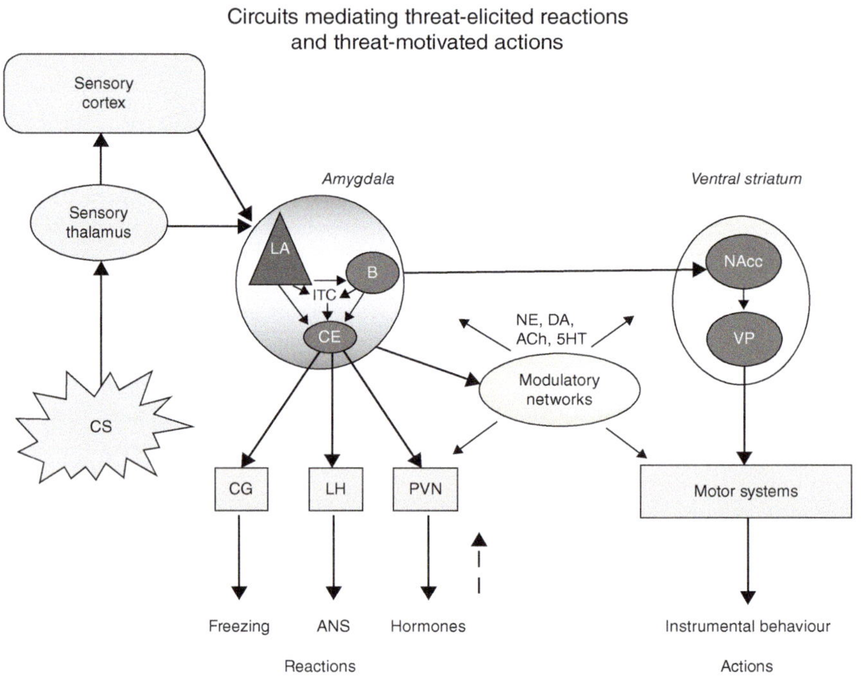

FIGURE 18.3 A schematic diagram of what is sometimes called the "fear circuit," which LeDoux (2012a) frames here as the threat-processing circuit. The CS, which is most often a tone or a light, is first registered in the sensory thalamus (e.g., the MGN or LGN) and then conveyed to the lateral nucleus of the amygdala (LA) via two routes, the putative direct "low road" and the cortical "high road." (The former presumably carries only low-resolution, magnocellular-dominated signals but is central to many models of amygdala function; some, however, have disputed its existence.) Within the amygdala complex are the lateral (LA), basal (B), and central (CE) nuclei, as well as the GABAergic intercalated cells (ITCs). The CE sends outputs to regions that produce the body's internal reactions to fear: the central gray (CG); the lateral hypothalamus (LH; which, in turn, activates the autonomic nervous systems [ANS]); and the paraventricular nucleus (PVN) of the hypothalamus. The basal nucleus sends outputs to the nucleus accumbens (NAcc) and ventral pallidum (VP) of the basal ganglia, thereby influencing motor actions. "Modulatory networks" refer to subcortical nuclei that innervate the brain to deliver the modulatory neurotransmitters listed (see Figure 2.5).

Source: Michael et al., 2012a / with permission of Elsevier.

Okay, now that you've familiarized yourself with LeDoux's diagram, here's his summary of fear conditioning. Fasten your seatbelt:

> CS and US convergence occurs in the lateral nucleus of the amygdala (LA), and specifically in the dorsal subregion of the LA. This convergence leads to synaptic plasticity and the formation of a CS–US association. Damage to LA, inactivation of LA, or manipulation of a variety of molecular pathways in LA prevents fear conditioning. A second important region is the central nucleus of the amygdala (CE). Manipulations of this region also disrupt conditioning. LA and CE are connected directly and by way of various intra-amygdala pathways. Once the CS–US association is formed, later exposure to the CS results in the retrieval of the learned association formed by CS–US convergence during conditioning. Information then flows from LA to CE, which then connects to hypothalamic and brainstem areas that control behavioral, autonomic, and hormonal responses that help the organism cope with the threat. Plasticity also occurs in CE, and in CS processing regions and motor control regions (LeDoux, 2012a, p. 435).

As noted by LeDoux, this is a simplified description that omits many details. Should one want more details, two places to begin are LeDoux (2000) and Davis and Whalen (2001), both listed in the *Further reading* section. Here, we will limit ourselves to just some key concepts.

First, the necessary locus of LTP, without which fear conditioning does not occur, is the LA nucleus. Among the manipulations of LA that block fear conditioning is the administration of protein synthesis inhibitors, which block the formation of new synapses within the LA and between the LA and other amygdala nuclei. This is an evolutionarily ancient form of learning, observable in many invertebrate organisms with much simpler nervous systems. (These animals have neither amygdalae nor LA nuclei. However, synaptic plasticity underlying Pavlovian conditioning in these animals results from very similar, if not identical, intracellular molecular cascades that are triggered by the network-level convergence of signals relating to the CS and the US.)

Second, downstream from synaptic changes in LA, (at least) two different kinds of learning are supported by (at least) two pathways in the amygdala. Most of our attention in this chapter will focus on Pavlovian fear conditioning, which is mediated by circuits connecting LA to CE, and expressed via CE's outputs to systems that implement the innate "Reactions" (bottom left of *Figure 18.3*). A second pathway, from LA to the basal nucleus, implements a different kind of learning, **avoidance learning**.

Distinguishing Avoidance Learning from Fear Conditioning Avoidance learning refers to context-dependent skeletomotor behaviors that, when engaged, enable the organism to avoid the adverse outcome predicted by the CS. One laboratory example of an avoidance behavior would be if the floor of the testing chamber has two different textures, and the rat learns to avoid a footshock by, each time a tone is played, moving to the "safe zone" in the chamber. An avoidance behavior from everyday life is illustrated during this author's daily walk home from work. Having been unpleasantly startled more than once by the aggressive dog who is sometimes (fenced in) outdoors in front of a particular house, he has learned to turn left at the intersection preceding this house so as to avoid the unpleasant encounter.

There are three points to emphasize about the amygdala-mediated "instrumental behavior" (*Figure 18.3*, lower right), of which avoidance learning is a subtype. First is that it entails engaging the motor system via the basal nucleus-to-ventral striatum efferent pathway of the amygdala (i.e., a different pathway from LA to CE). Second is its context dependence. If I'm on a sailboat on Lake Mendota and suddenly I see a large motorboat bearing down on me, the notion of *turning left at the intersection of Kendall St. and Prospect Ave. in order to avoid this threat* doesn't even make sense – that learned behavior is only relevant in the context of avoiding the dog on the walk home from work. Third is that the behaviors acquired via avoidance learning aren't emotional per se. Returning again to my pedestrian commute, if, on my way home from work, I need to pick up my son at his friend Alex's house, I would also turn left at that same intersection, because that's the way to get to Alex's house. This is in contradistinction to fear conditioning, in which the CS triggers the same innate, hardwired defense mechanisms as does an unconditioned stimulus. Thus, for example, when a dog suddenly barks and lunges (an unconditioned stimulus), one's first responses are to freeze and to activate the autonomic nervous system (i.e., the "fight or flight" reflex). Similarly, when the sailor suddenly sees the large motorboat bearing down on them (also an unconditioned stimulus), their first response is also to freeze and to activate the autonomic nervous system. (It is only "a split second" after this initial stereotyped response that they engage the contextually appropriate response of grabbing the tiller to steer the sailboat out of the path of the oncoming motorboat.)

Emotional Content in Declarative Memories

Pharmacological Interference with Norepinephrine

The two types of memory summarized in the preceding section, fear conditioning and avoidance learning, are nondeclarative – they do not depend on the integrity of the hippocampus or neocortex of the MTL. However, declarative memories can also have an emotional component. Is the amygdala involved in these? Before answering this question, we'll first revisit the study of pharmacological interventions with emotional declarative memory. Recall from section *Reconsolidation, Chapter 11*, that administration of the β-adrenergic antagonist propranolol at the time of retrieval of an emotional memory "knocks down" the emotional content of the memory on subsequent retrievals. This finding provided evidence that reconsolidation under normal circumstances entails the activation of the subcortical "modulatory networks" illustrated in *Figure 18.3*. Those reconsolidation studies considered in *Chapter 11* built on the earlier work performed by neurobiologists Larry Cahill and colleagues, as summarized here. In one celebrated study, Cahill, Bruce Prins, Michael Weber, and James McGaugh (1994) used 12 images to construct a story with two variants, one emotionally arousing and one emotionally neutral. Both involved a mother and son leaving home, a hospital emergency room, and hailing a taxi. In the neutral story, the mother and son walk to the hospital where the father works, passing automobile wreckage in a junkyard along the way. They observe an emergency preparedness drill (which includes a brain scan and simulated injuries created by a makeup artist), and the mother phones the day care facility where her younger child is enrolled, then hails a taxi in order to pick up this child. The arousing story begins the same way, but then the boy is critically injured by a collision between cars while he and the mother are crossing the street, the brain scan and gore at the hospital are described as medical procedures undertaken to save the boy's life, and the phone call and taxi are the same.

For their experiment, Cahill et al. (1994) divided their subjects into four groups. An hour prior to hearing the story, subjects in two of the groups were administered propranolol, and those in the other two were administered a placebo. Subsequently, subjects in one of the two propranolol groups and in one of the two placebo groups heard the arousing version of the story, and those in the remaining two groups heard the neutral version. On the surprise memory test administered 1 week later, the *arousing-story/placebo* group (A/P in *Figure 18.4*) showed the expected benefit that emotional content gives to memory performance. Such emotion-related enhancement was not present, however, for the *arousing-story/propranolol* (A/BB) group, whose memory performance for the middle part of the story didn't differ from that of the two neutral-story groups (*Figure 18.4.A*). Notably, however, the A/BB did not differ from the A/P group with regard to how emotional they found the story to be when asked to rate it immediately after having heard it. This latter finding suggests that the effect of propranolol was specific to emotional memory encoding and had minimal, if any, effect on the experience of emotion at the time that the story was presented.

Emotional Declarative Memory in Patients with Amygdala Lesions

Now, you may be wondering why the description of the Cahill et al. (1994) experiment is presented in this section of this chapter that is focused on the amygdala. After all, propranolol administration in this study was systemic, and so antagonism of β-adrenergic receptors was likely to have occurred throughout the brain, as well as in the periphery. The reason for including it in this section is because a subsequent study used the same experimental materials and procedure to test the emotional memory of patients with bilateral amygdala lesions. In it, a team led by Ralph Adolphs, and including Larry Cahill, found that the performance of amygdala-lesioned

FIGURE 18.4 Effect of propranolol on emotional memory encoding.
Source: Cahill et al., 1994 / Springer Nature.

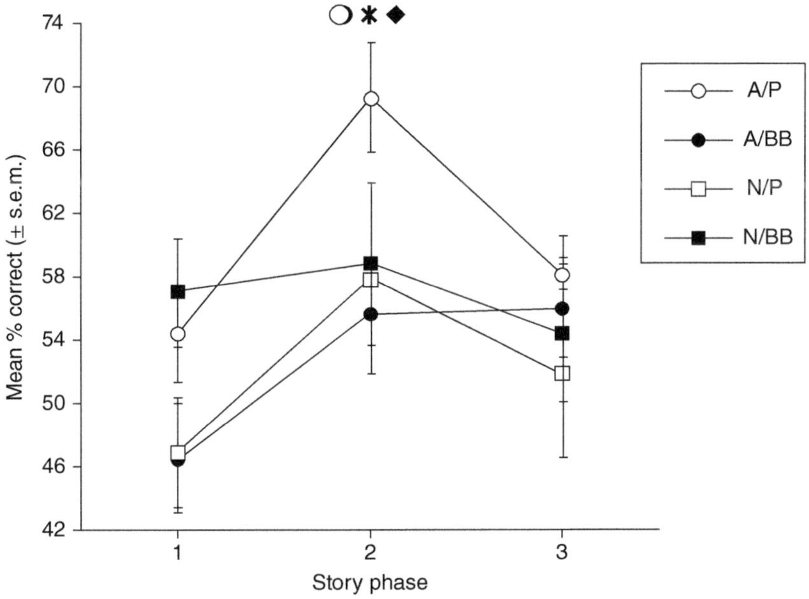

FIGURE 18.4.A Performance of four groups of subjects on a surprise memory test administered 1 week after hearing either the emotionally arousing (A) or neutral (N) version of a story, prior to which they had been administered either a placebo (P) or the drug propranolol (a "beta blocker" [BB]). These factors were fully crossed in a 2 × 2 between-subjects design. Story phases 1 and 3 were identical. The A/P group, but not the A/BB group, demonstrated superior memory performance for story phase 2, which contained the emotionally arousing content. The A/BB group's performance did not differ from that of the groups that heard the emotionally neutral version of the story.

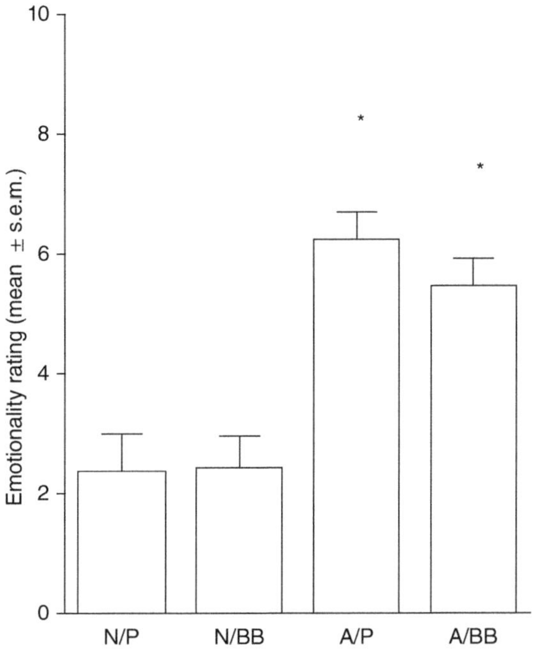

FIGURE 18.4.B Immediately after hearing the story, subjects were asked to rate on a 1–10 scale how emotional they found the story. Both groups that had heard the emotionally arousing version of the story rated it to be more emotional than did the groups that had heard the emotionally neutral version.

patients was very similar to that of healthy individuals who had been administered propranolol: First, just like the A/BB subjects in *Figure 18.4.A*, their declarative memory was selectively impaired for emotional portions of the story; second, like the A/BB subjects in *Figure 18.4.B*, their immediate rating of the emotionality of the story was comparable to that of control subjects(!). This certainly came as a surprise to this author. Does this mean that amygdala isn't necessary for the experience of emotion?!? Anecdotally, Adolphs, Cahill, Rina Schul, and Ralf Babinsky (1997) note that one of the two patients

> explained that she had found the slide with the surgically repaired legs quite emotional and unpleasant, a comment she also made spontaneously when she first saw the slides. She has made similarly appropriate comments in regard to her experience of a large number of emotionally charged stimuli we have shown her, as well as in regard to emotional events from her own life.
>
> Then, they go on to conclude that
>
> It may thus be that the experience of emotional events does not depend essentially on the amygdala. The amygdala's function in humans appears to be rather more subtle, serving to mediate between the evaluation and experience of emotional events, on the one hand, and their acquisition and consolidation into long-term memory, on the other (p. 298).

Other findings, from other groups, are consistent with this idea of a distinction between the experience of emotion and the incorporation of emotional content into memory. For example, a PET study by Cahill et al. (1996) suggested that activity in the amygdala correlated more strongly with memory for emotionally arousing stimuli than with subjects' subjective reports of their state of emotional arousal while in the scanner. Thus, we may need to look beyond the amygdala to get a fuller picture of how emotion is represented while we experience it "in real time," and how it influences ongoing cognition and behavior. In doing so, we need to keep in mind, however, the dictum of which we've periodically been reminded, which is that one's introspection is a notoriously poor indicator of what processes are actually unfolding between the ears. For example, earlier in this chapter, we've reviewed evidence of the unconscious influence of the amygdala on decisions related to trustworthiness and to racial bias. Thus, one caveat to keep in mind is whether, despite their reports on a single subjective measure of emotionality, patients with bilateral amygdala damage are truly experiencing the full richness of the emotional response to an evocative story that control subjects are experiencing. The same holds for subjects with propranolol in their systems.

And so, to recap, our understanding at this point in this chapter is that the amygdala can influence our decisions, and possibly our emotions, implicitly. Additionally, however, there's reason to think that our explicit, subjective experience of emotions "in the moment" is supported, at least in part, by systems outside of the amygdala proper.

The Amygdala's Influence on Other Brain Systems

As a transition toward considering the processing of emotion outside of the amygdala, we can start by considering how the amygdala influences other brain systems. For example, one possible explanation of the findings from the emotional memory studies that we have just reviewed (Adolphs et al., 1997; Cahill et al., 1994) is that the amygdala's activation of the locus coeruleus (one of the "Modulatory networks" in *Figure 18.3*), and the consequent increase in norepinephrine levels in many parts of the brain, results in enhanced memory consolidation. If β-adrenergic receptors are blocked by a pharmacological agent, then the emotional memory effect is blocked. Similarly, if there is no amygdala to trigger the increased release of norepinephrine, then enhanced consolidation will not take place. Note that, unlike the midbrain dopaminergic nuclei A8–A10, whose output is focused on the basal ganglia and PFC, the locus coeruleus sends projections diffusely throughout the cortical mantle and to several subcortical targets (see *Figure 2.5*). Further, β-adrenergic receptors are found throughout the brain, most densely in hippocampus, but also in cerebellum, basal ganglia, thalamus,

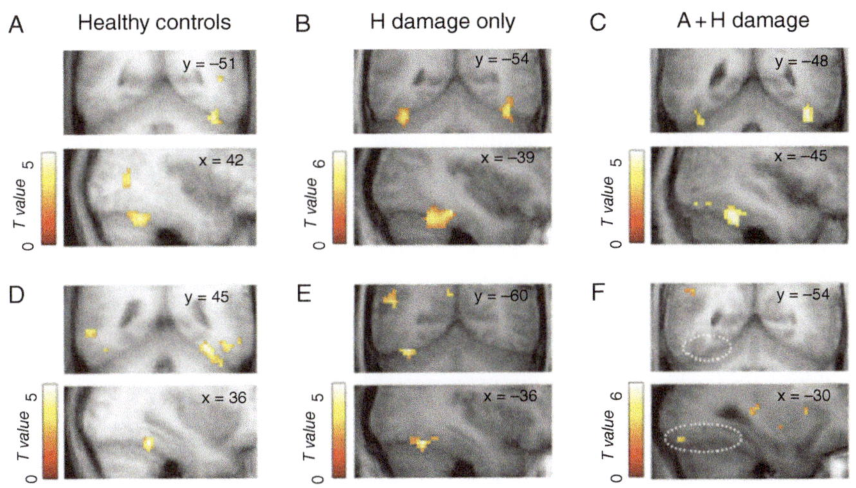

FIGURE 18.5 Activity evoked by attention to faces vs. houses, in control subjects, patients with medial temporal lobe damage encompassing the hippocampus, but not the amygdala ("H damage only"), and in patients with damage encompassing the hippocampus and amygdala ("A + H damage"). On each trial, two faces and two houses were presented, and, depending on the attentional cue, subjects had to decide whether either the two faces or the two houses were the same or different. Orthogonal to the factor of attention was the fact that half of the trials presented neutral faces and half presented fearful faces. **A–C** show that the response in fusiform gyrus for attention to faces was comparable across the three groups. **D–F**, in contrast, show a selective reduction of activity to fearful vs. neutral faces, regardless of whether subjects were attending to faces or houses, for the A + H group.

Source: Reproduced with permission from Vuilleumier et al. (2004) / Springer Nature.

midbrain, and cerebral cortex. Thus, it is difficult to know how anatomically localized or diffuse are the effects of propranolol that blocks the consolidation of memory for the emotional components of a story.

Consistent with the caveat about the interpretation of self-reports of the subjective experience of emotion, there is fMRI evidence that damage to the amygdala does, indeed, influence the processing of emotional stimuli. As illustrated in *Figure 18.5*, the fMRI response of the midfusiform gyrus to the visual presentation of faces, relative to houses, is no different in patients with amygdala damage relative to control subjects. Where these patients differ, however, is in the comparison of the response to fearful vs. neutral faces. In the inferior temporal and occipital regions shown in *Figure 18.5*, as well as in primary visual cortex and superior temporal sulcus (not shown), patients with amygdala lesions do not show the robust increase in activity for fearful vs. neutral faces that is seen in healthy control subjects, as well as in patients whose lesions compromise the hippocampus but spare the amygdala. And so our understanding of the functions of the amygdala does, indeed, need to be nuanced.

The Control of Emotions

Recall from the beginning of this chapter that Davidson and Irwin (1999) have suggested that positive emotions involve appetitive and approach-related behaviors, whereas negative emotions involve aversive and withdrawal-related behaviors. Davidson and colleagues have associated positive, approach-related emotions with elevated activity in the left PFC and negative, withdrawal-related emotions to elevated activity in the right PFC. This is seen in mood-induction studies, in which subjects who are made to feel happy or sad reliably produce greater activity in the left or right PFC, respectively. Further, in the resting EEG, when subjects are sitting quietly and not performing a task, alpha-band power over the PFC is relatively higher over the left than the right hemisphere in patients with depression, suggesting a relative hyperactivation of the right PFC. Finally, damage to the left frontal cortex is more likely to produce depression than a frank lesion of any other part of the brain.

The fact that one can carry out a "mood induction study" is a demonstration of something that each of us has experienced several times throughout our lives: external circumstances can *make* us feel a certain way, thereby influencing our emotional state. In this section, we will consider how, and under what circumstances, we exert (internal) control over our emotions. As you make your way through this section, keep in mind that the questions it addresses are of keen interest to those who study psychopathology and mental health.

Extinction

As important as it can be to an organism to learn that a particular stimulus, or context, represents a threat, and should be avoided, it can be equally important to extinguish this association once the threat no longer exists. There is, regrettably, a real-world example of this fact that will be familiar to almost any reader of this book, regardless of where on the planet they live. For a soldier who is in an active combat zone, it is highly adaptive to take evasive action when there is an unexpected loud noise. Often, this is produced by an explosion or by gunfire, and the soldier needs to protect themself and/or do what's necessary to repel the attackers. Once decommissioned and back in civilian life, however, it is no longer adaptive for the ex-soldier to respond in the same way to an unexpected loud sound. The sound is highly likely to be the result of something innocuous, like a car backfiring or the crash of a garbage can knocked over by a dog. "Hitting the dirt" or running for cover in the civilian context can interfere with family and other social relations, can make it difficult to obtain or hold a job, and so on. Further along, we'll see that at pathological levels, an inability to extinguish no-longer-relevant conditioned fear can result in post-traumatic stress disorder (PTSD), and possibly other anxiety-related disorders.

Research in the Rodent Fear extinction refers to the gradual decrement in conditioned fear responses that occur with repeated presentation of a CS without the accompanying US. Extinction was originally thought by Pavlov and his contemporaries to be an inhibitory phenomenon, akin to "unlearning," or forgetting, the CS–US association. Research from physiological psychology has long since established, however, that extinction of conditioned fear is better understood as the result of learning a new association with the CS, one that competes with the previously learned CS–US association. Behavioral phenomena such as spontaneous recovery and rapid relearning provide evidence against an "unlearning" mechanism. Consistent with the "new learning" account of extinction is the finding that fear extinction requires the participation of NMDA receptors in the basolateral nucleus of the amygdala. The principles and mechanisms that govern fear extinction have now been well worked out in the rodent, and translating these to the human, including into potential treatment strategies, are currently the focus of intensive research activity.

The Roles of Midline Frontal Cortex As indicated above, the basal nucleus of the amygdala has been identified as an important locus for learning a new association for the CS that was previously associated with a threatening US. Learning the new association presumably entails the pairing of sensory information representing the CS with a representation of the context in which extinction trials are administered. (Extinction is more quickly learned if extinction trials – i.e., trials presenting the CS in the absence of the threat-related US – are carried out in a different context from the one in which the fear memory was acquired.) Additionally, however, there are top-down control signals that adjudicate between the older CS–fear association and the newer CS–neutral association. The sources of this top-down control are the midline frontal regions illustrated in *Figure 18.6*. Interestingly, the two seem to operate in an antagonistic, "push me-pull you" fashion.

The role for the infralimbic (IL) cortex of the rodent in prioritizing the newer CS–neutral association (often referred to as the "extinction memory") has been demonstrated in a series of elegant studies by neurobiologist Gregory Quirk and his colleagues, while based at the University of Puerto Rico. The first experiments in the series demonstrated that whereas lesions of IL did not interfere with extinction on day 1 of the experiment, they did interfere with

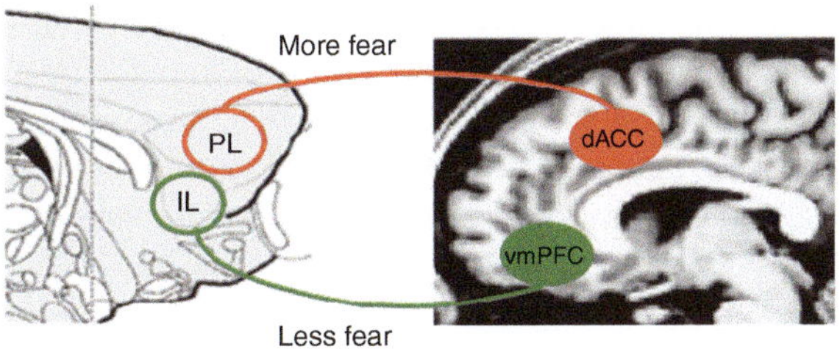

FIGURE 18.6 Anteromedial regions in the rat and the human are believed to play homologous roles in the control of conditioned fear memories. PL = paralimbic; IL = infralimbic.

Source: Reproduced with permission from Milad, Mohammed R., and Gregory J. Quirk. (2012) / Annual Reviews.

retrieval of this newer CS–neutral association on day 2. That is, the animal's behavior on day 2 was similar to what it would have been had it not gone through extinction learning on day 1. At face value, this could either reflect a deficit in the consolidation of the newly learned CS–neutral association or an impairment in the newer memory's retrieval. Evidence in favor of the latter account came from recording studies indicating that although IL neurons responded to the CS (a tone) during neither the initial acquisition of the fear memory nor during its extinction, they did respond to the CS during retrieval of the new CS–neutral memory on day 2 of extinction. Furthermore, the magnitude of these "extinction memory" responses was inversely correlated with the amount of freezing at the retrieval test, suggesting that the strength of this IL signal was determining the influence of the newer CS–neutral memory on the animal's behavior. Causal evidence for this interpretation was produced by microstimulation of the IL neurons that represented the CS during retrieval of the extinction memory – microstimulation enhanced the expression of the newer CS–neutral memory over the older CS–US fear memory.

As alluded to earlier, a second region along the frontal midline, the prelimbic (PL) cortex (*Figure 18.6*), seems to play the opposite role. First, inactivation of PL has been shown to reduce the expression of conditioned fear (i.e., the duration of time that the animal freezes upon hearing the tone). Second, neurons in PL show sustained increases in firing rate in response to presentation of the CS, and the time course of this activity closely mirrors the duration of the freezing behavior itself. This sustained activity seems to be the product of activity in a recurrent network linking PL with the amygdala, in that the onset of the CS is first detected by the amygdala, which sends a transient "fear signal" to PL. PL then converts this into a sustained signal that feeds back onto the amygdala, resulting in sustained amygdala output to the systems that implement the freezing response (*Figure 18.3*). Finally, as they have done with the IL circuit, Quirk's group has demonstrated that microstimulation of PL neurons has the effect of increasing freezing responses to the CS and of interfering with extinction.

Fear Conditioning and Extinction in the Human As suggested previously in the text and diagrammed explicitly in *Figure 18.6*, there seem to be important parallels from the rodent work that we have just reviewed and findings with related behaviors in humans. In particular, activity in human vmPFC seems to support functions that are analogous to those of the rodent IL: during fear conditioning, activity in vmPFC is suppressed relative to baseline; during extinction learning, activity in vmPFC increased; and during retrieval of the extinction memory, the magnitude of vmPFC activity predicts the subject's success at inhibiting conditioned responding. In addition to these functional studies, analysis of structural MRI data suggests that individual differences in the thickness of cortex in the vmPFC (as measured with voxel-based morphometry [VBM; section *Voxel-based morphometry, Chapter 4*]) are positively correlated with the strength of extinction learning.

With regard to the establishment and maintenance of conditioned fear memories, there's good evidence that the human dorsal ACC supports functions analogous to those of the rodent PL (*Figure 18.6*): activity in this region correlates with behavioral and skin-conductance correlates of fear conditioning, and there's also a large body of evidence indicating that this region is highly responsive to aversive unconditioned stimuli (e.g., the delivery of pain, or an unexpected and loud noise). (Skin conductance measures increased activity in sweat glands in the skin, an [automatic] autonomic response to fear, stress, or anxiety.) Interestingly, the omission of an expected US also produces increased activity in this region, an effect that likely reflects a role for error prediction signals in fear conditioning.

The Volitional Regulation of Emotion Any particular emotion can influence us for varying lengths of time. Davidson and Begley (2013) summarize it as such: "The smallest, most fleeting unit of emotion is an emotional *state* . . . a feeling that . . . persist[s] over minutes or hours or even days, is a *mood* . . . And a feeling that characterizes you . . . for years is an emotional *trait*" (p. xi). In contrast to acquisition and extinction of conditioned fear, processes of which we are typically unaware, and which contribute implicitly to our emotional and personality traits, emotional states and moods are amenable to volitional control. One model of the cognitive control of emotion, which social cognitive neuroscientist Kevin Ochsner and colleagues have been building and refining for over a decade, is illustrated in *Figure 18.7*. In effect, the model posits that many of the same principles and mechanisms that we use for cognitive control are also used for emotion regulation.

In the model of emotion regulation illustrated in *Figure 18.7*, individual mechanisms that implement emotion regulation each act on one of the steps in emotion generation that are illustrated in panel A of *Figure 18.7*. "Situation selection" and "situation modification" are strategies for avoiding an encounter with a potentially aversive situation. "Attentional selection" and its complement, "attentional filtering," control what information is gated into or out of the emotion generation process. "Cognitive change" refers to a collection of processes and strategies that act on the process of emotional appraisal. The most widely studied of this is "cognitive reappraisal," which entails reinterpreting the meaning or significance of the triggering event, so as to change one's emotional response to it. Finally, the processes that act on the expression of emotion ("Response" in *Figure 18.7*) fall under the rubric of "response modulation." The most commonly studied of these is expressive suppression – controlling the muscles of one's face to disguise from observers what emotion one is experiencing (e.g., the "poker face").

Meditation as Mental Training in Emotion Regulation Our emotional states, moods, and traits are arguably the most important factors in determining our quality of life. A growing body of promising findings indicates that through intensive, scientifically informed training, one can become more skilled at regulating one's emotional states and reap collateral cognitive benefits to boot. One example, which we'll consider here, is meditation. With an introduction seemingly more fitting for this book's *Chapter 9* than *Chapter 18*, here's how cognitive neuroscientist Heleen Slagter et al. (2007; including senior author Richard Davidson) set up their meditation study:

> A major limitation in human information processing arises from the time required to consciously identify and consolidate a visual stimulus in short-term memory . . . This process can take more than a half-second before it is free for a second stimulus, as is revealed by the attentional-blink paradigm: If the second target stimulus (T2) of two target stimuli is presented within 500 ms of the first one (T1) in a rapid sequence of distracters, it is often not detected . . . This deficit . . . is believed to result from competition between the two targets for limited attentional resources . . . : When many attentional resources are devoted to the processing of T1, too few may be available for T2 . . . Yet, the attentional blink does not reflect a general, immutable bottleneck, because most individuals are able to identify T2 on at least a portion of trials . . . suggest[ing] that some control . . . over the allocation of attentional resources is possible (p. 1).

In the study by Slagter et al. (2007), subjects performed the attentional-blink task, with concurrent EEG, immediately prior to beginning, and immediately upon completing, a

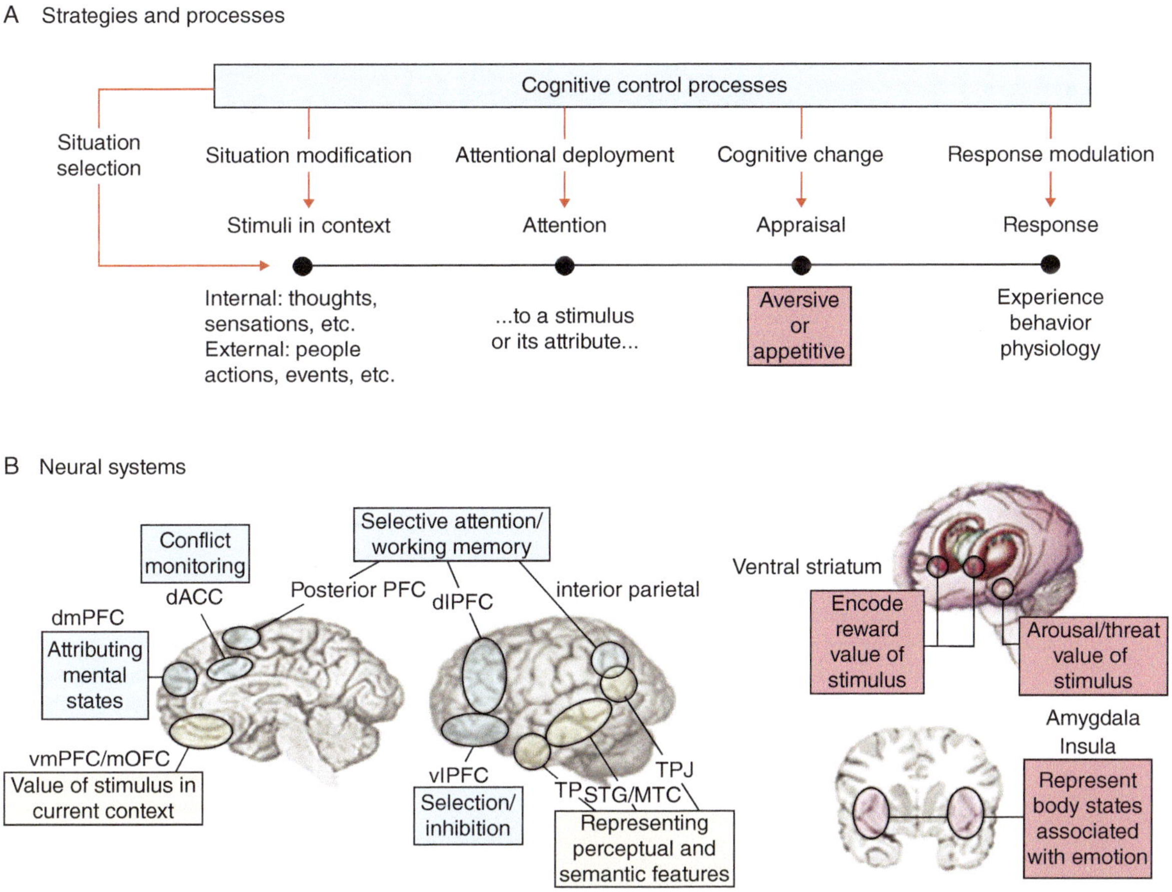

FIGURE 18.7 Ochsner's model of the cognitive control of emotion. In **A**, the four black dots represent the stages involved in generating an emotional state. First, a triggering event occurs, be it a spontaneous thought or an external event. Second, attention is drawn to all or just a part of the representation of the triggering event. Third, a process of appraisal happens, whereby a determination is made about the valence (positive or negative) of this event. There are many theories about the processes that may underlie emotional appraisal, and the neural bases of some processes that may be important appear in blue in panel **B**; here, Ochsner, Silvers, and Buhle (2012) have simplified the appraisal step into a binary classification of "aversive or appetitive." (Note that this has parallels with Davidson's "avoid/approach" distinction.) Finally, the "Response" stage corresponds to "translating these appraisals into changes in experience, emotion-expressive behavior, and autonomic physiology" (p. e3). The control processes that can influence each of these stages are elaborated in the text. Panel B summarizes mental processes and neural systems proposed to be involved in appraisal (blue), generating responses (pink), and systems with "an undefined or intermediary role in reappraisal" (p. e3; yellow).

Source: Ochsner et al., 2012 / John Wiley & Sons.

3-month retreat during which they meditated for 10–12 hours per day with Vipassana meditation. With this technique, one starts by focusing or stabilizing concentration on an object such as breath, and subsequently broadens one's focus, cultivating a "nonreactive" form of sensory awareness, meaning that one does not respond emotionally to the foci of attention. Control subjects were individuals who were interested in learning about meditation; they were given a 1-hour class and meditated for 20 minutes daily for the week prior to each EEG session.

Behavioral results showed a greater reduction of the attentional blink post- vs. pre-training for the meditation group relative to the control group. Notably, however, both groups improved slightly at T1 detection on session 2 vs. session 1, and the control group also showed a modest (though significantly smaller) improvement at T2 detection. This highlights the

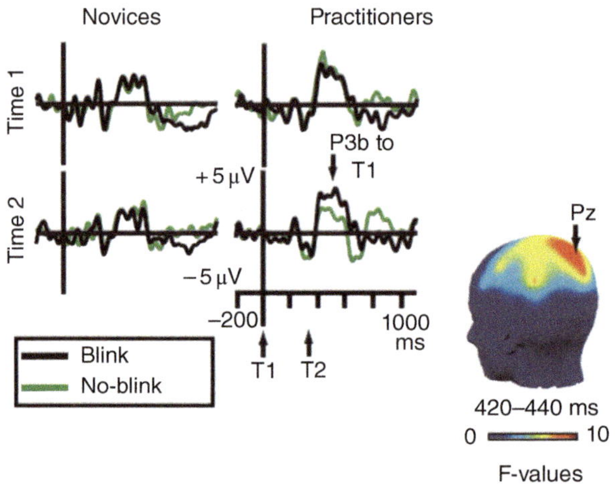

FIGURE 18.8 Comparison of the P3b ERP component evoked by the T1 stimulus as a function of group (Novices [i.e., controls]; Practitioners [i.e., meditation training group]); pre- vs. post-training session ("Time 1" and "Time 2," respectively) and, in each plot, whether the following T2 stimulus was detected ("No-blink") or missed ("Blink"). The P3b is associated with the allocation of attentional resources. The finding of a lower P3b to "No-blink" T1 stimuli in the post-training session for Practitioners, but not Novices, therefore, is interpreted as evidence that, as a result of training, they were able to devote fewer attentional resources to T1, thereby leaving more resources available for detection of T2. Also consistent with this interpretation was the fact that the individuals who showed the largest Time 1-to-Time 2 reductions in P3b were those who showed the largest reductions in attentional blink from Time 1 to Time 2.

Source: Slagter et al., 2007 / PLoS / CC BY 4.0.

importance of including a control group in training studies. Without one, one cannot rule out effects of learning the task, or some other factor that may have nothing to do with the training procedure itself. The ERP data, illustrated in *Figure 18.8*, also showed a selective effect of meditation training.

Although other studies have shown that intensive performance of a task can produce similar reductions in the attentional blink, noteworthy about the present finding from Slagter et al. (2007) was that the benefits of training resulted from *purely mental* activity – subjects weren't pointing a video-game gun, controlling a joystick, or performing any other overtly sensorimotor task; they were "just thinking." ("Just thinking," of course, in a particularly disciplined, focused way.) Subsequent studies from Davidson and colleagues have demonstrated impressive effects with other types of mental training. One example is that 2 weeks of compassion training (relative to a reappraisal control group) alters performance on a neuroeconomic game entailing the altruistic redistribution of funds, a behavioral change accompanied by changes in task-related functional connectivity between dorsolateral PFC and the nucleus accumbens (Weng et al., 2013).

The Role of Awareness One interpretation of the results from Slagter et al. (2007) is that intensive training on increasing awareness of one's body and one's thoughts can help one become more aware of events in the outside world that one might otherwise have missed. Here we'll look at the idea that the volitional control of one's emotional state may depend on awareness of the event that put one in that state. The study was led by Regina Lapate, then a graduate student with Richard Davidson. Lapate et al. (2016) used an affect misattribution task in which an emotionally evocative stimulus can bias the assessment of a subsequently encountered neutrally valenced stimulus. This is typically demonstrated in the laboratory by presenting the emotional stimulus under perceptually challenging conditions, and the typical finding is that the misattribution effect is strongest when subjects aren't aware of having perceived the emotional stimulus. For this study, Lapate et al. (2016)

scanned subjects with fMRI while presenting fearful faces under conditions of "continuous flash suppression" (CFS), a technique whereby a stimulus can be presented to a subject, but not detected by them, if it is presented at low contrast to the nondominant eye while a series of high-contrast colorful stimuli (here, "Mondrian" patterns) are simultaneously presented to the dominant eye. Six-to-nine seconds later, a neutral face was presented, and subjects rated "How much do you like this person?" on a 1–4 scale. Neutral priming stimuli were images of flowers, and both fearful faces and flowers were also shown in blocks without CFS, during which they were visible.

Behavioral results indicated that there was considerable intersubject variability in the size of the emotion misattribution effect (indexed by subtracting neutral-face ratings on flower trials from neutral-face ratings on fearful-face trials). Ignoring these individual differences, univariate analyses showed two primary effects of interest: first, BOLD signal was greater on *aware* (CFS-absent) than *unaware* (CFS-present) trials, collapsing over fearful faces and flowers, in dorsolateral PFC (areas 9/46/45), dorsomedial PFC (areas 6/8), and fusiform and lateral occipital cortex (*Figure 18.9*); second, the central nucleus of the amygdala in the right hemisphere (identified a priori as an ROI) responded more strongly to fearful faces than to flowers on both *aware* and *unaware* trials. Notably, when individual differences in the emotion misattribution effect were taken into account, it was only in the unaware condition that the intensity of the amygdala response to fearful faces predicted the size of an individual's emotion misattribution effect (*Figure 18.10*). "Therefore," the authors noted, "when unchecked by conscious awareness, greater amygdala responses to fear cues were associated with a negative bias towards later-shown neutral stimuli—i.e., greater affective coloring" (p. 3).

Now, onto the question of primary interest to us (and to the authors): the neural mechanisms associated with the control of emotional misattribution. Panel A in *Figure 18.11* shows the regions in left dorsolateral PFC and medial PFC for which a decrease in the value of functional connectivity with the right amygdala predicted a smaller emotion misattribution effect, effects consistent with the idea that PFC-based control signals play an important role in emotion regulation. That may need some unpacking. If two regions are involved in a process, let's say face perception, it makes sense to think that increased efficacy of that process would be associated with an increase in functional connectivity between these regions. If we consider V1 and the FFA, for example, the presentation of high-contrast faces might be expected to produce greater functional connectivity between V1 and FFA than would the presentation of low-contrast faces. That is, the correlation between these two regions would be higher. But what if we consider another circuit in the brain where one region has an inhibitory effect on the other – let's say the substantia nigra pars reticulata (SNpr) and the superior colliculus (SC;

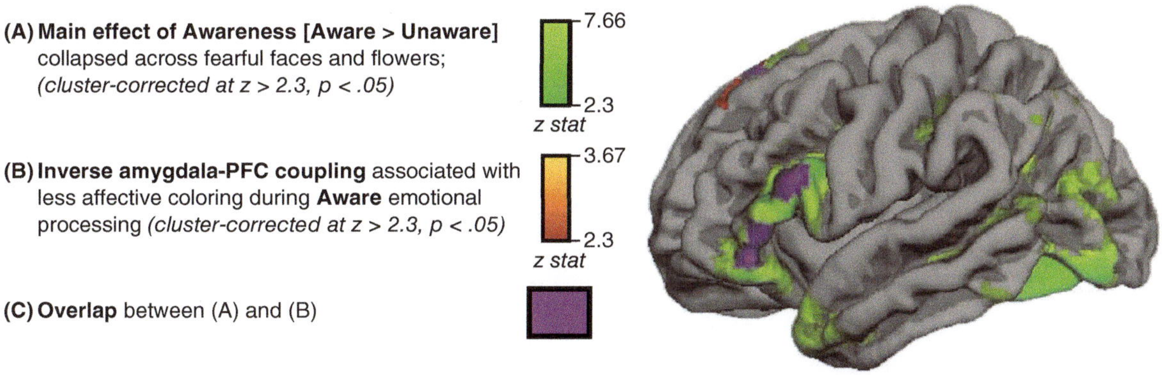

FIGURE 18.9 Lateral left-hemisphere view of regions showing a greater response to the 1-second binocular presentation of faces and flowers than to continuous flash suppression (1-second presentation of face/flower to nondominant eye plus concurrent 1.5-second presentation of 10-Hz Mondrian patterns to dominant eye).

Source: Lapate et al., 2016 / Springer Nature / CC BY 4.0.

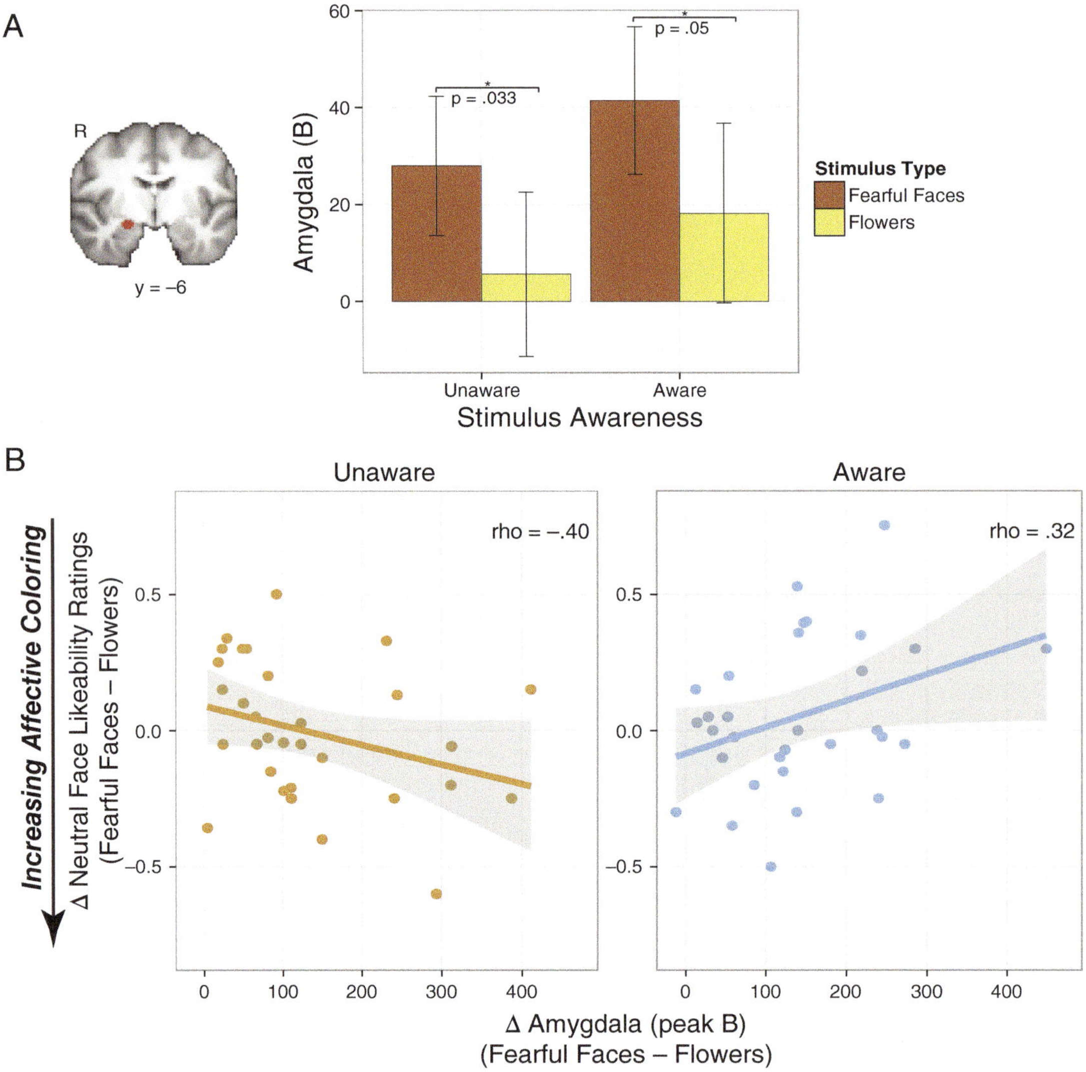

FIGURE 18.10 Amygdala responses to perceived vs. not-perceived fearful faces (and flowers), and their relation to emotion misattribution. **A.** Right-hemisphere central amygdala ROI, and its mean BOLD response to priming stimuli as a function of awareness condition. (BOLD values are in units of beta values from the GLM analysis.) **B.** The differential response of the amygdala to fearful faces vs. flowers (abscissa) plotted against the emotion misattribution effect ("affective coloring", ordinate). In each plot, each dot corresponds to 1 of the 31 subjects in the study. The plot on the left shows the significant trend for *unaware* trials, whereby greater amygdala activity for fearful faces relative to flowers predicts a greater emotion misattribution effect. The plot on the right shows a trend in the opposite direction for *aware* trials, although this effect did not exceed the threshold for significance. (The *unaware* vs. *aware* regression lines are significantly different from each other.)

Source: Lapate et al., 2016 / Springer Nature / CC BY 4.0.

section *The superior colliculus, Chapter 9*). Because activity in these two structures is negatively correlated, the functional connectivity between them will be negative. Using this same logic, the more negative is the functional connectivity between the PFC and the amygdala, the more effective is the inhibitory control of the latter by the former.

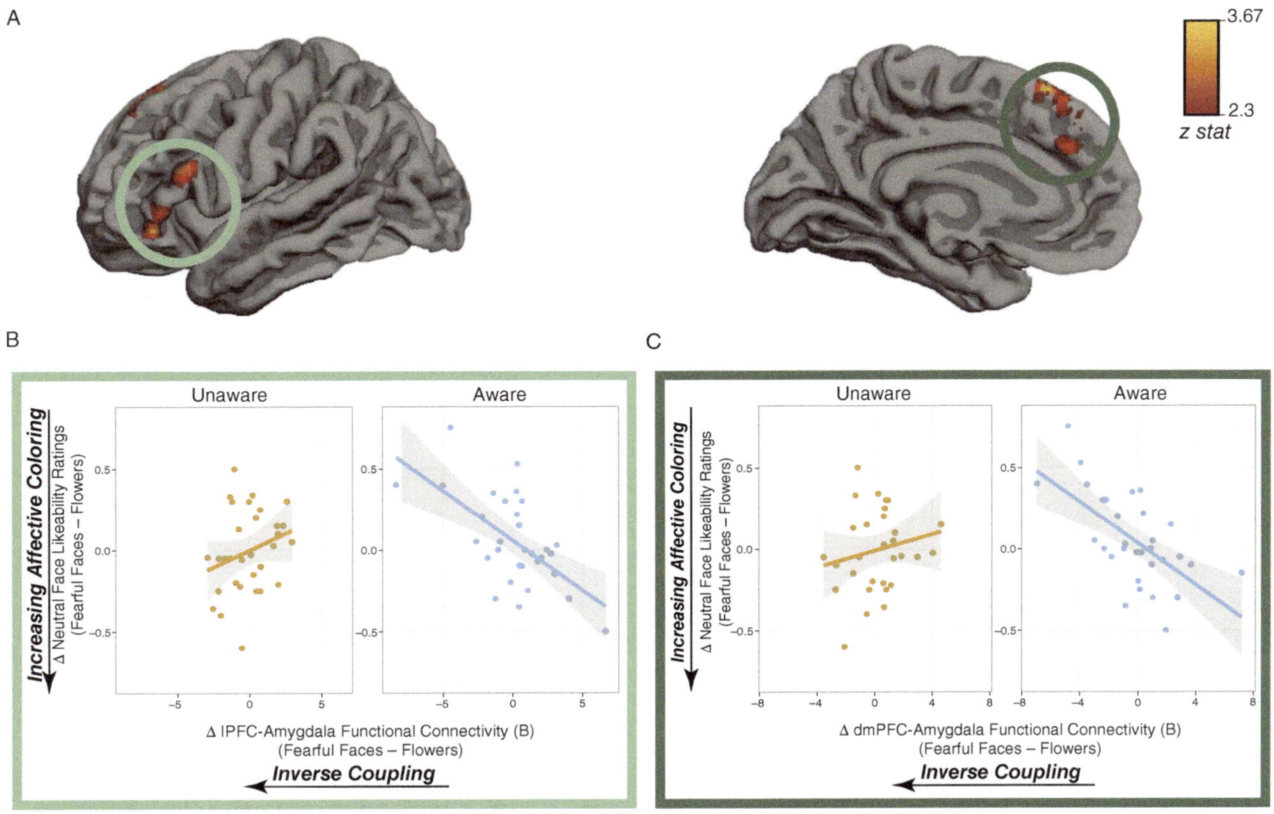

FIGURE 18.11 Emotion regulation by PFC control of amygdala responses to fearful faces. **A.** The cortical regions in the left hemisphere that show an inverse coupling with amygdala. (Dorsomedial PFC in the right hemisphere also showed this effect.) **B** and **C** illustrate that, for both of these regions, the effect is only seen on *aware* trials.

Source: Lapate et al., 2016 / Springer Nature / CC BY 4.0.

How Does That Make You Feel?

Emotion processing – at least negative emotion processing, which is what we focused on in this chapter – is strongly associated with the amygdala. Although the amygdala can play a role in the top-down modulation of visual processing, it doesn't seem to be necessary for real-time assessment of the emotional content of a situation. It does seem to play a key role, however, in long-term memory for such information. Research indicates that learning to control your emotions can make you "more aware," and that, conversely, being aware of what's affecting your mood might be important for being able to control it. With mental health being such a large, and growing, concern for our society, further expansion of our understanding of the neural bases of emotion and its regulation can't happen too soon.

End-of-Chapter Questions

1. In what way(s) does it make sense to think of faces and the information that they convey – about emotion, trustworthiness, and race – as conditioned stimuli?
2. Trace the circuitry that underlies fear conditioning. Is this same or different from the circuitry underlying avoidance learning?
3. Fear conditioning and avoidance learning are both types of nondeclarative memory. Is the amygdala also involved in processing the emotional component of declarative memories? If so, through what mechanism(s)?
4. How, and under what circumstances, does the amygdala influence visual processing?
5. What is an emotion? How are emotions different, neurobiologically, from the domains of cognition that we have studied up through this point in the book?
6. Is the role of the vmPFC in fear extinction best understood as learning the new CS, or retrieving it after it is learned? Contrast this with the role of the ACC.
7. How do the processes of emotion regulation differ from extinction? What brain systems and mechanisms are associated with emotion regulation?
8. How is emotion regulation related to psychopathology?
9. What's the role of awareness in emotion regulation?

References

Adolphs, Ralph, Larry Cahill, Rina Schul, and Ralf Babinsky. 1997. "Impaired Declarative Memory for Emotional Material Following Bilateral Amygdala Damage in Humans." *Learning & Memory* 4 (3): 291–300. doi: 10.1101/lm.4.3.291.

Adolphs, Ralph, Daniel Tranel, and Antonio R. Damasio. 1998. "The Human Amygdala in Social Judgment." *Nature* 393: 470–474. doi: 10.1038/30982.

Cahill, Larry, Bruce Prins, Michael Weber, and James L. McGaugh. 1994. "β-Adrenergic Activation and Memory for Emotional Events." *Nature* 371 (6499): 702–704. doi: 10.1038/371702a0.

Cahill, Larry, Richard J. Haier, James Fallon, Michael T. Alkire, Cheuk Tang, David Keator, . . . James L. McGaugh. 1996. "Amygdala Activity at Encoding Correlated with Long-Term, Free Recall of Emotional Information." *Proceedings of the National Academy of Sciences of the United States of America* 93 (15): 8016–8021. doi: 10.1073/pnas.93.15.8016.

Davidson, Richard J., and Sharon Begley. 2013. *The Emotional Life of Your Brain: How Its Unique Patterns Affect the Way You Think, Feel, and Live – and How You Can Change Them.* New York: Plume.

Davidson, Richard J., and William Irwin. 1999. "The Functional Neuroanatomy of Emotion and Affective Style." *Trends in Cognitive Sciences* 3 (1): 11–21. doi: 10.1016/S1364-6613(98)01265-0.

Engell, Andrew D., James V. Haxby, and Alexander Todorov. 2007. "Implicit Trustworthiness Decisions: Automatic Coding of Face Properties in the Human Amygdala." *Journal of Cognitive Neuroscience* 19 (9): 1508–1519.

Lapate, Regina C., B. Rokers, D. P. M. Tromp, N. S. Orfali, J. A. Oler, S. T. Doran, . . . R. J. Davidson. 2016. "Awareness of Emotional Stimuli Determines the Behavioral Consequences of Amygdala Activation and Amygdala-Prefrontal Connectivity." *Scientific Reports* 6: 25826. doi: 10.1038/srep25826.

LeDoux, Joseph E. 2012a. "Evolution of Human Emotion: A View through Fear." In *Evolution of the Primate Brain: From Neuron to Behavior*, edited by Michael A. Hofman and Dean Falk (pp. 431–442). Amsterdam: Elsevier. doi: 10.1016/B978-0-444-53860-4.00021-0. vol. 195 of Progress in Brain Research, edited by Stephen G. Waxman, Donald G. Stein, Dick F. Swaab, and Howard L. Fields.

LeDoux, Joseph E. 2012b. "Rethinking the Emotional Brain." *Neuron* 73 (4): 653–676. doi: 10.1016/j.neuron.2012.02.004.

Milad, Mohammed R., and Gregory J. Quirk. 2012. "Fear Extinction as a Model for Translational Neuroscience: Ten Years of Progress." *Annual Review of Psychology* 63: 129–151. doi: 10.1146/annurev.psych.121208.131631.

Nahm, Frederick K. D., and Karl H. Pribram. 1998. "Heinrich Klüver 1897–1979." In *Biographical Memoirs 73: 1–19*. Washington, DC: National Academies Press.

Ochsner, Kevin N., Jennifer A. Silvers, and Jason T. Buhle. 2012. "Functional Imaging Studies of Emotion Regulation: A Synthetic Review and Evolving Model of the Cognitive Control of Emotion." *Annals of the New York Academy of Sciences* 1251: e1–e24. doi: 10.1111/j.1749-6632.2012.06751.x.

Phelps, Elizabeth A., Kevin J. O'Connor, William A. Cunningham, E. Sumie Funayama., J. Christopher Gatenby, John C. Gore, and Mahzarin R. Banaji. 2000. "Performance on Indirect Measures of Race Evaluation Predicts Amygdala Activation." *Journal of Cognitive Neuroscience* 12 (5): 729–738. doi: 10.1162/089892900562552.

Slagter, Heleen A., Antoine Lutz, Lawrence L. Greischar, Andrew D. Francis, Sander Nieuwenhuis, James M. Davis, and Richard J. Davidson. 2007. "Mental Training Affects Distribution of Limited Brain Resources." *PLoS Biology* 5 (6): e138. doi: 10.1371/journal.pbio.0050138.

Vuilleumier, Patrik, Mark P. Richardson, Jorge L. Armony, Jon Driver, and Raymond J. Dolan. 2004. "Distant Influences of Amygdala Lesion on Visual Cortical Activation during Emotional Face Processing." *Nature Neuroscience* 7 (11): 1271–1278. doi: 10.1038/nn1341.

Weng, Helen Y., Andrew S. Fox, Alexander J. Shackman, Diane E. Stodola, Jessica Z. K. Caldwell, Matthew C. Olson, . . . Richard J. Davidson. 2013. "Compassion Training Alters Altruism and Neural Responses to Suffering." *Psychological Science* 24 (7): 1171–1180. doi: 10.1177/0956797612469537.

Other Sources Used

Adolphs, Ralph, Daniel Tranel, Hanna Damasio, and Antonio R. Damasio. 1994. "Impaired Recognition of Emotion in Facial Expressions following Bilateral Damage to the Human Amygdala." *Nature* 372 (6507): 669–672. doi: 10.1038/372669a0.

Cunningham, William A., Marcia K. Johnson, Carol L. Raye, J. Chris Gatenby, John C. Gore, and Mahzarin R. Banaji. 2004. "Separable Neural Components in the Processing of Black and White Faces." *Psychological Science* 15 (12): 806–813. doi: 10.1111/j.0956-7976.2004.00760.x.

Davidson, Richard J. 1998. "Affective Style and Affective Disorders: Perspectives from Affective Neuroscience." *Cognition and Emotion* 12 (3): 307–330. doi: 10.1080/026999398379628.

Demos, Kathryn E., William M. Kelley, S. L. Ryan, and Paul J. Whalen. 2008. "Human Amygdala Sensitivity to the Pupil Size of Others." *Cerebral Cortex* 18 (12): 2729–2734. doi: 10.1093/cercor/bhn034.

Hariri, Ahmad R., and Paul J. Whalen. 2011. "The Amygdala: Inside and Out." *F1000 Biology Reports* 3: 2. doi: 10.3410/B3-2.

Heller, Aaron S., Tom Johnstone, Alexander J. Shackman, Sharee N. Light, Michael J. Peterson, Gregory G. Kolden, . . . Richard J. Davidson. 2009. "Reduced Capacity to Sustain Positive Emotion in Major Depression Reflects Diminished Maintenance of Fronto-Striatal Brain Activation." *Proceedings of the National Academy of Sciences of the United States of America* 106 (52): 22445–22450. doi: 10.1073/pnas.0910651106.

Johnstone, Tom, Carien M. van Reekum, Heather L. Urry, Ned H. Kalin, and Richard J. Davidson. 2007. "Failure to Regulate: Counterproductive Recruitment of Top-Down Prefrontal-Subcortical Circuitry in Major Depression." *Journal of Neuroscience* 27 (33): 8877–8884. doi: 10.1523/JNEUROSCI.2063-07.2007.

Klüver, Heinrich. 1926. "Mescal Visions and Eidetic Vision." *American Journal of Psychology* 37 (4): 502–515.

Klüver, Heinrich. 1928. *Mescal: The "Divine" Plant and Its Psychological Effects.* London: Kegan Paul, Trench, Trubner.

Klüver, Heinrich, and Paul C. Bucy. 1937. "'Psychic Blindness' and Other Symptoms following Bilateral Temporal Lobectomy in Rhesus Monkeys." *American Journal of Physiology* 119 (2): 352–353.

LeDoux, Joseph E. 2013. "The Slippery Slope of Fear." *Trends in Cognitive Sciences* 17 (4): 155–156. doi: 10.1016/j.tics.2013.02.004.

Nitschke, Jack B., Issidoros Sarinopoulos, Desmond J. Oathes, Tom Johnstone, Paul J. Whalen, Richard J. Davidson, and Ned H. Kalin. 2009. "Anticipatory Activation in the Amygdala and Anterior Cingulate in Generalized Anxiety Disorder and Prediction of Treatment Response." *American Journal of Psychiatry* 166 (3): 302–310. doi: 10.1176/appi.ajp.2008.07101682.

OED Online. 2019. "emotion, n." Oxford University Press, September 2019, www.oed.com/view/Entry/61249. Accessed December 2, 2019.

Phan, K. Luan, Mike Angstadt, Jamie Golden, Ikechukwu Onyewuenyi, Ana Popovska, and Harriet de Wit. 2008. "Cannabinoid Modulation of Amygdala Reactivity to Social Signals of Threat in Humans." *Journal of Neuroscience* 28 (10): 2313–2319. doi: 10.1523/JNEUROSCI.5603-07.2008.

Reznikoff, Glen A., C. Scott Manaker, Harker Rhodes, Andrew Winokur, and Thomas C. Rainbow. 1986. "Localization and Quantification of Beta-Adrenergic Receptors in Human Brain." *Neurology* 36 (8): 1067–1073. doi: 10.1212/WNL.36.8.1067.

Vuilleumier, Patrik, Jorge L. Armony, Jon Driver, and Raymond J. Dolan. 2001. "Effects of Attention and Emotion on Face Processing in the Human Brain: An Event-Related fMRI Study." *Neuron* 30 (3): 829–841. doi: 10.1016/S0896-6273(01)00328-2.

Vuilleumier, Patrik. 2005. "How Brains Beware: Neural Mechanisms of Emotional Attention." *Trends in Cognitive Sciences* 9 (12): 585–594. doi: 10.1016/j.tics.2005.10.011.

Further Reading

Bavelier, Daphne, and Richard J. Davidson. 2013. "Brain Training: Games to Do You Good." *Nature* 494 (7438): 425–426. doi: 10.1038/494425a.

Leading experts in the training of attention and emotion, respectively, consider the question of "Because gaming is clearly here to stay, . . . how to channel people's love of screen time towards positive effects on the brain and behavior."

Davidson, Richard J., and Sharon Begley. 2013. *The Emotional Life of Your Brain: How Its Unique Patterns Affect the Way You Think, Feel, and Live – and How You Can Change Them.* New York: Plume.

An engrossing, authoritative "users' manual" for understanding and controlling one's emotional style, interwoven with facts from affective neuroscience and anecdotes from the career of one of its leading scholars.

Davis, Michael, and Paul J. Whalen. 2001. "The Amygdala: Vigilance and Emotion." *Molecular Psychiatry* 6 (1): 13–34.

A detailed review of the anatomy, physiology, and pharmacology of conditioning in the amygdala.

Greenwald, Anthony G., and Mahzarin R. Banaji. 1995. "Implicit Social Cognition: Attitudes, Self-Esteem, and Stereotypes." *Psychological Review* 102 (1): 4–27. doi: 10.1037/0033-295X.102.1.4.

This paper lays out the theoretical background for understanding implicit bias and stereotyping from a social psychology perspective.

Kubota, Jennifer T., Mahzarin R. Banaji, and Elizabeth A. Phelps. 2012. "The Neuroscience of Race." *Nature Neuroscience* 15 (7): 940–948. doi: 10.1038/nn.3136.

A review of exciting, vitally important research that has revealed "overlap in the neural circuitry of race, emotion and decision-making."

LeDoux, Joseph E. 2000. "Emotion Circuits in the Brain." *Annual Review of Neuroscience* 23: 155–184.

Provocative argument by one of the leading scientists of fear conditioning for reconceptualizing emotion research as research on survival circuits.

Milad, Mohammed R., and Gregory J. Quirk. 2012. "Fear Extinction as a Model for Translational Neuroscience: Ten Years of Progress." *Annual Review of Psychology* 63: 129–151. doi: 10.1146/annurev.psych.121208.131631.

A review of the truly pioneering research, much of it performed by the authors, on the neural bases of extinction learning.

Ochsner, Kevin N., and Matthew D. Lieberman. 2007. "The Emergence of Social Cognitive Neuroscience." *American Psychologist* 56 (9): 717–734. doi: 10.1037//0003-066X.56.9.717.

As told by two of the field's leading practitioners.

CHAPTER 19

Language

KEY THEMES

- Language, with its ubiquity in our lives, and its uniqueness to our species, is the focus of strongly debated theories that get at the core of what it means to be human.
- Nineteenth-century neurological models posited a network comprising posterior temporal cortex (Wernicke's area), temporoparietal regions, posterior inferior frontal gyrus (Broca's area), and, critically, the connections bguetween them, that still influences contemporary ideas of the neural organization of language.
- EEG indicates that the earliest cortical generators of the AEP begin segregating speech from nonspeech sounds, probably bilaterally.
- The idea that there may exist a single "grammar gene" has prompted considerable excitement and research, but it is probably "too good to be true."
- More than 150 years after Broca's first report of language impairment following damage to inferior PFC, the function(s) attributable to "his" area are still the focus of contentious debate.
- EEG and MEG suggest that predictive coding is an important principle governing language processing, both its comprehension and its production.

CONTENTS

Companion Website: www.wiley.com/go/postle/cognitiveneuroscience3e

A System of Remarkable Complexity

> A human language is a system of remarkable complexity . . . A normal child acquires this knowledge on relatively slight exposure and without specific training. He can then quite effortlessly make use of an intricate structure of specific rules and guiding principles to convey his thoughts and feelings to others, arousing in them novel ideas and subtle perceptions and judgments. (Chomsky, 1975, p. 4)

Language is, indeed, a most remarkable element of human cognition. It is the medium through which culture is transmitted, technology propagated, and knowledge about topics as rich and complex as, say, *cognitive neuroscience*, is taught, updated, debated, refined, and so on. It also seems to be a uniquely human faculty. Although some other species have sophisticated means of communication, and some can be taught some rudimentary elements of human language, none has a system of communication whereby a finite number of elements can be recombined in an infinite number of ways to generate an infinite number of messages. This is referred to as the generative property of human language.

Perhaps it is because language is so uniquely human, and so intertwined with virtually everything that we do as individuals and as societies, that it is the most intensively studied domain of human cognition.[1] One consequence of this intense interest is that there are many theoretical debates about, for example, how language is learned, the rules of grammar (indeed, whether there even exist rules of grammar), and the extent to which language depends on neural structures that are unique to our species. Although these debates can be rich and fascinating, and often get at core questions about human nature, many of them are simply outside the remit of this book. Nonetheless, when appropriate, theoretical motivations and/or implications of particular studies that we will consider will be flagged.

[1] This author is Editor-in-Chief of the *Journal of Cognitive Neuroscience* (i.e., a journal devoted to the topic of this book [wink emoji]), and it is unquestionably the case that language is the domain of cognition about which the *Journal of Cognitive Neuroscience* receives the most submissions.

Wernicke–Lichtheim: The Classical Core Language Network

The Aphasias

In *Chapter 1,* we introduced the work of Broca, including with his famous patient "Tan," as an important demonstration, alongside roughly contemporaneous research on motor control and vision, of localization of function in the brain. In his famous and influential paper from 1970, the neurologist Norman Geschwind (1926–1984) pointed out another important feature of this work: "The aphasias were . . . the first demonstrations of the fact that selective damage to the brain could affect one class of *learned behavior* while sparing other classes" (p. 940, emphasis added). That is, the first evidence that an unequivocally cognitive function (as contrasted with motor control and vision) could be localized to a particular part of the brain. But "the aphasias"? Broca only described one. What Geschwind was also referring to was the work of neurologist Carl Wernicke (1848–1904), who, in 1874, proposed a model for the neural bases of two classes of aphasia. Here's how Geschwind (1970) summarized them:

> The aphasic of the Broca's type characteristically produces little speech, which is emitted slowly, with great effort, and with poor articulation . . . Characteristically the small grammatical words and endings are omitted . . . These patients invariably show a comparable disorder in their written output, but they may comprehend spoken and written language normally. In striking contrast to these performances, the patient may retain his musical capacities. It is a common but most dramatic finding to observe a patient who produces single substantive words with great effort and poor articulation and yet sings a melody correctly and even elegantly.

This contrasts with Geschwind's summary of the aphasia first described by Wernicke in 1874:

> The Wernicke's aphasi[a] . . . patient usually has no paralysis of the opposite side, a fact which reflects the difference in the anatomical localization of his lesion. The speech output can be rapid and effortless, and in many cases the rate of production of words exceeds the normal. The output has the rhythm and melody of normal speech, but it is remarkably empty and conveys little or no information. The patient uses many filler words, and the speech is filled with circumlocutions. There may be many errors in word usage, which are called paraphasias . . . The Wernicke's aphasic may, in writing, produce well-formed letters, but the output exhibits the same linguistic defects which are observed in the patient's speech. He shows a profound failure to understand both spoken and written language, although he suffers from no elementary impairment of hearing or sight (pp. 940–941).

The loci of the regions described by Broca and by Wernicke, and redescribed by Geschwind (1970), are illustrated in *Figure 19.1*. Broca's area is located at the posterior end of the inferior frontal gyrus of the left hemisphere of the PFC, immediately anterior to premotor cortical regions that control the face, tongue, lips, palate, and vocal cords. Classically, because of the characteristics of Broca's aphasia, Broca's area has been presumed to be the neural seat of language production (but see Dronkers, 2000, *Further reading*). Wernicke's area is located in the posterior superior temporal gyrus (STG) in the left hemisphere, occupying a portion of auditory parabelt cortex (*Figure 3.10*). It is, therefore, anatomically proximal to auditory cortex, and receives projections from A1 and belt cortex, as well as direct projections from the medial geniculate nucleus (MGN). Its function has classically been associated with the comprehension of spoken language.

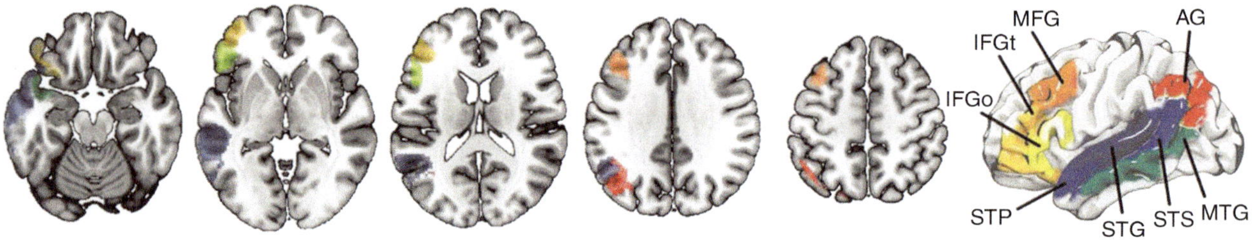

FIGURE 19.1 Cortical regions of the left hemisphere involved in language functions. Broca's area is traditionally localized to the IFGo and the IFGt, and Wernicke's area to the caudal portion of STG. AG = angular gyrus; MFG = middle frontal gyrus; IFGt = inferior frontal gyrus pars triangularis; IFGo = IFG pars opercularis; STP = superior temporal pole; STG = superior temporal gyrus; STS = superior temporal sulcus; MTG = middle temporal gyrus.

Source: Reproduced with permission from John Del Gaizo et al. (2017) / Society for Neuroscience / CC BY 4.0.

The Functional Relevance of the Connectivity of the Network

Although Geschwind didn't include him in the 1970 review, a third important nineteenth-century contributor to our understanding of the brain bases of language function is the neurologist Ludwig Lichtheim (1845–1928). Lichtheim is famous for his "house model," which diagrammatically predicted how interruptions of connections between input, semantic, and output regions would produce aphasias that would differ in subtle ways from those resulting from frank damage that was limited to Wernicke's or Broca's area (*Figure 19.2*). Remarkably, over the next century, each of the aphasias predicted by Wernicke and by Lichtheim came to be identified by subsequent generations of neurologists. To name just one example, conduction aphasia presents as fluent but **paraphasic speech**, but in the presence of *intact* language comprehension. (Wernicke's aphasia, in contrast, would present as fluent but paraphasic speech, but with severely *impaired* language comprehension.) It is most often associated with damage to the inferior parietal cortex – "AG" in *Figure 19.1* and corresponding to "3" in *Figure 19.2.A* – and is explained by damage to the arcuate fasciculus, a white matter

FIGURE 19.2 Lichtheim's (1885) "house model" of the neural substrates of language.

Source: Compston and Alastair, 2006 / Oxford University.

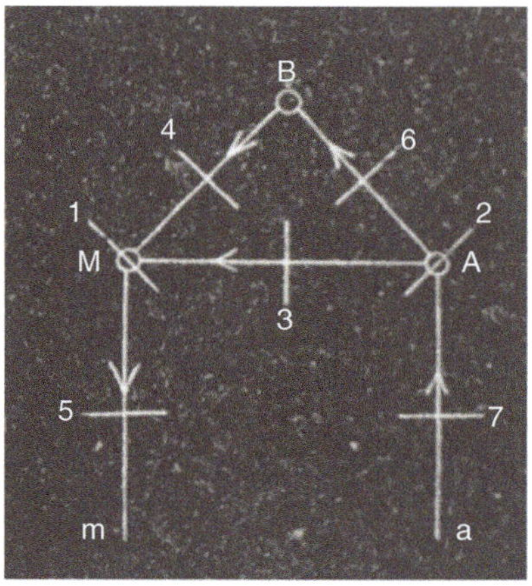

FIGURE 19.2.A "a" and "m" correspond to auditory inputs and motor outputs, respectively; "A" to Wernicke's area and "M" to Broca's. "B" is a stand-in for the neural representation of the semantic content carried by language (see *Figure 19.2.B* for more elaboration on "B"). The numerals indicate lesioning points, each known (1, 2) or (accurately) predicted (3–7) to produce a different aphasia: 1 = Broca's; 2 = Wernike's; 3 = conduction; 4 = transcortical motor; 5 = subcortical motor; 6 = transcortical sensory; 7 = subcortical sensory. Details on these can be found in Alexander (1997, *Further Reading*).

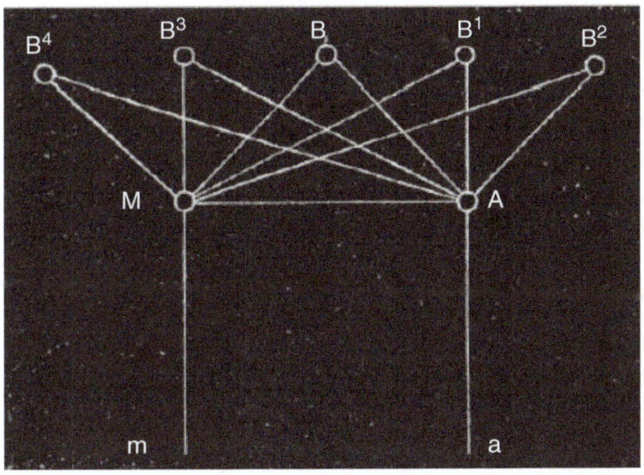

FIGURE 19.2.B Lichtheim's strikingly modern conceptualization of the distributed nature of the brain's representation of knowledge and its anatomical interfaces with Broca's and Wernicke's areas.

pathway connecting, among others, Wernicke's and Broca's areas. Damage to the arcuate fasciculus has the effect of leaving both Wernicke's and Broca's areas intact, but interrupting the fibers that connect them.

Thus, this Wernicke–Lichtheim model provides a framework from which we can start examining language functions more closely, beginning with speech perception, and then proceeding to grammar and production.

Speech Perception

Segregation of the Speech Signal

In *Chapter 3*, we considered in some detail the processes of the transduction of acoustic energy into a neural code, and the stages of processing of the auditory signal from brainstem to MGN to cortex that are discernible in the auditory-evoked potential (AEP). This gives us a starting point to think about speech perception and, in particular, where and how auditory signal that is related to speech is identified and extracted from the auditory stream for its presumably specialized processing as language. A straightforward way to get at this question would clearly be to contrast the processing of speech sounds vs. nonspeech sounds while measuring sound-evoked activity, and determining how the two physiological signals differ. Before just jumping in, however, there are some basic facts that we need to understand about the signal that we want to study. First, what are the elements of spoken language? Second, at what level of organization do we want to study it? Finally, what are some fundamental physical and psychophysical properties of the speech signal itself?

The Elements of Language One way to think about the organization of spoken language is as a hierarchy. At the lowest level are **phonemes**, the smallest unit of sound in a language that, when changed, can change the meaning of an utterance. For example, as we shall see in the next section, in US English, the words "doll" and "tall" only differ by one phoneme, even though they differ by two letters. Note that, with a few exceptions, phonemes do not, by themselves, convey meaning. Rather, phonemes are assembled to create words. All human languages use many fewer phonemes than there are possible sounds that can be made with the articulatory apparatus (i.e., the diaphragm, vocal cords, tongue, jaw, and lips). Although the number of phonemes differs across languages, and often differs across dialects within a language, no natural language is believed to contain more than 150. The next level in the hierarchy is *words*. Words are the smallest element of the language that have inherent meaning. The mental representation of words is referred to as the mental lexicon, and the mental lexicon of the typical adult comprises anywhere between 50,000 and 75,000 words. The meaning of a word can be changed by the addition of one or more *morphemes*: prefixes and suffixes that modify words. For example, in English, adding an "s" to the end of a regular noun makes it plural, and adding "un" to the front of one adds negation or "the opposite of."

The next level is the *clause*. A clause is constructed of words, and it is at this level of language that grammar comes into play. For example, it is the rules of grammar that determine that different orderings of the same three words can have different meanings (e.g., "Dog bites man" vs. "Man bites dog"), or no meaning (e.g., "Bites dog man"). Within the two grammatical clauses just given, the meaning was changed by changing which noun filled the role of *noun phrase* and which the role of *verb phrase*. These two clauses are also each a *sentence*.

Sentences can consist of single clauses or of a combination of two or more clauses. Indeed, it was to the infinite "combine-ability" of clauses into grammatically legal, information-conveying sentences that Chomsky (1975) was referring to as "an intricate structure of specific rules and guiding principles." Collectively, these rules are referred to as "syntax" or "grammar."

Finally, there is *discourse*, which comprises any collection of sentences that can be construed as comprising a unit of communication (e.g., a paragraph, a song, and a book).

If we're interested in understanding how speech is processed differently from nonspeech sounds, it makes sense to start at the most basic level, the phoneme. Studying the perception of words, for example, risks confounding neural signals associated with processing the meaning of the word vs. neural signals associated with detecting and processing a speech sound, per se. Of course, as we're about to see, limiting oneself to just studying phoneme perception doesn't mean that one's task will be easy.

The Speech Signal Speech perception presents several difficult engineering problems. One of them has been summarized as the "lack of invariance" problem. That is, to understand spoken language, we need to be able to categorize sounds as corresponding to specific phonemes. However, the same phoneme can often be carried by acoustic patterns that are physically different from one another. When hearing the English words "doll" and "deal," for example, one needs to categorize the initial sound from both words as being the same: /d/. (Mistakenly categorizing one of them as /t/, for example, would lead to mistakenly hearing those words as "tall" or as "teal.") The problem of the lack of invariance, however, is that the acoustic signals when one is saying [da] vs. [di] are quite different (*Figure 19.3*). Indeed, there are no invariant cues to the identity of any phoneme. (One reason for lack of invariance of speech sounds is the phenomenon of coarticulation: the way that we shape and move our speech apparatus to utter the current phoneme is influenced by preparations already underway for the next phoneme to be spoken.)

Although lack of invariance can pose problems for the auditory system, it creates opportunities for scientists. Consider the following. A complement to the property illustrated in *Figure 19.3* is the fact there exist pairs of phonemes whose acoustic properties are very similar, yet they are perceived differently. The most studied examples are phonemes that differ only along one physical dimension, and depending on where along that dimension the sound falls, it is perceived as one or the other. A famous example from English is the phonemes [da] and [ta]. The consonants /d/ and /t/ are from a class of consonants called "stop consonants," whose utterance requires a momentary blockage of the vocal tract, typically with the tongue. The voice onset timing (VOT) of a stop consonant refers to the latency between the release of the stop and the onset of vibration in the vocal cords. [da] and [ta] differ from each other only in that [da] has a VOT of 0 msec and [ta] a VOT of approximately 70 msec. Experimentally, it has been shown that if one begins with [da] and gradually modifies the sound by increasing the VOT from 0 msec out to 70 msec [ta] in, say, 5-msec intervals, subjects do not hear a smooth transition of sounds incrementally changing from [da] to [ta]. Rather, what they hear is a series of undifferentiated "[da]"s until, at one point (typically around a VOT of 35 msec), they suddenly begin hearing a series of undifferentiated "[ta]"s. What this means is that the physical stimulus is changing continuously, but the percept has only two states. Finding the first station in the auditory system that tracks the percept, as opposed to tracking the physical signal, would be a candidate for the first area that processes speech sounds differently than nonspeech sounds.

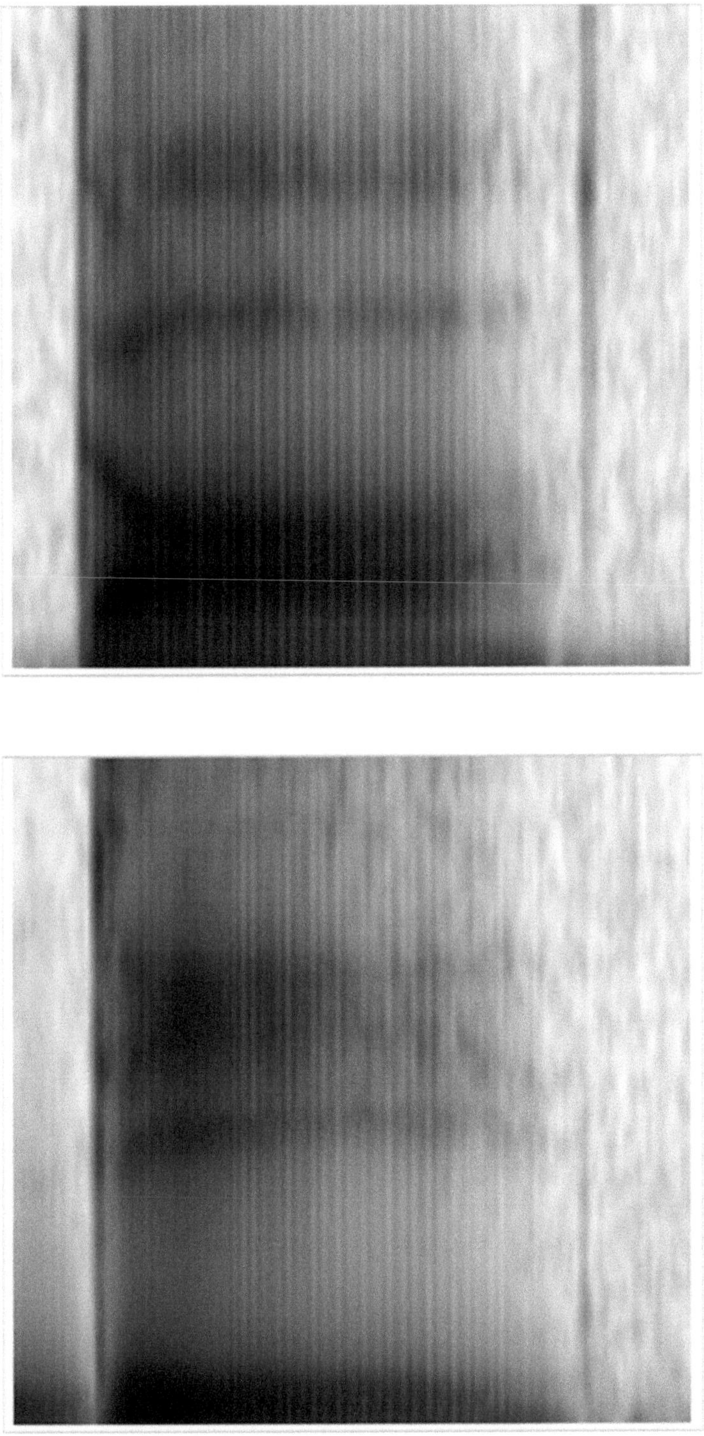

FIGURE 19.3 Spectrograms from an individual uttering the phonemes [da] (top) and [di] (bottom). The vertical axis is frequency (scale of 0–5000 Hz) and the horizontal axis is time (scale of 0–300 msec), with darker gray representing greater power. Note how the early portion of the speech signals differ, even though both are perceived as /d/. The "dark bands" of sustained, elevated oscillatory power that are visibly evident in these spectrograms are called formants. Formants are labeled from low to high frequency, with the first formant also known as the **fundamental frequency** of the signal.

Source: Bradley R. Postle.

Neural Correlates of Speech Perception In 2005, a team led by Ghislaine Dehaene-Lambertz published a study that followed a logic similar to the one just described. Specifically, it employed a mismatch paradigm, which is one of the most commonly used to study differences in the auditory/language processing system. The stimuli that Dehaene-Lambertz et al. (2005) presented to subjects were "synthetic sinewave analogues of speech" that could be interpreted as either whistles or as the phonemes [ba] or [da]. Without prompting, most hear them as whistles. Subjects in this study were native speakers of French, so instead of varying VOT (which differentiates [da] vs. [ta] in English), they varied the place of articulation – the physical location in the mouth where the tongue applies the blockage that makes the /b/ and /d/ stop consonants – to create the continuum along which [ba] vs. [da] differ in French. Varying **place of articulation** influences the acoustic signal by changing the frequency of its **formants** (see *Figure 19.3*). The stimuli were labeled according to their phonemic identity for French speakers and according to the onset frequency of the second formant: ba975, ba1250, da1525, and da1800. (Note that, to achieve such precise and replicable acoustic properties in the stimuli, it's common for speech perception research to use synthesized, rather than natural stimuli.)

Stimuli were presented in groups of four (*Figure 19.4*). In repetition trials, one of the four stimuli was repeated four times. In within-category change (WC) trials, the last stimulus differed from the previous three, but still fell on the same side of the phonemic boundary (e.g., *ba975, ba975, ba975, ba1250* or *da1800, da1800, da1800, da1525*). In across-category change (AC) trials, the last stimulus fell on the other side of the phonemic boundary (e.g., *da1525, da1525, da1525, ba1250* or *ba1250, ba1250, ba1250, da1525*). Thus, the acoustical distance between the last stimulus and the preceding ones was identical in the two types of change, the only difference being that, when the stimuli were perceived as speech sounds, the change in AC trials would be perceived as a change of phonemic category. This created the critical contrast whereby a change in the auditory percept could be dissociated from changes in the acoustic signal. This comparison was implemented experimentally by performing the experiment in two stages. In "Nonspeech mode," which always came first, the stimuli were referred to as "whistles," and subjects were instructed to indicate whether or not the fourth whistle of each trial differed from the others in pitch. Prior to the second stage – "Speech mode" – the speech-like nature of the stimuli was explained to subjects, and they were played the two most distinctively different sounds until they could identify them as [ba] and [da]. Then the procedure was repeated.

Results from the ERP study (*Figure 19.4.A*) indicated that the identical physical change (of 275 Hz) produced significantly greater changes in the ERP for AC vs. WC changes, only in speech mode, beginning with the P1 component. Because the P1 has been localized to parabelt cortex of the STG, this suggests that speech is segregated from nonspeech at a very early stage of cortical processing. When the same experimental procedure was repeated, with different subjects, during fMRI scanning, three patterns emerged (*Figure 19.4.B*): (1) midline and lateral frontal areas, insula, and subcortical regions were sensitive to any change of stimulus; (2) the posterior portion of the superior temporal sulcus was sensitive to mode of perception (i.e., speech > whistle); and (3) supramarginal gyrus was sensitive to a change of phoneme (i.e., AC > WC).

The ERP findings from Dehaene-Lambertz et al. (2005), indicating that the earliest cortical AEPs discriminate speech signals from nonspeech ones, led them to hypothesize that the two rely on "partially distinct neural processes" (p. 29). Although they don't speculate about the origin of these processes, they do note that "Further research should determine to what extent this organization is laid down in the course of language acquisition and to what extent it is already present early in infancy" (p. 32). In the ensuing years, Dehaene-Lambertz and colleagues performed some of this "further research," with one more recent finding, using near-infrared spectroscopy (NIRS; also known as "optical imaging") on preterm infants (28–32 weeks gestational age) coming down decidedly on the side of "already present" (see Mahmoudzadeh et al., 2013, *Further reading*).

FIGURE 19.4 Dissociating speech perception from nonspeech perception.

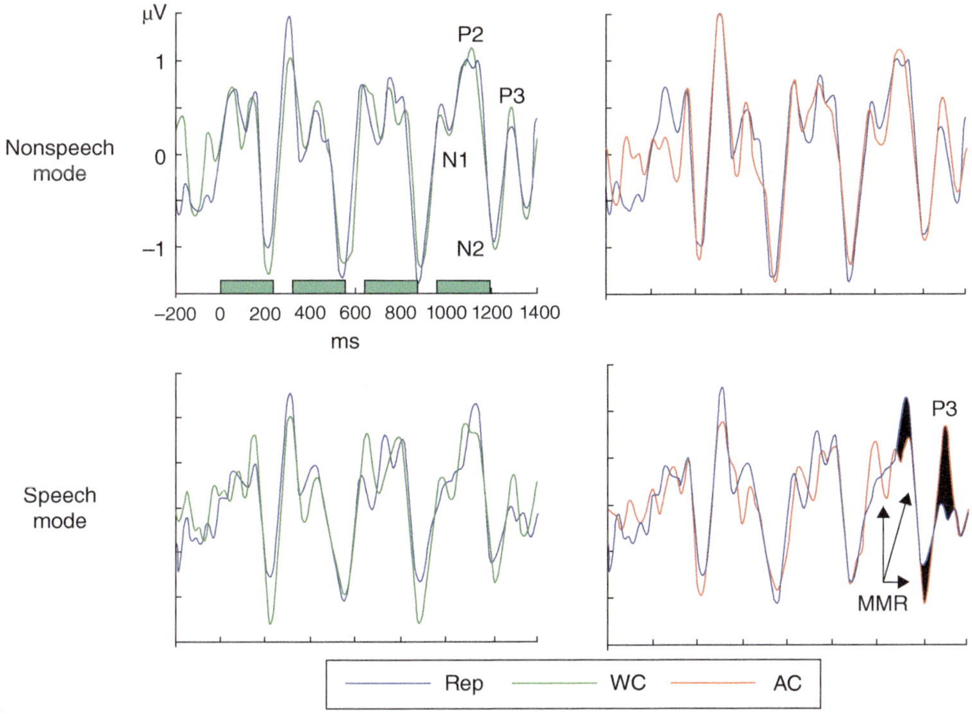

FIGURE 19.4.A ERPs from the Fz electrode for repeat trials (Rep), collapsed across stimuli, plotted with each of the two types of mismatch trials. Along the abscissa of the plot in the upper left, the timing and duration of each stimulus are illustrated with green blocks. The mismatch response (MMR) was prominent, beginning with P1, for stimuli in speech mode that produced an across-category (AC) change.

Source: Dehaene-Lambertz et al., 2005 / with permission of Elsevier.

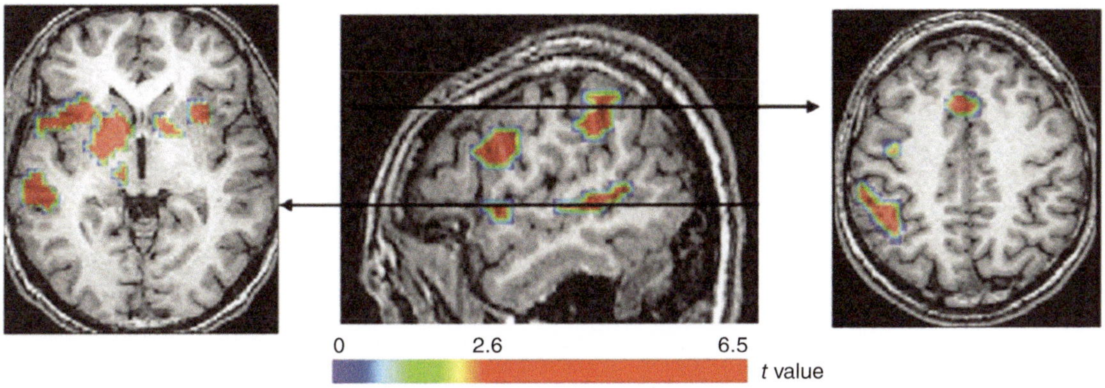

FIGURE 19.4.B Differential sensitivity of these regions to specific contrasts identified with fMRI as showing greater signal for AC vs. Rep in speech mode.

Source: Reproduced with permission from Dehaene et al. (2005) / Elsevier.

Dual Routes for Speech Processing

One model for speech perception that is generally consistent with the network of regions illustrated in *Figure 19.4.B*, and with the white matter tracts illustrated in *Figure 19.6*, is a "dual-route" model advocated by Hickok and Poeppel (2000) whereby "the posterior–superior temporal lobe, bilaterally, is the primary substrate for systems involved in constructing sound-based representations of heard speech" (p. 134), and processing then bifurcates into a ventral and a dorsal stream. The ventral stream is proposed to subserve auditory comprehension via connections that support "interfacing sound-based representations in auditory cortex with conceptual–semantic information [represented in] multimodal cortical fields in the vicinity of the left temporal-parietal-occipital junction" (p. 134). Note that these "multimodal cortical fields" correspond to portions of the temporal and occipital lobe areas that we studied in considerable detail in *Chapter 13, Semantic long-term memory*. Further, Hickok and Poeppel readily acknowledge that their model draws heavily on ideas first proposed by Wernicke and by Lichtheim. Thus, their ventral stream can be understood as corresponding to the pathway *A–B–M* as portrayed in *Figure 19.2.A*, and magnified in *Figure 19.2.B*. (We'll consider a modern-day depiction of this pathway in the upcoming section on grammar.)

The dorsal stream is proposed to act as an "auditory-motor interface" that, in effect, follows the course of the arcuate fasciculus, but with at least some fibers synapsing in inferior parietal cortex. The argument is that posterior temporal regions, as well as inferior parietal regions, contribute to assembling articulatory codes for speech. One consequence of this is the involvement of "dorsal stream" regions, particularly in inferior parietal cortex, in processing phonetic segments, such as stimuli of the kind featured in the study from Dehaene-Lambertz et al. (2005) that we just reviewed.

Note that although *Figure 19.4.B* does not show evidence of elevated right hemisphere activity for the "AC > Rep" contrast illustrated from the Dehaene-Lambertz et al. (2005) study, Hickok and Poeppel (2000) review several neuropsychological and neuroimaging studies that implicate right STG in at least some aspects of speech perception. Although beyond the scope of this book, reviews of data and theories relating to the lateralization of processing of speech and other acoustical signals are provided in the *Further reading* from Zatorre and Gandour (2008), as is an alternative dual-route model from Scott and Johnsrude (2003).

Grammar

Up until this point, we have focused on the perception of speech sounds and referenced our earlier treatments of single-word comprehension in *Chapter 4* and *Chapter 13*. Now, let's turn to the decoding of the language signal. After all, it's one thing to understand the meaning of the individual words *dog*, *bites*, and *man*, but with this knowledge alone, one couldn't know who was the perpetrator and who the victim.

Genetics

Here is a partial summary of impairments of four individuals diagnosed with a developmental language disorder:

> They took a long time to name pictures of objects with which they were familiar, and tended to use approximate words, for example "glass" or "tea" for cup, and "sky" for star. Comprehension was also delayed, especially the understanding of comparatives. "The knife is longer than the pencil" was poorly understood. "The girl is chased by the horse" became "the girl is chasing the horse," and "the boy chasing the horse is fat" was interpreted as being the same as "a thin boy chasing a fat horse." Most of those affected, especially the children, could not retain three items in the correct sequence. Many were unintelligible and reluctant to offer spontaneous conversation (Hurst et al., 1990, p. 354).

The striking thing about these four is that they were all drawn from three generations of the same family (the "KE family," as Hurst and colleagues refer to them): "The affected members of this family all have the same type of speech and language difficulty, but to varying degrees of severity. The unaffected members have no speech and language difficulties and all attended normal schools" (p. 354). This was a remarkable finding because, as Jane Hurst et al. (1990) noted,

> Few speech disorders are inherited in a simple Mendelian way, and when familial clustering does occur, both genetic and environmental factors are involved. The genetic contribution in most cases involves more than one gene (polygenic inheritance), although a dominant gene with reduced penetrance is possible. In practice, it is unusual to find full penetrance of a speech disorder occurring in a regular manner over generations (p. 352).

Let's unpack this statement. Inspection of the KE family's pedigree (*Figure 19.5*) indicates that, beginning with the first generation on record, each child has had a 50% chance of acquiring the disorder. This is a hallmark of autosomal dominant transmission of a mutation in a single gene. That is, in one parent, one of two alleles of this single gene carries a mutation. As a consequence, because the sperm and the egg each contribute one allele from each gene, there is a 50% chance that any child produced by that couple will inherit the mutation. The mutation is dominant, meaning that it determines the transcription and translation of that gene. (For eye color, a brown allele is dominant over blue, such that if a child inherits a blue allele from Mom and a brown allele from Dad, the child's eyes will be brown.) "Penetrance" refers to the likelihood that, if one does inherit the mutation, it will be expressed in that individual's phenotype; *Figure 19.5* indicates that the disorder is fully penetrant. Autosomes are all chromosomes that are not the sex chromosomes – that is, the *X* and the *Y* – and therefore an autosomal disorder can be inherited by either male or female offspring. (For a primer on inheritance of single-gene disorders, see Chial, 2008, *Further reading*.) That's the elementary

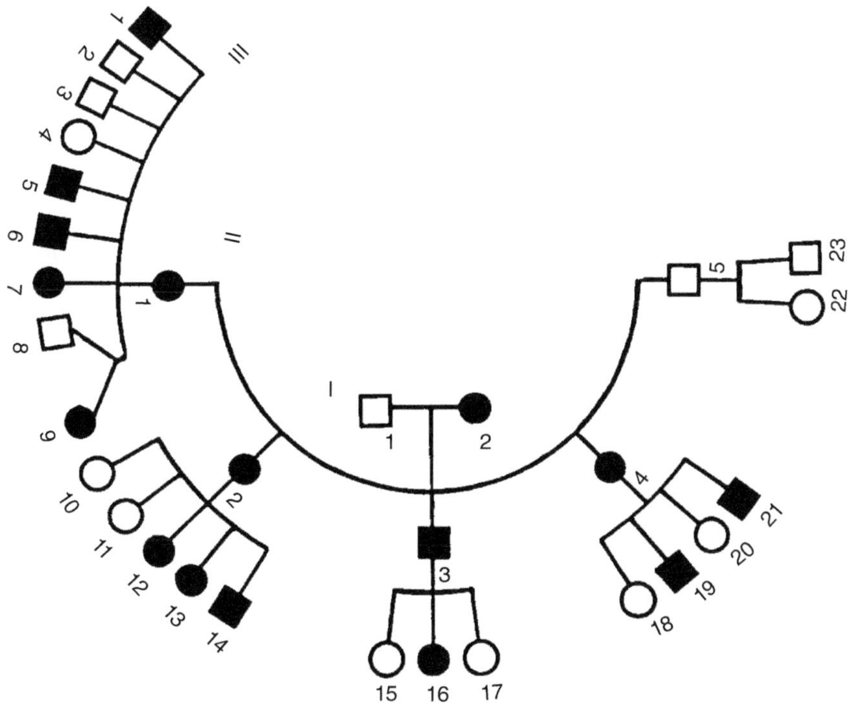

FIGURE 19.5 The pedigree of the KE family. Squares represent males; filled symbols represent affected individuals. Roman numerals identify the three generations of the family, Arabic numerals the pedigree number of an individual within a generation.

Source: Hurst et al., 1990 / John Wiley & Sons.

Mendelian genetics. What's most striking about this case is that it indicates that a single gene is responsible for the KE family's disorder!

Autosomal dominant disorders are uncommon. (Your author just looked up a list of exemplars, and the only one he's confident that he recognizes is Huntington's disease.) They are almost unheard of for purely cognitive disorders. Thus, considerable excitement, and controversy, was generated by the linguist Myrna Gopnik, and subsequently by others, when she proposed that the function of the mutated gene is to "affect the capacity to acquire language" (Gopnik, 1990b, p. 26). In the interpretation of some (including Pinker, 1994), this was evidence for a "grammar gene."

Is There a Grammar Gene? The reason the initial summary of KE family deficits was qualified as "partial" is because the initial report from Hurst et al. (1990) also included the fact that, for example, "Articulation was also defective, and [the affected family members had] . . . a moderate to severe degree of dyspraxia. They could position the tongue and lips for simple movements, but failed when a sequence of movements was required" (p. 354). These would be considered by many to extend beyond grammar per se. Nonetheless, where grammar ends and where extra-grammatical, but nonetheless "language related," processes begin is not well defined.

Gopnik's original (1990a) report on the KE family prompted immediate objections to her interpretation that noted, for example, that the impairments of affected family members were much broader than portrayed, and also included "impairment in repeating phonemes, words, nonwords, and sentences . . . [and in] aspects of language that are unrelated to syntax[, including] semantic errors in naming . . . [and poor] receptive vocabulary" (Vargha-Khadem and Passingham, 1990, p. 226). Gopnik's reply to these objections, in turn, was that

> What really is at stake here are not the data, but rather how to account for them. My explanation hypothesizes that the subjects are impaired because they cannot construct language rules at the necessary level of abstraction. [Fletcher (1990) and Vargha-Khadem and Passingham (1990)] prefer an explanation which hypothesizes that the subjects are impaired because they cannot hear or cannot pronounce certain sounds, and this indirectly affects the grammar carried by these sounds (Gopnik, 1990b, p. 26).

When confronted with such a case of "he said-she said," what is one to do? The answer, of course, is that one is to perform studies that are carefully designed to assess the key questions of the debate. This additional research proceeded along two paths: one behavioral and one genetic. The behavioral, pursued by Faraneh Vargha-Khadem et al. (1995), elaborated on the arguments that they had raised in their initial response, and also established that affected members had significantly lower verbal and nonverbal IQ, with the score of many being below the value "commonly considered an exclusionary criterion for classification of a subject as having a specific language impairment" (p. 932).

Perhaps the most compelling evidence against the "grammar gene" position, however, arrived with the identification of the gene itself. In 2001, geneticists Cecilia Lai and Simon Fisher, working in the laboratory of Anthony Monaco at Oxford University, reported the identification of the mutated gene as FOXP2. This was an important breakthrough because the functions of the gene could then be studied, independent of the KE family or others carrying the mutation. From research that both preceded and followed the report of Lai et al. (2001), we know that FOXP2 acts as a regulator (primarily a repressor) of the transcription of other genes. Sarah Graham and Simon Fisher (2013) have noted that "FoxP2 is likely to be present in all vertebrates, and is highly conserved in neural expression pattern and amino-acid coding sequence . . . Thus, ancestral versions contributed to brain development long before language appeared" (p. 44). In mice, the mutation is associated with impaired motor learning and electrophysiological abnormalities in the striatum.

The cumulative effect of the findings summarized here is that, in this "post-FOXP2 era," most would endorse the statement that a complex cognitive faculty like grammar is unlikely to be isolable to a single gene. At a different level, another lesson that one can take away from the saga of FOXP2 is that, for some developmental disabilities, it is not uncommon for there to be disagreement about what constitutes a fundamentally linguistic impairment vs. a more general cognitive impairment. (This is also seen, for example, with so-called specific language impairment [SLI] and with dyslexia.) If we want to address the cognitive neuroscience of grammar head-on, then let's move to a different literature.

Rules in the Brain?

Grammar refers to the systematic ways by which one can combine and modify words to encode (if speaking) or decode (if listening) a precise message. One property of grammar is that it is combinatorial. For example, the phrase structure of grammar allows one to go from "The boy is fat" to "The boy chasing the horse is fat," to "The boy chasing the horse on the reduced-calorie diet is fat," with nary any uncertainty about which organism's body type is being called out. Another property of grammar is that it allows one to convey temporal context by changing verb tense: "The boy was fat" vs. "The boy is fat" vs. "The boy will be fat." These are descriptions of grammar that no one would contest as untrue. Where there is contention, however, is whether these operations – combinatorial recursion and verb inflection – depend on rules.

Steven Pinker and Michael Ullman (2002a) have summarized it as follows:

> The [English] past tense is of theoretical interest because it embraces two strikingly different phenomena. Regular inflection, as in walk-walked and play-played, applies predictably to thousands of verbs and is productively generalized to neologisms such as spam-spammed and mosh-moshed, even by preschool children. Irregular inflection, as in come-came and feel-felt, applies in unpredictable ways to some 180 verbs, and is seldom generalized; rather, the regular suffix is often overgeneralized by children to these irregular forms, as in holded and breaked. A simple explanation is that irregular forms must be stored in memory, whereas regular forms can be generated by a rule that suffixes -ed to the stem. (p. 456)

Indeed, they go on to argue that "rules are indispensable for explaining the past tense, and by extension, language and cognitive processes" (p. 456). Although Pinker, a cognitive psychologist/psycholinguist (we'll define this in a later section), originally made this argument on theoretical and behavioral grounds, his former student, and subsequently collaborator, Michael Ullman added a neural implementation of this "Words-and-Rules" theory: whereas the past-tense forms of irregular verbs are stored in lexical memory (i.e., posterior temporoparietal cortex), past tense forms of regular verbs are computed online by a concatenation rule ("add *-ed*") implemented by the cortico-basal ganglia-thalamic loop that includes Broca's area. Evidence that Ullman and colleagues have marshaled in support of this model has included two demonstrations of neuropsychological double dissociations. In one, a patient with a nonfluent (for our purposes, Broca's) aphasia was shown to have a selective impairment at generating the past tense with regular verbs, whereas a patient with a fluent (for our purposes, Wernicke's) aphasia had a selective impairment with irregular verbs. In a second, patients with Parkinson's disease, which is characterized by progressive deafferentation of the neostriatum from its supply of midbrain dopamine, and thus by progressive striatal dysfunction, have selective difficulty inflecting regular verbs, whereas patients with Alzheimer's disease, associated with episodic and semantic memory loss, have selective difficulty inflecting irregular verbs.

An alternative view has been advanced by McClelland and colleagues. For example, James McClelland and Karalyn Patterson (2002a), in response to Pinker and Ullman (2002a), wrote that the parallel distributed processing (PDP) framework holds that "Acquisition of language and other abilities occurs via gradual adjustment of the connections among simple processing units. Characterizations of performance as 'rule-governed' are viewed as approximate descriptions of patterns of language use; no actual rules operate in the processing of language" (p. 465). Although much of their argument derives from computational modeling, McClelland and Patterson (2002a) also appeal to neural data as consistent with their perspective. For example, they note that among the findings of Vargha-Khadem et al. (1995) was the fact that affected members of the KE family (see the section *Is there a language gene?*) showed comparable levels of impaired past-tense processing of regular and irregular verbs. Further, with Helen Bird, Matthew Lambon-Ralph, and Mark Seidenberg, they have argued that a key difference between regular and irregular verbs in English is that "relative to most irregular past-tense forms, regular past-tense English verbs place greater demands on the phonological system, because the transformation from regular stem to past always involves the addition of extra phonemes whereas this is rarely the case for irregular verbs" (Bird et al., 2003; p. 503). They suggest that some studies, including the double dissociations invoked by Pinker and Ullman (2002a), may thus be explainable in terms of patients with anterior lesions having more difficulty with items with greater phonological complexity. Further, Bird et al. (2003) demonstrated in 10 nonfluent (i.e., Broca's) aphasics that "the apparent disadvantage for the production of regular past tense forms disappeared when phonological complexity was controlled" (p. 502).

"Immediate" replies to the two positions summarized here can be found at Pinker and Ullman (2002b) and McClelland and Patterson (2002b), and in many ensuing publications. The debate about whether the brain truly represents rules, or, alternatively, rule-like patterns that are emergent from complex network dynamics, seems unlikely to end in a consensus agreement during the career of this author (but at this point the reader should know enough to be able to pick a side ;-)). In the meantime, with this context, let's consider some perspectives on the functions of Broca's area.

Broca's Area

The classical view from behavioral neurology, as embodied by the Wernicke–Lichtheim model, is that Broca's area is critical for syntactic processing – that is, for the grammatical decoding of heard sentences, as well as the grammatical encoding of spoken sentences. For example, patients with Broca's aphasia have difficulty understanding sentences like "It was the squirrel that the raccoon chased," from which meaning can't be derived just from knowledge of the meaning of the individual words. Despite this fact, however, others have shown that even though these patients don't understand these sentences, they can make correct grammaticality judgments about them, suggesting that at least some grammatical knowledge may reside elsewhere in the brain. And so, what is the function of Broca's area?

The Connectivity of Broca's Area Actually, before we dive into function, let's peel back the overlay and take a closer look at structure, specifically, at white matter tracts underlying perisylvian cortex. *Figure 19.6* is taken from a paper by Pascale Tremblay and Anthony Steven Dick (2016) titled "Broca and Wernicke are dead, or moving past the classic model of language neurobiology." Indeed, this figure contrasts (in drab gray scale) the authors' characterization of the "obsolete" view of language-critical white matter tracts espoused by Geschwind (1970), with (in popping color) the "emerging picture" of pathways contributing to language function. Certainly, in the "emerging" image, one can see that the inferior fronto-occipital fasciculus and the uncinate fasciculus provide a substrate for the ventral stream of dual-route models. This figure also makes clear how dorsal and ventral anatomical pathways converge in an inferior frontal region of the brain.

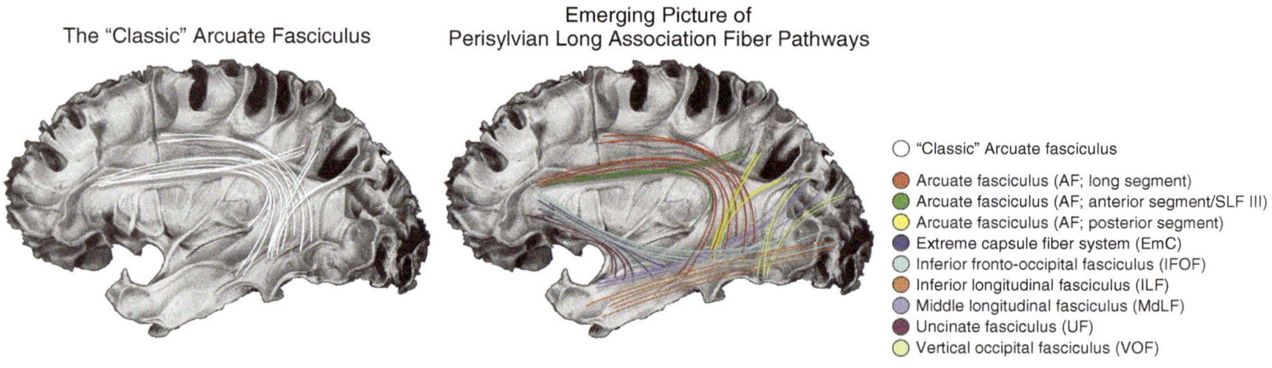

FIGURE 19.6 "Classic" vs. contemporary views of the perisylvian connectivity underlying language functions.

Source: Reproduced with permission from Tremblay, P. et al. (2016) / Elsevier.

Functional Accounts of Broca's Area Readers who have made it this far through the book won't be surprised to learn that the classical view of Broca's area as the neural seat of grammar has, over the past quarter century, been called into question by many investigators. There's not room here to detail every alternative account, but some prominent ones are verbal short-term memory (STM), cognitive control, and "unification," a hypothesized process of integrating information from phonological, lexical, syntactic, and semantic levels in the service of language comprehension and production (Hagoort, 2005; this concept will also be relevant for the upcoming section on *The electrophysiology of grammar*). Although these alternative accounts differ in terms of the extent to which each may or may not generalize to domains of cognition outside of language, what they have in common is that they propose non-syntactic functions for this region. Two responses to these non-syntactic models have argued that there may be a finer-grained functional organization of Broca's area, such that some subregions do, indeed, support syntactic functions, and others may support non-syntactic ones. This style of reasoning is similar in spirit to one that we saw in relation to the question of whether theory-of-mind (ToM) mentalization can be localized to the right temporoparietal junction (TPJ), in *Chapter 17*. Indeed, one of the proponents of one "subregional specialization" model of Broca's area is none other than Nancy Kanwisher, whose intellectual fingerprints are also on the ToM debate, in addition, of course, to that of face processing in ventral temporal cortex. Evelina Fedorenko, John Duncan, and Nancy Kanwisher (2012) summarize what's at stake in this debate as follows:

> In 1861, Paul Broca stood up before the Anthropological Society of Paris and announced that the left frontal lobe was the seat of speech. Ever since, Broca's eponymous brain region has served as a primary battleground for one of the central debates in the science of the mind and brain: Is human cognition produced by highly specialized brain regions, each conducting a specific mental process, or instead by more general-purpose brain mechanisms, each broadly engaged in a wide range of cognitive tasks? (p. 2059)

Two "subregional specialization" models of Broca's area, defined with univariate analyses of fMRI data, are illustrated in *Figure 19.7*.

FIGURE 19.7 Two models advocating a functional compartmentalization of Broca's area.

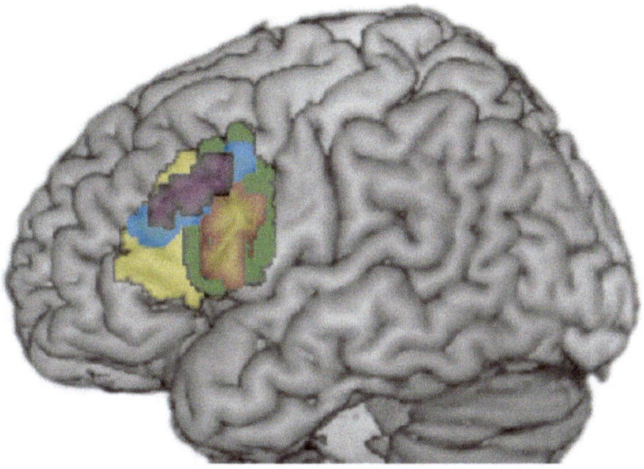

FIGURE 19.7.A fMRI evidence for subregions of Broca's area sensitive to syntactic complexity (orange) vs. working memory load (teal) of sentences. Syntactic complexity was manipulated by varying hierarchical structure, such as the presence of center-embedded clauses, in sentences. Working memory was manipulated by the number of words separating a subject noun from its respective verb, and the region sensitive to this contrast is illustrated in teal. Regions in purple showed elevated connectivity with PO during more syntactically demanding sentence processing, and are interpreted as evidence for increased working-memory support for difficult sentence processing. Yellow is anatomically identified BA 45/IFGt; green is anatomically identified BA 44/IFGo.

Source: Reproduced with permission from Makuuchi et al. (2009) / Proceedings of the National Academy of Sciences PNAS.

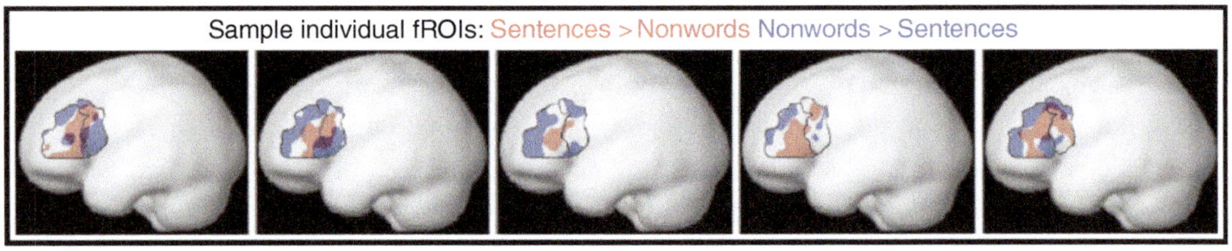

FIGURE 19.7.B Data from Broca's area of five individual subjects, with black outlines corresponding to BA 45/IFGt and BA 44/IFGo. Regions in red responded with greater fMRI signal intensity during sentence-reading, followed by a single-word recognition probe, and regions in blue during nonword viewing, followed by a single-nonword recognition probe. Subsequently, the sentence-sensitive regions were shown to respond only minimally to tests of mental arithmetic, spatial and verbal STM, and three tests of cognitive control, whereas the nonword-sensitive regions responded with significantly greater signal intensity to difficult vs. easy versions of many of these tasks.

Source: Reproduced with permission from Fedorenko et al. (2012) / Elsevier.

Pyrrhic Battles? Broca's area has, indeed, been a hotly contested piece of territory in a number of scientific skirmishes. Just one other example that has used martial metaphors is "The Battle for Broca's Region" (Grodzinsky and Santi, 2008) and "Broca's Region: Battles Are Not Won by Ignoring Half of the Facts" (Willems and Hagoort, 2009). So, not to be left out, this author will introduce a martial metaphor of his own: Some neuropsychological research suggests that these "Battles for Broca's area" might end up being viewed rather like the D-Day (June 6, 1944) assault by US Army Rangers on the Pointe du Hoc–after fierce fighting and heavy losses, the US soldiers took the position, only to find that the objective of their attack, large artillery guns, had been disassembled and moved days earlier.

Traditional approaches to neuropsychology, although valuable in many instances, can be susceptible to bias. One is to group patients by locus of lesion. A potential source of bias with this method is that the existence of multiple functional subregions may be obscured if many of the patients have lesions that span these subregions. (An analogous caveat about TMS was raised in *Chapter 17*'s treatment of the rTMS study featured in the section *Challenges to the Challenges to the Specificity of Right TPJ for ToM*.) A second traditional method is to select patients based on their symptoms; after identifying individuals with similar behavioral impairments, one looks for a locus of lesion overlap that might explain the syndrome. The potential bias with this approach relates to specificity: when employing a symptom-based approach, one necessarily only selects patients whose behavior manifests the symptom(s) that one is interested in. Thus, even if area X is damaged in each patient in one's sample, one cannot know whether, in recruiting patients, one may have overlooked a comparable number who also have lesions of area X, but who don't manifest the symptom(s) of interest (see also section *Experimental neuropsychology*, Chapter 4.).

A method known as voxel-based lesion-symptom mapping (VLSM) avoids these two sources of bias by allowing for the study of deficit–lesion correlations without requiring the categorization of patients, either in terms of lesion location or in terms of behavior. Rather, both can be treated as continuous variables, and the procedure evaluates the relation of tissue integrity to behavior on a voxel-by-voxel basis. Thus, it is effectively the same approach that is used in massively parallel univariate analysis of functional neuroimaging data, the difference being that there is no variation in the neural data over time.

A study by Elizabeth Bates et al. (2003), in a team anchored by Nina Dronkers, applied VSLM to 101 patients who had suffered left-hemisphere strokes and showed some degree of consequent language impairment. Behavioral measures of verbal fluency and auditory comprehension were acquired from subtests of a standard clinical assessment tool, the Western Aphasia Battery. Each patient's fluency score summarized performance on articulatory, word-finding, and sentence-production tasks, and the auditory comprehension score summarized performance on yes/no questions, single-word recognition, and enactment of one-, two-, and three-part commands. Lesion maps were transformed into a common space, and each voxel was then binarized for each subject as "intact" or "lesioned." (That is, tissue integrity was not treated as a continuous variable in this study, although one could do so, as is done with voxel-based morphometry [VBM] data; see Chapter 4 section *Voxel-Based Morphometry*.)

The results, illustrated in *Figure 19.8*, suggest a more prominent role for insular cortex than Broca's area for fluency and a more prominent role for middle temporal gyrus than superior temporal gyrus for comprehension. For arguments supporting these two findings, see Dronkers (2000) and Binder (2003) in the list of *Further readings*.

A caveat not unique to VSLM, but salient here, is that stroke damage is often correlated across regions, because one arterial branch typically feeds multiple regions. Thus, for example, it could be that the identification of the superior longitudinal fasciculus, which primarily connects posterior parietal cortex with PFC, is incidental to concurrent damage to the arcuate fasciculus, which actually does contribute importantly to production.

(Note that we also saw this approach in *Figure 7.3*, where it was used to determine regions whose damage was associated with acute vs. chronic unilateral neglect.)

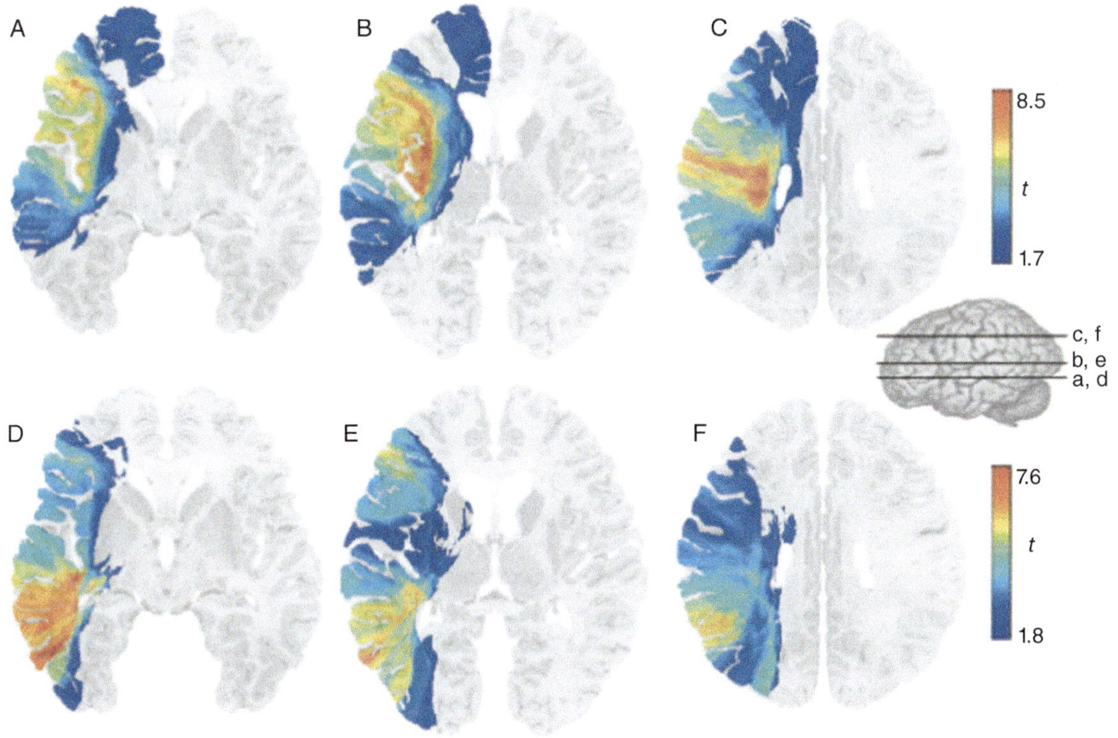

FIGURE 19.8 Voxel-based lesion-symptom maps (VLSM) from 101 left-hemisphere stroke patients. The top row illustrates the voxel-by-voxel association between lesion status and verbal fluency performance, and the lower row between lesion status and auditory comprehension. The color at each voxel corresponds to its *t*-value for that contrast, just as it does for univariate functional imaging maps. Thus, warmer colors indicate regions where lesions are more strongly associated with behavioral impairment. The faintly visible gray line on each color bar indicates the Bonferroni-corrected significance cutoffs (in the teal range for fluency, and near the teal–yellow transition for auditory comprehension. These analyses suggest that lesions of Broca's area (**A**), insula (**B**), and white matter encompassing both the arcuate and superior longitudinal fasciculi (**C**) had the greatest impact on fluency, whereas lesions of the middle (**D**) and superior (**E**) temporal gyri, and parietal association cortex (**F**), had the greatest impact on auditory comprehension.

Source: Reproduced with permission from Bates et al. (2003) / Springer Nature.

The Electrophysiology of Grammar

Explicit in the arrows drawn onto Lichtheim's house model (*Figure 19.2.A*), as well as in many more recent accounts, is the assumption that sentence processing is carried out in a feedforward (or "bottom-up") manner: the first stage is the identification of phonemes; followed by word recognition; followed by syntactic decoding of the spoken utterance. ERP studies of sentence processing, however, have provided evidence for high levels of interactivity within the system. For example, *Figure 19.9* illustrates the results from a study by Jos Van Berkum et al. (2005).

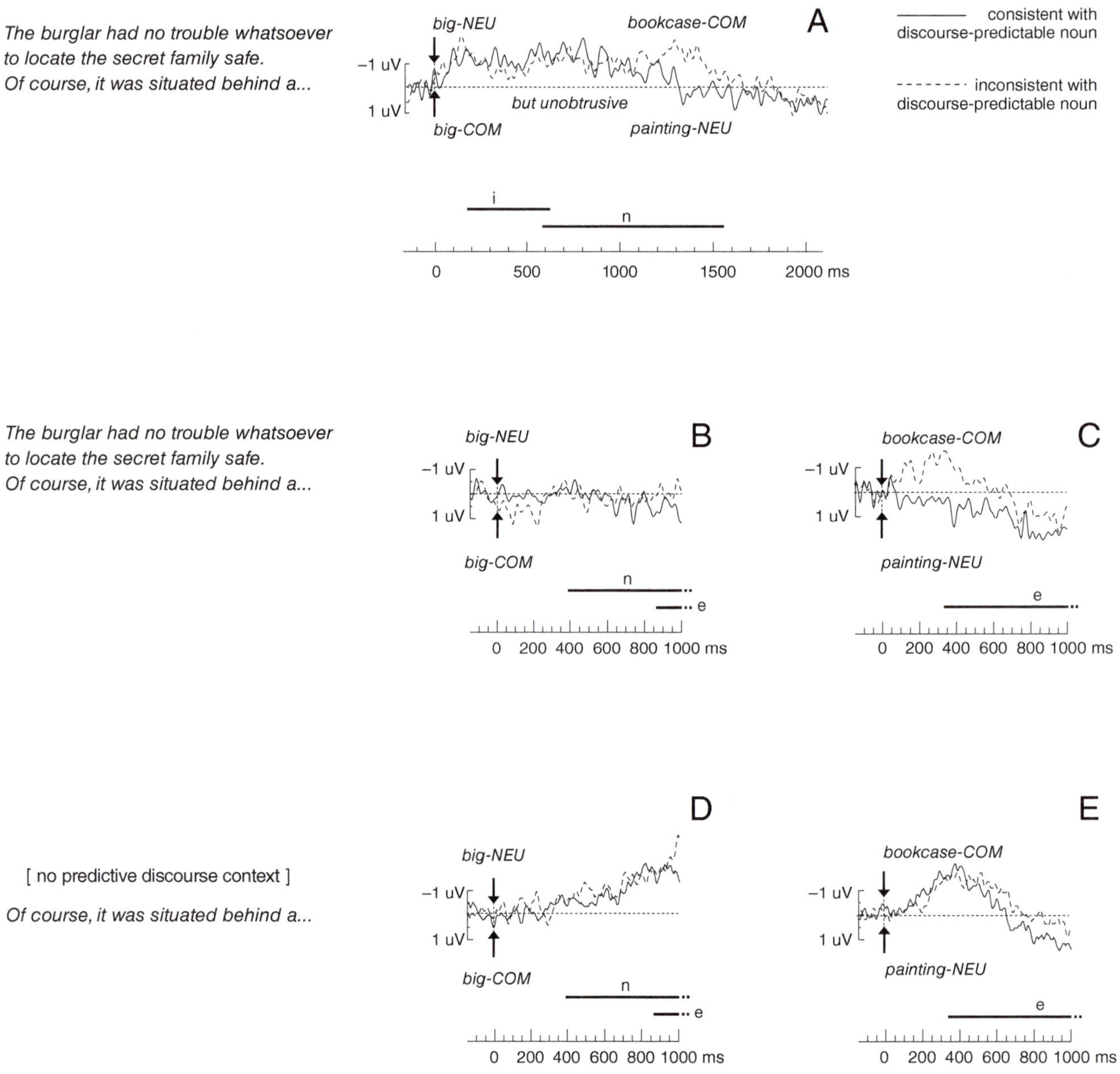

FIGURE 19.9 ERPs time-locked to the adjective that preceded the critical noun that either was (solid waveform) or was not (dotted waveform) consistent with subjects' predictions. The negative-going deviation related to the inconsistent (and, presumably, unpredictable) noun is the N400 ERP component. The data are averaged over several two-sentence stories, each with a different onset time of the inflected adjective that preceded the critical noun ("i" above the time axis in plot A), of the critical noun itself ("n" above the time axis in panels A, B, and D) and of the end of the sentence ("e" above time axis in panels B, C, D, and E), which accounts for the "smeary-ness" of the N400 in this figure.

Source: Van Berkum et al., 2005 / American Psychological Association.

In it, subjects listened to a series of stories that were crafted to lead subjects to predict a particular word. The key manipulation was whether or not the expected word or another grammatically and semantically valid, but unexpected, word was actually spoken. The researchers' goal was "to determine whether listeners can use their knowledge of the wider discourse to rapidly predict specific upcoming words as a sentence is unfolding" (p. 446).

The dependent measure of interest in the study of Van Berkum et al. (2005) was the N400, an ERP component previously shown to be sensitive to the processing of meaning in several contexts, including spoken, written, and signed language, mathematical symbols, and videos with social content. As the name implies, it typically peaks later than ERP components associated with sensory and perceptual processing. Marta Kutas and Kara Federmeier (2011) interpret findings like these as follows: "Because, in the absence of prediction, these [critical] words constitute equally good fits to the accrued contextual information, N400 reductions when the words matched as opposed to mismatched the predicted target showed clearly that information about likely upcoming words has shaped the system in advance" (p. 634). That is, one perspective on the grammatical decoding of language is to understand it as another example of the principle of predictive coding (*Chapter 5*, section *Predictive coding*). This perspective will also carry through to the final section of this chapter, on speech production.

Speech Production

The physical production of speech is an exquisitely complicated motor control problem. We have seen this, for example, in the fact that an offset of a few tens of milliseconds in the coordination of the release of the tongue from the palate relative to the contraction of the diaphragm to force air over the vocal cords can make the difference in whether one produces the word "doll" or "tall." Further, we saw with the KE family that dysfunction in the control of the articulatory apparatus can produce profound impairments in the ability to communicate. Our focus here, however, will be on the neural control of speech production. Recall that with Broca's aphasia, for example, the patients are no better able to produce language with a pen or a keyboard than with their voice. Thus, there's a level of language production that is abstracted from the effectors that will actually generate the output. (Having said this, however, it will be most expedient in this brief chapter to stick with spoken language.)

A Psycholinguistic Model of Production

Within the study of language, a distinction is often made between the fields of *linguistics* and *psycholinguistics*. Although no single definition will please everyone, it's a fair generalization to say that linguistics concerns itself primarily with computational and theoretical questions about the structures and rules of language, whereas psycholinguistics addresses how humans process and use language in everyday circumstances. As a general rule, the discipline of psycholinguistics tends to be more associated with designing and carrying out experiments. Almost all the topics that we've covered in this chapter fall under the rubric of psycholinguistics.

According to one influential model, speech production occurs via a series of stages, beginning with the formulation of a message, followed by lexical retrieval (mapping an abstract, conceptual message onto words), phonological encoding (specifying the speech sounds that comprise the words), articulatory planning (formulation of a sequential motor plan for speech output), and articulation (Peter Indefrey and Willem Levelt, 2004). It is likely that many of these processes recruit systems that we have already considered. For example, repetitive transcranial magnetic stimulation (rTMS) of left posterior STG, timed to interfere with the phonological encoding stage of production, does, indeed, produce errors in spoken output (Daniel Acheson et al., 2011). The area targeted for rTMS in this study overlapped with the region of STG highlighted in *Figure 19.4.B*, and the processes disrupted by rTMS likely overlapped with those discussed earlier in the context of articulatory coding functions of the speech perception system (i.e., the "dorsal stream").

Forward Models for the Control of Production

Decades of psycholinguistic research on speech production indicate that it, too, is a highly dynamic and interactive process. In particular, our production of speech is very sensitive to our online assessment of it. Here's a summary from John Houde et al. (2002):

> Adding noise to a speaker's auditory feedback results in an elevation of voice volume . . . Delaying a speaker's auditory feedback by more than about 50 msec produces noticeable disruptions in speech . . . Shifting the spectrum of auditory feedback causes shifts in the spectrum of produced speech . . . Perturbing perceived pitch causes the subject to alter his pitch to compensate for those perturbations . . . Altering perceived formants induces compensating changes in the production of vowels (p. 1125).

These findings have given rise to the idea that speech production may involve the construction of a neural **forward model** of the planned utterance, against which the actual speech output is compared. Recall that we have already seen the same principle at work in *Chapter 8*, in the context of the "internal models" of movements represented in the cerebellum, and their use in fine-tuning skeletomotor control. (For our purposes, the terms "forward model" and "internal model" are interchangeable.)

To test this idea, Houde et al. (2002) recorded the magnetoencephalogram (MEG) while subjects uttered a single vowel and heard its real-time playback, and when they passively listened to the acoustically identical signal (i.e., to a recording of themselves from the speaking session). The data illustrated in *Figure 19.10* showed a marked attenuation of the auditory-evoked response in the speaking condition, which the authors attributed to "a comparison between the incoming signal and an internally generated prediction of what that signal would be" (p. 1131). When the match was high, they reasoned, the "error" would be minimal, and so, too, would be the neural response. To rule out any possible confounds due to the fact that one condition involved actual production and one did not, they performed a control study that was identical to what was just described, with the exception that the auditory feedback of their voice was convolved with white noise. Thus, the auditory signal was perfectly matched to the timing of hearing one's own voice, but it was a signal that the auditory system could not predict that it would hear. The result, comparable responses in both conditions, ruled out many confounding alternative explanations to the "forward model" interpretation. (Conceptually similar results have also been demonstrated with fMRI, implicating bilateral STG in processing mismatches between expected and actual auditory signals [Tourville, Reilly, and Guenther, 2008].)

In effect, what Houde et al. (2002) describe is a predictive coding account of speech production, whereby auditory-evoked responses are construed as signaling mismatches between the brain's expectation about the environment and the actual state of the environment. In relation to this section of this chapter, the studies reviewed here suggest that production is a highly interactive process that recruits many levels of neural representation of sound, meaning, and syntax.

Prediction

The experiment discussed in the previous section highlights the important role that prediction plays in speech production. Here we bring it full circle by illustrating research that emphasizes a role for prediction in the perception of others' speech. Starting with the rationale that the brain needs a mechanism to parse the continuous speech stream into decodable units, David Poeppel and colleagues have noted that the rate at which syllables unfold in speech falls into the delta (~1–4 Hz) and theta (~4–8 Hz) range of neural oscillatory frequencies, and these oscillations may provide a substrate for "pars[ing] the continuous speech signal into the necessary chunks for decoding." The scheme that they and others have explored is that resets of the ongoing oscillations implement an ongoing process of "sliding and resetting" oscillatory

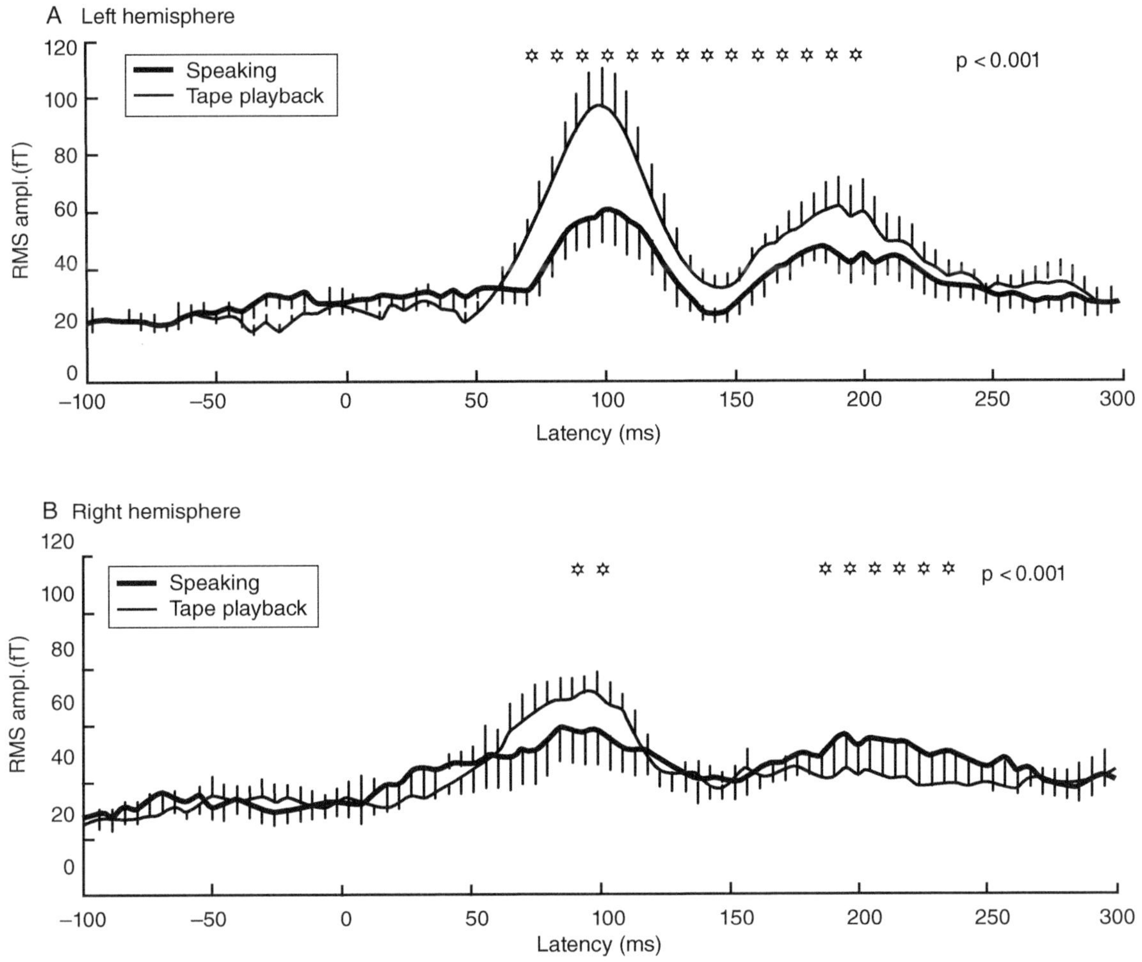

FIGURE 19.10 MEG responses to hearing one's own speech. MEG-evoked responses (in A. the left hemisphere and B. the right hemisphere), time-locked to sound onset, from subjects hearing their own utterance of a vowel while speaking it ("Speaking") and while passively listening to it "Tape playback"). The response is significantly attenuated in the speaking condition.

Source: Houde et al., 2002 / MIT Press.

cycles that act as temporal integration windows that optimize the initial processing of the speech signal (Poeppel, 2014, pp. 146–147). This is sometimes referred to as entrainment of activity in the auditory system to the speech signal.

To fully appreciate the proposed mechanisms and how analyses were carried out to generate the results portrayed in *Figure 19.11*, it may be helpful to revisit section *Analysis of time-varying signals*, *Chapter 4,* and accompanying figures. For example, panel A of *Figure 19.11* uses filtering analogous to the technique that generated the "alpha-filtered gamma amplitude" from *Figure 4.11* to generate the envelope of time-varying fluctuations in power in the MEG signal from 2 to 8 Hz, which is shown in the blue trace in panel A of *Figure 19.11*. It is evident from visual inspection that these fluctuations in the neural signal are closely following the fluctuations in energy in the concurrent speech signal (red trace). How does the brain accomplish this? In the experiment from Keith Doelling et al. (2014), from which panels A, B, and C of *Figure 19.11* are taken, the researchers used a synthesized speech signal in which they controlled whether or not transitions between syllables were accompanied by abrupt changes in the amplitude of the signal, a measure referred to as *sharpness*. (*Sharpness* is computed as the first derivative of the speech envelope over time – i.e., its rate of change.) A key finding was that decreasing the sharpness in the speech signal markedly decreased how closely the neural signal tracked the otherwise identical speech signal, and a concomitant

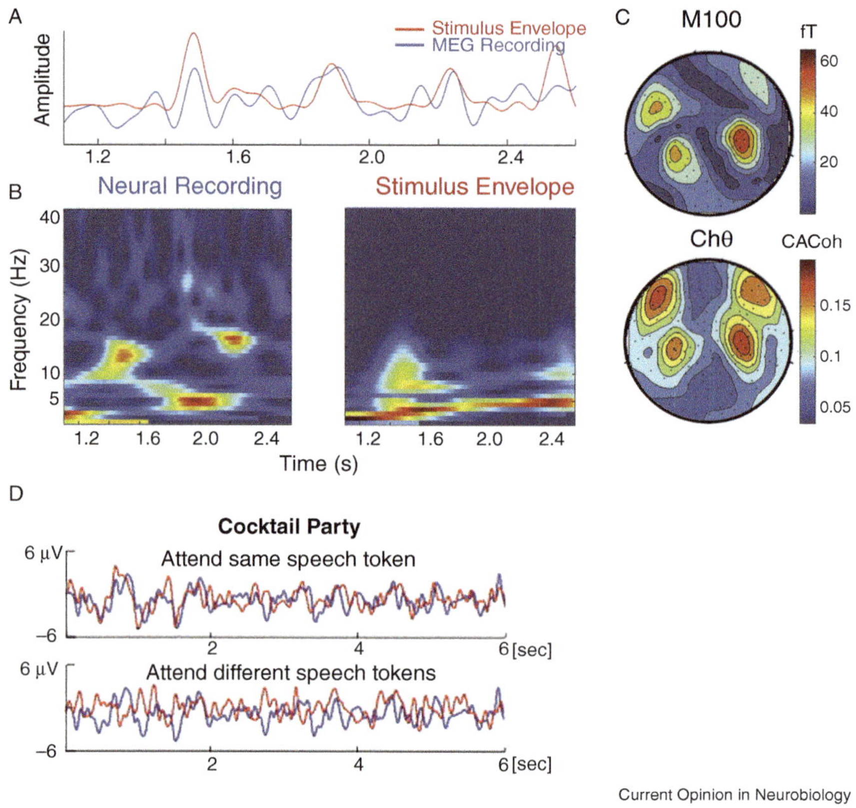

FIGURE 19.11 Synchronization of neural rhythms to incoming speech. **A.** Results from the study of Doelling et al. (2014) showing the close tracking of fluctuations in the speech signal ("Stimulus Envelope," red trace) by the auditory system ("MEG Recording," blue trace). **B.** Time–frequency representations (TFRs) of the data from panel **A**. **C.** Comparison of topography of the M100 with the onset of a pure tone (top) vs. the similarly timed-evoked response to the Chθs, the syllabic transitions in the synthesized speech signal (bottom). Because the M100 is known to be generated by auditory cortex, the similarity between the two validates the interpretation that it is the processing of Chθs in the auditory system that drives the synchronization illustrated in **A**. (M100 is the MEG analogue to the N1 AEP that is measured with EEG (see *Figure 5.4*). fT = femotesla (10^{-15} tesla); CACoh = cerebro-acoustic coherence, a measure of phase locking between the neural and acoustic signals. **D.** Data from one ECoG electrode from the study by Zion Golumbic et al. (2013). The top figure shows two different trials when the subject is viewing and listening to the same snippet of two people talking simultaneously, and on both trials, attending to the speech being spoken by the same person. The bottom shows the same trace from one of these two trials (blue), but now compared to a trace from third trial in which the patient viewed the same snippet, but was attending to the other talker.

Source: Reproduced with permission from Poeppel, D. (2014) / Elsevier.

decrease in the intelligibility of the speech. Therefore, transients in the amplitude envelope of the speech signal may provide the triggers that the auditory system uses to reset the phase of its low-frequency oscillations.

One can imagine that an entrainment-to-speech mechanism like the one proposed here would be most helpful in an environment in which there are multiple sources of acoustic input, and one needs to be able to isolate and track the signal coming from just one source – say, to follow a single conversation taking place at a crowded cocktail party. (Recall from *Chapter 3* that situations like this, which are characteristic of the vast majority of situations that we encounter every day, present a major challenge for the auditory system because the mechanical elements at the front end of the auditory system combine all incoming acoustic signals into a single complex pattern of vibration.) This is a problem formally similar to the one that confronts a visual system wanting to track the location and movements of a single object of interest in a crowded scene; one that we know requires endogenously controlled attention. To test whether auditory entrainment could help solve what psychologists call "the cocktail party problem," a team led by Elana Zion Golumbic asked epilepsy patients with subdural grids placed within and near the Sylvian fissure to follow a narrative being spoken by one of two individuals who were talking simultaneously. The data shown in panel D of *Figure 19.11* suggests that the entrainment-to-speech mechanism can, indeed, be guided by attention.

Integration

The final sections of this chapter provide the kind of synergy that a textbook author lives for! It demonstrates that the same principle of building, then updating, predictive models of the world – first introduced in *Chapter 3*'s treatment of visual perception – also applies to the production and the perception of speech. In this chapter's example, this plays out on a very fast timescale – at the speed of speech – with model updates needed each time the cadence of the talker's output changes. Like other examples that we've seen, however, this system of model building and updating is hierarchically nested. Representations of who are the talkers, what are the rules governing what I should be doing in this situation, and so on, are encoded at higher levels of representation than A1, and shifts of attention between different talkers take place much less frequently than do changes in the cadence of any one talker's output. Nonetheless, the mechanism for resetting the phase angle of oscillation in corticothalamic circuits of the auditory system is the same regardless of whether the system is adjusting to a change within one speech train or switching to a different one. Furthermore, it's likely that a mechanism very similar to the signals from primary cortex to first-order thalamus that we covered in considerable detail in section *Information processing in primary visual cortex – interactivity, Chapter 3,* is also important for implementing the real-time "sliding and resetting" of cortical oscillations that implement the mechanism of entrainment to speech.

End-of-Chapter Questions

1. Draw Lichtheim's house model, and indicate how lesions of three different areas would produce three kinds of aphasia.

2. What level of language processing was of interest in the study of Dehaene-Lambertz et al. (2005) that varied place of articulation of stimuli?

3. What anatomical systems comprise the dual routes of language processing? What are their proposed functions?

4. What conclusions can be drawn from the "story" of FOXP2, with regard to genetic contributions to language function?

5. There are at least four distinct accounts of the functions of Broca's area that we reviewed in this chapter. Summarize them and propose an account that you think best fits the current state of knowledge.

6. Explain the concept of predictive coding as it applies to sentence processing. What is the evidence for it?

7. Explain the proposed role of forward models in speech production and the evidence for it.

8. Can speech perception and speech production both be interpreted within the framework of predictive coding? If so, how?

References

Acheson, Daniel J., Massihullah Hamidi, Jeffrey R. Binder, and Bradley R. Postle. 2011. "A Common Neural Substrate for Language Production and Verbal Working Memory." *Journal of Cognitive Neuroscience* 23 (6): 1358–1367. doi: 10.1162/jocn.2010.21519.

Bates, Elizabeth, Stephen M. Wilson, Ayse Pinar Saygin, Frederic Dick, Martin I. Sereno, Robert T. Knight, and Nina F. Dronkers. 2003. "Voxel-Based Lesion-Symptom Mapping." *Nature Neuroscience* 6 (5): 448–450. doi: 10.1038/nn1050.

Bird, Helen, Matthew A. Lambon Ralph, Mark S. Seidenberg, James L. McClelland, and Karalyn Patterson. 2003. "Deficits in Phonology and Past-Tense Morphology: What's the Connection?." *Journal of Memory and Language* 48 (3): 502–526. doi: 10.1016/S0749-596X(02)00538-7.

Chomsky, Noam. 1975. *Reflections on Language*. New York: Pantheon.

Compston, Alastair. 2006. "On Aphasia. By L. Lichtheim, MD, Professor of Medicine in the University of Berne. *Brain* 1885; 7: 433–484." *Brain* 129 (6): 1347–1350. doi: 10.1093/brain/awl134.

Dehaene-Lambertz, Ghislaine, Christophe Pallier, Willy Serniclaes, Liliane Sprenger-Charolles, Antoinette Jobert, and Stanislas Dehaene. 2005. "Neural Correlates of Switching from Auditory to Speech Perception." *NeuroImage* 24 (1): 21–33. doi: 10.1016/j.neuroimage.2004.09.039.

Del Gaizo, John, Julius Fridriksson, Grigori Yourganov, Argye E. Hillis, Gregory Hickok, Bratislav Misic, . . . Leonardo Bonilha. 2017. "Mapping Language Networks Using the Structural and Dynamic Brain Connectomes." *eNeuro* 4: e0204-0217.2017. doi: 10.1523/ENEURO.0204-17.2017.

Doelling, Keith B., Luc H. Arnal, Oded Ghitza, and David Poeppel. 2014. "Acoustic Landmarks Drive Delta-Theta Oscillations to Enable Speech Comprehension by Facilitating Perceptual Parsing." *NeuroImage* 85: 761–768.

Fedorenko, Evelina, John Duncan, and Nancy Kanwisher. 2012. "Language-Selective and Domain-General Regions Lie Side by Side within Broca's Area." *Current Biology* 22 (21): 2059–2062. doi: 10.1016/j.cub.2012.09.011.

Fletcher, Paul. 1990. "Speech and Language Deficits." *Nature* 346 (6281): 226. doi: 10.1038/346226c0.

Geschwind, Norman. 1970. "The Organization of Language and the Brain: Language Disorders after Brain Damage Help in Elucidating the Neural Basis of Verbal Behavior." *Science* 170 (3961): 940–944. doi: 10.1126/science.170.3961.940.

Gopnik, Myrna. 1990a. "Feature-Blind Grammar and Dysphasia." *Nature* 344 (6268): 715. doi: 10.1038/344715a0.

Gopnik, Myrna. 1990b. "Genetic Basis of Grammar Defect." *Nature* 347 (6288): 26. doi: 10.1038/347026a0.

Graham, Sarah A., and Simon E. Fisher. 2013. "Decoding the Genetics of Speech and Language." *Current Opinion in Neurobiology* 23: 43–51. doi: 10.1016/j.conb.2012.11.006.

Grodzinsky, Yosef, and Andrea Santi. 2008. "The Battle for Broca's Region." *Trends in Cognitive Sciences* 12 (12): 474–480. doi: 10.1016/j.tics.2008.09.001.

Hagoort, Peter. 2005. "On Broca, Brain, and Binding: A New Framework." *Trends in Cognitive Sciences* 9 (9): 416–423. doi: 10.1016/j.tics.2005.07.004.

Hickok, Gregory, and David Poeppel. 2000. "Towards a Functional Neuroanatomy of Speech Perception." *Trends in Cognitive Sciences* 4 (4): 131–138. doi: 10.1016/S1364-6613(00)01463-7.

Houde, John F., Srikantan S. Nagarajan, Kensuke Sekihara, and Michael M. Merzenich. 2002. "Modulation of the Auditory Cortex during Speech: An MEG Study." *Journal of Cognitive Neuroscience* 14 (8): 1125–1138.

Hurst, Jane A., Elizabeth Michael Baraitser, Frances Graham Auger, and Staffan Norell. 1990. "An Extended Family with a Dominantly Inherited Speech Disorder." *Developmental Medicine and Child Neurology* 32 (4): 352–355. doi: 10.1111/j.1469-8749.1990.tb16948.

Indefrey, Peter, and Willem J. M. Levelt. 2004. "The Spatial and Temporal Signatures of Word Production Components." *Cognition* 92 (1–2): 101–144. doi: 10.1016/j.cognition.2002.06.001.

Kutas, Marta, and Kara D. Federmeier. 2011. "Thirty Years and Counting: Finding Meaning in the N400 Component of the Event-Related Brain Potential (ERP)." *Annual Review of Psychology* 62: 621–647. doi: 10.1146/annurev.psych.093008.131123.

Lai, Cecilia S. L., Simon E. Fisher, Jane A. Hurst, Faraneh Vargha-Khadem, and Anthony P. Monaco. 2001. "A Forkhead-Domain Gene Is Mutated in a Severe Speech and Language Disorder." *Nature* 413.

Makuuchi, Michiru, Jörg Bahlmann, Alfred Anwander, and Angela D. Friederici. 2009. "Segregating the Core Computational Faculty of Human Language from Working Memory." *Proceedings of the National Academy of Sciences of the United States of America* 106 (20): 8362–8367. doi: 10.1073/pnas.0810928106.

McClelland, James L., and Karalyn Patterson. 2002a. "Rules or Connections in Past-Tense Inflections: What Does the Evidence Rule Out?." *Trends in Cognitive Sciences* 6 (11): 465–472. doi: 10.1016/S1364-6613(02)01993-9.

McClelland, James L., and Karalyn Patterson. 2002b. "'Words *or* Rules' Cannot Exploit the Regularity in Exceptions." *Trends in Cognitive Sciences* 6 (11): 464–465. doi: 10.1016/S1364-6613(02)02012-0.

Pinker, Steven. 1994. *The Language Instinct: How the Mind Creates Language*. New York: William Morrow and Company.

Pinker, Steven, and Michael T. Ullman. 2002a. "The Past and Future of the Past Tense." *Trends in Cognitive Sciences* 6 (11): 456–463. doi: 10.1016/S1364-6613(02)01990-3.

Pinker, Steven, and Michael T. Ullman. 2002b. "Combination and Structure, Not Gradedness, Is the Issue." *Trends in Cognitive Sciences* 6 (11): 472–474. doi: 10.1016/S1364-6613(02)02013-2.

Poeppel, D. 2014. "The Neuroanatomic and Neurophysiological Infrastructure from Speech and Language." *Current Opinion in Neurobiology* 28: 142–149.

Tourville, Jason A., Kevin J. Reilly, and Frank H. Guenther. 2008. "Neural Mechanisms Underlying Auditory Feedback Control of Speech." *NeuroImage* 39 (3): 1429–1443. doi: 10.1016/j.neuroimage.2007.09.054.

Tremblay, P., and A. S. Dick. 2016. "Broca and Wernicke Are Dead, or Moving Past the Classic Model of Language Neurobiology." *Brain & Language* 162: 60–71.

Van Berkum, Jos J. A., Colin M Brown, Pienie Zwitserlood, Valesca Kooijman, and Peter Hagoort. 2005. "Anticipating Upcoming Words in Discourse: Evidence from ERPs and Reading Times." *Journal of Experimental Psychology: Learning, Memory, and Cognition* 31: 443–467.

Vargha-Khadem, Faraneh, and Richard E. Passingham. 1990. "Speech and Language Deficits." *Nature* 346 (6281): 226. doi: 10.1038/346226c0.

Vargha-Khadem, Faraneh, Kate Watkins, Katie Alcock, Paul Fletcher, and Richard E. Passingham. 1995. "Praxic and Nonverbal Cognitive Deficits in a Large Family with a Genetically Transmitted Speech and Language Disorder." *Proceedings of the National Academy of Sciences of the United States of America* 92 (3): 930–933. doi: 10.1073/pnas.92.3.930.

Willems, Roel M., and Peter Hagoort. 2009. "Broca's Region: Battles Are Not Won by Ignoring Half of the Facts." *Trends in Cognitive Sciences* 13 (3): 101. doi: 10.1016/j.tics.2008.12.001.

Zion Golumbic, Elana M., Nai Ding, Stephan Bickel, Peter Lakatos, Catherine A. Schevon, Guy M. McKhann, . . . Charles E. Schroeder. 2013. "Mechanisms Underlying Selective Neuronal Tracking of Attended Speech at a 'Cocktail Party'." *Neuron* 77: 980–991.

Other Sources Used

Boatman, Dana. 2002. "Neurobiological Bases of Auditory Speech Processing." In *The Handbook of Adult Language Disorders: Integrating Cognitive Neuropsychology, Neurology, and Rehabilitation*, edited by Argye E. Hillis (pp. 269–291). New York: Psychology Press.

Carroll, John B. 1958. "Communication Theory, Linguistics, and Psycholinguistics." *Review of Educational Research* 28 (2): 79–88. doi: 10.2307/1168862.

Chomsky, Noam. 1959. "A Review of B. F. Skinner's *Verbal Behavior*." *Language* 35 (1): 26–58. doi: 10.2307/411334.

Fedorenko, Evelina, and Nancy Kanwisher. 2011. "Some Regions within Broca's Area Do Respond More Strongly to Sentences Than to Linguistically Degraded Stimuli: A Comment on Rogalsky and Hickok." *Journal of Cognitive Neuroscience* 23 (10): 2632–2635. doi: 10.1162/jocn_a_00043.

Gabrieli, John D. E. 2009. "Dyslexia: A New Synergy Between Education and Cognitive Neuroscience." *Science* 325 (5938): 280–283. doi: 10.1126/science.1171999.

Goswami, Usha. 2010. "A Temporal Sampling Framework for Developmental Dyslexia." *Trends in Cognitive Sciences* 15 (1): 3–10. doi: 10.1016/j.tics.2010.10.001.

Hauser, Marc D., Noam Chomsky, and W. Tecumseh Fitch. 2002. "The Faculty of Language: What Is It, Who Has It, and How Did It Evolve?." *Science* 298 (5598): 1569–1579. doi: 10.1126/science.298.5598.1569.

Hickok, Gregory, and Corianne Rogalsky. 2011. "What Does Broca's Area Activation to Sentences Reflect." *Journal of Cognitive Neuroscience* 23 (10): 2629–2631. doi: 10.1162/jocn_a_00044.

Pinker, Steven, and Ray Jackendoff. 2005. "The Faculty of Language: What's Special about It?." *Cognition* 95 (2): 201–236. doi: 10.1016/j.cognition.2004.08.004.

Samet, Jerry. 1999. "History of Nativism." In *The MIT Encyclopedia of the Cognitive Sciences*, edited by Robert A. Wilson and Frank C. Keil (pp. 586–588). Cambridge, MA: MIT Press.

Serniclaes, Willy, Liliane Sprenger-Charolles, Rene Carre, and Jean-Francois Demonet. 2001. "Perceptual Discrimination of Speech Sounds in Developmental Dyslexia." *Journal of Speech, Language, and Hearing Research* 44 (2): 384–397. doi: 10.1044/1092-4388(2001/032).

Skinner, B. F. 1957. *Verbal Behavior*. Acton, MA: Copley.

Wernicke, Carl. 1874. *Der Aphasische Symptomencomplex: Eine Psychologische Studie Auf Anatomischer Basis*. Breslau: Cohn and Weigert.

Further Reading

Alexander, Michael P. 1997. "Aphasia: Clinical and Anatomic Issues." In *Behavioral Neurology and Neuropsychology*, edited by Todd E. Feinberg and Martha J. Farah (pp. 133–149). New York: McGraw-Hill.

Authoritative overview of the eight classical aphasia syndromes.

Binder, Jeffrey R. 2003. "Wernicke Aphasia: A Disorder of Central Language Processing." In *Neurological Foundations of Cognitive Neuroscience*, edited by Mark D'Esposito (pp. 175–238). Cambridge, MA: MIT Press.

Exhaustive review of the neuropsychological and neuroimaging literature, which concludes that "Wernicke's aphasia, simply put, consists of [a] combination of . . . syndromes and results from a larger lesion that encompasses both lexical-semantic and phoneme output systems" (p. 226).

Chial, Heidi. 2008. "Mendelian Genetics: Patterns of Inheritance and Single-Gene Disorders." *Nature Education* 1 (1). http://www.nature.com/scitable/topicpage/mendelian-genetics-patterns-of-inheritance-and-single-966.

Primer on inheritance of single-gene disorders.

Dehaene, Stanislas. 2009. *Reading in the Brain: The Science and Evolution of a Human Invention*. New York: Viking.

A thorough, reader-friendly introduction to the cognitive neuroscience of reading.

Dronkers, Nina F. 2000. "The Gratuitous Relationship between Broca's Aphasia and Broca's Area." *Behavioral and Brain Sciences* 23 (1): 30–31. doi: 10.1017/S0140525X00322397.

A succinct argument, thoroughly referenced, against a grammar-specific view of Broca's area.

Herholz, Sibylle C., and Robert J. Zatorre. 2012. "Musical Training as a Framework for Brain Plasticity: Behavior, Function, and Structure." *Neuron* 76 (3): 486–502. doi: 10.1016/j.neuron.2012.10.011.

A comprehensive overview of the effects of musical training on the brain.

Mahmoudzadeh, Mahdi, Ghislaine Dehaene-Lambertz, Marc Fournier, Guy Kongolo, Sabrina Goudjil, Jessica Dubois, . . . Fabrice Wallois. 2013. "Syllabic Discrimination in Premature Human Infants prior to Complete Formation of Cortical Layers." *Proceedings of the National Academy of Sciences of the United States of America* 110 (12): 4846–4851. doi: 10.1073/pnas.1212220110.

Technically impressive demonstration of speech-like functions in the brains of prematurely delivered infants whose cortices are still dramatically underdeveloped.

Salimpoor, Valorie N., Iris van den Bosch, Natasa Kovacevic, Anthony Randal McIntosh, Alain Dagher, and Robert J. Zatorre. 2013. "Interactions between the Nucleus Accumbens and Auditory Cortices Predict Music Reward Value." *Science* 340 (6129): 216–219. doi: 10.1126/science.1231059.

Integrates content from Chapter 15, Chapter 16, and Chapter 18 with "music appreciation": "aesthetic rewards arise from the interaction between mesolimbic reward circuitry and cortical networks involved in perceptual analysis and valuation."

Scott, Sophie K., and Ingrid S. Johnsrude. 2003. “The Neuroanatomical and Functional Organization of Speech Perception.” *Trends in Neurosciences* 26 (2): 100–107. doi: 10.1016/S0166-2236(02)00037-1.

Presents an alternative dual-route model of perception, with a greater emphasis on homologies with the monkey auditory system.

Zatorre, Robert J., and Jackson T. Gandour. 2008. “Neural Specializations for Speech and Pitch: Moving beyond the Dichotomies.” *Philosophical Transactions of the Royal Society of London, Series B: Biological Sciences* 363 (1493): 1087–1104. doi: 10.1098/rstb.2007.2161.

A detailed consideration of what factors may underlie the lateralized processing of some sounds.

CHAPTER 20

Consciousness

KEY THEMES

- Consciousness can be construed at many levels, and the three that we'll consider here are physiological (What physiological conditions are necessary to support consciousness?), content based (What neural processes determine whether or not one is aware of a specific stimulus?), and theoretical (What are the neurobiological principles that make consciousness possible?).
- The neurological syndrome of coma indicates that elevated activity in the brainstem reticular activating system is necessary for an individual to be conscious, but the persistent vegetative state/unresponsive wakefulness syndrome (UWS) indicates that elevated brainstem activity is not sufficient for consciousness.
- Lesions of the ventral pons can produce the diabolical locked-in syndrome (LIS), in which the patient is fully conscious but only able to blink and produce vertical eye movements. LIS patients are often initially misdiagnosed as vegetative state/UWS.
- Perturbation of the brain with TMS, when coupled with EEG recording, reveals a systematic reduction of effective connectivity accompanying the loss of consciousness experienced during non-REM sleep, or while under general anesthesia.
- When visual stimuli are presented at the threshold of detection, V1 activity more closely tracks the subjective judgment of whether or not one has seen a target than the objective reality of whether or not a target was presented.
- In the monkey, detection of a target stimulus seems to depend not on the initial "feedforward sweep" of information from the retina and up through the visual hierarchy, but rather on reentrant, feedback signals to V1 after the feedforward sweep has been registered in higher-level visual areas.
- Studies using visual masking, as well as studies of the attentional blink, have been interpreted to suggest that widespread activation of high-level cortical areas corresponding to a putative "global neuronal workspace" might be necessary for awareness of a stimulus.
- One theory of consciousness, Integrated Information Theory, has given rise to an empirical measure, the Perturbational Complexity Index (PCI), which discriminates levels of consciousness associated with neurological syndromes, level of anesthesia, and stage of sleep.

CONTENTS

Companion Website: www.wiley.com/go/postle/cognitiveneuroscience3e

---

The Most Complex Object in the Universe

> Natural evolution, as brilliantly revealed by Charles Darwin (1809–1882), over these many million years gave rise to nervous systems as complex as the human brain, arguably the most complex object in the universe. And somehow, through the interactions among its 100 billion neurons, connected by trillions of synapses, emerges our conscious experience of the world and ourselves (Laureys and Tononi, 2009 , p. ix).

In 2005, to mark its 125th anniversary, *Science* magazine published a feature on "What don't we know?," posing 125 questions that science has yet to satisfactorily answer. Twenty-five of these were allocated a page in the journal, and, although they weren't explicitly rank ordered, one of them necessarily had to appear on the first page of the section, and one on the 25th. Coming in at number two (and thereby reconfirming that "just because it appeared in *Science* doesn't make it so") was *What is the Biological Basis of Consciousness?* Number one had something to do with the origin of the universe. What?!? I mean, come on, without consciousness, the notion of what a universe is, not to mention that it can have an origin, wouldn't exist . . .

What is it that gives you that ineffable sense of knowing that you are who you are, that you are presently reading a cognitive neuroscience textbook, that you are engrossed/tired/hungry/relaxed/stressed/however it is that you currently feel? These are the questions at which we will take a crack in this, our final chapter together. AND IT'S GOING TO BE AWESOME!

Different Approaches to the Problem

Even though we all experience it, there's an "unmeasurable" quality to consciousness that makes its study different from every other aspect of cognition that we have considered up to this point. There aren't obvious ways in which behavioral measures such as reaction time or accuracy of a response can index consciousness in the way that we can use these to study visual perception, or attention, or emotion, or sentence processing. Nor are there a priori neural signatures that everyone would agree on as being indisputably related to consciousness, short of some basal level of physiological functioning in at least some parts of the brain. But even for these, as we'll soon see, their invocation leads immediately to questions of the necessity vs. the sufficiency of activity in the systems in question. Nobody said that this would be simple.

The approach that we will take is to group cognitive neuroscience studies of consciousness into three categories: *physiological*, *content-based*, and *theoretical*. Physiological approaches to understanding consciousness will include quantitative measurement of metabolic or electrical activity of the brain during states of consciousness that can be independently validated, typically by a physician with specialized training. One area of study that has produced an enormous amount of knowledge about physiological bases of consciousness is coma and stages of recovery from coma. Two other models that are also yielding valuable information about relations between various physiological states and states of consciousness are sleep and anesthesia. Note that, for the "physiological/content-based" distinction to be useful, the former will be limited to physiological states that persist for minutes, hours, or longer. Shorter-lived, momentary states, such as the instantaneous phase of an oscillation in a particular frequency band in the EEG, will be grouped under the content-based approach to consciousness. Finally, as we consider physiological bases of consciousness, it will be important to distinguish what Christoph Koch et al. (2016) refer to as "true neural correlates of consciousness" from "background conditions" that contribute to, and may even be necessary for, consciousness, but that aren't directly involved in determining what the contents of consciousness will be at any moment in time. "For example, global enabling factors, such as blood flow or oxygen supply to the cortex, are obviously essential for consciousness, but they do not contribute directly to its contents" (p. 9604). Although this particular example may seem uncontroversial, we'll see further along that there are other phenomena that Koch and colleagues will also classify as "background conditions," a designation with which other reasonable and smart people will disagree.

What we'll call "content-based" approaches to consciousness are those that assess trial-by-trial awareness of specific stimuli or events and seek to infer from trials with, vs. trials without, awareness of the item in question, what are the neural correlates of awareness of that item/event? One such study that we have already considered was the phosphene induction study featured all the way back in *Chapter 3, The relation between visual processing and the brain's physiological state*. Recall that the finding was that the likelihood that transcranial magnetic stimulation (TMS) of the occipital cortex would induce a phosphene was predicted by the power in the alpha band of the EEG during the 500 msec prior to the TMS pulse. This tells us something about how the instantaneous state of V1 relates to visual awareness.

Finally, there are theoretical approaches, and here, we will limit ourselves to cognitive- and systems-level neuroscience theories and models of how the brain might give rise to consciousness. Of course, it is invariably the case that tests of these theories will, themselves, be classifiable in our scheme as either "physiological" or "content-based" experiments, and so for some of this final section we'll be considering how research that we had reviewed earlier in this chapter fits into theory X as opposed to theory Y.

The Physiology of Consciousness

Physiological states are objective, measurable phenomena, and so provide objective, measurable anchoring points to which we can remain tethered during our exploration of consciousness, and to which we can periodically return as things get progressively more abstract.

Neurological Syndromes

From the syndromes of coma and the sequelae of minimally conscious state and locked-in syndrome, we can gain insight into which neuroanatomical and neurochemical systems are necessary for consciousness. From the vegetative state/unresponsive wakefulness syndrome (UWS), we can begin cataloguing physiological states that are not sufficient. (Due to the pejorative connotations, in everyday language, of the term "vegetative" [despite its technical appropriateness], there has been a movement underway to adopt the term "unresponsive wakefulness syndrome [UWS]" in the place of "vegetative state" [Laureys et al., 2010]. Because much of the literature cited here predates 2010, however, there will necessarily be some switching back and forth.)

Coma Coma is a state of unarousable unconsciousness, characterized by a failure of the arousal/alerting system of the brain, the ascending reticular activating system. For practical purposes, this includes failure of eye opening to stimulation, a motor response no better than simple withdrawal-type movements, and a verbal response no better than simple vocalization of nonword sounds. This presupposes that the motor pathways and systems that would allow the person to respond if they were conscious are intact (Young, 2009, p. 138).

"Ascending reticular activating system" is a name given to a collection of nuclei in the brainstem that are necessary for arousal from sleep and for maintenance of wakefulness. In particular, two nuclei located in the pons (the "bridge" [from Latin] of the brainstem) deliver the neurotransmitters acetylcholine (ACh) and glutamate to targets in the thalamus via a dorsal pathway, and to the basal forebrain and posterior hypothalamus via a ventral pathway. Neurons in these structures, in turn, project diffusely throughout the brain, including cortex, releasing the excitatory/arousing neurochemicals glutamate, norepinephrine, histamine, and hypocretin/orexin. These pontine cholinergic nuclei, together with the cholinergic nuclei of the basal forebrain and the glutamatergic interlaminar nuclei of the thalamus, fire at high rates in wakefulness and during the rapid-eye-movement (REM) stage of sleep, but decrease or stop firing during non-REM stages of sleep. Thus, coma and related neurological states of compromised consciousness are often due to abnormal functioning of the brainstem. Due to the redundancy of nuclei and ascending fibers from the reticular activating system, recovery/transition from the initial state of coma often occurs within three weeks of coma onset.

At this point, we can provisionally say that elevated activity in the reticular activating system seems to be necessary for consciousness, as a background condition.

Vegetative State/UWS The syndrome of vegetative state/UWS demonstrates, all too cruelly, that an activated state of the reticular activating system is not sufficient for consciousness. As summarized by neurologist Steven Laureys (2005):

> Vegetative patients have their eyes wide open but are considered – by definition – to be unaware of themselves or their surroundings. They may grimace, cry or smile (albeit never contingent upon specific external stimuli) and move their eyes, head and limbs in a meaningless "automatic" manner. The vegetative state is often, but not always, chronic (the "persistent vegetative state"). Given proper medical care (i.e., artificial hydration and nutrition) patients can survive for many years (p. 556).

Vegetative state/UWS is the state into which patients transition from coma. How is it determined that these patients lack consciousness? The absence of consciousness is inferred from the absence of any of the following signs across repeated neurological examinations that are ideally performed at different times of the day: no meaningful response to external stimuli, including threats and noxious (i.e., painful) stimuli; no control over bladder or bowels; no sustained visual-pursuit eye movements, nor volitional fixation; and no purposeful limb withdrawal, or localization of a stimulus with a limb. By the classical terminology, the diagnosis transitions to persistent vegetative state if present for longer than one month.

Because the transition out of coma necessarily entails a recovery of at least some of the functions of the reticular activating system, UWS is often accompanied by a daily cycle of opening and closing of the eyes. Even during periods of "wakefulness," however, global brain metabolic activity in UWS rarely surpasses 50% of the level that is typical for the healthy awake state. For comparison, this 50%-of-normal level is similar to what is observed when healthy individuals are under general anesthesia or deep states of non-REM sleep.

The diagnosis of vegetative state/UWS inescapably has a dissatisfying, equivocal element because short of brain death, one can never know with absolute certainty that there isn't some residual, difficult-to-detect spark of awareness "somewhere in there." Indeed, the reality of the neurological syndromes of minimally conscious state and locked-in syndrome plays into this. For this author, it's analogous to (although, of course, much more consequential than) a failure to reject the null hypothesis in classical hypothesis testing – because one can never "prove" the null, one can never know with certainty that a "true" difference isn't lurking somewhere in those data, but just too subtle to detect.

Locked-In Syndrome *What is it like to be conscious but paralyzed and voiceless?* (A question posed by Laureys et al., 2005.) It's horrifying to even contemplate, right? In this author's pre-science days, ideas that pushed him toward his current career included the musing that one can lose an arm, or a leg, or both and still be the same person. Lose just a tiny piece of brain from the wrong spot, however, or tweak its function with a pharmacological agent, and one's very essence could be dramatically altered. (And this was long before he had encountered the expression "He was no longer Gage" . . .) What if one were to take this hypothetical exercise in a different direction, losing the use of *all* of one's body, but leaving the brain intact? Unfortunately, this is not just an idle, lay-philosophical question for patients with locked-in syndrome (LIS).

LIS typically results from damage to the corticospinal and corticobulbar pathways, most often due to stroke at the level of the ventral pons. We learned about the former pathway in *Chapter 8*; the latter pathway carries fibers from the motor cortex to motor neurons controlling the muscles of the face, head, and neck (i.e., the lower cranial nerves). An authoritative definition of LIS comes from a seminal neurology text by Fred Plum and Jerome Posner:

> a state in which selective supranuclear motor de-efferentation produces paralysis of all four limbs and the last cranial nerves without interfering with consciousness. The voluntary motor paralysis prevents the subjects from communicating by word or body movement. Usually, but not always, the anatomy of the responsible lesion in the brainstem is such that locked-in patients are left with the capacity to use vertical eye movements and blinking to communicate their awareness of internal and external stimuli (Plum and Posner, 1983, p. 9).

Despite the sparing of vertical eye movements and blinking in most cases of LIS, upon transition from coma, many patients with LIS go misdiagnosed as UWS for extended periods of time. One celebrated case, the Frenchman Jean-Dominique Bauby, who dictated a bestselling memoir after his stroke (1997), founded the Association for LIS (ALIS). Laureys et al. (2005) cite a survey of 44 patient-members of ALIS, which indicated that the average time between insult and diagnosis of LIS was 78 days, and for some, more than four years! Just imagine being the patient who has written that the doctors believed he was a "vegetable and treated him as such" (Laureys et al., 2005, p. 500). The same ALIS survey indicated that family members made the initial observation that their loved one might be conscious in 55% of the cases, while doctors did so in only 23% of cases. Therapists are also often credited with making the discovery. In one case, a therapist was testing the gag reflex of a presumed vegetative patient, and the patient bit the therapist. As the therapist cursed and withdrew his finger, the patient managed a grin. The now-suspicious therapist asked, "How much is 2 + 2?" and the patient blinked four times.

The eloquent writing of many patients with LIS leaves no doubt about their level of consciousness. Bauby (1997) dictated his book letter by letter, blinking each time his therapist spoke the desired letter from a frequency-ordered list. Phillipe Vigand, the finger biter, composed his (2000) book on software controlled by eye movements tracked with an infrared camera.

Detecting Awareness in the Vegetative State One of the first in the series of fMRI studies by Adrian Owen and colleagues – which has perhaps garnered more attention in the popular press than any other cognitive neuroscience research program, ever – was an fMRI study of a 23-year-old traumatic brain injury patient who had been in a persistent vegetative state for five months. First, it was observed that for spoken sentences vs. acoustically matched noise sequences, activity in posterior STG and MTG was greater for speech vs. noise. A tantalizing result, but not definitive, as it could possibly be attributable to automatic activation of auditory/language cortex spared by the accident. The second task was devised to require a volitional, internally generated response: the patient was asked, at specific times during the scan, to either "imagine yourself playing tennis," or "imagine yourself walking around your house, visiting each room." The results, illustrated in *Figure 20.1*, indicated that the patient's neural activity in response to these two sets of instructions was comparable to that of the control subjects.

Now, of course, this is an analytically simplistic example of "brain reading" in comparison to the sophisticated MVPA methods that we've discussed in previous chapters. Indeed, had this patient been scanned absent any comparison, it would be inferentially problematic to visually inspect activity from the scan and conclude that she was imagining tennis vs. navigating her house. However, that's not the point here. The point is that this study indicated that this patient, who was believed to be vegetative, was, in fact, able to modulate her brain activity "on command," in more or less the same way as did unequivocally conscious control subjects. Thus, one might reasonably conclude that she, too, was conscious, despite also being fully locked in, such that she was deprived of even volitional eye movements or blinks.

In a subsequent study, Martin Monti and (many, many) colleagues (2010) scanned 54 patients with disorders of consciousness and found five who could willfully modulate their brain activity in this way. With one patient, they took the further step of telling him that he'd be asked a series of autobiographical questions, and that he was to respond "yes" by imagining tennis, or "no" by imagining navigating through his house. In response to the question "Is your father's name Alexander?," for example, he correctly responded "yes" by producing elevated activity in predefined "tennis regions." To the question "Is your father's name Thomas?" he correctly responded "no" by producing elevated activity in navigation regions.

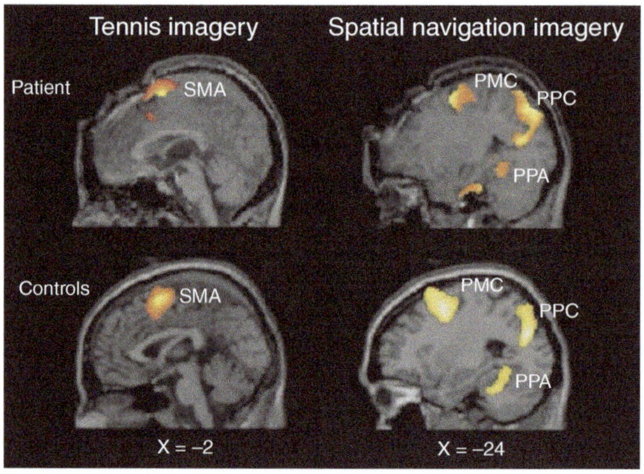

FIGURE 20.1 fMRI responses to imagery instructions, in a patient diagnosed as being in a persistent vegetative state (top row) and in the group average of 12 control subjects.

Source: Reproduced with permission from Owen et al. (2006) / American Association for the Advancement of Science - AAAS.

Recovery of Consciousness from Coma or UWS In some fortunate instances, patients in a coma or UWS experience substantial recovery of function. Such cases offer unique opportunities to assess the changes in the brain that accompany recovery of conscious awareness. Of course, doing so requires having thoroughly documented the patient's condition prior to recovery, something that is not a standard procedure at most hospitals. One notable exception is the Coma Science Group, under the direction of Steven Laureys, at the Université de Liège in Belgium, which has produced a prodigious amount of groundbreaking research on the neurology of consciousness. Their work indicates that, although the UWS is associated with widespread metabolic dysfunction, measures of global metabolic activity, alone, lack both the sensitivity and the specificity that one would want in a "consciousness meter": there are cases of patients who have recovered from UWS without significant changes in brain metabolism, and there are neurologically healthy volunteers whose global brain metabolism levels are as low as those of UWS patients.

At least one intriguing case suggests that more diagnostic precision might be found in patterns of connectivity than in measures of raw metabolic activity. A patient was scanned with $H_2{}^{15}O$ PET two weeks after the onset of UWS, and again, at rest, four months after recovery of consciousness and "partial autonomy." While in UWS, functional connectivity between the thalamus and several regions of lateral PFC (BAs 8, 9, and 10) and anterior cingulate cortex (BAs 24 and 32) was reduced relative to 18 control subjects; after clinical recovery, thalamocortical connectivity was also recovered to normal levels. Further consistent with the disconnection idea is that UWS patients (who, unfortunately, have not recovered) show "'Functional disconnections' in long-range cortico–cortical (between latero-frontal and midline-posterior areas) and cortico–thalamo–cortical (between nonspecific thalamic nuclei and lateral and medial frontal cortices) pathways" (Laureys, 2005, p. 557).

Two Dimensions Along Which Consciousness Can Vary This review of neurological syndromes has introduced the idea of two dissociable dimensions along which states of consciousness can vary. One, which seems to be necessary but is clearly not sufficient, is the level of physiological arousal of the brain. This is portrayed as the horizontal axis in the diagram in *Figure 20.2*. The second, for the time being, we can label as the "level of awareness."

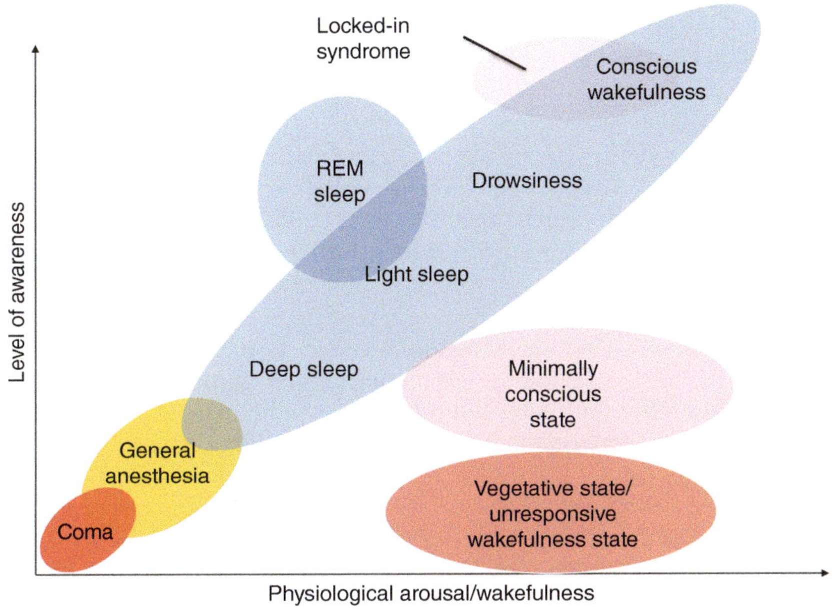

FIGURE 20.2 A depiction of neurophysiological states as they fall along two dimensions that are related to consciousness: arousal (horizontal axis) and awareness (vertical axis). The blue region corresponds to normal physiological states, pink to pathological coma, and orange to pharmacologically induced coma (a state from which patients cannot be awakened).

Source: Adapted from Laureys et al., 2005.

Different clinical states that we just discussed, and physiological states that we're about to take up in the next two subsections, can be portrayed in terms of where they fall in this 2-D space. The label of, and the idea behind, the second dimension is not satisfactory, because it's just a descriptive term. Ideally, to really understand the neural bases of consciousness, one would want to know what measurable, physical property varies along that axis, "bringing awareness along with it." Indeed, one way to construe the third section of this chapter, on theoretical approaches to consciousness, will be to evaluate each theory in terms of how well its explanatory factor would do if plugged into the label for the vertical axis of this plot. (To make this concrete, the implication of one theory will be that the physical property that varies along the vertical axis is connectivity – greater levels of connectivity within the brain, coupled with greater levels of physiological arousal, result in higher levels of awareness.)

In the next two subsections, on sleep and anesthesia, we will introduce a different technique for relating physiological state to consciousness: estimating effective connectivity from the TMS-evoked response in the EEG. Once we have established an understanding of this technique, the final subsection of this section on physiological state will return to coma, and summarize how the recovery of consciousness is paralleled by a recovery of large-scale connectivity within the brain.

Sleep

Sleep offers another fascinating window on consciousness. As discussed previously, sleep results from an inhibition of arousing signals to thalamus and cortex from the brainstem and basal forebrain. In the absence of these signals, two phenomena come about. First, there is a marked reduction in long-range connectivity between brain areas. Second, there is a marked increase in local homogeneity of activity across populations of cortical neurons whose waking activity is typically not correlated, certainly not for extended periods of time. At the level of the EEG, the first change to occur at the transition between quiet eyes-closed wakefulness and sleep is the replacement of the prominent "high-voltage" alpha rhythm (*Figure 3.5*) with low-voltage oscillations in the theta band. Then, the EEG gradually comes to be dominated by the large-amplitude low-frequency (~1–2 Hz) "slow waves" of so-called "slow-wave sleep." High-density EEG recordings have revealed slow waves to be traveling waves that sweep across the cortical surface, typically from anterior to posterior, in a manner very reminiscent of the expanding, concentric rings produced by a single stone dropped into the proverbial flat pond: an expanding arc of neuronal depolarization, and, hence, "lock-step" elevated firing, followed by a prolonged, few-hundred millisecond period of hyperpolarization, during which synaptic activity is reduced to almost nil. Upon falling asleep, one typically progresses through three stages of ever-deeper non-REM sleep, with only infrequent slow waves during stage N1, roughly 5 per minute in N2, and more than 10 per minute in N3. After a bout of several, if not tens of, minutes in N3 (longer at the beginning of the night, progressively shorter as the night wears on), one transitions back into N2, and then "pops" into REM.

REM sleep shares many characteristics with wakefulness, in that it entails high activity in the reticular activating system, basal forebrain, and thalamus. These, in turn, arouse the cortex via release of ACh and glutamate, just as in wakefulness. The difference between REM sleep and wakefulness is that additional neurotransmitter systems, also driven by the reticular activating system during wakefulness – including norepinephrine, histamine, hypocretin/orexin, and serotonin – remain inhibited during REM. Additionally, a set of neurons in the dorsal pons applies tonic inhibition that counteracts descending cortical motor signals, thus keeping muscle tone flaccid.

REM is, of course, the stage of sleep during which we experience our most vivid dreams. Dreams can be construed as "sleep consciousness," and offer yet another window through which consciousness can be studied (see Yuval Nir and Giulio Tononi, 2010, *Further reading*).

Studying Sleep (and Consciousness) with Simultaneous TMS-EEG

> Using TMS/EEG to investigate critical differences in the functioning of the waking and sleeping brain offers several advantages. Unlike sensory stimulation, direct cortical stimulation does not activate the reticular formation and bypasses the thalamic gate. Thus, it directly probes the ability of cortical areas to interact, unconfounded by peripheral effects (Massimini et al., 2005, p. 2229).

Marcello Massimini and colleagues ran their experiments late at night, when subjects would more readily fall sleep. Subjects were fitted with an electrode cap connected to an EEG amplifier that, when triggered by the TMS stimulator, would momentarily divert the signal coming from the electrodes, such that the amplifier would not saturate in response to the TMS pulse (see *Figure 4.2*). (The voltage transient produced by a pulse of TMS exceeds the range within which a conventional EEG amplifier, configured to detect exquisitely small voltage fluctuations on the scalp, can detect signals. The resulting "saturation" would render the amplifier insensitive to voltage fluctuations for hundreds of milliseconds or longer, meaning that much, if not all, of the neural response evoked by the TMS pulse would not be recorded.)

Figure 20.3 illustrates the EEG response to a TMS pulse delivered to the right premotor cortex of a single subject before falling asleep (A–C) and during non-REM sleep (A′–C′). A and A′ show the traces from all 60 electrodes in the cap, all plotted on the same timeline (a "butterfly plot"), and color-coded red during periods when the signal deviated significantly from baseline. Comparison across the two conditions illustrates that (1) the initial TMS-evoked response was roughly twofold larger in magnitude during non-REM sleep than during wakefulness and (2) the TMS-evoked response was of considerably longer duration during wakefulness than during non-REM sleep. The reason for the latter is evident from C and C′: whereas in wakefulness the initial response of the region directly under the coil was followed by responses in contralateral and posterior regions, then again in right PMC and then again in

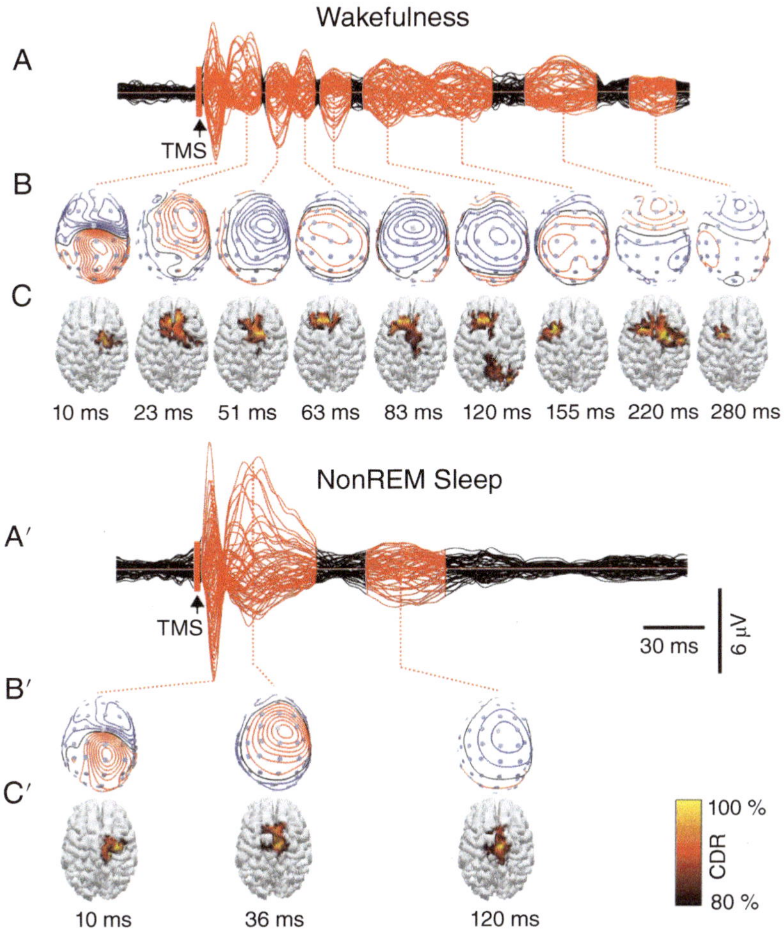

FIGURE 20.3 TMS-EEG from a single subject during wakefulness and non-REM sleep. Rows A and A′ are "butterfly plots" in which the trace from each electrode is plotted along the same time axis. B and B′ show the scalp distribution of voltages associated with the peak of each significant excursion of the signal. C and C′ show the source solutions of the maps from B and B′, displayed on the subject's MRI. CDR = current density reconstruction.

Source: Reproduced with permission from Massimini et al. (2005) / American Association for the Advancement of Science - AAAS.

the left, during non-REM sleep, the response stayed local. Thus, during wakefulness, the ERP was "kept alive" longer because activity in proximal areas triggered activity in distal areas, which then reactivated the proximal area, which then reactivated the distal area. There was greater effective connectivity during wakefulness. (Recall that *functional connectivity* refers to correlated activity between two regions, whereas *effective connectivity* refers to one region exerting a causal influence over activity in another.)

Why was the initial response of such greater magnitude during non-REM sleep? One possibility is that, because proximal neurons are more tightly synchronized during non-REM sleep, the response to TMS in the region that was directly stimulated was also more synchronized. A second is that thalamic neurons are more likely to respond in burst mode (section *Setting the state of thalamic neurons: tonic mode vs. burst mode, Chapter 3*) during non-REM sleep, because they are in a hyperpolarized state.

The point emphasized by the authors is that the fading of consciousness as we fall asleep is accompanied by a breakdown of long-range connectivity.

Anesthesia

> "[M]any aspects of an EEG of anaesthesia are really consistent with patients who are in a coma. The key difference is that anaesthesia is reversible . . . If you came in for an operation and I told you I was going to put you into a coma, you would probably get up and run away! [But] the idea of being put to sleep is a euphemism . . . For your surgery, you need to be in a state of general anaesthesia, not sleep." (Anesthesiologist and neuroscientist Emery Brown, quoted in Heathcoat, 2011.)

Anesthesia refers to a chemically induced, reversible loss of sensation, and general anesthesia, of interest to us here, to a chemically induced loss of consciousness. As detailed by Emery Brown, Ralph Lydic, and Nicholas Schiff (2010, *Further reading*), and illustrated in *Figure 20.2*, general anesthesia is, indeed, a physiological state more akin to coma than to sleep. One can be shaken awake from even the deepest sleep, but not so with anesthesia (or coma). Furthermore, with one exception, systemically administered anesthesia causes a decline in overall brain glucose metabolism, as assessed with PET. The effects of anesthesia are dose-dependent. For example, the anesthesiologist Michael Alkire (2009) describes a patient for whom a small dose of desflurane lowered global cerebral metabolism by 5–10% from baseline, rendering the patient sedated, but still able to generate a movement on request. The patient lost consciousness at a larger dose, which reduced global cerebral metabolism by 30%. (The exception is the anesthetic agent ketamine, which is "dissociative" in that it lowers awareness, and affects different brain regions in different ways, but, overall, causes an increase in global brain metabolic activity. Further, not unlike the dissociated neurological states that we have considered, including UWS, the eyes remain open during ketamine anesthesia).[1]

There are two additional findings from anesthesia that we will consider here, the first relating to a "breakdown of effective connectivity" reminiscent of what is seen with sleep. The second, neuroimaging evidence for why this might happen.

Studying Anesthesia with TMS/EEG A second study by Tononi's group, led by psychiatrist Fabio Ferrarelli and including anesthesiologist Robert Pearce, replicated the general procedures of the study of Massimini et al. (2005), but did so while subjects were administered the anesthetic agent midazolam. Midazolam is a benzodiazepine whose anesthetic properties derive from activating $GABA_A$ receptors, and thus imposing widespread inhibition in the brain. The effects of midazolam on the TMS-evoked response were virtually identical to those seen with non-REM sleep: the immediate response under the TMS coil was of greater magnitude, but the overall response was markedly reduced in terms of anatomical spread and temporal duration. Thus, anesthesia-induced loss of consciousness is also associated with drastic reduction of effective connectivity.

[1] Over the past several years there has been increasing buzz about a possible application of ketamine as an antidepressant.

Studying Anesthesia with Surface EEG and Deep Brain EEG Despite the considerable advantages of the TMS/EEG approach that we have described, it is limited, as are all extracranial (a.k.a., "scalp") EEG studies, by the fact that it can't directly "see inside" the brain. This problem has been addressed by a team led by anesthesiologist Lionel Velly, that has studied the effects of general anesthesia on patients with Parkinson's disease (PD) who have electrodes chronically implanted in the subthalamic nucleus of the basal ganglia (see *Figures 8.2 and 8.3*). Signal from the in-dwelling electrodes provided subcortical field potential recordings, referred to as electrosubcorticography (ESCoG), that can be thought of as a "subcortical EEG." They performed two analytically independent analyses, one being a fairly conventional spectral analysis of the electrical signals, the second being a nonlinear measure based on deterministic chaos theory. "Schematically," as Velly et al. (2007) explain it, dimensional activation (D_a) estimates "the complexity of EEG and ESCoG signals: The more alert the patient is, the more complex the EEG is, and the higher the D_a is; the deeper the sleep or anesthetic state is, the simpler the EEG is, and the lower the D_a is" (pp. 204–205).

The findings from this study, illustrated in *Figure 20.4*, are striking and clear: anesthesia-induced loss of consciousness is associated with a precipitous drop in oscillatory power at frequencies above the theta range, and a comparably precipitous drop in D_a, in the cortical EEG. Measures of subcortical activity, in contrast, begin a gradual decline with anesthesia onset. This suggests that anesthesia-related loss of consciousness, and perhaps also the commensurate loss of effective connectivity reported in the TMS/EEG study of Ferrarelli et al. (2010), is primarily due to effects in the cortex. More recently studies in nonhuman primates (NHP) have extended these findings by, for example, measuring the effects anesthesia on intercortical and cortical-subcortical connectivity with laminar electrode recordings from multiple areas (see *Further readings* from Bastos et al., 2021; Bhattacharya et al., 2022; Eisen et al., 2024; Lundqvist et al., 2023; Redinbaugh et al., 2022; Redinbaugh et al., 2020; Redinbaugh & Saalmann, 2024; Tauber et al., 2024; Whyte et al., 2024).

Summary Across Physiological Studies

Let's take a moment to consolidate what we've learned about the "physiology of consciousness." First, a factor that is necessary, but not sufficient, for conscious awareness is elevated activity in the reticular activating system, which, in turn, drives the state of arousal in thalamus and cortex. When this system is in an inactive state, whether due to neurological dysfunction

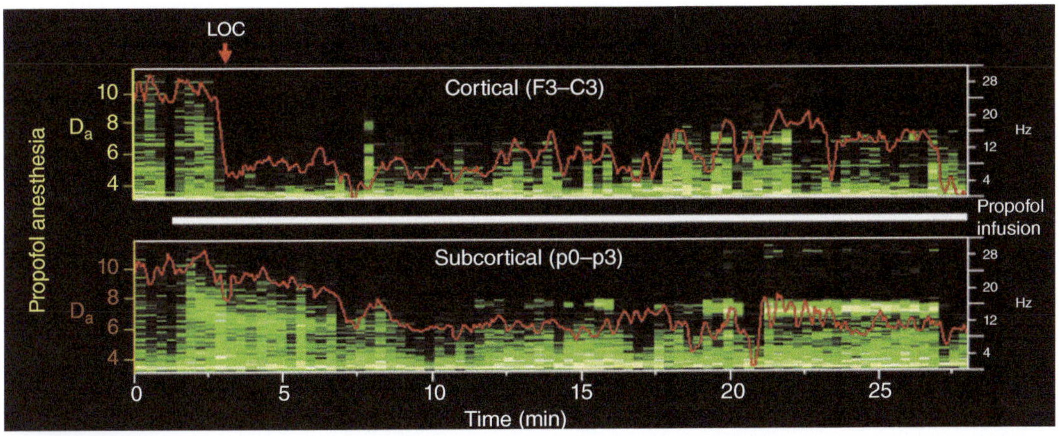

FIGURE 20.4 The time course of propofol anesthesia-induced loss of consciousness ("LOC"), as indexed by electrical activity measured from scalp EEG ("Cortical [F3–C3]") and from electrodes implanted in the subthalamic nuclei ("Subcortical [p0–p3]"). Red traces indicate level of dimensional activation (D_a) computed from the electrical signals (see text), with D_a axis on left-hand side of graphs, and green-to-white horizontal bars indicate spectral power in the EEG in 20-second time steps, with axis for the spectrograms on the right-hand side of the graphs.

Source: Reproduced with permission from Velly et al. (2007) / Wolters Kluwer Health, Inc.

(e.g., coma), sleep state, or anesthesia, one does not experience conscious awareness. The fact that elevated levels of physiological arousal are not sufficient to support consciousness, however, is seen in vegetative state/UWS, as well as in circumstances that we have not discussed, sleepwalking and epileptic seizures. What do UWS patients, and patients under anesthesia, lack that individuals who are conscious (REM sleep, LIS, healthy wakefulness) seem to have? Complex cortical activity and substantial cortico-cortical and cortico-thalamic connectivity. In the final section of this chapter, we will consider some theoretical explanations for why these aspects of brain activity might be important for consciousness.

As a "farewell to physiology," *Figure 20.5* illustrates the evolution of the TMS/EEG response as subjects recover from coma, indicating that, just as with sleep and with anesthesia, a return to consciousness in these patients is accompanied by an increase in complex, interconnected activity.

FIGURE 20.5 Tracking recovery from coma with TMS/EEG.

Source: Rosanova et al., 2012 / Oxford University Press.

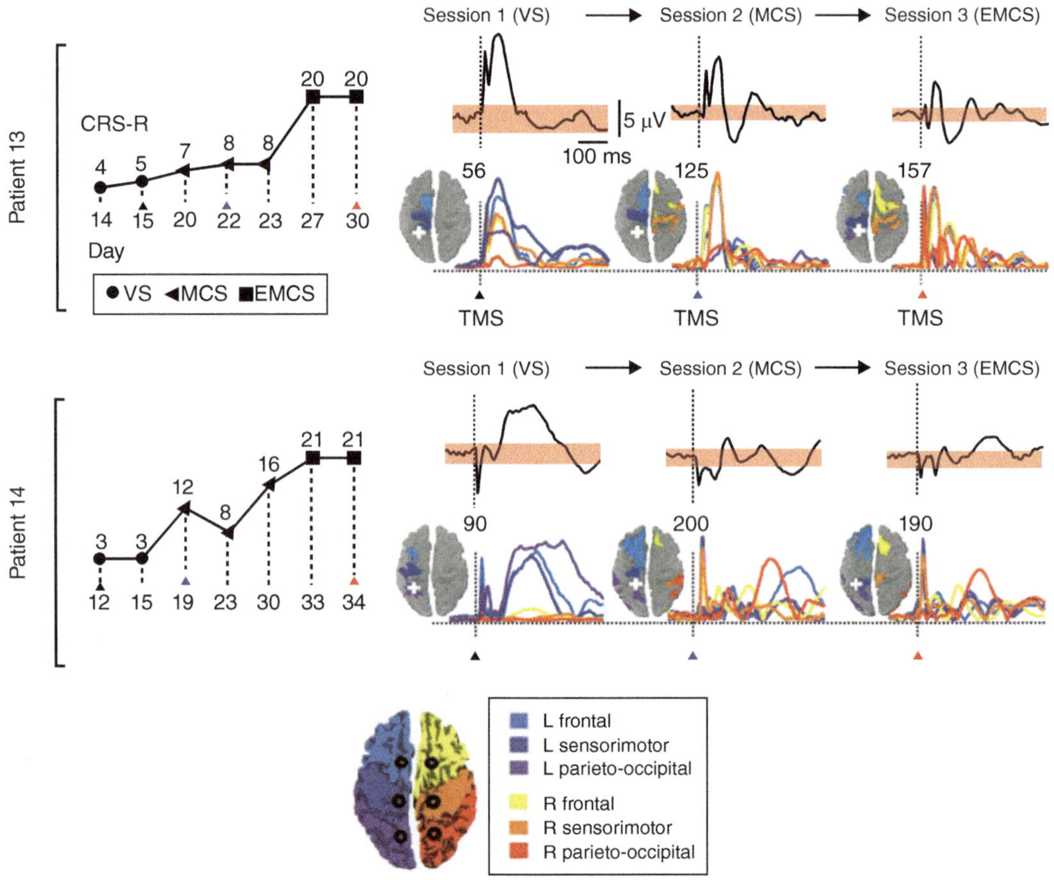

FIGURE 20.5.A Two patients whose recovery transitioned from coma to vegetative state (VS) to minimally conscious state (MCS) to emerged-from-MCS (EMCS), at which point they had recovered the ability to communicate and were classified as "recovered" by the Coma Recovery Scale-Revised (CRS-R), a standard diagnostic assessment. CRS-R score is tracked as a function of day post-trauma, with arrows indicating day of each TMS/EEG session (black = first; blue = second; red = third). At the top of the diagram for each session is the TMS-evoked response from the electrode under the coil. Lower left illustrates TMS target (white "+") and brain regions from which a TMS-evoked response occurred, color coded as per the legend. Plots to the right of each brain show the estimated TMS-evoked current from each of the six sources identified with black circles in the legend. The numbers between the two plots (e.g., 56, 125, and 157 for Patient 13) indicate the number of vertices in the cortical mesh from the source solution at which a significant TMS-evoked response was detected.

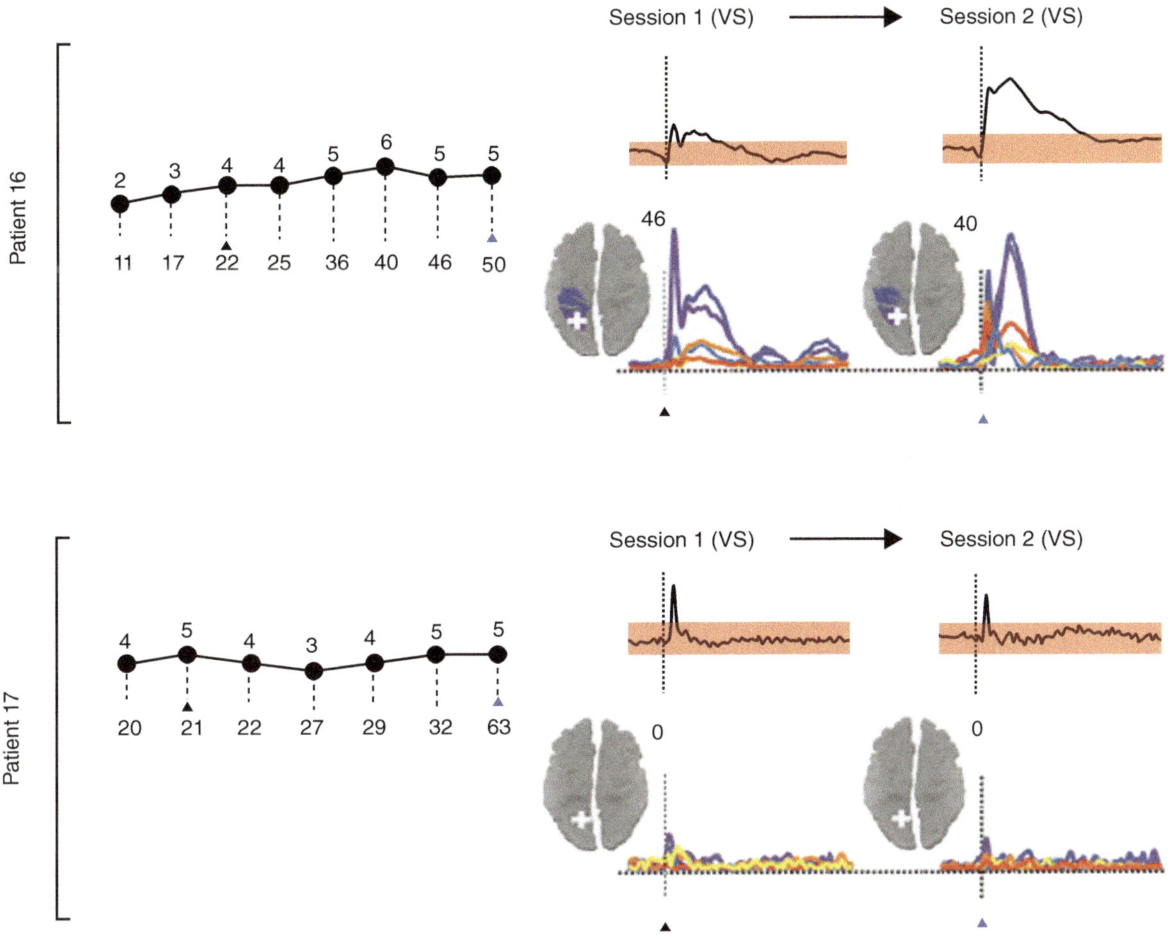

FIGURE 20.5.B Data from two patients who did not emerge from VS.

Brain Functions Supporting Conscious Perception

Up until now, we've considered what factors underlie the state of being conscious. Now we turn to a different question: *What determines the contents of our conscious awareness at any given moment?* As I lift my eyes from my computer screen and look out from my front patio, what neural functions underlie my becoming aware of that sign across the street, or the hawk that's perched up in the tree? It's presumably not "just" the visual processes that we considered earlier in this book, because, as we saw with the phenomenon of the attentional blink (section *Meditation as mental training in emotion regulation, Chapter 18*), one can be presented with the same stimulus under identical external conditions and sometimes one becomes aware of it and other times one doesn't. And so minimally, we would need to specify what is different about the state of the visual system during trials when we are aware of the stimulus vs. during trials when we are not. And then there's the question of attention. Patients with unilateral neglect are not aware of stimuli on the left side of space, so surely attention and consciousness are closely linked? Undoubtedly they are, but one of the claims that we'll consider in this section is that the two can be dissociated.

Research that addresses these kinds of questions is often referred to as the study of the neural correlates of consciousness (NCC). As alluded to in the previous paragraph, studies of the NCC often use the strategy of presenting subjects with a series of identical trials, under conditions when they may or may not be aware of the stimulus. After the experiment, trials are sorted as a function of whether the target was or was not detected, and trials from the two types are compared for differences. Although we will restrict ourselves here to the visual modality, we'll see that there are many domains of cognition that are implicated in this research.

Are We Conscious of Activity in Early Sensory Cortex?

The first question we might want to address when thinking about visual awareness is: what level(s) of the system *can* potentially support it? Let's say, for example, we had some way of determining that areas V1–V4 in the ventral stream are very machine-like, in that although the output of their processing is raw material that is needed for visual awareness, they don't actually contribute to the generation of visual awareness. If we knew this to be true, then we could focus our attention on higher-level visual areas and not worry about fluctuations in signal in the earlier areas – these might relate to something like signal strength but couldn't tell us about awareness per se.

There are two classes of experimental procedures that have been used extensively to address this question. The one that we will consider in detail is, in a way, the simplest: it consists in presenting a single item on each trial, and comparing brain activity from trials in which the stimulus was seen vs. from trials in which it wasn't. A second experimental strategy for addressing this question takes advantage of the phenomenon of **binocular rivalry**: when a different image is presented to each of the two eyes, the percept is of seeing just one of the two, with frequent seemingly spontaneous "switches" between which of the two one is currently seeing. Because it explicitly dissociates the information being processed by the retina from the percept that we are consciously aware of, this procedure has been used extensively in studies of the NCC in both humans and monkeys. It's a rich and nuanced literature to which we can't do justice here, but that can be explored via publications by Leopold and Logothetis (1996), Crick (1996), Engel et al. (1999), and Blake and Tong (2008), all listed under *Further reading*.

Now, back to "single-item" studies. The first that we will consider in some detail is a very simple, very elegant fMRI study by cognitive neuroscientists David Ress and David Heeger (2003). It was designed to ask, in effect, *does activity in early visual cortex correspond to the external stimulus from which photons are impacting our retinae, or does it correspond to our subjective ("internal") experience?* Subjects fixated centrally, and every two seconds, a ring of "background" visual noise would appear for one second, and on a randomly determined 17% of trials, a target (a sinusoidal grating, i.e., parallel lines) would be superimposed on the background (*Figure 20.6.A*). Subjects responded "yes" or "no" on every trial, and target contrast was adjusted for each subject such that they would detect it on roughly 80% of trials. Each trial could have one of four outcomes: the target is present and the subject detects it (a "hit"); the target is present and the subject does not detect it (a "miss"); the target is absent and the subject reports detecting it (a "false alarm"); or the target is absent and the subject does not detect it (a "correct rejection"). It was assumed that hits would produce a robust stimulus-evoked response in V1, and correct rejections were treated as the baseline. The questions of interest, then, were how V1 would respond on trials in which the physical display and the subject's perception were at odds. If the fMRI response to misses resembled that of hits, and the fMRI response to false alarms resembled that of correct rejections, then visual cortex activity would be congruent with the objective state of the visual world. If, on the other hand, the reverse were true, then visual cortex activity would be congruent with the subject's subjective percept. Drum roll please . . . *Figure 20.6.B* indicates that V1 activity was congruent with the percept! The implication for consciousness research, then, is that regions as early as primary sensory cortex may contribute to our conscious awareness of sensory perception.

If you stop to think about this result for a moment, it might be somewhat unsettling for your sense of agency. Is it not an implication of the result from false-alarm trials that our visual system may sometimes "show us what we want to see," rather than what is really out in the world? Perhaps. But keep in mind that subjects were performing under atypically difficult conditions – low-contrast targets, continuous target presentation, speeded responses, and no feedback. Additionally, isn't it at least somewhat reassuring to encounter an effect in this, our last chapter together, that reinforces principles that we've encountered earlier in the book, in this instance the hypothesis-testing idea articulated by Sillito and colleagues all the way back in *Chapter 3* and, more generally, that of predictive coding?

FIGURE 20.6 Does V1 activity correspond to the external world or to our conscious perception of it?
Source: Reproduced with permission from Ress et al. (2003) / Springer Nature.

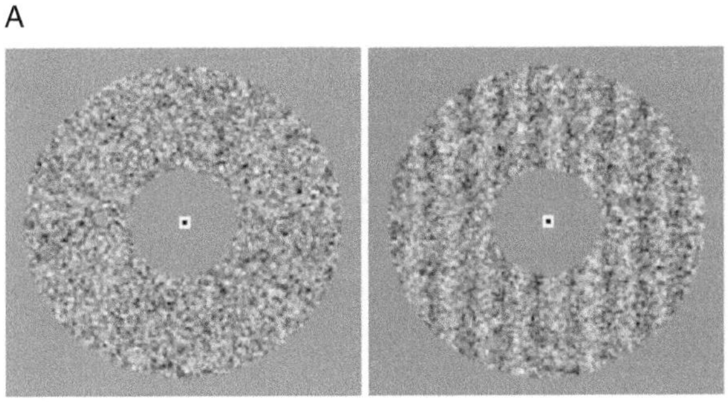

FIGURE 20.6.A A stimulus without the target vertical grating (left), and with it (right).

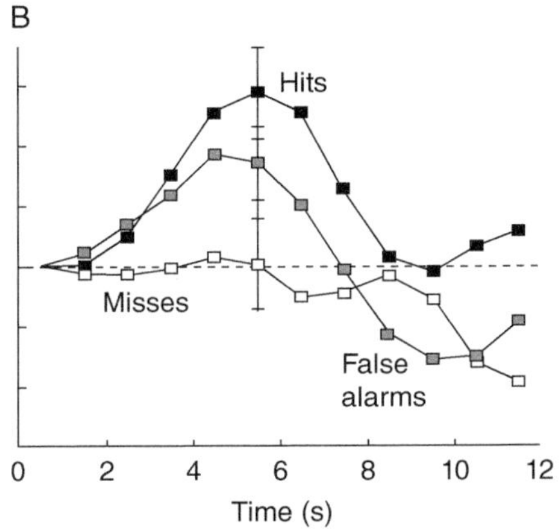

FIGURE 20.6.B fMRI responses from V1 of a single subject, time locked to stimulus onset, as a function of behavioral response. Correct-rejection trials were treated as the baseline for this analysis, meaning that the activity during misses did not differ from activity during correct rejections. (Each tick mark on the vertical axis corresponds to 0.1% signal change from baseline.)

Although the false-alarm trials from Ress and Heeger (2003) might be spookier, for the reasons just discussed, we also need to come up with a satisfactory account for the miss trials from this study. We'll address this first, and then return to the false alarms.

What Intrinsic Factors Influence Conscious Visual Perception? If one takes a deterministic view of the brain (which we do), there must have been one or more factors that differed in the momentary state of subjects' brains during miss trials vs. during hit trials from the Ress and Heeger (2003) study. One possibility that was raised at the beginning of this chapter is the spontaneous fluctuation in posterior alpha-band power. The study from Romei et al. (2008; section *The relation between visual processing and the brain's physiological state, Chapter 3*) demonstrated that the excitability of visual cortex varies systematically with spontaneous fluctuations of power in the alpha band. A second factor that influences near-threshold visual stimulus detection is the phase of low-frequency oscillations during which a stimulus is presented. Kyle Mathewson et al. (2011) have proposed that oscillations in the alpha band implement a "pulsed inhibition" of neuronal activity, such that the phase of the ongoing alpha-band oscillation at which a stimulus is presented can determine how effectively it is processed. Relatedly, several groups have provided evidence for periodic attentional sampling that flits between targets at a rate corresponding to the theta band. One interesting exercise would be to revisit this evidence for periodic "up" and "down" states ("open" and "closed"?) of our perceptual awareness after reading the final section of this chapter, on theories of consciousness, and to try to interpret these phenomena in the context of the theories that we're about to review.

Bottom-Up and Top-Down Influences on Conscious Visual Perception

Now we turn to the false-alarm finding from Ress and Heeger (2003), that the V1 "response" to an absent target was almost as robust as its response to real targets, but only on the trials when subjects thought that they had seen a target. One possible explanation is that the conditions of this experiment promoted noisy retino-geniculo-striate signaling, such that on some target-absent trials, there was simply more afferent input to V1 than on others. By this account, target-absent trials with randomly higher input to V1 would have produced greater V1 physiological responses, which, in turn, would trigger false-alarm behavioral responses. This explanation follows the logic that we saw in the microstimulation studies described in *Chapter 16*'s treatment of perceptual decision making. That is, from the perspective of the signal-detection theory of perceptual decision making, perhaps there was more afferent "momentary evidence" on false-alarm trials than on correct-rejection trials.

By the logic of signal detection theory, false alarms are necessarily trials in which, due to noise, stimulus information is greater than it is for misses. So it is logically possible that the pattern of correct rejections < misses < false alarms is entirely driven by varying levels of noise in the feedforward signaling from retina to V1. Were this the case, however, one might expect to see an orderly progression between these three trial types. Instead, to this author's eye, the responses in V1 appear to be categorical, with correct rejections and misses almost identical, and false alarms quite similar to hits. Thus, it's at least plausible that intrinsic, top-down factors, such as predictions, account for at least part of the response on false-alarm trials. (This would be consistent with the IEM reconstruction of stimulus information on 0% contrast trials, from early visual cortex (Yu and Postle, 2021) (*Figure 5.9*).) In *Chapter 3,* we considered anatomical and physiological substrates for such top-down influence on V1 (and LGN) processing of an afferent motion signal. Next, we consider a study whose results suggest a physiological basis for this top-down account of perceptual awareness.

The Role of Reentrant Signals to V1 For the experiment whose results are shown in *Figure 20.7*, the team of Hans Supèr, Henk Spekreijse, and Victor Lamme (2001) recorded from V1 of monkeys performing a target-detection task with many similarities to that of Ress and Heeger (2003): each trial presented a full-screen "background" of small scratch-like lines all oriented in the same direction, with the to-be-detected "figure" defined by rotating the orientation of every line within a square-shaped region by 90°. The figure appeared in each of three locations on 26.7% of trials, the remaining 20% being catch trials with no figure. The first thing to notice from *Figure 20.7* is that the neural detection of the figure (i.e., the "modulation") lagged behind the initial, nonspecific, stimulus-evoked ramp-up of activity by roughly 90 msec. This effect is reminiscent of the effects of object-based attention reported by Chelazzi, Duncan, Miller, and Desimone (1998; *Figure 7.15.B*), in that both show a delayed boost in activity that corresponds to the discrimination between two visual elements in the display. The effect in the Supèr, Spekreijse, and Lamme (2001) data must derive from a different source, however, because its "boost" comes much earlier than the earliest that selective attention effects are seen in V1, which is 200–250 msec after stimulus onset. (Note that the 120–175 msec latencies reported in Chelazzi et al. [1998; section *Object-based attention, Chapter 7*] were recorded from vAIT.)

The monkeys' performance was such that there were too few unambiguous false-alarm responses to analyze. What's shown in *Figure 20.7*, panel B, however, is that activity on miss (i.e., "Not seen") trials completely lacks any evidence of the figure-related modulation. (Thus, had Supèr, Spekreijse, and Lamme [2001] portrayed their data in a manner analogous to how Ress and Heeger [2003] did theirs, by subtracting baseline [i.e., "Ground"] from target-present [i.e., "Figure"] trials, V1 activity on the miss [i.e., "Not seen"] trials from *Figure 20.7*, panel B, would also have been a flat line with a value of 0.) Supèr, Spekreijse, and Lamme (2001) suggested that the source of figure detection-related modulation of V1 was a reentrant (i.e., feedback) signal coming from a higher station in extrastriate cortex. We will also return to this idea in the final section on theories of consciousness.

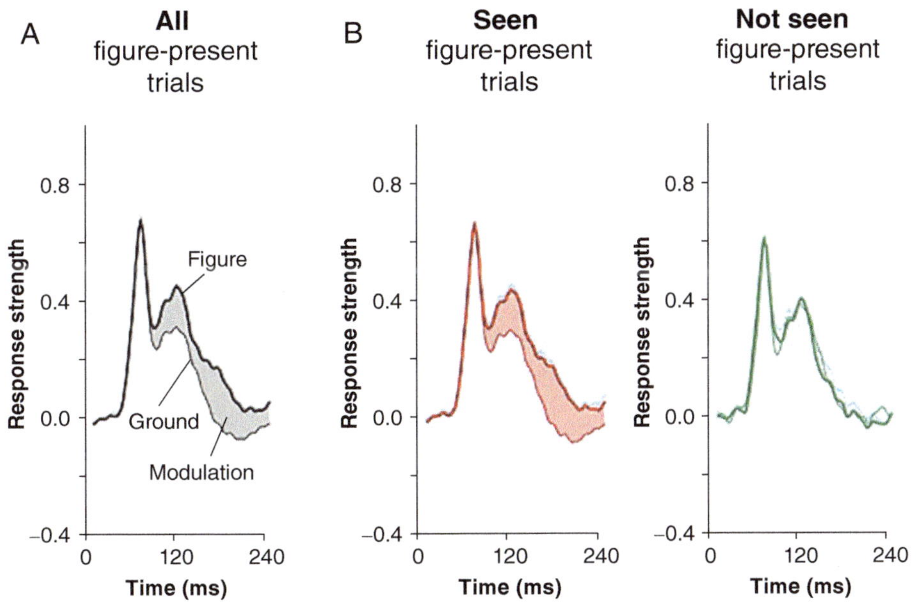

FIGURE 20.7 Normalized spiking activity ("Response strength") from V1 neurons in a monkey performing a target-detection task. Each trial began with the onset of a full-field textured "background" within which a figure (defined by differently oriented texture) was embedded in one of three locations. These plots show the response of V1 neurons when only the background fell into their receptive fields ("Ground"; light lines) and when the figure fell into their receptive fields (heavy lines). **A** the results from all trials when a figure was present somewhere on the screen (20% of trials, not shown here, were catch trials in which no figure was presented). **B** the same data, but broken into hits ("Seen") and misses ("Not seen").

Source: Supèr et al., 2001 / Springer Nature.

Next, we turn to a study whose logic relies on extrinsic, rather than intrinsic, factors to control whether or not subjects are aware of a given stimulus.

Manipulating Extrinsic Factors to Study Conscious vs. Unconscious Vision

The cognitive neuroscientist Stanislaus Dehaene has made important contributions to at least three subdisciplines within the field: numerical cognition, reading (see *Chapter 19, Further reading*), and consciousness. The study that we'll consider here combines the latter two interests. In it, Dehaene et al. (2001) explored the phenomenon that words presented very briefly and backward masked, such that they are not consciously perceived, can nonetheless produce robust repetition priming effects. (This is reminiscent of the emotional face presentation studies that we considered in *Chapter 18*, section *The role of awareness.*) While in the fMRI scanner, subjects viewed a serial stream of jumbled masks, each for a duration of 71 msec, with a mask periodically replaced by one or two 71-msec blank screens. Embedded in these streams were words presented for 29 msec that were either immediately preceded and followed by a blank screen ("unmasked") or immediately preceded and followed by a mask.

Behavioral data from Dehaene et al. (2001) indicated that masked words went undetected on >99.3% of trials, whereas unmasked words were detected on >90% of trials. Despite subjects' lack of awareness that masked words had been presented, there was evidence in both the behavioral and fMRI data that they were processed to at least the level of the mental lexicon. The behavioral evidence came in the form of repetition priming: when a masked word was followed by the 500-msec (i.e., clearly visible) presentation of a target word about which subjects had to make a "natural/manmade" judgment, responses were significantly faster when the target word was the same as had been the masked word. This was even true when the masked word was presented in an ALL CAPS typeface and the target word in lower case, meaning that it was a relatively high-level representation of the word that had been accessed, not just a low-level visual representation of what the letters physically looked like. The fMRI evidence that masked words were processed to a fairly high level came from the fact that repetition suppression (section *Repetition effects and fMRI adaptation, Chapter 13*) was observed in left fusiform gyrus, in the "visual word form area" (labeled "word selective" in *Figure 10.5*), for 500-msec target words that were preceded by masked presentation of the same word, relative to 500-msec target words preceded by masked presentation of a different word.

As illustrated in *Figure 20.8*, the fMRI response evoked by unmasked 29-msec words was markedly stronger than that for masked 29-msec words, both in terms of signal intensity and in terms of the number of regions responding at above-threshold levels. Unmasked words

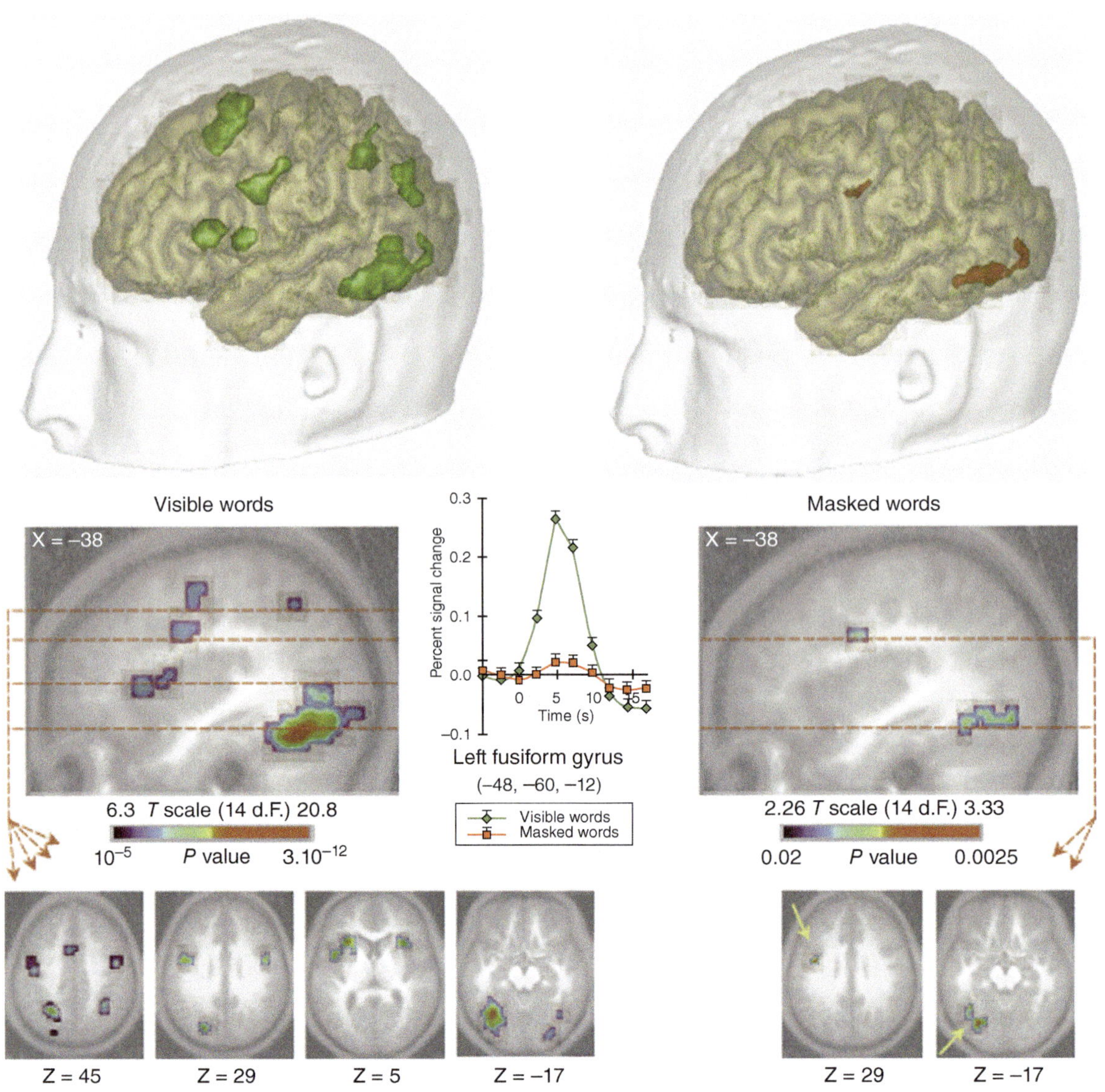

FIGURE 20.8 fMRI activity associated with words that were unmasked, and therefore visible (left-hand column), vs. words that were masked, and therefore not detected (right-hand column). The plot in the center compares the group-averaged response to visible vs. masked words in left fusiform gyrus.

Source: Reproduced with permission from Dehaene et al. (2001) / Springer Nature.

evoked responses in several regions, including fusiform gyrus, parietal cortex, posterior inferior PFC/anterior insula, anterior cingulate, precentral cortex, and supplementary motor area, bilaterally. Masked words, in contrast, evoked above-threshold responses only in left fusiform gyrus and in left precentral sulcus. Further, when signal intensity in "commonly activated" areas was compared, the response to masked words was only 8.6% as strong as the response to unmasked words in fusiform gyrus, and 5.2% as strong in left precentral sulcus. Finally, for many of the regions listed here, functional connectivity was significantly greater during the presentation of unmasked than masked words. In summarizing their findings, the authors foreshadowed one of the theories that we'll be considering in the final section of this chapter: "unmasking the words enabled the propagation of activation and the ignition of a large-scale correlated cerebral assembly" (Dehaene et al., 2001, p. 757).

Are Attention and Awareness the Same Thing?

(This is an interesting question, and one that offers a nice transition between the preceding section on empirical studies of consciousness and the upcoming one on theories of consciousness.)

This author's intuition certainly tells him that they are. He is aware of that to which he pays attention and, conversely, how would it be possible for him to be aware of something to which he's not attending? The classic example is one considered earlier in the book: the feeling of the pressure of the chair that you're currently sitting in pressing against your body. The sensory information coming from your legs, etc., was no different 10 seconds ago than it is now, yet without attending to it, you weren't aware of it. But there are at least two really smart groups of people who have given this question considerable thought, and who would disagree.

Neuroscientist Victor Lamme, whose study of visual awareness in the monkey is featured in *Figure 20.7*, has argued that we can be aware of much more information than we can attend to. While the capacity of the number of items we can simultaneously attend to is limited to 4 ± 1, we can be consciously aware of much more information. One example that he points to is iconic memory. The classic demonstration is from the psychologist George Sperling (1960), in which a 4×3 array of letters is briefly flashed (50 msec). If subjects are asked to write down as many letters as they can remember seeing (the so-called "full report" procedure), they typically only recall three or four items. If, however, after the offset of the array, a high-, medium-, or low-pitched tone is played, indicating which row is to be "read out" from memory, subjects will typically remember three items from that row. Because they did not know prior to the tone which row would be cued, it must be the case that, for that brief moment, subjects had at least nine items in mind. Part of Lamme's (2003) argument is that attentional selection is necessary for any kind of overt response, and that it's the attentional selection of items from conscious awareness into the focus of attention that is the capacity-limiting step, during which the representation of nine items shrinks to three. More generally, he argues that attentional selection is the process whereby one (or a few) mental representations that are competing to control behavior get selected for that purpose. Conscious awareness of visual representations arises through other processes (to be considered in the next section), independent of whether or not they will be selected by attention to influence behavior.

Naotsugu Tsuchiya and Christoph Koch (2009) have also argued that these two constructs can be shown to operate independently. An example of attention without consciousness comes from a variant of the task used by Dehaene et al. (2001). In it, Lionel Naccache, Elise Blandin, and Stanislaus Dehaene (2002) demonstrate that the priming for masked words (i.e., for words for which subjects have no awareness) only occurs when they are attending to the display. As an example of consciousness without attention, they point to dual-task studies in which subjects' attention is focused on a central task, yet they are able to identify each time a briefly flashed image in the periphery contains an animal, information that they became aware of without attending to it (Fei Fei Li et al., 2002).

Theories of Consciousness

"It is remarkable that most of the work in both cognitive science and the neurosciences makes no reference to consciousness (or 'awareness'), especially as many would regard consciousness as the major puzzle confronting the neural view of the mind and indeed at the present time it appears deeply mysterious to many people. This attitude is partly a legacy of behaviorism and partly because most workers in these areas cannot see any useful way of approaching the problem" (Crick and Koch, 1990, p. 263).

A great deal has changed in the 35+ years since those words were written. Indeed, much of the early energy, the ideas, and the cheerleading driving consciousness research came from this duo, the Nobel Laureate molecular biologist, codiscoverer of the structure of DNA, and the young computational neuroscientist. Today, in contrast to 1990, there is an Association for the Scientific Study of Consciousness, and a handful of journals devoted to the topic.

In this final section, we'll summarize just a small number of neural theories of consciousness, working backward through this chapter up to this point, to highlight how theoretical and empirical work on this problem are interwoven.[2]

Global Neuronal Workspace Theory

Global Neuronal Workspace Theory was first developed by Bernard Baars, based on global workspace computer architecture with a distributed set of knowledge sources, which could cooperatively solve problems that no single constituent could solve alone. Considerable theoretical and empirical work with this model has been carried out by Dehaene and colleagues, in whose hands it has become Global Neuronal Workspace Theory (GNWT). In 2003 Stanislaus Dehaene, Claire Sergent, and Jean-Pierre Changeux published a neural network model proposing that "the step of conscious perception, referred to as access awareness, is related to the entry of processed visual stimuli into a global brain state that links distant areas including the prefrontal cortex through reciprocal connections, and thus makes perceptual information reportable by multiple means" (p. 8520). This step of access awareness corresponds to the "ignition of a large-scale correlated cerebral assembly" triggered by the presentation of unmasked words in the Dehaene et al. (2001) study that we considered in the previous section.

A key component of the model is competition among stimulus representations for representation in the global neuronal workspace. The global neuronal workspace itself is implemented as high-level cortical areas (representing prefrontal, parietal, temporal, and cingulate) that implement "brain-scale propagation of stimulus information," which results in its accessibility for consciousness. There are several distinctive features to this model. A central tenet that differentiates it from many other models is the all-or-none property of conscious awareness of a representation:

> According to the present model, the primary correlate of conscious access is a sudden self-amplifying bifurcation leading to a global brain-scale pattern of activity. This leads to several critical predictions for neuroimaging and pharmacological experiments. First, in experiments with a continuously varying and increasingly visible stimulus, we predict a sudden nonlinear transition toward a state of globally

[2]The week that the final draft of this 3rd edition of this book were sent to the publisher, a paper reporting the results of a large adversarial collaboration testing empirical predictions of two of the three theories presented here – Global Neuronal Workspace Theory (GNWT) and of Integrated Information Theory (IIT) – appeared in the journal *Nature* (Cogitate Consortium et al., 2025). (An adversarial collaboration entails preregistration of an experimental design, plus predicted outcomes, that is agreed to by each of two or more parties advocating different models or theories; in this case the experiments and analyses were carried out by research groups with no overt commitment to either theory.) With regard to the outcomes, this author takes the position of the authors of Cogitate Consortium et al. (2025): "[R]eaders might expect a definitive verdict on the . . . theories under evaluation. Instead, we invite readers to weigh the evidence themselves—considering the support for each preregistered prediction, the breadth of the data, the sophistication of the methods and analyses, and the cognitive biases that shape interpretation" (p. 9). Having read this book, the reader will be well-equipped to assess the data (generated by fMRI, MEG, and iEEG), the analyses (multivariate decoding, RSA, and synchronization analyses), and the interpretations offered by those who carried out the experiments and by the "adversaries."

> increased brain activity ("ignition"), particularly evident in prefrontal, cingulate, and parietal cortices, accompanied by a synchronous amplification of posterior perceptual activation and by thalamo-cortical brain-scale synchrony in the [gamma] range (20–100 Hz) (Dehaene, Sergent, and Changeux, 2003, p. 8525).

This "all-or-noneness" is illustrated in *Figure 20.9*, in which the simulated attentional blink effectively prevents any representation of T2 in the global workspace. Further, in simulations with the model, when long-distance top-down connections within areas C and D of the global workspace and between C and D and earlier sensory levels of the model were removed, weakened by 50%, or reduced to only short-range connections, the attentional blink no longer occurred (i.e., T2 gained access to the global workspace). An empirical demonstration that the authors point to is the finding illustrated in *Figure 20.8*: unmasked words, which were consciously perceived, evoked robust activity in a broadly distributed array of cortical areas; masked words, in contrast, of which patients were unaware, evoked relatively weaker activity, and only in a narrow set of regions that is automatically engaged by the visual presentation of words.

Recurrent Processing Theory

Victor Lamme, whose group's empirical work is illustrated in *Figure 20.7*, has assembled a theoretical account from his analysis of the neurophysiology of visual perception:

> When a new image hits the retina, it is processed through successive levels of visual cortex, by means of feedforward connections, working at an astonishing speed. Each level takes only 10 ms of processing, so that in about 100–150 ms the whole brain "knows" about the new image before our eyes, and potential motor responses are prepared. From the very first action potentials that are fired, neurons exhibit complex tuning properties such as selectivity for motion, depth, color or shape, and even respond selectively to faces. Thus, the feedforward sweep enables a rapid extraction of complex and meaningful features from the visual scene, and lays down potential motor responses to act on the incoming information.
>
> Are we conscious of the features extracted by the feedforward sweep? Do we see a face when a face-selective neuron becomes active? It seems not. Many studies, in both humans and monkeys, indicate that no matter what area of the brain is reached by the feedforward sweep, this in itself is not producing (reportable) conscious experience. What seems necessary for conscious experience is that neurons in visual areas engage in so-called recurrent (or re-entrant or resonant) processing . . ., where high- and low-level areas interact. This would enable the widespread exchange of information between areas processing different attributes of the visual scene, and thus support perceptual grouping. . . . In addition, when recurrent interactions span the entire sensorimotor hierarchy, or involve the frontoparietal areas, potential motor responses could modify the visual responses, which would form the neural equivalent of task set, attention, etc. (Lamme, 2006, pp. 496–497).

Thus, although the Recurrent Processing and Global Neuronal Workspace models both emphasize a critical role for recurrent processing, they also differ in important ways, as illustrated in *Figure 20.10*. First, by the Recurrent Processing view, activation by the feedforward sweep is not sufficient, in and of itself, to trigger conscious awareness. For example, the initial feedforward sweep of visual information could activate parietal and frontal oculomotor centers so as to trigger an eye movement toward a target without the subject being consciously aware of the stimulus (*Figure 20.10*, Panel A). Second, as illustrated in *Figure 20.10, B*, recurrent processing that is restricted to ventral-stream processing areas would be sufficient to support conscious awareness in the absence of selective attention. Examples of this type of awareness are highlighted in the arguments raised both by Lamme (2003) and Tsuchiya and Koch (2009) in the earlier section *Are attention and awareness the same thing?* Lamme has noted that the distinction between consciousness without attention (*Figure 20.10.B*) and consciousness with attention (*Figure 20.10.C*) maps onto the distinction made by philosopher Ned Block (1996) between "phenomenal awareness" and "access awareness."

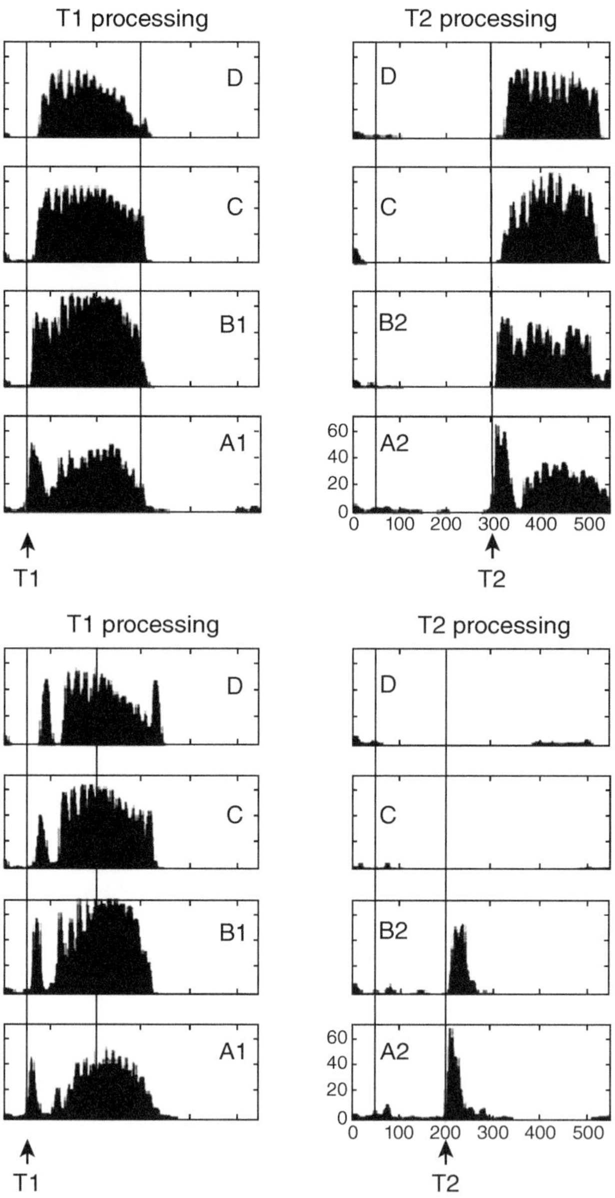

FIGURE 20.9 Simulation of two trials from the attentional blink task in a neural network model of Global Neuronal Workspace Theory. In both groups, each rectangle corresponds to a level in the model, A1 and B1 being sensory channels that process the T1 stimulus; A2 and B2 being sensory channels that process the T2 stimulus. C and D are higher-level areas in which the stimulus must compete for representation. Activity within each level represents firing rate. The trial illustrated in the upper panels simulates a long lag (250 msec) between the two stimuli, and as a result, T2 is presented at a time when the sustained activity evoked by T1 has decayed. T2 is therefore able to invade all cortical levels and elicits long-lasting activity comparable to T1. The trial illustrated in the lower panels simulates a "blink" trial that featured a shorter (150 msec) T1–T2 lag. Because T1 is still dominating the workspace when T2 arrives, T2 is blocked from entering, and therefore fails to evoke neural activity beyond an initial bottom-up activation in areas A and B.

Source: Dehaene et al., 2003 / National Academy of Sciences.

An important distinction between the Recurrent Processing and Global Neuronal Workspace models, therefore, is that the former allows for quantitatively graded levels of consciousness, whereas the latter treats consciousness as an all-or-none proposition. Recurrent Processing Theory also argues, based on neurophysiological evidence, that there can be states in which we are aware of information, but this information is not accessible to overt report. This relates to Lamme's (2006) argument that when behavioral/psychological evidence (e.g., a subject's overt report or performance, or even one's subjective experience) diverges from neurophysiological evidence, the latter should be given equal weight with regard to evidence for conscious awareness of the stimulus in question. Otherwise, he reasons, our construal of consciousness reduces to the cognitive functions necessary for behavior and/or subjective experience – language, motor control, attention, and working memory – and we are no longer studying consciousness per se.

Important challenges for the Recurrent Processing model include specifying what it is about recurrent processing, per se, that gives rise to conscious awareness. Is the activation of certain layers of cortex critical, or the synchronized coactivation of two or more specific layers? Are there different neurotransmitter receptors whose activation is crucial (e.g., AMPA receptors by feedforward glutamate signaling vs. NMDA receptors by feedback)? What are the implications for consciousness of recurrent processing in brain regions whose activity seems to be inaccessible to overt awareness on the part of patients, such as in the right hemisphere of split-brain patients or in the right hemisphere of patients suffering from unilateral neglect?

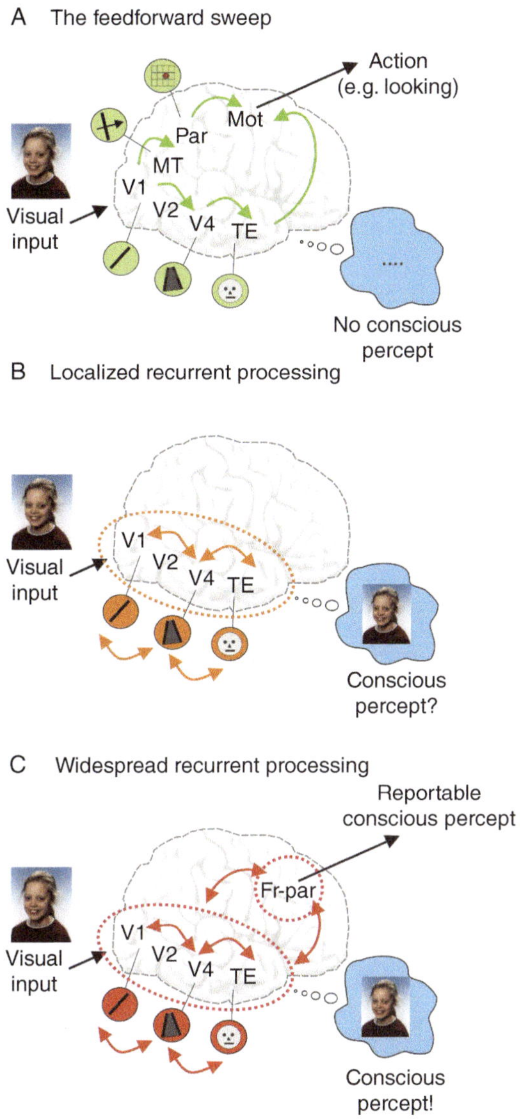

FIGURE 20.10 Three scenarios considered by Lamme's (2006) Recurrent Processing framework. In **A**, the presentation of a stimulus triggers a feedforward sweep along the ventral and dorsal processing streams of the visual system, the icons representing the features that are extracted at each level. **B** corresponds to highly interactive recurrent processing that is nonetheless restricted to the ventral stream. **C** illustrates a state of widespread recurrent processing, which is equivalent to ignition of the global neuronal workspace, as specified in Global Neuronal Workspace Theory.

Source: Reproduced with permission from Lamme et al. (2006) / Elsevier.

Integrated Information Theory

To convey the gist of his Integrated Information Theory (IIT),[3] Giulio Tononi (2008) invites us to consider the following:

> You are facing a blank screen that is alternately on and off, and you have been instructed to say "light" when the screen turns on and "dark" when it turns off. A photodiode – a simple light-sensitive device – has also been placed in front of the screen . . . The first problem of consciousness reduces to this: when you distinguish between the screen being on or off, you have the subjective experience of seeing light or dark. The photodiode can also distinguish between the screen being on or off, but presumably it does not have a subjective experience of light and dark. What is the key difference between you and the photodiode?
>
> . . . the difference has to do with how much information is generated when that distinction is made. Information is classically defined as reduction of uncertainty: the more numerous the alternatives that are ruled out, the greater the reduction of uncertainty, and thus the

[3] In the few years leading up to the preparation of this 3rd edition of this book, IIT has been at the center of considerable controversy. Recent summaries can be found as Further Readings: (Gomez-Marin & Seth, 2025; IIT-Concerned et al., 2025; Tononi et al., 2025). The gist of this controversy is that the preliminary announcement of results from the adversarial collaboration reported by Cogitate Consortium et al. (2025) prompted a large group of scientists and philosophers, with varying levels of scholarly involvement in the study of consciousness per se (and many of whom appear elsewhere in this book, including in this chapter), labeled IIT "pseudo-science" (IIT-Concerned et al., 2023). Without seeking to take a position on this controversy in this book, the author feels obliged to state explicitly that it is his considered opinion that the concerns expressed in (IIT-Concerned et al., 2023; IIT-Concerned et al., 2025) relate to factors that are outside the scope of this cognitive neuroscience textbook—some of them philosophical, some pertaining to the sociology of science and the communication of science in the popular press—and that none of these concerns provide any basis for questioning the integrity of the empirical methods and results of experiments reviewed here. Indeed, their inclusion signifies that this author judges them to be "particularly effective for explicating the concept[s] in question." (If nothing else, they will be helpful preparation for anyone interested in reading Cogitate Consortium et al. (2025).)

> greater the information . . . When the blank screen turns on, . . . the photodiode . . . reports "light." . . . When you see the blank screen turn on, on the other hand, the situation is quite different . . . [because] you are in fact discriminating among a much larger number of alternatives, thereby generating many more bits of information.
>
> This is easy to see. Just imagine that, instead of turning light and dark, the screen were to turn red, then green, then blue, and then display one after the other, every frame from every movie that was ever produced. The photodiode, inevitably, would go on signaling whether the amount of light for each frame is above or below its threshold: to a photodiode, things can only be one of two ways . . . For you, however, a light screen is different not only from a dark screen, but from a multitude of other images, so when you say "light," it really means this specific way versus countless other ways, such as a red screen, a green screen, a blue screen, this movie frame, that movie frame, and so on for every movie frame (not to mention for a sound, smell, thought, or any combination of the above). Clearly, each frame looks different to you, implying that some mechanism in your brain must be able to tell it apart from all the others. So when you say "light," whether you think about it or not (and you typically won't), you have just made a discrimination among a very large number of alternatives (pp. 217–218).

And so, according to this theory, effective connectivity is key because the number of potential alternative states that the brain can take on determines the amount of information contained in the brain's present state. Tononi calls this measure of integrated information "phi," and quantitative models for computing the value of phi can be found, for example, in David Balduzzi and Giulio Tononi (2008, 2009) and in Larissa Albantakis and colleagues (2023). Many of the facts and findings that were reviewed in the first section of this chapter can be interpreted from the perspective of IIT. Instead of running through these, however, we'll conclude with a set of reanalyses of data from some of these, plus other studies, that demonstrate how something so seemingly abstract and recondite as a quantitative theory of consciousness can have practical applications.

A Practical Application of Integrated Information Theory A problem that we considered earlier in this chapter is determining whether patients diagnosed with UWS truly lack all conscious awareness. A team co-led by Adenauer Casali and Olivia Gosseries has sought to address this problem by applying the following rationale:

> Phenomenologically, each conscious experience is both differentiated – that is, it has many specific features that distinguish it from a large repertoire of other experiences – and integrated – that is, it cannot be divided into independent components. Neurophysiologically, these fundamental properties of subjective experience rely on the ability of multiple, functionally specialized areas of the thalamocortical system to interact rapidly and effectively to form an integrated whole . . . Hence, an emerging idea in theoretical neuroscience is that consciousness requires an optimal balance between functional integration and functional differentiation in thalamocortical networks – otherwise defined as brain complexity . . . This kind of complexity should be high when consciousness is present and low whenever consciousness is lost in sleep, anaesthesia or coma (Casali et al., 2013, n.p.).

To assay IIT-inspired complexity in real brains, Casali et al. (2013) developed a measure inspired by phi, called the Perturbational Complexity Index (PCI). From one perspective, it's an approach that's similar in spirit to the "dimensional activation" estimate of complexity in the EEG that was used by Velly et al. 2007 (*Figure 20.4*). However, because the PCI is derived from TMS-evoked signal in the EEG, it is (1) potentially more sensitive (because perturbation of a system with an exogenous force can sometimes reveal properties of a system that aren't evident just by observing it) and (2) not as susceptible to variability in the state of the brain at the time of measurement (because it is computed as a difference score between baseline EEG and the TMS-evoked response in the EEG). (For example, if an individual is experiencing pain or not experiencing pain at the time of EEG measurement, these measurements will be quite different. However, [TMS/EEG_{pain} – EEG_{pain}] is likely to be comparable to [$TMS/EEG_{no\ pain}$ – $EEG_{no\ pain}$].) "[O]perationally, PCI is defined as the normalized Lempel–Ziv complexity of the spatiotemporal pattern of cortical activation triggered by a direct TMS perturbation," and those who want to dig into the details are directed to Casali et al. (2013).

Figure 20.11 illustrates the PCI derived from patients suffering from the neurological syndromes that we reviewed in the first section of this chapter, as well as from individuals in different states of consciousness produced by anesthesia or by sleep. Perhaps most impressively, and most promisingly, it shows the PCI to be sensitive to different levels of consciousness, as associated, for example, with pre-anesthesia wakefulness vs. intermediate levels of anesthesia vs. deep levels. This holds out the promise of a clinically practical procedure, and one far less expensive than fMRI, to objectively, quantitatively, confirm the diagnosis, for example, of persistent vegetative state/UWS.

FIGURE 20.11 The PCI applied to anesthesia, sleep, and neurological syndromes of consciousness.

Source: From Casali, Adenauer G., Olivia Gosseries, Mario Rosanova, Mélanie Boly, Simone Sarasso, Karina R. Casali, Marcello Massimini. 2013. "A Theoretically Based Index of Consciousness Independent of Sensory Processing and Behavior." *Science Translational Medicine* 5 (198): 198ra105. Reproduced with permission of American Association for the Advancement of Science - AAAS.

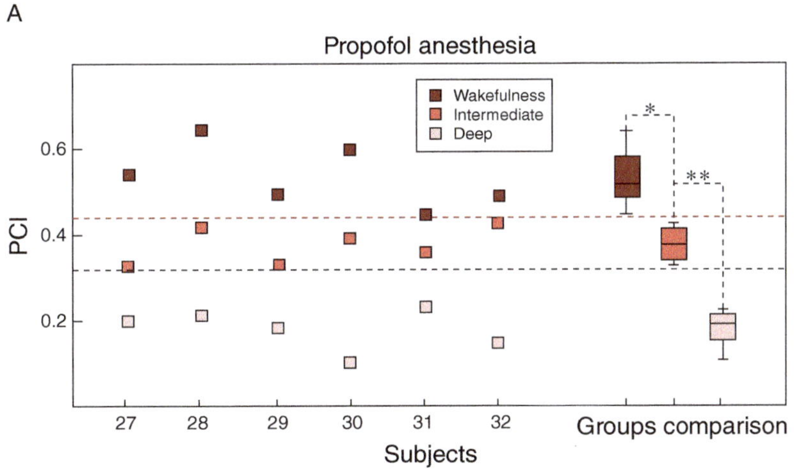

FIGURE 20.11.A PCI is sensitive to graded changes in the level of propofol anesthesia; data from six individual subjects.

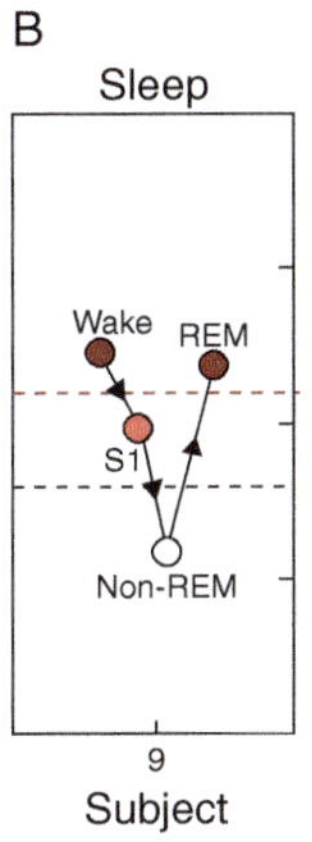

FIGURE 20.11.B PCI is sensitive to changes in sleep state, as illustrated in a single subject transitioning from wakefulness to sleep stage N1 (S1) to non-REM sleep to REM sleep.

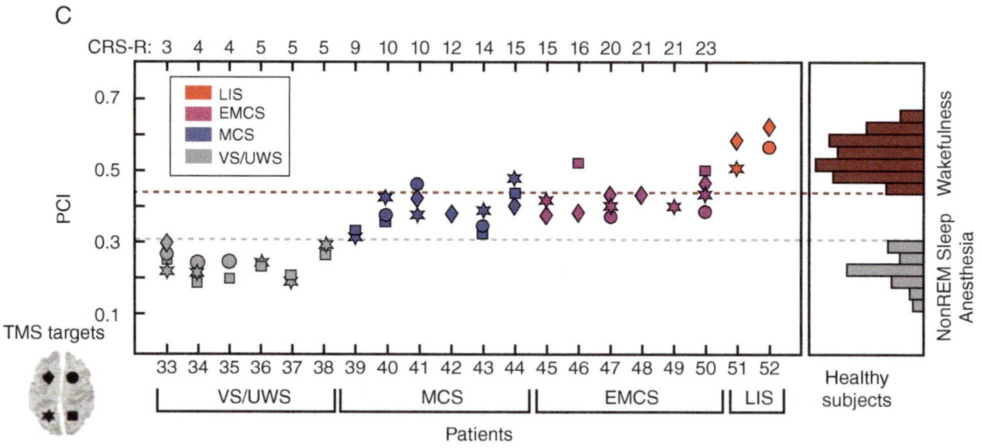

FIGURE 20.11.C PCI, estimated from TMS delivered to each of the four locations indicated on the legend, discriminates vegetative state/unresponsive wakefulness syndrome (VS/UWS) from minimally conscious state (MCS) and emerging-from-MCS (EMCS) from locked-in syndrome (LIS). For comparison, to the right are histograms showing the distribution of PCI scores from healthy individuals in non-REM sleep or under deep general anesthesia, and in wakefulness.

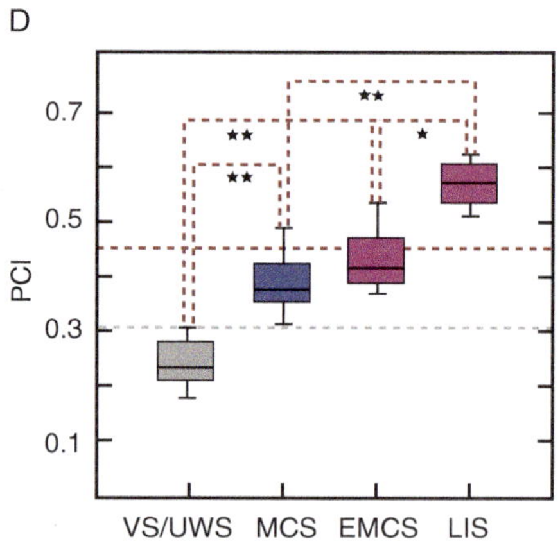

FIGURE 20.11.D Group data from the four neurological groups.

Updating the Consciousness Graph

At the conclusion of this chapter, although we haven't definitively answered the question *What is the Biological Basis of Consciousness?* (not to mention the Origin of the Universe; nor, for that matter, the Meaning of Life . . .), we are, at least, in a position to put some more satisfactory labels on the vertical axis of our two-dimensions-of-consciousness graph (*Figure 20.2*): the level of awareness seems to depend on connectivity, particularly of lateral and feedback projections, and the complexity of cortical activity that these connections underlie. Of course, there's so much more that we don't yet understand. But amazing discoveries about the neural bases of cognition are being made practically every day. And who knows? Perhaps, gentle reader, it will be you who one day solves the puzzle of the biological bases of consciousness!

End-of-Chapter Questions

1. What factors – physiological and behavioral – differentiate coma from persistent vegetative state/unresponsive wakefulness syndrome? From locked-in syndrome?

2. Describe the role of the reticular activating system in physiological arousal. How does its activity vary in wakefulness vs. non-REM vs. REM sleep?

3. Are the effects of general anesthesia – physiologically and behaviorally – more akin to coma or to sleep? What physiological change occurs abruptly at the point of anesthesia-induced loss of consciousness?

4. How have scientists addressed the question of whether activity in early sensory cortex more closely reflects events in the outside world or our subjective experience of events in the outside world? And what have they learned?

5. Two sets of studies have emphasized two distinct kinds of physiological response that seem to correspond to whether or not one will be consciously aware of a visually presented stimulus; summarize these.

6. What are the key tenets of Global Neuronal Workspace Theory? Of Recurrent Processing Theory? Of Integrated Information Theory? Is it possible that more than one of these could be "right"?

7. What are the biological bases of consciousness?

References

Alkire, T. Michael. 2009. "General Anaesthesia and Consciousness." In *The Neurology of Consciousness: Cognitive Neuroscience and Neuropathology*, edited by Steven Laureys and Giulio Tononi (pp. 118–134). Amsterdam: Elsevier.

Balduzzi, David, and Giulio Tononi. 2008. "Integrated Information in Discrete Dynamical Systems: Motivation and Theoretical Framework." *PLoS Computational Biology* 4 (6): e1000091. doi: 10.1371/journal.pcbi.1000091.

Balduzzi, David, and Giulio Tononi. 2009. "Qualia: The Geometry of Integrated Information." *PLoS Computational Biology* 5 (8): e1000462. doi: 10.1371/journal.pcbi.1000462.

Bauby, Jean-Dominique. 1997. *The Diving Bell and the Butterfly*. Translated by Jeremy Leggatt. New York: Knopf.

Block, Ned. 1996. "How Can We Find the Neural Correlate of Consciousness?." *Trends in Neurosciences* 19 (11): 456–459. doi: 10.1016/S0166-2236(96)20049-9.

Casali, Adenauer G., Olivia Gosseries, Mario Rosanova, Mélanie Boly, Simone Sarasso, Karina R. Casali, . . . Marcello Massimini. 2013. "A Theoretically Based Index of Consciousness Independent of Sensory Processing and Behavior." *Science Translational Medicine* 5 (198): 198ra105. doi: 10.1126/scitranslmed.3006294.

Chelazzi, Leonardo, John Duncan, Earl K. Miller, and Robert Desimone. 1998. "Responses of Neurons in Inferior Temporal Cortex during Memory-Guided Visual Search." *Journal of Neurophysiology* 80 (6): 2918–2940. http://wexler.free.fr/library/files/chelazzi%20(1998)%20responses%20of%20neurons%20in%20inferior%20temporal%20cortex%20during%20memory-%20guided%20visual%20search.pdf.

Cogitate Consortium, Oscar Ferrante, Urszula Gorska-Klimowska, Simon Henin, Rony Hirschhorn, Aya Khalaf, . . . Lucia Melloni. 2025. "Adversarial Testing of Global Neuronal Workspace and Integrated Information Theories of Consciousness." *Nature*. doi: 10.1038/s41586-025-08888-1.

Crick, Francis, and Christof Koch. 1990. "Towards a Neurobiological Theory of Consciousness." *Seminars in the Neurosciences* 2: 263–275. http://authors.library.caltech.edu/40352/1/148.pdf.

Dehaene, Stanislas, Lionel Naccache, Laurent Cohen, Denis Le Bihan, Jean-François Mangin, Jean-Baptiste Poline, and Denis Rivière. 2001. "Cerebral Mechanisms of Word Masking and Unconscious Repetition Priming." *Nature Neuroscience* 4 (7): 752–758. doi: 10.1038/89551.

Dehaene, Stanislas, Claire Sergent, and Changeux Jean-Pierre. 2003. "A Neuronal Network Model Linking Subjective Reports and Objective Physiological Data during Conscious Perception." *Proceedings of the National Academy of Sciences of the United States of America* 100 (14): 8520–8525. doi: 10.1073/pnas.1332574100.

Ferrarelli, Fabio, Marcello Massimini, Simone Sarasso, Adenauer Casali, Brady A. Riedner, Giuditta Angelini, . . . Robert A. Pearce. 2010. "Breakdown in Cortical Effective Connectivity during Midazolam-Induced Loss of Consciousness." *Proceedings of the National Academy of Sciences of the United States of America* 107 (6): 2681–2686. doi: 10.1073/pnas.0913008107.

Heathcote, Elizabeth. 2011. "Emery Brown: 'Aspects of Anaesthesia Are Consistent with Patients in a Coma'." *The Observer* (April 9). http://www.theguardian.com/technology/2011/apr/10/anaesthesia-coma-sleep-emery-brown.

Koch, C., M. Massimini, M. Boly, and G. Tononi. 2016. "Neural Correlates of Consciousness: Progress and Problems." *Nature Reviews Neuroscience* 17: 307–321.

Lamme, Victor A. F. 2003. "Why Visual Attention and Awareness Are Different." *Trends in Cognitive Sciences* 7 (1): 12–18. doi: 10.1016/S1364-6613(02)00013-X.

Lamme, Victor A. F. 2006. "Towards a True Neural Stance on Consciousness." *Trends in Cognitive Sciences* 10 (11): 494–501. doi: 10.1016/j.tics.2006.09.001.

Laureys, Steven. 2005. "The Neural Correlate of (Un)Awareness: Lessons from the Vegetative State." *Trends in Cognitive Sciences* 9 (12): 556–559. doi: 10.1016/j.tics.2005.10.010.

Laureys, Steven, and Giulio Tononi, eds. 2009. *The Neurology of Consciousness*. Amsterdam: Elsevier.

Laureys, Steven, Frédéric Pellas, Philippe Van Eeckhout, Sofiane Ghorbel, Caroline Schnakers, Favien Perrin, . . . Serge Goldman. 2005. "The Locked-In Syndrome: What Is It Like to Be Conscious but Paralyzed and Voiceless?." *Progress in Brain Research* 150: 495–511. doi: 10.1016/S0079-6123(05)50034-7.

Laureys, Steven, Gastone G. Celesia, Francois Cohadon, Jan Lavrijsen, José León-Carrión, Walter G. Sannita, . . . European Task Force on Disorders of Consciousness. 2010. "Unresponsive Wakefulness Syndrome: A New Name for the Vegetative State or Apallic Syndrome." *BMC Medicine* 8 (1): 68. doi: 10.1186/1741-7015-8-68.

Li, Fei, Rufin Van Rullen, Christof Koch, and Pietro Perona. 2002. "Rapid Natural Scene Categorization in the Near Absence of Attention." *Proceedings of the National Academy of Sciences of the United States of America* 99 (14): 9596–9601. doi: 10.1073/pnas.092277599.

Massimini, Marcello, Fabio Farrarelli, Reto Huber, Steve K. Esser, Harpreet Singh, and Giulio Tononi. 2005. "Breakdown of Cortical Effective Connectivity during Sleep." *Science* 309 (5744): 2228–2232. doi: 10.1126/science.1117256.

Mathewson, Kyle E., Alejandro Lleras, Diane M. Beck, Monica Fabiani, Tony Ro, and Gabriele Gratton. 2011. "Pulsed Out of Awareness: EEG Alpha Oscillations Represent a Pulsed-Inhibition of Ongoing Cortical Processing." *Frontiers in Psychology* 2: 99. doi: 10.3389/fpsyg.2011.00099.

Monti, Martin M., Audrey Vanhaudenhuyse, Martin R. Coleman, Melanie Boly, John D. Pickard, Luaba Tshibanda, . . . Steven Laureys. 2010. "Willful Modulation of Brain Activity in Disorders of Consciousness." *New England Journal of Medicine* 362 (7): 579–589. doi: 10.1056/NEJMoa0905370.

Naccache, Lionel, Elise Blandin, and Stanislas Dehaene. 2002. "Unconscious Masked Priming Depends On Temporal Attention." *Psychological Science* 13 (5): 416–424. doi: 10.1111/1467-9280.00474.

Owen, Adrian M., Martin R. Coleman, Melanie Boly, Matthew H. Davis, Steven Laureys, and John D. Pickard. 2006. "Detecting Awareness in the Vegetative State." *Science* 212 (5792): 1402. doi: 10.1126/science.1130197.

Plum, Fred, and Jerome B. Posner. 1983. *The Diagnosis of Stupor and Coma*. Philadelphia, PA: F. A. Davis.

Ress, David, and David J. Heeger. 2003. "Neural Correlates of Perception in Early Visual Cortex." *Nature Neuroscience* 6 (4): 414–420. doi: 10.1038/nn1024.

Romei, Vincenzo, Verena Brodbeck, Christoph Michel, Amir Amedi, Alvaro Pascual-Leone, and Gregor Thut. 2008. "Spontaneous Fluctuations in Posterior [alpha]-Band EEG Activity Reflect Variability in Excitability of Human Visual Areas." *Cerebral Cortex* 18 (9): 2010–2018. doi: 10.1093/cercor/bhm229.

Rosanova, Mario, Olivia Gosseries, Silvia Casarotto, Mélanie Boly, Adenauer G. Casali, Marie-Aurélie Bruno, . . . Marcello Massimini. 2012. "Recovery of Cortical Effective Connectivity and Recovery of Consciousness in Vegetative Patients." *Brain* 135 (4): 1308–1320.

Sperling, George. 1960. "The Information Available in Brief Visual Presentations." *Psychological Monographs* 74 (11): 1–29. doi: 10.1037/h0093759.

Supèr, Hans, Henk Spekreijse, and Victor A. F. Lamme. 2001. "Two Distinct Modes of Sensory Processing Observed in Monkey Primary Visual Cortex (V1)." *Nature Neuroscience* 4 (3): 304–310. doi: 10.1038/85170.

Tononi, Giulio. 2008. "Consciousness as Integrated Information: A Provisional Manifesto." *Biological Bulletin* 215 (3): 216–242. doi: 10.2307/25470707.

Tsuchiya, Naotsugu, and Christof Koch. 2009. "The Relationship Between Consciousness and Attention." In *The Neurology of Consciousness: Cognitive Neuroscience and Neuropathology*, edited by Steven Laureys and Giulio Tononi (pp. 63–77). Amsterdam: Elsevier.

Velly, Lionel J., Marc F. Rey, Nicolas J. Bruder, François A. Gouvitsos, Tatiana Witjas, Jean Marie Regis, . . . François M. Gouin. 2007. "Differential Dynamic of Action on Cortical and Subcortical Structures of Anesthetic Agents during Induction of Anesthesia." *Anesthesiology* 107 (2): 202–212. doi: 10.1097/01.anes.0000270734.99298.b4.

Vigand, Phillipe, and Stephane Vigand. 2000. *Only the Eyes Say Yes: A Love Story. English* language edition. New York: Arcade.

Young, G. Brian. 2009. "Coma." In *The Neurology of Consciousness: Cognitive Neuroscience and Neuropathology*, edited by Steven Laureys and Giulio Tononi (pp. 137–150). Amsterdam: Elsevier.

Yu, Q., and B. R. Postle. 2021. "The Neural Codes Underlying Internally Generated Representations in Visual Working Memory." *Journal of Cognitive Neuroscience 33*: 1142–1157. doi: 10.1162/jocn_a_01702.

Other Sources Used

Albantakis L., Barbosa L., Findlay G., Grasso M., Haun A. M., Marshall W., Mayner W. G. P., Zaeemzadeh A., Boly M., Juel B. E., Sasai S., Fujii K., David I., Hendren J., Lang J. P., and Tononi G. 2023. "Integrated information theory (IIT) 4.0: formulating the properties of phenomenal existence in physical terms." *PLoS Comput Biol 19:* e1011465. https://doi.org/10.1371/journal.pcbi.1011465 pmid:37847724.

Baars, Bernard J. 2005. "Global Workspace Theory of Consciousness: Toward a Cognitive Neuroscience of Human Experience?." *Progress in Brain Research* 150: 45–53. doi: 10.1016/S0079-6123(05)50004-9.

Boly, Melanie, Marcello Massimini, Naotsugu Tsuchiya, Bradley R. Postle, Christof Koch, and Giulio Tononi. 2017. "Are the Neural Correlates of Consciousness in the Front or in the Back of the Cerebral Cortex?." *The Journal of Neuroscience* 37: 9603–9613.

Gosseries, Olivia, Marie-Aurélie Bruno, Audrey Vanhaudenhuyse, Steven Laureys, and Caroline Schnakers. 2009. "Consciousness in the Locked-In Syndrome." In *The Neurology of Consciousness: Cognitive Neuroscience and Neuropathology*, edited by Steven Laureys and Giulio Tononi (pp. 191–203). Amsterdam: Elsevier.

Lau, Hakwan. 2011. "Theoretical Motivations for Investigating the Neural Correlates of Consciousness." *WIREs Cognitive Science* 2 (1): 1–7. doi: 10.1002/wcs.93.

Laureys, Steven, Maryliese E. Faymonville, Maurice Lamy AndréLuxen, George Franck, and Pierre Maquet. 2000. "Restoration of Thalamocortical Connectivity after Recovery from Persistent Vegetative State." *Lancet* 355 (9217): 1790–1791. doi: 10.1016/S0140-6736(00)02271-6.

Laureys, Steven, Christian Lemaire, Pierre Maquet, Christophe Phillips, and George Franck. 1999. "Cerebral Metabolism during Vegetative State and after Recovery to Consciousness." *Journal of Neurology, Neurosurgery, and Psychiatry* 67 (1): 121–122. doi: 10.1136/jnnp.67.1.121.

Shannon, Claude E. 1948. "A Mathematical Theory of Communication." *Bell System Technical Journal* 27 (3): 379–423. doi: 10.1002/j.1538-7305.1948.tb01338.x.

Tononi, Giulio. 2009. "Sleep and Dreaming." In *The Neurology of Consciousness: Cognitive Neuroscience and Neuropathology*, edited by Steven Laureys and Giulio Tononi (pp. 89–107). Amsterdam: Elsevier.

Van, Rullen, Niko A. Rufin, Jan Drewes Busch, and Julien Dubois. 2011. "Ongoing EEG Phase as a Trial-by-Trial Predictor of Perceptual and Attentional Variability." *Frontiers in Psychology* 2. doi: 10.3389/fpsyg.2011.00060.

Further Reading

An authoritative and succinct summary of the history of the study of this intriguing phenomenon.

Brown, Emery N, Ralph Lydic, and Nicholas D Schiff. 2010. "General Anesthesia, Sleep, and Coma." *New England Journal of Medicine* 363 (27): 2638–2650. doi: 10.1056/NEJMra0808281.

Authoritative review by prominent clinician-scientists focusing on the neural mechanisms of unconsciousness induced by selected intravenous anesthetic drugs.

Crick, Francis. 1994. *The Astonishing Hypothesis: The Scientific Search for the Soul.* New York: Scribner.

Francis Crick's influential book is among the publications that contributed to making consciousness a respectable topic for study by mainstream cognitive neuroscientists.

Crick, Francis. 1996. "Visual Perception: Rivalry and Consciousness." *Nature* 379 (6565): 485–486. doi: 10.1038/379485a0.

A succinct statement of why and how the study of binocular rivalry has important implications for understanding the neural correlates of consciousness.

Engel, Andreas K., Pascal Fries, Peter König, Michael Brecht, and Wolf Singer. 1999. "Temporal Binding, Binocular Rivalry, and Consciousness." *Consciousness and Cognition* 8 (2): 128–151. doi: 10.1006/ccog.1999.0389.

Summary of the influential view that oscillatory synchrony among anatomically distal brain areas is of central importance to conscious experience; also reviews binocular rivalry, a phenomenon that is often used in the study of visual awareness.

Laureys, Steven, Olivia Gosseries, and Giulio Tononi, eds. 2015. *The Neurology of Consciousness*, 2nd ed. Amsterdam: Elsevier.

A volume containing chapters by a proverbial "veritable who's-who" of scientific and clinical experts on disorders of consciousness.

Leopold, David A., and Nikos K. Logothetis. 1996. "Activity Changes in Early Visual Cortex Reflect Monkeys' Percepts during Binocular Rivalry." *Nature* 379 (6565): 549–553. doi: 10.1038/379549a0.

An empirical paper that Crick (1996) declared "among the opening salvos of a concerted attack on the baffling problem of consciousness."

Nir, Yuval, and Giulio Tononi. 2010. "Dreaming and the Brain: From Phenomenology to Neurophysiology." *Trends in Cognitive Sciences* 14 (2): 88–100. doi: 10.1016/j.tics.2009.12.001.

Overview of this fascinating arena from which to study consciousness.

Seager, William. 2007. "A Brief History of the Philosophical Problem of Consciousness." In *The Cambridge Handbook of Consciousness*, edited by Philip David Zelazo, Morris Moscovitch, and Evan Thompson (pp. 9–33). New York: Cambridge University Press.

This chapter offers a nice overview for the nonphilosopher.

Tononi, Giulio. 2012. *Phi: A Voyage from the Brain to the Soul.* New York: Pantheon Books.

A literary, fantastical dream in which Galileo, alternately guided by Francis Crick, Alan Turing, and Charles Darwin, encounters a variety of neurological patients whose syndromes define the parameters of consciousness.

Recent studies of cell-electrophysiological bases of anesthetic loss of consciousness include the following:

Bastos, André M., Jacob A. Donoghue, Scott L. Brincat, Meredith Mahnke, Jorge Yanar, Josefina Correa, . . . Miller, Earl K. (2021). Neural Effects of Propofol-Induced Unconsciousness and Its Reversal Using Thalamic Stimulation. *eLife, 10*. doi: 10.7554/eLife.60824.

Bhattacharya, Sayak, Jacob A. Donoghue, Meredith Mahnke, Scott L. Brincat, Emery N. Brown, and Earl K. Miller. 2022. "Propofol Anesthesia Alters Cortical Traveling Waves." *Journal of Cognitive Neuroscience 34* (7): 1274–1286. doi: 10.1162/jocn_a_01856.

Eisen, Adam J., Leo Kozachkov, Andre M. Bastos, Jacob A. Donoghue, Meredith K. Mahnke, Scott L. Brincat, . . . Miller, Earl K. (2024). Propofol Anesthesia Destabilizes neural Dynamics Across Cortex. *Neuron, 112*(16), 2799–2813 e2799. doi: 10.1016/j.neuron.2024.06.011.

Gomez-Marin, Alex, and Anil K. Seth. 2025. "A Science of Consciousness Beyond Pseudo-Science and Pseudo-Consciousness." *Nature Neuroscience 28* (4): 703–706. doi: 10.1038/s41593-025-01913-6.

IIT-Concerned, Fleming, Stephen, Chris D. Frith, Mel Goodale, Hakwan Lau, Joseph E. LeDoux, . . . Slagter, Heleen A. (2023). The Integrated Information Theory of Consciousness as Pseudoscience. *PsyArXiv Preprints, version 1 (Original Publication Date 2023-09-15).* doi: https://doi.org/10.31234/osf.io/zsr78.

IIT-Concerned, Michal Klincewicz, Tong Cheng, Michael Schmitz, Migual A. Sebastián, and Joel S. Snyder. 2025. "What Makes a Theory of Consciousness Unscientific?." *Nature Neuroscience 28*: 689–693. doi: doi-org.ezproxy.library.wisc.edu/10.1038/s41593-025-01881-x.

Lundqvist, Mikael, Scott L. Brincat, Jonas Rose, Melissa R. Warden, Timothy J. Buschman, Earl K. Miller, and Pawel Herman. 2023. "Working Memory Control Dynamics Follow Principles of Spatial Computing." *Nature Communications 14* (1): 1429. doi: 10.1038/s41467-023-36555-4.

Redinbaugh, Michelle J., Mohsen Afrasiabi, Jessica M. Phillips, Niranjan A. Kambi, Sounak Mohanta, Aeyal Raz, and Yuri B. Saalmann. 2022. "Thalamic Deep Brain Stimulation Paradigm to Reduce Consciousness: Cortico-Striatal Dynamics Implicated in Mechanisms of Consciousness." *PLoS Computational Biology 18* (7): e1010294. doi: 10.1371/journal.pcbi.1010294.

Redinbaugh, Michelle J., Jessica M. Phillips, Niranjan A. Kambi, Sounak Mohanta, Samantha Andryk, Gaven L. Dooley, . . . Yuri B. Saalmann. 2020. "Thalamus Modulates Consciousness via Layer-Specific Control of Cortex." *Neuron 106* (1): 66–75 e12. doi: 10.1016/j.neuron.2020.01.005.

Redinbaugh, Michelle J., and Yuri B. Saalmann. 2024. "Contributions of Basal Ganglia Circuits to Perception, Attention, and Consciousness." *Journal of Cognitive Neuroscience 36* (8): 1620–1642. doi: 10.1162/jocn_a_02177.

Tauber, John M., Scott L. Brincat, Emily P. Stephen, Jacob A. Donoghue, Leo Kozachkov, Emery N. Brown, and Earl K. Miller. 2024. "Propofol-Mediated Unconsciousness Disrupts Progression of Sensory Signals through the Cortical Hierarchy." *Journal of Cognitive Neuroscience 36* (2): 394–413. doi: 10.1162/jocn_a_02081.

Tononi, Giulio, Larissa Albantakis, Leonardo Barbosa, Melanie Boly, Chiara Cirelli, Renzo Comolatti, . . . Zaeemzadeh, Alireza (2025). Consciousness or Pseudo-Consciousness? A Clash of Two Paradigms. *Nature Neuroscience, 28*(4), 694–702. doi: 10.1038/s41593-025-01880-y.

Whyte, Christopher J., Michelle J. Redinbaugh, James M. Shine, and Yuri B. Saalmann. 2024. "Thalamic Contributions to the State and Contents of Consciousness." *Neuron 112* (10): 1611–1625. doi: 10.1016/j.neuron.2024.04.019.

Debate about the scientific status of IIT

Blake, Randolph, and Frank Tong. 2008. "Binocular Rivalry." *Scholarpedia* 3 (12): 1578. doi: 10.4249/scholarpedia.1578.

Gomez-Marin, Alex. 2023. "The Consciousness of Neuroscience." *eNeuro 10* (11): ENEURO.0434-23.2023. doi: 10.1523/ENEURO.0434-23.2023.

Gomez-Marin, Alex, and Anil K. Seth. 2025. "A Science of Consciousness Beyond Pseudo-Science and Pseudo-Consciousness." *Nature Neuroscience 28* (4): 703–706. doi: 10.1038/s41593-025-01913-6.

IIT-Concerned, Fleming, Stephen, Chris D. Frith, Mel Goodale, Hakwan Lau, Joseph E. LeDoux, . . . Slagter, Heleen A. (2023). The Integrated Information Theory of Consciousness as Pseudoscience. *PsyArXiv Preprints, version 1 (Original Publication Date 2023-09-15).* doi: https://doi.org/10.31234/osf.io/zsr78.

This is the original "pseudoscience" letter. The definitive, archival statement of this argument was published as IIT-Concerned et al. (2025).

IIT-Concerned, Michał Klincewicz, Tony Cheng, Michael Schmitz, Miguel Ángel Sebastián, and Joel S. Snyder. 2025. "What makes a theory of consciousness unscientific?." *Nature Neuroscience 28*: 689–693. doi: doi-org.ezproxy.library.wisc.edu/10.1038/s41593-025-01881-x.

Tononi, Giulio, Larissa Albantakis, Leonardo Barbosa, Melanie Boly, Chiara Cirelli, Renzo Comolatt, . . . Zaeemzadeh, Alireza (2025). Consciousness or Pseudo-Consciousness? A Clash of Two Paradigms. *Nature Neuroscience, 28*(4), 694-702. doi: 10.1038/s41593-025-01880-y

Glossary

acoustic energy The movement of and collisions between molecules of the gases that make up the air that's all around us; or, when underwater, collisions between and movement of molecules of water (and all that is dissolved in it).

action An isolated movement, or a coordinated series of movements intended to achieve some behavioral goal.

affective neuroscience The study of the neural bases of emotions. Because disorders of emotional processing are often characteristic of, if not at the root of, many types of psychopathology (e.g., depression, addiction, generalized anxiety disorder), there is considerable overlap between affective neuroscience and clinical psychology. (Affective is the adjectival form of the noun affect, a synonym for emotion.)

allocentric localization The representation of space in an environment-centered coordinate system (e.g., "the cup is on the table" is a property of the cup that does not change as you move from one room to another).

AMPA receptor Glutamate-gated sodium channel.

anatomical specificity This refers to the degree to which a particular effect on behavior is attributable to only a particular anatomical region.

anions A general term for negatively charged ions.

anomia An inability to produce the appropriate verbal label for objects (i.e., an inability to "name" things).

anoxia Deprivation of oxygen to brain tissue.

anterior Used as a term of direction, it refers to the front (a synonym, introduced in *Chapter 2*, is "rostral").

antisaccade task A task requiring a speeded saccade in the opposite direction of a target; it requires cognitive control to overcome the prepotent tendency to saccade to the salient onset of a stimulus in the environment.

aperture problem The small size of receptive fields at early stages of the visual system can result in ambiguities when local information present within the aperture is inconsistent with global information in the scene.

aphasia An inability to use language following brain damage.

attention deficit hyperactivity disorder A neurological condition associated with difficulty sustaining attention, difficulty controlling behavior, and, in some cases, hyperactivity.

attention The prioritization of the processing of a subset of the information that is available at any given moment in time.

auditory nerve The bundle of axons that carry auditory information from the cochlear nucleus to the brainstem auditory nuclei.

autism spectrum disorder A developmental disorder characterized by deficits in social communication and social interaction, and often accompanied by restricted, repetitive patterns of behavior, interests, or activities.

avoidance learning Context-dependent skeletomotor behaviors that, when engaged, enable an organism to avoid the adverse outcome predicted by a conditioned stimulus (CS).

axon hillock Region of the cell body from which the axon emerges. The membrane of the hillock is dense with voltage-gated Na^+ channels, such that it can powerfully initiate action potentials.

axonal transport Intracellular mechanisms for transporting proteins from the cell body to locations along the axon, often to presynaptic terminals.

axons The branches via which a neuron sends signals to other neurons. Most axons have many "collateral" arms splitting off from the main branch, thereby enabling a single neuron to influence hundreds, thousands, and in some cases tens of thousands of other neurons.

barrel cortex The region of rodent somatosensory cortex containing groupings of neurons in layer IV – "barrels" – that, together, represent somatosensory signals coming from a single whisker.

basilar membrane The membrane within the cochlea whose vibrations effect the spectral transformation of acoustic energy, which is subsequently encoded in the cochlear nucleus's place code. The base of the basilar membrane is the portion nearest the oval window and is maximally displaced by high frequencies. The apex is the "far end" of the basilar membrane and is maximally displaced by low frequencies.

binding problem The fact that anatomically distinct parts of the brain encode what an object is vs. where it is, yet our perception is of an object occupying (i.e., "bound to") a location.

binocular rivalry The phenomenon that when a different image is presented to each eye, one sees only one of the two at any given point of time, and the perceived image alternates, stochastically, between the two.

blood oxygen level-dependent (BOLD) signal The signal most commonly detected by fMRI, measured via T2* relaxation.

blood–brain barrier The layer of endothelial cells lining the inside walls of blood vessels that prevents the diffusion from capillaries of many substances carried in the bloodstream.

brain The organ of the body responsible for the control of all other systems of the body, and thus for the control of behavior. In anatomical terms, the brain is composed of the brainstem, cerebellum, and cerebrum (see *Chapter 2*).

brainstem auditory nuclei The many subcortical nuclei that process the auditory signal prior to the inferior colliculus, medial geniculate nucleus, and primary auditory cortex.

brainstem oculomotor nuclei Neurons located at the rostrocaudal level of the superior colliculus, whose axons innervate the muscles that control the position and movements of the eyes (the "extraocular muscles").

cations A general term for positively charged ions.

central nervous system Comprises the brain plus the spinal cord and the motor neurons that leave the cord to innervate the muscles of the body.

cerebellum The highly folded structure that lies "below" the "back" of the cerebral cortex. (See *Figure 1.2*; technically precise terms of direction are introduced in Chapter 2.)

cerebral hemisphere The cerebrum is the largest part of the brain (in volume), sitting atop the brainstem. It is divided into two roughly symmetrical halves, each referred to as a hemisphere.

cerebrospinal fluid (CSF) The fluid that circulates through the ventricles (thereby inflating the brain) and also along the exterior surface of the CNS (thereby providing a medium in which the brain floats).

cerebrum Also referred to as the forebrain, the cerebrum is the anterior-most part of the brain, and the largest in volume. Deriving from the embryonic telencephalon, it comprises the thalamus plus all the tissue that is rostral to it. Major elements include the five lobes of the cerebral cortex, basal ganglia, hippocampus, thalamus, and all the white matter connecting these structures.

choice probability A measure derived by relating variations in neuronal activity evoked by sensory signals to variations in behavioral choices prompted by those same sensory signals.

cognition Thinking. This word derives from Ancient Greek and Latin words meaning "to know" or "to learn" and, in some translations, "to recognize."

cognitive neuroscience The studies of the neural bases (e.g., anatomical, physiological, pharmacological, genetic) of cognition and the behaviors that have traditionally fallen under the purview of cognitive psychology.

cognitive psychology Cognitive psychology is the study of the information processing that intervenes between sensory inputs and motoric outputs. Domains of mental activity and behavior that it covers include those covered in this book, beginning with *Chapter 6*.

conjugate eye movements Movements of the two eyes in parallel (i.e., with the same vector).

consolidation In the context of long-term memory, consolidation is the hypothesized process whereby, over time, memories become more resistant to disruption.

construct validity The extent to which there is a principled basis for asserting the existence of a psychological, or physiological, construct.

contralateral delay activity (CDA) An ERP component that scales with the amount of information being held in visual working memory and that asymptotes at the subject's estimated visual working memory capacity.

convolution (*n.*; to convolve, *v.*) The transformation of a function (e.g., a time-varying signal) that results from passing it through a filter.

coordinate transformations The conversion of spatial information from one reference frame to another, such as when re-representing a location initially encoded in eye-centered coordinates into head-centered coordinates.

corpus callosum (Latin for "tough body," presumably because, relative to other structures, it is difficult for the anatomist to cut through or pull apart.) The corpus callosum is made up of millions of axons that project between neurons in the two hemispheres.

cortex Refers to the layer of tissue containing cell bodies and, thus, is often synonymous with "gray matter." Cortex is the Latin name for "rind," and thus the name references the outer covering of many types of fruit, such as melons or citrus fruit. The cerebrum and cerebellum each have a cortex.

cortical column A group of neurons that are stacked, as though in an imaginary tube that is oriented orthogonal to the cortical surface. Neurons within a cortical column are more strongly interconnected, and, therefore, share more functional properties, than are physically adjacent neurons that are not within the same column.

cortical magnification The phenomenon that higher-resolution regions of a sensory-transduction surface, or more finely controlled muscles, are represented by larger areas of cortex.

cotransport Process whereby more than one molecule is simultaneously carried across a cell membrane, as with neurotransmitter reuptake.

covert attention Attention deployed toward an object or location without looking directly at it.

craniotomy Surgical procedure of removing a portion of the cranium (skull) in order to expose a portion of the underlying brain tissue.

decision variable A hypothesized representation of all the accruing information related to a decision.

declarative memory Long-term memory that entails conscious retrieval of information from one's past. Synonymous with explicit memory.

deep neural networks (DNNs) A class of artificial neural networks with a feedforward architecture and multiple serially connected hidden layers, which are particularly adept at classification (e.g., of visual images, or of speech sounds).

degrees of visual angle When foveating an object in the environment, the surface area of retina that that object occupies can be expressed as an angle anchored in the fovea, and whose imaginary sides project to the left and right edges (or top and bottom edges) of the object. At a given distance from the retina, the larger the object, the wider the degrees of visual angle that it occupies.

delay discounting The tendency to assign less value to a reward if its delivery will occur at some point in the future, rather than immediately.

delayed match-to-sample (DMS) A recognition memory test in which memory for a previously presented sample stimulus is assessed at test by re-presenting it along with one or more foil stimuli.

delayed recognition A recognition memory test in which memory for one or more previously presented sample stimuli is assessed at test by decision of whether or not a single probe item was presented as a sample. (Although this definition also applies if memory is tested by re-presentation of the entire array of sample items, and judgement of whether or not the test array is identical to the sample array, such a procedure is more commonly referred to as "change detection.")

dementia A progressive impairment of intellect and behavior that, over time, dramatically alters and restricts normal activities of daily living. Although typically compromising memory, dementia differs from amnesia in that it also affects at least one other domain of cognition (e.g., language, motor control, visual perception, . . .).

dendrites The branches of a neuron that receive signals from other neurons see, for example, (Figure 2.6).

depolarize To make the membrane potential of a cell more positive. Typically, because the resting state of neurons is negative, this is equivalent to making the membrane potential less negative.

Diencephalon commonly referred to as the thalamus. Large collection of nuclei located near the center of the cerebrum, straddling the midline and immediately rostral (see *Figure 1.2*) to the midbrain. First-order thalamic nuclei serve as relay points between peripheral sensory information and the cerebral cortex; higher-order thalamic nuclei link nonprimary cortical areas, in some cases by projecting "back to cortex" as the final stage in a cortico-basal ganglia-thalamic loop.

diffusion tensor imaging A type of MRI that measures the diffusion of water to infer information about white-matter tracts.

dipole An object with a positive charge at one end and a negative charge at the other.

distributed system A system in which functions arise from the contribution of many processing elements performing simple computations (i.e., carrying out simple functions) that often bear little surface resemblance to the function in question. These elements may or may not be anatomically distant from each other.

double dissociation of function A pattern of results in which damage to area A affects performance on task X, but not on task Y; whereas damage to area B affects performance on task Y, but not on task X.

dynamics The forces and torques that produce movement or motion.

dysphasia An impairment in the ability to communicate following brain damage (compare with aphasia).

efference copy The principle of sending a copy of the motor command (see **motor efferent**), via a recurrent projection to a circuit (often in a different brain region) that is not directly involved in motor execution.

egocentric localization The representation of space in a body-centered coordinate system (e.g., "the cup is to my right; if I rotate in place by 180° the cup will be to my left").

electrocorticography (ECoG) Electrical recordings made from the surface of the cortex.

emergent property A property that is characteristic of a system, but that is not reducible to the properties of the system's constituent elements.

encoding In the context of neural function, the representation of a piece of information via a change in the activity and/or connectivity of a population of neurons; in the context of memory, encoding refers to the processing of newly encountered information such that it can be stored and later retrieved.

engram The hypothetical physical representation of a memory in the brain.

ensembles From the French for "together," this term is often used to refer to a group of neurons that are "working together" as a functional unit. One analogy is to a musical ensemble, such as a string quartet.

epilepsy A chronic condition characterized by repeated seizures.

epileptogenic Brain tissue with a low threshold for initiating seizure activity, as is the case of tissue that is a source of origination of seizure activity in epilepsy.

episodic memory Declarative memory that includes a representation of the context associated with the episode being remembered (e.g., the place where an event happened, the time that the event happened (e.g., time of day, and/or time of the year), and/or the social circumstances that were in place, and/or the people who were present, etc.).

equipotentiality The idea that any given piece of cortical tissue has the potential to support any brain function.

etiology The cause of a disease.

excitatory neurotransmitter A neurotransmitter whose effect on the postsynaptic membrane is to depolarize it.

explicit memory Long-term memory that entails conscious retrieval of information from one's past. Synonymous with declarative memory.

express saccades A very short-latency saccade, typically triggered by the abrupt appearance of an unexpected stimulus.

extinction A phenomenon often accompanying unilateral neglect, whereby a patient can be aware of a single object presented on their left when it appears in isolation, but will be unaware of it if a second item is simultaneously present on their right.

extracellular recording Electrical recordings made from an electrode located in extracellular space. Such recordings can be sensitive to action potentials and/or LFPs.

extrapersonal space Those portions of perceived space that are further than we can reach with hand or foot.

extrastriate cortex Cortex that is part of the visual system, but not a part of striate cortex (i.e., it is "beyond" or "outside of" primary visual cortex).

familiarity In recognition memory, the subjective experience that accompanies correctly recognizing an item on a recognition memory test (or, in real life, perhaps recognizing the face of a person on the bus) without a memory for the context in which that item was previously experienced. Hypothesized in some models to correspond to a neural signal and/or process that is qualitatively different from recollection.

feature detector An element in a sensory processing array whose function is to signal each time it detects the presence of the feature for which it is tuned.

fMRI adaptation The experimental procedure of habituating the response of a region to repeated exposure to a stimulus (or class of stimuli), then varying the stimuli along a dimension of interest and measuring whether there is a "release from habituation," which would indicate that the region in question is sensitive to change along the dimension being varied.

foraging decision The more-or-less-continual decision of whether to persist in one's current mode of behavior or whether to change to a different mode of behavior, often in the context of reducing a physiological drive (e.g., hunger, thirst, reproduction). Compare with perceptual decision and value-based decision.

formants Bands of sustained, elevated oscillatory power in a spectrogram of speech.

fornix The bundle of fibers leaving the hippocampus, in the primate initially in the caudal direction, and arcing dorsally and rostrally to synapse on targets in the hypothalamus and basal forebrain. It is generally understood that these fibers are important for maintaining the physiological state of the hippocampus (e.g., maintenance and regulation of hippocampal theta rhythm) rather than carrying the "informational output" of the hippocampus, which, instead, is carried by projections to entorhinal cortex.

forward model A model that predicts the consequences of an action.

Fourier transform The transformation of a time-varying waveform into the set of sine and cosine waves that can represent it.

fovea Region of the retina most densely packed with photoreceptors and, thus, supporting highest resolution vision.

frontal lobe The rostral-most of the five lobes of the cerebral cortex.

functional connectivity A state in which the activity of two or more regions is correlated, and they are therefore presumed to be "working together." (Note that the existence of a "structural connection" need not imply that two or more structurally connected areas are functionally connected in a particular context.)

functional magnetic resonance imaging (fMRI) The application of MRI that is sensitive to physiological signals (specifically to blood oxygenation) as opposed to anatomical structure.

fundamental frequency The lowest frequency formant of an utterance.

fundus The "bottom" of a sulcus, typically where its two banks meet.

GABA (*adj.* GABAergic) The abbreviated name of γ-aminobutyric acid, the most common inhibitory neurotransmitter in the CNS.

gamma frequency band Neural oscillations in the range of 30–80 Hz.

ganglion (pl. -glia) Ganglion is a synonym for nucleus. The basal ganglia, for example, are a group of nuclei located near the base of the cerebrum, and anterior and lateral to the thalamus. Their function is considered first in *Chapter 8*.

gating The process of selectively allowing certain signals to enter, or exit, a circuit.

generalized anxiety disorder (GAD) A psychiatric condition characterized by incessant, excessive worry.

gestalt psychology A school of thought, originating with the study of perception, that emphasized recognition of whole objects as being more important than feature-level processes.

glial cells Glial cells (or "glia") is the designation given to cells in the brain that are not themselves neurons but can be construed as playing supporting roles that are necessary for the normal functioning of neurons. Two types of glia mentioned in Chapter 2 are oligodendrocytes (responsible for myelin in the CNS) and astrocytes.

glutamate (*n.*; glutamatergic), *adj.* Also referred to as "glutamic acid," glutamate is the excitatory neurotransmitter released by cortical pyramidal cells and, thus, the primary chemical medium for information transmission in the brain.

grand mal epileptic seizure A seizure producing a loss of consciousness and violent muscle contractions (sometimes also referred to as tonic–clonic).

gray matter Informal, but widely used, term for the cortex. Derives from fact that cell bodies in the cortex lack myelin, and thus it appears darker to the naked eye than does the myelin-rich white matter.

gyri (*plural*; gyrus, *sing*). From the Latin for "circles," convex ridges on the surface of the cerebral cortex. Each gyrus is bounded by sulci on each side.

hidden unit layer A layer in a computational model (e.g., a parallel-distributed processing (PDP) model) that neither receives direct external input from nor sends direct output to, the environment.

high-level cognition An informal, but widely used, classification for most mental functions other than sensory perception, motor control, and some aspects of memory and attention. Examples include language, problem solving, reasoning, and metacognition (thinking about thinking).

hippocampus A subcortical structure of the cerebrum that, in the primate, is surrounded by the cortex of the temporal lobe and lies parallel to this lobe's long axis. The term is Latin for seahorse, of which its shape is suggestive.

homunculus A "little human" in the brain. In the context of somatosensory and motor neuroscience, the homunculus refers to the somatotopic representation of the post- and precentral gyri, respectively; in the context of psychology, the homunculus refers to a hypothetical little person inside the brain who is responsible for one's cognitive functions.

horizontal meridian The imaginary horizontal line that divides the visual field into upper and lower quadrants.

hypercolumn A hypothesized functional unit of cortical columns in V1, the totality of which represents every possible feature that could be presented to a specific V1 receptive field.

hyperpolarize To make the membrane potential of a cell more negative. (I.e., the opposite of depolarize.)

implicit memory The influence of past experience on present behavior that is accompanied by awareness of neither this influence nor the past experience. Synonymous with nondeclarative memory.

individual differences The study of factors underlying why individuals in a sample or population differ from each other. In studies of brain–behavior relationships, for example, a between-subject correlation between levels of some neurobiological dependent measure (e.g., neuroimaging signal in Region x) and variation in a behavioral measure (e.g., RT on Task y) is taken as compelling evidence for a role for x in performance of y.

information theory A set of mathematical formalisms for understanding how messages (i.e., information) can be transmitted over a noisy channel and understood by a receiver.

inhibitory interneurons After pyramidal cells, the second major class of neurons in the cerebral cortex. Although there are many types of inhibitory interneuron, this book will primarily refer to the generic interneuron: a GABAergic cell with only local projections to nearby neurons.

inhibitory neurotransmission Of a neurotransmitter whose effect on the postsynaptic membrane potential is to hyperpolarize it, that is, to make it more negative.

inhibitory surround A mechanism for increasing the signal-to-noise ratio of a neural representation by inhibiting activity corresponding to adjacent, but irrelevant, information.

inner hair cells Cells that are attached to the basilar membrane, the vibration of which causes them to release neurotransmitter onto a neuron of the cochlear nucleus, thereby effecting the transduction of acoustic energy into a neural signal.

innervate To connect to a neuron via one or more synaptic connections.

intention When used in contradistinction to attention, intention refers to the processes required to prepare for (or, sometimes, just to contemplate) performing an action.

interaural intensity difference (IID) The phenomenon that the acoustic energy from a single sound source, if not positioned in direct alignment with the midline of the head, will be of greater intensity for one ear than the other. This provides a useful cue for sound localization.

interaural timing difference (ITD) The phenomenon that the time of arrival of the acoustic energy emanating from a single sound source, if not positioned in direct alignment with the midline of the head, will be earlier for one ear than the other. This provides a useful cue for sound localization.

intertemporal choice A situation in which an individual must choose to receive a reward delivered at two different points in time (often immediate vs. delayed reward), and often producing the phenomenon of delay discounting.

intracellular recording Synonymous with "whole-cell recording." Electrical recordings made with a hollow-tube electrode that punctures the membrane of a cell (and forms a tight seal between membrane and electrode) so that fluctuations of voltage within that individual neuron can be measured.

invariant The property of not responding to changes along a particular dimension.

inverse problem For EEG, the fact that there is an infinite number of possible source solutions for any pattern of voltages distributed across the scalp.

isoluminant A display in which all objects, plus the background, are presented with the same luminance (i.e., brightness), and so only color information can be used to segment the scene.

kinematics The dynamics of movement or motion without consideration of the forces that impel it.

laminar "Lamina" is another word for layer; although derived from Latin, the plural form is "laminas" or "laminae." It is often used as an adjective when referring to layer-specific (i.e., "laminar") organization within cortex.

lateral inhibition When the activity of a neuron in area X inhibits the activity of other neurons in area X; that is, the source of the inhibition is neither feedback nor feedforward, but "feed-sideways"/ "feed-laterally."

lesion Used as a noun, it refers to either damage or an abnormality. It is a general term, in that it does not specify either the nature or the cause. Thus, a region of dead or otherwise compromised tissue can be referred to as a lesion regardless of whether it was caused by, for example, viral encephalitis (swelling), by anoxia (deprivation of oxygen, such as could happen as a result of a stroke), or by the experimental injection of ibotenic acid, a chemical that kills the soma of neurons, but not fibers of passage. (Note that each of these causes would produce a different pattern of damage.)

ligand A substance, typically a molecule, that binds to a specific site on a protein, thereby triggering some process. In the context of neurotransmission, the ligand is the neurotransmitter that binds with a binding site on the postsynaptic receptor.

local field potential (LFP) The fluctuating electrical potential recorded from extracellular space that reflects the moment-to-moment aggregation of voltages from all dendritic trees in the vicinity of the electrode.

localization of function The idea that a behavioral or cognitive function can arise from a discrete (i.e., "localized") anatomical region of the brain.

machine learning A branch of computer science that studies how computer algorithms can learn about structure in a set of data.

major depressive disorder (MDD) A mood state characterized by sadness, poor concentration, and loss of interest in daily activities that can also be accompanied by fatigue, insomnia, and loss of appetite.

mass action The idea that behavioral and cognitive functions cannot be understood as arising from discrete anatomical regions of the brain.

mechanoreceptors Somatosensory receptors in the skin that respond to mechanical forces: pressure, texture, flutter, vibration, and stretch.

mental lexicon The subset of semantic memory corresponding to all the words that one knows the meaning of.

motor effector The part of the body that actually carries out an action – most often used to refer to, depending on the context, the limbs, the digits, or the eyes.

motor efferent An efferent fiber is a fiber projecting away from a region (an afferent is a fiber projecting into a region). The term "motor efferents" refers to fibers leaving the cortex and synapsing in the spinal cord.

myelin The cholesterol-laden sheath that insulates axons. Myelin is formed by branches from a type of glial cell, called an oligodendrocyte that wraps the axon in several layers.

Na^+/K^+ pump (spoken aloud as "sodium-potassium pump") Also known as "ATPase," because it is an enzyme that requires ATP for its operation. The Na^+/K^+ pump is a membrane-spanning complex that actively restores the electrochemical gradients of Na^+ and K^+ that are decreased by the mechanisms of the action potential and of neurotransmitter reuptake.

natural language Any human language commonly used for verbal or written communication that has arisen in an unpremeditated fashion. Computer-programming languages and languages used in formal logic are not natural languages.

neural code The way that the nervous system represents information via action potentials and neurochemicals.

neurodegenerative disease A disease characterized by progressive loss of brain tissue.

neuroeconomics The study of the neural bases of value-based decision making.

neurons The cells in the brain that generate electrical and chemical signals that control all other systems of the body. The typical neuron has three distinct regions—dendrites, cell body, axon—with postsynaptic terminals located primarily on dendrites and presynaptic terminals located primarily on axons (see *Chapter 2*).

neurophysiology The study of the functioning of the brain. Two broad classes of neurophysiological technique are stimulation and measurement.

neuropsychology The analysis of the behavioral consequences resulting from damage to a particular brain structure. Neuropsychology can be conducted either by experimentally producing a surgical lesion in an animal or by observing the effects on behavior of brain damage incurred by humans.

nigrostriatal tract The bundle of axons, originating from the substantia nigra pars compacta, responsible for the release of dopamine in the neostriatum.

nondeclarative memory The influence of past experience on present behavior that is accompanied by awareness of neither this influence nor the past experience. Synonymous with implicit memory.

nucleus (*pl.* *-clei*) In the context of the cell, the nucleus is the central structure containing DNA. In the context of gross anatomy, a nucleus is a subcortical group of neurons, often visible to the naked eye when viewing an image acquired from an in-vivo brain or a dissection of ex-vivo tissue.

ontogeny The development of an organism; in the case of vertebrates, from fertilization through birth and the entirety of the lifespan.

outer hair cells Cells anchored at one end to the basilar membrane, and at the other to the cochlea; their coordinated activity can dampen the vibrations of the basilar membrane in precise areas.

overt attention Attention deployed toward an object or location by looking directly at it.

paraphasic speech Speech including unintended/inappropriate syllables, words, or phrases.

perception The identification of important features of the item or information being sensed.

perceptual decision A categorical decision about a perceived stimulus (e.g., Is it moving up or down?, Is this tone louder or softer than the previous one?). In effect, what is the state of this specific part of my environment? Compare with value-based decision and foraging decision.

peripersonal space The space surrounding one's body that is within one's grasp, or kickable, or otherwise touchable.

peripheral nervous system The peripheral nervous system (sometimes abbreviated PNS) is made up of all neurons in the body whose cell bodies are located outside of the central nervous system. These include somatosensory (i.e., "touch") neurons whose cell bodies are in the skin and that send signals via axons that project into the spinal cord, and neurons that control autonomic functions of many organ systems of the body.

perseveration The persistent selection of a previously reinforced response (or type of response) after having received feedback that this pattern of behavior is no longer appropriate.

phase precession Precession is the rotation of an axis of rotation, such as the "wobble" of a spinning top. Phase precession occurs when a dot painted on the cylinder of the top is facing in a progressively different direction each time the spinning axis completes one cycle of its wobble. In neurophysiology, it refers to the phenomenon of a single spike (or burst of spiking) occurring at a progressively earlier or at a progressively later phase angle of a reference oscillation.

phase synchronization The phase of a sinusoid refers to the location within its cycle (e.g., the peak, or the trough). To synchronize the phase of two oscillators is to adjust them such that, whenever one is at a particular phase in its cycle (say, the peak), the other will always be at the same phase in its (this could also be the peak, or it could be any other phase, so long as its stable across cycles).

phase–amplitude coupling (PAC) The periodic waxing and waning of the amplitude of a high-frequency signal (either spiking or an oscillation) that is synchronized with the phase of a lower-frequency oscillating signal.

phoneme The smallest unit of sound in a language that, when changed, can change the meaning of an utterance.

phototransduction The conversion of energy from the electromagnetic spectrum ("visible light") into neural signals.

phrenology The practice, initiated by Franz Josef Gall (1758–1828), of divining mental traits from patterns of convexities and concavities on the skull.

phylogeny The evolutionary history of organismal lineage.

pinwheel The actual physical layout, discovered with optical imaging, of the cortical columns in area V1 that accomplish the function that had previously been proposed for the hypercolumn.

place code In audition, the scheme whereby the representation of frequency (pitch) in the cochlear nucleus is laid out in a linear fashion, from high to low. For navigation, can refer to the coding properties of place cells in the hippocampus.

place of articulation The physical location in the mouth where the tongue applies the blockage of airflow that produces stop consonants.

plasticity The property of neural tissue that its structure and function can modify as a consequence of processing information that corresponds to regularities in the structure of the environment. Neural plasticity is widely believed to be the physical basis of learning.

posterior Used as a term of direction, posterior refers to the back (a synonym, introduced in *Chapter 2*, is "caudal").

post-traumatic stress disorder (PTSD) A pathological condition resulting from traumatic experience. Symptoms can include re-experiencing the traumatic event (including "flashbacks" and nightmares); avoidance symptoms; and hyperarousal (includes being easily startled and feeling tense).

power spectrum A representation of the magnitude of each frequency resulting from a spectral transform.

power The magnitude of an oscillatory component in a signal.

predictive coding The idea that a core function of the brain is to construct, and constantly update, a model of the current state of the external world.

premotor theory of attention The idea that attention may be a consequence of motor planning, covert attention resulting from the processing of a motor plan that never gets realized as an actual movement (sometimes referred to as a "subthreshold" motor plan).

primary visual cortex (also referred to as V1) The site of the initial cortical processing of signals originating in the retina and conveyed to it via projections from the LGN of the thalamus.

principal component analysis (PCA) A statistical procedure for summarizing a dataset by identifying the elements (the components) that account for the most variance. PCA is a common way to carry out dimensionality reduction on a dataset.

priority map A neural representation of the stimuli and/or locations in space that are currently the most relevant for behavior.

proprioception The sense of where different parts of the body are positioned relative to one another.

pyramidal cells Glutamate-releasing neurons with pyramid-shaped cell bodies that are the most common excitatory neurons in the neocortex and hippocampus.

random walk A mathematical formalization of a process that proceeds via stochastic steps.

rate code A neural code whereby information about a change in some metric property is conveyed by a change in the rate at which a neuron fires.

receiver operating characteristic (ROC) A graph plotting hits vs. false alarms as a function of criterion (often operationalized as "confidence"). Deriving from signal detection theory, this measure is intended to capture the strength of a percept (or, in memory research, of a subject's memory) independent of decision criteria.

receptive field The portion of the sensory-transduction surface to which a neuron responds.

recollection In the context of memory retrieval, the act of remembering the context in which a fact was learned or an event occurred. Hypothesized in some models to correspond to a neural signal and/or process that is qualitatively different from familiarity.

recurrent circuit A circuit carrying feedback signals.

recurrent neural network (RNN) An artificial neural network in which interactivity between units in the hidden layer allows for the processing of information over time, making them well-suited for modeling neural information processing that evolves over time, and/or for processing inputs that vary over time (e.g., speech).

region of interest (ROI) In neuroimaging, a region from which signal is extracted for analysis.

reinforcement learning (RL) A process by which an agent learns to optimize its behavior based on its past experience with gaining rewards or other desired outcomes. It is a form of unsupervised learning. Robots and other artificial agents can be built to be controlled by RL algorithms, and many models of memory and decision making in biological organisms (including humans) hypothesize that at least some aspects of these phenomena are governed by principles of RL.

resonant frequency The frequency at which oscillations are most readily induced in a system, and at which it will oscillate at the greatest amplitude.

retinal ganglion cells The neurons in the retina that send visual signals to the thalamus.

retinotopic organization, or retinotopy The property of reinstating the spatial organization of the retina in the spatial organization of visual regions of the brain, such that, for example, adjacent regions of the retina are represented by adjacent regions of visual cortex.

reuptake The active process of removing molecules of neurotransmitter, or their catabolites, from the synaptic cleft by transporting them into a cell, either the presynaptic neuron or an adjacent astrocyte.

saccade A French word for a fast, ballistic, eye movement that "jumps" from point A to point B, with "no interest" in what is between the two points. Saccadic eye movements differ from smooth-pursuit eye movements, in which the eye follows the movement of an object in the environment.

salience map A neural representation of the location of stimuli that have the most energy (e.g., the brightest, or the loudest). Compare with priority map.

scotoma A small area of blindness in the visual field surrounded by normal visual sensation.

seizure An incidence of abnormal brain functioning that can last from seconds to minutes and can occur as an isolated event or as a chronic condition of repeating seizures (i.e., epilepsy). Positive manifestations of seizure can include the perception of flashing light or the uncontrolled, involuntary jerking of a limb; negative manifestations can be a transient blindness or paralysis. Seizures result from stereotypical, abnormal patterns of activity in brain cells (neurons).

semantic memory Knowledge that was acquired through learning, but for which one cannot remember the context (e.g., place, situation, who was present) at the time that the initial encoding of that information occurred.

sensation The detection of energy in the external world via one of the sensory organs (eyes, ears, skin, nose, tongue), or of the state of an internal organ via visceral sensors.

sensorimotor circuits Neural pathways connecting the processing of sensory information (i.e., having to do with vision, audition, touch, smell, or taste) with the motor system, which controls the movement of the body. The most basic sensorimotor circuits are reflex circuits that afford, for example, rapid withdrawal of the hand from a hot surface.

signal detection theory A framework in which decision-making factors are explicitly taken into account in tests of perception and recognition memory. Entails categorizing each response as a hit, false alarm, miss, or correct rejection.

social cognitive neuroscience One of many terms used to refer to the study of the neural bases of social cognition.

somatotopy This word derives from soma (Greek for body) and -topy (of or pertaining to a place). The principle of somatotopy is that adjacent parts of the body (e.g., the upper lip and the nose) are represented in adjacent parts of the brain. Note that the "map" created by a somatotopically organized portion of cortex need not bear close physical resemblance to the parts of the body being represented – there will typically be distortions and discontinuities.

spectrogram A representation of how a power spectrum evolves over time.

striate cortex Another name for V1, so named for its striped appearance when viewed in just the right way.

stroke Disruption of the supply of blood to a region of the brain, either due to blockage (occlusive stroke) or bleeding from a vessel (hemorrhagic stroke).

sulci (*sing.* sulcus) Latin for "furrows," fissures on the cortical surface.

superior temporal polysensory (STP) area The region in the superior temporal gyrus of the monkey that receives inputs from visual, auditory, and somatosensory regions, and in which many neurons respond to more than one sensory modality.

synapse Name introduced by Nobel Laureate Charles Sherrington (1857–1952) for the location at which one neuron passes a signal to another cell (within the CNS, it is typically to the dendrite of another neuron; at the neuromuscular junction, it is to a muscle cell). The name is derived from the Greek for "to clasp."

synaptic cleft The gap between the presynaptic and postsynaptic terminals, across which neurotransmitter diffuses from pre to post.

systems neuroscience The study of how neural circuits and brain regions give rise to functions of the brain (e.g., behavior, or the regulation of autonomic functions).

thermoreceptors Receptors in the skin that are tuned to detect heat or cold.

tonotopy The organization of primary auditory cortex by frequency, which derives from the place code originating in the cochlear nucleus.

topographic organization The principle that adjacent parts of some aspect of the external world are represented in adjacent parts of the brain. Thus, somatotopy is one example of topographic organization. Other examples include the representation of the visual field, as projected onto the retina, by the visual cortex ("retinotopy"), the representation of sound in a continuous map from low to high frequencies ("tonotopy"), and the scheme for the representation of geometric space by "grid cells" of the entorhinal cortex.

transduction The translation of physical energy from the environment into a neural code that represents the properties of that energy.

traveling wave A wave that propagates energy through a medium. In the case of the cochlea, it characterizes the propagation of vibrational energy from the oval window along the length of the basilar membrane.

type vs. token These two words are used to distinguish a category of stimulus (e.g., the category of faces) from a specific exemplar from within that category (e.g., my father's face is a specific token drawn from the type of objects known as faces).

typically developed (or "–ing") Refers to individuals who do not have a neurological or psychiatric diagnosis. In the context of studies of developmental disorders (e.g., autism spectrum disorder or fragile X syndrome), this term is often preferred to the synonym "normal," to avoid the pejorative connotations of the label "abnormal."

utilization behavior An exaggerated tendency for one's behavior to be determined by the external environment.

value-based decision Selecting between two (or more) items when faced with a choice (as, e.g., when at the store, or when deciding how to spend one's Saturday evening). The purview of neuroeconomics; compare with perceptual decision and foraging decision.

ventricle A hollow chamber inside the brain within which cerebrospinal fluid (CSF) circulates. Like a chain of lakes connected by canals, the ventricles are part of a continuous system of CSF that extends to the caudal end of the spinal cord.

vertical meridian The imaginary vertical line that divides the visual field in half, thereby defining the boundary between the two hemifields.

viral encephalitis Acute inflammation of the brain due to viral infection.

visual field The full extent of what one can see while holding the eyes still, measured as degrees of angle from the point of fixation to the edge of what is visible.

visual hemifield The half of the visual field represented in V1 of one hemisphere.

voxel A 3D image element, the smallest unit of data in a PET or fMRI dataset; 2D "picture elements" having earned the nickname "pixel," these "pixels with volume" have been dubbed "voxels."

white matter Made up of billions of myelin-sheathed axons, the white matter makes up the majority of the volume of the cerebrum.

Index

Note: Page numbers in *italic* refer to figures.

D

E

Q

R

S

X

Y